THE JUSTICES OF THE UNITED STATES SUPREME COURT 1789–1978

Their Lives and Major Opinions

THE JUSTICES OF THE UNITED STATES SUPREME COURT
Their Lives and Major Opinions

VOLUMES I–IV
1789–1969
LEON FRIEDMAN & FRED L. ISRAEL
EDITORS
with an Introduction by
LOUIS H. POLLAK
Dean, Yale University Law School

VOLUME V
THE BURGER COURT
1969–1978
LEON FRIEDMAN
EDITOR

VOLUME I
THE JUSTICES OF THE UNITED STATES SUPREME COURT 1789–1978
Their Lives and Major Opinions

LEON FRIEDMAN & FRED L. ISRAEL
EDITORS

CHELSEA HOUSE PUBLISHERS
NEW YORK & LONDON
1980

First published 1969 in association with the R.R. Bowker Company
First paperback edition 1980
Printed in the United States of America

Library of Congress Cataloging in Publication Data (Revised)
Friedman, Leon, comp.
The justices of the United States Supreme Court, 1789–1969, their lives and major opinions.

Includes bibliographies.
Vol. 5: 1969-1978.
1. United States. Supreme Court—Biography. 2. Judges—United States—Biography.
I. Israel, Fred L., joint comp. II. Title.
KF8744.F75 347'.73'2634 [B] 69-13699
ISBN 0-8352-0217-8
ISBN 0-87754-130-2 (pbk.)

Chelsea House Publishers

Harold Steinberg, Chairman & Publisher Andrew E. Norman, President
Susan Lusk, Vice President
A Division of Chelsea House Educational Communications, Inc.
70 West 40th Street, New York 10018

Preface

THIRTY YEARS AGO Henry Steele Commager observed: "We know shockingly little about our judges. Of some fourscore judges who have sat upon the Supreme Court we have biographies of perhaps a dozen and acceptable biographies of half that number." Felix Frankfurter, writing about the same time, noted: "American legal history has done very little to rescue the Court from the limbo of impersonality . . . Until we have penetrating studies of the influence of [the Justices who shaped American Constitutional doctrines] we shall not have an adequate history of the Supreme Court and therefore of the United States."

In the decades since these words were written, not much has been done to rescue the Justices of the Supreme Court from the shadows of history. Excellent biographies of some recent Court members and a handful of the nineteenth-century Justices have been published. But so little has been written on fully half the men who have wielded the nation's highest judicial power—even though they were important political figures in their own time, friends and advisers to Presidents, and leaders of the bar in a society traditionally deferential to its lawyers—that today many legal scholars hardly recognize their names. Many of these "unknown" jurists authored key constitutional decisions, or at least, as collaborators or opponents, helped shape the great opinions of the judicial giants such as Marshall, Story, Taney, Bradley and Holmes. Who were these men? How did they rise to the top of the judicial ladder? Why have they been forgotten? Why did they support or oppose the more luminous stars of the Court? What role did they play in the development of the most powerful judicial institution in world history? These ninety-seven essays attempt to answer these questions.

Since the entire Court participated in each important decision, some of these essays necessarily deal with the same event from differing vantage points. It is impossible to ignore each Justice's role in the Dred Scott decision, the

1894 Income Tax case or the crucial New Deal opinions of the 1930's. Since the thirty-eight contributors to these volumes represent not only various viewpoints but different disciplines—law, political science, history—the multiplicity of approach broadens the understanding of the Supreme Court as a social and political force. Included with each essay are one or more representative opinions of each Justice. Some are, of course, well known to students of constitutional law. Others, including some circuit court or state court opinions, are not. Publishing these opinions with each biographical essay shows the jurist in action and illustrates that impersonal words from the bench come from a living man whose personal history helped mold his contribution to the law.

In the preparation of this work, we have incurred many agreeable debts of gratitude. Our contributors graciously cooperated with us through the various stages in preparing the final manuscript. Mrs. Anne Richter, Miss Elizabeth Geiser and Miss Marilyn Joffe of R. R. Bowker Co. gave their encouragement and assistance through many crises; Miss Nina Flannery offered valuable editorial assistance and our research aides Lauren Kaplan, Evan Fetterman and Martin Silver patiently solved our library queries.

LEON FRIEDMAN
FRED L. ISRAEL

New York City
August, 1969

Introduction

by LOUIS H. POLLAK

Dean, Yale University Law School

I

"THE GOVERNMENT of the United States has been emphatically termed a government of laws, and not of men." So spoke John Marshall in *Marbury* v. *Madison,* 1 Cranch 137 (1803) and in that famous case went on, through the force of his own will and wisdom, to turn a moribund tribunal into the Supreme Court of the United States, a new political institution powerful enough to chastise and limit Congresses and Presidents. In the name of man's subordination to law, Marshall proved what Bishop Hoadly told George I almost a century before:

> *Whoever hath an absolute authority to interpret written or spoken laws; it is he who is truely the lawgiver to all intents and purposes and not the person who wrote or spoke them.*

These volumes are biographical essays on the ninety-seven lawgivers who have been Justices of the Supreme Court, and to the extent that each is in fact a valid historical appraisal of a man and his life in the law, the ninety-seven critical biographies contained in this edition constitute a unique resource. For—apart from several book-length studies, of varying worth and interest, of some of the leading Justices—there has been little biographical attention given to the members of the Court. And this dearth of scholarly enterprise reflects the kind of narrow historical perspective which sees the Court's work only in terms of those Justices who have made judicial headlines. Primary interest of course centers on Marshall; on Taney; on Miller and Field and the elder Harlan; on Holmes and Hughes and Brandeis; on Frankfurter and Black. But to ignore Cushing or Duvall or Grier or Brown or Moody or Minton is to put out of sight one of the most distinctive facts about the Court—that it is a *collective* institution, whose achievements, for good or ill, are the achievements of men who *jointly* wield the "judicial power."

Nor is the relevant partnership simply the nine (or six, or seven, or ten) Justices who shared the bench on any given opinion day. Justice Black (as John Frank tellingly reminds us) has served with a fourth of all the ninety-seven Justices; Chief Justice Hughes, in two terms on the Court, served with a fifth of all the Justices. Yet the partnership relates back farther still. The Court's "we" is cumulative, going back almost four hundred volumes to the first of Dallas' *Reports*. Elections punctuate the life-cycles of the other departments of government: the waning days of 1968 have marked the passing of a Congress (the ninetieth) and a Presidency (the thirty-sixth). But there remains in unbroken continuity the third department established by the Constitution—"one supreme Court."

The longevity of the Court—which is to say, the longevity of our constitutional republic—has long since ceased to surprise. But, at the launching of the Constitution, Americans gave no hostages to perpetuity. They had done so in drafting the "Articles of Confederation and perpetual Union"—and managed under the Articles for a scant eleven years. The Constitution-makers proposed to build a "more perfect Union," not a perpetual one. They did not, in the Constitution, seek to plant the American flag on infinite horizons. But they did lay a moderate claim upon the future. The last-named and all-comprehensive objective of the charter was "to secure the Blessings of Liberty to ourselves and our Posterity. . . ."

In one important respect the Constitution did not give to the Justices as substantial a role in defining national policy—which is to say, promoting liberty for "ourselves and our Posterity"—as Madison had hoped. The Convention rejected Madison's plan to join judges with the executive in a Council of Revision vested with a veto power over Congress. But one of the central objections to the plan—namely, that conditioning the enactment of national legislation on the assent of judges would vastly complicate the Court's subsequent and independent review of the laws assented to, as those laws were sought to be applied in actual "cases and controversies"—is in itself important testimony of the understanding of many of the Framers that due exercise of the "judicial power" encompassed the authority to determine not only the meaning but the validity of national laws.

The unwillingness of the Convention to acquiesce in another of Madison's proposals—in this instance, a proposal that would have aggrandized Congress as against the so-called "sovereign" states—by indirection gave further scope to the judicial power: Madison pushed hard in the Convention for a constitutional provision vesting in Congress the authority to review state laws with a view to disallowing those which ran counter to paramount national policy. He thought this defensive authority essential to the smooth maintenance of a federal system keyed to the exercise of national power in pursuit of national objectives. When his fellow delegates balked at this explicit subordination of the state legislatures to Congress, Madison admonished the Convention that, in default of this procedure, the judiciary alone would have the opportunity and obligation to defend national power against subversion by the parochial excesses of one or more of the states. And thus, when the Constitution was adopted and the new national government was established, one of the first Congress' first steps was to enable the Court to fulfill that obligation: Section 25 of the Judiciary Act of 1789 gave to the Court the appellate authority, which it has ever since retained, to review—and, if need be, reverse—state court judgments in cases in which state laws and national laws (including treaties, and the Constitution itself) are assertedly in conflict.

Although he was doubtful that the Court could alone fully protect national interests against the states, Madison saw the Court as uniquely equipped to prevent Congress and the other branches of the national government from infringing (whether inadvertently or by design) upon those "Blessings of Liberty" which the Constitution was intended to foster. In urging that Congress approve, for submission to the states, those proposed constitutional amendments which were to become the Bill of Rights, Madison argued the case to his fellow members of the House in the following terms:

> *It may be thought that all paper barriers against the power of the community are too weak to be worthy of attention. . . . If they are incorporated into the constitution, independent tribunals of justice will consider themselves in a peculiar manner the guardians of those rights; they will be an impenetrable bulwark against every assumption of power in the legislative or executive; they will be naturally led to resist every encroachment upon rights expressly stipulated for in the constitution by the declaration of rights.* [I ANNALS OF CONGRESS, 449 *et seq.*]

The Convention debates; the text of the Constitution and the early amendments; the *Federalist* papers of Madison and his great collaborators—these were the preliminary (and often fuzzy) plans of the judicial power. The Judiciary Act of 1789 turned the plans into an initial blueprint of a high tribunal. But it took a master builder to construct a Supreme Court.

This was Marshall's work. The decision in *Marbury v. Madison,* establishing the authority of judges to invalidate national laws *judicially perceived* to conflict with the Constitution, was the first great step. And it is a matter of some irony that Madison was at once a winning litigant and a losing partisan in the case which first vindicated his expectation that "independent tribunals of justice . . . will be an impenetrable bulwark against every assumption of power in the legislative or executive. . . ."

Strengthened by the first step, Marshall proceeded to take the further steps which Madison had contemplated.

In *McCulloch v. Maryland,* 4 Wheat. 316 (1819) and again in *Gibbons v. Ogden,* 9 Wheat. 1 (1824) Marshall resolutely struck down exercises of state power found to be inconsistent with national economic policy (as such national economic policy was *judicially perceived* to have been set down by Congress and/or the Constitution).

And two years before the end of his epochal term, Marshall declared the Court's readiness, in an appropriate case, to prevent the United States from infringing upon those liberties of the individual which Madison had embodied, and for which he sought judicial protection, in the Bill of Rights:

> *These Amendments demanded security against the apprehended encroachments of the General Government. . . . The great revolution which established the Constitution of the United States was not effected without immense opposition. Serious fears were extensively entertained that those powers, which the patriot statesmen who then watched over the interests of our country deemed essential to Union, and to the attainment of those invaluable objects for which Union was sought, might be exercised in a manner dangerous to liberty.* Barron *v.* Baltimore, *7 Pet. 243 (1833).*

Nor did Marshall only decide the great cases. In his thirty-four years of service, he wrote almost one-half of his Court's eleven hundred opinions.

Justice Story, writing about his friend and colleague, was at once fulsome and right:

> *Chief Justice Marshall was the growth of a century. Providence grants such men to the human family only on great occasions to accomplish its own great end. Such men are found only when our need is the greatest.*

No one judge has so dominated the Court and its work since Marshall's time. But even Marshall was not the sole proprietor of the judicial power. Justice Story was the author of *Martin v. Hunter's Lessee,* 1 Wheat. 304 (1816) which established for all time the constitutionality of the Court's jurisdiction to review state courts. (Marshall, virtually a litigant in the case, did not participate.) And Justice William Johnson—as he demonstrated, for example, in his concurrences in *Gibbons v. Ogden* and *Fletcher v. Peck,* 6 Cranch 87 (1810)—was not hesitant to defend even higher ground than that taken by his Chief. Even in Marshall's time, the exercise of the judicial power was a joint and several venture.

II

The paramount purpose of the judicial venture was and remains what Madison and his fellow-delegates declared to be the paramount purpose of the constitutional system—"to secure the Blessings of Liberty to ourselves and our Posterity. . . ." The phrase carries a double implication: (1) if liberty perishes, the Constitution perishes, whether or not the confederation of the states persists for other purposes; and (2) the principal way to " 'preserve, protect and defend the Constitution' " is to foster the liberty of the American people.

The lessons involved are more than rhetorical. They are hard political truths, going directly to the conditions of national survival. It is the burden of this Introduction that we must learn and live by these truths; for if we do not, these biographical studies of the Justices will be memorial volumes, not the living history of an on-going Court umpiring a free society.

We very nearly failed of survival once. However many causes underlay the Civil War, the prime cause was our inability, through established governmental processes, to limit slavery. The "peculiar institution," given limited sufferance by the Framers, had not withered as Madison and Jefferson and their colleagues had confidently anticipated; it had flourished—to the ever-increasing hazard of liberty: And then, in 1857, in *Dred Scott* v. *Sandford,* 19 How. 393, Chief Justice Taney by fiat declared that Congress could not limit the spread of slavery in the vast and beckoning western territories. The Constitution had turned its back on its central purposes; and elected officials were assertedly without power—even had they had the will—to save the Constitution and the country. The election of a President who thought *Dred Scott* wrong triggered secession: And war. And the death of half a million Americans (at least fifty, perhaps a hundred, times as many as had perished in the Revolution). And the death of the Constitution as it had been.

The end came, for that Constitution, when the aging Chief Justice, after the outbreak of hostilities in 1861, sought to enforce that constitutional liberty he felt was paramount—the writ of habeas corpus—in aid of one John Merryman, a civilian, taken from his Maryland home by Union soldiers and thereafter kept in military custody. Taney directed that a copy of his writ, and his supporting opinion, be transmitted to the President of the United States:

> *The answer* [*wrote Attorney General Robert H. Jackson, in a book published shortly before he ascended the bench*], *if any, was drowned out by the measured tread of marching feet. Judicial power was all but extinct. Nothing but the indispensable necessity for its function could bid it rise again.*
>
> *Did the lonely and frustrated Chief Justice recall the tragic part that he, more than any other had played in starting that march? Only four years before he had read the opinion in the* Dred Scott *case, in which his Court had held the Missouri Compromise to be unconstitutional. The Missouri Compromise itself had ceased to be important. But there was still hope that American forbearance and statesmanship would prove equal to finding some compromise between the angry forces that were being aroused by the slave issue. That hope vanished when the Supreme Court held that the Constitution would allow no compromise about the existence of slavery in the territories. Taney had attempted to forestall the anticipated verdict of coming elections—the verdict that came with the election of 1860. Now the weary and weatherbeaten old Chief Justice was overmastered by the violence of forces that he had himself turned away from compromise in legislative halls and had huried toward war.* [*Jackson,* The Struggle for Judicial Supremacy, *326–27.*]*

Taney's death, three years later, was posthumous.

The remaking of our constitutional covenant was built less upon faith in our constitutional processes than upon the armed might which had prevailed in Merryman's home and at Appomattox. Under the remade covenant, blacks and whites, and citizens and states and nation, were placed in new relation with one another. The touchstones of that liberty whose blessings were now to be secured for "ourselves and our Posterity" were freedom and "the equal protection of the laws."

* *It seems that Merryman was, in fact, released from military custody to civilian custody (to be indicted, but ultimately never tried, for treason). Apparently, the President neither formally acquiesced in nor formally ignored Taney's writ. See Pollak,* The Constitution and the Supreme Court: A Documentary History, Vol. II, pp. 122–24.

But within a generation of the adoption of the Thirteenth and Fourteenth Amendments, the Supreme Court (1) in the *Civil Rights Cases,* 109 U.S. 3 in 1883, denied Congress authority to *forbid* racial segregation or exclusion in public places, and (2) in *Plessy* v. *Ferguson,* 163 U.S. 537 in 1896, upheld state power to *require* racial segregation in public places. The rationale of the *Civil Rights Cases* was that federal protective remedies were unwarranted except where racial distinctions were ordained or fostered by state law (rather than by the individual or aggregate business decisions of the white entrepreneurs who governed the public market place). The rationale of *Plessy* was that racial segregation ordained by law was not a denial of the equal protection of the laws: if "the enforced separation of the races stamps the colored race with a badge of inferiority . . . it is not by reason of anything found in the act, but solely because the colored race chooses to put that construction upon it."

In fact, of course, only the *Plessy* majority was discerning enough to see that racial segregation was a neutral social policy. Whites and blacks not blessed with the sophistication of those in high judicial station uniformly understood that the central purpose of Jim Crow laws was exactly to "stamp the colored race with a badge of inferiority":

> *Those laws* [*as C. Vann Woodward has put it*] *backed up the Alabamian who told the disfranchising convention of his state that no Negro in the world was the equal of "the least, poorest, lowest-down white man I ever knew of"; . . . The Jim Crow laws put the authority of the state or city in the voice of the street car conductor, the railway brakeman, the bus driver, the theater usher, and also into the voice of the hoodlum of the public parks and playgrounds. They gave free rein and the majesty of the law to mass aggressions that might otherwise have been curbed, blunted, or deflected. . . .*
>
> *The Jim Crow laws, unlike feudal laws, did not assign the subordinate group a fixed status in society. They were constantly pushing the Negro further down* [*Woodward,* The Strange Case of Jim Crow, *93*].

To the elder Justice Harlan, the sole dissenter in *Plessy,* "the judgment this day rendered will, in time, prove to be quite as pernicious as the decision made by this tribunal in the *Dred Scott* case." *Plessy* has not generated a civil war—not yet, at least. But it took fifty-eight years—from 1896 to 1954, when *Brown* v. *Board of Education,* 347 U.S. 483 was decided—before the Court undertook to redress the nation's broken commitment to equality. And meanwhile, for two generations, white Americans "were constantly pushing the Negro farther down."

For the last fifteen years the Court has taken the lead in redeeming the nation's promises. But the apparent constitutional objective seems more remote today than in 1954. Our towns and cities have fast become conglomerates of hostility: black areas of dole, rats, wretched schools and desperation; white areas of higher per capita income and intolerance.

The sources of our public and private ineptitude and irresolution are multiple: We have squandered lives and treasure and moral resolve in dubious foreign conflict rather than risk committing our full energies to fighting the main battle for constitutional principle in our own land. Killers have taken our bravest, our most devoted, leaders. Many whites (millions of whom, in 1968, supported a know-nothing third-party candidate) neither want nor understand a free society. And some blacks have lost faith in the will and capacity of our society to become free.

It is not hard to understand why some blacks have lost faith. It is perhaps harder to understand why many blacks have any faith left that the nation can at last undertake to "secure the Blessings of Liberty to ourselves and our Posterity."

That there remains such faith—and in a time of unexampled peril to our Constitution that faith is our last best hope—is made plain in the closing words of a speech Dick Gregory gave, in December of 1967, to the Yale senior class:

> *You see, America ain't nothing but a cigarette machine now: you can't communicate with her. You know if you're running through the airport and put 40 cents in the cigarette machine, pull it and you don't get cigarettes, that's a funny feeling when you can't talk to that machine. You go up to the ticket counter, and you say, "Look, I just put my money in the cigarette machine," and the girl says, "Look, I work for TWA, I just write tickets, I have nothing to do with that machine." You say, "Well, look miss, somebody tell me." She says, "Well, look, go back and look at the little mirror there, you see yourself and there's a little message to tell you what to do if you blow your dough." And you go back and there it is. "Welcome to Hartford, Connecticut. In case of problems with this machine, call Giddings Jones, Kansas City, Missouri." Now you hear the last call for your flight and you stand there looking at that cigarette machine that you can't relate with and that's got your 40 cents and your flight's leaving, so you do the normal thing—you kick that machine—pow. You didn't get no money, but you see that old dent in it and you feel pretty good. You go on down there and get your plane feeling, well, you feel mellow. Let me tell you something, when you kick that machine, if that machine had kicked you back, you would have cancelled your flight and taken that damn machine outside and torn it up in little pieces. Now, let's see if this is funny. America is a cigarette machine to us. We didn't put 40 cents in it to get something that was going to make us sick, we put 400 years of our lives in that machine, baby, to get something that was going to make us well, and we didn't get nothing, man, and we went to every ticket counter and they kept sending us to Kansas City, so in the form of Detroit, Watts, and Chicago we kicked that machine and in the form of the National Guard and the police that machine kicked us back, and we're going to do the same thing you would. We say, cancel the flight, we're going to break this machine up in little, bitty pieces, that's what we say.*
>
> *A free man is nothing but a man with no fears. If a man fears me living in his neighborhood, eating in his restaurants, dating his daughter, going to his schools, he's my slave whether he wants to be one or not. And he's more my slave than my ancestors ever were to his, because when my forefathers broke that chain off the black ankle and split to Canada they were free. Once you become enslaved in your head, you never get free. A white cracker from America can go to Moscow, Russia, man, and see a nigger with a white woman,*

and he goes crazy because he takes his enslavement with him all over the world.

I go all over but this is the first time I've talked to a group where 98 per cent is fixing to be dumped into the system, and that's why I feel it's so extremely important. I'm very bitter, and I'm very angry. I don't hate America. I don't go for "isms." I imagine if I was born in Russia, I'd probably be fighting just as hard to clean Russia up, but this is my home and I don't intend to go anywhere. But I do see all the mistakes that we left on you, and I hope that you will rectify them. It's a hell of a thing to ask you, but I hope you will for the benefit of the whole world, because the Constitution of the United States is a good piece of paper. No one has ever made it work right yet, and I say, let's do make it right. We might decide to tear it up after we do it, but let's first make it right. [*Gregory, "Let's First Make it Right,"* Yale Alumni Magazine *(February, 1968) 37.*]

III

As these biographical studies of ninety-seven Justices go to press, the centennial year of the Fourteenth Amendment has just passed. It was an anniversary to be observed; we are not yet entitled to celebrate it.

In the Fall of 1968, there was televised a filmed interview of Justice Hugo Black. He spoke of many things. At one point he had this to say:

I do know that a study of history convinces me that nations have risen, their stars have gone up, and then they begin to grow dimmer. Particularly if they get too big and try to run the world. I hope this nation will have a longer life than all of them. Nobody knows.

Table of Contents

VOLUME I

VOLUME II

VOLUME III

VOLUME IV

See Volume V, p. vii for Volume V Table of Contents

THE JUSTICES OF THE UNITED STATES SUPREME COURT 1789-1969

Their Lives and Major Opinions

John Jay

☆ 1745–1829 ☆

APPOINTED BY

GEORGE WASHINGTON

YEARS ON COURT

1789–1795

John Jay

by
IRVING DILLIARD

FEW MEN have participated as fully in the public life of their time as John Jay. Possessed of one of the great provincial fortunes, he was a handsome and graceful man, regarded by his contemporaries as modest and cultivated. The first Chief Justice left to that office and to his country an extraordinary record of public service: the only notable office in the colonial, state, and federal governments that Jay was not called upon to fill was that of Chief Executive. Yet, although a term in the Presidency would have given Jay a more prominent place in political history, he made many worthy contributions in the areas of policy formation, lawmaking, administration, diplomacy, and jurisprudence.

In his political and judicial career, one major assignment followed another with kaleidoscopic variety and swiftness. Already a member of the New York Committee of Correspondence, John Jay was twenty-nine when he served as delegate to the First Continental Congress in 1774, and a year later he was returned to serve in the Second Continental Congress. During the next two years, 1776–1777, he was a delegate to the New York Provincial Congress (The New York Convention). In 1777 he left that post to become Chief Justice of the Supreme Court of New York, and served on its bench until 1779. In 1778, during a grave phase of the Revolutionary War, Jay served as president of the Continental Congress, the chief civilian post in the rebelling colonies.

In less than a year the Continental Congress selected Jay as Minister to Spain, in the hope that he could win diplomatic recognition and assistance for the new government. Many diplomatic missions followed until, in 1782, Jay became a Joint Commissioner at the peace conference in Paris to negotiate the treaty with Great Britain which ended the Revolutionary War.

IRVING DILLIARD, former reporter and editor of the St. Louis Post-Dispatch *editorial page, is Ferris Professor and Senior Fellow in the Council of the Humanities at Princeton University. He is a former trustee of the University of Illinois. He has published numerous articles and is the author of books on Supreme Court Justices Brandeis and Black and Judge Learned Hand.*

Abroad for most of the next two years, Jay returned home in 1784 to find that the Continental Congress had elected him Secretary for Foreign Affairs and Secretary of State *ad interim*. He held this post until the new government abolished it in 1789. Jay had collaborated with James Madison and Alexander Hamilton in late 1787 and early 1788 in writing *The Federalist Papers,* key documents in the adoption of the federal Constitution. When the Constitution was ratified and the infant nation established, George Washington chose Jay to be the first Chief Justice of the United States, and Jay headed the Supreme Court during the crucial formative years of its existence. His tenure on the Court was interrupted in 1794, when he was sent to England to resolve diplomatic conflicts which threatened renewed hostilities. In 1795 Jay returned home and resigned from the Chief Justiceship in order to become governor of New York. He administered this most populous of the new states through two terms, from 1795 to 1801. In 1800 Jay declined a formal renomination to the post of Chief Justice by President John Adams, and the appointment then went to John Marshall.

The patriot who compiled this record of service to his country did not seek a public career. It was truly thrust upon him. The one post that he actively and successfully sought was appointment to a commission as colonel in the New York State Militia. He might have preferred his own law practice and the enjoyments of private life as a member of the colonial aristocracy, but the Jays had traditionally associated themselves with the struggle for freedom. John Jay's great grandfather was Pierre Jay, a Huguenot merchant of La Rochelle, France. When the Edict of Nantes was revoked in 1685 and most of his property taken from him, Pierre Jay went to England in voluntary exile where he found hospitality and refuge until his death. His son Augustus, John Jay's grandfather, arrived in New York in 1686. There he married Anna Maria Bayard, a descendant of a French professor of theology who had left Paris for the sake of his Protestant faith and had lived in Holland.

Augustus Jay became a prosperous merchant engaged in importing, exporting, and retailing. Peter, his son and John Jay's father, did so well with a partnership in the family business that he could retire at the age of forty, "a gentleman of opulence, character and reputation." By 1740 Peter Jay's name was on the roll of the Aldermen of New York. His wife was Mary Van Cortlandt, daughter of Jacobus Van Cortlandt and a member of one of New York's most influential Dutch families. Five of John Jay's great grandparents were Dutch and three were French; it is a notable fact that not one of his immediate ancestors was English.

The life of Peter and Mary Van Cortlandt Jay was mildly political and devoutly religious. In a letter to John's older brother James, the father wrote: "Let us endeavor to adhere to the worship of God, and, observing his holy ordinances as the rule of our lives, let us disregard the wicked insinuations of libertines, who not only deride our most Holy Religion and the professors of it, but also endeavor to gain prosilites to their detestable notions, and so rob the Almighty of the honour and adoration that is due to him from his creatures."

John Jay, the sixth son and eighth child in the family, was born in the city of New York on December 12, 1745. The father retired from business that year and the family moved to the Jay farmstead at Rye. The old house was "a long, low building, but one room deep," the rooms being added as a growing family required. John survived serious childhood illnesses that caused the death or blindness of three of his siblings. His mother taught him English and Latin grammar. His father described him at seven as "of a very grave disposition." He noted that the boy "gives me a very pleasing prospect," and further that "he seems to be endowed with a very good capacity" and "quite of his brother James' disposition for books."

John's first formal school was conducted by the pastor of the French Huguenot Church at New Rochelle, the Swiss Reverend Peter Stoope. The language of the village of refugees as well as that of the parsonage was French and young John learned it well during the three years that he lived in the minister's home and school. At fourteen, John entered King's College (forerunner of Columbia University) for which his brother James had raised funds in England. He had already determined to pursue law as a career when, shortly before graduation in 1764, he was charged with disobedience for not informing on fellow students who had destroyed college property. In defense of his refusal to testify, Jay pointed out that the college rules did not obligate him to inform against students with whom he associated. Even though he appeared to have the proper interpretation of the rules on his side, the school suspended him and then allowed him to return for the commencement exercises at which he spoke on the benefits of peace. In the audience were General Gage, the King's Council, and other notable representatives of the Colonial authority of George III.

Jay's future at the bar was so promising that he was taken into the prominent law office of Benjamin Kissam. One of his young colleagues, Lindley Murray, recalling their student days together, later wrote: "He was remarkable for strong reasoning powers, comprehensive views, indefatigable application, and uncommon firmness of mind." Jay was admitted to practice in 1768. He formed a short-term partnership with Robert R. Livingston, but often assisted Kissam in legal matters. Kissam took a strong liking to his young clerk and the relationship was a happy one. Long afterward Jay, in a letter presenting a son of Kissam to John Adams, wrote that young Kissam's father was "one of the best men I have ever known, as well as one of the best friends I ever had."

By the early 1770's Jay was an established lawyer enjoying the spirited cultural life of New York. There he met and fell in love with the beautiful Sarah Van Brugh Livingston, whose father, William Livingston, was to become Governor of New Jersey during the Revolution. The marriage, which took place April 28, 1774 at "Liberty Hall," Elizabeth, New Jersey, brought together two prominent colonial families. In the wedding reports Jay, although only twenty-eight years old, was called "an eminent barrister." The description borrowed from the future, but not too heavily, for by this time Jay had already entered his first public service. In 1773 he had become secretary of a royal commission established to adjudicate a boundary dispute between New York and New Jersey. A study of Jay's later diplomatic work showed him using mixed commissions which he first saw employed in the arbitration between these two colonies.

This service for the colonies actually foretold the end of Jay's private practice of law. With the coming of the Revolution, he ceased to work for himself and his family and devoted himself to public eauses. His position on relations with the mother country was that of a moderate, although his fellow members of the New York Committee of Correspondence regarded him as a conservative. But Jay moved with events, and from 1774 to 1776 events moved unmistakably toward independence.

More than most men, Jay remained sensitive to the wide diversity of opinion among his fellow colonists. Indeed he was so considerate of the views of others that he protested when a motion was made to open the First Continental Congress with prayer. Jay was probably as devoutly religious as any delegate, but he objected, as John Adams wrote, "because we were so divided in religious sentiments." Though Jay's caution did not prevail on that occasion, the incident illustrated the regard of the young New Yorker for all shades of opinion.

Jay's name did not appear among the signers of the Declaration of Independence because he was in the New York Provincial Congress at the time, helping draft that state's constitution. He did, however, work for approval of the Declaration by the New York Congress. A few days after his return to the Continental Congress in December, 1778 Jay was elected its president and in less than a year he was sent on the mission to Spain. At the outset there was almost no prospect of substantial success in persuading Spain to recognize the independence of the colonies or in obtaining economic aid on a large scale. But Spain did continue secretly its modest assistance in arms and money and so some small benefit was gained even though it could not be pointed to publicly. The experience provided training for Jay in negotiation and international affairs.

That generally unrewarding diplomatic venture came to an end in 1782 when Franklin called Jay to Paris as joint commissioner to work out a peace treaty with the British. Jay's first contribution was a significant one although it held up the start of serious deliberations on terms: he took the position that the designation "colonies" be dropped and that Great Britain recognize that it must deal with "the United States." He won his point even though it did not seem important at first to Franklin. Jay had the ear of the Earl of Shelburne, then Prime Minister, and was able to make his voice heard from time to time in the negotiations. These were complicated, involving not only the United States and Britain and delicate boundary problems in the New World, but also France and Spain and Gibraltar. Jay and the other members of the negotiating groups patiently persisted in their efforts, and the result was the 1783 Treaty of Paris.

The war with Britain officially ended, Jay planned to return to private law practice and live again with his family. This dream vanished when he found, on his return from Europe in mid-1784, that the Continental Congress had voted him Secretary for Foreign Affairs. Once again he fell to work. He learned quickly that the treaty he had helped negotiate with the British had to be enforced. Accords had to be achieved with other countries on commercial and diplomatic exchanges.

From these international dealings with Britain, France and particularly Spain, the new Secretary of Foreign Affairs recognized the weakness of the Articles of Confederation and foresaw the need for a new government that would bring the colonies, now called states, into a closer, more dependable union.

Through the summer of 1787, while the Constitutional Convention deliberated in Philadelphia, Jay continued to serve in the important post of Secretary of Foreign Affairs for the confederated colonies. But by late September, almost as soon as the proposed national charter was completed, signed by the delegates, and submitted for ratification to the colonial conventions, Jay joined James Madison and Alexander Hamilton in an imaginative enterprise crucial to the Constitution's adoption. The three men took part in writing one of the most significant documents in American history.

The need for a series of expository essays like these on the philosophy behind the provisions of the Constitution could hardly have been plainer. For although the handiwork of Washington, Franklin, Madison, Randolph, Wilson, and the other delegates had many devoted supporters, a relatively large number of adversaries denounced it. Some of these were sincere opponents of a strong central government, but others engaged in ill-informed and intemperate attacks for partisan if not merely selfish reasons. Approval of the Constitution by a required nine of the thirteen Colonies was not at all assured. Jay's home colony of New York was sharply divided: New York City and Long Island were Federalist and therefore pro-Constitution; rural upper New York bitterly opposed the Constitution and even spoke of lower New York as a separate governmental entity.

Jay was the perfect collaborator in several ways. As a New Yorker he knew well his fellow colonists. He was not a delegate to the Constitutional Convention like Hamilton and Madison—so he could contribute to the project detachment and perspective. He was experienced in the judiciary of New York and in foreign relations under the Articles of the Confederation, topics that required exposition. In the years of the Revolution he was essentially a moderate whose views developed in part with the trend of events. Lawyer, judge, and diplomat, he was trained in writing clearly, precisely, and persuasively.

To answer the verbal assaults on the Constitution which began to appear in the journals of New York and vicinity, the three collaborators prepared and printed *The Federalist Papers* in the New York press. They remained in New York City throughout the fall, winter and spring, 1787–1788, developing their arguments. These answering essays were addressed "To the People of the State of New York" and were signed "Publius." Their manifest purpose was to convince the citizens of New York and their delegates of the necessity for approving the Constitution when it came before them for action. But although the essays were reprinted first in New York, they soon appeared in other journals throughout the states. In time, the arguments of Jay and his colleagues reached to remote places, including even backwoods regions.

The first essay, by Hamilton, appeared on October 27, 1787, in the New York semi-weekly, *The Independent Journal.* Jay wrote Nos. 2 through 5 and No. 64. Madison and Hamilton contributed the others, though several are not clearly identifiable by author. The names of the three writers soon became known.

Jay's first paper followed Hamilton's by only four days. It described the existing government as "deficient and inadequate" to serve "this one connected country, this one united people" who "by their joint counsels, arms and efforts, fighting side by side throughout a long and bloody war, have nobly established their general Liberty and Independence." In Nos. 3, 4 and 5, Jay took up aspects of national security and relations with other countries. Though mild in manner, Jay was firm and realistic in his attitudes. In *Federalist* No. 5 he sounded a warning that "in America, as in Europe, neighboring nations, acting under the impulse of opposite interest, and unfriendly passions, would frequently be found taking different sides."

Jay was not robust, and illness, perhaps the dyspepsia which troubled him throughout his life, interrupted his participation in *The Federalist Papers.* But after an interval he returned to write one of the most urgent of the arguments. In No. 64 he addressed himself to those critics whose "fears and apprehensions" arose from the provision in the Constitution for the conduct of foreign affairs by the President including the power to make treaties "by and with the consent of the Senate." To opponents of the Constitution who said that treaties should not be supreme laws of the land, but "like acts of the assembly, should be repealable at pleasure," Jay replied:

> *These gentlemen would do well to reflect that a treaty is only another name for a bargain; and that it would be impossible to find a nation who would make any bargain with us, which should be binding on them* absolutely, *but on us only so long and so far as we may think proper to be bound by it.*

The contention of some critics that the President and Senate could not be trusted with authority which could potentially so control the lives of the people, Jay answered clearly and wisely:

> *In proportion as the United States assume a national form, and a national character, so will the good of the whole be more and more an object of attention; and the government must be a weak one indeed, if it should forget that the good of the whole can only be promoted by advancing the good of each of the parts or members which compose the whole. It will not be in the power of the President and Senate to make any treaties, by which they and their families and estates will not be equally bound and affected with the rest of the community; and having no private interest distinct from that of the nation, they will be under no temptation to neglect the latter.*

To increase their circulation still further, the authors collected *The Federalist Papers* in book form, a first volume of thirty-six essays on March 22, 1788 and a second of forty-nine on May 28. Meantime the states began the ratifying process with Delaware leading the way on December 7, 1787. The process in New York went much more slowly. In its behalf, Jay, who had been overwhelmingly elected a delegate to the state convention by New York City voters in April, prepared and issued on his own initiative, but without his signature, an "Address to the People of the State of New York." This single pamphlet, simply and logically written, summarized the case for the Constitution in compact form. Franklin was so impressed by it that he urged Jay to disclose his authorship for additional impact. Jay's reply was characteristic: "If the reasoning is sound, it will have its effect on candid and discerning minds; if weak and inconclusive, my name will not render it otherwise." Without his name, Jay's summary and conclusion, so a contemporary observer wrote, had "a most astonishing influence in converting anti-Federalists to a knowledge and belief that the new Constitution was their only salvation."

The struggle in the New York convention at Poughkeepsie lasted forty days. It was an ordeal for Jay and Hamilton, but finally, on July 26, their efforts produced a victorious result even though by the close margin of thirty to twenty-seven. From Mount Vernon, Washington wrote to Jay: "With peculiar pleasure I now congratulate you on the success of your labors to obtain an unconditional ratification." With the perspective of more than a quarter century, John Adams wrote in 1815: "I forbore to mention one of more importance than any of the rest, indeed of almost as much weight as all the rest. I mean Mr. Jay. That gentlemen had as much influence in the preparatory measures in digesting the Constitution, and obtaining its adoption, as any man in the nation. His known familiarity with Madison and Hamilton, his connection with all the members of the old Congress, have given to these writings [*The Federalist*] more consideration than both the other writers could have given to them." Had it not been for that memorable series of political essays and also for Jay's work prior to and during the New York convention, New York and probably several other close states would have voted against the Constitution. Clearly, Jay contributed a service of inestimable value to the new plan of government at its most critical time.

The ratification of the Constitution by the ninth state set machinery in motion for the selection of presidential electors by the states. Again Jay was involved, his time as one of the Federalist leaders on whom the responsibiilty for suggestion and counsel rested. When the electors met in January, 1789 to choose the President and Vice President, major attention centered on the preeminent hero of the Revolutionary War, General Washington, who had so recently concluded his duties as president of the Constitutional Convention. Washington received all sixty-nine of the presidential votes in the Electoral College; John Adams received the largest number of second-place votes, thirty-four, and so became Vice President.

In the interval between the election and the inauguration of the new government, Washington relied heavily on the advice of John Jay. The President particularly sought Jay's opinions on the organization of the Department of State and offered him the post of Secretary. Suited though the position was to his talents and experience, Jay declined.

After designating Jefferson as Secretary of State, Washington returned to Jay to fill the new post of Chief Justice of the United States. Notwithstanding their lack of experience with such an office, a substantial field of applicants either urged themselves on the President or were strongly recommended to him by their friends: James Wilson of Pennsylvania proposed himself, supporters of John Rutledge of South Carolina set forth his qualifications. Some backed Robert R. Livingston of New York, while still others advanced Robert Hanson Harrison of Maryland. But Washington decided not to take any unnecessary risks in selecting the chief judge of the highest court. If the Supreme Court was to interpret the laws and the actions of executive officials, the judiciary might well become a center of controversy between the Federalists and Antifederalists over a strong central government. As to this issue, the position of Jay was unmistakable, and so Washington selected his New York friend for the Chief Justiceship.

The organic Judiciary Act of the First Congress provided the "one Supreme Court" with six members, the Chief Justice and five Associate Justices. Washington signed the bill into law on September 24, 1789 and on the same day nominated Jay to be the first Chief Justice. Confirmation came two days later. Addressing Jay as Chief Justice "with singular pleasure" and enclosing his commission, Washington wrote to his forty-three year old friend and adviser:

> *In nominating you for the important station which you now fill, I not only acted in conformity to my best judgment, but I trust I did a grateful thing to the good citizens of these United States; and I have a full confidence that the love which you bear to our country, and a desire to promote the general happiness, will not suffer you to hesitate a moment to bring into action the talents, knowledge and integrity which are so necessary to be exercised at the head of that department which must be considered as the keystone of our political fabric.*

To this strong and moving testimonial from President Washington, Jay replied:

> *When distinguished discernment and patriotism unite in selecting men for stations of trust and dignity, they derive honor not only from their offices, but from the hand which confers them. With a mind and a heart impressed with these reflections and their correspondent sensations, I assure you that the sentiments expressed in your letter of yesterday and implied by the commission it enclosed, will never cease to excite my best endeavours to fulfill the duties imposed by the latter, and as far as may be in my power, to realize the expectations which your nominations especially to important places, must naturally create.*

Washington was so pleased to have Jay in the Chief Justiceship that he wrote to Lafayette that the appointment of Jay to the Supreme Court and of Jefferson, Hamilton and Knox as members of his Cabinet "generally have given perfect satisfaction to the public."

Chief Justice Jay and two of his five colleagues, Associate Justices William Cushing of Massachusetts and James Wilson of Pennsylvania, attended the convening of the Supreme Court, February 1, 1790, in the Royal Exchange

Building at the foot of Broad Street in New York City. A quorum was obtained the next day with the arrival of Associate Justice John Blair from Virginia, along with the first Attorney General, Edmund Randolph. The jurists were in proper robes and the high Bench met before a throng of spectators including both bar and laity. The ranks of the Associate Justices were completed with the subsequent participation of Washington's other appointee, James Iredell of North Carolina, successor to the seat of Robert Hanson Harrison who had declined the federal post to be Chancellor of Maryland. (John Rutledge of South Carolina, the senior Associate Justice, never attended a meeting of the Court and resigned in 1791 to be replaced by Thomas Johnson of Maryland.)

Although Washington could not have foreseen the ultimate importance of the Supreme Court, it is manifest from his selections and letters to Jay and the others that he gave his judicial choices the most thoughtful consideration. All the men he chose had been intimately associated with the drafting or ratification of the Constitution. Three of the six, Wilson, Blair, and Rutledge, were delegates to the Philadelphia Convention and signed its charter of government. Jay, Wilson, Cushing, and Iredell led campaigns for approval in their states. Jay and three of the others had sat on colonial courts. The Justices were at the peak of their powers, the ages of the six ranging from thirty-eight to fifty-seven.

With no case before it, the first session was largely ceremonial, and after ten days Chief Justice Jay and his colleagues adjourned for six months. The newspapers of New York and Philadelphia, however, displayed much interest in the new judiciary, reporting that the press devoted more attention to the first session of the Supreme Court than to "any other event connected with the new Government." Newspapers throughout the new nation reprinted these dispatches.

Although the Chief Justice, John Jay also had to perform circuit court duty established by the first Judiciary Act of Congress. His territory included New York and New England, a circuit bench consisting of two Justices of the Supreme Court and one district court judge. Jay made one of his most notable judicial pronouncements in a charge to a grand jury on federal circuit in New York on April 4, 1790. He spoke on that occasion these memorable words:

> *Let it be remembered that civil liberty consists not in a right to every man to do just what he pleases; but it consists in an equal right to all the citizens to have, enjoy, and do, in peace, security and without molestation, whatever the equal and constitutional laws of the country admit to be consistent with the public good.*

The Chief Justice was most hospitably received as he went on his circuit. Friends and admirers showered him with invitations for entertainment. These he graciously but firmly declined, unwilling to contend with even the appearance of embarrassing obligations. He did accept an honorary doctorate degree from Harvard College in the belief that this properly recognized his federal position. After the second term, which opened on August 2, 1790, and also had almost no case work, he rode circuit again with sessions in Albany, Hartford, Providence, Boston and Exeter. Jay and the Associate Justices listed as the first case on their docket, *Van Staphorst* v. *State of Maryland* in the February, 1791 term when the seat of government moved from New York to Philadelphia. The case, however, did not go to a decision from the bench as the contending parties settled their differences by agreement.

Since the Supreme Court remained virtually without cases during its first year or so, it is remarkable that Chief Justice Jay and his colleagues found it necessary as early as they did to assert the jurisdiction of the Supreme Court over both state and federal legislation. Application of the federal judiciary's authority in the field of state legislation came as early as May, 1791 in the circuit court rather than the Supreme Court. In that first instance, the federal circuit court held in an unreported case that an act of the Connecticut Legislature violated the terms of the peace treaty with England. A contemporary newspaper account said that the case presented "the great and much litigated question whether obligations in favor of real British subjects or those who had joined the armies of Great Britain during the war, should draw interest during the time the creditors were inaccessible by reason of the war. In this case, the Court adjudged that the statute law of Connecticut enabling the state courts to add interest in such cases was an infringement of the treaty of peace, and that upon common law principles interest was recoverable. The learned and ingenious arguments from the bench on this question were highly interesting and gave general satisfaction."

Chief Justice Jay, Justice Cushing, and District Judge Henry Marchant, sitting as a circuit court in Rhode Island, unanimously reaffirmed this supremacy of the federal authority over state law a year later. In June, 1792, in the case of *Champion and Dickason* v. *Casey* (referred to in 1 Warren *The Supreme Court in United States History*, 67) they invalidated a Rhode Island law as a violation of the constitutional provision against impairing the obligation of contracts. A Rhode Island debtor had petitioned the legislature for an extension of three years for the satisfaction of his obligations to his creditors, including immunity from arrests and penalties during the extension. A newspaper report of the decision by Jay and his two colleagues on the circuit court said that they held that "the legislature of a state have no right to make a law to exempt an individual from arrests and his estate from attachments for his private debts, for any term of time, it being clearly a law impairing the obligation of contracts, and therefore contrary to the Constitution of the United States."

In the eyes of the Chief Justice, an act of Congress had to pass the same test of constitutionality. In April, 1791, as he presided on circuit in New York City, Jay, without dissent from his colleagues, rejected an act of Congress which called on Supreme Court Justices on circuit to pass on applications for invalid pensions. Jay and his fellow judges took the position that Congress did not have the authority to assign to the courts "any duties but such as are properly judicial, and to be performed in a judicial manner." That opinion of the circuit court over which Jay presided anticipated Chief Justice John Marshall's famous 1803 decision in *Marbury* v. *Madison* by saying:

> *. . . the duties assigned to the Circuit Courts by this act are not of that description . . . inasmuch as it subjects the decisions of these courts, made pursuant to those duties, first to the consideration and suspension of the Secretary at War, and then to the revision of the Legislature; whereas, by the Constitution, neither the Secretary at War, nor any other executive officer, nor even the Legislature, are authorized to sit as a court of errors on the judicial acts or opinions of this Court.*

The issue of the constitutionality of this assignment by Congress to the circuit courts came before the Supreme Court in *Hayburn's Case,* 2 Dall. 410 (1792), where the earlier circuit court opinion of Chief Justice Jay, Justice Cushing, and District Judge Duane was also recorded. But by that time Congress had "provided, in another way," for the relief of the pensioners, and so solved the problem it had created. Constitutional history was made in this controversy and made because the Supreme Court Justices and their district court colleagues held respectfully but firmly to the separation of the national government into three co-ordinate branches. In so doing, the judges of Chief Justice Jay's tenure erected the signpost that John Marshall was to follow more than a decade later.

Clear and staunch in his views that the Supreme Court could and should declare an act of Congress unconstitutional if the occasion arose, Jay was equally ready to take a strong stand against an executive plea which he also considered to be in violation of the Constitution. The specific question in the latter instance was whether the Supreme Court should render an advisory opinion upon request from the executive branch or issue no opinion unless the Court had first heard a duly accepted case brought up through the courts by parties to a suit at law.

Hamilton, as Secretary of the Treasury, strenuously opposed the critical resolutions passed by the Virginia House of Representatives with respect to federal responsibility for state and public debts. The Virginia legislators resolved officially that a congressional bill for assumption of the debts of the states was "repugnant to the Constitution." A companion resolution denounced a proposal for federal redemption of the public debt as "dangerous to the rights and subversive of the interests of the people." Hamilton turned to Jay and, in effect, asked for the support of the Supreme Court. Writing to the Chief Justice on November 13, 1790 he said:

> *This is the first symptom of a spirit which must either be killed or it will kill the Constitution of the United States. I send the resolutions to you that it may be considered what ought to be done. Ought not the collective weight of the different parts of the Government to be employed in exploding the principles they contain? This question arises out of sudden and undigested thought.*

Jay, by contrast, remained calm and deliberate and wholly unafraid. His answer to Hamilton was a model of restraint. As Chief Justice, he replied:

> *Having no apprehension of such measures, what was to be done appeared to me to be a question of some difficulty as well as importance; to treat them as very important might render them more so than I think they are. The assumption will do its own work; it will justify itself and not want advocates. Every*

indecent interference of State Assemblies will diminish their influence; the National Government has only to do what is right, and, if possible, be silent. If compelled to speak, it should be in a few words, strongly envinced of temper, dignity and self-respect.

Jay was so firm in his belief in the separation of powers, and hence the complete independence of the judiciary, that he later declined President Washington's request for advice on the European war and how to maintain peace in the United States in the following blunt words to Secretary of State Jefferson:

Owing to the duties of the Supreme Court and the executive branch of the government. . . . Supreme Court Justices would not give him [*the President*] *any advice about the war in Europe and they believed that under the Constitution he ought to get that advice from the heads of the departments, that is the cabinet members.*

And so the first Chief Justice, and with him the Supreme Court, took at the outset a stand against responding to requests from the Executive Department for advisory opinions.

Although these decisions voiding acts of Congress or state legislatures were of precedent-setting importance in the life of the new nation, historians have paid most attention to Jay's part in a case overridden by the Eleventh Amendment. This latter decision came in *Chisholm* v. *Georgia,* 2 Dall. 419 (1793). The question was whether a state could be sued by individual citizens of another state. It grew out of a lawsuit by the estate of Alexander Chisholm to force Georgia to pay claims of the Chisholm executors which they contended were due from the state of Georgia. The constitutional basis of the suit was the provision in the Constitution, Article III, Section 2, which extended the jurisdiction of United States cases to include those "between a State and Citizens of another State."

The Salem (S.C.) *Gazettee* of March 6, 1793, described the facts of the case as follows:

A citizen of Georgia had left America prior to the Revolution and removed to Great Britain, after settling a partnership account with two partners in trade whose bonds he took for the balance due. After his decease, his executors (*who were citizens of South Carolina*) *on making application for payment found that these two persons who had given their joint bonds had been inimical to the cause of liberty in the United States and that their property was confiscated. The executors, alleging that the bonds were given previous to the Revolution, applied to the State of Georgia for relief.*

When the case went before the Supreme Court, Attorney General Edmund Randolph appeared on behalf of the Chisholm heirs, but Georgia, refusing to become a party to the suit, presented only a "remonstrance and protestation" that the Supreme Court lacked jurisdiction. In the face of widespread opposition in the states, the Court sustained the right of citizens of one state to sue another state. Chief Justice Jay and four other members of the Court made up the majority, Justice Iredell being the only dissenter. Although the Supreme Court seemingly had the language of the Constitution on its side, the fact remained that when opposition to the clause at issue arose in the conventions held in the states for the purpose of passing on the Constitution, the Federalists had promised their critics that the words would not be interpreted to mean that a citizen of one state might sue another state. Marshall, for example, had assured the Virginia Convention that it was "not rational to suppose that the sovereign power should be dragged before a court. The intent is to enable states to recover claims of [against] individuals residing in other states."

Jay used the occasion to analyze the nature of the Union and its constitutional compact which bound the states into a federal whole. He said:

> *Every State Constitution is a compact made by and between the citizens of a State to govern themselves in a certain manner; and the Constitution of the* United States *is likewise a compact made by the people of the* United States *to govern themselves as to general objects in a certain manner. . . . The sovereignty of the nation is* [*in*] *the people of the nation, and the residuary sovereignty of each state* [*is*] *in the people of each State.*

The Chief Justice continued, saying that the people of the United States, "acting as sovereigns of the whole country," established a "Constitution by which it was their will, that the State Governments should be bound, and to which the State Constitutions should be made to conform."

It was clear in Jay's mind that the words of the Constitution were intended to permit just such a suit as that filed by the Chisholm heirs. He reasoned that if the Constitution permitted all the people of a state to sue another state, "it plainly follows that suability and State sovereignty are not incompatible." He further contended that if it was the intention of the Constitution to limit the jurisdiction of the United States in "controversies between a State and citizens of another State," to disputes with the state as a plaintiff, it was "inconceivable that it should have attempted to convey that meaning in words . . . so incompetent." He wrote in the opinion: "Words are to be understood in their ordinary and common acceptation, and the word party, being in common usage applicable to both plaintiff and defendant, we cannot limit it to one of them. . . . If that [party plaintiff] only was meant, it would have been easy to have found words to express it."

The governor of Georgia did not wait for the decision to begin a campaign to overturn it. While the case was pending in the Supreme Court, he called on the legislature of his state to invite other states to join Georgia in proposing a constitutional amendment to forbid such suits. As similar suits had been filed in Maryland, Massachusetts, New York, South Carolina, and Virginia, the invitation from Georgia met a wide welcome. Immediately after the decision a resolution to amend the Constitution was introduced in Congress, its language expressly declaring that "the judicial power of the United States shall not be construed to extend to any suit in law or equity, commenced or prosecuted against one of the United States by citizens of another state, or by citizens or subjects of any foreign State." This rejection of the decision—the congressional resolution was declared ratified and became the Eleventh Amendment in 1798—was a setback to the Supreme Court and it took time to recover the lost prestige.

Chief Justice Jay, however, was not devastated by the resort of Congress and the states to the amending process as a means of overturning the *Chisholm* decision. He believed the duty of the Supreme Court was to interpret and apply the Constitution and to leave it to Congress and the states to use their own best judgment in determining constitutional changes. And so he went on to other work in hand. The ink was hardly dry on *Chisholm* before he was deep in the international issue that produced, in all probability, Jay's most important Supreme Court opinion. The essential question in *Glass* v. *The Sloop Betsey,* 3 Dall. 6 (1794) was whether the United States courts had jurisdiction over prize vessels captured and brought into its ports or whether foreign consuls stationed in the United States had this authority on American soil.

Feelings were running high between French and British sympathizers in the infant nation in 1793 when a French privateer captured *The Betsey,* owned by neutral Swedes, and with a cargo belonging to neutral Swedish citizens and the United States, and took her to Baltimore as a prize. The owners filed a complaint against the action and asked the United States District Court to function as a court of admiralty and to entertain the complaint. The French consul contended he had international right to adjudicate the seized ship and cargo as a prize. When the United States District Court in Maryland held that it was without jurisdiction over French prizes, it undercut President Washington's policy of strict neutrality in the French-British struggle. Because of the importance of the question, the case was appealed at once to the Supreme Court where it attracted much attention. Outstanding counsel argued the case over most of a week.

In his opinion for a unanimous Court which reversed the district court, Chief Justice Jay said that "besides the question of jurisdiction as to the District Court, another question fairly arose upon the record, whether any foreign nation had a right without the positive stipulation of a treaty, to establish in this country, an admiralty jurisdiction for taking cognizance of prizes captured on the high seas, by its subjects or citizens, from its enemies." On the latter question, the Jay opinion held "that the admiralty jurisdiction which has been exercised in the United States by the Consuls of France, not being so warranted, is not of right." When he took his long look at the history of the Supreme Court, Charles Warren wrote of *Glass* v. *The Sloop Betsey:* "No decision of the Court ever did more to vindicate our international rights, to establish respect amongst other nations for the sovereignty of this country, and to keep the United States out of international complications."

In the same term, Jay spoke for the Court in *Georgia* v. *Brailsford,* 3 Dall. 1 (1794), which, like the *Chisholm* case, also concerned the sovereignty of Georgia. The alien plaintiff was a British creditor who brought suit against a citizen of Georgia in the United States circuit court to require payment of a debt sequestrated by Georgia. In the *Brailsford* case the position of Georgia was substantially different from its position in *Chisholm.* In *Chisholm* Georgia resisted being made a party to the suit brought by non-residents of Georgia. But in the *Brailsford* case, Georgia sought to become a party to the suit, claiming it owned the debt through the operation of its sequestration law, but the Court initially ruled against it. The Supreme Court apparently disliked to rule against Georgia a second time in such a short span and so arranged for trial on the merits before a special jury. Chief Justice Jay's devotion to a just settlement was plain from his charge to the jury:

> *Some stress has been laid on a consideration of the different situations of the parties to the cause: The State of Georgia sues three private persons. But what is it to justice, how many, or how few; how high, or how low; how rich, or how poor; the contending parties may chance to be? Justice is indiscriminately due to all, without regard to numbers, wealth or rank. Because to the State of Georgia, composed of many thousands of people, the litigated sum cannot be of great moment, you will not for this reason be justified, in deciding against her claim; if the money belongs to her, she ought to have it; but on the other hand, no consideration of the circumstances or of the comparative insignificance of the defendants, can be a ground to deny them the advantage of a favourable verdict, if in justice they are entitled to it.*

With this strong charge to do justice bearing upon it, the jury ruled for Brailsford, the alien creditor. The claim of Georgia was rejected, the holding being that debts were not confiscated by a sequestration law, neither was title vested in a state by such a law. Even so there must have been reassurance for the states in Jay's words that justice was the first goal of the federal judiciary.

In 1792, Jay was persuaded by his friends to run for governor of New York against George Clinton who had been chief executive of the state for fifteen years. To keep his candidacy from embarrassing his position as Chief Justice, Jay set the condition that he would not campaign in any way for the office. Nevertheless he soon found it necessary to refute a political charge that he intended, in the slave-holding state of New York, immediately to free the slaves, not a few of whom were held by the Dutch landowners. On emancipation, Jay said:

> *Every man, of every color and description, has a natural right to freedom, and I shall ever acknowledge myself to be an advocate for the manumission of slaves in such a way as may be consistent with the justice due to them, with the justice due their masters, and with the regard due to the actual state of society. These considerations unite in convincing me that the abolition of slavery must necessarily be gradual.*

Clinton's followers did not scruple to describe Jay as a Washington-backed aristocrat, living on the generous salary of a judge, while depicting the governor as a man of hard work, representative of the people. During much of the campaign, Jay presided over circuit courts out of New York State. In the end Clinton was reelected but not without the major help of an unfair Board of Election Canvassers which resorted to technicalities to disallow many ballots cast for Jay.

The first Chief Justice did not attend a Supreme Court session after 1793, as he accepted a mission to England in 1794 to settle the continuing differences with Great Britain which again had assumed warlike proportions. Although Hamilton had much to do with the American proposals, it was Jay who worked out the precise accord with Lord Grenville in London and the resulting agreement came to be known as Jay's Treaty. Among its provisions were these: the British would withdraw their soldiers from the Northwest Territory; boundary disputes with the British would be adjusted by commissions, as would claims by the United States and the private debts of the British; and freedom of navigation on the Mississippi would be guaranteed. But England would not give up its practice of impressing American seamen captured on the high seas and insisted on restrictions on American trade with the West Indies.

Many citizens believed that the terms were not favorable enough to the United States, and criticized Jay when the provisions became known. A picture of Jay and a copy of the treaty were set afire in a demonstration in New York City. One representation showed Jay with the treaty and a bag of gold in a scales and speaking the words: "Come up to my price, and I will sell you my country." As usual Jay faced the abuse unperturbed. He thought he had done his duty and was willing to abide by the results. A reasonable view of Jay's Treaty found it justified as the means by which the Federalists maintained the peace and relative financial stability at a crucial time.

On returning from England in 1795, Jay learned that his friends, in his long absence, not only had put him up again for governor, but this time had brought about his election. Under these circumstances and partly also because he disliked the arduous task of traveling about the circuit, Jay resigned as Chief Justice and took over the administration of his native state. Serving two three-year terms, he conducted the office in a solid, thoroughly honest and generally conservative manner, marked throughout by exceptionally high standards. He supported and signed the bill that established a procedure for gradual freeing of slaves in the state. Jay himself bought slaves from time to time, trained them to care for themselves and then granted them their freedom.

When the governor of Connecticut took up with Jay the matter of executive clemency for a youth with prominent family connections who had been found guilty of forgery in New York, Governor Jay replied: "Justice cannot look with more favorable eye on those who become criminal in spite of a good education and of good examples than of those other offenders who from infancy have lived destitute of those advantages." Jay showed much interest in the care of prisoners and on his recommendation, New York constructed a model penitentiary. He led in the revision of New York's criminal code and in the reduction of the list of crimes for which the death penalty could be exacted. Jay opposed political change as a basis for public employment, and as governor, retained many qualified state employees from the preceding administration, practicing, in effect, the idea of a career civil service.

Republican-Democratic successes in local and state contests in early 1800 made the Federalists increasingly fearful of a victory for Jefferson in the approaching presidential election. Expecting New York to determine the outcome and hopeful of creating a new advantage for the Federalists, Hamilton reversed himself on the constitutional argument and supported a plan for choosing New York's presidential electors by vote in districts rather than by the state at large, as was the established method. To accomplish the change in time, Hamilton wrote Jay on May 7 and proposed that the governor call a special session of the outgoing Federalist legislature so it could rewrite the law before its authority ran out on July 1. Leading Federalists generally put pressure on Jay, Philip Schuyler, for example, advising him: "Your friends will justify it as the only means to save a nation from more disasters, which it must and probably will experience from the misrule of a man who has given such strong evidence that he was opposed to the salutary measures of those who have been heretofore at the helm, and who is in fact pervaded with the mad French philosophy."

Although Jay believed in Federalist principles more strongly than many of his colleagues, he also believed in abiding by the agreed rules. His decision as governor with respect to this highly political proposal was contained in a single comment that he wrote on the letter from Hamilton: "Proposing a measure for party purposes which I think it would not become me to adopt." It was not an insignificant fact that when the electoral votes were counted that year, New Jersey, Connecticut, Delaware and Rhode Island had cast all or some of their votes for John Jay for President of the United States.

The Federalists called on Jay to stand again for governor, but he had made up his mind to retire. He held firmly to this resolve when he learned that President John Adams in December, 1800, near the end of his Administration, had sent Jay's name to the Senate in a nomination that would have returned the former Chief Justice to the head of the federal judiciary. The letter from Adams was most commendatory: "I had no permission from you to take this step, but it appeared to me that Providence had thrown in my way an opportunity, not only of marking to the public the spot where, in my opinion, the greatest mass of worth remained collected in one individual, but of furnishing my country with the best security its inhabitants afforded against the increasing dissolution of morals."

In responding, Jay addressed himself not to the thought that the President raised, but rather to the deficiencies of the Supreme Court as the first Chief Justice had seen them. With complete candor he stated his reasons for resigning five years earlier:

> *I left the bench perfectly convinced that under a system so defective it would not obtain the energy, weight, and dignity which was essential to its affording due support to the national government; nor acquire the public confidence and respect which, as the last resort of the justice of the nation, it should possess. Hence I am induced to doubt both the propriety and the expediency of my returning to the bench under the present system. Independently of these considerations, the state of my health removes every doubt.*

Another consideration in Jay's decision not to return to the Court was the fact that in the five years after his resignation, two successor Chief Justices had been named by President Washington. Although one of these, former Associate Justice John Rutledge, was not confirmed and served only briefly on a recess appointment, Oliver Ellsworth, who was confirmed, resigned following a tenure shorter than Jay's. The date of Jay's second appointment as Chief Justice was December 18, 1800 and he was confirmed the next day. As the date of his declination was January 2, 1801, he was, in effect, confirmed in the seat of Chief Justice for approximately two weeks, but without having taken up any of its duties.

If Jay had accepted Adams' nomination of him, in December, 1800, to be Chief Justice a second time, there would have been no vacancy in the Court for the President to appoint John Marshall. Jay must have reflected on this more than once as word of Marshall's great decisions penetrated to the fields and orchards and woods of Westchester to which he retired. For if John Marshall reared a constitutional edifice, and to be sure he did, then certainly he built it on foundation stones that John Jay had done much to lay so early and so well.

Jay had lived out two spans of twenty-eight years each. The first, from 1745 to 1773, comprised years of preparation and development. The second, ending in 1801, had consisted of unbroken public service. He now embarked on still a third such span—in retirement until the end of his life in 1829. In particular he looked forward to companionship with his wife from whom he had so often and regretfully been parted by his European missions and the circuit-riding duties of the bench. But this anticipated association of the heart was denied him, for she died in 1802. Fortunately he was close to his two sons and five daughters, and some of them lived with their father on the 800-acre estate near Bedford, in Westchester County.

Here Jay tested out his agricultural ideas, kept up an extensive correspondence with friends at home and abroad, and replied to frequent requests for counsel on issues of the day. Affiliating with a Federalist peace group, he opposed the War of 1812 and commended expression of dissent to it. But he also pointed out that since "the war has been constitutionally declared, the people are evidently bound to support it in the manner which constitutional laws do or shall prescribe." As the years passed he grew more strongly opposed to slavery. When "the Missouri question" came to the fore, he wrote in 1819: "The obvious dictates of both morality and policy teach us, that our free nation cannot encourage the extension of slavery, nor the multiplication of slaves, without doing violence to their principles, and without depressing their power and prosperity." He took part in selecting the district assemblyman and otherwise performed the duties of citizenship at the local level. A substantial part of his time he devoted to religious pursuits, both for the Episcopal Church of which he was a member, and for non-denominational organizations, including Bible and Sunday School societies and an association that sought to lead young men into the pastorate. He helped establish the American Bible Society and in 1821 was its president.

During the morning he might plant trees for future generations to enjoy, as he himself had walked in the shade of trees set out by his father. The afternoon might see him receiving such a visitor as James Fenimore Cooper and relating personal experiences that would appear later in the pages of *The Spy*. At night he listened as some member of the family read aloud. He outlived so many of his contemporaries that he became the last survivor of the First Continental Congress. When a question of authorship of Washington's Farewell Address arose because a copy was found in Hamilton's handwriting, Jay could explain. Washington had sent the address to both Hamilton and Jay for comments and each had copied it and returned the original to the outgoing President.

To the end, prudence, compassion, gratitude and fairness marked the career of John Jay. Above all fairness ruled his life, for as far back as the Revolution he could be fair even to an England from which came repressive rule. "I view a return to the domination of Britain with horror, and would risk all for independence," he had written in the midst of the war. "But that point ceded, I would give them advantageous commercial terms. The destruction of Old England would hurt me; I wish it well; it afforded my ancestors an asylum from persecution."

Not all viewers of the American past have seen Jay in this light. Gustavus Myers, in his *History of the Supreme Court of the United States* (1911), found Jay to be a key figure in a land-owning combine of colonial aristocrats who protected the interests of their own class against the popular rank and file. But his experience was the experience of many of the other Revolutionary leaders and Founding Fathers. If Washington and Jay trusted each other in part because their backgrounds and outlooks were similar, there was nothing either strange or necessarily wrong about that.

The survivor of the mutually trusting pair died of the "infirmities of age" at Bedford on May 17, 1829, in his eighty-fifth year. After simple services, he was buried in the Jay cemetery at Rye. Expressly directing in his will that certain usual funeral customs be omitted, he announced instead that "I give two hundred dollars to any one deserving widow or orphan of this town, whom my children shall select." In his last hours he still was considerate, thoughtful, ready to depart from practice for good reason.

SELECTED BIBLIOGRAPHY

The extensive and long-needed Jay letters, papers, reports and diary entries were not assembled until in the 1960's when the project was undertaken at Columbia University with Professor Richard B. Morris as editor. Pending publication of the previously unpublished papers and a description of the collection as a whole, the editor prepared a series of three articles for *American Heritage,* beginning in February, 1968, which dealt with major aspects of Jay's life and career. Morris's own important contribution, *The Peacemakers* (New York, 1965), recounted the steps and negotiations that led to the Treaty of Paris. Samuel F. Bemis treated Jay as diplomat in *The American Secretaries of State and Their Diplomacy* (Vol. I, 1927). The earlier edition of Jay's correspondence and papers was edited by H. P. Johnston (4 vols., New York, 1890–93). Frank Monaghan produced the fullest biography in *John Jay* (New York, 1935), while that by George Pellew, a descendant, *John Jay* (Boston, 1890) in the American Statesman Series, still has much to commend it. Jay's son, William, wrote his father's life in two volumes in 1833. For the period of the Constitutional Convention and the ratification process see Carl Van Doren, *The Great Rehearsal* (New York, 1948) and Jacob E. Cooke, ed., *The Federalist* (Middletown, Connecticut, 1961). Charles Warren, *The Supreme Court in United States History* (revised edition, 2 vols., Boston, 1932), has the most detailed account of Jay's appointment and work on the Supreme Court, but Mathis Doyle, "Chisholm v. Georgia: Background and Settlement," 54 *Journal of American History* (June, 1967), makes changes in Warren's statement of the facts of Jay's best-known decision. For the Supreme Court period see also: Hampton L. Carson, *The Supreme Court of the United States: Its History* (Vol. 1, Philadelphia, 1892); Charles Grove Haines, *The Role of the Supreme Court in American Government and Politics: 1789–1835* (Berkeley, 1944); and Gustavus Myers, *History of the Supreme Court of the United States,* rev. ed. (Chicago, 1925). For the politics of the times consult John C. Miller, *The Federalist Era* (New York, 1960), and Carl L. Becker, "The History of Political Parties in the Province of New York, 1760–1776," *Bulletin of the University of Wisconsin Historical Series* (New York, 1960).

John Jay

REPRESENTATIVE OPINIONS

CHISHOLM v. GEORGIA, 2 DALL. 419 (1793)

In the first major decision by the Supreme Court the issue was, as Chief Justice Jay said, whether a state was suable by individual citizens of another state. This question arose when the heirs of one-time Georgian Alexander Chisholm, themselves citizens of South Carolina, sued the state of Georgia to require Georgia to pay claims of the Chisholm estate held by its executors to be due it from the state of Georgia. The sued state refused to become a party to the suit by defending it, but Georgia did present a "remonstrance and protestation" that the Court was without jurisdiction. Applying Article III, Section 2 of the United States Constitution, the Supreme Court sustained the right of citizens of one state to sue another state. Of the six judges, only Justice Iredell dissented. A movement to amend the Constitution developed immediately and with the ratification of the Eleventh Amendment in 1798 such suits were expressly prohibited.

JAY, *Chief Justice:*—The question we are now to decide has been accurately stated, viz., Is a state suable by individual citizens of another state?

It is said, that Georgia refuses to appear and answer to the plaintiff in this action, because she is a sovereign state, and therefore not liable to such actions. In order to ascertain the merits of this objection, let us enquire, 1st. In what sense Georgia is a sovereign state. 2d. Whether suability is incompatible with such sovereignty. 3d. Whether the constitution (to which Georgia is a party) authorizes such an action against her.

Suability and suable are words not in common use, but they concisely, correctly convey the idea annexed to them.

1st. In determining the sense in which Georgia is a sovereign state, it may be useful to turn our attention to the political situation we were in, prior to the revolution, and to the political rights which emerged from the revolution: All the country now possessed by the United States was then a part of the dominions appertaining to the crown of Great Britain. Every acre of land in this country was then held mediately or immediately by grants from that crown. All the people of this country were then, subjects of the king of Great Britain, and owed allegiance to him: and all the civil authority then existing or exercised here, flowed from the head of the British Empire. They were in strict sense, fellow subjects, and in a variety of respects, one people. When the revolution commenced, the patriots did not assert that only the same affinity and social connection subsisted between the people, of the colonies, which subsisted between the people of Gaul, Britain and Spain, while Roman provinces, viz., only that affinity and social connection which result from the mere circumstances of being governed by the same prince; different ideas prevailed, and gave occasion to the congress of 1774 and 1775.

The revolution or rather the Declaration of Independence, found the people already united for general purposes, and at the same time providing for their more domestic concerns by state conventions, and other temporary arrangements. From the crown of Great Britain, the sovereignty of their country passed to the people of it; and it was then not an uncommon opinion, that the unappropriated lands, which belonged to that crown, passed not to the people of the colony or states within whose limits they were situated, but to the whole people; on whatever principles this opinion rested, it did not give way to the other, and thirteen sovereignties were considered as emerged from the principles of the revolution, combined with local convenience and considerations; the people nevertheless continued to consider themselves, in a national point of view, as one people; and they continued without interruption to manage their national concerns accordingly; afterwards, in the hurry of the war, and in the warmth of mutual confidence, they made a confederation of the states, the basis of a general government. Experience disappointed the expectations they had formed from it; and then the people, in their collective and national capacity, established the present constitution. It is remarkable that in establishing it, the people exercised their own rights, and their own proper sovereignty, and conscious of the plentitude of it, they declared with becoming dignity, "We the people of the United States do ordain and establish this constitution." Here we see the people acting as sovereigns of the whole country; and in the language of sovereignty, establishing a constitution by which it was their will, that the state governments should be bound, and to which the state constitutions should be made to conform. Every state constitution is a compact made by and between the citizens of a state to govern themselves in a certain manner; and the constitution of the United States is likewise a compact made by the people of the United States to govern themselves as to general objects, in a certain manner. By this great compact however, many prerogatives were transferred to the national government, such as those of making war and peace, contracting alliances, coining money, etc. etc.

If then it be true, that the sovereignty of the nation is the people of the nation, and the residuary sovereignty of each state, in the people of each state, it may be useful to compare these sovereignties, with those in Europe, that we may thence be enabled to judge, whether all the prerogatives which are allowed to the latter, are so essential to the former. There is reason to suspect that some of the difficulties which embarrass the present question, arise from inattention to differences which subsist between them.

It will be sufficient to observe briefly, that the sovereignties in Europe, and particularly in England, exsit on feudal principles. That system considers the prince as the sovereign, and the people as his subjects; it regards his person as the object of allegiance, and excludes the idea of his being on an equal footing with a subject, either in a court of justice or elsewhere. That system contemplates him as being the fountain of honor and authority; and from his grace and grant derives all franchises, immunities and privileges; it is easy to perceive that such a sovereign could not be amenable to a court of justice, or subjected to judicial control and actual constraint. It was of necessity, therefore, that suability, became incompatible with such sovereignty. Besides, the prince having all the executive powers, the judgment of the courts would, in fact, be only monitory, not mandatory to him, and a capacity to be advised, is a distinct thing from a capacity to be sued. The same feudal ideas run through all their jurisprudence, and constantly remind us of the distinction between the prince and the subject. No such ideas obtain here; at the revolution, the sovereignty devolved on the people; and they are truly the sovereigns of the country, but they are sovereigns without subjects (unless the African slaves among us may be so called) and have none to govern but themselves; the citizens of America are equal as fellow citizens, and as joint tenants in the sovereignty.

From the differences existing between feudal sovereignties and governments founded on compacts, it necessarily follows that their respective prerogatives must differ. Sovereignty is the right to govern; a nation or state-sovereign is the person or persons in whom that resides. In Europe the sovereignty is generally ascribed to the prince; here it rests with the people; there, the sovereign actually administers the government; here, never in a single instance; our governors are the agents of the people, and at most stand in the same relation to their sovereign, in which regents in Europe stand to their sovereigns. Their princes have personal powers, dignities, and pre-eminences, our rulers have none but official; nor do they partake in the sovereignty otherwise, or in any other capacity, than as private citizens.

2d. The second object of enquiry now presents itself, viz., whether suability is compatible with state sovereignty:

Suability, by whom? Not a subject, for in this country there are none; not an inferior, for all the citizens being as to civil rights perfectly equal, there is not, in that respect, one citizen inferior to another. It is agreed, that one free citizen may sue another; the obvious dictates of justice, and the purposes of society demanding it. It is agreed, that one free citizen may sue any number on whom process can be conveniently executed; nay, in certain cases one citizen may sue forty thousand; for where a corporation is sued all the members of it are actually sued, though not personally sued. In this city there are forty odd thousand free citizens, all of whom may be collectively sued by any individual citizen. In the state of Delaware, there are fifty odd thousand free citizens, and what reason can be assigned why a free citizen who has demands against them should not prosecute them? Can the difference between forty odd thousand, and fifty odd thousand make any distinction as to right? Is it not as easy, and as convenient to the public and parties, to serve a summons on the governor and attorney general of Delaware, as on the mayor or other officers of the corporation of Philadelphia? Will it be said, that the fifty odd thousand citizens in Delaware being associated under a state government, stand in a rank so superior to the forty odd thousand of Philadelphia, associated under their charter, that although it may become the latter to meet an individual on an equal footing in a court of justice, yet that such a procedure would not comport with the dignity of the former?—In this land of equal liberty, shall forty odd thousand in one place be compellable to do justice, and yet fifty odd thousand in another place be privileged to do justice only as they may think proper? Such objections would not correspond with the equal rights we claim; with the equality we profess to admire and maintain, and with that popular sovereignty in which every citizen partakes. Grant that the governor of Delaware holds an office of superior rank to the major of Philadelphia, they are both nevertheless the officers of the people; and however more exalted the one may be than the other, yet in the opinion of those who dislike aristocracy, that circumstance cannot be a good reason for impeding the course of justice.

If there be any such incompatibility as is pretended, whence does it arise? In what does it consist? There is at least one strong undeniable fact against this incompatibility, and that is this, any one state in the union may sue another state, in this court, that is, all the people of one state may sue all the people of another state. It is plain then, that a state may be sued, and hence it plainly follows, that suability and state sovereignty are not incompatible. As one state may sue another state in this court, it is plain that no degradation to a state is thought to accompany her appearance in this court. It is not therefore to an appearance in this court that the objection points. To what does it point? It points to an appearance at the suit of one or more citizens. But why it should be more incompatible, that all the people of a state should be sued by one citizen, then by one hundred thousand, I cannot perceive, the process in both cases being alike; and the consequences of a judgment alike. Nor can I observe any greater inconveniences in the one case than in the other, except what may arise from the feelings of those who may regard a lesser number in an inferior light. But if any reliance be made on this inferiority as an objection, at least one half of its force is done away by this fact, viz., that it is conceded that a state may appear in this court as plaintiff against a single citizen as defendant; and the truth is, that the state of Georgia is at this moment prosecuting an action in this court against two citizens of South Carolina.[1]

The only remnant of objection therefore that remains is, that the state is not bound to appear and answer as a defendant at the suit of an individual: but why it is unreasonable that she should be so bound, is hard to conjecture: That rule is said to be a bad one, which does not work both ways; the citizens of Georgia are content with a right of suing citizens of other states; but are not content that citizens of other states should have a right to sue them.

Let us now proceed to enquire whether Georgia has not, by being a party to the national compact, consented to be suable by

[1] Georgia *v*. Brailsford, et al. *Ant. 402*.

individual citizens of another state. This enquiry naturally leads our attention. 1st. To the design of the constitution. 2d. To the letter and express declaration in it.

Prior to the date of the constitution, the people had not any national tribunal to which they could resort for justice; the distribution of justice was then confined to state judicatories, in whose institution and organization the people of the other states had no participation, and over whom they had not the least control. There was then no general court of appellate jurisdiction, by whom the errors of state courts, affecting either the nation at large or the citizens of any other state, could be revised and corrected. Each state was obliged to acquiesce in the measure of justice which another state might yield to her, or to her citizens; and that even in cases where state considerations were not always favorable to the most exact measure. There was danger that from this source animosities would in time result; and as the transition from animosities to hostilities was frequent in the history of independent states, a common tribunal for the termination of controversies became desirable, from motives both of justice and of policy.

Prior also to that period, the United States had, by taking a place among the nations of the earth, become amenable to the laws of nations; and it was their interest as well as their duty to provide, that those laws should be respected and obeyed; in their national character and capacity, the United States were responsible to foreign nations for the conduct of each state, relative to the laws of nations, and the performance of treaties: and there the inexpediency of referring all such questions to state courts, and particularly to the courts of delinquent states became apparent. While all the states were bound to protect each, and the citizens of each, it was highly proper and reasonable, that they should be in a capacity, not only to cause justice to be done to each, and the citizens of each; but also to cause justice to be done by each, and the citizens of each; and that, not by violence and force, but in a stable, sedate, and regular course of judicial procedure.

These were among the evils against which it was proper for the nation, that is, the people of all the United States, to provide by a national judiciary, to be instituted by the whole nation, and to be responsible to the whole nation.

Let us now turn to the constitution. The people therein declare, that their design in establishing it, comprehended six objects. 1st. To form a more perfect union. 2d. To establish justice. 3d. To ensure domestic tranquillity. 4th. To provide for the common defence. 5th. To promote the general welfare. 6th. To secure the blessings of liberty to themselves and their posterity. It would be pleasing and useful to consider and trace the relations which each of these objects bears to the others; and to shew that they collectively comprise every thing requisite, with the blessing of Divine Providence, to render a people prosperous and happy: on the present occasion such disquisitions would be unreasonable, because foreign to the subject immediately under consideration.

It may be asked, what is the precise sense and latitude in which the words "to establish justice," as here used, are to be understood? The answer to this question will result from the provisions made in the constitution on this head. They are specified in the 2d. section of the 3d article, where is ordained, that the judicial power of the United States shall extend to ten descriptions of cases, viz. 1st. To all cases arising under this constitution; because the meaning, construction, and operation of a compact ought always to be ascertained by all the parties, or by authority derived only from one of them. 2d. To all cases arising under the laws of the United States; because as such laws constitutionally made, are obligatory on each state, the measure of obligation and obedience ought not to be decided and fixed by the party from whom they are due, but by a tribunal deriving authority from both the parties. 3d. To all cases arising under treaties made by their authority; because, as treaties are compacts made by, and obligatory on, the whole nation, their operation ought not to be affected or regulated by the local laws or courts of a part of the nation. 4th. To all cases affecting ambassadors, or other public ministers and consuls; because, as these are officers of foreign nations, whom this nation are bound to protect and treat according to the laws of nations, cases affecting them ought only to be cognizable by national authority. 5th. To all cases of admiralty and maritime jurisdiction; because, as the seas are the joint property of nations, whose right and privileges relative thereto, are regulated by the law of nations and treaties, such cases necessarily belong to national jurisdiction. 6th. To controversies to which the United States shall be a party; because in cases in which the whole people are interested, it would not be equal or wise to let any one state decide and measure out the justice due to others. 7th. To controversies between two or more states; because domestic tranquillity requires, that the contentions of states should be peaceably terminated by a common judicatory; and, because, in a free country justice ought not to depend on the will of either of the litigants. 8th. To controversies between a state and citizens of another state; because in case a state (that is all the citizens of it) has demands against some citizens of another state, it is better that she should prosecute their demands in a national court, than in a court of the state to which those citizens belong; the danger of irritation and criminations arising from apprehensions and suspicions of partiality, being thereby obviated. Because, in cases where some citizens of one state have demands against all the citizens of another state, the cause of liberty and the rights of men forbid, that the latter should be the sole judges of the justice due to the latter; and true republican government requires that free and equal citizens should have free, fair, and equal justice. 9th. To controversies between citizens of the same state, claiming lands under grants of different states, because, as the rights of the two states to grant the land, are drawn into question, neither of the two states ought to decide the controversy. 10th. To controversies between a state, or the citizens thereof; and foreign states, citizens or subjects; because, as every nation is responsible for the conduct of its citizens towards other nations; all questions touching the justice due to foreign nations, or people, ought to be ascertained by, and depend on national authority. Even this cursory view of the judicial powers of the United States, leaves the mind strongly impressed with the importance of them to the preservation of the tranquility, the equal sovereignty, and the equal right of the people.

The question now before us renders it necessary to pay particular attention to that part of the 2d section, which extends the judicial power "to controversies between a state and citizens of another state." It is contended, that this ought to be construed to reach none of these controversies, excepting those in which a state may be plaintiff. The ordinary rules for construction will easily decide whether those words are to be understood in that limited sense.

This extension of power is remedial, because it is to settle controversies. It is therefore, to be construed liberally. It is politic, wise, and good, that, not only the controversies, in which a state is plaintiff, but also those in which a state is defendant, should be settled, both cases, therefore, are within the reason of the remedy; and ought to be so adjudged, unless the obvious, plain, and literal sense of the words forbid it.. If we attend to the words, we find them to be express, positive, free from ambiguity, and without room for such implied expressions: "The judicial power of the United States shall "extend to controversies between a state and citizens of another state." If the Constitution really meant to extend these powers only to those controversies in which a state might be plaintiff, to the exclusion of those in which citizens had demands against a state, it is inconceivable that it should have attempted to convey that meaning in words, not only so incompetent, but also repugnant to it; if it meant to exclude a certain class of these controversies, why were they not expressly excepted; on the contrary, not even an intimation of such intention appears in any part of the Constitution. It cannot be pretended that where citizens urge and insist upon demands against a state, which the state refuses to admit and comply with, that there is no controversy between them. If it is a controversy between them, then it clearly falls not only within the spirit, but the very words of the Constitution. What is it to the cause of justice, and how can it affect the definition of the word, controversy, whether the demands which cause the dispute, are made by a state against citizens of another state, or by the latter against the former? When power is thus extended to a controversy, it necessarily, as to all judicial purposes, is also extended to those, between whom it subsists.

The exception contended for, would contradict and do violence to the great and leading principles of a free and equal national government, one of the great objects of which is, to insure justice to all. To the few against the many, as well as to the many against the few. It would be strange, indeed, that the joint and equal sovereigns of this country, should, in the very Constitution by which they professed to establish justice, so far deviate from the plain path of equality and impartiality, as to give to the collective citizens of one state, a right as suing individual citizens of another state, and yet deny to those citizens a right of suing them. We find the same general and comprehensive manner of expressing the same ideas, in a subsequent clause; in which the Constitution ordains, that "in all cases affecting ambassadors, other public ministers and consuls, and those in which a state shall be a party, the Supreme Court shall have original jurisdiction." Did it mean here party-plaintiff? If that only was meant, it would have been easy to have found words to express it. Words are to be understood in their ordinary and common acceptation, and the word, party, being in common usage applicable both to plaintiff and defendant, we cannot limit it to one of them in the present case. We find the Legislature of the United States expressing themselves in the like general and comprehensive manner; they speak in the 13th section of the judicial act, of controversies where a state is a party, and as they do not impliedly or expressly apply that term to either of the litigants, in particular, we are to understand them of speaking of both. In the same section they distinguish the cases where ambassadors are plaintiffs, from those in which ambassadors are defendants, and make different provisions respecting those cases; and it is not unnatural to suppose, that they would in like manner have distinguished between cases where a state was plaintiff, and where a state was defendant, if they had intended to make any difference between them, or if they had apprehended that the constitution had made any difference between them.

I perceive, and therefore candor urges me to mention, a circumstance, which seems to favor the opposite side of the question. It is this: the same section of the constitution which extends the judicial power to controversies "between a state and the citizens of another state," does also extend that power to controversies to which the United States are a party. Now, it may be said, that if the word, party, comprehends both plaintiff and defendant, it follows, that the United States may be sued by any citizen, between whom and them there may be a controversy. This appears to me to be fair reasoning; but the same principles of candor which urge me to mention this objection, also urge me to suggest an important difference between the two cases. It is this: in all cases of actions against states or individual citizens, the national courts are supported in all their legal and Constitutional proceedings and judgments, by the arm of the executive power of the United States; but in cases of actions against the United States, there is no power which the courts can call to their aid. From this distinction important conclusions are deducible, and they place the case of a state and the case of the United States, in very different points of view.

I wish the state of society was so far improved, and the science of government advanced to such a degree of perfection, as that the whole nation could in the peaceable course of law, be compelled to do justice, and be sued by individual citizens. Whether that is, or is not, now the case, ought not to be thus collaterally and incidentally decided: I leave it a question.

As this opinion, though deliberately formed, has been hastily reduced to writing between the intervals of the daily adjournments, and while my mind was occupied and wearied by the business of the day, I fear it is less concise and connected than it might otherwise have been. I have made no references to cases, because I know of none that are not distinguishable from this case: nor does it appear to me necessary to show that the sentiments of the best writers on government and the rights of men, harmonize with the principles which direct my judgment on the present question. The acts of the former Congresses, and the acts of many of the state conventions are replete with similar ideas; and to the honor of the United States, it may be observed, that in no other country are subjects of this kind better, if so well, understood. The attention and attachment of the Constitution to the equal rights of the people are discernable in almost every sentence of it; and it is to be regretted that the provision in it which we have been considering, has not in every instance received the approbation and acquiescence which it merits. Georgia has in language advocated the cause of republican equality; and there is reason to hope that the people of that state will yet perceive that it would not have been consistent with that equality, to have exempted the body of her citizens from that suability which they are at this moment exercising against citizens of another state.

For my own part, I am convinced that the sense in which I understand and have explained the words "controversies between states and citizens of another state," is the true sense. The extension of the judiciary power of the United States to such controversies, appears to me to be wise, because it is honest, and because it is useful. It is honest, because it provides for doing justice without respect of persons, and by securing individual citizens as well as states, in their respective rights, performs the promise which every free government makes to every free citizen, of equal justice and protection. It is useful, because it is honest, because it leaves not even the most obscure and friendless citizen without means of obtaining justice from a neighboring state; because it obviates occasions of quarrels between states on account of the claims of their respective citizens; because it recognizes and strongly rests on this great moral truth, that justice is the same whether due from one man or a million, or from a million to one man; because it teaches and greatly appreciates the value of our free republican national government, which places all our citizens on an equal footing, and enables each and every one of them to obtain justice without any danger of being overborne by the weight and number of their opponents; and, because it brings into action, and enforces this great and glorious principle, that the people are the sovereign of this country, and consequently that fellow citizens and joint sovereigns cannot be degraded by appearing with each other in their own courts to have their controversies determined. The people have reason to prize and rejoice in such valuable privileges; and they ought not to forget, that nothing but the free course of constitutional law and government can insure the continuance and enjoyment of them.

For the reasons before given, I am clearly of opinion, that a state is suable by citizens of another state: but lest I should be understood in a latitude beyond my meaning, I think it necessary to subjoin this caution, viz.: That such suability may nevertheless not extend to all the demands, and to every kind of action; there may be exceptions. For instance, I am far from being prepared to say that an individual may sue a state on bills of credit issued before the Constitution was established, and which were issued and received on the faith of the state, and at a time when no ideas or expectations or judicial interposition were entertained or contemplated.

The following order was made:—BY THE COURT. It is ordered, that plaintiff in this cause do file his declaration on or before the first day of March next,

Ordered, that certified copies of the said declaration be served on the governor and attorney general of the state of Georogia, on or before the first day of June next.

Ordered, that unless the said state shall either in due form appear, or show cause to the contrary in this court, by the first day of next term, judgment by default shall be entered against the said state.

GLASS v. THE SLOOP BETSEY, 3 DALL. 6 (1794)

President Washington's policy of strict neutrality in foreign controversies was brought into serious question by a decision of the Federal District Court for Maryland which held that the United States admiralty court was without jurisdiction over a French prize captured at sea and then taken into port at Baltimore. In an opinion by Chief Justice Jay, the Supreme Court, to which the government appealed, upheld the jurisdiction of the admiralty court. But it went further, declaring that the admiralty jurisdiction which has been exercised in the United States by the consuls of France "was unwaranted in law" and "not of right." The decision, which came at a crucial moment in the new nation's life, vindicated its international rights, increased respect for its sovereignty among other nations and spared it dangerous foreign involvements. Although the decision in *Chisholm* v. *Georgia* is far better known, *Glass* v. *The Sloop Betsey* doubtless was Jay's most important opinion as Chief Justice.

THE COURT, having kept the cause under advisement for several days, informed the counsel, that besides the question of jurisdiction as to the district court, another question fairly arose upon the record,—whether any foreign nation had a right, without the positive stipulations of a treaty, to establish in this country, an admiralty jurisdiction for taking cognizance of prizes captured on the high seas, by its subjects or citizens, from its enemies?

Though this question had not been agitated, the court deemed it of great public importance to be decided; and, meaning to decide it, they declared a desire to hear it discussed. *Du Ponceau,* however, observed, that the parties to the appeal did not conceive themselves interested in the point; and that the French ministers had given no instructions for arguing it. Upon which, JAY, *Chief Justice,* proceeded to deliver the following unanimous opinion:

BY THE COURT:—The judges being decidedly of opinion, that every district court in the United States, possesses all the powers of a court of admiralty, whether considered as an instance, or as a prize court, and that the plea of the aforesaid appellee, Pierre Arcade Johannenc, to the jurisdiction of the district court of Maryland, is insufficient. Therefore it is considered by the supreme court aforesaid, and now finally decreed and adjudged by the same, that the plea be, and the same is hereby overruled and dismissed, and that the decree of the said district court of Maryland, founded thereon, be, and the same is hereby revoked, reversed and annulled.

And the said supreme court being further clearly of opinion, that the district court of Maryland aforesaid, has jurisdiction competent to inquire, and to decide, whether, in the present case, restitution ought to be made to the claimants, or either of them, in whole or in part (that is whether such restitution can be made consistently with the laws of nations and the treaties and laws of the United States) therefore it is ordered and adjudged that the said district court of Maryland do proceed to determine upon the libel of the said Alexander S. Glass, and others, agreeably to law and right, the said plea to the jurisdiction of the said court, notwithstanding.

And the said supreme court being further of opinion, that no foreign power can of right institute, or erect, any court of judicature of any kind, within the jurisdiction of the United States, but such only as may be warranted by, and be in pursuance of treaties, it is therefore decreed and adjudged that the admiralty jurisdiction, which has been exercised in the United States by the consuls of France, not being so warranted, is not of right.

It is further ordered by the said supreme court, that this cause be, and it is hereby, remanded to the district court, for the Maryland district, for a final decision, and that the several parties to the same do each pay their own costs.

John Rutledge

☆ 1739–1800 ☆

APPOINTED BY

GEORGE WASHINGTON

ASSOCIATE JUSTICE: 1789–1791

CHIEF JUSTICE: 1795

John Rutledge

by

LEON FRIEDMAN

JOHN RUTLEDGE *of South Carolina* holds more dubious distinctions than any other Justice in the history of the Supreme Court. No other Justice resigned from the Court to take a judicial post on a state court, and no Justice served for a shorter period of active service—one month in his second term on the Bench. He was the only Chief Justice nominee rejected by the Senate and the only recess appointee to issue opinions and then not to serve. Rutledge was the first Justice to resign and be reappointed to the Court, the first not confirmed by the Senate, and the first to become insane.*

As these laurels indicate, Rutledge's renown in history is not due to his Supreme Court activities. He made his mark as a delegate to all the important colonial congresses, president and governor of South Carolina during the Revolutionary War, member of the Philadelphia Constitutional Convention, and chief justice of South Carolina's highest courts—the acknowledged leader of the planter aristocracy whose support was crucial for independence and federation but whose narrow defense of its economic interests has dimmed the luster of its spokesmen.

John Rutledge was born in Charleston (then Charles Town), South Carolina in 1739, probably in late September. His mother, Sarah Hext Rutledge, was then but fifteen years old, having married Dr. John Rutledge the preceding December when only fourteen. There seems little doubt that Andrew Rutledge, Dr. John's older brother, had arranged the match since he had previously married

* *Robert Harrison of Maryland declined his appointment by Washington in 1789 to become Chancellor of Maryland. President Ulysses Grant withdrew two of his nominations for Chief Justice (George H. Williams and Caleb Cushing) before any vote was taken, after adverse criticism of the nominees developed in the Senate. By a forty-five to forty-three vote (less than the required two-thirds) the Senate refused to cut off debate on the nomination of Abe Fortas as Chief Justice.*

LEON FRIEDMAN practices law in New York, and is the editor of Southern Justice *and* The Civil Rights Reader.

Sarah's mother, a wealthy woman also called Sarah, and the young Sarah was the wealthiest heiress in South Carolina. Thus Andrew was young John Rutledge's uncle and grandfather as well as his mentor after Dr. John died in 1750, leaving a family of seven children and a still beautiful and wealthy widow of twenty-six. Rutledge studied law in his uncle's law office and statecraft in the South Carolina Commons House of Assembly where Andrew Rutledge served as speaker. When Andrew died in 1755, Rutledge read law for two years with James Parsons (later Speaker of the House). In keeping with the practice of the great families of the province, Rutledge travelled to the old country where he studied law at Middle Temple and was called to the English bar in 1760.

Success was assured Rutledge on his return to South Carolina in 1761 at the age of twenty-one. His mother's wealth, his uncle's political achievements, his education and intelligence brought him instant political office (he was elected to the Assembly within three months of his return) and sizeable legal fees (early in 1763 he announced he would not even look into a case for a retainer of less than one hundred pounds). Rutledge brought and won the first breach of promise action in the colonies and had no difficulty mastering the legal ropes of his time. With Charles Pinckney (the father of C. C. Pinckney and later chief justice of the province) and James Parsons, Rutledge dominated the local bar, and from that position the triumvirate came close to governing the province itself. The three represented most of the wealthy merchants and landowners and spoke for them not only in the courts but also in the Assembly.

The South Carolina House had veto power over the appointment of the governor's councillors as well as traditional power over local taxes. In 1762 Christopher Gadsden, later the radical leader in the state and Rutledge's principal opponent, was elected to the Assembly. The king's governor, Thomas Boone, refused to take the oath of allegiance from Gadsden, already known as a noxious reformer who was corresponding with Samuel Adams in Boston, on the ground that he had not properly qualified. Whatever their feelings about Gadsden's politics, the members of the Assembly, with Rutledge already one of its leaders, insisted on its right "to examine and determine the validity of the election of its own members." Boone then dissolved the Assembly; a new Assembly almost identical to the earlier one convened and refused to vote any taxes, pay the governor's salary, or conduct any business. Both the governor and the Assembly claimed to speak for the province. The stalemate continued for almost three years until Boone left for England in May, 1764. The government in London decided to take no vigorous action that would threaten the profitable rice and indigo trade with South Carolina. Early in 1764, before leaving for England, Boone appointed Rutledge, then twenty-four years old, attorney general of the province, apparently to win him to the king's side. Rutledge served for ten months but did not compromise the Assembly's position.

In 1763 George Grenville replaced Lord Bute as Prime Minister and tried to raise taxes from the colonies to pay for part of the crown's expenses in the French and Indian Wars. The Stamp Tax (1765)—an impost for the specially stamped paper to be affixed to or used for all legal documents and each issue of every newspaper as well—aroused the Americans since it imposed a direct tax on the colonies without their consent, required payment in specie during a time of economic stagnation and currency constriction, and gave admiralty courts sitting without a jury the right to try violations of the law. James Otis of Massachusetts called for an immediate "congress" of all the colonies to be held in New York in October, 1765. Although North Carolina, Georgia, and Virginia did not attend, the leaders of the South Carolina Assembly decided to send a three-man delegation; Gadsden, Thomas Lynch, and John Rutledge, at twenty-five, the youngest delegate. Gadsden reflected the more advanced feeling in the Congress by calling for a united "stand on the broad and common ground of natural and inherent rights . . . There ought to be no more New England men, no New Yorkers . . . but all of us Americans." Rutledge stood with the rear guard, as he was to do in almost all the colonial congresses and conventions. As the chairman of the Committee on Resolutions, he drafted a respectful memorial to the House of Lords requesting repeal of the act. (John Dickinson of Pennsylvania wrote a more forceful but not intemperate Declaration of Rights and Grievances to the Commons.) Surprised by the vehement American reaction and severely hurt by their nonimportation boycott, London merchants pressed Lord Rockingham, the new Prime Minister, for repeal of the tax which took place on March 18, 1766.

From 1765 to 1774, Rutledge continued his prosperous law practice. In 1763 he married Elizabeth Grimké, the daughter of an old but not wealthy Charleston family and the aunt of the famous Grimké sisters who achieved notoriety as leading abolitionists and reformers in the 1830's and 1840's. Ten children were born to the couple, including John Rutledge, Jr., a member of the House of Representatives from 1797 to 1803. One of John Rutledge's brothers, Andrew, married Gadsden's daughter Elizabeth in 1767; another brother, Edward, a signer of the Declaration of Independence and later governor of South Carolina, married the very rich Henrietta Middleton; and a third brother, Hugh, joined the South Carolina bar. Rutledge in his own right, and through his family, became the leading citizen of the province although his wealth, close ties to the planter aristocracy, and loyalty toward the home country made him suspect among the Sons of Liberty in the colonies. His reputation with the radicals increased after his successful defense in 1771 of Dr. John Haley, a Gadsden ally accused of murder for killing one De Lancey, son of the Chief Justice of New York, in a duel.

In 1773–74, a controversy arose over the tea duty, and the designation of specific merchants to sell tea as a monopoly in America. In South Carolina, unlike Boston, local patriots did not destroy the tea but put pressure on local consignees not to accept it. The provincial leaders called a series of General Meetings consisting of representatives from all sections of South Carolina who later formed the Revolutionary state government. The radicals under Gadsden had a majority in the meetings and voted to send a delegation to the First

Continental Congress (September, 1774) with wide power to approve any steps taken there. The conservative planters, concerned that the northern colonies would press for commercial nonintercourse with England which would be disastrous for their interests, managed to elect Rutledge as chairman of the delegation to support their views in Philadelphia. The other delegates included Gadsden, Edward Rutledge, Thomas Lynch and Henry Middleton, Edward's father-in-law.

The debates in Philadelphia reflected all the hesitations, doubts, and confusions of the time. Only radicals like Gadsden, Patrick Henry and Samuel Adams pressed for extreme measures. Joseph Galloway of Pennsylvania, strongly supported by Rutledge, proposed a conciliatory plan for administrative separation of the colonies which was only narrowly defeated. (Galloway remained loyal to England during the war.) The Congress adopted a Declaration of Rights and Liberties complaining of the injustice of various acts passed since 1763, indicating that the delegates initially wished only to reestablish the political structure of the early 1760's.

Rutledge with the other conservatives avoided any suggestion of separation or independence. In the debates he insisted on basing the Declaration of Rights on the British Constitution (to show the colonies' continued status under the Crown) instead of relying on the Law of Nature as Richard Henry Lee of Virginia proposed. Patrick Henry, who spoke highly of Rutledge's oratory—the most important measure of a political man in those days—derided the caution of the conservatives. John Adams reported that Henry "has a horrid view of Galloway, Jay, and the Rutledges. Their System he says would ruin the Cause of America." Adams described Rutledge at the first Congress in his diary: ". . . his appearance is not very promising. There is no keenness in his eye. No depth in his countenance. Nothing of the profound, sagacious, brilliant or sparkling in his first appearance." Elsewhere he noted, "Rutledge dont [sic] exceed in learning or oratory, tho he is a rapid speaker."

Adams showed little enthusiasm for Rutledge because of his consistent concern for South Carolina's economic welfare. In all the excitement and idealism of the Congress, Rutledge coolly pressed for maintaining the trade advantages of his home province. While other delegates prepared for danger and sacrifice, proposing a nonconsumption, nonimportation and nonexportation "Association" against England, Rutledge led his delegation out when Congress would not permit South Carolina to continue to sell its indigo and rice as before. He accused the northern delegates of devising "a commercial scheme among the flour colonies to find a better vent for their flour through the British Channel by preventing, if possible, any rice from being sent to these markets." To achieve unaninimity, the delegates had to concede something to Rutledge, and they finally permitted only one commodity to be sold outside the Association—rice, South Carolina's principal product.

On his return to South Carolina, the Gadsden radicals and the indigo planters condemned Rutledge for the rice exemption. He claimed that South

Carolina's exports to England were larger than those of any colony, its economic well-being required some market for its rice, and ruin was the alternative. The northern colonies would continue to sell their fish and flour to the Continent despite the Association, Rutledge said, and South Carolina had to do the same. He insisted that the rice planters could pay compensation to the other planters from the benefits they secured from exemption. The Assembly was sufficiently persuaded by Rutledge's argument to send him back as the chairman of the delegation to the Second Continental Congress.

At the Second Congress beginning in May, 1775, the current toward independence became strong enough to carry Rutledge at least partially. As chairman of the Committee on Government, he suggested a uniform procedure for forming new state governments. He recommended a plan for building an American fleet and proposed obstruction of the Hudson River to block British ships from using it. He supported the nomination of George Washington as Commander-in-Chief of the American forces. In the Committee on Trade, Rutledge noted that "the Consequences will be dreadfull [sic], if we ruin the merchants," but he supported the Association as established in 1774, that is, with the rice exemption.

While Rutledge stayed on in Philadelphia, William Henry Drayton assumed control over the Committee of Public Safety, the new governing body in South Carolina, and acted as commander of the local militia. Rutledge returned to Charleston in late December, 1775, and helped to draft a new constitution for the Republic of South Carolina which provided for a lower house chosen by a restricted electorate, an upper house elected by the lower house, and a president as chief executive officer, chosen by both houses and possessing absolute veto power over the legislature. The new Assembly met in March, 1776, and immediately chose John Rutledge as the first president. The move from loyal servant of the king to president of an independent republic was made in less than two years. But Rutledge held to some lingering doubts about complete independence. Before taking office as president, he told the moderates in the Assembly that the republic was only temporary "until an accommodation of the unhappy differences between Great Britain and America can be obtained." Perhaps he still believed it in March.

Rutledge immediately organized the militia and asked for help from the Continental Congress for the inevitable attack on Charleston. Washington sent General Charles Lee who was to contribute almost nothing in the coming battles. In late June, 1776, a British fleet under Sir Henry Clinton and Peter Parker anchored off Fort Sullivan, a partially completed, palmetto log fortification north of the city. Lee thought the fort would be easily destroyed by the British guns and ordered it evacuated. Countermanding Lee's order, Rutledge told Colonel William Moultrie that the fort was Charleston's best protection and had to be defended. Bad planning and seamanship by the British, the resiliency of the palmetto logs which easily absorbed the English shot, and accurate cannon fire by the Carolinians under Moultrie led to the sinking of one British ship and the killing of hundreds of troops on board the others. Parker and Clinton sailed away. The defeat drove the British from the South for almost three years. Rutledge's bold move in defending the fort led to the American's first great victory over the British. In Philadelphia one week later, Edward Rutledge, acting chairman of the South Carolina delegation in the absence of his brother, signed the Declaration of Independence.

Military operations against the Cherokees occupied Rutledge through 1776 and 1777. In March, 1778, a new constitution was proposed disestablishing the Anglican Church, changing the republic to a state and the president to a governor, providing for popular election of both the Senate and the Assembly and removing the executive's absolute veto. Rutledge, never a democrat, vetoed the plan: "However unexceptional democratic power may appear at first view," he said, "its effects have been found arbitrary, severe, and destructive." He also claimed that the new constitution would make accommodation with Great Britain impossible—an anomalous position to take in 1778. Rather than stalemate the legislature, Rutledge then resigned as president, the new constitution passed, and Rawlins Lowndes was elected governor.

A year later (February, 1779) the Assembly returned Rutledge to the chief executive post with wide, almost dictatorial powers to meet the invasion of the state by British troops under General Augustine Prevost. The first attack on Charleston (May, 1779) led to an offer by Rutledge to surrender the city and guarantee the state's neutrality until the war decided the fate of all the colonies—another example of Rutledge's anglophilia or vacillation. Before the offer was acted upon, word of the imminent arrival of General Benjamin Lincoln with a relieving force drove Prevost from the city. In May, 1780, a larger British army under Sir Henry Clinton succeeded in capturing Charleston in the heaviest American defeat of the war—5,000 men and four ships captured against only nominal British losses. The rest of the state fell soon after. British forces burned and plundered and hanged many suspected patriots, creating violently anti-British feeling among the inhabitants and leaders of the state. Rutledge escaped to North Carolina and made his way to Philadelphia to obtain military aid. General Horatio Gates and then Nathanael Greene led the Continental Army in the Carolinas in frequent battles with Lord Cornwallis' troops. With the help of local militia under Francis Marion, Andrew Pickens, and Thomas Sumter, Greene's forces defeated the British at King's Mountain (October, 1780) and Cowpens (January, 1781). Cornwallis took his troops out of the Carolinas to Yorktown, Virginia, where the end came in October, 1781.

Rutledge worked efficiently to reestablish civil authority in the state. Loyalists were pardoned if they joined the militia, British property was confiscated in an orderly manner, indigo replaced depreciated paper currency as legal tender, and elections took place in late 1781. Rutledge could not succeed himself as governor but he was elected to Congress from 1782 to 1784. He declined a position on the federal court set up under the Articles of Confederation and also refused an appointment to be minister to the Netherlands.

In 1784 Rutledge took his first judicial post. A new court of chancery had been established by the South Carolina legislature in March, 1784, and Rutledge was appointed its chief judge. The cases heard by the court involved the day to day affairs of the state: the value of depreciated currency circulated during the war, *Hunter* v. *Boykin,* 1 Desaussure (S.C.) 108 (1784); a suit for the purchase price of a brig which the seller claimed was "sound and good, British built and British bottom" which turned out to be "American built, worn out and unsound," *Neilson and Sarrazin* v. *Dickenson,* 1 Desaussure (S.C.) 133 (1786); and a fight over the estate of John Izard brought by his cousin Ralph Izard (later South Carolina's first United States Senator) who was represented by Edward Rutledge and C. C. Pinckney, *Izard* v. *Middleton,* 1 Desaussure (S.C.) 115 (1785). John Rutledge could hardly recuse himself when one of his brothers argued a case before him since Edward or Hugh Rutledge appeared as counsel in almost every one of the suits he heard. The decisions were reported *en banc* and Rutledge's personal role in their solution is impossible to determine.

Rutledge's brother-in-law, John Mathews, succeeded him as governor, and in 1786 Thomas Pinckney, Edward Rutledge's law partner and C. C. Pinckney's brother, succeeded Mathews. The Pinckney-Rutledge control over the state's affairs led to the appointment of Rutledge, C. C. Pinckney, and Charles Pinckney (a cousin of C.C. and at twenty-nine the new leader of the South Carolina bar) as delegates to the Philadelphia Convention in 1787, along with Pierce Butler.

Rutledge came to Philadelphia with long experience in governing and a strong aversion to democracy. Gadsden had always made unnecessary difficulties for him in South Carolina and the various colonial congresses. The radicals under Drayton had changed his oligarchic republic into a more democratic state and then dispensed with his services. But although Rutledge had vetoed the 1778 constitution as too democratic, it guaranteed control of the state by the wealthy landowners, merchants, and lawyers of the Charleston area. Senators, though popularly elected, had to own a freehold worth £2000 free of debt. The debtor class of small farmers from the western part of the state were under-represented in the Assembly and not at all represented in the South Carolina delegation to Philadelphia. Charles Beard had suggested that "our fundamental law was not the product of an abstraction known as 'the whole people' but of a group of economic interests which must have expected beneficial results from its adoption." Whatever the validity of his thesis for the rest of the colonies, it had much force when one looks at the South Carolina delegation.

Rutledge had a place of honor in the convention from the start. A French observer of the proceedings noted that Rutledge had been employed "in all the great events" of the time, and that he was eloquent but the most proud and imperious of the delegates. (3 Farrand, *Records,* 238.) William Pierce described him as "highly mounted . . . a distinguished rank among the American Worthies . . . a Gentleman of distinction and fortune . . . but too rapid in his public speaking to be denominated an agreeable orator." Rutledge seconded George Washington's nomination as president of the Convention and with

Robert Morris of Pennsylvania accompanied Washington to the chairman's seat.

Oliver Ellsworth reportedly said to his son that Rutledge played as important a role as himself, James Wilson, Alexander Hamilton, and James Madison in the convention, and Madison's biographer Irving Brant gives him credit with both Madison and Wilson for the "actual construction of the government." There is some justification for these claims. Rutledge was the South Carolina delegate to the select committee which brought in the Great Compromise, giving the states equal voice in the Senate, with the lower house apportioned according to population (five slaves considered three persons) and requiring all revenue measures to originate in the lower house. He proposed the supremacy clause in substantially the form in which it stands in the Constitution. He also served as chairman of the Committee on Detail which composed the first draft of the Constitution.

But a reading of the debates shows that Rutledge again lagged behind the other delegates, pressing for his class' interests rather than for the common good and willing to concede no more to democracy than his home state's constitution had allowed. Soon after the convention opened, Edmund Randolph introduced the Virginia plan: lower house elected by the people, upper house by the lower, and.executive by both. The South Carolina delegation objected to popular election of the lower house. C. C. Pinckney pointed out the danger of democracy: "A majority of the people in South Carolina were notoriously for paper money as a legal tender; the Legislature has refused . . . [since it] had some sense of character." Rutledge claimed that the people could act just as well through their agents, the state legislature, in choosing a national Congress. He supported the Virginia plan to have the upper house chosen by the lower, which was defeated seven states to three.

Rutledge also suggested that the number of representatives in the lower house be determined according to the taxes paid by each state toward the general revenue since "property was certainly the principal object of Society." (1 Farrand, 534.) The South Carolina delegation eventually switched to the population and three-fifths formula. Rutledge also proposed that members of the upper house not be paid any salary, thus insuring membership by the wealthy. He seconded Charles Pinckney's suggestion for a property qualification for all members of the national government, or at the least that the qualifications be the same as those prevailing in their home state legislatures.

Rutledge spoke of the need for a strong executive to be elected by the upper house for one term of seven years. But he opposed the selection of the national judiciary by the President since "the people will think we are leaning too much toward monarchy." Madison reported him as "against establishing any national tribunal except a single supreme one. The State Tribunals [are most proper] to decide in all cases in the first instance." (1 Farrand, 119.) Rutledge moved that the Constitution provide only for a Supreme Court and no inferior tribunals. But James Wilson suggested that Congress be given the power to establish other inferior national courts in its discretion and his proposal was accepted.

Rutledge did not support the type of states' rights program later associated with his fellow Carolinian John C. Calhoun. It is true that he opposed any veto by Congress over state legislation (a plan proposed by Charles Pinckney and supported by James Wilson). ". . . This alone would damn and ought to damn the Constitution. Will any state ever agree to be bound hand and foot in this manner?" (2 Farrand, 391.) But he introduced a strongly worded supremacy clause, supported a vigorous executive, and called for wide powers to the national Congress. He sought to interpose the state legislature between the national government and the voters not because he wished more power in the states but because he wanted less power in the people. The large debtor class clamoring for paper money and insolvency laws was the danger the Constitution had to guard against, and the national government should be as far away from them as possible.

Rutledge's Committee on Detail brought in a draft of the final Constitution. It contained a clause forbidding any tax on exports or any law against the "migration or importation . . . of such persons as the several States shall think proper to admit." Luther Martin of Maryland opposed the inclusion of a ban on the slave trade; it was "inconsistent with the principles of the Revolution and dishonourable to the American character to have such a feature in the Constitution." Rutledge wasted no words on the morality of the ban, saying that the true question was whether the southern states should or should not be parties to the union. If the convention thought North Carolina, South Carolina, and Georgia would ever agree to the Constitution "unless their right to import slaves be untouched, the expectation is vain." (2 Farrand, 373.) Finally a compromise was reached allowing the slave trade to continue until 1808.

With this agreement, the convention moved swiftly to its end. C. C. Pinckney still insisted on a two-thirds requirement in Congress for all "navigation acts," i.e., tariffs or other regulations on trade which the southerners feared would be passed against their interest. But even Rutledge deserted him. He did not think the power to regulate trade would be abused by the northern states. The great object was to secure the "West India trade" to this country, and navigation acts would help foster such commerce. Rutledge, who missed signing the Declaration of Independence because of the battle of Charleston, was the first of his delegation to sign the Constitution. The South Carolina legislature convened on January 10, 1788, to consider ratification. Rutledge answered many of the questions raised by Rawlins Lowndes, the Anti-Federalist leader. A ratifying convention met in the spring and a substantial majority, including Rutledge, ratified on May 23, 1788.

When the first electoral college met early in 1789, Washington won all the votes for President. The South Carolina electors cast their votes for Vice-President for Rutledge, in acknowledgment of all his efforts for his state and the new nation. Washington had known and worked with Rutledge since 1775. His choice for the first Chief Justice centered on John Jay, James Wilson, and Rutledge. Wilson was probably the best lawyer, but not enough of a statesman to lead the Supreme Court. There was no doubt of Washington's personal feelings toward Rutledge. However, with so many southerners in positions of prominence in the government, the selection of Jay seemed desirable. Washington offered Rutledge a seat as senior Associate Justice in a warm personal letter: ". . . I concluded that I should discharge the duty which I owe the public by nominating to this important office a person whom I judged best qualified to execute its functions, and you will allow me to repeat the wish that I may have the pleasure to hear of your acceptance of the appointment."

Although Rutledge did accept the appointment, he never sat as a Justice in this initial period. In the first four terms of the Court, from February, 1790 until August, 1791, no case was argued. The Justices convened for only a few days to admit lawyers and swear in clerks. Rutledge came to New York for the August, 1790 term but was incapacitated by gout and did not attend any Court meeting. However, he did participate at least second hand in a decision relating to circuit court duties. Since the Justices in riding circuit would be swearing in lawyers before the federal courts, it seemed desirable that they be inhabitants of the circuit to which they were assigned, and thus have an independent view of the attorney's qualifications. Rutledge passed his assent to the plan through James Iredell of North Carolina who later complained bitterly about its unfairness to the southern Justices who had the longest distances to travel.

Rutledge and Iredell rode the first southern circuit together. In Charleston they swore in C. C. Pinckney, John E. Calhoun (a cousin of John C.), and four others as members of the federal bar. In company with Iredell on the long trip through the South, Rutledge was most charming and friendly. Iredell wrote to his wife, "He is one of the most agreeable men I was ever acquainted with, and his wife seems a truly respectable and amiable woman." Iredell's letters show that despite the long travels there were moments of peace and pleasure. "I arrived here [in Savannah] in company with Mr. Rutledge, from whom I continue to receive the greatest attention . . . The last part of the way we came down by water, chiefly on Savannah River, in a canoe with four of Mr. Rutledge's hands, as he has a plantation on the way. Mr. R. carried me to some excellent private houses on the road, and we lay by as much as we could in the heat of the day, so that the journey has been on the whole agreeable . . ."

During the same period (1790) Rutledge sat with Justices Wilson and Blair in the Circuit Court of North Carolina in an action which produced the first conflict between the state and federal courts. Some years before, an action had been initiated in the North Carolina Court of Equity at Edenton by the executor and various beneficiaries (who were British subjects) under the will of one Redmond Cunningham. The defendants included James Iredell himself. After the case had been twice argued and various interlocutory orders issued, the British plaintiffs sought to remove the action to the federal courts which after the Judiciary Act of 1789 had jurisdiction of actions brought by aliens. Rutledge's circuit court panel issued a writ of certiorari to the North Carolina court directing the judges to transfer the action to it. The judges refused, claiming that as a court of "original, general, supreme and unlimited jurisdiction" they were not amenable to the authority of any judiciary, "much less by that of a court of inferior and limited jurisdiction." Furthermore they said no act of Congress permitted such removal. The North Carolina judges then wrote to the legislature of their state about the matter. There was strong anti-federalist sentiment in the state and even federalists like W. R. Davie spoke out against the power given to the Supreme Court to review state court decisions by writ of error. The North Carolina legislature, on December 15, 1790, supported the judges in their refusal to obey the federal writ, and did "commend and approve of the conduct of the Judges of the courts of law and courts of equity in this particular." (State Records of North Carolina, Vol. XXI, p. 1054, 1080) The case greatly disturbed Iredell since he was a defendant and the Circuit Court was in his jurisdiction. He begged Jay to assign him elsewhere until the dispute resolved itself.

A combination of pique at not being selected Chief Justice, the lack of activity by the Court, and the long distances required to travel made Rutledge rethink his decision to leave South Carolina. In his home state he was a leading citizen, whereas in Philadelphia he had a secondary role on a secondary institution. Robert Harrison pointed the way by refusing his appointment to the Supreme Court in order to become Chancellor of Maryland. In February, 1791, Rutledge decided his talents would be put to better use in his home state, and he resigned in March to become Chief Justice of the South Carolina Court of Common Pleas. To replace him Washington made one of the most unusual offers in the history of the Court. He wrote a joint letter to Edward Rutledge and C. C. Pinckney about the vacancy. "Will either of you two Gentlemen accept it? And in that case, which of you?" Both declined, also in a joint letter.

The cases Rutledge heard in Common Pleas in law were not appreciably different from those he had decided earlier at equity in Chancery, and they show the grist that went through the legal mill of the day. In his first case, *State* v. *Washington,* 1 Bay (S.C.) 120 (1791), Rutledge sentenced a forger to death after dismissing various technical defenses he had raised:

> *His honor the Chief Justice then (calling him prisoner) briefly stated to him the crime for which he had been indicted; the deliberate trial thereupon, in which he had the assistance of able counsel, and that he had been duly convicted by the oaths of twelve of his peers; that he had afterwards appealed to the court upon several legal exceptions in arrest of judgment; that those exceptions had also been ably argued by his counsel, patiently attended to, and maturely considered by the court, and for the substantial reasons this day stated by them, had also been overruled. That having now nothing further to offer, it was incumbent on the court to pronounce the sentence of the law against him. That the laws of his country demanded no less than his life as the penalty of his crime. His honour then dilated upon the enormity and ruinous tendency of this crime, in all countries, and especially in a commercial community, and strongly painted the heinousness of the guilt, in a civil, a moral, and a religious view. That as a citizen, he had grossly infringed the public rights; as a man, he had broken*

through the obligations of honour and integrity; and as a christian, he had violated the most wholesome precepts of religion. That from a person of his education and habits, better things were to have been expected. That the court pitied his delusion, and hoped that he felt on that solemn occasion as he ought to feel; recommending to him, in a very pathetic manner, to employ that little interval of life which remained, in making his peace with that God whose law he had offended; and suggesting, as an additional motive, that from the malignity of his offense, the court could not flatter him with any hope of pardon. He then concluded an affecting address, and sentenced him, the prisoner at the bar, to be taken to the place from whence he came, from thence to the place of execution, and there, on Wednesday, the 23d of the present month, between the hours of ten and two, to be hanged by the neck until his body is dead, and prayed that the Lord might have mercy on his soul!

The reporter then noted:

He was executed according to sentence, but not on the 23d of March, as the court had granted him one week's respite in order to settle his private affairs, which had been complicated, and in a great state of derangement.

In later cases, Rutledge held that calling a white man a mulatto constituted defamation since the party would be deprived of all his legal rights if the statement were true. *Eden* v. *Legare,* 1 Bay (S.C.) 171 (1791). In the case of *Guardian of Sally* v. *Beaty,* 1 Bay (S.C.) 260 (1792), a Negro woman had acquired a considerable amount of money by hiring herself out with the permission of her master. She paid him a monthly sum in return for the privilege. With her extra money, she purchased the freedom of a young Negro girl, Sally. The master claimed Sally as his, citing a provision of the Civil Law that property acquired by a slave belonged to the master. In rebuttal, the attorney for Sally's guardian claimed that her act "was so singular and extraordinary in itself, so disinterested in its nature, and so replete with kindness and benevolence, that to thwart or defeat the wench's intention would be doing violence to some of the best qualities of the human heart." Rutledge charged the jury in Sally's favor and they returned a verdict for her without retiring from their box.

After four years of hearing cases on dower, mortgages, and sureties, Rutledge evidently regretted his resignation from the Supreme Court which had started to decide cases of national importance. His wife had died in 1792 and he lived alone in Charleston. He also encountered serious financial problems, investing in merchant ships which had to be sold at a loss. In June, 1795, John Jay resigned as Chief Justice after being elected governor of New York. Before the official resignation, Rutledge wrote to Washington about the possible vacancy:

Finding that Mr. Jay is elected Governor of New York and presuming that he will accept the office, I take the liberty of intimating to you privately, *that if he shall, I have no objection to take the place which he holds . . . Several of my friends . . .* [*thought*] *that my pretensions to the office of Chief Justice were at least equal to Mr. Jay's in point of law-knowledge, with the additional weight of much longer experience and much greater practice . . .* [*When*] *the office of Chief Justice of the United States becomes vacant, I feel that the duty which I owe to my children should impel me to accept it, if offered, tho, more arduous and troublesome than my present station, because more respectable and honorable.*

Washington replied immediately on July 1, 1795, tendering the appointment, telling Rutledge that an official letter would be sent by Secretary of State Edmund Randolph, and requesting Rutledge to preside over the August term of the Court. Mail between Philadelphia and Charleston took from one to two weeks. On July 16, 1795, shortly after the letter arrived,* Rutledge committed the most serious political gaffe of his career which doomed his new appointment.

The Jay Treaty had been signed on November 19, 1794. It called for British evacuation of the northwestern forts and referred all boundary disputes and the problem of British debts to various commissions. But Jay also agreed to insulting restrictions on American trade with the West Indies, which were struck out by the Senate, and the British would not yield their right to impress American seamen or recognize international maritime law in their dealings with American ships. Nor would they compensate slave owners for Negroes taken away by British evacuating armies after the war. But Washington was determined to have peace even at that price, the Federalists closed ranks and the Senate grudgingly confirmed the treaty with not one vote to spare on June 24, 1795.

The Treaty was published in the Philadelphia *Aurora* on June 30, 1795 and elsewhere around the country in succeeding days. Economic disappointment and political humiliation produced a wave of resentment and anger. In South Carolina anti-British feeling had been strong since the occupation and plundering of 1780–81. A public meeting was called in Charleston for July 16, 1795. Rutledge assumed the leadership of the meeting and spoke for at least an hour on the treaty. He called it a surrender of American privileges and a "prostitution of the dearest rights of free men." He attacked the language of the treaty as too supplicatory. " 'His Majesty will withdraw his troops . . .' WILL . . . implied it as a favor. It should have been SHALL withdraw his troops." Any doubt as to boundary lines he called the "grossest absurdities." While payment of the debts was just, Rutledge said "to take the power of deciding upon those claims from our state courts, to deny to trust the Supreme Court of the United States and submit the causes to a few commissioners was ridiculous and inadmissible." The only clause with a pretense of reciprocity—the one allowing open trade with the West Indies—was vitiated by the conditions attached to it. Finally he said that he would rather the President should die, dearly as he loved him, than that he should sign the treaty.

* *There is some dispute whether the letter came before or after Rutledge's speech. Charles Warren claims it came later. But Henry Flanders states that the provisions of the Jay Treaty were published on June 30 in the Philadelphia* Aurora *from which the Charleston* Daily Gazette *obtained the text which it printed on July 12. Edmund Randolph insisted his letter must have arrived before July 16, 1795, when the speech was made. It would certainly appear that a letter from the President or Secretary of State would travel as fast as a Philadelphia newspaper.*

As intemperate as his remarks were, Federalist newspapers exaggerated them further. The party leaders could not allow such disloyalty, particularly by one so well known and respected, to be rewarded by public office. Oliver Wolcott of Connecticut wrote to Randolph, "I hope, . . . however disagreeable it may be to imply an error of judgment in the President in appointing Mr. Rutledge, that he will not be confirmed in his office." Another problem with the appointment was soon being discussed: Rutledge's mental condition. Randolph wrote to Washington, "The conduct of the intended Chief Justice is so extraordinary that Mr. Wolcott and Col. Pickering conceive it to be a proof of the imputation of insanity . . ." Attorney General William Bradford wrote to Alexander Hamilton, "The crazy speech of Mr. Rutledge joined to certain information that he is daily sinking into debility of mind and body, will probably prevent him from receiving the appointment."

The suggestion of insanity spread quickly. Hamilton wrote to Senator Rufus King of New York that he would vote to confirm if only Rutledge's opposition to the treaty were involved. "But if it be really true that he is sottish, or that his mind is otherwise deranged, or that he had exposed himself by improper conduct in pecuniary transactions, the bias of my judgment would be to negative." Despite Washington's continued confidence and pressure from southern friends, the Senate rejected Rutledge by a vote of fourteen to ten on December 15, 1795. It was the first important executive nomination turned back by the Senate.

The Republicans took up Rutledge's defense. The Philadelphia *Aurora* commented:

> *There is a remarkable occurrence in our affairs, the refusal of the Senate to confirm the President's nomination of Mr. Rutledge as Chief Justice of the United States—It is the first instance in which they have differed from him in any nomination of importance, and what is remarkable in this case, is that the minority of the members on the Treaty were the minority on this nomination. The face of the thing exhibited a well-digested plan, and as common decency made a nomination necessary, management with the Senate must have rendered the appointment abortive—Senators who had been in a uniform habit of acting with the President would hardly have abandoned him of a sudden, had not the thing been well understood.*

Jefferson saw the rejection as a "declaration that [the administration] will receive none but tories" into the government. An anonymous Anti-Federalist spokesman wrote that the incident showed "the violence of party spirit, the force of stock-jobbing influence and the prejudice of . . . Anglo-men here . . ."

Before the Senate's rejection, Rutledge presided over the August, 1795 term of the Court. Two cases were heard and decided in that month: *United States* v. *Richard Peters,* 3 Dall. 121, and *Talbot* v. *Jansen,* 3 Dall. 133. Both cases dealt with the practice of the French enlisting Americans and fitting out or authorizing armed ships to seize British goods in North American waters. Although the Neutrality Act of 1794 and subsequent laws forbade any Americans from joining the French, many renounced their American citizenship to escape the laws and continued to prey on British ships. Citizen Edmond Genêt and his successors as French ministers ignored the prohibitions against arming French ships in American ports, relying on the strong pro-French feeling throughout the country, particularly in the South.

In the first case, the American schooner *William Lindsey,* loaded with rum and flour taken on at the British possession of St. Thomas, was seized by a French corvette, the *Cassius* (owned by the government and not a privateer), commanded by Samuel Davis, an American citizen acting under the authority of a French commission. The *Lindsey* was taken to a French prize court in Port de Paix and condemned. When the *Cassius* docked later in Philadelphia, James Yard, owner of the *Lindsey,* libelled her, claiming the seizure was illegal. Davis defended his acts, citing the French treaty and international maritime law which permitted the condemning of neutral ships carrying a belligerent's products. Going straight to the Supreme Court, Davis moved for a prohibition to the District Court judge, Richard Peters, requiring him to dismiss the libel. Rutledge speaking for a majority of the Court issued the prohibition, stating that French ships owned by the sovereign could not be libelled by private persons under the French treaty. However the government subsequently filed an information against the *Cassius* since it had been outfitted with arms in United States territory in violation of the neutrality laws of 1794. After protesting, the French government abandoned the ship and discharged the crew.

In the *Talbot* case, the Dutch brigantine *Magdalena,* commanded by Joost Jansen, was captured on May 16, 1794 by a French privateer, *L'Ami de la Liberté,* commanded by Edward Ballard who had no commission of any kind authorizing him to capture neutral ships. (Ballard was later tried for piracy in Charleston but the jury acquitted him.) The following day Ballard met another armed schooner, *L'Ami de la Point à Petre,* commanded by William Talbot who claimed to be a naturalized French citizen since December, 1793. Talbot had received a commission from the French government to capture neutral ships. Talbot rather than Ballard brought the *Magdalena* to Charleston, hoping to have the French consul condemn her. However, Janson immediately libelled both ships, praying for restitution of his vessel and asserting that both Ballard and Talbot were American citizens whose ships were illegally outfitted as armed privateers in America contrary to the neutrality laws. The district court found for Jansen and the circuit court affirmed that decision. Justices Paterson, Iredell, Cushing and Rutledge considered the appeal from the circuit court.

Paterson first considered the effect of the capture by Ballard. Although Ballard had effectively renounced his Virginia citizenship in accordance with its laws, he was still an American citizen since he had taken no oath of allegiance elsewhere. Paterson stated:

> *Ballard was, and still is, a citizen of the United States; unless, perchance, he should be a citizen of the world. The latter is a creature of the imagination and far too refined for any republic of ancient or modern times. If, however, he be a citizen of the world, the character bespeaks universal benevolence and breathes*

> *peace on earth and good will to man; it forbids roving on the ocean in quest of plunder and implies amenability to every tribunal.*

The capture by Ballard's ship—not proved to be sailing under French authority—was in violation of American treaties and laws. As for Talbot, he acted in collusion with Ballard, gave him cannon contrary to the terms of his French commission, and his fraudulent cooperation could not change the character of the initial illegal capture.

Iredell took up the question of Talbot's citizenship. Since Congress had not passed any laws on expatriation, the Court had to have strong and conclusive evidence that Talbot had severed all his ties with the United States. Iredell felt that taking an oath of allegiance to France was an equivocal act and could have been done merely as an excuse to commit piracy. "It surely is impossible to say, he meant a real expatriation, when his conduct *prima facie* as much indicates a crime as any thing else."

Cushing also considered Talbot and Ballard to be in collusion. As for expatriation, Cushing felt there should be, at the very least, physical removal into another country of an emigrant's family and effects.

Rutledge issued his short opinion last, as Chief Justice. He felt there was no proof of Talbot's desire to relinquish his American citizenship since "a man may, at the same time, enjoy the rights of citizenship under two governments." Talbot's ship continued to be American and his capture was thus illegal under the treaty with the Netherlands. Restitution was ordered to Jansen.

Rutledge's decision in the *Talbot* case was his last official utterance. He started to ride circuit in November, 1795. On his way from Augusta, Georgia, to North Carolina he became ill and returned to Charleston. After hearing of his rejection by the Senate, he attempted to drown himself by jumping off a wharf into Charleston Bay on December 26, 1795. Two passing Negro slaves saved him.

For the next five years Rutledge became a recluse. How serious his mental condition became is uncertain. Richard Barry, his biographer, writes there was no basis whatever to the charge of insanity and that critics even labelled John Marshall mad at varying points in his career. However, there are too many contemporaneous references to specific incidents of derangement to substantiate Barry's claim that the rumor was based only on political jealousy and the speech against the treaty. Even before the suicide attempt, Ralph Izard wrote to Jacob Read (South Carolina's other senator in 1795) that after the death of Rutledge's wife in 1792 "his mind was frequently deranged so as to be in a great measure deprived of his senses." Benjamin Moodie, a Charleston lawyer, wrote to Read in December, 1795, "Poor man. I am sorry to say that my ideas were too true with respect to the deranged state of his mind as on the morning of the 26th I am credibly informed that he made an attempt to drown himself at old Cap Blake's wharf, South Bay." However, both Izard and Read voted to confirm Rutledge as Chief Justice, indicating they did not consider the disorder serious or the position particularly important.

On occasion, Rutledge returned to a normal existence. Iredell, riding circuit in Charleston in May, 1798, reported him as "perfectly recovered and in such high spirits that he, and another gentleman and myself outsat all the rest of the company at a friend's house, till near 11 o'clock." The next day Rutledge accompanied Iredell to Roger Smith's house: "This gentleman is married to a sister of Mr. Rutledge's and has a very large and agreeable family . . . Mr. Rutledge has lived so much in retirement that, though very fond of his sister, and the whole family, they had not seen him for a long time; and it was truly affecting to witness their meeting, and how happy they all seemed to be."

Rutledge died on June 21, 1800, a few months after his brother Edward. Though he participated in all the great events of his time, he lacked the vision, ability, and power of Hamilton, Madison, Jefferson, or even of Jay and Adams. Only as the wartime commander of his state did he show the consistent strength required by the times of its leaders. While many members of the Virginia aristocracy concerned themselves with the general welfare of the nation, the South Carolinian leaders looked only to their own constituents. As a broker between what the rest of the colonies were willing to concede and what the South was prepared to accept, Rutledge did his job well. But history demands more of its elected.

SELECTED BIBLIOGRAPHY

Many of Rutledge's personal papers are held by the Charleston Library Society. Only one full-length biography has been prepared: Richard Barry's *Mr. Rutledge of South Carolina* (New York, 1942), which is uneven and exaggerates all of Rutledge's accomplishments. Henry Flanders' *The Lives and Times of the Chief Justices* (New York, 1875) is useful. A few valuable articles have appeared: George S. McCowan, "Chief Justice John Rutledge and the Jay Treaty," 52 *South Carolina Historical Magazine* 10 (Jan., 1961); and Robert W. Barnwell, "Rutledge, 'The Dictator,'" 7 *Journal of Southern History* 215 (May, 1941).

John Rutledge

REPRESENTATIVE OPINIONS

STATE v. WASHINGTON, 1 BAY (S.C.) 120 (1791)

Rutledge's Supreme Court output was extremely meager: three short paragraphs in *Talbot* v. *Janson,* 3 Dall. 133 (1795), and an order in *United States* v. *Richard Peters,* 3 Dall. 121 (1795). However he sat as a state court judge for a number of years and his opinions on the South Carolina bench show his credentials as a legal scholar were quite impressive. In *State* v. *Washington* the defendant was accused of forging an indented certificate of the state by signing the name of the state treasurer to it, forging the name of a prior bearer, and selling the certificate to a Charleston merchant. The jury found him guilty. On appeal, certain technical defenses to the indictment were made which Rutledge had no difficulty in dismissing.

RUTLEDGE, Ch. J. The indictment against the prisoner is very specially drawn, and contains several counts. It charges him in the words of the act of assembly, with having falsely made, forged and counterfeited; with having caused and procured to be falsely made, forged and counterfeited; and with having willingly assisted in the false making, forging, and counterfeiting a writing obligatory, which is commonly called, and well known by the name of an indent of this state; the writing is set forth *verbatim*. It also charges him with having uttered as *true,* a forged and counterfeit writing obligatory, purporting to be an indent, and set forth *verbatim,* knowing it to be so. And it charges him in like manner with forging, with procuring to be forged, and with assisting in the forgery of several receipts for *money,* on the said indent; and with uttering as true, such forged receipts for money on said indent, knowing such receipts to be forged. And all these acts are laid to be done with intent to defraud the several persons mentioned in the indictment, and contrary to the act of assembly, in such case made and provided. The prisoner being found guilty, has offered, in arrest of judgment, the following objections. [Mr. *Chief Justice* here stated the several objections, precisely as they had been laid down by the counsel for the prisoner.] These several points have been argued with ability and ingenuity, at the bar; we have heard them with great attention, and have since maturely considered them. With regard to the first objection, we consider it as we did at the argument, as of no weight. The indictment, had it stopped at the word *"same,"* would have been faulty, and not as the constitution directs. It directs, that all prosecutions shall be carried on in the name, and by the authority of the state of *South-Carolina,* and conclude against the peace and dignity of the *same.* In this clause of the constitution, *state* is the antecedent to the word *same,* to which it refers, and there was no need to add the word *state.* But towards the end of this indictment, *act of assembly,* not *state,* is the antecedent. There was a necessity, therefore, to add the word *state* after the word *same;* otherwise the conclusion would have been against the peace and dignity (not of the state, but) *of the act of assembly.* Another objection was, that the acquittance and receipt charged, was not such as come within the act. This act, which was passed the 5th of *March,* 1736, was made, as the title declares, for putting in force part of the statutes of 2 and 7 *Geo.* II. and incorporates such parts thereof as relates to this offence. And the third clause, on which the present indictment is founded, is in these words. [Here Mr. *Chief Justice* read the clause; which being lengthy, I refer the reader to the public laws.] The arguments in support of this objection, were substantially as follows: That to make forgery, felony within this act, it must be done with intention to defraud; and that these receipts were not intended to defraud. Who, say they, were to be defrauded? Not the treasurers, because several years interest were released: not the party to whom the indent was transferred, because he took it with the receipts upon it, and, consequently, had no right to the interest which appeared to have been paid. That the law means a receipt, the forging of which would tend to deprive some person of his right; but this is only a relinquishment by the prisoner, of his claim on the treasury for so much interest; therefore, that the receipt could only injure himself. The forging such a receipt was compared to the case of *Rex* v. *Knight, Salk.* 375. Another ground was, that if the counts on the indent itself be not felony (which they had before contended, on the ground of its not being a *writing obligatory,* within the act) those on the receipts cannot be felony; for it cannot be more criminal to counterfeit the receipts, than the indent; unconnected with which, the receipt is perfectly innocent. The last ground was, that the receipts were neither for *money* nor *goods,* which the act requires they should be. But special indents are paid for the interest on general indents; therefore, the receipts must be considered for special indents only, and they are not for money. That money has no *ear-mark,* which special indents have; neither are they *goods.* The receipt, therefore, being neither for *money* nor *goods,* comes not within the act. These arguments rest on three grounds; 1. That the receipt was not given with intention to defraud. 2. That if it was not felony to counterfeit the indent, it could not be felony to forge the receipt. 3. That the receipt was not given for *money* or *goods.* Although these arguments may at first view appear ingenious and plausible, yet, on examination, they will be found altogether destitute of solidity. The only point on which we agree with the prisoner's counsel, is, that to make forgery, felony under this act, it must be done with *intention to defraud.* It surely must. It is the essence of the crime. But they say these receipts were not intended to defraud either the *treasurers* or *Vale.* But the jury have found that it was with intent to defraud *both.* They were the judges of that fact: we cannot say they were mistaken. It is of no consequence whether any person was actually defrauded or not; if the forgery was done with intention to defraud, it is sufficient, and that is found. We will cite some leading cases, which warrant this opinion. From 1 *Hawk. P. C.* c. 70. s. 2. "The notion of forgery doth not seem so much to consist in the counterfeiting a man's hand, which may often be done innocently, but *in the endeavouring to give an appearance of truth to a mere deceit and falsity; and to impose that upon the world as the solemn act of another, which he is no way privy to,"* &c. This was the idea of forgery at common law; it is the same under the statute. *Strange,* 747. *Ward's* case. It is not necessary to shew an actual *prejudice;* a possibility is enough. And a case from *Stiles,* p. 12. is there referred to, of an indictment at common law, for forgery of a letter of credit to raise money; and no body, says the book, imagined that the indictment did not lie, though it was not said that he actually received money on the letter of credit. 2 *Black. Rep.* 787. That it is sufficient to aver a general intention to defraud a certain person, which intention must be made out by facts at the trial. It is not necessary to set forth particularly the manner in which the fraud is to operate. Solemnly adjudged by all the judges at Lord *Mansfield's* chambers.

The case quoted by the prisoner's counsel, that of erasing the word "pounds" in a bond, and inserting *marks,* is not a forgery, because the sum is thereby *lessened,* which cannot injure the obligor, but affects only the obligee, will be found, on examination, not to have any avail in a case like this. The law there laid down is good; but the reason on which it is grounded does not apply here. 1 *Hawk*. c. 70. s. 4. (2 *Bac*. 567.) "It is no forgery in one who raseth the word *libris* in a bond given to himself, and inserts *marcis;* because here is no appearance of a fraudulent design to cheat another, the alteration being prejudicial to him who makes it. But it would be forgery, if by the circumstances of the case, it should any way appear to have been done with an eye of gaining an advantage to the party himself, who makes it, or of defrauding a third person." This was the case of a good bond; of a bond made to the man himself; it was a case at common law; yet there it was said it would be forgery, if done with an intention to defraud. *Leech,* 189. *Harrison's* case. Prisoner was convicted on the statute of 2 *Geo*. II. c. 25. and 31 *Geo*. II. c. 22. (which extends the former to corporations,) for forging a receipt for money, with intention to defraud the *London Assurance Company*. He was accountant to the company, who kept their cash at the bank of *England,* where they had paid 210*l.* which was entered by *Clifford,* a cashier at the bank, in *their* bank book thus: "1777, *June* 16th. Bank notes. *Clifford.* 210*l.*" The prisoner altered this entry by prefixing the figure 3, which made it read 3,210*l.* The question referred to the twelve judges was, whether this was a receipt within the meaning of the statute? And they were unanimously of opinion it was. I mention this case to shew, that although it might have been urged, that this could not have been done with intention to defraud the *London Assurance Company,* because it appeared to be for their advantage to have credit for 3,000*l.* more than they had paid; yet no such objection was made, or it was not regarded. They could have no right to credit for more than they had paid; and the conviction was held to be legal. From these cases, and a variety of others that might be adduced, it is clear, that in order to make forgery felony under this act, it is only necessary that it should be done *mala fide,* with intention to defraud some person. It is not necessary to lay or to prove, that any person was actually defrauded. And this upon good reasons; because the forgery may be discovered, and the party apprehended for prosecution, before the fraud intended could be thoroughly effected. *The intention constitutes the crime.*

The counsel for the prisoner contended further, that if the counterfeiting the indent was not felony, counterfeiting the *receipts* could not be felony; for it cannot be more criminal to counterfeit the receipt, than the indent; and unconnected with the indent, the receipt is perfectly innocent. But this we conceive to be false and inconclusive reasoning; and that the transactions of counterfeiting the indent, and forging the receipt, may be considered and determined upon, as totally independent of each other. The charge with respect to the receipt is for *forging a receipt for money, with intention to defraud certain persons.* And it is of no consequence *on what* those receipts were written; whether on the back of an indent, on the back of a lottery ticket, on a sheet of paper, or on the margin of a newspaper. If the receipt was for money; if it was forged; if it was forged with intention to defraud any person, that is sufficient to constitute it felony under the act. It was further alleged, that these receipts are not for money or goods, but must be considered as given for *special indents,* which are neither one nor the other. It is clear that the receipts are not for goods; but it is laid in the indictment that they were for money; and the fact is so found by the jury. There are two modern cases that shew, that the court have not been very strict on this head, where the intention to defraud has been manifest, always keeping that in view as the foundation of every thing. The one was the case of *James Elliott,* in 1777, *Leech,* 185. He was indicted for forging a bank note, whereby *Thomas Thompson,* for the governor and company of the bank of *England, promised to pay Joseph Crooke, or bearer, on demand,* fifty; and the indictment charged it to be a promissory note for the payment of money. It was contended for the prisoner, that the word *pounds* being omitted in the body of the note, it was not a note for payment of money; or if it was, it was totally uncertain what coin, whether pounds or shillings; and that on such an uncertainty in a declaration, a plaintiff would be nonsuited. The judge left it with the jury to consider, whether the word *fifty* imported pounds; and they found the prisoner guilty on that count which charged him with *having forged a promissory note for payment of money, with intention to defraud the bank of England.* And on this objection being renewed, by way of motion in arrest of judgment, before the judges at *Serjeants-Inn,* they were unanimously of opinion the verdict was legal. The other case was that of *John Taylor,* 1779,

Leech, 214. He was indicted for that having in his possession, a bill of exchange drawn by *Thomas Harper* on *Joseph Cuff,* for 20*l.* he forged a receipt and acquittance *for the said sum,* as follows, viz. "Rec'd. *William Wilson,*" with intent to defraud the said *Joseph Cuff.* He was convicted; and the twelve judges were of opinion the conviction was legal. With respect to the special indents, the tax act under which they were issued made them redeemable or exchangeable at the treasury, for gold or silver, at certain periods, &c. that the man who had them, might probably, if he kept them by him, get the full amount. But if he chose to part with them, he could at any time *get money* for them, though he could not dispose of them *at par.* However, *it does not appear,* that special indents were paid. They might have been, and they might not have been considered as money. The fact we suppose is, that neither money nor special indents were paid, because the receipt is charged to be *forged,* and found so. It is said to be for two years' interest; but it is also said to be for 86*l.* 2*s.* 6*d.* making total two years' interest. Though the receipt is for those sums, in figures, the operation is the same as if it had been in words at length. We are, therefore, of opinion, that this objection must be overruled. It is immaterial to consider any of the other objections which have been offered; because the first and last objection being overruled, it follows, that the prisoner is lawfully convicted of having forged a receipt for money, with intention to defraud the persons mentioned in the indictment; and that such a forgery is, by the act of assembly, felony without benefit of clergy. We would not, however, be understood, as according to the doctrine laid down by the prisoner's counsel in their other objections. We have been more diffuse in delivering this opinion than is usual, or perhaps was necessary. But this being a case of great importance to the public and to the prisoner, and his counsel appearing to lay great stress on this objection, we considered it proper to state thus fully the reasons upon which our decision is founded.

The prisoner being asked by the clerk, what he had further to offer why sentence of death should not be pronounced against him according to law; replied, that he had nothing further to offer.

His honor the Chief Justice then (*calling him prisoner**) briefly stated to him the crime for which he had been indicted; the deliberate trial thereupon, in which he had the assistance of able counsel, and that he had been duly convicted by the oaths of twelve of his peers; that he had afterwards appealed to the court upon several legal exceptions in arrest of judgment; that those exceptions had also been ably argued by his counsel, patiently attended to, and maturely considered by the court, and for the substantial reasons this day stated by them, had also been overruled. That having now nothing further to offer, it was incumbent on the court to pronounce the sentence of the law against him. That the laws of his country demanded no less than his life as the penalty of his crime. His honour then dilated upon the enormity and ruinous tendency of this crime, in all countries, and especially in a commercial community, and strongly painted the heinousness of the guilt, in a civil, a moral, and a religious view. That as a citizen, he had grossly infringed the public rights; as a man, he had broken through the obligations of honour and integrity; and as a christian, he had violated the most wholesome precepts of religion. That from a person of his education and habits, better things were to have been expected. That the court pitied his delusion, and hoped that he felt on that solemn occasion as he ought to feel; recommending to him, in a very pathetic manner, to employ that little interval of life which remained, in making his peace with that God whose law he had offended; and suggesting, as an additional motive, that from the malignity of his offence, the court could not flatter him with any hope of pardon. He then concluded an affecting address, and sentenced him, the prisoner at the bar, to be taken to the place from whence he came, from thence to the place of execution, and there, on *Wednesday,* the 23d of the present month, between the hours of ten and two, to be hanged by the neck until his body is dead, and prayed that the Lord might have mercy on his soul!

He was executed according to sentence, but not on the 23d of *March,* as the court had granted him one week's respite in order to settle his private affairs, which had been complicated, and in a great state of derangement.

* *The reader must have observed, that he was indicted under several names. He had long gone by the name of* Washington; *but it had often been suspected, and from circumstances latterly transpired, is not now doubted to have been an assumed name. It is said that his real name was* Welch.

TALBOT v. JANSEN, 3 DALL. 133 (1795)

Jansen, the master of a Dutch schooner, libelled Edward Ballard and William Talbot who together had brought his ship into Charleston to be condemned as a French prize—Ballard had captured the ship but Talbot alone had a French commission to seize neutral merchants. Since the neutrality laws forbade any Americans from engaging in such captures, both claimed not to be American citizens, and in fact Talbot had taken an oath of allegiance to France before the episodes complained of. Talbot claimed his ship was not owned by any American, but the documents he presented to prove it were inconclusive at the least. All the Justices found for Jansen, Rutledge speaking last in a short opinion.

RUTLEDGE, *Chief Justice*. The merits of the cause are so obvious, that I do not conceive there is much difficulty in pronouncing a fair and prompt decision, for affirming the decree of the Circuit Court.

The doctrine of expatriation is certainly of great magnitude; but it is not necessary to give an opinion upon it, in the present case, there being no proof, that Captain *Talbot's* admission as a citizen of the *French* Republic, was with a view to relinquish his native country; and a man may, at the same time, enjoy the rights of citizenship under two governments.

It appears, upon the whole, that *Ballard's* vessel was illegally fitted out in the *United States;* and the weight of evidence satisfies my mind, that *Talbot's* vessel, which was originally *American* property, continued so at the time of the capture, notwithstanding all the fraudulent attempts to give it a different complexion. The capture, therefore, was a violation of the law of nations, and of the treaty with *Holland*. The court has a clear jurisdiction of the cause, upon the express authority of *Pelaches's* Case. 4 *Inst*. And every motive of good faith and justice must induce us to concur with the Circuit Court, in awarding restitution.

The Decree of the Circuit Court affirmed.

William Cushing

☆ 1732–1810 ☆

APPOINTED BY

GEORGE WASHINGTON

YEARS ON COURT

1789–1810

William Cushing

by

HERBERT ALAN JOHNSON

WILLIAM CUSHING might well have adopted the Psalmist David's prayer of thanksgiving, "Yea, I have a goodly heritage" as the motto for his varied and eventful life. For Cushing was truly most fortunate in his family and its political connections. Opportunities for advancement came to young Cushing more as a result of the accident of birth than because of his natural abilities. In the maternal line he could trace his genealogy to Reverend John Cotton, the theological giant of seventeenth century Massachusetts. His father, and his grandfather before him, had been members of the Governor's Council and sat as judges in the Superior Court of the province of Massachusetts Bay. Social and political connections being an important aspect of office holding in the Bay Colony, it was a foregone conclusion that one day young William would succeed to the positions of his ancestors as one of the leaders of his native province.

One of the remarkable aspects of William Cushing's career was his ability to survive the upheaval of the American Revolution in Massachusetts that so profoundly upset the social and political order to which he fell heir. At his father's insistence and because of the senior Cushing's political power, William was appointed to the high post of Associate Justice of the Superior Court in 1772. The elder Cushing had deferred his resignation until he could be certain that Lieutenant Governor Thomas Hutchinson would appoint William to the seat he left vacant upon the bench. Hutchinson delayed and there is good reason to believe that William Cushing was his second choice for the judgeship. Nevertheless, his ultimate choice was forced upon him and the Lieutenant Governor could comfort himself with the thought that, if nothing else, young Cushing would be a reliable supporter of the Crown and the established order in the

HERBERT A. JOHNSON, Associate Editor of the John Marshall Papers, Institute of Early American History and Culture, has written The Law Merchant and Negotiable Instruments in Colonial New York, 1664–1730.

province. Indeed, William Cushing more than most other Massachusetts judges was dependent upon his judicial office for his livelihood and hence more amenable to gubernatorial influence; as we shall see later, the young man had not been very successful in the first forty years of his life, and a place upon the bench was an excellent source of guaranteed income, provided one did not offend the colonial executive or the imperial administrators in London.

Scarcely a year after Cushing's appointment to the Superior Court the partisan controversy that was to lead to the American Revolution broke in upon his protected bailiwick and demanded that he choose between the interests of the province and those of the Crown. Lieutenant Governor Hutchinson precipitated a conflict with the legislature concerning the manner in which the justices of the Superior Court were to be paid. The previous practice had been that the legislature would appropriate funds for this purpose, but Hutchinson proposed that the judges' salaries were properly chargeable to Crown revenues and that they should thereafter receive their perquisites from the Crown. At this critical juncture Cushing and his fellow judges demurred from choosing either alternative, and the patriot party in the legislature threatened impeachment to any judge of the Superior Court who remained uncommitted or who chose the Crown grant. Throughout the controversy Hutchinson had considered William Cushing to be a "friend of government" who would choose loyalty to the Crown and the established authorities of the province. Judge Cushing remained silent until Chief Justice Peter Oliver was forced to announce his decision, which was to refuse the legislative salary in favor of the Crown grant. Immediately the patriot party commenced impeachment proceedings, and at the same time demanded Cushing's public avowal concerning his intentions. His informants in the legislature urged him to elect the legislative appropriation, and at the last moment before impeachment proceedings were commenced against him, he took their advice. On February 5, 1774, Judge Cushing announced his willingness to accept his pay from the province and to refuse a grant from the Crown for the same purpose. With that single choice he left the protection of the ruling powers of Massachusetts and cast his lot with the patriot party. The choice was clearly too late to be an entirely voluntary one, yet it alienated Cushing from Hutchinson and for this reason raised him in the esteem of the legislature. During the summer of 1774 he was denied a seat on the Governor's Council because of Hutchinson's animosity and the contempt of Chief Justice Peter Oliver. When this became known it only tended to reassert his position as a silent supporter of the patriot cause. Thus it was that William Cushing moved from a favored place in the "Court party" of Hutchinson to an ambivalent position as a reluctant supporter of American liberties against the Crown.

Throughout the controversy Cushing continued to ride the Superior Court circuit, thereby keeping the royal courts open for business. His associates were either ill, or in the case of Chief Justice Oliver, too frightened to ride the circuit, and two justices were required to open the court and retain a semblance of order in a province rapidly approaching revolution. With the successful impeachment of Oliver the possibility of obtaining a quorum of two justices was further reduced, but Cushing persisted in executing his circuit duties. Once hostilities broke out between the provincial and British forces, the commissions of all royal officials were declared revoked effective September 19, 1775; only then did William Cushing lay aside his elaborate justice's wig and cease to ride the circuit travelled by his ancestors.

One month after his royal commission expired, Cushing was again on the circuit bouncing along the roads in his Padduck curricle with a commission as senior Associate Justice of the Superior Court of the independent Commonwealth of Massachusetts. This transfer of allegiance was a matter of utmost circumspection, for to the very last days of royal government Cushing had executed his sworn duty under his royal commission. In fact his determination to continue terms of the Superior Court served to perpetuate the semblance of royal authority long after his native province had embarked upon the path toward armed revolt against the British authorities. Holding circuits at the risk of his personal safety, Cushing did much to maintain the authority of the Crown in the critical period from 1774 to 1775. Well might his detractors point to this service as an indication that the "Brahman" Cushing was loyal to the interests of his class and the Crown. On the other hand, Cushing's decision to accept a salary grant from the province, and his exclusion from a seat at the Council board because of this choice, marked him as one who had suffered a loss of office and dignities for his adherence to the patriot cause, or at the least, the cause of Massachusetts fiscal autonomy. This ambivalent stance has been aptly described by his biographer, John D. Cushing, as a deft piece of political tightrope walking. It is still a mystery whether Cushing himself ever made an election to follow the patriot party, or if the circumstances of the time and Hutchinson's actions did not force him to that reluctant step.

While William Cushing's dedication to the American Revolution can be seriously questioned, there can be little doubt that his popularity with the new rulers of Massachusetts Bay was sufficient to place him back upon the Superior Court as an associate justice. Thereafter he worked devotedly toward restoring orderly government in the province. In his earliest decisions as a state justice he held firmly against property seizures made in admiralty cases that were not in accordance with due process of law. In treason trials he insisted that the same procedural rights be afforded defendants that were provided by British precedents. While the land was rife with rebellion against the Crown, William Cushing took care that the rule of law was not subverted.

The task of giving law to a rebellious people was not a peaceful one, as Cushing discovered in his brush with the Berkshire rioters in 1779. This group, also known as the Berkshire Constitutionalists, objected to the government of Massachusetts Bay under the 1692 charter, claiming that that document was illegal and that the 1629 charter should form the basis of government. When Cushing arrived to open the Superior Court in 1779 they refused to permit him to sit in accordance with the provisions of the 1692 charter, and he and his associates were compelled to meekly withdraw under the threat of physical violence.

Fresh from the humiliation suffered at the hands of the Berkshire rioters in the spring of 1779, Cushing joined his associates on the bench to meet at the Massachusetts Constitutional Convention. There they helped to draft an instrument of government that would partially remove the Berkshire Constitutionalists' objections to the first revolutionary government under the 1692 charter. Despite this concession to the constitutional demands of western Massachusetts, the tendency in that region toward violent obstruction of justice was to lead inevitably to Shay's Rebellion in 1786. Cushing's steadfastness in the face of these and other similar disorders, point quite clearly to the service he rendered to Massachusetts by his maintenance of the law in the province during the American Revolution.

At the Constitutional Convention, Cushing, who had succeeded John Adams as Chief Justice of the Superior Court in 1777, played a minor role. At one time his boredom led him to jot down a list of materials that he would need to make a new suit of clothes. Very likely the debates upon the nature of the state, the allocation of political power between the branches of government, and the relationship of citizen to government, were of little concern to him, and he left such matters to others of a more philosophical bent. His own court was renamed the Supreme Judicial Court, but except for the change of name, remained substantially the same tribunal that it had been under the royal government. There is no record of Cushing's participating in the floor debates or the committee work of the convention. On the other hand, once the document was in final form, he worked strenuously to obtain its ratification. During his charges to the juries on his circuits, Cushing rarely lost occasion to extol the merits of the new constitution, and his support may have done much to insure its ratification by the people of Massachusetts.

In spite of the ostensible ease with which William Cushing had weathered the political storm of the Revolution and retained his high judicial office, Cushing was not a particularly gifted lawyer. As noted above, the constitutional debates of 1779–1780 fatigued him to the extent that he doodled at the convention. Before his appointment to the royal court of the province, his practice had been far from successful. After a thorough classical training at Harvard from 1747 to 1751, he taught for one year at Roxbury before commencing his clerkship with Jeremy Gridley, one of the leaders of the Boston bar. Admitted to practice upon Gridley's motion in 1755, he began his professional career in his native town of Scituate. There he found it difficult to make his way in the highly competitive bar, and in 1760 he moved to Pownalborough in the province of Maine. Despite an appointment to be the justice of peace of the quorum for that town, and a subsequent commission to be judge of probates for the surrounding county of Lincoln, Cushing was scarcely more successful in Maine. He had been charged with the legal affairs of the Kennebec and Pemaquid proprietary companies when he left for Pownalborough, and the nature of Maine land titles was such that this could have been a source of activity and profits. Despite these professional advantages, he achieved more success in business ventures than in practice, and even in business he made so little that he could not arrange a marriage until two years after he had been appointed to the Superior Court bench. Eventually Cushing lost his corporate clients to other attorneys. It is not without significance that when a matter was to be argued on appeal at the bar of the Superior Court, his clients removed it from Cushing's care or insisted that he accept co-counsel in the presentation of the case. Among Cushing's private papers there is ample evidence that the suspicions of his clients were not without adequate foundation, for he continually wrote to his father, to Jeremy Gridley, and even to his contemporaries at the bar, requesting their advice upon law or procedure. Throughout his life Cushing was unsure of the law; decision for him was thus a consultative rather than a deliberative process. Without powerful family connections and a winning personality, such an attorney would never have survived in the highly educated and articulate bar that produced a practitioner of the caliber of John Adams.

As Chief Justice of the Superior Court from 1777 to 1780, and Chief Justice of the Supreme Judicial Court from 1780 to 1789, William Cushing was assigned numerous tasks of legislative draftsmanship. For the most part his performance in shaping the law of the Commonwealth was undistinguished. A member of the commission to revise the laws, he had an excellent opportunity to contribute to the future jurisprudence of Massachusetts. Among the bills drawn by the Chief Justice and later enacted by the legislature were those for the establishment of a naval office, for the regulation of seamen, and for the alteration of the grounds and procedures for obtaining a divorce. Only the latter bill, providing a judicial rather than a legislative procedure for divorce actions, had any substantial effect upon the law, and it remains the basic outline for Massachusetts divorce law to the present day. For the most part, Cushing worked slowly and painfully upon the subjects assigned to him. Burdened by the other duties of office, he failed to bring energy and direction to his own work, and significantly, he also failed to inspire his colleagues upon the law revision commission with the need to restate the laws in a clear and unequivocal form. As a result, the attempt at law revision and reform was for the most part abortive.

Undoubtedly the most famous litigation which came before Cushing as Chief Justice of the Supreme Judicial Court was the series of cases which are known to historians as the Quock Walker Case. As John Cushing has clearly shown, these were no less than six related cases during the course of which the Chief Justice did not render an opinion. Nevertheless the historical tradition is that in the course of this controversy William Cushing decided that the clause in the 1780 Massachusetts constitution that declared all men free and equal was, in effect, the equivalent of abolishing slavery in Massachusetts. As Cushing points out, the law in Massachusetts at this time was stated by the jury and not in opinions of the court. It is in the case of *Commonwealth* v. *Jennison* that the Chief Justice charged the jury concerning the status of slavery in Massachusetts;

although the charge did not mean the immediate abolition of the institution, it did in the opinion of Jeremy Belknap result in the inevitable weakening and eventual death of slavery in the Bay State.

The complex series of cases concerning Quock Walker began when the slave fled from his master, Nathaniel Jennison, in 1781. Sheltered by one Caldwell, Walker was eventually discovered by Jennison and a fracas ensued, in the course of which both Walker and Caldwell were assaulted by Jennison. Both sued in civil actions for assault and battery, and in both cases Jennison entered the defense that he was merely attempting to recover his runaway slave. To this Walker and Caldwell replied that Walker could not be a slave because the 1780 Massachusetts Constitution had abolished slavery. When the case reached the Supreme Court in the latter part of 1781, the issue of slavery was debated at great length but Cushing was absent because of illness. Not until 1783, when the trial of a criminal indictment was brought before the Supreme Court *en banc,* did Cushing sit upon the case. This resulted in his famous charge to the jury referred to above. The strong likelihood is that Cushing did not himself have any strong convictions concerning slavery, for even after the Quock Walker cases he was quite willing to restore slaves to their masters provided the master was not a Massachusetts resident. On the other hand, slavery was a dying institution and Cushing's charge in *Commonwealth* v. *Jennison* was a well-devised attempt at euthanasia.

One other incident brought Cushing and his court to public attention in the period between the end of the War for Independence and the ratification of the federal Constitution in 1788. This was the 1786 uprising of debtors in western Massachusetts which has been named Shay's Rebellion—for lack of a better descriptive term. Part of the reason for the outbreak of disorder was the fact that the Supreme Court frequently rode the circuit without the two justices necessary to constitute a quorum; as a result, collection of debts by judgment was not possible and the debtors, far from benefitting by the delay, were required to pay more in interest when the justices arrived and held court. For the most part, however, the economic difficulties of the western portion of the state were the principal cause of the riots, and the delays in obtaining justice only aggravated an already tense situation.

Cushing was not a stranger to riots in western Massachusetts; as noted above, he had been forced to meekly retire from his confrontation with the Berkshire rioters in 1779. In the April term of 1782 he had travelled to the same region and tried Samuel Ely, a leader of debt rioters, in spite of the surly temper of the community. Before convening the Court he had dismissed a petition from the people asking that Ely be released without trial since he had led opposition to an unjust and inequitable law. This application he rejected and suggested that the proper means of obtaining redress was to address such a request to the legislature which alone could alter the laws. Wisely enough, after Ely was convicted, Chief Justice Cushing pronounced a rather lenient sentence.

These incidents had somewhat prepared Cushing for the crisis in September of 1786 when the Supreme Court met at its Springfield session under the protection of the state militia. The troops had seized the county courthouse before the rioters could do so, but both grand and petit jurors were terrorized into ignoring the venire writs of the sheriff. This compelled Cushing and his colleagues to suspend the proceedings. Nevertheless he appears to have exhibited considerable personal courage in the course of the riots, and certainly the legend reported by Flanders must have some basis in fact.

> *As* [*Cushing*] *advanced, the crowd opened before him, but slowly and sullenly; muskets rattled, and some bayonets rapped upon his breast; quietly and firmly, however, he moved on, reached the courthouse, and the court was regularly opened.*

Six months later he was to return to this very courthouse, there to preside over the treason trials of the leaders of Shay's Rebellion.

The disorders in Massachusetts were the last in a series of causes that drove many to support the movement toward a stronger national government. From his firsthand knowledge of these events, Cushing must have been even more strongly motivated, for when the ratification of the Constitution of the United States was debated in Massachusetts, he no longer spent his time contemplating the necessary components of a new suit of clothes. Instead he served as vice-president of the ratifying convention, and for most of that body's proceedings acted as the presiding officer in the absence of its president, John Hancock. When Hancock finally appeared at the Convention, Cushing stepped down from the chair and prepared an oration he wished to deliver in support of the Constitution. Although the speech was never given, it survives in manuscript and is a valuable indication of the view Cushing took concerning the contemplated alterations in the federal government.

Sharp debate had occurred in the convention sessions concerning the right of the federal government to maintain a standing army. This departure from the provisions of the Articles of Confederation William Cushing defended as being entirely in accord with similar power granted to the government of Massachusetts under the 1780 constitution. In regard to demands that the members of the House of Representatives should be reelected on a yearly basis and that they should not be permitted to succeed themselves, Cushing again supported the longer term in the constitutional proposals from Philadelphia, and he also pointedly commented that rotation of legislators had not been particularly useful in saving Rome from consular dictatorship. It had prevented the states, under the Articles of Confederation, from freely electing men they wished to represent them. Nothing good could be accomplished by rotation being written into the legislative provisions of the Philadelphia document, and it was actually an intrusion upon the free choice of the people.

Upon the questions of federal and state power, Cushing demonstrated that he had few fears that the national government would usurp the functions of state agencies. After all, did not the President and the Senate of the national government gain their positions through the indirect electoral processes which functioned through the states? Without state governments these important officials of the proposed federal government could never be elected to office. On the other hand experience under the Articles of Confederation had indicated that the states would undermine the authority of the general government and take to themselves its powers and authority, and the likelihood was that government under the Philadelphia document would do so also.

Cushing's view of the clause that has become known to political scientists as the "elastic clause" is surprising in the retrospection of history. And yet, like so much of Cushing's thought, it represents a comfortable simplification of a prickly problem of law and statutory construction. He felt that objections to the "necessary and proper" clause were pointless, in fact the clause itself was somewhat superfluous. Obviously the grant of express powers to the Congress carried with it the authority to enact such means as were necessary to effectuate the express powers. Constitutions must be construed to uphold the orderly administration of government; this Cushing had demonstrated once before when he delivered an advisory opinion concerning the 1780 Massachusetts constitution and upheld the temporary appointment of members of the Governor's Council until such time as the vacant council seat could be filled by election as the constitution required. Otherwise, Cushing pointed out, the government would come to a standstill for lack of a quorum on the Governor's Council. Likewise with the proposed federal Constitution, why should powers be granted if the legislature which received them was deprived of the techniques by which they could be carried out?

One further evidence of Cushing's nationalist position is his view of the locus of sovereignty that would exist under the proposed Constitution. There was really no reason to include an amendment concerning the "reserved powers" of the states. In fact those powers which were not granted to the federal government under the new frame of government would be reserved either to the states or to the people, the ultimate repositories of all sovereign power. The federal problem for Cushing was not whether the states or federal government took the residue of sovereignty to themselves, for that was clearly deposited with the people, and, without an express constitutional grant to either federal or state governments, sovereignty remained in the people. In this he anticipated some of the constitutional theories of James Wilson, and clearly indicates that the power of the federal government was not in his opinion derived from the grant of the several states.

Since Cushing never delivered the above constitutional views to his colleagues at the ratifying convention, we have no way of determining what impact these thoughts may have had upon them. Undoubtedly his views were known to most of the members of that body, and the prestige of his office may have aided the advocates of the new constitution to achieve their narrow majority of 187 to 168 in favor of ratification.

Once the federal Constitution was ratified and put into effect, Cushing performed two final services for his native state. Despite protests that judges were forbidden by the 1780 Massachusetts constitution from serving as presidential electors, Cushing and his associate justices were members of the Massachusetts delegation to the Electoral College in 1788 and cast their votes for George Washington as first President of thc United States. In September of 1789 Cushing was commissioned an Associate Justice of the Supreme Court of the United States, but before he accepted the appointment he performed his final duty as Chief Justice of the Massachusetts Supreme Judicial Court. He rode the circuit, thereby insuring that there was a quorum of judges to handle the business at hand, and after this arduous duty was completed, he accepted the appointment as a Supreme Court Justice and resigned as Chief Justice in Massachusetts.

When William Cushing took his seat upon the Supreme Court bench in February of 1790, he was in his fifty-eighth year. A man of slight build and medium height, he was of a fair complexion. His eyes were blue but the most conspicuous feature of his countenance was his aquiline nose, which was somewhat large, and about which he was somewhat sensitive. His one objection to a portrait of himself by Sharpless was that the artist had been too brutally honest concerning the nose. Flanders reports the anecdote that when Cushing arrived for the first sitting of the Court in New York City he wore his old-fashioned full-bottomed judicial wig. About one hundred little boys followed him down the street, watching him with curiosity and awe. The crowd grew and gradually it dawned upon the Justice that he was the object of unusual attention, although he did not know the reason why. Finally a sailor was astonished into exclaiming, "My eyes! What a wig!" The new Associate Justice of the Supreme Court returned to his hotel room, ordered a peruke maker to prepare a more fashionable headpiece for him, and was never again seen in his judge's wig.

In moving to the federal bench Cushing left behind more than his judicial wig, for the duties imposed on a Supreme Court Justice altered to his detriment many of the customs which he had followed in riding the Massachusetts Supreme Court circuit. There he had travelled in a carriage, at first a Padduck curricle, later in a phaeton. Always accompanied by a lady to serve as his hostess, he travelled in luxury and sociable comfort. While a bachelor he had taken his unmarried sister Hannah with him, and after his marriage in 1774 his wife, the former Hannah Phillips, went with him. As they rode she read to him from the large store of books he kept in special receptacles he had designed for them in his phaeton. The distances involved in the circuits of the Supreme Court of the United States did not allow such slow and luxurious travel, and he spent most of his days in the saddle riding the rocky New England roads with Chief Justice John Jay, a man who gloried in the medicinal effects of long rides on horseback. Perhaps the wig was the least of Cushing's sacrifices for his elevation to the highest court in the land.

Cushing's twenty-one years upon the Supreme Court ran from the date he accepted his commission, November 26, 1789, to the date of his death on September 13, 1810. During this period he wrote but nineteen opinions in the Supreme Court. All are modest, straightforward discussions of the cases before the Court; some are brief to the point of being abrupt, most are careful, if uninspired, treatments of the issues involved. His biographer, John D. Cushing, notes with truth that more of the man's constitutional philosophy emerges from his speech before the Massachusetts ratifying convention than in all of his opinions from the Supreme Court bench.

For one week Cushing held Washington's commission naming him to be Chief Justice of the United States, the appointment having been tendered immediately after John Rutledge had been rejected by the Senate in 1795. The only recorded function that Cushing performed as Chief Justice was to attend one of President Washington's dinner parties, at which he was given the place of honor due to him as the principal Justice of the Court. A few days thereafter he declined the Chief Justiceship upon grounds of ill health, but retained his seat upon the Bench as an Associate Justice. A student of his judicial career, F. William O'Brien, has commented that Cushing was "the only human bridge between the weak judicial institution of the Jay Court and the firm and respected structure of the Marshall era." This was the second transition of Cushing's life; a royal justice had made his way into the judiciary of the independent Commonwealth of Massachusetts, and now a Justice from the Jay Court was to survive to see the commencement of Supreme Court authority and power under the guiding hand of Chief Justice John Marshall.

Justice Cushing's propensity to simplify complex issues has already been illustrated from events in his career before he became a Supreme Court Justice. This continued when he wrote his opinions from the federal bench. An example is his two sentence decision in the case of *Calder* v. *Bull,* 3 Dall. 386 (1798), in which the Court had under consideration a Connecticut statute that denied probate to an otherwise valid will. His colleagues struggled with the serious questions of constitutionality that were involved. Did the federal Constitution offer protection to the property rights of the dispossessed legatees and devisees? Did the Connecticut law fall within the prohibition of the *ex post facto* clause of the federal Constitution? Their opinions were long and careful analyses of the constitutional problem and the impact of the federal Constitution upon state action in this field. For Cushing the case was "clear of all difficulty," for the *ex post facto* provision applied only to criminal and not to civil matters. In *Ware* v. *Hylton,* 2 Dall. 282 (1796), Cushing went immediately to the intent and phraseology of the 1783 peace treaty to decide the issue of British creditors collecting from their pre-Revolutionary debtors. Again his "instinct for the jugular vein" was sure, and the problem ultimately resolved itself upon the single issue that Cushing raised, but the tendency to ignore the broader implications and technical problems of federalism is readily apparent. Were William Cushing not so clear in his analysis of the case and simple in his statement of the central issue, one would suspect that the more subtle aspects of arguments of counsel and the discussions of his fellow jurists were lost upon him. Yet if one looks for a judge who understood how to dispose of a case as tersely as possible, it is hard to find a man on the Supreme Court of the United States who surpasses William

Cushing. Although he may not have been the most profound thinker to serve upon the Supreme Court, his dogged determination to resolve a case upon the one vital issue it raised must have made him a joy to the attorneys who appeared before him and the commentators who digested his laconic opinions.

Among Cushing's constitutional opinions two stand out as most prominent, *Chisholm* v. *Georgia,* 2 Dall. 467 (1793), and *Ware* v. *Hylton.* Both intimately involved questions of federal and state sovereignty and both were the basis for hotly debated political contests in their own day. The *Chisholm* case was based upon a rather large debt which the state of Georgia had incurred in purchasing military supplies from Chisholm's testator, a citizen of South Carolina. After the ratification of the federal Constitution and the opening of the federal courts, Chisholm brought action against the Georgia authorities in the United States Circuit Court, but the procedures in that tribunal were ineffective and Chisholm turned to the alternative measure of suing the state of Georgia in the Supreme Court of the United States, as part of that Court's original jurisdiction. Although Georgia failed to appear in the case before the Supreme Court, the Court itself requested counsel for Chisholm to direct his argument to the question of its jurisdiction over the state of Georgia. The decision of the Court was delivered *seriatim,* and Cushing joined a majority of the Court in his opinion that the state of Georgia was amenable to process issued by the Court at the instance of a citizen of another state. Cushing's opinion follows that of Associate Justice John Blair, who also argued that it was clear that states could be made defendants in all actions before the Supreme Court. Since a state could sue a state before the Court, it was apparent that in such an action a state was a defendant; thus there was no reason why a state could not be made a party defendant if the opposing party was a citizen of another state. There was just as much danger of interstate strife if a citizen could not sue a neighboring state, as there would be if the states could not resolve their own disputes by recourse to law.

Shortly after the decision in *Chisholm* v. *Georgia* the requisite number of state legislatures ratified the Eleventh Amendment to the federal Constitution which reversed the *Chisholm* case and protected states from being hauled before the bar of the Supreme Court by citizens of other states. William Cushing, despite the fact that his opinion was rather sterile of the comments upon political science that studded other opinions on the Court, was nevertheless caught in the voter backlash against *Chisholm* v. *Georgia.* In 1794 he was induced to run for the office of governor of Massachusetts and was defeated by the resounding plurality of two to one. Even the judge who refrained from attacks upon state sovereignty and wrote his opinion upon the basis of a simple analogy, was not immune from political reprisals.

Ware v. *Hylton* raised for the Supreme Court's consideration the problem of state legislation during the American Revolution that had confiscated the obligations which Americans owed to British merchants. A 1777 statute of Virginia had provided a method by which citizens of that state could discharge their debts by paying the amount into the state treasury. Under the terms of the

1783 peace treaty, which the federal Constitution adopted as part of the law of the land, there were to be no impediments to the collection of debts owned to British subjects. The issue before the Court was whether the ratification of the Constitution repealed *ab initio* the Virginia statute. Cushing held that the Virginia legislature was competent to make whatever law it chose during the Revolution, but that the return of peace and the ratification of the 1783 treaty obliged her to make no laws impeding debt collections and to consider annulled any laws she had passed which by their terms conflicted with the provisions of the treaty. This in itself was adequate to make the British debts collectable despite the debtor's payment into the Virginia treasury. However, the adoption of the federal Constitution gave the treaty additional force as the supreme law of the land. Now there could be no question that the British creditor could collect from his American debtors. Cushing pointed out that Virginia, since her legislative act had compelled her citizens to pay the debts twice, should, in equity and good conscience, indemnify those Virginians who had taken advantage of the 1777 statutory provision and were damaged by their reliance upon it.

With the *Ware* case Cushing made his first public statement on federal supremacy in the field of international affairs. At the Massachusetts ratifying convention he had prepared his speech to support federal authority in the field of tariffs and commercial treaties, but as noted above, that speech was not delivered to the convention. F. William O'Brien has indicated that there was no point in Cushing's career on the Massachusetts bench when he was called upon to decide the question of state laws and federal supremacy, nor even the question of state laws and congressional treaty-making powers under the Articles of Confederation. In an unreported opinion on the federal circuit in Connecticut, Cushing had joined Chief Justice Jay to invalidate a state statute that suspended the accrual of interest on obligations payable to British creditors. By 1796 the Federalists were sufficiently certain of Cushing's attitude toward the supremacy of treaties over state statutes that the Senate had confirmed his nomination to be Chief Justice. A short while previously the same body had rejected John Rutledge because of his public attacks upon the 1794 Jay Treaty with Great Britain. Cushing's decision in *Ware* v. *Hylton* makes it clear that he was firmly in the Federalist camp and that he supported the broad interpretation of the treaty-making power that was advanced by the Federalist party and was to become the prevailing position of the Supreme Court, whether Federalist, Jeffersonian, or New Deal. Thus the position adopted by Cushing and his fellow Justices remains the rule today in the field of treaty-making powers of the federal government.

Familiarity with the early jurisprudence of the American states made Cushing a natural choice when decisions were to be written upon the questions of loyalist property rights. These deserve some passing attention in any comments upon the contributions of William Cushing to the activities of the Supreme Court. In *Cooper* v. *Telfair,* 4 Dall. 14 (1800), he upheld the right of the state of Georgia to banish a citizen by a statute passed in 1782, contending that the Court should not declare such a law unconstitutional although it had the undoubted power to do so. Subsequently, in *M'Ilvaine* v. *Coxe's Lessee,* 4 Cranch 209 (1808), he upheld the title to realty standing in the name of a loyalist who had fled from New Jersey after serving in the British army fighting the American revolutionaries. Coxe had been declared a traitor, and Cushing held that by insisting upon his allegiance and declaring him a traitor, the state of New Jersey had refused to consider the man an alien. Nothing that he could do would alter Coxe's relationship to New Jersey, for only the legislature could alter his citizenship. Since New Jersey had not declared him an alien he remained a citizen, and thus he was not barred from holding title to real estate because of alienage. From these cases, Cushing's position on citizenship emerges quite clearly. All persons subject to the authority of the provincial congress on the date the states declared their independence were citizens of those states unless subsequently declared aliens by act of the state legislatures. In holding that citizenship was a matter for determination by the political authorities of the states during the American Revolution, and that all denizens of the states were citizens of those states unless the contrary was enacted into law, Cushing provided guidelines upon which the future development of American naturalization law would take place.

Another contribution of Cushing to the jurisprudence of the Supreme Court should be considered, not because of the constitutional importance of the opinion, but rather because of the simple method by which a large number of cases that might have been brought before the Court as original jurisdiction matters were relegated to the circuit courts for initial proceedings and trial. In *Fowler* v. *Lindsay,* 3 Dall. 411 (1799), the Court was called upon to resolve a problem of land titles between two citizens who claimed under grants of different states. Under the old Articles of Confederation such cases were referred to the same boundary arbitration courts that tried titles and boundary disputes between the states. The position of the provision in the federal Constitution, granting federal courts power to hear such disputes, seemed to indicate that this was part of the original jurisdiction of the Supreme Court. For the Court, Cushing very wisely held that such cases were to be tried in circuit courts; however if a state appeared as a party to the case, it might bring the case to the Supreme Court for trial. This was a significant step in reducing the number of possibilities that would compel the Supreme Court to resort to the ponderous procedure of trying disputed land titles before the Court *en banc.* Cushing made a noteworthy contribution to a more efficient federal court system through the application of this decision.

As senior Associate Justice of the Supreme Court, Cushing was called upon to preside in the absence of the Chief Justice and to deliver certain opinions on behalf of the Court. His assignments in opinion writing in the Marshall court seem to have been limited to cases involving technicalities of law or procedure, but as *Fowler* v. *Lindsay* demonstrates, many of those cases had a significance far beyond the immediate points in issue. For all of his shortcomings Cushing was an able judge who throughout his life discharged his duties conscientiously and with dignity. As he aged, the circuit duties began to take their toll on his health and he considered retirement as a possibility. This was complicated by the fact that he had been on the Bench for so long that he had no private fortune and was dependent upon his salary as a judge to maintain himself in the necessities of life. One of his biographers claims that he began to lose his mental faculties and that toward the end of his life his mind became deranged. By September of 1810 he was faced with the impossible choice of an impecunious retirement or death from riding the circuit. As in 1775 - and 1776, he was undecided and delayed his decision as long as possible; again, circumstances made his choice more one of chance than decision, for he died at Scituate on September 13, 1810, the last of Washington's original appointees to remain in continual service upon the Supreme Court.

SELECTED BIBLIOGRAPHY

The most comprehensive study of Cushing to date is John D. Cushing, "A Revolutionary Conservative: The Public Life of William Cushing, 1732–1810," unpublished doctoral dissertation, Clark University, 1960. Henry Flanders, *The Lives and Times of the Chief Justices* (New York, 1875), II, 11–51, contains valuable materials. Also of use are John D. Cushing, "The Cushing Court and the Abolition of Slavery in Massachusetts," 5 *American Journal of Legal History* 118 (1961); Arthur P. Rugg, "William Cushing," 30 *Yale Law Journal* 128 (1920); F. William O'Brien, "Justice William Cushing and the Treaty-Making Power," 10 *Vanderbilt Law Review* 351 (1957); and F. William O'Brien, "Justice Cushing's Undelivered Speech on the Federal Constitution," 15 *William and Mary Quarterly,* 3rd Series 74 (1958).

William Cushing

REPRESENTATIVE OPINIONS

CHISHOLM v. GEORGIA, 2 DALL. 467 (1793)

A South Carolinian's estate sued the state of Georgia for the purchase price of military supplies delivered during the Revolutionary War. Georgia refused to appear and denied that the Supreme Court had jurisdiction. Plaintiff was directed to argue the jurisdictional issue. Justice Cushing's opinion (one of five in the case) analyzed the phraseology and intent of the judiciary article of the federal Constitution. He held that under the grant of original jurisdiction to the Court, such actions were proper. "The rights of individuals and the justice due to them, are as dear and precious as those of states," he said. The precedent established by this case was nullified by the ratification of the Eleventh Amendment in 1798.

CUSHING, JUSTICE. The grand and principal question in this case is, whether a state can, by the federal constitution, be sued by an individual citizen of another state?

The point turns not upon the law or practice of England, although, perhaps, it may be in some measure elucidated thereby, nor upon the law of any other country whatever; but upon the constitution established by the people of the United States; and particularly, upon the extent of powers given to the federal judiciary in the 2d section of the 3d article of the constitution. It is declared, that "the judicial power shall extend to all cases in law and equity arising under the constitution, the laws of the United States, or treaties made or which shall be made under their authority; to all cases affecting ambassadors or other public ministers and consuls; to all cases of admiralty and maritime jurisdiction; to controversies, to which the United States shall be a party; to controversies between two or more states and citizens of another state; between citizens of different states; between citizens of the same state, claiming lands under grants of different states; and between a state and citizens thereof and foreign states, citizens or subjects." The judicial power, then, is expressly extended to "controversies between a state and citizens of another state." When a citizen makes a demand against a state, of which he is not a citizen, it is as really a controversy between a state and a citizen of another state, as if such state made a demand against such citizen. The case, then, seems clearly to fall within the letter of the constitution. It may be suggested, that it could not be intended to subject a state to be a defendant, because it would affect the sovereignty of states. If that be the case, what shall we do with the immediate preceding clause—"controversies between two or more states," where a state must of necessity be defendant? If it was not the intent, in the very next clause also, that a state might be made defendant, why was it so expressed, as naturally to lead to and comprehend that idea? Why was not an exception made, if one was intended?

Again, what are we to do with the last clause of the section of judicial powers, *viz.,* "controversies between a state, or the citizens thereof, and foreign states or citizens." Here again, states must be suable or liable to be made defendants by this clause, which has a similar mode of language with the two other clauses I have remarked upon. For if the judicial power extends to a controversy between one of the United States and a foreign state, as the clause expresses, one of them must be defendant. And then, what becomes of the sovereignty of states so far as suing affects it? But although the words appear reciprocally to affect the state here and a foreign state, and put them on the same footing so far as may be, yet ingenuity may say, that the state here may sue, but cannot be sued; but that the foreign state may be sued, but cannot sue. We may touch foreign sovereignties, but not our own. But I conceive, the reason of the thing, as well as the words of the constitution, tend to show that the federal judicial power extends to a suit brought by a foreign state against any one of the United States. One design of the general government was, for managing the great affairs of peace and war and the general defence, which were impossible to be conducted, with safety, by the states separately. Incident to these powers, and for preventing controversies between foreign powers or citizens from rising to extremities and to an appeal to the sword, a national tribunal was necessary, amicably to decide them, and thus ward off such fatal, public calamity. Thus, states at home and their citizens, and foreign states and their citizens, are put together without distinction, upon the same footing, so far as may be, as to controversies between them. So also, with respect to controversies between a state and citizens of another state (at home), comparing all the clauses together, the remedy is reciprocal; the claim to justice equal. As controversies between state and state, and between a state and citizens of another state, might tend gradually to involve states in war and bloodshed, a distinterested civil tribunal was intended to be instituted to decide such controversies, and preserve peace and friendship. Further, if a state is entitled to justice in the federal court, against a citizen of another state, why not such citizen against the state, when the same language equally comprehends both? The rights of individuals and the justice due to them, are as dear and precious as those of states. Indeed, the latter are founded upon the former; and the great end and object of them must be, to secure and support the rights of individuals, or else, vain is government.

But still it may be insisted, that this will reduce states to mere corporations, and take away all sovereignty. As to corporations, all states whatever are corporations or bodies politic. The only question is, what are their powers? As to individual states and the United States, the constitution marks the boundary of powers. Whatever power is deposited with the Union by the people, for their own necessary security, is so far a curtailing of the power and prerogatives of states. This is, as it were, a self-evident proposition; at least, it cannot be contested. Thus, the power of declaring war, making peace, raising and supporting armies for public defence, levying duties, excises and taxes, if necessary, with many other powers, are lodged in congress; and are a most essential abridgement of state sovereignty. Again, the restrictions upon states: "No state shall enter into any treaty, alliance or confederation, coin money, emit bills of credit, make anything but gold and silver a tender in payment of debts, pass any law impairing the obligations of contracts"; these, with a number of others, are important restrictions of the power of states, and were thought necessary to maintain the Union; and to establish some fundamental uniform principles of public justice, throughout the whole Union. So that, I think, no argument of force can be taken from the sovereignty of states. Where it has been abridged, it was thought necessary for the greater indispensable good of the whole. If the constitution is found inconvenient in practice, in this or any other particular, it is well that a regular mode is pointed out for amendment. But while it remains, all officers, legislative, executive and judicial, both of the states and of the Union, are bound by oath to support it.

One other objection has been suggested, that if a state may be sued by a citizen of another state, then the United States may be sued by a citizen of any of the states, or, in other words, by any of their citizens. If this be a necessary consequence, it must be so. I doubt the consequence, from the different wording of the different clauses, connected with other reasons. When speaking of the United States, the constitution says, "controversies to which the United States shall be a party," not controversies between the United States and any of their citizens. When speaking of states, it says, "controversies between two or more states; between a state and citizens of another state." As to reasons for citizens suing a different state, which do not hold equally good for suing the United States; one may be, that as controversies between a state and citizens of another state, might have a tendency to involve both states in contest, and perhaps in war, a common umpire to decide such controversies, may have a tendency to prevent the mischief. That an object of this kind was had in view, by the framers of the constitution, I have no doubt, when I consider the clashing interfering laws which were made in the neighboring states, before the adoption of the constitution, and some affecting the property of citizens of another state, in a very different manner from that of their own citizens. But I do not think it necessary to enter fully into the question, whether the United States are liable to be sued by an individual citizen in order to decide the point before us. Upon the whole, I am of opinion, that the constitution warrants a suit against a state, by an individual citizen of another state.

A second question made in the case was, whether the particular action of *assumpsit* could lie against a state? I think *assumpsit* will lie, if any suit; provided a state is capable of contracting.

The third question respects the competency of service, which I apprehend is good and proper; the service being by summons and notifying the suit to the governor and the attorney-general; the governor, who is the supreme executive magistrate and representative of the state, who is bound by oath to defend the state, and by the constitution to give information to the legislature of all important matters which concern the interest of the state; the attorney-general, who is bound to defend the interests of the state in courts of law.

WARE v. HYLTON, 3 DALL. 282 (1796)

This case brought before the Court the question of the validity of a 1777 Virginia statute that sequestered debts Virginians owed to British creditors. The 1783 peace treaty guaranteed the collectability of such debts, and the treaty had been declared the law of the land by the federal Constitution. Mr. Justice Cushing held that the 1783 nullified *ab initio* the 1777 Virginia statute and that the British creditors were not barred from recovering from the original obligor. The people of the United States had received valuable inducements at the peace negotiations in return for their guarantees of debt collection. It was not odious to enforce honest obligations in accordance with the intent of the parties, he said. However it would be just and equitable for Virginia to indemnify those of her citizens who had acted to their detriment in reliance upon the 1777 act.

CUSHING, JUSTICE. My state of this case will, agreeable to my view of it, be short. I shall not question the right of a state to confiscate debts. Here is an act of the assembly of Virginia, passed in 1777, respecting debts; which, contemplating to prevent the enemy deriving strength by the receipt of them during the war, provides, that if any British debtor will pay his debt into the loan-office, obtain a certificate and receipt as directed, he shall be discharged from so much of the debt. But an intent is expressed in the act not to confiscate, unless Great Britain should set the example. This act, it is said, works a discharge and a bar, to the payer. If such payment is to be considered as a discharge, or a bar, so long as the act had force, the question occurs—was there a power, by the treaty, supposing it contained proper words, entirely to remove this law, and this bar, out of the creditor's way? This power seems not to have been contended against, by the defendant's counsel; and indeed, it cannot be denied; the treaty having been sanctioned, in all its parts, by the constitution of the United States, as the supreme law of the land.

Then arises the great question, upon the import of the fourth article of the treaty: And to me, the plain and obvious meaning of it goes to nullify, *ab initio,* all laws, or the impediments of any law, so far as they might have been designed to impair or impede the creditor's right or remedy against his original debtor. "Creditors on either side shall meet with no lawful impediment to the recovery of the full value, in sterling money, of all *bonâ fide* debts heretofore contracted."

The article, speaking of creditors, and *bonâ fide* debts heretofore contracted, plainly contemplates debts, as originally contracted, and creditors and original debtors; removing out of the way all legal impediments; so that a recovery might be had, as if no such laws had particularly interposed. The words—"recovery of the full value, in sterling money," if they have force or meaning, must annihilate all tender laws, making anything a tender but sterling money; and the other words, or, at least, the whole taken together, must, in like manner, remove all other impediments of law aimed at the recovery of those debts.

What has some force to confirm this construction, is the sense of all Europe, that such debts could not be touched by states, without a breach of public faith: and for that, and other reasons, no doubt, this provision was insisted upon, in full latitude, by the British negotiators. If the sense of the article be as stated, it obviates, at once, all the ingenious, metaphysical reasoning and refinement upon the words, debt, discharge, extinguishment, and affords an answer to the decision made in the time of the *interregnum*—that payment to sequestrators, was payment to the creditor.

A state may make what rules it pleases; and those rules must necessarily have place within itself. But here is a treaty, the supreme law, which overrules all state laws upon the subject, to all intents and purposes; and that makes the difference. Diverse objections are made to this construction: that it is an odious one, and as such, ought to be avoided: that treaties regard the existing state of things: that it would carry an imputation upon public faith: that it is founded on the power of eminent domain, which ought not to be exercised, but upon the most urgent occasions: that the negotiators themselves did not think they had power to repeal laws of confiscation; because they, by the 5th article, only agreed, that congress should recommend a repeal to the states.

As to the rule respecting odious constructions; that takes place where the meaning is doubtful, not where it is clear, as I think it is, in this case. But it can hardly be considered as an odious thing, to enforce the payment of an honest debt, according to the true intent and meaning of the parties contracting; especially, if, as in this case, the state, having received the money, is bound in justice and honor, to indemnify the debtor, for what it in fact received. In whatever other lights this act of assembly may be reviewed, I consider it in one, as containing a strong implied engagement on the part of the state, to indemnify every one who should pay money under it, pursuant to the invitation it held out. Having never confiscated the debt, the state must, in the nature and reason of things, consider itself as answerable to the value. And this seems to be the full sense of the legislators upon this subject, in a subsequent act of assembly; but the treaty holds the original debtor answerable to his creditor, as I understand the matter. The state, therefore, must be responsible to the debtor.

These considerations will, in effect, exclude the idea of the power of eminent domain; and if they did not, yet there was sufficient authority to exercise it, and the greatest occasion that perhaps could ever happen. The same considerations will also take away all ground of imputation upon public faith.

Again, the treaty regarded the existing state of things, by removing the laws then existing, which intended to defeat the creditor of his usual remedy at law.

As to the observations upon the recommendatory provision of the 5th article; I do not see that we can collect the private opinion of the negotiators, respecting their powers, by what they did not do: and if we could, this court is not bound by their opinion, unless the reasons on which it was founded, being known, were convincing. It would be hard upon them, to suppose they gave up all, that they might think they strictly had a right to give up. We may allow somewhat to skill, policy and fidelity.

With respect to confiscations of real

and personal estates, which had been completed, the estates sold, and perhaps, passed through the hands of a number of purchasers, and improvements made upon real estates, by the then possessors; they knew, that to give them up absolutely, must create much confusion in this country. Avoiding that (whether from an apprehension of want of power does not appear from the instrument), they were led only to agree, that congress should recommend a restitution, or composition. The 4th article, which is particularly and solely employed about debts, makes provision, according to the doctrine then held sacred by all the sovereigns of Europe.

Although our negotiators did not gain an exemption for individuals, from *bonâ fide* debts, contracted in time of peace, yet they gained much for this country: as rights of fishery, large boundaries, a settled peace, and absolute independence, with their concomitant and consequent advantages: all which, it might not have been prudent for them to risk, by obstinately insisting on such exemption, either in whole or in part, contrary to the humane and meliorated policy of the civilized world, in this particular.

The 5th article, it is conceived, cannot affect or alter the construction of the 4th article. For, first, it is against reason, that a special provision made respecting debts by name, should be taken away immediately after, in the next article, by general words, or words of implication, which words, too, have, otherwise, ample matter to operate upon. 2d. No implication from the 5th article can touch the present case, because that speaks only of actual confiscations, and here was no confiscation. If we believe the Virginia legislators, they say, "We do not confiscate—we will not confiscate debts, unless Great Britain sets the example"—which it is not pretended she ever did.

The provision, that "creditors shall meet with no lawful impediment," &c., is an absolute, unconditional and peremptory, as words can well express, and made not to depend on the will and pleasure, or the optional conduct, of any body of men whatever.

To effect the object intended, there is no want of proper and strong language; there is no want of power, the treaty being sanctioned as the supreme law, by the constitution of the United States, which nobody pretends to deny to be paramount and controlling to all state laws, and even state constitutions, wheresoever they interfere or disagree. The treaty, then, as to the point in question, is of equal force with the constitution itself; and certainly, with any law whatsoever. And the words, "shall meet with no lawful impediment," &c., are as strong as the wit of man could devise, to avoid all effects of sequestration, confiscation, or any other obstacle thrown in the way, by any law, particularly pointed against the recovery of such debts.

I am, therefore, of opinion, that the judgment of the circuit court ought to be reversed.

By the Court. All and singular the premises being seen by the court here and fully understood, and mature deliberation had thereon, because it appears to the court now here, that in the record and process aforesaid, and also in the rendition of the judgment aforesaid, upon the demurrer to the rejoinder of the defendants in error, to the replication of the second plea, it is manifestly erred, it is considered, that the said judgment, for those errors and others in the record and process aforesaid, be revoked and annulled, and altogether held for nought, and it is further considered by the court here, that the plaintiff in error recover against the defendants, 2976*l.* 11*s.* 6*d.* good British money, commonly called sterling money, his debt aforesaid, and his costs by him about his suit in this behalf expended, and the said defendants, in mercy, &c. But this judgment is to be discharged by the payment of the sum of $596, and interest thereon, to be computed after the rate of five per cent. *per annum,* from the 7th day of July 1782, until payment, besides the costs, and by the payment of such damages as shall be awarded to the plaintiff in error, on a writ of inquiry to be issued by the circuit court of Virginia, to ascertain the sum really due to the plaintiff in error, exclusively of the said sum of $596, which was found to be due to the plaintiff in error, upon the trial in the said circuit court, on the issue joined upon the defendant's plea of payment, at a time when the judgment of the said circuit court on the said demurrer was unreversed and in full force and vigor; and for the execution of the judgment of the court, the cause aforesaid is remanded to the said circuit court of Virginia.

James Wilson

☆ 1742–1798 ☆

APPOINTED BY

GEORGE WASHINGTON

YEARS ON COURT

1789–1798

James Wilson

by

ROBERT G. McCLOSKEY

JAMES WILSON was born in Fifeshire, Scotland, the eldest son of James Wilson, a hard-working but unprosperous farmer, and Alison Lansdale Wilson, a pious but barely literate woman. From these modest beginnings in the Old World he advanced to a position of rare eminence in the New. As the years went on he was to become: a brilliant and prescient contributor to the American colonists' pre-Revolutionary pamphlet war with Great Britain; a delegate to the Second Continental Congress and a signer of the Declaration of Independence; a highly successful Pennsylvania lawyer; a delegate to the Federal Convention of 1787, playing a part second only to James Madison in the deliberations of that historic conclave; a force in Pennsylvania politics, heavily influential in securing his state's ratification of the new federal Constitution and in shaping the important Pennsylvania Constitution of 1790; a daring and—for a time—successful business speculator, regarded as one of the richest men in America; an Associate Justice of the first Supreme Court of the United States; a legal scholar widely recognized as the most learned and gifted in the nation, Professor of Law in the College of Philadelphia, author of a massive and erudite commentary on the political theory and law of the Republic.

Nor does this partial list of Wilson's objective accomplishment exhaust his claims to distinction. When we look beyond the quantity of his exploits to their quality, we detect an attribute that sets him apart, even among the illustrious company of the American founding fathers. In the ideas he held and the causes he espoused, he showed himself to be more in tune with what America was to become than any of his celebrated contemporaries. Not one of them—not Hamilton, or Jefferson, or Adams, or Madison, or Marshall—anticipated so

ROBERT G. McCLOSKEY, Professor of Government at Harvard University, is the author of American Conservatism in the Age of Enterprise, The American Supreme Court *and* Essays in Constitutional Law *as well as numerous articles on the Supreme Court.*

clearly the future contours of the American polity, reflected so faithfully the complex pattern of motives and values that have shaped our national history. His modernity, his continuing relevance to the continuing development of the Republic, was documented again as late as 1964 when Mr. Justice Black cited Wilson in support of the "one-man–one-vote" principle in legislative apportionment (*Wesberry* v. *Sanders,* 376 U.S. 1). Wilson was the only really helpful eighteenth century authority the Justice could invoke for the very good reason that he was the only one of the framers who had unequivocally expressed himself in favor of the principle.

With all these worldly attainments to his credit, with all posterity's vindications of his insights, it might be thought that Wilson must have been in life a happy and self-fulfilled man, and in death a figure much remembered and revered by the country he served. But on the contrary there is reason to believe that his career was a series of disappointments; and there is no doubt at all that his final years, when he should have been able to bask in accumulated honors, were bleakly tragic. As for his future fame, it is fair to say that few statesmen who did so much have been recompensed so little by a nation's memory. Among constitutional historians indeed his importance has been acknowledged, though even they have had little enough to say about it, beyond the bare acknowledgment. But by the general educated public he has been, almost since the time of his death, virtually forgotten.

The explanation of these paradoxes is buried in the nature and history of the man and his times. It begins with certain qualities of intellect and character that can be already dimly seen in what little we know about his Scottish youth. His parents were devout Calvinists, and from the first they resolved that James, their first-born, should be a minister of the Kirk. To attain that end he must be well-educated, and although money was scarce (the farm was not large, and there were six other children) enough was scraped together so that he could go first to a nearby parish school, then at the age of fourteen with the help of a bursary scholarship, to St. Salvator College in the University of St. Andrews. He studied Latin, Greek, mathematics, and philosophy; and we can be sure, not only because of his election to the bursarship but on the basis of the scholarly bent he revealed throughout his life, that he studied them hard. In his fifth year at the University he transferred to the divinity school at St. Mary's College, but his father's death caused him to break off from both the University and the commitment to the ministry, and he never returned to them. His only further Scottish education seems to have been a brief course in accounting in Edinburgh when he was twenty-three. Meanwhile after leaving St. Andrews he had found a post as a private tutor, but the rewards and prospects of such a career were small, nor were there other open avenues in Scotland that seemed more promising. He decided that the New World was the place for him and set sail for America in 1765.

When the character of the mature man is read back into the bare facts of this youthful record, a living individual begins to emerge. The record might seem ordinary enough. But there was almost nothing about Wilson that was ordinary. Every characteristic he had, he had in abundance, sometimes to the point of excess; and his rich and varied propensities must have made him a remarkable young man. To begin with, he was energetic, ambitious, and optimistic far beyond the common lot. Throughout his life he poured an apparently unlimited store of vitality into diverse, demanding, and simultaneous projects conceived in his restless brain or thrust upon him by the course of events. Throughout his life he yearned and strove for the highest rewards the world could offer: recognition as a selfless and preeminent founder-statesman, as the father of American law; political power; professional success and riches beyond the dreams of avarice. Throughout his life he persistently believed, against all evidence, that he could have all these things and the many others his heart desired, and would have them when he rounded the next corner. The optimism was not perhaps wholly unreasonable, for in addition to the character traits just canvassed, he also possessed intellectual resources of a very high order. Though his time at St. Andrews had been interrupted, he had attended long enough to acquire a solid educational background and, equally important, to be fired by the intellectual excitement of the Scottish Enlightenment. He was a lover of books, and ideas had for him a reality and allure that most men associate with material things. Above all he was endowed with that priceless but often dangerous quality, creative imagination: his mind reached out and grasped concepts beyond the horizons of orthodox belief.

Most of these qualities are at least conjecturally discernible in his pre-American years. His ambition and his optimism are reflected in his decision to emigrate, for he was not one of those who were forced by grinding penury to cast their lot in the New World. Life in his homeland would have been constricted but tolerable, but he wanted and dared to seek a more spacious future. His decision, in repudiation of his dead father's wish, to abandon a career in the Kirk suggests further that his thirst for worldly prizes was already strong. His apparent academic success suggests the tireless scholarly drive that was always to distinguish him. Add to this the fact that the man's outward personality was stiff, dour, and somewhat forbidding; and the supposition that the boy's demeanor probably foreshadowed these traits. On this point all observers seem to agree about the mature Wilson, though Waln suggests that his stern air was owing to extreme shortsightedness. It is clear from his portrait that his spectacles fit him badly, and this might have accounted for his carriage, which was described as "stooping backward." He seems to have been tall for his time—about six feet—and inclined to be heavy in body as well as in manner. The combination of all these characteristics provides us with an idea of the sort of youth who landed in New York in the autumn of 1765, and with some inklings to explain his future in America.

He went directly to Philadelphia where, with the help of a letter of introduction and his unusual educational credentials, he quickly found a job as tutor in the College of Philadelphia. But though his taste for scholarly life was always strong, it was never all-absorbing. He aspired to a more spectacular success than the library and classroom could offer, and the law must have immediately struck him as a calling nicely adapted to his talents and ambitions. It was both scholarly and worldly. Wilson's erudite background and propensities would serve him well in the law; and by happy chance the legal profession was at this very time developing the prestige and importance that were to elevate lawyers to such a vital place in the history of America. He made an arrangement to read law under John Dickinson, one of the luminaries of the colonial bar who had himself studied at the London Inns of Court, and by 1767 Wilson was ready to begin practice in the town of Reading.

His first ventures into public affairs concurred with the launching of his professional career, and this was appropriate, for thereafter the two concerns always vied for his attention. His mentor, Dickinson, had published in 1767–1768 the *Farmer's Letters,* challenging Parliament's right to tax the colonies for the raising of revenue, but conceding the authority to regulate external trade and to levy duties for controlling imperial commerce. This comparatively moderate viewpoint was characteristic of native polemicists at the time. Though relations between the colonists and the mother country were growing tense, there was little disposition in America to press the colonial argument to extremes. Wilson's interest in the matter was doubtless quickened by his association with Dickinson, perhaps by ambition to make a name for himself, and certainly by his congenital fascination with an intellectual problem. He sat down, as he tells us, "with the view and expectation of being able to trace some constitutional line between those cases in which we ought, and those in which we ought not, to acknowledge the power of parliament over us." (3 *Works* 201.) But Wilson was, unlike Dickinson, an immigrant, and a very recent one at that. He may have felt, as immigrants sometimes do, a special need to assert his patriotic *bona fides* to his adopted country; he may have enjoyed, as late comers sometimes do, a special clarity of vision about her problems. Moreover he was naturally endowed with imaginative insight beyond ordinary bounds and with an inclination to follow ideas where they led him. He found himself concluding, somewhat to his own surprise he says, that the power of Parliament over the colonies must be denied *"in every instance,"* and he embodied the argument for this precocious view in one of the most noteworthy of pre-Revolutionary pamphlets, *Considerations on the Nature and Extent of the Legislative Authority of the British Parliament*.

The conception Wilson had seized upon was nothing less than the principle of dominion status which was to be accepted in the middle nineteenth century as the working basis that preserved the British Commonwealth—i.e., the understanding that the members were bound together only by their common allegiance to the Crown. Starting from the premise drawn from "the law of nature" that government must rest on consent, and observing that the colonists had no means of choosing or influencing the Parliament, he moved inexorably to the conclusion that Parliament should have no voice whatever in the affairs of the colonies. This viewpoint became an American dogma in the 1770's; John Adams gave it classic expression in his *Novanglus* in 1774. But Wilson drafted his *Considerations* in 1768, and can thus be credited, as a biographer has said, "with formulating the idea of dominion status six years ahead of [Adams] and some seventy years ahead of the British Foreign Office." (Smith, 58.)

However, while it was characteristic that Wilson's mind should outpace his contemporaries in reaching a conclusion, it is also revealing that he did not in fact publish his *Considerations* until six years after it was composed. A friend suggested in 1768 that its publication might impair his prospects as a rising young lawyer, and whether for this reason or another, Wilson held it back until 1774 when the drift of opinion made it seem far less radical. Though he had a taste for syllogisms and daring intellectual leaps, he also had always a taste for getting on, and particularly for getting rich, and he had begun to arrange a life designed to achieve that end. His law practice developed gratifyingly. He had started to establish good relations with the solid, affluent folk of Pennsylvania. This was always the kind of company he preferred. In the future one of the things that would make it hard for the populace to accept his democratic protestations was the fact that his friends were so largely drawn from the moneyed "aristocracy." In 1771 he married Rachel Bird, and while there is no reason to doubt that this was a love match, it is also true that her father had built the Hay Creek ironworks and that her family were plainly on the way to a position of power in state financial affairs. By this time he had moved from Reading to Carlisle in order to expand his legal practice further. The move was evidently a resounding success. The developing economy of the region, and especially the growth of trading in land, provided endless occasions for litigation, and Wilson quickly became one of the busiest attorneys in that part of Pennsylvania. He had already come a long way from the little farm in Fifeshire.

But now the smooth course of his professional progress was ruffled by the intrusion of history. The American Revolution was in the making, and in 1774 Wilson was chosen as a deputy from Carlisle to attend a gathering of Pennsylvania leaders in Philadelphia. He was not elected to the First Continental Congress. But he had begun to make a statewide impression as a man of talent and influence devoted to the colonial cause, and when the Second Continental Congress was called in 1775, Wilson was a delegate. There he met and formed friendships with the men from other colonies who were emerging as the leaders of the emerging Republic. Wilson impressed them, for he was always at his best in such gatherings where industry and erudition were at a premium. But his attachment to his Pennsylvania colleagues, especially of course to Dickinson, was also strong, and they were on the whole proponents of moderation in the controversy with Britain. Although a *de facto* state of war already existed, they and many others clung to the hope that outright separation could still be avoided. In February, 1776, Wilson drafted a manifesto for the Congress to issue, stating that the purpose of the Americans was not independence, but the "Defense and Re-establishment of the Constitutional Rights of the Colonies." (4 *Journals of Continental Cong.* 141.) He said privately that he hoped by it to prepare the public mind for the idea of ultimate independence, but the public mind was already moving fast along this road, and the manifesto with its comparatively moderate language was dropped (*Ibid.*, 146). As the months went on, Wilson and the Pennsylvania delegation were slow to change their public stand, partly because of lingering reluctance to dissolve the political bands with the mother country, partly because they felt bound by their Assembly's instructions to oppose separation. After those instructions were altered, Wilson finally did vote for independence and signed the Declaration, unlike his friends Dickinson and Robert Morris who never gave in. But Wilson's tardiness earned him a reputation as a foe of independence, and even in 1829, long after his death, Goodrich felt called upon in his *Lives of the Signers* to refute the slander.

It was also at this time that he began to be stigmatized by the rising radical faction in Pennsylvania as an enemy of democracy, and this charge too pursued him throughout his career. It was in fact grossly unjust. The truth is that he believed in popular rule at least as ardently as his populist critics, believed in it to a degree that must have seemed eccentric to the conservatives he hobnobbed with. To be sure even they, or most of them, accepted the premise of popular consent as the foundation of government; by 1776 only Tories dared repudiate it. But after making his initial concession, the solid citizens began to hedge and to look for ways to dilute and check the operation of the "democratical principle." Wilson did not share these misgivings. Just as he had been unable, once the premise was granted, to find a line distinguishing the legitimate from the illegitimate colonial powers of parliament, so he was unable to recognize a logical stopping point for the principle of popular rule. Perhaps the explanation for this idiosyncrasy is to be found partly in the social structure he had known in his boyhood: the gap between rich and poor, between laird and commoner, had not been wide in Fifeshire. Perhaps it is to be found in his exposure to the Scottish "common sense philosophy" which was taking form when he was at St. Andrews and which emphasized the reliability of intuition and the general benevolence of human nature. But whatever the origins of his conviction, Wilson was unmistakably a democrat.

However, the populace never found this easy to credit, for to them it seemed incompatible with his other propensities. In Pennsylvania politics they saw him constantly allied with men of conservative hue. He had joined Dickinson, Morris, Benjamin Rush, and George Ross to oppose the Pennsylvania Constitution of 1776. That document, blessed by Benjamin Franklin and Tom Paine, was regarded as the very symbol of democracy and, with its test oath to disfranchise rich Quakers and crypto-Tories, as "a mighty stumbling block in the way of our gentry." (Brunhouse, 20.) In the view of populists like George Bryan and William Findley, to oppose the constitution was to favor oligarchy and despise the people. Wilson certainly did oppose it; he was one of the principal leaders in a long and ultimately successful battle to wipe it from the books. But in truth it was in many ways a poorly conceived instrument of government, and even its vaunted democracy was open to question, for it had never been submitted to popular approval, and the test-oath requirements were nicely calculated to prevent the formation of an anti-Radical majority. Moreover its provisions for a unicameral legislature and a feeble executive flouted the principle of separation of powers which was already an American article of faith for democrats no less than for their opponents. Wilson could find plenty to object to in the constitution of 1776 without in the least compromising his belief in political democracy. Nevertheless to the "honest well-meaning Country men" (*Ibid.*, 13) his position in this matter, and in state politics generally, identified him as an opponent of the popular cause.

This identification seemed further confirmed in the years after independence by Wilson's powerful commitment to nationalism. Again we can only guess at the origins of this predilection. Perhaps it was easier for Wilson than for some of his contemporaries to think in nationalistic terms, because he was as a newcomer unencumbered by a heritage of local allegiances and jealousies. No doubt his wartime experience in Congress, where he watched a supposedly national legislature being rendered nearly impotent by localism, served to confirm his pro-union leanings. No doubt too he was influenced somewhat by the considerations that helped generate the movement toward union among so many propertied men in the post-Revolutionary years. Most such men believed that a stronger national government would stimulate commerce and strengthen the position of property-holders. Wilson was already making money, and he hoped to make a lot more: he was probably not indifferent to the effect of centralization on his present security and future prospects.

But at all events he was an outspoken nationalist, and this fact made it all the more difficult for public opinion to accept that he was also a democrat. American politics had already begun to spawn the illusion that was to plague it for many years to come: that the states' rights position was linked to democracy, while nationalism was linked to elitism. This was the polarization that later hardened into a dogma during the ratification controversy and was to be represented in the 1790's by the rivalry between the Jeffersonian and Hamiltonian persuasions. The idea of *democratic nationalism,* which Wilson professed, was so unusual that it seemed incongruous. It is not surprising that the populace found it hard to believe in the sincerity of a man who professed it.

And finally Wilson's professional and financial involvements compounded the problem of belief still further. Even before the Revolution, in Carlisle, he had begun some modest land speculations to augment the income from his growing legal practice. But his congressional experience in 1775–76 had brought him into contact with ambitious entrepreneurs throughout the colonies—men like Silas Deane, Charles Carroll, William Duer, and above all Robert Morris—and he like so many of his contemporaries became half-intoxicated by the vast commercial prospects that he saw unfolding with the birth of the nation. The imaginative gift, the taste for daring intellectual flights, was potentially disastrous when applied to business affairs. Speculation, chiefly in land but also in various other commercial adventures, obsessed him continually for the remainder of his life, robbed him of time and energy he might have devoted to statesmanship or scholarship, clouded his repute beyond remedy, and finally helped, quite literally, to drive him to the grave.

Carlisle was too small to hold him, and in 1778 he moved to Philadelphia where he quickly built up an enormously successful legal practice, and where he was better able to consolidate his connections with the business world. In the courtroom he defended Quaker Tories against prosecutions by professional patriots, writing thereby the beginning of a significant chapter in the history of American treason law, but also earning the further suspicion of the radicals—together, of course, with the gratitude of the defendants and their wealthy friends. He represented a variety of other rich and powerful clients. And as the fees poured in he poured them back into an endless train of grandiose business schemes. Though the schemes were manifold, land was his passion, and he plunged in his land speculations with the rashness, optimism, and growing desperation of a compulsive gambler. As time went on and the house of cards became increasingly precarious, his measures to survive became more and more reckless and less and less scrupulous. They also became notorious and further nourished public doubts about his democratic pretensions.

His defense of the Bank of North America provides an excellent example of the way in which Wilson's personal interests and political convictions intertwined, and it also illustrates the foresight, the capacity for "brilliant conceits" (McMaster and Stone, 759) which so often distinguished his political thinking. The Bank had been chartered in 1781 by both the Continental Congress and the Assembly of Pennsylvania, and it soon became the center of a political controversy very like the one that swirled about the Bank of the United States some years later. When the Bank's enemies proposed in 1785 that the Assembly revoke its state charter, the management called on Wilson to help repel the onslaught, and he composed a pamphlet "Considerations on the Bank of North America." (3 *Works* 397.) This pamphlet is a remarkable document; it certainly belongs in any list of America's distinguished state papers; there is no doubt that it represented Wilson's sincere convictions about public policy. But he would have been in no position to decline the Bank's invitation to defend it, even if he had wished, for not only was he its attorney and a member of its board of directors, he also, characteristically, owed it a large sum of money.

His objectives in the pamphlet were two: to persuade readers that the congressional charter alone was enough to preserve the Bank's lawful existence; and to persuade them that in any event the Assembly ought not revoke the state charter. As to the first point, the difficulty was that the Articles of Confederation seemed to grant no congressional power to incorporate the Bank in the first place, and that Article II reserved to the states all powers not expressly delegated to the Congress. But Wilson boldly argued that the states never possessed the power to legislate for national objects and hence the reserved powers clause was here irrelevant. In fact, he continued, Congress enjoys, in addition to the powers specifically delegated, "general powers . . . resulting from the union of the whole"; it is authorized to accomplish any general objects that the individual states are incompetent to effect. This contention not only prefigures the "implied powers" conception of *McCulloch* v. *Maryland,* 4 Wheat. 316 (1819); it will further suggest to students of constitutional history the "inherent powers" doctrine of such relatively modern decisions as *Missouri* v. *Holland,* 252 U.S. 416 (1920) and *United States* v. *Curtiss-Wright,* 299 U.S. 304 (1936). Indeed the logic of Wilson's argument implies that the supposedly feeble Confederation Congress possessed wider national powers than did the Congress of the United States as late as 1935 before the scope of the general welfare clause was first explicitly recognized! As for the second point, Wilson advanced a contention that came very close to anticipating Marshall's opinion in *Fletcher* v. *Peck,* 6 Cranch 87 (1810) more than twenty years later. He had, of course, no contract clause to aid him, but he did rather well without it, hinting strongly that the Assembly's repealing act would be a nullity because it would violate "the rules and maxims, by which compacts are governed."

In spite of its ingenuity, the defense failed; the charter was repealed. Wilson's role might have suggested guidelines for the Republic sometime in the future; but for the present it chiefly served to strengthen the popular impression that he was not a disinterested democratic patriot, but a self-seeker "who can bewilder the truth in all the mazes of sophistry." (McMaster and Stone, 642.) Nevertheless in spite of all difficulties he managed to remain a force in Pennsylvania politics. A shift in the political breezes deprived him of his congressional seat in 1777, and in 1779 he was forced to flee Philadelphia in order to escape violence from a "patriotic" mob. But by 1782 the Pennsylvania conservatives began to recapture the political favor they had lost to the radicals during the Revolution. Wilson was again elected to Congress, and he served in it thereafter off and on throughout the Articles of Confederation period. The associations and proclivities that undermined his popularity were always to some extent counterbalanced by widespread respect for his virtues: his intellect, his erudition, his industry. Moreover, then as always, wealth and patrician associates were not an unmixed disadvantage to a politician. As the movement toward union began to wax in the 1780's, Wilson was hand-in-glove with its promoters, and when the federal Convention was called in 1787, he was chosen by the legislature as a Pennsylvania delegate.

The "assembly of demigods" would have felt his absence; the nation would be poorer if a change in the Pennsylvania political climate had kept Wilson out of the Convention. No one, except perhaps Madison, worked harder at the business of statesmanship during that hot Philadelphia summer; no one, again except Madison, contributed more to the Convention's deliberations. Manifestly both Wilson and Madison were in their element in such a small and sober conclave, where the need was for men who would speak to the point rather than to galleries, who would do their homework, who had thought deeply about the art of government.

Wilson had already progressed by 1787 to a set of views that were in themselves a kind of synthesis of the Convention's divided mind. The delegates' problem was to reconcile the need for a more perfect union with the stubborn fact of localism, the need to protect property rights and commercial stability with the rise of democracy. Wilson had achieved such a reconciliation on his own account. He had, as has been said, fully accepted the notion of popular democracy. But, as a convinced nationalist, he thought of the electorate not in terms of the states but in terms of the whole: as a single, sovereign entity, "the people of the United States." (1 Farrand, *Records* 52, 69.) His confidence in the benevolence and good judgment of a free electorate immunized him against excessive fears of popular transgressions, and the idea that the electorate transcended state lines provided him with a basis for belief in vigorous national government. Moreover he had faced and resolved to his own satisfaction a question that confused many: the relative positions of the nation and the states. His answer was that the states should remain supreme within their own spheres, but that as to the purposes of the union "should be considered as having no existence" (1 Farrand, 406): the general government should be supreme. This was the conception that was to become a keystone of American constitutional law when Marshall later enunciated it in such decisions as *McCulloch* v. *Maryland* and *Cohens* v. *Virginia,* 6 Wheat. 264 (1821).

With these principles in mind, he worked to steer the Convention on all points toward democratic nationalism, as he understood it, and he was more consistently true to that ideal than any other delegate. Not only did he join the other large-state representatives in urging popular election of the first branch of the legislature, but he insisted, with less support, that the second branch should be similarly chosen, so that the legislature would be "the most exact transcript of the whole Society." (1 Farrand, 132.) He was almost alone in contending that the executive should also be popularly elected. He opposed the two-thirds rule for Senate ratification of treaties on the ground that it would grant a minority undue power. When Madison proposed a freehold qualification for voting, Wilson spoke against it. He rejected restrictions on the admission of new states, based on fears that the democratic western area might grow in population and dominate the union: "The majority of people wherever found ought in all questions to govern the minority." (*Ibid.,* 605.) He joined with Madison and others in successfully urging that the proposed Constitution be submitted to popularly elected conventions in each state, a policy that has been called "the most audacious and altogether unqualified appeal to the notion of popular sovereignty that had ever been made, even in America." (Corwin, *Doctrine of Judicial Review,* 106.)

At the same time he pressed with equal single-mindedness for measures that would strengthen the national government and its powers. His attachment to the principle of popular election of both political branches grew from his awareness that the government would be strong and effective in proportion as it found its roots in the support of the people. He fought for a single, powerful executive; and even proposed that the President be provided with an absolute veto to augment his authority. During the 1780's Wilson had already recognized the need for a national judiciary as an instrument of national unity, and he supported the measure authorizing Congress to establish inferior federal courts. He was one of those whose acceptance of the idea of judicial review was unmistakable (2 Farrand, 73, 391). As has been said earlier, he had developed long before the Convention a view, strikingly modern in its expansiveness, of national legislative authority.

None of these views, taken separately, was surprising or unique. It is in combination that they distinguish Wilson as one of the remarkable men of his generation: a Federalist with an almost doctrinaire devotion to popular sovereignty; a democrat who believed in a potent government and a firm union. And in combination they illustrate the foreknowledge that was his most striking characteristic. The frame of government that emerged from the Convention's deliberations was not identical to the one that Wilson had advocated. The presidency was strong, but not as strong as he would have preferred; the electoral college arrangement fell short of the direct popular election he advocated. The House was to be popularly elected; but the Senate was not. The position of the states in the Union was left ambiguous; the full scope of national powers was not spelled out. In all these matters Wilson had succeeded in moving, or helping to move, the Convention toward his own ideal. But he had not succeeded in moving it all the way. As perhaps the most active member of the important Committee of Detail, and the probable draftsman of its final report, he had been forced to accept provisions that denied or modified some of his cherished principles.

However, with respect to some of the most central of those principles, Wilson had the last word after all: posterity ratified what contemporaries had rejected. The presidency in short order did become a popularly elected office and the President the tribune of the people Wilson contended for. In 1913 the Seventeenth Amendment vindicated Wilson's argument that the Senate should also be popularly elected. His latitudinarian notion of national legislative authority evolved slowly in practice, but by the 1940's Congress was conceded to have something like the range of power Wilson had thought it should have. By the 1960's his idea of representation was given constitutional sanction in the form of the "one-man-one-vote" principle. Most important of all his belief in a strong national union based on popular sovereignty took form as the central and progressively developing concept of American constitutionalism. Marshall's great nationalist decisions, Webster's Reply to Hayne, the Gettysburg Address, and Theodore Roosevelt's New Nationalism were all "Wilsonian," though only Roosevelt acknowledged an indebtedness.

For the moment, however, the problem of Wilson and his fellow constitution-makers was to secure ratification of the instrument of government they had hammered out. The approval of Pennsylvania was essential, and Wilson threw his intellectual and political energies into the task of obtaining it. The issue was settled for practical purposes when the Assembly set an early date for the election of delegates to the ratifying convention, and the Federalists won a solid majority. But Wilson as the only member who had also attended the federal Convention inherited the position of chief spokesman for ratification and was recognized as the leading figure in engineering the result. His speeches probably changed no votes, but they constituted one of the ablest reasoned defenses of the Constitution. Also, although they were full of apostrophes to "the people" and of protestations that the Constitution would establish a "democracy," they did not alter his entrenched popular image. In the eyes of his radical opponents, he was irremediably "James the Caledonian, Leut. Gen. of the Myrmidons of power." (McMaster and Stone, 631.)

It even seems unlikely that this image was much modified by his work in drafting and securing approval for the Pennsylvania Constitution of 1790, though it must have been hard to explain why an anti-democrat would fight for direct popular election of state senators and accept a negligible property qualification for voters. It was in this state convention that Wilson summed up in one sentence his political principles: "To render Government efficient, Power must be given liberally: to render it free as well as efficient, those Powers must be drawn from the People as directly and immediately as possible." (Smith, 302.) But under the tyranny of contemporary political stereotypes it continued to seem incredible that an exponent of strong and centralized government, a declared Federalist, a rich business speculator, could also be a sincere democrat.

Meanwhile the national government which he had done so much to form was getting under way, and Wilson, endlessly ambitious, hoped to scale new heights of fame as one of its founder-statesmen. He no doubt realized that he lacked the qualities for high elective office. But he was already widely acclaimed as a legal scholar, and with his characteristic insight, he was able to foresee the part that law would play in America's future. He knew that his best chance for acknowledged greatness lay in the field of jurisprudence. He proposed himself to Washington for the Chief Justiceship of the new Supreme Court, explaining that he spoke so that the President would be spared the embarrassment of offering the post to one who would scorn it (*Calendar of Applications and Recommendations for Office under the Presidency of George Washington,* ed. by Gaillard Hunt, Washington, 1901). When the honor was tendered instead to John Jay, Wilson consoled himself with an associate justiceship and looked about for other ways to augment his celebrity. The College of Philadelphia appointed him to its first professorship of law, and Wilson patently hoped that the course of lectures he gave there would lay the foundation for a distinctively American system of law based on Wilsonian principles. They represented the major written work of his life, his pretension to challenge the renown of the *Federalist Papers,* but extending to a far wider terrain. Wilson planned them to be so extensive in fact—embracing *inter alia* epistemology, political philosophy, natural law, the law of nations, the common law, as well as commentaries on the constitutions of the United States and Pennsylvania—that he was unable to finish their delivery in the winter of 1790–91. He broke off in order to attend to his circuit duties as a Supreme Court Justice and to his myriad business affairs. But a few months later he had not only taken them up again but had absorbed himself in two other vast schemes: to produce by his own hand full digests of the laws of Pennsylvania and the United States. He solicited the Pennsylvania legislature and President Washington to commission him for these herculean tasks, but Washington seems to have turned him down, and the Pennsylvania digest, though begun, was never completed.

The lectures on law were published after Wilson's death, and although prolix and uneven, they touch on many of the great issues of political philosophy and jurisprudence, and are the most nearly full treatment we have of those matters by an eminent American of the founders' generation. As we have seen, Wilson was heavily committed to the ideal of popular rule, and had succeeded in transcending the contemporary conflict between that ideal and nationalism—between Jeffersonian and Hamiltonian prepossessions—by invoking a national popular will as the basis for national government. The other great tension of contemporary political thought was that between the will of the people and the rule of law, for it was hard to see how the popular will could be supreme if it were restrained by law, yet equally hard to see how the great western notion of fundamental law could survive if the will of the people were unlimited. Though the lectures on law range over many subjects, their chief problem is to resolve this difficulty, for Wilson was as much a legalist as he was a democrat or a nationalist. It was necessary to him that these values be reconciled, and he thought he knew how to do it.

He began with two premises: a concept of natural law and a concept of human nature. Natural law, he argued, is ordained by God and imposes obligations on men and nations. But God, having willed such a rule to guide human conduct, has not been so inconsiderate as to withhold from men the means of apprehending it, or the inclination to obey it. He has endowed them with conscience or intuition, reason, and scriptural revelation; and the combination of these benefactions enables most men—not merely a favored few—to know what the natural law commands. Moreover, He has also instilled in them the propensity to obey its mandates, to conform themselves to His design. In America this great truth, so long unknown, has now been discovered. Therefore America can and must reject the Blackstonian definition of law as a rule prescribed by a superior. The true basis of law is "the consent of those whose obedience the law requires." (1 *Works* 99.) For, given the premise of an innately moral and essentially social human nature, it follows that popular consent will tend to reflect God's natural law.

God's will then as interpreted by popular consent is the source of legal obligation. Sovereignty resides not in states or in governments, but in the free and independent man. In practice, this freeman's consent to the law may be expressed in compacts, in majority votes, or—most importantly of all—in custom. The great virtue of the English common law is that it is such a customary law, representing the consent of those it affects, and conforming by innumerable adjustments to the needs and desires of the people. America, which is uniquely dedicated to the "revolution principle" of popular consent, should therefore adopt the *method* of the common law, but should scrutinize its precedents and reject many of them, fashioning an *American* common law on American needs. She must also reject Blackstone's doctrine of legislative supremacy, for in America all branches of government represent the people: the pronouncements of the judiciary, no less than the enactments of the legislature, speak with the sovereign authority of that "free and independent man" who has consented to be bound by them.

Wilson obviously hoped that the lectures, when published for the world to see, would lay the basis for American jurisprudence and establish their author as the Republic's premier lawgiver. The scholarship they displayed was impressive, and their central theme did anticipate a central truth about the American legal system: that it would grow by the accretion of custom and acceptance rather than by the fiat of legislators; that popular government and the rule of law would be more complementary than antithetical. But they did not bring Wilson the fame he wanted and in some degree deserved, partly because he was prevented by other distractions from casting them in finished form, or even in publishable form in his own lifetime. As always, he was trying to do too many things at once, and that made it hard to do any of them perfectly.

His first wife had died in 1786 after bearing six children. In 1793, Wilson, now in his fifties, married Hannah Gray of Boston, who was not yet twenty. Meanwhile his business affairs were deteriorating ominously, absorbing more and more of the time and energy he might have devoted to other concerns. And finally, of course, there were his duties as a Justice of the Supreme Court. Here, it might be thought, was one more chance to stamp his name indelibly in the American memory. If he could not be a Jefferson, a Hamilton, or a Madison, perhaps he could be a John Marshall.

But the mention of Marshall suggests why this aspiration too was unrealizable. To begin with of course he never attained the Chief Justiceship. Washington bypassed him not only at the time of Jay's appointment, but again in 1795 and 1796 when John Rutledge and Oliver Ellsworth were chosen. The reasons for such presidential preferences are seldom clear, but it is at least plausible that Wilson's growing reputation for reckless financial adventuring hurt his chances. However, quite apart from the question of the Chief Justiceship, he lacked some of the personal gifts that made Marshall the leader of his Court and the primary spokesman of our constitutional tradition. Unlike Marshall, who charmed all who knew him, Wilson was always handicapped by his stiff, forbidding manner. And although he was far more learned in the law and a deeper thinker than Marshall, he could not match the lucidity, simplicity, and persuasiveness of Marshall's prose style. His own prose was alternately heavy and florid; and he seldom resisted the temptation to display his learning in erudite and tenuously relevant digressions.

Beyond all that, the most decisive fact is that Wilson did not really have Marshall's opportunity for juristic greatness: the occasion was not ripe during his time on the Bench. The status of the federal judiciary in the 1790's was ambiguous and, for the moment, comparatively minor. The great pyramid of subordinate courts and causes leading up to the Supreme Court was still in the process of formation. The paramount governmental tasks were legislative and executive. The nation was not ready for the judicial leadership of later years.

Within this limited range Wilson did what he could to earn a place in America's legal Pantheon, but the range must have seemed constricting to a man of his ambitions, and the occasions were tantalizingly few. The total of his written opinions on the Supreme Court sums up to little more than twenty pages in the *Reports;* and even when added to the cases in which he cast a vote without opinion, the record is slim. With one exception, his judicial decisions provide us with little inkling of his stature.

To be sure, his role in "The First Hayburn Case," 2 Dall. 409 (1792) has a certain historical interest. Congress had in 1792 directed circuit courts to act as pension commissioners, and a controversy had arisen over the question whether this was a function the courts could constitutionally perform. Wilson and two of his brethren in the Pennsylvania circuit directed a letter to Washington (probably composed by Wilson) explaining why they had refused to proceed in a pension case. "To be obliged to act contrary, either to the obvious direction of Congress, or to a constitutional principle in our judgment equally obvious, excited feelings in us, which we hope never to experience again." Their refusal to act, in spite of those feelings, marks what seems to be the first holding by a federal court that a congressional act was unconstitutional. Wilson of course had long since made it plain that he envisioned the power of judicial review. In the Hayburn case he was acting on that basis, and in *Hylton* v. *United States,* 3 Dall. 171 (1796) he seconded the rest of the Court in confirming it once again by implication and at the same time upholding a broad interpretation of national powers. This case, involving a national tax that was important to Hamilton's fiscal program had come before Wilson in circuit court where it had been upheld against constitutional attack. He refrained therefore from joining in the Supreme Court's similar judgment, merely remarking that his "sentiments in favor of the constitutionality of the tax . . . have not been changed." Of course by considering the question of constitutionality at all, even to decide it affirmatively, both courts were assuming that they had authority to disallow an act of Congress.

Wilson's short opinion in *Ware* v. *Hylton,* 3 Dall. 199 (1796) is also moderately interesting. The case raised the important question whether a 1777 Virginia law confiscating and sequestrating debts due British citizens was valid against the 1783 treaty with Great Britain, i.e., whether the national treaty power was paramount to state law. Wilson of course joined the Court in upholding national supremacy and went a step beyond his fellow Justices by intimating that, even without the treaty, the Virginia statute might have been invalid as a violation of "the law of nations in its modern state of purity and refinement."

But the only case that gave Wilson a fair chance to show his mettle was *Chisholm* v. *Georgia,* 2 Dall. 419 (1793). It presented one of the most heated constitutional questions of the Federalist period: whether a state was amenable in federal courts to a suit by a citizen of another state. In the ratification controversy, champions of the Constitution had offered assurances that no such incongruity was contemplated by the loose language of Article III, but soon after the new government was established two South Carolina citizens did bring a suit for debt against Georgia. Underlying the suability issue was of course a much greater one: whether the Constitution had created a nation or a league of sovereign states.

Wilson had already thought deeply about the question whether states should be exempt from suit on the ground that they were "sovereign." In his law lectures he had argued that sovereignty resides not in states but in the people, and that if a man can submit himself without loss of dignity to the courts, the state can claim no greater immunity. In *Chisholm* these ideas were reinforced by his belief in the need for a potent national judiciary to cement national union. He joined in a four-to-one holding that the suit could be entertained and wrote in defense of the holding his only really substantial Supreme Court opinion.

The opinion contains, either explicitly or impliedly, most of the major ideas that had been ripening in his mind since the days at St. Andrews. His intellectual debt to Scottish common sense philosophy is suggested by an opening reference to Thomas Reid. His democratic bias is revealed in his contention that the state is subordinate to the people who create it and that the people of Georgia have not surrendered sovereignty to the state or its government, but have retained it in their own hands. His nationalism is revealed in the conclusion that the people, exercising this sovereign power, had willed a truly national government: "as to the purposes of the Union, therefore, Georgia is not a sovereign state." And the whole opinion is of course a testimonial to his belief in the need for an American jurisprudence based on anti-Blackstonian principles and to his conviction that such a democratically rooted legal system can be viable and effective.

It was a noteworthy effort. But one fine opinion in one famous case is not enough to establish immortality, and it turned out that this first opportunity to cast his ideas in the form of memorable judicial statement was also to be his last. Already in 1793 the clouds that darkened his final years were beginning to gather. His financial commitments were outrunning his capacities to meet them, yet nothing could dissuade him from contracting new ones and further multiplying his difficulties. He had bought on mortgage the Birdsboro ironworks that once belonged to his first wife's father. In 1794 he conceived and began to develop an extensive industrial complex on Lake Wallenpaupack, including sawmills, cloth mills, and dye works. The lure of land and more land—in Pennsylvania, in Carolina, in Virginia, in the West—continued to entice him. The shaky structure rose higher and higher, and he was repeatedly forced to turn away from his judicial duties and his scholarly pursuits to cope with a procession of crises.

Such crises were nothing new. He had been encountering them for years, and somehow by a process of borrowing and postponement he had managed to forestall disaster. But at last in 1796 the game neared its grim end. American speculators had counted on a flow of European money and immigrants, but the war in Europe cut that flow off. Wilson and many another rich Federalist were trapped in a calamitous credit squeeze. In the same year, as he desperately sought for means to hold his world together, his young wife bore him a son.

Wilson's remaining life was a nightmare of penury, harassment, imprisonment, and failing health. He who had dreamed of princely riches lacked now the money to clothe and feed his family adequately. He who had hoped for and earned a place near the forefront of America's hall of fame now found himself denounced and derided. Even while he rode circuit as a Justice of the Supreme Court, clamoring business associates and creditors pursued him, threatening scandal and debtors' prison. "Hunted like a wild beast," (Smith, 387), he hid from them in Bethlehem. But they apprehended him and had him imprisoned in Burlington, New Jersey. His eldest son managed to provide bail, and Wilson fled to a squalid temporary retreat in Edenton, North Carolina. But he owed Pierce Butler $197,000, and Butler's agents found him and jailed him again. Meanwhile his formerly robust health had begun to deteriorate. In July, 1798, still in Edenton, he caught malaria. A few weeks later he suffered a stroke. And on August 21, with only his young wife at his side, he died.

Those last years must have been unbearable for a man of Wilson's ego and ambition. The fact that he had risen so far since his Fifeshire days only heightened the tragedy of his fall at the end. He had coveted vast wealth, contemporary esteem, and undying fame. The first two had been only half-attained at best and were now beyond the reach of even his optimism. If he had any hopes left, they must have centered on the third: that his merits and services would be cherished in the future by "a just and grateful country." But even this posthumous consolation was to be denied him like the others, partly because of his own character and partly because of the character of America, then and in years to come.

He had many of the qualities we might look for in a great constitutional statesman-judge: learning, industry, insight, all far beyond the common measure. If he lacked some of the others that a man like Marshall had, those deficiencies might have been overcome, in the right time and place, by the sheer force of his abilities. But he wanted too many things, and he seemed congenitally unable to choose between them, or even to believe that choice was necessary. He wanted to be, not a freebooting financier, or a politician, or a revered constitutional statesman, but all three.

This may be too much for any man to ask at any time. It was certainly too much for a man like Wilson to ask in the time Providence had chosen for him. If he had lived twenty years longer, or later, he might have shared in the great expansion of judicial power that we identify with the Marshall Era. The nation might have been somewhat readier then to accept this curious blend of a democrat, a nationalist, and a legalist. But even of that there is room for doubt. Wilson was unappreciated by his own time because he was too far ahead of it. Perhaps he has been unappreciated by the future, because America, though following in his footsteps, has never quite caught up with him.

SELECTED BIBLIOGRAPHY

The main body of Wilson's papers is held by the Historical Society of Pennsylvania, but few enlightening personal items have survived. Wilson's own works, including the lectures on law and many of his essays and addresses, have been published in three editions: Bird Wilson, ed., 3 vols. (Philadelphia, 1804); J. D. Andrews, ed., 2 vols. (Chicago, 1896); R. G. McCloskey, ed., 2 vols. (Cambridge, 1967). The only full biography is C. P. Smith, *James Wilson, Founding Father: 1742–1798* (Chapel Hill, 1956). R. G. Adams, *Selected Political Essays of James Wilson* (New York, 1930) includes an introductory essay on Wilson's political thought and a useful bibliography. Other references are: J. B. McMaster and F. D. Stone, eds., *Pennsylvania and the Federal Constitution* (Philadelphia, 1888); R. L. Brunhouse, *The Counter-Revolution in Pennsylvania, 1776–1790* (Harrisburg, 1942); Robert Waln, "James Wilson" in John Sanderson, ed., *Biography of the Signers of the Declaration of Independence,* vol. 6 (Philadelphia, 1823); C. A. Goodrich, *Lives of the Signers to the Declaration of Independence* (New York, 1829); A. B. Leavelle, "James Wilson and the Relation of Scottish Metaphysics to American Political Thought," 57 *Political Science Quarterly* 394 (1942); A. C. McLaughlin, "James Wilson in the Philadelphia Convention," 12 *Political Science Quarterly* 1 (1897).

James Wilson

REPRESENTATIVE OPINIONS

CHISHOLM v. GEORGIA, 2 DALL. 419 (1793)

This was an action of *assumpsit,* brought by two citizens of South Carolina, executors of a British creditor, against the state of Georgia. Georgia refused to appear, but presented a written "remonstrance and protestation," arguing that the Court had no jurisdiction to hear the suit. The Attorney General, Edmund Randolph, appeared as counsel for the plaintiff. The Court, by a vote of four-to-one, sustained the right of a citizen of one state to bring a suit in the Supreme Court against another state. Opinions were delivered *seriatim,* only Justice Iredell arguing that the action could not lie. Judgment by default was entered against Georgia. The decision was received with widespread consternation and not a little indignation. During the ratification controversy, defenders of the proposed Constitution had expressly repudiated the interpretation of Article III that was now adopted by the Court. It was feared that the decision would expose the states to numerous and harassing claims and threaten their financial solvency. A writ of inquiry of damages was awarded in the February term, 1794, but it was never executed. A movement to amend the Constitution began in Congress the day after the *Chisholm* decision was handed down, and by March 4, 1794, both the Senate and House had overwhelmingly endorsed a resolution that: "The judicial power of the United States shall not be construed to extend to any suit in law or equity, commenced or prosecuted against one of the United States by Citizens of another State, or by Citizens or Subjects of any Foreign State." On January 8, 1798, the necessary number of states having ratified, this became the Eleventh Amendment.

WILSON, *Justice.* This is a case of uncommon magnitude. One of the parties to it is a state; certainly respectable, claiming to be sovereign. The question to be determined, is, whether this state, so respectable, and whose claim soars so high, is amenable to the jurisdiction of the supreme court of the United States? This question, important in itself, will depend on others, more important still; and, may, perhaps, be ultimately resolved into one, no less radical than this—"do the people of the United States form a nation?"

A cause so conspicuous and interesting should be carefully and accurately viewed from every possible point of sight. I shall examine it, 1st. By the principles of general jurisprudence. 2d. By the laws and practice of particular states and kingdoms. From the law of nations little or no illustration of this subject can be expected. By that law the several states and governments spread over our globe, are considered as forming a society, not a nation. It has only been by a very few comprehensive minds, such as those of Elizabeth and the fourth Henry, that this last great idea has been even contemplated. 3dly. and chiefly, I shall examine the important question before us, by the Constitution of the United States, and the legitimate result of that valuable instrument.

I. I am, first to examine this question by the principles of general jurisprudence. What I shall say upon this head, I introduce by the observation of an original and profound writer, who, in the philosophy of mind, and all the sciences attendant on this prime one, has formed an era not less remarkable, and far more illustrious, than that formed by the justly celebrated Bacon, in another science, not prosecuted with less ability, but less dignified as to its object; I mean the philosophy of matter. Dr. Reid, in his excellent enquiry into the human mind, on the principles of common sense, speaking of the sceptical and illiberal philosophy, which under bold, but false pretensions to liberality, prevailed in many parts of Europe before he wrote, makes the following judicious remark: "The language of philosophers, with regard to the original faculties of the mind, is so adapted to the prevailing system, that it cannot fit any other; like a coat that fits the man for whom it was made, and shows him to advantage, which yet will fit very awkward upon one of a different make, although as handsome and well-proportioned. It is hardly possible to make any innovation in our philosophy concerning the mind and its operations, without using new words and phrases, or giving a different meaning to those that are received." With equal propriety may this solid remark be applied to the great subject, on the principles of which the decision of this court is to be founded. The perverted use of genus and species in logic, and of impressions and ideas in metaphysics, have never done mischief so extensive or so practically pernicious, as has been done by states and sovereigns, in politics and jurisprudence; in the politics and jurisprudence even of those, who wished and meant to be free. In the place of those expressions I intend not to substitute new ones; but the expressions themselves I shall certainly use for purposes different from those, for which hitherto they have been frequently used; and one of them I shall apply to an object still more different from that to which it has hitherto been more frequently, I may say almost universally applied. In these purposes, and in this application, I shall be justified by example the most splendid, and by authority the most binding; the example of the most refined as well as the most free nation known to antiquity; and the authority of one of the best constitutions known to modern times. With regard to one of the terms—state—this authority is declared: With regard to the other—sovereign—the authority is implied only: But it is equally strong: For, in an instrument well drawn, as in a poem well composed, silence is sometimes most expressive.

To the Constitution of the United States the term sovereign, is totally unknown. There is but one place where it could have been used with propriety. But, even in that place it would not, perhaps, have comported with the delicacy of those, who ordained and established that constitution. They might have announced themselves "sovereign" people of the United States: But serenely conscious of the fact, they avoided the ostentatious declaration.

Having thus avowed my disapprobation of the purposes, for which the terms, state and sovereign, are frequently used, and of the object to which the application of the last of them is almost universally made; it is now proper that I should disclose the meaning which I assign to both, and the application, which I make of the latter. In doing this, I shall have occasion incidently to evince, how true it is, that states and governments were made for man; and at the same time how true it is, that his creatures and servants have first deceived, next vilified, and at last, oppressed their master and maker.

Man, fearfully and wonderfully made, is the workmanship of his all perfect creator: A state, useful and valuable as the contrivance is, is the inferior contrivance of man; and from his native dignity derives all its acquired importance. When I speak of a state as an inferior contrivance, I mean that it is a contrivance inferior only to that, which is divine: Of all human contrivances, it is certainly most transcendently excellent. It is concerning this contrivance that Cicero says so sublimely, "Nothing, which is exhibited upon our globe, is more acceptable to that divinity, which governs the whole universe, than those communities and assemblages of men, which, lawfully associated, are denominated states."[1]

Let a state be considered as subordinate to the people: But let everything else be subordinate to the state. The latter part of this position is equally necessary with the former. For in the practice, and even at length, in the science of politics there has very frequently been a strong current against the natural order of things, and an inconsiderate or an interested disposition to sacrifice the end to the means. As the state has claimed precedence of the people; so, in the same inverted course of things, the government has often claimed precedence of the state; and to this perversion in the second degree, many of the volumes of confusion concerning sovereignty owe their existence. The ministers, dignified very properly by the appellation of the magistrates, have wished, and have succeeded in their wish, to be considered as the sovereigns of the state. This second degree of perversion is confined to the old world, and begins to diminish even there: but the first degree is still too prevalent even in the several states, of which our union is composed. By a state I mean, a complete body of free persons united together for their common benefit, to enjoy peaceably what is their own, and to do justice to others. It is an artificial person. It has its affairs and its interests: It has its rules: It has its rights: And it has its obligations. It may acquire property distinct from that of its members. It may incur debts to be discharged out of the public stock, not out of the private fortunes of individuals. It may be bound by contracts; and for damages arising from the breach of those contracts. In all our contemplations, however, concerning this feigned and artificial person, we should never forget, that, in truth and nature, those who think and speak and act, are men.

[1] *Som. Sup. c. 3.*

Is the foregoing description of a state a true description? It will not be questioned, but it is. Is there any part of this description, which intimates in the remotest manner, that a state, any more than the men who compose it, ought not to do justice and fulfil engagements? It will not be pretended that there is. If justice is not done; if engagements are not fulfilled; is it upon general principles of right, less proper, in the case of a great number, than in the case of an individual, to secure, by compulsion, that, which will not be voluntarily performed? Less proper it surely cannot be. The only reason, I believe why a free man is bound by human laws, is, that he binds himself. Upon the same principles, upon which he becomes bound by the laws, he becomes amenable to the courts of justice, which are formed and authorized by those laws. If one free man, an original sovereign, may do all this, why may not an aggregate of free men, a collection of original sovereigns, do this likewise? If the dignity of each singly, is undiminished, the dignity of all jointly must be unimpaired. A state, like a merchant, makes a contract: A dishonest state, like a dishonest merchant, wilfully refuses to discharge it: The latter is amenable to a court of justice: Upon general principles of right shall the former when summoned to answer the fair demands of its creditor, be permitted, proteus-like, to assume a new appearance, and to insult him and justice, by declaring, I am a sovereign state? Surely not. Before a claim, so contrary, in its first appearance, to the general principles of right and equality, be sustained by a just and impartial tribunal, the person, natural or artificial, entitled to make such claim, should certainly be well known and authenticated. Who, or what, is a sovereignty? What is his or its sovereignty? On this subject, the errors and the mazes are endless and inexplicable. To enumerate all, therefore, will not be expected: To take notice of some will be necessary to the full illustration of the present important cause: In one sense, the term sovereign, has for its correlative, subject. In this sense, the term can receive no application; for it has no object in the Constitution of the United States. Under that constitution there are citizens, but no subjects. "Citizens of the United States."[1] "Citizens of another state," "Citizens of different states." "A state or citizen thereof."[2] The term, subject, occurs,

[1] *Art. 1, s. 2.*
[2] *Art. 3, s. 3.*

indeed, once in the instrument; but to mark the contrast strongly, the epithet "foreign"[3] is prefixed. In this sense, I presume the state of Georgia has no claim upon her own citizens: In this sense, I am certain, she can have no claim upon the citizens of another state.

In another sense, according to some writers,[4] every state, which governs itself without any dependence on another power, is a sovereign state. Whether, with regard to her own citizens, this is the case of the state of Georgia; whether those citizens have done, as the individuals of England are said, by their late instructors, to have done, surrendered the supreme power to the state or government, and reserved nothing to themselves; or whether like the people of other states, and of the United States, the citizens of Georgia have reserved the supreme power in their own hands: and on that supreme power have made the state dependent, instead of being sovereign; these are questions, to which, as a judge in this cause, I can neither know nor suggest the proper answer; though, as a citizen of the union, I know, and am interested to know, that the most satisfactory answers can be given. As a citizen, I know the government of that state to be republican; and my short definition of such a government is,—one constructed on this principle, that the supreme power resides in the body of the people. As a judge of this court, I know, and can decide upon the knowledge, that the citizens of Georgia, when they acted upon the large scale of the union, as a part of the "People of the United States," did not surrender the supreme or sovereign power to that state; but, as to the purposes of the union, retained it to themselves. As to the purposes of the union, therefore, Georgia is not a sovereign state. If the judicial decision of this case forms one of those purposes; the allegation, that Georgia is a sovereign state, is unsupported by the fact. Whether the judicial decision of this cause is, or is not, one of those purposes, is a question which will be examined particularly in a subsequent part of my argument.

There is a third sense, in which the term sovereign, is frequently used, and which it is very material to trace and explain, as it furnishes a basis for what I presume to be one of the principal objections against the jurisdiction of this court over the state of Georgia. In this sense, sovereignty is derived from a feudal source; and like many other parts of that system so degrading to man, still retains its influence over our sentiments and conduct, though the cause, by which that influence was produced, never extended to the American states. The accurate and well informed President *Henault,* in his excellent chronological abridgment of the history of France, tells us, that, about the end of the second race of kings, a new kind of possession was acquired, under the name of fief. The governors of cities and provinces usurped equally the property of land, and the administration of justice; and established themselves as proprietary seigniors over those places, in which they had been only civil magistrates or military officers. By this means, there was introduced into the state, a new kind of authority, to which was assigned the appellation of sovereignty. In process of time the feudal system was extended over France, and almost all the other nations of Europe: And every kingdom became, in fact, a large fief. Into England this system was introduced by the Conqueror: And to this era we may, probably, refer the English maxim, that the king or sovereign is the fountain of justice. But, in the case of the king, the sovereignty had a double operation. While it vested him with jurisdiction over others, it excluded all others from jurisdiction over him. With regard to him, there was no superior power; and, consequently, on feudal principles, no right of jurisdiction. "The law," says Sir William Blackstone, "ascribes to the king the attribute of sovereignty; he is sovereign and independent within his own dominions; and owes no kind of subjection to any other potentate upon earth. Hence, it is, that no suit or action can be brought against the king, even in civil matters; because no court can have jurisdiction over him: for all jurisdiction implies superiority of power." This last position is only a branch of a much more extended principle, on which a plan of systematic despotism has been lately formed in England, and prosecuted with unwearied assiduity and care. Of this plan the author of the commentaries was, if not the introducer, at least the great supporter. He has been followed in it by writers later and less known; and his doctrines have, both on the other and this side of the Atlantic, been implicitly and generally received by those who neither examined their principles nor their consequences. The principle is, that all human law must be prescribed by a supe-

[3] *Art. 3, s. 3.*
[4] *Vatt. B. 1, c. s. 4.*

rior. This principle I mean not now to examine. Suffice it at present to say, that another principle, very different in its nature and operations, forms, in my judgment, the basis of sound and genuine jurisprudence; laws derived from the pure source of equality and justice must be founded on the consent of those, whose obedience they require. The sovereign, when traced to his source, must be found in the man.

I have now fixed, in the scale of things, the grade of a state; and have described its composure: I have considered the nature of sovereignty; and pointed its application to the proper object. I have examined the question before us, by the principles of general jurisprudence. In those principles, I find nothing, which tends to evince an exemption of the state of Georgia, from the jurisdiction of the court. I find every thing to have a contrary tendency.

II. I am, in the second place, to examine this question by the laws and practice of different states and kingdoms. In ancient Greece, as we learn from Isocrates, whole nations defended their rights before crowded tribunals: Such occasions as these, excited, we are told, all the powers of persuasion; and the vehemence and enthusiasm of the sentiment was gradually infused into the Grecian language, equally susceptible of strength and harmony. In those days, law, liberty, and refining science, made their benign progress in strict and graceful union: The rude and degrading league between the bar and feudal barbarism was not yet formed.

When the laws and practice of particular states have any application to the question before us; that application will furnish what is called an argument *a fortiori;* because all the instances produced will be instances of subjects instituting and supporting suits against those who were deemed their own sovereigns. These instances are stronger than the present one; because between the present plaintiff and defendant no such unequal relation is alleged to exist.

Columbus achieved the discovery of that country, which, perhaps, ought to bear his name. A contract made by Columbus furnished the first precedent for supporting, in his discovered country, the cause of injured merit against the claims and pretensions of haughty and ungrateful power. His son, Don Diego wasted two years in incessant, but fruitless, solicitation at the court of Spain, for the rights which descended to him in consequence of his father's original capitulation. He endeavored, at length, to obtain by a legal sentence, what he could not procure from the favor of an interested monarch. He commenced a suit against Ferdinand before the council, which managed Indian affairs; and that court, with integrity which reflects honor on their proceedings, decided against the king, and sustained Don Diego's claim.

Other states have instituted officers to judge the proceedings of their kings: Of this kind were the Ephori of Sparta; of this kind also was the mayor of the palace, and afterwards, the constable of France.

But of all the laws and institutions relating to the present question, none is so striking as that described by the famous Hottoman, in his book entitled Francogallia. When the Spaniards of Arragon elect a king, they represent a kind of play, and introduce a personage, whom they dignify by the name of law, *la justiza* of Arragon. This personage they declare, by a public decree, to be greater and more powerful than their king; and then address him in the following remarkable expressions. "We, who are of as great worth as you, and can do more than you can do, elect you to be our king, upon the conditions stipulated: But between you and us, there is one of greater authority than you."

In England, according to Sir William Blackstone, no suit can be brought against the king, even in civil matters. So, in that kingdom, is the law, at this time, received. But it was not always so. Under the Saxon government, a very different doctrine was held to be orthodox. Under that government, as we are informed by the Mirror of Justice, a book, said by Sir Edward Coke, to have been written, in part, at least, before the conquest; under that government it was ordained, that the king's court should be open to all plaintiffs, by which, without delay, they should have remedial writs as well against the king, or against the queen, as against any other of the people.[1] The law continued to be the same for some centuries after the conquest. Until the time of Edward I. the king might have been sued as a common person. The form of the process was even imperative. *"Præcipe Henrico Regi Angliæ"* etc. "Command Henry King of England" etc.[2] Bracton, who wrote in the time of Henry III., uses these very remarkable expressions concerning the king; *"in justitia*

[1] *4 C. A. N. 487.*

[2] *Brac. 107. Com. 104.*

recipienda, minimo de regno suo comparetur"—"in receiving justice, he should be placed on a level with the meanest person in the kingdom."[3] True it is, that now in England the king must be sued in his courts by petition; but even now, the difference is only in the form, not in the thing. The judgments or decrees of those courts will substantially be the same upon a precatory as upon a mandatory process. In the courts of justice, says the very able author of the considerations on the laws of forfeiture, the king enjoys many privileges; yet not to deter the subject from contending with him freely.[4] The judge of the high court of admiralty in England made, in a very late cause, the following manly and independent declaration. "In any case, where the crown is a party, it is to be observed, that the crown can no more withhold evidence of documents in its possession, than a private person. If the court think proper to order the production of any public instrument; that order must be obeyed. It wants no insignia of an authority derived from the crown."[5]

"Judges ought to know, that the poorest peasant is a man as well as the king himself; all men ought to obtain justice; since in the estimation of justice, all men are equal; whether the prince complain of a peasant, or a peasant complain of the prince."[6] These are the words of a king, of the late Frederic of Prussia. In his courts of justice, that great man stood upon his native greatness; and disdained to mount upon the artificial stilts of sovereignty.

Thus much concerning the laws and practice of other states and kingdoms. We see nothing against, but much in favor of, the jurisdiction of this court over the state of Georgia, a party to this cause.

III. I am, thirdly, and chiefly, to examine the important question now before us, by the Constitution of the United States, and the legitimate result of that valuable instrument. Under this view, the question is naturally subdivided into two others. 1. Could the Constitution of the United States vest a jurisdiction over the state of Georgia? 2. Has that constitution vested such jurisdiction in this court? I have already remarked, that in the practice, and even in the science of politics, there has been frequently a strong current against the natural order of things; and an inconsiderate or an interested disposition to sacrifice the end to the means. This remark deserves a more particular illustration. Even in almost every nation, which has been denominated free, the state has assumed a supercilious pre-eminence above the people who have formed it: Hence the haughty notions of state independence, state sovereignty, and state supremacy. In despotic governments, the Government has usurped, in a similar manner, both upon the state and the people: Hence all arbitrary doctrines and pretensions concerning the supreme, absolute, and incontrolable, power of government. In each, man is degraded from the prime rank, which he ought to hold in human affairs: In the latter, the state as well as the man is degraded. Of both degradations, striking instances occur in history, in politics, and in common life. One of them is drawn from an anecdote, which is recorded concerning Louis XIV. who has been styled the grand monarch of France. This prince, who diffused around him so much dazzling splendor, and so little vivifying heat, was vitiated by that inverted manner of teaching and of thinking, which forms kings to be tyrants, without knowing or even suspecting that they are so. The oppression, under which he held his subjects, during the whole course of his long reign, proceeded chiefly from the principles and habits of his erroneous education. By these, he had been accustomed to consider his kingdom as his patrimony, and his power over his subjects as his rightful and undelegated inheritance. These sentiments were so deeply and strongly imprinted on his mind, that when one of his ministers represented to him the miserable condition, to which those subjects were reduced, and in the course of his representation, frequently used the word, *L'État*, the state, the king, though he felt the truth and approved the substance of all that was said, yet was shocked at the frequent repetition of the expression, *L'Etat;* and complained of it as an indecency offered to his person and character. And indeed, that kings should imagine themselves the final causes for which men were made, and societies were formed, and governments were instituted, will cease to be a matter of wonder or surprise, when we find that lawyers, and statesmen, and philosophers, have taught or favored principles, which necessarily lead to the same conclusion. Another instance, equally strong, but still more astonishing, is drawn from the British government, as described by Sir William Blackstone and his

3 *Com. 104.*
4 *G. F. 124.*
5 *Col. Jur. 68.*
6 *War. 343.*

followers. As described by him and them, the British is a despotic government. It is a government without a people. In that government, as so described, the sovereignty is possessed by the parliament: In the parliament therefore, the supreme and absolute authority is vested:[7] In the parliament resides that incontrolable and despotic power, which, in all governments, must reside somewhere. The constituent parts of the parliament are the king's majesty, the lord's spiritual, the lord's temporal, and the commons. The king and these three estates together form the great corporation or body politic of the kingdom. All these sentiments are found; the last expressions are found verbatim[1] in the commentaries upon the laws of England.[2] The parliament form the great body politic of England! What then, or where, are the people? Nothing! No where! They are not so much as even the "baseless fabric of a vision!" From legal contemplation they totally disappear! Am I not warranted in saying, that, if this is a just description; a government, so, and justly so described, is a despotic government? Whether this description is or is not a just one, is a question of very different import.

In the United States, and in the several states which compose the union, we go not so far: but still we go one step farther than we ought to go in this unnatural and inverted order of things. The states, rather than the people, for whose sakes the states exist, are frequently the objects which attract and arrest our principal attention. This, I believe, has produced much of the confusion and perplexity, which have appeared in several proceedings and several publications on state politics, and on the politics too, of the United States. Sentiments and expressions of this inaccurate kind prevail in our common, even in our convivial, language. Is a toast asked? "The United States" instead of the "People of the United States," is the toast given. This is not politically correct. The toast is meant to present to view the first great object in the union: It presents only the second: It presents only the artificial person, instead of the natural persons, who spoke it into existence. A state I cheerfully admit, is the noblest work of man: But man himself, free and honest, is, I speak as to this world, the noblest work of God.

Concerning the prerogative of kings, and concerning the sovereignty of states, much has been said and written; but little has been said and written concerning a subject much more dignified and important, the majesty of the people. The mode of expression, which I would substitute in the place of that generally used, is, not only politically, but also (for between true liberty and true taste there is a close alliance) classically more correct. On the mention of Athens, a thousand refined and endearing associations rush at once into the memory of the scholar, the philosopher, and the patriot. When Homer, one of the most correct, as well as the oldest of human authorities, enumerates the other nations of Greece, whose forces acted at the siege of Troy, he arranges them under the names of their different kings or princes: But when he comes to the Athenians, he distinguishes them by the peculiar appellation of the people[3] of Athens. The well known address used by Demosthenes, when he harangued and animated his assembled countrymen, was, "O men of Athens." With the strictest propriety, therefore, classical and political, our national scene opens with the most magnificent object which the nation could present. "The people of the United States" are the first personages introduced. Who were those people? They were the citizens of thirteen states, each of which had a separate constitution and government, and all of which were connected together by articles of confederation. To the purposes of public strength and felicity, that confederacy was totally inadequate. A requisition on the several states terminated its legislative authority: Executive or judicial authority it had none. In order, therefore, to form a more perfect union, to establish justice, to ensure domestic tranquillity, to provide for common defense, and to secure the blessings of liberty, those people among whom were the people of Georgia, ordained and established the present constitution. By that constitution legislative power is vested, executive power is vested, judicial power is vested.

The question now opens fairly to our view; could the people of those states, among whom were those of Georgia, bind those states, and Georgia among the others, by the legislative, executive, and judicial power so vested? If the principles, on which I have founded myself, are just and true, this question must unavoidably receive an

[7] *1 Bl. Com. 46–52, 147, 160–162.*
[1] *1 Bl. Com. 153.*
[2] *1 Bl. Com. 153.*

[3] *Il. 1. 2. v. 54, Demos. Pol. 12, one of the words of which democracy is compounded.*

affirmative answer. If those states were the work of those people; those people, and, that, I may apply the case closely, the people of Georgia, in particular, could alter, as they pleased, their former work: To any given degree, they could diminish as well as enlarge it. Any or all of the former state powers they could extinguish or transfer. The inference, which necessarily results, is, that the constitution ordained and established by those people; and, still closely to apply the case, in particular by the people of Georgia, could vest jurisdiction or judicial power over those states and over the state of Georgia in particular.

The next question under this head, is.—Has the constitution done so? Did those people mean to exercise this, their undoubted power? These questions may be resolved, either by fair and conclusive deductions, or by direct and explicit declarations. In order, ultimately, to discover, whether the people of the United States intended to bind those states by the judicial power vested by the national constitution, a previous enquiry will naturally be: Did those people intend to bind those states by the legislative power vested by that constitution? The articles of confederation, it is well known, did not operate upon individual citizens; but operated only upon states. This defect was remedied by the national constitution, which, as all allow, has an operation on individual citizens. But if an opinion, which some seem to entertain, be just; the defect remedied, on one side, was balanced by a defect introduced on the other. For they seem to think, that the present constitution operates only on individual citizens, and not on states. This opinion, however, appears to be altogether unfounded. When certain laws of the states are declared to be "subject to the revision and control of the Congress,"[4] it cannot surely, be contended that the legislative power of the national government was meant to have no operation on the several states. The fact, uncontrovertibly established in one instance, proves the principle in all other instances, to which the facts will be found to apply. We may then infer, that the people of the United States intended to bind the several states, by the legislative power of the national government.

In order to make the discovery, at which we ultimately aim, a second previous enquiry will naturally be—Did the people of the United States intend to bind the several states by the executive power of the national government? The affirmative answer to the former question directs, unavoidably, an affirmative answer to this. Ever since the time of Bracton, his maxim, I believe, has been deemed a good one—*"Supervacuum esset leges condere, nisi esset qui leges tueretur."*[1] "It would be superfluous to make laws, unless those laws, when made, were to be enforced." When the laws are plain and the application of them is uncontroverted, they are enforced immediately by the executive authority of government. When the application of them is doubtful or intricate, the interposition of the judicial authority becomes necessary. The same principle, therefore, which directed us from the first to the second step will direct us from the second to the third and last step of our deduction. Fair and conclusive deduction, then, evinces that the people of the United States did vest this court with jurisdiction over the state of Georgia. The same truth may be deduced from the declared objects, and the general texture of the constitution of the United States. One of its declared objects is, to form a union more perfect than before that time, had been formed. Before that time, the union possessed legislative, but uninforced legislative power over the states. Nothing could be more natural than to intend that this legislative power should be enforced by powers executive and judicial. Another declared object is "to establish justice." This points, in a particular manner, to the judicial authority. And when we view this object in conjunction with the declaration, "that no state shall pass a law impairing the obligation of contracts;" we shall probably think, that this object points, in a particular manner, to the jurisdiction of the court over the several states. What good purpose could this constitutional provision secure, if a state might pass a law impairing the obligation of its own contracts; and be amenable, for such a violation of right, to no controling judiciary power? We have seen, that on the principles of general jurisprudence, a state, for the breach of a contract, may be liable for damages. A third declared object is—"to ensure domestic tranquillity." This tranquillity is most likely to be disturbed by controversies between states. These consequences will be most peaceably and effectually decided by the establishment and by the exercise of a superintending judicial authority.

[4] *Ar. 1, s. 10.*

[1] *Brac. 107.*

By such exercise and establishment, the law of nations; the rule between contending states; will be enforced among the several states, in the same manner as municipal law.

Whoever considers, in a combined and comprehensive view, the general texture of the constitution, will be satisfied, that the people of the United States intended to form themselves into a nation for national purposes. They instituted for such purposes, a national government, complete in all its parts, with powers legislative, executive, and judiciary; and in all those powers extending over the whole nation. Is it congruous, that, with regard to such purposes, any man, or body of men, any person, natural or artificial, should be permitted to claim successfully an entire exemption from the jurisdiction of the national government? Would not such claims, crowned with success, be repugnant to our very existence as a nation? When so many trains of deduction coming from different quarters, converge and unite, at last, in the same point; we may safely conclude, as the legitimate result of this constitution, that the state of Georgia is amenable to the jurisdiction of this court.

But, in my opinion, this doctrine rests not upon the legitimate result of fair and conclusive deduction from the constitution: It is confirmed beyond all doubt, by the direct and explicit declaration of the constitution itself. "The judicial power of the United States shall extend, to controversies between two states."[1] Two states are supposed to have a controversy between them: This controversy is supposed to be brought before those vested with the judicial power of the United States: Can the most consummate degree of professional ingenuity devise a mode by which this "controversy between two states" can be brought before a court of law; and yet neither of those states be a defendant? "The judicial power of the United States shall extend to controversies, between a state and citizens of another state." Could the strictest legal language; could even that language, which is peculiarly appropriated to an art, deemed, by a great master, to be one of the most honorable, laudable, and profitable things in our law; could this strict and appropriated language, describe, with more precise accuracy, the cause now depending before the tribunal? Causes and not parties to causes, are weighed by justice in her equal scales: On the former solely, her attention is fixed: To the latter, she is as she is painted, blind.

I have now tried this question by all the touchstones, to which I proposed to apply it. I have examined it by the principles of general jurisprudence; by the laws and practice of states and kingdoms; and by the constitution of the United States. From all, the combined inference is, that the action lies.

[1] *Art. 3, s. 2.*

John Blair, Jr.

☆ 1732–1800 ☆

APPOINTED BY

GEORGE WASHINGTON

YEARS ON COURT

1789–1796

John Blair, Jr.

by

FRED L. ISRAEL

BORN IN Williamsburg, Virginia in 1732, John Blair, Jr. was the son of one of colonial Virginia's leading statesmen. His father had served in the House of Burgesses, 1734–1740; as a member of the Governor's Council, 1745–1770; and Acting Governor in 1758 and again in 1768. John Blair, Jr., one of ten children, had the benefits of a fine education, graduating from William and Mary College with honors in 1754—Blair's great-uncle James Blair (1655–1743) had established the College of William and Mary while he served as the Virginia Deputy of the Anglican Bishop of London. The large family fortune, which included enormous land holdings in western Virginia, enabled young Blair to study law at London's Middle Temple, 1755–1756. While in London he was the guest and protégé of former Governor Robert Dinwiddie, who had long been a warm friend of his father. Upon returning to Williamsburg, he began practicing in the General Court "where he enjoyed a respectable share of the business before that tribunal."

Blair's own career as a statesman started in 1765 when, at the age of thirty-three, his college alma mater chose him to represent them in the House of Burgesses. Conservative in his thinking, he moved among the select of Williamsburg where, as one contemporary described, "he preserved to the last that strict attention to dress which was the characteristic of the colonial régime." In the Burgesses, Blair opposed Patrick Henry's 1765 Stamp Act resolutions as premature, reasoning that every peaceful means should be exhausted in protesting the Act before boldly defying the English ministry. When the Crown dissolved the Burgesses in 1769, Blair, with George Washington, Richard Bland, and Robert Carter Nicholas, drafted the nonimportation agreement. And in 1770, when the Crown again dissolved the Burgesses, Blair was among those who revised the agreement under which leading Virginia merchants boycotted speci-

FRED L. ISRAEL, Associate Professor of History at the City College of New York, is the author of Nevada's Key Pittman.

fied British goods until Parliament repealed the import taxes on tea, paper, and paint. In the fall of 1770, Blair resigned from the Burgesses to become Clerk of the Governor's Council. As events led to separation from Great Britain, Blair sided with those merchants and landowners who favored independence. When the Virginia Convention met on May 6, 1776 to formulate a constitution for the new Commonwealth, Blair served as a delegate from William and Mary College. During this famous convention, Blair held many important committee assignments and was one of twenty-eight eminent Virginia men assigned to prepare a plan of government. Upon the adoption of their report, Blair was chosen a member of the new Governor's Council on June 30, 1776. With the creation of a Virginia judicial system—which included Chancery, General, and Admiralty Courts—in October, 1777, a joint legislature ballot selected him to be one of five General Court judges. He was chosen Chief Justice in 1779. On November 23, 1780, Blair was elevated to Chancellor of the three member High Court of Chancery. Because of his judicial positions, Blair also served on Virginia's first Court of Appeals when it was organized in May, 1779. In the celebrated case of *The Commonwealth of Virginia* v. *Caton et al.,* 4 Call. 5 (1782), Blair and one other Appeal judge declared that the Court had power to nullify an unconstitutional legislative act. This is one of the first cases in which the validity of a law enacted by a duly constituted legislature was presented to a judicial tribunal for review. The enunciating principle of their opinions could have been in John Marshall's mind as he framed his 1803 landmark decision in *Marbury* v. *Madison,* 5 Cranch 137 (1803).

On December 4, 1786, the Virginia legislature chose Blair as a delegate to represent the state at the Constitutional Convention which met in Philadelphia the following June. Virginia's seven man delegation included some of the most illustrious colonial figures—George Washington, Edmund Randolph, James Madison, George Mason, and George Wythe. Judges Blair and Wythe, owing to the "badness of their cavalry, were furnished with a state boat to convey them to the head of the Chesapeake Bay," and they sailed from Yorktown on May 7, 1787. According to the Madison and Yates records of the Convention, Blair never delivered a speech during the sessions, but William Pierce of Georgia observed that "his good sense, sound judgement, and excellent principles overbalanced any oratorical deficiency." When the question of a single or plural Chief Executive arose, Virginia voted for the single person plan although Randolph and Blair opposed it in the Virginia caucus. Choosing the Chief Executive provoked a long debate as to whether he should be elected directly by the people or by the national legislature. On the vote, six states favored election by the legislature, three opposed it, one state was absent, and the Virginia delegation divided—Washington and Madison opposed legislative election while Blair and Mason favored it. The ensuing general compromise created the electoral college. When the final draft of the Constitution was ready, Blair, convinced that absolute perfection could never be achieved and delay would be ruinous, voted with Washington and Madison for adoption. The three signed the document for Virginia on September 17, 1787.

Blair returned to Virginia and resumed his judicial duties. When the Virginia Convention was called in 1788 to discuss ratifying the federal Constitution, York County had Blair as its delegate and he again voted for adoption. In November, 1787, the case of *Commonwealth* v. *Posey,* 4 Call. 109 (1787), came before the Court of Appeals. The prisoner stood indicted for arson but claimed the benefit of clergy. Judge Blair and his colleagues, in denying the accused the benefit of clergy, relied on *Powlter's* case which had been decided more than two hundred years before and upon which English statutes relative to the question had long since been construed. This decision is important because a settled English construction of a statute was adhered to by the Virginia Court forming a precedent for future cases. The following year, the Virginia judicial system was reorganized and the legislature chose Blair as one of five judges for the Supreme Court of Appeals of Virginia. This new Court held its first meeting on June 20, 1789. Blair served but three months in this office before President Washington requested his services on the national judiciary.

The Judiciary Act, which Washington signed on September 24, 1789, provided that the United States Supreme Court should consist of a Chief Justice and five Associate Justices. On the same day, Washington sent to the Senate the names of his Supreme Court appointees—for Chief Justice, John Jay; for Associate Justices, John Rutledge, James Wilson, William Cushing, Robert Harrison (who declined), and John Blair. "Impressed with a conviction that the due administration of justice is the firmest pillar of good Government, I have considered the first arrangement of the Judicial department as essential to the happiness of our Country, and to the stability of its political system," Washington wrote Edmund Randolph, "hence the seletcion of the fittest characters to expound the laws, and dispense justice, has been an invariable object of my anxious concern." To each Justice, the President addressed letters stating that he considered "the Judicial System as the chief Pillar upon which our national Government must rest," and he asked that "the love which you bear to our Country, and a desire to promote general happiness, will lead you to a ready acceptance of the enclosed Commission." The appointment came as a surprise to Blair but he accepted immediately and resigned from the Virginia Supreme Court of Appeals.

The first Supreme Court meeting was held in New York, then the United States capital, on February 1, 1790. Chief Justice Jay and Justices Cushing and Wilson appeared in the old Federal Hall but, as the required quorum was lacking, they adjourned. Blair arrived with Attorney General Edmund Randolph later that day and the following morning the first formal Supreme Court meeting convened and each Justice qualified according to law. During the first years of its existence, the Supreme Court docket remained comparatively light, with organizational and procedural matters being the principal business. A. J. Dallas even records how "malignant fever" which raged in Philadelphia during August, 1793 "dispersed the great body of its inhabitants, and . . . interrupted, likewise, the business of the courts; and I cannot trace, that any important cause was agitated in the present term." 2 Dall. 480 (1793). Because of the sparse Court calendar as well as his wife's chronic ill health, Blair did not attend all Court terms. He remained on the Court, though, through the August, 1795 session, resigning on January 27, 1796.

In August, 1792, the Supreme Court decided its first important case—*Georgia* v. *Brailsford,* 2 Dall. 402 (1792). Brailsford, a British creditor, had sued a Georgia citizen in the United States Circuit Court for a Revolutionary debt which the state of Georgia had sequestrated. Georgia had requested the Circuit Court for permission to intervene as an interested party in order to establish title to the property. The court refused and when judgment was entered for the plaintiff, Georgia sought a Supreme Court injunction to stay the lower court proceedings. The Court granted the injunction. Each Justice wrote an opinion—with Justices Thomas Johnson, who had replaced Rutledge, and Cushing, dissenting. Wrote Blair in explaining his decision:

> *It appears to me to be too early, to pronounce an opinion upon the titles in collision; since it is enough, on a motion of this kind, to show a colorable title. The state of Georgia has set up her confiscation act, which certainly is a fair foundation for future judicial investigation; and that an injury may not be done, which it may be out of our power to repair, the injunction ought, I think, to issue, till we are enabled, by a full inquiry, to decide upon the whole merits of the case* (*2 Dall. 407*).

The case was eventually tried before a special jury in 1794—one of the very few times in the history of the Supreme Court when it empaneled a jury—and the jury found in favor of Brailsford; Georgia's claim was denied on the ground that the state's sequestration law did not confiscate the British debt or give the state title to it. The Brailsford case is interesting historically because it is the first recorded Supreme Court case in which all Justices present submitted written opinions—and these were read in reverse order of seniority with Blair following Johnson and James Iredell, who had received Harrison's commission. Also, the case is important because when it did go to the special jury, Chief Justice Jay's charge for the Court strongly asserted federal supremacy, intimating that a state law could not conflict with a United States treaty; that is, the 1783 Treaty of Paris removed all legal impediments for the recovery of bona fide debts, and "the treaty is the supreme law of the land, by virtue of the federal constitution." 3 Dall. 3 (1794).

Blair delivered his most important decision during his seven years on the Court in the case of *Chisholm* v. *Georgia,* 2 Dall. 419 (1793). In 1792, three years after the launching of the new government, the Supreme Court found itself compelled to analyze the very nature of the Union in an attempt to deal with a fundamental question not solved by the Founding Fathers. That year, a man named Chisholm, executor for a citizen of South Carolina, brought suit in the United States Supreme Court to enforce a claim against the state of Georgia. The constitutional basis for this unprecedented action was the provision in Article III, Section 2 which included within the jurisdiction of the federal judiciary those cases "between a State and Citizens of another State." In several state ratifying conventions, Anti-Federalists had challenged this clause but had been assured by Federalists that it would never be construed so as to permit the citizen of one state to sue another state. As a member of the Virginia Ratifying Convention, John Marshall stated that it was "not rational to suppose that the sovereign power should be dragged before a court. The intent is, to enable states to recover claims of [against] individuals residing in other states." In Number 81 of the *Federalist,* Hamilton echoed this view. "It is inherent in the nature of sovereignty," he wrote, "not to be amenable to the suit of an individual without its own consent."

The Chisholm case came before the Court in August, 1792. As no one appeared on behalf of Georgia, Attorney General Edmund Randolph requested that judgment be entered for Chisholm unless Georgia was represented by counsel at the February, 1793 term. In December, 1792, the Georgia legislature denounced the proceedings as "unconstitutional and extrajudicial," declaring that it would not be bound by the Supreme Court decision. The following February, the Court delivered its opinion but also allowed a delay in execution until August, 1793, when, unless Georgia appeared in court, judgment by default in favor of Chisholm would be entered. Five Justices wrote opinions—Iredell, Wilson, Cushing, Jay, and Blair. Only Iredell thought that a state could not be sued in a federal court without its consent. The other four ruled against the Georgia contention, clearing the way for such suits against states in federal courts as citizens of other states might see fit to institute. But the hostility aroused by this decision led to an effective movement for an Eleventh Amendment which took the matter out of the federal courts' jurisdiction before any attempt at collection was made. The amendment swept from the Court docket the Chisholm case and all other individual suits by citizens of one state against another state. See *Hollingsworth, et al.* v. *Virginia,* 3 Dall. 378 (1798).

The five opinions in the Chisholm case deal with the issue of state sovereignty and immunity from suit. Chief Justice Jay's opinion is perhaps the most elaborate of his judicial utterances as he emphasized that a nation's sovereignty was in the people of the nation, who were "sovereigns without subjects." In his opinion, Blair undertook neither a lengthy treatise on political theory, as did Jay and Wilson, nor the exhaustive research into the antecedent law which Iredell performed. Referring to the analogy which Attorney General Randolph had drawn from European confederations, Blair held the Constitution to be the sole governing authority to which recourse should be had in determining the issue. Blair observed that the Constitution clearly conferred on the Court jurisdiction in such cases as *Chisholm* v. *Georgia* and he agreed with Randolph that the mere word order in Article III, Section 2—"controversies between a State and Citizens of another State"—did not limit the Court's jurisdiction only to cases where a state was plaintiff. His decision is based on the Constitution's explicit judicial provisions. "Is then," he asked, "the case before us one of that description?"

> *Undoubtedly it is, unless it may be a sufficient denial to say, that it is a controversy between a citizen of one State and another State. Can this change of order be an essential change in the thing intended? And is this alone a sufficient ground from which to conclude that the jurisdiction of this Court reaches the case where a State is plaintiff, but not where it is defendant? In this latter case, should any man be asked, whether it was not a controversy between a State and a citizen of another State, must not the answer be in the affirmative? A dispute between A and B is surely a dispute between B and A.*

Blair also discussed the nature of sovereignty. The full text of his decision is reprinted below. Although the Eleventh Amendment was proposed on February 20, 1793, but two days after the Court gave its decision, the importance of the several opinions remains. This was the first clear national judicial opinion in American history which referred to an indissoluble Union and which enunciated a definition of state sovereignty.

The early Court sessions had little business to transact, but the Justices, nevertheless, found themselves fully employed attempting to fulfill their duties as detailed in the 1789 Judiciary Act. The nation had been divided into thirteen judicial districts with a district judge presiding over each. The act provided for three circuits (the Eastern, Middle, and Southern), to each of which two Supreme Court Justices were assigned and directed to hold court twice a year in each district together with the district judge. These circuit courts had both original and appellate jurisdiction from the district courts. (This system was revised by the Judiciary Acts of 1801 and 1802.) Justices Blair and Wilson presided over the Middle Circuit which consisted of New Jersey, Pennsylvania, Delaware, Maryland, and Virginia. Few records of these early circuit courts are extant, although many Justices found their energies taxed to the limit by "riding the circuit." During the April, 1792 term, the case of *Collet* v. *Collet,* 2 Dall. 294 (1792), came before the Middle Circuit Court from the Pennsylvania District Court. The issue presented was whether a state had a right to naturalize an alien, and if so, whether under the Constitution, the authority to naturalize is exclusive or concurrent. Justices Blair and Wilson, with District Judge Peters, unanimously stated that the states have a concurrent authority but that a state cannot contravene rules established by Congress, and a state cannot exclude from citizenship those who have been naturalized by the federal government. "We are of the opinion, then, that the states, individually, still enjoy a concurrent authority upon this subject; but that their individual authority cannot be exercised so as to contravene the rule established by the authority of the Union. . . . The true reason for investing Congress with the power of naturalization has been assigned at the bar:—It was to guard against too narrow instead of too liberal a mode of conferring the rights of citizenship." The federal Naturalization Act of 1795 generally superseded this decision but it is interesting for its concept of federalism espoused by those who set the new government in operation.

Blair found riding the circuit increasingly more difficult, especially as chronic headaches lasted longer and became more frequent. His general ill health, aggravated by his wife's death, forced him to resign from the Court on January 27, 1796—his wife, Jean Balfour, and at least two of their daughters had been "afflicted with Hysteria." "I have been a good deal distressed myself by almost continual cholics," Blair wrote to a sister shortly after his retirement, "yet I have a good appetite and eat I believe more than is good for me; that and the want of teeth to masticate my food properly are probably the cause of my malady." Blair retired to the seclusion of his Williamsburg home. On July 5, 1799, in a shaky handwriting, he detailed his ill health to a younger sister: "I was on 5th Nov 1797, struck with a strange disorder to which I knew not how to give a name . . . the effects of which are to me most melancholy depriving me of nearly all the powers of mind. The effect was very sudden and instantaneous. I happened to be employed in some algebraical exercises (of which kind of amusement I was very fond) when all at once a torpid numbness seized my whole face and I found my intellectual powers much weakened and all was confusion. My tongue partook of the distress and some words I was not able to articulate distinctly and a general difficulty of remembering words at all. There are intervals when all these distresses abate considerably; but there are times when I am unable to read and am obliged to lay aside a newspaper or whatever else I may happen to be engaged in." Blair died on August 31, 1800. Contemporaries have described Blair as nearly six feet in height "of slight frame, but with an astonishing breadth of brow, particularly between the eyes, which were brown in color, surmounted by a bald forehead fringed with scanty locks of red hair, which fell over his ears. His lower lip protruded in a singular way, like the bill of a bird. . . . Amiable in disposition, blameless and pious, possessed of great benevolence and goodness of heart." Upon hearing of Blair's retirement in 1796, William Plumer, later Senator from New Hampshire, wrote: "I consider him as a man of good abilities, not indeed a Jay, but far superior to Cushing, a man of firmness, strict integrity and of great candour."

SELECTED BIBLIOGRAPHY

A good scholarly biographical article of Blair is J. Elliott Drinard, "John Blair, Jr.," 39 *Proceedings of the Virginia State Bar Association* 436 (1927). See also Fredrick Horner, *History of the Blair, Banister and Braxton Families* (Philadelphia, 1898), and Hampton L. Carson, *History of the Supreme Court of the United States* (Philadelphia, 1892).

John Blair, Jr.

REPRESENTATIVE OPINIONS

CHISHOLM v. GEORGIA 2 DALL. 419 (1793)

Under the United States Constitution as construed by the Court in the *Chisholm* case, a state could be sued by a citizen of another state, in *assumpsit.* Although the Court upheld this right only to have the Eleventh Amendment (1798) negate their decision, the five opinions in the *Chisholm* case are important because they discuss divergent theories of state sovereignty. In his opinion, Blair held that the Court must literally interpret the Constitution and, therefore, the issue before the Court was not to pass judgment on the merits of a citizen of one state suing a sovereign state, but to carry out the provisions enunciated in the Constitution. "It seems to me," wrote Blair, "that if this Court should refuse to hold jurisdiction of a case where a State is Defendant, it would renounce part of the Authority conferred, and, consequently, part of the duty imposed on it by the Constitution."

BLAIR, Justice. In considering this important case, I have thought it best to pass over all strictures which have been made on the various European confederations; because, as, on the one hand, their likeness to our own is not sufficiently close to justify any analogical application; so, on the other, they are utterly destitute of any binding authority here. The constitution of the United States is the only fountain from which I shall draw; the only authority to which I shall appeal. Whatever be the true language of that, it is obligatory upon every member of the Union; for no state could have become a member, but by an adoption of it by the people of that state. What then do we find there, requiring the submission of individual states to the judicial authority of the United States? This is expressly extended, among other things, to controversies between a state and citizens of another state. Is, then, the case before us one of that description? Undoubtedly, it is, unless it may be a sufficient denial to say, that it is a controversy between a citizen of one state and another state. Can this change of order be an essential change in the thing intended? And is this alone a sufficient ground from which to conclude, that the jurisdiction of this court reaches the case where a state is plaintiff, but not where it is defendant? In this latter case, should any man be asked, whether it was not a controversy between a state and citizen of another state, must not the answer be in the affirmative? A dispute between A. and B. is surely a dispute between B. and A. Both cases, I have no doubt, were intended; and probably, the state was first named, in respect to the dignity of a state. But that very dignity seems to have been thought a sufficient reason for confining the sense to the case where a state is plaintiff. It is, however, a sufficient answer to say, that our constitution most certainly contemplates, in another branch of the cases enumerated, the maintaining a jurisdiction against a state, as defendant; this is unequivocally asserted, when the judicial power of the United States is extended to controversies between two or more states; for there, a state must, of necessity, be a defendant. It is extended also to controversies between a state and foreign states; and if the argument taken from the order of designation were good, it would be meant here, that this court might have cognisance of a suit, where a state is plaintiff, and some foreign state a defendant, but not where a foreign state brings a suit against a state. This, however, not to mention that the instances may rarely occur, when a state may have an opportunity of suing, in the American courts, a foreign state, seems to lose sight of the policy which, no doubt, suggested this provision, viz., that no state in the Union should, by withholding justice, have it in its power to embroil the whole confederacy in disputes of another nature. But if a foreign state, though last named, may, nevertheless, be a plaintiff against an individual state, how can it be said, that a controversy between a state and a citizen of another state means, from the mere force of the order of the words, only such cases where a state is plaintiff? After describing, generally, the judicial powers of the United States, the constitution goes on to speak of it distributively, and gives to the supreme court original jurisdiction, among other instances, in the case where a state shall be a *party;* but is not a state a party as well in the condition of a defendant, as in that of a plaintiff? And is the whole force of that expression satisfied, by confining its meaning to the case of a plaintiff-state? It seems to me, that if this court should refuse to hold jurisdiction of a case where a state is defendant, it would renounce part of the authority conferred, and consequently, part of the duty imposed on it by the constitution; because, it would be a refusal to take cognisance of a case, where a state is a party.

Nor does the jurisdiction of this court, in relation to a state, seem to me to be questionable, on the ground, that congress has not provided any form of execution, or pointed out any mode of making the judgment against a state effectual; the argument *ab inutile* may weigh much, in cases depending upon the construction of doubtful legislative acts, but can have no force, I think, against the clear and positive directions of an act of congress and of the constitution. Let us go on so far as we can; and if, at the end of the business, notwithstanding the powers given us in the 14th section of the judicial law, we meet difficulties insurmountable to us, we must leave it to those departments of government which have higher powers; to which, however, there may be no necessity to have recourse. Is it altogether a vain expectation, that a state may have other motives than such as arise from the apprehension of coercion, to carry into execution a judgment of the supreme court of the United States, though not conformable to their own ideas of justice? Besides, this argument takes it for granted that the judgment of the court will be against the state; it possibly may be in favor of the state: and the difficulty vanishes. Should judgment be given against the plaintiff, could it be said to be void, because extra-judicial? If the plaintiff, grounding himself upon that notion, should renew his suit against the state, in any mode in which she may permit herself to be sued in her own courts, would the attorney-general for the state be obliged to go again into the merits of the case, because the matter, when here, was *coram non judice?* Might he not rely upon the judgment given by this court, in bar of the new suit? To me, it seems clear, that he might. And if a state may be brought before this court, as a defendant, I see no reason for confining the plaintiff to proceed by way of petition; indeed, there would even seem to be an impropriety in proceeding in that mode. When sovereigns are sued in their own courts, such a method may have been established, as the most respectful form of demand but we are not now in a state court; and if sovereignty be an exemption from suit, in any other than the sovereign's own courts, it follows, that when a state, by adopting the constitution, has agreed to be amenable to the judicial power of the United States, she has, in that respect, given up her right of sovereignty.

With respect to the service of the summons to appear, the manner in which it has been served, seems to be as proper as any which could be devised for the purpose of giving notice of the suit, which is the end proposed by it, the governor being the head of the executive department, and the attorney-general the law officer, who generally represents the state in legal proceedings: and this mode is the less liable to exception, when it is considered, that in the suit brought in this court, by the state of *Georgia* against *Brailsford* and others, (*a*) it is conceived in the name of the governor in behalf of the state. If the opinion which I have delivered, respecting the liability of a state to be sued in this court, should be the opinion of the court, it will come, in course, to consider, what is the proper step to be taken for inducing appearance, none having been yet entered in behalf of the defendant. A judgment by default, in the present state of the business, and writ of inquiry for damages, would be too precipitate in any case, and too incompatible with the dignity of a state in this. Further opportunity of appearing to defend the suit ought to be given. The conditional order moved for the last term, the consideration of which was deferred to this, seems to me to be a very proper mode; it will warn the state of the meditated consequence of a refusal to appear, and give an opportunity for more deliberate consideration. The order, I think, should be thus: "Ordered, that unless the state of Georgia should, after due notice of this order, by a service thereof upon the governor and attorney-general of the said state, cause an appearance to be entered in behalf of the state, on the 5th day of the next term, or then show cause to the contrary, judgment be then entered up against the state, and a writ of inquiry of damages be awarded."

James Iredell

☆ 1751–1799 ☆

APPOINTED BY

GEORGE WASHINGTON

YEARS ON COURT

1790–1799

James Iredell

by

FRED L. ISRAEL

JAMES IREDELL was born at Lewes, Sussex County, England, on October 5, 1751, the eldest of five sons. His father, Francis, a Bristol merchant, married Margaret McCulloch of Dublin on August 1, 1750. There is a tradition in the Iredell family that they are collateral descendants of Henry Ireton, son-in-law of Oliver Cromwell; and that after the Restoration, prudence dictated that the family change its name to escape the royalist fury.

Francis Iredell was stricken with a "paralysis" in the early 1760's. Unable to supervise his business, he was reduced to poverty and through family connections, his wife's relatives purchased a government position in the colonies for their eldest son. "My father desires me to inform you," wrote a cousin to seventeen-year-old James, "that you must for the present, at least, give up your hopes of going to India, as he finds every vacancy long filled. . . . You may assure yourself he has it much at heart to give you a good opening into life, and he directs me to inform you that he has thought of the Comptroller of the Customs place at New Bern in North Carolina, for you. It is an office to be created, none having been yet appointed,—he has reserved it in view for a near friend in Carolina, but his desires to serve you preponderate with him." The position created was at Edenton, North Carolina, with an annual salary of £30 which was to be paid directly to the elder Iredell. James' personal salary would come from "fees," estimated "near £100 per annum now." "You may at first view object to the country," his cousin cautioned, "but permit me to assure you life may be passed there very happily, without too great an exercise of philosophy: another thing is, that if your genius leads to the bar or trade—the first especially, you may promise yourself a fair field for success, as it is a most growing country. Add to this, that the natural weight which my father's property

FRED L. ISRAEL, Associate Professor of History at the City College of New York, is the author of Nevada's Key Pittman.

and my connections give us there, shall be of service to you." And, another relative informed the ailing elder Iredell that James "cannot, unless it is his own fault, miss of doing extremely well, and we are the more pleased, as it may put him in a situation to be of the greatest service to you."

In October, 1768, James Iredell sailed for North Carolina to be Comptroller of His Majesty's Customs at Edenton, North Carolina. Edenton, situated on the north shore of Albemarle Sound, was then but a village of a few hundred inhabitants, but in and around it lived many wealthy and cultured families who would be the leaders in the forthcoming Revolution. Iredell, described as "of pleasing appearance and winning manners, and educated in the best schools of England, was kindly received and warmly welcomed." For the next six years, Iredell kept all the custom house accounts—the books and papers are still in existence—and supervised the Carolina lands and business of his British relatives.

In addition, young Iredell found time to study law with Samuel Johnston, the leading community figure, whose sister Hannah he married on July 18, 1773. In his journal entry for August 22, 1770, Iredell, not yet nineteen, noted: "Indolence in any is shameful, but in a young man quite inexcusable. Let me consider for a moment whether it will be worth my while to attempt making a figure in life, or whether I will be content with mediocrity. . . . Nothing is to be acquired without industry; and indolence is an effectual bar to improvement. . . . I have not done as much as I ought to have done; read a little in Lyttleton's *Tenures* and stopped in the middle of his Chapter on Rents; whereas I ought to have gone through it; it would have been better than losing three or four games at billiards." In another journal entry, Iredell reflected his strong Episcopal upbringing as well as his reading tastes. "Resumed my Spectator; read a great many entertaining and improving things, particularly Mr. Addison's Discourses on Fame, in the fourth volume, which are incomparably elegant and sublime. Surely the writings of such great, learned and good men are more than a counterpoise to the libertine writings of professed Deists, whose immoral lives made them dread an encounter hereafter." If Iredell's journal is accurate, every free moment was devoted to his legal studies or to reading works calculated to refine and improve himself. On July 31, 1771, he asked his father for a set of Blackstone's *Commentaries on the Laws of England* "by the first opportunity. I have, indeed, read them by the favor of Mr. Johnston, who lent them to me, but it is proper that I should read them frequently and with great attention. They are books admirably suited for a young student, and indeed may interest the most learned. . . . I would take leave to add one more desire that you would be pleased to send me the Tatlers and Guardians—the Spectators I have, and these, with the others, will afford me agreeable desultory reading."

Within two years of his arrival in North Carolina, on December 14, 1770, Iredell received a license from Governor William Tyron to practice law in all the inferior courts of the province and the following November Governor Josiah Martin approved his application for practice in the superior courts. As the dispute between the Royal Governors and the people of North Carolina intensified, Iredell, although a King's officer, became convinced that his future was intertwined with the American leaders. His letters during this period certainly do not favor separation from England but express the advanced American position. (Although when the Regulators in western North Carolina complained of unequal taxation, excessive court fees, land administration in the interest of eastern North Carolina politicians, and demanded freer paper money and the trial of debt cases without lawyers by a jury of freeholders, Iredell supported Governor Tyron and the provincial militia's suppression of this group at the "Battle of Alamance" in May, 1771. "How horrid are the miseries of civil war, but how much more horrid to have property insecure and lives held at the will of a parcel of banditti!")

Iredell became Collector of the Port at Edenton in May, 1774, and he held this post through the spring of 1776. Although not an effective public speaker as he tended to lisp, Iredell nevertheless entered actively into political affairs through an extensive correspondence with the leading Carolina politicians—his letter file was so extensive that one friend described him as "the letter writer of the war." Many of his anonymously written essays have been preserved and, together with his letters, it is clear that he had a lucid, candid, and popular style. As early as September, 1773, he published his first political essay, the theme summarized in the concluding sentence: "I have always been taught and, till I am better informed, must continue to believe, that the Constitution of this country is founded on the Provincial Charter, which may well be considered the original contract between the King and the inhabitants."

When the Committees on Correspondence suggested in May, 1774 that a general congress of the colonies assemble to bring about united action in the growing conflict with England, the Governor of North Carolina, Josiah Martin, refused to sanction a legislative meeting to elect delegates. Local leaders promptly summoned a provincial congress independent of the Governor, which met at New Bern on August 25, 1774, giving a practical demonstration that government originated with the people. Resolutions passed claiming the rights of Englishmen without abridgment, and that no subject should be taxed without his consent or that of his legal representative. The congress condemned the several Parliamentary acts which imposed duties on the colonies, censured the Boston Port Bill, and approved the conduct of Massachusetts, declaring that unless grievances were redressed before October 1, 1775, the colony would halt exports of tobacco, pitch, tar, and turpentine to Great Britain. In addition, of course, this was a striking defiance of royal authority. Iredell's friends were conspicuous members—Richard Caswell, Joseph Hewes, Thomas Jones, William Hooper, as well as his brother-in-law Samuel Johnston. Iredell fought the battle on paper. His address "To the Inhabitants of Great Britain" published in September, 1774, elaborately defended the American cause by tracing the settlements, the various charter provisions, and their subsequent violations by the King and his Parliament. "I am concerned to find you so full of politics," his uncle and benefactor wrote in January, 1775. "I am sure they can be of no use to you as a king's officer, at the head of the Customs in the province you live in. The people of America are certainly mad. . . . Let me desire you will keep yourself perfectly neuter in these disputes, both in words and actions, unless you choose to see yourself adrift with it." Young Iredell, however, had made his irrevocable decision by settling his account books and resigning from his position. But although he remained hopeful for reconciliation with England as late as June, 1776, Iredell's fortunes now became linked with the Revolutionary cause.

After July 4, 1776, Iredell became deeply interested in the form of government to be adopted by North Carolina. When the election for a state constitutional convention was held in October, he supported the conservative Whigs led by Samuel Johnston. This group wanted few changes from the old royal government, favoring a strong state executive, an independent judiciary with life tenure, adequate protection of property rights with a property qualification for voting and officeholding. Their opponents, the Radicals, advocated "a simple democracy" in which a weak executive would be subordinate to a strong legislature. The North Carolina Constitution, adopted in November, 1776, was a compromise of short and ambiguous statements which future legislatures were left to detail, with the salient feature being the shift to legislative predominance and away from the executive supremacy of colonial days. The convention had demonstrated that there were two major groups in North Carolina politics—Conservatives and Radicals, a division closely related to social classes, economic interests, and geography. Lawyers, merchants, shippers, large planters, slaveholders, and land speculators tended to be conservative. Most of the educated and wealthy were in this party, which consisted of a minority of the population mainly living in the coastal section. Iredell clearly sided with this group. The Radicals, on the other hand, constituted the overwhelming majority of North Carolinians—the farmers and workers, many of them poor and in debt. This party division played a significant role in the struggle for the adoption of the federal Constitution in 1787—a struggle in which Iredell played a leading part.

After the break with England, Iredell assisted in drafting and revising the laws necessary for the new status of North Carolina. The following year, in November, 1777, the Assembly created a state judicial system with six districts and three superior court judges—on December 20, Samuel Ashe, Samuel Spencer, and Iredell were chosen to be the judges. Iredell reluctantly accepted—"Politics I am really quite sick of," he wrote his wife. "They have got into a most melancholy train. The best cause, and the most promising one, is grossly injured by many of its conductors in this country." Knowing of Iredell's indecision, his friend William Hooper, who had signed the Declaration of Independence, apologetically wrote: "You will be at a loss to conjecture how I have been accessory to this step, after you had been so explicit to me on the subject. Be assured that I was not inattentive to your objections, nor did I fail to mention them and urge them with sincerity to every person who mentioned you for the office to which you are now designated. . . . I expostulated with them upon the impropriety of electing one who, in all probability might decline. . . . Their reasoning prevailed and you have now the satisfaction of an unrestricted choice. The appointment has been imposed upon you, and therefore you are at perfect liberty to act or not." Archibald Maclaine, a member of the Assembly, confided to Iredell: "The Assembly, in appointing you, thought, with great reason, that they effectually served themselves and their constituents. As to myself, I confess I was actuated by duty to the public, having been taught that your promotion would more effectually serve them than you." And so at the age of twenty-seven, Iredell, a resident of the state for but ten years, had the honor of being chosen, unsought and against his inclination, to North Carolina's highest judicial position.

The first meeting of the Superior Court of North Carolina was held on January 13, 1778, at New Bern. Iredell rode one circuit for the Court and resigned on June 15, 1778. His letters to his wife Hannah during that circuit give an interesting account of the country through which he traveled, as well as a vivid description of the trials and tribulations of a judge on circuit—"I shall leave this cursed place to-day," he wrote from Salisbury in western North Carolina. "We take the Moravian town in our way, and shall endeavor to while away the time, till Hillsborough court, in as amusing a manner as possible. O! how long every hour seems to me." And from Hillsborough, he complained about "a most dirty and rascally tavernkeeper who told us fifty lies about what he had in his house . . . nothing could have made this ride supportable but the agreeable company we had." Finally, from New Bern: "I cannot tell you particularly *when* I shall be at home; I can only say that it shall be with as much expedition as possible after Wilmington Court. This place even shall not have charms to detain me one day. *I am fully determined on the point of my resignation.*" Iredell resumed his private law practice which apparently was a prosperous one. Records of one case at Currituck Court indicate he "made £160 inclusive of a fee raised by volunteers among the people, amounting to £100. Mr. Iredell's fees would have been more numerous, but he declined any new business."

On July 8, 1779, Governor Richard Caswell, with the advice and consent of his Council, appointed Iredell as Attorney General; the Assembly confirmed him on November 20. Iredell accepted, telling his niece: "Things of more consequence seem to hang in awful suspense. The operations of war are rather menacing than active, and the prospect for peace more gloomy than could be wished for." Hooper, expressing pleasure that Iredell had consented to accept, wrote: "I have the happiness to assure you that the leading characters in this part of the country [Cape Fear] speak of you as a capital acquisition to our courts, and exult that there is a prospect of offenders being brought to due punishment without the passions of party or the prejudice of individuals swaying the prosecution." Iredell resumed travelling the circuit, attending courts throughout the state in the discharge of his duties. His letters to Mrs. Iredell again give an interesting and often amusing account of his experiences. He resigned from this office in 1781. Writing to his brother in July, 1783, he said: "Since then I have been only a private lawyer, but with a show of business very near equal to any lawyers in the country."

After the ratification of the 1783 Treaty of Peace and the withdrawal of British troops from North Carolina, the people began the work of restoring their fortunes and enacting laws suited to the new political condition. Differences, more or less fundamental, which had manifested themselves during the war, became more menacing. Iredell concurred with the conservatives, Johnston, Hooper, Maclaine, William Davie, Richard Spaight, and others, in opposition to Willie Jones, Thomas Person, Samuel Spencer, and their followers. The former insisted that North Carolina should carry out in good faith the Treaty terms and adopt such measures for that purpose as well as enforce contracts and maintain a strong government. Nevertheless, the state legislature continued to sell confiscated Tory property, violating the Treaty of Paris provision. A 1783 report revealed that such property amounting to £583,643 had been sold and a later study estimated that an additional £284,452 was realized from sales between 1784–1790. The 1785 legislature even passed a law prohibiting suits for the recovery of property which was subsequently sold under the Confiscation Acts. While Iredell neither held nor sought any public position, he did maintain an exhaustive correspondence with conservative state leaders. He continued to devote himself to his private practice and ranked easily with the leaders of the state bar.

In "An Address to the Public" in 1786, Iredell set forth his views regarding the enforcement of constitutional limitations upon the legislature. Referring to the November, 1776 convention which framed the state constitution, he said:

> *It was of course to be considered how to impose restrictions on the Legislature, that might still leave it free to all useful purposes, but at the same time guard against the abuse of unlimited power, which was not to be trusted without the most imminent danger, to any man or body of men on earth. We had not only been sickened and disgusted for years with the high and almost impious language from Great Britain, of the omnipotent power of the British Parliament, but had severely smarted under the effects. We felt, in all its rigor, the mischiefs of an absolute and unbounded authority, claimed by so weak a creature as man, and should have been guilty of the basest breach of trust, as well as the grossest folly, if in the same moment, when we spurned at the insolent despotism of Great Britain, we had established a despotic power among ourselves. . . . I have no doubt but that the power of the Assembly is limited and defined by the Constitution. It is the creature of the Constitution.*

Writing to Richard Spaight on August 26, 1787, Iredell further clarified his views on legislative power and the need for judicial review. "I confess it has ever been my opinion, that an act inconsistent with the Constitution was void; and that the judges, consistently with their duties, could not carry it into effect. The Constitution appears to me to be a fundamental law, limiting the powers of the legislature, and with which every exercise of those powers must, necessarily, be compared." It should be noted that Iredell's argument advanced to Spaight, who was then a member of the Constitutional Convention at Philadelphia, affirming judicial review of statutes passed in violation of a Constitution, was considered unique in 1787.

When the Philadelphia Convention submitted their work to the state legislatures in September, 1787, Iredell at once began working for its adoption by North Carolina. In January, 1788, over the signature of "Marcus," he wrote "Answers to Mr. Mason's Objections to the New Constitution Recommended by the Late Convention at Philadelphia," a tract which received national attention and which appeared contemporaneously with the earliest issues of the *Federalist.* Iredell, a member of the Governor's Council since November, 1787, stated each of George Mason's eleven objections to the federal Constitution and, in the same order, gave his "answer," answers which brilliantly supported and upheld the new document. Undoubtedly, this pamphlet made a very favorable impression upon national Federalist leaders and strongly affected Iredell's future career.

The North Carolina Convention called for ratifying the Constitution met at Hillsboro on July 21, 1788. The Anti-Federalists had an overwhelming majority —the election for delegates had been bitter with opponents of the Constitution maintaining the document would establish an "aristocratic tyranny or a monarchy." One Lemuel Burkitt predicted that its adoption would make of the national capital a walled city with a standing army of 50,000 or more to be used for "crushing the liberties of the people." Nevertheless, Federalist leaders conducted an able campaign, attempting to show that ratification would best serve the interests of both North Carolina and the nation. Iredell and other Federalist leaders made long, impassioned arguments for adoption but, after eleven days of debate, ratification failed by a sweeping 184–84 vote. The Convention declared, instead, that a bill of rights "asserting and securing from encroachment the great Principles of civil and religious Liberty, and the inalienable rights of the People, together with Amendments," ought to be passed by Congress and then another North Carolina ratifying convention be held. A second convention was held at Fayetteville and finally acceded to the document on November 21, 1789, seven months after the formal launching of the new government.

Iredell's acknowledged leadership of the state's ratification forces brought him added recognition which extended beyond the borders of North Carolina. Senator Pierce Butler of South Carolina declared in August, 1789, that "Southern interests call aloud for such men as Mr. Iredell to represent it—to do it justice." Hugh Williamson, who had signed the Constitution for North Carolina, wrote from New York: "The North Carolina debates are considerably read in this State especially by Congress members; some of whom, who formerly had little knowledge of the citizens of North Carolina, have lately been *very minute in their inquiries concerning Mr. Iredell."*

Iredell's vigorous Federalist activities impressed Washington: "The President enquired particularly after you and spoke of you in a manner that gave me great pleasure," wrote Samuel Johnston from New York. And, when Robert Harrison declined his Supreme Court appointment, the President noted in his diary of February 6, 1790: "The resignation of Mr. Harrison as an Associate

Judge making a nomination of some other character to supply his place necessary, I determined, after contemplating every character which presented itself to my view, to name Mr. Iredell of North Carolina; because, in addition to the reputation he sustains for abilities, legal knowledge and respectability of character, he is of a State of some importance in the Union that has given no character to a federal office. In ascertaining the character of this gentleman, I had recourse to every means of information in my power and found them all concurring in his favor." On February 10, 1790, Washington appointed Iredell to the Court. That same day, Senator Pierce Butler wrote: "You have this day been nominated by the President and *unanimously* appointed by the Senate. . . . I congratulate the States on the appointment, and you on this mark of their well-merited opinion of you." When the presidential commission arrived by special post, Iredell acknowledged graciously: "In accepting this dignified trust, I do it with all the diffidence becoming the humble abilities I possess; but, at the same time, with the most earnest resolution to endeavor by unremitting application a faithful discharge of all of its duties in the best manner in my power." Iredell was assigned to the Southern Circuit and began his work immediately. At the Supreme Court's August term (August 2, 1790) he formally presented himself to his colleagues and, after the reading of his commission, and the admitting of two counselors, the Court adjourned because of the lack of business. James Iredell, at thirty-nine, became the sixth Justice of the Supreme Court and its youngest member.

The Southern Circuit included South Carolina and Georgia—and North Carolina after that state joined the Union in November, 1789. Riding the circuit, especially the Southern one, proved extremely difficult, but Iredell's initial enthusiasm is captured in a series of charming letters to his wife, who had moved to New York with their children—the third and last was born in 1792. The Justice exuberantly described the warm hospitality which greeted him as he moved along his appointed rounds. "I have met with such extreme attention and politeness in this country," he wrote from South Carolina, "that I cannot avoid feeling some degree of pain in parting from it. . . . Had the weather not been so hot, my circuit would have been quite a jaunt of pleasure, for I have been everywhere received by everybody, with the utmost kindness and distinction and by many of the first families in South Carolina with a degree of unaffected politeness which was gratifying indeed." But, in a very short time, the exhausting labor and weary travel on the circuit gave way to letters of complaint. "I will venture to say no Judge can conscientiously undertake to ride the Southern Circuit constantly, and perform the other parts of his duty," Iredell wrote Jay in March, 1792, "Besides the danger his health must be exposed to, it is not conceivable that accidents will not often happen to occasion a disappointment of attendance at the Courts. I rode upon the last Circuit 1900 miles: the distance from here and back again is 1800. Can any man have a probable chance of going that distance twice a year, and attending at particular places punctually on particular days?" "The Circuits press hard upon us all," agreed the Chief Justice, "and your share of the task has hitherto been more than in due proportion." When Iredell described his circuit duties to his younger brother living in England, the latter compared them to "the life of a Postboy." Congress did amend the Judiciary Act in 1792 to allow for rotation in the circuit "most distant from the seat of the Government" but, nevertheless, Iredell rode the Southern Circuit five times between 1790 and 1794. "The fatigue of so long a journey twice a year is more than the strength of any man can bear," Georgia District Judge Nathaniel Pendleton sympathetically told Iredell. Although Congress made several modifications, riding the circuit remained a Supreme Court Justice's duty until the end of the nineteenth century.

At the June, 1792 term of the Circuit Court at Raleigh, North Carolina, Justice Iredell and District Judge John Sitgreaves were confronted with an important but delicate point in constitutional law. On March 23, 1792, Congress enacted a statute which required circuit court judges to serve as pension commissioners and grant pension certificates, subject to review by the Secretary of War. Convinced these new duties were not judicial, and therefore not authorized by the Constitution which had carefully separated the powers of each governmental division, Iredell protested to President Washington and explained the unconstitutionality of the act: "The high respect we entertain for the Legislature, our feelings as men for persons whose situation requires the earliest, as well as the most effectual relief, and our sincere desire to promote, whether officially or otherwise, the just and benevolent views of Congress, so conspicuous on this, as well as on many other occasions, have induced us to reflect, whether we could be justified in acting under this act personally in the character of Commissioners during the session of a Court; and could we be satisfied that we had authority to do so we would cheerfully devote such part of our time as might be necessary for the perfermance of the service." Other Justices addressed similar letters to the President, and Congress eventually "made other provisions for the relief of pensioners." Iredell, nevertheless, mainly out of humanitarian reasons, did agree to hear a number of pension petitions. He wrote his wife from Connecticut on September 30, 1792: "We have a great deal of business to do here, particularly as I have reconciled myself to the propriety of doing the invalid business out of court." Iredell's protest, though, is certainly one of the several precedents for Marshall's landmark decision in *Marbury* v. *Madison,* 1 Cranch 137 (1803). Sixty years later, Chief Justice Roger Taney praised Iredell's remonstrance, writing: "The repeal of the act clearly shows that the President and Congress acquiesced in the correctness of the decision that it was not a judicial power," *United States* v. *Ferreira,* 13 How. 52 (1852).

At the February, 1792 term, the Court postponed a controversial suit by a citizen of South Carolina against the state of Georgia, *Chisholm* v. *Georgia,* 2 Dall. 419 (1793). Attorney General Edmund Randolph moved that unless Georgia made an appearance at the next term or showed cause to the contrary (August, 1792), judgment then should be entered against the state. But, by granting Georgia "time to deliberate on the measures she ought to adopt," the

Court deferred action until February, 1793. The state of Georgia again refused to appear and, further, denied the jurisdiction of the Supreme Court. On February 18, the Court delivered five opinions; four sustained the right of a citizen of one state to sue in federal court another state for breach of contract. Following reverse seniority, Chief Justice Jay called on Iredell to deliver his decision the first. It took the Justice an hour and a quarter to deliver the only dissenting opinion in the case.

While the majority opinions were concerned with a state's liability in general to suits by citizens of other states, Iredell confined himself to the narrow and technical issue of a state's liability to actions in *assumpsit* and the Supreme Court's right to decide the issue. Basically, Iredell's position was that irrespective of what authority the Court might possess potentially under the Constitution, congressional legislation giving the Court specific authority was essential and formed a precedent to the exercise by the Court of such authority. In response to Attorney General Randolph's argument "that the moment a Supreme Court is formed, it is to exercise all the judicial power vested in it by the Constitution by its own authority, whether the legislature has prescribed methods of doing so or not," Iredell replied: "My conception of the Constitution is entirely different," and proceeded to explain that Congress has power to "make all laws which shall be necessary and proper for carrying into execution" the powers vested by the Constitution "in the Government of the United States, or in any department or officer thereof" and therefore congressional legislation was necessary to give the judicial authority its proper effect—"This appears to me to be one of those cases, with many others, in which an article of the constitution cannot be effectuated, without the intervention of the legislative authority. . . . The constitution intended this article so far, at least, to be the subject of a legislative act. Having a right thus to establish the court, and it being capable of being established in no other manner, I conceive it necessarily follows, that they are also to direct the manner of its proceedings." Having affirmed to his own satisfaction the absolute necessity for congressional action to supplement and effectuate the judicial authority granted in the Constitution before the Court could act in any matter, Iredell then argued that the necessary legislative authorization to proceed in the *Chisholm* case had not been granted. By quoting the 1789 Judiciary Act, Iredell could not find the necessary power that the majority opinions assumed the Supreme Court possessed. In common law, continued Iredell, the only part that could have any application to suits against a state was that which concerned actions against the British Crown. Since he could find no precedent in common law—"a law which I presume is the groundwork of the laws in every state in the Union"—he concluded that therefore "every state in the Union in every instance where its sovereignty has not been delegated to the United States, I consider to be as completely sovereign, as the United States are in respect to the powers surrendered. The United States are sovereign as to all the powers of government actually surrendered, therefore each state in the Union is sovereign as to all the powers reserved." Iredell limited his opinion to what he conceived to be the law pertinent to and controlling the determination of the issue—namely, the Constitution, the 1789 Judiciary Act, and the pre-existing common law. Fundamental to his argument was the proposition that neither the Constitution nor the Judiciary Act invested jurisdiction in the federal courts over cases between states and citizens of other states and the framers of both did not intend any such all-embracing grant of authority which would deprive the sovereign states of their prior immunity to compulsory actions against them for the recovery of money.

In shaping his famous dissent, which is reprinted below, Iredell was undoubtedly aware of the states' rights sentiment in his own state of North Carolina and the real fear of the possible intervention by the federal courts in the states' financial affairs. Perhaps this dominant local feeling caused him to avoid the extreme nationalistic position taken by his judicial colleagues. Professor J. G. de Roulhac Hamilton described Iredell as a "states' rights Federalist" and perhaps this is a just description. Indeed, Iredell's dissenting opinion represented the view far more generally held at the time the Constitution was adopted. His opinion reflected not an extreme states' rights position but rather his sober judgment as to the sound and practical limits of federal authority and his concern over the danger to the new nation from defiance by the states. Certainly this decision does not mark him as the forerunner of the extreme states' rights philosophy as it later developed, but simply as a firm supporter of the divided sovereignty concept common to his generation and shared by both Federalists and Anti-Federalists. Iredell's decision represented the concept of Union held by most Americans, while that of the majority represented an extreme nationalistic viewpoint which, as Charles Warren phrased it, "fell upon the country with a profound shock"—the rapid adoption of the Eleventh Amendment is the proof.

In national affairs, Iredell was always a federalist and an unwavering advocate of a strong central government and perhaps the foremost champion in the North Carolina fight over ratifying the Constitution. The sincerity of Iredell's federalism was strikingly demonstrated during the interim of North Carolina's separation from the Union (April–November, 1789) when he moved to New York to accept a judgeship under the new government. Whether in public or private, Iredell vigorously supported Washington's policies—the controversial financial programs, the Neutrality Proclamation, Jay's Treaty, and the suppression of the Whiskey Rebellion. In praising Washington's forthright stand in the Whiskey Rebellion, Iredell said: "The whole scene has exhibited a lesson for government and people, which never before was displayed on the theatre of the world. God grant it may not be without its effect on other times and other countries nor ever be obliterated from the memory of our own." In Iredell's last charge to a grand jury convened in Philadelphia on April 11, 1799, he expressed the typical federalist view upholding the Alien and Sedition Act. Deeply impressed that the French "philosophy of revolution" was finding American defenders, the Justice expressed the fear that the French doctrines could threaten the Union and lead only to America's destruction. As a federalist, he distrusted the French leaders and their principles, warning Americans against involving themselves in French affairs. Never a rich man, he had been disinherited by his wealthy uncle for his stand against the Crown. Iredell died at his home in Edenton on October 20, 1799, two weeks past his forty-eighth birthday, and less than ten years after he had taken his seat on the federal bench.

SELECTED BIBLIOGRAPHY

The University of North Carolina Press has announced intentions to publish the Iredell papers, which have been deposited with the North Carolina Historical Society. The most important work on Iredell is Griffith J. McRee, *Life and Correspondence of James Iredell,* 2 vols. (New York, 1857). (Concerning McRee's editorial "liberties," see Julian P. Boyd to the Editor, 7 *William and Mary Quarterly,* Third Series, 317 [1951].) See also H. G. Connor, "James Iredell: Lawyer, Statesman, Judge, 1751–1799," 60 *University of Pennsylvania Law Review* 225 (1911–1912); Jeff B. Fordham, "Iredell's Dissent in *Chisholm* v. *Georgia,*" 8 *North Carolina Historical Review* 155 (1931); Kemp Plummer Yarborough, "*Chisholm* v. *Georgia;* A Study of the Minority Opinion," unpublished doctoral dissertation (Columbia University, 1963) and Hugh Talmage Lefler and Albert Ray Newsome, *North Carolina* (Chapel Hill, 1954).

James Iredell

REPRESENTATIVE OPINIONS

CHISHOLM v. GEORGIA, 2 DALL. 419 (1793)

In the only dissenting opinion written in the *Chisholm* case, Iredell argued that the states were sovereign and could not be sued by citizens of another state. The question arose upon an action of *assumpsit* begun in the Supreme Court against the state of Georgia, process being served upon the Governor and the state's Attorney General. The state refused to be represented but filed a protest against the Court's jurisdiction. The Attorney General of the United States, Edmund Randolph, argued before the Court that, since Georgia was not represented, default judgment should be entered. The Court upheld Randolph's arguments and, therefore, a citizen's right to sue a sovereign state. In his dissent, Iredell embraced the divided sovereignty concept common to his generation rather than the extreme nationalistic viewpoint taken by the Court's majority. A resolution designed to counteract the majority opinion was introduced into the House of Representatives on February 19, 1793, the day after the *Chisholm* decision. This resolution eventually became the forerunner of the Eleventh Amendment which was ratified in 1798. Thus, Iredall's explanation of divided sovereignty eventually became part of the Constitution.

IREDELL, Justice. This great cause comes before the court, on a motion made by the attorney-general, that an order be made by the court to the following effect: "That unless the state of Georgia shall, after reasonable notice of this motion, cause an appearance to be entered on behalf of the said state, on the fourth day of next term, or show cause to the contrary, judgment shall be entered for the plaintiff, and a writ of inquiry shall be awarded." Before such an order be made, it is proper that this court should be satisfied it hath cognisance of the suit; for, to be sure, we ought not to enter a conditional judgment (which this would be), in a case where we were not fully persuaded we had authority to do so.

This is the first instance wherein the important question involved in this cause has come regularly before the court. In the Maryland case, it did not, because the attorney-general of the state voluntarily appeared. We could not, therefore, without the greatest impropriety, have taken up the question suddenly. That case has since been compromised; but had it proceeded to trial, and a verdict been given for the plaintiff, it would have been our duty, previous to our giving judgment, to have well considered whether we were warranted in giving it. I had then great doubts upon my mind, and should, on such a case, have proposed a discussion of the subject. Those doubts have increased since, and after the fullest consideration I have been able to bestow on the subject, and the most respectful attention to the able argument of the attorney-general, I am now decidedly of opinion, that no such action as this before the court can legally be maintained.

The action is an action of *assumpsit*. The particular question then before the court, is, will an action of *assumpsit* lie against a state? This particular question (abstracted from the general one, viz., whether, a state can in any instance be sued?) I took the liberty to propose to the consideration of the attorney-general, last term. I did so, because I have often found a great deal of confusion to arise from taking too large a view at once, and I had found myself embarrassed on this very subject, until I considered the abstract question itself. The attorney-general has spoken to it, in deference to my request, as he has been pleased to intimate, but he spoke to this particular question slightly, conceiving it to be involved in the general one; and after establishing, as he thought, that point, he seemed to consider the other followed of course. He expressed, indeed, some doubt how to prove what appeared so plain. It seemed to him (if I recollect right), to depend principally on the solution of this simple question; can a state assume? But the attorney-general must know, that in England, certain judicial proceedings, not inconsistent with the sovereignty, may take place against the crown, but that an action of *assumpsit* will not lie. Yet, surely, the King can assume as well as a state. So can the United States themselves, as well as any state in the Union: yet, the attorney-general himself has taken some pains to show, that no action whatever is maintainable against the United States. I shall, therefore, confine myself, as much as possible, to the particular question before the court, though every thing I have to say upon it will effect every kind of suit, the object of which is to compel the payment of money by a state.

The question, as I before observed, is—will an action of *assumpsit* lie against a state? If it will, it must be in virtue of the constitution of the United States, and of some law of congress conformable thereto. The part of the constitution concerning the judicial power, is as follows, viz.: Art. III., §2. The judicial power shall extend, (1) To all cases, in law and equity, arising under the constitution, the laws of the United States, and treaties made, or which shall be made, under their authority: (2) To all cases affecting ambassadors, or other public ministers and consuls: (3) To all cases of admiralty and maritime jurisdiction: (4) To all controversies to which the United States shall be a party: (5) To controversies between two or more states; between a state and citizens of another state; between citizens of different states; between citizens of the same state, claiming lands under grants of different states; and between a state or the citizens thereof, and foreign states, citizens or subjects. The constitution, therefore, provides for the jurisdiction wherein a state is a party, in the following instances: 1st. Controversies between two or more states: 2d. Controversies between a state and citizens of another state: 3d. Controversies between a state, and foreign states, citizens or subjects. And it also provides, that in all cases in which a state shall be a party, the supreme court shall have original jurisdiction.

The words of the general judicial act, conveying the authority of the supreme court, under the constitution, so far as they concern this question, are as follows: §13. "That the supreme court shall have exclusive jurisdiction of all controversies of a civil nature, where a state is a party, except between a state and its citizens; and except also, between a state and citizens of other states or aliens, in which latter case, it shall have original, but not exclusive jurisdiction. And shall have, exclusively, all jurisdiction of suits or proceedings against ambassadors or other public ministers, or their domestics or domestic servants, as a court of law can have or exercise consistently with the law of nations; and original, but not exclusive jurisdiction, of all suits brought by ambassadors or other public ministers, or in which a consul or vice-consul shall be a party."

The supreme court hath, therefore, *first*, exclusive jurisdiction in every controversy of a civil nature: 1st. Between two or more states: 2d. Between a state and a foreign state: 3d. Where a suit or proceeding is depending against ambassadors, other public ministers, or their domestics or domestic servants. *Second,* original, but not exclusive jurisdiction, 1st. Between a state and citizens of other states: 2d. Between a state and foreign citizens or subjects: 3d. Where a suit is brought by ambassadors or other public ministers: 4th. Where a consul or vice-consul is a party. The suit now before the court (if maintainable at all) comes within the latter description, it being a suit against a state by a citizen of another state.

The constitution is particular in expressing the parties who may be the objects of the jurisdiction in any of these cases, but in respect to the subject matter upon which such jurisdiction is to be exercised, used the word "controversies" only. The act of congress more particularly mentions civil controversies, a qualification of the general word in the constitution, which I do not doubt every reasonable man will think well warranted, for it cannot be presumed, that the general word "controversies" was intended to include any proceedings that relate to criminal cases, which in all instances that respect the same governor only, are uniformly considered of a local nature, and to be decided by its particular laws. The word "controversy" indeed, would not naturally justify any such construction, but nevertheless it was perhaps a proper instance of caution in congress to guard against the possibility of it.

A general question of great importance here occurs. What controversy of a civil nature can be maintained against a state by an individual? The framers of the constitution, I presume, must have meant one of two things—Either, 1. In the conveyance of that part of the judicial power which did not relate to the execution of the other authorities of the general government (which it must be admitted are full and discretionary, within the restrictions of the constitution itself), to refer to antecedent laws for the construction of the general words they use: or, 2. To enable congress in all such cases to pass all such laws as they might deem necessary and proper to carry the purposes of this constitution into full effect, either absolutely at their discretion, or, at least, in cases where prior laws were deficient for such purposes, if any such deficiency existed.

The attorney-general has indeed suggested another construction, a construction, I confess, that I never heard of before, nor can I now consider it grounded on any solid foundation, though it appeared to me to be the basis of the attorney-general's argument. His construction I take to be this: "That the moment a supreme court is formed, it is to exercise all the judicial power vested in it by the constitution, by its own authority, whether the legislature has prescribed methods of doing so, or not." My conception of the constitution is entirely different. I conceive, that all the courts of the United States must receive, not merely their *organization* as to the number of judges of which they are to consist; but all their authority, as to the manner of their proceeding, from the legislature only. This appears to me to be one of those cases, with many others, in which an article of the constitution cannot be effectuated, without the intervention of the legislative authority. There being many such, at the end of the special enumeration of the powers of congress in the constitution, is this general one: "To make all laws which shall be necessary and proper for carrying into execution the foregoing powers, and all other powers vested by this constitution in the government of the United States, or in any department or officer thereof." None will deny, that an act of legislation is necessary to say, at least, of what number the judges are to consist; the President, with the consent of the senate, could not nominate a number at their discretion. The constitution intended this article so far, at least, to be the subject of a legislative act. Having a right thus to establish the court, and it being capable of being established in no other manner, I conceive it necessarily follows, that they are also to direct the manner of its proceedings. Upon this authority, there is, that I know, but one limit; that is, "that they shall not exceed their authority." If they do, I have no hesitation to say, that any act to that effect would be utterly void, because it would be inconsistent with the constitution, which is a fundamental law, paramount to all others, which we are not only bound to consult, but sworn to observe; and therefore, where there is an interference, being superior in obligation to the other, we must unquestionably obey that in preference. Subject to this restriction, the whole business of organizing the courts, and directing the methods of their proceeding, where necessary, I conceive to be in the discretion of congress. If it shall be found, on this occasion, or on any other, that the remedies now in being are defective, for any purpose, it is their duty to provide for, they no doubt will provide others. It is their duty to *legislate,* so far as is necessary to carry the constitution into effect. It is *ours* only to *judge*. We have no reason, nor any more right to distrust their doing their duty, than they have to distrust that we all do ours. There is no part of the constitution that I know of, that authorizes this court to take up any business where they left it, and in order that the powers given in the constitution may be in full activity, supply their omission by making *new laws* for *new cases;* or, which I take to be the same thing, applying *old principles* to *new cases* materially different from those to which they were applied before.

With regard to the attorney-general's doctrine of incidents, that was founded entirely on the supposition of the other I have been considering. The authority contended for is certainly not one of those necessarily incident to all courts merely as such.

If therefore, this court is to be (as I consider it) the organ of the constitution and the law, not of the *constitution* only, in respect to the manner of its proceeding, we must receive our directions from the legislature in this particular, and have no right to constitute ourselves an *officina brevium,* or take any other short method of doing what the constitution has chosen (and, in my opinion, with the most perfect propriety) should be done, in another manner.

But the act of congress has not been altogether silent upon this subject. The 14th section of the judicial act, provides in the following words: "All the before-mentioned courts of the United States shall have power to issue writs of *scire facias, habeas corpus,* and all other writs not specially provided for by statute, which may be necessary for the exercise of their respective jurisdictions, and agreeable to the principles and usages of law." These words refer as well to the supreme court as to the other courts of the United States. Whatever writs we issue, that are necessary for the exercise of our jurisdiction, must be agreeable to the principles and usages of law. This is a direction, I apprehend, we cannot supersede, because it may appear to us not sufficiently extensive. If it be not, we must wait until other remedies are provided by the same authority. From this it is plain, that the legislature did not choose to leave to our own discretion the path to justice, but has prescribed one of its own. In doing so, it has, I think, wisely, referred us to principles and usages of law, already well known, and by their precision calculated to guard against that innovating spirit of courts of justice, which the attorney-general, in another case, reprobated with so much warmth, and with whose sentiments in that particular, I most cordially join. The principles of law to which reference is to be had, either upon the general ground I first alluded to, or upon the special words I have above cited, from the judicial act, I apprehend, can be, either, 1st. Those of the particular laws of the state, against which the suit is brought. Or 2d. Principles of law, common to all the states. I omit any consideration arising from the word "usages," though a still stronger expression. In regard to the principles of the particular laws of the state of Georgia, if they in any manner differed, so as to affect this question, from the principles of law, common to all the states, it might be material to inquire, whether, there would be any propriety or congruity in laying down a rule of decision which would induce this consequence, that an action would lie in the supreme court against some states, whose laws admitted of a compulsory remedy against their own governments, but not against others, wherein no such remedy was admitted, or which would require, perhaps, if the principle was received, fifteen different methods of proceeding against states, all standing in the same political relation to the general government, and none having any pretence to a distinction in its favor, or justly liable to any distinction to its prejudice. If any such difference existed in the laws of the different states, there would seem to be a propriety, in order to induce uniformity (if a constitutional power for that purpose exists), that congress should prescribe a rule, fitted to this new case, to which no equal, uniform and impartial mode of proceeding could otherwise be applied.

But this point, I conceive, it is unnecessary to determine, because I believe there is no doubt, that neither in the state now in question, nor in any other in the Union, any particular legislative mode, authorizing a compulsory suit for the recovery of money against a state, was in being, either when the constitution was adopted, or at the time the judicial act was passed. Since that time, an act of assembly for such a purpose has been passed in Georgia. But that surely could have no influence in the construction of an act of the legislature of the United States, passed before.

The only principles of law, then, that can be regarded, are those common to all the states. I know of none such, which can affect this case, but those that are derived from what is properly termed "the common law," a law which I presume is the groundwork of the laws in every state in the Union, and which I consider, so far as it is applicable to the peculiar circumstances of the country, and where no special act of legislation controls it, to be in force in each state, as it existed in England (unaltered by any statute), at the time of the first settlement of the country. The statutes of England that are in force in America differ perhaps in all the states; and therefore, it is probable, the common law in each is in some respects different. But it is certain, that in regard to any common-law principle which can influence the question before us, no alteration has been made by any statute, which could occasion the least material difference, or have any partial effect. No other part of the common law of England, it appears to me, can have any reference to this subject, but that part of it which prescribes remedies against the crown. Every state in the Union, in every instance where its sovereignty has not been delegated to the United States, I consider to be as completely sovereign, as the United States are in respect to the powers surrendered. The United States are sovereign as to all the powers of government actually surrendered: each state in the Union is sovereign, as to all the powers reserved. It must necessarily be so, because the United States have no claim to any authority but such as the states have surrendered to them: of course, the part not surrendered must remain as it did before. The powers of the general government, either of a legislative or executive nature, or which particularly concerns treaties with foreign powers, do for the most part (if not wholly) affect individuals, and not states: they require no aid from any state authority. This is the great leading distinction between the old articles of confederation, and the present constitution. The judicial power is of a peculiar kind. It is indeed commensurate with the ordinary legislative and executive powers of the general government, and the power which concerns treaties. But it also goes further. Where certain parties are concerned, although the subject in controversy does not relate to any of the special objects of authority of the general government, wherein the separate sovereignties of the states are blended in one common mass of supremacy, yet the general government has a judicial authority in regard to such subjects of controversy, and the legislature of the United States may pass all laws necessary to give such judicial authority its proper effect. So far as states, under the constitution, can be made legally liable to this authority, so far, to be sure, they are subordinate to the authority of the United States, and their individual sovereignty is in this respect limited. But it is limited no further than the necessary execution of such authority requires. The authority extends only to the decision of controversies in which a state is a party, and providing laws necessary for that purpose. That surely can refer only to such controversies in which a state *can* be a party; in respect to which, if any question arises, it can be determined, according to the principles I have supported, in no other manner than by a reference either to pre-existent laws, or laws passed under the constitution and in conformity to it.

Whatever be the true construction of the constitution in this particular; whether it is to be construed as intending merely a transfer of jurisdiction from one tribunal to another, or as authorizing the legislature to provide laws for the decision of all possible controversies in which a state may be involved with an individual, without regard to any prior exemption; yet it is certain, that the legislature has in fact proceeded upon the former supposition, and not upon the latter. For, besides what I noticed before, as to an express reference to principles and usages of law, as the guide of our proceeding, it is observable, that in instances like this before the court, this court hath a *concurrent jurisdiction* only; the present being one of those cases where, by the judicial act, this court hath *original* but not *exclusive* jurisdiction. This court, therefore, under that act, can exercise no authority, in such instances, but such authority as, from the subject-matter of it, may be exercised in some other court. There are no courts with which such a concurrence can be suggested but the circuit courts, or courts of the different states. With the former, it cannot be, for admitting that the constitution is not to have a restrictive operation, so as to confine all cases in which a state is a party, exclusively to the supreme court (an opinion to which I am strongly inclined), yet, there are no words in the definition of the powers of the circuit court, which give a color to an opinion, that where a suit is brought against a state, by a citizen of another state, the circuit court could exercise any jurisdiction at all. If they could, however, such a jurisdiction, by the very terms of their authority, could be only concurrent with the courts of the several states. It follows, therefore, unquestionably, I think, that looking at the act of congress, which I consider is on this occasion the limit of our authority (whatever further might be constitutionally enacted), we can exercise no authority, in the present instance, consistently with the clear intention of the act, but such as a proper state court would have been, at least, competent to exercise, at the time the act was passed.

If, therefore, no new remedy be provided (as plainly is the case), and consequently, we have no other rule to govern us, but the principles of the pre-existent laws, which must remain in force until superseded by others, then it is incumbent upon us to inquire, whether, previous to the adoption of the constitution (which period, or the period of passing the law, in respect to the object of this inquiry, is perfectly equal), an action of the nature like this before the court could have been maintained against one of the states in the Union, upon the principles of the common law, which I have shown to be alone applicable. If it could, I think, it is now maintainable here: if it could not, I think, as the law stands at present, it is not maintainable; whatever opinion may be entertained, upon the construction of the constitution as to the power of congress to authorize such a one. Now, I presume, it will not be denied, that in every state in the Union, previous to the adoption of the constitution, the only common-law principles in regard to suits that were in any manner admissible in respect to claims against the state, were those which, in England, apply to claims against the crown; there being certainly no other principles of the common law which, previous to the adoption of this constitution, could, in any manner, or upon any color, apply to the case of a claim against a state, in its own courts, where it was solely and completely sovereign, in respect to such cases, at least. Whether that remedy was strictly applicable or not, still, I apprehend, there was no other. The only remedy, in a case like that before the court, by which, by any possibility, a suit can be maintained against the crown, in England, or, at any period from which the common law, as in force in America, could be derived, I believe, is that which is called a *Petition of right*. It is stated, indeed, in Com. Dig. 105, that "until the time of Edward I., the King might have been sued in all actions, as a common person." And some authorities are cited for that position, though it is even there stated as a doubt. But the same authority adds—"but now, none can have an action against the King, but one shall be put to sue to him by petition." This appears to be a quotation or abstract from Theloall's Digest, which is also one of the authorities quoted in the former case. And this book appears (from the law catalogue) to have been printed so long ago as the year 1579. The same doctrine appears (according to a quotation in Blackstone's Commentaries, 1 vol. 243) to be stated in Finch's Law 253, the first edition of which, it seems, was published in 1579. This also more fully appears in the case of *The Bankers,* and particularly from the celebrated argument of SOMERS, in the time of Wm. III., for, though that case was ultimately decided against Lord SOMERS's opinion, yet, the ground on which the decision was given, no way invalidates the reasoning of that argument, so far as it respects the simple case of a sum of money demandable from the King, and not by him secured on any particular revenues. The case is reported in Freeman, vol. 1, p. 331; 5 Mod. 29; Skin. 601; and lately very elaborately in a small pamphlet published by Mr. Hargrave, which contains all the reports at length, except Skinner's, together with the argument at large of Lord Somers; besides some additional matter.

The substance of the case was as follows: King Charles II. having received large sums of money from bankers, on the credit of the growing produce of the revenue, for the payment of which, tallies and orders of the exchequer were given (afterwards made transferable by statute), and the payment of these having been afterwards postponed, the King at length, in order to relieve the bankers, in 1677, granted annuities to them out of the hereditary excise, equal to six per cent. interest on their several debts, but redeemable on payment of the principal. This interest was paid until 1683, but it then became in arrear, and continued so at the revolution; and the suits which were commenced to enforce the payment of these arrears, were the subject of this case. The bankers presented a petition to the barons of the exchequer, for the payment of the arrears of the annuities granted; to which petition the attorney-general demurred. Two points were made: First, whether the grant out of the excise was good; second, whether a petition to the barons of the exchequer was a proper remedy. On the first point, the whole court agreed, that, in general, the King could alienate the revenues of the crown; but Mr. Baron Lechmere differed from the other barons, by thinking that this particular revenue of the excise, was an exception to the general rule. But all agreed, that the petition was a proper remedy. Judgment was, therefore, given for the petition, by directing payment to the complainants, at the receipt of the exchequer. A writ of error was brought on this judgment, by the attorney-general, in the exchequer-chamber. There, all the judges who argued held the grant out of the excise good. A majority of them, including Lord Chief Justice Holt, also approved of the remedy by petition to the barons. But Lord Chief Justice Treby was of opinion, that the barons of the exchequer were not authorized to make order for payments on the receipt of the exchequer, and therefore, that the remedy by petition to the barons was inapplicable. In this opinion, Lord Somers concurred. A doubt then arose, whether the Lord Chancellor and Lord High Treasurer were at liberty to give judgment, according to their own opinion, in opposition to that of a majority of the attendant judges; in other words, whether the judges called by the Lord Chancellor and Lord High Treasurer were to be considered as mere assistants to them, without voices. The opinion of the judges being taken on this point, seven against three, held, that the Lord Chancellor and Lord Treasurer were not concluded by the opinions of the judges, and therefore, that the Lord Keeper, in the case in question, there being then no Lord Treasurer, might give judgment according to his own opinion. Lord Somers concurring in this idea, reversed the judgment of the court of exchequer. But the case was afterwards carried by error into parliament, and there the Lords reversed the judgment of the exchequer-chamber, and affirmed that of the exchequer. However, notwithstanding this final decision in favor of the bankers and their creditors, it appears by a subsequent statute, that they were to receive only one-half of their debts; the 12 & 14 *Wm. III.*, after appropriating certain sums out of the hereditary excise for public uses, providing that in lieu of the annuities granted to the bankers and all arrears, the hereditary excise should, after the 26th of December 1601, be charged with annual sums equal to an interest of three per cent., until redeemed by payment of one moiety of the principal sums. *Hargrave's Case of the Bankers,* 1, 2, 3.

Upon perusing the whole of this case, these inferences naturally follow: 1st. That admitting the authority of that decision, in its fullest extent, yet, it is an authority only in respect to such cases, where letters-patent from the crown have been granted for the payment of certain sums out of a particular revenue. 2d. That such relief was grantable in the exchequer, upon no other principle than that that court had a right to direct the issues of the exchequer as well after the money was deposited there, as while (in the exchequer language) it was *in transitu.* 3d. That such an authority could not have been exercised by any other court in Westminster Hall, nor by any court, that, from its particular constitution, had no control over the revenues of the kingdom. Lord C. J. Holt, and Lord Somers (though they differed in the main point) both agreed in that case, that the court of King's bench could not send a writ to the treasury. Hargrave's case, 45, 89. Consequently, no such remedy could, under any circumstances, I apprehend, be allowed in any of the American states, in none of which it is presumed any court of justice hath any express authority over the revenues of the state such as has been attributed to the court of exchequer in England.

The observations of Lord Somers, concerning the general remedy by petition to the King, have been extracted and referred to by some of the ablest law characters since; particularly, by Lord C. Baron Comyns, in his digest. I shall, therefore, extract some of them, as he appears to have taken uncommon pains to collect all the material learning on the subject; and indeed is said to have expended several hundred pounds in the procuring of records relative to that case. Hargrave's Preface to the Case of the Bankers.

After citing many authorities, Lord Somers proceeds thus: "By all these authorities, and by many others, which I could cite, both ancient and modern, it is plain, that if the subject was to recover a rent or annuity, or other charge from the crown; whether it was a rent or annuity, originally granted by the King, or issuing out of lands, which by subsequent title came to be in the King's hands; in all cases, the remedy to come at it was, by petition to the person of the King; and no other method can be shown to have been practised at common law. Indeed, I take it to be generally true, that in all cases where the subject is in the nature of a plaintiff, to recover anything from the King, his only remedy, at common law, is to sue by petition to the person of the King. I say, where the subject comes as a plaintiff. For, as I said before, when, upon a title found for the King by office, the subject comes in to traverse the King's title, or to show his own right, he comes in the nature of a defendant; and is admitted to interplead in the case, with the King, in defence of his title, which otherwise would be defeated by finding the office. And to show that this was so, I would take notice of several instances. That, in cases of debts owing by the crown, the subject's remedy was by petition, appears by *Aynesham's Case,* Ryley, 251, which is a petition for 19*l.* due for work done at Carnarvon castle. So, Ryley 251, the executors of John Estrateling petition for 132*l.* due to the testator, for wages. The answer is remarkable; for there is a latitude taken, which will very well agree with the notion that is taken up in this case; *habeant bre. de liberate in canc. thes. et camerar, de* 32*l. in partem solutionis.* So, the case of *Yerward de Galeys,* for 56*l.* Ryley 414. In like manner, in the same book, 253 (33 *Edw. I.*), several parties sue by *petition* for money and goods taken for the King's use; and also for wages due to them; and for debts owing to them by the king. The answer is, *rex ordinavit per concilium thesaurarii et baronum de scaccario, quod satisfiet iis quam citius fieri poterit; ita quod contertos se tenebunt.* And this is an answer given to a petition presented to the king in parliament; and therefore, we have reason to conclude it to be warranted by law. They must be content, and they shall be paid, *quam citius fieri poterit.* The parties, in these cases, first go to the King by petition: it is by him they are sent to the exchequer; and it is by writ under the great seal, that the exchequer is impowered to act. Nor can any such writ be found (unless in a very few instances, where it is mere matter of account), in which the treasurer is not joined with the barons. So far was it from being taken to be law at that time, that the barons had any original power of paying the King's debts; or of commanding annuities, granted by the King or his progenitors, to be paid, when the person applied to them for such payment. But, perhaps, it may be objected, that it is not to be inferred, because petitions were brought in these cases, that, therefore, it was of necessity, that the subject should pursue that course, and could take no other way. It might be reasonable to require from those who object thus, that they should produce some precedents, at least, of another remedy taken. But I think, there is a good answer to be given to this objection. All these petitions which I have mentioned, are after the Stat. 8 *Edw. I.* (Ryley 442), where notice is taken that the business of parliament is interrupted by a multitude of petitions, which might be redressed by the chancellor and justices. Wherefore, it is thereby enacted, that petitions which touch the seal shall come first to the chancellor; those which touch the exchequer, to the exchequer; and those which touch the justices, or the law of the land, should come to the justices; and if the business be so great, or *fi de grace,* that the chancellor, or others, cannot do them without the King, then the petitions shall be brought before the King, to know his pleasure; so that no petitions come before the King and his council, but by the hands of the chancellor, and other chief ministers; that the King and his council may attend the great affairs of the King's realm, and his sovereign dominions. This law being made; there is reason to conclude, that all petitions brought before the King or parliament, after this time, and answered there, were brought according to the method of this law; and were of the nature of such petitions as ought to be brought before the person of the King. And that petitions did lie for a chattel, as well as for a freehold, does appear, 37 Ass. pl. ii.; Bro. Pet. 17. If tenant by the statute-merchant be ousted, he may have petition, and shall be restored. *Vide* 9 *Hen. IV.*, 4; Bro. Pet. 9; 9 *Hen. VI.,* 21; Bro. Pet. 2. If the subject be ousted of his term, he shall have his petition. 7 *Hen. VII.,* 2. Of a chattel real, a man shall have his petition of right, as of his freehold. 34 *Hen. VI.,* 51; Bro. Pet. 3. A man shall have a petition of right, for goods and chattels, and the King indorses it in the usual form. It is said, indeed, 1 *Hen. VII.,* 3; Bro. Pet. 19, that a petition will not lie on a chattel. And admitting there was any doubt as to that point, in the present suit, we are in the case of a freehold." Lord Somers's argument in Hargrave's Case of the Bankers, 103–105.

The solitary case, noticed at the conclusion of Lord Somers's argument, "that a petition will not lie of a chattel," certainly is deserving of no consideration, opposed to so many other instances mentioned, and unrecognised (as I believe it is) by any other authority, either ancient or modern, whereas, the contrary, it appears to me, has long been received and established law. In Comyn's Dig. 4 vol. 458, it is said, expressly, "suit shall be to the king by petition, for goods as well as for land." He cites Staundf.

Præer. 75 *b,* 72 *b,* for his authority, and takes no notice of any authority to the contrary. The same doctrine is also laid down, with equal explicitness, and without noticing any distinction whatever, in Blackstone's Commentaries, 3 vol. 256, where he points out the petition of right as one of the common-law methods of obtaining possession or restitution from the crown, either of real or personal property; and says expressly, the petition of right "is of use, where the King is in full possession of any hereditaments or chattels, and the petitioner suggests such a right as controverts the title of the crown, grounded on facts disclosed in the petition itself."

I leave out of the argument, from which I have made so long a quotation, everything concerning the restriction on the exchequer, so far as it concerned the case then before the court, as Lord Somers (although more perhaps by weight of authority than reasoning) was overruled in that particular. As to all others, I consider the authorities on which he relied, and his deduction from them, to be unimpeached.

Blackstone, in the first volume of his Commentaries (p. 203), speaking of demands in point of property upon the King, state the general remedy thus: "If any person has, in point of property, a just demand upon the King, he must petition him in his court of chancery, where his chancellor will administer right, as a matter of grace, though not upon compulsion." (For which he cites Finch L. 255.) "And this is exactly consonant to what is laid down by the writers on natural law. A subject, says Puffendorf, so long as he continues a subject, hath no way to oblige his prince to give him his due when he refuses it; though no wise prince will ever refuse to stand to a lawful contract. And if the prince gives the subject leave to enter an action against him upon such contract, in his own courts, the action itself proceeds rather upon natural equity than upon the municipal laws. For the end of such action is not to compel the prince to observe the contract, but to persuade him."

It appears, that when a petition to the person of the King is properly presented, the usual way is, for the King to indorse or to underwrite *soit droit fait al partie* (let right be done to the party); upon which, unless attorney-general confesses the suggestion, a commission is issued to inquire into the truth of it; after the return of which, the King's attorney is at liberty to plead in bar, and the merits shall be determined upon issue or demurrer, as in suits between subject and subject. If the attorney-general confesses the suggestion, there is no occasion for a commission, his admission of the truth of the facts being equally conclusive, as if they had been found by a jury. See 3 Blackstone's Commentaries, 256; and 4 Com. Dig. 458, and the authorities there cited. Though the above-mentioned indorsement be the usual one Lord Somers, in the course of his voluminous search, discovered a variety of other answers to what he considered were unquestionable petitions of right, in respect to which he observes: "The truth is, the manner of answering petitions to the person of the King was very various; which variety did sometimes arise from the conclusion of the party's petition; sometimes, from the nature of the thing; and sometimes, from favor to the person; and according as the indorsement was, the party was sent into chancery or the other courts. If the indorsement was general, *soit droit fait al partie,* it must be delivered to the chancellor of England, and then a commission was to go, to find the right of the party, and that being found, so that there was a record for him, thus warranted, he is let in to interplead with the King; but if the indorsement was special, then the proceeding was to be according to the indorsement in any other court. This is fully explained by Staundfort in his treatise of the Prerogative, c. 22. The case Mich. 10 *Hen. IV.*, No. 4, 8, is full as to this matter. The King recovers in a *quare impedit,* by default, against one who was never summoned; the party cannot have a writ of deceit, without a petition. If, then, says the book, he concludes his petition generally *"que le Roy lui face droit"* (that the King will cause right to be done), and the answer be general, it must go into the chancery, that the right may be inquired of by commission; and upon the inquest found, an original writ must be directed to the justices, to examine the deceit, otherwise, the justices before whom the suit was, cannot meddle. But if he conclude his petition especially, that it may please his highness to command his justices to proceed to the examination, and the indorsement be accordingly, *that* had given the justices a jurisdiction. They might, in such case, have proceeded upon the petition, without any commission or any writ to be sued out, the petition and answer indorsed giving a sufficient jurisdiction to the court to which it was directed. And as the book I have mentioned proves this, so many other authorities may be cited. He, accordingly, mentions many other instances, immaterial to be recited here, particularly remarking a very extraordinary difference in the case belonging to the revenue, in regard to which he said, he thought there was not an instance, to be found, where petitions were answered, *soit droit fait aux parties* (let right be done to the parties). The usual reference appears to have been to the treasurer and barons, commanding them to do justice. Sometimes, a writ under the great seal was directed to be issued to them for that purpose: sometimes, a writ from the chancery directing payment of money immediately, without taking notice of the barons. And other varieties appear to have taken place. See Hargrave's Case of the Bankers, p. 73, *et seq.* But in all cases of petition of right, of whatever nature is the demand, I think it is clear, beyond all doubt, that there must be some indorsement or order of the King himself, to warrant any further proceedings. The remedy, in the language of Blackstone, being a matter of grace and not on compulsion.

In a very late case in England, this point was incidentally discussed. The case I refer to, is that of *Macbeath* v. *Haldimand,* reported 1 T. R. 172. The action was against the defendant, for goods furnished by the defendant's order, in Canada, when the defendant was governor of Quebec. The defence was, that the plaintiff was employed by the defendant, in his official capacity, and not upon his personal credit, and that the goods being therefore, furnished for the use of government, and the defendant not having undertaken personally to pay, he was not liable. The defence was set up at the trial, on the plea of the general issue, and the jury, by Judge BULLER's direction, found a verdict for the defendant. Upon a motion for a new trial, he reported particularly all the facts given in evidence, and said, his opinion had been at the trial, that the plaintiff should be nonsuited; "but the plaintiff's counsel appearing for their client, when he was called, he left the question to the jury, telling them that they were bound to find for the defendant in point of law. And upon their asking him whether, in the event of the defendant not being liable, any other person was, he told them, that was no part of their consideration, but being willing to give them any information, he added, that he was of opinion, that if the plaintiff's demands were just, his proper remedy was by a petition of right to the crown. On which, they found a verdict for the defendant. The rule for granting a new trial was moved for, on the misdirection of two points. 1st. That the defendant had, by his own conduct, made himself liable, which question should have been left to the jury. 2d. That the plaintiff had no remedy against the crown, by a petition of right, on the supposition of which the jury had been induced to give their verdict." "Lord MANSFIELD, Chief Justice, now declared, that the court did not feel it necessary for them to give any opinion on the second ground. His lordship said, that great difference had arisen, since the revolution, with respect to the expenditure of the public money. Before that period, all the public supplies were given to the King, who, in his individual capacity, contracted for all expenses. He alone had the disposition of the public money. But since that time, the supplies had been appropriated by parliament to particular purposes, and now, whoever advances money for the public service, trusts to the faith of parliament. That according to the tenor of Lord Somers's argument in the *Banker's case,* though a petition of right would lie, yet it would probably produce no effect. No benefit was ever derived from it in the *Banker's case;* and parliament was afterwards obliged to provide a particular fund for the payment of those debts. Whether, however, this alteration in the mode of distributing the supplies had made any difference in the law upon this subject, it was necessary to determine; at any rate, if there were a recovery against the crown, application must be made to parliament, and it would come under the head of supplies for the year." The motion was afterwards argued on the other ground (with which I have at present nothing to do), and rejected.

In the old authorities, there does not appear any distinction between debts that might be contracted personally by the King, for his own private use, and such as he contracted in his political capacity, for the service of the kingdom. As he had, however, then, fixed and independent revenues, upon which depended the ordinary support of government, as well as the expenditure for his own private occasions, probably, no material distinction, at that time, existed, or could easily be made. A very important distinction may, however, perhaps, now subsist between the two cases, for the reasons intimated by Lord MANSFIELD; since the whole support of government depends now on parliamentary provisions, and except in the case of the civil list, those for the most part annual.

Thus, it appears, that in England, even in the case of a private debt contracted by the King, in his own person, there is no remedy but by petition, which must receive his express sanction, otherwise there can be no proceeding upon it. If the debts contracted be avowedly for the public uses of government, it is at least doubtful, whether that remedy will lie, and if it will, it remains afterwards in the power of parliament to provide for it, or not, among the current supplies of the year.

Now, let us consider the case of a debt due from a state. None can, I apprehend, be directly claimed but in the following instances. 1st. In case of a contract with the legislature itself. 2d. In case of a contract with the executive, or any other person, in consequence of an express authority from the legislature. 3d. In case of a contract with the executive, without any special authority. In the first and second cases, the contract is evidently made on the public faith alone. Every man must know that no suit can lie against a legislative body. His only dependence, therefore, can be, that the legislature, on principles of public duty, will make a provision for the execution of their own contracts, and if that fails, whatever reproach the legislature may incur, the case is certainly without remedy in any of the courts of the state. It never was pretended, even in the case of the crown in England, that if any contract was made with parliament or with the crown, by virtue of an authority from parliament, that a petition to the crown would in such case lie. In the third case, a contract with the governor of a state, without any special authority. This case is entirely different from such a contract made with the crown in England. The crown there has very high prerogatives; in many instances, is a kind of trustee for the public interest; in all cases, represents the sovereignty of the kingdom, and is the only authority which can sue or be sued in any manner, on behalf of the kingdom, in any court of justice. A governor of a state is a mere executive officer; his general authority very narrowly limited by the constitution of the state; with no undefined or disputable prerogatives; without power to effect one shilling of the public money, but as he is authorized under the constitution, or by a particular law; having no color to represent the sovereignty of the state, so as to bind it in any manner, to its prejudice, unless specially authorized thereto. And therefore, all who contract with him, do it at their own peril, and are bound to see (or take the consequence of their own indiscretion) that he has strict authority for any contract he makes. Of course, such contract, when so authorized, will come within the description I mentioned, of cases where public faith alone is the ground of relief, and the legislative body, the only one that can afford a remedy, which, from the very nature of it, must be the effect of its discretion, and not of any compulsory process. If, however, any such cases were similar to those which would entitle a party to relief, by petition to the King, in England, that petition being only presentable to him, as he is the sovereign of the kingdom, so far as analogy is to take place, such petition in a state could only be presented to the sovereign power, which surely the governor is not. The only constituted authority to which such an application could, with any propriety, be made, must undoubtedly be the legislature, whose express consent, upon the principle of analogy, would be necessary to any further proceeding. So that this brings us (though by a different route) to the same goal—the discretion and good faith of the legislative body.

There is no other part of the common law, besides that which I have considered, which can, by any person, be pretended, in any manner, to apply to this case, but that which concerns corporations. The applicability of this, the attorney-general, with great candor, has expressly waived. But as it may be urged on other occasions, and as I wish to give the fullest satisfaction, I will say a few words to that doctrine. Suppose, therefore, it should be objected, that the reasoning I have now used, is not conclusive, because, inasmuch as a state is made subject to the judicial power of congress, its sovereignty must not stand in the way of the proper exercise of that power, and therefore, in all such cases (though in no other), a state can only be considered as a subordinate corporation merely. I answer: 1st. That this construction can only be allowed, at the utmost, upon the supposition that the judicial authority of the United States, as it respects states, cannot be effectuated, without proceeding against them in that light: a position, I by no means admit. 2d. That according to the principles I have supported in this argument, admitting that states ought to be so considered for that purpose, an act of the legislature is necessary to give effect to such a construction, unless the old doctrine concerning corporations will naturally apply to this particular case. 3d. That as it is evident, the act of congress has not made any special provision in this case, grounded on any such construction, so it is to my mind perfectly clear, that we have no authority, upon any supposed analogy between the two cases, to apply the common doctrine concerning corporations, to the important case now before the court. I take it for granted, that when any part of an ancient law is to be applied to a new case, the circumstances of the new case must agree in all essential points with the circumstances of the old cases to which that ancient law was formerly appropriated. Now, there are, in my opinion, the most essential differences between the old cases of corporations, to which the law intimated has reference, and the great and extraordinary case of states separately possessing, as to everything simply relating to themselves, the fullest powers of sovereignty, and yet, in some other defined particulars, subject to a superior power, composed out of themselves, for the common welfare of the whole. The only law concerning corporations, to which I conceive the least reference is to be had, is the common law of England on that subject. I need not repeat the observations I made in respect to the operation of that law in this country. The word "corporations," in its largest sense, has a more extensive meaning than people generally are aware of. Any body politic (sole or aggregate), whether its power be restricted or transcendent, is in this sense, "a corporation." The king, accordingly, in England, is called a corporation. 10 Co. 29 *b*. So also, by a very respectable author (Sheppard, in his Abridgement, 1 vol. 431), is the parliament itself. In this extensive sense, not only each state singly, but even the United States may, without impropriety, be termed "corporations." I have, therefore, in contradistinction to this large and indefinite term, used the term "subordinate corporations," meaning to refer to such only (as alone capable of the slightest application, for the purpose of the objection) whose creation and whose powers are limited by law.

The differences between such corporations, and the several states in the Union, as relative to the general government, are very obvious, in the following particulars. 1st. A corporation is a mere creature of the king, or of parliament; very rarely, of the latter; most usually, of the former only. It owes its existence, its name, and its laws (except such laws as are necessarily incident to all corporations merely as such), to the authority which create it. A state does not owe its origin to the government of the United States, in the highest or in any of its branches. It was in existence before it. It derives its authority from the same pure and sacred source as itself: the voluntary and deliberate choice of the people. 2d. A corporation can do no act but what is subject to the revision either of a court of justice, or of some other authority within the government. A state is altogether exempt from the jurisdiction of the courts of the United States, or from any other exterior authority, unless in the special instances where the general government has power derived from the constitution itself. 3d. A corporation is altogether dependent on that government to which it owes its existence. Its charter may be forfeited by abuse: its authority may be annihilated, without abuse, by an act of the legislative body. A state, though subject, in certain specified particulars, to the authority of the government of the United States, is, in every other respect, totally independent upon it. The people of the state created, the people of the state can only change, its constitution. Upon this power, there is no other limitation but that imposed by the constitution of the United States; that it must be of the republican form. I omit minuter distinctions. These are so palpable, that I never can admit that a system of law, calculated for one of these cases, is to be applied, as a matter of course, to the other, without admitting (as I conceive) that the distinct boundaries of law and legislation may be confounded, in a manner that would make courts arbitrary, and, in effect, makers of a new law, instead of being (as certainly they alone ought to be) expositors of an existing one. If still it should be insisted, that though a state cannot be considered upon the same footing as the municipal corporations I have been considering, yet, as relative to the powers of the general government, it must be deemed in some measure dependent; admitting that to be the case (which to be sure is, so far as the necessary execution of the powers of the general government extends), yet, in whatever character this may place a state, this can only afford a reason for a new law, calculated to effectuate the powers of the general government in this new case: but it affords no reason whatever for the court admitting a new action to fit a case, to which no old ones apply, when the *applica-*

tion of law, not the *making* of it, is the sole province of the court.

I have now, I think, established the following particulars. 1st. That the constitution, so far as it respects the judicial authority, can only be carried into effect, by acts of the legislature, appointing courts, and prescribing their methods of proceeding. 2d. That congress has provided no new law in regard to this case, but expressly referred us to the old. 3d. That there are no principles of the old law, to which we must have recourse, that in any manner authorize the present suit, either by precedent or by analogy. The consequence of which, in my opinion, clearly is, that the suit in question cannot be maintained, nor, of course, the motion made upon it be complied with.

From the manner in which I have viewed this subject, so different from that in which it has been contemplated by the attorney-general, it is evident, that I have not had occasion to notice many arguments offered by the attorney-general, which certainly were very proper, as to his extended view of the case, but do not affect mine. No part of the law of nations can apply to this case, as I apprehend, but that part which is termed, "The conventional Law of Nations"; nor can this any otherwise apply, than as furnishing rules of interpretation, since, unquestionably, the people of the United States had a right to form what kind of union, and upon what terms they pleased, without reference to any former examples. If, upon a fair construction of the constitution of the United States, the power contended for really exists, it undoubtedly may be exercised, though it be a power of the first impression. If it does not exist, upon that authority, ten thousand examples of similar powers would not warrant its assumption. So far as this great question affects the constitution itself, if the present afforded, consistently with the particular grounds of my opinion, a proper occasion for a decision upon it, I would not shrink from its discussion. But it is of extreme moment, that no judge should rashly commit himself upon important questions, which it is unnecessary for him to decide. My opinion being, that even if the constitution would admit of the exercise of such a power, a new law is necessary for the purpose, since no part of the existing law applies, this alone is sufficient to justify my determination in the present case. So much, however, has been said on the constitution, that it may not be improper to intimate, that my present opinion is strongly against any construction of it, which will admit, under any circumstances, a compulsive suit against a state for the recovery of money. I think, every word in the constitution may have its full effect, without involving this consequence, and that nothing but express words, or an insurmountable implication (neither of which I consider, can be found in this case), would authorize the deduction of so high a power. This opinion, I hold, however, with all the reserve proper for one, which, according to my sentiments in this case, may be deemed in some measure extra-judicial. With regard to the policy of maintaining such suits, that is not for this court to consider, unless the point in all other respects was very doubtful. Policy might then be argued from, with a view to preponderate the judgment. Upon the question before us, I have no doubt. I have, therefore, nothing to do with the policy. But I confess, if I was at liberty to speak on that subject, my opinion on the policy of the case would also differ from that of the attorney-general. It is, however, a delicate topic. I pray to God, that if the attorney-general's doctrine, as to the law, be established by the judgment of this court, all the good he predicts from it may take place, and none of the evils with which, I have the concern to say, it appears to me to be pregnant.

Thomas Johnson

☆ 1732–1819 ☆

APPOINTED BY

GEORGE WASHINGTON

YEARS ON COURT

1791–1793

Thomas Johnson

by

HERBERT ALAN JOHNSON

FEW MEN have so conducted their lives to escape historical study better than Thomas Johnson of Maryland. Born on November 4, 1732, he was among that generation marked for destiny, the group from which the revolutionaries and "Founding Fathers" were to be drawn who gained immortal fame in the decades between 1760 and 1790. Most men in this group of leaders were much aware that their words and deeds would bear the study and be subjected to the evaluation not only of their contemporaries but of succeeding generations of Americans as well. Not so Thomas Johnson. Undoubtedly entitled to rank as a "Founding Father," Johnson was significantly absent when the foremost events in our national history took place.

With twelve years' experience as a colonial legislator to his credit, Johnson was already a man of power and influence when his native Maryland began to drift toward revolution and sent her first delegation to the Continental Congress that met at Philadelphia in 1774. Indeed, he had served on the committee of the House of Delegates which nearly a decade before had issued instructions to Maryland's representatives at the historic Stamp Act Congress in New York City. Thomas Johnson himself went to the First Continental Congress at Philadelphia's Carpenter's Hall, and there took part in the committee work that was concerned with drafting the petition to the king. In 1775 he returned to the Second Continental Congress and was appointed to the sensitive Secret Committee of Correspondence, the group charged with soliciting foreign support for the position of Britain's colonies in North America. It was Thomas Johnson who placed George Washington's name in nomination for the post of commander-in-chief of the armies surrounding Boston. But for the great event which would have marked his name for historic attention, the passage of the resolution for

HERBERT A. JOHNSON, Associate Editor of the John Marshall Papers, Institute of Early American History and Culture, has written The Law Merchant and Negotiable Instruments in Colonial New York, 1664–1730.

independence and the signature of the Declaration, Thomas Johnson was absent—he had left the congressional session and returned to Annapolis, there to help raise Maryland's quota of militia.

Ten years later Johnson was again absent when the commercial aspects of the Articles of Confederation were debated at Mount Vernon and Annapolis. He did not attend the Constitutional Convention, and did not witness the 1787 "Miracle at Philadelphia." Rather he was in retirement at Frederick, Maryland when the Constitution was taking form. He emerged from his preoccupations with his iron foundry only to take part in the lackluster Maryland ratifying convention the following year. By every test of economic interest or personal conviction, Johnson should have been at Philadelphia in the eventful summer of 1787. As early as 1770 he had acted in concert with George Washington to encourage improvements that would open the Potomac to east-west commerce. Johnson was Washington's opposite number in a widespread movement to obtain joint Maryland-Virginia legislation that would increase trade upon the river. In his attempts to persuade his fellow members of the House of Delegates to vote for the plan, Johnson was defeated by the opposition of powerful Baltimore interests. Now, with the change of government and greater emphasis upon the role of the West, the situation was far more favorable to launch such a venture. In addition, Johnson now had an economic stake in the navigation of the Potomac since this would provide a cheap mode of transportation for his ironware from the foundry he had established at Frederick. Thomas Johnson nevertheless was absent—from the Mount Vernon meeting, the Annapolis Convention, and also the Constitutional Convention at Philadelphia—and another chance for fame passed him by.

At the end of his public career, Johnson was appointed an Associate Justice of the Supreme Court of the United States. He demurred at taking the post because of the onerous nature of the circuit duties required of Justices. The Judiciary Act of 1789 had provided that the Circuit Courts of the United States were to be composed of two Justices of the Supreme Court and one district judge. The Northern Circuit embraced New England and New York; the Middle Circuit included New Jersey, Pennsylvania, Delaware, and Maryland; the huge Southern Circuit covered all the territorial area of the United States south of the Potomac River. Because of his age and health, Thomas Johnson doubted the wisdom of accepting the hardships of circuit riding. Chief Justice John Jay assured him that he would be given every possible consideration. President Washington, anxious to have Johnson accept the nomination, belittled his objections and pointed out that steps were even then being taken to set up distinct circuit courts that would relieve the members of the Supreme Court from these duties. With these high-level guarantees Johnson finally acquiesced and accepted the appointment. He was commissioned on November 7, 1791, but it was not until August 6, 1792 that he took his place upon the Supreme Court bench.

As a Supreme Court Justice on circuit, and as a member of the Supreme Court *en banc,* Thomas Johnson had numerous opportunities to express his views concerning the nature of federalism and the new Constitution. Yet as a Circuit Justice he wrote no opinions, and as a Supreme Court Justice, his one reported opinion was a vote with the minority upon a mere procedural point. He resigned from his judicial post after fourteen months upon the Bench, leaving nary a trace of his legal philosophy for future generations.

One wonders whether Thomas Johnson consciously avoided fame or whether it continually slipped from his grasp. The record is clear that Thomas Johnson was a man who contributed much to the success of the American Revolution. However, because those deeds of leadership were performed at state rather than national level, he is little known except to students of Maryland history. In the years following the Revolution he had several opportunities to grow to the stature of a national statesman, but in each instance he demurred and resigned before the tasks set for him could be completed. How else can one explain his retirement from the political scene when navigation of the Potomac was within the grasp of commercially minded nationalists? Why also the failure to participate in the opinion writing tasks of the General Court of Maryland, the Circuit Courts of the United States, and the Supreme Court of the United States?

One approach to analyzing Thomas Johnson's career and actions is through his association and collaboration with George Washington. Their joint interest in the navigation of the Potomac during the 1770's has already been noted, and after the War for Independence was won, the two men combined their talents and influence to successfully launch the Potomac Company. This corporation, chartered by both the state of Maryland and Virginia, was set up to improve the river through the use of bypass canals and dredging. Ultimately it was hoped that navigation into western Maryland would provide a passageway to the West that would bring farm products down river to the ports of Chesapeake Bay. George Washington was elected first president of the Potomac Company at its organization meeting in May of 1785; Thomas Johnson was elected a director of the corporation. He later succeeded to the presidency of the company when Washington was elected President of the United States.

Johnson's biographer, Judge Edward S. Delaplaine, notes the service that he rendered to Washington's army during the most trying months of the Revolution. Johnson had served three successive terms as governor from 1777 to 1779, and during that time he displayed an uncanny ability to supply men, arms, food, and supplies to the Continental Army. This must have required great persuasive and organizational skill, and certainly was a substantial contribution to the war effort. As President, Washington was quick to tender the first appointment as District Judge for Maryland to his friend Thomas Johnson, but Johnson declined to serve. Washington did convince Johnson to accept the office of commissioner for the planning of the national capital on the Potomac, and, of course, the post of Associate Justice of the Supreme Court. Undoubtedly the relationship was a close one, and there is even some evidence to believe that the two men were quite comradely in their dealings with each other. It is reported that when Johnson arrived at General Washington's camp with militia reinforcements in January of 1777, he was challenged by a sentinel guarding the commander's tent. Splattered with mud from the march, and diminutive of stature, Johnson looked anything but a brigadier general of militia. The guard told him that the general was occupied and had given orders that he was not to be disturbed. After Johnson's explosion of words, the man reported to General Washington that there was a filthy red-headed little man who demanded to see him and that the general's orders could be damned but he intended to see him. The Commander-in-Chief exclaimed, "Oh! It is Johnson of Maryland! Admit him at once!"

Powerful though Washington's friendship and support could be, it does not account for the popularity Thomas Johnson enjoyed within his home state. Legislative offices were his for the asking, and his election by the Maryland Senate to be the war-time governor of the state for three successive terms is ample testimony to the esteem in which he was held by his fellow legislators. He was not elected to a fourth term because he was forbidden by the constitution of Maryland to succeed himself. However, in 1789, he was again offered the governor's chair, but at that time declined to serve. During the formative years of Maryland state government, Johnson was called upon by the House of Delegates to serve upon the committee which prepared legislation conferring jurisdiction upon the state court of admiralty. This was a difficult task without precedent in American legislation, and Johnson's assignment is some indication of the value which the house attached to his legal training and ability. Immediately prior to Johnson's appointment to the Supreme Court of the United States he had served Maryland as Chief Judge of her General Court, an important post which required extensive legal ability in the execution of the court's function of appellate review of common law judgments in the lower courts.

Although Thomas Johnson had substantially retired from politics during the so-called Critical Period from 1783 to 1789, he was selected to serve as a judge in the territorial dispute between Massachusetts and New York. This conflict arose from the claim by Massachusetts that she held legal title to the lands lying to the west of the Genesee River by virtue of her sea-to-sea charter. New York, on the other hand, asserted her rights as successor to the Iroquois tribe and also as holder of sovereignty derived from the presumptive right of the crown to such lands. Matters were additionally complicated by the financial stake which the former president of the Continental Congress, Nathaniel Gorham of Massachusetts, had in the resolution of the issue. Ultimately the court, set up in accordance with the provisions of the Articles of Confederation, awarded sovereignty over the territory to the state of New York, but was careful to respect the property interests of Gorham. Johnson's service upon the court provided an interesting link between the old Confederation government's boundary adjustment courts and their successor, the Supreme Court of the United States. One of the attorneys who appeared before Johnson was John Jay, then agent for the state of New York, and subsequently Chief Justice of the United States.

It is plain that although Washington's friendship was a strong influence in Thomas Johnson's life, he did gain important positions when the general's opinions would either be ignored or given little weight. Johnson was a man of substance in his own right, one who could be and had been trusted with various offices of government. Upon his appointment to the Supreme Court, he brought prestige to that body, and it is safe to say that, like nearly every Federalist appointment to the Supreme Court bench, he was an able man, a good lawyer, and had the makings of a statesman. This he shared with his Federalist colleagues, and he also shared their limited view of the destiny of the nation and the Supreme Court which served as a vital link in its federal system.

By the time Thomas Johnson reached the Supreme Court of the United States, he had a wealth of experience in the practice of law and a year of valuable apprenticeship as Chief Judge of the General Court of Maryland. Trained in youth as a scrivener in the office of the Clerk of the Maryland Provincial Court, he worked his way to a place at the bar of colonial Maryland. From the writing desk of the clerk's office, he moved to another writing desk in the private law office of Stephen Bordley of Annapolis. There his duties were more closely related to actual practice, and we may judge from the fact that Bordley also trained William Paca, that some attention was paid to the learned aspects of the profession. Nevertheless the task of a law clerk was an arduous one, based upon assiduous attention to form books and the monotonous details of practice.

In 1760 Johnson was admitted to the bar at the relatively advanced age of twenty-seven. While he had spent many a busy day and night preparing himself for admission, he nevertheless found time to notice Ann Jennings, the daughter of his first employer, Thomas Jennings, who was clerk of the Maryland Provincial Court. By 1766 Johnson had achieved sufficient success at the practice of law that he could propose marriage to Miss Jennings, and they were married in that year. In the twenty-eight years of their marriage, the Johnsons had eight children, five girls and three boys, of whom all but one daughter survived infancy. Mrs. Johnson died in 1794, shortly after her husband had retired as commissioner to plan the national capital. Thereafter he did not accept another public office, and his principal public interest seems to have been to encourage the building of a suitable memorial to his friend, George Washington.

The fact that Johnson married the daughter of a lawyer should serve as strong persuasive evidence that he was a good lawyer. This supposition is reinforced by his appointment to the Maryland General Court on April 20, 1790. In many ways service upon the highest common law court in a state was the best place to study and decide the knotty problems of federal constitutional law that arose after 1789. State, and not federal, courts were the first to consider the implications of the new federal Constitution. They were called upon immediately to determine what state laws were altered by the new frame of government and to declare what was the law in the light of the new requirement that the Constitution of the United States be the supreme law of the land. Then, as now, more constitutional decisions occur at state rather than federal level; however, in the early 1790's there was no body of federal precedents to guide the state tribunals to their decisions. Hence, as Chief Judge of the Maryland General Court, Johnson stood at the forefront of jurists who were required to pass upon the constitutionality of state laws even before cases had reached the Supreme Court of the United States upon appeal.

The three reported decisions of the General Court of Maryland while Johnson was Chief Judge all bear upon the clash between Maryland and federal law. They touch upon those subjects which later students of the Constitution would term the commerce clause, the contract clause, vested rights, and the supremacy of federal treaties. Although Johnson wrote opinions in none of these cases, they deserve treatment because they show quite clearly the importance of the litigation in this court, and cast some light upon the legal thought of Johnson, if we assume that he concurred with the decisions and opinions in these matters.

In *Maryland* v. *Sluby,* 2 H. & McH. 480 (1790), Johnson's court was called upon to consider the validity of a Maryland tariff that antedated the ratification of the federal Constitution. The question was whether the tariff was rendered void by the constitutional provision, or whether it would continue in effect until the federal Congress acted under the commerce power bestowed upon it by the new Constitution. The Court, by a *per curiam* opinion, accepted the argument of Luther Martin, the Maryland Attorney General, who contended that if the federal Constitution was intended to repeal all state tariffs it should have done so by express provisions. The General Court judgment, on appeal to the Maryland Court of Appeals, was affirmed by that Court. In effect this early Maryland case represents an enunciation of what would ultimately become the theory of concurrent federal and state power concerning interstate commerce; or, to phrase the matter differently, Maryland here held that the Congress of the United States did not have exclusive power over interstate commerce, but that it would have to "occupy the field" before state legislation would be invalidated.

The contract clause of the federal Constitution also came before Johnson as Chief Judge; again he did not render an opinion, yet the argument in *Donaldson* v. *Harvey,* 3 H. & McH. 12 (1790) must have been followed closely by him as a former practitioner in colonial Maryland. The peculiar execution procedure, by which Maryland judgments were collected prior to the Revolution, was brought into focus by this case. Ordinarily property execution, by writ of *fieri facias,* was accomplished by the sheriff's seizure of the goods of the judgment debtor and his private sale of the property to obtain funds for the payment of the judgment. If public auction were required, the judgment creditor might secure the additional remedy of *venditioni exponas,* which permitted the sheriff to sell by this method. However, in 1716 the Maryland legislature had provided that an alternative mode of satisfying the judgment could be elected by the judgment debtor. Upon entry of the judgment against him, the debtor could have his goods appraised, and then tender to his creditor those goods which had been appraised as being equivalent to the money value of the judgment debt. In other words the judgment creditor could be compelled to accept goods rather than legal tender in satisfaction of the judgment outstanding in his favor.

It was the contention in *Donaldson* v. *Harvey* that the Constitution of the United States, through the operation of the obligations of contracts clause, repealed the 1716 Maryland act, since the legislation in effect provided that debts could be paid in goods rather than in money. The Court held that the federal Constitution did not apply to debts that had been contracted *prior* to its ratification; presumably, the Court had taken the position that as to debts contracted *after* the date of ratification, the 1716 act concerning executions no longer applied. Within the context of this case one may observe the early reasoning of a state court faced with the difficulty of determining complex issues of federal sovereignty, constitutional construction, and various aspects of vested property rights in commercial transactions.

Taken together, *Maryland* v. *Sluby* and *Donaldson* v. *Harvey* raised in a microcosm the much larger issues of federal constitutional law that were to be the primary concern of the Supreme Court of the United States for five decades to come. Thomas Johnson was fortunate to be a member of the court that first met these questions, and one wonders what would have been the impact of this experience upon the decisions of Thomas Johnson as Associate Justice had he remained upon the Court. There is a certain aspect of "dual sovereignty" in these cases, and Maryland even at this early date seems to have been tending in the direction that was to be taken by one of her most eminent sons upon the Court, then a young friend of Thomas Johnson, named Roger Brooke Taney.

Most significant of the three cases determined before the General Court during Johnson's tenure was the British debt case of *Dulany* v. *Wells,* 3 H. & McH. 20 (1790). In this instance Johnson must have contributed much to the conference discussion of the case, for his legislative experience in the 1780 session of the House of Delegates made him an expert on the history of the sequestration statute passed by Maryland for the seizure of British property within the state. An ardent patriot, Johnson had fought unsuccessfully for the inclusion of a provision that would have enumerated commercial debts among the types of property to be seized by the state of Maryland. The conservatism of the Maryland Senate frustrated this attempt, but Johnson was not one to forget the circumstances of the debate. He, above all other men in Maryland, was painfully aware that commercial debts owed to British subjects were specifically excepted from this confiscatory legislation as it was finally passed. Hence only tangible property, real or personal, belonging to British subjects, was amenable to seizure. Upon this point *Dulany* v. *Wells* was adjudicated, Johnson and his brethren on the bench awarding recovery to the British creditor. Their decision was later reversed by the Maryland Court of Appeals, which held that payment into the treasury was a valid discharge of the obligation (3 H. & McH. 83, 1795). Eventually the Supreme Court's decision in *Ware* v. *Hylton,* 3 Dall. 199 (1796), resolved the *Dulany* v. *Wells* question by reference to the provisions of the 1783 peace treaty and federal supremacy. Although the case involved a

Virginia sequestration statute, the provisions of that act were nearly identical to the Maryland act. Six years after the General Court's decision in the *Dulany* case, and four years after Thomas Johnson left the Supreme Court bench, the Supreme Court finally struck down the British debt legislation of the American States.

After his appointment as Associate Justice of the Supreme Court of the United States on November 7, 1791, Johnson was promptly requested to attend the Circuit Court scheduled to sit for the District of Virginia later in the month. The order book for the Virginia Circuit Court shows that he had taken his oath of office before Richard Potts, Chief Judge of the County Court for the Fifth District of Maryland. He then started south for Richmond where he met Associate Justice John Blair, and the two in conjunction with District Judge Cyrus Griffin, opened the court. During the course of this term, preliminary arguments in the case of *Ware* v. *Hylton* were heard, but the matter was continued and no decision was rendered by the court. Because of his prior acquaintance with the British debt issue, Johnson must have followed the points of counsel with interest. This case in the Virginia Circuit Court also prepared him for his one and only opinion as an Associate Justice of the Supreme Court.

This solitary opinion of Johnson was in the case of *Georgia* v. *Brailsford,* 2 Dall. 405 (1792), a British debt case that arose under the Georgia sequestration statute of 1782. The ordinary course of events, in which the British creditor sued his American debtor, who pleaded the state statute as a bar to recovery, was again taking place. Here the case was pending in a United States Circuit Court for Georgia, and the Attorney General of Georgia had been denied permission to appear as a party in the circuit court litigation. The case went to judgment against the Georgia debtor who had paid his obligation into the Georgia treasury as required by the statute. The situation was one which well could have been resolved by admitting the state of Georgia as a party to the circuit court case. This would in effect have been a waiver of sovereignty by Georgia and a submission of her interest in the case to the federal court for adjudication. Because of the refusal of the circuit court to permit such a joinder, the state of Georgia brought a petition to the Supreme Court of the United States requesting that the execution of the circuit court judgment be enjoined, and that the parties be ordered to submit their case to the Supreme Court, where the interest of Georgia as well as the private litigants, might be determined.

Johnson, supported by Justice William Cushing, felt that the state of Georgia was not entitled to an injunction because her remedy at law was adequate. The four other Supreme Court Justices were inclined to grant the injunction and voted accordingly. Chief Justice John Jay expressed serious misgivings and stated that he considered the proceeding to be a most unusual one; its one redeeming feature was that the interests of all parties were brought before the Supreme Court for resolution. Justice James Wilson advanced the opinion that jurisdiction by the Supreme Court should properly be by writ of error to the circuit court, as the circuit court had erred in deciding that a sovereign could not voluntarily submit itself to the jurisdiction of the courts of another sovereign power. Wilson referred to Pennsylvania cases in which the French monarch had submitted voluntarily to the jurisdiction of American courts, and contended that a state could follow the same procedure in regard to federal courts. However, Wilson agreed with the majority that no damage would be done by issuing the injunction and removing the case to the Supreme Court.

Over Thomas Johnson's dissent, the injunction was granted by the Supreme Court, and *Georgia* v. *Brailsford* was brought before the Supreme Court for trial before the Court and jury. Chief Justice Jay charged the jury concerning the issues of federal supremacy involved in the case, and without going from the bar, the jury returned a verdict for the original creditor. The holding of the Court and jury was that payment under the sequestration act was not a bar to recovery by the British creditor, and Georgia's claim was rejected. 3 Dall. 1, 4 (1794).

It was only with strong misgivings that Johnson had accepted his appointment to the Supreme Court, and the assurances of Jay and Washington had partially removed his reluctance on the basis of circuit duties. Riding the circuit had been a continual source of complaint by the Supreme Court Justices, yet Congress did not act to relieve this condition. As a junior member of the Court, Johnson found himself assigned to the far-flung Southern Circuit. He and Justice James Iredell, the other Justice for this circuit, hoped to persuade the Chief Justice that circuit duties should be rotated between the members of the Court. This would have made the occasional difficulties of the Southern Circuit more bearable, but Jay considered it unwise to rotate the judges between circuits. His point was that the number of issues upon which decision was reserved required that the same judges ride the circuit in successive terms. There was undoubtedly some self-interest involved in the matter also. Jay, for example, customarily rode the Northern Circuit with Justice William Cushing; however, in 1793 when the case of *Ware* v. *Hylton* was coming up for decision in the Virginia circuit, Jay managed to be there. Since it involved British debts, a matter which he had negotiated on the Peace Commission of 1782–1783 and an issue that was of vital interest to the foreign relations of the United States, Jay went to Virginia to defend his position and that of the federal government. It seems safe to conclude that Thomas Johnson was outmaneuvered by Jay and the other Justices with greater seniority. Finally, abandoning hope of legislative relief from circuit duties, he resigned from the Court on January 16, 1793.

Justice Johnson's connection with the federal government was not totally severed by his resignation from the Court, for he continued to serve as one of the commissioners appointed to plan the new national capital on the Potomac. He had been selected for this post by President Washington, and accepted the commission on January 22, 1791. With his fellow commissioners, he had selected the city plan submitted by Pierre L'Enfant, and had joined with them in their decision to name the city Washington, and the federal district the District of Columbia. In 1793 they chose Dr. William Thornton's design for the Capitol building, and the former Justice was one of the dignitaries present at the laying of the cornerstone in September of that year. When Johnson resigned from the commission in September of the following year (1794), the city was already beginning to take shape according to the French engineer's plan; Johnson, always the entrepreneur, purchased several lots along Rock Creek and then haggled over the price after he resigned from the commission.

Washington's affection for Johnson and respect for his abilities resulted in a final offer of public office; in August of 1795 the former Justice was offered the portfolio of the Department of State. Several years earlier the first President had thought of nominating Thomas Johnson for this important post when Thomas Jefferson retired to private life. At that time he felt that Johnson was not sufficiently trained in diplomacy to function in the position as Secretary of State. Nevertheless he earnestly wanted to include the Marylander in his Cabinet. Perhaps it was just as well for American foreign relations that Johnson declined this final tender of Washington's esteem, and refused to serve as Secretary of State. He remained retired at Frederick, where he continued to attend to his business ventures until his death on October 26th, 1819, at the venerable age of eighty-seven.

Although Thomas Johnson, it must be admitted, had fallen short of the fame that attached to so many members of his generation, he nevertheless had served the federal government well in the branch of political life he knew best—that of the executive. His work on the commission that planned and supervised the erection of the District of Columbia was an invaluable service. Presiding over the transition of a Maryland swamp into a federal city, he played a vital role in creating a territorial symbol of nationalism. And was it not a tribute to his foresight that this new national city was set upon the banks of the very Potomac upon which Johnson had based his 1770 dreams? Maryland was the scene of Johnson's greatness during the course of the War for Independence, and it was his destiny to work again in Maryland when he helped build the city of Washington. His native state was for him an adequate stage upon which to play his role of advancing the destiny of his state and nation. He had lived a full and active life, knew the great men of his time, and had seen the aspirations of his youth reach fruition in his old age.

SELECTED BIBLIOGRAPHY

Edward S. Delaplaine, *The Life of Thomas Johnson* (New York, 1927) is a thorough biographical study of Johnson although it bears the impress of the historiography of its period. Materials for a reconstruction of Johnson's career on the Supreme Court of the United States are in the Virginia State Library at Richmond (Circuit Court records), and in the microfilmed records of the Supreme Court of the United States available from the National Archives, Washington, D.C. Scattered papers are in the Washington Papers in the Library of Congress, and a small but important collection is at the C. Burr Artz Library, Frederick, Maryland.

Thomas Johnson

REPRESENTATIVE OPINIONS

GEORGIA v. BRAILSFORD, 2 DALL. 405 (1792)

Georgia, along with many other states, had passed a sequestration statute to collect debts owed by its citizens to British creditors. However, the Treaty of Paris ending the Revolutionary War had promised repayment of all such debts. When a British creditor sued his Georgia debtor in the federal courts and won a judgment, the state of Georgia sought to intervene, claiming it should collect this money under its law. The request for intervention was denied by the circuit court and Georgia then brought an original petition in the Supreme Court to enjoin execution of the judgment until its right to the debt could be determined. Johnson (along with William Cushing) voted to deny Georgia's petition. However, four other members decided the state should have its chance to assert its claim to the debt. Eventually the claim was tried before the Supreme Court sitting with a jury and a verdict rendered for the British creditor, 3 Dall. 1 (1794).

JOHNSON, Justice. In order to support a motion for an injunction, the bill should set forth a case of probable right, and a probable danger that the right would be defeated, without this special interposition of the court. It does not appear to me, that the present bill sufficiently claims such an interposition. If the state has a right to the debt in question, it may be enforced at common law, notwithstanding the judgment of the circuit court; and there is no suggestion in the bill, though it has been suggested at the bar, that the state is likely to lose her right by the insolvency either of Spalding, the original debtor, or of Brailsford, who will become her debtor for the amount, if he receives it, when in law he ought not to receive or retain it. Nor does the bill state any particular confederacy or fraud. The refusal to admit the attorney-general as a party on the record, was the act of a competent court; and it is not sufficient barely to allege, that the defendant has not chosen to sue out a writ of error. The case might, perhaps, be made better; but I can only know, at present, the facts which the bill alleges, and which the affidavit supports, it is my opinion, that there is not a proper foundation for issuing an injunction.

William Paterson

☆ 1745–1806 ☆

APPOINTED BY

GEORGE WASHINGTON

YEARS ON COURT

1793–1806

William Paterson

by

MICHAEL KRAUS

"TO BE A complete lawyer," William Paterson wrote to a friend, "is to be versed in the feudal system, and to say the truth I am not very fond of being entangled in the cobwebs of antiquity. *Sic lex est,* is what every plodding pettifogger can say but to dive into the spirit requires intense application and assiduity." Paterson was an earnest man, hard-working and thorough (mirthless, one suspects), and these virtues served him well in his important and exacting duties as a member of the Constitutional Convention of 1787, as a drafter of the Judiciary Act of 1789, and as a Supreme Court Justice.

Born on December 24, 1745, in County Antrim, Ireland, Paterson was brought as an infant of two to America. His parents, Richard and Mary Paterson, having moved from place to place, finally settled in May of 1750 in Princeton, New Jersey, where Richard supported his family by the manufacture of tin plate and general merchandising. Frugality and judicious real estate investment increased the family's means so that they could send their son to the College of New Jersey, later known as Princeton.

Paterson graduated from Princeton in 1763, took a master of arts in 1766 at the same time that he was studying law with Richard Stockton. His letters during this time, collected in *Glimpses of Colonial Society and the Life at Princeton College, 1766–1773,* showed him to be a lively correspondent, a gay companion, a young man deeply involved with and attached to his school. During these years, along with Oliver Ellsworth, Luther Martin (later colleagues at the Constitutional Convention), and others, Paterson founded the Well-Meaning Society (parent to the famous Cliosophic Club), a club where they could harangue and argue over the real and theoretical injustices of the Stamp Act of 1765 and other problems affecting colonial life.

MICHAEL KRAUS is Professor Emeritus, City University of New York. His many publications include The Atlantic Civilization: Eighteenth Century Origins; The Writing of American History; *and* The United States to 1865.

Admitted to the bar in 1769, Paterson began his practice in New Bromley, Hunterdon County, about thirty miles from Princeton. He wilted in "so retired a corner of the World, conversing with none but the dead," and returned in 1772 to Princeton. Life may have been gayer but he was still disgruntled at the slow progress of his practice. With grumbling impatience he confided to a friend that he knew "of no young lawyer, unless abetted by a Party of Influence, that has any run of Practice."

He seems to have established himself as a reputable lawyer and a prominent citizen more easily than he had anticipated. In 1775, at the outset of the American Revolution, he was sent as a deputy from Somerset County to the Provincial Congress of New Jersey where he was elected assistant secretary, and the following year he served as secretary to the Congress. In 1776, he was made a member of the convention that drew up the constitution for the state and in addition was appointed attorney general, in which office he served for five years. His list of public duties is long: he served for two years during the Revolution on the legislative council of New Jersey, he was a minute man in Somerset County, and a member of the Council of Safety. In that capacity he urged vigorous prosecution of Tories. He noted that people in New Jersey were hostile to Tories wishing to return after the Revolution; "a few of them came over but they were immediately hunted back." So arduous were his duties that he declined to serve in the Continental Congress after his election to it in 1780.

Paterson's law practice flourished. "I have full as much Business in the law way as I can manage," he wrote to his brother Tom, "and it is increasing daily in my hands." Characteristically he added, "It is a very slow way of making Money." He had married, in 1779, Cornelia Bell. They lived first in Raritan and later in New Brunswick. She died in childbirth in 1783, and shortly thereafter he married a close friend of hers, Euphemia White. A portrait painted during these years shows Paterson to be a short man, only five feet two, with a prominent nose and penetrating eyes. Physically he was not prepossessing, but nonetheless he impressed his colleagues: "[Paterson] never speaks but when he understands his subject well," William Pierce was to say in 1787. He is "one whose powers break in upon you and create wonder and astonishment. He is a man of great modesty, with looks that bespeak talents of no great extent, but he is a Classic, a Lawyer and an Orator. . . ."

The country, barely established, was beset by problems both practical and philosophical. What tradition there was had come out of a very short history, and assumptions that had been made in 1776 proved by the 1780's to be inadequate, especially in regard to matters of regulation and authority within the confederation of states. Paterson, now in his mid-thirties, had fully determined his political attitudes and opinions and was clear in his defense of republicanism. Republicanism, said he, "delights in virtue which is an active principle, and excites to honesty and industry, and of course is opposed to idleness and sloth. The equalizing of property by the strong hand of power would be a tax upon the active and industrious man for the support of the sluggard. That nation, however, [is most happy] in which property, especially if it be of a landed nature, is fairly equally diffused among the people." "One order of Citizens," he continued, "ought not to be preferred to another." Property should be secured and industry encouraged. The New Jersey lawyer, says the state's leading historian, Richard P. McCormick, was "a rigid republican in his political beliefs . . . conservative in his economic thinking," which eventually caused him to align himself with the staunchest of Federalists. In the 1780's Paterson took time out from the law to speak and write against the evils of paper money issues then plaguing the states.

When the Constitutional Convention of 1787, held in Philadelphia, was called, Paterson was a delegate from New Jersey. This gathering met primarily to revise the Articles of Confederation and to make workable a system which placed power neither in the Congress nor in the states. The preceding decade had shown a frightening increase in administrative confusion and jealous self-interest among the states, and there was no thought among the majority of delegates that the convention would propose any radical solution to the principles of confederation—in part because the members tended to be conservative and methodical, and in part because they were convinced that the country would not ratify any dramatic changes. It became clear, however, that the groupings of self-interest that existed among the states were well and accurately represented in the convention. George Washington, elected to preside over the convention because of his national popularity and prestige, early declared, "It is too probable that no plan we propose will be adopted. Perhaps another dreadful conflict is to be sustained. If to please the people, we offer what we ourselves disapprove, how can we afterwards defend our work? Let us raise a standard to which the wise and the honest can repair. The event is in the hand of God."

The first major issue was the character of the legislature—whether there would be a single chamber or an upper and lower house—and the method of election thereto. The large delegation from Virginia proposed that the legislature have two chambers, each made up of representatives chosen on the basis of population. For the small states, of course, this constituted a great threat, and in answer to the "Virginia Plan" Paterson drew up the "New Jersey Plan" (or as some called it, "Mr. Paterson's Plan"), which also favored government based on an executive, judiciary, and legislature. The latter, however, was to be a single chamber, representing states, not individuals, where every state had an equal vote regardless of population or wealth.

Paterson's position in this matter was that the convention had been called to revise the Articles of Confederation. To do otherwise, he said, would lay the delegates open to charges of "usurpation" by their constituents. Fearing the nationalizing tendencies of some colleagues (the term "federal" at this early stage in the convention conveyed the meaning only of confederation), he maintained that "we are met . . . for federal purposes. Can we consolidate their sovereignty and form one nation, and annihilate the sovereignties of our states who have sent us here for other purposes? . . . We have no power to go beyond the federal scheme; if we had, the people are not ripe for any other." With unwonted passion, he went on, "My self or my state will never submit to tyranny or despotism."

Strenuously concentrated efforts on the part of all delegates were devoted to the forming of the Constitution. The members, by and large, were practical rather than theoretical men, which meant that the debates were long and detailed. Paterson, alternately pessimistic and optimistic about the outcome in Philadelphia, asked his friend, Oliver Ellsworth, if the Convention "would agree upon a system energetic and effectual, or will they break up without doing anything to the purpose?" In a depressed mood he spoke of the gathering as "full of disputation and noisy as the wind." But, like most, he felt that out of the struggle would come a unifying and strong document. He wrote to his wife, "The business is difficult and unavoidably takes up much time, but I think we shall eventually agree upon and adopt a system that will give strength and harmony to the Union and render us a great and happy people. This is the wish of every good, and the interest of every wise man." The wish to succeed in this extraordinary undertaking resulted in the saving "great compromise": there would be two houses, the upper comprised of an equal number of representatives from each state, the lower being made up of numbers in proportion to the population of each state.

Paterson left Philadelphia for a time to attend to law business but returned to sign the new Constitution on September 17, 1787. According to Madison, the chronicler of the convention, Paterson and others with similar views, having won their demand for the small states of equal votes in the Senate, were thereafter ardent in granting powers to the national government. Paterson favored both the popular election of the President and the ratification of the Constitution by state legislatures. Max Farrand, the most serious scholar on the convention, said that Paterson and fellow-minded delegates "were not mere obstructionists. . . . The Constitution would not have assumed so satisfactory a form if it had not been for the part taken by them. Their best service was rendered in restraining the tendency of the majority to overrule the rights of states and individuals in endeavoring to establish a thoroughly strong government." In Madison's words, Paterson became, from this time on "a federalist of federalists."

Paterson worked diligently to get the Constitution ratified in the state of New Jersey, and for his good services was elected in March of 1789 to the Senate of the United States. It was in this capacity that he served perhaps his most useful function: he created, with Oliver Ellsworth and others (the first nine sections of the act are written in Paterson's hand, the bulk of the remainder in the hand of Oliver Ellsworth) the Judiciary Act of 1789—the base of the judiciary system as we know it which is, as Bryce said, "the living voice of the Constitution."

The Constitution specified only (Article III, Section 1) that "the judicial power of the United States, shall be vested in one supreme Court, and in such inferior Courts as the Congress may from time to time ordain and establish." This enlightened and prescient act went way beyond the generality of the Constitution and established an appellate system of three levels: thirteen district courts (one for every state) having original jurisdiction over all suits which, under the Constitution, could be brought in the federal courts, with the exception of those that could be brought directly to the Supreme Court; three circuit courts (whose judges during those days travelled throughout the country) comprised of two Supreme Court Justices and one district judge—two of the three making a quorum—hearing appeals from the district courts as well as having original jurisdiction in many civil and criminal cases; and the Supreme Court, made up of the Chief Justice and five Associate Justices, holding final jurisdiction in all appeals from the federal district courts as well as appeals from the highest state courts in matters of the federal Constitution or an act of Congress.

The arguments against the Judiciary Act were almost exclusively directed to Section 25 which, by allowing the Supreme Court to review final decisions of the state courts in all matters relating to Constitutional and federal rights, established the supremacy of federal law. There was much heat and debate over the amount of power this section gave to the Supreme Court. Roger Sherman of Connecticut, in support, declared the section necessary "to guard the rights of the Union against the States," whereas James Jackson of Georgia was convinced that "it swallows up every shadow of a judiciary." The debate, of course, did not dissipate itself with the passing of the act—the testing of the principle continued from *Ware* v. *Hylton,* 3 Dall. 199 (1796) through *Cohens* v. *Virginia,* 6 Wheat. 264 (1821).

As senator, Paterson was a declared supporter of Hamilton, enthusiastic enough to be listed by a hostile critic as a member of Hamilton's "gladiatorial band." Hamilton, as Secretary of the Treasury, had begun to implement his financial policies of a strong, centrally controlled economic structure, and Paterson was a member of the committee to consider the funding, at the hands of private creditors, of the federal debt and the assumption, by the federal government, of all state debts. He also, during his short term, took part in the compromise that moved the capital from New York to the shores of the Potomac.

But the activity of New York life did not agree with him, and when the Senate adjourned in September of 1789 he wrote to his wife, "Gay life has never been my wish: my disposition is naturally pensive. . . . I hope soon to take leave of my present situation and to return to private life." He was never to return to private life, but he did not long remain in the Senate. In November, 1790, he resigned his seat to become the governor and chancellor of New Jersey on the death of the incumbent William Livingston. Annually elected to this office until his appointment to the Supreme Court in 1793, Paterson performed the useful task of codifying the laws of New Jersey, published in 1800, as well as updating the rules of practice and procedure in the common law and chancery courts. These rules, approved by the state legislature in 1799, were afterward called "Paterson's Practice Laws." While governor, Paterson, along with Hamilton, planned an industrial city at the falls of the Passaic. They set up the Society for Establishing Useful Manufactures in 1791, purchased land adjacent to the falls, and named the proposed town "Paterson." But the enterprise at this time came to little.

Early in 1793 President Washington named Paterson to the Supreme Court to replace Thomas Johnson of Maryland. In proposing him for the Court Washington wrote to him (February 20, 1793), "I think it necessary to select a person who is not only professionally qualified to discharge that important trust, but one who is known to the public, and whose conduct meets their approbation. I shall have the satisfaction to believe that our country will be pleased with and benefited by the acquisition."

Paterson had been on the Bench but a short time when the Whiskey Rebellion in western Pennsylvania broke out. General grievances spread quickly in the back country: dislike of Hamilton's fiscal policies which tended to concentrate wealth in the upper class was the most specific irritation, but the inhabitants were angry over the failure to open the Mississippi River to navigation, the dilatory conduct of the Indian War, speculative land prices, ill-paid militia, and so forth. When, in 1791, an excise tax was levied on whiskey, the chief product of this part of the country (at once easily transportable and easily barterable), resentment grew still stronger and the citizens refused to cooperate. Distillers who did not comply with the tax had to go to York or Philadelphia to face trial, a journey causing them great financial deprivation. Unrest grew and in 1794 Alleghany County residents attacked a government official which resulted in the calling out of the militia in Pittsburgh. Nothing satisfactory came of the committee called to negotiate the grievances, and a militia army, which had been gathering in the East, was called into action to occupy in November of 1794 the western counties. Prisoners were sent east to Philadelphia to be tried—all, in fact, were acquitted, pardoned, or dismissed. Paterson at this time regretfully wrote to his wife, "It is probable that I shall be under the disagreeable necessity of trying the insurgents at this place [Philadelphia]." The insurrection resulted in strengthening Hamilton's political power, as well as that of the Federalists. Some hold that there is sufficient circumstantial evidence to say that Hamilton promoted the original misunderstanding in order to send the army west to consolidate his control over the fractious rural counties.

As a Supreme Court Justice Paterson was obliged to travel a great deal to serve on the circuit courts. Very little, at this time, was being decided in the Supreme Court: almost all the important decisions, mostly without precedent, were being decided in the circuit courts. (The amount of judicial interpretation that came from only a few men during the first decade in the history of the Court is staggering to consider.)

One of Paterson's first important decisions was *Talbot* v. *Jansen,* 3 Dall. 133 (1795). In this case, concerned with the restitution of a prize captured by a French privateer, itself illegally fitted out in this country, the Court held that no foreign power had a legal right to issue commissions in this country. The real issue, however, was the right of national expatriation which was considered but not decided upon. Paterson firmly held that a man might renounce his state citizenship under the provision of a state statute, but that no one could renounce his United States citizenship without taking more definite steps than merely leaving the country for a short period. He defined the American system of government as "sovereignties moving within a sovereignty. Of course there is complexity and difficulty in the system, which requires a penetrating eye to explore, and steady and masterly hands to keep in unison and order. A slight collision may disturb the harmony of the parts and endanger the machinery of the whole."

Anticipating John Marshall in *Marbury* v. *Madison,* Paterson, on circuit in 1795, in *Van Horne's Lessee* v. *Dorrance,* 2 Dall. 304, brought into question the validity of a state statute which contradicted the state constitution. In this case, the litigant's title to property depended on an act of the state legislature which, said Paterson, must be declared void because it violated the state constitution. "The Constitution," said he, "expressly declares that the right of acquiring, possessing and protecting property is natural, inherent and unalienable." He went on in his lengthy decision (often cited as a landmark) that "whatever may be the case in other countries, yet there can be no doubt that every act of the Legislature repugnant to the Constitution is absolutely void. . . . The Constitution is the basis of legislative authority; it lies at the foundation of all law and is a rule and commission by which both legislators and judges are to proceed. It is an important principle, which, in the discussion of questions of the present kind, ought never to be lost sight of, that the judiciary in this country is not a subordinate, but co-ordinate branch of the government. . . ."

Having declined an offer to serve as Secretary of State, Paterson was on the Court to rule on the important decision of *Ware* v. *Hylton,* 3 Dall. 199 (1796). The case ruled on the relation of the states to the federal government: whether state laws confiscating and sequestering debts due the British, or allowing their payment in depreciated currency, were valid against a federal treaty with Great Britain. (Politically, this was a tense issue as a number of states and individuals would be affected by the ruling. In Virginia alone it was estimated that there were more than $2 millions of British debts.) Paterson concurred with fellow Justices Cushing, Wilson, and Chase that British treaty provisions must prevail over state laws, that British creditors were entitled to recover, and in general that a treaty so far as it is compatible with the Constitution supersedes all state laws which derogate from its provisions.

The same year, the Court, for the first time, exercised its right to pass on the constitutionality of an act of Congress in *Hylton* v. *United States,* 3 Dall. 171 (1796), and upheld the right of the federal government to impose a carriage tax, defining a federal tax on carriages as a direct tax within the meaning of the Constitution. It was a curious and extraordinary case, brought from a split circuit court by Hylton who was "contesting the law" "merely to ascertain a constitutional point and not by any means to delay the payment of a public duty." Both sides, in signed statements, agreed that the facts were fictitious, the allegation being that the defendant kept 125 chariots "exclusively for the defendant's own private use and not to let out to hire." The government paid counsel on both side to bring the argument in the Court which ended by the case being decided by only three of the six Justices (Ellsworth had just been sworn in, Cushing was ill, and Wilson having sat in circuit could offer no opinion). Paterson was, by now, a strong nationalist who had made clear his belief in the supremacy of the Constitution and had upheld the necessity of the judiciary to maintain, as interpreter of the Constitution, its separateness and independence. It was "the duty of Judges to declare, and not to make the law," *Fowler* v. *Lindsay,* 3 Dall. 411 (1799), and to remain free from executive pressure, executive opinion having no legal base and therefore not admissible as evidence, *Ship Amanda, Talbot* v. *Seaman,* 1 Cranch 1 (1801).

The character of the Court was strongly Federalist, and its administration of the Sedition Law brought it under severe attack from infuriated Democratic-Republicans. The charges to grand juries made by these judges, said Jefferson, were "a perversion of the institution of the grand jury from a legal to a political engine." These judges, exclaimed a supporter of Jefferson, were "political partisans," giving "harangues throughout the United States." And neither was far wrong.

The best example is the case of Matthew Lyon, congressman from Vermont, who had predicted that the Sedition Bill was aimed at Democratic-Republican congressmen and that he would be its first victim. Having been a rabid critic of the Adams' administration, he was accused by Federalists of hoping that France would dominate the United States. In the first issue of his own newspaper (October 1, 1798), *The Scourge of Aristocracy and Repository of Important Political Truths,* he said the "Scourge will be devoted to politics, and shall commemorate the writings, essays and speeches . . . in the Republican interest." Two days later, at the convening of the Federal Circuit Court for the District of Vermont, Paterson charged the grand jury to pay close attention "to the seditious attempts of disaffected persons to disturb the government."

The jury in response said, "We solemnly feel what the Honorable Judge has so powerfully expressed, that licentiousness more endangers the liberties and independence of a free Government, than hosts of invading foes." The jurors went on to decry a situation where "our liberties . . . are abused to licentiousness." Believing that Lyon was a danger to the United States, they indicted him for sedition on October 5, 1798.

In charging the jury Paterson reminded them that they had but two points to decide: Was Lyon the author of the writings listed in the indictment? Had he written them seditiously, that is, with "bad intent?" The first question was answered by Lyon's own admission of authorship. As for the second point, Judge Paterson told the jury, "You will have to consider whether language such as that here complained of could have been uttered with any other intent than that of making odious or contemptible the President and Government, and bringing them both into disrepute. If you find such is the case, the offense is made out, and you must render a verdict of guilty." The judge, in this instance, was asking that the tendency of the words be made the test of intent. Though Paterson in these fevered times had a more judicial bearing than Justice Chase, he was not above assuming the function of prosecutor as well as judge. As a modern student, James M. Smith, expresses it, "At no time in his charge did Justice Paterson mention the concept of a legitimate political opposition, the fact that truth was a justification or even the fact that acquittal was possible." The jury took one hour to consider the case and found Lyon guilty.

In pronouncing sentence Paterson determined to single out Lyon for punishment as a warning to others not to abuse the government. That Congressman Lyon was a public official made his actions all the more culpable. Sternly addressing the offender, the judge said, "Matthew Lyon, as a member of the federal legislature, you must be well acquainted with the mischiefs which flow from an unlicensed abuse of government, and of the motives which led to the passage of the act under which this indictment is framed. No one, also can be better acquainted than yourself with the existence and the nature of the act." To fit the punishment to the dimensions of the crime, Federalist Judge Paterson sentenced Republican Congressman Lyon to four months in jail. In addition a fine of $1,000 was imposed, plus court costs of $60.96. Until the fine and court costs were paid Lyon was to remain imprisoned.

While Federalists approved the verdict and sentence, Republicans denounced judge and jury. Partisans of Lyon hailed him as a martyr in fighting for free speech and regretted that "the *tory* and *aristocratic* leaders of *write* and *wrong* . . . exult at having caught the Lyon in their toils." Jefferson wrote that he did not know what mortified him most, "that I should fear to write what I think or my country bear such a state of things. Yet Lyon's judges, and . . . jury . . . are objects of national fear." Supporters of Lyon raised $1,000 to pay his fine, and at the conclusion of his jail term he was released, February 9, 1799. Reelected to office while in prison, the Congressman was toasted by Republicans all the way from Vermont to Philadelphia where he returned in triumph to his seat in the House of Representatives.

Paterson gained the reputation, with his colleague Justice Chase, of being an avenger of the Federalist cause in a number of sedition trials. To a large extent they earned the abuse and criticism they received. Thomas Adams, editor of the Republican *Independent Chronicle,* criticized the policies of President Adams and excoriated the Alien and Sedition Laws as hostile to freedom. He challenged the government to prosecute him and they obliged by indicting him for sedition in October, 1798, Paterson presiding over the federal circuit court in Boston. Adams, who had been ill, died before he was brought to trial but Federalist animosity pursued him and one bitter opponent cried that he had been "finally arrested, not by the Marshal of the district, but by that grim messenger whose mandate strikes terror to the heart of the false and malicious libeller."

Journalists were ready victims for prosecution. William Duane, editor of the Philadelphia *Aurora,* the most influential Republican journal in the country, was arrested on July 30, 1799, for seditious libel. Federalists were fearful that

Duane's influence might determine the outcome of the election of 1800. "If the *Aurora* is not blown up," said one, "Jefferson will be elected in defiance of everything." Paterson, presiding, agreed to a postponement because of the absence of witnesses necessary to Duane's defense. With the election of Jefferson soon after and the expiration of the Sedition Law, prosecution of Duane was dropped. Another victim to be silenced before the 1800 election was Anthony Haswell, editor of the *Vermont Gazette*. A supporter of Jeffersonian views, a strong critic of the Alien and Sedition Laws, and a defender of Matthew Lyon (which defense won him threats of tarring and feathering), Haswell was also indicted.

Paterson, who had sentenced Lyon, presided in the trial of Haswell which began on May 5, 1800. In charging the jury, the Supreme Court Justice, in effect, restated the government's case. "You must look critically at the tendency of the whole libel laid before you and minutely scrutinize its parts." As in his remarks in the trial of Lyon, Paterson again emphasized the "bad tendency" of Haswell's words, rather than his "bad intent." The accused was linked with Lyon, "a seditious libeller of your government, a convict justly suffering the penalty of a mild law, that spares the lives of those who had aimed at the subversion of all lawful authority among you, hoping by unprecedented clemency, to have prevented base repetition of his crime, like that which you have now under consideration." Haswell, the judge went on, had labored "to overturn your constitution, the boast of liberty." It was the jury's task, said Paterson, to preserve the Constitution "from the malicious attacks of unprincipled sedition." In words tantamount to a declaration that Haswell was guilty of sedition, Paterson asked that the defendant be convicted. The jury was to decide whether the editor intended to defame the federal government. The verdict it rendered was "guilty." On May 9, 1800, Haswell was sentenced to two months in prison, fined $200, and charged with court costs. Like other imprisoned Republican editors, Haswell continued to uphold his cause from his cell and to be acclaimed a hero by his fellow Republicans in Vermont.

When, with Ellsworth's resignation, the office of Chief Justice fell vacant in 1800, it was widely supposed that Paterson would be appointed to the post. His close relationship to Alexander Hamilton, however, made him obnoxious to President Adams who was at odds with Hamiltonian Federalists. When Paterson was passed over in favor of John Marshall, Federalists delayed the latter's confirmation, hoping that the President would still name Paterson. Adams refused to yield. Paterson swallowed his disappointment with good grace, but his friends were indignant. Senator Jonathan Drayton, of New Jersey, wrote to him that "the eyes of all parties had been turned upon you, whose pretensions were in every respect the best, and who would have been most acceptable to the country." Adams, said Drayton, "was inflexible, . . . he would never nominate you."

To the great surprise and pleasure of the Republican Administration, on March 2, 1803, Paterson in the case of *Stuart* v. *Laird,* 1 Cranch 299, upheld the constitutionality of the Circuit Court Act of 1802. There were two serious constitutional questions in sustaining this act: first, the right of Congress, by repealing the Act of 1801, to abolish judicial positions created by it; and second, the right of Congress to impose upon Supreme Court Justices the duty of sitting on the new circuit courts. After the enactment in 1802 by Congress, Marshall had conferred with his Associate Justices, asking for their opinion as to whether they felt they could comply with the act. "This is a subject not to be lightly resolved on," he wrote Paterson. "The consequences of refusing to carry the law into effect may be very serious." Paterson, Cushing, and Bushrod Washington agreed, in replying to Marshall, that the act was constitutional since Supreme Court Justices had already agreed to serve on circuit courts under the Judiciary Act of 1789. Chase disagreed, believing it unconstitutional as well as feeling that the burden would undermine the concentration and energy of the Court. When the actual test in *Stuart* v. *Laird* came up, Federalist members of the Court, against their own wishes and inclinations, sustained the Republican act, thereby relieving what had grown to be a sharp political conflict. Congress, Paterson said, had "constitutional authority to establish from time to time, such inferior tribunals as they may think proper; and to transfer a cause from one tribunal to another."

Riding the circuit was no joy to Paterson. He and his colleagues complained of wearisome travel and uncomfortable lodgings. From Portsmouth, New Hampshire (May 19, 1800), he wrote to his wife that he had gone over very bad roads, "over stones and rocks and mountains." In three days he could only cover a hundred miles. The burden of going on circuit may have been less heavy a weight than the strain of Republican animosity. Judge Jeremiah Smith of New Hampshire said that Republicans hated Marshall and Paterson "worse than they hate Chase because they are men of better character." Ill health added to Paterson's difficulties. When horses bolted, upsetting his carriage, the judge suffered painful injuries. He wrote to Chase (February 1, 1804), that he would not be able to attend the next session of the Court. He was back on the Bench in 1805, though not well. His last judicial act was on circuit in New York, in the summer of 1806, in the trial of Samuel G. Ogden and William S. Smith, charged with violating neutrality laws in aiding the revolutionary activities of Francisco de Miranda, the South American patriot. Paterson differed so strongly with District Judge Tallmadge in conducting the trial that he left the bench, and Tallmadge carried on alone. The defendants were acquitted.

Failing health prompted Paterson to seek relief at Ballston Springs, New York, in September, 1806. He never reached it, dying en route in his daughter's home at Albany on September 9.

SELECTED BIBLIOGRAPHY

The most useful sources for biographical information are Gertrude S. Wood, *William Paterson of New Jersey 1745–1806,* unpublished doctoral dissertation (Columbia University, 1933) and Charles A. Shriner, *William Paterson* (Paterson, 1940), a condensation of Miss Wood's work. Invaluable material is found in Max Farrand, ed., *The Records of the Federal Convention 1787,* 4 vols. (New Haven, 1911–1937) as well as in his *The Framing of the Constitution of the United States* (New Haven, 1913). For Paterson's political and economic views, see Richard P. McCormick's *Experiment in Independence: New Jersey in the Critical Period, 1781–1789* (New Brunswick, 1950). James M. Smith, *Freedom's Fetters: The Alien and Sedition Laws and American Civil Liberties* (Ithaca, 1956) is a careful and scholarly treatment of those areas. For Princeton see: W. J. Mills, *Glimpses of Colonial Society and the Life at Princeton College, 1766–1773* (1903). Finally, the most recent work on Paterson's role in the Constitutional Convention is Catherine D. Bowen, *Miracle at Philadelphia* (Boston, 1966).

William Paterson

REPRESENTATIVE OPINIONS

HYLTON v. UNITED STATES, 3 DALL. 171 (1796)

In 1796, the Court first considered the constitutionality of a federal law. Congress had passed a tax on carriages which was challenged as a direct tax, forbidden by the Constitution unless apportioned according to population among the states. Paterson as a member of the Constitutional Convention outlined the reasons for the prohibition and had no difficulty upholding the law. One hundred years later, the dissenters in the *Pollock* case which declared void a federal income tax relied heavily on Paterson's opinion as the most authoritative explanation of the constitutional language on direct taxes.

PATERSON, Justice.—By the second section of the first article of the constitution of the United States, it is ordained, that representatives and direct taxes shall be apportioned among the states, according to their respective numbers, which shall be determined by adding to the whole number of free persons, including those bound to service for a term of years, and including Indians not taxed, three-fifths of all other persons. The eighth section of the said article, declares, that congress shall have power to lay and collect taxes, duties, imposts and excises; but all duties, imposts and excises shall be uniform throughout the United States. The ninth section of the same article provides, that no capitation or other direct tax shall be laid, unless in proportion to the census or enumeration before directed to be taken.

Congress passed a law, on the 5th of June 1794, entitled, "An act laying duties upon carriages for the conveyance of persons." Daniel Lawrence Hilton, on the 5th of June 1794, and therefrom to the last day of September next following, owned, possessed and kept one hundred and twenty-five chariots for the conveyance of persons, but exclusively for his own separate use, and not to let out to hire, or for the conveyance of persons for hire.

The question is, whether a tax upon carriages be a direct tax? If it be a direct tax, it is unconstitutional, because it has been laid pursuant to the rule of uniformity, and not to the rule of apportionment. In behalf of the plaintiff in error, it has been urged, that a tax on carriages does not come within the description of a duty, impost or excise, and therefore, is a direct tax. It has, on the other hand, been contended, that as a tax on carriages is not a direct tax, it must fall within one of the classifications just enumerated, and particularly, must be a duty or excise. The argument on both sides turns in a circle; it is not a duty, impost or excise, and therefore, must be a direct tax; it is not tax, and therefore, must be a duty or excise. What is the natural and common, or technical and appropriate, meaning of the words, duty and excise, it is not easy to ascertain; they present no clear and precise idea to the mind; different persons will annex different significations to the terms. It was, however, obviously the intention of the framers of the constitution, that congress should possess full power over every species of taxable property, except exports. The term taxes, is generical, and was made use of, to vest in congress plenary authority in all cases of taxation. The general division of taxes is into direct and indirect; although the latter term is not to be found in the constitution, yet the former necessarily implies it; indirect stands opposed to direct. There may, perhaps, be an indirect tax on a particular article, that cannot be comprehended within the description of duties, or imposts or excises; in such case, it will be comprised under the general denomination of taxes. For the term tax is the *genus,* and includes: 1. Direct taxes. 2. Duties, imposts and excises. 3. All other classes of an indirect kind, and not within any of the classifications enumerated under the preceding heads.

The question occurs, how is such tax to be laid, uniformly or apportionately? The rule of uniformity will apply, because it is an indirect tax, and direct taxes only are to be apportioned. What are direct taxes, within the meaning of the constitution? The constitution declares, that a capitation tax is a direct tax; and both in theory and practice, a tax on land is deemed to be a direct tax. In this way, the terms direct taxes, and capitation and other direct tax, are satisfied. It is not necessary to determine, whether a tax on the product of land be a direct or indirect tax. Perhaps, the immediate product of land, in its original and crude state, ought to be considered as the land itself; it makes part of it; or else the provision made against taxing exports would be easily eluded. Land, independently of its produce, is of no value. When the produce is converted into a manufacture, it assumes a new shape; its nature is altered; its original state is changed; it becomes quite another subject, and will be differently considered. Whether direct taxes, in the sense of the constitution, comprehend any other tax than a capitation tax, and tax on land, is a questionable point. If congress, for instance, should tax, in the aggregate or mass, things that generally pervade all the states in the Union, then, perhaps, the rule of apportionment would be the most proper, especially, if an assessment was to intervene. This appears by the practice of some of the states, to have been considered as a direct tax. Whether it be so, under the constitution of the United States, is a matter of some difficulty; but as it is not before the court, it would be improper to give any decisive opinion upon it. I never entertained a doubt, that the principal, I will not say, the only, objects, that the framers of the constitution contemplated, as falling within the rule of apportionment, were a capitation tax and a tax on land. Local considerations, and the particular circumstances, and relative situation of the states, naturally lead to this view of the subject. The provision was made in favor of the southern states; they possessed a large number of slaves; they had extensive tracts of territory, thinly settled, and not very productive. A majority of the states had but few slaves, and several of them a limited territory, well settled, and in a high state of cultivation. The southern states, if no provision had been introduced in the constitution, would have been wholly at the mercy of the other states. Congress in such case, might tax slaves, at discretion or arbitrarily, and land in every part of the Union, after the same rate or measure: so much a head, in the first instance, and so much an acre, in the second. To guard them against imposition, in these particulars, was the reason of introducing the clause in the constitution, which directs that representatives and direct taxes shall be apportioned among the states, according to their respective numbers.

On the part of the plaintiff in error, it has been contended, that the rule of apportionment is to be favored, rather than the rule of uniformity; and, of course, that the instrument is to receive such a construction, as will extend the former, and restrict the latter. I am not of that opinion. The constitution has been considered as an accommodating system; it was the effect of mutual sacrifices and concessions; it was the work of compromise. The rule of apportionment is of this nature; it is radically wrong; it cannot be supported by any solid reasoning. Why should slaves, who are a species of property, be represented more than any other property? The rule, therefore, ought not to be extended by construction.

Again, numbers do not afford a just estimate or rule of wealth. It is, indeed, a very uncertain and incompetent sign of opulence. This is another reason against the extension of the principle laid down in the constitution.

The counsel on the part of the plaintiff in error, have further urged, that an equal participation of the expense or burden by the several states in the Union, was the primary object, which the framers of the constitution had in view; and that this object will be effected by the principle of apportionment, which is an operation upon states, and not on individuals; for each state will be debited for the amount of its *quota* of the tax, and credited for its payments. This brings it to the old system of requisitions. An equal rule is doubtless the best: but how is this to be applied to states or to individuals? The latter are the objects of taxation, without reference to states, except in the case of direct taxes. The fiscal power is exerted certainly, equally, and effectually on individuals; it cannot be exerted on states. The history of the United Netherlands, and of our own country, will evince the truth of this position. The government of the United States could not go on, under the confederation, because congress were obliged to proceed in the line of requisition. Congress could not, under the old confederation, raise money by taxes, be the public exigencies ever so pressing and great; they had no coercive authority—if they had, it must have been exercised against the delinquent states, which would be ineffectual, or terminate in a separation. Requisitions were a dead letter, unless the state legislatures could be brought into action; and when they were, the sums raised were very disproportional. Unequal contributions or payments engendered discontent, and fomented state jealousy. Whenever it shall be thought necessary or expedient to lay a direct tax on land, where the object is one and the same, it is to be apprehended, that it will be a fund not much more productive than that of requisition under the former government. Let us put the case. A given sum is to be raised from the landed property in the United States. It is easy to apportion this sum, or to assign to each state its *quota*. The constitution gives the rule. Suppose the proportion of North Carolina to be $80,000. This sum is to be laid on the landed property in the state, but by what rule, and by whom? Shall every acre pay the same sum, without regard to its quality, value, situation or productiveness? This would be manifestly unjust. Do the laws of the different states furnish sufficient *data* for the purpose of forming one common rule, comprehending the quality, situation and value of the lands? In some of the states, there has been no land-tax for several years, and where there has been, the mode of laying the tax is so various, and the diversity in the land is so great, that no common principle can be deduced, and carried into practice. Do the laws of each state furnish *data* from whence to extract a rule, whose operation shall be equal and certain in the same state? Even this is doubtful. Besides, sub-divisions will be necessary; the apportionment of the state, and perhaps, of a particular part of the state, is again to be apportioned among counties, townships, parishes or districts. If the lands be classed, then a specific value must be annexed to each class. And there a question arises, how often are classifications and assessments to be made? Annually, triennally, septennially? The oftener they are made, the greater will be the expense; and the seldomer they are made, the greater will be the inequality and injustice. In the process of the operation, a number of persons will be necessary to class, to value and assess the land; and after all the guards and provisions that can be devised, we must ultimately rely upon the discretion of the officers in the exercise of their functions. Tribunals of appeal must also be instituted, to hear and decide upon unjust valuations, or the assessors will act *ad libitum,* without check or control. The work, it is to be feared, will be operose and unproductive, and full of inequality, injustice and oppression. Let us, however, hope, that a system of land taxation may be so corrected and matured by practice, as to become easy and equal in its operation, and productive and beneficial in its effects.

But to return. A tax on carriages, if apportioned, would be oppressive and pernicious. How would it work? In some states, there are many carriages, and in others, but few. Shall the whole sum fall on one or two individuals in a state, who may happen to own and possess carriages? The thing would be absurd and inequitable. In answer to this objection, it has been observed, that the sum, and not the tax is to be apportioned; and that congress may select, in the different states, different articles or objects from whence to raise the apportioned sum. The idea is novel. What? shall land be taxed in one state, slaves in another, carriages in a third, and horses in a fourth? or shall several of these be thrown together, in order to levy and make the quotated sum? The scheme is fanciful. It would not work well, and perhaps is utterly impracticable. It is easy to discern, that great, and perhaps insurmountable, obstacles must arise in forming the subordinate arrangements necessary to carry the system into effect; when formed, the operation would be slow and expensive, unequal and unjust. If a tax upon land, where the object is simple and uniform throughout the states, is scarcely practicable, what shall we say of a tax attempted to be apportioned among, and raised and collected from, a number of dissimilar objects. The difficulty will increase with the number and variety of the things proposed for taxation. We shall be obliged to resort to intricate and endless valuations and assessments, in which everything will be arbitrary, and nothing certain. There will be no rule to walk by. The rule of uniformity, on the contrary, implies certainty, and leaves nothing to the will and pleasure of the assessor. In such case, the object and the sum coincide, the rule and the thing unite, and, of course, there can be no imposition. The truth is, that the articles taxed in one state should be taxed in another; in this way, the spirit of jealousy is appeased, and tranquillity preserved; in this way, the pressure on industry will be equal in the several states, and the relation between the different objects of taxation duly preserved. Apportionment is an operation on states, and involves valuations and assessments, which are arbitrary, and should not be resorted to but in case of necessity. Uniformity is an instant operation on individuals, without the intervention of assessments, or any regard to states, and is at once easy, certain and efficacious. All taxes on expenses or consumption are indirect taxes; a tax on carriages is of this kind, and of course, is not a direct tax. Indirect taxes are circuitous modes of reaching the revenue of individuals, who generally live according to their income. In many cases of this nature, the individual may be said to tax himself. I shall close the discourse, with reading a passage or two from Smith's Wealth of Nations.

"The impossibility of taxing people in proportion to their revenue, by any capitation, seems to have given occasion to the invention of taxes upon consumable commodities; the state, not knowing how to tax directly and proportionably the revenue of its subjects, endeavors to tax it indirectly, by taxing their expense, which it is supposed, in most cases, will be nearly in proportion to their revenue. Their expense is taxed, by taxing the consumable commodities upon which it is laid out. 3 Vol. page 331.

"Consumable commodities, whether necessaries or luxuries, may be taxed in two different ways; the consumer may either pay an annual sum, on account of his using or consuming goods of a certain kind, or the goods may be taxed, while they remain in the hands of the dealer, and before they are delivered to the consumer. The consumable goods, which last a considerable time before they are consumed altogether, are most property taxed in the one way; those of which the consumption is immediate, or more speedy, in the other: the coach-tax and plate-tax are examples of the former method of imposing; the greater part of the other duties of excise and customs of the latter." 3 Vol. page 341.

I am, therefore, of opinion, that the judgment rendered in the circuit court of Virginia ought to be affirmed.

If any state had no carriages, there could be no apportionment at all. This mode is too manifestly absurd to be supported, and has not even been attempted in debate.

But two expedients have been proposed, of a very extraordinary nature, to evade the difficulty.

TALBOT v. JANSEN, 3 DALL. 133 (1795)

The undeclared war between France and the United States in the 1790's led to frequent captures of neutral ships carrying British goods by French privateers, often captained by Americans who had renounced their citizenship to escape the neutrality laws. Two Americans, Ballard and Talbot, captured a Dutch ship whose owner brought libel proceedings against them in an American court. Paterson found the captors and their ships were still American, the capture was therefore illegal under our laws and restitution was ordered.

PATERSON, Justice.—The libel in this cause was exhibited by Joost Jansen, master of the Vrouw Christiana Magdalena, a Dutch brigantine, owned by citizens of the United Netherlands; and its prayer is, that Edward Ballard, and all others having claim, may be compelled to make restitution. The district court directed restitution; the circuit court affirmed the decree; and the cause is now before this court for revision. The Magdalena was captured by Ballard, or by Ballard and Talbot, and brought into Charleston. The general question is, whether the decree of restitution was well awarded. In discussing the question, it will be necessary to consider the capture as made—1. By Ballard. 2. By Ballard and Talbot.

I. By Ballard. This ground not being tenable, has been almost abandoned in argument. It is, indeed, impossible to suggest any reason in favor of the capture on the part of Ballard. Who is he? A citizen of the United States: for although he had renounced his allegiance to Virginia, or declared an intention of expatriation, and admitting the same to have been constitutionally done, and legally proved, yet he had not emigrated to, and become the subject or citizen of any foreign kingdom or republic. He was domiciliated within the United States, from whence he had not removed and joined himself to any other country, settling there his fortune and family. From Virginia, he passed into South Carolina, where he sailed on board the armed vessel called the *Ami de la Liberte.* He sailed from, and returned to, the United States, without so much as touching at any foreign port, during his absence. In short, it was a temporary absence, and not an entire departure from the United States; an absence with intention to return, as has been verified by his conduct and the event, and not a departure with intention to leave this country, and settle in another. Ballard was, and still is, a citizen of the United States; unless, perchance, he should be a citizen of the world. The latter is a creature of the imagination, and far too refined for any republic of ancient or modern times.[1] If however, he be a citizen of the world, the character bespeaks universal benevolence, and breathes peace on earth and good will to man; it forbids roving on the ocean in quest of plunder, and implies amenability to every tribunal. But what is conclusive on this head is, that Ballard sailed from this country with an iniquitous purpose, *cum dolo et culpa,* in the capacity of a cruiser against friendly powers. The thing itself was a crime. Now, it is an obvious principle, that an act of illegality can never be construed into an act of emigration or expatriation. At that rate, treason and emigration, or treason and expatriation, would, in certain cases, be synonymous terms. The cause of removal must be lawful; otherwise, the emigrant acts contrary to his duty, and is justly charged with a crime. Can that emigration be legal and justifiable, which commits or endangers the neutrality, peace or safety of the nation of which the emigrant is a member?

As we have no statute of the United States, on the subject of emigration, I have taken up the doctrine respecting it, as it stands on the broad basis of the law of nations, and have argued accordingly. That law is in no wise applicable to the present case; for, Ballard, at the time of his taking the command of the *Ami de la Liberte,* and of his capturing the Magdalena, was a citizen of the United States; he was domiciliated within the same, and not elsewhere; and besides, his cause of departure, supposing it to have been a total departure from and abandonment of his country, was unwarrantable, as he went from the United States, in the character of an illegal cruiser. The act of the legislature of Virginia does not apply. Ballard was a citizen of Virginia, and also of the United States. If the legislature of Virginia pass an act specifying the causes of expatriation, and prescribing the manner in which it is to be effected by the citizens of that state, what can be its operation on the citizens of the United States? If the act of Virginia affects Ballard's citizenship, so far as respects that state, can it touch his citizenship, so far as it regards the United States? Allegiance to a particular state is one thing; allegiance to the United States is another. Will it be said, that the renunciation of allegiance to the former, implies or draws after it a renunciation of allegiance to the latter? The sovereignties are different; the allegiance is different; the right, too, may be different. Our situation being new, unavoidably creates new and intricate questions. We have sovereignties moving within a sovereignty. Of course, there is complexity and difficulty in the system, which requires a penetrating eye fully to explore, and steady and masterly hands to keep in unison and order. A slight collision may disturb the harmony of the

[1] *See* Rabaud *v.* D'Wolf, *1 Paine 580; S. C. 1 Pet. 485.*

parts, and endanger the machinery of the whole. A statute of the United States, relative to expatriation, is much wanted; especially, as the common law of England is, by the constitution of some of the states, expressly recognised and adopted. Besides, ascertaining by positive law the manner in which expatriation may be effected, would obviate doubts, render the subject notorious and easy of apprehension, and furnish the rule of civil conduct on a very interesting point.

But there is another ground, which renders the capture on the part of Ballard altogether unjustifiable. The *Ami de la Liberte* was built in Virginia, and is owned by citizens of that state; she was fitted out as an armed sloop of war, in, and as such, sailed from, the United States, under the command of Ballard, and cruised against and captured vessels belonging to the subjects of European powers, at peace with the said states. Such was her predicament, when she took the Magdalena. It is idle to talk of Ballard's commission; if he had any, it was not a commission to cruise as a privateer, and if so, it was of no validity, because granted to an American citizen, by a foreign officer, within the jurisdiction of the United States. We are not, however, to presume, that the French admiral or consul would have issued a commission of the latter kind, because it would have been a flagrant violation of the sovereignty of the United States; and of course, incompatible with his official duty. Therefore, it was not, and indeed, could not, have been a war commission. It is not necessary, at present, to determine, whether acting under color such a commission would be a piratical offence. Every illegal act or transgression, committed on the high seas, will not amount to piracy. A capture, although not piratical, may be illegal, and of such nature as to induce the court to award restitution.[1]

It has been urged in argument, that the *Ami de la Liberte* is the property of the French republic. The assertion is not warranted by the evidence; and if it was, would not, perhaps, be of any avail, so as to prevent restitution by the competent authority. The proof is clear and satisfactory, that she was an American vessel, owned by citizens of the United States, and still continues to be so. The evidence in support of her being French property is extremely weak and futile; it makes no impression; it merits no attention. But if the *Ami de la Liberte* be the property of the French republic, it might admit of a doubt, whether it would be available, so as to legalize her captures and prevent restoration; because she was, after the sale (if any took place) to the republic, and before her departure from, and while she remained in, the United States, fitted out as an armed vessel of war; from whence, in such capacity, and commanded by Ballard, an American citizen, she set sail, and made capture of vessels belonging to citizens of the United Netherlands. The United States would, perhaps, be bound, both by the law of nations and an express stipulation in their treaty with the Dutch, to restore such captured vessels, when brought within their jurisdiction, especially, if they had not been proceeded upon to condemnation, in the admiralty of France. On this, however, I give no opinion. The United States are neutral in the present war; they take no part in it; they remain common friends to all the belligerent powers, not favoring the arms of one, to the detriment of the others. An exact impartiality must mark their conduct towards the parties at war; for if they favor one to the injury of the other, it would be a departure from pacific principles, and indicative of an hostile disposition. It would be a fraudulent neutrality. To this rule, there is no exception, but what arises from the obligation of antecedent treaties, which ought to be religiously observed. If, therefore, the capture of the Magdalena was effected by Ballard alone, it must be pronounced to be illegal, and of course, the decree of restitution is just and proper. This leads us—

II. To consider the capture as having been made by Ballard and Talbot. Talbot commanded the privateer *L'Ami de la Point-a-Pitre*. The question is, as the Magdalena struck to and was made prize of by Ballard, and as Talbot, who knew his situation, aided in his equipment, and acted in confederacy with him, afterwards had a sort of joint possession, whether Talbot can detain her as prize, by virtue of his French commission? To support the validity of Talbot's claim, it is contended, that Ballard had no commission, or an inadequate one, and therefore, his capture was illegal: that it was lawful for Talbot to take possession of the ship so

[1] *So, a seizure as prize, is no trespass, though it may be wrongful; the authority and intention with which it is done, deprive the act of the character which would otherwise be impressed upon it; the tort is merged in the capture as prize.* Stoughton *v.* Taylor, *2 Paine 655.*

captured, being a Dutch bottom, as the United Netherlands were at open war and enmity with the French republic, and Talbot was a naturalized French citizen, acting under a regular commission from the governor of Guadaloupe. It has been already observed, that Ballard was a citizen of the United States; that the *Ami de la Liberte,* of which he had the command, was fitted out and armed as a vessel of war in the United States; that as such she sailed from the United States, and cruised against nations at peace and in amity with the said states. These acts were direct and daring violations of the principles of neutrality, and highly criminal by the law of nations. In effecting this state of things, how far was Talbot instrumental and active? What was his knowledge, his agency, his participation, his conduct in the business? It appears in evidence, that Talbot expected Ballard at Tybee; that he waited for him there several days; that he set sail without him, and in a short time, returned to his former station. This indicates contrivance and a previous communication of designs. At length, Ballard appeared; on his arrival, Talbot put on board the *Ami de la Liberte,* in Savannah river, and confessedly within the jurisdiction of the United States, four cannon, which he had brought for the purpose. Were these guns furnished by order of the French consul? The insinuation is equally unfounded and dishonorable. They also fired a salute, and hailed Sinclair, a citizen of the United States, as an owner: an incident of this kind, at such a moment, has the effect of illumination. Talbot knew Ballard's situation, and in particular, aided in fitting out the *Ami de la Liberte,* by furnishing her with guns. Without this assistance, she would not have been in a state for war. An essential part of the outfit, therefore, was provided by Talbot. The equipment being thus completed, the two privateers went to sea. When on the ocean, they acted in concert; they cruised together, they fought together, they captured together. Talbot knew that Ballard had no commission; he so states it in his claim: the facts confirm the statement; for, about an hour after Ballard had captured the Magdalena, he came up, and took a joint possession, hoping to cover the capture by his commission, and thus to legalize Ballard's spoliation. How silly and contemptible is cunning —how vile and debasing is fraud! In furnishing Ballard with guns, in aiding him to arm and outfit, in co-operating with him on the high seas, and using him as the instrument and means of capturing vessels, Talbot assumed a new character, and instead of pursuing his commission, acting in opposition to it. If he was a French citizen, duly naturalized, and if, as such, he had a commission, fairly obtained, he was authorized to capture ships belonging to the enemies of the French republic, but not warranted in seducing the citizens of neutral nations from their duty, and assisting them in committing depredations upon friendly powers. His commission did not authorize him to abet the predatory schemes of an illegal cruiser on the high seas; and if he undertook to do so, he unquestionably deviated from the path of duty. Talbot was an original trespasser, for he was concerned in the illegal outfit of the *Ami de la Liberte*. Shall he then reap any benefit from her captures, when brought within the United States? Besides, it is in evidence, that Ballard took possession first of the Magdalena, and put on board of her a prize-master and some hands; Talbot, in about an hour after, came up, and also put on board a prize-master, and other men. The possession in the first instance was Ballard's; he was not ousted of it; the prey was not taken from him; indeed, it was never intended to deprive him of it. So far from it, that it was an artifice to cover the booty. Talbot's possession was gained by a fraudulent co-operation with Ballard, a citizen of the United States, and was a mere fetch or contrivance, in order to secure the capture. Ballard still continued in possession. The Magdalena, thus taken and possessed, was carried into Charleston. Can there be a doubt with respect to restoration? Stating the case, answers the question. It has been said, that Ballard had a commission, and acted under it. The point has already been considered, and indeed is not worth debating; the commission, if any, was illegal, and of course, the seizures were so. But then, what effect has this upon Talbot? Does it make his case better or worse? The truth is, that Talbot knew that Ballard had no commission, and he also knew the precise case and situation of the *Ami de la Liberte;* to whom she belonged, where fitted out, and for what purpose. Talbot gave Ballard guns, within the jurisdiction of the United States, and thus aided in making him an illegal cruiser; he consorted and acted with him, and was a participant in the iniquity and fraud. In short, Ballard took the Magdalena, had the possession of her, and kept it; Talbot was in, under Ballard, by connivance and fraud, not with a view to oust him of the prize, but to cover and secure it; not with a view to bring him into judgment as a transgressor against the law of nations, but to intercept the stroke of justice and prevent his being punished. If Talbot procured possession of the Magdalena, through the medium of Ballard, a citizen of the United States, and then brought her within the jurisdiction of the said states, would it not be the duty of the competent authority, to order her to be restored? The principle deducible from the law of nations is plain—you shall not make use of our neutral arm, to capture vessels of your enemies, but of our friends. If you do, and bring the captured vessels within our jurisdiction, restitution will be awarded. Both the powers, in the present instance, though enemies to each other, are friends of the United States; whose citizens ought to preserve a neutral attitude; and should not assist either party in their hostile operations. But if, as is agreed on all hands, Ballard first took possession of the Magdalena, and if he continued in possession, and brought her within the jurisdiction of the United States, which I take to be the case, then no question can arise with respect to the legality of restitution. It is an act of justice, resulting from the law of nations, to restore to the friendly power the possession of his vessel, which a citizen of the United States illegally obtained, and to place Joost Jansen, the master of the Magdalena, in his former state, from whence he had been removed by the improper interference, and hostile demeanor of Ballard. Besides, it is right to conduct all cases of this kind, in such a manner, as that the persons guilty of fraud, should not gain by it. Hence, the efficacy of the legal principle, that no man shall set up his own fraud or iniquity as a ground of action or defence. This maxim applies forcibly to the present case, which, in my apprehension, is a fraud upon the principles of neutrality, a fraud upon the law of nations, and an insult, as well as a fraud, against the United States, and the republic of France.

I am, therefore, of opinion, that the decree of the circuit court ought to be affirmed. Being clear on the preceding points, it supersedes the necessity of deciding upon other great questions in the cause; such as, whether Redick and Talbot were French citizens; whether the bill of sale was colorable and fraudulent; whether Redick, if a French citizen, did not lend his name as a cover; and whether the property did not continue in Sinclair and Wilson, citizens of the United States.

Samuel Chase

☆ 1741–1811 ☆

APPOINTED BY

GEORGE WASHINGTON

YEARS ON COURT

1796–1811

Samuel Chase

by

IRVING DILLIARD

ONLY ONE MEMBER of the United States Supreme Court has ever been impeached by vote of the national House of Representatives and tried in the United States Senate on charges of "high crimes and misdemeanors" under the provisions of the Constitution. That Justice was Samuel Chase, vehement foe of the Stamp Act, fiery insurrectionist of the Revolution, proud signer of the Declaration of Independence, active opponent of the Constitution, stern enforcer of the Sedition Act, and surprise appointee to the federal judiciary by President George Washington. No doubt he was the most turbulent soul ever to serve on the Nation's highest bench.

This Revolutionary Spirit was born at Princess Anne, in Somerset County, Maryland, on April 17, 1741. His parents were the Reverend Thomas Chase, an Episcopal clergyman who ministered to the parish of St. Paul's in Baltimore for many years and Martha Walker Chase, the daughter of Maryland farm folk.

His mother died when Samuel was still a small boy and he was educated by his father, primarily in classical languages and studies. After his private tutoring, chiefly at home, young Chase was invited in 1759 into the law office of Hammond and Hall in Annapolis. He was then eighteen years old. Following two years of legal study he was admitted to the bar, his first practice being in the Mayor's Court of Annapolis. In two years, his practice extended to chancery and the courts of the county around Annapolis.

The Supreme Court's early historian, Hampton L. Carson, wrote that Chase's "remarkable personal traits soon brought him distinction." Describing the young lawyer at the outset of his career, Carson gave him generous praise:

> *His abilities were of the highest order; industry, intrepidity, intense convictions, energetic eloquence, added to a sonorous voice and imposing stature, made*

IRVING DILLIARD, former reporter and editor of the St. Louis Post-Dispatch *editorial page, is Ferris Professor and Senior Fellow in the Council of the Humanities at Princeton University. He is a former trustee of the University of Illinois. He has published numerous articles and is the author of books on Supreme Court Justices Brandeis and Black and Judge Learned Hand.*

him conspicuous as a leader in the Colonial Legislature, where he became known as "the Maryland Demosthenes."

Chase's tenure in the Maryland General Assembly began in 1764 when he was only twenty-three, and continued for an even twenty years. Meanwhile he committed himself deeply to related public services. When the First Continental Congress met in Philadelphia, September–October, 1774, Chase was there as one of the five delegates from Maryland. He continued as a Maryland delegate through 1778, by which time sessions had been held in Baltimore, Lancaster, and York, Pennsylvania. After an interval when he did not attend, he was returned to the Continental Congress for the 1784–85 sessions which met in Trenton, New Jersey and New York City.

The true nature of Chase's contributions in those early years can not be told from a factual recital of the official positions he shared with many of his fellow citizens in their own colonial legislatures and in the Continental Congress. It was what Chase did rather than where he was that set him apart from his colleagues.

He had no sooner entered the Maryland Assembly in 1764 than he lined up irrevocably against the Crown-appointed Governor of the Colony. He even went so far in his opposition to the Governor's policies and program as to work and vote for a bill regulating the pay of the clergy, one consequence of which was to reduce the salary of his father by one half. Outraged by the Stamp Act of 1765, he joined the organization of demonstrators known as the Sons of Liberty.

Although at thirty-three Chase was one of the youngest members of the Continental Congress, he did not hesitate to press ideas however extreme on his senior associates. At the heart of his anti-British program was an economic boycott. He insisted that, if the Colonists refused to ship to them, the British would be brought to their knees commercially and would be forced to yield to their demands.

To accomplish this goal, Chase advocated not only an economic association but a political confederation of the Colonies. They must join together governmentally in a concerted attack on common problems and needs, so he contended.

Chase's opposition to the ruling authority was so violent that the Mayor of Annapolis and its Board of Aldermen officially condemned him for his attitude and conduct. They called him a "busy, restless incendiary, a ringleader of mobs, a foul-mouthed and inflaming son of discord." Chase was more than ready to reply on the same terms. He dismissed the lot of his denouncers in words equally as harsh, calling them "despicable tools of power, emerged from obscurity and basking in proprietary sunshine."

Ordinary channels moved too slowly for Samuel Chase. Forced to perform within the normal framework, he sought the most challenging mission, the virtually impossible goal of persuading Canada to free herself from Great Britain and unite with the Colonies in a North American Revolution.

Serving with Benjamin Franklin and Charles Carroll of Carrollton, Chase was a member of the commission that arrived in Montreal in April, 1776. He joined in presenting the case for a new union and a joint effort on a continental basis. The mission made little impression in Canada and so was of short duration. Its members reported back to Philadelphia in June.

As Maryland had instructed its delegates to the Continental Congress to vote against independence, Chase hurried to Annapolis to launch a campaign to persuade the Maryland Assembly to reverse its position. In this ambitious and critical undertaking, Chase was a phenomenal success. Immediately after the vote to reverse carried, Chase rushed back to Philadelphia where, after a two-day ride of 100 miles plus, he arrived with the new instructions just in time for the vote on independence. He himself became a signer of the Declaration as enrolled on August 2.

A sensational episode in Chase's early career was his bitter condemnation of his fellow delegate to the Continental Congress, the Rev. Dr. John Joachim Zubly of Georgia. Zubly, who distrusted the republic as a form of government, represented an area in which Loyalist sympathies dominated. When the group that included Chase called for independence, Zubly declared his unwillingness to join with them. In October, 1775, Chase unloosed what was perhaps his most extreme denunciation. He publicly accused Zubly of disloyalty and, branding the Georgian a Judas, shouted that he was unfit to remain in the Continental Congress.

Chase's indictment of his fellow delegate was so severe that Zubly hastily quit the Continental Congress and returned to Savannah, his explanation being that he was "greatly indisposed." Whether Chase was wholly fair in his unrestrained attack on Zubly, the consequence was that, even in Georgia, the Council of Safety soon afterward took Zubly into custody. Later Zubly was banished and half his property confiscated. Eventually Chase's victim was allowed to return to preaching in Savannah where in 1781 he died. Zubly's career would indicate that although he did not help the Revolution, neither was he the utterly unprincipled character that Chase made him out to be.

Chase was so full of energy and industry, and so zealous to push the cause of independence, that he apparently had a hand in almost everything the Continental Congress did. He was a member of twenty-one committees of the Congress of 1777 and the next year he was a member of no fewer than thirty. With Gouverneur Morris and Richard Henry Lee he served on a special committee whose purpose was to turn public opinion against the peace proposals that Britain advanced in 1778. The dissection of the British tender, which took the form of a widely circulated pamphlet, was prepared chiefly by Chase. It was the kind of uncompromising task that delighted his rebellious temperament.

About this time Chase entered a sorely clouded period of his life. Taking advantage of official information available to the Continental Congress, he joined with a few others in an effort to corner the flour market. The scheme became known and for it Chase was attacked in the *New York Journal* as having "the peculiar privilege of being universally despised." The excoriation, which bore the signature of "Publius," was plainly the work of Alexander Hamilton who was outraged by such conduct in the midst of the Revolutionary War.

Maryland showed its disapproval by dropping Chase from its delegation to the Continental Congress for two years. However, the Governor of Maryland returned him at least partially to public life in 1783 by dispatching him to England to retrieve Maryland's pre-Revolutionary shares in the Bank of England which two Loyalists had taken to Britain. The generally fruitless mission kept Chase abroad for a year when absence was to his benefit.

Chase's more regular business ventures also brought him trouble and embarrassment. He invested extensively in coal and iron properties that were confiscated as a result of the Revolution. He also entered into partnerships for the purpose of buying and selling war supplies. For one reason or another, these enterprises failed financially and Chase found himself lacking the means to meet his obligations. Finally in 1789 he took the extreme step of formally asking the Maryland legislature to declare him bankrupt. His petition was granted, but with conditions set by the legislature concerning divestiture of the partnerships.

Chase represented Maryland at the bi-state convention that met in 1785 for the purpose of working out the trade differences between his State and Virginia. The main result was an interstate compact relating to shipping on the Potomac. In 1786 Chase moved from Annapolis to Baltimore where he began the judicial career that continued to the end of his life a quarter century later. In 1788 he took up the post of Judge of the Baltimore Criminal Court. Three years later, in 1791, he also became Chief Judge of the General Court of Maryland.

As a signer of the Declaration of Independence, Chase might have been counted a supporter of the Constitution, but in fact he was not. The proposed charter that issued from Philadelphia did not suit him. His chief criticism was that it would lead to a government of the few, that is, of the rich. In the Maryland ratifying conventions he claimed that Congress would not represent the farmers or mechanics of the state, but only the rich merchants. He wrote to a friend: "I consider the Constitution as radically defective in this essential: the bulk of the people can have nothing to say to it. The government is *not* a government of the people." Coming from Chase, whose close contacts with the merchant class were well known, these sentiments must have raised many eyebrows. They are even more surprising in the light of his later anti-democratic speeches as a Justice.

Chase not only opposed the document signed and submitted by the Founders but even wrote articles against its adoption. Using the pen name of "Caution", he put himself at least nominally in competition with Madison, Hamilton, and Jay as the authors of *The Federalist Papers*. When the Constitution went before the Maryland Convention, of which Chase was a member, he was one of the minority of eleven that voted against his state's ratification, which carried with sixty-three favorable votes. Chase offered the additional objection that the Constitution failed to protect the freedom of the press and trial by jury. To remedy that defect he served on a committee of the Maryland Convention that drew up amendments for the Constitution in the area of individual liberties.

The fact that Chase held several public positions, including the two judgeships, and his frequently bullying manners on the bench, brought increasing criticism. Finally a motion was introduced in the Maryland Assembly to remove him from all his public offices. A majority voted for the ouster, but lacked the two-thirds necessary to carry.

Notwithstanding the reputation for controversy and turbulence that Chase had been acquiring from his earliest public days, the Maryland jurist was strongly recommended to President Washington for a federal appointment. Indeed Chase had in effect commended himself to Washington at the time of the Continental Congress by holding firm against anti-Washington maneuvers among some of the delegates.

For if Chase had his critics, he also had staunch supporters including James McHenry of Maryland, Washington's friend, and Secretary of War. McHenry urged Washington to name Chase to a governmental position. In mid-1795 McHenry wrote to Washington of Chase's "past errors" which he said existed "no longer" and were in any case far overbalanced by his many favorable points.

For a time the office of Attorney General appeared to be a likelihood, but the President came to believe that a seat on the bench was more suited to Chase's talents. After the resignation of Associate Justice John Blair of Virginia, one of Washington's first Supreme Court appointees, the President nominated Chase to the vacancy on January 26, 1796. The Senate confirmed the appointment without opposition one day later and Chase was immediately commissioned and seated. A new era of turbulence had quietly begun.

If Chase had any premonition of greater trouble he kept it to himself. He wrote Secretary McHenry confidently that "the President shall never have reason to regret the nomination." Convinced, the Cabinet officer relayed that reassurance to Washington.

Others were less certain and some even outspokenly negative on the choice of Chase. Oliver Wolcott of Connecticut, Washington's Secretary of the Treasury following the resignation of Hamilton, wrote that he had "but an unworthy opinion" of Chase, while William Plumer, Speaker of the New Hampshire House of Representatives and another leading Federalist, expressed an equally unfavorable view. Plumer wrote that the appointment did "not encrease the respectability and dignity of the judiciary." Justice James Iredell of North Carolina, an earlier appointee of Washington to the Supreme Court, was far from ready to welcome Chase to the highest bench. He wrote: "I have no personal acquaintance with Mr. Chase, but am not impressed with a very favorable opinion of his moral character, whatever his professional abilities may be."

Samuel Chase had no more than taken his seat on February 4, 1796 when the Supreme Court of which he now was a part found itself with important work on its hands. A new term opened that month during which Oliver Ellsworth of Connecticut was seated as Chief Justice. Of the five cases heard that term, three were not notable, but the two others were of outstanding significance and called for thoughtful and far-seeing judicial solutions. The significant two were *Hylton*

v. *United States,* 3 Dall. 171 and *Ware* v. *Hylton,* 3 Dall. 199, both decided in March, 1796. In each the newest Associate Justice wrote an opinion that made it plain he would do his own thinking on the Bench.

The circumstances surrounding *Hylton* v. *United States* were all the more unusual because of the record against advisory opinions dating back to the Supreme Court's earliest days. A half dozen years before Chase was appointed, John Jay, as the first Chief Justice, rejected a request from Alexander Hamilton that the Supreme Court give an advisory opinion on an executive matter that the Secretary of the Treasury considered to be of primary importance. The position of Chief Justice Jay was that it would be improper and unwise for the Supreme Court to attempt to formulate an opinion other than through the normal procedure after a case had come up through the lower courts and had been duly accepted and argued in the Supreme Court, with qualified litigants and counsel taking part.

Probably no subsequent case quite matched *Hylton* v. *United States* in its odd conditions. Hylton claimed that an act of Congress in 1794 which levied a tax on each carriage was a direct tax and must be laid in proportion to the population. But since Hylton owned only one carriage on which the tax and penalty would have been only $16, he took the position that he was not seeking to hinder the payment of a public duty, but to determine a constitutional question, namely, whether the tax was a direct levy and therefore subject to apportionment among the states. Rules as to jurisdiction required that a sum of at least $2,000 be involved, and so, by agreement with the government, Hylton was allowed to enter a fictitious statement that he owned 125 carriages for his own personal use and not for hire. That supposed set of facts brought the case within the jurisdiction of the trial court.

It was also agreed that if the outcome went against Hylton and he was adjudged "liable to pay the tax and fine for not doing so and for not entering the carriages, then judgment shall be entered for the plaintiff for $2,000 to be discharged by the payment of sixteen dollars, the amount of duty and penalty." The Government also agreed to pay the costs of counsel on both sides as a further assistance in getting the issue through the courts and to a judicial determination. The circuit court decided against Hylton's claim and he obtained a review on the same agreed fictitious facts.

Other aspects of the "carriage case" brought it to public notice. In taking the case for decision, the Supreme Court, while not guaranteeing a ruling on the constitutionality of an act of Congress, raised the possibility that such a decision might be handed down. The argument of the case attracted more spectators than was usual in the Supreme Court chamber. Attorney General Charles Lee presented the government's side. Alexander Hamilton, lately retired from the Cabinet, was special government counsel. Justice Iredell sensed the importance of the occasion when he wrote:

"Mr. Hamilton spoke in our Court, attended by the most crowded audience I ever saw there, both Houses of Congress being almost deserted on the occasion.

Though he was in ill health, he spoke with astonishing ability, and in a most pleasing manner, and was listened to with the profoundest attention."

Still another circumstance excited public interest. The Supreme Court was without an effective Chief Justice so far as the case at hand was concerned. Oliver Ellsworth had just taken the oath of office, but since he had not heard the arguments in the preceding month, he did not sit with the Justices who were to consider and decide the case. Justice Cushing did not hear the arguments either, as he was sick at the time. And a third member, Justice Wilson, took part in the case in the circuit court. This meant that, according to custom, he did not participate at the Supreme Court level. Thus only three Justices, Iredell, Paterson, and Chase, the latter almost as much of a newcomer as Chief Justice Ellsworth, made up the deciding Bench.

On March 8, 1796, less than two weeks after the crowded courtroom listened to opposing counsel, the three Justices read their opinions, that of Justice Chase, as the junior Associate Justice, coming first. He presented his views in major part as follows:

> *"It appears to me, that a tax on carriages cannot be laid by the rule of apportionment, without very great inequality and injustice. For example: suppose, two states, equal in census, to pay $80,000 each, by a tax on carriages, of eight dollars on every carriage; and in one State, there are 100 carriages, and in the other 1,000. The owners of carriages in one State would pay ten times the tax of owners in the other. A. in one State, would pay for his carriage eight dollars, but B. in the other State, would pay for his carriage, eighty dollars. . . .*
>
> *"I think, an annual tax on carriages for the conveyance of persons, may be considered as within the power granted to Congress to lay duties. The term* duty, *is the most comprehensive, next to the general term* tax; *and practically, in Great Britain (whence we take our general ideas of taxes, duties, imposts, excises, customs, &c.), embraces taxes on stamps, tolls for passage, &c., and is not confined to taxes on importation only. It seems to me, that a tax on expense is an indirect tax; and I think, an annual tax on a carriage for conveyance of persons, is of that kind; because a carriage is a consumable commodity; and such annual tax on it, is on the expense of the owner.*
>
> *"I am inclined to think, but of this I do not give a judicial opinion, that the direct taxes contemplated by the Constitution, are only two, to wit, a capitation or poll tax simply, without regard to property, profession or any other circumstance; and a tax on land. I doubt, whether a tax, by a general assessment of personal property, within the United States, is included within the term direct tax. . . ."*

Justices Iredell and Paterson also took the view that the carriage tax was in the nature of an excise or duty rather than a direct tax and so the question of constitutionality was not faced. As to this point, Chase said in his opinion: "It is unnecessary for me at this time to determine whether this Court constitutionally possesses the power to declare an act of Congress void."

Hylton v. *United States,* decided by Chase and two of his colleagues, went into judicial history, therefore, as the first case in which the Supreme Court expressly reviewed an act of Congress, but having done that, deliberately refrained from saying that it had the authority to void an act of the national legislature as a violation of the Constitution. Yet the signpost was up and it pointed the way that a future Chief Justice, John Marshall, and his associates would follow in *Marbury* v. *Madison,* 1 Cranch 137 (1803), six years later.

The decision in *Ware* v. *Hylton*—evidently the same Daniel Lawrence Hylton of Virginia as in *Hylton* v. *United States*—was still more important. No less a constitutional scholar than the late Edward S. Corwin said of Chase's opinion in *Ware* v. *Hylton* that it "remains to this day the most impressive assertion of the supremacy of national treaties over State laws." The point at issue was whether the provisions of the treaty with Britain, following the Revolutionary War, took precedence over the laws of states that confiscated and sequestrated debts owed to British subjects or arranged for their payment in depreciated paper money.

By the time the controversy was decided by the Supreme Court, it had compiled a substantial history. The question was first heard on circuit in Virginia, in September, 1791, with Justices Blair and Johnson and District Judge Griffin making up the bench. Then in May, 1793, it was re-argued before Chief Justice Jay, Justice Iredell and Judge Griffin, also on circuit. Nearly three years more had passed when four Justices of the Supreme Court—Chase, Paterson, Cushing, and Wilson—heard arguments and took the case for decision in February, 1796.

So much judicial attention to the issue was a measure of the division in the new nation over the solution. Political and financial stakes were high. Both the states and many of their residents were involved financially in such debts. The total of obligations to the British in the state of Virginia, for example, was said to be upwards of $2,000,000. The public tended to divide, in the post-Revolutionary years, into pro-British and pro-French segments and that affected attitudes on the confiscated debts. Since this bore on the fortunes of the Federalist Party, soon to seek its third presidential term in office, Attorney General Edmund Randolph reported to President Washington:

"The late debates concerning British debts have served to kindle a wide-spreading flame. The debtors are associated with the Anti-Federalists, and they range themselves under the standard of Mr. [Patrick] Henry, whose ascendancy has risen to an immeasurable height."

The arguments before Justice Chase and his three fellow judges in *Ware* v. *Hylton* were made the more notable by the appearance of John Marshall of Virginia as counsel for the debtors. Pointing out that this was Marshall's only argument in the Supreme Court, historian Charles Warren found it "interesting to note that Marshall, in arguing against the binding force of the treaty over the state legislation, referred to 'those who wish to impair the sovereignty of Virginia,' thus employing the very phrase which the ardent State-Rights adherents used so frequently in after years in attacking his own decisions as Chief Justice."

Spectators hung on Marshall's words, but Justices Chase, Paterson, Cushing, and Wilson decided in two weeks for the national position and against the contentions of Marshall for the states and the individual debtors. Thus, Justice Chase helped determine only a half dozen years after the inauguration of the new government that a constitutional treaty stood above the laws of states. And thus, as Warren wrote, "was settled forever one of the fundamental doctrines of American law."

Chase made a memorable contribution with his opinion in *Calder* v. *Bull,* 3 Dall. 386 (1798). In it he achieved a definition of the term *ex post facto* law and an interpretation of its meaning within the Constitution that have remained a part of our constitutional heritage. He concluded that the Constitutional prohibitions applied only in criminal cases, not in civil matters such as the *Calder* suit. Chase noted in passing that any law "contrary to the *great first principles* of the *social compact*" must be declared void. Corwin found this approach of great significance "for its suggestion that there are unwritten, inherent limitations on legislative powers," a doctrine that "may be fairly regarded as the germ of the modern doctrine of due process of law as 'reasonable law'."

An example of how an early statement by a Justice may extend far into the future came from Chase in *Hollingsworth* v. *Virginia,* 3 Dall. 378 (1798). He said in a footnote concerning resolutions of Congress for amending the Constitution: "The negative of the President applies only to the ordinary cases of legislation: He has nothing to do with the proposition, or adoption, of amendments to the Constitution." If anything else was said on this point by any member of the Supreme Court for a century and a quarter, it escaped scrupulous search.

The matter of the power of the Supreme Court to declare an act of Congress void was the subject of further remarks by Chase in *Cooper* v. *Telfair,* 4 Dall. 14 (1800). He sought to summarize the attitude of the lawyers by saying:

> *"Although it is alleged that all acts of the legislature, in direct opposition to the prohibitions of the Constitution, would be void; yet, it still remains a question, where the power resides to declare it void. It is, indeed, a general opinion, it is expressly admitted by all this bar, and some of the Judges have individually in the Circuits, decided, that the Supreme Court can declare an act of Congress unconstitutional, and therefore invalid; but there is no adjudication of the Supreme Court itself upon the point."*

Still other early cases of more than passing interest in which Chase took part include *United States* v. *La Vegeance,* 3 Dall. 297, *Hunter* v. *Fairfax Devisee,* 3 Dall. 305, and *Moodie* v. *The Ship Phoebe Anne,* 3 Dall. 319, all decided in 1796. Chase delivered perhaps his most notable opinion on circuit in *United States* v. *Worrall,* 2 Dall. 384 (1798) in which, going against some of his colleagues, he asserted that federal courts do not have jurisdiction over crimes at common law. Chase's position was adopted by the Supreme Court in *United States* v. *Hudson and Goodwin,* 7 Cranch 32 (1812).

Meantime Chase was sinking deeper and deeper into water that was growing more and more hot. In the very year that he was seated on the Court, he made partisan speeches for John Adams' presidential campaign, an activity which set off complaints that he not only ignored judicial propriety, but also neglected his duties on the bench. Even worse, Chase agitated for passage of the odious Alien and Sedition Acts, primarily the latter, and then threw himself into the forefront of the Federalist judges who pushed hard for enforcement.

Hardly less than the prosecutors, Chase demanded indictments and verdicts of guilty from juries. He, more than anyone else, was responsible for the indictment of James Thomson Callender of Virginia, a strong supporter of Jefferson who had attacked President Adams in print. After obtaining Callender's indictment for sedition, Chase directed the marshal to keep off the jury all Anti-Federalists. The biased Judge then proceeded to try Callender and sentence him to prison for nine months and to fine him $200.

On circuit Chase was so dogmatic and high-handed that his performance as judge was almost indistinguishable from that of the prosecution. In Baltimore and Wilmington, for example, he bent every energy to bring about the indictment of Republican editors because of their Anti-Federalist opinions in print. He imposed the severest sentences under the act, sending David Brown of Dedham, Massachusetts to jail for eighteen months for speaking and writing in opposition to the Adams administration.

Chase's conduct was even more reprehensible when he presided over the treason trial of John Fries of Pennsylvania, a soldier and insurgent, who was also a strong supporter of Jefferson. The Judge permitted as jurors only those who made known their prejudice against Fries. Although the defendant was without the assistance of counsel in a criminal proceeding that carried a possible death sentence, Chase offered Fries no more protection than to inform him, in interrogating the Court or witnesses, to "be careful to ask no questions wherein you may possibly criminate yourself, for remember, whatever you say to your own crimination, is evidence with the jury; but if you say anything to your justification, it is not evidence." It was no wonder that the lawyers of Philadelphia investigated Chase's prejudiced handling of the Fries trial and then jointly agreed not to practice before him when he came to their city on circuit. Fries was found guilty and Chase sentenced him to be put to death. However President Adams in an act of clemency, set aside the sentence against the advice of his Cabinet.

When the question of responsibility for declaring an act of Congress unconstitutional came up in the *Callender* case, Chase showed a much firmer opinion than he had previously held. Callender's counsel took the position that since the common law gave the jury the right to determine the law, the jury in the instant case, if it so believed, had the duty to declare the Sedition Act invalid under the Constitution, and to refuse to find the defendant guilty. Chase strongly opposed this argument. Setting out his views in a detailed statement, he rejected the idea that a "jury can rightfully exercise the power granted by this Constitution to the Federal judiciary." Putting his belief into the plainest possible words, he concluded "that the judicial power of the United States is the only proper and competent authority to decide whether any statute made by Congress (or any of the State Legislatures) is contrary to, or in violation of, the Federal Constitution." To prevent this view from being dismissed as an unusual or personal interpretation, Chase said firmly: "I believe that it has been the general and prevailing opinion in all the Union, that the power now wished to be exercised by a jury, belongs properly to the Federal Courts."

Chase took part in hearing and deciding *Marbury* v. *Madison,* 1 Cranch 137 (1803). Thus he shared with Chief Justice John Marshall and the other Federalist Justices the hostility engendered by that historic ruling which first voided a provision of Congress. Republicans saw in the *Marbury* decision a partisan assault on Thomas Jefferson, who had won the presidency in 1800 but did not take office until after Marshall's confirmation to the Supreme Court. However, Chase did more than share the hostility of the Republicans and became largely the center of it because his abusive speech and arbitrary conduct made him the most vulnerable of all the political Federalist judges.

On May 2, 1803, Chase committed what undoubtedly was his gravest offense against judicial propriety. He charged a United States grand jury in Baltimore in the most intemperate terms, denouncing democracy and condemning the principles of the Republican Party. Outraged by the repeal of the Federalist-sponsored Judiciary Act of 1801, which related to the operations of the United States circuit courts, Chase said the Jeffersonians had undertaken a course that shook the independence of the courts to their very foundations.

Chase's state of Maryland had approved suffrage for males and this also disturbed him deeply. A voting democracy, he told the grand jurors, would "rapidly destroy all protection to property, and all security to personal liberty, and our Republican Constitution [would] sink into mobocracy, the worst of all possible governments." As for the cause of such troubles, Chase was certain he knew beyond the slightest question. Making an obvious reference to the Republicans, he said: "The modern doctrines by our late reformers, that all men in a state of society are entitled to enjoy equal liberty and equal rights, have brought this mighty mischief upon us, and I fear that it will rapidly destroy progress, until peace and order, freedom and property shall be destroyed."

That was too much for Jefferson. On May 13, he sent a printed report and summary of Chase's tirade to Representative Joseph H. Nicholson of Maryland with the inquiry: "Ought this seditious and official attack on the principles of our Constitution, and the proceedings of a State, go unpunished? And to whom more pointedly than yourself will the public look for the necessary measures?"

The second question was a reference to Representative Nicholson's responsibility as one of the managers of the successful impeachment proceedings against Judge John Pickering of the federal district court in New Hampshire. With the Pickering removal as precedent—the proven charge finally was insanity—the Republicans decided to follow up on Chase. On January 6, 1804, the House named a committee to inquire into Chase's judicial conduct and to report whether or not it required "the interposition of the constitutional power of the House." In short, was impeachment in order?

The special committee decided that impeachment was indeed justified, and on March 12 the House supported the report by a vote of 73 to 32. Six of the eight articles of impeachment charged Chase with specific instances of misconduct is presiding over the Callender and Fries trials. A seventh charge concerned his attempt to obtain an indictment against the Republican editor in Wilmington. The charge that weighed most heavily, however, was the final one that dealt with his political harangue before the grand jury in Baltimore.

For months the case was debated in the press, the party affiliation of the editor dictating the newspaper's point of view. Typical of the pro and con was the reaction of the *Independent Chronicle* that "never, never was the bench so disgraced as by Judge Chase; talk of Jeffries [the hanging judge], and in comparison with Chase, he was a faithful officer and honest man." Balanced with this was the *Connecticut Courant's:* "Behold this aged patriot, one of the pillars of our Revolutionary struggle rudely dragged by a Virginia stripling before the national tribunal."

The House having impeached Chase, the proceedings moved to the Senate. There the trial officially opened on January 3, 1805, but not much was done until February 9. Chase had a battery of capable lawyers, including Luther Martin, Joseph Hopkinson, Philip Barton Key, Charles Lee, and Robert Goodloe Harper, who conducted an exceptional defense. His attorneys were disappointed though by the testimony of John Marshall. The Chief Justice, called as a witness for Chase, said it was unusual not to hear arguments of counsel in the Callender case that the Sedition Act was unconstitutional.

Chase did not deny that he had spoken out on public issues in his grand jury charge, but he did deny strenuously that he had said anything that was improper for a Judge. He was after all, he said, a friend of his country as his life demonstrated, and he believed strongly in both the federal and state systems of government. Behind the scenes Jefferson used his presidential power on behalf of Chase's conviction, an end that did not appear to be impossible since Jefferson's party held twenty-five of the Senate's thirty-four seats.

In the end the crux of the case came in the meaning of the Constitution's words "High crimes and misdemeanors." The voting occurred on March 1 and on each charge the question was put in this form: "Is Samuel Chase guilty or not guilty of a high crime or misdemeanor as charged in the article just read?"

It soon became clear that some Senators would agree that Chase had used poor judgment, as indeed many other early jurists had, but would not vote to convict him of a high crime. One of the eight articles did not have the support of a single Senator. Five received fewer than a simple majority. None obtained the two-thirds required for conviction. The vote most unfavorable to Chase was 19 to 15 on the charge dealing with his performance before the Baltimore grand jury.

The failure to convict Chase on even one count was a major setback to the political plans of the Republicans. Senator John Quincy Adams informed his father, the immediate past President, that "the assault upon Judge Chase . . .

was unquestionably intended to pave the way for another prosecution, which would have swept the Supreme Judicial Bench clean at a stroke." From Jefferson came later the admission that the attempted ouster turned out to be no more than "a mere scarecrow." Representative John Randolph of Virginia, who bore much of the blame for the collapse of the prosecution, sought unsuccessfully, before the dust of battle had settled, to recoup by proposing a constitutional amendment providing that "the Judges of the Supreme Court and all other courts of the United States shall be removed from office by the President on the joint address of both Houses of Congress requesting the same."

Jefferson's party was not without gains in the controversy over Chase. Thereafter Judges generally were more careful in what they did and how they spoke. If the exoneration of Chase kept down a similar attack and possible conviction of Marshall, and some were certain that it did, then failure of the case against Chase was of abiding historical consequence. Whether the Republican intentions went as far as Senator Adams reported to his father, there can be no question about the deep feeling in Jefferson's differences with the Marshall Court. Chase's acquittal, less on his account than for the role of the Supreme Court, was a major contribution to the independence of the judiciary at a critical time.

Marshall's biographer Albert J. Beveridge described six-footer Chase as having a large head with a wide brow, a broad and massive face, colored a brownish-red that caused contemporaries in the Maryland legal profession to call him "Bacon face." In latter years his hair, still thick, was snow white.

After the impeachment and trial Chase went into the shadows. He was sixty-four years old and had been a lawyer for forty years. After 1801 Marshall dominated the Court. He spoke for it a large part of the time and in important decisions almost always. Chase was seldom heard in that period. Indeed his reputation rested far more on the half dozen years from 1796 to 1801 than on the full decade from 1801 to 1811. Moreover, Chase was frequently ill with gout and unable to participate in the later deliberations. The work of the Court was at a low ebb during 1811 when Chase died, on June 19, in his seventy-first year. He had married first Anne Baldwin on May 21, 1762, and, after her death, Hannah Kilty Giles on March 3, 1784.

A fair appraisal of Justice Chase is far from simple. He was an intense patriot given his lights. He was a man of ability, skill, learning, and intellect. But he also was unrestrained, autocratic, violent, and headstrong. He was more the advocate than the judge, although on occasion he could be wholly judicious. District Judge Richard Peters of Pennsylvania spoke for many others as well as himself when he said: "I never sat with him without pain, as he was forever getting into some intemperate and unnecessary squabble." And he aided and abetted the police state era of the Alien and Sedition Acts, that "reign of witches," as Jefferson called the dark and ugly years. One Samuel Chase on the Supreme Court of the United States may be said to have been enough.

SELECTED BIBLIOGRAPHY

A century and a half after Chase's death this dramatic, turbulent figure still lacks major, full-length biographical treatment. Edward S. Corwin's fair, balanced, and accurate article on Chase in the *Dictionary of American Biography* 20 vols. (1930) included a list of major sources then available. For background and early years consult John Sanderson, *Biography of the Signers of the Declaration of Independence* (1817), J. T. Scharf, *History of Maryland* (1879), Edmund C. Burnett, *The Continental Congress* (New York, 1941), *Journals of the Continental Congress* (1904–08), and J. H. Hazelton, *The Declaration of Independence—Its History* (New York, 1906). Chase's business dealings were reported in part in "Journals and Correspondence of the State Council of Maryland, 1778–80," 21, 43 *Archives of Maryland.* For Chase's years on the Supreme Court see Charles Warren, *The Supreme Court in United States History,* rev. ed. 2 vols. (Boston, 1937), Charles G. Haines, *The Role of the Supreme Court in American Government and Politics, 1789–1835* (Berkeley, 1944), Homer C. Hockett, *The Constitutional History of the United States, 1776–1826* (New York, 1939), Albert J. Beveridge, *Life of John Marshall,* 4 vols. (New York, 1919) and Gustavus Myers, *History of the Supreme Court of the United States* (Chicago, 1925). Chase's Supreme Court opinions range from 2 Dallas to 6 Cranch. The official record of the impeachment proceedings was printed in *Senate Document No. 876,* 62nd Congress, 2nd Session. William Plumer's report of the trial in *Memorandum of Proceedings in the United States Senate, 1803–07* (1923) was edited by E. S. Brown. Henry Adams recounted the congressional action on the charges against Chase in *History of the United States During the Administrations of Thomas Jefferson and James Madison,* 9 vols. (1889–91). Jane Elsmere's doctoral dissertation, *The Impeachment Trial of Justice Samuel Chase* (1962), is in the Indiana University Library, Bloomington, Ind. The early years of the new government, including the Alien and Sedition period, are covered in John C. Miller's excellent *Crisis in Freedom* (Boston, 1951), the same author's *The Federalist Era: 1789–1801* (New York, 1960) and James M. Smith's *Freedom's Fetters* (Ithaca, 1956). Main events in Chase's career are in *Biographical Directory of the American Congress, 1774–1961* (1961).

Samuel Chase

REPRESENTATIVE OPINIONS

WARE v. HYLTON, 3 DALL. 199 (1796)

The problem of British debts plagued the government long after the Treaty of Paris (1783) guaranteed repayment to British creditors. Many states had sequestered such debts during the Revolution and the debtors refused to pay a second time. When a Virginia law seizing the debts was challenged, the Supreme Court held that the Treaty prevailed over any state law on the subject. Chase's opinion follows.

THE COURT, after great consideration, delivered their opinions, *seriatim,* as follow:

CHASE, *Justice.*—The Defendants in error, on the 7th day of *July*, 1774, passed their penal bond to *Farrell* and *Jones,* for the payment of £2,976 11 6, of good *British* money; but the condition of the bond, or the time of payment, does not appear on the record.

On the 20th of *October,* 1777, the legislature of the commonwealth of *Virginia,* passed a law to *sequester British* property. In the 3d section of the law, it was enacted, "that it should be *lawful* for any citizen of *Virginia,* owing money to a subject of *Great Britain,* to *pay* the same, or any part thereof, from time to time, as he should think fit, into the loan office, taking thereout a certificate for the *same,* in the *name* of the *creditor,* with an indorsement, under the hand of the commissioner of the said office, expressing the name of the *payer*; and shall deliver such certificate to the governor and the council, *whose receipt* shall *discharge him* from so much of the debt. And the governor and the council shall, in like manner, lay before the General Assembly, once in every year, an account of these *certificates,* specifying the names of the persons *by,* and *for* whom they were *paid;* and shall see to the safe keeping of the *same; subject to the future directions of the legislature:* provided, that the governor and the council may make such allowance, as they shall think reasonable, out of the INTEREST of the money so paid into the loan office, to the wives and children, residing in the state, of *such creditor*.

On the 26th of *April,* 1780, the Defendants in error, paid into the loan office of *Virginia, part* of their debt, to wit, 3,111 1–9 dollars, equal to £933 14 0 *Virginia* currency; and obtained a certificate from the commissioners of the loan office, and a receipt from the governor and the council of *Virginia,* agreeably to the above, in part recited law.

The Defendants in error being sued, on the above bond, in the Circuit Court of *Virginia,* pleaded the above law, and the payment above stated, in bar of so much of the Plaintiff's debt. The plaintiff, to avoid this bar, replied the fourth article of the Definitive Treaty of Peace, between *Great Britain* and the *United States,* of the 3d of *September,* 1783. To this replication there was a great demurrer and joinder. The Circuit Court allowed the demurrer, and the plaintiff brought the present writ of error.

The case is of very great importance, not only from the property that depends on the decision, but because the effect and operation of the treaty are necessarily involved. I wished to decline sitting in the cause, as I had been counsel, some years ago, in a suit in *Maryland,* in favour of *American debtors;* and I consulted with my brethren, who unanimously advised me not to withdraw from the bench. I have endeavored to divest myself of all *former* prejudices, and to form an opinion with impartiality. I have diligently attended to the arguments of the learned counsel, who debated the several questions, that were made in the cause, with great legal abilities, ingenuity and skill. I have given the subject, since the argument, my deliberate investigation, and shall, (as briefly as the case will permit,) deliver the result of it with great dissidence, and the highest respect for those, who entertain a different opinion. I solicit, and I hope I shall meet with, a candid allowance for the many imperfections, which may be discovered in observations hastily drawn up, in the intervals of attendance in court, and the consideration of other very important cases.

The *first* point raised by the counsel for the Plaintiff in error was, "that the legislature of *Virginia* had no *right* to make the law, of the 20th *October,* 1777, above in part recited. If this objection is established, the judgment of the Circuit Court must be reversed; because it destroys the Defendants plea in bar, and leaves him without defence to the Plaintiff's action.

This objection was maintained on *different* grounds by the Plaintiff's counsel. One of them (*Mr. Tilghman*) contended, that the legislature of *Virginia* had *no right* to confiscate *any British* property, because *Virginia* was *part* of the *dismembered empire* of *Great Britain,* and the Plaintiff and Defendants were, all of them, *members* of the *British* nation, *when the debt was contracted,* and therefore, that the laws of independant nations do not apply to the case; and, if applicable, that the legislature of *Virginia* was not justified by the *modern* law and practice of European nations, in confiscating private debts. In support of this opinion, he cited *Vattel Lib.* 3. *c.* 5. *s.* 77, who expresses himself thus: "The sovereign has naturally the *same* right over what his subjects may be indebted to enemies. Therefore, he may confiscate *debts of this nature,* if the term of payment happen in the time of war. But *at present,* in regard to the advantage of safety of *Commerce,* all the sovereigns of Europe have departed from *this rigour;* and, as this *custom* has been *generally* received, he, who should act contrary to it, would injure the *public faith;* for strangers trusted *his* subjects, only from a firm persuasion, that the *general custom* would be observed."

The other counsel for the Plaintiff in error (Mr. *Lewis*) denied any power in the *Virginia* legislature, to confiscate *any British* property, because all such power belonged *exclusively* to Congress; and he contended, that if *Virginia* had a power of confiscation, yet, it did not extend to the confiscation of *debts* by the *modern* law and practice of nations.

I would premise that this objection against the *right* of the *Virginia* legislature to confiscate *British* property, (and especially *debts*) is made on the part of *British* subjects, and *after the treaty of peace,* and not by the government of the *United States.* I would also remark, that the law of *Virginia* was made *after* the declaration of independence by *Virginia,* and also by Congress; and several years *before* the Confederation of the *United States,* which, although agreed to by Congress on the 15th of *November,* 1777, and assented to by ten states, in 1778, was only *finally* completed and ratified on the 1st of *March,* 1781.

I am of opinion that the *exclusive right* of confiscating, during the war, *all and every species of British property,* within the territorial limits of *Virginia,* resided only in the Legislature of that commonwealth. I shall hereafter consider whether the law of the 20th of *October* 1777, operated to *confiscate* or *extinguish British* debts, contracted before the war. It is worthy of remembrance, that Delegates and Representatives were elected, by the people of the several counties and corporations of *Virginia,* to meet in *general convention,* for the purpose of framing a NEW government, by the authority of *the people only;* and that the said Convention met on the 6th of *May,* and continued in session until the 5th of *July* 1776; and, in virtue of their *delegated* power, established a constitution, or form of government, to regulate and determine by *whom,* and in *what manner,* the authority of *the people* of *Virginia* was *thereafter* to be executed. As *the people* of that country were the genuine source and fountain of *all* power, that could be *rightfully* exercised within its limits; they had therefore an unquestionable *right* to grant it to whom they pleased, and under what restrictions or limitations they thought proper. *The people of Virginia,* by their Constitution or *fundamental* law, granted and delegated all their Supreme civil power to a *Legislature,* an *Executive,* and a *Judiciary;* The *first* to make; the *second* to execute; and the last to declare or expound, the laws of the Commonwealth. This abolition of the *Old* Government, and this establishment of a *new* one was the highest act of power, that any people can exercise. From the moment *the people* of *Virginia* exercised *this power,* all dependence on, and connection with *Great Britain* absolutely and forever ceased; and no *formal* declaration of Independence was necessary, although a decent respect for the opinions of mankind required a declaration of the causes, which impelled the separation; and was proper to give notice of the event to the nations of *Europe.*—I hold it as unquestionable, that the *Legislature* of *Virginia* established as I have stated by the authority of the people, was for ever thereafter invested with the *supreme and sovereign power of the state,* and with authority to make any *Laws* in their discretion, to affect the *lives, liberties,* and *property* of all the citizens of that Commonwealth, *with this exception only,* that such laws should not be repugnant to the *Constitution,* or *fundamental* law, which could be subject only to the controul of the *body of the nation,* in cases not to be defined, and which *will always* provide for themselves. The *legislative* power of every nation can only be restrained by its *own constitution:* and it is the duty of its courts of justice not to question the *validity* of any law made in pursuance of the constitution. There is no question but the act of the *Virginia* Legislature (of the 20th of *October* 1777) was within the authority granted to them by *the people* of that country; and this being admitted, it is a necessary result, that the law is obligatory on the courts of *Virginia,* and, in my opinion, on the courts of the *United States.* If *Virginia* as a sovereign State, violated the ancient or modern law of nations, in making the law of the 20th of *October* 1777, she was answerable in her *political* capacity to the *British* nation, whose subjects have been injured in consequence of that law. Suppose a general right to confiscate *British* property, is admitted to be in Congress, and Congress had confiscated all *British* property within the *United States,* including private debts: would it be permitted to contend in any court of the *United States,* that Congress had no power to confiscate such *debts,* by the *modern* law of nations? If the *right* is conceded to be in Congress, it necessarily follows, that she is the judge of the exercise of the right, as to the *extent, mode,* and *manner.* The same reasoning is strictly applicable to *Virginia,* if considered a *sovereign nation;* provided she had not delegated such power to Congress, before the making of the law of *October* 1777, which I will hereafter consider.

In *June* 1776, the Convention of *Virginia formally* declared, that *Virginia* was a free, sovereign, and independent state; and on the 4th of *July,* 1776, following, the *United States,* in Congress assembled, declared the *Thirteen United Colonies* free and independent states; and that as *such,* they had full power to levy war, conclude peace, &c. I consider this as a declaration, not that the United Colonies *jointly,* in a *collective* capacity, were independent states, &c. but that *each* of them was a sovereign and independent state, that is, that *each* of them had a right to govern itself by its own authority, and its own laws, without any controul from any other power upon earth.

Before these solemn acts of separation from the Crown of *Great Britain,* the war between *Great Britain* and the United Colonies, *jointly,* and *separately,* was *a civil* war; but *instantly,* on that great and ever memorable event, the war changed its *nature,* and became a PUBLIC war between *independent governments;* and immediately thereupon ALL the *rights* of *public* war (and all the other rights of an independent nation) attached to the government of *Virginia;* and all the *former political* connexion between *Great Britain* and *Virginia,* and also between their respective subjects, were totally dissolved; and not only the *two nations,* but all the subjects of each, were in a state of war; precisely as in the present war between *Great Britain* and *France. Vatt. Lib.* 3. *c.* 18, *s.* 292. to 295. *lib.* 3. *c.* 5. *s.* 70. 72 and 73.

From the 4th of *July,* 1776, the *American* States were *de facto,* as well as *de jure,* in the possession and actual exercise of all the *rights* of independent governments. On the 6th of *February,* 1778, the King of France entered into a treaty of *alliance* with the *United States;* and on the 8th of *Oct.* 1782, a treaty of Amity and Commerce was concluded between the *United States* and the States General of the *United Provinces.* I have ever considered it as the established doctrine of the *United States,* that their independence originated from, and commenced with, the declaration of Congress, on the 4th of *July,* 1776; and that *no other period* can be fixed on for its commencement; and that all laws made by the legislatures of the several states, *after* the declaration of independence, were the laws of sovereign and independent governments.

That *Virginia* was part of the dismembered *British* empire, can, in my judgment, make no difference in the case. No such distinction is taken by *Vattell* (or any other writer) but *Vattell,* when considering the *rights of war* between *two parties* absolutely independent, and no longer acknowledging a common superior (precisely the case in question) thus expresses himself, *Lib.* 3. *c.* 18 *s.* 295. "In *such* case, the state is dissolved, and the war between the *two parties,* in *every respect,* is the same with that of a *public war* between *two different nations.*" And *Vattell* denies, that *subjects* can acquire *property* in things taken during a CIVIL war.

That the *creditor* and *debtor* were members of the same *empire, when the debt was contracted, cannot* (in my opinion) distinguish the case, for the *same* reasons. A most arbitrary claim was made by the parliament of *Great Britain,* to make laws to bind the people of *America,* in *all cases whatsoever,* and the King of *Great Britain,* with the approbation of parliament, employed, not only the national forces, but hired foreign mercenaries to compel submission to this absurd claim of *omnipotent* power. The resistance against this claim was *just,* and independence became necessary; and the people of the *United States* announced to the people of *Great Britain,* "that they would hold them, as the rest of mankind, *enemies in war, in peace, friends.*" On the declaration of independence, it was in the option of any subject of *Great Britain,* to join their brethren in *America,* or to remain subjects of *Great Britain.* Those who joined us were entitled to all the benefits of our freedom and independence; but those who elected to continue subjects of *Great Britain,* exposed themselves to any loss, that might arise therefrom. By their adhering to the enemies of the *United States,* they *voluntarily* became parties to the injustice and oppression of the *British* government; and they also contributed to carry on the war, and to enslave their former fellow citizens. As members of the *British* government, from their own choice, they became *personally* answerable for the conduct of that government, of which they remained a part; and their property, wherever found (on land or water) became liable to confiscation. On this ground, Congress on the 24th of *July,* 1776, confiscated *any British* property taken on the *seas.* See 2 *Ruth. Inst. lib.* 2. *c.* 9. *s.* 13. *p.* 531. 559. *Vatt. lib.* 2. *c.* 7. *s.* 81. *& c.* 18. *s.* 344. *lib.* 3. *c.* 5. *s.* 74. *& c.* 9. *s.* 161 *&* 193.

The *British* creditor, by the conduct of his sovereign, became an *enemy* to the commonwealth of *Virginia;* and thereby his debt was forfeitable to that government, as a compensation for the damages of an *unjust* war.

It appears to me, that every nation at *war* with another is justifiable, *by the general and strict law of nations,* to seize and confiscate all *moveable* property of its enemy, (of any kind or nature whatsoever) *wherever found,* whether within its territory, or not. *Bynkershoek Q. I. P. de rebus bellicis. Lib.* 1. *c.* 7. *p.* 175. thus delivers his opinion. "*Cum ea sit belli conditia ut bostes sint, omni jure, spoliati proscriptique, rationis est, quascunque res bostium, apud hostes inventas, Dominum mutare, et Fisco cedere.*" "Since it is a condition of war, that enemies, by *every right,* may be plundered, and seized upon, it is reasonable that whatever effects of the enemy are found with us who are his enemy, should change their master, and be confiscated, or *go into the treasury.*" S. P. *Lee on Capt. c.* 8. *p.* 111. *S. P.* 2. *Burl. p.* 209. *s.* 12. *p.* 219. *s.* 2. *p.* 221. *s.* 11. *Bynekershoek* the same book, and chapter, *page* 177. thus expresses himself: "*Quod dixi de actionibus recte publicandis ita demum obtinet. Si quod subditi nostri hostibus nostris debent, princeps a subditis suis, revera exegerit: Si exegerit recte solutum est, si non exegerit, pace facta, reviviscit jus pristinum creditoris; quia occupatio, quæ bello sit, magis in facto, quam in potestate juris consistit. Nomina igitur, non exacta, tempore belli quodammodo intermori videntur, sed per pacem, genere quodam postliminii, ad priorem dominum reverti. Secùndum hæ inter gentes sere convenit ut nominibus bello publicatis, pace deinde facta, exacta censeantur periisse, et maneant extincta; non autem exacta reviviscant, et restituantur veris creditoribus.*"

"What I have said of *things in action* "*being rightfully* confiscated, holds thus: "If the prince truly *exacts* from his subjects, "what they owed to the enemy; if he shall "have exacted it, it is *rightfully* paid, if he "shall not have exacted it, peace being made, "the *former* right of the creditor *revives;* "because the seizure, which is made during "war, consists more in *fact* than in right. "Debts, therefore, not exacted, seem as it "were to be forgotten in time of war, but "upon peace, *by a kind of postliminy,* return "to their former proprietor. Accordingly, it "is for the most part agreed among nations, "*that things in action,* being confiscated in "war, the peace being made, those which "were *paid* are deemed to have *perished,* "and remain *extinct;* but those *not paid* "revive, and are restored to their true "creditors. *Vatt. lib.* 4. *s.* 22. *S. P. Lee an* "*Capt. c.* 8. *p.* 118."

That this is the law of nations, as held in *Great Britain,* appears from Sir *Thomas Parker's Rep. p.* 267 (11 *William* 3*d*) in which it was determined, that *choses in action* belonging to an *alien enemy* are *forfeitable* to the crown of *Great Britain;* but there must be a commission and inquisition to entitle the crown; and if peace is concluded *before* inquisition taken, *it discharges the cause of forfeiture.*

The *right* to confiscate the property of enemies, during war, is derived from *a state of war,* and is called the *rights of war.* This right originates from *self-preservation,* and is adopted as one of the means to weaken an enemy, and to strengthen ourselves. *Justice,* also, is another pillar on which it may rest; to wit, a right to reimburse the expence of an *unjust* war. *Vatt. lib.* 3. *c.* 8. *s.* 138, *& c.* 9. *s.* 161.

But it is said, if *Virginia* had a right to confiscate *British property,* yet by the *modern* law, and practice of *European* actions, she was not justified in confiscating *debts* due from her citizens to subjects of *Great Britain;* that is, private debts. *Vattell* is the only author relied on (or that can be found) to maintain the distinction between confiscating *private* debts, and *other property* of an enemy. He admits the *right* to confiscate *such debts,* if the term of payment happen in the time of war; but this limitation on the right is no where else to be found. His opinion alone will not be sufficient to restrict the right to that case only. It does not appear in the present case, whether the time of payment happened before, or during the war. If this restriction is just, the Plaintiff ought to have shewn the fact. *Vattell* adds, "at present, in regard to the advantages and safety of *commerce, all* the sovereigns of Europe have departed from *this rigour;* and this *custom* has been *generally* received, and he who should act contrary to it (the custom) would injure the public faith." From these expressions it may be fairly inferred, that, by the rigour of the law of nations, *private debts* to enemies might be confiscated, as well as any other of their property; but that a *general custom* had prevailed in Europe to the contrary; founded on *commercial* reasons. The law of nations may be considered of three kinds, to wit, *general, conventional,* or *customary.* The *first* is *universal,* or established by the general consent of mankind, and binds *all nations.* The *second* is founded on *express* consent, and is not universal, and only binds those nations that have assented to it. The *third* is founded on TACIT consent; and is only obligatory on those nations, who have adopted it. The relaxation or departure from the *strict rights of war* to confiscate private debts, by the *commercial* nations of Europe, was not binding on the state of *Virginia,* because founded *on custom only;* and she was at liberty to reject, or adopt the *custom,* as she pleased. The conduct of nations at war, is generally governed and limited by their exigencies and necessities. *Great Britain* could not claim from the *United States,* or any of them, any relaxation of the *general* law of nations, *during the late war,* because she did not consider it, as a *civil* war, and much less as a *public* war, but she gave it the odious name of *rebellion;* and she refused to the citizens of the *United States* the *strict rights of ordinary* war.

It cannot be forgotten, that the Parliament of *Great Britain,* by statute (10 *Geo.* 3. *c.* 5. *in* 1776) declared, that the vessels and cargoes belonging to the people of *Virginia,* and the twelve other colonies, found and taken on the high seas, should be liable to seizure and confiscation, as the property of open enemies; and, that the mariners and crews should be taken and considered as having *voluntarily* entered into the service of the King of *Great Britain;* and that the killing and destroying the persons and property of the *Americans, before* the passing this act, was *just and lawful:* And it is well known that, in consequence of this statute, very considerable property of the citizens of *Virginia* was seized on the high seas, and confiscated; and that other considerable property, found within that Commonwealth, was seized and applied to the use of the *British* army, or navy. *Vattel lib.* 3. *c.* 12. *sec.* 191. says, and reason confirms his opinion, "That whatever is lawful for one nation to do, in time of war, is lawful for the other." The law of nations is part of the municipal law of *Great Britain,* and by her laws all *moveable* property of enemies, found within the kingdom, is considered as forfeited to the crown, as the head of the nation; but if no inquisition is taken to ascertain the owners to be *alien enemies, before peace* takes place, the cause of forfeiture is discharged, by the peace *ipso facto. Sir Thomas Parker's Rep. pa.* 267. This doctrine agrees with *Bynk. lib.* 1. *c.* 7. *pa.* 177. and *Lee on Capt. ch.* 8. *p.* 118. that *debts* not confiscated and *paid,* revive on peace. *Lee* says, "Debts, therefore, which are not *taken hold of,* seem, as it were, suspended and forgotten in time of war; but by a peace return to their former proprietor by a *kind of postliminy.*" Mr. *Lee,* who wrote since *Vattel,* differs from him in opinion, that *private debts* are not confiscable, *pag.* 114. He thus delivers himself: "By the law of nations, *Rights and Credits* are not less in our power than *other goods;* why, therefore, should we *regard the rights of war* in regard to *one,* and not as to the *other?* And when nothing occurs, which gives room for a proper distinction; the *general* law of nations ought to prevail." He gives many examples of *confiscating debts,* and concludes, (*p.* 119). "All which prove, that not only *actions,* but all other things whatsoever, are forfeited in time of war, and are often exacted."

Great Britain does not consider herself bound to depart from the rigor of the *general* law of nations, because the *commercial* powers of Europe wish to adopt a more *liberal* practice. It may be recollected, that it is an established principle of the law of nations, "that the goods of a *friend* are free in an *enemy's* vessel; and an *enemy's* goods lawful prize in the vessel of a *friend.*" This may be called the *general law* of nations. In 1780 the Empress of Russia proposed a relaxation of this rigor of the laws of nations, "That all the effects belonging to the subjects of the *belligerent powers* shall be free on board *neutral* vessels, except only *contraband* articles." This proposal was acceded to by the *neutral* powers of *Sweden, Denmark,* the *States General of the United Provinces, Prussia* and *Portugal; France* and *Spain,* two of the powers at war, did not *oppose* the principle, and *Great Britain* only declined to adopt it, and she still adheres to the *rigorous* principle of the law of nations. Can this conduct of *Great Britain* be objected to her as an *uncivilized and barbarous practice?* The confiscating *private debts* by *Virginia* has been branded with those terms of reproach, and very improperly in my opinion.

It is admitted, that *Virginia* could not confiscate *private debts* without a violation of the *modern* law of nations, yet is in *fact,* she has so done, the law is obligatory on all the citizens of *Virginia,* and on her Courts of Justice; and, in my opinion, on all the Courts of the *United States.* If *Virginia* by such conduct violated the law of nations, she was answerable to *Great Britain,* and *such injury could only be redressed in the treaty of peace.* Before the establishment of the national government, *British* debts could only be sued for in the *state* court. This, alone, proves that the several states possessed a power over debts. If the crown of *Great Britain* had, according to the *mode* of proceeding in that country, confiscated, or forfeited *American debts,* would it have been permitted in any of the courts of *Westminster Hall,* to have denied the *right* of the crown, and that its power was restrained by the *modern* law of nations? Would it not have been answered, that the *British* nation was to justify her own conduct; but that her courts were to obey her laws.

It appears to me, that there is another and conclusive ground, which effectually precluded any objection, *since the peace,* on the part of *Great Britain, as a nation,* or on the part of any of *her subjects,* against the *right* of *Virginia* to confiscate *British debts,* or any other *British* property, during the war; even on the admission that such confiscation was in violation of the ancient or *modern* law of nations.

If the Legislature of *Virginia confiscated* or *extinguished* the debt in question, by the law of the 20th of *October* 1777, as the Defendants in error contend, this *confiscation* or *extinguishment,* took place in 1777, *flagrante Bello;* and the definitive treaty of peace was ratified in 1783. What effects flow from a treaty of peace, even if the *confiscation,* or *extinguishment* of the debt was contrary to the law of nations, *and* the stipulation in the 4th article of the treaty does *not* provide for the recovery of the debt in question?

I apprehend that the treaty of peace abolishes the *subject* of the war, and that after peace is concluded, neither the matter in dispute, nor the *conduct* of either party, during the war, can ever be revived, or brought into contest again. All violencies, injuries, or damages sustained by the government, or people of either, during the war, are buried in oblivion; and *all those things* are *implied* by the very treaty of peace; and therefore not necessary to be expressed. Hence it follows, that the restitution of, or compensation for, *British* property confiscated, or extinguished, during the war, by any of the *United States,* could only be provided for by the treaty of peace; and if there had been no provision, respecting these subjects, in the treaty, they could not be agitated *after the treaty,* by the *British* government, much less by her subjects in courts of justice. If a nation, during a war, conducts herself contrary to the law of nations, and no notice is taken of such conduct in the *treaty of peace,* it is thereby *so far* considered *lawful,* as never afterwards to be revived, or to be a subject of complaint.

Vattel lib. 4. *sect.* 21. *p.* 121. says, "The state of things at the *instant* of the treaty, is held to be *legitimate,* and any change to be made in it requires an *express specification* in the treaty; consequently, all things not mentioned in the treaty, are to remain as they were at the conclusion of it.—All the *damages* caused during the war are likewise buried in oblivion; and no plea is allowable for those, the reparation of which is *not mentioned* in the treaty: *They are looked on as if they had never happened.*" The *same* principle applies to *injuries* done by one nation to another, on occasion of, and during the war. *See Grotius lib.* 3. *c.* 8. *sect.* 4.

The Baron *De Wolfuis,* 1222, says, *"De quibus nibil dictum ea manent quo sunt loco."* Things of which nothing is said remain in the state in which they are.

It is the opinion of the celebrated and judicious Doctor *Rutherforth,* that a nation in a *just war* may seize upon any *moveable* goods of an enemy, (and he makes no distinction as to *private* debts) but that whilst the war continues, the nation has, *of right,* nothing but the *custody* of the goods taken; and if the nation has granted to *private* captors (as privateers) the property of goods taken by them, and on peace, *restitution* is agreed on, that the *nation* is obliged to make restitution, and not the *private* captors; and if on peace no restitution is stipulated, that the *full property* of *moveable* goods, taken from the enemy during the war, passes, by *tacit* consent, to the nation that takes them. This I collect as the *substance* of his opinion in *lib.* 2. *c.* 9, from *p.* 558 to 573.

I shall conclude my observations on the *right* of *Virginia* to confiscate *any British* property, by remarking, that the *validity* of such a law would not be questioned in the Court of Chancery of *Great Britain;* and I confess the doctrine seemed strange to me in an *American* Court of Justice. In the case of *Wright and Nutt,* Lord Chancellor *Thurlow* declared, that he considered an act of the State of *Georgia,* passed in 1782, for the confiscation of the real and personal estate of *Sir James Wright,* and also his *debts,* as a law of an *independent country;* and concluded with the following observation, that the law of every country, must be *equally* regarded in the Courts of Justice of *Great Britain,* whether the law was a *barbarous* or *civilised* institution, or wise or foolish. *H. Black. Rep. p.* 149. In the case of *Folliot* against *Ogden, Lord Loughborough,* Chief Justice of the Court of Common Pleas, in delivering the judgment of the court, declared "that the act of the State of *New York,* passed in 1779, for attaining, forfeiting, and confiscating the real and personal estate of *Folliott,* the Plaintiff, was certainly of as *full validity,* as the act of any independent State. *H. Black. Rep. p.* 135. On a writ of error *Lord Kenyon,* Chief Justice of the Court of King's Bench, and Judge *Grose,* delivered direct contrary sentiments; but Judges *Ashurst* and *Buller* were silent. 3 *Term Rep. p.* 726.

From these observations, and the authority of *Bynkersboek, Lee, Burlamaque,* and *Rutherforth,* I conclude, that *Virginia* had a *right,* as a sovereign and independent nation, to confiscate *any British* property *within its territory, unless* she had *before* delegated that power to Congress, which Mr. *Lewis* contended she had done. The proof of the allegation that *Virginia* had transferred this authority to Congress, lies on those who make it; because if she had parted with such power it must be conceded, that she once *rightfully* possessed it.

It has been enquired what powers Congress possessed from the *first* meeting, in *September* 1774, until the ratification of the articles of confederation, on the 1st of *March,* 1781? It appears to me, that the powers of Congress, *during that whole period,* were derived from *the people* they represented, expressly given, through the medium of their State Conventions, or State Legislatures; *or* that after they were exercised they were impliedly ratified by the acquiescence and obedience of the people. After the confederacy was compleated, the powers of Congress rested on the authority of the *State Legislatures,* and the *implied ratifications of the people;* and was a *government* over *governments.* The powers of Congress originated from necessity, and arose out of, and were only limited by, events or, in other words, they were *revolutionary* in their very nature. Their extent depended on the exigencies and necessities of public affairs. It was absolutely and indispensably necessary that Congress should possess the power of *conducting* the war against *Great Britain,* and therefore if not expressly given by all, (as it was by some of the States) I do not hesitate to say, that Congress did rightfully possess *such* power. The authority to make *war,* of necessity implies the power to make *peace;* or the war must be perpetual, I entertain this general idea, that the several States retained all *internal sovereignty;* and that Congress properly possessed the great *rights* of *external sovereignty:* Among others, the right to make treaties of commerce and alliance; as with *France* on the 6th of *February* 1778. In deciding on the powers of Congress, and of the several States, BEFORE the confederation, I see but one safe rule, namely, that all the powers ACTUALLY exercised by Congress, *before* that period were *rightfully* exercised, on the presumption not to be controverted, that they were so authorized by the people they represented, by an *express,* or *implied grant;* and that all the powers exercised by the State Conventions or State Legislatures were also *rightfully* exercised, on the *same presumption* of authority from the people. That Congress did not possess *all* the powers of *war* is self-evident from this consideration alone, that she never attempted to lay any kind of *tax* on the people of the *United States,* but relied altogether on the State Legislatures to impose taxes, to raise money to carry on the war, and to sink the emissions of all the paper money issued by Congress. It was expressly provided, in the 8th article of the confederation, that "all *charges of war* (and all other expences for the common defence and general welfare) and allowed by Congress, shall be defrayed out of a common Treasury, *to be supplied by the several States* in proportion to the value of the land in each State; and *the taxes for paying the said proportion, shall be levied by the Legislatures of the several States.*" In every free country the power of laying taxes is considered a *legislative* power over the *property* and *persons* of the citizens; and this power the people of the *United States,* granted to their State Legislatures, and they neither could, nor did transfer it to Congress; but on the contrary they expressly stipulated that it should remain with them. It is an incontrovertible *fact* that Congress never attempted to confiscate any kind of *British* property within the *United States* (except what their army, or vessels of war captured) and thence I conclude that Congress did not conceive the power was vested in them. Some of the states did exercise this power, and thence I infer, they possessed it. —On the 23d of *March,* 3d of *April,* and 24th of *July,* 1776, Congress confiscated *British* property, taken on the high *seas.**

The *second* point made by the council for the Plaintiff in error was, "if the legislature of *Virginia* had a *right* to confiscate *British debts,* yet she did *not* exercise that right by the act of the 20th *October,* 1777." If this objection is well founded, the Plaintiff in error must have judgment for the money covered by the plea of that law, and the payment under it. The preamble recites, that the public faith, and the law and the usage of nations require, that *debts* incurred, during the connexion with *Great Britain,* should *not be confiscated.* No language can possibly be stronger to express the opinion of the legislature of *Virginia,* that *British* debts ought *not* to be confiscated, and if the words or effect and operation, of the enacting clause, are ambiguous or doubtful, such construction should be made as not to extend the provisions in the enacting clause, beyond the intention of the legislature, so clearly expressed in the preamble; but if the words in the enacting clause, in their nature, import, and common understanding, are not ambiguous, but plain and clear, and their operation and effect certain, there is no room for *construction.* It is not an uncommon case for a legislature, in a preamble, to declare their intention to provide for *certain cases,* or to punish *certain offences,* and in enacting clauses to include other cases, and *other* offences. But I believe *very few* instances can be found in which the legislature declared that a thing ought not to be

* *See the Ordinance of the 30th of November, 1781. See, also, the Resolution of the 23d of November, 1781, in which Congress recommended to the states, to pass laws to punish infractions of the law of nations.*

done, and afterwards did the very thing they reprobated. There can be no doubt that strong words in the enacting part of a law may extend it beyond the preamble. If the preamble is contradicted by the enacting clause, as to the *intention* of the legislature, it must prevail, on the principle that the legislature changed their intention.

I am of opinion, that the law of the 20th of *October,* 1777, and the payment in virtue thereof, amounts either to *a confiscation,* or *extinguishment,* of so much of the *debt* as was paid into the loan office of *Virginia.* 1st. The law makes *it lawful* for a citizen of *Virginia* indebted to a subject of *Great Britain* to pay the *whole,* or *any part,* of his debt, into the loan office of that commonwealth. 2d. It directs the *debtor* to take a certificate of his payment, and to deliver it to the governor and the council; and it declares that the *receipt* of the governor and the council for the certificate shall discharge him (the debtor) from so much of the *debt* as he paid into the loan office. 3d. It enacts that the certificate shall be subject to the future direction of the legislature. And 4thly, it provides, that the governor and council *may* make such allowance, as they shall think reasonable, out of the INTEREST of the money paid, to the wives and children, residing within the state, of such *creditor.* The payment of the *debtor* into the loan office is made a *lawful* act. The public receive the money, and they discharge the *debtor,* and they make the certificate (which is the evidence of the payment) subject to their direction; and they benevolently appropriate *part* of the money paid, to wit, the *interest* of the debt, to such of the family of the *creditor* as may live within the state. *ALL* these acts are plainly a legislative *interposition* between the creditor and debtor; annihilates the right of the creditor; and is an exercise of the right of *ownership* over the money; for the giving *part* to the family of the creditor, under the restriction of being residents of the state, or to a stranger, can make no difference. The government of *Virginia* had precisely the *same* right of dispose of the *whole,* as of *part* of the debt. Whether *all these acts* amount to a *confiscation* of the debt, or not, may be disputed according to the different ideas entertained of the proper meaning of the word *confiscation.* I am inclined to think that all these acts, *collectively* considered, are substantially a confiscation of the debt. The verb confiscate is derived from the latin, con *with, and* Fiscus a basket, or hamper, in which the Emperor's treasure was *formerly* kept. The meaning of the word to *confiscate* is to transfer property from PRIVATE to *public* use; or to forfeit property to the prince, or state. In the language of Mr. *Lee,* (*page* 118) *the debt was taken hold of;* and this he considers as confiscation. But if strictly speaking, the debt was not *confiscated,* yet it certainly was *extinguished* as between the creditor and debtor; the debt was *legally* paid, and of consequence *extinguished.* The state interfered and received the debt, and discharged the debtor from his *creditor;* and not from the *state,* as suggested. The debtor owed nothing to the state of *Virginia,* but she had a right to take the debt or not at her pleasure. To say that the discharge was from the *state,* and not from the *debtor,* implies that the debtor was under some obligation or duty to pay the state, what he owed his *British* creditor. If the debtor was to remain charged to his creditor, notwithstanding his payment; not one farthing would have been paid into the loan office. Such a construction, therefore, is too vilent and not to be admitted. If *Virginia* had confiscated *British* debts, and received the debt in question, and said nothing more, the debtor would have been discharged by the *operation of the law.* In the present case, there is an *express* discharge on payment, certificate, and receipt.

It appears to me that the plea, by the Defendant, of the act of Assembly, and the payment agreeably to its provisions, which is admitted, is a bar to the plaintiff's action, for *so much* of his debt as he paid into the loan office; unless the plea is avoided, or destroyed, by the Plaintiff's replication of the fourth article of the Definitive Treaty of Peace, between *Great Britain* and the *United States,* on the 3d of *September,* 1783.

The question then may be stated thus: Whether the 4th article of the said treaty *nullifies* the law of Virginia, passed on the 20th of *October,* 1777; destroys the payment made under it; and revives the debt, and gives a right of recovery thereof, against *the original debtor?*

It was doubted by one of the counsel for the Defendants in error (Mr. *Marshall*) whether Congress had a *power* to make a treaty, that could operate to *annul* a *legislative* act of any of the states, and to destroy *rights* acquired by, or vested in individuals, in virtue of such acts. Another of the Defendant's council (Mr. *Campbell*) expressly, and with great zeal, denied that Congress possessed such *power.*

But a few remarks will be necessary to shew the inadmissibility of this objection to the power of Congress.

1st. The legislatures of all the states, have often exercised the power of taking the property of its citizens for the use of the public, but they uniformly compensated the proprietors. The principle to maintain this right is for the public good, and to that the interest of individuals must yield. The instances are many; and among them are lands taken for forts, magazines, or arsenals; or for public roads, or canals; or to erect towns.

2d. The legislatures of all the states have *often* exercised the power of divesting rights vested; and even of impairing, and, in some instances, of almost annihilating the obligation of *contracts,* as by tender laws, which made an offer to pay, and a refusal to receive, paper money, for a *specie* debt, an *extinguishment,* to the amount tendered.

3d. If the Legislature of *Virginia* could, by a law, *annul* any former law; I apprehend that the effect would be to destroy all rigths acquired under the law so nullified.

4th. If the Legislature of *Virginia* could not by *ordinary acts of legislation,* do these things, yet possessing the supreme sovereign power of the state, she certainly could do them, by a *treaty of peace;* if she had not parted with the power or making such treaty. If *Virginia* had such power *before* she delegated it to Congress, it follows, that *afterwards* that body possessed it. Whether *Virginia* parted with the power of making treaties of peace, will be seen by a perusal of the 9th article of the Confederation (ratified by all the states, on the 1st of *March,* 1781,) in which it was declared, "that the *United States* in Congress assembled, shall have the *sole and exclusive right and power* of determining on *peace,* or *war,* except in the two cases mentioned in the 6th article; and of entering into treaties and alliances, with a *proviso,* when made, respecting *commerce.*" This grant has no restriction, nor is there any limitation on the power in any part of the confederation. A right to make peace, necessarily includes the power of determining *on what terms peace shall be* made. A power to make *treaties* must of necessity imply a power, to decide the terms on which they shall be made: A war between two nations can only be concluded by *treaty.*

Surely, the sacrificing *public,* or *private,* property, to obtain *peace* cannot be the cases in which a treaty would be *void. Vatt. lib.* 2 *c.* 12. *s.* 106. 161. *p.* 173. *lib.* 6. *c.* 2. *s.* 2. It seems to me that treaties made by Congress, according to the Confederation, were superior to the laws of the states; because the Confederation made them obligatory on all the states. They were so declared by Congress on the 13th of April, 1787; were so admitted by the legislatures and executives of most of the states; and were so decided by the judiciary of the general government, and by the judiciaries of some of the state governments.

If *doubts* could exist *before* the establishment of the present national government, they must be *entirely* removed by the 6th article of the Constitution, which provides "That all treaties *made,* or which shall be made, under the authority of the *United States,* shall be the *Supreme law of the land;* and the Judges in every State shall be bound thereby, any thing in the *Constitution,* or *laws,* of any State to the contrary notwithstanding." There can be no limitation on the power of *the people* of the *United States.* By their authority the State Constitutions were made, and by their authority the Constitution of the *United States* was established; and they had the power to change or abolish the State Constitutions, or to make them yield to the general government, and to treaties made by their authority. A treaty cannot be the *Supreme law* of the land, that is of all the *United States,* if any act of a *State Legislature* can stand in its way. If the Constitution of a State (which is the *fundamental* law of the State, and paramount to its Legislature) must give way to a treaty; and fall before it; can it be questioned, whether the *less* power, an act of the State Legislature, must not be prostrate? It is the declared will of *the people* of the *United States* that every treaty made, by the authority of the *United States,* shall be superior to the *Constitution* and *laws* of *any individual State;* and their will alone is to decide.—If a law of a State, contrary to a treaty, is not void, but *voidable only* by a repeal, or nullification by a State Legislature, this certain consequence follows, that the will of a *small part* of the *United States* may controul or defeat the will of the *whole. The people of America* have been pleased to declare, that all treaties made *before* the establishment of the National *Constitution,* or *laws* of any of the States, contrary to a treaty, shall be disregarded.

Four things are apparent on a view of this 6th article of the National Constitution.

1st. That it is *Retrospective,* and is to be considered in the *same* light as if the Constitution had been established before the making of the treaty of 1783. 2d. That the Constitution, or laws, of any of the States so far as either of them shall be found contrary to that treaty are by force of the said article, prostrated before the treaty. 3d. That consequently the treaty of 1783 has superior power to the *Legislature* of any State, because no Legislature of any State has any kind of power over the Constitution, which was its *creator.* 4thly. That it is the declared duty of the State Judges to determine any Constitution, or laws of any State, contrary to that treaty (or any other) made under the authority of the *United States, null and void.* National or Federal Judges are bound by duty and oath to the time conduct*.

The argument, that Congress had not power to make the 4th article of the treaty of peace, if its intent and operation was to *annul* the laws of any of the States, and to destroy *vested* rights (which the Plaintiff's Council contended to be the object and effect of the 4th article) was unnecessary, but on the supposition that this court possess a power to decide, whether this article of the treaty is within the authority delegated to that body, by the articles of confederation. Whether this court constitutionally possess such a power is not necessary now to determine, because I am fully satisfied that Congress were invested with the authority to make the stipulation in the 4th article. If the court possess a power to declare treaties *void,* I shall never exercise it, but in a very clear case indeed. One further remark will shew how very circumspect the court ought to be before they would decide against the *right* of Congress to make the stipulation objected to. If Congress had no power (under the confederation) to make the 4th article of the treaty, and for want of power that article is void, would it not be in the *option* of the crown of *Great Britain* to say, whether the *other* articles, in the *same* treaty, shall be obligatory on the *British* nation?

I will now proceed to the consideration of the treaty of 1783. It is evident on a perusal of it what were the great and principal objects in view by *both* parties. There were *four* on the part of the *United States,* to wit. 1st. An acknowledgment of their independence, by the crown of *Great Britain.* 2d. A settlement of their *western* bounds. 3d. The right of fishery: and 4thly. The free navigation of the *Mississippi.* There were *three* on the part of *Great Britain,* to wit, 1st. A recovery by *British* Merchants, of the value in *sterling* money, of debts contracted, by the citizens of *America, before* the treaty. 2d. Restitution of the confiscated property of *real British* subjects, and of persons residents in districts in possession of the *British* forces, and who had not borne arms against the *United States;* and a *conditional* restoration of the confiscated property of all *other persons*: and 3dly. A prohibition of all *future* confiscations, and *prosecutions.* The following facts were of the most public notoriety, at the time when the treaty was made, and therefore must have been very well known to the gentlemen who assented to it. 1st. That *British* debts, to a great amount, had been paid into some of the State Treasuries, or loan offices, in paper money of very little value, either under laws confiscating debts, or under laws authorising payment of such debts in paper money, and discharging the *debtors.* 2d. That tender laws had existed in all the states; and that by some of those laws, a tender and a refusal to accept, by principal or *factor,* was declared an *extinguishment of the debt.* From the knowledge that *such* laws had existed there was good reason to *fear* that *similar* laws, with the *Same* or less consequences, might be again made, (and the fact really happened) and prudence required to guard the British creditors against them. 3d. That in some of the States property, of any kind, might be paid, *at an appraisement,* in discharge of any execution. 4th. That laws were in force in some of the States, at the time of the treaty, which prevented suits by *British* creditors. 5th. That laws were in force in other of the States, at the time of the treaty, to prevent suits by *any person* for a *limited time.* All these laws created *legal impediments,* of one kind or another, to the recovery of many *British* debts, contracted *before* the war; and in many cases compelled the receipt of property instead of gold and silver.

To secure the recovery of *British debts,* it was by the latter part of the 5th article, agreed as follows, "That all persons who have any interest in *confiscated lands,* by DEBTS, should meet with no *lawful impediment* in the prosecution of their just rights."

* *See the oath in the act of the 24th of September, 1789. 1 vol. p. 53. f. 8. Swift's edition.*

This provision clearly related to *debts* secured by mortgages on lands in fee simple, which were afterwards confiscated; or to *debts* on judgments, which were a *lien* on lands, which also were afterwards confiscated, and where such debts on mortgages, or judgments, had been paid into the State Treasuries, and the debtors discharged. This stipulation was absolutely necessary if *such debts* were intended to be paid. The pledge, or security by *lien,* had been confiscated and sold. *British* subjects being *aliens,* could neither recover the possession of the lands by ejectment, nor foreclose the equity of redemption; nor could they claim the money secured by a mortgage, or have the benefit of a *lien* from a judgment, if the debtor had paid his debt into the Treasury, and been discharged. If a British subject, either of those cases, prosecuted his just right, it could only be in a court of justice, and if any of the above causes were set up as a *lawful impediment,* the courts were bound to decide, whether this article of the treaty nullified the laws confiscating the lands, and also the purchases made under them, or the laws authorizing payment of such debts to the State; or whether *aliens* were enabled, by this article, to hold lands mortgaged to them before the war. In all these cases, it seems to me, that the courts, in which the cases arose, were the only proper authority to decide, whether the case was within this article of the treaty, and the operation and effect of it. One instance among many will illustrate my meaning. Suppose a mortgagor paid the mortgage money into the public Treasury, and *afterwards* sold the land, would not the *British* creditor, under this article, be entitled to a remedy against the mortgaged lands?

The 4th article of the treaty is in these words: "It is agreed that *creditors,* on either side, shall meet with no *lawful impediment* to the recovery of the full value, in sterling money, of all *bona fide* debts, *heretofore contracted.*"

Before I consider this article of the treaty, I will adopt the following remarks, which I think applicable, and which may be found in Dr. *Rutherforth* and *Vattel.* (2 *Ruth.* 307 *to* 315. *Vattel lib.* 2. *c. sect,* 263 *and* 271.) The intention of the framers of the treaty, must be collected from a view of the *whole* instrument, and from the *words* made use of by them to express their intention, or from *probable* or *rational conjectures.* If the words express the meaning of the parties *plainly, distinctly,* and *perfectly,* there ought to be no other means of interpretation; but if the words are *obscure,* or *ambiguous,* or *imperfect,* recourse must be had to *other* means of interpretation, and in these *three* cases, we must collect the meaning from the words or from *probable or rational conjectures,* or from *both.* When we collect the intention from the *words only,* as they lie in the writing before us, it is a *literal interpretation;* and indeed if the *words,* and the construction of a writing, are *clear* and *precise,* we can scarce call it interpretation to collect the intention of the writer from thence. The *principal* rule to be observed in *literal interpretation,* is to follow that sense, in respect both of the *words,* and the *construction,* which is agreeable to common use.

If the recovery of the present debt is not within the clear and manifest *intention* and *letter* of the 4th article of the treaty, and if it was not intended by it to *annul* the law of *Virginia,* mentioned in the plea, and to destroy the payment under it, and to *revive* the right of the *creditor* against his *original debtor;* and if the treaty cannot effect *all* these things, I think the court ought to determine in favour of the Defendants in error. Under this impression, it is altogther unnecessary to notice the several rules laid down by the Council for the Defendants in error, for the *construction* of the treaty.

I will examine the 4th article of the treaty in its *several parts;* and endeavour to affix the plain and natural meaning of each part.

To take the 4th article in order as it stands.

1st. "It is agreed," that is, it is *expressly* contracted; and it appears from what follows, that *certain* things shall *not* take place. This stipulation is *direct.* The distinction is self-evident, between a thing that shall *not* happen, and an agreement that a third power shall prevent a certain thing being done. The *first* is obligatory on the *parties contracting.* The *latter* will depend on the will of *another;* and although the parties contracting, had power to lay him under a *moral* obligation for compliance, yet there is a very great difference in the two cases. This diversity appears in the treaty.

2d. "That creditors on either side," without doubt meaning *British and American creditors.*

3d. "Shall meet with no *lawful impediment,*" that is, with no obstacle (or bar) arising from the common law, or acts of Parliament, or acts of Congress, or acts of any of the States, then in existence, or thereafter to be made, that would, in any manner, operate to prevent the recovery of *such* debts, as the treaty contemplated. A *lawful* impediment to prevent a recovery of a debt can only be *matter of law* pleaded in bar to the action. If the word *lawful* had been omitted, the impediment would not be confined to matter of *law*. The prohibition that *no lawful* impediment shall be *interposed,* is the same as that *all* lawful impediment shall be *removed*. The meaning cannot be satisfied by the removal of *one* impediment, and leaving *another;* and *a fortiori* by taking away the *less* and leaving the *greater*. These words have both a *retrospective* and *future aspect*.

4th. "To the recovery," that is, to the right of action, judgment, and execution, and receipt of the money, without impediments in courts of justice, which could only be by plea, (as in the present case) or by proceedings, *after judgment,* to compel receipt of paper money, or property, instead of sterling money. The word *recovery* is very comprehensive, and operates, in the present case, to give remedy from the commencement of suit, to the receipt of the money.

5th. "In the full value in *sterling* money," that is, *British* creditors shall not be obliged to receive *paper money,* or *property at a valuation,* or any thing else but the full value of their debts, according to the exchange with *Great Britain*. This provision is clearly *restricted* to *British* debts, *contracted before the treaty,* and cannot relate to debts contracted *afterwards,* which would be dischargeable according to *contract,* and the laws of the State where entered into. This provision has also a *future* aspect in this particular, namely, that no *lawful* impediment, no law of any of the States made *after* the treaty, shall oblige *British* creditors to receive their debts, *contracted before* the treaty, in *paper* money, or *property at appraisement,* or in any thing but the value in sterling money. The obvious intent of these words was to prevent the operation of *past* and *future tender laws;* or *past and future* laws, authorizing the discharge of *executions* for such debts by *property at a valuation*.

6th. "Of all *bona fide* debts," that is, debts of every species, kind, or nature, whether by mortgage, if a covenant therein for payment; or by *judgments,* specialties, or simple *contracts*. But the debts contemplated were to be *bona fide debts,* that is, *bona fide contracted before* the peace, and contracted with good faith, or honestly, and without covin, and not kept on foot fraudulently. *Bona fide* is a *legal technical* expression; and the law of *Great Britain* and this country has annexed a certain idea to it. It is a term used in statutes in *England,* and in acts of Assembly of all the States, and signifies a thing done *really,* with a *good faith,* without *fraud,* or *deceit,* or *collusion,* or *trust*. The words *bona fide* are *restrictive,* for a debt may be for a valuable *consideration,* and yet not *bona fide*. A debt must be *bona fide* at the *time of its commencement,* or it never can become so *afterwards*. The words *bona fide,* were not *prefixed* to describe the *nature* of the debt *at the time of the treaty,* but the *nature* of the debt *at the time it was contracted*. Debts created *before* the war, were almost the only debts in the contemplation of the treaty; although debts contracted *during the war* were covered by the general provision, taking in debts from the most distant period of time, to the date of the treaty. The recovery, where no *lawful* impediments were to be interposed, was to have *two* qualifications: 1st. The debts were to be *bona fide contracted;* and, 2d, they were to be contracted *before the peace*.

7th. "Heretofore contracted," that is, entered into at any period of time *before the date of the treaty;* without regard to the length or distance of time. These words are *descriptive* of the *particular* debts that might be recovered; and *relate back to the time such debts were contracted*. The *time* of the *contract* was plainly to designate the *particular* debts that might be recovered. A debt entered into *during the war,* would not have been recoverable, unless under this description of a debt contracted at *any time before the treaty*.

If the words of the 4th article taken *separately,* truly bear the meaning I have given them, their sense *collectively,* cannot be mistaken, and must be the *same*.

The next enquiry is, whether the debt in question, is one of those, described in this article. It is very clear that the article contemplated *no debts* but those contracted *before the treaty;* and *no debts* but only *those* to the recovery whereof some *lawful* impediment might be interposed. The present debt was contracted *before* the war, and to the recovery of it a *lawful* impediment, to wit, a law of *Virginia* and payment under it, is pleaded in bar. There can be no doubt that the debt sued for, is within the *description,* if I have given a proper interpretation of the words. If the treaty had been silent as *to debts,* and the law of *Virginia* had *not* been made, I have already proved that debts would, on peace, have *revived* by the *law of nations.* This alone shews that the *only impediment* to the recovery of the debt in question, is the *law* of *Virginia,* and the payment under it; and the treaty relates to *every kind of legal impediment.*

But it is asked, did the 4th article intend to *annul* a *law* of the states? and destroy rights acquired under it?

I answer, that the 4th article did intend to destroy all *lawful impediments, past* and *future;* and that the law of *Virginia,* and the payment under it, is a lawful impediment; and would bar a recovery, if not destroyed by this article of the treaty. This stipulation could not intend only to repeal laws that created legal impediments, to the recovery of the debt (without respect to the mode of payment) because the *mere repeal* of a law would not destroy acts done, and rights acquired, under the law, *during its existence and before the repeal.* This right to repeal was only admitted *by the council for the Defendants in error,* because a repeal would not affect their case; but on the same ground that a treaty can repeal a law of the state, it can *nullify* it. I have already proved, that a treaty can *totally annihilate* any part of the *Constitution* of any of the individual states, that is contrary to a treaty. It is admitted that the treaty intended and did annul some laws of the states, to wit, any laws, *past* or *future,* that authorised a tender of *paper money* to extinguish or discharge the debt, and any laws, *past* or *future,* that authorized the discharge of executions by paper money, or delivery of property at appraisement; because if the words *sterling money* have not this effect, it cannot be shewn that they have any other. If the treaty could nullify *some* laws, it will be difficult to maintain that it could not equally *annul* others.

It was argued, that the 4th article was necessary to revive debts which had not been paid, as it was *doubtful,* whether debts *not paid* would revive on peace by the *law of nations.* I answer, that the 4th article was not necessary on *that account,* because there was *no doubt* that debts not paid do revive by the *law of nations;* as appears from *Bynkershoek, Lee,* and Sir *Thomas Parker.* And if necessary, this article would not have this effect, because it revives no debts, but only those to which some *legal* impediment might be interposed, and there could be no legal impediment, or bar, to the recovery, after peace, of debts *not paid,* during the war to the state.

It was contended, that the provision is, that CREDITORS shall recover, &c. and there was no *creditor* at the time of the *treaty,* because there was then no *debtor,* he having been legally discharged. *The creditors described* in the treaty, were not creditors generally, but only those with whom debts had been contracted, at some time before the treaty; and is a description of *persons,* and not of their *rights.* This adhering to the *letter,* is to destroy the plain meaning of the provision; because, if the treaty does not extend to debts paid into the state treasuries, or loan offices, it is very clear that *nothing* was done by the treaty as to those debts, not even so much as was stipulated *for Royalists,* and *Refugees,* to wit, a *recommendation of restitution.* Further, by this construction, nothing was done for *British creditors,* because the law of nations secured a recovery of their debts, which had not been confiscated and paid to the states; and if the debts paid in paper money, of little value, into the state treasuries, or loan offices, were not to be paid to them, the article was of no kind of value to them, and they were deceived. The article relates either to debts *not paid,* or, to debts *paid* into the treasuries, or loan offices. It has no relation to the *first,* for the reasons above assigned; and if it does not include the latter it relates to nothing.

It was said that the treaty secured *British* creditors from payment in paper money. This is admitted, but it is by force and operation of the words, *"in sterling money;"* but then the words, *"heretofore contracted,"* are to have *no effect whatsoever;* and it is those very words, and those only, that secure the recovery of the debts, paid to the states; because no lawful impediment is to be allowed to prevent the recovery of *debts contracted at any time before the treaty.*

But it was alledged, that the 4th article only stipulates, that there shall be no *lawful impediment,* &c. but that a law of the state was first necessary to *annul* the law creating such impediment; and that the state is under a *moral* obligation to pass such a law; but until it is done, the impediment remains.

I consider the 4th article in this light, that it is not a stipulation that *certain* acts shall be done, and that it was necessary for the legislatures of individual states, to do those acts; but that it is an express agreement, that certain things shall *not* be permitted the *American* courts of justice; and that it is a contract, on behalf of those courts, that *they* will not allow such acts to be pleaded in bar, to prevent a recovery of certain *British* debts. "Creditors are to meet with no lawful impediment, &c." As creditors can only sue for the recovery of their debts, in courts of justice; and it is only in courts of justice that a *legal* impediment can be set up by way of plea, in bar of their actions; it appears to me, that *the courts* are bound to overrule every *such* plea, if contrary to the treaty. A recovery of a debt can only be prevented *by a plea in bar to the action*. A recovery of a debt in sterling money, can only be prevented by a like plea in bar to the action, as tender and refusal, to operate as an extinguishment. *After* judgment, payment thereof in *sterling* money can only be prevented by some proceedings under some law, that authorises the debtor to discharge an *execution* in paper money, or in property, at a valuation. In all these, and similar cases, it appears to me, that the *courts* of the *United States* are bound, by the treaty, to interfere. No one can doubt that a treaty may stipulate, that certain acts shall be done by the Legislature; that other acts shall be done by the Executive; and others by the Judiciary. In the 6th article it is provided, that no *future prosecutions* shall be commenced against any person, for or by reason of the *part* he took in the war. Under this article the American courts of justice discharged the prosecutions, and the persons, on receipt of the treaty, and the proclamation of Congress. 1 *Dall. Rep*. 233.

If a law of the State to *annul* a former law was *first* necessary, it must be either on the ground that *the treaty* could not *annul* any *law* of a State; or that the words used in the treaty were not explicit or effectual for that purpose. Our Federal Constitution establishes the power of a treaty over the constitution and laws of any of the States; and I have shewn that the words of the 4th article were intended, and are sufficient to *nullify* the *law* of *Virginia,* and the payment under it. It was contended that *Virginia* is interested in this question, and ought to compensate the Defendants in error, if obliged to pay the Plaintiff under the treaty. If *Virginia* had a *right* to receive the money, which I hope I have clearly established, by what law is she obliged to return it? The treaty only speaks of the *original debtor,* and says nothing about a recovery from any of the States.

It was said that the defendant ought to be *fully indemnified,* if *the treaty* compels him to pay his debt over again; as his rights have been sacrificed for the *benefit of* the *public.*

That Congress had the power to sacrifice the *rights* and *interests* of *private* citizens to secure the *safety* or prosperity of the public, I have no doubt; but the immutable principles of justice; the public faith of the States, that confiscated and received *British* debts, pledged to the debtors; and the rights of the debtors violated by the treaty; all combine to prove, that ample compensation ought to be made to all the debtors who have been injured by the treaty for the benefit of the *public*. This principle is recognized by the Constitution, which declares, "that *private* property shall not be taken for *public* use without *just compensation*". See *Vattel. lib.* 1. *c.* 20. *s.* 244.

Although *Virginia* is not bound to make compensation to the debtors, yet it is evident that they ought to be indemnified, and it is not to be supposed, that those whose duty it may be to make the compensation, will permit the *rights* of our citizens to be sacrificed to a *public object,* without the fullest indemnity.

On the best investigation I have been able to give the 4th article of the treaty, I cannot conceive, that the wisdom of men could express their meaning in more accurate and intelligible words, or in words more proper and effectual to carry their *intention* into execution. I am satisfied, that the words, in their natural import, and common use, give a recovery to the *British* creditor from his original *debtor* of the debt contracted *before* the treaty, notwithstanding the payment thereof into the public treasuries, or loan offices, under the authority of any State law; and, therefore, I am of opinion, that the judgment of the Circuit Court ought to be reversed, and that judgment ought to be given, on the demurrer, for the Plaintiff in error; with the costs in the Circuit Court, and the costs of the appeal.

CALDER v. BULL, 3 DALL. 386 (1798)

After the time for appeal had already expired on a probate matter, the Connecticut legislature passed a special law giving the losing litigant additional time to lodge his appeal. The opposing party claimed that the legislation was an *ex post facto* law, forbidden by the Constitution. The Supreme Court disagreed, stating that only criminal statutes making prior conduct a crime were covered by the clause. Chase also made the broadest claim for testing the constitutionality of legislation, making the test whether the law in question was in keeping with the first great principles of the social compact. His view was rejected in a concurring opinion by Justice Iredell who established the words of the Constitution as the only test.

CHASE, *Justice*. The decision of *one* question determines (in my opinion) the present dispute. I shall, therefore, state from the record no more of the case, than I think necessary for the consideration of that question only.

The Legislature of *Connecticut*, on the 2d *Thursday* of *May* 1795, passed a resolution or law, which, for the reasons assigned, set aside a *decree* of the court of *Probate for Hartford,* on the 21st of *March* 1793, which decree *disapproved* of the will of *Normand Morrison* (the grandson) made the 21st of *August* 1779, and refused to *record* the said will; and granted a new hearing *by the said Court of Probate,* with liberty of appeal therefrom, in six months. A new hearing was had, in virtue of the resolution, or law, before the *said Court of Probate*, who, on the 27th of *July* 1795, *approved* the said will, and ordered it to be recorded. At *August* 1795, appeal was then had to the *Superior* court at *Hartford,* who at *February* term 1796, *affirmed* the decree of the *Supreme Court of errors* of *Connecticut,* who, in *June* 1796, adjudged *that there were no errors.* More than 18 months elapsed from the decree of the Court of *Probate* (on the 1st of *March* 1793) and thereby *Caleb Bull* and wife were barred of all rights *of appeal,* by a statute of *Connecticut.* There was no law of that State whereby a *new* hearing, or trial, before the said Court of Probate might be obtained. *Calder* and wife claim the premises in question, in right of his wife, as heiress of *N. Morrison,* physician; *Bull* and wife claim under the will of *N. Morrison,* the grandson.

The Council for the Plaintiffs in error, contend, that the said resolution or law of the *Legislature* of *Connecticut,* granting a *new hearing,* in the above case, is *an ex post facto law,* prohibited by the *Constitution of the United States;* that any law of the Federal government, or of any of the State governments, contrary to the *Constitution of the United States,* is *void;* and that this court possesses the power to declare *such* law *void.*

It appears to me a self-evident proposition, that the several State Legislatures *retain* all the powers of *legislation,* delegated to them by the State Constitutions; which are not EXPRESSLY taken away by the Constitution of the *United States.* The establishing courts of justice, the appointment of Judges, and the making regulations for the administration of justice, *within such State,* according to its laws, *on all subjects not entrusted to the Federal Government,* appears to me to be the *peculiar* and *exclusive* province, and duty of the *State Legislatures*: *All* the powers delegated by *the people* of the *United States* to the *Federal* Government are defined, and NO CONSTRUCTIVE powers can be exercised by it, and *all* the powers that *remain* in the State Governments are *indefinite;* except only in the Constitution of *Massachusetts.*

The *effect* of the resolution or law of *Connecticut,* above stated, is to *revise* a decision of one of its Inferior Courts, called the Court of *Probate for Hartford,* and to direct a *new* hearing of the case by the *same Court of Probate,* that passed the decree *against* the will of *Normand Morrison.* By the *existing* law of *Connecticut a right to recover certain property* had vested in *Calder* and wife (the appellants) in consequence of a decision of a *court of justice,* but, in virtue of a subsequent resolution or law, *and the new hearing* thereof, *and the decision* in subsequence, this right to recover certain property was divested, and the right to the property declared to be in *Bull* and wife, the appellees. The *sole* enquiry is, whether this resolution or law of *Connecticut,* having *such operation,* is an *ex post facto law,* within the *prohibition* of the *Federal* Constitution?

Whether the Legislature of any of the States can revise and correct by law, a decision of any of its Courts of Justice, although not prohibited by the Constitution of the State, is a question of very great importance, and not necessary NOW to be determined; *because the resolution or law in question does not go so far.* I cannot subscribe to the *omnipotence of a State Legislature,* or that it is *absolute and without controul;* although its authority should not be *expressly* restrained by the *Constitution,* or *fundamental law,* of the State. The people of the *United States* erected their Constitutions, or forms of government, to establish justice, to promote the general welfare, to secure the blessings of liberty; and to protect their *persons* and *property* from violence. The purposes for which men enter into society will determine the *nature* and *terms* of the *social* compact; and as *they* are the foundation of the *legislative* power, *they* will decide what are the *proper* objects of it: The *nature,* and *ends* of *legislative* power will limit the *exercise* of it. This *fundamental* principle flows from the very nature of our free *Republican* governments, that no man should be compelled to do what the laws do *not* require; *nor to refrain from acts which the laws permit.* There are acts which the *Federal,* or *State,* Legislature cannot do, *without exceeding their authority.* There are certain *vital* principles in our *free Repubican governments,* which will determine and over-rule an *apparent and flagrant* abuse of *legislative* power; as to authorize *manifest injustice by positive law;* or to take away that security for *personal liberty,* or *private property,* for the protection whereof the government was established. An ACT of the Legislature (for I cannot call it a *law*) contrary to the *great first principles* of the *social compact,* cannot be considered a *rightful exercise* of *legislative* authority. The obligation of a law in governments established on *express compact, and on republican principles,* must be determined by the *nature* of the *power,* on which it is founded. A few instances will suffice to explain what I mean. A law that punished a citizen for an *innocent* action, or, in other words, for an act, which, when done, was in violation of no *existing* law; a law that destroys, or impairs, the *lawful private* contracts of citizens; a law that makes a man *a Judge in his own cause;* or a law that takes *property* from A. and gives it to B: It is against all reason and justice, for a people to entrust a Legislature with SUCH powers; and, therefore, it cannot be presumed that they have done it. The *genius,* the *nature,* and the *spirit,* of our State Governments, amount to a prohibition of *such acts of legislation;* and the *general principles of law and reason* forbid them. The Legislature may enjoin, permit, forbid, and punish; they may declare *new* crimes; and establish rules of conduct for *all* its citizens in *future* cases; they may *command* what is right, and *prohibit* what is wrong; but they cannot change *innocence* into *guilt;* or punish *innocence* as a *crime;* or violate the right of an *antecedent lawful private contract;* or the *right of private property.* To maintain that our Federal, or State, Legislature possesses *such powers,* if they had not been *expressly* restrained; would, in my opinion, be a *political heresy,* altogether inadmissible in our *free republican governments.*

ALL the restictions contained in the Constitution of the *United States* on the power of the *State Legislatures,* were provided in favour of the authority of the *Federal* Government. The prohibition against their making *any ex post facto laws* was introduced for *greater* caution, and very probably arose from the knowledge, that *the Parliament of Great Britian* claimed and exercised a power to pass *such laws,* under the denomination of *bills of attainder,* or *bills of pains and penalties;* the *first* inflicting *capital,* and the other *less,* punishment. *These acts were legislative judgments; and an exercise of judicial power.* Sometimes they respected the *crime,* by declaring acts to be treason, which were *not* treason, when committed;* at other times, they violated the rules of evidence (to supply a deficiency of legal proof) by admitting *one* witness, when the *existing* law required *two;* by receiving evidence without *oath;* or the oath of the *wife* against the *husband;* or other testimony,

* *The case of the Earl of Strafford, in 1641.*

which the courts of justice would not admit;† at other times they inflicted *punishments,* where the party was not, by *law,* liable to *any punishment*;‡ and in *other* cases, they inflicted *greater* punishment, than the law annexed to the offence§— The ground for the exercise of such *legislative* power was this, that the *safety* of the kingdom depended on the death, or other punishment, of the offender: as if traitors, when *discovered,* could be so formidable, or the government so insecure! With very few exceptions, the advocates of *such* laws were stimulated by ambition, or personal resentment, and vindictive malice. To prevent such, and similar, acts of violence and injustice, I believe, the Federal and State Legislatures, were prohibited from passing any bill of *attainder;* or any *ex post facto law.*

The Constitution of the *United States,* article 1, section 9, prohibits the Legislature of the *United States* from passing any *ex post facto law;* and, in section 10, lays several restrictions on the authority of the *Legislatures* of the several *States;* and, among them, "that no state shall pass any *ex post facto law.*"

It may be remembered, that the legislatures of several of the states, to wit, *Massachusetts, Pennsylvania, Delaware, Maryland,* and *North* and *South Carolina,* are expressly prohibited, by their state *Constitutions,* from passing any *ex post facto law.*

I shall endeavour to shew *what law* is to be considered an *ex post facto law,* within the words and meaning of the prohibition in the *Federal* Constitution. The prohibition, "that no state shall pass any *ex post facto law,*" necessarily requires some explanation; for, naked and without explanation, it is unintelligible, and means nothing. *Literally,* it is only, *that a law shall not be passed concerning,* and *after the fact, or thing done, or action committed.* I would ask, *what fact;* or what *nature,* or *kind;* and by *whom* done? That *Charles* 1st king of *England,* was beheaded, that *Oliver Cromwell* was Protector of England; that *Louis* 16th, late King of *France,* was guillotined; are all *facts,* that have happened; but it would be nonsense to suppose, that the States were prohibited from making any *law after either of these events, and with reference thereto.* The prohibition, in the *letter,* is not to pass any law *concerning, and after the fact;* but the plain and obvious meaning and intention of the prohibition is this; *that the Legislatures of the several states, shall not pass laws, after a fact done by a subject, or citizen, which shall have relation to such fact, and shall punish him for having done it.* The prohibition considered in this light, is an *additional* bulwark in favour of the personal security of the subject, to protect his person from *punishment by legislative acts,* having a retrospective operation. I do not think it was inserted to secure the citizen in his *private rights,* of either *property,* or *contracts.* The prohibitions not to make any thing but gold and silver coin a tender in payment of *debts,* and not to pass any laws impairing the obligation of contracts, were inserted to secure *private rights;* but the restriction not to pass any *ex post facto law,* was to secure the *person* of the subject from injury, or *punishment,* in consequence of *such law.* If the prohibition against making *ex post facto laws* was intended to secure *personal rights* from being affected, or injured, by such laws, and the prohibition is sufficiently extensive for that object, the *other* restraints, I have enumerated, were unnecessary, and therefore improper; for both of them are *retrospective.*

I will state *what laws* I consider *ex post facto laws,* within the *words* and the *intent* of the prohibition. 1st. Every law that makes an action done before the passing of the law, and which was *innocent* when done, criminal; and punishes such action. 2d. Every law that *aggravates* a *crime,* or makes it *greater* than it was, when committed. 3d. Every law that *changes the punishment,* and inflicts a *greater punishment,* than the law annexed to the crime, when committed. 4th. Every law that alters the *legal* rules of *evidence,* and receives less, or different, testimony, than the law required at the time of the commission of the offence, *in order to convict the offender.* All these, and similar laws, are manifestly *unjust and oppressive.* In my opinion, the true distinction is between *ex post facto laws,* and *retrospective laws.* Every *ex post facto law* must necessarily be *retrospective;*

† *The case of Sir John Fenwick, in 1696.*

‡ *The banishment of Lord Clarendon, 1669* (*19* Ca. *2.* c. *10.*) *and of the Bishop of Atterbury, in 1723,* (*9* Geo. *1.* c. *17.*)

§ *The Coventry act, in 1670,* (*22* & *23 Car. 2 c. 1.*)

but every *retrospective law* is not an *ex post facto law:* The former, only, are prohibited. Every law that takes away, or impairs, *rights vested,* agreeably to existing laws, is retrospective, and is generally unjust, and may be oppressive; and it is a good general rule, that a law should have no *retrospect*: but there are cases in which laws may justly, and for the benefit of the community, and also of individuals, relate to a time antecedent to their commencement; as statutes of oblivion, or of *pardon.* They are certainly *retrospective,* and literally both *concerning, and after, the facts committed.* But I do not consider any law *ex post facto,* within the prohibition, that mollifies the rigor of the *criminal* law; but only those that *create,* or *aggravate,* the *crime;* or encrease the punishment, or change the rules of evidence, *for the purpose of conviction.* Every law that is to have an operation before the making thereof, as to commence at an antecedent time; or to save time from the statute of limitations; or to excuse acts which were unlawful, and before committed, and the like; is *retrospective.* But such laws may be proper or necessary, as the case may be. There is a great and apparent difference between making an UNLAWFUL act LAWFUL; and the making an *innocent* action *criminal,* and punishing it as a CRIME. The expressions *"ex post facto laws,"* are *technical,* they had been in use long before the Revolution, and had acquired an appropriate meaning, by *Legislators, Lawyers,* and *Authors.* The celebrated and judicious *Sir William Blackstone,* in his commentaries, considers an *ex post facto law* precisely in the *same* light I have done. His opinion is confirmed by his successor, *Mr. Wooddeson;* and by the author of *the Federalist,* who I esteem superior to *both,* for his extensive and accurate knowledge of the *true principles of Government.*

I also rely greatly on the definition, or explanation of EX POST FACTO LAWS, as given by the Conventions of *Massachusetts, Maryland,* and *North Carolina;* in their several Constitutions, or forms of Government.

In the declaration of rights, by the convention of *Massachusetts,* part 1st. sect. 24, "Laws made to *punish actions done before the existence of such laws,* and which have not been declared CRIMES by preceeding laws, are unjust, &c."

In the declaration of rights, by the convention of *Maryland,* art. 15th, "Retrospective laws punishing *facts* committed before the existence of *such* laws, and by them only declared *criminal,* are oppressive, &c."

In the declaration of rights by the convention of *North Carolina,* art. 24th, I find the same definition, precisely in the same words, as in the *Maryland* constitution.

In the declaration of Rights by the convention of *Delaware,* art. 11th, the same definition was clearly intended, but *inaccurately* expressed; by saying "laws punishing *offences* (instead of actions, or facts) committed before the existence of such laws, are oppressive, &c."

I am of opinion, that the *fact,* contemplated by the prohibition, and not to be affected by a *subsequent* law, was *some fact to be done by a Citizen, or Subject.*

In 2nd *Lord Raymond* 1352, *Raymond,* Justice, called the stat. 7 *Geo. 1st. stat. 2 par. 8,* about registering Contracts for South Sea Stock, an *ex post facto law;* because it affected *Contracts* made *before* the statute.

In the present case, *there is no fact done by Bull* and *wife* Plaintiffs in Error, that is in any manner affected by the law or resolution of *Connecticut:* It does not *concern,* or *relate* to, *any act done by them. The decree of the Court of Probate* of *Hartford* (on the 21st, *March*) in consequence of which *Calder* and wife claim a right to the property in question, was given *before* the said law or resolution, and in that sense, was affected and set aside by it; and in consequence of the law allowing a hearing and the decision in favor of the will, they have lost, what they would have been entitled to, if the Law or resolution, and the decision in consequence thereof, had not been made. *The decree of the Court* of probate is the only *fact,* on which the law or resolution operates. In my judgment the case of the Plaintiffs in Error, is not within the *letter* of the prohibition; and, for the reasons assigned, I am clearly of opinion, that it is not within the *intention* of the prohibition; and if within *the intention,* but out of *the letter,* I should not, therefore, consider myself justified to *continue* it within the prohibition, and therefore that the whole was void.

It was argued by the Counsel for the plaintiffs in error, that the *Legislature* of *Connecticut* had no *constitutional* power to make the resolution (or law) in question, granting a new hearing, &c.

Without giving an opinion, at this time, whether this Court has jurisdiction to decide that any law made by Congress, contrary to the Constitution of the *United States,* is void; I am fully satisfied that this court has no *jurisdiction* to determine that any law of any state *Legislature,* contrary to the Constitution of such *state,* is void. Further, if this court had *such* jurisdiction, yet it does not appear to me, that the resolution (or law) in question, is contrary to the charter of *Connecticut,* or its constitution, which is said by counsel to be composed of its charter, acts of assembly, and usages, and customs. I should think, that the courts of *Connecticut* are the proper tribunals to decide, whether laws, contrary to the constitution thereof, are void. In the present case they have, both in the inferior and superior courts, determined that the Resolution (or law) in question was *not* contrary to either their state, or the federal, constitution.

To shew that the resolution was contrary to the constitution of the *United States,* it was contended that the words, *ex post facto law,* have a precise and accurate meaning, and convey but *one idea* to *professional* men, which is, *"by matter of after fact; by something after the fact."* And *Co. Litt. 241. Fearnes Con. Rem.* (*Old Ed.*) 175 *and* 203. *Powell on Devises* 113, 133. 134. were cited; and the table to *Coke's* Reports (by *Wilson*) title *ex post facto,* was referred to. There is no doubt that a man may be a *trespasser* from the *beginning,* by matter *of after fact;* as where an entry is given by *law,* and the party abuses it; or where the law gives a *distress,* and the party kills, or works, *the distress.*

I admit, an act *unlawful* in the beginning may, in some cases, become lawful *by matter of after fact.*

I also agree, that the words *"ex post facto"* have the meaning contended for, and no other, in the cases cited, and in all *similar* cases; where they are used unconnected with, and without relation to, *Legislative* acts, or laws.

There appears to me a manifest distinction between the case where one *fact* relates to, and affects, *another fact,* as where an *after fact,* by *operation of law,* makes a *former fact,* either *lawful* or *unlawful;* and the case where a *law* made after a fact done, is to operate on, and to affect, *such fact.* In the *first* case *both* the acts are done by *private* persons. In the *second* case the *first* act is done by a *private* person, and the *second* act is done by the *legislature* to affect the *first* act.

I believe that but *one* instance can be found in which a *British* judge called a statute, that affected *contracts* made *before* the statute, an *ex post facto law;* but the judges of *Great Britain* always considered *penal* statutes, that created *crimes,* or encreased the punishment of them, as *ex post facto laws.*

If the term *ex post facto law* is to be *construed* to include and to prohibit the enacting *any law after a fact,* it will greatly restrict the power of the federal and state legislatures; and the consequences of such a *construction* may not be foreseen.

If the prohibition to make no *ex post facto law* extends *to all laws made after the fact,* the two prohibitions, not to make any thing but gold and silver coin a tender in payment of debts; and not to pass any law impairing the obligation of contracts, were improper and unnecessary.

It was further urged, that if the provision does not extend to prohibit the making *any law after a fact,* then all *choses in action;* all lands by *Devise;* all personal property by bequest, or distribution; by *Elegit;* by execution; by judgments, particularly on *torts;* will be unprotected from the legislative power of the states; *rights vested* may be divested at the will and pleasure of the state legislatures; and, therefore, that the true construction and meaning of the prohibition is, that the states pass *no law to deprive a citizen of any right vested in him by existing laws.*

It is not to be presumed, that the federal or state legislatures will pass laws to deprive citizens of *rights* vested in them by *existing* laws; unless for the benefit of the *whole* community; and on making full satisfaction. The restraint against making any *ex post facto laws* was not considered, by the framers of the constitution, as extending to prohibit the depriving a citizen even of a *vested right to property;* or the provision, "that *private* property should not be taken for PUBLIC use, without just compensation," was unnecessary.

It seems to me, that the *right of property,* in its origin, could only arise from *compact express, or implied,* and I think it the better opinion, that the *right,* as well as the *mode,* or *manner,* of acquiring property, and of alienating or transferring, inheriting, or transmitting it, is conferred by society; is regulated by *civil* institution, and is always subject to the rules prescribed *by positive law.* When I say that a *right* is vested in a citizen, I mean, that he has the *power* to do *certain actions;* or to possess *certain things, according to the law of the land.*

If any one has a right to *property* such right is a *perfect and exclusive right;* but no one can have *such* right before he has acquired a *better* right to the property, than any other person in the world: a right, therefore, only to *recover property* cannot be called a *perfect and exclusive right.* I cannot agree, that a *right to property* vested in *Calder* and *wife,* in consequence of the decree (of the 21st of *March* 1783) disapproving of the will of *Morrison,* the Grandson. If the will was valid, *Mrs. Calder* could have *no right,* as heiress of *Morrison,* the physician; but if the will was set aside, she had an undoubted title.

The resolution (or law) *alone* had no manner of effect on *any right whatever* vested in *Calder* and *wife.* The Resolution (or law) combined with the new hearing, *and* the decision, in virtue of it, took away their right to *recover* the property in question. But when combined they took away no *right of property* vested in *Calder* and *wife;* because the decree against the will (21st. *March* 1783) did not vest in or transfer *any property* to them.

I am under a necessity to give a *construction,* or explanation of the words, *"ex post facto law,"* because they have not any certain meaning attached to them. But I will not go farther than I feel myself bound to do; and if I ever exercise the jurisdiction I will not decide *any law to be void, but in a very clear case.*

I am of opinion, that the decree of the Supreme Court of Errors of *Connecticut* be affirmed, with costs.

Oliver Ellsworth

☆ 1745–1807 ☆

APPOINTED BY

GEORGE WASHINGTON

YEARS ON COURT

1796–1799

Oliver Ellsworth

by

MICHAEL KRAUS

"IF ANY ONE man can be called the founder, not of [the Supreme] Court only, but of the whole system of federal courts, . . . Ellsworth is the man." This praise, entirely merited, was bestowed on Oliver Ellsworth, commissioned Chief Justice, March 4, 1796, by his leading biographer, William G. Brown. Ellsworth was revered by his contemporaries for his intelligence, common sense, and his diligence, and took a major role in the Revolutionary period.

The Ellsworths came to America from Yorkshire, England, in the middle of the seventeenth century. Oliver Ellsworth was born on April 29, 1745, to Captain David Ellsworth (famous at the siege of Louisburg) and his wife Jemima Leavitt. They had settled on a farm in Windsor, Connecticut, and it was there that Oliver grew up. Little is known about his childhood other than that his father, encouraging his son to become a minister (like so many aspiring men in the American colonies), secured him a good education and entered him in Yale, in 1762, at the age of seventeen. But Oliver apparently found it difficult to assume the role of a decorous and mannerly gentleman and at the end of his sophomore year, under some pressure from the college (some allege he was dismissed), he left, due in part to complaints that he and others ran "and Halloed in the College Yard in contempt of the Law of the College."

Ellsworth soon after enrolled at Princeton. He was much taken with the activity and energy of the student body, many of whom, such as Benjamin Rush, William Paterson, Luther Martin, had already distinguished themselves as serious young men deeply committed to the problems of colonial life and politics. There was a greater portion of southern students than there had been at Yale and the worldliness and complication of imperial and colonial policies

MICHAEL KRAUS is Professor Emeritus, City University of New York. His many publications include The Atlantic Civilization: Eighteenth Century Origins; The Writing of American History; *and* The United States to 1865.

excited Ellsworth and his colleagues. The specific issue of the Stamp Act of 1765 lent them extra passion and heat. There was much debating of a formal and informal nature, and early on Ellsworth gained a reputation as a skilled and talented debater. Caution and compromise marked his character then and later.

Upon graduating in 1766, Ellsworth returned to Connecticut where he acceded to his father's wishes and for a year studied theology. But his interest was in law and he decided to study for the bar to which he was admitted in 1771. To pay off debts accumulated during this time (his father, apparently, refused him further funds for education when he stopped studying for the ministry), he cut and sold timber from a woodland tract he had acquired by gift or inheritance. Though he cleared the land and his debt, he was not well off during his early law practice—his professional earnings for the first three years were only three pounds, Connecticut currency. His constricted means did not, however, stop him from marrying in 1772 sixteen-year-old Abigail Wolcott, the daughter of a prosperous and distinguished East Windsor family.

The couple took over a farm belonging to Ellsworth's father. Because of their impoverished circumstances, Ellsworth did the heavy chores on the place and cut and split rails to fence the land. When court was in session he walked the ten miles to his office in Hartford, not being able to afford a horse. Physically strong—a robust man, six feet two, and broad shouldered—his portraits show a face with strong jaws and firm lips. "The interest of his life," writes William G. Brown, "is not to be found in dramatic exhibitions of his powers. It lies, rather, in the tasks which his hand found to do. . . ."

After a slow start, Ellsworth's law practise and reputation as a man of talent grew with exceptional rapidity. Windsor named him deputy to the Connecticut General Assembly in 1773, from which time, though still continuing his profession, he never relinquished public duties and responsibilities. His private practice grew, over the next few years, to be, probably, greater than any other in Connecticut—and so did his personal wealth. He bought land and houses, became a money-lender, and invested in diverse enterprises. His house in Windsor was imposing and his personal appearance always scrupulously elegant—he invariably wore a white, ruffled shirt, silk stockings, and silver knee-buckles. To discerning contemporaries, more significant than Ellsworth's prosperity was his character, his powers of application, and his eloquence. His friend, Dr. Timothy Dwight, president of Yale, noted his glowing images, "his style concise and strong, and his utterance vehement and overwhelming."

The onset of the Revolution in 1775 drew Ellsworth into the conflict. As a member of Connecticut's Assembly, he was named to a five-member Committee of the Pay Table to supervise expenditures and to audit accounts in the state's military efforts. Two years later he was chosen to be the state's attorney for Hartford County, which post he retained (though the fees were small) until 1785.

During the war years he also served as a delegate from Connecticut to the Continental Congress, representing his state over a period of six years. The

Congress was already being plagued by the problems which were to bring it to its knees. Its authority over unilateral action by the states was slight and was increasingly being challenged. Very little direct power had been given it; its duty was to administer and advise rather than to rule—the states, proud of their independence and jealous of their autonomy, were loathe to accord final jurisdiction to a central power. It is difficult to ascertain Ellsworth's role in the Congress with accuracy, for he served, like so many other delegates, on a large number of committees, among them the Board of Treasury and the Committee of Appeals. In the light of his subsequent judicial career, Ellsworth's membership on the Committee of Appeals is significant for the committee's activities marked the first exercise of federal jurisprudence and may, in that light, be considered as a forerunner of the Supreme Court.

In 1777 this committee was named by the Continental Congress to dispose of prizes captured by vessels sailing under its authority. Shortly after Ellsworth became a member of the committee, an appeal was made to it which had far-reaching implications for the relationship between the judicial authority of a state and of the United States. Gideon Olmstead and other Connecticut men had been put on board the British sloop *Active,* as captives. On the voyage from Jamaica to New York the Americans overpowered the captain and crew, and then steered for Egg Harbor, New Jersey. Within sight of port a Pennsylvania brig, *Convention,* commanded by Captain Houston, took possession of the *Active.* Houston brought the sloop to Philadelphia and, before the Pennsylvania Court of Admiralty, claimed her as lawful prize. The Connecticut men, led by Olmstead, interposed a claim to the vessel and its cargo.

A jury trial resulted in a decision to award one-quarter of the value of the prize to the Connecticut men, with three-fourths to go to Captain Houston and his crew. The Connecticut men then appealed to Congress which referred the case to the committee on which Ellsworth sat. A full hearing was held and the judgment of the Pennsylvania state court was reversed. The *Active* was adjudged the lawful prize of Olmstead and his companions. The case was remanded to the state court with instructions to execute the judgment. While the Pennsylvania judge recognized the authority of the committee, he refused to disregard the award of the jury. Again steps were taken to carry out the intent of the committee but they were frustrated by local Pennsylvania officials.

Here was a clear conflict between a state's judicial authority and that of a presumably superior body speaking for the United States. As one writer expressed it "the committee found itself as powerless to enforce its decree as Congress was to enforce its requisitions." Final disposition of the case did not come until some thirty years later, in 1809 (*United States* v. *Judge Peters,* 5 Cranch 115) in the court presided over by John Marshall.

The committee that handled the case of the *Active* was succeeded in 1780 by a special court to handle such matters. On the advice of General Washington, Congress resolved in January, 1780, "that a court be established for the trial of all appeals from the courts of admiralty in these United States, in cases of capture, to consist of three judges, appointed and commissioned by Congress."

Three lawyers were named for this first federal court which was called "The Court of Appeals in Cases of Capture." It remained in existence for six years, ceasing to function as no more cases were on its docket. Ellsworth's share in creating this court and his participation in the work of its predecessor were doubtless good training ground for the judicial post he was to hold.

Among Ellsworth's other duties in the Continental Congress was the task of getting supplies for the army from reluctant rebels. Robert Morris proposed to secure supplies by a subscription, with Congress guaranteeing repayment to the subscribers. (This in itself was a ticklish problem since the country's finances were rapidly weakening and it was increasingly difficult to collect money from the states.) Ellsworth was named head of the committee to cooperate with the army officers. He also served on committees dealing with international treaties, and showed wisdom in his appraisal of America's relation to England: "Neither the safety of this country or the balance of power of Europe requires that Great Britain should be at all more reduced than in fact she is." He was neither an anglophobe, like some of his colleagues, nor an idolater, like Hamilton, of the British system.

With Hamilton and Madison as associates, Ellsworth served on a committee "to provide a system for foreign affairs, for military and naval establishments, and also to carry into execution the regulation of weights and measures, and other articles of the Confederation not attended to during the war." In effect the committee was being asked to establish a comprehensive system of administration.

It was not easy for Ellsworth to move from his position of upholding states' rights to one supporting a stronger central government. But fiscal considerations and the influence of associates exerted enough pressure to move him in that direction. To Trumbull, governor of Connecticut, Ellsworth wrote: "There *must,* Sir, be a revenue somehow established, that can be relied on, and applied for national purposes as the exigencies arise, independent of the will or views of a single State, or it will be impossible to support national faith or national existence. The power of Congress must be adequate to the purposes of their constitution. It is possible, there may be abuses and misapplication, still it is better to hazard *something,* than to hazard all." Though privately Ellsworth expressed himself forcefully on the need for a more effective national government he played no significant part in the movement for a strong constitution. Advocates of a stronger union, apart from Noah Webster, were not conspicuous in Connecticut. On Ellsworth's retirement from Congress in 1783, he carried on his law practice and continued to serve his native state as a member of the governor's council.

In 1785, he served on the newly created Supreme Court of Errors in Connecticut, where he performed his first judicial functions. Soon afterward, he was chosen to the Superior Court, joining there his colleague and mentor, Roger Sherman, in the meantime resigning from the council, since it was illegal to sit simultaneously on both bodies. Ellsworth's performance on this court indicated his command of terse and trenchant language. He was, said an admirer, a man who "could be trusted with the ordering of society and the safeguarding of interests and rights."

When the time came to select delegates to the Federal Convention in 1787, Connecticut was so laggard that she made her choice on May 12, only two days before the meeting in Philadelphia. Sherman and William Samuel Johnson were elected with Ellsworth, who took his seat in Independence Hall on May 28, in time for the second sitting of the convention. Major William Pierce, a delegate from Georgia, characterizing Connecticut's trio, noted Ellsworth's "clear, deep, and copious understanding." He was "eloquent, and connected in debate, and always attentive to his duty. He is very happy in reply, and choice in selecting such parts of his adversary's arguments as he finds make the strongest impressions—in order to take off the force of them, so as to admit the power of his own." He was "a man much respected for his integrity, and venerated for his abilities."

Connecticut's delegates had gone to Philadelphia with the intention of amending the Articles of Confederation to correct their defects. However, they, as did others at the convention, gradually shifted their ground. The debate over the basis of representation in the proposed government became more complicated and heated, and Ellsworth and his colleagues were ready to compromise on the form of the new legislature. Instead of a single chamber, which they had favored, they were willing to accept a bicameral body, if in the second house each state had equal representation.

In Ellsworth's first lengthy speech at the convention, he said "we must build our general government on the strength and vigor of the state governments. Without their cooperation it would be impossible to support a republican government over so great an extent of country . . . We know that the people of the states are strongly attached to their own constitutions. If you hold up a system of general government destructive of their constitutional rights, they will oppose it . . . The only chance we have to support a general government is to graft it on the state governments. I want to proceed on this ground, as the safest, and I believe no other plan is practicable." Ellsworth was groping toward a partly national, partly federal system, a political conception not easily grasped by eighteenth century minds, and it was he who insisted upon the important rephrasing of "the national government" to "the government of the United States."

When other delegates despaired of reaching agreement on the nature of the new government, Ellsworth's was the counsel of hope that a satisfactory plan would be adopted. Though still expressing views voiced by small state delegations, Ellsworth asked that strong executive, judiciary, and legislative departments be created. The United States, he asserted, "are sovereign on one side of the line dividing their jurisdictions—the states on the other. Each ought to have power to defend their respective sovereignties." He cautioned that not too much be attempted, lest all be lost. "If this convention only chalked out lines of good government, we should do well." In general, he said, he was not a half-way man, yet he "preferred doing half the good he could, rather than do nothing at all."

When Madison, in debate, implied that Ellsworth's remarks reflected a parochial view, the Connecticut delegate rejoined that his state had been federally minded during the Revolution. The muster rolls, he said, showed that she had more troops in the field than Virginia. Connecticut went heavily into debt to support the war effort but, said Ellsworth, he defied anyone to show that his state had ever refused a federal requisition. The Connecticut delegation, speaking for compromise, urged the establishment of a federal nation. Extremists for small states on the one hand and the large states' representatives holding out for a strongly centralized government on the other were both, at length, beaten, and, in the victory, Sherman and Ellsworth shared honors.

Ellsworth was also active on the committee to establish the outlines of the judiciary branch of government. Though nowhere in the Constitution is it specifically stated that the Supreme Court holds the right to interpret the Constitution and to declare federal or state statutes null and void, it was assumed by many of the men most active at the convention that the highest Court would have this inherent jurisdiction. It was clear in Ellsworth's mind that this power did reside in the Court, and in addressing the Connecticut convention on January 7, 1788, to ratify the Constitution he made it clear:

> *This constitution defines the extent of the powers of the general government. If the general legislature should at any time overleap their limits, the judicial department is a constitutional check. If the United States go beyond their powers, if they make a law which the Constitution does not authorize, it is void; and the judicial power, the national judges, who, to secure their impartiality, are to be made independent, will declare it to be void.*

Ellsworth's duties on the Connecticut bench obliged him to leave Philadelphia before the convention ended, thus leaving him no chance to sign the Constitution. His part in its framing long lay in obscurity, yet few were more effective than he in creating the great document. Not as well known as most fellow members at the start of the convention, his will and wisdom brought him to a position of leadership among a group of remarkable men. In after years John C. Calhoun, upholding states' rights, paid special tribute to Ellsworth: "It is owing mainly to the states of Connecticut and New Jersey that we have a federal instead of a national government . . . Who are the men . . . to whom we are indebted for this excellent form of government? I will name them . . . They were Chief Justice Ellsworth and Roger Sherman of Connecticut, and Judge Paterson of New Jersey."

Ratification of the Constitution was by no means a sure thing. In Connecticut the convention met at Hartford, in January, 1788, to make its decision. At the opening Ellsworth rose to explain the document and urge its ratification. In strong and rapid speech he exhibited his mastery of the subject. "He was armed at all points," wrote an eyewitness. "Scarcely a single objection was made but what he answered. His energetic reasoning bore down all before it." He argued for a strong government to prevent the disunited American states from falling prey to foreign powers. "If we continue so, how easy it is for them to portion us out among them, as they did the Kingdom of Poland." With great power Ellsworth defined the new relation between the Union and the States, between the federal government and the individual citizen, between the federal and state judiciaries. Connecticut's ratification probably owed more to Ellsworth than to any other single individual.

Calhoun, it has been noted, found in Ellsworth support for his views. By a curious coincidence his opponent, Daniel Webster, went to the same source for aid. In the debate over nullification in 1833, Webster was thanked by Ellsworth's son, then a member of Congress, for upholding the Constitution against nullifiers. "Where do you think," said Webster, "I got my ideas on the subject? Among the most important sources of my knowledge have been the two speeches of your father before the Connecticut Convention." It was extraordinary to have won the homage of these two opposed giants.

Ellsworth's service to his state and nation continued with his selection to be one of Connecticut's first two senators, the other being William Samuel Johnson. In the Senate, a group small enough to gather near the fire on a chilly day, Ellsworth was in the company of men he had met in the Continental Congress or in the Federal Convention, and their efforts were employed to make this fledgling government that they had created effective and respectable. Ellsworth, busy on many Senate committees and participating in framing much legislation, was made head of the committee to draw up rules for the Senate. He suggested an economic boycott of Rhode Island in order to force the recalcitrant state to join the Union. He helped plan the organization of an army, a government post office, a census, and was a fierce supporter in the Senate of Hamilton's fiscal policies. From this time on, essentially, he abandoned his attachment to the doctrine of states' rights and his constant support went to the Federalists—to the extent, for instance, of supporting the Alien and Sedition Laws of 1798, though his straightforward and commonsensical New England character allowed him to avoid the extremism so common to that time. Throughout his career his organization and attention to detail was excellent, but nowhere did it serve him as well as it did in those demanding seven years he spent trying to establish a new and original government.

Ellsworth's outstanding achievement in the Senate was the Judiciary Act of 1789. As chairman of the committee responsible for drafting the bill, he won the later praise of Madison: the bill, organizing the judicial department, he said, originated in Ellsworth's draft (sections 10 through 23, in fact, are in Ellsworth's handwriting), and "it was not materially changed in its passage into law." To Richard Law, a Connecticut judge, Ellsworth outlined the judiciary system his committee was contemplating. The Supreme Court was to consist of six judges and hold two sessions annually. A district court with one judge resident in each state would have "jurisdiction in admiralty cases, smaller offenses and some other special cases." The country was to be divided into three circuits, a court to be held twice annually in each state consisting of two judges of the Supreme Court and the district judge. The circuit court would receive appeals from the district court, try high crimes "and have original jurisdiction in law and equity, in controversies between foreigners and citizens and between citizens of different states" in cases involving more than two thousand dollars. Senator Maclay of Pennsylvania, also a member of the committee, was not as impressed with Ellsworth as Madison. "This vile bill," he said, "is a child of his, and he defends it with the care of a parent."

After considerable debate in the Senate and House, the Judiciary Act was signed by President Washington on September 24, 1789. Several months later, on February 2, 1790, the Supreme Court was organized in New York City (the capital at that time), and the Judiciary Department became operative. Ellsworth and his colleagues, William Paterson of New Jersey in particular, succeeded in laying a firm but flexible base for the judiciary system, one that has changed little since its inception.

Ellsworth won reelection to the Senate to serve until 1797. During this period, in the conflicts spawned by the French Revolution, the senator from Connecticut had no sympathy for Gallican liberty. When many in the United States were clamoring for war with England because of her high-handed treatment of American shipping and her failure to abide by the peace treaty of 1783, Ellsworth kept his head. In January, 1794, he wrote to a friend, "As to the war between this country and England, so much dreaded by some and wished for by others, *I think it will not take place."* To ease the tension between the two countries Ellsworth, in concert with a small group of intimates, took steps that ultimately led to the choice of John Jay as envoy to England. The fight over the treaty brought back by Jay and Washington's delay in signing it left Ellsworth overwrought. He paced the hall of his Connecticut home in Windsor through long nights before the news came of the treaty's acceptance.

A measure of Ellsworth's influence upon his senatorial colleagues is the tribute paid him by an adversary. "If," said Aaron Burr, "Ellsworth had happened to spell the name of the Deity with two d's, it would have taken the Senate three weeks to expunge the superfluous letter." John Adams called Ellsworth "the firmest pillar" in the Senate during Washington's administration. The President, himself, it should be added, had a deep regard for the Senator from Connecticut.

In 1795 John Jay resigned his post of Chief Justice to become governor of New York. The Senate refused to confirm the appointment of John Rutledge to succeed him and William Cushing refused to serve as Chief Justice. Washington commissioned Ellsworth on March 4, 1796, and four days later he took his seat on the Bench. He gained no great reputation as Chief Justice—he served only three years and the Court handed down very few decisions during this period. He was not as learned in the law as some of his colleagues on the bench, notably James Wilson, but he subjected himself to a close study of those fields in which he felt inadequate. Ellsworth was an impressive figure as he presided over the

Court, and he was not loathe to assert the dignity of his office against any one, even a fellow judge, if offense was shown it.

Before March of 1796 was up, Ellsworth sailed for Savannah to go on the southern circuit. Travelling the circuits was a duty filled with physical hardship and fatigue, but it had the virtue of allowing the judges to see the country in all its diversity. A judge's opening charge to the grand jury was often a discourse on the nature of American institutions, with special emphasis on the role of the courts. Ellsworth's charges had clarity and force. His first was given at Savannah in April, 1796. "Your duty," he said, "may be deemed unpleasant, but it is too important not to be faithfully performed . . . Institutions without respect, laws violated with impunity are, to a republic, the symptoms and the seed of death . . . The national laws are the national ligatures and vehicles of life. Though they pervade a country as diversified in its habits as it is vast in extent, yet they give to the whole harmony of interest and unity of design . . . Admonished by the fate of republics which have gone before us, we should profit by their mistakes. Impetuosity in legislation, and instability in execution, are the rocks on which they perished . . . Let there be vigilance, constant diligence, and fidelity for the execution of laws—of laws made by all and having for their object the good of all. So let us rear an empire sacred to the rights of man and commend a government of reason to the nations of the earth."

The decisions Ellsworth himself wrote during his tenure as Chief Justice were few, but some dealt with very important questions. In the August term of 1796 the Court dealt with prize and admiralty cases, types that Ellsworth was well fitted to handle as they were the same matters that came before him on the Committee of Appeals of the Continental Congress.

In the first case that came before him on the Supreme Court, *United States* v. *La Vengeance,* 3 Dall. 297 (1796), the judges rendered an opinion which eventually served as the foundation for a considerable extension of federal admiralty jurisdiction to inland navigable rivers, to the Great Lakes, and elsewhere off the high seas. A vessel had been libelled for illegally exporting arms from Sandy Hook to French possessions. It was argued that the English common law should prevail, that an act committed not entirely on the high seas, but partly within the confines of a state, should be held to be outside admiralty jurisdiction. The Court held to the contrary, a bold decision asserting federal authority. Though frequently attacked in later years it remained a fundamental decision of American law.

Another admiralty case in the same year, *Moodie* v. *The Ship Phoebe Anne,* 3 Dall. 319 (1796), was a test of the court's impartiality, the judges being strongly disposed against France. A storm-tossed French privateer sought safety in an American port and made repairs there. It was libelled for breach of America's neutrality laws, counsel arguing "the impolicy and inconveniency of suffering privateers tc equip in our ports." Ellsworth, however, in a decision favoring France, said: "Suggestions of policy and conveniency cannot be considered in the judicial determination of a question of right: the treaty with France

. . . must have its effect. By the 19th article, it is declared that French vessels . . . may, on any urgent necessity, enter our ports, and be supplied with all things needful for repairs."

In 1797 and 1798 the few cases that were decided were of no great importance. In 1799, however, Ellsworth, in the Circuit Court for the District of Connecticut handed down a decision which had immense political and emotional repercussions. In *United States* v. *Isaac Williams,* Ellsworth, in supporting an indictment for violation of the law forbidding American-citizens from accepting commissions in the service of a foreign power, maintained that Americans had no right of expatriation. No such right existed under English common law which, said Ellsworth, was binding upon United States courts. The Chief Justice did not rest his argument solely on the tradition of the common law. In arguing against the right of an American to expatriate himself he appealed to the social compact. No member of the compact, said Ellsworth, can break his tie with the community unless the latter consents.

The *Williams* decision had stirred intense hostility, Republicans arguing that this was one of a series of partisan decisions aimed at them. Sympathizers of France had been evading the neutrality laws by swearing allegiance to her and privateering against English and neutral commerce. Newspapers denounced the opinion as one bending "our necks under a foreign yoke . . . We are not free, we are not an independent nation . . . It is an erroneous and dangerous doctrine, unwarrantable, iniquitous and illegal. The United States have no common law." The Chief Justice was called "a foe to republican principles and an advocate for monarchical principles." Republicans were convinced that the national judiciary was an annex to the Federalist party.

Anti-federalists, on general principle, were fearful of the spread of this doctrine of England's common law, but they also pointed to a specific danger to the United States. They asserted that it harmed America's opposition to England's claim to impress naturalized American seamen, a claim based on the common law denying the right of expatriation. It was forgotten then, and not remembered until the historian Charles Warren unearthed the fact, that Ellsworth, ordering an injunction in a circuit court, enforced the law against Great Britain as well. In a suit brought by the Spanish consul at Charleston, South Carolina, the Chief Justice enjoined the British consul from selling in the United States a Spanish ship, *Neustra Signora,* brought in by a British warship. To sell prizes without permission of the neutral state was, said Ellsworth, "incompatible with the sovereignty of the State."

On the day that Ellsworth came to the Supreme Court, the case of *Hylton* v. *United States,* 3 Dall. 171 (1796) was on trial. It involved the constitutionality of a carriage tax by an act of 1794. For the first time the Court passed upon the constitutionality of an act of Congress, upholding its right to levy a direct tax. As Ellsworth had not heard all the arguments he did not participate in the decision. Shortly afterward, the case of *Ware* v. *Hylton,* 3 Dall. 199 (1796) was tried. The fundamental issue was the relation of the states to the federal government—whether state laws confiscating and sequestrating debts owing to Englishmen or permitting payment in depreciated currency were in keeping with the peace treaty of 1783. The finances of states and many citizens were involved. British debts in Virginia alone amounted to some $2,000,000.

The Court seemed to find no great difficulty in declaring that federal treaty provisions must prevail over laws of individual states. British creditors were legally entitled to recover. Generally, said the Court, a treaty which is compatible with the Constitution supersedes state laws which derogate from its provisions. Though Ellsworth did not pass on the case of *Ware* v. *Hylton* he did agree with the decision as his opinion in a similar case indicated. In a circuit court in North Carolina he delivered an opinion which carefully discussed the bearing of the treaty on the rights of British creditors, *Hamiltons* v. *Eaton,* 2 Martin (N.C.) 83 (C.C.N.C. 1797). "As to the opinion that a treaty does not annul a statute, so far as there is an interference," said Ellsworth, "it is unsound. . . . A treaty, when it is in fact made, is, with regard to each nation that is a party to it, a national act; an expression of the national will, as much as a statute can be; and does, therefore, of necessity annul any prior statute, so far as there is an interference. The supposition that the public can have two wills, at the same time, repugnant to each other—one expressed by a statute and another by a treaty—is absurd."

Ellsworth and his associates on the Supreme Court in examining its relations with circuit and district courts and its appellate jurisdiction, set down important rules concerning writs of error and appeals. Ellsworth's clear distinction between the two has often been quoted. "An appeal," he said, "is a process of civil law origin, and removes a cause entirely, subjecting the facts as well as the law to review and retrial; but a writ of error is a process of common law origin, and it removes nothing for reexamination but the law," *Wiscart* v. *Dauchy,* 3 Dall. 321 (1796).

Ellsworth had not the intellectual power of his successor, John Marshall. Yet they had much in common. Their general views on the great public questions were similar. Ellsworth's few, brief judicial opinions suggest the tone and style of Marshall's. The man from Connecticut had a special gift for the terse phrase.

Like his predecessor, John Jay, who was plucked from the Court and sent to England as envoy to prevent an escalation into war, Ellsworth was asked by President Adams to go to France in an attempt to come to a new understanding with her, both countries being on the edge of an undeclared war. The intensely pro-British faction among the Federalists sought to dissuade Ellsworth from going on the mission whose success he doubted. But he went "from the necessity of preventing a greater evil." William Vans Murray of Maryland, and William R. Davie of North Carolina, were named envoys with him.

On November 3, 1799, Ellsworth embarked at Newport in the frigate *United States* for Europe. The ship touched at Lisbon and, after a fortnight's stay, set sail again for L'Orient in France. A great storm battered the frigate which had to make port again in Spain, near Corunna. From there the worn-out American made the overland journey to Paris, arriving in March of 1800, a physically broken man.

Ellsworth arrived in France when Napoleon had taken over the country. French ships were harassing American vessels which, by decree, were subject to capture and confiscation should their cargoes contain anything of British production. The American envoys were instructed to insist on reparation as a condition of a peaceable agreement. The Americans set forth other proposals, but Ellsworth, who directed negotiations for the United States, had little expectation of France accepting them as basis for a treaty. It was clear that France had no intention of indemnifying Americans for their losses.

Failing to achieve this objective the American envoys proposed a temporary provision for freedom of commerce between the two countries. The French minister, freed of the immediate need to pay indemnities, agreed to discuss the matter at a future time and accepted the American view on other controversial points. Contraband was defined more specifically to refer to military supplies. The procedure of captures was carefully regulated to prevent wanton destruction of property.

The American envoys felt they had come off well in negotiating this convention with France. Ellsworth had completed his last important service for the United States. To his brother David, he wrote on October 10, 1800, "Altho' our best and long continued efforts have not obtained all that justice required, yet enough is finally done . . . to restore peace to our country . . . to guard against further injuries, as well as they can be guarded against by engagements, and to disentangle our country from its former alliance and connections with France." The convention was ratified by the Senate on February 3, 1801.

Ellsworth's health was so badly broken he could not leave for home until the spring. Meanwhile, he resigned from the Supreme Court, feeling he would be unable to shoulder its burdens. On hearing lamentations from Federalists about Jefferson's victory in the election of 1800, Ellsworth took the view that the Republicans "must support the government while he administers it . . . the government may even be consolidated, and acquire new confidence."

Ellsworth left for home the end of March, sailing from Bristol. His ship made port in Boston and from there the wearied voyager went on to Windsor. The waiting family that had remembered him two years earlier as a robust person of impressive physique were shocked to see a pale, emaciated old man step from the carriage.

Ellsworth was fifty-six years old when he left the service of the nation. In retirement he remained intensely interested in politics, and promoted better agricultural methods in Connecticut, where he was recognized as his state's first citizen. He was a well-to-do man, and his estate, Elmwood, in Windsor, was the town's showplace. He died where he had wished to die, in his home, November 26, 1807.

SELECTED BIBLIOGRAPHY

For complete biographical information, see William G. Brown, *The Life of Oliver Ellsworth* (New York, 1905). A caustic observer of Ellsworth's contemporaries is E. S. Maclay, in *The Journal of William Maclay* (New York, 1890). Indispensable material is located in Edmund C. Burnett, *The Continental Congress* (New York, 1941) and in Max Farrand, ed., *The Records of the Federal Convention of 1787,* 4 vols., (New Haven, 1911–1937).

Oliver Ellsworth

REPRESENTATIVE OPINIONS

MOODIE v. THE SHIP PHOEBE ANNE, 3 DALL. 319 (1796)

Despite his own strong feelings against the French, Ellsworth upheld all her rights under applicable treaties. When the ship *Phoebe Anne,* a French privateer, put in for repairs at Charleston, South Carolina, she was libelled by the owner of a prize she had taken. However under the French treaty such ships were allowed access to American ports and Ellsworth dismissed the libel.

ERROR from the Circuit Court for the district of South Carolina.

The Phoebe Anne, a British vessel, had been captured by a French privateer, and sent into Charleston. The British consul filed a libel, claiming restitution of the prize, upon a suggestion, that the privateer had been illegally outfitted, or had illegally augmented her force, within the United States. On the proofs, it appeared, that the privateer had originally entered the port of Charleston, armed and commissioned for war; that she had there taken out her guns, masts and sails, which remained on shore, until the general repairs of the vessel were completed, when they were again put on board, with the same force, or thereabouts; and that, on a subsequent cruise, the prize in question was taken. The decrees in the district and circuit courts were both in favor of the captors; and on the return of the record into this court, *Reed,* having pointed out the additional repairs, argued, generally, on the impolicy and inconveniency of suffering privateers to equip in our ports.

ELLSWORTH, Chief Justice.—Suggestions of policy and convenience cannot be considered in the judicial determination of a question of right: the treaty with France, whatever that is, must have its effect. By the 19th article, it is declared, that French vessels, whether public and of war, or private and of merchants, may, on any urgent necessity, enter our ports, and be supplied with all things needful for repairs. In the present case, the privateer only underwent a repair; and the mere replacement of her force cannot be a material augmentation; even if an augmentation of force could be deemed (which we do not decide) a sufficient cause for restitution.

BY THE COURT.—Let the decree of the circuit court be affirmed.

WISCART v. DAUCHY, 3 DALL. 321 (1796)

In an action to set aside certain conveyances as fraudulent, the circuit court held that fraud had been proved by the plaintiff. The defendants brought the case to the Supreme Court by appeal instead of by writ of error. Ellsworth examined the difference between the two procedures, particularly as it bore on the conclusiveness of the circuit court findings. His distinction was important in the development of the Supreme Court's appellate jurisdiction.

ELLSWORTH, Chief Justice.—I will make a few remarks in support of the rule. The constitution, distributing the judicial power of the United States, vests in the supreme court, an original as well as an appellate jurisdiction. The original jurisdiction, however, is confined to cases affecting ambassadors, other public ministers and consuls, and those in which a state shall be a part. In all other cases, only an appellate jurisdiction is given to the court; and even the appellate jurisdiction is, likewise, qualified; inasmuch as it is given "with such exceptions, and under such regulations, as the congress shall make." Here, then, is the ground, and the only ground, on which we can sustain an appeal. If congress has provided no rule to regulate our proceedings, we cannot exercise an appellate jurisdiction; and if the rule is provided, we cannot depart from it. The question, therefore, on the constitutional point of an appellate jurisdiction, is simply, whether congress has established any rule for regulating its exercise?

It is to be considered, then, that the judicial statute of the United States speaks of an appeal and of a writ of error; but it does not confound the terms, nor use them promiscuously. They are to be understood, when used, according to their ordinary acceptation, unless something appears in the act itself, to control, modify or change the fixed and technical sense which they have previously borne. An appeal is a process of civil law origin, and removes a cause entirely; subjecting the fact, as well as the law, to a review and retrial: but a writ of error is a process of common-law origin, and it removes nothing for re-examination, but the law. Does the statute observe this obvious distinction? I think it does. In the 21st section, there is a provision for allowing an appeal in admiralty and maritime causes from the district to the circuit court; but it is declared, that the matter in dispute must exceed the value of $300, or no appeal can be sustained; and yet, in the preceding section, we find, that decrees and judgments in civil actions may be removed by writ of error from the district to the circuit court, though the value of the matter in dispute barely exceeds $50. It is unnecessary, however, to make any remark on this apparent diversity: the only question is, whether the civil actions here spoken of, include causes of admiralty and maritime jurisdiction? Now, the term civil actions would, from its natural import, embrace every species of suit, which is not of a criminal kind; and when it is considered, that the district court has a criminal as well as a civil jurisdiction, it is clear, that the term was used by the legislature, not to distinguish between admiralty causes and other civil actions, but to exclude the idea of removing judgments in criminal prosecutions, from an inferior to a superior tribunal. Besides, the language of the first member of the 22d section seems calculated to obviate every doubt. It is there said, that final *decrees* and judgments in civil actions in a district court may be removed into the circuit court, upon a writ of error; and since there cannot be a *decree* in the district court, in any case, except cases of admiralty and maritime jurisdiction, it follows, of course, that such cases must be intended, and that if they are removed at all, it can only be done by writ of error.

In this way, therefore, the appellate jurisdiction of the circuit court is to be exercised; but it remains to inquire, whether any provision is made for the exercise of the appellate jurisdiction of the supreme court; and I think, there is, by unequivocal words of reference. Thus, the 22d section of the act declares, that "upon a like process," that is, upon a writ of error, final judgments and decrees in civil actions (a description still employed in contradistinction to criminal prosecutions) and suits in equity, in the circuit court, may be here re-examined, and reversed or affirmed. Among the causes liable to be thus brought hither upn a writ of error, are such as had been previously removed into the circuit court, "by appeal from a district court," which can only be causes of admiralty and maritime jurisdiction.

It is observed, that a writ of error is a process more limited in its effects than an appeal; but whatever may be the operation, if an appellate jurisdiction can only be exercised by this court conformable to such regulations as are made by the congress, and if congress has prescribed a writ of error, and no other mode, by which it can be exercised, still, I say, we are bound to pursue that mode, and can neither make nor adopt another. The law may, indeed, be improper and inconvenient; but it is of more importance, for a judicial determination, to ascertain what the law is, than to speculate upon what it ought to be. If, however, the construction, that a statement of facts by the circuit court is conclusive, would amount to a denial of justice, would be oppressively injurious to individuals, or would be productive of any general mischief, I should then be disposed to resort to any other rational exposition of the law, which would not be attended with these deprecated consequences. But, surely, it cannot be deemed a denial of justice, that a man shall not be permitted to try his cause two or three times over. If he has one opportunity for the trial of all the parts of his case, justice is satisfied; and even if the decision of the circuit court had been made final, no denial of justice could be imputed to our government; much less, can the imputation be fairly made, because the law directs that in cases of appeal, part shall be decided by one tribunal, and part by another; the facts by the court below, and the law by this court. Such a distribution of jurisdiction has long been established in England.

Nor is there anything in the nature of a fact, which renders it impracticable or improper to be ascertained by a judge; and if there were, a fact could never be ascertained in this court, in matters of appeal. If, then, we are competent to ascertain a fact, when assembled here, I can discern no reason why we should not be equally competent to the task, when sitting in the circuit court; nor why it should be supposed, that a judge is more able, or more worthy, to ascertain the facts in a suit in equity (which, indisputably, can only be removed by writ of error), than to ascertain the facts in a cause of admiralty and maritime jurisdiction.

The statute has made a special provision, that the mode of proof, by oral testimony and examination of witnesses, shall be the same in all the courts of the United States, as well in the trial of causes in equity and of admiralty and maritime jurisdiction, as of actions at common law: but it was perceived, that although the personal attendance of witnesses could easily be procured in the district or circuit courts, the difficulty of bringing them from the remotest parts of the Union, to the seat of government, was insurmountable; and therefore, it became necessary, in every description of suits, to make a statement of the facts in the circuit court definitive, upon an appeal to this court.

If, upon the whole, the original constitutional grant of an appellate jurisdiction is to be enforced in the way that has been suggested, then all the testimony must be transmitted, reviewed, re-examined and settled here; great private and public inconvenience would ensue; and it was useless to provide that "the circuit courts should cause the facts on which they found their sentence or decree fully to appear upon the record."

But, upon the construction contained in the rule laid down by the court, there cannot, in any case, be just cause of complaint, as to the question of fact, since it is ascertained by an impartial and enlightened tribunal; and, as to the question of law, the re-examination in this court is wisely meant, and calculated to preserve unity of principle, in the administration of justice throughout the United States.(*a*)

On the 12th of August, the Chief Justice delivered the opinion of the court upon the point, whether there was, in this cause, such a statement of facts, as the legislature contemplated?

BY THE COURT.—The decree states, that certain conveyances are fraudulent; and had it stopped with that general declaration, some doubt might reasonably be entertained, whether it was not more properly an inference, than the statement of a fact; since fraud must always principally depend upon the *quo animo*. But the court immediately afterwards proceed to describe the fraud, or *quo animo*, declaring, that "the conveyances were intended to defraud the complainant, and to prevent his obtaining satisfaction for a just demand"; which is not an inference from a fact, but a statement of the fact itself. It is another fact, illustrative of this position, that "the grantee was a party and privy to the fraud."

We are, therefore, of opinion, that the circuit court have sufficiently caused the facts on which they decided, to appear from the pleadings and decree, in conformity to the act of Congress.

The decree affirmed.

Bushrod Washington

☆ 1762–1829 ☆

APPOINTED BY

JOHN ADAMS

YEARS ON COURT

1798–1829

Bushrod Washington

by

ALBERT P. BLAUSTEIN

and

ROY M. MERSKY

BUSHROD WASHINGTON had ability in large measure. And he had all or most of the other attributes which should have resulted in enduring fame: diligence, learning, modesty, and personal charm. His lineage was such that he could not be ignored, and he was given the opportunity of devoting most of his adult life to public service—including thirty-one years on the Supreme Court (1798 to 1829).

Yet Bushrod Washington is far from a famous name in American history; indeed, it is far from famous even in the history of the United States Supreme Court, primarily because Washington's tenure on the Bench coincided with that of his brilliant and forceful friend Chief Justice John Marshall. In mid-twentieth century, the first reaction to his name is to ask whether he was related to the first president. He was a nephew of the childless George Washington and as "favorite nephew" inherited the President's estate at Mount Vernon. His closeness to these two towering figures should not, however, obscure his genuine contribution to the development of constitutional law.

The background and early career of Bushrod Washington show a distinctive precocity and talent that cannot be explained simply by the influence of family. Born on June 5, 1762, the son of John Augustine and Hanna (Bushrod) Washington, young Bushrod Washington received an education typical of the

ALBERT P. BLAUSTEIN, Professor of Law at Rutgers University Law School at Camden, is author of Civil Rights and the American Negro *and is co-author of* The American Lawyer *and* Desegregation and the Law.

ROY MERSKY, Professor of Law and Director of Research at the University of Texas, is author of many articles on law and library science.

colonial Virginia aristocracy. He was born in Westmoreland County and was taught by tutors at home and in the house of Richard Henry Lee. He entered William and Mary College in 1775 and received his A.B. degree in 1778 at age sixteen. He apparently returned to his family home after graduation, remaining there until 1780.

It is possible that Washington first met John Marshall during the early days of the Revolution, but according to college records they were both students of George Wythe's law course at William and Mary. There both became founding members of the Phi Beta Kappa society, then a semi-secret fraternity. Marshall left college in August, 1780, after receiving his license to practice law. Washington, however, stayed on into the early fall, when in the final throes of the War of Independence Cornwallis invaded Virginia. Washington volunteered for service in the Continental Army and joined a cavalry troop headed by Colonel John F. Mercer and under the command of the Marquis de Lafayette. Serving as a private of dragoons, he stayed in action through the summer of 1781, when Cornwallis crossed the James River and no longer posed a threat to Virginia. Washington took part in the clash at Green Spring and later witnessed the surrender of Cornwallis at Yorktown.

Following the War of Independence Washington studied law for two years in the offices of the eminent Philadelphia attorney James Wilson, who was to become one of President Washington's original appointees to the Supreme Court. It was ironic that it was Wilson's seat to which Bushrod Washington succeeded when he was appointed to the Bench by President Adams in 1798. Neither Washington nor Marshall ever received a formal legal education culminating in a degree. The war with England had precluded study at the Inns of Court, and the fledgling American universities had not yet established law schools; Wythe taught law for only a few months at William and Mary. Extensive legal training thus took the form of an informal apprenticeship or "reading" in a lawyer's office. Using these criteria, Washington received unusually complete and excellent training, particularly in comparison to Marshall's meager six months with Wythe. Since Wilson was an outstanding practitioner, his reader's prospects, as well as his scholarship, must have benefited.

Washington began his law practice in Westmoreland County in 1784, later moving to Alexandria where he found "a wider sphere for the exercise of his talents." About 1790, and certainly by 1792, he moved again, this time to Richmond where Marshall had already been practicing for more than ten years. In 1785 he married Julia Ann Blackburn, daughter of Colonel Thomas Blackburn of Rippon Lodge, Virginia, the volunteer aide-de-camp to General Washington. (Blackburn, who was wounded at Germantown was once referred to by General Washington as belonging to "good old Federal fighting stock.") Mrs. Bushrod Washington was a delicate woman, a semi-invalid for some years, and though she and her husband were childless, they seemed to have been devoted to each other. She accompanied him everywhere, even on his rounds as a circuit judge, and maintained the elaborate hospitality required by the semi-official status of

Mount Vernon, the home and tomb of the first President. When Bushrod Washington died in Philadelphia in 1829, she survived him by three days.

The relationship between Bushrod Washington and his President uncle, influenced young Washington's early career. John Augustine Washington, Bushrod's father, was the closest brother to the President. A strong-minded but gentlemanly man, he served as a delegate in the state legislature of Virginia and as a magistrate in Westmoreland County. It must have been apparent to General Washington by 1780 that he would not have children of his own. At this point he chose the son of his closest brother as his eventual heir. No doubt the General-President aided his nephew's career, but far more notable was his admirable restraint in doing so. When Bushrod Washington went to Philadelphia to complete his law studies with James Wilson, his father paid for his board. But what of the cost of the education itself? The following note, written in Philadelphia on March 22, 1782, supplies at least a partial answer: "I promise to pay James Wilson, Esq: or order on demand one hundred guineas, his fee for receiving my nephew, Bushrod Washington, as a Student of Law in his office." It is signed, "G. Washington."

In a letter to Bushrod's father on January 16, 1783, George Washington wrote: "I have heard a favourable acct. of Bushrod, and doubt not but his prudence will direct him to a proper line of Conduct. I have given him my sentiments on his head, and persuade myself that, with the advice of Mr. Wilson, to whose friendship as well as instruction in his profession I recommended him and the admonition of others, he will stand as good a chance as most youth of his age to avoid the Vices of large Cities, which have their advantages and disadvantages in fitting a man for the great theatre of public Life."

In September, 1798, before Bushrod Washington was considered for a vacancy on the Supreme Court, the former President assisted his nephew in obtaining a seat in the Sixth Congress. Both John Marshall and Bushrod Washington had been invited to visit George Washington at Mount Vernon to discuss the forthcoming congressional elections. Bushrod Washington, it is reported, "readily agreed to offer himself for a seat," but Marshall consented to run only upon the ex-President's urgings.

George Washington, however, was not a man inclined to nepotism. When Bushrod once let himself be persuaded to ask his uncle, then President, for an appointment as district attorney for Virginia, Washington's reply was curt: "Do you think yourself worthy of the office, and even if you do, do you suppose I would use the patronage of my office for the benefit of anyone, however worthy, connected with me?" When young Washington wished to organize a "Patriotic Society to inquire into the state of public affairs" he received a cold reply from his uncle: "I have seen as much evil as good result from such societies as you describe . . ." Nor did Bushrod Washington bask in the reflected glory of his uncle. His name made him conspicuous, but his modest nature protected him from the jealous. Neither uncle nor nephew, in short, sought to circumvent the difficulties of a legal career by using the power so easily available to both of them.

It is also clear, as pointed out by Lawrence B. Custer, that the former President had not "used his influence with the Adams administration" to help his nephew obtain his seat on the Supreme Court. If either of the Washingtons had expected that the appointment was imminent, Custer reasons, they would have discussed it at their Mount Vernon meeting in September, and the following letter would have been completely unnecessary.

Richmond October 19th 1798

My dear Uncle

Upon my return to this place I met with a Commission from the President of the United States appointing me one of the Judges of the Supreme Court. This appointment I have accepted, and was induced thereto by the strongest motives.

I was very unwilling to abandon a profession, to which I was much attached, and to the study of which I had devoted the greatest part of my life. A situation which permits me to pursue it, and to improve the knowledge which I have acquired in this science, wihout endangering my sight (already considerably injured) could not fail to be agreeable to me.

Independent of this consideration, I could not upon a small piece of poor land in Westmoreland have paid debts which I owe, & supported my family.

Knowing the wish you had, that I should be a candidate for Congress, I have felt much uneasiness lest my acceptance of this appointment should be disagreeable to you. The desire of attempting to serve my Country in that line had also created in myself an anxiety for success in the election, altho' I foresaw the extreme inconvenience which could result from it, in my private affairs; I was however willing to make the sacrifice. I trust that this candid statement of my situation will be an apology with you for having relinquished my first intention, and I flatter myself that my services will not be less useful to my Country in the office which I now hold, than they would have been in the legislative Councils.—

I am just preparing to go upon the Southern Circuit, & shall if possible leave this place tomorrow.

From the best information which I could collect, there is very little doubt, but that a federal man will be sent from our district: whether Genl. [*Henry*] *Lee, or Mr. Landon Carter will offer is not certainly ascertained; but I believe it will be the latter.—*

Mrs. W. Joins me in love to my aunt & yourself, and believe me to be most sincerely

My dear Uncle
Your affect. Nephew
B. Washington

Bushrod Washington was the active executor of his uncle's will. He inherited the estate at Mount Vernon, including a considerable property in slaves. He also inherited the ex-President's public and private papers. Yet it was not Bushrod Washington who was to author the George Washington biography. About two months after the death of his uncle in 1800 he wrote, "A diffidence of my own talents for such an undertaking, together with weak eyes and want of time, will probably forbid me from attempting it; but I trust that the selection of a fit character may be in my power, and this I shall endeavor to make immediately." At Justice Washington's request and with his assistance, Marshall undertook the task which resulted in his five-volume *Life of Washington.*

On the lighter side is an anecdote told by Washington Irving—one which not only reflects the relationships between Justice Washington and both his uncle and John Marshall, but which even more reflects the contemporary knowledge of those relationships. In Irving's words: "They [Bushrod Washington and Marshall] were on their way to visit Mount Vernon, attended by a black servant, who had charge of a large portmanteau containing their clothes. As they passed through a wood near Mount Vernon, they stopped to make a hasty toilet, being covered with dust. They undressed while the servant opened the portmanteau. Out flew cakes of soap, and fancy articles of all kinds but no clothes. The man by mistake had changed portmanteaus with a Scotch pedlar at their last resting place. Gen. Washington happened to be near and attracted by the noise came up and was so overcome by their strange plight and the servant's dismay that he is said to have actually rolled on the grass with laughter."

During Washington's practice in Alexandria he specialized in chancery cases. His practice in Richmond was successful, though far from sensational. He was primarily the student and scholar. Many law students, including Henry Clay, were trained in his office. He also served as reporter of the Court of Appeals from 1700 to 1796 and devoted much effort toward writing two volumes of *Reports of Cases Argued in the Court of Appeals of Virginia.* (Four volumes of his *Reports of Cases Determined in the Circuit Court of the United States for the Third Circuit, 1803–27* were later prepared during his Supreme Court years.) In his role as attorney he defended the immunity of the Episcopal Church's land holdings from seizure by Virginia. His position in the "Glebe lands" controversy was determined both by his devotion to the Episcopal communion and by his basic political conservatism. In 1815 this argument would be echoed by his decision in *Terret* v. *Taylor,* 9 Cranch 43 (1815) that church lands were private property which Virginia could neither dispose of nor control.

As his son C. Bushrod Washington later wrote, "He continued a deep student of law, so absorbing and assimilating it into his nature that it became his possession. Sacrificing general literature, belles lettres, and all that pertained chiefly to adornment, for the weightier matters of the law, he became distinguished as a counselor-at-law rather than an advocate." His studies apparently resulted in physical toll as well. Timothy Pickering, then Secretary of State, wrote President Adams in 1798 that Washington's "indefatigable pursuit of knowledge and the business of his profession has deprived him of the sight of one eye; it will be happy if the loss does not make him perfectly the emblem of justice."

Politics necessarily involved Bushrod Washington. In 1787 he had, on his uncle's advice, run for the Virginia House of Delegates and had been elected. The following year he was a delegate to the state ratification convention, where he, Madison, and Marshall argued successfully for the adoption of the Constitution of the United States. At the convention his views foreshadowed the Federalist philosophy and his votes proved vitally important for ratification of the Constitution.

When Mr. Justice Wilson, who had been in bad health, died on August 21, 1798, five men were mentioned as possible successors—Jacob Rush, Samuel Sitgreaves, and Richard Peters of Pennsylvania, and Bushrod Washington and John Marshall of Virginia. President Adams determined that the appointment should go to Virginia, which had not been represented on the Court since John Blair's resignation in 1795. Adams wrote to Secretary of State Pickering that either Virginian was acceptable. "The reasons urged by Judge Iredell for an early appointment of a successor (to Wilson) are important. I am ready to appoint either General Marshall or Bushrod Washington. The former I suppose ought to have the preference. If you think so, send him a commission. If you think any other person more proper, please to mention him."

In his reply, Pickering paid due respect to Washington's talents, virtues, and general patriotism, but raised the question of his age: "He is young, not more, I believe, than three or four and thirty." (He was thirty-six.)

To this faint praise Adams answered: "The name, the connections, the character, the merit and abilities of Mr. Washington are greatly respected, but I still think that General Marshall ought to be preferred. Of the three envoys [involved in the XYZ Affair], the conduct of Marshall alone has been entirely satisfactory and ought to be marked by the most decided approbation of the public . . . He is older at the Bar than Mr. Washington, and I know by experience that seniority at the Bar is nearly as much regarded as in the army."

Marshall was offered the appointment but declined it to run for Congress. In his letter declining the nomination, he strongly recommended that Washington be offered the post instead. Adams then decided to fill the vacancy by the appointment of Bushrod Washington, and sent the commission to him October 6, 1798. He accepted the appointment and a recommission was made on December 20, when the Senate convened.

In the early days of the Supreme Court, the Justices heard trials as well as appeals. They frequently sat at *nisi prius,* with a jury, for the trial of issues of fact. Washington, as his letter to his uncle of October 19, 1798, indicated, was originally assigned to the Southern Circuit; but from 1803 until his death, he presided over the Third Circuit, in both Pennsylvania and New Jersey. In spite of his early specialization in cases in equity, he was attentive in court and lucid in his summations.

It was as a trial judge that Washington undoubtedly excelled. He received the extravagant and probably exaggerated accolades of David Paul Brown of the Philadelphia Bar, who had witnessed the judge in action. "Perhaps," said Brown, "the greatest *nisi prius* judge that the world has ever known, not excepting Chief Justice Holt or Lord Mansfield, was the late Justice Washington." Brown went on to laud his "great perspicuity and great-mindedness, exemplary self-possession and inflexible courage, all crowned by an honesty of purpose." During a trial he took few notes, keeping his eyes fixed on the witness or counsel.

He never addressed the audience or even seemed to know that they were present. Washington, it is reported, concentrated completely on the discharge of his official duties, thus severely limiting his further learning. Perhaps that is why Brown, in a less enthusiastic moment, commented that his "literary reading was so limited that it is questionable whether he ever knew who was the author of *Macbeth*."

By far the most noteworthy case which came before Washington as a Circuit Judge was *United States* v. *Bright,* 24 Fed. Cases 1232 (No. 14,647) (C.C.E.D. Pa. 1809). It was the culmination of what Charles Warren, in his *The Supreme Court in United States History,* called a "dangerous clash . . . between the Pennsylvania and the United States officials, in a dispute which had been in existence between the two sovereignties for about twenty-five years." Technically, the case involved the question of whether the Constitution gave federal courts exclusive jurisdiction of all admiralty and maritime cases. It also involved the consitituional power of a state to direct its governor to employ force to resist the execution of a federal court decree.

During the Revolutionary War, in 1778, Gideon Olmstead and three others captured a British sloop on which they were being held prisoner. They had been steering for a United States port when, within five miles of land, the sloop was seized as a prize by a brig belonging to the State of Pennsylvania. The disagreement over who was entitled to the prize money was heard in Philadelphia in a court of admiralty established by the Pennsylvania State Legislature. Only one-fourth of the prize money was awarded to Olmstead and his associates. Olmstead then turned to the court of appeals in prize causes, which had been established by Congress under the Articles of Confederation. The prize court reversed the decision of the Pennsylvania tribunal and awarded the whole prize to Olmstead and his companions.

The Pennsylvania court was directed to order the marshal to sell the vessel and cargo and pay over the net proceeds to the former prisoners of war, but it refused to acknowledge the jurisdiction of the congressional court. Instead, the marshal was directed to make the sale, and bring the proceeds into the state court. In 1779 the judge then turned over the state's money to the state treasurer.

In 1802 Olmstead filed suit against the treasurers' heirs in the district court of the United States, arguing that the earlier decree of the Articles of Confederation court should be executed. The federal court ruled in his favor in January, 1803.

The Pennsylvania legislature soon passed an act requiring the treasurer's representatives to turn the money over to the state treasury. At the same time, the governor was directed "to protect the just rights of the state by any further measures he might deem necessary." This was countered by an order of the Supreme Court directing the district court judge to execute the judgment in favor of Olmstead. The district court judge complied.

In response to the federal court order, the governor ordered General Michael Bright of the state militia "immediately to have in readiness such a portion of the militia under his command, as might be necessary to execute the orders, and to employ them to protect and defend the persons and the property of the treasurer's representatives from and against any process, founded on the decree of the . . . judge of the district court of the United States, . . ." A guard was then placed, which opposed with muskets and bayonets the efforts of the United States marshal to serve the appropriate court writ.

General Bright and other members of the militia were then indicted and brought to trial before Justice Washington and District Court Judge Richard Peters for resisting the process of a court of the United States.

The sentencing of General Bright was more than an act of courage. It was also the important judicial determination that "a state has no constitutional power . . . to employ force to resist the execution of a decree of a federal court, [even] though such decree is deemed to have been beyond the jurisdiction of the [federal] court to make . . ."

This trial put Justice Washington's judicial skill and high sense of duty to a severe test. It was surrounded by violent popular agitation. The states' rights faction disdained federal authority and threatened not to accept the judgment of a federal court. Many had felt that Justice Washington, a Virginian, would not have the presumption to charge against the Pennsylvania defendants, let alone convict and sentence them. But Washington showed a rare calm and wisdom in the midst of the turmoil. When counsel for both sides had concluded, the crowd that had come to relish the judge's expected embarrassment overflowed the small courtroom, but Washington only suggested that judgment be pronounced in a larger courtroom so that the citizens' legitimate curiosity about the result could be satisfied. When he reassembled the court, he found the defendant, a Pennsylvania militia general, guilty of obstructing the process of the federal courts and, in an eloquent speech, sentenced him to prison. Interest in the trial had died down somewhat a month later, and President Madison pardoned the offender just as his sentence was about to begin.

Despite his acknowledged judicial learning and austere temperament, Washington never "looked" his role as Supreme Court Justice. A small man, sallow, never in perfect health, and blind in one eye, he was an inveterate snuff taker and untidy dresser. Even his habits were respected, however. Once, when Henry Clay, his former student, boldly took a pinch of Justice Washington's snuff while arguing a case before the Court, Justice Story said, "I do not believe there is a man in the United States who could have done that, but Mr. Clay." Perhaps a more reliable guide to Washington's character can be found in his methodical habits. He filed all his correspondence according to date and author, preserving even seemingly worthless trifles, such as a letter from someone claiming to be his illegitimate son (endorsed "From some fool or knave claiming to be my son"), and another of bilingual vituperation signed "Votre implacable enemy" (annotated "Anonymous and sufficiently impudent").

Considerable correspondence concerning the Court, between Washington and Story and Marshall and Story, has survived, so the modern student can only assume that a similar body of correspondence between the closer friends Washington and Marshall must have existed, but was destroyed by the principals or their heirs.

During the period of Washington's service, many able Supreme Court Justices were relegated to virtual obscurity—overshadowed by the greater brilliance and force of Chief Justice Marshall and, to a lesser extent, of Justice Story. Nevertheless, as Justice Frankfurter has pointed out, "In William Johnson . . . Marshall had a colleague of intellectual independence and power," and "At least two other members of Marshall's Court, Bushrod Washington and Joseph Story, must have had views of their own . . ."

This was also the period in which there were comparatively few concurring and dissenting opinions; and Marshall wrote the bulk of the majority opinions. Since Washington practically never disagreed with Marshall, he seldom recorded his individual judicial views in the reports. The two Justices differed only three times during the twenty-nine years that they shared on the Supreme Court, and only once in *Dartmouth College* v. *Woodward,* 4 Wheat. 518 (1819), did Washington add his opinion to Marshall's decision.

The very modesty and amiability which made him so valuable a judge tended to conceal the greatness in him. In 1808 Justice Story commented on this paradox: "Nothing about him indicates greatness; he converses with simplicity and frankness. But he is highly esteemed as a profound lawyer, and I believe not without reason. His written opinions are composed with ability, and on the bench, he exhibits great promptitude and firmness in decision. It requires intimacy to value him as he deserves."

When death ended Washington's judicial service in 1829, Marshall said that "no man knew his worth better or deplores his death more than myself." He added: "I had few friends whom I valued so highly . . . or whose loss I should regret more sincerely. . . . We have been most intimate friends for more than forty years, and never has our friendship sustained the slightest interruption." Another contemporary eulogy extended the praise: "No learning however profound, no intelligence however cultivated, no patience however unwearied, no deportment however dignified, if this be wanting, can make a judge truly respectable. It is in their union that judicial excellence can alone be found. The late Judge Washington was a true exemplification of their blended influence . . . No man ever more truly appreciated or admired legal excellence and private worth. Such was the respect felt for his character and conduct, that the good uniformly treated him with respect and deference, because they revered him, and the turbulent were in his presence awed into decorum."

In his thirty-one years of tenure on the Court, Washington wrote seventy majority opinions, two concurrences, six *seriatim,* and, remarkably, only two dissents, or more exactly, one, in *Mason* v. *Haile,* 12 Wheat. 270 (1827). In that dissent he argued that, contrary to Story's and Marshall's opinion, a state could not retroactively abolish imprisonment for debt; the dissent was logical and grounded in precedent, but narrow and somewhat Draconian in outlook. He implicitly dissented from the majority decision in *United States* v. *Fisher,* 2 Cranch 358 (1804) by not taking part in the judgment.

The striking lack of dissents may well have constituted part of a deliberate effort by Washington to support Marshall's attempts to have the court speak as a single, well-defined judicial voice. On one occasion he convinced Justice Story to suppress a dissent on the grounds that, in Story's words, "delivering dissenting opinions on ordinary occasions weakens the authority of the Court, and is of no public benefit."

Since Washington's views on constitutional questions closely paralleled Marshall's Federalism, and since Marshall wrote most of the important constitutional opinions during their twenty-nine years together on the Supreme Court, there are few decisions by Mr. Justice Washington in this area. But at least three are significant.

The first of these is the carefully reasoned concurring opinion in *Dartmouth College* v. *Woodward* in 1819, which marked the only time that Washington felt called upon to add to Marshall's opinion. Here Washington warned against a wide interpretation of the decision. Justice Story had written a sweeping *obiter dictum* which brought all corporations under the contracts clause of the Constitution, and Washington undoubtedly wished to limit its effect.

In the celebrated case of *Ogden* v. *Saunders,* 12 Wheat. 213 (1827), Washington wrote the first part of the Court's opinion. The case involved the respective powers of Congress and the states in the field of bankruptcy. A contract had been made in New York by a New York debtor with a citizen of another state, *after* the passage of the New York insolvency law. The issues were: (1) whether a state bankruptcy law was valid as to contracts made after its passage; and (2) whether such a state insolvency law could discharge a contract of a citizen of another state.

The Supreme Court was closely divided on these questions. Did the federal government have exclusive powers over bankruptcy? Congress had been given the power under Art. I, Sec. 8 of the Constitution to establish "uniform Laws on the subject of Bankruptcies throughout the United States," but no law had as yet been enacted. Was the state insolvency statute a "Law impairing the Obligation of Contracts," as prohibited under Art. I, Sec. 10 of the Constitution?

In the first part of this two-part decision, Washington wrote the majority opinion, supported by three of his colleagues; Marshall spoke for the three dissenters. While Washington retained his previous belief that the power of congress over bankruptcy was exclusive, he upheld the constitutionality of the New York insolvency statutes on the narrow ground that they formed part of the contract when it was made and therefore did not impair its obligation. The decision did not overturn the veto which the Court had already imposed on state insolvency power applied retroactively in *Sturges* v. *Crowninshield,* 4 Wheat. 122 (1819). It is possible to argue that the *Ogden* opinion departed from Washington's own earlier stand on circuit in *Golden* v. *Prince,* 10 Fed. Cases 542 (No. 5,509) (C.C.E.D. Pa. 1814), but Washington's respect for Court decisions made him apply the *Crowninshield* decision unbendingly and since it had held that congressional power was not exclusive, he upheld the New York law.

In his opinion he defended the wisdom and good will of the state legislature. "[T]he question which I have been examining is involved in difficulty and doubt. But if I could rest my opinion in favor of the constitutionality of the law on which the question arises, on no other ground than this doubt so felt and acknowledged, that alone, would, in my estimation, be a satisfactory vindication of it. It is but a decent respect due to the wisdom, the integrity and the patriotism of the legislative body, by which any law is passed, to presume in favor of its validity, until its violation of the constitution is proved beyond all reasonable doubt." Thompson, Trimble, and Johnson agreed. Johnson, however, declared that the power of Congress was *not* exclusive, and that the state could enact retroactive insolvency laws applicable to contracts made before its passage as well as those made after it. The dissenters, Marshall, Story, and Duvall, denied that an insolvency law enacted prior to a contract became a part of such contract. They argued that the majority view made the bankruptcy clause of the Constitution meaningless. But did the state bankruptcy law discharge a contract of a citizen of *another* state? In the second part of this two-part decision, Justice Johnson spoke for the majority—again a four-man majority. He said that such a contract could not be discharged. Wrote Johnson: "[W]hen . . . the states pass beyond their own limits, and the rights of their own citizens, and act upon the rights of citizens of other states, there arises a conflict of sovereign power, and a collision with the judicial powers granted to the United States, which renders the exercise of such a power incompatible with the rights of other states, and with the constitution of the United States." Now Marshall, Story, and Duvall were part of the 4–3 majority; Washington, Thompson, and Trimble dissented.

The third of Washington's important constitutional law opinions is the majority opinion in *Green* v. *Biddle,* 8 Wheat. 1, 69 (1823)—another *cause célèbre.* Because of carelessly awarded patents and equally careless land surveys, Kentucky courts were plagued with conflicting land claims. In order to resolve this problem, the legislature had enacted statutes providing that the legal owner of a piece of property could not take possession until he had compensated the occupier of the land for any improvements. If he did not pay, the squatter could take the land upon payment of its value without improvements. The legal owners charged that the laws violated a compact made between Virginia and Kentucky when Kentucky became a state in 1791, assuring the maintenance of all private rights in the new state exactly as they had been maintained by the 1791 laws of Virginia. The state of Kentucky denied any violation, as did the occupiers of the land who were caught in the middle of the argument.

Speaking through Justice Story in 1821, in *Green* v. *Biddle,* 8 Wheat. 1 (1821), the Supreme Court declared the Kentucky statutes unconstitutional. But in October of that year, the Kentucky legislature passed a resolution denouncing the decision as "incompatible with the constitutional powers of this State," and Henry Clay was directed to ask for a reargument. In the second and final decision in 1823, it was Justice Washington who spoke for the Supreme Court, which again held the Kentucky laws unconstitutional.

It was not an easy or popular decision to make. Justice Washington recognized that when he wrote in his opinion: "[W]e hold ourselves answerable to God, our consciences, and our country, to decide this question according to the dictates of our best judgment, be the consequences of the decision what they may." It was typical of Washington's seriousness that he wished to include this avowal of honesty, but it was also typical that his opinion supported existing legislation and discouraged the novel reinterpretation of statutes.

In an interview in 1829, Justice Washington offered a summary of his constitutional law philosophy. His conservative Federalism sought to avoid direct conflicts with the rights of states. The Court, he said, had always assumed good will on the part of state legislatures, in order to avoid giving offense to individual states. Statutes were overruled only when they directly interfered with the operation of the central government. The states could not tax the salaries of federal officers because, however slight the tax might be initially, it opened the way to removing the financial encouragement of able men to work for the government; the same went for state attempts to tax stocks issued under the authority of the federal government. In both these examples, however, future decisions permitting state taxation of federal stocks and salaries proved Washington wrong.

Washington was not deaf to the rights of individual citizens. He made the first attempt to interpret the privileges and immunities clause of the Constitution. In *Corfield* v. *Coryell,* 6 Fed. Cases 546 (No. 3,230) (C.C.E.D. Pa. 1823), Washington upheld the validity of a New Jersey law forbidding dredging for oysters in its waters from May until December. The New Jersey authorities seized the ship of an out-of-state fisherman gathering oysters and he protested, claiming that his privileges and immunities as a United States citizen were being infringed. Washington made the following comments about the meaning of the terms:

> *The inquiry is, what are the privileges and immunities of citizens in the several states? We feel no hesitation in confining these expressions to those privileges and immunities which are, in their nature, fundamental; which belong, of right, to the citizens of all free governments; and which have, at all times, been enjoyed by the citizens of the several states which compose this Union, from the time of their becoming free, independent, and sovereign. What these fundamental principles are, it would perhaps be more tedious than difficult to enumerate. They may, however, be all comprehended under the following general heads: Protection by the government; the enjoyment of life and liberty, with the right to acquire and possess property of every kind, and to pursue and obtain happiness and safety; subject nevertheless to such retraints as the government may justly prescribe for the general good of the whole. The right of a citizen of one state to pass through, or to reside in any other state, for purposes of trade, agriculture, professional pursuits, or otherwise; to claim the benefit of the writ of habeas corpus; to institute and maintain actions of any kind in the courts of the*

state; to take, hold and dispose of property, either real or personal; and an exemption from higher taxes or impositions than are paid by the other citizens of the state; may be mentioned as some of the particular privileges and immunities of citizens, which are clearly embraced by the general description of privileges deemed to be fundamental: to which may be added, the elective franchise, as regulated and established by the laws or exercised.

This decision was the starting point for many later attempts to define the limits of these key words.

Three of Mr. Justice Washington's less known "common law" decisions are also worthy of comment. He stated an important principle of the law of contracts when he spoke for the Court in *Eliason* v. *Henshaw,* 4 Wheat. 225 (1819). Wrote the Justice: "[A]n offer of a bargain by one person to another imposes no obligation upon the former until it is accepted by the latter, according to the terms in which the offer was made. Any qualification of, or departure from, those terms, invalidates the offer, unless the same be agreed to by the person who [originally] made it."

Thornton v. *Wynn,* 12 Wheat. 183 in 1827, involved both the liability of an indorser of a promissory note and a warranty on the sale of personal property. The indorser knew that he had been discharged from his liability under the note, but he still made an unconditional promise to pay it. Under these circumstances it was held that the holder of the note had the right to recover against that indorser; and that the indorser had impliedly waived prior demand by the holder on the maker of the note and notice to himself. The warranty question was structured this way: In a suit brought by a seller against a purchaser for the purchase price, is it a valid defense that the article purchased was not as warranted? The answer according to Washington was "yes." The purchaser could not be held for payment.

The third case, *Buckner* v. *Finley,* 2 Pet. 586 (1829), was concerned with some of the technicalities of bills of exchange, but it involved more than that. "For all national purposes, embraced by the federal constitution," wrote Justice Washington, "the states and the citizens thereof are one, united under the same sovereign authority, and governed by the same laws. In all other respects, the states are necessarily foreign to, and independent of, each other." He concluded that bills of exchange are not within "national purposes" to be governed by "the same laws." Thus bills of exchange drawn in one state on persons living in another state, "partake of the character of foreign bills" rather than inland bills and must be so treated in the law.

Although Bushrod Washington did not face the necessity of deciding civil rights and slavery cases, as did his colleagues later in the century, his views on slavery provide a cautionary antidote to his otherwise admirable career. He was in favor of the abolition of slavery according to any plan that was just for the slaves and their owners both. When President Washington died he did not, like Jefferson, free his slaves; he left them to Justice Washington under the proviso that they were to be freed upon the death of Martha Washington. Washington took a practical stance on the subject and felt that the dilapidated state of Mt. Vernon (and the difficulty of settling freed Negroes) gave him the right to ignore his uncle's wishes.

In 1816, he was elected the first president of the American Colonization Society, an organization whose object was the colonizing of liberated Negroes on the African Coast. In November, 1821, Washington sold fifty-four slaves from the Mount Vernon estate to "two gentlemen of Louisiana," and in doing so separated some of the slaves from their immediate families. The result was a bitter attack on humanitarian grounds in the "journals of the day." Washington sought to answer the charges, and, on September 18, 1821, wrote a lengthy letter about the sale to the editors of the Baltimore *Federal Republican.*

He gave as reasons the fact that he was unable to support his slaves "from the produce of their (own) labor," that some of his slaves showed a "total disregard of all authority," not unusual in view of the fact that they had been denied their promised freedom, and that he "had good reason for anticipating the escape of all the laboring men of any value to the northern states." Furthermore, he added, slaves were property, pure and simple, and his disposal of them was solely his concern:

". . . I take the liberty, on my own behalf, and on that of my southern fellow citizens, to enter a solemn protest against the propriety of any person questioning our right, *legal or moral,* to dispose of property which is secured to us by sanctions equally valid with those by which we hold every other species of property; . . .

"I pass by the *insinuation,* that, because General Washington thought proper to emancipate his slaves, his nephew ought to do so likewise, with the single observation, that I do not admit the right of any person to decide for me on this point."

As the colleague and friend of Justice Story and Chief Justice Marshall, Washington was naturally grouped with them. Justice William Johnson once complained that Marshall and Washington "are commonly estimated as a single judge"; when Story joined the court he complained that the duo had expanded into a "triumvirate." Washington lacked Story's broad erudition and Marshall's brilliant analytic style, but he held his own on the Court. In later years he received honorary LL.D. degrees from Harvard, Princeton, and the University of Pennsylvania. His family connections afforded him minimal advancement; his career might well have run the same course had he been born under a different name. Most of all, Washington provided a voice for conservative Federalism on the early Supreme Court. His respect for *stare decisis* gave the court a backbone of precedent and a respect for it from which it could later draw, even if his respect tended to make him choose the narrower of any two interpretations.

Bushrod Washington died in Philadelphia on November 26, 1829. No account of Justice Washington's career on the Court can be complete without reference to Justice Story's famous eulogy at his death:

> *For thirty-one years, Judge Washington held the station of justice of the supreme court, with a constantly increasing reputation and usefulness. Few men, indeed, have possessed higher qualifications for the office, either natural or acquired. Few men have left deeper traces in their judicial career of everything which a conscientious judge ought to propose for his ambition, or his virtue, or his glory. His mind was solid, rather than brilliant; sagacious and searching, rather than quick or eager; slow, but not torpid; steady, but not unyielding; comprehensive, and at the same time cautious; patient in inquiry, forcible in conception, clear in reasoning. He was, by original temperament, mild, conciliating and candid; and yet was remarkable for an uncompromising firmness. Of him, it may be truly said, that the fear of man never fell upon him; it never entered into his thoughts, much less was it seen in his actions. In him the love of justice was the ruling passion—it was the master-spring of all his conduct. . . . His wisdom was the wisdom of the law, chastened, and refined, and invigorated by study, guided by experience, dwelling little on theory, but constantly enlarging itself by a close survey of principles.*
>
> *He was a learned judge. Not in that every-day learning which may be gathered up by a hasty reading of books and cases; but that which is the result of long-continued laborious services, and comprehensive studies. He read to learn, and not to quote; to digest and master, and not merely to display. He was not easily satisfied. If he was not as profound as some, he was more exact than most men. But the value of his learning was, that it was the keystone of all his judgments. He indulged not the rash desire to fashion the law to his own views; but to follow out its precepts, with a sincere good faith and simplicity. Hence, he possessed the happy faculty of yielding just the proper weight to authority; neither, on the one hand, surrendering himself to the dictates of other judges, nor, on the other hand, overruling settled doctrines upon his own private notions of policy or justice.*

Justice Story's emphasis on the balanced wisdom of Bushrod Washington's life and legal philosophy is interesting as a well-informed contemporary view; but it is also equally valuable today as a lucid assessment of this modest and devoted Justice.

SELECTED BIBLIOGRAPHY

There is no definitive life of Washington. Relatively brief memorials were written by Horace Binney (published in Philadelphia in 1830) and Justice Joseph Story (included in W. W. Story, ed., *Life and Letters of Joseph Story* [Boston, 1851]). A sketch also appears in the proceedings published at 3 Peters vii (1832). References also appear in Albert J. Beveridge, *Life of John Marshall* (Boston, 1919); P. J. Staudenraus, *The African Colonization Movement* (New York, 1961) and Richard B. Davis, *Intellectual Life in Jefferson's Virginia* (Chaptel Hill, 1964). C. Bushrod Washington wrote an article about the Justice in 9 *Green Bag* 329 (1897).

Bushrod Washington

REPRESENTATIVE OPINIONS

OGDEN v. SAUNDERS, 12 WHEAT. 213 (1827)

Ogden v. *Saunders* marked the only time Washington wrote a majority opinion on a constitutional question where he differed with John Marshall. The question presented was whether a New York insolvency law passed before the execution of a contract could be applied after the debtor became bankrupt. *Sturges* v. *Crowninshield* had held that laws passed after a contract was executed were invalid insofar as they tried to discharge the debt of one of the parties. But a law passed before a contract was made, Washington held, became part of that contract. His diffidence in disputing Marshall on this point pervades the opinion.

WASHINGTON, JUSTICE.—The first and most important point to be decided in this cause turns essentially upon the question, whether the obligation of a contract is impaired by a state bankrupt or insolvent law, which discharges the person and the future acquisitions of the debtor from his liability under a contract, entered into in that state after the passage of the act?

This question has never before been distinctly presented to the consideration of this court, and decided, although it has been supposed by the judges of a highly respectable state court, that it was decided in the case of *McMillan* v. *McNeill*, 4 Wheat. 209. That was the case of a debt contracted by two citizens of South Carolina, in that state, the discharge of which had a view to no other state. The debtor afterwards removed to the territory of Louisiana, where he was regularly discharged, as an insolvent, from all his debts, under an act of the legislature of that state, passed prior to the time when the debt in question was contracted. To an action brought by the creditor in the district court of Louisiana, the defendant plead in bar his discharge, under the law of that territory, and it was contended by the counsel for the debtor, in this court, that the law under which the debtor was discharged, having passed before the contract was made, it could not be said to impair its obligation. The cause was argued on one side only, and it would seem from the report of the case, that no written opinion was prepared by the court. The chief justice stated, that the circumstance of the state law, under which the debt was attempted to be discharged, having been passed before the debt was contracted, made no difference in the application of the principle, which had been asserted by the court in the case of *Sturges* v. *Crownin-*

shield. The correctness of this position is believed to be incontrovertible. The principle alluded to was, that a state bankrupt law, which impairs the obligation of a contract, is unconstitutional, in its application to such contract. In that case, it is true, the contract preceded, in order of time, the act of assembly, under which the debtor was discharged, although it was not thought necessary to notice that circumstance in the opinion which was pronounced. The principle, however, remained, in the opinion of the court, delivered in *McMillan* v. *McNeill*, unaffected by the circumstance that the law of Louisiana preceded a contract made in another state, since that law, having no extraterritorial force, never did at any time govern or affect the obligation of such contract. It could not, therefore, be correctly said to be prior to the contract, in reference to its obligation, since if, upon legal principles, it could affect the contract, that could not happen, until the debtor became a citizen of Louisiana, and that was subsequent to the contract. But I hold the principle to be well established, that a discharge under the bankrupt laws of one government, does not affect contracts made or to be executed under another, whether the law be prior or subsequent in the date to that of the contract; and this I take to be the only point really decided in the case alluded to. Whether the chief justice was correctly understood by the reporter, when he is supposed to have said, "that this case was not distinguishable in principle from the preceding case of *Sturges* v. *Crowninshield*," it is not material at this time to inquire, because I understand the meaning of these expressions to go no further than to intimate, that there was no distinction between the cases as to the constitutional objection, since it professed to discharge a debt contracted in another state, which, at the time it was contracted, was not within its operation, nor subject to be discharged by it. The case now to be decided, is that of a debt contracted in the state of New York, by a citizen of that state, from which he was discharged, so far as he constitutionally could be, under a bankrupt law of that state, in force at the time when the debt was contracted. It is a case, therefore, that bears no resemblance to the one just noticed.

I come now to the consideration of the question, which, for the first time, has been directly brought before this court for judgment. I approach it with more than ordinary sensibility, not only on account of its importance, which must be acknowledged by all, but of its intrinsic difficulty, which, every step I have taken in arriving at a conclusion with which my judgment could in any way be satisfied, has convinced me, attends it. I have examined both sides of this great question, with the most sedulous care, and the most anxious desire to discover which of them, when adopted, would be most likely to fulfil the intentions of those who framed the constitution of the United States. I am far from asserting that my labors have resulted in entire success; they have led me to the only conclusion by which I can stand with any degree of confidence; and yet, I should be disingenuous, were I to declare, from this place, that I embrace it, without hesitation, and without a doubt of its correctness. The most that candor will permit me to say upon the subject is, that I see, or think I see, my way more clear on the side which my judgment leads me to adopt, then on the other, and it must remain for others to decide, whether the guide I have chosen has been a safe one or not.

It has constantly appeared to me, throughout the different investigations of this question, to which it has been my duty to attend, that the error of those who controvert the constitutionality of the bankrupt law under consideration, in its application to this case, if they be in error at all, has arisen from not distinguishing accurately between a law which impairs a contract, and one which impairs its obligation. A contract is defined by all to be an agreement to do, or not to do, some particular act; and in the construction of this agreement, depending essentially upon the will of the parties between whom it is formed, we seek for their intention, with a view to fulfil it. Any law, then, which enlarges, abridges, or in any manner changes, this intention, when it is discovered, necessarily impairs the contract itself, which is but the evidence of that intention. The manner, or the degree, in which this change is effected, can in no respect influence this conclusion; for whether the law affect the validity, the construction, the duration, the mode of discharge, or the evidence of the agreement, it impairs the contract, though it may not do so to the same extent, in all the supposed cases. Thus, a law which declares that no action shall be brought whereby to charge a person upon his agreement to pay the debt of another, or upon an agreement relating to lands, unless the same be reduced to writing, impairs a contract made by parol, whether the law precede or follow the making of such contract; and, if the argument, that this law also impairs, in the former case, the obligation of the contract, be sound, it must follow, that the statute of frauds, and all other statutes which in any manner meddle with contracts, impair their obligation, and are, consequently, within the operation of this section and article of the constitution. It will not do, to answer, that, in the particular case put, and in others of the same nature, there is no contract to impair, since the pre-existing law denies all remedy for its enforcement, or forbids the making of it, since it is impossible to deny, that the parties have expressed their will in the form of a contract, notwithstanding the law denies to it any valid obligation.

This leads us to a critical examination of the particular phraseology of that part of the above section which relates to contracts. It is a law which impairs the obligation of contracts, and not the contracts themselves, which is interdicted. It is not to be doubted, that this term, *obligation,* when applied to contracts, was well considered and weighed by those who framed the constitution, and was intended to convey a different meaning from what the prohibition would have imported without it. It is this meaning of which we are all in search. What is it, then, which constitutes the obligation of a contract? The answer is given by the chief justice, in the case of *Sturges* v. *Crowninshield,* to which I readily assent now, as I did then; it is the law which binds the parties to perform their agreement. The law, then, which has this binding obligation, must govern and control the contract, in every shape in which it is intended to bear upon it, whether it affects its validity, construction or discharge.

But the question, which law is referred to in the above definition still remains to be solved. It cannot, for a moment, be conceded, that the mere moral law is intended, since the obligation which that imposes is altogether of the imperfect kind, which the parties to it are free to obey, or not, as they please. It cannot be supposed, that it was with this law the grave authors of this instrument were dealing. The universal law of all civilized nations, which declares that men shall perform that to which they have agreed, has been supposed by the counsel who have argued this cause for the defendant in error, to be the law which is alluded to; and I have no objection to acknowledging its obligation, whilst I must deny that it is that which exclusively governs the contract. It is upon this law, that the obligation, which nations acknowledge to perform their compacts with each other, is founded, and I, therefore, feel no objection to answer the question asked by the same counsel—what law it is which constitutes the obligation of the compact between Virginia and Kentucky? by admitting, that it is this common law of nations which required them to perform it. I admit further, that it is this law which creates the obligation of a contract made upon a desert spot, where no municipal law exists, and (which was another case put by the same counsel) which contract, by the tacit assent of all nations, their tribunals are authorized to enforce.

But can it be seriously insisted, that this, any more than the moral law upon which it is founded, was exclusively in the contemplation of those who framed this constitution? What is the language of this universal law? It is, simply, that all men are bound to perform their contracts. The injunction is as absolute as the contracts to which it applies. It admits of no qualification, and no restraint, either as to its validity, construction or discharge, further than may be necessary to develop the intention of the parties to the contract. And if it be true, that this is exclusively the law to which the constitution refers us, it is very apparent, that the sphere of state legislation upon subjects connected with the contracts of individuals, would be abridged beyond what it can for a moment be believed the sovereign states of this Union would have consented to; for it will be found, upon examination, that there are few laws which concern the general police of a state, or the government of its citizens, in their intercourse with each other, or with strangers, which may not in some way or other affect the contracts which they have entered into, or may thereafter form. For what are laws of evidence, or which concern remedies, frauds and perjuries, laws of registration, and those which affect landlord and tenant, sales at auction, acts of limitation, and those which limit the fees of professional men, and the charges of tavern-keepers, and a multitude of others which crowd the codes of every state, but laws which may affect the validity, construction, or duration or discharges of contracts? Whilst I admit, then, that this common law of nations, which has been mentioned, may form a part of the obligation of a contract, I must unhesitatingly insist, that this law is to be taken in strict subordination to the municipal laws of the land where the contract is made, or is to be executed. The former can be satisfied by nothing short of performance; the latter may affect and control the validity, construction, evidence, remedy, performance and discharge of the contract. The former is the common law of all civilized nations, and of each of them; the latter is the peculiar law of each, and is paramount to the former, whenever they come in collision with each other.

It is, then, the municipal law of the state, whether that be written or unwritten, which is emphatically the law of the contract made within the state, and must govern it throughout, wherever its performance is sought to be enforced. It forms, in my humble opinion, a part of the contract, and travels with it, wherever the parties to it may be found. It is so regarded by all the civilized nations of the world, and is enforced by the tribunals of those nations, according to its own forms, unless the parties to it have otherwise agreed, as where the contract is to be executed in, or refers to the laws of, some other country than that in which it is formed, or where it is of an immoral character, or contravenes the policy of the nation to whose tribunals the appeal is made; in which latter cases, the remedy which the comity of nations afford for enforcing the obligation of contracts wherever formed, is denied. Free from these objections, this law, which accompanies the contract as forming a part of it, is regarded and enforced everywhere, whether it affect the validity, construction or discharge of the contract. It is upon this principle of universal law, that the discharge of the contract, or one of the parties to it, by the bankrupt laws of the country where it was made, operates as a discharge everywhere. If then, it be true, that the law of the country where the contract is made, or to be executed, forms a part of that contract, and of its obligation, it would seem to be somewhat of a solecism, to say, that it does, at the same time, impair that obligation.

But it is contended, that if the municipal law of the state where the contract is so made, form a part of it, so does that clause of the constitution which prohibits the states from passing laws to impair the obligation of contracts; and consequently, that the law is rendered inoperative by force of its controlling associate. All this I admit, provided it be first proved, that the law, so incorporated with, and forming a part of the contract, does, in effect, impair its obligation; and before this can be proved, it must be affirmed, and satisfactorily made out, that if, by the terms of the contract, it is agreed, that, on the happening of a certain event, as, upon the future insolvency of one of the parties, and his surrender of all his property for the benefit of his creditors, the contract shall be considered as performed and at an end, this stipulation would impair the obligation of the contract. If this proposition can be successfully affirmed, I can only say, that the soundness of it is beyond the reach of my mind to understand.

Again it is insisted, that if the law of the contract forms a part of it, the law itself cannot be repealed, without impairing the obligation of the contract. This proposition, I must be permitted to deny. It may be repealed at any time, at the will of the legislature, and then it ceases to form any part of those contracts which may afterwards be entered into. The repeal is no more void, than a new law would be, which operates upon contracts to affect their validity, construction or duration. Both are valid (if the view I take of this case be correct), as they may affect contracts afterwards formed; but neither are so, if they bear upon existing contracts; and in the former case, in which the repeal contains no enactment, the constitution would forbid the application of the repealing law to past contracts, and to those only.

To illustrate this argument, let us take four laws, which either by new enactments, or by the repeal of former laws, may affect contracts as to their validity, construction, evidence or remedy. Laws against usury are of the first description. A law which converts a penalty, stipulated for by the parties, as the only atonement for a breach of the contract, into a mere agreement for a just compensation, to be measured by the legal rate of interest, is of the second. The statute of frauds, and the statute of limitations, may be cited as examples of the two last. The validity of these laws can never be questioned by those who accompany me in the view which I take of the question under consideration, unless they operate, by their express provisions, upon contracts previously entered into; and even then they are void only so far as they do so operate, because, in that case, and in that case only, do they impair the obligation of those contracts. But if they equally impair the obligation of contract subsequently made, which they must do, if this be the operation of a bankrupt law upon such contracts, it would seem to follow, that all such laws, whether in the form of new enactments, or of repealing laws, producing the same legal consequences, are made void by the constitution; and yet the counsel for the defendants in error have not ventured to maintain so alarming a proposition.

If it be conceded, that those laws are not repugnant to the constitution, so far as they apply to subsequent contracts, I am yet to be instructed how to distinguish between those laws, and the one now under consideration. How has this been attempted by the learned counsel who have argued this cause upon the ground of such a distinction? They have insisted, that the effect of the law first supposed, is to annihilate the contract in its birth, or rather to prevent it from having a legal existence, and, consequently, that there is no obligation to be impaired. But this is clearly not so, since it may legitimately avoid all contracts afterwards entered into, which reserve to the lender a higher rate of interest than this law permits. The validity of the second law is admitted, and yet this can only be in its application to subsequent contracts; for it has not, and I think it cannot, for a moment, be maintained, that a law which, in express terms, varies the construction of an existing contract, or which, repealing a former law, is made to produce the same effect, does not impair the obligation of that contract. The statute of frauds, and the statute of limitations, which have been put as examples of the third and fourth classes of laws, are also admitted to be valid, because they merely concern the modes of proceeding in the trial of causes. The former, supplying a rule of evidence, and the latter, forming a part of the remedy given by the legislature to enforce the obligation, and likewise providing a rule of evidence.

All this I admit. But how does it happen, that these laws, like those which affect the validity and construction of contracts, are valid as to subsequent, and yet void as to prior and subsisting contracts? For we are informed by the learned judge who delivered the opinion of this court in the case of *Sturges* v. *Crowninshield,* that, "if, in a state where six years may be pleaded in bar to an action of *assumpsit,* a law should pass, declaring that contracts already in existence, not barred by the statute, should be construed within it, there could be little doubt of its unconstitutionality." It is thus most apparent, that, whichever way we turn, whether to laws affecting the validity, construction or discharges of contracts, or the evidence or remedy to be employed in enforcing them, we are met by this overruling and admitted distinction, between those which operate retrospectively, and those which operate prospectively. In all of them, the law is pronounced to be void, in the first class of cases, and not so, in the second.

Let us stop, then, to make a more critical examination of the act of limitations, which, although it concerns the remedy, or, if it must be conceded, the evidence, is yet void or otherwise, as it is made to apply retroactively, or prospectively, and see, if it can, upon any intelligible principle, be distinguished from a bankrupt law, when applied in the same manner? What is the effect of the former? The answer is, to discharge the debtor, and all his future acquisitions, from his contract; because he is permitted to plead in bar of any remedy which can be instituted against him, and consequently, in bar or destruction of the obligation which his contract imposed upon him. What is the effect of a discharge under a bankrupt law? I can answer this question in no other terms than those which are given to the former question. If there be a difference, it is one which, in the eye of justice at least, is more favorable to the validity of the latter than of the former; for in the one, the debtor surrenders everything which he possesses towards the discharge of his obligation, and in the other, he surrenders nothing, and sullenly shelters himself behind a legal objection with which the law has provided him, for the purpose of protecting his person, and his present, as well as his future acquisitions, against the performance of his contract. It is said, that the former does not discharge him absolutely from his contract, because it leaves a shadow sufficiently substantial to raise a consideration for a new promise to pay. And is not this equally the case with a certificated bankrupt, who afterwards promises to pay a debt from which his certificate had discharged him? In the former case, it is said, the defendant must plead the statute, in order to bar the remedy, and to exempt him from his obligation. And so, I answer, he must plead his discharge under the bankrupt law, and his conformity to it, in order to bar the remedy of his creditor, and to secure to himself a like exemption. I have, in short, sought in vain or some other grounds on which to distinguish the two laws from each other, than those which were suggested at the bar. I can imagine no other, and I confidently believe that none exist, which will bear the test of a critical examination.

To the decision of this court, made in the case of *Sturges* v. *Crowninshield,* and to the reasoning of the learned judge who delivered that opinion, I entirely submit; although I did not then, nor can I now, bring my mind to concur in that part of it, which admits the constitutional power of the state legislatures to pass bankrupt laws, by which I understand, those laws which discharge the person and the future acquisitions of the bankrupt from his debts. I have always thought that the power to pass such a law was exclusively vested by the constitution in the legislature of the United States. But it becomes me to believe, that this opinion was, and is incorrect, since it stands condemned by the decision of a majority of this court, soelmnly pronounced.

After making this acknowledgment, I refer again to the above decision with some degree of confidence, in support of the opinion to which I am now inclined to come, that a bankrupt law, which operates prospectively, or in so far as it does so operate, does not violate the constitution of the United States. It is there stated, "that, until the power to pass uniform laws on the subject of bankruptcies be exercised by congress, the states are not forbidden to pass a bankrupt law, provided it contain no principle which violates the tenth section of the first article of the constitution of the United States." The question in that case was, whether the law of New York, passed on the 3d of April 1811, which liberates, not only the person of the debtor, but discharges him from all liability for any debt contracted previous, as well as subsequent to his discharge, on his surrendering his property, for the use of his creditors, was a valid law, under the constitution, in its application to a debt contracted prior to its passage? The court decided that it was not, upon the single ground, that it impaired the obligation of that contract. And if it be true, that the states cannot pass a similar law, to operate upon contracts subsequently entered into, it follows inevitably, either that they cannot pass such laws at all, contrary to the express declaration of the court, as before quoted, or that such laws do not impair the obligation of contracts subsequently entered into; in fine, it is a self-evident proposition, that every contract that can be formed, must either precede, or follow, any law by which it may be affected.

I have, throughout the preceding part of this opinion, considered the municipal law of the country, where the contract is made, as incorporated with the contract, whether it affects its validity, construction or discharge. But I think it quite immaterial to stickle for this position, if it be conceded to me, what can scarcely be denied, that this municipal law constitutes the law of the contract so formed, and must govern it throughout. I hold the legal consequences to be the same, in whichever view the law, as it affects the contract, is considered.

I come now to a more particular examination and construction of the section under which this question arises; and I am free to acknowledge, that the collocation of the subjects for which it provides, has made an irresistible impression upon my mind, much stronger, I am pursuaded, than I can find language to communicate to the minds of others. It declares, that "no state shall coin money, emit bills of credit, make anything but gold and silver coin to tender in payment of debts." These prohibitions, associated with the powers granted to congress "to coin money, and to regulate the value thereof, and of foreign coin," most obviously constitute members of the same family, being upon the same subject, and governed by the same policy. This policy was, to provide a fixed and uniform standard of value throughout the United States, by which the commercial and other dealings between the citizens thereof or between them and foreigners, as well as the moneyed transactions of the government, should be regulated. For it might well be asked, why vest in congress the power to establish a uniform standard of value, by the means pointed out, if the states might use the same means, and thus defeat the uniformity of the standard, and, consequently, the standard itself? And why establish a standard at all, for the government of the various contracts which might be entered into, if those contracts might afterwards be discharged by a different standard, or by that which is not money, under the authority of state tender laws? It is, obvious, therefore, that these prohibitions, in the 10th section, are entirely homogeneous, and are essential to the establishment of a uniform standard of value, in the formation and discharge of contracts. It is for this reason, independent of the general phraseology which is employed, that the prohibition, in regard to state tender laws, will admit of no construction which would confine it to state laws which have a retrospective operation.

The next class of prohibitions contained in this section, consists of bills of attainder, *ex post facto* laws, and laws impairing the obligation of contracts. Here, too, we observe, as I think, members of the same family brought together in the most intimate connection with each other. The states are forbidden to pass any bill of attainder or *ex post facto* law, by which a man shall be punished criminally or penally, by loss of life, of his liberty, property or reputation, for an act which, at the time of its commission, violated no existing law of the land. Why did the authors of the constitution turn their attention to this subject, which, at the first blush, would appear to be peculiarly fit to be left to the discretion of those who have the police and good government of the state under their management and control? The only answer to be given is, because laws of this character are oppressive, unjust and tyrannical; and, as such, are condemned by the universal sentence of civilized man. The injustice and tyranny which characterizes *ex post facto* laws, consists altogether in their retrospective operation, which applies with equal force, although not exclusively, to bills of attainder. But if it was deemed wise and proper to prohibit state legislation as to retrospective laws, which concern, almost exclusively, the citizens and inhabitants of the particular state in which this legislation takes place, how much more did it concern the private and political interests of the citizens of all the states, in their commercial and ordinary intercourse with each other, that the same prohibition should be extended civilly to the contracts which they might enter into? If it were proper to prohibit a state legislature to pass a retrospective law, which should take from the pocket of one of its own citizens a single dollar, as a punishment for an act which was innocent at the time it was committed; how much more proper was it to prohibit laws of the same character precisely, which might deprive the citizens of other states, and foreigners, as well as citizens of the same state, of thousands, to which, by their contracts, they were justly entitled, and which they might possibly have realized but for such state interference? How natural, then, was it, under the influence of these considerations, to interdict similar legislation in regard to contracts, by providing, that no state should pass laws impairing the obligation of past contracts? It is true, that the first two of these prohibitions apply to laws of a criminal, and the last to laws of a civil character; but if I am correct in my view of the spirit and motives of these prohibitions, they agree in the principle which suggested them. They are founded upon the same reason, and the application of it is at least as strong to the last, as it is to the first two prohibitions.

But these reasons are altogether inapplicable to laws of a prospective character. There is nothing unjust or tyrannical in punishing offences prohibited by law, and committed in violation of that law. Nor can it be unjust or oppressive, to declare by law, that contracts subsequently entered into, may be discharged in a way different from that which the parties have provided, but which they know, or may know, are liable, under certain circumstances, to be discharged in a manner contrary to the provisions of their contract.

Thinking, as I have always done, that the power to pass bankrupt laws was intended by the authors of the constitution to be exclusive in congress, or, at least, that they expected the power vested in that body would be exercised, so as effectually to prevent its exercise by the states, it is the more probable, that, in reference to all other interferences of the state legislatures upon the subject of contracts, retrospective laws were alone in the contemplation of the convention.

In the construction of this clause of the tenth section of the constitution, one of the counsel for the defendant supposed himself at liberty so to transpose the provisions contained in it, as to place the prohibition to pass laws impairing the obligation of contracts in juxtaposition with the other prohibition to pass laws making anything but gold and silver coin a tender in payment of debts, inasmuch as the two provisions relate to the subject of contracts. That the derangement of the words, and even sentences of a law, may sometimes be tolerated, in order to arrive at the apparent meaning of the legislature, to be gathered from other parts, or from the entire scope of the law, I shall not deny. But I should deem it a very hazardous rule to adopt, in the construction of an instrument so maturely considered, as this constitution was, by the enlightened statesmen who framed it, and so severly examined and criticised by its opponents in the numerous state conventions which finally adopted it. And if, by the construction of this sentence, arranged as it is, or as the learned counsel would have it to be, it could have been made out, that the power to pass prospective laws, affecting contracts, was denied to the states, it is most wonderful, that not one voice was raised against the provision, in any of those conventions, by the jealous advocates of state rights, nor even an amendment proposed, to explain the cause, and to exclude a construction which trenches so extensively upon the sphere of state legislation. But, although the transposition which is contended for may be tolerated, in cases where the obvious intention of the legislature can in no other way be fulfilled, it can never be admitted, in those where consistent meaning can be given to the whole clause, as its authors thought proper to arrange it, and where the only doubt is, whether the construction which the transposition countenances, or that which results from the reading which the legislature has thought proper to adopt, is most likely to fulfil the supposed intention of the legislature. Now, although it is true, that the prohibition to pass tender laws of a particular description, and laws impairing the obligation of contracts, relate, both of them, to contracts, yet the principle which governs each of them, clearly to be inferred from the subjects with which they stand associated, is altogether different; that of the first forming part of a system for fixing a uniform standard of value, and, of the last, being founded on a denunciation of retrospective laws. It is, therefore, the safest course, in my humble opinion, to construe this clause of the section according to the arrangement which the convention has thought proper to make of its different provisions. To insist upon a transposition, with a view to warrant one construction rather than the other, falls little short, in my opinion, of a begging of the whole question in controversy.

But why, it has been asked, forbid the states to pass laws making any thing but gold and silver coin a tender in payment of debts, contracted subsequent, as well as prior, to the law which authorizes it; and yet confine the prohibition to pass laws impairing the obligation of contracts to past contracts, or in other words, to future bankrupt laws, when the consequence resulting from each is the same, the latter being considered by the counsel as being, in truth, nothing less than tender laws in disguise. An answer to this question has, in part, been anticipated by some of the preceding observations. The power to pass bankrupt laws having been vested in congress, either as an exclusive power, or under the belief that it would certainly be exercised, it is highly probable that state legislation, upon that subject, was not within the contemplation of the convention; or, if it was, it is quite unlikely, that the exercise of the power by the state legislatures, would have been prohibited by the use of terms which, I have endeavored to show, are inapplicable to laws intended to operate prospectively. For had the prohibition been to pass laws impairing contracts, instead of the obligation of contracts, I admit, that it would have borne the construction which is contended for, since it is clear, that the agreement of the parties, in the first case, would be impaired as much by a prior, as it would be by a subsequent, bankrupt law. It has, besides, been attempted to be shown, that the limited restriction upon state legislation, imposed by the former prohibition, might be submitted to by the states, whilst the extensive operation of the latter would have hazarded, to say the least of it, the adoption of the constitution by the state conventions.

But an answer, still more satisfactory to my mind, is this: Tender laws, of the description stated in this section, are always unjust; and, where there is an existing bankrupt law, at the time the contract is made, they can seldom be useful to the honest debtor. They violate the agreement of the parties to it, without the semblance of an apology for the measure, since they operate to discharge the debtor from his undertaking, upon terms variant from those by which he bound himself, to the injury of the creditor, and unsupported, in many cases, by the plea of necessity. They extend relief to the opulent debtor, who does not stand in need of it; as well as to the one who is, by misfortunes, often unavoidable, reduced to poverty, and disabled from complying with his engagements. In relation to subsequent contracts, they are unjust, when extended to the former class of debtors, and useless, to the second, since they may be relieved by conforming to the requisitions of the state bankrupt law, where there is one. Being discharged by this law from all his antecedent debts, and having his future acquisitions secured to him, an opportunity is afforded him to become once more a useful member of society. If this view of the subject be correct, it will be difficult to prove, that a prospective bankrupt law resembles, in any of its features, a law which should make anything but gold and silver coin a tender in payment of debts.

I shall now conclude this opinion, by repeating the acknowledgment which candor compelled me to make in its commencement, that the question which I have been examining is involved in difficulty and doubt. But if I could rest my opinion in favor of the constitutionality of the law on which the question arises, on no other ground than this doubt so felt and acknowledged, that alone, would, in my estimation, be a satisfactory vindication of it. It is but a decent respect due to the wisdom, the integrity and the patriotism of the legislative body, by which any law is passed, to presume in favor of its validity, until its violation of the constitution is proved beyond all reasonable doubt. This has always been the language of this court, when that subject has called for its decision; and I know that it expresses the honest sentiments of each and every member of this bench. I am perfectly satisfied, that it is entertained by those of them from whom it is the misfortune of the majority of the court to differ on the present occasion, and that they feel no reasonable doubt of the correctness of the conclusion to which their best judgment has conducted them.

Alfred Moore

☆ 1755–1810 ☆

APPOINTED BY

JOHN ADAMS

YEARS ON COURT

1799–1804

Alfred Moore

by

LEON FRIEDMAN

ALFRED MOORE of North Carolina must surely be one of the most unnoticed men ever to sit on the Supreme Court. Charles Warren in his monumental study *The Supreme Court in United States History* notes only his arrival (in 1799) and his departure (in 1804). Although Moore sat with John Marshall for the first three years of his term as Chief Justice, he is mentioned only in a footnote in Albert Beveridge's multi-volume *Life of John Marshall,* and is called "Albert" rather than "Alfred." There is an almost total absence of any biographical studies of the man.

Yet Moore, like so many of the Federalist figures of his time, played a significant role in his state as a soldier, statesman, lawyer, and judge. Born on May 21, 1755, in Brunswick County, North Carolina, of one of the most respected families in the colony, he numbered among his ancestors Roger Moore, a leader of the Irish Rebellion of 1641, and James Moore, governor of South Carolina in 1700 and 1719–21. His father Maurice sat as one of the three colonial judges of North Carolina. Alfred was educated in Boston since rural North Carolina could not match its schools. He returned to his native state to read law under his father and in 1755, at the age of twenty, received his license to practice. When the Revolutionary War began, Moore obtained a captain's commission in the First North Carolina Continental Regiment, commanded by his uncle Colonel James Moore. His regiment fought a number of successful battles with the British and Loyalists, the most notable being the Battle of Moore's Creek Bridge (near Fayetteville) on February 27, 1776, where 500 of General Donald McDonald's Royal Highlanders were killed or captured with the loss of only two Continentals. Because of this victory and his participation in the successful defence of Charleston in June, 1776, James Moore (then a brigadier general) was appointed Commander-in-Chief of the Southern Depart-

LEON FRIEDMAN practices law in New York, and is the editor of Southern Justice *and* The Civil Rights Reader.

ment. But James died soon after in January, 1777. When Maurice Moore died early in 1777 and Alfred's brother was killed in another skirmish, Moore resigned his commission in March, 1777, to care for his mother and the family plantation. However, he continued some military activity, becoming a colonel in the militia which caused extensive damage in irregular encounters with British troops in the area. In retaliation, Moore's plantation was plundered and his house destroyed in 1781. Moore combined both his legal and military training to become judge advocate of the North Carolina forces shortly before hostilities ceased.

As one who had given much to the Revolutionary cause, Moore was elected to the North Carolina legislature in 1782. In June of that year he was appointed Attorney General of the state, replacing James Iredell. For the next eight years he showed great technical skill as the state's chief legal officer, and with W. R. Davie, became one of the leaders of the North Carolina bar. He prosecuted many cases of fraud, including one involving the forgery of war certificates that entitled the bearer to certain pensions. Among those accused of involvement in the scheme was Henry Montfort, a member of the North Carolina House who was defended by Iredell and Davie. (Montfort was acquitted on a technicality.)

Moore also defended the constitutionality of the North Carolina Confiscation Act in the celebrated case of *Bayard* v. *Singleton,* 1 Martin (N.C.) 42 (1787). The act, passed during the war, declared forfeit all land owned by the Tories who had fled North Carolina. Such property was then sold by a Commissioner of Forfeited Estates to third parties and the proceeds kept by the state. A successor to a Tory landowner (defended by Iredell and Davie) brought suit to reclaim some of this property after the war, and Moore defended the purchaser under the act. In 1785 the North Carolina legislature passed a law requiring the dismissal of all actions to determine the title of land conveyed under the provisions of the Confiscation Act. The three judge superior court leaned over backwards to avoid a clash with the legislature and urged the defendant to let the case go to a jury. He refused and the court reluctantly disregarded the dismissal law and the Confiscation Act and ordered the proceedings to continue. Moore finally won the case, however. He argued to the court that the original land owner, Cornell, had signed the deed to the land (under which the plaintiff claimed) in December, 1777, two years after he had left North Carolina to seek British protection. At that time he was an alien, and regardless of the Confiscation Act, it was firmly established under the common law that "aliens are incapacitated to hold lands." Thus, Moore argued, the state succeeded to the lands and could convey good title to a third party. The court accepted his argument and the jury found for the defendant on all issues. Twenty-seven similar cases were dismissed on the basis of the decision and the initial effort by Loyalist landowners to reclaim their lands or debts (though guaranteed by the 1783 peace treaty) was aborted.

The judge's initial decision upholding the power of a court to disregard or declare unconstitutional an act of the legislature—according to Louis Boudin (in *Government by Judiciary,* Vol. I, p. 63–66) the only genuine precedent for judicial review prior to *Marbury* v. *Madison*—created a furor in the state. Despite their favorable ruling on the merits, the judges were called to account (for refusing to dismiss the case) before a committee of the legislature headed by Richard Spaight, soon to be a delegate to the Philadelphia Convention which drafted the Constitution. Spaight strongly condemned the judges for their actions: "I do not pretend to vindicate the law which has been the subject of controversy; it is immaterial what law they have declared void; it is their usurpation of the authority to do it that I complain of, as I do most positively deny that they have any such power . . ." No disciplinary action was taken against the judges although they were upbraided for their actions. Moore supported the inquiry and Spaight's position. But sixteen years later, he played a significant role in John Marshall's decision in *Marbury* which firmly established the judicial power denied by Spaight.

Moore was a strong Federalist and the North Carolina legislature named him a commissioner to the Annapolis Convention in 1786, the first serious effort to strengthen the Confederation. He did not attend because of illness. A year later the legislature bypassed Moore and chose Davie, Spaight, Alexander Martin, William Blount, and Hugh Williamson as members of the North Carolina delegation to the Philadelphia Convention. Moore strongly pressed for ratification of the Constitution and stood for election to the ratifying convention at Hillsboro. Anti-federalist feeling was strong in North Carolina—the small farmers, a majority of the state's population, bitterly opposed the control long exercised by the eastern, conservative plantation owners who formed the Federalist party. Frightened at the prospects of even greater control by a distant federal government, these farmers tried to defeat the new Constitution. Moore lost his election to a virtually unknown candidate. When the Hillsboro convention met in July, 1788, with a majority of Anti-Federalists, nine states had already ratified the Constitution and two more did so while the convention met, leaving only North Carolina and Rhode Island as independent states. The delegates voted not to accept the Constitution as submitted but urged Congress to pass a federal bill of rights as soon as possible. The next year another convention was called, and hard campaigning by Iredell, Davie, and Moore produced a favorable majority for ratification which took place in November, 1789.

In 1791 Moore resigned as Attorney General. The North Carolina legislature had passed a law expanding the court system and creating the office of Solicitor General with the same powers and remuneration as that of Attorney General. Moore insisted this was an unconstitutional infringement upon the prerogatives of his office. The strain of both his official functions and his own profitable private practice was probably a more significant factor leading to his retirement to his plantation. Two years later, in 1792, he returned to public life, winning election as a representative in the legislature despite a Republican sweep in the state. In 1795 he ran for the United States Senate against the most popular Republican leader in the state, Timothy Bloodworth, who made a strong campaign issue of the Neutrality Act of 1794, which was highly unpopular among the pro-French North Carolinians. Nevertheless, Moore lost by only one vote in the legislature.

For a brief time in 1798, he acted as a federal commissioner to conclude a treaty with the Cherokee Indians. At the end of the year Federalist strength revived in the state, following French seizure of North Carolina ships and the XYZ affair, in which American representatives, including John Marshall, were insulted by a request for bribes by French ministers. Elected a judge of the North Carolina Superior Court in 1799, Moore served for one year in that position. The cases he heard were of no lasting importance but he handled them with intelligence and common sense. In one case, *Felts* v. *Foster and Williams,* 1 N.C. 58 (1799), the plaintiffs were entitled to certain property in the event the widow of the original owner remarried. The bill charged she had in fact remarried, which she denied. Moore concluded:

> *There is in this case no positive proof of a marriage, but there are circumstances advancing to create a belief that a marriage has taken place; they have lived together a long time, as man and wife, have had several children, and the witnesses say she was a woman of irreproachable character, before these things happened. If so, a presumption arises that she would not thus have cohabited with the defendant, unless a marriage had been previously solemnized.*

In another case, *State* v. *Hall,* 1 N.C. 76 (1799), the defendant had been indicted for stealing a slave under a law forbidding stealing or taking a slave with the intention of selling or using him. The defendant claimed an improper indictment because he had been charged only with stealing a slave, not with the intention of selling or using him. Moore, who had served in the legislature shortly after the law's passage and was chiefly responsible for its enforcement during his eight years as Attorney General, described the conditions leading to the act and its purpose before finding the defendant guilty:

> *With respect to the act of Assembly, it was passed in turbulent times, when a practice prevailed of carrying slaves away, under the pretence that they belonged to the public, as confiscated; or that they were owned by disaffected persons or the like: they were sometimes carried off privately and by stealth, at other times openly and by violence: the former case is embraced by the word steal: the words next following repress the mischief of carrying slaves away by open force, or by persuasion, or by any other means than by stealth, accompanied nevertheless with an intention to appropriate to the taker's own use. The word "steal" does not include* ex vi termini, *an intention to appropriate to his own use, or to sell and dispose of to another; and, therefore, the intention expressed in the act, if applied to the crime of stealing, is useless and redundant. But the other modes of taking away slaves, enumerated in the act, do not necessarily import the intention of selling them, or of appropriating them to their own use; nor are they, when unaccompanied by such intention, so detrimental or injurious. Of these offences, the intention forms a principal ingredient, and to them the words must be exclusively referred. I am consequently of opinion that the judgment ought not to be arrested.*

The problems of British debts continued to plague the state courts long after the signing of the 1783 peace treaty which guaranteed repayment. Many states had sequestered such debts and had given discharges to debtors who paid to the state treasuries the moneys owed. In *Ware* v. *Hylton,* 3 Dall. 199 (1796), the Supreme Court unanimously held that the treaty provisions took precedence over any state law on the subject, and that British creditors could recover all prior debts in full. Chief Justice Oliver Ellsworth had also specifically held on circuit in 1797 that the North Carolina Confiscation Act must bow to the treaty provisions: " . . . the treaty is now law in this State, and the Confiscation Act, so far as the treaty interferes with it, is annulled." *Hamiltons* v. *Eaton,* 2 Martin (N.C.) 83, 131 (C.C.D.N.C. 1797). The creditors then pressed not only for the principal amount but for interest on the debts, which in some cases was owed for more than twenty years. When such an action came before the North Carolina courts, *Anonymous,* 2 N.C. 263 (1799), Moore had no difficulty in dismissing the claim for interest. In passing he showed his strong distaste for the treaty provisions, despite his Federalist leanings.

> *This is an action brought by a British creditor, under the treaty of peace, for a debt contracted in this state before the war, which debt was effectually confiscated by a sovereign power, having a right to make the confiscation. A treaty has not the omnipotence attributed to it, that of taking a debt from the State which lawfully belongs to it; or that of re-charging a debtor who has actually paid into the treasury under the existing laws, and has procured a discharge agreeably to them before the treaty. And I would not now suffer such suitors to recover, but for the consideration that they may recover by suing in the Federal Court. As to the interest I am very clear it ought not to be allowed, but from the time the debt was demanded after the treaty; those creditors did not return till long after the war, most of them kept the bonds in their possession beyond sea, so that the debtor could not pay.*

On October 2, 1799, Justice James Iredell died. In keeping with the practice at the time, President John Adams sought a replacement for the vacated Supreme Court seat from Iredell's home state. Adams had been favorably impressed by Moore when he had acted as treaty commissioner in 1798. Although W. R. Davie had a better claim on the seat, he had just been appointed plenipotentiary to France (with Chief Justice Ellsworth), and the choice fell on Moore, who took his seat at the August, 1800 term of the Court.

Anti-French feeling was still high during Moore's first year on the Court, despite the appointment of Oliver Ellsworth as a minister to reestablish peaceful relations with France. The first significant case to come before Moore (and the only one in which he wrote any opinion in five years on the Court) resulted from the frequent collisions on the high seas between French armed ships and American merchant ships carrying British made goods, *Bas* v. *Tingy,* 4 Dall. 37 (1800). The American ship *Eliza* had been captured by the French early in 1799 and was recaptured by an American armed ship twenty days later. A March, 1799, law specified that the owner of American ships captured by "the enemy" and recaptured more than ninety-six hours later must pay one-half the value of the ship and the goods on board to the recaptor as salvage. However, if the ship was not taken by an "enemy" the owner had to pay only one-eighth.

Thus the Court had to define the status of France in terms of the statute in question.

Moore, as the junior member of the Court, gave his opinion first:

> *. . . if words are the representatives of ideas, let me ask, by what other word the idea of the relative situation of America and France could be communicated, than by that of hostility, or* war. *And how can the characters of the parties engaged in hostility or war, be otherwise described than by the denomination of enemies: . . . it is by that description alone, that either could justify or excuse, the scene of bloodshed, depredation and confiscation, which has unhappily occurred.*

Justices Bushrod Washington and Samuel Chase followed Moore's opinion in words that have a remarkably modern tone. Washington wrote:

> *It may, I believe, be safely laid down, that every contention by force between two nations, in external matters, under the authority of their respective governments, is not only war, but public war. If it be declared in form it is called solemn, and is of the perfect kind; because one whole nation is at war with another whole nation, and all the members of the nation declaring war, are authorized to commit hostilities against all the members of the other, in every place, and under every circumstance. In such a war all the members act under a general authority, and all the rights and consequences of war attach to their condition.*
>
> *But hostilities may subsist between two nations, more confined in its nature and extent; being limited as to places, persons, and things; and this is more properly termed imperfect war, because not solemn, and because those who are authorized to commit hostilities, act under special authority, and can go no farther than to the extent of their commission. Still, however, it is a public war, because it is an external contention by force between some of the members of the two nations, authorized by legitimate powers. It is a war between the two nations, though all the members are not authorized to commit hostilities such as in a solemn war, where the government restrain the general power.*

And Chase said:

> *Congress is empowered to declare a general war, or Congress may wage a limited war; limited in place, in objects, and in time. . . .*
>
> *What, then, is the nature of the contest subsisting between America and France? In my judgment, it is a limited, partial war. Congress has not declared war in general terms, but Congress has authorized hostilities on the high seas by certain persons in certain cases. . . . If Congress had chosen to declare a general war, France would have been a general enemy; having chosen to wage a partial war, France was, at the time of the capture, only a partial enemy; but still she was an enemy. . . .*
>
> *The acts of Congress have been analyzed to show that a war is not openly denounced against France, and that France is nowhere expressly called the enemy in America; but this only proves the circumspection and prudence of the legislature. . . .*

Justice Paterson also concluded that a limited and partial war existed between France and the United States and the Court thereby concluded that the former owner of the *Eliza* must pay one-half the value of the ship and her goods as salvage.

The decision had important political implications. The Federalists had passed a number of strong measures in 1798 and 1799 against the French and their sympathizers (including the hated Alien and Sedition Acts). These laws were justified, the Federalists claimed, by the undeclared state of war which existed between France and the United States. The Court's decision in *Bas* v. *Tingy* lent sanction to the Federalist position, a position roundly condemned by the Republicans. A leading anti-federalist newspaper, the *Aurora* stated: ". . . every Judge who asserted we were in a state of war, contrary to the rights of Congress to declare it, ought to be impeached."

The conflict with France figured in two more important decisions by the Court in 1801. In early 1799 the ship *Amelia,* owned by a Hamburg concern, sailed from Calcutta to a European port past the American coast. She was captured by a French corvette who replaced the crew with French sailors, armed her with cannon, and sailed her toward St. Domingo to a French prize court. Such action was in keeping with a French law condemning goods manufactured or grown in England or her possessions. The American frigate *Constitution,* later to be immortalized as "Old Ironsides" for her exploits during the War of 1812, captured the *Amelia* before she reached port and brought her to New York where she was libeled. Alexander Hamilton appeared for Talbot, captain of the *Constitution,* and Brockholst Livingston (later a Supreme Court Justice) along with Aaron Burr defended the Hamburg owner. Talbot argued that he was entitled to one-half the value of the ship and her goods as salvage under the provisions of various laws passed in 1798 and 1799 sanctioning the capture of French armed vessels. In addition a law of March 2, 1799, allowed Americans to recapture ships of nations "in amity with the United States" which had been taken by "the enemy," and provided for salvage of one-half the value of the ship and the goods on board to be paid to the recaptor. The circuit court found for Talbot on all issues.

On appeal, the case was argued first in the August, 1800 term under the title *Talbot* v. *Ship Amelia,* 4 Dall. 34 (1800), but was set over for reargument in the August, 1801 term when a more complete panel of the Court was available, *Talbot* v. *Seaman,* 1 Cranch 1 (1801). When counsel for the claimants offered to read President Adams' construction of the statutes in issue as conclusive of their meaning, the Court objected. Paterson noted he would hear what Adams had written, "but they will have no influence on my opinion. . . . We are willing to hear them as the opinion of [counsel] but not as the opinion of the Executive." Chief Justice John Marshall, in his first opinion for the Court (which, after his appointment, gave up its practice of reading *seriatim* opinions and thereafter spoke with one voice), held that Talbot lawfully took the ship since it looked like an armed vessel under French authority. The captain performed a meritorious service in recapturing the ship since a French prize court would most certainly have condemned her inasmuch as she carried goods from "Bengal," then a British possession. However, the Court rejected the claim to one-half the value of the goods. The law under which Talbot sought compensation had been designed to cover situations in which both the United States and the home country of the ship's owner were united in hostilities against the same enemy. In this case, Hamburg was neutral toward France and the United States, and the March 2, 1799 law did not apply. Talbot was entitled to a fair salvage, however, which the Court fixed at one-sixth.

In April, 1800, another French armed ship, the *Schooner Peggy,* was captured and brought into a Connecticut port for condemnation by the American ship *Trumbull.* The ship and goods aboard were sold and the proceeds held by the District Court clerk for payment as the Court directed. On September 23, 1800, the circuit court issued an order directing payment of one-half of the proceeds to the United States Treasury and the other half to the captain and crew of the *Trumbull,* in accordance with various laws similar to those invoked in *Bas* v. *Tingy* and the *Ship Amelia* case. However, on September 30, 1800, a convention was signed between France and the United States providing for the restoration of property not "definitively condemned" on the date of the convention. The French claimants appealed the decision of the circuit court and demanded the entire amount held on the grounds that no "definitive" order had been issued in the case prior to September 20, 1800. President Jefferson, soon after coming into office, ordered the United States Attorney for Connecticut, Pierpont Edwards, to have the money paid to the French as provided by the treaty. The clerk refused to comply and took the matter to the circuit court which supported him, stating that the money could be paid only by court order and not by the dictates of the President.

The case was then argued before the Supreme Court. Moore heard preliminary argument on the case in August, 1801, but was not present for final argument and the decision in December, 1801. Marshall held on the merits for Jefferson's position while protecting the Court's right to issue the final order in the case, *United States* v. *Schooner Peggy,* 1 Cranch 103 (1801). He stated that the decision of the circuit court had not definitively condemned the property since only a final order of a court of ultimate jurisdiction, in this case the Supreme Court, could do so. Until the Supreme Court acted, no definitive condemnation had taken place. In passing, Marshall upheld the reach and force of the Executive's treaty power and the Court's obligation to enforce all foreign agreements ratified in accordance with the Constitution.

The case was one of the first defining the treaty power of the government. It served as a precedent for the proposition that a treaty is self-executing, i.e., that a court is bound to take judicial notice of a treaty and to accept it as equivalent to a legislative enactment whether or not Congress passes any implementing legislation. It also established that a subsequent treaty prevails over earlier inconsistent statutory provisions passed by Congress (in this case, the disposition of prizes taken from the French) even without congressional repeal of the earlier laws. Moore, who as a state court judge had denigrated the federal treaty power, lost an opportunity to restrict or dissent from the Court's sweeping support of that power. It would not be the only time his absence was crucial in a constitutional decision of the Marshall court.

The *Schooner Peggy* episode was only the first confrontation between the federal courts and Jefferson. On the day before Marshall's decision was announced in that case, Charles Lee, Attorney General under Adams, served a preliminary motion for a rule to show cause upon James Madison, the Secretary of State, on behalf of his client, William Marbury, seeking a writ of *mandamus* to compel Madison to issue a commission to him as a justice of the peace for the District of Columbia. The next day Jefferson's Attorney General, Levi Lincoln, stated in court that he had received no instructions on the matter from the government since Madison had been served only the day preceding. On December 22, 1801, the Court set the case down for argument on the fourth day of the next term of court.

Marshall and his Court assumed that the next term would take place in June, 1802, as specified by the Circuit Court Act of 1801. That law, hurriedly passed by the Federalists after the 1800 Republican victory, provided for two new Court terms, June and December. It also completely reorganized the judicial system, relieving the Supreme Court Justices of the rigors of circuit court duty of which Jay had so bitterly complained and which had contributed to Iredell's early death. The law created six new circuit courts with sixteen circuit court judges, all filled by the departing Adams with Federalists.

Whatever the abstract merits of the new system, the Republicans saw it as a Federalist plot to capture the judiciary after having lost both Congress and the Presidency. When the new Republican Congress met in December, 1801, one of their first legislative acts repealed the 1801 law by an almost strict party line vote. The new act (April 29, 1802) established six new circuits to which one Supreme Court Justice and one district court judge were assigned. Under the original judiciary law, there were three circuit courts, consisting of two Justices and one district court judge, which would meet twice a year. Some modifications were made in 1792, and the 1802 law provided for only one annual circuit court meeting, thus halving the number of sessions and the travelling time for each Justice. Congress also provided for only one annual term for the Supreme Court which would convene in February. Thus, the Court did not meet at all during 1802. The *Marbury* case was not called until early in 1803.

In February, 1803, the Court met to hear argument on Marbury's suit. According to the minutes of the Court, witnesses were examined on February 10, 1803. Levi Lincoln, the Attorney General, answered certain written questions concerning his knowledge of the facts on February 11, and Charles Lee argued the cause for the plaintiff on the same day before Marshall, Paterson, Chase, and Washington. (The government did not present its side of the case.) Moore, making the long journey from North Carolina, did not arrive until February 12 and heard only a final witness. Not having heard any argument, Moore could not participate in the decision issued two weeks later, on February 24, 1803 which held that Marbury was entitled to the commission he demanded, that the law afforded him an appropriate remedy in the form of *mandamus,* that the 1789 Judiciary Act gave the Supreme Court the power to issue a writ of *mandamus,* but, unfortunately for Marbury, that that section of the Judiciary Act was void as being inconsistent with the constitutional grant of original jurisdiction to the Court. The Court, wrote Marshall, clearly had the responsibility to void any congressional enactment not authorized by the Constitution, and the provision in question must fall.

Marshall has been criticized for participating in the case at all. He had been Secretary of State at the time the commissions were issued, had sealed them after Adams had affixed his signature, and had arranged for his brother James Marshall to deliver some of them to the appointees in question. Charles G. Haines wrote: "Because of his personal responsibility and interest in the case, it might have been expected that Marshall would decline to act as a Judge in passing upon the application for a *mandamus.*" Marshall ignored the judicial proprieties, apparently because of the absence of Moore and Cushing. If he had excused himself, only three Justices of six would have been present to hear and decided the case. Rather than let the opportunity to attack Jefferson's Administration and add to the power of his Court slip by because of the absence of a quorum, Marshall may have decided to participate despite his earlier involvement. How Moore reacted, arriving a day too late to hear argument on the question of judicial review which he had fought against in the *Bayard* case many years earlier, is lost to history. He sat silently by as Marshall's decision was announced two weeks later.

During the irregular year of 1802 Marshall had not been idle. The Justices were required by the Circuit Court Act of 1802 to follow a new circuit court schedule prepared by the Republican Congress. Marshall wrote to each of his brother judges, asking them whether they should comply with the new statute, and indicating his own feeling that the Constitution required "distinct appointments and commissions for the Judges of the inferior courts from those of the Supreme Court." Only Justice Chase responded that the new law was unconstitutional. Letters from Paterson, Cushing, and Washington have been preserved, showing their support of the statute. Moore's response has not been found, but he evidently followed the view of the majority, as shown by his acquiescence in *Stuart* v. *Laird,* 1 Cranch 299 1803), in which two weeks after the Marbury decision the Court sanctioned the 1802 judiciary law. The defendant in that case had protested against the execution of a bond signed by Marshall as circuit court judge, complaining that the Constitution did not permit any such double function for a Supreme Court Justice. The Court, through Paterson, concluded that all doubts about the system must be set aside, citing the practice of the Supreme Court Justices performing circuit court duty since 1789. Historians have been fond of pointing out that the same kind of approach could have been taken in the *Marbury* case. Fred Rodell has written that: ". . . Had precisely the same reasoning [of acquiescence by practice] been used in *Marbury* . . . about the Court's power to issue writs of *mandamus*—which the Court had also been doing for several years—Marshall's most famous decision would have had to go the other way." However, the Court had never in fact issued a writ of *mandamus,* although it had issued a writ of prohibition under the same law. Three times before 1803 *mandamus* had been requested and both counsel and the Court assumed it could grant such relief, but the Court decided against its exercise. See 1 Cranch 148. Thus Marshall could quite properly reexamine the *mandamus* power without considering the matter closed by prior practice.

Stuart v. *Laird* closed the circuit court question for the government. But the hardship, though halved by the new law, still remained serious. Moore had the long Sixth Circuit to travel (Georgia and South Carolina) and the strain on him, like that on Iredell, was more than he could endure. In February, 1804, he resigned, citing ill health. Republican Senator William Plumer of New Hampshire wrote to a friend: "Judge Moore from a full conviction of a speedy removal by writ of *habeas corpus* returnable to Heaven's Chancery, has resigned his office." Jefferson now had his first chance to place a Republican on the bench and he chose William Johnson of South Carolina. Moore returned to North Carolina, where he devoted his energies to establishing the University of North Carolina. He died at the home of his son-in-law on October 15, 1810.

Moore's career made scarcely a ripple in American judicial history. He did his early legal work competently and earned his later judicial posts. Marshall, writing in 1827, stated that "I never heard Mr. Davie or Mr. Moore at the bar, but the impressions they both made on me in private circles were extremely favorable." When he finally reached the center stage, Moore was completely overshadowed by his brethren. One commentator (David Loth) notes: "His trim figure topped by a bald head made him not the least impressive on the bench, although he had the least influence." In his earlier days in North Carolina, he denied any power of judicial review over legislative acts, but years later, his arrival one day late in the *Marbury* case helped establish this power on a national scale. His failure to participate in the *Schooner Peggy* case may have been a contributing factor in expanding the national treaty power. Although Moore had taken prior judicial positions inconsistent with those of the Marshall Court, he apparently had no effect on his brother judges. Whether his absence on the key cases was crucial, or whether his views had in fact changed over the years, remains a mystery. Perhaps he was simply one of the first to feel the force of Marshall's persuasiveness in the conference room.

SELECTED BIBLIOGRAPHY

There are no full length biographical studies of Alfred Moore. On April 29, 1899, Junius Davis delivered a brief address about Moore and Iredell to the Sons of the American Revolution Chapter in North Carolina (reported in 124 N.C. 882). There are frequent references to Moore in North Carolina historical records of the Revolutionary period such as North Carolina Colonial Records and State Records of North Carolina as well as many histories of the period.

Alfred Moore

REPRESENTATIVE OPINIONS

BAS v. TINGY, 4 DALL. 37 (1800)

The sea war between France and the United States had reached its height in 1798 and 1799, based primarily on French claims of the right to capture all British-made or grown goods as prizes even if transported on American ships. To meet the situation Congress passed many laws permitting American armed ships to take French armed vessels or to recapture American merchant vessels seized by the French. A law of March 2, 1799, provided that the recaptor of an American ship would be allowed one-half the value of the ship and goods as salvage if the ship was retaken from "the enemy" more than ninety-six hours after the original capture. An earlier law of June 28, 1798, provided generally that one-eighth of the value of the ship would be paid to any recaptor as salvage.

Tingy was the commander of the public armed ship *Ganges*. On April 31, 1799, his ship had recaptured the ship *Eliza* (John Bas, master) after she had been taken by a French pirateer on March 31, 1799. Tingy argued that he was entitled to one-half the value of the ship since France was "an enemy." All four Justices hearing the case agreed in *seriatim* opinions (Washington, Chase, Paterson, and Moore). Moore's opinion, his only written effort for the Court, follows.

MOORE, JUSTICE.—This case depends on the construction of the act for the regulation of the navy. It is objected, indeed, that the act applies only to future wars; but its provisions are obviously applicable to the present situation of things, and there is nothing to prevent an immediate commencement of its operation.

It is, however, more particularly urged, that the word "enemy" cannot be applied to the French; because the section in which it is used, is confined to such a state of war, as would authorize a recapture of property belonging to a nation in amity with the United States, and such a state of war, it is said, does not exist between America and France. A number of books have been cited to furnish a glossary on the word enemy; yet, our situation is so extraordinary, that I doubt whether a parallel case can be traced in the history of nations. But if words are the representatives of ideas, let me ask, by what other word, the idea of the relative situation of America and France could be communicated, than by that of hostility or war? And how can the characters of the parties engaged in hostility or war, be otherwise described, than by the denomination of enemies? It is for the honor and dignity of both nations, therefore, that they should be called enemies; for it is by that description alone, that either could justify or excuse the scene of bloodshed, depredation and confiscation, which has unhappily occurred; and surely, congress could only employ the language of the act of June 13, 1798, towards a nation whom she considered as an enemy.

Nor does it follow, that the act of March 1799, is to have no operation, because all the cases in which it might operate, are not in existence at the time of passing it. During the present hostilities, it affects the case of recaptured property belonging to our own citizens, and in the event of a future war, it might also be applied to the case of recaptured property belonging to a nation in amity with the United States. But it is further to be remarked, that all the expressions of the act may be satisfied, even at this very time: for by former laws, the recapture of property, belonging to persons resident within the United States, is authorized; those residents may be aliens; and if they are subjects of a nation in amity with the United States, they answer completely the description of the law.

The only remaining objection, offered on behalf of the plaintiff in error, supposes, that, because there are no repealing or negative words, the last law must be confined to future cases, in order to have a subject for the first law to regulate. But if two laws are inconsistent (as, in my judgment, the laws in question are), the latter is a virtual repeal of the former, without any express declaration on the subject.

On these grounds, I am clearly of opinion, that the decree of the circuit court ought to be affirmed.

John Marshall

☆ 1755–1835 ☆

APPOINTED BY

JOHN ADAMS

YEARS ON COURT

1801–1835

John Marshall

by

HERBERT ALAN JOHNSON

"WHEN I WAITED on the President with Mr. Jay's letter declining appointment he said thoughtfully, 'Who shall I nominate now?' I replied that I could not tell, . . . After a few moments hesitation he said 'I believe I must nominate you.' I had never before heard myself named for the office and had not even thought of it. I was pleased as well as surprized, and bowed in silence." Thus did John Marshall, then Secretary of State, recollect the conversation with President John Adams which resulted in his becoming Chief Justice of the Supreme Court of the United States.

Marshall's bow of acquiescence was as pleasing to the President as it was to Marshall himself. The unexpected resignation of Chief Justice Oliver Ellsworth had presented Adams with an opportunity to nominate a successor before Adams himself left office. He offered the post first to John Jay, the first Chief Justice of the Court, who was finishing his term as governor of New York after being defeated in the Jeffersonian Republican landslide of 1800. Jay and Adams had been close friends ever since they had served together on the peace mission in Paris in 1782 and 1783. Jay declined after what seemed to be an interminable delay, giving as his reason the hardships of riding circuit. This brought renewed party pressure upon Adams to raise William Paterson, then an Associate Justice, to the post of Chief Justice. Marshall in his capacity as Secretary of State had been privy to these considerations, and in fact was one of those who strongly urged that the appointment go to Paterson on the basis of his seniority upon the Court.

As Kathryn Turner has demonstrated, these political niceties were greatly complicated by the impending passage of the Federalist-sponsored and short-lived Judiciary Act of 1801, which reduced the number of Supreme Court

HERBERT A. JOHNSON, Associate Editor of the John Marshall Papers, Institute of Early American History and Culture, has written The Law Merchant and Negotiable Instruments in Colonial New York, 1664–1730.

Justices from six to five. Once the approval of both houses was secured and the President signed the bill into law, as he undoubtedly would, his choice of a Chief Justice of necessity would be limited to the five Associate Justices then commissioned. This unusual set of circumstances was what precipitated the selection of John Marshall to be the fourth man to occupy the Chief Justiceship; it was one of those fortunate chances which ofttimes control the fate of men and nations that attended the bestowal of this office upon Marshall. To him, the post was to offer fame and renown, but he simultaneously would give to the office a dignity and power that it had never before known.

Marshall's qualifications for the post at the time of his nomination were twofold: he was a loyal, although at times independent, Federalist political leader, and secondly, he was an experienced and skillful lawyer who, as John Adams phrased it, "has the knowledge of the science fresh in his head." While Marshall may have owed his nomination to both qualities, it is undoubtedly true that although he never lost his skill as a politician, he did lose his partisan commitments after his party, including himself, abortively opposed the War of 1812. The death of the palsied Federalist party in effect liberated Marshall from the active political arena. Thereafter his political battles were to take place on the more exalted plane of constitutional interpretation, and the skills of the lawyer, learned in youth and perfected in middle age, were to pave his path to fame.

Prior to his acceptance of the chief judicial post in the federal government, Marshall had been an occasional officeholder, but had generally declined to enter upon public office despite continual urging to do so. As a young man he was perennially elected to the House of Delegates of Virginia (1782–85, 1787–90, 1795–96), and for a short time had a seat upon the Virginia Executive, or Privy, Council of State (1782–84). Simultaneously he held judicial office as Recorder of the Richmond City Hustings Court, where he and his colleagues dispensed justice in small claims and minor criminal causes (1785–88). The seat upon the Council undoubtedly came to the struggling young lawyer through the influence of his father-in-law Jaquelin Ambler, who was a councillor himself and also Treasurer of the Commonwealth. The other posts were elective, indicating John Marshall's popularity with the electorate. He filled each office with competence, at the same time carefully nurturing his law practice at Richmond to gain adequate sustenance for the large family that was to follow his marriage in 1783.

With the commencement of the new federal government in 1789 it was to be expected that Marshall would be tendered a post by the first administration under George Washington. In the Virginia ratifying convention, Marshall had been among the leaders in the fight for approval and had made an able and well received speech upon the judiciary provisions of the proposed constitution and the need for judicial review. In addition, President Washington was a close friend of the Marshall family. Upon the assurance of a mutual friend that Marshall would accept, Washington offered him a commission as the first Attorney of the United States for the District of Virginia. This was courteously and promptly refused, a procedure that the young Richmond attorney was to follow in regard to the numerous other positions that were to be offered him by Presidents Washington and Adams. In the years between 1789 and 1801, Marshall held only three offices in the federal government—one as Minister to France (1797–98), one as a Virginia member of the House of Representatives (1799–1800), and the last as Secretary of State in the divided and shaken Cabinet of John Adams (1800–1801).

Part of the explanation for Marshall's frequent refusal of public office and the attendant honors was the continued pressure of the debts he had incurred in regard to the purchase of the manor of Leeds from the devisee of Lord Fairfax. This extensive tract of land in the northern neck of Virginia was purchased by a syndicate of which Marshall was a member. Although the transaction was negotiated sometime in 1793 or 1794, it was not until 1796 that a compromise of claims was arranged with the Virginia General Assembly and title was formally vested in Marshall's group. From then until 1806 the need to meet the expiration dates of notes relating to the purchase dominated Marshall's life and financial situation. He was impelled to accept the ministry to France in 1797 by the possibility of a generous award from a grateful Congress. The XYZ Affair, in which unofficial emissaries of the French Directory demanded a bribe before the American diplomats would be received, doomed the mission to failure. But the enthusiasm of Congress for the American ministers' stubborn resistance to the French demands resulted in such a lavish grant to Marshall that the mission proved a great personal financial success. Despite this windfall of good fortune, Marshall continued to decline public office in favor of continuing his lucrative private practice at Richmond. In 1798 he refused a nomination to become Associate Justice of the Supreme Court, suggesting instead that Bushrod Washington be nominated in his place. Indeed even the initial plan of Marshall to write a biography of George Washington may at its inception have had the financial catalytic agent of the Fairfax purchase notes. There is no doubt that one of the prime motivations of Marshall's life in these years was the need to weather the financial storm into which his speculative ventures had driven him.

Significantly, however, Marshall had refused Washington's nomination and appointment to be Attorney for Virginia, even before the Fairfax land purchase had been arranged. From that time until his acceptance of the ministry to France, he remained at Richmond building his law practice and working patiently for the Federalist party in his native state. There is evidence in Marshall's papers that he served as an embryonic "political boss" of the Old Dominion during these years. Recently Harry Ammon has suggested, rather persuasively, the likelihood that Marshall was the author of the *Aristides* and *Gracchus* letters published in the Richmond *Virginia Gazette*. Appearing in 1793, these anonymous missives supported the Washington administration's rather unpopular stand against the violations of neutrality by the French minister, Citizen Genet. In short, Marshall was an important part of the Federalist "machine" in Virginia; that the apparatus was poorly constructed and rapidly depreciating does not detract from the contribution of the men who, through local political maneuver, supported the national administration in its enemy's stronghold of Virginia. While there is as yet insufficient evidence to evaluate Marshall's role in this regard, the indication seems to be that Marshall was a trusted and valued political ally during the period of Federalist rule, and that he was a sounding board for the Federalist leaders when they wished to obtain the sense of public opinion in Virginia. It is perhaps noteworthy that the most unpopular legislation of the Federalists, the hated Alien and Sedition Acts, were vigorously attacked by John Marshall on the floor of the House, to the dismay of his fellow partisans. Before accepting the office of Secretary of State, Marshall had been tendered the portfolio of the War Department; he declined this cup of hemlock which would have involved him in the saber-rattling of Inspector General Alexander Hamilton. The future Chief Justice understood the temper of the American people far better than his Federalist associates in New York and Washington. He had the politician's instinct for taking the safe stand on political issues, and an ability to attract popular support and confidence.

Notwithstanding these abstentions from the excessive behavior of his party, John Marshall was a loyal Federalist who demonstrated his fixity of purpose on many an occasion before he became Chief Justice. As a member of the House of Representatives he had successfully led the legislative defense of the administration's surrender of Jonathan Robbins, a British murderer delivered upon the demand of the British minister for trial in London. His acceptance of the post of Secretary of State was at a time when he could expect little reward from participation in Adams' administration, already repudiated by the Hamiltonian wing of the Federalist party. Thereafter he served Adams devotedly, taking to himself the burdens of everyday administration of the government while Adams was frequently absent in Braintree. In 1800 he supported Adams' renewed efforts to secure peace with France despite the fact that he personally had been humiliated by the behavior of Messrs. X, Y, and Z. Finally his devotion to Washington was unswerving. At the ex-President's request he ran for and won a seat in the House of Representatives in 1798, and after the leader's death undertook the task of writing a biography at the request of Martha Washington and the General's nephew, Bushrod Washington.

Such political loyalty and influence can easily make a man a federal judge, but no amount of popularity can make a judge so appointed a great jurist. Knowledge of the law, of its subtleties and variety; an understanding of the facts and circumstances involved in every conceivable human activity; in short, the training and experience of a practicing lawyer and man of affairs are the indispensable prerequisites to achieving fame upon the bench.

Judged by the standards of the present day, or even by those of eighteenth century colonial America, John Marshall was given a paltry foundation in the law. Six weeks of attendance at George Wythe's law lectures at William and Mary were supplemented by some common-placing from Bacon's *Abridgement*. Family tradition holds that he clerked for a time in the northwestern part of the state, but no documentary evidence of this has been found. Marshall for the most part was a lawyer who learned his law while he practiced it; this is not the best of situations from a client's point of view, but in the case of a capable and adaptable man it can produce a hardened, albeit battle-scarred, attorney who has obtained his knowledge under the pressure of litigation. Such a man is less likely to forget the law than the more fortunate legal scholar who absorbs the abstract principles in the seclusion of the classroom. Derision of classmates passes with time, but the humiliation of a non-suit or overruled demurrer remains a public record.

Initially Marshall was a penniless lawyer. William Swindler has shown that Marshall's law notes were essentially transcripts from the materials in Bacon's *Abridgement*. The very lack of variety indicates that young Marshall did not have many other law books at his disposal. Indeed since he spent so many hours copying from Bacon, it is apparent that he did not have a copy of his own from which to study the law. Undoubtedly the set of Blackstone's *Commentaries* which his father had ordered prior to the Revolution were lost in the intervening years. From this financial low point, Marshall began to develop his practice into one of the most lucrative in Richmond. Indeed after the bankruptcy of Robert Morris, he had no source of credit to sustain him in the Fairfax venture, and it was his private practice that provided funds to meet the demands of his speculative operations, as well as support for his substantial family. Marshall and his wife, Mary Willis Ambler Marshall, had seven sons and three daughters; five sons and one daughter survived to adulthood.

Ironically, much of John Marshall's success in practice and fame as an attorney came from his defense of Virginians against the collection of obligations due to their pre-Revolutionary British creditors. The institution of the federal court system had resulted in a plethora of actions against most of the leading figures in the commonwealth. Basing their cases upon the provisions of the 1783 peace treaty, the attorneys for the British merchants diligently began to protect their client's interests. While Marshall's retention to represent the defendants in the case that was to become *Ware* v. *Hylton,* 3 Dall. 199 (1796), was perhaps fortuitous, his management of that case in the circuit court before Chief Justice Jay brought the young Richmond attorney to public notice even before he carried the case on appeal to the Supreme Court of the United States where he lost his appeal in 1796. In the interim he had secured many a fee in similar cases, and the record books of the Circuit Court for the Virginia District are filled with the notation ". . . the defendant appears by his attorney, John Marshall. . . ." Thus did the man who was to be the advocate of strong nationalism on the Bench become a successful attorney through his representation of clients whose interests were diametrically opposed to the extension of federal judicial power.

Lack of early formal training, coupled with Marshall's early career at the bar, has led many of his biographers to evaluate him as a great statesman but a very poor lawyer. The impression, buttressed by the conclusions of Albert J. Beveridge's otherwise laudatory biography, is that Marshall excelled in enunciating the principles of law and left the problem of finding precedents to others. To a degree Marshall's constitutional opinions tend to support this rule of thumb, but, as we shall see later, for reasons quite apart from his ability as a lawyer. A cursory reading of John Marshall's opinions while on circuit reveals a judge who was superb at analyzing legal problems, and what is perhaps even more significant, had an uncanny facility in handling precedents that permitted him to reject out-of-hand those rules which to him did not seem appropriate to the circumstances of the cases at bar. In short, when private law was at issue, Marshall was brilliant in the conventional sense. That he chose to utilize other techniques in dealing with the great issues of public law that had to be resolved by his Court, should not detract from his unquestioned ability as a man highly learned in the law. Indeed Julius Goebel has laid to earth this persistent myth of Marshall's lack of erudition, but its persistence in the minds of scholars seems inevitable.

Ability in private law notwithstanding, it is in the area of constitutional interpretation that John Marshall achieved his everlasting fame and a place on the frieze surrounding the present Supreme Court chamber. It is impossible to reduce his constitutional thought to a simple formula, for in a very real sense he believed in a constitutional framework that was sufficiently flexible to leave room for judicial interpretation within the circumstances of each individual case. As long as the Supreme Court of the United States would sit as enunciator of the principles of constitutionalism, it could provide such rules of constitutional law as the times would require. Unlike his kinsman and rival, Thomas Jefferson, Marshall did not look to revolution as the process by which one generation would free itself from the constitutional and political forms of its predecessors. Rather he sought a gradual evolution of constitutional government through the case-by-case determinations of an ever changing and responsive Supreme Court. One can find within Marshall's constitutional doctrine points of departure which, if followed to their logical conclusion, would defeat the major premise of the very case in which they were enunciated. For example in *Gibbons* v. *Ogden,* 9 Wheat. 1 (1824), Marshall refers in passing to what would ultimately receive judicial recognition as the police powers of states. In *McCulloch* v. *Maryland,* 4 Wheat. 316 (1819), and later in *Brown* v. *Maryland,* 12 Wheat. 419 (1827), the Chief Justice commented upon the undoubted right of a state to tax under certain circumstances despite the existence of federal supremacy. Small wonder that the Taney Court found within Marshall's decisions sufficient material from which to erect their own precedents without violation of the rule of *stare decisis*! Marshall knew quite well that it was a constitution that he was expounding, and he was too good a lawyer and judge to be doctrinaire about such an important subject.

Through Marshall's constitutional thought there are several threads of jurisprudence which should be delineated despite the danger that their crystallization into words may render them far more rigid than the Chief Justice himself would have preferred. Primarily, he was a man who strongly supported the concept of federal supremacy over the states. This dominant theme is the focal point of *McCulloch* v. *Maryland,* yet it is the leitmotif of nearly every Marshall opinion in the constitutional field, and certainly of all those reprinted below. Next, his strong sense of an ordered and orderly society required that property rights be secured to individuals by their governments, and that should the states trespass upon those rights of their citizens, they might properly be restrained from doing so in accordance with the federal Constitution. Only with such a system of constitutionally guaranteed ownership might the economy of the United States expand. Finally all governments, both state and federal had to be effective if they were to gain respect and secure to their peoples the peace, tranquillity and prosperity which the Founding Fathers had intended. As a corollary to the last proposition, we should note that Marshall knew the intentions of the Founding Fathers not in the conventional historical sense, but rather as one who was personally acquainted with them and their works. He looked to the four corners of the Constitution for its meaning, but when forced to seek the intent of the Federal Convention he was inclined to consult his own recollection and declare their intentions *ex cathedra.*

Undoubtedly the best known opinion of Chief Justice Marshall is that of *Marbury* v. *Madison,* 1 Cranch 137 (1803), which is frequently cited as the federal case establishing judicial review. As we shall note later the doctrine of judicial review was not a new one in American courts, and Marbury's case is noteworthy primarily because it was the first clear enunciation of the principle by the Supreme Court of the United States. The controversy arose from the refusal of Secretary of State James Madison to deliver to William Marbury his commission as a justice of the peace for the District of Columbia. Marbury had been appointed by out-going President John Adams at the end of his term in office; he was one of the group of "Mid-night Judges" so named from the legend that Adams spent his last night in office appointing Federalists to judicial positions. Because of the confusion in the office of the Secretary of State, Marbury's commission had been signed and sealed but remained undelivered when Jefferson's Secretary of State took possession of the office and with it, Marbury's commission. If the land records of the District of Columbia be any index of wealth, William Marbury was a wealthy man who had no great need for such an office, but he was a loyal Federalist who felt duty bound to demand his commission. When he did so, Madison refused to deliver it and Marbury applied to the Supreme Court for the issuance of a writ of *mandamus.* This writ was traditional at common law and commanded a ministerial officer to perform his function as set forth by statute; it was not expressly a part of the jurisdiction of the Supreme Court under the terms of the Constitution, but the Judiciary Act of 1789 had empowered the Supreme Court to issue writs of *mandamus* as part of its original jurisdiction.

Marshall, who as Secretary of State to John Adams was perhaps too closely involved in the case by present-day standards of judicial restraint, undertook to write the opinion of the Court. He found that the appointment was complete upon the President's signature of the commission, and that the sealing and delivery by the Secretary of State were mere ministerial acts imposed upon the Secretary by statute. Thus the Secretary of State acted not in accordance with his discretion as an agent of the President, but rather in accordance with the ministerial and administrative duties imposed upon him as keeper of the Great Seal of the United States. Marbury had a property right in his office, was entitled to delivery of his commission, and a writ of *mandamus* was a proper remedy. The one issue that remained was whether the Judiciary Act of 1789 could constitutionally vest in the Supreme Court the original jurisdiction to issue the writ of *mandamus*. Here Marshall found a conflict between the words of the Constitution and the grant of power by Congress. In such a situation he held it to be the duty of a judge to compare the statute with the constitutional pattern, and it was "the very essence of judicial duty" that a judge faced with such a decision should uphold the Constitution which he had sworn an oath to support and deny efficacy to the statute which conflicted with it. Therefore, although Marbury was entitled in law and natural justice to receive his commission, he was stopped because he had requested the Supreme Court to issue a writ which was not within its power to grant or withhold.

The decision is notable more for its insight into Marshall's political acumen than as a case establishing judicial review. Because the opinion denied relief to William Marbury, there was no order to be enforced against the wishes of the executive branch of government. Hence the Jeffersonians were refused the opportunity to actively oppose the opinion of the Court. At the same time however, the decision firmly established the constitutional, rather than the legislative, source of the jurisdiction of the Supreme Court of the United States. And, perhaps most aggravating of all, it thoroughly entrenched judicial review in federal jurisprudence and undermined Jeffersonian insistence upon legislative supremacy. *Marbury* v. *Madison* stands as one of the most artful utilizations of judicial power in the history of the Supreme Court.

Far more significant in the pre–Civil War evolution of the Constitution of the United States was Marshall's fashioning of the contract clause of the Constitution into an instrument of federal control over state action. Initially the task was commenced by Marshall's opinion in *Fletcher* v. *Peck,* 6 Cranch 87 (1810), which dealt with the issue of title to land involved in the infamous Yazoo land fraud. Corrupt Georgia legislators had been bribed to obtain the legislature's consent to the purchase of the rich farmlands which now comprise the major portions of the states of Alabama and Mississippi. Exposure of the villainy resulted in the ouster of the entire Georgia legislature in the following year's election. The new legislators were pledged to repeal the land grant, and promptly proceeded to do so. One of the grantees in the chain of title from the land speculators sued his grantor upon the latter's warranty that he held good title to the land. Since the Georgia courts upheld the legislative revocation of the land grant, the matter came before the Supreme Court. Marshall for the Court held that the land grant by the Georgia legislature was in the nature of a contract between the state of Georgia and the recipients of the grant; consequently the grantees of the land speculators did in fact hold good title to the land, and this title was a vested right which might not be divested by legislative action since this would violate the contract clause.

Subsequently the Court was presented with a similar case involving the corporate charter of Dartmouth College, which had been granted by the Crown prior to the American Revolution. Here the litigation arose from the attempt by the New Hampshire legislature to revoke the charter and to appoint a new body of trustees for the college. The courts of New Hampshire upheld the action of the legislature, and *Dartmouth College* v. *Woodward,* 4 Wheat. 518 (1819) was brought before the Supreme Court on appeal from their decision. Daniel Webster argued the cause most eloquently for his alma mater, tradition having it that he broke into tears in the midst of his peroration. Marshall wrote the opinion for the Court, holding that there was a contractual relationship between the Crown, the benefactors of the college, and the trustees of the institution. The state of New Hampshire had succeeded to the position of the Crown by virtue of the Revolution, but otherwise the bonds of obligation and duty remained. One of those duties binding upon the state of New Hampshire as successor to the Crown was that it would permit the trustees of the college to manage and use the property given by the benefactors of Dartmouth College for the corporate uses designated in the charter. Absent any showing that the trustees had voided their grant through exceeding their powers, the state of New Hampshire could not in the light of the obligation of the contracts clause of the federal Constitution revoke the charter of Dartmouth College.

Dartmouth College v. *Woodward* is the high point of Marshall's enunciation of the contract clause of the Constitution. It could be, and for a time was, used as a precedent to protect all corporate charters from amendment or alteration by legislative action of the granting sovereignty. Although the opinion is sufficiently broad to permit such an interpretation, it seems likely that Marshall himself would have limited the binding effect of the case to corporations similar in nature to Dartmouth College. Thus he might well have been reluctant to apply the Dartmouth College rule to the situation in which a state legislature amended or altered a charter issued to a business corporation. At any rate, shortly after Chief Justice Marshall's opinion it became commonplace for all corporate charters to contain a clause reserving to the state legislature the right to amend them at any time. Through this means, states were again in a position to exercise effective control over all of their corporate grants, whether for charitable or business purposes. The impact of *Dartmouth College* v. *Woodward* was substantially reduced, but it nevertheless retains the preeminence of being the strongest defense of vested property rights to be enunciated by an ante-bellum federal court.

The same term of the Supreme Court which gave birth to *Dartmouth College* v. *Woodward* also witnessed the strong affirmation of federal primacy through Marshall's opinion for the Court in *McCulloch* v. *Maryland,* 4 Wheat.

316 (1819). Here the complicated issue of a Maryland tax upon the operations of the Bank of the United States branch at Baltimore was brought to the Supreme Court on appeal from the Maryland courts. The cashier of the bank had been held liable in the state courts for the amount of taxes payable under the state statute. In writing his opinion for the Court, Marshall first had to consider the nature of the Bank of the United States. Was it a constitutional exercise of the powers granted to the Congress by the federal Constitution? The Chief Justice held that it was because the chartering of such a bank was a necessary and proper means toward achieving the effective exercise of the powers delegated to Congress by express grant in the Constitution. To quote Marshall, "Let the end be legitimate, let it be within the scope of the Constitution, and all means which are appropriate, which are plainly adapted to that end, which are not prohibited, but consist with the letter and spirit of the Constitution, are constitutional . . ." Further, since the United States was a sovereign power, it followed that within the scope of its limited but sovereign powers it could charter corporations for federal purposes. Maryland's tax was one which fell upon an instrumentality of the federal government; it inhibited the action of the general government for the benefit of the people of *all* the states, and thus was inconsistent with the sovereignty of the federal government and the nature of the federal union. It clashed with the supremacy of the Constitution of the United States and statutes made pursuant to that Constitution, and hence the Maryland tax was unconstitutional in its application to the Bank of the United States.

More than any other Marshall opinion, with the possible exception of *Gibbons* v. *Ogden,* 9 Wheat. 1 (1824), *McCulloch* v. *Maryland* forms the basis upon which affirmative action by the federal government became possible. The cases we have discussed previously represent constitutional limitations either upon the power of the federal legislative branch or upon the state legislative branches. In other words they show the Court, through Marshall, acting as a restraint upon governmental action. *McCulloch,* while it restrains the action of state legislatures, also liberates the federal legislature by giving judicial sanction to the "loose construction" of the Constitution, and particularly of the "necessary and proper" clause. It is central to the jurisprudence of John Marshall, and very likely the most important decision the Chief Justice wrote.

Gibbons v. *Ogden* provided the Court with another opportunity to build this affirmative power of the federal government, particularly in the area of interstate commerce. Involving the constitutionality of a New York State monopoly over steamboat navigation on the Hudson River, the *Gibbons* case came to the Supreme Court on appeal from the decision of Chancellor James Kent which upheld the monopoly grant. For the Court, Marshall held that the congressional statute requiring that a federal coasting license be secured for such navigation constituted federal action under the commerce clause of the Constitution. Navigation, held Marshall, was clearly included within the term "commerce," and navigation that occurred among the various states fell within the regulatory powers of Congress. Consequently the New York statute was void because it conflicted with the power of Congress to regulate, a power they had exercised through the enactment of the Federal Coasting License Act of 1793. To deny one who held such a federal license the right to navigate the streams and coastal waters of any state, was to hinder congressional power to regulate interstate commerce.

In terms of the economic growth of the United States, *Gibbons* v. *Ogden* liberated interstate trade from trade barriers erected by the various states; it was a deadly blow at the growing danger of state oriented mercantilism. Navigation of the Hudson River was far from the most significant implication of the case, for behind Marshall's decision and the arguments of counsel there was the realization that should the state monopoly stand in New York, the states at the mouth of the Mississippi would hold the entire transmontane United States in an economic strangle hold. Marshall's opinion for the Court thus freed the Hudson to navigation and at the same time insured that all Americans could utilize the Father of Waters for commercial purposes, subject only to those regulations which the federal government might choose to impose upon this lucrative trade. For these reasons *Gibbons* v. *Ogden* was one of the few Marshall opinions that was widely acclaimed in Marshall's own day.

Upon the holding and dicta of *Gibbons* v. *Ogden* the entire body of federal regulation over interstate commerce is based. So detailed is the Chief Justice's consideration of the problem that one may find within the text of this opinion numerous suggestions concerning the future areas of decision in this field. Thus one may trace to Marshall the distinction between direct and indirect burdens upon interstate commerce, an analysis which was to find acceptance with later Supreme Court panels in their consideration of what state action might be acceptable in the exercise of state police powers. Within *Gibbons* Marshall sets forth a broad interpretation of the term commerce, and one may find a basis for the "flow of commerce" doctrine, used by later Courts to delineate that puzzling distinction between goods moving in commerce and goods which have come to a rest, and thus are no longer subject to congressional regulation and control. Precise in analysis and sweeping in its scope, *Gibbons* is a veritable *corpus juris* in its field. While *McCulloch* v. *Maryland* is undoubtedly the most significant of Marshall's opinions, and *Marbury* is the most artful in terms of political acumen, the premier Marshall opinion in its encyclopedic statement of the law is *Gibbons* v. *Ogden*.

As he established the foundations for American constitutional law, John Marshall was not unmindful of the authority and strength that his decisions conferred upon the Court over which he presided. *Marbury* springs to mind as an example of this aspect of Marshall's jurisprudence, and yet the most significant case conferring power upon the Court to maintain the supremacy of the federal government is *Cohens* v. *Virginia,* 6 Wheat. 264 (1821). This involved the authority of the federal Supreme Court to review the judgments of the judicial systems of the various states. Ostensibly the appellate power of the United State Supreme Court in "federal questions" had been settled in 1816 by *Martin* v.

Hunter's Lessee, 1 Wheat. 304. However, in the *Martin* case the Virginia Supreme Court of Appeals, under Chief Justice Spencer Roane, had defied the Supreme Court mandate and refused to conform its own judgment to that of the federal Supreme Court.

Cohens v. *Virginia* arose from the criminal prosecution of a partnership which had sold District of Columbia lottery tickets in the city of Norfolk. The Virginia statute provided that no appeals would be allowed from such a conviction, and hence the defendants after their conviction were prohibited from carrying their appeal to the highest court in Virginia. However, at the trial they had raised a "federal question," namely, they had asserted that the Virginia proceeding violated the Constitution and statutes of the United States. This was urged as a positive defense to the prosecution, and the partners argued that the section of the District of Columbia organic act which granted the right to conduct a lottery was, as a law made by Congress pursuant to the Constitution, entitled to precedence over state legislation and protected them from state penalties. The issues raised before the Supreme Court were thus two in number. Did the Supreme Court of the United States have power to issue a writ of error to a state court that was not the highest court of a state? And, if so, did the District of Columbia organic act, erecting the lottery, constitute such an exercise of federal authority that it was entitled to supremacy over the enactments of the various states?

The jurisdictional issue concerning the efficacy of the writ of error was the initial question to be considered by the Supreme Court, and also was the significant aspect of the litigation. What was at stake was the right of a state to limit appeals to the Supreme Court of the United States through the simple process of denying appeals on constitutional issues to the highest court in its state judicial system. If this power were to be conceded, the supremacy clause of the federal Constitution, at least as far as judicial review by the Supreme Court was concerned, would be effective only at the discretion of the legislatures of the various states.

Marshall proceeded to carefully analyze the intent of the Eleventh Amendment, and then to write an extended exposition of the Supreme Court's power to review all state judicial proceedings which brought into issue rights asserted under the Constitution, laws, and treaties of the United States. As far as the Eleventh Amendment was concerned, Marshall pointed out that its purpose was to protect a state from being sued as a party defendant, and that it did not prevent an individual convicted in a state criminal prosecution from bringing his case before the United States Supreme Court by writ of error. Noting that this also involved a distinction between the original and the appellate jurisdiction of the Supreme Court, he proceeded to the consideration that *Cohens* v. *Virginia* was distinguishable from *Chisholm* v. *Georgia,* 2 Dall. 419 (1793), in that the Supreme Court took jurisdiction in *Cohens* not by virtue of a state being a party, but rather because the case raised issues asserted under the federal Constitution. Such power in the federal Supreme Court was absolutely essential if the judicial interpretation of the federal Constitution was to be uniform throughout the

United States. Just as the supremacy clause was essential to the operation of the federal Union, so *Cohens* v. *Virginia* was necessary to insure the authority of the Supreme Court to protect that Union.

Having decided the jurisdictional issue in favor of federal Supreme Court review by writ of error, Marshall proceeded to hold that the lottery legislation was intended by Congress as merely local regulations for the government of the District of Columbia. Consequently, absent the express declaration of Congress, it should not be considered part of the "supreme law of the land," and therefore did not protect Cohens and his partner from prosecution for violation of the Virginia law concerning out-of-state lotteries. As in *Marbury,* the decision of the Court did not conflict with the political powers it challenged, and there was again no basis upon which Virginia or her supporters could oppose the assertion of jurisdiction by the Supreme Court.

One cannot overstress the importance of *Cohens* to the constitutional development of the United States. Because it upheld federal supremacy it was far more significant than *Marbury* v. *Madison,* which dealt with the division of powers within the branches of the federal government. It was a strong statement of the nature of the federal Union at a time when the seeds of dissension over slavery were beginning to sprout. Marshall thus gave expression to a principle of federal supremacy which his fellow Virginians would challenge with force of arms four decades later.

Marshall's opinions on constitutional law are unique in their formulation, and his unorthodox approach to reaching a decision is at times most disturbing to the lawyer who looks at one of Marshall's opinions in the light of present-day practice on the Court. Historical hindsight partially obscures the fact that when Marshall took his place as Chief Justice there was substantially little constitutional law to be consulted for precedents. The one major constitutional decision enunciated by the pre-Marshall Court had been *Chisholm* v. *Georgia,* and this ultra-nationalist decision was quickly reversed by the prompt ratification of the Eleventh Amendment. The Judiciary Act of 1789 provided guidelines for the Court in finding precedents in the laws of the various states in which the private disputes before them arose. Yet only the Court itself could state the rules of constitutional law that were to be derived from the common law, not of one state, certainly not of all of the states simultaneously, and clearly not that of England. Indeed this new federal government provided a factual situation which would permit the distinction upon the facts of nearly every previous American or English decision. As John Marshall was quite capable of distinguishing all rules that did not apply to the facts of the case before him, this skill could be turned to good use in the constitutional field to wipe the slate clean of all "precedents" offered by counsel. The framers of the federal Constitution had created a situation unique in the history of the common law. First, they had drawn up a constitution which was to be a written body of law superior to both federal and state statutes, thereby implicitly subordinating ordinary legislation. Henceforth American legislatures were to be limited in authority, despite the fact that

Parliament, and perhaps the colonial assemblies also, had operated under no such restriction. Secondly, the framers had divided sovereignty between a federal state and its various component states, leaving to a large degree unresolved the problem of allocating to each sovereign a portion of the hitherto unitary sovereign power. Thirdly, all of this had been done in terms of republican rather than monarchial institutions. To hew closely to English public law would be absurd. To choose one state's common law in preference to others would be foolhardly. Decision upon the basis of natural law, right reason, and constitutional intent was the only true course. In taking the latter alternative, Marshall set forth, not precise rules of constitutional law, but rather the broad general outlines upon which future generations would evolve more explicit constitutional doctrines. America needed such a spacious outline of constitutional theory and interpretation before the Court would be able to proceed to evolve a highly articulated constitutional law; the jurisprudence of John Marshall was merely the architect's sketch or rough grand plan, and he left to future generations of judges the task of developing the working drawings from which the constitutional structure would take its pattern.

Committed as he was to the development of the general outlines of constitutional doctrine, and that, as we have noted, upon extremely flexible lines, John Marshall wrote opinions that are long, wordy, and at times unnecessarily involved. Occasionally he exhibited a rare literary flourish which proved sufficiently impressive to find its way into the opinions of his own and other Courts. He struggled with his opinions, attempting always to make them full treatments of all relevant subjects. As a result there is much in the Chief Justice's opinions that might be considered dicta, or what is even worse from the lawyer's point of view, *obiter dicta*. And yet these terms are the catchwords of the law student, which Marshall was for only a brief period of time. His practical experience as an advocate before the bar led Marshall to realize that one day's dictum or dissent can be the next day's law. One need only read Marshall's opinions carefully to discover a remarkable number of irrelevent or unnecessary statements which, at some future date, the Supreme Court elevated from the category of Marshall dictum to a precedent, forming the basis for decision in the case at bar. The very length and complexity of Marshall's opinions are therefore another reason for his greatness as a judge. His approach was to consider the issues from every conceivable point of view, and in this his colleagues undoubtedly lent their own analysis. Much that emerged was technically dictum, but taken together with the holding, it constituted an encyclopedic treatment of the subject.

Marshall's economic position as it emerges from his decisions is that of a conservative, or more properly, according to Clinton Rossiter, a "right of center" conservative. While Max Lerner has accused Marshall of being the ". . . strategic link between capitalism and constitutionalism," this is a gross simplification of the Chief Justice's position in matters economic. He certainly did not consider it to be his chosen mission to erect constitutional barricades behind which business might isolate itself from the power of government. True, he had created a powerful constitutional safeguard for businesses with corporate charters through the *Dartmouth College* decision reprinted below, but in his relatively unknown decision of *Providence Bank* v. *Billings,* 4 Pet. 514 (1830), he held that corporate charters to business corporations must be strictly construed in favor of the people as sovereigns who granted the charter. In the development of commerce and industry Marshall saw a bright future for the United States, and although he recognized the social problems that would arise in an industrialized society, he sought means to alleviate those difficulties rather than methods to forestall the approach of an industrial age. Even as he appreciated the advantages which economic growth had to offer, Marshall feared that the employment of capital would be unwise or speculative, and that society would be disrupted by the process, *Craig* v. *Missouri,* 4 Pet. 410 (1830). For this reason he sought to utilize the powers of government, limited though they might be under the Constitution, to control business activity or at the least to channel it into directions that were conducive to the public good. Although opposed to price fixing, he supported state inspection of the tobacco crop and various quarantine and common carrier laws. He had served on the congressional committee that reported the first federal bankruptcy law, but was opposed to state insolvency laws because he felt they would encourage speculation. *Ogden* v. *Saunders,* 12 Wheat. 213 (1827). John Marshall seems to have been in step with the leading businessmen of his time, and although he realized that the opportunities which American life offered had to be secured to men through a highly developed constitutional protection of property, he was nevertheless not a man to cast aside the responsibilities of government for a system of *laissez-faire.*

The Chief Justice who extended constitutional protection to property rights did so in strict regard for the proper balance of state and federal power. Thus in *Barron* v. *Baltimore,* 7 Pet. 243 (1833), Marshall declined to extend Fifth Amendment due process guarantees to actions taken by individual states against their citizens. Had he done so and the precedent had survived the dual sovereignty propensities of the Taney Court, the Fourteenth Amendment as far as due process is concerned, might have been rendered superfluous. Marshall found the principal restrictions upon state activities in the commerce and contract clauses. These he used to combat an incipient state-oriented mercantilism on the one hand, and legislative supremacy on the other. Even in these areas the balance of federal-state powers was to be maintained. *Gibbons* v. *Ogden* must be read in the light of *Willson* v. *Black Bird Creek Marsh Company,* 2 Pet. 245 (1829), just as *Dartmouth College* v. *Woodward* needs *Providence Bank* v. *Billings* for a chaser. One must note in passing that Marshall understood the contract clause to be much broader than would the legal scholar of today. The technical rules of contract law were only beginning to be evolved when he studied law, and a fully defined principle of consideration did not find its way into American jurisprudence until after his death. Thus he was not in the least embarrassed to paraphrase Blackstone that a land grant is a contract, *Fletcher* v. *Peck,* 6 Cranch 87 (1810), in defiance of the as yet unformulated principle of consideration.

Likewise, *Dartmouth College* did not present to Marshall any problems of privity of contract or third party beneficary. It is perhaps fortunate that Marshall took such a liberal and non-technical view of the term "contract," for the contract clause as such would have been far less effective without this interpretation.

Although the Chief Justice is not famous for his decisions in the area of civil liberties, or rather, the relationship of the individual citizen to the sovereign power, his contributions in this area deserve mention. The treason trial of Aaron Burr at the federal Circuit Court for Virginia (1807) reaffirmed the constitutional definition of the crime and eliminated the possibility of constructive treason from American criminal law. In his decisions on motions in the Burr case, Marshall upheld procedural due process in spite of the pressure of the Executive branch of government and the weight of public opinion. Worthy of mention also, is Marshall's valiant attempt to apply law and reason to the question of the removal of the civilized Indian tribes from the old Southwest Territory by the officials of the state of Georgia. In this the Chief Justice knew that he challenged the power of the President of the United States, and that he would in effect have to rule upon the treaty rights of the Indians in a manner that would be diametrically opposed to the intentions of the Jackson administration. Finally presented with a case of which he had to take jurisdiction, Marshall in *Worcester* v. *Georgia,* 6 Pet. 515 (1832), wrote an appealing and forceful defense of the right of the Cherokees to hold their lands independent of Georgia sovereignty. Jackson's defiance of the Supreme Court's decision sent the Cherokees off on their "Trail of Tears" to Oklahoma, and thoroughly humiliated Marshall and his Court for upholding their treaty rights.

To some degree Marshall's opinions for the Court bear the impress of other men's ideas. No case more fully illustrates this point than *Marbury* v. *Madison,* which was a synopsis of the thought on judicial review ranging from Sir Edward Coke through James Otis to the early state decisions upholding review of state statutes. There is much of Hamilton's opinion on the Bank of the United States in *McCulloch* v. *Maryland,* including both the so-called loose construction of the necessary and proper clause and the justification of the granting of corporate charters as a power inherent in federal sovereignty. Marshall was also capable of accepting some ideas of others, even as he rejected other concepts advanced by the same men. Daniel Webster, never accused of humility, claimed with some element of truth that the Chief Justice merely copied his argument in *Gibbons* v. *Ogden.* And yet Felix Frankfurter shows very clearly that what Marshall did was to accept much of the "mighty Daniel's" argument, but to reject his theory that an exclusive power to regulate commerce was vested in the Congress of the United States by the Constitution.

Much controversy has arisen in the past decade concerning the unanimity which Marshall imposed upon his Court by inducing them to abandon *seriatum* opinions in favor of a single opinion of the Court. Not only did he achieve this procedural alteration, but he then proceeded to become spokesman for the Court in approximately half of all the opinions handed down during the course of his

Chief Justiceship. He himself was forced into dissent in only one constitutional decision, that of *Ogden* v. *Saunders,* 12 Wheat. 213 (1827). The traditional interpretation had always been that Marshall so dominated his brethren on the Court that they calmly acquiesced in his preeminent role as law-giver to the nation. William W. Crosskey challenges this viewpoint on several grounds, some of which have validity. Without questioning the greatness of Marshall, he asserts that Marshall demonstrated his abilities not by imposing his will upon his associates, but rather by achieving a consensus with them by which he gained the right to act as spokesman for the Court. Crosskey asserts that Marshall thus became the scrivener for Jeffersonian justices, but did so that, in the process of reducing the joint opinion of the Court to writing, he might have the chance to insert Federalist doctrines into their constitutional decisions. In short, the Jeffersonian justices did not acquiesce in the dominance of an intellect they respected, but rather were tricked into permitting Marshall to express their joint opinions in terms that were unfavorable to the political principles of their party.

By way of contrast Donald G. Morgan, biographer of the frequent dissenter William Johnson, finds that although Marshall's influence in the conferences of the Court gradually diminished and reached a low point in the years from 1831 to 1835, nevertheless, through the most active decades of his court, Marshall was able to channel their decisions in the paths he wished to follow. This seems a more accurate analysis of what happened in the conferences of the Supreme Court, and yet all who venture into this area are met with the problem that there is little positive evidence of the weight that Marshall's opinions had with each of his Associate Justices.

While it is difficult to disagree with Professor Crosskey's statement that the unanimity of the Marshall Court is a myth that discourages study, his contentions are inconsistent with the character of John Marshall and rather insulting to the intelligence of the Associate Justices of the Supreme Court. Throughout his lifetime Marshall demonstrated a remarkable degree of intellectual honesty, as well as a tenacity of purpose. Crosskey suggests that Marshall took the opportunity of his position as Chief Justice to gain for himself the privilege of writing the Court's opinions. Then he acquiesced in opinions, many of which were contrary to his own convictions, and wrote them as far as possible in accordance with principles that were in conflict with those of his associates. In short, Marshall was a man who would cheat at solitaire! Concede that the man was so devious and designing that he so sacrificed his own deeply felt opinions, thereby gaining a chance to undermine the strength of the Jeffersonian Justices' arguments—and such a concession is a difficult one to jibe with Crosskey's reaffirmation that Marshall was a great man, no less a great judge. Concede that all other Justices of the Supreme Court during the Marshall period were incredibly stupid, and totally immune to the hostility of public opinion that greeted nearly every significant opinion written by the Chief Justice. Concede finally that all of the Presidents of the United States from Adams to Jackson were so inept that they selected legally trained men who failed to recognize that their opinions had been altered in the writing by a wily Chief Justice. If one is willing to believe this, and then agree that Marshall himself was capable of such duplicity, then certainly this Rasputin of Richmond was the worst scoundrel in American history!

A simpler and more plausible analysis would seem to proceed along the lines first of studying the parallels between Marshall's constitutional thought and that of his Jeffersonian brethren, and secondly of weighing carefully the impression which Marshall's personality made not only upon the Justices of his Court but upon men in all walks and stations of life. As to the first proposition, it seems to me that after 1815 Marshall's nationalism and economic policies were in tune with the temper of the times; they were aspirations he shared with Jefferson's appointees to the bench. Neither Marshall nor his associates were impressed with the rising sentiment for free competition in the economic sphere, nor did they concur in the sectionalism inherent in the incipient Jacksonian movement. It has been suggested at the beginning of this essay that the end of the War of 1812 freed the Chief Justice from political ties to the moribund Federalist party; one might argue that Marshall was no longer a Federalist in politics. Along with many of his fellow partisans he drifted through the era noted for its good feelings, but by the middle years of the 1820's he found himself well within that group of Jeffersonian Republicans who were in due course to become the Whig party. Whether Marshall joined the Jeffersonians or they joined Marshall is largely a matter of an historian's semantics and point of view.

An indeterminate quantity in analyzing Marshall's capacity to minimize dissent is the personality of the Chief Justice himself, for of this we know but little. We know from descriptions that he was an awkward, ungainly man whose face appeared too small for his frame. He was accused of being careless in dress, and numerous anecdotes confirm his humility in manner. Although a "log cabin boy" by birth, he was not the frontiersman Beveridge depicts, and he would have been puzzled by his biographer's describing him as the prototype of that paragon of all backwoodsmen, Abraham Lincoln. Marshall was a man of well-developed tastes who enjoyed the salon and carefully attended to his supply of wines. His father moved to Kentucky, and his sons moved to the mountains of western Virginia and the fertile lands in Alabama and Mississippi, but the Chief Justice remained in the city of Richmond. There he frequented a club where the members of the bench and bar banqueted, played tenpins and quoits, and discussed events of the day. A Mason, he was Master of his Richmond lodge and for several years Grand Master of the Commonwealth of Virginia. He served as an official in the American Colonization Society, which was dedicated to the transportation and settlement of free Negroes in Africa; he belonged to the Washington Historical Monument Society, a society for the encouragement of military knowledge, and several literary societies. There can be no doubt that Marshall found happiness in the company of his fellow men. They in turn found him a charming and interesting companion, and few in number were those who, after meeting the Chief Justice, did not become his friends even though they strongly opposed his political and constitutional views.

Yet we know too little about the man who was Chief Justice Marshall. He lives too much in the words of his judicial opinions for us to judge with any degree of accuracy the power his personality may have given him over the thoughts of men, and particularly those men who sat with him on the Supreme Court. Gradually his papers are being assembled, and they reveal a man who wrote free and forceful letters, many of which are studded with humorous expressions or comments upon the times. More than most men of his generation, he was, even with subordinates, never stiffly formal. One finds him a truly likeable person, and some of his endearing qualities are preserved in his correspondence and private papers; yet a man does not live, nor influence, by letters alone, and hence we can never fully assess the persuasive powers that might have been the principal weapon of John Marshall as he strove for unanimity on his Supreme Court.

As a warm and intense human being, Marshall deeply resented personal attacks and reacted angrily to them. Goaded by Spencer Roane (1762–1822, then Chief Justice of the Supreme Court of Appeals of Virginia) in 1819, the Chief Justice of the United States Supreme Court dropped his judicial detachment, and Marshall the man wrote a stinging anonymous response, defending the opinions of his Court in *McCulloch* v. *Maryland* and *Dartmouth College* v. *Woodward*. Resentment still unquenched, Marshall used his influence to prevent Roane's articles from appearing in a prominent Philadelphia journal for the legal profession. Quick to anger, he was also deep in his family attachments and utterly devoted to his "Dearest Polly," to whom he had been married in 1783 and upon whom he showered a lifetime of affection and devotion. When away from Richmond he wrote unceasingly to his wife, and doted upon her through her lifetime of chronic illness and attendant nervousness. One year after her death he could contain himself no longer and poured forth his acute sadness and loneliness in the pathetic monologue of an old man who had never aged until her death. "I have lost her! And with her I have lost the solace of my life! Yet she remains still the companion of my retired hours,—still occupies my inmost bosom. When I am alone and unemployed, my mind turns unceasingly to her."

Blessed with vigorous health, Marshall was to live on until just three months short of eighty. The surgery of Philip Syng Physick had successfully treated stones in the bladder, but age was nevertheless pressing down upon the "Silver Heels" who had run so fleetly through the encampment of Washington's army at Valley Forge. Failing in health and strength, Marshall continued to serve as Chief Justice, hoping to the end that the Jacksonian administration would either be repudiated or else become reconciled with his view of the Constitution and the destiny of America. In both he proved mistaken, but still his sense of duty carried him forward. He refused to resign his office, and, characteristically, John Marshall was the first Chief Justice of the United States Supreme Court to die in office. In this too, he established a precedent.

SELECTED BIBLIOGRAPHY

Albert J. Beveridge, *The Life of John Marshall,* 4 vols. (Boston, 1916–1919) remains the standard biographical treatment of John Marshall, but should be read in conjunction with the criticism by Landon C. Bell, "Albert J. Beveridge as a Biographer of Marshall," 12 *Virginia Law Register,* n.s. 641 (1927); and Max Lerner, "John Marshall and the Campaign of History," 39 *Columbia Law Review* 396 (1939). A shorter and more vigorous treatment is Edward S. Corwin, *John Marshall and the Constitution* (New Haven, 1919). The most useful collection of interpretive essays to date is W. Melville Jones, ed., *Chief Justice John Marshall: A Reappraisal* (Ithaca, 1956). On Marshall's constitutional decisions see the appropriate sections of Benjamin F. Wright, *The Contract Clause of the Constitution* (Cambridge, 1938) and Felix Frankfurter, *The Commerce Clause Under Marshall, Taney and Waite* (Chapel Hill, 1937). The best treatment of the Burr episode is Thomas P. Abernethy, *The Burr Conspiracy* (New York, 1954). On Marshall's personal life see Frances Norton Mason, *My Dearest Polly* (Richmond, 1961). An excellent bibliography of primary and secondary sources is James A. Servies, *A Bibliography of John Marshall* (Washington, D.C., 1956).

John Marshall

REPRESENTATIVE OPINIONS

MARBURY v. MADISON, 1 CRANCH 137 (1803)

A fully executed but undelivered commission of a "mid-night judge" caused the appointee to request a writ of *mandamus* from the Supreme Court to compel delivery. Chief Justice Marshall for the Court postponed decision of the jurisdictional issue, finding that the appointee was legally entitled to delivery, that *mandamus* was the proper remedy, and that such a writ was authorized by the Judiciary Act of 1789. However, since the writ was not included within the constitutional grant of original jurisdiction to the Supreme Court, the Judiciary Act conflicted with the Constitution. In such cases he held that the Court was bound to follow the Constitution and to ignore the statute; consequently it was without power to issue a *mandamus* as part of its original jurisdiction. The case placed the Court's imprimatur upon the evolving principle of judicial review of federal statutes and firmly established that the Court's jurisdiction was based upon the Constitution and only secondarily upon legislative authorizations.

Opinion of the Court. At the last term, on the affidavits then read and filed with the clerk, a rule was granted in this case, requiring the secretary of state to show cause why a *mandamus* should not issue, directing him to deliver to William Marbury his commission as a justice of the peace for the county of Washington, in the district of Columbia.

No cause has been shown, and the present motion is for a *mandamus*. The peculiar delicacy of this case, the novelty of some of its circumstances, and the real difficulty attending the points which occur in it, require a complete exposition of the principles on which the opinion to be given by the court is founded. These principles have been, on the side of the applicant, very ably argued at the bar. In rendering the opinion of the court, there will be some departure in form, though not in substance, from the points stated in that argument.

In the order in which the court has viewed this subject, the following questions have been considered and decided: 1st. Has the applicant a right to the commission he demands? 2d. If he has a right, and that right has been violated, do the laws of his country afford him a remedy? 3d. If they do afford him a remedy, is it a *mandamus* issuing from this court?

The first object of inquiry is—Has the applicant a right to the commission he demands? His right originates in an act of congress passed in February 1801, concerning the district of Columbia. After dividing the district into two counties, the 11th section of this law enacts, "that there shall be appointed in and for each of the said counties, such number of discreet persons to be justices of the peace, as the president of the United States shall, from time to time, think expedient, to continue in office for five years.

It appears, from the affidavits, that, in compliance with this law, a commission for William Marbury, as a justice of peace for the county of Washington, was signed by John Adams, then President of the United States; after which, the seal of the United States was affixed to it; but the commission has never reached the person for whom it was made out. In order to determine whether he is entitled to this commission, it becomes necessary to inquire, whether he has been appointed to the office. For if he has been appointed, the law continues him in office for five years, and he is entitled to the possession of those evidences of office, which, being completed, became his property.

The 2d section of the 2d article of the constitution declares, that "the president shall nominate, and by and with the advice and consent of the senate, shall appoint ambassadors, other public ministers and consuls, and all other officers of the United States, whose appointments are not otherwise provided for." The 3d section declares, that "he shall commission all the officers of the United States."

An act of congress directs the secretary of state to keep the seal of the United States, "to make out and record, and affix the said seal to all civil commissions to officers of the United States, to be appointed by the president, by and with the consent of the senate, or by the president alone; provided, that the said seal shall not be affixed to any commission, before the same shall have been signed by the president of the United States."

These are the clauses of the constitution and laws of the United States, which affect this part of the case. They seem to contemplate three distinct operations: 1st. The nomination: this is the sole act of the president, and is completely voluntary. 2d. The appointment: this is also the act of the president, and is also a voluntary act, though it can only be performed by and with the advice and consent of the senate. 3d. The commission: to grant a commission to a person appointed, might, perhaps, be deemed a duty enjoined by the constitution. "He shall," says that instrument, "commission all the officers of the United States."

1. The acts of appointing to office, and commissioning the person appointed, can scarcely be considered as one and the same; since the power to perform them is given in two separate and distinct sections of the constitution. The distinction between the appointment and the commission, will be rendered more apparent, by adverting to that provision in the second section of the second article of the constitution, which authorizes congress "to vest, by law, the appointment of such inferior officers, as they think proper, in the president alone, in the courts of law, or in the heads of departments;" thus contemplating cases where the law may direct the president to commission an officer appointed by the courts, or by the heads of departments. In such a case, to issue a commission would be apparently a duty distinct from the appointment, the performance of which, perhaps, could not legally be refused.

Although that clause of the constitution which requires the president to commission all the officers of the United States, may never have been applied to officers appointed otherwise than by himself, yet it would be difficult to deny the legislative power to apply it to such cases. Of consequence, the constitutional distinction between the appointment to an office and the commission of an officer who has been appointed, remains the same, as if, in practice, the president had commissioned officers appointed by an authority other than his own. It follows, too, from the existence of this distinction, that if an appointment was to be evidenced by any public act, other than the commission, the performance of such public act would create the officer; and if he was not removable at the will of the president, would either give him a right to his commission, or enable him to perform the duties without it.

These observations are premised, solely for the purpose of rendering more intelligible those which apply more directly to the particular case under consideration.

This is an appointment made by the president, by and with the advice and consent of the senate, and is evidenced by no act but the commission itself. In such a case, therefore, the commission and the appointment seem inseparable; it being almost impossible to show an appointment, otherwise than by providing the existence of a commission; still the commission is not necessarily the appointment, though conclusive evidence of it.

But at what stage, does it amount to this conclusive evidence? The answer to this question seems an obvious one. The appointment being the sole act of the president, must be completely evidenced, when it is shown that he has done everything to be performed by him. Should the commission, instead of being evidence of an appointment, even be considered as constituting the appointment itself; still, it would be made, when the last act to be done by the president was performed, or, at farthest, when the commission was complete.

The last act to be done by the president is the signature of the commission: he has then acted on the advice and consent of the senate to his own nomination. The time for deliberation has then passed: he has decided. His judgment, on the advice and consent of the senate, concurring with his nomination, has been made, and the officer is appointed. This appointment is evidenced by an open unequivocal act; and being the last act required from the person making it, necessarily excludes the idea of its being, so far as respects the appointment, an inchoate and incomplete transaction.

Some point of time must be taken, when the power of the executive over an officer, not removable at his will, must cease. That point of time must be, when the constitutional power of appointment has been exercised. And this power has been exercised, when the last act, required from the person possessing the power, has been performed: this last act is the signature of the commission. This idea seems to have prevailed with the legislature, when the act passed converting the department of foreign affairs into the department of state. By that act, it is enacted, that the secretary of state shall keep the seal of the United States, "and shall make out and record, and shall affix the said seal to all civil commissions to officers of the United States, to be appointed by the president;" "provided, that the said seal shall not be affixed to any commission, before the same shall have been signed by the President of the United States; nor to any other instrument or act, without the special warrant of the president therefor."

The signature is a warrant for affixing the great seal to the commission; and the great seal is only to be affixed to an instrument which is complete. It attests, by an act, supposed to be of public notoriety, the verity of the presidential signature. It is never to be affixed, until the commission is signed, because the signature, which gives force and effect to the commission, is conclusive evidence that the appointment is made.

The commission being signed, the subsequent duty of the secretary of state is prescribed by law, and not to be guided by the will of the president. He is to affix the seal of the United States to the commission, and is to record it. This is not a proceeding which may be varied, if the judgment of the executive shall suggest one more eligible; but is a precise course accurately marked out by law, and is to be strictly pursued. It is the duty of the secretary of state, to conform to the law, and in this he is an officer of the United States, bound to obey the laws. He acts, in this respect, as has been very properly stated at the bar, under the authority of law, and not by the instructions of the president. It is a ministerial act, which the law enjoins on a particular officer for a particular purpose.

If it should be supposed, that the solemnity of affixing the seal is necessary, not only to the validity of the commission, but even to the completion of an appointment, still, when the seal is affixed, the appointment is made, and the commission is valid. No other solemnity is required by law; no other act is to be performed on the part of government. All that the executive can do, to invest the person with his office, is done; and unless the appointment be then made, the executive cannot make one without the co-operation of others.

After searching anxiously for the principles on which a contrary opinion may be supported, none have been found, which appear of sufficient force to maintain the opposite doctrine. Such as the imagination of the court could suggest, have been very deliberately examined, and after allowing them all the weight which it appears possible to give them, they do not shake the opinion which has been formed. In considering this question, it has been conjectured, that the commission may have been assimilated to a deed, to the validity of which delivery is essential. This idea is founded on the supposition, that the commission is not merely evidence of an appointment, but is itself the actual appointment; a supposition by no means unquestionable. But for the purpose of examining this objection fairly, let it be conceded, that the principle claimed for its support is established.

The appointment being, under the constitution, to be made by the president, personally, the delivery of the deed of appointment, if necessary to its completion, must be made by the president also. It is not necessary, that the delivery should be made personally to the grantee of the office: it never is so made. The law would seem to contemplate, that it should be made to the secretary of state, since it directs the secretary to affix the seal to the commission after it shall have been signed by the president. If, then, the act of delivery be necessary to give validity to the commission, it has been delivered, when executed and given to the secretary, for the purpose of being sealed, recorded and transmitted to the party.

But in all cases of letters-patent, certain solemnities are required by law, which solemnities are the evidences of the validity of the instrument: a formal delivery to the person is not among them. In cases of commissions, the sign manual of the president, and the seal of the United States are those solemnities. This objection, therefore, does not touch the case.

It has also occurred as possible, and barely possible, that the transmission of the commission, and the acceptance thereof, might be deemed necessary to complete the right of the plaintiff. The transmission of the commission is a practice, directed by convenience, but not by law. It cannot, therefore, be necessary to constitute the appointment, which must precede it, and which is the mere act of the president. If the executive required that every person appointed to an office should himself take means to procure his commission, the appointment would not be the less valid on that account. The appointment is the sole act of the president; the transmission of the commission is the sole act of the officer to whom that duty is assigned, and may be accelerated or retarded by circumstances which can have no influence on the appointment. A commission is transmitted to a person already appointed; not to a person to be appointed or not, as the letter inclosing the commission should happen to get into the post-office and reach him in safety, or to miscarry.

It may have some tendency to elucidate this point, to inquire, whether the possession of the original commission be indispensably necessary to authorize a person, appointed to any office, to perform the duties of that office. If it was necessary, then a loss of the commission would lose the office. Not only negligence, but accident or fraud, fire or theft, might deprive an individual of his office. In such a case, I presume, it could not be doubted, but that a copy from the record of the office of the secretary of state would be, to every intent and purpose, equal to the original: the act of congress has expressly made it so. To give that copy validity, it would not be necessary to prove that the original had been transmitted and afterwards lost. The copy would be complete evidence that the original had existed, and that the appointment had been made, but not that the original had been transmitted. If, indeed, it should appear, that the original had been mislaid in the office of state, that circumstance would not affect the operation of the copy. When all the requisites have been performed, which authorize a recording officer to record any instrument whatever, and the order for that purpose has been given, the instrument is, in law, considered as recorded, although the manual labor of inserting it in a book kept for that purpose may not have been performed. In the case of commissions, the law orders the secretary of state to record them. When, therefore, they are signed and sealed, the order for their being recorded is given; and whether inserted in the book or not, they are in law recorded.

A copy of this record is declared equal to the original, and the fees to be paid by a person requiring a copy are ascertained by law. Can a keeper of a public record erase therefrom a commission which has been recorded? Or can he refuse a copy thereof to a person demanding it on the terms prescribed by law? Such a copy would, equally with the original, authorize the justice of peace to proceed in the performance of his duty, because it would, equally with the original, attest his appointment.

If the transmission of a commission be not considered as necessary to give validity to an appointment, still less is its acceptance. The appointment is the sole act of the president; the acceptance is the sole act of the officer, and is, in plain common sense, posterior to the appointment. As he may resign, so may he refuse to accept: but neither the one nor the other is capable of rendering the appointment a nonentity.

That this is the understanding of the

government, is apparent from the whole tenor of its conduct. A commission bears date, and the salary of the officer commences, from his appointment; not from the transmission or acceptance of his commission. When a person appointed to any office refuses to accept that office, the successor is nominated in the place of the person who has declined to accept, and not in the place of the person who had been previously in office, and had created the original vacancy.

It is, therefore, decidedly the opinion of the court, that when a commission has been signed by the president, the appointment is made; and that the commission is complete, when the seal of the United States has been affixed to it by the secretary of state.

Where an officer is removable at the will of the executive, the circumstance which completes his appointment is of no concern; because the act is at any time revocable; and the commission may be arrested, if still in the office. But when the officer is not removable at the will of the executive, the appointment is not revocable, and cannot be annulled: it has conferred legal rights which cannot be resumed. The discretion of the executive is to be exercised, until the appointment has been made. But having once made the appointment, his power over the office is terminated, in all cases where, by law, the officer is not removable by him. The right to the office is then in the person appointed, and he has the absolute unconditional power of accepting or rejecting it.

Mr. Marbury, then, since his commission was signed by the president, and sealed by the secretary of state, was appointed; and as the law creating the office, gave the officer a right to hold for five years, independent of the executive, the appointment was not revocable, but vested in the officer legal rights, which are protected by the laws of his country. To withhold his commission, therefore, is an act deemed by the court not warranted by law, but violative of a vested legal right.

2. This brings us to the second inquiry; which is: If he has a right, and that right has been violated, do the laws of his country afford him a remedy? The very essence of civil liberty certainly consists in the right of every individual to claim the protection of the laws, whenever he receives an injury. One of the first duties of government is to afford that protection. In Great Britain, the king himself is sued in the respectful form of a petition, and he never fails to comply with the judgment of his court.

In the 3d vol. of his Commentaries (p. 23), Blackstone states two cases in which a remedy is afforded by mere operation of law. "In all other cases," he says, "it is a general and indisputable rule, that where there is a legal right, there is also a legal remedy by suit, or action at law, whenever that right is invaded." And afterwards (p. 109, of the same vol.), he says, "I am next to consider such injuries as are cognisable by the courts of the common law. And herein I shall, for the present, only remark, that all possible injuries whatsoever, that did not fall within the exclusive cognisance of either the ecclesiastical, military or maritime tribunals, are, for that very reason, within the cognisance of the common-law courts of justice; for it is a settled and invariable principle in the laws of England, that every right, when withheld, must have a remedy, and every injury its proper redress."

The government of the United States has been emphatically termed a government of laws, and not of men. It will certainly cease to deserve this high appellation, if the laws furnish no remedy for the violation of a vested legal right. If this obloquy is to be cast on the jurisprudence of our country, it must arise from the peculiar character of the case.

It behooves us, then, to inquire whether there be in its composition any ingredient which shall exempt it from legal investigation, or exclude the injured party from legal redress. In pursuing this inquiry, the first question which presents itself is, whether this can be arranged with that class of cases which come under the description of *damnum absque injuria;* a loss without an injury. This description of cases never has been considered, and it is believed, never can be considered, as comprehending offices of trust, of honor or of profit. The office of justice of peace in the district of Columbia is such an office; it is, therefore, worthy of the attention and guardianship of the laws. It has received that attention and guardianship: it has been created by special act of congress, and has been secured, so far as the laws can give security, to the person appointed to fill it, for five years. It is not, then, on account of the worthlessness of the thing pursued, that the injured party can be alleged to be without remedy.

Is it in the nature of the transaction? Is the act of delivering or withholding a commission to be considered as a mere political act, belonging to the executive department alone, for the performance of which entire confidence is placed by our constitution in the supreme executive; and for any misconduct respecting which, the injured individual has no remedy? That there may be such cases is not to be questioned; but that every act of duty, to be performed in any of the great departments of government, constitutes such a case, is not to be admitted.

By the act concerning invalids, passed in June 1794 (1 U. S. Stat. 392), the secretary at war is ordered to place on the pension list, all persons whose names are contained in a report previously made by him to congress. If he should refuse to do so, would the wounded veteran be without remedy? Is it to be contended, that where the law, in precise terms, directs the performance of an act, in which an individual is interested, the law is incapable of securing obedience to its mandate? Is it on account of the character of the person against whom the complaint is made? Is it to be contended that the heads of departments are not amenable to the laws of their country? Whatever the practice on particular occasions may be, the theory of this principle will certainly never be maintained. No act of the legislature confers so extraordinary a privilege, nor can it derive countenance from the doctrines of the common law. After stating that personal injury from the king to a subject is presumed to be impossible, Blackstone (vol. 3, p. 255), says, "but injuries to the rights of property can scarcely be committed by the crown, without the intervention of its officers; for whom the law, in matters of right, entertains no respect or delicacy; but furnishes various methods of detecting the errors and misconduct of those agents, by whom the king has been deceived and induced to do a temporary injustice."

By the act passed in 1796, authorizing the sale of the lands above the mouth of Kentucky river (1 U. S. Stat. 464), the purchaser, on paying his purchase-money, becomes completely entitled to the property purchased; and on producing to the secretary of state the receipt of the treasurer, upon a certificate required by the law, the president of the United States is authorized to grant him a patent. It is further enacted, that all patents shall be countersigned by the secretary of state, and recorded in his office. If the secretary of state should choose to withhold this patent; or, the patent being lost, should refuse a copy of it; can it be imagined, that the law furnishes to the injured person no remedy? It is not believed, that any person whatever would attempt to maintain such a proposition.

It follows, then, that the question, whether the legality of an act of the head of a department be examinable in a court of justice or not, must always depend on the nature of that act. If some acts be examinable, and others not, there must be some rule of law to guide the court in the exercise of its jurisdiction. In some instances, there may be difficulty in applying the rule to particular cases; but there cannot, it is believed, be much difficulty in laying down the rule.

By the constitution of the United States, the president is invested with certain important political powers, in the exercise of which he is to use his own discretion, and is accountable only to his country in his political character, and to his own conscience. To aid him in the performance of these duties, he is authorized to appoint certain officers, who act by his authority, and in conformity with his orders. In such cases, their acts are his acts; and whatever opinion may be entertained of the manner in which executive discretion may be used, still there exists, and can exist, no power to control that discretion. The subjects are political: they respect the nation, not individual rights, and being entrusted to the executive, the decision of the executive is conclusive. The application of this remark will be perceived, by adverting to the act of congress for establishing the department of foreign affairs. This officer, as his duties were prescribed by that act, is to conform precisely to the will of the president: he is the mere organ by whom that will is communicated. The acts of such an officer, as an officer, can never be examinable by the courts. But when the legislature proceeds to impose on that officer other duties; when he is directed peremptorily to perform certain acts when the rights of individuals are dependent on the performance of those acts; he is so far the officer of the law; is amenable to the laws for his conduct; and cannot, at his discretion, sport away the vested rights of others.

The conclusion from this reasoning is, that where the heads of departments are the political or confidential agents of the executive, merely to execute the will of the president, or rather to act in cases in which the executive possesses a constitutional or legal discretion, nothing can be more perfectly clear, than that their acts are only politically examinable. But where a specific duty is assigned by law, and individual rights depend upon the performance of that duty, it seems equally clear, that the individual who considers himself injured, has a right to resort to the laws of his country for a remedy.

If this be the rule, let us inquire, how it applies to the case under the consideration of the court. The power of nominating to the senate, and the power of appointing the person nominated, are political powers, to be exercised by the president, according to his own discretion. When he has made an appointment, he has exercised his whole power, and his discretion has been completely applied to the case. If, by law, the officer be removable at the will of the president, then a new appointment may be immediately made, and the rights of the officer are terminated. But as a fact which has existed, cannot be made never to have existed, the appointment cannot be annihilated; and consequently, if the officer is by law not removable at the will of the president, the rights he has acquired are protected by the law, and are not resumable by the president. They cannot be extinguished by executive authority, and he has the privilege of asserting them in like manner, as if they had been derived from any other source.

The question whether a right has vested or not, is, in its nature, judicial, and must be tried by the judicial authority. If, for example, Mr. Marbury had taken the oaths of a magistrate, and proceeded to act as one; in consequence of which, a suit has been instituted against him, in which his defence had depended on his being a magistrate, the validity of his appointment must have been determined by judicial authority. So, if he conceives that, by virtue of his appointment, he has a legal right either to the commission which has been made out for him, or to a copy of that commission, it is equally a question examinable in a court, and the decision of the court upon it must depend on the opinion entertained of his appointment. That question has been discussed, and the opinion is, that the latest point of time which can be taken as that at which the appointment was complete, and evidenced, was when, after the signature of the president, the seal of the United States was affixed to the commission.

It is, then, the opinion of the Court: 1st. That by signing the commission of Mr. Marbury, the President of the United States appointed him a justice of peace for the county of Washington, in the district of Columbia; and that the seal of the United States, affixed thereto by the secretary of state, is conclusive testimony of the verity of the signature, and of the completion of the appointment; and that the appointment conferred on him a legal right to the office for the space of five years. 2d. That, having this legal title to the office, he has a consequent right to the commission; a refusal to deliver which is a plain violation of that right, for which the laws of his country afford him a remedy.

3. It remains to be inquired whether he is entitled to the remedy for which he applies? This depends on—1st. The nature of the writ applied for; and 2d. The power of this court.

1st. The nature of the writ. Blackstone, in the 3d volume of his Commentaries, page 110, defines a *mandamus* to be "a command issuing in the king's name, from the court of king's bench, and directed to any person, corporation or inferior court of judicature, within the king's dominions, requiring them to do some particular thing therein specified, which appertains to their office and duty, and which the court of king's bench has previously determined, or at least supposes, to be consonant to right and justice."

Lord MANSFIELD, in 3 Burr. 1267, in the case of *The King* v. *Baker et al.*, states, with much precision and explicitness, the cases in which this writ may be used. "Whenever," says that very able judge, "there is a right to execute an office, perform a service, or exercise a franchise (more especially if it be in a matter of public concern, or attended with profit), and a person is kept out of possession, or dispossessed of such right, and has no other specific legal remedy, this court ought to assist by *mandamus*, upon reasons of justice, as the writ expresses, and upon reasons of public policy, to preserve peace, order and good government." In the same case, he says, "this writ ought to be used upon all occasions where the law has established no specific remedy, and where in justice and good government there ought to be one." In addition to the authorities now particularly cited, many others were relied on at the bar, which show how far the practice has conformed to the general doctrines that have been just quoted.

This writ, if awarded, would be directed to an officer of government, and its mandate to him would be, to use the words of Blackstone, "to do a particular thing therein specified, which appertains to his office and duty, and which the court has previously determined, or at least supposes, to be consonant to right and justice." Or, in the words of Lord MANSFIELD, the applicant, in this case, has a right to execute an office of public concern, and is kept out of possession of that right. These circumstances certainly concur in this case.

Still, to render the *mandamus* a proper remedy, the officer to whom it is to be directed, must be one to whom, on legal principles, such writ may be directed; and the person applying for it must be without any other specific and legal remedy.

1. With respect to the officer to whom it would be directed. The intimate political relation subsisting between the president of the United States and the heads of departments, necessarily renders any legal investigation of the acts of one of those high officers peculiarly irksome, as well as delicate; and excites some hesitation with respect to the propriety of entering into such investigation. Impressions are often received, without much reflection or examination, and it is not wonderful, that in such a case as this, the assertion, by an individual, of his legal claims in a court of justice, to which claims it is the duty of that court to attend, should at first view be considered by some, as an attempt to intrude into the cabinet, and to intermeddle with the prerogatives of the executive.

It is scarcely necessary for the court to disclaim all pretensions to such a jurisdiction. An extravagance, so absurd and excessive, could not have been entertained for a moment. The province of the court is, solely, to decide on the rights of individuals, not to inquire how the executive, or executive officers, perform duties in which they have a discretion. Questions in their nature political, or which are, by the constitution and laws, submitted to the executive, can never be made in this court.

But, if this be not such a question; if, so far from being an intrusion into the secrets of the cabinet, it respects a paper which, according to law, is upon record, and to a copy of which the law gives a right, on the payment of ten cents; if it be no intermeddling with a subject over which the executive can be considered as having exercised any control; what is there, in the exalted station of the officer, which shall bar a citizen from asserting, in a court of justice, his legal rights, or shall forbid a court to listen to the claim, or to issue a *mandamus,* directing the performance of a duty, not depending on executive discretion, but on particular acts of congress, and the general principles of law?

If one of the heads of departments commits any illegal act, under color of his office, by which an individual sustains an injury, it cannot be pretended, that his office alone exempts him from being sued in the ordinary mode of proceeding, and being compelled to obey the judgment of the law. How then, can his office exempt him from this particular mode of deciding on the legality of his conduct, if the case be such a case as would, were any other individual the party complained of, authorize the process?

It is not by the office of the person to whom the writ is directed, but the nature of the thing to be done, that the propriety or impropriety of issuing a *mandamus* is to be determined. Where the head of a department acts in a case, in which executive discretion is to be exercised; in which he is the mere organ of executive will; it is again repeated, that any application to a court to control, in any respect, his conduct would be rejected without hesitation. But where he is directed by law to do a certain act, affecting the absolute rights of individuals, in the performance of which he is not placed under the particular direction of the president, and the performance of which the president cannot lawfully forbid, and therefore, is never presumed to have forbidden; as, for example, to record a commission or a patent for land, which has received all the legal solemnities; or to give a copy of such record; in such cases, it is not perceived, on what ground the courts of the country are further excused from the duty of giving judgment that right be done to an injured individual, than if the same services were to be performed by a person not the head of a department.

This opinion seems not now, for the first time, to be taken up in this country. It must be well recollected, that in 1792, an act passed, directing the secretary at war to place on the pension list such disabled officers and soldiers as should be reported to him, by the circuit courts, which act, so far as the duty was imposed on the courts, was deemed unconstitutional;[1] but some of the judges, thinking that the law might be executed by them in the character of commissioners, proceeded to act, and to report in that character. This law being deemed unconstitutional, at the circuits, was repealed,

[1] *Hayburn's case, 2 Dall. 410 n.*

and a different system was established; but the question whether those persons who had been reported by the judges, as commissioners, were entitled, in consequence of that report, to be placed on the pension list, was a legal question, properly determinable in the courts, although the act of placing such persons on the list was to be performed by the head of a department.

That this question might be properly settled, congress passed an act, in February 1793, making it the duty of the secretary of war, in conjunction with the attorney-general, to take such measures as might be necessary to obtain an adjudication of the supreme court of the United States on the validity of any such rights, claimed under the act aforesaid. After the passage of this act, a *mandamus* was moved for, to be directed to the secretary of war, commanding him to place on the pension list, a person stating himself to be on the report of the judges. There is, therefore, much reason to believe, that this mode of trying the legal right of the complainant was deemed, by the head of a department, and by the highest law-officer of the United States, the most proper which could be selected for the purpose. When the subject was brought before the court, the decision was, not that a *mandamus* would not lie to the head of a department, directing him to perform an act, enjoined by law, in the performance of which an individual had a vested interest; but that a *mandamus* ought not to issue in that case; the decision necessarily to be made, if the report of the commissioners did not confer on the applicant a legal right. The judgment, in that case, is understood to have decided the merits of all claims of that description; and the persons, on the report of the commissioners, found it necessary to pursue the mode prescribed by the law, subsequent to that which had been deemed unconstitutional, in order to place themselves on the pension list. The doctrine, therefore, now advanced, is by no means a novel one.

It is true, that the *mandamus,* now moved for, is not for the performance of an act expressly enjoined by statute. It is to deliver a commission; on which subject, the acts of congress are silent. This difference is not considered as affecting the case. It has already been stated, that the applicant has, to that commission, a vested legal right, of which the executive cannot deprive him. He has been appointed to an office, from which he is not removable at the will of the executive; and being so appointed, he has a right to the commission which the secretary has received from the president for his use. The act of congress does not indeed order the secretary of state to send it to him, but it is placed in his hands for the person entitled to it; and cannot be more lawfully withheld by him, than by any other person.

It was at first doubted, whether the action of *detinue* was not a specific legal remedy for the commission which has been withheld from Mr. Marbury; in which case, a *mandamus* would be improper. But this doubt has yielded to the consideration, that the judgment in *detinue* is for the thing itself, *or* its value. The value of a public office, not to be sold, is incapable of being ascertained; and the applicant has a right to the office itself, or to nothing. He will obtain the office by obtaining the commission, or a copy of it, from the record.

This, then, is a plain case for a *mandamus,* either to deliver the commission, or a copy of it from the record; and it only remains to be inquired, whether it can issue from this court?

The act to establish the judicial courts of the United States authorizes the supreme court, "to issue writs of *mandamus,* in cases warranted by the principles and usages of law, to any courts appointed or persons holding office, under the authority of the United States." The secretary of state, being a person holding an office under the authority of the United States, is precisely within the letter of this description; and if this court is not authorized to issue a writ of *mandamus* to such an officer, it must be because the law is unconstitutional, and therefore, absolutely incapable of conferring the authority, and assigning the duties which its words purport to confer and assign.

The constitution vests the whole judicial power of the United States in one supreme court, and such inferior courts as congress shall, from time to time, ordain and establish. This power is expressly extended to all cases arising under the laws of the United States; and consequently, in some form, may be exercised over the present case; because the right claimed is given by a law of the United States.

In the distribution of this power, it is declared, that "the supreme court shall have original jurisdiction, in all cases affecting ambassadors, other public ministers and consuls, and those in which a state shall be a party. In all other cases, the supreme court shall have appellate jurisdiction." It has been insisted, at the bar, that as the original grant of jurisdiction to the supreme and inferior courts, is general, and the clause, assigning original jurisdiction to the supreme court, contains no negative or restrictive words, the power remains to the legislature, to assign original jurisdiction to that court, in other cases than those specified in the article which has been recited; provided those cases belong to the judicial power of the United States.

If it had been intended to leave it in the discretion of the legislature, to apportion the judicial power between the supreme and inferior courts, according to the will of that body, it would certainly have been useless to have proceeded further than to have defined the judicial power, and the tribunals in which it should be vested. The subsequent part of the section is mere surplusage—is entirely without meaning, if such is to be the construction. If congress remains at liberty to give this court appellate jurisdiction, where the constitution has declared their jurisdiction shall be original; and original jurisdiction where the constitution has declared it shall be appellate; the distribution of jurisdiction, made in the constitution, is form without substance. Affirmative words are often, in their operation, negative of other objects than those affirmed; and in this case, a negative or exclusive sense must be given to them, or they have no operation at all.

It cannot be presumed, that any clause in the constitution is intended to be without effect; and therefore, such a construction is inadmissible, unless the words require it. If the solicitude of the convention, respecting our peace with foreign powers, induced a provision that the supreme court should take original jurisdiction in cases which might be supposed to affect them; yet the clause would have proceeded no further than to provide for such cases, if no further restriction on the powers of congress had been intended. That they should have appellate jurisdiction in all other cases, with such exceptions as congress might make, is no restriction; unless the words be deemed exclusive of original jurisdiction.

When an instrument organizing, fundamentally, a judicial system, divides it into one supreme, and so many inferior courts as the legislature may ordain and establish; then enumerates its powers, and proceeds so far to distribute them, as to define the jurisdiction of the supreme court, by declaring the cases in which it shall take original jurisdiction, and that in others it shall take appellate jurisdiction, the plain import of the words seems to be, that in one class of cases, its jurisdiction is original, and not appellate; in the other, it is appellate, and not original. If any other construction would render the clause inoperative, that is an additional reason for rejecting such other construction, and for adhering to their obvious meaning. To enable this court, then, to issue a *mandamus,* it must be shown to be an exercise of appellate jurisdiction, or to be necessary to enable them to exercise appellate jurisdiction.

It has been stated at the bar, that the appellate jurisdiction may be exercised in a variety of forms, and that if it be the will of the legislature that a *mandamus* should be used for that purpose, that will must be obeyed. This is true, yet the jurisdiction must be appellate, not original. It is the essential criterion of appellate jurisdiction, that it revises and corrects the proceedings in a cause already instituted, and does not create that cause. Although, therefore, a *mandamus* may be directed to courts, yet to issue such a writ to an officer, for the delivery of a paper, is, in effect, the same as to sustain an original action for that paper, and therefore, seems not to belong to appellate, but to original jurisdiction. Neither is it necessary in such a case as this, to enable the court to exercise its appellate jurisdiction. The authority, therefore, given to the supreme court by the act establishing the judicial courts of the United States, to issue writs of *mandamus* to public officers, appears not to be warranted by the constitution; and it becomes necessary to inquire, whether a jurisdiction so conferred can be exercised.

The question, whether an act, repugnant to the constitution, can become the law of the land, is a question deeply interesting to the United States; but, happily, not of an intricacy proportioned to its interest. It seems only necessary to recognise certain principles, supposed to have been long and well established, to decide it. That the people have an original right to establish, for their future government, such principles as, in their opinion, shall most conduce to their own happiness, is the basis on which the whole American fabric has been erected. The exercise of this original right is a very great exertion; nor can it, nor ought it, to be frequently repeated. The principles, therefore, so established, are deemed fundamental: and as the authority from which they proceed is supreme, and can seldom act, they are designed to be permanent.

This original and supreme will organizes the government, and assigns to different departments their respective powers. It may either stop here, or establish certain limits not to be transcended by those departments. The government of the United States is of the latter description. The powers of the legislature are defined and limited; and that those limits may not be mistaken or forgotten, the constitution is written. To what purpose are powers limited, and to what purpose is that limitation committed to writing, if these limits may, at any time, be passed by those intended to be restrained? The distinction between a government with limited and unlimited powers is abolished, if those limits do not confine the persons on whom they are imposed, and if acts prohibited and acts allowed, are of equal obligation. It is a proposition too plain to be contested, that the constitution controls any legislative act repugnant to it; or that the legislature may alter the constitution by an ordinary act.

Between these alternatives, there is no middle ground. The constitution is either a superior paramount law, unchangeable by ordinary means, or it is on a level with ordinary legislative acts, and, like other acts, is alterable when the legislature shall please to alter it. If the former part of the alternative be true, then a legislative act, contrary to the constitution, is not law: if the latter part be true, then written constitutions are absurd attempts, on the part of the people, to limit a power, in its own nature, illimitable.

Certainly, all those who have framed written constitutions contemplate them as forming the fundamental and paramount law of the nation, and consequently, the theory of every such government must be, that an act of the legislature, repugnant to the constitution, is void. This theory is essentially attached to a written constitution, and is, consequently, to be considered, by this court, as one of the fundamental principles of our society. It is not, therefore, to be lost sight of, in the further consideration of this subject.

If an act of the legislature, repugnant to the constitution, is void, does it, notwithstanding its invalidity, bind the courts, and oblige them to give it effect? Or, in other words, though it be not law, does it constitute a rule as operative as if it was a law? This would be to overthrow, in fact, what was established in theory; and would seem, at first view, an absurdity too gross to be insisted on. It shall, however, receive a more attentive consideration.

It is, emphatically, the province and duty of the judicial department, to say what the law is. Those who apply the rule to particular cases, must of necessity expound and interpret that rule. If two laws conflict with each other, the courts must decide on the operation of each. So, if a law be in opposition to the constitution; if both the law and the constitution apply to a particular case, so that the court must either decide that case, conformable to the law, disregarding the constitution; or conformable to the constitution, disregarding the law; the court must determine which of these conflicting rules governs the case: this is of the very essence of judicial duty. If then, the courts are to regard the constitution, and the constitution is superior to any ordinary act of the legislature, the constitution, and not such ordinary act, must govern the case to which they both apply.

Those, then, who controvert the principle, that the constitution is to be considered, in court, as a paramount law, are reduced to the necessity of maintaining that courts must close their eyes on the constitution, and see only the law. This doctrine would subvert the very foundation of all written constitutions. It would declare that an act which, according to the principles and theory of our government, is entirely void, is yet, in practice, completely obligatory. It would declare, that if the legislature shall do what is expressly forbidden, such act, notwithstanding the express prohibition, is in reality effectual. It would be giving to the legislature a practical and real omnipotence, with the same breath which professes to restrict their powers within narrow limits. It is prescribing limits, and declaring that those limits may be passed at pleasure. That it thus reduces to nothing, what we have deemed the greatest improvement on political institutions, a written constitution, would, of itself, be sufficient, in America, where written constitutions have been viewed with so much reverence, for rejecting the construction. But the peculiar expressions of the constitution of the United States furnish additional arguments in favor of its rejection. The judicial power of the United States is extended to all cases arising under the constitution. Could it be the intention of those who gave this power, to say, that in using it, the constitution should not be looked into? That a case arising under the constitution should be decided, without examining the instrument under which it arises? This is too extravagant to be maintained. In some cases, then, the constitution must be looked into by the judges. And if they can open it at all, what part of it are they forbidden to read or to obey?

There are many other parts of the constitution which serve to illustrate this subject. It is declared, that "no tax or duty shall be laid on articles exported from any state." Suppose, a duty on the export of cotton, of tobacco or of flour; and a suit instituted to recover it. Ought judgment to be rendered in such a case? ought the judges to close their eyes on the constitution, and only see the law?

The constitution declares "that no bill of attainder or *ex post facto* law shall be passed." If, however, such a bill should be passed, and a person should be prosecuted under it; must the court condemn to death those victims whom the constitution endeavors to preserve?

"No person," says the constitution, "shall be convicted of treason, unless on the testimony of two witnesses to the same *overt* act, or on confession in open court." Here, the language of the constitution is addressed especially to the courts. It prescribes, directly for them, a rule of evidence not to be departed from. If the legislature should change that rule, and declare one witness, or a confession out of court, sufficient for conviction, must the constitutional principle yield to the legislative act?

From these, and many other selections which might be made, it is apparent, that the framers of the constitution contemplated that instrument as a rule for the government of courts, as well as of the legislature. Why otherwise does it direct the judges to take an oath to support it? This oath certainly applies in an especial manner, to their conduct in their official character. How immoral to impose it on them, if they were to be used as the instruments, and the knowing instruments, for violating what they swear to support!

The oath of office, too, imposed by the legislature, is completely demonstrative of the legislative opinion on this subject. It is in these words: "I do solemnly swear, that I will administer justice, without respect to persons, and do equal right to the poor and to the rich; and that I will faithfully and impartially discharge all the duties incumbent on me as ——, according to the best of my abilities and understanding, agreeably to the constitution and laws of the United States." Why does a judge swear to discharge his duties agreeably to the constitution of the United States, if that constitution forms no rule for his government? if it is closed upon him, and cannot be inspected by him? If such be the real state of things, this is worse than solemn mockery. To prescribe, or to take this oath, becomes equally a crime.

It is also not entirely unworthy of observation, that in declaring what shall be the supreme law of the land, the constitution itself is first mentioned; and not the laws of the United States, generally, but those only which shall be made in pursuance of the constitution, have that rank.

Thus, the particular phraseology of the constitution of the United States confirms and strengthens the principle, supposed to be essential to all written constitutions, that a law repugnant to the constitution is void; and that courts, as well as other departments, are bound by that instrument.

The rule must be discharged.

GIBBONS v. OGDEN, 9 WHEAT. 1 (1824)

A monopoly of steamboat navigation upon the Hudson River was granted to the licensees of Robert Fulton by the New York legislature. Previously Congress had required that federal coasting licenses be obtained by all vessels navigating the coastal and interstate waters of the United States. This case raised for the first time questions concerning the nature and scope of Congressional authority in regulating interstate commerce. For the Court Chief Justice Marshall stated that interstate navigation was clearly included in the term "interstate commerce" and that the Constitution had granted its regulation to Congress. Those powers had been exercised in the Federal Coasting Act, and the New York law creating the monopoly conflicted both with the federal act and the Constitution of the United States. Thus the New York monopoly was in violation of the federal Constitution and invalid. He declined to adopt the theory, urged by Webster for the appellant, and stated by Justice William Johnson in his concurring opinion, that the control of interstate commerce was vested exclusively in the federal Congress, and that powers in this area unexercised by Congress remained "dormant" and not subject to state legislative action.

MR. Chief Justice MARSHALL delivered the opinion of the Court, and, after stating the case, proceeded as follows:

The appellant contends that this decree is erroneous, because the laws which purport to give the exclusive privilege it sustains, are repugnant to the constitution and laws of the United States.

They are said to be repugnant—

1st. To that clause in the constitution which authorizes Congress to regulate commerce.

2d. To that which authorizes Congress to promote the progress of science and useful arts.

The State of New-York maintains the constitutionality of these laws; and their Legislature, their Council of Revision, and their Judges, have repeatedly concurred in this opinion. It is supported by great names—by names which have all the titles to consideration that virtue, intelligence, and office, can bestow. No tribunal can approach the decision of this question, without feeling a just and real respect for that opinion which is sustained by such authority; but it is the province of this Court, while it respects, not to bow to it implicitly; and the Judges must exercise, in the examination of the subject, that understanding which Providence has bestowed upon them, with that independence which the people of the United States expect from this department of the government.

As preliminary to the very able discussions of the constitution, which we have heard from the bar, and as having some influence on its construction, reference has been made to the political situation of these States, anterior to its formation. It has been said, that they were sovereign, were completely independent, and were connected with each other only by a league. This is true. But, when these allied sovereigns converted their league into a government, when they converted their Congress of Ambassadors, deputed to deliberate on their common concerns, and to recommend measures of general utility, into a Legislature, empowered to enact laws on the most interesting subjects, the whole character in which the States appear, underwent a change, the extent of which must be determined by a fair consideration of the instrument by which that change was effected.

This instrument contains an enumeration of powers expressly granted by the people to their government. It has been said, that these powers ought to be construed strictly. But why ought they to be so construed? Is there one sentence in the constitution which gives countenance to this rule? In the last of the enumerated powers, that which grants, expressly, the means for carrying all others into execution, Congress is authorized "to make all laws which shall be necessary and proper" for the purpose. But this limitation on the means which may be used, is not extended to the powers which are conferred; nor is there one sentence in the constitution, which has been pointed out by the gentlemen of the bar, or which we have been able to discern, that prescribes this rule. We do not, therefore, think ourselves justified in adopting it. What do gentlemen mean, by a strict construction? If they contend only against that enlarged construction, which would extend words beyond their natural and obvious import, we might question the application of the term, but should not controvert the principle. If they contend for that narrow construction which, in support of some theory not to be found in the constitution, would deny to the government those powers which the words of the grant, as usually understood, import, and which are consistent with the general views and objects of the instrument; for that narrow construction, which would cripple the government, and render it unequal to the objects for which it is declared to be instituted, and to which the powers given, as fairly understood, render it competent; then we cannot perceive the propriety of this strict construction, nor adopt it as the rule by which the constitution is to be expounded. As men, whose intentions require no concealment, generally employ the words which most directly and aptly express the ideas they intend to convey, the enlightened patriots who framed our constitution, and the people who adopted it, must be understood to have employed words in their natural sense, and to have intended what they have said. If, from the imperfection of human language, there should be serious doubts respecting the extent of any given power, it is a well settled rule, that the objects for which it was given, especially when those objects are expressed in the instrument itself, should have great influence in the construction. We know of no reason for excluding this rule from the present case. The grant does not convey power which might be beneficial to the grantor, if retained by himself, or which can enure solely to the benefit of the grantee; but is an investment of power for the general advantage, in the hands of agents selected for that purpose; which power can never be exercised by the people themselves, but must be placed in the hands of agents, or lie dormant. We know of no rule for construing the extent of such powers, other than is given by the language of the instrument which confers them, taken in connexion with the purposes for which they were conferred.

The words are, "Congress shall have power to regulate commerce with foreign nations, and among the several States, and with the Indian tribes."

The subject to be regulated is commerce; and our constitution being, as was aptly said at the bar, one of enumeration, and not of definition, to ascertain the extent of the power, it becomes necessary to settle the meaning of the word. The counsel for the appellee would limit it to traffic, to buying and selling, or the interchange of commodities, and do not admit that it comprehends navigation. This would restrict a general term, applicable to many objects, to one of its significations. Commerce, undoubtedly, is traffic, but it is something more: it is intercourse. It describes the commercial intercourse between nations, and parts of nations, in all its branches, and is regulated by prescribing rules for carrying on that intercourse. The mind can scarcely conceive a system for regulating commerce between nations, which shall exclude all laws concerning navigation, which shall be silent on the admission of the vessels of the one nation into the ports of the other, and be confined to prescribing rules for the conduct of individuals, in the actual employment of buying and selling, or of barter.

If commerce does not include navigation, the government of the Union has no direct power over that subject, and can make no law prescribing what shall constitute American vessels, or requiring that they shall be navigated by American seamen. Yet this power has been exercised from the commencement of the government, has been exercised with the consent of all, and has been understood by all to be a commerical regulation. All America understands, and has uniformly understood, the word "commerce," to comprehend navigation. It was so understood, and must have been so understood, when the constitution was framed. The power over commerce, including navigation, was one of the primary objects for which the people of America adopted their government, and must have been contemplated in forming it. The convention must have used the word in that sense, because all have understood it in that sense; and the attempt to restrict it comes too late.

If the opinion that "commerce," as the word is used in the constitution, comprehends navigation also, requires any additional confirmation, that additional confirmation is, we think, furnished by the words of the instrument itself.

It is a rule of construction, acknowledged by all, that the exceptions from a power mark its extent; for it would be absurd, as well as useless, to except from a granted power, that which was not granted —that which the words of the grant could not comprehend. If, then, there are in the constitution plain exceptions from the power over navigation, plain inhibitions to the exercise of that power in a particular way, it is a proof that those who made these exceptions, and prescribed these inhibitions, understood the power to which they applied as being granted.

The 9th section of the 1st article declares, that "no preference shall be given, by any regulation of commerce or revenue, to the ports of one State over those of another." This clause cannot be understood as applicable to those laws only which are passed for the purposes of revenue, because it is expressly applied to commercial regulations; and the most obvious preference which can be given to one port over another, in regulating commerce, relates to navigation. But the subsequent part of the sentence is still more explicit. It is, "nor shall vessels bound to or from one State, be obliged to enter, clear, or pay duties, in another." These words have a direct reference to navigation.

The universally acknowledged power of the government to impose embargoes, must also be considered as showing, that all America is united in that construction which comprehends navigation in the word commerce. Gentlemen have said, in argument, that this is a branch of the war-making power, and that an embargo is an instrument of war, not a regulation of trade.

That it may be, and often is, used as an instrument of war, cannot be denied. An embargo may be imposed for the purpose of facilitating the equipment or manning of a fleet, or for the purpose of concealing the progress of an expedition preparing to sail from a particular port. In these, and in similar cases, it is a military instrument, and partakes of the nature of war. But all embargoes are not of this description. They are sometimes resorted to without a view to war, and with a single view to commerce. In such case, an embargo is no more a war measure, than a merchantman is a ship of war, because both are vessels which navigate the ocean with sails and seamen.

When Congress imposed that embargo which, for a time, engaged the attention of every man in the United States, the avowed object of the law was, the protection of commerce, and the avoiding of war. By its friends and its enemies it was treated as a commercial, not as a war measure. The persevering earnestness and zeal with which it was opposed, in a part of our country which supposed its interests to be vitally affected by the act, cannot be forgotten. A want of acuteness in discovering objections to a measure to which they felt the most deep rooted hostility, will not be imputed to those who were arrayed in opposition to this. Yet they never suspected that navigation was no branch of trade, and was, therefore, not comprehended in the power to regulate commerce. They did, indeed, contest the constitutionality of the act, but, on a principle which admits the construction for which the appellant contends. They denied that the particular law in question was made in pursuance of the constitution, not because the power could not act directly on vessels, but because a perpetual embargo was the annihilation, and not the regulation of commerce. In terms, they admitted the applicability of the words used in the constitution to vessels; and that, in a case which produced a degree and an extent of excitement, calculated to draw forth every principle on which legitimate resistance could be sustained. No example could more strongly illustrate the universal understanding of the American people on this subject.

The word used in the constitution, then, comprehends, and has been always understood to comprehend, navigation within its meaning; and a power to regulate navigation, is as expressly granted, as if that term had been added to the word "commerce."

To what commerce does this power extend? The constitution informs us, to commerce "with foreign nations, and among the several States, and with the Indian tribes."

It has, we believe, been universally admitted, that these words comprehend every species of commercial intercourse between the United States and foreign nations. No sort of trade can be carried on between this country and any other, to which this power does not extend. It has been truly said, that commerce, as the word is used in the constitution, is a unit, every part of which is indicated by the term.

If this be the admitted meaning of the word, in its application to foreign nations, it must carry the same meaning throughout the sentence, and remain a unit, unless there be some plain intelligible cause which alters it.

The subject to which the power is next applied, is to commerce "among the several States." The word "among" means intermingled with. A thing which is among others, is intermingled with them. Commerce among the States, cannot stop at the external boundary line of each State, but may be introduced into the interior.

It is not intended to say that these words comprehend that commerce, which is completely internal, which is carried on between man and man in a State, or between different parts of the same State, and which does not extend to or affect other States. Such a power would be inconvenient, and is certainly unnecessary.

Comprehensive as the word "among" is, it may very properly be restricted to that commerce which concerns more States than one. The phrase is not one which would probably have been selected to indicate the completely interior traffic of a State, because it is not an apt phrase for that purpose; and the enumeration of the particular classes of commerce to which the power was to be extended, would not have been made, had the intention been to extend the power to every description. The enumeration presupposes something not enumerated; and that something, if we regard the language or the subject of the sentence, must be the exclusively internal commerce of a State. The genius and character of the whole government seem to be, that its action is to be applied to all the external concerns of the nation, and to those internal concerns which affect the States generally; but not to those which are completely within a particular State, which do not affect other States, and with which it is not necessary to interfere, for the purpose of executing some of the general powers of the government. The completely internal commerce of a State, then, may be considered as reserved for the State itself.

But, in regulating commerce with foreign nations, the power of Congress does not stop at the jurisdictional lines of the several States. It would be a very useless power, if it could not pass those lines. The commerce of the United States with foreign nations, is that of the whole United States. Every district has a right to participate in it. The deep streams which penetrate our country in every direction, pass through the interior of almost every State in the Union, and furnish the means of exercising this right. If Congress has the power to regulate it, that power must be exercised whenever the subject exists. If it exists within the States, if a foreign voyage may commence or terminate at a port within a State, then the power of Congress may be exercised within a State.

This principle is, if possible, still more clear, when applied to commerce "among the several States." They either join each other, in which case they are separated by a mathematical line, or they are remote from each other, in which case other States lie between them. What is commerce "among" them; and how is it to be conducted? Can a trading expedition between two adjoining States, commence and terminate outside of each? And if the trading intercourse be between two States remote from each other, must it not commence in one, terminate in the other, and probably pass through a third? Commerce among the States must, of necessity, be commerce with the States. In the regulation of trade with the Indian tribes, the action of the law, especially when the constitution was made, was chiefly within a State. The power of Congress, then, whatever it may be, must be exercised within the territorial jurisdiction of the several States. The sense of the nation on this subject, is unequivocally manifested by the provisions made in the laws for transporting goods, by land, between Baltimore and Providence, between New-York and Philadelphia, and between Philadelphia and Baltimore.

We are now arrived at the inquiry—What is this power?

It is the power to regulate; that is, to prescribe the rule by which commerce is to be governed. This power, like all others vested in Congress, is complete in itself, may be exercised to its utmost extent, and acknowledges no limitations, other than are prescribed in the constitution. These are expressed in plain terms, and do not affect the questions which arise in this case, or which have been discussed at the bar. If, as has always been understood, the sovereignty of Congress, though limited to specified objects, is plenary as to those objects, the power over commerce with foreign nations, and among the several States, is vested in Congress as absolutely as it would be in a single government, having in its constitution the same restrictions on the exercise of the power as are found in the constitution of the United States. The wisdom and the discretion of Congress, their identity with the people, and the influence which their constituents possess at elections, are, in this, as in many other instances, as that, for example, of declaring war, the sole restraints on which they have relied, to secure them from its abuse. They are the restraints on which the people must often rely solely, in all representative governments.

The power of Congress, then, comprehends navigation, within the limits of every State in the Union; so far as that navigation may be, in any manner, connected with "commerce with foreign nations, or among the several States, or with the Indian tribes." It may, of consequence, pass the jurisdictional line of New-York, and act upon the very waters to which the prohibition now under consideration applies.

But it has been urged with great earnestness, that, although the power of Congress to regulate commerce with foreign nations, and among the several States, be co-extensive with the subject itself, and have no other limits than are prescribed in the constitution, yet the States may severally exercise the same power, within their respective jurisdictions. In support of this argument, it is said, that they possessed it as an inseparable attribute of sovereignty, before the formation of the constitution, and still retain it, except so far as they have surrendered it by that instrument; that this principle results from the nature of the government, and is secured by the tenth amendment; that an affirmative grant of power is not exclusive, unless in its own nature it be such that the continued exercise of it by the former possessor is inconsistent with the grant, and that this is not of that description.

The appellant, conceding these postulates, except the last, contends, that full power to regulate a particular subject, implies the whole power, and leaves no residuum; that a grant of the whole is incompatible with the existence of a right in another to any part of it.

Both parties have appealed to the constitution, to legislative acts, and judicial decisions; and have drawn arguments from all these sources, to support and illustrate the propositions they respectively maintain.

The grant of the power to lay and collect taxes is, like the power to regulate commerce, made in general terms, and has never been understood to interfere with the exercise of the same power by the States; and hence has been drawn an argument which has been applied to the question under consideration. But the two grants are not, it is conceived, similar in their terms or their nature. Although many of the powers formerly exercised by the States, are transferred to the government of the Union, yet the State governments remain, and constitute a most important part of our system. The power of taxation is indispensable to their existence, and is a power which, in its own nature, is capable of residing in, and being exercised by, different authorities at the same time. We are accustomed to see it placed, for different purposes, in different hands. Taxation is the simple operation of taking small portions from a perpetually accumulating mass, susceptible of almost infinite division; and a power in one to take what is necessary for certain purposes, is not, in its nature, incompatible with a power in another to take what is necessary for other purposes. Congress is authorized to lay and collect taxes, &c. to pay the debts, and provide for the common defence and general welfare of the United States. This does not interfere with the power of the States to tax for the support of their own governments; nor is the exercise of that power by the States, an exercise of any portion of the power that is granted to the United States. In imposing taxes for State purposes, they are not doing what Congress is empowered to do. Congress is not empowered to tax for those purposes which are within the exclusive province of the States. When, then, each government exercises the power of taxation, neither is exercising the power of the other. But, when a State proceeds to regulate commerce with foreign nations, or among the several States, it is exercising the very power that is granted to Congress, and is doing the very thing which Congress is authorized to do. There is no analogy, then, between the power of taxation and the power of regulating commerce.

In discussing the question, whether this power is still in the States, in the case under consideration, we may dismiss from it the inquiry, whether it is surrendered by the mere grant to Congress, or is retained until Congress shall exercise the power. We may dismiss that inquiry, because it has been exercised, and the regulations which Congress deemed it proper to make, are now in full operation. The sole question is, can a State regulate commerce with foreign nations and among the States, while Congress is regulating it?

The counsel for the respondent answer this question in the affirmative, and rely very much on the restrictions in the 10th section, as supporting their opinion. They say, very truly, that limitations of a power, furnish a strong argument in favour of the existence of that power, and that the section which prohibits the States from laying duties on imports or exports, proves that this power might have been exercised, had it not been expressly forbidden; and, consequently, that any other commercial regulation, not expressly forbidden, to which the original power of the State was competent, may still be made.

That this restriction shows the opinion of the Convention, that a State might impose duties on exports and imports, if not expressly forbidden, will be conceded; but that it follows as a consequence, from this concession, that a State may regulate commerce with foreign nations and among the States, cannot be admitted.

We must first determine whether the act of laying "duties or imposts on imports or exports," is considered in the constitution as a branch of the taxing power, or of the power to regulate commerce. We think it very clear, that it is considered as a branch of the taxing power. It is so treated in the first clause of the 8th section: "Congress shall have power to lay and collect taxes, duties, imposts, and excises;" and, before commerce is mentioned, the rule by which the exercise of this power must be governed, is declared. It is, that all duties, imposts, and excises, shall be uniform. In a separate clause of the enumeration, the power to regulate commerce is given, as being entirely distinct from the right to levy taxes and imposts, and as being a new power, not before conferred. The constitution, then, considers these powers as substantive, and distinct from each other; and so places them in the enumeration it contains. The power of imposing duties on imports is classed with the power to levy taxes, and that seems to be its natural place. But the power to levy taxes could never be considered as abridging the right of the States on that subject; and they might, consequently, have exercised it by levying duties on imports or exports, had the constitution contained no prohibition on this subject. This prohibition, then, is an exception from the acknowledged power of the States to levy taxes, not from the questionable power to regulate commerce.

"A duty of tonnage" is as much a tax, as a duty on imports or exports; and the reason which induced the prohibition of those taxes, extends to this also. This tax may be imposed by a State, with the consent of Congress; and it may be admitted, that Congress cannot give a right to a State, in virtue of its own powers. But a duty of tonnage being part of the power of imposing taxes, its prohibition may certainly be made to depend on Congress, without affording any implication respecting a power to regulate commerce. It is true, that duties may often be, and in fact often are, imposed on tonnage, with a view to the regulation of commerce; but they may be also imposed with a view to revenue; and it was, therefore, a prudent precaution, to prohibit the States from exercising this power. The idea that the same measure might, according to circumstances, be arranged with different classes of power, was no novelty to the framers of our constitution. Those illustrious statesmen and patriots had been, many of them, deeply engaged in the discussions which preceded the war of our revolution, and all of them were well read in those discussions. The right to regulate commerce, even by the imposition of duties, was not controverted; but the right to impose a duty for the purpose of revenue, produced a war as important, perhaps, in its consequences to the human race, as any the world has ever witnessed.

These restrictions, then, are on the taxing power, not on that to regulate commerce; and presuppose the existence of that which they restrain, not of that which they do not purport to restrain.

But, the inspection laws are said to be regulations of commerce, and are certainly recognised in the constitution, as being passed in the exercise of a power remaining with the States.

That inspection laws may have a remote and considerable influence on commerce, will not be denied; but that a power to regulate commerce is the source from which the right to pass them is derived, cannot be admitted. The object of inspection laws, is to improve the quality of articles produced by the labour of a country; to fit them for exportation; or, it may be, for domestic use. They act upon the subject before it becomes an article of foreign commerce, or of commerce among the States, and prepare it for that purpose. They form a portion of that immense mass of legislation, which embraces every thing within the territory of a State, not surrendered to the general government: all which can be most advantageously exercised by the States themselves. Inspection laws, quarantine laws, health laws of every description, as well as laws for regulating the internal commerce of a State, and those which respect turnpike roads, ferries, &c., are component parts of this mass.

No direct general power over these objects is granted to Congress; and, consequently, they remain subject to State legislation. If the legislative power of the Union can reach them, it must be for national purposes; it must be where the power is expressly given for a special purpose, or is clearly incidental to some power which is expressly given. It is obvious, that the government of the Union, in the exercise of its express powers, that, for example, of regulating commerce with foreign nations and among the States, may use means that may also be employed by a State, in the exercise of its acknowledged powers; that, for example, of regulating commerce within the State. If Congress license vessels to sail from one port to another, in the same State, the act is supposed to be, necessarily, incidental to the power expressly granted to Congress, and implies no claim of a direct power to regulate the purely internal commerce of a

State, or to act directly on its system of police. So, if a State, in passing laws on subjects acknowledged to be within its control, and with a view to those subjects, shall adopt a measure of the same character with one which Congress may adopt, it does not derive its authority from the particular power which has been granted, but from some other, which remains with the State, and may be executed by the same means. All experience shows, that the same measures, or measures scarcely distinguishable from each other, may flow from distinct powers; but this does not prove that the powers themselves are identical. Although the means used in their execution may sometimes approach each other so nearly as to be confounded, there are other situations in which they are sufficiently distinct to establish their individuality.

In our complex system, presenting the rare and difficult scheme of one general government, whose action extends over the whole, but which possesses only certain enumerated powers; and of numerous State governments, which retain and exercise all powers not delegated to the Union, contests respecting power must arise. Were it even otherwise, the measures taken by the respective governments to execute their acknowledged powers, would often be of the same description, and might, sometimes, interfere. This, however, does not prove that the one is exercising, or has a right to exercise, the powers of the other.

The acts of Congress, passed in 1796 and 1799,[1] empowering and directing the officers of the general government to conform to, and assist in the execution of the quarantine and health laws of a State, proceed, it is said, upon the idea that these laws are constitutional. It is undoubtedly true, that they do proceed upon that idea; and the constitutionality of such laws has never, so far as we are informed, been denied. But they do not imply an acknowledgment that a State may rightfully regulate commerce with foreign nations, or among the States; for they do not imply that such laws are an exercise of that power, or enacted with a view to it. On the contrary, they are treated as quarantine and health laws, are so denominated in the acts of Congress, and are considered as flowing from the acknowledged power of a State, to provide for the health of its citizens. But, as it was apparent that some of the provisions made for this purpose, and in virtue of this power, might interfere with, and be affected by the laws of the United States, made for the regulation of commerce, Congress, in that spirit of harmony and conciliation, which ought always to characterize the conduct of governments standing in the relation which that of the Union and those of the States bear to each other, has directed its officers to aid in the execution of these laws; and has, in some measure, adapted its own legislation to this object, by making provisions in aid of those of the States. But, in making these provisions, the opinion is unequivocally manifested, that Congress may control the State laws, so far as it may be necessary to control them, for the regulation of commerce.

[1] *2* U. S. L. *p. 545. 3* U. S. L. *p. 126.*

The act passed in 1803,[1] prohibiting the importation of slaves into any State which shall itself prohibit their importation, implies, it is said, an admission that the States possessed the power to exclude or admit them; from which it is inferred, that they possess the same power with respect to other articles.

If this inference were correct; if this power was exercised, not under any particular clause in the constitution, but in virtue of a general right over the subject of commerce, to exist as long as the constitution itself, it might now be exercised. Any State might now import African slaves into its own territory. But it is obvious, that the power of the States over this subject, previous to the year 1808, constitutes an exception to the power of Congress to regulate commerce, and the exception is expressed in such words, as to manifest clearly the intention to continue the pre-existing right of the States to admit or exclude, for a limited period. The words are, "the migration or importation of such persons as any of the States, now existing, *shall* think proper to admit, shall not be prohibited by the Congress prior to the year 1808." The whole object of the exception is, to preserve the power to those States which might be disposed to exercise it; and its language seems to the Court to convey this idea unequivocally. The possession of this particular power, then, during the time limited in the constitution, cannot be admitted to prove the possession of any other similar power.

It has been said, that the act of August 7, 1789, acknowledges a concurrent power in the States to regulate the conduct of pilots,

[1] *3* U. S. L. *p. 529.*

and hence is inferred an admission of their concurrent right with Congress to regulate commerce with foreign nations, and amongst the States. But this inference is not, we think, justified by the fact.

Although Congress cannot enable a State to legislate, Congress may adopt the provisions of a State on any subject. When the government of the Union was brought into existence, it found a system for the regulation of its pilots in full force in every State. The act which has been mentioned, adopts this system, and gives it the same validity as if its provisions had been specially made by Congress. But the act, it may be said, is prospective also, and the adoption of laws to be made in future, presupposes the right in the maker to legislate on the subject.

The act unquestionably manifests an intention to leave this subject entirely to the States, until Congress should think proper to interpose; but the very enactment of such a law indicates an opinion that it was necessary; that the existing system would not be applicable to the new state of things, unless expressly applied to it by Congress. But this section is confined to pilots within the "bays, inlets, rivers, harbours, and ports of the United States," which are, of course, in whole or in part, also within the limits of some particular state. The acknowledged power of a State to regulate its police, its domestic trade, and to govern its own citizens, may enable it to legislate on this subject, to a considerable extent; and the adoption of its system by Congress, and the application of it to the whole subject of commerce, does not seem to the Court to imply a right in the States so to apply it of their own authority. But the adoption of the State system being temporary, being only "until further legislative provision shall be made by Congress," shows, conclusively, an opinion that Congress could control the whole subject, and might adopt the system of the States, or provide one of its own.

A State, it is said, or even a private citizen, may construct light houses. But gentlemen must be aware, that if this proves a power in a State to regulate commerce, it proves that the same power is in the citizen. States, or individuals who own lands, may, if not forbidden by law, erect on those lands what buildings they please; but this power is entirely distinct from that of regulating commerce, and may, we presume, be restrained, if exercised so as to produce a public mischief.

These acts were cited at the bar for the purpose of showing an opinion in Congress, that the States possess, concurrently with the Legislature of the Union, the power to regulate commerce with foreign nations and among the States. Upon reviewing them, we think they do not establish the proposition they were intended to prove. They show the opinion, that the States retain powers enabling them to pass the laws to which allusion has been made, not that those laws proceed from the particular power which has been delegated to Congress.

It has been contended by the counsel for the appellant, that, as the word "to regulate" implies in its nature, full power over the thing to be regulated, it excludes, necessarily, the action of all others that would perform the same operation on the same thing. That regulation is designed for the entire result, applying to those parts which remain as they were, as well as to those which are altered. It produces a uniform whole, which is as much disturbed and deranged by changing what the regulating power designs to leave untouched, as that on which it has operated.

There is great force in this argument, and the Court is not satisfied that it has been refuted.

Since, however, in exercising the power of regulating their own purely internal affairs, whether of trading or police, the States may sometimes enact laws, the validity of which depends on their interfering with, and being contrary to, an act of Congress passed in pursuance of the constitution, the Court will enter upon the inquiry, whether the laws of New-York, as expounded by the highest tribunal of that State, have, in their application to this case, come into collision with an act of Congress, and deprived a citizen of a right to which that act entitles him. Should this collision exist, it will be immaterial whether those laws were passed in virtue of a concurrent power "to regulate commerce with foreign nations and among the several States," or, in virtue of a power to regulate their domestic trade and police. In one case and the other, the acts of New-York must yield to the law of Congress; and the decision sustaining the privilege they confer, against a right given by a law of the Union, must be erroneous.

This opinion has been frequently expressed in this Court, and is founded, as well on the nature of the government as on the words of the constitution. In argument, however, it has been contended, that if a law passed by a State, in the exercise of its acknowledged sovereignty, comes into conflict with a law passed by Congress in pursuance of the constitution, they affect the subject, and each other, like equal opposing powers.

But the framers of our constitution foresaw this state of things, and provided for it, by declaring the supremacy not only of itself, but of the laws made in pursuance of it. The nullity of any act, inconsistent with the constitution, is produced by the declaration, that the constitution is the supreme law. The appropriate application of that part of the clause which confers the same supremacy on laws and treaties, is to such acts of the State Legislatures as do not transcend their powers, but, though enacted in the execution of acknowledged State powers, interfere with, or are contrary to the laws of Congress, made in pursuance of the constitution, or some treaty made under the authority of the United States. In every such case, the act of Congress, or the treaty, is supreme; and the law of the State, though enacted in the exercise of powers not controverted, must yield to it.

In pursuing this inquiry at the bar, it has been said, that the constitution does not confer the right of intercourse between State and State. That right derives its source from those laws whose authority is acknowledged by civilized man throughout the world. This is true. The constitution found it an existing right, and gave to Congress the power to regulate it. In the exercise of this power, Congress has passed "an act for enrolling or licensing ships or vessels to be employed in the coasting trade and fisheries, and for regulating the same." The counsel for the respondent contend, that this act does not give the right to sail from port to port, but confines itself to regulating a pre-existing right, so far only as to confer certain privileges on enrolled and licensed vessels in its exercise.

It will at once occur, that, when a Legislature attaches certain privileges and exemptions to the exercise of a right over which its control is absolute, the law must imply a power to exercise the right. The privileges are gone, if the right itself be annihilated. It would be contrary to all reason, and to the course of human affairs, to say that a State is unable to strip a vessel of the particular privileges attendant on the exercise of a right, and yet may annul the right itself; that the State of New-York cannot prevent an enrolled and licensed vessel, proceeding from Elizabethtown, in New-Jersey, to New-York, from enjoying, in her course, and on her entrance into port, all the privileges conferred by the act of Congress; but can shut her up in her own port, and prohibit altogether her entering the waters and ports of another State. To the Court it seems very clear, that the whole act on the subject of the coasting trade, according to those principles which govern the construction of statutes, implies, unequivocally, an authority to licensed vessels to carry on the coasting trade.

But we will proceed briefly to notice those sections which bear more directly on the subject.

The first section declares, that vessels enrolled by virtue of a previous law, and certain other vessels, enrolled as described in that act, and having a license in force, as is by the act required, "and no others, shall be deemed ships or vessels of the United States, entitled to the privileges of ships or vessels employed in the coasting trade."

This section seems to the Court to contain a positive enactment, that the vessels it describes shall be entitled to the privileges of ships or vessels employed in the coasting trade. These privileges cannot be separated from the trade, and cannot be enjoyed, unless the trade may be prosecuted. The grant of the privilege is an idle, empty form, conveying nothing, unless it convey the right to which the privilege is attached, and in the exercise of which its whole value consists. To construe these words otherwise than as entitling the ships or vessels described, to carry on the coasting trade, would be, we think, to disregard the apparent intent of the act.

The fourth section directs the proper officer to grant to a vessel qualified to receive it, "a license for carrying on the coasting trade;" and prescribes its form. After reciting the compliance of the applicant with the previous requisites of the law, the operative words of the instrument are, "license is hereby granted for the said steam-boat, Bellona, to be employed in carrying on the coasting trade for one year from the date hereof, and no longer."

These are not the words of the officer; they are the words of the legislature; and convey as explicitly the authority the act intended to give, and operate as effectually, as if they had been inserted in any other part of the act, than in the license itself.

The word "license," means permission, or authority; and a license to do any particular thing, is a permission or authority to do that thing; and if granted by a person having power to grant it, transfers to the grantee the right to do whatever it purports to authorize. It certainly transfers to him all the right which the grantor can transfer, to do what is within the terms of the license.

Would the validity or effect of such an instrument be questioned by the respondent, if executed by persons claiming regularly under the laws of New-York?

The license must be understood to be what it purports to be, a legislative authority to the steam-boat Bellona, "to be employed in carrying on the coasting trade, for one year from this date."

It has been denied that these words authorize a voyage from New-Jersey to New-York. It is true, that no ports are specified; but it is equally true, that the words used are perfectly intelligible, and do confer such authority as unquestionably, as if the ports had been mentioned. The coasting trade is a term well understood. The law has defined it; and all know its meaning perfectly. The act describes, with great minuteness, the various operations of a vessel engaged in it; and it cannot, we think, be doubted, that a voyage from New-Jersey to New-York, is one of those operations.

Notwithstanding the decided language of the license, it has also been maintained, that it gives no right to trade; and that its sole purpose is to confer the American character.

The answer given to this argument, that the American character is conferred by the enrolment, and not by the license, is, we think, founded too clearly in the words of the law, to require the support of any additional observations. The enrolment of vessels designed for the coasting trade, corresponds precisely with the registration of vessels designed for the foreign trade, and requires every circumstance which can constitute the American character. The license can be granted only to vessels already enrolled, if they be of the burthen of twenty tons and upwards; and requires no circumstance essential to the American character. The object of the license, then, cannot be to ascertain the character of the vessel, but to do what it professes to do—that is, to give permission to a vessel already proved by her enrolment to be American, to carry on the coasting trade.

But, if the license be a permit to carry on the coasting trade, the respondent denies that these boats were engaged in that trade, or that the decree under consideration has restrained them from prosecuting it. The boats of the appellant were, we are told, employed in the transportation of passengers; and this is no part of that commerce which Congress may regulate.

If, as our whole course of legislation on this subject shows, the power of Congress has been universally understood in America, to comprehend navigation, it is a very persuasive, if not a conclusive argument, to prove that the construction is correct; and, if it be correct, no clear distinction is perceived between the power to regulate vessels employed in transporting men for hire, and property for hire. The subject is transferred to Congress, and no exception to the grant can be admitted, which is not proved by the words or the nature of the thing. A coasting vessel employed in the transportation of passengers, is as much a portion of the American marine, as one employed in the transportation of a cargo; and no reason is perceived why such vessel should be withdrawn from the regulating power of that government, which has been thought best fitted for the purpose generally. The provisions of the law respecting native seamen, and respecting ownership, are as applicable to vessels carrying men, as to vessels carrying manufactures; and no reason is perceived why the power over the subject should not be placed in the same hands. The argument urged at the bar, rests on the foundation, that the power of Congress does not extend to navigation, as a branch of commerce, and can only be applied to that subject incidentally and occasionally. But if that foundation be removed, we must show some plain, intelligible distinction, supported by the constitution, or by reason, for discriminating between the power of Congress over vessels employed in navigating the same seas. We can perceive no such distinction.

If we refer to the constitution, the inference to be drawn from it is rather against the distinction. The section which restrains Congress from prohibiting the migration or importation of such persons as any of the States may think proper to admit, until the year 1808, has always been considered as an exception from the power to regulate commerce, and certainly seems to class migration with importation. Migration applies as appropriately to voluntary, as importation does to involuntary, arrivals; and, so far as an exception from a power proves its existence, this section proves that the power to regulate commerce applies equally to the regulation of vessels employed in transporting men, who pass from place to place voluntarily, and to those who pass involuntarily.

If the power reside in Congress, as a portion of the general grant to regulate commerce, then acts applying that power to vessels generally, must be construed as comprehending all vessels. If none appear to be excluded by the language of the act, none can be excluded by construction. Vessels have always been employed to a greater or less extent in the transportation of passengers, and have never been supposed to be, on that account, withdrawn from the control or protection of Congress. Packets which ply along the coast, as well as those which make voyages between Europe and America, consider the transportation of passengers as an important part of their business. Yet it has never been suspected that the general laws of navigation did not apply to them.

The duty act, sections 23 and 46, contains provisions respecting passengers, and shows, that vessels which transport them, have the same rights, and must perform the same duties, with other vessels. They are governed by the general laws of navigation.

In the progress of things, this seems to have grown into a particular employment, and to have attracted the particular attention of government. Congress was no longer satisfied with comprehending vessels engaged specially in this business, within those provisions which were intended for vessels generally; and, on the 2d of March, 1819, passed "an act regulating passenger ships and vessels." This wise and humane law provides for the safety and comfort of passengers, and for the communication of every thing concerning them which may interest the government, to the Department of State, but makes no provision concerning the entry of the vessel, or her conduct in the waters of the United States. This, we think, shows conclusively the sense of Congress, (if, indeed, any evidence to that point could be required,) that the pre-existing regulations comprehended passenger ships among others; and, in prescribing the same duties, the Legislature must have considered them as possessing the same rights.

If, then, it were even true, that the Bellona and the Stoudinger were employed exclusively in the conveyance of passengers between New-York and New-Jersey, it would not follow that this occupation did not constitute a part of the coasting trade of the United States, and was not protected by the license annexed to the answer. But we cannot perceive how the occupation of these vessels can be drawn into question, in the case before the Court. The laws of New-York, which grant the exclusive privilege set up by the respondent, take no notice of the employment of vessels, and relate only to the principle by which they are propelled. Those laws do not inquire whether vessels are engaged in transporting men or merchandise, but whether they are moved by steam or wind. If by the former, the waters of New-York are closed against them, though their cargoes be dutiable goods, which the laws of the United States permit them to enter and deliver in New-York. If by the latter, those waters are free to them, though they should carry passengers only. In conformity with the law, is the bill of the plaintiff in the State Court. The bill does not complain that the Bellona and the Stoudinger carry passengers, but that they are moved by steam. This is the injury of which he complains, and is the sole injury against the continuance of which he asks relief. The bill does not even allege, specially, that those vessels were employed in the transportation of passengers, but says, generally, that they were employed "in the transportation of passengers, or otherwise." The answer avers, only, that they were employed in the coasting trade, and insists on the right to carry on any trade authorized by the license. No testimony is taken, and the writ of injunction and decree restrain these licensed vessels, not from carrying passengers, but from being moved through the waters of New-York by steam, for any purpose whatever.

The questions, then, whether the conveyance of passengers be a part of the coasting trade, and whether a vessel can be protected in that occupation by a coasting license, are not, and cannot be, raised in this case. The real and sole question seems to be, whether a steam machine, in actual use, deprives a vessel of the privileges conferred by a license.

In considering this question, the first idea which presents itself, is, that the laws of Congress for the regulation of commerce, do not look to the principle by which vessels are moved. That subject is left entirely to individual discretion; and, in that vast and complex system of legislative enactment concerning it, which embraces every thing that the Legislature thought it necessary to notice, there is not, we believe, one word respecting the peculiar principle by which vessels are propelled through the water, except what may be found in a single act, granting a particular privilege to steam boats. With this exception, every act, either prescribing duties, or granting privileges, applies to every vessel, whether navigated by the instrumentality of wind or fire, of sails or machinery. The whole weight of proof, then, is thrown upon him who would introduce a distinction to which the words of the law give no countenance.

If a real difference could be admitted to exist between vessels carrying passengers and others, it has already been observed, that there is no fact in this case which can bring up that question. And, if the occupation of steam boats be a matter of such general notoriety, that the Court may be presumed to know it, although not specially informed by the record, then we deny that the transportation of passengers is their exclusive occupation. It is a matter of general history, that, in our western waters, their principal employment is the transportation of merchandise; and all know, that in the waters of the Atlantic they are frequently so employed.

But all inquiry into this subject seems to the Court to be put completely at rest, by the act already mentioned, entitled, "An act for the enrolling and licensing of steam boats."

This act authorizes a steam boat employed, or intended to be employed, only in a river or bay of the United States, owned wholly or in part by an alien, resident within the United States, to be enrolled and licensed as if the same belonged to a citizen of the United States

This act demonstrates the opinion of Congress, that steam boats may be enrolled and licensed, in common with vessels using sails. They are, of course, entitled to the same privileges, and can no more be restrained from navigating waters, and entering ports which are free to such vessels, than if they were wafted on their voyage by the winds, instead of being propelled by the agency of fire. The one element may be as legitimately used as the other, for every commercial purpose authorized by the laws of the Union; and the act of a State inhibiting the use of either to any vessel having a license under the act of Congress, comes, we think, in direct collision with that act.

As this decides the cause, it is unnecessary to enter in an examination of that part of the constitution which empowers Congress to promote the progress of science and the useful arts.

The Court is aware that, in stating the train of reasoning by which we have been conducted to this result, much time has been consumed in the attempt to demonstrate propositions which may have been thought axioms. It is felt that the tediousness inseparable from the endeavour to prove that which is already clear, is imputable to a considerable part of this opinion. But it was unavoidable. The conclusion to which we have come, depends on a chain of principles which it was necessary to preserve unbroken; and, although some of them were thought nearly self-evident, the magnitude of the question, the weight of character belonging to those from whose judgment we dissent, and the argument at the bar, demanded that we should assume nothing.

Powerful and ingenious minds, taking, as postulates, that the powers expressly granted to the government of the Union, are to be contracted by construction, into the narrowest possible compass, and that the original powers of the States are retained, if any possible construction will retain them, may, by a course of well digested, but refined and metaphysical reasoning, founded on these premises, explain away the constitution of our country, and leave it, a magnificent structure, indeed, to look at, but totally unfit for use. They may so entangle and perplex the understanding, as to obscure principles, which were before thought quite plain, and induce doubts where, if the mind were to pursue its own course, none would be perceived. In such a case, it is peculiarly necessary to recur to safe and fundamental principles to sustain those principles, and, when sustained, to make them the tests of the arguments to be examined.

McCULLOCH v. MARYLAND, 4 WHEAT. 316 (1819)

A Maryland tax statute directed against the operations of the Bank of the United States in that state came before the Court for review in this case. The appeal from the state court decision upholding the statute raised the issue of the constitutionality of the Bank as well as that of federal immunity from state taxation. For the Court, Chief Justice Marshall held that the establishment of a bank was a proper exercise of the federal sovereignty and also constitutional under a broad definition of the "necessary and proper" clause of the Constitution. He held it unreasonable and unconstitutional for state tax measures to impede activities of the federal government that were for the general benefit of all of the states. Consequently the Maryland tax law, under which the cashier of the bank had been fined, was held unconstitutional and the fine was ordered refunded.

MARSHALL, *Ch. J.*, delivered the opinion of the court:

In the case now to be determined, the defendant, a sovereign state, denies the obligation of a law enacted by the legislature of the Union, and the plaintiff, on his part, contests the validity of an act which has been passed by the legislature of that state. The constitution of our country, in its most interesting and vital parts, is to be considered; the conflicting powers of the government of the Union and of its members, as marked in that constitution, are to be discussed; and an opinion given, which may essentially influence the great operations of the government. No tribunal can approach such a question without a deep sense of its importance, and of the awful responsibility involved in its decision. But it must be decided peacefully, or remain a source of hostile legislation, perhaps of hostility of a still more serious nature; and if it is to be so decided, by this tribunal alone can the decision be made. On the Supreme Court of the United States has the constitution of our country devolved this important duty.

The first question made in the cause is, has Congress power to incorporate a bank?

It has been truly said that this can scarcely be considered as an open question, entirely unprejudiced by the former proceedings of the nation respecting it. The principle now contested was introduced at a very early period of our history, has been recognized by many successive legislatures, and has been acted upon by the judicial department, in cases of peculiar delicacy, as a law of undoubted obligation.

It will not be denied that a bold and daring usurpation might be resisted, after an acquiescence still longer and more complete than this. But it is conceived that a doubtful question, one on which human reason may pause, and the human judgment be suspended, in the decision of which the great principles of liberty are not concerned, but the respective powers of those who are equally the representatives of the people, are to be adjusted; if not put at rest by the practice of the government, ought to receive a considerable impression from that practice. An exposition of the constitution, deliberately established by legislative acts, on the faith of which an immense property has been advanced, ought not to be lightly disregarded.

The power now contested was exercised by the first Congress elected under the present constitution. The bill for incorporating the bank of the United States did not steal upon an unsuspecting legislature, and pass unobserved. Its principle was completely understood, and was opposed with equal zeal and ability. After being resisted, first in the fair and open field of debate, and afterwards in the executive cabinet, with as much persevering talent as any measure has ever experienced, and being supported by arguments which convinced minds as pure and as intelligent as this country can boast, it became a law. The original act was permitted to expire; but a short experience of the embarrassments to which the refusal to revive it exposed the government, convinced those who were most prejudiced against the measure of its necessity and induced the passage of the present law. It would require no ordinary share of intrepidity to assert that a measure adopted under these circumstances was a bold and plain usurpation, to which the constitution gave no countenance.

These observations belong to the cause; But they are not made under the impression that, were the question entirely new, the law would be found irreconcilable with the constitution.

In discussing this question, the counsel for the state of Maryland have deemed it of some importance, in the construction of the constitution, to consider that instrument not as emanating from the people, but as the act of sovereign and independent states. The powers of the general government, it has been said, are delegated by the states, who alone are truly sovereign; and must be exercised in subordination to the states, who alone possess supreme dominion.

It would be difficult to sustain this proposition. The convention which framed the constitution was indeed elected by the state legislatures. But the instrument, when it came from their hands, was a mere proposal, without obligation, or pretensions to it. It was reported to the then existing Congress of the United States, with a request that it might "be submitted to a convention of delegates, chosen in each state by the people thereof, under the recommendation of its legislature, for their assent and ratification." This mode of proceeding was adopted; and by the convention, by Congress, and by the state legislatures, the instrument was submitted to the people. They acted upon it in the only manner in which they can act safely, effectively, and wisely, on such a subject, by assembling in convention. It is true, they assembled in their several states—and where else should they have assembled? No political dreamer was ever wild enough to think of breaking down the lines which separate the states, and of compounding the American people into one common mass. Of consequence, when they act, they act in their states. But the measures they adopt do not, on that account, cease to be the measures of the people themselves, or become the measures of the state governments.

From these conventions the constitution derives its whole authority. The government proceeds directly from the people; is "ordained and established" in the name of the people; and is declared to be ordained, "in order to form a more perfect union, establish justice, insure domestic tranquillity, and secure the blessings of liberty to themselves and to their posterity." The assent of the states, in their sovereign capacity, is implied in calling a convention, and thus submitting that instrument to the people. But the people were at perfect liberty to accept or reject it; and their act was final. It required not the affirmance, and could not be negatived, by the state governments. The constitution, when thus adopted, was of complete obligation, and bound the state sovereignties.

It has been said that the people had already surrendered all their powers to the state sovereignties, and had nothing more to give. But, surely, the question whether they may resume and modify the powers granted to government does not remain to be settled in this country. Much more might the legitimacy of the general government be doubted, had it been created by the states. The powers delegated to the state sovereignties were to be exercised by themselves, not by a distinct and independent sovereignty, created by themselves. To the formation of a league, such as was the confederation, the state sovereignties were certainly competent. But when, "in order to form a more perfect union," it was deemed necessary to change this alliance into an effective government, possessing great and sovereign powers, and acting directly on the people, the necessity of referring it to the people, and of deriving its powers directly from them, was felt and acknowledged by all.

The government of the Union, then (whatever may be the influence of this fact on the case), is, emphatically, and truly, a government of the people. In form and in substance it emanates from them. Its powers are granted by them, and are to be exercised directly on them, and for their benefit.

This government is acknowledged by all to be one of enumerated powers. The principle, that it can exercise only the powers granted to it, would seem too apparent to have required to be enforced by all those arguments which its enlightened friends, while it was depending before the people, found it necessary to urge. That principle is now universally admitted. But the question respecting the extent of the powers actually granted, is perpetually arising, and will probably continue to arise, as long as our system shall exist.

In discussing these questions, the conflicting powers of the general and state governments must be brought into view, and the supremacy of their respective laws, when they are in opposition, must be settled.

If any one proposition could command the universal assent of mankind, we might expect it would be this—that the government of the Union, though limited in its powers, is supreme within its sphere of action. This would seem to result necessarily from its nature. It is the government of all; its powers are delegated by all; it represents all, and acts for all. Though any one state may be willing to control its operations, no state is willing to allow others to control them. The nation, on those subjects on which it can act, must necessarily bind its component parts. But this question is not left to mere reason; the people have, in express terms, decided it by saying, "this constitution, and the laws of the United States, which shall be made in pursuance thereof," "shall be the supreme law of the land," and by requiring that the members of the state legislatures, and the officers of the executive and judicial departments of the states shall take the oath of fidelity to it.

The government of the United States, then, though limited in its powers, is supreme; and its laws, when made in pursuance of the constitution, form the supreme law of the land, "anything in the constitution or laws of any state to the contrary notwithstanding."

Among the enumerated powers, we do not find that of establishing a bank or creating a corporation. But there is no phrase in the instrument which, like the articles of confederation, excludes incidental or implied powers; and which requires that everything granted shall be expressly and minutely described. Even the 10th amendment, which was framed for the purpose of quieting the excessive jealousies which had been excited, omits the word "expressly," and declares only that the powers "not delegated to the United States, nor prohibited to the states, are reserved to the states or to the people;" thus leaving the question, whether the particular power which may become the subject of contest has been delegated to the one government, or prohibited to the other, to depend on a fair construction of the whole instrument. The men who drew and adopted this amendment had experienced the embarrassments resulting from the insertion of this word in the articles of confederation, and probably omitted it to avoid those embarrassments. A constitution, to contain an accurate detail of all the subdivisions of which its great powers will admit, and of all the means by which they may be carried into execution, would partake of a prolixity of a legal code, and could scarcely be embraced by the human mind. It would probably never be understood by the public. Its nature, therefore, requires, that only its great outlines should be marked, its important objects designated, and the minor ingredients which compose those objects be deduced from the nature of the objects themselves. That this idea was entertained by the framers of the American constitution, is not only to be inferred from the nature of the instrument, but from the language. Why else were some of the limitations, found in the ninth section of the 1st article, introduced? It is also, in some degree, warranted by their having omitted to use any restrictive term which might prevent its receiving a fair and just interpretation. In considering this question, then, we must never forget that it is a constitution we are expounding.

Although, among the enumerated powers of government, we do not find the word "bank" or "incorporation," we find the great powers to lay and collect taxes; to borrow money; to regulate commerce; to declare and conduct a war; and to raise and support armies and navies. The sword and the purse, all the external relations, and no inconsiderable portion of the industry of the nation, are entrusted to its government. It can never be pretended that these vast powers draw after them others of inferior importance, merely because they are inferior. Such an idea can never be advanced. But it may with great reason be contended, that a government, entrusted with such ample powers, on the due execution of which the happiness and prosperity of the nation so vitally depends, must also be entrusted with ample means for their execution. The power being given, it is the interest of the nation to facilitate its execution. It can never be their interest, and cannot be presumed to have been their intention, to clog and embarrass its execution by withholding the most appropriate means. Throughout this vast republic, from the St. Croix to the Gulf of Mexico, from the Atlantic to the Pacific, revenue is to be collected and expended, armies are to be marched and supported. The exigencies of the nation may require that the treasure raised in the north should be transported to the south, that raised in the east conveyed to the west, or that this order should be reversed. Is that construction of the constitution to be preferred which would render these operations difficult, hazardous, and expensive? Can we adopt that construction (unless the words imperiously require it) which would impute to the framers of that instrument, when granting these powers for the public good, the intention of impeding their exercise by withholding a choice of means? If, indeed, such be the mandate of the constitution, we have only to obey; but that instrument does not profess to enumerate the means by which the powers it confers may be executed; nor does it prohibit the creation of a corporation, if the existence of such a being be essential to the beneficial exercise of those powers. It is, then, the subject of fair inquiry, how far such means may be employed. It is not denied that the powers given to the government imply the ordinary means of execution. That, for example of raising revenue, and applying it to national purposes, is admitted to imply the power of conveying money from place to place, as the exigencies of the nation may require, and of employing the usual means of conveyance. But it is denied that the government has its choice of means; or, that it may employ the most convenient means, if, to employ them, it be necessary to erect a corporation.

On what foundation does this argument rest? On this alone: The power of creating a corporation, is one appertaining to sovereignty, and is not expressly conferred on Congress. This is true. But all legislative powers appertain to sovereignty. The original power of giving the law on any subject whatever, is a sovereign power; and if the government of the Union is restrained from creating a corporation, as a means for performing its functions, on the single reason that the creation of a corporation is an act of sovereignty; if the sufficiency of this reason be acknowledged, there would be some difficulty in sustaining the authority of Congress to pass other laws for the accomplishment of the same objects.

The government which has a right to do an act, and has imposed on it the duty of performing that act, must, according to the dictates of reason, be allowed to select the means; and those who contend that it may not select any appropriate means, that one particular mode of effecting the object is excepted, take upon themselves the burden of establishing that exception.

The creation of a corporation, it is said, appertains to sovereignty. This is admitted. But to what portion of sovereignty does it appertain? Does it belong to one more than to another? In America, the powers of sovereignty are divided between the government of the Union, and those of the States. They are each sovereign, with respect to the objects committed to it, and neither sovereign with respect to the objects committed to the other. We cannot comprehend that train of reasoning which would maintain that the extent of power granted by the people is to be ascertained, not by the nature and terms of the grant, but by its date. Some state constitutions were formed before, some since that of the United States. We cannot believe that their relation to each other is in any degree dependent upon this circumstance. Their respective powers must, we think, be precisely the same as if they had been formed at the same time. Had they been formed at the same time, and had the people conferred on the general government the power contained in the constitution, and on the states the whole residuum of power, would it have been asserted that the government of the Union was not sovereign with respect to those objects which were entrusted to it, in relation to which its laws were declared to be supreme? If this could not have been asserted, we cannot well comprehend the process of reasoning which maintains that a power appertaining to sovereignty cannot be connected with that vast portion of it which is granted to the general government, so far as it is calculated to subserve the legitimate objects of that government. The power of creating a corporation, though appertaining to sovereignty, is not, like the power of making war, or levying taxes, or of regulating commerce, a great substantive and independent power, which cannot be implied as incidental to other powers, or used as a means of executing them. It is never the end for which other powers are exercised, but a means by which other objects are accomplished. No contributions are made to charity for the sake of an incorporation, but a corporation is created to administer the charity; no seminary of learning is instituted in order to be incorporated, but the corporate character is conferred to subserve the purposes of education. No city was ever built with the sole object of being incorporated, but is incorporated as affording the best means of being well governed. The power of creating a corporation is never used for its own sake, but for the purpose of effecting something else. No sufficient reason is, therefore, perceived, why it may not pass as incidental to those powers which are expressly given, if it be a direct mode of executing them.

But the constitution of the United States has not left the right of Congress to employ the necessary means for the execution of the powers conferred on the government to general reasoning. To its enumeration of powers is added that of making "all laws which shall be necessary and proper, for carrying into execution the foregoing powers, and all other powers vested by this constitution, in the government of the United States, or in any department thereof."

The counsel for the State of Maryland have urged various arguments, to prove that this clause, though in terms a grant of power, is not so in effect; but is really restrictive of the general right, which might otherwise be implied, of selecting means for executing the enumerated powers.

In support of this proposition, they have found it necessary to contend, that this clause was inserted for the purpose of conferring on Congress the power of making laws. That, without it, doubts, might be entertained whether Congress could exercise its powers in the form of legislation.

But could this be the object for which it was inserted? A government is created by the people, having legislative, executive, and judicial powers. Its legislative powers are vested in a Congress, which is to consist of a senate and house of representatives. Each house may determine the rule of its proceedings; and it is declared that every bill which shall have passed both houses, shall, before it becomes a law, be presented to the President of the United States. The 7th section describes the course of proceedings, by which a bill shall become a law; and, then, the 8th section enumerates the powers of Congress. Could it be necessary to say that a legislature should exercise legislative powers in the shape of legislation? After allowing each house to prescribe its own course of proceeding, after describing the manner in which a bill should become a law, would it have entered into the mind of a single member of the convention that an express power to make laws was necessary to enable the legislature to make them? That a legislature, endowed with legislative powers, can legislate, is a proposition too self-evident to have been questioned.

But the argument on which most reliance is placed, is drawn from the peculiar language of this clause. Congress is not empowered by it to make all laws, which may have relation to the powers conferred on the government, but such only as may be "necessary and proper" for carrying them into execution. The word "necessary" is considered as controlling the whole sentence, and as limiting the right to pass laws for the execution of the granted powers, to such as are indispensable, and without which the power would be nugatory. That it excludes the choice of means, and leaves to Congress, in each case, that only which is most direct and simple.

Is it true that this is the sense in which the word "necessary" is always used? Does it always import an absolute physical necessity, so strong that one thing, to which another may be termed necessary, cannot exist without that other? We think it does not. If reference be had to its use, in the common affairs of the world, or in approved authors, we find that it frequently imports no more than that one thing is convenient, or useful, or essential to another. To employ the means necessary to an end, is generally understood as employing any means calculated to produce the end, and not as being confined to those single means, without which the end would be entirely unattainable. Such is the character of human language, that no word conveys to the mind, in all situations, one single definite idea; and nothing is more common than to use words in a figurative sense. Almost all compositions contain words, which, taken in their rigorous sense, would convey a meaning different from that which is obviously intended. It is essential to just construction, that many words which import something excessive should be understood in a more mitigated sense—in that sense which common usage justifies. The word "necessary" is of this description. It has not a fixed character peculiar to itself. It admits of all degrees of comparison; and is often connected with other words, which increase or diminish the impression the mind receives of the urgency it imports. A thing may be necessary, very necessary, absolutely or indispensably necessary. To no mind would the same idea be conveyed by these several phrases. This comment on the word is well illustrated by the passage cited at the bar, from the 10th section of the 1st article of the constitution. It is, we think, impossible to compare the sentence which prohibits a state from laying "imposts or duties on imports or exports, except what may be absolutely necessary for executing its inspection laws," with that which authorizes Congress "to make all laws which shall be necessary and proper for carrying into execution" the powers of the general government, without feeling a conviction that the convention understood itself to change materially the meaning of the word "necessary," by prefixing the word "absolutely." This word, then, like others, is used in various senses; and, in its construction, the subject, the context, the intention of the person using them, are all to be taken into view.

Let this be done in the case under consideration. The subject is the execution of those great powers on which the welfare of a nation essentially depends. It must have been the intention of those who gave these powers, to insure, as far as human prudence could insure, their beneficial execution. This could not be done by confiding the choice of means to such narrow limits as not to leave it in the power of Congress to adopt any which might be appropriate, and which were conducive to the end. This provision is made in a constitution intended to endure for ages to come, and, consequently, to be adapted to the various crises of human affairs. To have prescribed the means by which government should, in all future time, execute its powers, would have been to change, entirely, the character of the instrument, and give it the properties of a legal code. It would have been an unwise attempt to provide, by immutable rules, for exigencies which, if foreseen at all, must have been seen dimly, and which can be best provided for as they occur. To have declared that the best means shall not be used, but those alone without which the power given would be nugatory, would have been to deprive the legislature of the capacity to avail itself of experience, to exercise its reason, and to accommodate its legislation to circumstances. If we apply this principle of construction to any of the powers of the government, we shall find it so pernicious in its operation that we shall be compelled to discard it. The powers vested in Congress may certainly be carried into execution, without prescribing an oath of office. The power to exact this security for the faithful performance of duty, is not given, nor is it indispensably necessary. The different departments may be established; taxes may be imposed and collected; armies and navies may be raised and maintained; and money may be borrowed, without requiring an oath of office. It might be argued, with as much plausibility as other incidental powers have been assailed, that the convention was not unmindful of this subject. The oath which might be exacted—that of fidelity to the constitution—is prescribed, and no other can be required. Yet, he would be charged with insanity who should contend that the legislature might not superadd, to the oath directed by the constitution, such other oath of office as its wisdom might suggest.

So, with respect to the whole penal code of the United States: whence arises the power to punish in cases not prescribed by the constitution? All admit that the government may, legitimately, punish any violation of its laws; and yet, this is not among the enumerated powers of Congress. The right to enforce the observance of law, by punishing its infraction, might be denied with the more plausibility because it is expressly given in some cases. Congress is empowered "to provide for the punishment of counterfeiting the securities and current coin of the United States," and "to define and punish piracies and felonies committed on the high seas, and offenses against the law of nations." The several powers of Congress may exist, in a very imperfect state, to be sure, but they may exist and be carried into execution, although no punishment should be inflicted in cases where the right to punish is not expressly given.

Take, for example, the power "to establish post-offices and post-roads." This power is executed by the single act of making the establishment. But, from this has been inferred the power and duty of carrying the mail along the post-road, from one post-office to another. And, from this implied power, has again been inferred the right to punish those who steal letters from the post-office, or rob the mail. It may be said, with some plausibility, that the right to carry the mail, and to punish those who rob it, is not indispensably necessary to the establishment of a post-office and post-road. This right is indeed essential to the beneficial exercise of the power, but not indispensably necessary to its existence. So, of the punishment of the crimes of stealing or falsifying a record or process of a court of the United States, or of perjury in such court. To punish these offenses is certainly conducive to the due administration of justice. But courts may exist, and may decide the causes brought before them, though such crimes escape punishment.

The baneful influence of this narrow construction on all the operations of the government, and the absolute impracticability of maintaining it without rendering the government incompetent to its great objects, might be illustrated by numerous examples drawn from the constitution, and from our laws. The good sense of the public has pronounced, without hesitation, that the power of punishment appertains to sovereignty, and may be exercised whenever the sovereign has a right to act, as incidental to his constitutional powers. It is a means for carrying into execution all sovereign powers, and may be used, although not indispensably necessary. It is a right incidental to the power, and conducive to its beneficial exercise.

If this limited construction of the word "necessary" must be abandoned in order to punish, whence is derived the rule which would re-instate it, when the government would carry its powers into execution by means not vindictive in their nature? If the word "necessary" means "needful," "requisite," "essential," "conducive to," in order to let in the power of punishment for the infraction of law; why is it not equally comprehensive when required to authorize the use of means which facilitate the execution of the powers of government without the infliction of punishment?

In ascertaining the sense in which the word "necessary" is used in this clause of the constitution, we may derive some aid from that with which it is associated. Congress shall have power "to make all laws which shall be necessary and proper to carry into execution" the powers of the government. If the word "necessary" was used in that strict and rigorous sense for which the counsel for the state of Maryland contend, it would be an extraordinary departure from the usual course of the human mind, as exhibited in composition, to add a word, the only possible effect of which is to qualify that strict and rigorous meaning; to present to the mind the idea of some choice of means of legislation not straightened and compressed within the narrow limits for which gentlemen contend.

But the argument which most conclusively demonstrates the error of the construction contended for by the counsel for the state of Maryland, is founded on the intention of the convention, as manifested in the whole clause. To waste time and argument in proving that without it Congress might carry its powers into execution, would be not much less idle than to hold a lighted taper to the sun. As little can it be required to prove, that in the absence of this clause, Congress would have some choice of means. That it might employ those which, in its judgment, would most advantageously effect the object to be accomplished. That any means adapted to the end, any means which tended directly to the execution of the constitutional powers of the government, were in themselves constitutional. This clause, as construed by the state of Maryland, would abridge, and almost annihilate this useful and necessary right of the legislature to select its means. That this could not be intended, is, we should think, had it not been already controverted, too apparent for controversy. We think so for the following reasons:

1st. The clause is placed among the powers of Congress, not among the limitations on those powers.

2d. Its terms purport to enlarge, not to diminish the powers vested in the government. It purports to be an additional power, not a restriction on those already granted. No reason has been, or can be assigned for thus concealing an intention to narrow the discretion of the national legislature under words which purport to enlarge it. The framers of the constitution wished its adoption, and well knew that it would be endangered by its strength, not by its weakness. Had they been capable of using language which would convey to the eye one idea, and, after deep reflection, impress on the mind another, they would rather have disguised the grant of power than its limitation. If, then, their intention had been, by this clause, to restrain the free use of means which might otherwise have been implied, that intention would have been inserted in another place, and would have been expressed in terms resembling these. "In carrying into execution the foregoing powers, and all others," &c., "no laws shall be passed but such as are necessary and proper." Had the intention been to make this clause restrictive, it would unquestionably have been so in form as well as in effect.

The result of the most careful and attentive consideration bestowed upon this clause is, that if it does not enlarge, it cannot be construed to restrain the powers of Congress, or to impair the right of the legislature to exercise its best judgment in the selection of measures to carry into execution the constitutional powers of the government. If no other motive for its insertion can be suggested, a sufficient one is found in the desire to remove all doubts respecting the right to legislate on that vast mass of incidental powers which must be involved in the constitution, if that instrument be not a splendid bauble.

We admit, as all must admit, that the powers of the government are limited, and that its limits are not to be transcended. But we think the sound construction of the constitution must allow to the national legislature that discretion, with respect to the means by which the powers it confers are to be carried into execution, which will enable that body to perform the high duties assigned to it, in the manner most beneficial to the people. Let the end be legitimate, let it be within the scope of the constitution, and all means which are appropriate, which are plainly adapted to that end, which are not prohibited, but consist with the letter and spirit of the constitution, are constitutional.

That a corporation must be considered

as a means not less usual, not of higher dignity, not more requiring a particular specification than other means, has been sufficiently proved. If we look to the origin of corporations, to the manner in which they have been framed in that government from which we have derived most of our legal principles and ideas, or to the uses to which they have been applied, we find no reason to suppose that a constitution, omitting, and wisely omitting, to enumerate all the means for carrying into execution the great powers vested in government, ought to have specified this. Had it been intended to grant this power as one which should be distinct and independent, to be exercised in any case whatever, it would have found a place among the enumerated powers of the government. But being considered merely as a means, to be employed only for the purpose of carrying into execution the given powers, there could be no motive for particularly mentioning it.

The propriety of this remark would seem to be generally acknowledged by the universal acquiescence in the construction which has been uniformly put on the 3d section of the 4th article of the constitution. The power to "make all needful rules and regulations respecting the territory or other property belonging to the United States," is not more comprehensive, than the power "to make all laws which shall be necessary and proper for carrying into execution" the powers of the government. Yet all admit the constitutionality of a territorial government, which is a corporate body.

If a corporation may be employed indiscriminately with other means to carry into execution the powers of the government, no particular reason can be assigned for excluding the use of a bank, if required for its fiscal operations. To use one, must be within the discretion of Congress, if it be an appropriate mode of executing the powers of government. That it is a convenient, a useful, and essential instrument in the prosecution of its fiscal operations, is not now a subject of controversy. All those who have been concerned in the administration of our finances, have concurred in representing the importance and necessity; and so strongly have they been felt, that statesmen of the first class, whose previous opinions against it had been confirmed by every circumstance which can fix the human judgment, have yielded those opinions to the exigencies of the nation. Under the confederation, Congress, justifying the measure by its necessity, transcended perhaps its powers to obtain the advantage of a bank; and our own legislation attests the universal conviction of the utility of this measure. The time has passed away when it can be necessary to enter into any discussion in order to prove the importance of this instrument, as a means to effect the legitimate objects of the government.

But, were its necessity less apparent, none can deny its being an appropriate measure; and if it is, the degree of its necessity, as has been very justly observed, is to be discussed in another place. Should Congress, in the execution of its powers, adopt measures which are prohibited by the constitution; or should Congress, under the pretext of executing its powers pass laws for the accomplishment of objects not entrusted to the government, it would become the painful duty of this tribunal, should a case requiring such a decision come before it, to say that such an act was not the law of the land. But where the law is not prohibited, and is really calculated to effect any of the objects entrusted to the government, to undertake here to inquire into the degree of its necessity, would be to pass the line which circumscribes the judicial department, and to tread on legislative ground. This court disclaims all pretensions to such a power.

After this declaration, it can scarcely be necessary to say that the existence of state banks can have no possible influence on the question. No trace is to be found in the constitution of an intention to create a dependence of the government of the Union on those of the states, for the execution of the great powers assigned to it. Its means are adequate to its ends; and on those means alone was it expected to rely for the accomplishment of its ends. To impose on it the necessity of resorting to means which it cannot control, which another government may furnish or withhold, would render its course precarious; the result of its measures uncertain, and create a dependence on other governments, which might disappoint its most important designs, and is incompatible with the language of the constitution. But were it otherwise, the choice of means implies a right to choose a national bank in preference to state banks, and Congress alone can make the election.

After the most deliberate consideration, it is the unanimous and decided opinion of this court that the act to incorporate the bank of the United States is a law made in pursuance of the constitution, and is a part of the supreme law of the land.

The branches, proceeding from the same stock, and being conducive to the complete accomplishment of the object, are equally constitutional. It would have been unwise to locate them in the charter, and it would be unnecessarily inconvenient to employ the legislative power in making those subordinate arrangements. The great duties of the bank are prescribed; those duties require branches; and the bank itself may, we think, be safely trusted with the selection of places where those branches shall be fixed; reserving always to the government the right to require that a branch shall be located where it may be deemed necessary.

It being the opinion of the court that the act incorporating the bank is constitutional, and that the power of establishing a branch in the state of Maryland might be properly exercised by the bank itself, we proceed to inquire:

2. Whether the state of Maryland may, without violating the constitution, tax that branch?

That the power of taxation is one of vital importance; that it is retained by the states; that it is not abridged by the grant of a similar power to the government of the Union; that it is to be concurrently exercised by the two governments: are truths which have never been denied. But, such is the paramount character of the constitution that its capacity to withdraw any subject from the action of even this power, is admitted. The states are expressly forbidden to lay any duties on imports or exports, except what may be absolutely necessary for executing their inspection laws. If the obligation of this prohibition must be conceded—if it may restrain a state from the exercise of its taxing power on imports and exports—the same paramount character would seem to restrain, as it certainly may restrain, a state from such other exercise of this power, as is in its nature incompatible with, and repugnant to, the constitutional laws of the Union. A law, absolutely repugnant to another, as entirely repeals that other as if express terms of repeal were used.

On this ground the counsel for the bank place its claim to be exempted from the power of a state to tax its operations. There is no express provision for the case, but the claim has been sustained on a principle which so entirely pervades the constitution, is so intermixed with the materials which compose it, so interwoven with its web, so blended with its texture, as to be incapable of being separated from it without rending it into shreds.

This great principle is, that the constitution and the laws made in pursuance thereof are supreme; that they control the constitution and laws of the respective states, and cannot be controlled by them. From this, which may be almost termed an axiom, other propositions are deduced as corollaries, on the truth or error of which, and on their application to this case, the cause has been supposed to depend. These are, 1st. that a power to create implies a power to preserve. 2d. That a power to destroy, if wielded by a different hand, is hostile to, and incompatible with these powers to create and to preserve. 3d. That where this repugnancy exists, that authority which is supreme must control, not yield to that over which it is supreme.

These propositions, as abstract truths, would, perhaps, never be controverted. Their application to this case, however, has been denied; and, both in maintaining the affirmative and the negative, a splendor of eloquence, and strength of argument seldom, if ever, surpassed, have been displayed.

The power of Congress to create, and of course to continue, the bank, was the subject of the preceding part of this opinion; and is no longer to be considered as questionable.

That the power of taxing it by the states may be exercised so as to destroy it, is too obvious to be denied. But taxation is said to be an absolute power, which acknowledges no other limits than those expressly prescribed in the constitution, and like sovereign power of every other description, is trusted to the discretion of those who use it. But the very terms of this argument admit that the sovereignty of the state, in the article of taxation itself, is subordinate to, and may be controlled by the constitution of the United States. How far it has been controlled by that instrument must be a question of construction. In making this construction, no principle not declared can be admissible, which would defeat the legitimate operations of a supreme government. It is of the very essence of supremacy to remove all obstacles to its action within its own sphere, and so to modify every power vested in subordinate governments as to exempt its own operations from their own influence. This effect need not be stated in terms. It is so involved in the declaration of supremacy, so necessarily implied in it, that the expression of it could not make it more certain. We must, therefore, keep it in view while construing the constitution.

The argument on the part of the state of Maryland is, not that the states may directly resist a law of Congress, but that they may exercise their acknowledged powers upon it, and that the constitution leaves them this right in the confidence that they will not abuse it.

Before we proceed to examine this argument, and to subject it to the test of the constitution, we must be permitted to bestow a few considerations on the nature and extent of this original right of taxation, which is acknowledged to remain with the states. It is admitted that the power of taxing the people and their property is essential to the very existence of government, and may be legitimately exercised on the objects to which it is applicable, to the utmost extent to which the government may choose to carry it. The only security against the abuse of this power is found in the structure of the government itself. In imposing a tax the legislature acts upon its constituents. This is in general a sufficient security against erroneous and oppressive taxation.

The people of a state, therefore, give to their government a right of taxing themselves and their property, and as the exigencies of government cannot be limited, they prescribe no limits to the exercise of this right, resting confidently on the interest of the legislator, and on the influence of the constituents over their representative, to guard them against its abuse. But the means employed by the government of the Union have no such security, nor is the right of a state to tax them sustained by the same theory. Those means are not given by the people of a particular state, not given by the constituents of the legislature, which claim the right to tax them, but by the people of all the states. They are given by all, for the benefit of all—and upon theory, should be subjected to that government only which belongs to all.

It may be objected to this definition, that the power of taxation is not confined to the people and property of a state. It may be exercised upon every object brought within its jurisdiction.

This is true. But to what source do we trace this right? It is obvious that it is an incident of sovereignty, and is co-extensive with that to which it is an incident. All subjects over which the sovereign power of a state extends, are objects of taxation; but those over which it does not extend, are, upon the soundest principles, exempt from taxation. This proposition may almost be pronounced self-evident.

The sovereignty of a state extends to everything which exists by its own authority, or is introduced by its permission; but does it extend to those means which are employed by Congress to carry into execution—powers conferred on that body by the people of the United States? We think it demonstrable that it does not. Those powers are not given by the people of a single state. They are given by the people of the United States, to a government whose laws, made in pursuance of the constitution, are declared to be supreme. Consequently, the people of a single state cannot confer a sovereignty which will extend over them.

If we measure the power of taxation residing in a state, by the extent of sovereignty which the people of a single state possess, and can confer on its government, we have an intelligible standard, applicable to every case to which the power may be applied. We have a principle which leaves the power of taxing the people and property of a state unimpaired; which leaves to a state the command of all its resources, and which places beyond its reach, all those powers which are conferred by the people of the United States on the government of the Union, and all those means which are given for the purpose of carrying those powers into execution. We have a principle which is safe for the states, and safe for the Union. We are relieved, as we ought to be, from clashing sovereignty; from interfering powers; from a repugnancy between a right in one government to pull down what there is an acknowledged right in another to build up; from the incompatibility of a right in one government to destroy what there is a right in another to preserve. We are not driven to the perplexing inquiry, so unfit for the judicial department, what degree of taxation is the legitimate use, and what degree may amount to the abuse of the power. The attempt to use it on the means employed by the government of the Union, in pursuance of the constitution, is itself an abuse, because it is the usurpation of a power which the people of a single state cannot give.

We find, then, on just theory, a total failure of this original right to tax the means employed by the government of the Union, for the execution of its powers. The right never existed, and the question whether it has been surrendered, cannot arise.

But, waiving this theory for the present, let us resume the inquiry, whether this power can be exercised by the respective states, consistently with a fair construction of the constitution.

That the power to tax involves the power to destroy; that the power to destroy may defeat and render useless the power to create; that there is a plain repugnance, in conferring on one government a power to control the constitutional measures of another, which other, with respect to those very measures, is declared to be supreme over that which exerts the control, are propositions not to be denied. But all inconsistencies are to be reconciled by the magic of the word CONFIDENCE. Taxation, it is said, does not necessarily and unavoidably destroy. To carry it to the excess of destruction would be an abuse, to presume which, would banish that confidence which is essential to all government.

But is this a case of confidence? Would the people of any one state trust those of another with a power to control the most insignificant operations of their state government? We know they would not. Why, then, should we suppose that the people of any one state should be willing to trust those of another with a power to control the operations of a government to which they have confided the most important and most valuable interests? In the legislature of the Union alone, are all represented. The legislature of the Union alone, therefore, can be trusted by the people with the power of controlling measures which concern all, in the confidence that it will not be abused. This, then, is not a case of confidence, and we must consider it as it really is.

If we apply the principle for which the state of Maryland contends, to the constitution generally, we shall find it capable of changing totally the character of that instrument. We shall find it capable of arresting all the measures of the government, and of prostrating it at the foot of the states. The American people have declared their constitution, and the laws made in pursuance thereof, to be supreme; but this principle would transfer the supremacy, in fact, to the states.

If the states may tax one instrument, employed by the government in the execution of its powers, they may tax any and every other instrument. They may tax the mail; they may tax the mint; they may tax patent-rights; they may tax the papers of the custom-house; they may tax judicial process; they may tax all the means employed by the government, to an excess which would defeat all the ends of government. This was not intended by the American people. They did not design to make their government dependent on the states.

Gentlemen say they do not claim the right to extend state taxation to these objects. They limit their pretensions to property. But on what principle is this distinction made? Those who make it have furnished no reason for it, and the principle for which they contend denies it. They contend that the power of taxation has no other limit than is found in the 10th section of the 1st article of the constitution; that, with respect to everything else, the power of the states is supreme, and admits of no control. If this be true, the distinction between property and other subjects to which the power of taxation is applicable, is merely arbitrary, and can never be sustained. This is not all. If the controlling power of the states be established; if their supremacy as to taxation be acknowledged; what is to restrain their exercising this control in any shape they may please to give it? Their sovereignty is not confined to taxation. That is not the only mode in which it might be displayed. The question is, in truth, a question of supremacy; and if the right of the states to tax the means employed by the general government be conceded, the declaration that the constitution, and the laws made in pursuance thereof, shall be the supreme law of the land, is empty and unmeaning declamation.

In the course of the argument, *The Federalist* has been quoted; and the opinions expressed by the authors of that work have been justly supposed to be entitled to great respect in expounding the constitution. No tribute can be paid to them which exceeds their merit; but in applying their opinions to the cases which may arise in the progress of our government, a right to judge of their correctness must be retained; and, to understand the argument, we must examine the proposition it maintains, and the objections against which it is directed. The subject of those numbers, from which passages have been cited, is the unlimited power of taxation which is vested in the general government. The objection to this unlimited power, which the argument seeks to remove, is stated with fullness and clearness. It is, "that an indefinite power of taxation in the latter (the government of the Union) might, and probably would, in time, deprive the former (the government of the states) of the means of providing for their own necessities; and would subject them entirely to the mercy of the national legislature. As the laws of the Union are to become the supreme law of the land; as it is to have power to pass all laws that may be necessary for carrying into execution the authorities with which it is proposed to vest it; the national government might at any time abolish the taxes imposed for state objects, upon the pretense of an interference with its own. It might allege a necessity for doing this, in order to give efficacy to the national revenues; and thus all the resources of taxation might, by degrees, become the subjects of federal monopoly, to the entire exclusion and destruction of the state governments."

The objections to the constitution which are noticed in these numbers, were to the undefined power of the government to tax, not to the incidental privilege of exempting its own measures from state taxation. The consequences apprehended from this undefined power were, that it would absorb all the objects of taxation, "to the exclusion and destruction of the state governments." The arguments of *The Federalist* are intended to prove the fallacy of these apprehensions; not to prove that the government was incapable of executing any of its powers, without exposing the means it employed to the embarrassments of state taxation. Arguments urged against these objections, and these apprehensions, are to be understood as relating to the points they mean to prove. Had the authors of those excellent essays been asked, whether they contended for that construction of the constitution, which would place within the reach of the states those measures which the government might adopt for the execution of its powers; no man, who has read their instructive pages, will hesitate to admit that their answer must have been in the negative.

It has also been insisted, that, as the power of taxation in the general and state governments is acknowledged to be concurrent, every argument which would sustain the right of the general government to tax banks chartered by the states, will equally sustain the right of the states to tax banks chartered by the general government.

But the two cases are not on the same reason. The people of all the states have created the general government, and have conferred upon it the general power of taxation. The people of all the states, and the states themselves, are represented in Congress, and, by their representatives, exercise this power. When they tax the chartered institutions of the states, they tax their constituents; and these taxes must be uniform. But, when a state taxes the operations of the government of the United States, it acts upon institutions created, not by their own constituents, but by people over whom they claim no control. It acts upon the measures of a government created by others as well as themselves, for the benefit of others in common with themselves. The difference is that which always exists, and always must exist, between the action of the whole on a part, and the action of a part on the whole—between the laws of a government declared to be supreme, and those of a government which, when in opposition to those laws, is not supreme.

But if the full application of this argument could be admitted, it might bring into question the right of Congress to tax the state banks, and could not prove the right of the states to tax the Bank of the United States.

The court has bestowed on this subject its most deliberate consideration. The result is a conviction that the states have no power, by taxation or otherwise, to retard, impede, burden, or in any manner control the operations of the constitutional laws enacted by Congress to carry into execution the powers vested in the general government. This is, we think, the unavoidable consequence of that supremacy which the constitution has declared.

We are unanimously of opinion that the law passed by the legislature of Maryland, imposing a tax on the Bank of the United States, is unconstitutional and void.

This opinion does not deprive the states of any resources which they originally possessed. It does not extend to a tax paid by the real property of the bank, in common with the other real property within the state, nor to a tax imposed on the interest which the citizens of Maryland may hold in this institution, in common with other property of the same description throughout the state. But this is a tax on the operations of the bank, and is, consequently, a tax on the operation of an instrument employed by the government of the Union to carry its powers into execution. Such a tax must be unconstitutional.

DARTMOUTH COLLEGE v. WOODWARD, 4 WHEAT. 518 (1819)

The royal corporate charter of Dartmouth College was altered by act of the New Hampshire legislature and a new board of trustees appointed. This case raised the issue of the power of a state legislature to take this action in light of the "obligation of contract" clause of the federal Constitution. Chief Justice Marshall for the Court held that New Hampshire succeeded to the contractual obligations of the Crown and that it was bound to abide by the Crown's contractual guarantees to the trustees and benefactors of Dartmouth College. He said that Dartmouth was a private and not a public corporation, and hence it was not subject to the general direction of the legislature. While the trustees of Dartmouth College continued to function under the terms of the royal charter, any legislative act by the state that altered its board of trustees impaired the obligation of contract and violated the federal Constitution. From this opinion, Justice Gabriel Duvall dissented without opinion.

The opinion of the court was delivered by MARSHALL, *Ch. J.:*

This is an action of trover, brought by the trustees of Dartmouth College against William H. Woodward, in the State Court of New Hampshire, for the book of records, corporate seal, and other corporate property, to which the plaintiffs allege themselves to be entitled.

A special verdict, after setting out the rights of the parties, finds for the defendant, if certain acts of the legislature of New Hampshire, passed on the 27th of June, and on the 18th of December, 1816, be valid, and binding on the trustees without their assent, and not repugnant to the constitution of the United States; otherwise, it finds for the plaintiffs.

The Superior Court of Judicature of New Hampshire rendered a judgment upon this verdict for the defendant, which judgment has been brought before this court by writ of error. The single question now to be considered is, do the acts to which the verdict refers violate the constitution of the United States?

This court can be insensible neither to the magnitude nor delicacy of this question. The validity of a legislative act is to be examined; and the opinion of the highest law tribunal of a state is to be revised: an opinion which carries with it intrinsic evidence of the diligence, of the ability, and the integrity, with which it was formed. On more than one occasion this court has expressed the cautious circumspection with which it approaches the consideration of such questions; and has declared that, in no doubtful case would it pronounce a legislative act to be contrary to the constitution. But the American people have said, in the constitution of the United States, that "no state shall pass any bill of attainder, *ex post facto* law, or law impairing the obligation of contracts." In the same instrument they have also said, "that the judicial power shall extend to all cases in law and equity arising under the constitution." On the judges of this court, then, is imposed the high and solemn duty of protecting, from even legislative violation, those contracts which the constitution of our country has placed beyond legislative control; and, however irksome the task may be, this is a duty from which we dare not shrink.

The title of the plaintiffs originates in a charter dated the 13th day of December, in the year 1769, incorporating twelve persons therein mentioned, by the name of "The Trustees of Dartmouth College," granting to them and their successors the usual corporate privileges and powers, and authorizing the trustees, who are to govern the college, to fill up all vacancies which may be created in their own body.

The defendant claims under three acts of the legislature of New Hampshire, the most material of which was passed on the 27th of June, 1816, and is entitled, "an act to amend the charter, and enlarge and improve the corporation of Dartmouth College." Among other alterations in the charter, this act increases the number of trustees to twenty-one, gives the appointment of the additional members to the executive of the state, and creates a board of overseers, with power to inspect and control the most important acts of the trustees. This board consists of twenty-five persons. The president of the senate, the speaker of the house of representatives, of New Hampshire, and the Governor and Lieutenant-Governor of Vermont, for the time being, are to be members *ex officio*. The board is to be completed by the Governor and council of New Hampshire, who are also empowered to fill all vacancies which may occur. The acts of the 18th and 26th of December are supplemental to that of the 27th of June, and are principally intended to carry that act into effect.

The majority of the trustees of the college have refused to accept this amended charter, and have brought this suit for the corporate property, which is in possession of a person holding by virtue of the acts which have been stated.

It can require no argument to prove that the circumstances of this case constitute a contract. An application is made to the crown for a charter to incorporate a religious and literary institution. In the application, it is stated that large contributions have been made for the object, which will be conferred on the corporation as soon as it shall be created. The charter is granted, and on its faith the property is conveyed. Surely in this transaction every ingredient of a complete and legitimate contract is to be found.

The points for consideration are:

1. Is this contract protected by the constitution of the United States?

2. Is it impaired by the acts under which the defendant holds?

1. On the first point it has been argued, that the word "contract," in its broadest sense, would comprehend the political relations between the government and its citizens, would extend to offices held within a state for state purposes, and to many of those laws concerning civil institutions, which must change with circumstances, and be modified by ordinary legislation; which deeply concern the public, and which, to preserve good government, the public judgment must control. That even marriage is a contract, and its obligations are affected by the laws respecting divorces. That the clause in the constitution, if construed in its greatest latitude, would prohibit these laws. Taken in its broad unlimited sense, the clause would be an unprofitable and vexatious interference with the internal concerns of a state, would unnecessarily and unwisely embarrass its legislation, and render immutable those civil institutions which are established for purposes of internal government, and which, to subserve those purposes, ought to vary with varying circumstances. That as the framers of the constitution could never have intended to insert in that instrument a provision so unnecessary, so mischievous, and so repugnant to its general spirit, the term "contract" must be understood in a more limited sense. That it must be understood as intended to guard against a power of at least doubtful utility, the abuse of which had been extensively felt; and to restrain the legislature in future from violating the right to property. That anterior to the formation of the constitution, a course of legislation had prevailed in many, if not in all, of the states, which weakened the confidence of man in man, and embarrassed all transactions between individuals, by dispensing with a faithful performance of engagements. To correct this mischief, by restraining the power which produced it, the state legislatures were forbidden "to pass any law impairing the obligation of contracts," that is, of contracts respecting property, under which some individual could claim a right to something beneficial to himself; and that since the clause in the constitution must in construction receive some limitation, it may be confined, and ought to be confined, to cases of this description; to cases within the mischief it was intended to remedy.

The general correctness of these observations cannot be controverted. That the framers of the constitution did not intend to restrain the states in the regulation of their civil institutions, adopted for internal government, and that the instrument they have given us is not to be so construed, may be admitted. The provision of the constitution never has been understood to embrace other contracts than those which respect property, or some object of value, and confer rights which may be asserted in a court of justice. It never has been understood to restrict the general right of the legislature to legislate on the subject of divorces. Those acts enable some tribunal, not to impair a marriage contract, but to liberate one of the parties because it has been broken by the other. When any state legislature shall pass an act annulling all marriage contracts, or allowing either party to annul it without the consent of the other, it will be time enough to inquire whether such an act be constitutional.

The parties in this case differ less on general principles, less on the true construction of the constitution in the abstract, than on the application of those principles to this case, and on the true construction of the charter of 1769. This is the point on which the cause essentially depends. If the act of incorporation be a grant of political power, if it create a civil institution to be employed in the administration of the government, or if the funds of the college be public property, or if the state of New Hampshire, as a government, be alone interested in its transactions, the subject is one in which the legislature of the state may act according to its own judgment, unrestrained by any limitation of its power imposed by the constitution of the United States.

But if this be a private eleemosynary institution, endowed with a capacity to take property for objects unconnected with government, whose funds are bestowed by individuals on the faith of the charter; if the donors have stipulated for the future disposition and management of those funds in the manner prescribed by themselves, there may be more difficulty in the case, although neither the persons who have made these stipulations nor those for whose benefit they were made, should be parties to the cause. Those who are no longer interested in the property, may yet retain such an interest in the preservation of their own arrangements as to have a right to insist that those arrangements shall be held sacred. Or, if they have themselves disappeared, it becomes a subject of serious and anxious inquiry, whether those whom they have legally empowered to represent them forever may not assert all the rights which they possessed, while in being; whether, if they be without personal representatives who may feel injured by a violation of the compact, the trustees be not so completely their representatives, in the eye of the law, as to stand in their place, not only as respects the government of the college, but also as respects the maintenance of the college charter.

It becomes, then, the duty of the court most seriously to examine this charter, and to ascertain its true character.

From the instrument itself, it appears that about the year 1754, the Rev. Eleazar Wheelock established at his own expense, and on his own estate, a charity-school for the instruction of Indians in the Christian religion. The success of this institution inspired him with the design of soliciting contributions in England for carrying on, and extending, his undertaking. In this pious work he employed the Rev. Nathaniel Whitaker, who, by virtue of a power of attorney from Dr. Wheelock, appointed the Earl of Dartmouth and others, trustees of the money which had been, and should be, contributed; which appointment Dr. Wheelock confirmed by a deed of trust authorizing the trustees to fix on a site for the college. They determined to establish the school on Connecticut River, in the western part of New Hampshire; that situation being supposed favorable for carrying on the original design among the Indians, and also for promoting learning among the English; and the proprietors in the neighborhood having made large offers of land, on condition that the college should there be placed. Dr. Wheelock then applied to the crown for an act of incorporation, and represented the expediency of appointing those whom he had, by his last will, named as trustees in America, to be members of the proposed corporation. "In consideration of the premises," "for the education and instruction of the youth of the Indian tribes," &c., "and also of English youth, and any others," the charter was granted, and the trustees of Dartmouth college were by that name created a body corporate, with power, for the use of the said college, to acquire real and personal property, and to pay the president, tutors, and other officers of the college, such salaries as they shall allow.

The charter proceeds to appoint Eleazar Wheelock, "the founder of said college," president thereof, with power by his last will to appoint a successor, who is to continue in office until disapproved by the trustees. In case of vacancy, the trustees may appoint a president, and in case of the ceasing of a president, the senior professor or tutor, being one of the trustees, shall exercise the office, until an appointment shall be made. The trustees have power to appoint and displace professors, tutors, and other officers, and to supply any vacancies which may be created in their own body, by death, resignation, removal, or disability; and also to make orders, ordinances, and laws, for the government of the college, the same not being repugnant to the laws of Great Britain, or of New Hampshire, and not excluding any person on account of his speculative sentiments in religion, or his being of a religious profession different from that of the trustees.

This charter was accepted, and the property, both real and personal, which had been contributed for the benefit of the college, was conveyed to, and vested in, the corporate body.

From this brief review of the most essential parts of the charter, it is apparent that the funds of the college consisted entirely of private donations. It is, perhaps, not very important who were the donors. The probability is, that the Earl of Dartmouth, and the other trustees in England, were, in fact, the largest contributors. Yet the legal conclusion, from the facts recited in the charter, would probably be, that Dr. Wheelock was the founder of the college.

The origin of the institution was, undoubtedly, the Indian charity-school, established by Dr. Wheelock, at his own expense. It was at his instance, and to enlarge this school, that contributions were solicited in England. The person soliciting these contributions was his agent; and the trustees, who received the money, were appointed by, and act under, his authority. It is not too much to say that the funds were obtained by him, in trust, to be applied by him to the purposes of his enlarged school. The charter of incorporation was granted at his instance. The persons named by him in his last will, as the trustees of his charity school, compose a part of the corporation, and he is declared to be the founder of the college, and its president for life. Were the inquiry material, we should feel some hesitation in saying that Dr. Wheelock was not, in law, to be considered as the founder[1] of this institution, and as possessing all the rights appertaining to that character. But be this as it may, Dartmouth College is really endowed by private individuals, who have bestowed their funds for the propagation of the Christian religion among the Indians, and for the promotion of piety and learning generally. From these funds the salaries of the tutors are drawn; and these salaries lessen the expense of education to the students. It is, then, an eleemosynary,[2] and, as far as respects its funds, a private corporation.

Do its objects stamp on it a different character? Are the trustees and professors public officers, invested with any portion of political power, partaking in any degree in the administration of civil government, and performing duties which flow from the sovereign authority?

That education is an object of national concern, and a proper subject of legislation, all admit. That there may be an institution founded by government, and placed entirely under its immediate control, the officers of which would be public officers, amenable exclusively to government, none will deny. But is Dartmouth College such an institution? Is education altogether in the hands of government? Does every teacher of youth become a public officer, and do donations for the purpose of education necessarily become public property, so far that the will of the legislature, not the will of the donor, becomes the law of the donation? These questions are of serious moment to society, and deserve to be well considered.

Doctor Wheelock, as the keeper of his charity-school, instructing the Indians in the art of reading, and in our holy religion; sustaining them at his own expense, and on the voluntary contributions of the charitable, could scarcely be considered as a public officer, exercising any portion of those duties which belong to government; nor could the legislature have supposed that his private funds, or those given by others, were subject to legislative management, because they were applied to the purposes of education. When, afterwards, his school was enlarged, and the liberal contributions made in England, and in America, enabled him to extend his cares to the education of the youth of his own country, no change was wrought in his own character, or in the nature of his duties. Had he employed assistant tutors with the funds contributed by others, or had the trustees in England established a school with Dr. Wheelock at its head, and paid salaries to him and his assistants, they would still have been private tutors; and the fact that they were employed in the education of youth could not have converted them into public officers, concerned in the administration of public duties, or have given the legislature a right to interfere in the management of the fund. The trustees, in whose care that fund was placed by the contributors, would have been permitted to execute their trust uncontrolled by legislative authority.

Whence, then, can be derived the idea that Dartmouth College has become a public institution, and its trustees public officers, exercising powers conferred by the public for public objects? Not from the source

[1] *1 Bl. Com. 481.*
[2] *1 Bl. Com. 471.*

whence its funds were drawn; for its foundation is purely private and eleemosynary. Not from the application of those funds; for money may be given for education, and the persons receiving it do not, by being employed in the education of youth, become members of the civil government. Is it from the act of incorporation? Let this subject be considered.

A corporation is an artificial being, invisible, intangible, and existing only in contemplation of law. Being the mere creature of law, it possesses only those properties which the charter of its creation confers upon it, either expressly or as incidental to its very existence. These are such as are supposed best calculated to effect the object for which it was created. Among the most important are immortality, and, if the expression may be allowed, individuality; properties by which a perpetual succession of many persons are considered as the same, and may act as a single individual. They enable a corporation to manage its own affairs, and to hold property without the perplexing intricacies, the hazardous and endless necessity, of perpetual conveyances for the purpose of transmitting it from hand to hand. It is chiefly for the purpose of clothing bodies of men, in succession, with these qualities and capacities, that corporations were invented, and are in use. By these means, a perpetual succession of individuals are capable of acting for the promotion of the particular object, like one immortal being. But this being does not share in the civil government of the country, unless that be the purpose for which it was created. Its immortality no more confers on it political power, or a political character, than immortality would confer such power or character on a natural person. It is no more a state instrument than a natural person exercising the same powers would be. If, then, a natural person, employed by individuals in the education of youth, or for the government of a seminary in which youth is educated, would not become a public officer, or be considered as a member of the civil government, how is it that this artificial being, created by law, for the purpose of being employed by the same individuals for the same purposes, should become a part of the civil government of the country? Is it because its existence, its capacities, its powers, are given by law? Because the government has given it the power to take and to hold property in a particular form, and for particular purposes, has the government a consequent right substantially to change that form, or to vary the purposes to which the property is to be applied? This principle has never been asserted or recognized, and is supported by no authority. Can it derive aid from reason?

The objects for which a corporation is created are universally such as the government wishes to promote. They are deemed beneficial to the country; and this benefit constitutes the consideration, and, in most cases, the sole consideration of the grant. In most eleemosynary institutions, the object would be difficult, perhaps unattainable, without the aid of a charter of incorporation. Charitable, or public-spirited individuals, desirous of making permanent appropriations for charitable or other useful purposes, find it impossible to effect their design securely, and certainly, without an incorporating act. They apply to the government, state their beneficent objects, and offer to advance the money necessary for its accomplishment, provided the government will confer on the instrument which is to execute their designs the capacity to execute them. The proposition is considered and approved. The benefit to the public is considered as an ample compensation for the faculty it confers, and the corporation is created. If the advantages to the public constitute a full compensation for the faculty it gives, there can be no reason for exacting a further compensation, by claiming a right to exercise over this artificial being a power which changes its nature, and touches the fund, for the security and application of which it was created. There can be no reason for implying in a charter, given for a valuable consideration, a power which is not only not expressed, but is in direct contradiction to its express stipulations.

From the fact, then, that a charter of incorporation has been granted, nothing can be inferred which changes the character of the institution, or transfers to the government any new power over it. The character of civil institutions does not grow out of their incorporation, but out of the manner in which they are formed, and the objects for which they are created. The right to change them is not founded on their being incorporated, but on their being the instruments of government, created for its purposes. The same institutions, created for the same objects, though not incorporated, would be public institutions, and, of course, be controllable by the legislature. The incorporating act neither gives nor prevents this control. Neither, in reason, can the incorporating act change the character of a private eleemosynary institution.

We are next led to the inquiry, for whose benefit the property given to Dartmouth College was secured. The counsel for the defendant have insisted that the beneficial interest is in the people of New Hampshire. The charter, after reciting the preliminary measures which had been taken, and the application for an act of incorporation, proceeds thus: "Know ye, therefore, that we, considering the premises, and being willing to encourage the laudable and charitable design of spreading Christian knowledge among the savages of our American wilderness, and, also, that the best means of education be established, in our province of New Hampshire, for the benefit of said province, do, of our special grace," &c. Do these expressions bestow on New Hampshire any exclusive right to the property of the college, any exclusive interest in the labors of the professors? Or do they merely indicate a willingness that New Hampshire should enjoy those advantages which result to all from the establishment of a seminary of learning in the neighborhood? On this point we think it impossible to entertain a serious doubt. The words themselves, unexplained by the context, indicate that the "benefit intended for the province" is that which is derived from "establishing the best means of education therein;" that is, from establishing in the province Dartmouth College, as constituted by the charter. But, if these words, considered alone, could admit of doubt, that doubt is completely removed by an inspection of the entire instrument.

The particular interests of New Hampshire never entered into the mind of the donors, never constituted a motive for their donation. The propagation of the Christian religion among the savages, and the dissemination of useful knowledge among the youth of the country, were the avowed and the sole objects of their contributions. In these, New Hampshire would participate; but nothing particular or exclusive was intended for her. Even the site of the college was selected, not for the sake of New Hampshire, but because it was "most subservient to the great ends in view," and because liberal donations of land were offered by the proprietors, on condition that the institution should be there established. The real advantages from the location of the college, are, perhaps, not less considerable to those on the west than to those on the east side of Connecticut River. The clause which constitutes the incorporation, and expresses the objects for which it was made, declares those objects to be the instruction of the Indians, "and also of English youth, and any others." So that the objects of the contributors, and the incorporating act, were the same; the promotion of Christianity, and of education generally, not the interests of New Hampshire particularly.

From this review of the charter, it appears that Dartmouth College is an eleemosynary institution, incorporated for the purpose of perpetuating the application of the bounty of the donors, to the specified objects of that bounty; that its trustees or governors were originally named by the founder, and invested with the power of perpetuating themselves; that they are not public officers, nor is it a civil institution, participating in the administration of government; but a charity school, or a seminary of education, incorporated for the preservation of its property, and the perpetual application of that property to the objects of its creation.

Yet a question remains to be considered, of more real difficulty, on which more doubt has been entertained than on all that have been discussed. The founders of the college, at least those whose contributions were in money, have parted with the property bestowed upon it, and their representatives have no interest in that property. The donors of land are equally without interest, so long as the corporation shall exist. Could they be found, they are unaffected by any alteration in its constitution, and probably regardless of its form, or even of its existence. The students are fluctuating, and no individual among our youth has a vested interest in the institution, which can be asserted in a court of justice. Neither the founders of the college nor the youth for whose benefit it was founded complain of the alteration made in its charter, or think themselves injured by it. The trustees alone complain, and the trustees have no beneficial interest to be protected. Can this be such a contract as the constitution intended to withdraw from the power of state legislation? Contracts, the parties to which have a vested beneficial interest, and those only, it has been said, are the objects about which the constitution is solicitous, and to which its protection is extended.

The court has bestowed on this argument the most deliberate consideration, and the result will be stated. Dr. Wheelock, acting for himself, and for those who, at his solicitation, had made contributions to his school, applied for this charter, as the instrument which should enable him, and them, to perpetuate their beneficent intention. It was granted. An artificial, immortal being, was created by the crown, capable of receiving and distributing forever, according to the will of the donors, the donations which should be made to it. On this being, the contributions which had been collected were immediately bestowed. These gifts were made, not, indeed, to make a profit for the donors, or their posterity, but for something in their opinion of inestimable value; for something which they deemed a full equivalent for the money with which it was purchased. The consideration for which they stipulated, is the perpetual application of the fund to its object, in the mode prescribed by themselves. Their descendants may take no interest in the preservation of this consideration. But in this respect their descendants are not their representatives. They are represented by the corporation. The corporation is the assignee of their rights, stands in their place, and distributes their bounty, as they would themselves have distributed it, had they been immortal. So with respect to the students who are to derive learning from this source. The corporation is a trustee for them also. Their potential rights, which, taken distributively, are imperceptible, amount collectively to a most important interest. These are, in the aggregate, to be exercised, asserted and protected, by the corporation. They were as completely out of the donors, at the instant of their being vested in the corporation, and as incapable of being asserted by the students, as at present.

According to the theory of the British constitution, their parliament is omnipotent. To annul corporate rights might give a shock to public opinion, which that government has chosen to avoid; but its power is not questioned. Had parliament, immediately after the emanation of this charter, and the execution of those conveyances which followed it, annulled the instrument, so that the living donors would have witnessed the disappointment of their hopes, the perfidy of the transaction would have been universally acknowledged. Yet then, as now, the donors would have had no interest in the property; then, as now, those who might be students would have had no rights to be violated; then, as now, it might be said, that the trustees, in whom the rights of all were combined, possessed no private, individual, beneficial interest in the property confided to their protection. Yet the contract would at that time have been deemed sacred by all. What has since occurred to strip it of its inviolability? Circumstances have not changed it. In reason, in justice, and in law, it is now what it was in 1769.

This is plainly a contract to which the donors, the trustees, and the crown (to whose rights and obligations New Hampshire succeeds), were the orignal parties. It is a contract made on a valuable consideration. It is a contract for the security and disposition of property. It is a contract, on the faith of which real and personal estate has been conveyed to the corporation. It is then a contract within the letter of the constitution, and within its spirit also, unless the fact that the property is invested by the donors in trustees for the promotion of religion and education, for the benefit of persons who are perpetually changing, though the objects remain the same, shall create a particular exception, taking this case out of the prohibition contained in the constitution.

It is more than possible that the preservation of rights of this description was not particularly in the view of the framers of the constitution when the clause under consideration was introduced into that instrument. It is probable that interferences of more frequent recurrence, to which the temptation was stronger, and of which the mischief was more extensive, constituted the great motive for imposing this restriction on the state legislatures. But although a particular and a rare case may not, in itself, be of sufficient magnitude to induce a rule, yet it must be governed by the rule, when established, unless some plain and strong reason for excluding it can be given. It is not enough to say that this particular case was not in the mind of the convention when the article was framed, nor of the American people when it was adopted. It is necessary to go farther, and to say that, had this particular case been suggested, the language would have been so varied, as to exclude it, or it would have been made a special exception. The case being within the words of the rule, must be within its operation likewise, unless there be something in the literal construction so obviously absurd, or mischievous, or repugnant to the general spirit of the instrument, as to justify those who expound the constitution in making it an exception.

On what safe and intelligible ground

can this exception stand. There is no exception in the constitution, no sentiment delivered by its contemporaneous expounders, which would justify us in making it. In the absence of all authority of this kind, is there, in the nature and reason of the case itself, that which would sustain a construction of the constitution, not warranted by its words? Are contracts of this description of a character to excite so little interest that we must exclude them from the provisions of the constitution, as being unworthy of the attention of those who framed the instrument? Or does public policy so imperiously demand their remaining exposed to legislative alteration, as to compel us, or rather permit us to say that these words, which were introduced to give stability to contracts, and which in their plain import comprehend this contract, must yet be so construed as to exclude it?

Almost all eleemosynary corporations, those which are created for the promotion of religion, of charity, or of education, are of the same character. The law of this case is the law of all. In every literary or charitable institution, unless the objects of the bounty be themselves incorporated, the whole legal interest is in trustees, and can be asserted only by them. The donors, or claimants of the bounty, if they can appear in court at all, can appear only to complain of the trustees. In all other situations, they are identified with, and personated by, the trustees; and their rights are to be defended and maintained by them. Religion, Charity, and Education, are, in the law of England, legatees or donees, capable of receiving bequests or donations in this form. They appear in court, and claim or defend by the corporation. Are they of so little estimation in the United States that contracts for their benefit must be excluded from the protection of words which, in their natural import, include them? Or do such contracts so necessarily require new-modeling by the authority of the legislature that the ordinary rules of construction must be disregarded in order to leave them exposed to legislative alteration?

All feel that these objects are not deemed unimportant in the United States. The interest which this case has excited proves that they are not. The framers of the constitution did not deem them unworthy of its care and protection. They have, though in a different mode, manifested their respect for science, by reserving to the government of the Union the power "to promote the progress of science and useful arts, by securing for limited times to authors and inventors the exclusive right to their respective writings and discoveries." They have so far withdrawn science, and the useful arts, from the action of the state governments. Why, then, should they be supposed so regardless of contracts made for the advancement of literature as to intend to exclude them from provisions made for the security of ordinary contracts between man and man? No reason for making this supposition is perceived.

If the insignificance of the object does not require that we should exclude contracts respecting it from the protection of the constitution, neither, as we conceive, is the policy of leaving them subject to legislative alteration so apparent as to require a forced construction of that instrument in order to effect it. These eleemosynary institutions do not fill the place, which would otherwise be occupied by government, but that which would otherwise remain vacant. They are complete acquisitions to literature. They are donations to education; donations which any government must be disposed rather to encourage than to discountenance. It requires no very critical examination of the human mind to enable us to determine that one great inducement to these gifts is the conviction felt by the giver, that the disposition he makes of them is immutable. It is probable that no man ever was, and that no man ever will be, the founder of a college, believing at the time that an act of incorporation constitutes no security for the institution; believing that it is immediately to be deemed a public institution, whose funds are to be governed and applied, not by the will of the donor, but by the will of the legislature. All such gifts are made in the pleasing, perhaps delusive hope, that the charity will flow forever in the channel which the givers have marked out for it. If every man finds in his own bosom strong evidence of the universality of this sentiment, there can be but little reason to imagine that the framers of our constitution were strangers to it, and that, feeling the necessity and policy of giving permanence and security to contracts, of withdrawing them from the influence of legislative bodies, whose fluctuating policy, and repeated interferences, produced the most perplexing and injurious embarrassments, they still deemed it necessary to leave these contracts subject to those interferences. The motives for such an exception must be very powerful, to justify the construction which makes it.

The motives suggested at the bar grow out of the original appointment of the trustees, which is supposed to have been in a spirit hostile to the genius of our government, and the presumption that, if allowed to continue themselves, they now are, and must remain forever, what they originally were. Hence is inferred the necessity of applying to this corporation, and to other similar corporations, the correcting and improving hand of the legislature.

It has been urged repeatedly, and certainly with a degree of earnestness which attracted attention, that the trustees deriving their power from a regal source, must necessarily partake of the spirit of their origin; and that their first principles, unimproved by that resplendent light which has been shed around them, must continue to govern the college, and to guide the students. Before we inquire into the influence which this argument ought to have on the constitutional question, it may not be amiss to examine the fact on which it rests. The first trustees were undoubtedly named in the charter by the crown; but at whose suggestion were they named? By whom were they selected? The charter informs us. Dr. Wheelock had represented "that, for many weighty reasons, it would be expedient that the gentlemen whom he had already nominated in his last will, to be trustees in America, should be of the corporation now proposed." When, afterwards, the trustees are named in the charter, can it be doubted that the persons mentioned by Dr. Wheelock in his will were appointed? Some were probably added by the crown, with the approbation of Dr. Wheelock. Among these is the doctor himself. If any others were appointed at the instance of the crown, they are the governor, three members of the council, and the speaker of the house of representatives of the colony of New Hampshire. The stations filled by these persons ought to rescue them from any other imputation than too great a dependence on the crown. If, in the revolution that followed, they acted under the influence of this sentiment, they must have ceased to be trustees; if they took part with their countrymen, the imputation which suspicion might excite would no longer attach to them. The original trustees, then, or most of them, were named by Dr. Wheelock, and those who were added to his nomination, most probably with his approbation, were among the most eminent and respectable individuals in New Hampshire.

The only evidence which we possess of the character of Dr. Wheelock is furnished by this charter. The judicious means employed for the accomplishment of his object, and the success which attended his endeavors, would lead to the opinion that he united a sound understanding to that humanity and benevolence which suggested his undertaking. It surely cannot be assumed that his trustees were selected without judgment. With as little probability can it be assumed, that, while the light of science, and of liberal principles, pervades the whole community these originally benighted trustees remain in utter darkness, incapable of participating in the general improvement; that, while the human race is rapidly advancing, they are stationary. Reasoning *a priori,* we should believe that learned and intelligent men, selected by its patrons for the government of a literary institution, would select learned and intelligent men for their successors; men as well fitted for the government of a college as those who might be chosen by other means. Should this reasoning ever prove erroneous in a particular case, public opinion, as has been stated at the bar, would correct the institution. The mere possibility of the contrary would not justify a construction of the constitution which should exclude these contracts from the protection of a provision whose terms comprehend them.

The opinion of the court, after mature deliberation, is, that this is a contract, the obligation of which cannot be impaired without violating the constitution of the United States. This opinion appears to us to be equally supported by reason, and by the former decisions of this court.

2. We next proceed to the inquiry whether its obligation has been impaired by those acts of the legislature of New Hampshire to which the special verdict refers.

From the review of this charter, which has been taken, it appears that the whole power of governing the college, of appointing and removing tutors, of fixing their salaries, of directing the course of study to be pursued by the students, and of filling up vacancies created in their own body, was vested in the trustees. On the part of the crown it was expressly stipulated that this corporation, thus constituted, should continue forever; and that the number of trustees should forever consist of twelve, and no more. By this contract the crown was bound, and could have made no violent alteration in its essential terms, without impairing its obligation.

By the revolution, the duties, as well as the powers, of government devolved on the people of New Hampshire. It is admitted, that among the latter was comprehended the transcendent power of parliament, as well as that of the executive department. It is too clear to require the support of argument, that all contracts, and rights, respecting property, remained unchanged by the revolution. The obligations, then, which were created by the charter to Dartmouth College, were the same in the new that they had been in the old government. The power of the government was also the same. A repeal of this charter at any time prior to the adoption of the present constitution of the United States, would have been an extraordinary and unprecedented act of power, but one which could have been contested only by the restrictions upon the legislature, to be found in the constitution of the state. But the constitution of the United States has imposed this additional limitation, that the legislature of a state shall pass no act "impairing the obligation of contracts."

It has been already stated that the act "to amend the charter, and enlarge and improve the corporation of Dartmouth College," increases the number of trustees to twenty-one, gives the appointment of the additional members to the executive of the state, and creates a board of overseers, to consist of twenty-five persons, of whom twenty-one are also appointed by the executive of New Hampshire, who have power to inspect and control the most important acts of the trustees.

On the effect of this law, two opinions cannot be entertained. Between acting directly, and acting through the agency of trustees and overseers, no essential difference is perceived. The whole power of governing the college is transferred from trustees appointed according to the will of the founder, expressed in the charter, to the executive of New Hampshire. The management and application of the funds of this eleemosynary institution, which are placed by the donors in the hands of trustees named in the charter, and empowered to perpetuate themselves, are placed by this act under the control of the government of the state. The will of the state is substituted for the will of the donors, in every essential operation of the college. This is not an immaterial change. (The founders of the college contracted, not merely for the perpetual application of the funds which they gave, to the objects for which those funds were given; they contracted also to secure that application by the constitution of the corporation.) They contracted for a system which should, as far as human foresight can provide, retain forever the government of the literary institution they had formed, in the hands of persons approved by themselves. This system is totally changed. The charter of 1769 exists no longer. It is re-organized; and re-organized in such a manner as to convert a literary institution, moulded according to the will of its founders, and placed under the control of private literary men, into a machine entirely subservient to the will of government. This may be for the advantage of this college in particular, and may be for the advantage of literature in general, but it is not according to the will of the donors, and is subversive of that contract, on the faith of which their property was given.

In the view which has been taken of this interesting case, the court has confined itself to the right possessed by the trustees, as the assignees and representatives of the donors and founders, for the benefit of religion and literature. Yet it is not clear that the trustees ought to be considered as destitute of such beneficial interest in themselves as the law may respect. In addition to their being the legal owners of the property, and to their having a freehold right in the powers confided to them, the charter itself countenances the idea that trustees may also be tutors with salaries. The first president was one of the original trustees; and the charter provides, that in case of vacancy in that office, "the senior professor or tutor, being one of the trustees, shall exercise the office of president, until the trustees shall make choice of, and appoint a president." According to the tenor of the charter, then, the trustees might, without impropriety, appoint a president and other professors from their own body. This is a power not entirely unconnected with an interest. Even if the proposition of the counsel for the defendant were sustained; if it were admitted that those contracts only are protected by the constitution, a beneficial interest in which is vested in the party, who appears in court to assert that interest; yet it is by no means clear that the trustees of Dartmouth College have no beneficial interest in themselves.

But the court has deemed it unnecessary to investigate this particular point, being of opinion, on general principles, that in these private eleemosynary institutions, the body corporate, as possessing the whole legal and equitable interest, and completely representing the donors, for the purpose of executing the trust, has rights which are protected by the constitution.

It results from this opinion, that the acts of the legislature of New Hamsphire, which are stated in the special verdict found in this cause, are repugnant to the constitution of the United States; and that the judgment on this special verdict ought to have been for the plaintiffs. The judgment of the State Court must therefore be reversed.

William Johnson

☆ 1771–1834 ☆

APPOINTED BY

THOMAS JEFFERSON

YEARS ON COURT

1804–1834

William Johnson

by

DONALD MORGAN

WILLIAM JOHNSON of South Carolina was Thomas Jefferson's first appointee to the Supreme Court. His thirty-year term (1804–1834) spanned nearly the whole of Chief Justice John Marshall's. Of all the fifteen Justices who sat on the Marshall Court, he was, at least until 1830, the most independent and the most vocal in advancing opinions different from Marshall's. For his part in winning acceptance for dissenting opinions and for his contributions—critical and creative—to the constitutional doctrines of the Court, he has achieved a degree of immortality.

William Johnson was the second of eleven children born to William Johnson of Charleston, blacksmith and Revolutionary patriot. A native of New York, the father had come south in the early 1760's. His marriage in 1769 to Sarah Nightingale brought him properties at the death of her father, Thomas Nightingale, saddler and race-track owner, and related him through her mother with the English family of Amory. Although the first Johnson to immigrate, in 1659, was probably a native of Holland, most of the Justice's ancestors were English in origin.

The elder Johnson not only gave his son a model of civic involvement—he served nearly two decades after 1775 in the state legislature—but exposed him to both the intellectual ferment and physical hardships of the Revolution. As early as 1766 the blacksmith had met with other mechanics and artisans under a great oak to hear Christopher Gadsden, merchant and delegate to the recent Stamp Act Congress, denounce British claims to parliamentary supremacy. Gadsden favored united colonial action for American rights; his hearers received his address with "silent but profound devotion"; "with linked hands, the whole party pledged themselves to resist." Johnson continued a leader of this Liberty Tree party until independence.

DONALD G. MORGAN, Professor of Political Science at Mount Holyoke College, wrote Congress and the Constitution *and* Justice William Johnson, the First Dissenter.

War brought suffering to the Johnson family. When the British finally took Charleston after a third siege, they arrested the elder Johnson and then released him on parole. Later they sent him and some seventy other Charlestonians to detention in St. Augustine, Florida. After some months, a prisoner exchange freed him to sail for Philadelphia, where he rejoined his family, also now in exile. After a winter at the new capital, the refugees undertook the hazardous overland journey to Charleston. Wrote Joseph, younger brother of the Justice, of their return to the family plantation on Goose Creek:

> *It was a joyful home to us—far beyond our expectations in many of the dark and gloomy periods of our absence. It was a reunion with our family, and our affectionate faithful servants, after an absence of eighteen months, and of my father's absence two and a half years.*

Justice Johnson was to devote much attention to the veterans of the War of Independence. In an 1812 oration, he would describe the Revolution as a great effort to improve the conditions of man, "a 'pillar of fire,' to conduct man to that high destiny for which his powers are calculated."

Johnson must have pursued his studies in spite of wartime and postwar turmoil, for at Princeton he won honors for scholarship. President John Witherspoon had enriched the curriculum with new subjects including ethics, politics and government, and had made the college a school for national leaders. Johnson won a sophomore Latin prize and in 1790 stood at the head of the graduating class.

In Charleston again, Johnson read law with the Federalist leader, Charles Cotesworth Pinckney. Pinckney was one of several ornaments of the Charleston bar who had studied at the Inns of Court; at this time he was building a rich practice and serving as an adviser to President Washington. Johnson later lauded him for his profound knowledge of law and for "every quality that can render man amiable and estimable." Johnson was admitted to the bar in 1793.

Johnson was married in 1794 to Sarah Bennett of Charleston, sister of Thomas, a political associate of the Justice and later governor of the state. Of the eight children born to the Johnson's, only two lived to maturity; but when the servile revolt in Santo Domingo flooded the city with refugees, they adopted two additional children, John and Madeleine L'Engle.

Johnson's brief but meteoric political career began in 1794. His town and country properties, including slaves, were enough to qualify him to run for the state House of Representatives. At the October balloting, he succeeded, not as a Federalist, but as a Republican. In South Carolina Charles Pinckney, young cousin of the Federalist leader, was making Jefferson's new party a vehicle both for city mechanics in their democratic clubs and for upcountry farmers and planters. Johnson's victory doubtless resulted from his talents, his connections and his budding legal practice.

In the legislature he served three consecutive two-year terms. By 1797 he was serving on a three-man steering committee for the House and by 1798 as its Speaker. The 1790 state constitution gave the legislature a dominant role in the governmental structure and the times gave the Republican majority openings to institute reforms. Accordingly, Johnson's legislative experience was rich and varied. Penal laws, the militia system, the powers of the governor, the Jay Treaty with England on commerce, and most tenaciously the judicial system were among the matters that faced Johnson. When the court reform act enabled the legislature in 1799 to elect three judges to the state's highest court, William Johnson received one of the posts.

On this Court of Common Pleas, or Constitutional Court, Johnson spent the next four years. In some respects his experience on the state bench foreshadowed that on the federal. Thus, the court act, by instituting circuit-riding among the twenty-eight new judicial districts of the state, hardened Johnson for the rigors of travel throughout the federal Sixth Circuit, comprising South Carolina and Georgia. In addition, a case in the Sumter District posed problems he would confront later. One Pitman was indicted under a state law for counterfeiting the notes of the United States Bank. Pitman's counsel argued against trial in the state courts, asserting that the offense could exist only under federal law and could be tried only in federal courts. Johnson denied the objection insisting:

> *The national government may pass such laws as may be proper and necessary to avoid the mischiefs arising from the counterfeiting, and passing, as true, the forged bills of credit of the bank of the nation; but it cannot be maintained that the several State governments may not also pass such laws, as they shall deem necessary, to the welfare of their internal concerns, in relation to the same subject. The power and authority which may be used and exercised by each, in this behalf, is by no means incompatible, but perfectly reconcilable and consistent.* [State *v.* Pitman, *1 Brevard S.C. 32, 34 (1801)*.]

The statement is noteworthy in blending support of federal implied power to create a bank and issue bank notes with support of state concurrent power over the same subject pending federal preemption.

In other respects, Johnson's situation on the state court was in contrast to what followed. The Republican members of the state court enjoyed a majority, and due perhaps to the absence of a strong chief judge, a striking freedom of expression. Two-fifths of the decisions reported during Johnson's tenure came down in the form of *seriatim* opinions, each judge rendering his own.

Throughout the decade in state office, he remained an active citizen. Even while a state judge, he served *ex officio* as a trustee of the incipient South Carolina College at Columbia. As Board President (1802–1804) he was instrumental in digesting plans, supervising construction, and hiring faculty. In helping found what was to become the University of South Carolina, he revealed an interest in education and letters, a restless activism, and an impatience with judicial detachment that would be lifelong.

On March 22, 1804, the Senate took up President Jefferson's nomination of Johnson as Associate Justice. In April, the state judge received notification of the appointment and his commission. The offer, he soon wrote Secretary of State James Madison, was entirely unexpected.

Clearly the appointment was part of an on-going party and doctrinal struggle. The elections of 1800 had given Congress and the presidency to the Republicans. Before the turnover took place on March 4, 1801, the Federalist Congress had reorganized the federal courts, adding numerous judgeships, and President John Adams had nominated fellow partisans to fill them. He had also secured the appointment of John Marshall of Virginia to be Chief Justice. Marshall in turn had taken command of the one branch of government remaining Federalist and begun to equip it for the task of constitutional exposition, mainly along Federalist lines. The Court's unanimous decision in *Marbury* v. *Madison,* 1 Cranch 137 (1803), irritated Jefferson and the Republicans by its strictures on executive misconduct; more important, it established persuasively the principle of judicial review. Furthermore Marshall was now the voice of the Court; previously the Justices had enjoyed a wide freedom of expression, nearly one-fifth of the pre-Marshall decisions having appeared with *seriatim* opinions. Between Marshall's advent and the appearance of Johnson, every decision was unanimous, *seriatim* opinions vanished, Marshall authored all but two of the Court's opinions and only once was there a separate concurring opinion. Marshall had made himself the mouthpiece of defiant Federalism.

From his inauguration on, Jefferson directed the campaign of the Republicans. The Federalist's court act was repealed and a Republican reform substituted for it; District Judge John Pickering was impeached and removed and a similar though unsuccessful attempt directed against Samuel Chase, the most offensively partisan of the Federalist justices. The Judiciary had become an issue of national politics, and the Republicans sought ways to bring that branch into line with Republican doctrine. Johnson's appointment gave the party its first toehold in the Supreme Court.

In selecting his man, Jefferson put loyalty to party doctrine high on the list of qualifications. From two leading South Carolinians in Congress he received this appraisal of Johnson: "a state judge . . . an excellent lawyer, prompt, eloquent, of irreproachable character, Republican connections, and of good nerves in his political principles . . . was speaker some years." A Federalist Senator acknowledged that Johnson was able and honest and had risen to office "without the aid of family, friends, or connections, by his talents and persevering industry." The same Senator nevertheless labeled Johnson "a zealous democrat."

Events were to confirm Jefferson's confidence in Johnson's courage, independence and tenacity of opinion. The young Justice also brought to his task knowledge of other fields besides law. A zest for history, as well as for literary fame, led him to prepare and to publish in 1822 a two-volume life of General Nathanael Greene. This study of Washington's second-in-command served to some degree as a Republican antidote to Marshall's earlier *Washington* with its Federalist overtones. Johnson's blending of law, history and political experience with a high native intelligence helped fit him to view the constitutional trends of his time with prophetic insight.

Yet courage and independence sometimes turned into imprudence and precipitancy. To one lawyer, Charles J. Ingersoll, he seemed "bold, independent, eccentric, and sometimes harsh," and John Quincy Adams described him as "restless," "turbulent," and "hot-headed." At his death, the Charleston bar paid tribute to his "great power of analysis, and very acute discrimination," but the Rev. John Bachman found imperfections in his character:

he may have been at times too strenuous in the maintenance of the opinions he had adopted, and unwilling sufficiently to allow that others, who were investigating the same subject, and sought for truth equally with himself, could come to different conclusions without the imputation of weakness or obstinacy. . . .

Johnson's appearance reflected his character. In 1824 a reporter found him, "a large, athletic, well built man of sixty or upwards, with a full, ruddy and fair countenance, with thin white hair, and partially bald." Yet portraits give credence to Jonathan Elliott's comment that the judge was not known for a "fascinating exterior." The face is stern, reserved, and contemplative, even forbidding, with a smoldering fire in the eyes.

Such was the man who took the oath at the Savannah Circuit Court in May, 1804. He would need independence. At thirty-two and of modest origins, he would soon join a tribunal otherwise solidly Federalist whose members topped his age by an average of fourteen years and whose party carried the prestige of long office-holding and social standing. The Court's makeup would change. In 1807, Henry Brockholst Livingston of New York and in 1808 a seventh justice, Thomas Todd of Kentucky, joined Johnson on the bench. By 1812, the appointment of Gabriel Duval of Maryland and Joseph Story of Massachusetts gave the Republicans five seats as against the two held by Marshall and Bushrod Washington. Yet the Chief Justice employed his talents and prerogatives to win over the recruits. He would try to make sure that anyone bold enough to differ from him remained in the minority.

Four years after Johnson took the oath, he thrust himself into his first major constitutional controversy. His decision in *Gilchrist* v. *Collector of Charleston,* 10 Fed. Cas. 355 No. 5420 (C.C.D.S.C. 1808) soon gained fame as a front-rank example of judicial independence. It asserted a key role for the courts in defending individual rights from executive encroachment. And this at a time when the Jefferson Administration's unsuccessful attempt to convict Aaron Burr for treason before John Marshall was to many a bitter memory, and when the fundamental relations between executive and judicial branches under the law were still being forged.

The background of the case was as follows: the previous year Jefferson had sought to keep the country out of the Napoleonic Wars through the unilateral adoption of trade sanctions. Britain and France had each been seizing American vessels trading with the other, and American involvement in the war seemed likely. In December, Congress passed Jefferson's Embargo, banning American ships from foreign commerce. It followed this act with successive amendments to plug loopholes in the system. One of these authorized collectors in the various American ports "to detain any vessel ostensibly bound with a cargo to some other port of the United States, whenever in their opinions the intention is to violate or evade . . . [the] embargo, until the decision of the President of the United States be had thereupon." In May the Treasury sent a circular to all collectors warning them to watch for excessive shipments of certain provisions such as flour and declaring such shipments adequate cause for detention of the vessels. The circular recommended that "every shipment of the above articles for a place where they cannot be wanted for consumption, should be detained." By this request, coupled with an order for weekly reporting of vessels and cargoes, the President was seemingly attempting to direct the decisions of his subordinates.

In Charleston, Adam Gilchrist, owner of a ship laden with cotton and rice destined so he said for Baltimore, applied to the Collector for clearance papers. When that official refused under the President's order, he petitioned Justice Johnson in the federal Circuit Court for a writ of *mandamus* ordering the Collector to permit the vessel to sail. The Collector conceded that he had no reason to suspect the shipment, but insisted that under the executive order it was his duty to refuse. In his quandary he turned the issue over to the Court. Had he disobeyed the orders he would have been subject to removal by the Executive; had he obeyed them he might have been liable for damages, since in *Little* v. *Barreme,* 2 Cranch 170 (1804), the Supreme Court had held executive subordinates financially responsible for enforcing illegal orders of superiors.

Justice Johnson, by family legend, took his walking-stick, boarded Gilchrist's ship and others similarly situated, and issued sailing orders to the captains. In any event, his decision of May 28, 1808, is emphatic. In granting *mandamus* for a clearance, it held that Congress had not authorized detention in such a case, and that the Collector was not "justified by the instructions of the executive, in increasing restraints upon commerce." He made this bold assertion of the rule of law:

> *The officers of our government, from the highest to the lowest, are equally subjected to legal restraint; and it is confidently believed that all of them feel themselves equally incapable, as well from law as inclination, to attempt an unsanctioned encroachment upon individual liberty.*

This assertion of judicial power brought an immediate response. Federalists hailed it as proof of the value of an independent judiciary and Republicans deplored it as a fresh instance of judicial interventionism. Jefferson felt dismay at this rebuff by his own appointee and soon wrote his Attorney General Caesar A. Rodney, warning that the decision had "too many important bearings on the constitutional organization of our government" to be ignored. Rodney thereupon published a legal opinion rebutting Johnson's argument. By circulating this opinion among Collectors and federal marshals the Administration evidently hoped to counteract in other circuits the effect of the Gilchrist decision. Rodney aimed his main attack at Johnson's weakest point, his want of jurisdiction to issue *mandamus*. Rodney could find no grant of such jurisdiction in either Constitution or statutes and denied that the acquiescence of the Collector in the jurisdiction could confer it. He warned of a judicial meddling with executive affairs:

> . . . *there appears to be a material and obvious distinction, between a course of proceeding which redresses a wrong committed by an executive officer, and an interposition by a mandatory writ, taking the executive authority out of the hands of the president, and prescribing the course, which he and the agents of any department must pursue. In one case the executive is left free to act in his proper sphere, but it is held to strict responsibility; in the other all responsibility is taken away; and he acts agreeably to judicial mandate.*

Decisions such as Gilchrist, Rodney thought, would foster conflicts of policy among the various ports and districts and destroy the accountability of the Executive to Congress and the nation.

Publication of Rodney's opinion gave Johnson a justification for replying. That autumn the press carried his lengthy rejoinder. (The two statements appear in 10 Fed. Cas. 357.) He rested his decision solidly on the independent judiciary as protector of individual rights. Everyone had as great a right to carry on commerce between American ports unless restricted by law as "to the air that he breathes, or the food that he consumes." No official could restrain him without express statutory authority. The embargo laws gave discretion to the Collector and no authority to the President to lay down general rules to control that discretion. In such a case judicial power must be available. Said he,

> *In a country where laws govern, courts of justice necessarily are the medium of action and reaction between the government and the governed. The basis of individual security and the bond of union between the ruler and the citizen must ever be found in a judiciary sufficiently independent to disregard the will of power, and sufficiently energetic to secure to the citizen the full enjoyment of his rights.*

The statute had been badly drafted, so as to hamper presidential policy direction. Courts could apply only those restraints found in the laws, and Johnson continued, echoing Marshall's opinion in *Marbury,* "of these laws the courts are the constitutional expositors; and every department of government must submit to their exposition." The rule of law might at times prove inconvenient, Johnson conceded, but this was "certainly very consistent with the nature of our government." To rely solely on Congress for protection against executive injustice would be folly. In spite of doubts about his own jurisdiction, Johnson concluded his defense:

> *There never existed a stronger case for calling forth the powers of a court; and whatever censure the executive sanction may draw upon us, nothing can deprive us of the consciousness of having acted with firmness, impartiality and an honest intention to discharge our duty.*

In time Johnson conceded from the Supreme Court Bench that he had erred in taking jurisdiction in the Gilchrist case, *M'Intire* v. *Wood,* 7 Cranch 504, 506 (1813). In general he shared Rodney's insistence that courts proceed only where the Constitution or statutes expressly permitted. Nevertheless the decision of 1808 came to buttress executive responsibility to the law. It prompted the Jefferson administration itself to secure from Congress new legislation clearly empowering the President to lay down general rules governing detentions and incidentally defining individual access to district courts for relief. Elsewhere Johnson spoke of Congress as the appropriate body to devise remedies for executive infractions. The supremacy of law for executives meant in large part the supremacy of congressional law.

The 1812 term brought Justice Johnson another issue of moment and a colleague with whom he would spar on that issue the rest of his career. The case of *United States* v. *Hudson and Goodwin* posed the question whether the federal courts possessed a power to try offences made criminal by the English common-law, 7 Cranch 32 (1812). More broadly, it concerned the status and function of the federal judiciary in the novel and complex federal system. Granted that the courts were protectors of individuals from government wrongdoing and also served as potential umpires of conflicts between federal and state authorities, yet great doubt enveloped the issue whether the judges should have a free hand under constitutional grants to assert their power and jurisdiction or alternatively should look to Congress for clear and express assignments before proceeding. The issue, as Rodney had shown, divided the two parties, and Johnson, in spite of the Gilchrist precedent, would pursue a Republican course of decision on the matter.

Justice Joseph Story took a different line. Story was like Johnson in having served as Republican speaker of his state legislature and even in coming to the Supreme Court at thirty-two, but he lacked Johnson's previous judicial experience. It is likely that region more than party dictated his reading of the judicial article.

Partisan politics produced the Hudson case, for in Connecticut Federalists were virulent in their criticisms of the Jefferson administration. Jefferson's prosecuting attorney brought them to the federal courts on charges of criminal libel. The trial of two editors of the *Connecticut Courant* raised the question whether the federal courts, in the absence of statutes clearly conferring such jurisdiction, could try offenses made criminal at the common law. On a division between the judges below, the question was certified to the Supreme Court. Federalist judges of the 1790's had generally endorsed such a jurisdiction, yet use of the jurisdiction in connection with the Sedition Act prosecutions and the ensuing Republican campaign denunciations had brought a reaction.

Johnson spoke for the majority of the Court. Judicial power, he declared, was among the powers which the states had expressly conceded to the United States:

> *. . . that power is to be exercised by Courts organized for the purpose, and brought into existence by an effort of the legislative power of the Union. Of all the Courts which the United States may, under their general powers, constitute, one only, the Supreme Court, possesses jurisdiction derived immediately from the constitution, and of which the legislative power cannot deprive it. All other Courts created by the general Government possess no jurisdiction but what is*

given them by the power that creates them, and can be vested with none but what the power ceded to the general Government will authorize them to confer.

In affirming a power in Congress to control jurisdiction, Johnson was acceding to the doctrine of implied powers. It was less to the judges than to the legislators, however, that he assigned such powers, and Johnson laid down the cardinal rule of federal criminal jurisdiction: "The legislative authority of the Union must first make an act a crime, affix a punishment to it, and declare the Court that shall have jurisdiction of the offense." Courts could claim by implication only minimal implied powers. Thus, "to fine for contempt—imprison for contumacy—inforce the observance of order, etc." were inherent in courts because they were needed for the exercise of all other powers. Yet he seemed to regard jurisdiction, except where the Constitution expressly assigned it to the courts, as subject to control by Congress.

Justice Story continued to doubt the correctness of the Hudson decision. Like all the Justices of that time he wished to strengthen the arms of the nation, and, like many, to foster commercial interests. Yet he believed intensely in the potentialities of the judicial branch as a self-directing instrument for advancing national ends. Four years after the Hudson case, he was backing legislation to strengthen the judicial establishment and was seeking a fresh look at that decision, an effort which the majority, again through Johnson, rejected in *United States* v. *Coolidge*, 1 Wheat. 415 (1816).

Johnson lost out to Story in the handling of other forms of jurisdiction. In construing the scope of admiralty jurisdiction, which Congress under Article III had vested in the district courts, Story applied an expansive reading as suggested by his researches into early English law. Johnson saw that expansion as endangering the state common law courts and trial by jury. The British Parliament had ultimately cut down the jurisdiction of the admiralty courts. His statement in 1827 was an indirect criticism of Story's approach to jurisdiction:

> *The study of the history of the admiralty jurisdiction in England, in common with that of all the Courts of that kingdom, except the common law Courts, presents an instructive lesson on the necessity of watching the advancement of judicial power, in common with all power; inasmuch as it shows in what small beginnings, and by what indirect and covert means, aided by perseverance and ingenuity, originated the mighty structures against which, ultimately, the legislative and judicial power of the country had to exert the full force of their united efforts.* [Ramsay *v.* Allegre, *12 Wheat. 611, 616 (1827)*.]

And, he asked, in case the judges wanted to inflate their jurisdiction in admiralty, "who is to issue a prohibition to us?"

Another aspect of jurisdiction in which Story prevailed was that respecting corporations as parties. Johnson's comment in 1808, opposing access by the United States Bank to lower courts was indicative of his point of view. In spite of his lifelong support of the Bank, he denied that a corporation could be considered a "citizen" within the terms of Article III without an excessive "liberality of construction." See *Bank of United States* v. *Deveaux,* 2 Fed. Cas.

692, 693 (No. 916) (C.C.D.Ga. 1808). See also dissenting opinions in *Bank of the United States* v. *Planters' Bank of Georgia,* 9 Wheat. 904 (1824) and *Osborn* v. *Bank of the United States,* 9 Wheat. 738 (1824). Finally, Johnson tended increasingly to look closely at the Court's review of state laws and decisions in the interest of congressional control and state judicial autonomy. He concurred with the opinion in *Martin* v. *Hunter's Lessee,* 1 Wheat. 304 (1816) and *Cohens* v. *Virginia,* 6 Wheat. 264 (1821) affirming appellate jurisdiction over state courts. Yet in the Martin case he took issue with Story's reasoning. Story's opinion for the majority insisted that Article III operated as a mandate, obligating Congress to vest in federal courts the whole range of judicial power. "Our conclusions," observed Johnson, "are most satisfactory to ourselves when arrived at in our own way" and accordingly he stated his own reasons. Congress had given only part of the jurisdiction delegated by Article III to federal courts and left the remainder initially to state courts. Congress, not the courts, should implement the constitutional grant. Johnson had less faith than Story in the infallibility of federal judges and in the omnicompetence of federal courts. See especially their opinions in *Cherokee Nation* v. *Georgia,* 5 Pet. 1 (1831).

The divergence between Johnson and Story exposed an enduring issue in American jurisprudence. Johnson's view placed the courts in a position somewhat subordinate to the representatives. It rested on Jeffersonian assumptions about the deliberative capacity of the legislature and the sagacity and alertness of public opinion. Story's view emphasized the independence of the judges, not only in reaching decisions free from political interference, but also in determining their own scope of jurisdiction and power where national interests seemed to demand it. It placed its trust in the judicial process and in the vigilance of the organized bar.

The 1819 and succeeding terms brought to Johnson and the Court a series of tests of national power, including powers vested in Congress. Doctrines of state sovereignty furnished local or regional interests with plausible grounds for resisting hostile federal laws or enacting protective state measures. The extinction of the Federalist Party after the War of 1812 gave the Republicans a free hand, and a strong wing of the party pressed for national reforms to unify the nation, among them a national bank, internal improvements, and a protective tariff. In *McCulloch* v. *Maryland,* 4 Wheat. 316 (1819), the Supreme Court defended the United States Bank from a Maryland tax, upholding both implied powers and the supremacy of federal laws. In *Gibbons* v. *Ogden,* 9 Wheat. 1 (1824), it struck down the New York steamboat monopoly and asserted a sweeping federal control over foreign and interstate commerce. That Marshall wrote the opinions in these and other nationalizing decisions, usually for an undivided Court, has invited the notion that the six other justices were pawns in his hands.

William Johnson acquiesced in these decisions but for reasons of his own. He was a promoter not only of agricultural improvements but of canals, steamboats, and railroads, in order to develop South Carolina's economy and to link that state with the nation. Restive on the bench, he had twice tried to obtain an executive appointment. The 1819 term, however, brought increases both in judicial salaries and in the importance of pending issues and Johnson decided to remain on the Court.

Johnson's espousal of implied powers in Congress suggested a departure from the doctrines of Republicanism. From Monticello, Jefferson was rallying other Virginians to denounce the Court as a tool of the money power and promoter of consolidation. Johnson, however, was able to rest his defense of powers in Congress in part at least on Republican tenets. From the beginning he had attributed a broad discretion to the legislature. By 1822 he was confiding to President Monroe that all of the judges supported certain forms of internal improvements and urging the President to distribute Marshall's *McCulloch* opinion throughout the country.

It was in 1821, in *Anderson* v. *Dunn,* 6 Wheat. 204, that he elaborated his conception of congressional power. Colonel John Anderson had offered a House committee chairman a "gift" of five hundred dollars for the trouble it would cause him to secure favorable action on certain claims. The House thereupon sent its sergeant-at-arms, Thomas Dunn, to arrest Anderson and bring him before its bar on a charge of a breach of its privileges and contempt of its authority. At length Anderson was reprimanded and then discharged. Later he sued Dunn for assault and battery and false imprisonment, contending that the Constitution gave the House no power to punish nonmembers for contempt. The case was crucial to the effective functioning of the legislature and its investigating committees.

Johnson spoke for a unanimous Court. In upholding a contempt power in Congress, he defended legislative discretion. Every grant of constitutional power drew with it others "not expressed, but vital to its exercise; not substantive and independent, indeed, but auxiliary and subordinate." He continued:

> *No one is so visionary as to dispute the assertion that the sole end and aim of all our institutions is the safety and happiness of the citizen. But the relation between the action and the end, is not always so direct and palpable as to strike the eye of every observer. The science of government is the most abstruse of all sciences; if, indeed, that can be called a science which has but few fixed principles, and practically consists in little more than the exercise of a sound discretion, applied to the exigencies of the state as they arise. It is the science of experiment.*

Johnson associated implied powers essentially with the people, their needs and their ultimate control of government. The "interests and dignity" of the people required in legislatures a range of choice among measures. Security against abuse of discretion rested on responsibility and appeals to the people. Individual liberty stood in little danger "where all power is derived from the people, and public functionaries, at short intervals, deposit it at the feet of the people, to be resumed again only at their will."

Congress was checked in its use of the contempt power in other ways. The limits of that power had been long known and settled. The Constitution was made for "an advanced state of society" and rested throughout "on received opinions and fixed ideas." Furthermore, one had to rely on a moral sense in officials. Even in a tyranny there was need of popular confidence in officials, and that need was greater in a government whose only basis was the "sound morals, moderation and good sense" of those composing it. Strict construction was hence inappropriate for the powers of Congress. Every individual depended on an effectively functioning legislature. Johnson's image of Congress was exalted: "a deliberate assembly, clothed with the majesty of the people," "composed of the most distinguished citizens," "whose decisions must be clothed with all that sanctity which unlimited confidence in their wisdom and purity can inspire." It was wild to suggest that such a body could not protect itself from rudeness or insult.

Johnson's endorsement of implied powers and his acquiescence in nationalizing decisions doubtless antagonized Jefferson. In October, 1822, the retired President opened a correspondence with Johnson that continued into the following summer and explored these matters in depth. Jefferson commended the judge on his biography of General Greene, which had just appeared, and which he hoped would help to vindicate the Republicans from the charges of Federalist critics and historians. Jefferson complained, however, that the Federalists had won over Republicans, even on the Court, and infected them with doctrines of consolidation. Moreover, he deplored Marshall's practice of having a single opinion, preferably his own, state the views of all the Justices. It shielded individual Justices from having to study the briefs, make up their own minds, formulate their own reasons, and present them before the public. The practice might suit "the lazy, the modest, and the incompetent," but it frustrated the operation of public responsibility. A return to *seriatim* opinions would help enforce such responsibility. Moreover, the alternative lines of reasoning which separate opinions would provide would clarify the weight to be attached to precedents and make it possible for dissenting opinions, by their cogency, to become in later times the law of the land.

Johnson's reply of December 10, 1822, was long and revealing. The endorsement of his *Life of Greene* brought solace, for the critics had bitterly attacked his style, his use of evidence, and especially his handling of such Revolutionary leaders as Gouverneur Morris. The book has value, however, in its treatment of military campaigns and in its disclosure of Johnson's own views. He had tried to associate Republicanism with neither states' rights nor centralization of power. "State rights, or United States' rights," he observed in an appendix, "are nothing, except as they contribute to the safety and happiness of the people." He denied Jefferson's charge that Federalists were now pursuing consolidation. Instead, they were seeking to dissolve the Union. A growing assertiveness in some of the states was driving many Republicans to espouse implied powers —"that bane of our civil tranquillity." He himself favored a constitutional amendment to explain and modify clauses concerned with legislative power and the obligation of contracts, but no system could be perfect. "Our security must be found at last, in the virtue and intelligence of the people, and in the firmness and purity of their rulers." He challenged Jefferson to point out defects in the decisions, as distinguished from the language, of the Court. Jefferson responded by furnishing two canons by which to interpret the line between federal and state powers. First, to leave with the states all matters concerning their own citizens exclusively and give the nation control of matters arising between these citizens and citizens of foreign or other states; and second, to read the Constitution not merely literally, but with a view to the times and spirit of the framers. Johnson came to apply this dual formula, but in his own distinct way.

He also took seriously Jefferson's criticisms of opinion practice. As a matter of fact, Johnson had spoken frequently; from his advent through 1822 he had written 12 of the 24 separate concurring opinions and 16 of the 32 dissenting opinions of the Court. He told Jefferson he had found the Supreme Court no "bed of roses." Marshall had insisted on giving all the opinions in cases in which he sat, even when contrary to his own position—ostensibly as a sign of respect to the presiding judge, but really because of the lethargy or incompetence of most of the other judges. Johnson continued:

> *At length I found that I must either submit to circumstances or become such a cypher in our consultations as to effect no good at all. I therefore bent to the current, and persevered until I got them to adopt the course they now pursue, which is to appoint someone to deliver the opinion of the majority, but leave it to the discretion of the rest of the judges to record their opinions or not* ad libitum.

This exposé is significant. It reveals not only Marshall's policy of unanimity, but also Johnson's resistance. His success in securing a tolerance for dissent was important and permanent. When Jefferson renewed his plea for *seriatim* opinions, Johnson capitulated. He agreed to speak out alone, on all matters of general interest, especially constitutional issues.

Johnson made good his promise to Jefferson. At the next session he opened his concurring opinion in the *Gibbons* case by stating, ". . . I feel my duty to the public best discharged, by an effort to maintain my opinions in my own way." At eleven terms from 1823 on, he gave 9 out of 11 concurring and 18 out of 42 dissenting opinions.

Six months before the *Gibbons* decision Johnson met similar issues in Charleston. In *Elkison* v. *Deliesseline,* 8 Fed. Cas. 493 (No. 4366), (C.C.D. S.C. 1823), he held the South Carolina Negro Seaman Act void as a violation of the federal commerce power and of a treaty. The state law resulted from public alarm the previous year over a plot by a free Negro, Denmark Vesey, and certain slaves to overthrow white rule in Charleston. A special court had tried the suspects and sentenced thirty-five to death and thirty-two to deportation. Citizen Johnson had incurred disfavor by publishing an article warning of hysteria and obliquely criticizing arbitrary features of the trials. The legislature had thereafter sought to curb agitation among slaves by requiring that colored seamen entering port be housed it jail and, if not properly claimed by ship captains, sold into slavery.

When Henry Elkison, a Negro sailor and British subject, asked the federal court to order his release from the sheriff, Johnson declared the state law invalid. As in the Gilchrist controversy, he sought to safeguard commerce from interference, this time by the state. He conceded that jurisdiction was lacking, yet took this occasion to describe the federal commerce power as "paramount and exclusive." The Constitution, "the most wonderful instrument ever drawn by the hand of man," contained no ban on state regulation of foreign commerce. None was needed, "for the words of the grant sweep away the whole subject, and leave nothing for the states to act upon." The treaty-making power, too, was paramount; a commercial convention guaranteed Great Britain access to American ports. If states could determine the necessity of restrictive laws, the Union, like the Confederation, would become "a mere rope of sand."

The opinion produced an instant response. Johnson wrote Jefferson for the last time, enclosed a copy of his opinion and complained that disunion, "that greatest of evils," was losing its terrors in Charleston. He denounced as Federalists those who had enforced the state act and who were desperate enough to adopt the most extreme measures regardless of their effect on the Union. For two full months, Johnson sparred with these adversaries in the press, and under the pseudonym "Philonimus," developed his views at length, particularly in relation to the treaty power.

All this was rehearsal for the Steamboat case. Marshall's great opinion in *Gibbons* v. *Ogden* went to integrate the economy of the nation and create legal principles for the long future. The whole Court, except for a late arrival, Smith Thompson of New York, the first new Justice in twelve years, approved the decision, but Johnson's separate opinion has a special interest. He followed Jefferson's advice by advocating a reading of the Constitution according to its original intent and purposes rather than to its verbiage. Where the "simple, classical, precise, yet comprehensive language" left room for maneuver, men should consult the overriding purpose: "to unite this mass of wealth and power, for the protection of the humblest individual; his rights, civil and political, his interests and prosperity, are the sole *end;* the rest are nothing but the *means*." Chief of those means was "the independence and harmony of the States," bodies whose purpose was to cherish and protect the various "families of this great republic."

In applying these guidelines, Johnson made three major points. He read the commerce power broadly. The simplest meaning of commerce was an exchange of commodities; but with social advancement, "labour, transportation, intelligence, care, and various mediums of exchange" became commodities and partook of commerce. The "subject, the vehicle, the agent, and their various operations" became objects of regulation and any nation unable to regulate such matters lacked power to regulate commerce. Not for fifty years would industrialization impose on Congress the necessity of wielding such powers in peacetime.

Second, he reiterated his *Elkison* contention that the power was exclusive in Congress. The states had relinquished all power over commerce *per se*. Since the power to lay down limits to the freedom of commerce necessarily implied a power to decide what should remain unlimited, that power logically must be exclusive.

Third, he found ample powers in the states to provide for their internal concerns. The same commodity or vessel that was the object of commercial regulation might also be the carrier of disease; the state health laws that required them to be detained and aired were not meant to regulate commerce any more than federal laws permitting importation were meant to introduce disease into the community. Difference of purpose furnished the key to difference of power, and no collision could be expected where powers were "frankly exercised." Yet some collisions, as he knew from bitter experience, were inevitable, and the only practical remedy where two governments applied distinct power to the same individuals and objects was "a frank and candid co-operation for the general good." He himself had tried unsuccessfully through negotiations with state officials to avert the *Elkison* confrontation. His formula of cooperation, however, was to become the rule in the federal system of the twentieth century.

In depicting powers of Congress in broad and even exclusive terms, Johnson had surpassed even Marshall. He had spoken out for federal powers at the cost of his reputation with his own community and with Jefferson. A war-ravaged childhood and studies in history had impressed him with the need for national unity and national power. Yet his concern for national power as furthering individual dignity and freedom and his campaign for free expression by the Justices were Jeffersonian.

This endorsement of powers in Congress had a parallel, especially from 1823 on, in Johnson's conception of state powers. Generally speaking, the Marshall Court asserted a broad reviewing power to strike down state laws, particularly as these affected vested rights. It tended to read congressional power and legislation and prohibitions on state powers to their fullest possible extent so as to confine states within narrow limits. But Johnson, under the pressure of economic stress in Charleston, his readings in history, Jefferson's admonitions, and other forces increasingly resisted this trend. In so doing, he developed a conception of American federalism in many ways unique. Ironically, this chief spokesman of state rights on the Marshall Court met in his own state the sharpest challenge yet made to the Union.

As late as January 3, 1822, Johnson was writing J. R. Poinsett of Charleston that the mounting attacks on the Court gave him no uneasiness. He thought the people supported the *Cohens* decision which, he said, had affirmed that the United States would "prevent the states from trampling on individual rights." In other cases, he went on, the Court had defended the rights of out-of-state citizens from "tyrannical and corrupt" state laws, whether on debtors, land titles or state-bank notes. In none of the eight decisions annulling state laws prior to 1823 did Johnson dissent, and in only one did he file a concurring opinion.

By contrast, from 1823 on, Johnson clearly concurred in only two out of eight similar decisions, both under the commerce power. In two others he concurred only in denying the laws an extraterritorial application, and in three he dissented. In one his position is unclear. This new spirit appears in a separate opinion in *Green* v. *Biddle,* 8 Wheat. 1 (1823). Kentucky had tried to legislate order into a chaos of conflicting land titles by enabling occupying claimants to receive compensation from original title holders for improvements or obtain title by payments to original holders. The majority found the laws violated an interstate compact and accordingly that clause which prohibits laws "impairing the obligation of contracts." Johnson said the decision chained Kentucky down to a condition of "hopeless imbecility" and prevented any power on earth from making those accommodations to the "ever-varying state of human things, which the necessities or improvements of society may require."

In 1827 Johnson spoke with a majority in the landmark case of *Ogden* v. *Saunders,* 12 Wheat. 213 (1827). A citizen of Kentucky sued a citizen of Louisiana in the latter state on bills of exchange drawn in New York. The defendant raised as bar to the action a discharge obtained under a New York bankruptcy law passed prior to the contracts. Did the contract clause prohibit "insolvent debtor laws" as applied to subsequent contracts? Marshall, with the endorsement of Story and Duvall, gave a rare dissenting opinion, arguing the invalidity of the law under natural law and the contract clause.

But Johnson, Washington, Thompson, and Robert Trimble upheld the law, speaking *seriatim.* Johnson had acquiesced in earlier contract clause decisions voiding state laws, especially *Fletcher* v. *Peck,* 6 Cranch 87 (1810), *Dartmouth College* v. *Woodward,* 4 Wheat. 518, and *Sturges* v. *Crowninshield,* 4 Wheat. 122 (1819). Now he objected to construing that clause literally. The Constitution, he declared, was made for an advanced society, in which contracts should receive a "relative" rather than "positive" reading. "The rights of all must be held and enjoyed in subserviency to the good of the whole." The state construed, applied, and controlled contracts and decided how far the "social exercise" of the rights created by contracts could be asserted with justice. Government had to consider debtors as well as creditors. Determination of when the community had met its duties to creditor and when further pursuit of debtor would destroy him without aiding creditor lay with "the common guardian of the rights of both." Johnson was anxious to safeguard state powers over contracts, as part of the administration of justice, and later spoke for the Court in affirming statutes of limitation, *Hawkins* v. *Barney's Lessee,* 5 Pet. 457 (1831) and state power over remedy, *Lessee of Livingston* v. *Moore,* 7 Pet. 469 (1883). Except for a few general safeguards, the Constitution let stand the functions of the states "as to their own citizens, and as to all internal concerns," *Ogden* v. *Saunders, supra* at 281. State legislatures, like Congress, operated within the limits of a moral sense and the control of the electorate.

In a second opinion in the *Ogden* case Johnson insisted that to avoid conflict of law and disharmony among the states, the New York debtor law and others like it should be confined to the state's territory and citizens. In his view it lay with Congress, not the Court, to provide a system for interstate transactions through its bankruptcy power. Except on matters such as treaty-making, commerce, naturalization and admiralty, he tended to assign broad concurrent powers to the states and to expect Congress clearly to express its will to preempt when the nation needed to occupy the field. (See concurring opinions in *Martin* v. *Hunter's Lessee,* 1 Wheat. 304, 375–376 [1816], *Houston* v. *Moore,* 5 Wheat. 1, 45–46 [1820], and *Bill to Establish an Uniform System of Bankruptcy . . .*, sec. 33, 1820, unsigned pamphlet.) Both governments served the people and cooperation was an essential ingredient in the system.

While Johnson was defending state autonomy between 1823 and 1833, his own state moved inexorably toward a clash with federal authority. The Elkison opinion and ensuing "Philonimus" papers of 1823 were directed at the emerging doctrines of state sovereignty and strict construction. When Robert J. Turnbull, as "Brutus," gave the Nullification Movement its manifesto in his *Crisis* papers of 1827, Johnson replied under the pseudonym "Hamilton." This little-known pamphlet is a rich commentary on the constitutional controversies of four decades and a preview of subsequent interpretations. Johnson said the realities of government had compelled every administration from 1789 on to employ implied powers. Warning of civil war, he declared, "every thing that makes this country worth a wise man's love, is bound up in the Union of these States." (*Review of a Late Pamphlet under the Signature of "Brutus,"* 1828, 5.) In 1830 he finally forsook anonymity and published an eight-point rebuttal to proposals to nullify the Tariff of 1828. Nullification he called folly, and the peaceable results expected of it "all a silly and wicked delusion." Subsequently he rejected an effort on appeal to submit the validity of the tariff to a Charleston jury. *Holmes* v. *United States, C.C.D.S.C.* (1832), (Charleston *City Gazette,* June 9, 1832).

After this final controversy, Johnson died following surgery in Brooklyn on August 4, 1834.

Johnson brought knowledge, learning and a keen intelligence to the judicial task. He stood with Marshall in supporting national power to meet the unforeseeable needs of the future. For nearly two decades, he also shared much of Marshall's esteem for a powerful judiciary, particularly as an instrument for enforcing property rights against the states. Yet increasingly he drew on Jefferson; government, federal or state, was a tool for serving the needs of various classes of persons. In his final decade he looked to the states for economic and social regulation. The most distinctive of his tenets was his exaltation of Congress. The national representatives had implied powers not only to meet a variety of national problems but also to implement constitutional provisions for an executive and a judiciary. Like a later dissenter, he saw legislatures as important "guardians of the liberties and the welfare of the people." See Justice Holmes, in *Missouri, Kansas & Texas Railway Company* v. *May,* 194 U.S. 267, 270 (1904), a conception which emphasized the responsibility as well as the power of the representatives.

The courage and impetuosity which impelled Johnson into controversies and sometimes reduced his effectiveness as a judge, also prompted him to speak his mind. In the resulting struggle for free expression he got dissenting opinions established as regular Court practice. In setting forth his own views on congressional power, government regulation of property rights, and federal-state cooperation, he foreshadowed later constitutional developments.

SELECTED BIBLIOGRAPHY

The only book-length biography of Johnson is Donald G. Morgan *Justice William Johnson, the First Dissenter: the Career and Constitutional Philosophy of a Jeffersonian Judge* (Columbia, 1954). Johnson's own papers have never been discovered, but a note in the foregoing book lists the more than a dozen libraries and collections containing his correspondence. It also lists numerous articles and pamphlets. The Judge's state court opinions appear in 2 Bay (S.C.) and 1 Brevard (S.C.). Some of his federal circuit court opinions not included in *Federal Cases* appear in Charleston and Savannah newspapers, and others in the minute-books of the Court for the Districts of South Carolina and Georgia, on file in Charleston and Savannah. His major non-judicial writing was the two-volume *Sketches of the Life and Correspondence of Nathanael Greene* . . . (Charleston, 1822). Among his pamphlets were *Eulogy on Thomas Jefferson* . . . (Charleston, 1826), Hamilton (pseud.), *Review of a Late Pamphlet under the Signature of "Brutus"* (Charleston, 1828), *Nugae Georgicae* . . . (Charleston, 1815), *An Oration Delivered in St. Philip's Church* . . . (Charleston, 1813), *Remarks Critical and Historical* . . . (Charleston, 1825), and *To the Public of Charleston* (Charleston, 1822). Johnson was the subject of little more than brief sketches until 1944. In that year Morgan published his "Mr. Justice William Johnson and the Constitution," 57 *Harvard Law Review* 328 and A. J. Levin "Mr. Justice William Johnson and the Unenviable Dilemma," first of a series to appear in seven issues between 42 and 47 *Michigan Law Review* (1944–1949). Levin's articles examine Johnson's work from the standpoints of modern psychology and legal philosophy. Another treatment, largely constitutional, is Oliver Schroeder, Jr., "Life and Judicial Work of Justice William Johnson, Jr.," 95 *University of Pennsylvania Law Review* 164 (1946–1947). Johnson's views on the treaty-making power as developed in the "Philonimus" papers are treated by Donald Morgan, "Justice William Johnson on the Treaty-Making Power," 22 *George Washington Law Review* 187 (1953) and his struggle for free expression in Donald Morgan, "The Origin of Supreme Court Dissent," 10 *William and Mary Quarterly* 3d series 353 (1953). For a study of Johnson's political activities see Irwin F. Greenberg's article, "Justice William Johnson: South Carolina Unionist, 1823–1830," 36 *Pennsylvania History* (1969).

William Johnson

REPRESENTATIVE OPINIONS

GILCHRIST v. COLLECTOR OF CHARLESTON, 10 FED. CAS. 355 (NO. 5420) (C.C.D.S.C. 1808)

The Embargo Act of 1807 was designed to force France and England to cease their interference with American shipping by banning American trade with all foreign countries. To enforce the law, a succeeding enactment of April, 1808, required customs collectors to detail any vessel supposedly sailing to an American port if "in their opinions the intention is to violate or evade . . . [the] . . . embargo . . ." To close any escape hatch, the Secretary of the Treasury issued a circular to all collectors directing them to detain all ships loaded with provisions "for a place where they cannot be wanted for consumption." One of the first victims of the circular was Adam Gilchrist of Charleston, South Carolina, owner of a ship loaded with cotton and rice bound for Baltimore. He petitioned for a writ of *mandamus* from the Circuit Court to compel the Collector of the port to issue clearance papers claiming that the circular went beyond the law. Johnson sitting on circuit granted the *mandamus* in an opinion that had wide political reverberations.

JOHNSON, Circuit Justice. The affidavit, upon which this motion is founded, states that the ship Resource is ballasted with 140 barrels of rice, under a load of cotton, and is destined for the port of Baltimore. The collector, in his return to the rule, acknowledges, that he believes the port of Baltimore to be her real destination; and that, if he had no other rule of conduct but the 11th section of the act supplementary to the embargo act, he would not detain her; but urges in excuse, for refusing her a clearance, a letter from the secretary of the treasury. It is not denied that if the petitioners be legally entitled to a clearance, this court may interpose its authority, by the writ of mandamus, to compel the collector to grant it. The only questions, therefore, will be, whether the section of the act alluded to, authorizes the detention of the vessel; and if it does not, whether the instructions of the president, through the secretary of the treasury, unsupported by act of the congress, will justify the collector in that detention. On the latter question there can be no doubt. The officers of our government, from the highest to the lowest, are equally subjected to legal restraint; and it is confidently believed that all of them feel themselves equally incapable, as well from law as inclination, to attempt an unsanctioned encroachment upon individual liberty. In the letter alluded to, Mr. Gallatin speaks only in the language of recommendation, not of command; at the utmost the collector could only plead the influence of advice, and not the authority of the treasury department in his justification. In the act of congress there is no ambiguity. The object is to prevent evasions of the embargo act, by vessels which sail ostensibly for some port in the United States, when their real destination is to some other port or place. The granting of clearances is left absolutely to the discretion of the collector; the right of detaining in cases which excite suspicion is given him, with a reference to the will of the executive. Congress might have vested this discretion in the president, the secretary of the treasury, or any other officer, in which they thought proper to vest it; but, having vested the right of granting or refusing in the collector, with an appeal to the president only in case of refusal—the right of granting clearances remains in him unimpaired and unrestricted.

It does not appear to us that the instructions from the treasury department are intended to reach this case. The recommendation not to grant clearances on shipments of provisions appears by the context to be restricted by two provisos, evidently pointed at by the reasons assigned for that recommendation. First, if intended for a place where they are not wanted for comsumption, or we suppose, where supplies of the same article can be had from the state or neighbourhood in which such place is situated. Secondly, for a port that usually exports that article. Now with regard to the article of rice, it is impossible to say how much the city of Baltimore will want for its consumption, as they have no internal supplies, and as the three Southern states alone are exporters of that article. Shipments of rice from Baltimore to Charleston might create suspicion, but not such shipments from Charleston to Baltimore. We are of opinion that the act of congress does not authorize the detention of this vessel. That without the sanction of law, the collector is not justified by the instructions of the executive, in increasing restraints upon commerce, even if this case had been contemplated by the letter alluded to; but that from a temperate consideration of that letter, this case does not appear to come within the spirit and meaning of the instructions which it contains.

ANDERSON v. DUNN, 6 WHEAT. 204 (1821)

John Anderson was found guilty of contempt by Congress for attempting to bribe a member of the House to favor certain legislation. After the Congressional sergeant-at-arms, Thomas Dunn, had brought Anderson before the bar of the House to answer the charges, he was sued by Anderson for assault and false imprisonment. The power of Congress to punish non-members for contempt was thus brought before the Supreme Court and upheld in an eloquent opinion by Johnson.

March 2d, 1821. JOHNSON, Justice, delivered the opinion of the court.—Notwithstanding the range which has been taken by the plaintiff's counsel, in the discussion of this cause, the merits of it really lie in a very limited compass. The pleadings have narrowed them down to the simple inquiry, whether the house of representatives can take cognisance of contempts committed against themselves, under any circumstances? The duress complained of was sustained under a warrant issued to compel the party's appearance, not for the actual infliction of punishment for an offence committed. Yet it cannot be denied, that the power to institute a prosecution must be dependent upon the power to punish. If the house of representatives possessed no authority to punish for contempt, the initiating process issued in the assertion of that authority must have been illegal; there was a want of jurisdiction to justify it.

It is certainly true, that there is no power given by the constitution to either house, to punish for contempts, except when committed by their own members. Nor does the judicial or criminal power given to the United States, in any part, expressly extend to the infliction of punishment for contempt of either house, or any one co-ordinate branch of the government. Shall we, therefore, decide, that no such power exists?

It is true, that such a power, if it exists, must be derived from implication, and the genius and spirit of our institutions are hostile to the exercise of implied powers. Had the faculties of man been competent to the framing of a system of government which would have left nothing to implication, it cannot be doubted, that the effort would have been made by the framers of the constitution. But what is the fact? There is not in the whole of that admirable instrument, a grant of powers which does not draw after it others, not expressed, but vital to their exercise; not substantive and independent, indeed, but auxiliary and subordinate. The idea is Utopian, that government can exist without leaving the exercise of discretion somewhere. Public security against the abuse of such discretion must rest on responsibility, and stated appeals to public approbation. Where all power is derived from the people, and public functionaries, at short intervals, deposit it at the feet of the people, to be resumed again, only at their will, individual fears may be alarmed by the monsters of imagination, but individual liberty can be in little danger. No one is so visionary as to dispute the assertion, that the sole end and aim of all our institutions is the safety and happiness of the citizen. But the relation between the action and the end, is not always so direct and palpable as to strike the eye of every observer. The science of government is the most abstruse of all sciences; if, indeed, that can be called a science, which has but few fixed principles, and practically consists in little more than the exercise of a sound discretion, applied to the exigencies of the state as they arise. It is the science of experiment.

But if there is one maxim which necessarily rides over all others, in the practical application of government, it is, that the public functionaries must be left at liberty to exercise the powers which the people have intrusted to them. The interests and dignity of those who created them, require the execution of the powers indispensable to the attainment of the ends of their creation. Nor is a casual conflict with the rights of particular individuals any reason to be urged against the exercise of such powers. The wretch beneath the gallows may repine at the fate which awaits him, and yet it is no less certain, that the laws under which he suffers were made for his security. The unreasonable murmurs of individuals against the restraints of society, have a direct tendency to produce that worst of all despotisms, which makes every individual the tyrant over his neighbor's rights. That "the safety of the people is the supreme law," not only comports with, but is indispensable to, the exercise of those powers in their public functionaries without which that safety cannot be guarded. On this principle it is, that courts of justice are universally acknowledged to be vested, by their very creation, with power to impose silence, respect and decorum in their presence, and submission to their lawful mandates, and as a corollary to this proposition, to preserve themselves and their officers from the approach and insults of pollution.

It is true, that the courts of justice of the United States are vested, by express statute provision, with power to fine and imprison for contempts; but it does not follow, from this circumstance, that they would not have exercised that power, without the aid of the statute, or not in cases, if such should occur, to which such statute provision may not extend; on the contrary, it is a legislative assertion of this right, as incidental to a grant of judicial power, and can only be considered, only as an instance of abundant caution, or a legislative declaration, that the power of punishing for contempt shall not extend beyond its known and acknowledged limits of fine and imprisonment.

But it is contended, that if this power in the house of representatives is to be asserted on the plea of necessity, the ground is too broad, and the result too indefinite; that the executive, and every co-ordinate, and even subordinate, branch of the government, may resort to the same justification, and the whole assume to themselves, in the exercise of this power, the most tyrannical licentiousness. This is, unquestionably, an evil to be guarded against, and if the doctrine may be pushed to that extent, it must be a bad doctrine, and is justly denounced. But what is the alternative? The argument obviously leads to the total annihilation of the power of the house of representatives to guard itself from contempts, and leaves it exposed to every indignity and interruption, that rudeness, caprice, or even conspiracy, may meditate against it. This result is fraught with too much absurdity, not to bring into doubt the soundness of any argument from which it is derived. That a deliberate assembly, clothed with the majesty of the people, and charged with the care of all that is dear to them; composed of the most distinguished citizens, selected and drawn together from every quarter of a great nation; whose deliberations are required, by public opinion, to be conducted under the eye of the public, and whose decisions must be clothed with all that sanctity which unlimited confidence in their wisdom and purity can inspire; that such an assembly should not possess the power to suppress rudeness, or repel insult, is a supposition too wild to be suggested. And accordingly, to avoid the pressure of these considerations, it has been argued, that the right of the respective houses to exclude from their presence, and their absolute control within their own walls, carry with them the right to punish contempts committed in their presence; while the absolute legislative power given to congress within this district, enables them to provide by law against all other insults against which there is any necessity for providing.

It is to be observed, that so far as the issue of this cause is implicated, this argument yields all right of the plaintiff in error to a decision in his favor; for, *non constat,* from the pleadings, but that this warrant issued for an offence committed in the immediate presence of the house. Nor is it immaterial, to notice what difficulties the negation of this right in the house of representatives draws after it, when it is considered, that the concession of the power, if exercised within their walls, relinquishes the great grounds of the argument, to wit, the want of an express grant, and the unrestricted and undefined nature of the power here set up. For why should the house be at liberty to exercise an ungranted, an unlimited, and undefined power, within their walls, any more than without them? If the analogy with individual right and power be resorted to, it will reach no further than to exclusion, and it requires no exuberance of imagination, to exhibit the ridiculous consequences which might result from such a restriction, imposed upon the conduct of a deliberative assembly.

Nor would their situation be materially relieved, by resorting to their legislative power within the district. That power may, indeed, be applied to many purposes, and was intended by the constitution to extend to many purposes indispensable to the security and dignity of the general government; but they are purposes of a more grave and general character than the offences which may be denominated contempts, and which, from their very nature, admit of no precise definition. Judicial gravity will not admit of the illustrations which this remark would admit of. Its correctness is easily tested by pursuing, in imagination, a legislative attempt at defining the cases to which the epithet contempt might be reasonably applied.

But although the offence be held undefinable, it is justly contended, that the punishment need not be indefinite. Nor is it so. We are not now considering the extent to which the punishing power of congress, by a legislative act, may be carried. On that subject, the bounds of their power are to be found in the provisions of the constitution. The present question is, what is the extent of the punishing power which the deliberative assemblies of the Union may assume and exercise on the principle of self-preservation?

Analogy, and the nature of the case, furnish the answer—"the least possible power adequate to the end proposed;" which is the power of imprisonment. It may, at first view, and from the history of the practice of our legislative bodies, be thought to extend to other inflictions. But every other will be found to be mere commutation for confinement; since commitment alone is the alternative, where the individual proves contumacious. And even to the duration of imprisonment a period is imposed, by the nature of things, since the existence of the power that imprisons is indispensable to its continuance: and although the legislative power continues perpetual, the legislative body ceases to exist, on the moment of its adjournment or periodical dissolution. It follows, that imprisonment must terminate with that adjournment.

This view of the subject necessarily sets bounds to the exercise of a caprice which has sometimes disgraced deliberative assemblies, when under the influence of strong passions or wicked leaders, but the instances of which have long since remained on record only as historical facts, not as precedents for imitation. In the present fixed and settled state of English institutions, there is no more danger of their being revived, probably, than in our own. But the American legislative bodies have never possessed, or pretended to, the omnipotence which constitutes the leading feature in the legislative assembly of Great Britain, and which may have led occasionally to the exercise of caprice, under the specious appearance of merited resentment.

It it be inquired, what security is there, that with an officer avowing himself devoted to their will, the house of representatives will confine its punishing power to the limits of imprisonment, and not push it to the infliction of corporal punishment, or even death, and exercise it in cases affecting the liberty of speech and of the press? the reply is to be found in the consideration, that the constitution was formed in and for an advanced state of society, and rests at every point on received opinions and fixed ideas. It is not a new creation, but a combination of existing materials, whose properties and attributes were familiarly understood, and had been determined by reiterated experiments. It is not, therefore, reasoning upon things as they are, to suppose that any deliberative assembly, constituted under it, would ever assert any other rights and powers than those which had been established by long practice, and conceded by public opinion. Melancholy, also, would be that state of distrust, which rests not a hope upon a moral influence. The most absolute tyranny could not subsist, where men could not be trusted with power, because they might abuse it, much less a government which has no other basis than the sound morals, moderation, and good sense of those who compose it. Unreasonable jealousies not only blight the pleasures, but dissolve the very texture of society.

But it is argued, that the inference, if any, arising under the constitution, is against the exercise of the powers here asserted by the house of representatives; and to expel them, by the application of a familiar maxim, raises an implication against the power to punish any other than their own members. This argument proves too much; for its direct application would lead to the annihilation of almost every power of congress. To enforce its laws upon any subject, without the sanction of punishment, is obviously impossible. Yet there is an express grant of power to punish in one class of cases, and one only, and all the punishing power exercised by congress, in any cases, except those which relate to piracy and offences against the laws of nations, is derived from implication. Nor did the idea ever occur to any one, that the express grant in one class of cases repelled the assumption of the punishing power in any other. The truth is, that the exercise of the powers given over their own members, was of such a delicate nature, that a constitutional provision became necessary to assert or communicate it. Constituted, as that body is, of the delegates of confederated states, some such provision was necessary to guard against their mutual jealousy, since every proceeding against a representative would indirectly affect the honor or interests of the state which sent him.

In reply to the suggestion, that, on this same foundation of necessity, might be raised a superstructure of implied powers in the executive, and every other department, and even ministerial officer, of the government, it would be sufficient to observe, that neither analogy nor precedent would support the assertion of such powers in any other than a legislative or judicial body. Even corruption anywhere else would not contaminate the source of political life. In the retirement of the cabinet, it is not expected, that the executive can be approached by indignity or insult; nor can it ever be necessary to the executive, or any other department, to hold a public deliberative assembly. These are not arguments; they are visions which mar the enjoyment of actual blessings, with the attack or feint of the harpies of imagination.

As to the minor points made in this case, it is only necessary to observe, that there is nothing on the face of this record, from which it can appear on what evidence this warrant was issued. And we are not to presume, that the house of representatives would have issued it, without duly establishing the fact charged on the individual. And as to the distance to which the process might reach, it is very clear, that there exists no reason for confining its operation to the limits of the district of Columbia; after passing those limits, we know no bounds that can be prescribed to its range but those of the United States. And why should it be restricted to other boundaries? Such are the limits of the legislating powers of that body; and the inhabitant of Louisiana or Maine may as probably charge them with bribery and corruption, or attempt, by letter, to induce the commission of either, as the inhabitant of any other section of the Union. If the inconvenience be urged, the reply is obvious: there is no difficulty in observing that respectful deportment which will render all apprehension chimerical.

Judgment affirmed.

GIBBONS v. OGDEN, 9 WHEAT. 1 (1824)

New York had granted a monopoly in steam navigation on its own waters. Under this franchise Ogden had sought and obtained a state injunction restraining Gibbons from plying between New York and New Jersey ports in competition with him. Gibbons had appealed to the Supreme Court resting his defense chiefly on the commerce clause and a federal coasting license. John Marshall speaking for the Court took a cautious step forward in interpreting the commerce clause. He held that Congress my passing the Federal Coasting Law had precluded any state law in conflict with it. Johnson, however, pressed for a wider interpretation, claiming that the federal commerce power was exclusive even without any congressional action.

MR. JUSTICE JOHNSON. The judgment entered by the Court in this cause, has my entire approbation; but having adopted my conclusions on views of the subject materially different from those of my brethren, I feel it incumbent on me to exhibit those views. I have, also, another inducement: in questions of great importance and great delicacy, I feel my duty to the public best discharged, by an effort to maintain my opinions in my own way.

In attempts to construe the constitution, I have never found much benefit resulting from the inquiry, whether the whole, or any part of it, is to be construed strictly, or literally. The simple, classical, precise, yet comprehensive language, in which it is couched, leaves, at most, but very little latitude for construction; and when its intent and meaning is discovered, nothing remains but to execute the will of those who made it, in the best manner to effect the purposes intended. The great and paramount purpose, was to unite this mass of wealth and power, for the protection of the humblest individual; his rights, civil and political, his interests and prosperity, are the sole *end;* the rest are nothing but the *means.* But the principal of those means, one so essential as to approach nearer the characteristics of an end, was the independence and harmony of the States, that they may the better subserve the purposes of cherishing and protecting the respective families of this great republic.

The strong sympathies, rather than the feeble government, which bound the States together during a common war, dissolved on the return of peace; and the very principles which gave rise to the war of the revolution, began to threaten the confederacy with anarchy and ruin. The States had resisted a tax imposed by the parent State, and now reluctantly submitted to, or altogether rejected, the moderate demands of the confederation. Every one recollects the painful and threatening discussions, which arose on the subject of the five per cent. duty. Some States rejected it altogether; others insisted on collecting it themselves; scarcely any acquiesced without reservations, which deprived it altogether of the character of á national measure; and at length, some repealed the laws by which they had signified their acquiescence.

For a century the States had submitted, with murmurs, to the commercial restrictions imposed by the parent State; and now, finding themselves in the unlimited possession of those powers over their own commerce, which they had so long been deprived of, and so earnestly coveted, that selfish principle which, well controlled, is so salutary, and which, unrestricted, is so unjust and tyrannical, guided by inexperience and jealousy, began to show itself in iniquitous laws and impolitic measures, from which grew up a conflict of commercial regulations, destructive to the harmony of the States, and fatal to their commercial interests abroad.

This was the immediate cause, that led to the forming of a convention.

As early as 1778, the subject had been pressed upon the attention of Congress, by a memorial from the State of New-Jersey; and in 1781, we find a resolution presented to that body, by one of the most enlightened men of his day,[a] affirming, that "it is indispensably necessary, that the United States, in Congress assembled, should be vested with a right of superintending the commercial regulations of every State, that none may take place that shall be partial or contrary to the common interests." The resolution of Virginia,[b] appointing her commissioners, to meet commissioners from other States, expresses their purpose to be, "to take into consideration the trade of the United States, to consider how far an uniform system in their commercial regulations, may be necessary to their common interests and their permanent harmony." And Mr. Madison's resolution, which led to that measure, is introduced by a preamble entirely explicit to this point: "Whereas, the relative situation of the United States has been found, on trial, to require uniformity in their commercial regulations, as the only effectual policy for obtaining, in the ports of foreign nations, a stipulation of privileges reciprocal to those enjoyed by the subjects of such nations in the ports of the United States, for preventing animosities, which cannot fail to arise among the several States, from the interference of partial and separate regulations," &c. "therefore, resolved," &c.

The history of the times will, therefore, sustain the opinion, that the grant of power over commerce, if intended to be commensurate with the evils existing, and the purpose of remedying those evils, could be only commensurate with the power of the States over the subject. And this opinion is supported by a very remarkable evidence of the general understanding of the whole American people, when the grant was made.

There was not a State in the Union, in which there did not, at that time, exist a variety of commercial regulations; concerning which it is too much to suppose, that the whole ground covered by those regulations was immediately assumed by actual legislation, under the authority of the Union. But where was the existing statute on this subject, that a State attempted to execute? or by what State was it ever thought necessary to repeal those statutes? By common consent, those laws dropped lifeless from their statute books, for want of the sustaining power, that had been relinquished to Congress.

And the plain and direct import of the words of the grant, is consistent with this general understanding.

The words of the constitution are, "Congress shall have power to regulate commerce with foreign nations, and among the several States, and with the Indian tribes."

It is not material, in my view of the subject, to inquire whether the article *a* or *the* should be prefixed to the word "power." Either, or neither, will produce the same result: if either, it is clear that the article *the* would be the proper one, since the next preceding grant of power is certainly exclusive, to wit: "to borrow money on the credit of the United States." But mere verbal criticism I reject.

My opinion is founded on the application of the words of the grant to the subject of it.

The "power to regulate commerce," here meant to be granted, was that power to regulate commerce which previously existed in the States. But what was that power? The States were, unquestionably, supreme; and each possessed that power over commerce, which is acknowledged to reside in every sovereign State. The definition and limits of that power are to be sought among the features of international law; and, as it was not only admitted, but insisted on by both parties, in argument, that, *"unaffected by a state of war, by treaties, or by municipal regulations, all commerce among independent States was legitimate,"* there is no necessity to appeal to the oracles of the *jus commune* for the correctness of that doctrine. The law of nations, regarding man as a social animal, pronounces all commerce legitimate in a state of peace, until prohibited by positive law. The power of a sovereign state over commerce, therefore, amounts to nothing more than a power to limit and restrain it at pleasure. And since the power to prescribe the limits to its freedom, necessarily implies the power to determine what shall remain unrestrained, it follows, that the power must be exclusive; it can reside but in one potentate; and hence, the grant of this power carries with it the whole subject, leaving nothing for the State to act upon.

And such has been the practical construction of the act. Were every law on the subject of commerce repealed to-morrow, all commerce would be lawful; and, in practice, merchants never inquire what is permitted, but what is forbidden commerce. Of all the endless variety of branches of foreign commerce, now carried on to every

[a] *Dr. Witherspoon.*
[b] *January 21, 1786.*

quarter of the world, I know of no one that is permitted by act of Congress, any otherwise than by not being forbidden. No statute of the United States, that I know of, was ever passed to permit a commerce, unless in consequence of its having been prohibited by some previous statute.

I speak not here of the treaty making power, for that is not exercised under the grant now under consideration. I confine my observation to *laws* properly so called. And even where freedom of commercial intercourse is made a subject of stipulation in a treaty, it is generally with a view to the removal of some previous restriction; or the introduction of some new privilege, most frequently, is identified with the return to a state of peace. But another view of the subject leads directly to the same conclusion. Power to regulate *foreign commerce,* is given in the same words, and in the same breath, as it were, with that over the commerce of the States and with the Indian tribes. But the power to regulate *foreign* commerce is necessarily exclusive. The States are unknown to foreign nations; their sovereignty exists only with relation to each other and the general government. Whatever regulations foreign commerce should be subjected to in the ports of the Union, the general government would be held responsible for them; and all other regulations, but those which Congress had imposed, would be regarded by foreign nations as trespasses and violations of national faith and comity.

But the language which grants the power as to one description of commerce, grants it as to all; and, in fact, if ever the exercise of a right, or acquiescence in a construction, could be inferred from contemporaneous and continued assent, it is that of the exclusive effect of this grant.

A right over the subject has never been pretended to in any instance, except as incidental to the exercise of some other unquestionable power.

The present is an instance of the assertion of that kind, as incidental to a municipal power; that of superintending the internal concerns of a State, and particularly of extending protection and patronage, in the shape of a monopoly, to genius and enterprise.

The grant to Livingston and Fulton, interferes with the freedom of intercourse among the States; and on this principle its constitutionality is contested.

When speaking of the power of Congress over navigation, I do not regard it as a power incidental to that of regulating commerce; I consider it as the thing itself; inseparable from it as vital motion is from vital existence.

Commerce, in its simplest signification, means an exchange of goods; but in the advancement of society, labour, transportation, intelligence, care, and various mediums of exchange, become commodities, and enter into commerce; the subject, the vehicle, the agent, and their various operations, become the objects of commercial regulation. Ship building, the carrying trade, and propagation of seamen, are such vital agents of commercial prosperity, that the nation which could not legislate over these subjects, would not possess power to regulate commerce.

That such was the understanding of the framers of the constitution, is conspicuous from provisions contained in that instrument.

The first clause of the 9th section, not only considers the right of controlling personal ingress or migration, as implied in the powers previously vested in Congress over commerce, but acknowledges it as a legitimate subject of revenue. And, although the leading object of this section undoubtedly was the importation of slaves, yet the words are obviously calculated to comprise persons of all descriptions, and to recognise in Congress a power to prohibit, where the States permit, although they cannot permit when the States prohibit. The treaty making power undoubtedly goes further. So the fifth clause of the same section furnishes an exposition of the sense of the Convention as to the power of Congress over navigation: "nor shall vessels bound to or from one State, be obliged to enter, clear, or pay duties in another."

But, it is almost labouring to prove a self-evident proposition, since the sense of mankind, the practice of the world, the contemporaneous assumption, and continued exercise of the power, and universal acquiescence, have so clearly established the right of Congress over navigation, and the transportation of both men and their goods, as not only incidental to, but actually of the essence of, the power to regulate commerce. As to the transportation of passengers, and passengers in a steam boat, I consider it as having been solemnly recognised by the State of New-York, as a subject both of commercial regulation and of revenue. She has imposed a transit duty upon steam boat passengers arriving at Albany, and unless this be done in the exercise of her control over personal intercourse, as incident to internal commerce, I know not on what principle the individual has been subjected to this tax. The subsequent imposition upon the steam boat itself, appears to be but a commutation, and operates as an indirect instead of a direct tax upon the same subject. The passenger pays it at last.

It is impossible, with the views which I entertain of the principle on which the commercial privileges of the people of the United States, among themselves, rests, to concur in the view which this Court takes of the effect of the coasting license in this cause. I do not regard it as the foundation of the right set up in behalf of the appellant. If there was any one object riding over every other in the adoption of the constitution, it was to keep the commercial intercourse among the States free from all invidious and partial restraints. And I cannot overcome the conviction, that if the licensing act was repealed to-morrow, the rights of the appellant to a reversal of the decision complained of, would be as strong as it is under this license. One half the doubts in life arise from the defects of language, and if this instrument had been called an *exemption* instead of a license, it would have given a better idea of its character. Licensing acts, in fact, in legislation, are universally restraining acts; as, for example, acts licensing gaming houses, retailers of spiritous liquors, &c. The act, in this instance, is distinctly of that character, and forms part of an extensive system, the object of which is to encourage American shipping, and place them on an equal footing with the shipping of other nations. Almost every commercial nation reserves to its own subjects a monopoly of its coasting trade; and a countervailing privilege in favour of American shipping is contemplated, in the whole legislation of the United States on this subject. It is not to give the vessel an American character, that the license is granted; that effect has been correctly attributed to the act of her enrolment. But it is to confer on her American privileges, as contradistinguished from foreign; and to preserve the government from fraud by foreigners, in surreptitiously intruding themselves into the American commercial marine, as well as frauds upon the revenue in the trade coastwise, that this whole system is projected. Many duties and formalities are necessarily imposed upon the American foreign commerce, which would be burdensome in the active coasting trade of the States, and can be dispensed with. A higher rate of tonnage also is imposed, and this license entitles the vessels that take it, to those exemptions, but to nothing more. A common register, equally entitles vessels to carry on the coasting trade, although it does not exempt them from the forms of foreign commerce, or from compliance with the 16th and 17th sections of the enrolling act. And even a foreign vessel may be employed coastwise, upon complying with the requisitions of the 24th section. I consider the license, therefore, as nothing more than what it purports to be, according to the 1st section of this act, conferring on the licensed vessel certain privileges in that trade, not conferred on other vessels; but the abstract right of commercial intercourse, stripped of those privileges, is common to all.

Yet there is one view, in which the license may be allowed considerable influence in sustaining the decision of this Court.

It has been contended, that the grants of power to the United States over any subject, do not, necessarily, paralyze the arm of the States, or deprive them of the capacity to act on the same subject. That this can be the effect only of prohibitory provisions in their own constitutions, or in that of the general government. The *vis vitæ* of power is still existing in the States, if not extinguished by the constitution of the United States. That, although as to all those grants of power which may be called aboriginal, with relation to the government, brought into existence by the constitution, they, of course, are out of the reach of State power; yet, as to all concessions of powers which previously existed in the States, it was otherwise. The practice of our government certainly has been, on many subjects, to occupy so much only of the field opened to them, as they think the public interests require. Witness the jurisdiction of the Circuit Courts, limited both as to cases and as to amount; and various other instances that might be cited. But the license furnishes a full answer to this objection; for, although one grant of power over commerce, should not be deemed a total relinquishment of power over the subject, but amounting only to a power to assume, still the power of the States must be at an end, so far as the United States have, by their legislative act, taken the subject under their immediate superintendence. So far as relates to the commerce coastwise, the act under which this license is granted, contains a full expression of Congress on this subject. Vessels, from five tons upwards, carrying on the coasting trade, are made the subject of regulation by that act. And this license proves, that this vessel has complied with that act, and been regularly ingrafted into one class of the commercial marine of the country.

It remains, to consider the objections to this opinion, as presented by the counsel for the appellee. On those which had relation to the particular character of this boat, whether as a steam boat or a ferry boat, I have only to remark, that in both those characters, she is expressly recognised as an object of the provisions which relate to licenses.

The 12th section of the act of 1793, has these words: "That when the master of any ship or vessel, *ferry boats* excepted, shall be changed," &c. And the act which exempts licensed steam boats from the provisions against alien interests, shows such boats to be both objects of the licensing act, and objects of that act, when employed exclusively within our bays and rivers.

But the principal objections to these opinions arise, 1st. From the unavoidable action of some of the municipal powers of the States, upon commercial subjects.

2d. From passages in the constitution, which are supposed to imply a *concurrent* power in the States in regulating commerce.

It is no objection to the existence of distinct, substantive powers, that, in their application, they bear upon the same subject. The same bale of goods, the same cask of provisions, or the same ship, that may be the subject of commercial regulation, may also be the vehicle of disease. And the health laws that require them to be stopped and ventilated, are no more intended as regulations on commerce, than the laws which permit their importation, are intended to inoculate the community with disease. Their different purposes mark the distinction between the powers brought into action; and while frankly exercised, they can produce no serious collision. As to laws affecting ferries, turnpike roads, and other subjects of the same class, so far from meriting the epithet of commercial regulations, they are, in fact, commercial facilities, for which, by the consent of mankind, a compensation is paid, upon the same principle that the whole commercial world submit to pay light money to the Danes. Inspection laws are of a more equivocal nature, and it is obvious, that the constitution has viewed that subject with much solicitude. But so far from sustaining an inference in favour of the power of the States over commerce, I cannot but think that the guarded provisions of the 10th section, on this subject, furnish a strong argument against that inference. It was obvious, that inspection laws must combine municipal with commercial regulations; and, while the power over the subject is yielded to the States, for obvious reasons, an absolute control is given over State legislation on the subject, as far as that legislation may be exercised, so as to affect the commerce of the country. The inferences, to be correctly drawn, from this whole article, appear to me to be altogether in favour of the exclusive grants to Congress of power over commerce, and the reverse of that which the appellee contends for.

This section contains the positive restrictions imposed by the constitution upon State power. The first clause of it, specifies those powers which the States are precluded from exercising, even though the Congress were to permit them. The second, those which the States may exercise with the consent of Congress. And here the sedulous attention to the subject of State exclusion from commercial power, is strongly marked. Not satisfied with the express grant to the United States of the power over commerce, this clause negatives the exercise of that power to the States, as to the only two objects which could ever tempt them to assume the exercise of that power, to wit, the collection of a revenue from imposts and duties on imports and exports; or from a tonnage duty. As to imposts on imports or exports, such a revenue might have been aimed at *directly*, by express legislation, or *indirectly*, in the form of inspection laws; and it became necessary to guard against both. Hence, first, the consent of Congress to such imposts or duties, is made necessary; and as to inspection laws, it is limited to the minimum of expenses. Then, the money so raised shall be paid into the treasury of the United States, or may be sued for, since it is declared to be for their use. And lastly, all such laws may be modified, or repealed, by an act of Congress. It is impossible for a right to be more guarded. As to a tonnage duty, that could be recovered in but one way; and a sum so raised, being obviously necessary for the execution of health laws, and other unavoidable port expenses, it was intended that it should go into the State treasuries; and nothing more was required, therefore, than the consent of Congress. But this whole clause, as to these two subjects, appears to have been introduced *ex abundanti cautela,* to remove every temptation to an attempt to interfere with the powers of

Congress over commerce, and to show how far Congress might consent to permit the States to exercise that power. Beyond those limits, even by the consent of Congress, they could not exercise it. And thus, we have the whole effect of the clause. The inference which counsel would deduce from it, is neither necessary nor consistent with the general purpose of the clause.

But instances have been insisted on, with much confidence, in argument, in which, by municipal laws, particular regulations respecting their cargoes have been imposed upon shipping in the ports of the United States; and one, in which forfeiture was made the penalty of disobedience.

Until such laws have been tested by exceptions to their constitutionality, the argument certainly wants much of the force attributed to it; but admitting their constitutionality, they present only the familiar case of punishment inflicted by both governments upon the same individual. He who robs the mail, may also steal the horse that carries it, and would, unquestionably, be subject to punishment, at the same time, under the laws of the State in which the crime is committed, and under those of the United States. And these punishments may interfere, and one render it impossible to inflict the other, and yet the two governments would be acting under powers that have no claim to identity.

It would be in vain to deny the possibility of a clashing and collision between the measures of the two governments. The line cannot be drawn with sufficient distinctness between the municipal powers of the one, and the commercial powers of the other. In some points they meet and blend so as scarcely to admit of separation. Hitherto the only remedy has been applied which the case admits of; that of a frank and candid co-operation for the general good. Witness the laws of Congress requiring its officers to respect the inspection laws of the States, and to aid in enforcing their health laws; that which surrenders to the States the superintendence of pilotage, and the many laws passed to permit a tonnage duty to be levied for the use of their ports. Other instances could be cited, abundantly to prove that collision must be sought to be produced; and when it does arise, the question must be decided how far the powers of Congress are adequate to put it down. Wherever the powers of the respective governments are frankly exercised, with a distinct view to the ends of such powers, they may act upon the same object, or use the same means, and yet the powers be kept perfectly distinct. A resort to the same means, therefore, is no argument to prove the identity of their respective powers.

I have not touched upon the right of the States to grant patents for inventions or improvements, generally, because it does not necessarily arise in this cause. It is enough for all the purposes of this decision, if they cannot exercise it so as to restrain a free intercourse among the States.

Brockholst Livingston

☆ 1757–1823 ☆

APPOINTED BY

THOMAS JEFFERSON

YEARS ON COURT

1806–1823

Brockholst Livingston

by

GERALD T. DUNNE

HENRY BROCKHOLST LIVINGSTON was born in New York City on November 25, 1757, the son of William Livingston and Susanna (French) Livingston. A member of the so-called Manor branch of the distinguished New York Livingstons, he was one of three men who had belonged to that powerful family through either birth or marriage to serve on the Supreme Court. The other two were his brother-in-law and the first Chief Justice, John Jay, and Smith Thompson, who was his immediate successor and who was married not once but twice to Livingstons.

While Brockholst Livingston was destined to have a long and close connection with New York City, much of his early years was spent in New Jersey. His distinguished father had removed to that state in 1772 and served as governor during the American Revolution. Possibly as a consequence of this residence and possibly because his father had strenuously opposed the foundation of Columbia, he attended Princeton where he was a fellow student of James Madison, the man who was to appoint him to the Supreme Court. Completing his studies in 1774, he returned home apparently to live the life of an heir of the aristocracy on his father's estate, "Liberty Hall," near Elizabethtown. In January of 1776, while still living at home, he took part in the interception and capture of a British supply ship. He subsequently joined the American army as a captain on General Schuyler's staff and served with Arnold against Burgoyne. The latter assignment involved complications, for Livingston's immense admiration for Arnold reputedly provoked the displeasure of General Gates. The high point of his military career, spent largely in staff capacities, was his selection to carry the news of the victory at Bennington to Congress. Doubtless his family's stature

GERALD T. DUNNE is Vice-President of the Federal Reserve Bank, St. Louis. He is the author of Monetary Decisions of the Supreme Court *and occasional contributions to various periodicals on American legal history.*

assisted his rapid rise, which saw him commissioned a major at nineteen and subsequently elevated to the rank of lieutenant colonel.

In 1779 he exchanged military for diplomatic duties and went to Spain as secretary to the American Minister John Jay, his brother-in-law. Probably it was in this period that one of the strongest influences of his life developed in the form of a personal antipathy toward Jay, notwithstanding (or perhaps because of) his personal and financial obligations toward his brother-in-law. In any event Livingston was a constant irritation to his brother-in-law both by reason of his undiplomatic criticism of the Continental Congress and his combining with other secretaries of the mission in intrigues against its head. Doubtless all involved were relieved when the association ended in 1782 as Jay was appointed one of the commissioners to negotiate the treaty ending the Revolutionary War and departed for Paris. Livingston was sent home with dispatches, but on the return voyage his ship was taken by the British, and he (after destroying the dispatches) was made a prisoner of war. Upon subsequently giving his parole to Sir Guy Carleton—an action which caused him to write a long letter of explanation to George Washington—he was released. Thereafter he studied law under Peter Yates at Albany, and was admitted to the bar in 1783.

Livingston returned to New York City after the British evacuation and dropped the "Henry," possibly to avoid confusion with two cousins also named Henry Livingston. He entered politics at the same time he began the practice of law and also acquired something of a reputation as a speculator in banking and securities. In 1786 he was elected to the twelfth session of the New York Assembly in what was to be the first of three tours in that body. During his early professional career he was occasionally associated with Alexander Hamilton. He was one of the committee which proposed and procured the Trumbull painting of Hamilton. Like his distinguished associate, legal and political activities were closely intertwined in his life. The coincidence was particularly suggested by the case of *Rutgers* v. *Waddington* where he served with Hamilton as defense counsel for a former Tory and pleaded the nullity of anti-Tory legislation on the grounds of conflict with the treaty of peace, a conciliatory position generally held by the nationalist-aristocratic faction soon to become the New York Federalists. Another famous case of his law practice in which he was co-counsel for the defense with Hamilton and Aaron Burr was "The Manhattan Well Mystery," a *cause célèbre* involving the discovery of the body of a young woman in a well and the subsequent trial and acquittal of her fiancé for her murder in a proceeding at which seventy-five witnesses were heard and the jury was out five minutes.

During this period he gradually rose to leadership in his own "Manor" branch of the family as he represented it in a complex land dispute with the "Clermont" branch headed by Chancellor Robert R. Livingston. Both branches gradually and for a variety of reasons passed from a federalist to an anti-federalist position. Brockholst Livingston seems to have been in the van of the transition with one study indicating that he began to hold conflicting allegiances as early as 1788. Conceivably his conversion to anti-federalism could have been effected by his Princeton schoolmate, James Madison, on the latter's famous visit to New York in 1791. On the other hand, his evolving political views were not of such a character or conspicuousness as to deprive him of the honor of delivering the first Independence Day oration under the Constitution to the most distinguished audience of his times. Actually delivered on Monday, July 5, 1789, Livingston made the speech in St. Paul's Church in the presence of President Washington, the members of Congress, the Order of the Cincinnati (of which he was an original member), the state and municipal officers and the Grand Sachem and Fathers of St. Tammany.

Livingston's anti-federalism became unequivocally and irrevocably manifested, however, as a response to John Jay's decision to seek the New York governorship in 1792. In fact, as early as 1787, Hamilton was writing Jay of his painful observation of "the progress of the transactions, which have excited irritations between Mr. Livingston and yourself. . . ." In the campaign Livingston proved he had not forgotten the antipathy as he showed himself to be truly "the toughest and the most persistent" member of his branch of the family and, according to a contemporary observer, strove "almost like a madman" to deny on a technicality, but, successfully as things turned out, a critical bloc of votes to his brother-in-law. The measure of his opposition can be found in the distress of Sarah Livingston Jay, his sister and Jay's wife ("Oh, how is the name of Livingston to be disgraced. . . ."). These very sharp and unconscionable tactics could well have contributed to a public sense of resentment which led to Jay's victory at the following election in 1795. The event occurred when the victor was absent in England on diplomatic service, and the excitement attending the bitter election had scarcely died away when a fresh storm came with disclosure of the apparently disastrous treaty which Jay had negotiated.

Writing under classical pseudonym, as he had previously done in the bitter election of 1792, Livingston attacked Jay and the treaty with vigor. One of his most effective weapons was the sentimental memory of a French assistance during the Revolution, and he used it to assail the Jay treaty with Britain. Notwithstanding current Franco-American difficulties, he was especially eloquent on the ninth anniversary of the French alliance in the toast: "May the present coolness between France and America produce like the quarrels of lovers, a renewal of love." During this period he also calmly witnessed Jay burned in effigy and was present in the mob which stoned and wounded Hamilton upon the latter's attempt to speak in defense of the treaty.

His brother-in-law's successful administration and easy reelection in 1798 slowed Livingston's rise to power. The eclipse, however, was but temporary, for at the turn of the century he was immersed in helping forge the Burr-Clinton-Livingston coalition, of which Henry Adams later wrote that contemporary judgment of principles or morals inclined to Burr as the least selfish of the lot. The emerging Anti-Federalist alliance gave powerful support to the Jefferson-Burr ticket in the election of 1800 and triumphed in the New York governorship contest the following year. Livingston shared in the triumph, being successively elected to the twenty-fourth and twenty-fifth sessions of the Assembly. His success, however, had just begun. The post-electoral disintegration of the coalition worked to his especial advantage, for the Livingstons took the lion's share of a division of the spoils which came as the Burr faction was given short shrift and the Federalists were removed from office "down to the auctioneer"—Edward Livingston was appointed mayor of New York, a Livingston in-law, Thomas Tillotson, became Secretary of State of New York, and two others, Morgan Lewis and Smith Thompson, became, respectively, Chief Justice and Associate Justice of the New York Supreme Court. Brockholst Livingston was promised the next vacancy on that tribunal.

Appointed a puisne judge of that Court in 1802, Livingston turned out to be a vigorous, energetic magistrate. Sitting alongside Kent, who was at the beginning of his work of bringing the "Grand Style" to an emergent body of commercial law, Livingston found himself on a court settling the disputes of a vigorous and enterprising society. It was a stimulating experience, and a modern observer, possibly overstressing the character of *seriatim* opinions, notes how the reports of the Court during the period abounded in controversy. Thus the first volume of Johnson shows only forty-eight *per curiam* opinions, and in it Livingston led with the greatest number of individual expressions of views. Typical of his vigorous independence were concurrences like that in *Lowry* v. *Lawrence,* 1 Cai. R. 69 (1803), and dissents such as that in *Jackson* v. *Bailey,* 2 Johns. R. 17 (1806). His constructive work in this period came on commercial law points such as that in *Russell* v. *Ball,* 2 Johns. R. 50 (1806). Little constitutional law was litigated before the Court; Livingston's essentially eclectic constitutional positions (discussed *infra*) were suggested by his nationalist view of the application of the full faith and credit clause to out-of-state judgments in *Hitchcock* v. *Aicken,* 1 Cai. R. 460 (1803), (forecasting his concurrence in *Mills* v. *Duryee,* 7 Cranch 481 [1813]) and his traditionalist attitude toward seditious libel indicated in *People* v. *Croswell,* 3 Johns. C. 337 (1804). The doctrine of seditious libel split the New York Supreme Courts into equal parts (one judge did not sit). Livingston held with Chief Justice Morgan Lewis that the truth of an utterance and the good faith with which it was made were irrelevant in a charge of seditious libel. This view was consistent both with a stinted attitude toward civil liberties, on one hand, and, on the other, a Jeffersonian distaste toward amendment of legal doctrine by judicial legislation. With equal ambiguity Smith Thompson, his future successor on the United States Supreme Court, joined Kent in an opinion to the contrary (i.e., that good faith was a relevant factor), a position which was validated in the following year by an enactment of the New York legislature.

One significant foreshadowing of Livingston's constitutional views came in his somewhat desultory service on the Council of Revision, that unique New York body which united the executive and judiciary in a veto power over the legislature. For it was on the Council that Livingston joined in disapproving a bill on the ground that "charters of incorporation . . . were not to be essentially affected without the consent of the parties concerned." A somewhat related item was Livingston's unsuccessful but vigorous *laissez faire* effort at the Council to secure its disapproval of a bill restraining unincorporated banking.

Despite the press of judicial duties—Livingston wrote 149 opinions in four years—he seems to have kept his hand in politics, and in 1803, DeWitt Clinton, seeking to succeed to the mayoralty of New York City, found it advantageous to report that Livingston, among others, had "waived their pretension in my favor." Conceivably, even at this early date, Livingston had designs on, and even a half-promise of, a seat on the United States Supreme Court, and this position produced an attitude of indifference to lesser and local honors. Significantly, careful consideration was given his name in 1804 with Jefferson's first opportunity to appoint a Justice to that Bench. Notwithstanding an appraisal as "first in point of talents" from his section of the country, a variety of reasons caused him to be passed over. The appointment went instead to William Johnson of South Carolina; on the death of Justice William Paterson in 1806, however, Livingston was appointed to the highest federal bench. He resigned from the New York tribunal in January, 1807, and first took his seat on the Supreme Court at the February, 1807 term.

A description of Livingston during his early years on the Court is contained in a letter written by his future colleague, Joseph Story, when in Washington on a lobbying assignment:

> *Livingston has a fine Roman face; an aquiline nose, high forehead, bald head, and projecting chin, indicate deep research, strength, and quickness of mind. I have no hesitation in pronouncing him a very able and independent Judge. He evidently thinks with great solidity and seizes on the strong points of argument. He is luminous, decisive, earnest and impressive on the bench. In private society he is accessible and easy, and enjoys with great good humor the vivacities, if I may coin a word, of the wit and moralist. [1 W. W. Story,* The Life and Letters of Joseph Story *167 (1851).]*

Livingston's affable geniality, noted by Story and almost every other observer, doubtless made him a particularly easy target for John Marshall's compelling charm, and indeed Livingston can serve as an illustrative example of how the Federalist Chief Justice dominated and made dominant a tribunal largely appointed by his political opponents. To be sure, in Livingston's case there was an abundant cluster of factors suggesting the hardening conservatism which he would show on the high court—the aristocratic background, the essentially opportunistic nature of his Jeffersonianism, his long participation in the familial-oligarchic New York government and the long association with Kent.

In fact, Livingston's two judicial careers can be said to be marked by the common pattern of an initial period of independence followed by an orchestral participation in a tribunal headed by a dominating chief. Thus he began his federal judgeship with a sprightly footnote asserting what the law of New York was, *Rhinelander* v. *The Insurance Company of Pennsylvania,* 4 Cranch 29, 37 (1807), and the following term suggested a restiveness with John Marshall's *per curiams* through an extraordinarily terse concurrence, *Rose* v. *Himely,* 4

Cranch 241, 281 (1808), and an opinionless dissent, *Higginson* v. *Mein,* 4 Cranch 415 (1808).

Yet if Livingston's career on the Supreme Court has a discernible pattern, it would be a regression to the federalism of his youth. If a point of inflexion is to be noted, perhaps it might be *United States* v. *Coolidge,* 1 Wheat. 415 (1816), where (in a reprise of *Croswell*) he announced his willingness to hear argument on the existence of common law federal crimes notwithstanding the apparent earlier settlement of doctrine to the contrary. This position, however, should not obscure his authentically libertarian strain, possibly inherited from his father, or possibly acquired from Jeffersonian associations, for as far back as 1803 while on the state bench, he indicated a sympathy for imprisoned debtor relief legislation (*Manhattan Co.* v. *Smith,* 1 Cai. R. 67 [1803]). A libertarian construction of the treason clause of the Constitution was set out in his jury charge in *United States* v. *Hoxie,* 26 Fed. Cas. 397 (No. 15,407) (C.C.D. Vt. 1808). And a particular sensitivity is suggested with a dissent on what was nominally an issue of statutory construction. "In a case affecting life," he noted, as he disagreed with Justice Story on a matter within Story's particular competence in international law, "no apology can be necessary for expressing my dissent. . . ." *United States* v. *Smith,* 5 Wheat. 153, 164 (1820).

Indeed a distinct Jeffersonian note appears in his assertion that his circuit court would not "take upon itself the high and delicate office of pronouncing any law of the United States unconstitutional unless the case were so clearly so that it were scarcely possible for any two men to differ in sentiment on the subject," *The Elizabeth,* 8 Fed. Cas. at 469–470 (No. 4,352) (C.C.D. N.Y. 1810). Yet notwithstanding this declaration against judicial activism in constitutional matters, Livingston gradually came round to, and was prepared to enforce by rigorous judicial veto, a view of the contract clause of the Constitution close to that of John Marshall. The one divergence lay in its application to state insolvency legislation, an exception possibly arising from his view of commercial necessity or perhaps only from a desire to maintain his judicial consistency.

For by a somewhat ironic coincidence these conflicting concepts traversed each other at almost the same moment of time. Thus in *Adams* v. *Storey,* 1 Fed. Cas. 141 (No. 66) (C.C.D. N.Y. 1817), he wrote an opinion of extraordinary sweep, upholding the retroactive and extraterritorial application of the New York insolvency law against claims that the statute transgressed not only the contract clause but the preempted federal bankruptcy jurisdiction as well. He accordingly had little choice but to disagree with the conclusion of the Supreme Court when two years later the retroactive aspect of the statute was declared an unconstitutional impairment of the obligation of contract in *Sturges* v. *Crowninshield,* 4 Wheat. 122 (1819). Significantly, however, Livingston did not formally dissent from the opinion of the Court, and we are aware of his disagreement only through Justice Story's private correspondence. This shift of attitude, so covertly suggested in *Sturges,* was more luminously shown in another controversy decided at the same term. In the famous *Dartmouth College* v.

Woodward, 4 Wheat. 518 (1819), Livingston, in a reprise of his membership on the Council of Revision, concurred in three opinions holding New Hampshire's attempted reformation of Dartmouth College unconstitutional—that of the Court, written by Chief Justice Marshall, the concurrence of Justice Story extending the principles of the decision to business corporations, and the concurrence of Justice Washington confining the decision of the Court to the facts before it. In addition, he seems to have prepared but declined to publish a concurring opinion of his own.

Livingston's position in *Dartmouth* vividly suggests the critical importance of the case in the evolution of his own views and of constitutional law generally. He was without opinion after argument, and as shrewd an observer of the Court as Daniel Webster was unwilling to forecast his final position. Reportedly the views of Chancellor Kent suggesting the unconstitutionality of the New Hampshire legislation were communicated to him extra-judicially. More influential, as his correspondence indicates, were those portions of Story's concurrence which dealt explicitly with the application of the contract clause to civil institutions partaking of a contractual nature but traditionally reserved to state control. He was criticized for accepting honorary degrees from Princeton and Harvard while the *Dartmouth* case was under advisement, but apparently encountered no adverse comment for sitting on the case notwithstanding his position as a trustee of Columbia.

The asserted extrajudicial communication of Kent's views, if such occurred, was not Livingston's only known breach of judicial decorum. At the second Madison inaugural ball he confidentially disclosed the forthcoming disposition of the Yazoo lands case, *Fletcher* v. *Peck,* 6 Cranch 87 (1810), to John Quincy Adams, one of the counsel therein. Ironically, on one occasion when he was criticized in the press for his judicial behavior, the comment came on a matter in which his position was beyond reproach. This was in one aspect of the "Batture" litigation, *Livingston* v. *Dorgenois,* 7 Cranch 577 (1813), which involved the suit of his distant cousin, Edward Livingston, over certain land near New Orleans. The *Louisiana Courier,* in an editorial reprinted in the *National Intelligencer* (December 11, 1813), asserted Edward Livingston's suit could not fail because "the plan had been concerted with his family [and] one of the members of that very family occupied a seat on the tribunal which was to consider the spoilation. . . ." Three days later the *National Intelligencer* printed a virtual apology, disclaiming any "indecorous insinuation against the uprightness of a high and, we believe, deservedly respected judicial officer." Possibly the *Intelligencer*'s apology was due to belated recognition of the fact that Livingston had taken no part in the decision under discussion, although nonparticipation seems to have been more coincidental than deliberate. Self-disqualification on such matters was not compelled by contemporary standards, and his famous cousin, Chancellor Robert R. Livingston, frequently sat on the affairs of relatives.

The incident, however, raises the interesting question whether Livingston would have participated in the final conclusion of the long and extensive case of *Gibbons* v. *Ogden,* 9 Wheat. 1 (1824), which involved the legitimacy of the steamboat monopoly granted to Robert Fulton and the "Clermont" branch of the Livingston family. But not only did it involve Brockholst Livingston's family; the case actually began in his circuit court where he dismissed the initial proceeding for lack of jurisdiction, *Livingston* v. *Van Ingen,* 15 Fed. Cas. 697 (No. 8, 420) (C.C.D. N.Y. 1811). However, Livingston never had to face the question of self-disaqualification in the final proceeding, for he sickened and died at the preceding term of the Supreme Court.

Livingston was the first member of the long-time "Marshall Court" to die, and reports of strict constructionist Nathaniel Macon as the possible successor were especially alarming to Marshall and Story. The succession, however, went to Smith Thompson, a political and judicial coadjutor from New York and a relative by marriage twice over. A more unusual development, *post mortem,* concerned Livingston's position on the Kentucky "occupying claimant" law which required occupying claimants of land in Kentucky to be paid for any improvements made while they were in possession. The statute had been invalidated by a three-to-one vote, *Green* v. *Biddle,* 8 Wheat. 1 (1823), on the ground that it was inconsistent with the compact made between Kentucky and Virginia when the former was accorded statehood, and the fact that an unusually undermanned Court decided the case was due in part to Livingston's absence during his final illness. The controversial nature of the decision and the fact that a minority of the Justices struck down the state statute provoked much criticism. On January 6, 1826, Congressman Mercer, speaking in defense of the Court, insisted that Livingston, now in his "silent but honored grave," had regarded the statute as unconstitutional and thereby made the decision *de facto* that of a majority of the Court.

It is perhaps appropriate that Livingston's last reported judicial views should be those which carried a view of the contract clause to a height considerably apart from his early views and, moreover, were those which constituted an essentially passive concurrence in another's judicial work. Certainly the product of Livington's sixteen years on the Supreme Court—thirty-eight majority opinions, eight dissents and six concurrences—sharply contrasts with his record on the New York bench. Moreover, none of his Supreme Court work is particularly noteworthy for a juristic or constitutional dimension. On the other hand, he did bring to the Court, particularly before the accession of Justice Story, a needed insight and feeling for the flexibility of commercial and prize law. Moreover, his genial and ebullient personality and his concern for the tribunal on which he sat helped make the Marshall Court a "band of brothers," and thus assisted in the Court's institutional evolution at a critical period of its history.

Livingston's opinions have a surprisingly modern ring to the late twentieth century reader—terse, crisp, unobtrusively learned, fact-oriented and, occasionally, delightful. Stylistically, he seemed to be at his best when stating independent views in either concurrence or dissent. One commentator, noting Livingston's dissent on the New York bench in *Pierson* v. *Post,* 3 Cai. R. 175 (1805), observed that he could tread "the verge of refined drollery" in the manner of Charles Lamb. And on the Supreme Court he from time to time showed the same touch, such as when he stated his separate views in a dry-as-dust patent case: "At this late period, when the patentee is in his grave, and his patent has expired a natural death, we are called on to say whether his patent ever had a legal existence . . ." *Evans* v. *Eaton,* 7 Wheat. 356, 435 (1822). To be sure, he could lapse into the tedious prolixity common to the style of his day, *United States* v. *Giles,* 9 Cranch 212 (1815), and *Brown* v. *Jackson,* 7 Wheat. 218 (1822), but generally his opinions are quite brief, sometimes surprisingly so, *Rose* v. *Himely; Maryland Insurance Co.* v. *Wood,* 7 Cranch 402 (1813), and *Young* v. *Grundy,* 7 Cranch 548 (1813).

Substantively, Livingston's significant work was undoubtedly done on the New York bench. In fact, Kent paid a left-handed tribute to his younger colleague's knowledge of European jurisprudence in the comment that Livingston was the only judge capable of resisting when he [Kent] waved his wand in the fields of French and civil law. And the New York reports support a suggestion of expertise, for Livingston's concurrence in *Nash* v. *Tupper,* 1 Cai. R. 402, 413 (1803), carries the reporter's note of the "great force in the reasoning of the learned judge."

While there was little opportunity to use these talents on the Supreme Court, he did bring to its Bench two related but distinct talents. One was a feel for the strengths and weaknesses of commercial law, particularly in negotiable instruments, e.g., *Lenox* v. *Prout,* 3 Wheat. 520 (1818), and *Dugan* v. *United States,* 3 Wheat. 172 (1818). Occasionally, however, he was unable to bring the Court around to his point of view, *Oliver* v. *Maryland Insurance Company,* 7 Cranch 487, 493 (1813). The other, as the phrase goes, was an ear nicely tuned for facts which went hand in hand with a great economy in the use of citations, e.g., *United States* v. *Tyler,* 7 Cranch 285 (1812); *Hall* v. *Leigh,* 8 Cranch 50 (1814); and the unusually long but characteristically citation-free *Spring* v. *South Carolina Insurance Company,* 8 Wheat. 268 (1823), which was probably his last opinion.

The foregoing qualities doubtless account for the number of opinions in the plastic and fact-oriented field of prize law which came from his pen, e.g., *The Euphrates,* 8 Cranch 385 (1814); *The St. Lawrence, Id.* at 434; *The Struggle,* 9 Cranch 71 (1815); *The Hazard* v. *Campbell, Id.* at 205; *The Rugen,* 1 Wheat. 62 (1816); *The Aeolus,* 3 Wheat. 392 (1818); and *The Estrella,* 4 Wheat. 298 (1819). In fact, during the law practice his reputation in prize law seems indicated by his having been retained as counsel for the French prizes brought into American ports.

As a consequence of the overshadowing figures of his associates in both New York and Washington, Livingston remains essentially an elusive and half-glimpsed figure of his age. He was married successively to Catharine Keteltas,

Ann Ludlow and Catharine Kortright, and had five children by the first marriage, three by the second and three by the third. His geniality has a multitude of testimonials, and his correspondence suggests that he was a good family man and fine friend; the record nonetheless occasionally shows a somewhat unattractive side. This is particularly true in his relationship with Jay. Dangerfield, a generally charitable observer, finds him "somewhat given to duplicity" and notes that in his early days he had "been distrusted by the whole Manor family."

Another collateral observation testifies to both Livingston's nose, "a regular Roman triumph," and to his "explosive temprement and rambunctious sense of humor." Overtones of violence tincture much of his career. An attempt was made to assassinate him in 1785 with the Common Council of New York City posting a $125.00 award for the assailant. And in 1798 he killed a man in a duel (fought in "Hobuck in New Jersey"). This was not his first resort to the field of honor. He fought at least one duel in the Burgoyne campaign, and family correspondence suggests that there were more. For when he accompanied John Jay to Spain, a female relative wrote his sister: "Tell Harry to beware of engaging in a quarrel with the Dons in Spain. This duelling is a very foolish way of putting oneself out of the world." Whatever may have been the circumstances elsewhere, in the New York affair he had some provocation—his assailant, an obscure Federalist named Jones, angered by Livingston's published barbs, "caught him by the nose & struck him" while Livingston had been promenading innocently on the Battery. The duel has been compared quite unfavorably to the Burr-Hamilton encounter. ("[N]o one thought of indicting Mr. Livingston for murder, presumably because Mr. Jones was not sufficiently important.") On the other hand, in Livingstone's favor it should be noted that, when on the New York bench, he had been prompt to issue his restraining order forbidding resort to the code of violence.

An attractive facet of Livingston's vigorous and outgoing nature was shown by many public services. These would include his longtime service to Columbia, which he served as trustee and treasurer from 1784 until his death. He was also concerned with elementary education and was instrumental in establishing New York City's first efforts at free public schools. Also typical of the same interest was his work as co-founder and officer of the New York Historical Society.

Perhaps his best testimonials, however, come from his judicial colleagues. One is from James Kent, who served with him on the New York bench and for whom he had a lifelong veneration. It was Livingston who secured the Columbia LL.D. for Kent in 1797, and many years later the old chancellor returned the compliment in a tribute calling Livingston's work "copious, fluid, abounding in skillful criticism, and beautiful allusions." A more extended one came from Justice Story, who found in Livingston "a loved and valued friend" and who, according to the correspondence of the Court's reporter, composed virtually all of the eulogy which prefaces the Court's reports (8 Wheat.) for the term at which he died:

On the 18th of March, a few days after the close of the present term, died the Honorable Brockholst Livingston, an Associate Justice of this court, in the sixty-sixth year of his age. He was appointed in 1806, being at that time a Judge of the Supreme Court of New York, and having before occupied an eminent rank at the bar of that state. He had served his country with distinguished military reputation during the war of the revolution, and subsequently filled several important civil stations at home and abroad. He was an accomplished classical scholar, and versed in the elegant languages and literature of the southern nations of Europe. At the bar he was an ingenious and learned advocate, fruitful in invention, and possessing a brilliant and persuasive elocution. On the bench, his candor and modesty were no less distinguished than his learning, acuteness and discrimination. His genius and taste had directed his principal attention to the maritime and commercial law; and his extensive experience gave to his judgments in that branch of jurisprudence a peculiar value, which was enhanced by the gravity and beauty of his judicial eloquence. In private life he was beloved for his amiable manners and general kindness of disposition, and admired for all those qualities which constitute the finished gentleman. He died with the deep regret of all who knew him; leaving behind him the character of an upright, enlightened and humane judge, a patriotic citizen, and a bright ornament of the profession. Isque et oratorum in numero est habendus, et fuit reliquis rebus ornatus, atque elegans.

SELECTED BIBLIOGRAPHY

Livingston's career runs in a close and meaningful connection through some singular episodes of American history—the military and diplomatic aspects of the Revolution, the evolution of the first political parties, the emergence of an authentically American *corpus* of commercial law, and the institutional development of the Supreme Court under a Federalist Chief Justice with Democratic-Republican associates. Yet notwithstanding the historic vantage point afforded by his life and times, as well as his unusual character and personality, his biography is yet to be written. Ironically, the overshadowing stature which his cousin, Chancellor Robert Livingston, held during their lifetimes continues to obtain, for the best picture of Brockholst Livingston is had in the fragmentary and episodic asides in George Dangerfield, *Chancellor Robert R. Livingston* (New York, 1960). A similar profile is contained in E. B. Livingston, *The Livingstons of Livingston Manor* (New York, 1910).

A view of his days in Spain and his beginnings in New York may be found in the Lewis Littlepage biography, C. C. Davis, *The King's Chevalier* (New York, 1961). Also, New York political history of the beginning of the nineteenth century cannot be written without some mention of him, and, hence, the standard works on the subject, e.g., D. S. Alexander, 1 *A Political History of the State of New York* (New York, 1906) will contain occasional references. An indication of his relationships on that Marshall Court is in G. Dunne, "The

Story-Livingston Correspondence, 1812–1822," 10 *American Journal of Legal History* 224 (1966).

Livingston's opinions on the New York bench may be found in the first three volumes of the New York Common Law Reports which carry the several original reporter series—Johnson's Reports and Cases, Caines Reports and Cases, and Coleman and Caines—containing his opinions. His Supreme Court opinions are contained in the fourth volume of Cranch to the eighth of Wheaton. His circuit court opinions are in the first volume of Paine, which is keyed to the Federal Cases series opposite page 2460 in its thirtieth (appendix) volume.

Brockholst Livingston

REPRESENTATIVE OPINIONS

PIERSON v. POST, 3 CAI. R. 175 (1805)

Occasionally the circumstances of the career of a member of the United States Supreme Court has resulted in his most memorable opinions being written on another bench. Such is the case of at least two Justices, Brockholst Livingston and Benjamin N. Cardozo, who, in a singular series of coincidences, were both learned in the law, both inimitable (though very different) stylists in their prose, and both of whom left their best work in the New York reports rather than those of the United States Supreme Court. In Cardozo's case this resulted from a long career on one bench and a short one on another. For Livingston the result was a consequence of Chief Justice Marshall's dominance of the opinion-writing function during that period of the Supreme Court's history.

If Cardozo put a supple yet stately elegance into his legal writing, Brockholst Livingston endowed his with a quality perhaps even rarer in incidence if not as lofty in *genre*. This was judicial wit. Probably the best example of this talent was his dissent on the New York Supreme Court in *Pierson* v. *Post,* 3 Cai. R. 175, and indeed this appears to be his only opinion to be carried in modern casebooks (see, e.g., E. Fraser, Cases and Readings on Personal Property 12 [1954]). Its subject matter is a fox, hotly pursued by one hunter but slain and taken by another. Smith Thompson, Livingston's future colleague on the United States Supreme Court, wrote the opinion reversing a jury verdict for the frustrated huntsman, while Livingston himself dissented to protest the latter's right to his quarry.

LIVINGSTON, J. My opinion differs from that of the court. Of six exceptions, taken to the proceedings below, all are abandoned except the third, which reduces the controversy to a single question.

Whether a person who, with his own hounds, starts and hunts a fox on waste and uninhabited ground, and is on the point of seizing his prey, acquires such an interest in the animal as to have a right of action against another, who in view of the huntsman and his dogs in full pursuit, and with knowledge of the chase, shall kill and carry him away.

This is a knotty point, and should have been submitted to the arbitration of sportsmen, without poring over Justinian, Fleta, Bracton, Puffendorf, Locke, Barbeyrac, or Blackstone, all of whom have been cited: they would have had no difficulty in coming to a prompt and correct conclusion. In a court thus constituted, the skin and carcass of poor Reynard would have been properly disposed of, and a precedent set, interfering with no usage or custom which the experience of ages has sanctioned, and which must be so well known to every votary of Diana. But the parties have referred the question to our judgment, and we must dispose of it as well as we can, from the partial lights we possess, leaving to a higher tribunal the correction of any mistake which we may be so unfortunate as to make. By the pleadings it is admitted that a fox is a "wild and noxious beast." Both parties have regarded him, as the law of nations does a pirate, *"Hostem humani generis,"* and although *"de mortuis nil nisi bonum"* be a maxim of our profession, the memory of the deceased has not been spared. His depredations on farmers and on barnyards, have not been forgotten; and to put him to death wherever found, is allowed to be meritorious, and of public benefit. Hence it follows, that our decision should have in view the greatest possible encouragement to the destruction of an animal, so cunning and ruthless in his career. But who would keep a pack of hounds; or what gentleman, at the sound of the horn, and at peep of day, would mount his steed, and for hours together, *"sub jove frigido,"* or a vertical sun, pursue the windings of this wily quadruped, if, just as night came on, and his stratagems and strength were nearly exhausted, a saucy intruder, who had not shared in the honors or labors of the chase, were permitted to come in at the death, and bear away in triumph the object of pursuit? Whatever Justinian may have thought of the matter, it must be recollected that his code was compiled many hundred years ago, and it would be very hard indeed, at the distance of so many centuries, not to have a right to establish a rule for ourselves. In his day, we read of no order of men who made it a business, in the language of the declaration in this cause, "with hounds and dogs to find, start, pursue, hunt, and chase," these animals, and that, too, without any other motive than the preservation of Roman poultry; if this diversion had been then in fashion, the lawyers who composed his institutes, would have taken care not to pass it by, without suitable encouragement. If anything, therefore, in the digests or pandects shall appear to militate against the defendant in error, who, on this occasion, was the fox hunter, we have only to say *tempora mutantur;* and if men themselves change with the times, why should not laws also undergo an alteration?

It may be expected, however, by the learned counsel, that more particular notice be taken of their authorities. I have examined them all, and feel great difficulty in determining, whether to acquire dominion over a thing, before in common, it be sufficient that we barely see it, or know where it is, or wish for it, or make a declaration of our will respecting it; or whether, in the case of wild beasts, setting a trap, or lying in wait, or starting, or pursuing, be enough; or if an actual wounding, or killing, or bodily tact and occupation be necessary. Writers on general law, who have favored us with their speculations on these points, differ on them all; but, great as is the diversity of sentiment among them, some conclusion must be adopted on the question immediately before us. After mature deliberation, I embrace that of Barbeyrac as the most rational and least liable to objection. If at liberty, we might imitate the courtesy of a certain emperor, who, to avoid giving offense to the advocates of any of these different doctrines, adopted a middle course, and by ingenious distinctions, rendered it difficult to say (as often happens after a fierce and angry contest) to whom the palm of victory belonged. He ordained, that if a beast be followed with large dogs and hounds, he shall belong to the hunter, not to the chance occupant; and in like manner, if he be killed or wounded with a lance or sword; but if chased with beagles only, then he passed to the captor, not to the first pursuer. If slain with a dart, a sling, or a bow, he fell to the hunter, if still in chase, and not to him who might afterwards find and seize him.

Now, as we are without any municipal regulations of our own, and the pursuit here, for aught that appears on the case, being with dogs and hounds of imperial stature, we are at liberty to adopt one of the provisions just cited, which comports also with the learned conclusion of Barbeyrac, that property in animals *feræ naturæ* may be acquired without bodily touch or manucaption, provided the pursuer be within reach, or have a reasonable prospect (which certainly existed here) of taking what he has thus discovered an intention of converting to his own use.

When we reflect also that the interest of our husbandmen, the most useful of men in any community, will be advanced by the destruction of a beast so pernicious and incorrigible, we cannot greatly err in saying that a pursuit like the present, through waste and unoccupied lands, and which must inevitably and speedily have terminated in corporeal possession, or bodily seisin, confers such a right to the object of it, as to make any one a wrong-doer who shall interfere and shoulder the spoil. The justice's judgment ought, therefore, in my opinion, to be affirmed.

RIGGS v. LINDSAY, 7 CRANCH 500 (1813)

Livingston's specialty on the Supreme Court was prize law. It represented the wartime face of a mercantilistic age wherein governmental functions were subcontracted out to enfranchised, small-scale entrepreneurs. This area of law reached its zenith around the beginning of the nineteenth century and then faded to insignificance as the industrial revolution began to take its impact on war at sea. Hence, while some of Livingston's prize opinions, cited *supra,* should be consulted for an overview of his work on the Supreme Court, they are of wholly antiquarian interest, and one more relevant to modern concerns is set out below. A commercial law case, it illustrates Livingston's concern for the realities of business practice and for the paramountcy of facts. Note also the vigorous style and the absence of citations.

MR. JUSTICE LIVINGSTON delivered the opinion of the Court.

This was an action brought by the defendant in error, in the circuit court of the United States for the District of Columbia, against William Stewart, Charles J. Nourse, Aquila Beall, and the plaintiff in error, Elisha Riggs, as co-partners, to recover from them the amount of certain bills of exchange, and damages, which had been drawn on them by the defendant in error, to reimburse him for certain salt which he had purchased on their account, and which bills, being protested for non-payment, were afterwards paid, with damages, by the plaintiffs below. The defendant, Beall, was not found; the defendants, Nourse and Stewart, confessed judgment, and the other defendant, Riggs, pleaded the general issue.

The declaration contained several counts on the bills of exchange; and two general counts, one for money laid out, expended, and paid, the other for money had and received, under which last counts a verdict was found for the plaintiff.

It appeared in evidence, that some time in November, 1809, Stewart and Beall, two of the defendants below, wrote a letter to the plaintiff, ordering a purchase of salt, and stating that two other persons were concerned in the said order. This letter directed him to purchase from ten to thirty thousand bushels, and authorised him to draw for the amount of such purchases on the defendants, Stewart and Beall, or on George Price & Co. of Baltimore. Purchases of salt were accordingly made by Lindsay, who, from time to time, apprised Stewart and Beall of the same. On the 4th of January, 1810, one of the defendants wrote to Lindsay as follows:

"Sir: You will hold up what salt you may have purchased, and send us a statement of your purchases. You have no doubt received Stewart and Beall's orders, requesting no further purchase. We shall some time hence direct you as to the disposal of the quantity purchased. In the mean time you may draw upon us, or upon Stewart and Beall, for the amount," &c.

It appears that Lindsay afterwards drew several bills of exchange on the parties who had subscribed the last mentioned letter, and who were the defendants, in favour of certain persons therein named, including his commission for purchasing. These bills were presented to the drawees, who refused to accept or pay the same, on which they were protested, and returned to Lindsay, who took them up. By the laws of South Carolina ten per cent. damages are allowed on the return of such bills under protest, and there was proof that these damages had also been paid by Lindsay. After the return of these bills, and payment of them by Lindsay, he sold the salt, and the proceeds on such resale were stated by Lindsay's counsel at the trial to the jury, who were desired to deduct the same from his demand against Riggs, which was done, and a verdict given for the balance. There was no other evidence of the proceeds than such admission, and the defendant, Riggs, denied that the sum stated by Lindsay's counsel was the amount thereof.

In the course of the trial, the counsel of Riggs produced a letter from Nourse to the plaintiffs, which, as he supposed, contained a statement favourable to his client. To discredit this statement the plaintiff produced certain interrogatories, which had been exhibited to Nourse, with his answers, which were at variance with the letter produced by Riggs.

The first exception taken, at the trial, to the conduct of the court, was of its admission of proof of the several bills which had been drawn by Lindsay, and protested and paid by him, and the instruction which it gave to the jury, that under the count for money paid, laid out, and expended, Lindsay might recover, not his commissions, which were included in the bills, but the ten per cent. damages, if the jury were satisfied that they had been actually paid by him.

Neither in the admission of this testimony, nor in the instructions given on it, was any error committed by the circuit court. As Lindsay was expressly authorised to draw, by the letter of the 4th of January, 1810, he certainly had a right to do so; and whether the defendants accepted his bills or not, so as to render themselves liable to the holders of them, there can be no doubt that, as between Lindsay and them, it was their duty, and that they were bound in law to pay them. Not having done so, and Lindsay, in consequence of their neglect, having taken them up, he must be considered as paying their debt, and as this was not a voluntary act on his part, but resulted from his being their surety (as he may well be considered from the moment he drew the bills) it may well be said that in paying the amount of these bills, which ought to have been paid, and was agreed to be paid by the drawees, he paid so much money for their use. Nor can any good reason be assigned for distinguishing the damages from the principal sum; for if it were the duty of the defendants to pay such principal sum, it is as much so to reimburse Lindsay for the damages which, by the law of South Carolina, he was compelled to pay, and which may therefore also be considered as part of the debt due by the defendant in consequence of the violation of their promise, contained in the letter which has just been mentioned.

The second exception which appears on the record is to the admission of certain interrogatories which had been propounded to the defendant, Nourse, with his answers to the same, having an indorsement upon the same, purporting to be an acknowledgment of Nourse that the same were correct.

In the opinion of this court, this paper was rendered proper evidence by the conduct of the defendant, Riggs, who had read as evidence for himself a letter from Nourse to Lindsay, dated the 14th of April, 1810, containing, as he supposed, some matters favourable to his defence. This letter having been thus produced by Riggs himself, it was certainly right to allow Lindsay to discredit the representations made in that letter, by showing that Nourse had himself at another time given a very different account of the same transaction.

The other opinions of the court below, to which exceptions were taken, may be comprised in these two; that the court erred in thinking the defendants jointly liable as co-partners, and that the resale of the salt did not destroy the plaintiff's right of action. In both these opinions this court concurs with the circuit court.

It is perhaps as clear a case of joint liability as can well be conceived. Whatever doubt there might be independent of the letter of the 4th of January, 1810, most certainly that letter puts this question at rest. Every one of the defendants signed it, and there is now no escape from the responsibility which they all thereby incurred to the plaintiff. Nor did Lindsay's selling the salt, after he had taken up these bills, destroy his right of action against the defendants. If he has acted irregularly in so doing, he will be liable, in a proper action, for the damages which the defendants have sustained by such conduct; but such sale could not be pleaded or set up in bar to the present suit. Nor will the defendant, under the circumstances of this case, be injured by the sum which the jury have discounted from Lindsay's demand, if it shall hereafter appear that as much was not allowed the defendant on that account as ought to have been.

The judgment of the circuit court is affirmed, with costs.

Thomas Todd

☆ 1765–1826 ☆

APPOINTED BY

THOMAS JEFFERSON

YEARS ON COURT

1807–1826

Thomas Todd

by

FRED L. ISRAEL

IN FEBRUARY, 1807, Congress amended the Judiciary Act of 1789 by creating a Seventh or Western Circuit composed of Tennessee, Kentucky, and Ohio. A sixth Associate Justice was also added to the Supreme Court to preside over this circuit. President Thomas Jefferson, in considering his choice for the position, asked each of the Tennessee, Kentucky, and Ohio Congressmen to inform him of their preferences from among the lawyers of these states. Thomas Todd was either the first or second candidate of every Congressman, and so Jefferson, without ever having met Todd, nominated him, the Senate unanimously confirmed, and on March 3, 1807, Todd received his commission which made him the first Supreme Court Justice from west of the Appalachian Mountains. The lack of manuscript material available about this quiet, introspective judicial statesman has made Todd one of the least known Supreme Court Justices.

Todd was born in King and Queen County, Virginia, on January 23, 1765, the youngest son of Richard and Elizabeth (Richards) Todd. According to Todd family genealogy tables, Thomas Todd was a direct descendant of the Thomas Todd who settled in Norfolk County, Virginia, in 1669. Hening's *Virginia Statutes At Large* describes the elder Thomas Todd as "formerly of the county of Gloucester, *gentleman,* was in his lifetime seized of a considerable estate in lands, and, among others, of a large and valuable tract lying on the Mattapong river in the county of King and Queen, and of another tract, containing about one thousand acres, lying on the Dragon swamp, in the parish of St. Stephen, in the said county of King and Queen." Much of these land tracts remained intact and eventually passed to Justice Todd's father, Richard, who died when Thomas was eighteen months old. Under the law of primogeniture which existed in the

FRED L. ISRAEL, Associate Professor of History at the City College of New York, is the author of Nevada's Key Pittman.

colony, the estate devolved upon the oldest son, William Todd. Todd's mother also died before he reached maturity. Raised by a guardian who "through mismanagement lost most of the property left him," young Todd, according to old Kentucky histories, obtained a "good English education, and the foundation of one in classics."

In 1781, during the British invasion of Virginia, Todd, then sixteen, served six months as a private in the American army. Returning to his studies after Yorktown, he graduated from Liberty Hall, Lexington, Virginia, in 1783 (later Washington and Lee University). A Presbyterian academy stressing the classics and mathematics, Liberty Hall, formerly Augusta Academy, had just relocated to a site at Lexington, a site donated by three farmers, each giving a portion of their land. Although Todd attended Liberty Hall for more than one year, there are no records of his scholastic or school activities.

After leaving Liberty Hall, Harry Innes, a distinguished lawyer and member of the Virginia Legislature and later Kentucky District Judge, 1784–1816, invited young Todd to live with the Innes family in Bedford County, Virginia. In return for room, board, and instruction in law, Todd tutored the Innes daughters. At this time, the Kentucky section of Virginia began to petition for admission to the Union as a separate state and Innes actively participated in this movement. In the spring of 1784, Innes received a commission to establish a district court in the Kentucky area, and so he moved his family, with Todd accompanying them, across the Appalachians to Danville. Through Innes' connections, Todd served as clerk of the 1784 Danville Convention called by General Benjamin Logan. This was the first of five conventions seeking separation from Virginia held between 1784 and the establishment of the state in 1792—and Todd acted as secretary-clerk for each convention. The last of these drew up the first Kentucky constitution; the original of that document is in Todd's handwriting and is displayed in the Kentucky State Historical Society Library.

Todd was admitted to the Virginia bar in 1788 and soon had a thriving practice specializing in land titles. "He made his first effort at Madison old Court-House," recalled a contemporary. "His slender outfit at the beginning of the term consisted of his horse and saddle and thirty-seven and a half cents in money, but when the Court rose he had enough to meet his current expenses, and returned home with the bonds for two cows and calves." At this time, the Virginia system of public land disposition was very confusing and often led to litigations involving priority and superiority of conflicting and overlapping entries and surveys—sometimes as many as five different surveys embracing the same land. Virginia had insisted that the Compact of Separation with the new state of Kentucky preserve to her entrants and those claiming under them, the same rights that would have protected them in Virginia courts and under Virginia law. Rapidly increasing immigration to Kentucky (the population grew from 73,600 in 1790 to 221,000 in 1800), as well as the desirable quality of this new area of great forests and fertile soil, multiplied the land title perplexities. Todd rapidly achieved a statewide reputation for his knowledge of land law and his practice grew accordingly. From 1792 to 1801, Todd had the additional responsibility of serving as secretary to the new Kentucky legislature as well as federal district court clerk. Upon the creation of Kentucky's Supreme Court (Court of Appeals) under the state's second constitution in 1799, Todd was appointed its chief clerk. The first three men selected for this new court were chosen because of their long and tried experience on the bench. But in 1801, the legislature sensed the desirability of infusing younger blood into the court and so a "Fourth Judge" of the Court of Appeals was created. On December 19, 1801, Governor James Garrard appointed Thomas Todd, then thirty-six, to this new post. Five years later, with the retirement of Chief Justice George Muter, Governor Greenup elevated Todd to that office. He held this post until Jefferson selected him for the Supreme Court the following year.

During Todd's six years on the Kentucky Court of Appeals, decisions were not signed but, according to contemporaries of Todd, he wrote almost all of the land title opinions. The Kentucky Reports contemporaneous with Todd's tenure are the volumes of Sneed and Hardin, beginning at page 106 of Sneed's Reports (May 31, 1804) and ending with page 77 of Hardin's Reports (November 1, 1806). Most of the Court's records from 1801 to May 31, 1804 were destroyed by fire in 1804. The overwhelming majority of cases dealt with by the Court of Appeals during this period involved land titles but in many of the cases it is difficult to determine the point decided because of the lack of sufficient factual statements upon which the opinion rested. The framers of the 1779 Virginia Land Law did not provide for a general state survey but authorized every owner of a land-warrant to make his own entry and survey. The owner, of course, located his land-warrant wherever he chose, but was required to do so in such a way that a subsequent locater could enter the adjoining land. This registration system proved monstrously defective. And, it was with the greatest difficulty that a title could be established at all. As a consequence, interminable disputes and litigation followed. As Kentucky was part of Virginia until 1792 and since the Compact of Separation recognized claims under Virginia laws, most of these disputed land claims came before Todd and the Kentucky Supreme Court. Todd's reputation for fairly adjusting titles in these difficult cases spread throughout the region and it is therefore not surprising that Congressmen from neighboring states urged Jefferson to appoint him to the nation's highest tribunal.

Todd received his Supreme Court commission on March 3, 1807 and he took his seat at the February, 1808 term. He delivered no opinions that session and he missed the 1809 term. "I set out last winter for the Federal City," he wrote his son Charles in May, 1809, "but owing to the extreme high freshlets, which had removed every bridge between Lexington & Chillicothe & almost every bridge & causeway between the latter place & Wheelin, I went no farther than to Chillicothe. Your Mama's ill health when I left her had also considerable influence to induce me to return." Todd's first opinion—five dissenting lines—occurred during the 1810 term in the case of *Finley* v. *Lynn,* 6 Cranch 238 (1810). Marshall, speaking for the Court, ruled that an indemnity bond executed after a partnership agreement, may, in equity, be restrained by that agreement and that a complainant may have relief, although he did not seek this in his suit. In dissenting, Todd wrote "that the complainant was not entitled to a relief" because he had in effect waived financial redress by not requesting it. This was Todd's only dissenting opinion during his Supreme Court service.

Todd remained on the Court until his death in 1826, although personal affairs and illness prevented him from attending the 1809, 1813, 1815, 1819, and 1825 sessions. During his nineteen years as a Justice, the Supreme Court delivered opinions in 644 cases. Todd, throughout this entire period, delivered but fourteen opinions—eleven majority, two concurring, and one dissenting. Ten of his eleven majority opinions involved disputed land and survey claims. One of the more interesting of these cases was *Preston* v. *Browder,* 1 Wheat. 115 (1816). In November, 1777, the North Carolina Assembly established offices in the several counties for receiving land claim entries. But the Assembly did not authorize entries within Indian territory so defined by the Treaty of the Long Island of Holston (July 20, 1777). The state, in an attempt to maintain the sanctity of this treaty, refused to validate entries made contrary to it. Todd upheld the right of the state to make such land claim restrictions. This decision is included below because it illustrates the complicated, but important, land claim cases decided by Todd both on the Kentucky Court and while on the Supreme Court. Likewise, Todd's decision in *Watts* v. *Lindsey's Heirs et al.,* 7 Wheat. 158 (1822), is reprinted because Todd, in his opinion explains the confusing and complicated land title problem which plagued the early settlers. Todd's only Court opinion which did not involve land law was his last. In *Riggs* v. *Taylor,* 9 Wheat. 483 (1824), the Justice made the important procedural ruling, now taken for granted, that "if it is intended to use an original document as evidence, then the original must be produced. But, if the original is in the possession of the other party to the suit, who refuses to produce it, or if the original is lost or destroyed, then secondary evidence will be admitted."

Under the system then prevailing, the Supreme Court Justices had to ride the circuit, in addition to sitting in Washington. Todd's new Seventh or Western Circuit included the then frontier states of Tennessee, Kentucky, and Ohio. Twice a year, except when prevented by illness, Todd held court in Nashville, Frankfort, and Chillicothe. Unfortunately, most of his circuit opinions have disappeared. Several though for the District of West Tennessee have been preserved. See e.g., 1 Overton (Tenn.) 273 (1808), 465 (1809); 1 Cooke (Tenn.) 110–160 (1812), 344–374 (1813); 2 Overton (Tenn.) 110, 118 (1811). Land disputes dominated the court calendar and Todd tended to liberally interpret the several state land laws—"the law should be construed so as to advance the remedy and suppress the mischief," *Dougherty's Heirs* v. *Edmiston,* 1 Cooke (Tenn.) 136 (1812).

In Washington, Chief Justice Marshall dominated the Court. He persuaded his colleagues to reduce the number of their separate decisions in deciding cases in favor of single opinions for the Court as an entity and he strove to achieve unanimity among his fellow Justices. Above all, Marshall succeeded in molding the Court to his own image through his persuasive leadership qualities. Todd served on the Supreme Court during a period which involved the Court in great issues of the day. Marshall's dominance, however, forced most of his colleagues, including Todd, to be but echoes of their Chief. Todd undoubtedly agreed with Marshall's tenets of economic conservatism and with his belief in a strong Union. Although a resident of Kentucky, an area which often threatened to defy Marshall's nationalist doctrines, and even though as a Kentucky Judge he had chastised the federal circuit system in 1802 because "foreigners" decided local issues, Todd now gave his Chief complete and unwavering support. Great policy issues gave rise to cases in which the Court, through Marshall, asserted the supremacy of the national government over claims of state power. Few of Marshall's opinions escaped bitter criticism—and although Jefferson's two other Court appointees, William Johnson and Brockholst Livingston, often disagreed with the Chief, no such dissent came from Todd.

Contemporary accounts describe Todd as "a dark complexioned, good-looking, substantial man . . . patient and candid in investigation, clear and sagacious in judgment, with a just respect for authority, and at the same time, with well-settled views of his own as to the law; never affecting to possess that which he did not know, but with learning of a solid and useful cast. . . . Justice Thomas Todd was an amiable, generous man, of kind heart and popular manners." Todd married Elizabeth Harris in 1788. To them were born five children—their second son, Charles Stewart, was Minister to Russia, 1841–1845. Mrs. Todd died in 1811. The following year Justice Todd married Lucy Payne, a sister of Dolly Madison and the widow of George Steptoe Washington, the President's nephew. The ceremony took place in the East Room of the White House, the first event of this kind to be celebrated in the Executive Mansion. Of this union, three children were born. The Todd family lived in Danville until 1801 and then in Frankfort. Until his death on February 7, 1826, the Judge was involved in local and state civic affairs—he was a charter member of the Kentucky River Company, the first company formed to promote navigation of Kentucky waterways. An inventory of his estate disclosed he was also the owner of Kentucky Turnpike shares, the first publicly improved highway west of the Alleghenys, as well as shares in the Frankfort toll bridge which spanned the Kentucky River. In addition to his Frankfort home, Todd owned more than 7200 acres of land scattered throughout the state and some twenty-odd pieces of real estate in Frankfort. After having provided for his children "their full proportion," as he expressed it, the remainder of his estate was valued at more than $70,000—indeed a sizable sum for this period.

SELECTED BIBLIOGRAPHY

No biography of Todd exists and material about his life must be gleaned from Kentucky state and county histories and from biographical accounts of his Court colleagues. Two brief scholarly articles about Todd are: "Letters of Judge Thomas Todd of Kentucky to His Son at College," 22 *William and Mary Quarterly* 20 (1913); Edward C. O'Rear, "Justice Thomas Todd," 38 *Register of the Kentucky State Historical Society* 113 (1940). In addition, the Supreme Court tribute to Todd is in 13 Pet. iii (1839).

Thomas Todd

REPRESENTATIVE OPINIONS

PRESTON v. BROWDER, 1 WHEAT. 115 (1816)

With the rapid expansion of the United States, it was inevitable that complicated land title and survey disputes would reach the federal courts. *Preston* v. *Browder* illustrates the type of case which Todd decided both on the Kentucky Court of Appeals and during his Supreme Court tenure. The question involved the validity of a North Carolina Assembly Act of April, 1778 which prohibited land entries within the "Indian boundary." North Carolina, attempting to maintain the sanctity of treaties made with the Indians as well as attempting an ordered disposal of the public domain, refused to validate land entries made contrary to these Indian treaties—in this instance the Treaty of the Long Island of Holston, July 20, 1777. Todd in speaking for the Court, upheld the right of North Carolina to make such land restrictions.

TODD, J., delivered the opinion of the court, and, after stating the facts, proceeded as follows:

The question now to be decided by the court is, whether the charge and instructions required by the plaintiff's counsel ought to have been given, and whether the one given was correct.

In the construction of the statutory or local laws of a state, it is frequently necessary to recur to the history and situation of the country, in order to ascertain the reason, as well as the meaning, of many of the provisions in them, to enable a court to apply, with propriety, the different rules for construing statutes. It will be found, by a recurrence to the history of North Carolina, at the time of passing this act, that she had, but a short time before, shaken off her colonial government, and assumed a sovereign independent one of her own choice; that, during the colonial system, by instructions and proclamations of the governor, the citizens were restrained and prohibited from extending their settlements to the westward, so as to encroach on lands set apart for the Indian tribes; that these encroachments had produced hostilities; and that, on the 20th of July, 1777, a treaty of peace had been concluded at fort Henry, on Holston river, near the Long Island, between commissioners from the state of North Carolina and the chiefs of that part of the Cherokee nation called the *Overhill* Indians; and that a boundary between the state and the said Indians was established. When the legislature of North Carolina were passing the act of November, 1777, establishing offices for receiving entries of claims for lands in the several counties within the state, it is improbable that the foregoing circumstances were not contemplated by them; and hence must have arisen the restriction in the act, as to lands "which have accrued, or shall accrue, to this state, by treaty or conquest." If this be not the ground or reason of the provision, it will be difficult to find one on which it can operate. It may be asked, where was the land which was to accrue by *treaty or conquest,* if not within the chartered limits of that state? If it was in a foreign country, or from a sister state, the restriction was unnecessary, because, in either case, it was not within the limits of *any* county within that state, and, of course, not subject to be entered for. The restriction must apply, then, to lands within the chartered limits of the state, which it contemplated would be acquired, by treaty or conquest, from the Indian tribes, for none other can be imagined. It is not to be presumed, that the legislature intended, so shortly after making the treaty, to violate it, by permitting entries to be made west of the line fixed by the treaty. From the preamble of the act, as well as other parts of it, it is clearly discernible that the legislature intended "to parcel out their vacant lands to industrious people, for the settlement thereof, and increasing the strength and number of the people of the country, and affording a comfortable and easy subsistence for families." Would these objects be attained by permitting settlements encroaching on the lands lately set apart, by treaty, for the use of the Indian tribes? by provoking hostilities with these tribes, and diminishing the strength of the country by a cruel, unnecessary, and unprofitable warfare with them? Surely not. However broad and extensive the words of the act may be, authorizing the entry takers of any county to receive claims for *any lands* lying in such county, under certain restrictions, yet, from the whole context of the act, the legislative intention, to prohibit and restrict entries from being made on lands reserved for Indian tribes, may be discerned. And this construction is fortified and supported by the act of April, 1778, passed to amend and explain the act of November, 1777; the 5th section of which expressely forbids the entering or surveying any lands within the Indian hunting grounds, recognises the western boundary as fixed by the above-mentioned treaty, and declares void all entries and surveys which have been, or shall thereafter be made within the Indian boundary.

It is objected, that the act of April, 1778, so far as it relates to entries made before its passage, is unconstitutional and void.

If the reasoning in the previous part of this opinion be correct, that objection is not well founded. That reasoning is founded upon the act of 1777, and the history and situation of the country at that time. The act of 1778 is referred to, as a legislative declaration, explaining and amending the act of 1777. It is argued that there is no recital in the act of 1778, declaring, that the act of 1777 had been misconstrued or mistaken by the citizens of the state; or, that entries had been made on lands, contrary to the meaning and intention of that act; and, that the 5th section is an exercise of legislative will, declaring null and void rights which had been acquired under a previous law. Although the legislature may not have made the recital and declaration in the precise terms mentioned, nor used the most appropriate expressions to communicate their meaning, yet it will be seen, by a careful perusal of the act, that they profess to *explain,* as well as to amend, the act of 1777. Upon a full review of all the acts of the legislature of North Carolina, respecting the manner of appropriating their vacant lands, and construing them *in pari materia,* there is a uniform intention manifested to prohibit and restrict entries from being made on lands included within the Indian boundaries. Therefore, this court unanimously affirms the decision of the circuit court with costs.

WATTS v. LINDSEY'S HEIRS ET AL., 7 WHEAT. 158 (1822)

In *Watts* v. *Lindsey's Heirs et al.,* Todd in speaking for the Court, ruled that a party must prove his case on the strength of his own land title and not on the weakness of his adversary's land claim.

Disputes such as this were frequently decided by the state as well as federal courts in the early part of the nineteenth century. This case illustrates Todd's pragmatic reasoning, so characteristic of his many land claim opinions.

Mr. Justice TODD delivered the opinion of the Court.

This controversy arises from entries for lands in the Virginia military reservation, lying between the Scioto and Little Miami Rivers, in the district of Ohio.

The plaintiff in the court below (Watts,) exhibited his bill in Chancery for the purpose of compelling the respondents to surrender the legal title, acquired under an elder grant founded on a surveyor's entry, than the one under which he derives his title.

The entry, set forth in the bill, and claimed by the plaintiff, is in the following words: "7th August, 1787. Captain Ferdinand O'Neal enters 1000 acres, &c. on the waters of the Ohio, beginning at the northwest corner of Stephen T. Mason's entry, No. 654, thence with his line, east 400 poles, north 400 poles, west 400 poles, south 400 poles."

The entry of Stephen T. Mason, referred to in the above entry, is in the following words:

7th August, 1787. Stephen T. Mason, assignee, &c. enters 1000 acres of land on part of a military warrant, No. 2012, on the waters of the Ohio, beginning 640 poles north from the mouth of the *third creek* running into the Ohio above the mouth of the Little Miami River; thence running west 160 poles; north 400 poles; east 400 poles; south 400 poles; thence to the beginning."

The respondents, in their answers, deny the validity of O'Neal's entry; allege that it is vague and uncertain, and that the survey made on it includes no part of the land described in the entry, and if properly surveyed would not interfere with any part of the land to which they claim title; that the creek selected by the complainant as the *third creek*, in the entry of Mason, on which that of O'Neal depends, is not in truth and in fact, the *third creek* running into the Ohio above the mouth of the Little Miami River; but that another is.

The depositions of several witnesses were taken, and other exhibits filed in the cause. Upon a final hearing in the Circuit Court, a decree was pronounced dismissing the plaintiff's bill.

The cause is now brought into this Court by appeal, and the *principal question* to be decided is, whether from the allegations and proofs in the cause, the entry claimed by the plaintiff can be sustained upon sound construction, and legal principles arising out of the land laws applicable thereto.

Before we go into an examination of that question, we will dispose of some preliminary objections made by the counsel for the respondents. They were that attested copies of the entries and patent referred to, and made exhibits in the bill are not in the record: that there does not appear in the record any assignment, or proof of an assignment from O'Neal to the plaintiff. Nor does it appear from the platt where the entry of O'Neal was actually surveyed, nor does it designate the creeks running into the Ohio above the mouth of the Little Miami River, so as to ascertain the *third creek*.

Some of these objections seem to be well founded, and might induce the Court to dismiss the bill, but such dismission should be without prejudice to the commencing of any other suit the party might choose to bring; the effect of which would be only turning the parties out of Court, without deciding the merits of the cause. We have therefore attentively examined the record, and are of opinion it contains enough to get at and decide the merits.

It has been long and well established as a rule of law and equity, that a party must recover on the strength of his own title, and not on the weakness of his adversary's title.

In order to uphold and support an entry, it is incumbent on the party claiming under it, to show that the objects called for in it are so sufficiently described, or so notorious, that others, by using reasonable diligence, could readily find them.

As O'Neal's entry is dependent on Mason's, if the objects called for in the latter can be ascertained, the position of the former can be precisely and certainly fixed.

The Ohio and Little Miami Rivers, from general history, the one having been used before, at, and since the time when these entries were made, as the great highway in going from the eastern to the western country, and each of them having been referred to in general laws, and designated as boundaries of certain districts of country, we consider must be deemed and taken as being identified and notorious, without further proof.

The *third creek,* running into the Ohio above the mouth of the Little Miami River, is then the only and principal object to be ascertained, to fix the entry of Mason, with specialty and precision. The plaintiff has assumed what is now called *Cross Creek* for the beginning, to run the 640 poles north from the mouth of the *third creek,* as called for in Mason's entry. The respondents contend, that what is now called Muddy Creek, and sometimes Nine Mile, is "the third creek."

It seems to be admitted, in argument, that *Cross Creek* is not, in truth and in fact, numerically the third creek above the mouth of the Little Miami. But the counsel for the plaintiff contends that the early explorers of the country, when the entries were made, designated Muddy Creek as the second. That streams then called *creeks,* have since been degraded into *runs,* and other streams, then called *runs,* are now termed *creeks.*

If this argument was supported by the proofs in the cause, it would be entitled to great consideration; but upon a careful and minute examination, there is a great preponderance of testimony against it: there is the deposition of one witness that affords some foundation for it; there are also the depositions of many witnesses who contradict it. But waiving this testimony, and examining this entry upon its face, it is obvious that subsequent locators and explorers commencing their researches at the mouth of the Little Miami River, would examine the creeks emptying into the Ohio above, according to their *numerical* order. The words "the third creek," emphatically applies to that order; nor would they depart from it, unless another stream, by general *reputation* or *notoriety,* had been so considered. It has however never been held that *reputation* or *notoriety* could be established by a single witness; and it may be further observed, that the other witness, whose deposition has been taken on the part of the plaintiff, states, that he had meandered the Ohio, and in his connection, had laid down Muddy, or Nine Mile Creek, as the third, and that he so considered it, until the year 1806, or 1807, when from the information of the other witness, and an examination of the entries and surveys on the books of the principal surveyor, he was induced to change his opinion. It is also in proof that the plaintiff and the last mentioned witness, in searching for O'Neal's entry, claimed a different creek as being the *third,* and directed the survey to be commenced from it. If, then, a locator and deputy surveyor, who had meandered the Ohio, and designated Muddy Creek as the *third,* and had so considered it for nearly ten years, it is surely a strong circumstance to show negatively, that *Cross Creek* was not in fact numerically, nor by general reputation or notoriety, considered as "the third creek." If an examination of the records in the principal surveyor's office would shew that the streams were designated and numbered differently, it was incumbent on the party to exhibit at least so much thereof as would conduce to prove the fact. It is incompetent to prove it by parol.

Upon mature consideration of the whole case, it is the unanimous opinion of the Court, that the decree of the Circuit Court be

Affirmed with costs.

Gabriel Duvall

☆ 1752–1844 ☆

APPOINTED BY

JAMES MADISON

YEARS ON COURT

1812–1835

Gabriel Duvall

by

IRVING DILLIARD

THERE COULD BE no question about the identity of two of the strongest public personalities in the new United States of America in the second decade of the nineteenth century. One was staunch, determined John Marshall of Virginia, Chief Justice of the United States and expounder of the Constitution. Another was granite-faced, golden-voiced Daniel Webster of New England, member of Congress and, excepting possibly only John C. Calhoun, the greatest American orator of the generation.

To break with either Marshall or Webster would have been an act of outstanding boldness. To go up against both would have taken courage to a rare degree. To have done the latter in an important Supreme Court case would have increased still further the strength of character required. Yet that is exactly what Gabriel Duvall (1752–1844), Associate Justice of the Supreme Court, did in the *Dartmouth College* case of 1819.

Webster was counsel for the historic college in New Hampshire from which he was graduated and which he had grown to love as if it were his second home. And Marshall, as Chief Justice, wrote the decision in the case that limited the power of the state legislature in dealing with contracts and thus became one of the early judicial landmarks in the development of the young federal system.

Justice Duvall generally supported Chief Justice Marshall's constitutional views, but here he parted company with the presiding officer of his Court. He did not write out his contrary opinion. The record in *Dartmouth College* v. *Woodward,* 4 Wheat. 518 (1819), states simply but also flatly: "Mr. Justice DUVALL dissented."

IRVING DILLIARD, former reporter and editor of the St. Louis Post-Dispatch, *has taught at Princeton and is currently a member of the Board of Trustees at the University of Illinois. He has published numerous articles and books including* One Man's Stand for Freedom; Mr. Justice Black and The Bill of Rights.

If it is to be assumed that by not taking the time or space to produce a detailed formal dissenting opinion, Justice Duvall showed what he thought of Webster's long oratorical plea before the bench and of Chief Justice Marshall's pioneering decision for the Supreme Court, then the blunt entry on behalf of Justice Duvall becomes even the more remarkable.

The Associate Justice who had this courage came of an old Maryland family. He was born on December 6, 1752, at "Marietta," the ancestral seat and plantation on the South River in Prince George's County, near Buena Vista. The land had been patented by Lord Baltimore to Martin DuVal, great-grandfather of Gabriel Duvall.

Marin DuVal, written more frequently as Mareen Duval, was born in Normandy, France, about 1630. He was a Huguenot planter and merchant who left Nantes to escape religious persecution. Emigrating by way of England, where he stayed a short time, he settled in Anne Arundel County, Maryland, before 1659. He died in August, 1694, leaving among other things a state of confusion as to the spelling of both his first and last names.

"The name was certainly in the French Marin," wrote James Loder Raymond in "Some Colonial Families: Duvall and DuVall of Maryland," in the *American Historical Register* (August, 1895) pp. 1474–76. Raymond stated that the earliest mention he found for the name was to a "Richard Du Val, Normandy, 1261." He quoted the Huguenot historian, Charles W. Baird, as accepting the name "Marin" and asserting that "the original of the name du Val was probably in Lorraine from la Ville Remiremont (Vosges)."

Genealogist Raymond cited the changes in Marin and DuVall as especially interesting to members of his historical-biographical lineage profession "as showing how names are changed and misspelled in documents and records." He noted that descendents of the original DuVal and founder of the family in the American colonies came to spell their last name DuVal, DuVall, and Duvall. There doubtless were other variations, for as George Norbury Mackenzie, the editor, noted in *Colonial Families of the U.S.A.* Vol. 1 (1907, 1966), pp. 142–151, it was also in earlier times "du Val."

The exact year of Marin DuVal's arrival from England is not known. Mackenzie's work is authority for the statement that he appeared in Anne Arundel County "about the year 1655." Colonial land records show that on August 25, 1659, the South River tract was surveyed and assigned to him with title. The land thus acquired by the French voluntary exile was called "LaVal" or "DuVal."

To the several hundred acres with which he started, this first American DuVal joined other tracts whenever opportunities arose with the result that his total accumulation of land reached into the thousands of acres. This made him one of the important landholders of colonial Maryland.

But Marin DuVal was more than a landowner and planter. He responded to calls of public service and necessity. Thus he contributed to the cost of an expedition against the Nanticoke Indians in 1678. When the General Assembly of the colony in 1683 appointed a commission to purchase sites and lay out towns, it turned to Marin DuVal as one of its members. Mackenzie's description of DuVal as "a prominent and useful citizen of Anne Arundel County, Maryland," was fully justified.

Marin DuVal was married three times and possibly a fourth, although the evidence for a union beyond the third is scant. Mackenzie did not name the first wife at all and about the second remarked only that she was "Susanna ———, who died about 1692." He named the third as Mary Stanton and said that she died between 1761 and 1782.

Raymond expanded on this somewhat by writing that for his second wife DuVal chose "an English lady by whom he had also six children." This placement of the children by the two marriages came from a family historian, Mary R. Duval of Baltimore.

Twelve children of Marin DuVal, six sons and six daughters by the two marriages, were living at the time of his death at his home, "Middle Plantation," on the South River. These second generation descendants were referred to by him in his will, dated August 2, 1694, whereby he devised his property to his widow and the sons and daughters. Listed probably in the order of their birth, the will named them as: Mareen, John, Eleanor, Samuel, Susannah, Lewis, Mareen, Catharine, Mary, Elizabeth, Johanna, and Benjamin.

The repetition of the name Mareen is explained by the fact that the father was so pleased with his name that he used it for his first son by the earlier marriage and also for a son in the next marriage.

The Marin or Mareen of this later union was born in 1678 and was married October 21, 1701, to Elizabeth Jacob. This Mareen—and it becomes necessary at this point if not earlier to shift the spelling—and his wife, according to genealogist Raymond, had a large family, including a son Benjamin, born April 4, 1711. This Benjamin married Susanna Tyler, daughter of Colonel Robert Tyler of Queen Ane Town. Benjamin and Susanna Tyler Duvall—and now change in the spelling of the last name is also in order—were the parents of Gabriel Duvall who became the Supreme Court Justice.

While the fact of Gabriel Duvall's parentage is unquestioned, it is stated in J. D. Warfield's *The Founders of Anne Arundel and Howard Counties, Maryland* (Baltimore, 1905) p. 105, that "Benjamin and Sophia Griffith Duvall were the parents of the Benjamin Duvall who married Susanna Tyler and had issue, Gabriel, who became Judge of the United States Supreme Court." That would put two Benjamins as well as two Marins or Mareens ahead of Justice Gabriel Duvall in direct male line in the colonies.

There are two reasons why this much space has been taken up with a description of Justice Duvall's family, its origin, its coming to the colonies, and its development in succeeding generations.

First, it is easy for the reader to be confused by the name changes on the one hand and by the repetitions on the other, and the need therefore is for the account to be as accurate as possible. Second, it is only through a presentation of some detail that the character and quality of Justice Duvall's family background becomes apparent.

The family of Benjamin and Susanna Tyler Duvall also was a large one. Gabriel, whose name had been borne by an uncle in the preceding generation, was sixth among ten children and the second son. Born late in 1752, he grew to manhood in the years leading to the Revolutionary War. Thus he was in his early twenties at the time of the Declaration of Independence.

Young Gabriel Duvall was first educated, as were his contemporaries with means, in the classics. Then he was trained for the law and was admitted to the bar in 1778. But before that he had gotten into public life in April, 1775, as the appointed clerk of the Maryland Convention. He served as well as clerk of the Council of Safety, the executive body of the Convention. He held the latter post until 1777, at which time the Maryland state government was created, whereupon he was designated as clerk of the state House of Delegates.

Busy as he was with his education and preparation for the legal profession, he answered the call to arms in the Revolutionary War. He was chosen mustermaster and commissary of stores for the armed forces of Maryland on January 3, 1776. Later he was a private in the Maryland militia at Morristown and Brandywine.

In the latter years of the war, beginning in 1781, he served as one of the commissioners to control and protect confiscated British property in the colonies. Before the war was over, he was elected on November 15, 1782, to the Maryland State Council. He was re-elected in 1783 and held the post, save for a brief period, until his term expired in 1785.

Prior to 1787 he had established residence in Annapolis in order to be close to the Maryland Superior Court situated there. In that year he was elected to the Maryland House of Delegates to represent the voters of Annapolis and he served in that capacity until 1794 when he was elected to the United States House of Representatives.

Meantime, on April 23, 1787, he was selected as one of the first group of five Maryland delegates to the Constitutional Convention at Philadelphia. At that time Duvall was thirty-five years old. However, although he might have been a party to the historic assemblage that drafted and submitted the federal Constitution, he did not serve at the Convention. He joined the four others, including Charles Carroll of Carrollton and Robert Hanson Harrison, in the decision not to attend. Subsequently five other Maryland delegates were selected, three of whom signed the completed document.

After the Constitution was ratified and the new nation came into being, Duvall was an early member of Congress. When John Francis Mercer, one of Maryland's first representatives resigned, Duvall was elected as a Republican-Democrat to fill the vacancy. He took his seat on November 11, 1794, as a member of the Third Congress, and subsequently was returned by the voters to the Fourth Congress. He himself resigned on March 28, 1796, to accept a seat as Chief Justice of the General Court of Maryland, on April 2 of the same year. He was elected Judge of the Court of Appeals of Maryland on January 16, 1806, but declined to serve.

Duvall's duties as Judge on the Maryland Court permitted him also to serve as Recorder of the Mayor's Court in Annapolis. In this latter post, he heard Roger Brooke Taney, later Chief Justice of the United States, make his maiden speech in 1799 as a member of the bar.

Duvall was chosen to be a member of the Electoral College in the Adams-Jefferson election of 1796 and again in 1800 when Jefferson became President. When Jefferson was called on to fill the new post of comptroller of the Treasury, he picked Duvall for it, on December 15, 1802. Duvall worked diligently in this position until Jefferson's successor in the presidency, James Madison, nominated the now widely experienced Marylander to be an Associate Justice of the United States Supreme Court.

Duvall was appointed to the nation's highest tribunal on November 15, 1811, and occupied the seat of Associate Justice Samuel Chase, who had died on June 19, 1811. Duvall's nomination was confirmed only three days later, November 18, and came at the same time as the confirmation of Justice Joseph Story to succeed William Cushing. Justice Duvall took up his new duties at the opening of the next term of the Supreme Court, February 3, 1812. He was then three months beyond his fifty-ninth birthday.

With Justices Duvall and Story seated on the Court, the majority was passed to members of the Republican-Democratic Party of Jefferson and Madison. But throughout Justice Duvall's tenure of nearly twenty-five years, John Marshall was the Chief Justice. And John Marshall dominated the high bench—not only its work, but also the men who sat on it.

Chief Justice Marshall's influence held particularly with respect to the work of the judges when they sat together. It was necessarily less true when the Associate Justices rode their circuits which they did much of the time. Justice Duvall's circuit took him to sittings in Maryland and Delaware.

Although Justices Duvall and Story were confirmed the same day, Justice Duvall outranked Justice Story in seniority. The full complement of Supreme Court Justices was listed at the outset of the February term, 1812, by William Cranch, then Supreme Court reporter as well as Chief Judge of the Circuit Court of the District of Columbia, as follows:

Honorable John Marshall, Chief Justice.
Honorable Bushrod Washington,
Honorable William Johnson,
Honorable Brockholst Livingston,
Honorable Thomas Todd, } Justices.
Honorable Gabriel Duvall,
Honorable Joseph Story,

Justice Duvall's prior service on the Maryland Supreme Court enabled him to assume his share of the work of the United States Supreme Court from the start. His first substantial work came in his opinion for the Court in *Archibald*

Freeland v. *Heron, Lenox and Company,* 7 Cranch 147 (1812). The case involved a straightforward commercial problem of a disputed account between a Virginia Company and a London supplier who sued on a long-standing debt. Duvall in a direct and simple decision found for the London creditor, noting that the Americans had not disputed the account for two years and only then began to complain about it.

The work of the Supreme Court in its early years in adjusting controversies arising under the application of federal authority was illustrated by Justice Duvall's opinion in 1813 in *United States* v. *January and Patterson,* 7 Cranch 572. In that case a federal collector of revenue had given two bonds for his official conduct at different periods and with different sureties. On the settlement of his accounts, a shortage was found. His supervisor promised to apply whatever money was available exclusively to the discharge of the first bond although some of the payments were for money collected and paid after the second bond was given. The government sought to hold both sureties responsible and was upheld by the Court. Justice Duvall said in the Supreme Court's opinion:

> *In this case a majority of the Court is of opinion that the rule adopted in ordinary cases is not applicable to a case circumstanced as this is; where the receiver is a public officer not interested in the event of the suit, and who receives on account of the United States, where the payments are indiscriminately made, and where different sureties, under distinct obligations, are interested. It will be generally admitted that monies arising due, and collected subsequently in the execution of the second bond, cannot be applied to the discharge of the first bond, without manifest injury to the surety in the second bond; and* vice versa, *justice between the different sureties can only be done by reference to the collector's books, and the evidence which they contain may be supported by parol testimony, if any in the possession of the parties interested.* Judgement reversed.

In *Prince* v. *Bartlett,* 8 Cranch 431 (1814), Duvall wrote the Court's decision in an important federal-state conflict. The United States had obtained a judgment against two Massachusetts merchants for duties on goods they had imported. After judgment, the merchants' goods were seized by a local sheriff to satisfy debts of other individuals. Prince, a federal marshal, broke into the sheriff's warehouse and seized the goods on the basis of the prior judgment, acting under a federal law giving the government priority "in all cases of insolvency." Duvall held that a formal petition of bankruptcy had to be filed before the law could be applied and therefore the property had to be returned to the sheriff for the benefit of local creditors:

> *The property in question being in the possession of the sheriff by virtue of legal process, before the issuing the writ on behalf of the United States, was bound to satisfy the debts for which it was taken; and the rights of the individual creditors thus acquired could not be defeated by the process on the part of the United States subsequently issued.*

In its early terms, the Supreme Court dealt with a large proportion of maritime and port cases. One of these was *The Frances and Eliza. Coates,*

Claimant, 8 Wheat. 398 (1823), for which Justice Duvall wrote the Court's unanimous opinion. The *Frances and Eliza* sailed from London, in February, 1819, for South America with 170 men aboard "for service of the patriots," under Simon Bolivar. At one point in the voyage the ship stood off the coast of Falmouth, in the island of Jamaica (owned by Great Britain), while the Captain, Coates, went into Falmouth in his boat for provisions. He returned the next day for more supplies, landed a passenger at Falmouth and took two on board for New Orleans. Under the Navigation Act passed in 1818, any British ship coming from or touching at a British port closed to American ships was liable to forfeit on reaching the United States. The question was whether the continuity of the voyage was broken under the terms of the Navigation Act.

Justice Duvall, again finding for the foreign plaintiff, stated:

> *The Frances and Eliza did not enter the port of Falmouth, but stood off and on, four or five miles from the harbour, for a few days, during which time the master went on shore to get provisions, of which he was in want. Whether he endeavoured to produce freight there, is a fact not ascertained by the testimony. It is certain that he did not obtain it, because it is admitted that the vessel sailed in ballast to New-Orleans. His real object in going on shore at Falmouth, appears to have been to procure provisions, of which the ship's crew were much in want. And there is no evidence of any act done by him, which can be construed into a breach of the act concerning navigation. The policy of that act, without doubt, was to counteract the British colonial system of navigation; to prevent British vessels from bringing British goods from the islands, in exclusion of vessels of the United States on a footing of reciprocity with British vessels. The system of equality was what was aimed at. The landing a passenger there, who casually got employment, and for that reason chose to remain on the island; and the taking in two passengers there, one of which was a boy and a relative, and the other taken, passage free, to New-Orleans, are not deemed to be acts in contravention of the true construction of the navigation act.*

As the issue of slavery came to the fore in the country, it also rose, in aspects at least, in the Supreme Court. In *Le Grand* v. *Darnall,* 2 Pet. 664 (1829), Justice Duvall declared for the Court the rule that the devise of property by a master to his slave entitled the slave to his freedom by necessary implication. The master, in this case, had attempted to set free his ten-year-old son, born of a slave woman. However, a Maryland law provided that the manumission of any slave under forty-five years old was not effective. Nevertheless the Supreme Court held the son was free since other property had been deeded to him and under Maryland law this had the effect of freeing him.

In another slavery case, Justice Duvall cited Maryland practice with which he was very familiar in dissenting from the holding of the Court in *Mima Queen and Child, Petitioners for Freedom* v. *Hepburn,* 7 Cranch 290 (1812), in which Chief Justice Marshall excluded hearsay evidence tending to establish the freedom of two slaves. Marshall felt that the intrinsic unworthiness of hearsay evidence made it inadmissible unless it fit within a well-known exception, such as pedigree or custom. Duvall objected, stating:

> *In Maryland the law has been for many years settled that on a petition for freedom where the petitioner claims from an ancestor who has been dead for a great length of time, the issue may be proved by hearsay evidence, if the fact is of such antiquity that living testimony cannot be procured. Such was the opinion of the judges of the General Court of Maryland, and their decision was affirmed by the unanimous opinion of the judges of the High Court of Appeals in the last resort, after full argument by the ablest counsel at the bar. I think the decision was correct. Hearsay evidence was admitted upon the same principle, upon which it is admitted to prove a custom, pedigree and the boundaries of land;—because from the antiquity of the transactions to which these subjects may have reference, it is impossible to produce living testimony. To exclude hearsay in such cases, would leave the party interested without remedy. It was decided also that the issue could not be prejudiced by the neglect or omission of the ancestor. If the ancestor neglected to claim her right, the issue could not be bound by length of time, it being a natural inherent right. It appears to me that the reason for admitting hearsay evidence upon a question of freedom is much stronger than in cases of pedigree or in controversies relative to the boundaries of land. It will be universally admitted that the right to freedom is more important than the right of property.*
>
> *And people of color from their helpless condition under the uncontrolled authority of a master, are entitled to all reasonable protection. A decision that hearsay evidence in such cases shall not be admitted, cuts up by the roots all claims of the kind, and puts a final end to them, unless the claim should arise from a fact of recent date, and such a case will seldom, perhaps never, occur.*

Although Justice Duvall differed from Chief Justice Marshall notably in the historic case of *The Trustees of Dartmouth College* v. *Woodward,* 4 Wheat 518 (1819), the Federalist Chief Justice and the Republican-Democratic Associate Justice stood together on more than one significant occasion. Such a time came in 1827 with a sharply divided bench in the important decision in *Ogden* v. *Saunders,* 12 Wheat. 213. The issue concerned the extent to which Congress, in establishing uniform laws on the subject of bankruptcies throughout the United States, had excluded or otherwise affected the right of the states to legislate on the same subject. That was one of the few times when Chief Justice Marshall found himself on the losing side in a constitutional controversy. Justice Duvall, joined by Justice Story, supported the Chief Justice against an overriding majority.

A large number of other significant cases were heard and decided during Justice Duvall's tenure. Among these were: *Martin* v. *Hunter's Lessee,* 1 Wheat. 304 (1816); *McCulloch* v. *Maryland,* 14 Wheat 316 (1819); *Cohens* v. *Virginia,* 6 Wheat. 264 (1821); *Gibbons* v. *Ogden,* 9 Wheat. 1 (1824); *Brown* v. *Maryland,* 12 Wheat. 419 (1827); and *Buckner* v. *Finley and Van Lear,* 2 Pet. 586 (1829). In all of these cases, Duvall voted with Marshall to expand and define the power of the federal government or narrow a state's power over commerce. His own role was small but his voice and vote were consistently on the side of the national government. Only in the *Dartmouth College* case did he desert the Chief Justice.

Justice Duvall was one of the relatively small number of Supreme Court Judges throughout its history whose tenure approximated a quarter century. Ascending to the highest bench when he was almost sixty years of age, he served twenty-three years and two months, and resigned about January 10, 1835 in his eighty-third year.

As Justice Duvall advanced in years, members of the bar, court attendants and visitors saw him as "a venerable among the Justices." At the three-quarter century mark, he was described as "the oldest looking man on the bench," (*Early Indiana Trials; and Sketches: Reminiscences by Hon. O. H. Smith,* 1858, p. 138.) The visiting counsel further said of Justice Duvall's patriarchal mien: "His head was white as a snow-bank, with a long white cue hanging down to his waist."

The unfortunate and handicapping disability of impaired hearing overtook the aging jurist. Charles Sumner, then a young lawyer from Massachusetts only recently out of Harvard, attended the Supreme Court in 1834 and wrote of the experience: "Judge Duvall is eighty-two years old and is so deaf as to be unable to participate in conversation." After studying the affliction and its effect on the Supreme Court and its work during those years, historian Carl Brent Swisher wrote of Justice Duvall that "arguments before the Court meant little or nothing to him."

There is a touching line in the Marshall-Story correspondence on Justice Duvall's deafness and the concern of his colleagues as to its effect on the arguments before, and the deliberations of, the Court. In connection with the arrangements of the Chief Justice for rented rooms, a sympathetic, understanding Marshall wrote to Justice Story on June 26, 1831: "Brother Duvall must be with us or he will be unable to attend consultations."

Inevitably this situation produced difficulties and much embarrassment. On an earlier occasion, the present author wrote of it: "For perhaps a decade his resignation was expected almost from week to week and there was jealous speculation as to his successor. Apparently he held his seat, though incapacitated and not infrequently absent, to prevent the appointment of someone whom he thought 'too much of a politician' for the Court" (Irving Dilliard, "Gabriel Duvall," in the *Dictionary of American Biography,* Supplement One [1945] pp. 272–274). This assessment of Justice Duvall's motivation was the conclusion of Professor Swisher in his biography of Chief Justice Taney after a careful study of the Supreme Court during that period.

When at last it became necessary to rectify the situation, notwithstanding the old Judge's preferences, the clerk of the Court told him that President Andrew Jackson had in mind appointing fellow Marylander, Roger Brooke Taney, as soon as Justice Duvall submitted his own resignation. This was the assurance that Justice Duvall apparently wanted. He did resign, departed from Washington, and retired to "Marietta," his birthplace.

As a matter of fact, Roger B. Taney, a Roman Catholic, did not quite succeed Gabriel Duvall, descendant of a Huguenot Protestant refugee from

France. As Chief Justice Marshall, the only member of the Court to outrank Justice Duvall in seniority in 1835, served only a short time longer himself, it was to the Marshall seat at the center of the Court that President Jackson appointed Duvall's younger colleague from Maryland. Phillip Barbour of Virginia took Duvall's seat in 1836.

At "Marietta" he lived comfortably and pleasantly in old and familiar surroundings for close to another decade. He had survived two wives. His first wife, Mary Bryce, was the daughter of Captain Robert Bryce of Annapolis. They were married on July 24, 1787. She died on March 24, 1790, soon after the birth of their only son, Edmund Bryce Duvall, who enjoyed a military career and rose to the rank of colonel. The second wife was Jane Gibbon, daughter of Captain James Gibbon, to whom he was married on May 5, 1795. She died in April, 1834, less than a year before Justice Duvall's resignation from the bench.

In retirement Gabriel Duvall gave attention to the family history, to his son and nieces and nephews, and to the Maryland fields and woods cherished by his ancestors. After living quietly into his ninety-second year, he died near Glen Dale, Prince George County, on March 6, 1844, from the infirmities of his advanced age. His body was laid to rest in the private family cemetery at "Marietta." Memorial services were held in a number of places including the Supreme Court where Justice Story, confirmed on the same day as Justice Duvall, thirty-three years earlier, paid a warm tribute to his longtime colleague. The printed record of the Supreme Court notes that Justice Story spoke of Gabriel Duvall's "irbanity [*sic*], his courtesy, his gentle manners, his firm integrity and undependence [*sic*] and his sound judgment" (2 *Howard,* xi).

Ernest Sutherland Bates, in his book, *The Story of the Supreme Court* (1936), made a manifestly unfair judgment when he dismissed Gabriel Duvall as "probably the most insignificant of all Supreme Court Judges." But it is undoubtedly true that he has been one of the most neglected of them, perhaps the most neglected of all. For he was the only one eligible who was omitted from the original twenty volumes of the *Dictionary of American Biography,* a slight that was corrected with the publication of the first supplementary volume. The venerable jurist from Maryland would have been unperturbed.

SELECTED BIBLIOGRAPHY

There is no substantial biographical study of Duvall. The fullest prior account, so far as extensive search disclosed, is Irving Dilliard's article in the *Dictionary of American Biography,* Supplement One (New York, 1945), pp. 272–274. It corrected the *D. A. B.'s* omission of Duvall from its original twenty volumes.

In addition to sources cited in the text above consult: *Biographical Directory of the American Congress: 1774–1961* (Washington, 1961); *Maryland Archives,* vols. XI, XII, XVI, XXI, XLII, XLV, XLVII, and XLVIII (1892–

1931); *Proceedings of the Conventions of the Province of Maryland Held at the City of Annapolis in 1774, 1775 & 1776* (Annapolis, 1836); *Daily National Intelligencer* (Washington, March 9, 1844); *Western Law Journal* (Cincinnati, May, 1844); William Wentworth Story, *Life and Letters of Joseph Story,* 2 vols. (Boston, 1851); Hampton L. Carson, *The Supreme Court of the United States: Its History* (Philadelphia, 1891); Charles Warren, *The Supreme Court in United States History,* 2 vols. (Boston, 1926); Albert J. Beveridge, *The Life of John Marshall,* 4 vols. (Boston, 1919); H. F. Powell, *Tercentenary History of Maryland* (Baltimore, 1925); L. H. Welsh, *Ancestral Colonial Families: Genealogy of the Welsh and Hyatt Families of Maryland and Their Kin* (Baltimore, 1928); Carl B. Swisher, *Roger B. Taney* (New York, 1935), Ernest Sutherland Bates, *The Story of the Supreme Court* (Indianapolis, 1936); Mortimer D. Schwartz and John C. Hogan, *Joseph Story* (New York, 1959), and Walker Lewis, *Without Fear or Favor* (Boston, 1965).

Gabriel Duvall

REPRESENTATIVE OPINIONS

LE GRAND v. DARNALL, 2 PET. 664 (1829)

None of Duvall's opinions have impressed the constitutional historians. They were competent and straightforward, but since they did not deal with significant social or governmental problems, they are forgotten today. Typical was *Le Grand* v. *Darnall* involving the freedom of a boy born to a master and his slave. Duvall found that the boy had been freed by the acts of his master, and land had been validly conveyed by him to a third party.

MR. JUSTICE DUVALL delivered the opinion of the Court.

This case is brought up by appeal from a decree of the circuit court for the district of Maryland, sitting as a court of equity; and is submitted on written argument. The principal facts are the following.

Bennett Darnall, late of Anne Arundel county, Maryland, on the 4th day of August 1810, duly made and executed his last will and testament, and thereby devised to his son, the appellee, several tracts of land in fee, one of which was called Portland Manor, containing by estimation five hundred and ninety six acres. The mother of Nicholas Darnall was the slave of the testator, and Nicholas was born the slave of his father, and was between ten and eleven years old at the time of the death of the testator. Bennett Darnall, in his will, refers to and confirms two deeds of manumission executed by him; one bearing date in 1805, and the other in 1810. In both of those deeds, Nicholas Darnall and a number of other slaves were included, and emancipated after his decease. The testator died in the month of January 1814.

Nicholas Darnall, on his arrival to full age, took possession of the property devised to him, and on the 26th of April 1826 he entered into a contract with Le Grand the appellant for the sale of the tract called Portland Manor for the consideration of twenty-two dollars per acre, amounting to the sum of thirteen thousand one hundred and twelve dollars, payable by agreement, in six annual payments with interest. Le Grand passed his notes pursuant to the terms of the agreement, and received the bond of Darnall to convey to him the property in fee simple upon payment of the purchase money. Le Grand was thereupon put into possession of the land. At the time the contract was made, the parties believed the title to the land to be unquestionable. Soon afterwards, however, doubts were suggested to Darnall, and he communited them to Le Grand, and they entered into a supplementary and conditional agreement, without varying in substance the original contract. Darnall was not more than ten or eleven years of age at the time of the death of his father; and, by a law of the state of Maryland, it is provided that no manumission by last will and testament shall be effectual to give freedom to any slave, unless the said slave shall be under the age of forty-five years, and able to work and gain a sufficient maintenance and livelihood at the time the freedom intended to be given shall take place.

A decision had lately been made by the court of appeals of Maryland, in the case of *Hamilton* v. *Cragg*, that an infant (whose age did not exceed two years when his title to freedom commenced) was not able to work and gain a sufficient maintenance and livelihood, and was therefore adjudged to be a slave. This decision of the highest court of law in the state gave rise to doubts concerning the capability of the appellee to make a good title to the land which he had sold to the appellant. Darnall deposited the amount of the first payment, that is to say $3000, in the hands of Benjamin Tucker of Philadelphia, to be held with the consent of the appellant subject to the result of an examination into the title. In consequence of the decision of the court of appeals of Maryland, the heir at law of Bennett Darnall, the testator, made claim to the land, and threatened to commence suit for the recovery of it. Le Grand being alarmed about the title, refused to make any further payment; and an action was commenced against him, and judgment recovered for the second payment. To prevent an execution and to ascertain under all the circumstances of the case, whether the appellee could make a good title to the land which he had sold to him, he filed his bill of complaint in equity, in the circuit court, stating the circumstances, and obtained an injunction against any further proceedings at law. The appellee put in his answer, admitting all the facts stated in the bill, except that of his inability to gain a maintenance and livelihood by labour, when his right to freedom commenced. The case was submitted to the court upon the bill, answer, exhibits and proof which had been taken; and the court, upon due consideration, ordered the injunction to be dissolved, and decreed the bill to be dismissed. From this decree, an appeal was taken to this Court, and the cause is now to be finally decided.

There is one question only to be discussed. If the appellee, at the time of the death of the testator, was entitled to his freedom under the will and deeds of manumission before mentioned, then his title to the land sold was unquestionable. His claim to freedom under the instruments above referred to depends upon a just construction of the act of the legislature of Maryland, passed in the year 1796, ch. 47, sect. 13.

The words of the act are these: "that all persons capable in law to make a valid will and testament, may grant freedom to, and effect the manumission of any slave or slaves belonging to such person or persons, by his, her or their last will and testament; and such manumission of any slave or slaves may be made to take effect at the death of the testator or testators, or at such other period as may be limited in such last will and testament; provided always, that no manumission by last will and testament, shall be effectual to give freedom to any slave or slaves, if the same shall be to prejudice of creditors; nor unless the said slave or slaves shall be under the age of forty-five years, and *able to work and gain a sufficient maintenance and livelihood* at the time the freedom given shall commence." The *time* of the freedom of the appellee commenced immediately after the death of the testator, when, according to the evidence, he was about eleven years old. Four respectable witnesses of the neighbourhood were examined. They all agree in their testimony, that Nicholas was well grown, healthy and intelligent, and of good bodily and mental capacity: that he and his brother Henry could readily have found employment, either as house servant boys, or on a farm, or as apprentices: and that they were able to work and gain a livelihood. The testator devised to each of them real and personal estate to a considerable amount. They had guardians appointed, were well educated and Nicholas is now living in affluence. Experience has proved that he was able to work, and gain a sufficient maintenance and livelihood. No doubt as to the fact has ever been entertained by any who know him. Of course, he was capable in law to sell and dispose of the whole or any part of his estate, and to execute the necessary instruments of writing to convey a sufficient title to the purchase.

The court of appeals of Maryland, in the case of *Hale* v. *Mullin*, decided, that a devise of property real or personal by a master to his slave, entitles the slave to his freedom by necessary implication. This Court entertains the same opinion.

It is not the inclination of this Court to express any opinion as to the correctness of the decision of the court of appeals of Maryland, in the case of *Hamilton* v. *Cragg*. It is unnecessary in reference to the case under consideration.

The decree of the circuit court is affirmed; and by consent of parties without costs.

Joseph Story

☆ 1779–1845 ☆

APPOINTED BY

JAMES MADISON

YEARS ON COURT

1811–1845

Joseph Story

by

GERALD T. DUNNE

JOSEPH STORY, youngest man ever appointed to the Supreme Court of the United States and one of the great jurists of the western world, was born at Marblehead, Massachusetts, on September 18, 1779. His respectable and middle-class family was descended from Elisha Story, a cordwainer, who emigrated from England about 1700. His father, also named Elisha, was a physician, and his paternal grandfather, William, had been register of the (British) Vice Admiralty Court at Boston and later clerk of the American Navy Board there. In addition to the Justice, distinguished members of the Story family include his artist son William Wetmore Story (whose works include the statue of Marshall on the Capitol lawn), his artist grandson Julian Russell Story, and his cousins, the mathematician William E. Story, and the poet and writer Isaac Story.

Dr. Story, Revolutionary veteran and participant in the Boston Tea Party, had married twice. By his first wife, Ruth Ruddock (d. 1777), he had seven children, and by his second, Mehitable Pedrick, eleven. Joseph Story, the oldest child of the second marriage, once described his childhood home as reminiscent of that in *The Cotter's Saturday Night,* and contemporary description of Dr. Story and his large and handsome family verified the recollection. The same source, however, also suggested the hot-tempered readiness of the future Justice to resort to "fisty cuffs" (3 Bentley, *The Diary of William Bentley* 18 [1911]), a characteristic which probably underlay his first public intellectual achievement. Impelled "to chastise" a classmate at Marblehead Academy, young Story incurred severe tutorial punishment, quit school, and sought accelerated matriculation at Harvard. It was conditioned upon demonstrating an academic attainment equivalent to that of the incumbent freshman class and was accomplished largely

GERALD T. DUNNE is Vice-President of the Federal Reserve Bank, St. Louis. He is the author of Monetary Decisions of the Supreme Court *and occasional contributions to various periodicals on American legal history.*

by self-tutoring. The same studious dedication continued throughout Story's bookish and somewhat isolated college years, which culminated with graduation in 1798, second only in class ranking to William Ellery Channing.

Story wrote the class poem, and the affinity for poetry was particularly marked upon his return to his native fishing village of Marblehead. There he chafed against the lack of both appreciation and outlet for his talents, and began writing in the style of Pope a long, rococo poem, *The Power of Solitude*. In it he lamented:

Gone then sweet Friendship who in HARVARD'S bowers,
With calm enjoyment winged my youthful hours.

and seems to have turned to the law for the lack of opportunity in verse. It was a truly happy choice for both fields, for as Joseph Choate later said, with a lawyer's instinct to minimize the unfavorable, Story was not by talent a pre-eminent votary of the Muses. The law studies began under Samuel Sewell in Marblehead and finished in 1801 under Samuel Putnam in nearby Salem. The beginning was inauspicious enough, for Story found (what he would subsequently call) the unmethodical, interrupted, and desultory mode of law office instruction especially depressing, and the crabbed prose of Lord Coke literally reduced him to tears. Yet while the taste for poetics continued—Story, known locally as "the poet of Marblehead," continued to work on *The Power of Solitude*—the law exerted an increasing call. Perhaps it was the law as literature which proved decisive, for the future jurist found Blackstone's *Commentaries* most elegant, and pronounced Fearne's *Contingent Remainders and Devises* as deep and wondrous.

Story finished his apprenticeship in mid-1801, was admitted to the Essex County bar, and by that action also gained admittance to such as there was of an inner circle of the Republican-Democratic party in Massachusetts. The latter affiliation was far more an inheritance from his Jeffersonian father than a selection of his own, for any choice was virtually foreclosed in a society dominated by an all-encompassing Federalist establishment. Story did make an initial effort to avoid partisan characterization, but his neutralist effort was brushed aside, and he complained with much truth of Federalist persecution.

Indeed the persecution prompted him occasionally to look south to a possible removal to Baltimore, but a growing number of ties which came into focus around early 1805 held him fast at Salem. One was literary, as the tug and countertug which poetry and law still exerted in him led to publication of two very different books—the finally published *The Power of Solitude* and a legal tome, *A Selection of Pleadings in Civil Actions*. Another was election to the state legislature. A third was marriage to Mary Oliver, a clergyman's daughter, who shared Story's poetic interests and who, in fact, had contributed several items to *The Power of Solitude*.

Yet the year which began so auspiciously changed completely before it was half over. In June Mary Story suddenly died and Story lost his father shortly thereafter. The succession of tragedies drove him to the brink of moral disintegration, and he burned all the copies of *The Power of Solitude* he could get his hands on. Perhaps he did so as a symbol of life over and past or possibly only because the public reception had ranged from unenthusiastic to critical. In any event, he did not burn his copies of *A Selection of Pleadings in Civil Actions,* and he did find ultimate surcease to his sorrow with the therapy he would call on several times in future tragedies: unremitting attention to legal matters.

Already on the high road to professional success, Story's redoubled dedication only accelerated an inevitable rise in law practice and its natural concomitant, political influence. However, purposeful devotion to the law—for poetry henceforward was to be the most subordinate of avocations—in turn had its own consequence. This was a sharp break with party doctrine in the legislature where Story not only defended the Massachusetts Federalist bench against the assaults of his co-partisans, but actually counterattacked in successive efforts to raise the judiciary's power and prestige. This combination of independence and ability made an obvious impression on the Federalist establishment and persecution changed to patronage. In part due to these qualities and in part necessitated by the Democratic-Republican dominance of the national government, Story was retained to support the claims of the Massachusetts investors to the famous "Yazoo" lands. The lands had been successively sold by a corrupted Georgia legislature, snapped up by New England speculators, and the grant revoked by a reform act. This retainer brought Story to national prominence. His several trips to Washington in support of the New England claimants culminated in successfully pleading their case before the bar of the Supreme Court in *Fletcher* v. *Peck,* 6 Cranch 87 (1810), in which he began as an attorney the work he was to complete as a judge—a transformation of the contracts clause of the Constitution into a bastion for the rights of property with the materials of construction being drawn equally from natural law and national power.

Doubtless this interest, in part at least, underlay Story's brief career in 1808–1809 in the House of Representatives. He was elected without Federalist opposition in the summer of 1808 to an unexpired portion of the term of Jacob Crowninshield, and the great national issue was not the Yazoo land frauds, but, rather, Jefferson's embargo on foreign trade. The embargo represented the administration's response to British and French depredations and its hope of preserving American neutrality from European strife. Story's attitude and actions toward it and especially its collapse have been indelibly misstated both by Jefferson, who named Story as the instrument of its failure, and by Story, who willingly accepted the role.

Yet Story's position on the embargo was extraordinarily ambiguous. He had begun as a supporter, giving consideration to writing a pamphlet in defense and actually joining the United States Attorney, probably at party behest, to uphold the measure when formidable Federalist counsel brought it under constitutional attack, *United States* v. *The William,* 28 Fed. Cas. 614 (No. 16,700) (C.C.D. Mass. 1808). He also spoke publicly in its defense, but as the year wore on, his position developed so many reservations as to almost qualify it out of existence, and doubtless this ambiguous stance cost him the nomination to succeed himself for the full congressional term. To be sure, he may not have wanted it, but, in any event, Story was a "lame duck" when he departed for Congress. The demands of his flourishing law practice made him come late and leave early and in between do his part, probably peripheral, in ending the embargo. Jefferson, however, thought it decisive, and thus Story's fleeting congressional career was significant only in that it might have cost him a seat on the Supreme Court.

For when in 1810 the death of Justice Cushing vacated the New England seat on the Supreme Court, Jefferson, then retired from public life, advised Madison that the embargo episode should foreclose even consideration of Story as a possible successor and asserted that in addition to being a deserter on that issue, the New Englander was unquestionably a Tory and too young as well. The hostility turned out to be unavailing. Madison had been at Princeton with Story's uncle, Isaac Story, and he had formed his own opinion of the nephew during the latter's visits to Washington as lobbyist, lawyer and congressman. Presumably it was highly favorable, for Story's name appeared on the presidential list from almost the first, and it progressed from the bottom to the top in an extraordinary sequence of events. Madison made three successive nominations. The first and third, Levi Lincoln and John Quincy Adams, respectively, were both confirmed but refused to serve. In between, Alexander Wolcott was rejected by the Senate.

Story, the fourth nominee, was named and confirmed in mid-November of 1811. He had some preliminary reservations about the Bench. He now had family obligations, both from his second marriage in 1808 (Sarah Wetmore) and toward his widowed mother whom he helped to support, and the $3,500 judicial salary was well below his current income. Moreover, this income seemed but the forerunner of better things to come from his professional, political and banking activities. For notwithstanding a declaration on leaving Congress that he would not continue in the public councils even if he received an annual salary of $10,000, he promptly returned to his old seat in the lower house of the Massachusetts legislature and soon was elected its speaker. Hand in hand with political success went growing professional prominence, both at the bar and in a succession of editions of English works which came from his pen—Chitty's *Bills and Notes,* Abbott's *Ships and Shipping* and Lawes' *Assumpsit*. The writing was decisive, for appetite came with eating, and "the opportunity . . . to pursue what of all things I admire, juridical studies . . ." could not be foregone. (Joseph Story to Nathaniel Williams, November 30, 1811, 1 W. W. Story, *The Life and Letters of Joseph Story* 201 [1851] hereinafter cited as W. W. Story.) Accordingly, Story accepted the nomination and took his seat on the Court on February 3, 1812.

Story mounted the Bench together with Justice Gabriel Duvall of Maryland. Their accession gave for the first time a Supreme Court majority to the strict constructionist Democratic-Republican party, and the new character of the tribunal seemed apparent in the self-effacing decision in *United States* v. *Hudson and Goodwin,* 7 Cranch 32 (1812). There the Court, ending a fifteen year controversy, denied its capacity to define and punish common law crimes against the United States. Significantly, Story disagreed with the decision, but did not formally dissent. A more significant index of both the future course of the Court and Story's juridical philosophy came the following year when he wrote the opinion in *Fairfax's Devisee* v. *Hunter's Lessee,* 7 Cranch 603 (1813). It was a complex and many-sided case involving the Virginia confiscation legislation of the Revolution; the core issue was whether the Supreme Court held a supervening jurisdiction over the state tribunals in constitutional questions. Story held affirmatively on the jurisdictional point and sent the case back to the Virginia Court of Appeals with a reversing mandate.

An even more pronounced nationalist note appeared in Story's prize and confiscation opinions growing out of the War of 1812 where his ideas even outran those of Chief Justice Marshall. Likewise strengthening the powers of the federal judiciary and drawing immense vitality from the sense of nationalism awakened by the war was his circuit opinion in *DeLovio* v. *Boit,* 7 Fed. Cas. 418 (No. 3,776) (C.C.D. Mass. 1815), wherein he set the bounds of the exclusive federal admiralty jurisdiction at those of the English counterpart, not at the time of the adoption of the Constitution but, rather, at its medieval zenith.

The war-born nationalism was, however, not strong enough to support Story's effort to have the Supreme Court reverse itself and assert jurisdiction over common law crimes (*United States* v. *Coolidge,* 1 Wheat. 415 [1816]). His failure here, however, only underscored his greatest judicial pronouncement in the second *Fairfax* proceeding, *Martin* v. *Hunter's Lessee,* 1 Wheat. 304 (1816). It was in this case that Story expounded the Constitution in terms of a national, organic law rather than a federal compact and, coining one of his rare epigrams ("It is *the case,* then, and not *the Court,* that gives the jurisdiction." *Id.* at 338), pronounced the Supreme Court its final arbiter over all departments of government including state tribunals. Indeed it could be said that in *Martin* Story forged the instrument which Chief Justice John Marshall used with such compelling effect. For three years later in the great trilogy of nationalizing opinions of the 1819 term he used it in major part to expound the contracts clause of the Constitution and the doctrine of implied powers as a code protecting private rights and promoting national authority—*Dartmouth College* v. *Woodward,* 4 Wheat. 518 (1819), holding that a private corporate charter was protected from unilateral state modification; *Sturges* v. *Crowninshield,* 4 Wheat. 122 (1819), voiding a retrospective insolvency law; and *McCulloch* v. *Maryland,* 4 Wheat. 316 (1819), upholding the charter of the second Bank of the United States and outlawing an avowedly extirpatory state tax upon it.

The great trilogy of 1819 marked not only the institutional emergence of the Court but also served as a significant datum in the unfolding of Story's political and juridical philosophy. He had a surprising extra-judicial connection with each case, and the nature of the association showed how far he had already come from his Jeffersonian beginnings. Thus while he voted to sustain the second Bank of the United States, back in 1810 the Massachusetts House over which he presided petitioned for an end of the first bank. Similarly, the luckless insolvent in *Sturges* v. *Crowninshield,* who was thrown back to his creditors, had been a onetime associate in the Salem political wars. And, finally, Story had actually been tendered (and declined) appointment as a Dartmouth overseer under the very New Hampshire statute which he held unconstitutional in a monumental concurring opinion which brought private business corporations within the ambit of constitutional guaranties. In fact, for Story the *Dartmouth College* case could well have been the catalyst of a conservatism in which property and contract became the central institutions from which all the other values of civilization descended. He was without opinion when the case was first argued in 1818, and the resulting reflection and research probably accelerated the formulation of a systematic juridical overview. Whatever the cause, however, the conservatism which Story expounded at the 1819 term of the Supreme Court received an elaborate restatement the following year. Elected to the Massachusetts constitutional convention of 1820—and significantly in his electoral district he placed first on the Democratic-Republican and second on the Federalist tickets of delegates—he was outspoken in his defense of vested rights and pleaded for virtual disenfranchisement of the urban working classes.

Yet there was more to his unfolding views than a lapse into reaction. The concurrent issue of whether Missouri should be admitted as slave or free prompted him to break for the one and only time his judicial silence on political questions, and at the Salem town meeting, he bitterly denounced further extensions of slavery west of the Mississippi. His extra-judicial activities apparently extended much further, for southern protests suggested that he stirred up northern sensitivity by anti-slavery polemics cast in the form of charges to federal grand juries and carried a campaign of opposition into congressional cloakrooms. Hence, crowning these activities almost as a logical consequence was his circuit decision in *United States* v. *La Jeune Eugenie,* 26 Fed. Cas. 832 (No. 15,551) (C.C.D. Mass. 1822), holding the maritime slave trade against international law. The decision was a characteristically bold Story *coup* which mixed the old and the new in much the same manner as he had previously done in *Martin* v. *Hunter's Lessee, DeLovio* v. *Boit* and *Dartmouth College.* On the slave trade issue, however, his effort miscarried by reason of a still unready climate of opinion abroad and the irrepressible tensions over slavery at home. His holding was, in effect, overruled by the Supreme Court's decision (Story not dissenting) in *The Antelope,* 10 Wheat. 66 (1825). It was not the first time that the Marshall Court had undertaken to curb the judicial activism of its junior member. In *Green* v. *Biddle,* 8 Wheat. 1 (1823), Story's categorical natural law opinion outlawing a Kentucky tenant improvement statute was withdrawn in favor of one of Mr. Justice Washington which reached a like result on the basis of an interstate compact. And in *The Thomas Jefferson,* 10 Wheat. 428 (1825), Story himself was the instrument of retreat when he overruled the efforts of lower federal courts to use his *DeLovio* opinion to obtain admiralty jurisdiction over inland waters.

Yet even in retreat Story could lay the groundwork for a future advance. Thus his *Thomas Jefferson* opinion asserted that an inland admiralty might be granted by Congress under the commerce clause notwithstanding the historical limits attached to the judicial grant. Similarly, that same year of 1825 saw the passage of a prototype federal criminal code which had been drafted by Story and gave the national courts much of the authority he had sought previously through a common law criminal jurisdiction. And in an apparent foreshadowing of other successes, the year 1825 saw the Presidency assumed by John Quincy Adams whose constitutional views largely coincided with Story's own.

In fact, the first two years of John Quincy Adams' administration could well have been the happiest of Story's life. Felicitously, the period coincided with the golden anniversary of American independence, and Story marked it by one of his most powerful orations, *Characteristics of the Age,* delivered as the Phi Beta Kappa lecture at Harvard on August 31, 1826. It was truly characteristic of the age for the long declamation which passed over democracy, slavery, and sectionalism to stress a progressive, messianic sense of nationhood and drew heavily on the mystic significance of the deaths of Jefferson and Adams the preceding July 4:

> *We have just passed the jubilee of our independence, and witnessed the prayers and gratitude of millions, ascending to heaven, for our public and private blessings . . . We have been privileged yet more; we have lived to witness an almost miraculous event in the departure of two great authors of our independence on that memorable and blessed day of jubilee.* [*"Characteristics of the Age,"* Miscellaneous Writings of Joseph Story 373 (*W. W. Story ed., 1852*).]

The golden years ended abruptly with the off-year elections of 1826, which, for the first time in American history, returned a Congress avowedly hostile to the incumbent administration. Still nominally Republican-Democratic, the new Jacksonian Congress confronted President Adams as hostilely as the early Jeffersonians ever regarded his father. And within the Supreme Court itself the rising tide of change produced a judicial manifestation. Shortly after the convocation of the 1827 term, a long-awaited decision came down in *Ogden* v. *Saunders,* 12 Wheat. 213 (1827), which validated state insolvency laws that were prospective in nature and thereby sharply limited, although technically did not overrule, the *Sturges* v. *Crowninshield* case of 1819. Chief Justice Marshall dissented—his first and only dissent in a constitutional case—and was joined by Story and Justice Duvall.

The congressional contest of 1826 and the *Ogden* case proved accurate forecasts of the results of the following presidential election as the irresistible tide of Jacksonian democracy swept John Quincy Adams from the White House and swirled around the Supreme Court. Story felt a deep concern in the election, but his forebearance had improved since the Missouri controversy, and he scrupulously observed the proprieties demanded by his position. His attitude however, was epitomized in the one sentence—"The reign of 'King Mob' seemed triumphant"—which he used to describe the first Jackson inaugural and which has become perhaps the most widely quoted item of his writings. (Letter to Mrs. Story, March 7, 1829, in 1 W. W. Story 563)

Yet within a few months of the inaugural, Story launched an immensely significant countering effort in his own assumption of the Dane Professorship of law at Harvard. It was an appropriate homecoming to the university he had left so tearfully over thirty years before. Not that he had been far away for long in spirit, however. In 1816 he had served on the Committee on Theological Education in connection with establishment of the divinity school. In 1818 he had been named an overseer of the University, an appointment which provoked criticism, coming as it did with the *Dartmouth College* case under advisement. In 1821 he was awarded the Harvard LL.D. and in 1825 was elected a fellow of the corporation.

These associations involved far more than sequence of nominal honors. At the Massachusetts constitutional convention of 1820 Story enumerated his triumphs in terms of a defense of the rights of the judiciary and Harvard. After a virtual student revolt in 1823, he headed an overseers' committee which laid the groundwork for a comprehensive revision in administration and curriculum. Again toward the close of 1824 he took the lead in facing down a faculty remonstrance that the fellows of the corporation could only come from their own ranks, and did so by placing his already enormous juristic reputation behind the proposition that the protesting teachers had simply mistaken the law of the matter. And if some ambiguous comment can be believed, Story could well have had a hand in the 1828 replacement of Doctor Kirkland, the clergyman president of Harvard, by Josiah Quincy, Boston lawyer, who had been his colleague in the Tenth Congress.

Quincy's inaugural as president of Harvard also involved the renewal of a hitherto abortive effort to obtain Story's services as a faculty member. A new and successful effort came in 1829 when Nathan Dane dedicated the profits of his legal writings to a special professorship devoted to a fivefold teaching—natural law, international law, commercial law, federal law and federal equity. He conditioned his bounty on the stipulation that Story be made the first holder of the chair and further specified that the duties were to be tailored to the incumbent's special circumstances. As with Madison's nomination eighteen years before, Story's acceptance was preordained.

Leaving Salem for Cambridge, Story assumed his professorship in the summer of 1829, and the results of his appointment were almost immediately apparent. The law school, which had fallen to a handful of students, turned the corner with increased enrollments, and hand in hand with student increases came the nine commentaries. The works were products of the Dane Professorship, which also carried the obligation of publishing the lectures given under its auspices. Nathan Dane had estimated that these would run to perhaps four octavo volumes. What Story in fact produced was an outburst virtually unrivalled in the history of legal writings: *Bailments* (1832) running to nine editions; *Constitution* (1833) running to five editions as well as to French, Spanish and German translations; *Conflicts* (1834) running to eight editions; *Equity Jurisprudence* (1836) running to fourteen American and three English editions; *Equity Pleadings* (1838) ten editions; *Agency* (1839) nine editions; *Partnership* (1841) seven editions; *Bills of Exchange* (1843) four editions; and *Promissory Notes* (1845) seven editions.

The range, power and universality of this corpus of the law is perhaps best attested to by foreign, rather than American, testimonials. Thus, de Tocqueville's recently discovered worksheets hold a handsome acknowledgment to dependence upon Story's *Commentaries on the Constitution.* Dr. Haroldo Valladao, a Brazilian scholar, has traced the impact of the *Commentaries on Conflicts* into not only Latin American law, but also into Latin American treaties. The English legal historian Plucknett notes that while many legal writers have tried their hands on the subject of equity, "none of their works equalled in renown and longevity the *Commentaries on Equity Jurisprudence* of Judge Story, which first appeared in Boston in 1836 and was re-edited many times, the last being in London as late as 1920" (Plucknett, *A Concise History of the Common Law* 694 [Fifth ed., 1956]). And finally and again from England, a current to Story. . . ." (Davis, *The Law Relating to Commercial Letters of Credit* 1 [Third ed., 1963].)

In addition to these formidable contributions, two other classes of Story's writings must be noted. One is conventional—unsigned articles on legal subjects in Francis Lieber's *Encyclopedia Americana,* legal essays often in the form of book reviews in the *North American Review;* contributions to the *American Law Review;* a compilation, *Laws of the United States* (1827); and the fourth American edition of Abbott's *Shipping* (1829). Complementing and perhaps surpassing in this, however, was another medium in which Story's pen made a novel and significant contribution. This was to turn the judicial opinion from a *ratio decidendi* of a particular dispute to a comprehensive and systematic restatement of the law as received, transformed and applied. In Story's case there were some unhappy by-products as he became far more involved in the publication of reports than a later age might deem proper for a judge. Moreover, the typical Story opinion, as someone has observed, groans with learning like an overloaded Christmas tree and thereby carries a decidedly tedious character to an age unaccustomed to leisurely reading and writing. Nonetheless it came at a point when reported opinions were seldom printed and still less read. Indeed the "Story opinion" was an immensely important influence in the formation of an indigenous and authentic system of American law and in raising professional standards.

Foreshadowing modern criticism, Story's colleague, Justice William Johnson, forcefully protested the effort to turn the reports into an open-ended hornbook ("We are constituted to decide causes, and not to discuss themes, or digest systems," *United States* v. *Palmer,* 3 Wheat. 610, 641 [1818]), and his viewpoint as to style had its parallel as to substance. For unlike Story, Johnson, Jefferson's first appointee to the Court, had a profound commitment to his anti-federalist background. It appeared and reappeared in a variety of manifestations: the co-equal status of congress and the Supreme Court as interpreters of the Constitution, a wide degree of concurrence between the state and federal governments in the exercise of constitutional powers, a decided preference to common law procedures over juryless admiralty and, in general, a disposition to regard the popular assembly as fully the equal and possibly the superior of the judiciary in a capacity to do justice.

These attitudes were particularly seen in the early Jeffersonian period in proposals to keep judges on short tether with low salaries, popular elections, short terms and legislative recall—attitudes which prompted Story's first political rebellion—and they drew a new lease on life in the Jacksonian era in the codification movement which proposed reduction of the entire law to systematic, comprehensive and simple writing. Story was initially quite sympathetic to the concept but chilled somewhat as the controversy turned from one on the merits to an effort to check the judiciary. On the whole his attitude was balanced and even modern as he deprecated equally the offsetting enthusiasms of the admirers of the common law and the advocates of reform. In fact, in terms of bringing certainty and clarity to the law, Story almost single-handedly undertook his own codification movement. And, in fact, he himself served on the Massachusetts codification commission in 1836–1837 which recommended limited codification but reported adversely on a more expansive undertaking.

It was the combination of writing and restraint which blunted much of the purely juridical thrust of the Jacksonian revolution. And perhaps the ironic development here was the process of events whereby Jackson himself became the champion of the federal judicial power during the nullification controversy of 1828 and thus underscored Story's view of the federal judiciary as the cohesive and normative component of the federal design. For to effectuate its nullification of the hated tariff, the South Carolina legislature was also forced to nullify, *pari passu,* any federal judicial proceedings relevant thereto, and it was the latter action that Jackson particularly denounced in his nullification proclamation. And even more ironic, the latter incident produced at the end of Jackson's first term a warm rapport between the President and the Justice who saw the beginning of that term as the reign of "King Mob."

Yet the rapport was incidental and even accidental. Far more significant were the differences. One came in the unequal contest between Georgia and the hapless Cherokees, and, in addition to illuminating the differences between Story and the Jackson administration, it also produced one of Story's rare breaks with Marshall. The break came in *Cherokee Nation* v. *Georgia,* 5 Pet. 1 (1831), wherein Marshall held, Story and Smith Thompson dissenting, that the tribe was not a "nation" entitled to invoke the original jurisdiction of the Supreme Court. Not that the two were completely divided. On the substantive aspect of the controversy, *Worcester* v. *Georgia,* 6 Pet. 515 (1832), Story and Marshall stood together in helpless consensus as President Jackson reputedly remarked that the Chief Justice could personally enforce his judgment of unconstitutionality against the Georgia repression statutes.

In terms of Story's hostility toward the Jackson administration, the Cherokee cases were far overshadowed by the controversy concerning the rechartering of the second Bank of the United States. The two episodes also differed in that Story showed up a considerably less heroic figure as defender of the bank than he did as defender of the Indians. Contrary to today's notions of judicial isolation, he supplied material for Webster's pro-bank Senate speeches on an issue which might come before him as a judge. And on a lesser note, he intervened to keep government funds in the bank of which he served as president. In his defense, all that can be said is that crisis badly impaired his judgment. He had read his Gibbon all too well, and the analogy between the last days of the Roman Republic and the current times of the American one seemed marked. His private correspondence contained brooding references to the American dictator and to himself as an American Cicero. Epitomizing his apprehension were the closing lines of his *Commentaries on the Constitution* where, in a sharp contrast to the optimism of his earlier oratory, he cut short a panegyric on the American destiny with the warning that it "may perish in an hour by the folly of its only keepers, THE PEOPLE."

Characteristic of the lag in which constitutional doctrines appear as judicial decisions, the Jacksonian revolution was not written into ruling case law until Jackson's last weeks in the White House. Then beginning in February of 1837, another three opinions were announced which rivalled in importance the great trilogy of 1819. The second set of opinions did not overrule the first but sharply checked their implications and set the corpus of constitutional law on a new direction. The new direction came from a new Court. Given two appointments by statutory enlargement and five by death, Andrew Jackson virtually reconstituted the Court during his years in office. Among the appointments was that of Roger B. Taney to the Chief Justiceship in succession to John Marshall, a post which the bench and bar generally felt should have gone to Story. Appointment by Jackson (who reputedly called Story the most dangerous man in America) was out of the question, and Story was accordingly left to face the revolutionary term not only without the honor but as the only survivor of the Bench of 1819—"the last of the old race of Judges . . . their solitary representative, with a painted heart and a subdued confidence." (Letter to Harriet Martineau, April 7, 1837, in 2 W. W. Story 277.)

His performance on the Bench was far more spirited than despondent, however, for he responded to the first case of the Jacksonian trilogy, *Charles River Bridge* v. *Warren Bridge,* 11 Pet. 420 (1837), with one of his most powerful and brilliant opinions. Dissenting from the majority view that the vesting of a franchise did not carry of itself any implied guarantee against successive and competing grants, Story combined scholarship ("I stand upon the old law; upon law established more than three centuries ago . . .") and pragmatism (". . . I can conceive of no surer plan to arrest all public improvements, founded on private capital and enterprise, than to make the outlay of that capital uncertain and questionable, both as to security and as to productiveness"). (*Id.* at 598, 608)

Completing the trilogy of 1837 were *Briscoe* v. *The Bank of the Commonwealth of Kentucky,* 11 Pet. 257 (1837), and *City of New York* v. *Miln,* 11 Pet. 102 (1837). Both had been originally argued before Chief Justice Marshall. Both concerned points which seemed practically, if not technically, foreclosed by prior Marshall opinions expounding preemptive federal powers over currency and commerce. Yet in an extraordinary tribute to Marshall, the majority strained to find the disputed points still open to decision, and Story, disagreeing with such a conclusion, put on the record the posthumous dissents of the dead Chief Justice.

Yet for all of Story's apodictic certainty to the contrary, the Taney Court attempted no counterrevolution in terms of either property rights or national power. Thus, as has been pointed out as to the *Charles River Bridge* opinion, ". . . though it is compatible with agrarian doctrine, its real affinity is with *laissez faire* . . . Taney just as surely was on the side of *laissez faire* and rampant business individualism as Story . . . [was] on the side of economic and technical conservatism." (Hammond, *Banks and Politics in America,* 337 [1957].) And exemplifying the pattern of continuity was Taney's opinion in *Bronson* v. *Kinzie,* 1 How. 311 (1843). Here the Court voided as repugnant to the contracts clause an Illinois statute which was adopted in the wake of the Panic of 1837 and which revised enforcement procedures of real estate foreclosures. The ill and absent Story—for the 1843 term was the only one missed in his third of a century on the Supreme Court—sounded as if he were writing to Marshall when he commended Marshall's successor for his sound constitutional doctrines in support of the rights of property and of creditors.

On the whole Story's personal relationships on the Taney Court were friendly enough, and especial rapport developed between him and Justice McLean. Not all was complete harmony, however. Story had some skepticism as to the intellectual stature of some of his new colleagues, one of whom, the erratic Justice Baldwin, published an extensive rebuttal to his *Commentaries on the Constitution* in 1837 with an effort entitled *A General View of the Origin and Nature of the Constitution.* And perhaps most offensive of all was the summary change in reporters in 1843 (the term he missed), an event which made him seriously consider submitting his resignation.

In fact, the new composition of the Court and its constitutional atmosphere had prompted thoughts of resignation as early as the 1837 term with its trilogy of Jacksonian decisions. The desirability of such action was further enhanced by the attraction of fulltime teaching at the renascent Harvard Law School. Two countervailing considerations held him fast. One was his natural predilection for the business of judging, both on the Supreme Court in Washington and riding circuit in New England. The other was the insidious reflection that while on the Bench, if he could not stop the advance of new ideas, he could at least slow it with a spirited rearguard action, and, hence, to yield his place was merely to open the way for the appointment of yet another Jacksonian Democrat.

Compounding his problem was a rule of silence which he had adopted at the behest of Justice Washington many years before and which held that, on the Supreme Court, dissent, employed other than sparingly and then in the gravest cases, tended to weaken the tribunal from which it came. Hence, it was his custom when he had what he called the misfortune to differ from his brothers to suffer in silence unless a momentous principle was involved. Yet as the post-Marshall years wore on, he increasingly felt that his rule of self-restraint involved a pervasive acquiescence in a body of law with which he profoundly disagreed. Nonetheless this frustrating pattern which attended his last nine years on the Court had relatively little effect on the quality and temper of his opinions.

Noteworthy are those on slavery which perhaps attempted the impossible—to resolve disputed points within a libertarian framework while giving effect to the basic constitutional design and making the Court a composing rather than a disruptive element in the irrepressible conflict. Thus in *United States* v. *The Schooner Amistad,* 15 Pet. 518 (1841), he wrote the opinion of the Court holding that Negroes, born free but enslaved and imported into Cuba in violation of Spanish law, could not be returned there once they had regained their freedom by mutiny, including homicide, and reached the United States. Implicit in the case was the point he had made two decades before in the *Eugenie* case—that slavery had no status under international law but derived its sole force and effect from municipal enactment. And he reiterated the point more explicitly the following year when he wrote the opinion of the Court in *Prigg* v. *Pennsylvania,* 16 Pet. 539 (1842), when he upheld the Fugitive Slave Law and struck down all state legislation, friendly or hostile, which bore on the subject. Illustrative of the rising temper of the times, however, was the criticism of his opinion both South and North. Southern views denounced the prohibition of state cooperation; northern abolitionist sentiment protested the voiding of personal liberty laws, taxed Story with infamy, and he turned on his critics with charges of madness.

Also shaped by historical forces but of a different kind was his landmark opinion in *Vidal* v. *Girard's Executors,* 2 How. 127 (1844), validating the Girard will establishing a school for poor white orphans who were to be taught "the purest principles of morality" but without any benefit of clergy whatever. The will had come under a two-pronged attack. The clergyman exclusion clause was denounced as *contra bona mores* and therefore void. The trust itself was asserted to be invalid for lack of specificity of its beneficiaries. And the doctrine, following what seemed to be solid English precedent, had been asserted by the Supreme Court back in 1819 in *Baptist Association* v. *Hart's Executors,* 4 Wheat. 1 (1819), to which Story contributed a concurrence published at 3 Pet. 481 (1830). Yet typifying his talent for the uses of legal history, he adopted the research of counsel which proved that, historically, English equity had enforced such trusts—adding thereto a British citation which the brief had overlooked—and went on to uphold the entire testamentary plan.

The case is also significant for the light it casts on Story's moral and religious attitudes and for putting into perspective his differences with Jefferson, from whom Story liked to think he was removed by a philosophical gulf far more profound than that which had ever separated him from Jackson. Their specific difference on whether Christianity was part of the common law had been joined by the posthumous publication of Jefferson's correspondence, which also contained the references to Story as "Tory" and "pseudo-Republican". The personal references apparently came as a complete surprise, and doubtless the astonishment and resentment underlay Story's vigorous response on the legal issue, for he counterattacked vigorously. He denounced the general character of the correspondence as a scandal *à la* Voltaire, insisted both in writing and in his inaugural address at Harvard that Christianity *was* part of the common law, and studded his *Commentaries on the Constitution* with a series of hostile references to the third President.

Yet the ironic aspect of this controversy was that on the root issues of repressive orthodoxy and religious toleration, Story could sound almost as liberal as Jefferson himself. His somewhat conservative Unitarianism was in part a reaction against the ultra-Calvinism of his inheritance and environment, and a consistent concern for religious tolerance was as fully a hallmark of his life and works as was his immense scholarship. It was particularly exemplified in an oratorical passage where he asserted in remarkably Jeffersonian idiom:

> *I stand not up here the apologist for persecution, whether it be by Catholic or Protestant, by Puritan or Prelate, by Congregationalist or Covenanter, by Church or State, by the monarch or the people. Wherever, and by whomsoever, it is promulgated or supported, under whatever disguises, for whatever purposes, at all times, and under all circumstances, it is a gross violation of the rights of conscience, and utterly inconsistent with the spirit of Christianity. I care not, whether it goes to life, or property, or office, or reputation, or mere private comfort, it is equally an outrage upon religion and the unalienable rights of man.* [*"History and Influence of the Puritans,"* Miscellaneous Writings, *440.*]

Doubtless much of his attitude came from his longtime Unitarian allegiance (having served as president of the American Unitarian Association in 1844) and a resulting consciousness of the repressions and disabilities which could attend a law-enforced orthodoxy. Also significant perhaps could have been a contemporary British decision voiding a bequest on the ground that Unitarians could not be "pious and godly persons." Hence, Story found Webster's powerful arguments against the Girard bequest a theological polemic addressed to the prejudices of the clergy, and his opinion upholding the will could be said to almost follow.

But the superb judicial effort of Story's sunset years was his landmark opinion in *Swift* v. *Tyson,* 16 Pet. 1 (1842), which is reproduced as an appendix to this article. The gist of his holding can be quickly given: a federal court in passing on a question of "general commercial law" is not foreclosed by state judicial decisions. Compressed in this proposition are four complex infrastructures—the organic nature of the United States as a nation-state rather than a federated alliance, the specific consequences of this holding for the nation's judicial arm, the existence of a natural law—immanent in principle, ascertainable by rationality and verifiable by experience—and the attenuated length to which the natural law could be drawn. For in *Swift* v. *Tyson,* Story, speaking as national judge with a jurisdiction given by a national constitution, determined the character of a bill of exchange (as did Lord Mansfield *vis-à-vis* marine freight charges) on the basis of Cicero's explication of the timeless and immutable natural law of the Stoic tradition—that "the law" could not be one thing at Rome, another at Athens, one thing now and another tomorrow.

It is noteworthy that in coming to this decision Story not only crowned the work of a lifetime but disregarded and, indeed, declared irrelevant the decisions of the respected courts of New York and of the venerated Chancellor Kent. (For it was also typical of Story that he could seize on Coke, Blackstone or Marshall to support a point or just as readily explain their views away.) Even more noteworthy was that for almost a century *Swift* v. *Tyson* not only effectively ruled interstate commercial transactions but, notwithstanding formidable objections, spread into related but distinct fields. Then in 1938 its doctrine was declared unconstitutional in *Erie R. Co.* v. *Tompkins,* 304 U.S. 64 (1938). Seemingly interred, it now shows signs of rising from its grave in the form of a new "federal common law" as a consequence of the national welfare, security, and regulatory programs. And, in respect of a truly national law of commerce—Story's immediate goal in *Swift* v. *Tyson*—the result has in some measure come to pass in the widespread enactment of uniform laws and, particularly, the Uniform Commercial Code.

Two other opinions of Story's sunset years might well be mentioned. One came in dissent on *Cary* v. *Curtis,* 3 How. 236 (1845), where the Court held that Congress could and had foreclosed a claimant from suing a collector of customs for custom fees paid under protest to test the validity of the fees. The dissent prompted Congress to act where his colleagues did not, and the statute in question was appropriately amended within a matter of weeks. The other was a curious *reprise* of the posthumous opinion. For just as Story had cited the parallel views of the dead Chief Justice Marshall in his own dissent to the 1837 trilogy, so did the dissenting Justice McLean in *Fox* v. *Ohio,* 5 How. 410, 440 (1847), cite Story, *post mortem,* that both federal and state governments cannot constitutionally punish the same single act.

Both opinions were dissenting ones and, therefore, characteristic of Story's position on the bench, which he had increasingly thought of leaving as soon as a suitable successor was available. The accident of Harrison's death and Tyler's succession in 1841 foreclosed the possibility of Story's resigning in that year, but the Whig defeat of 1844 settled the issue. Story was then sixty-five, and he reluctantly concluded that it was unlikely that he would live to see a President who shared his views and inclined to appoint a successor of like attitude. Accordingly, he came to the 1845 term prepared to resign as soon as possible, but the momentum of unfinished business prodded by a lifetime of unflagging energy forced him to defer his separation. Ironically, for one who had done so much, he never effected the last task he set for himself. While still performing his judicial affairs with the preparation of circuit court opinions, he was suddenly stricken and after a brief illness, died on September 10, 1845.

He is buried in Mount Auburn Cemetery in Cambridge.

Story's death was marked by appropriate commemorative proceedings throughout the Union and noted abroad. All joined in saluting his enormous contribution to the systemization and harmonization of the law. In private correspondence Chief Justice Taney, who so often opposed him, expressed a typical American lament: "What a loss the court has sustained in the death of Judge Story! It is irreparable, utterly irreparable . . . for there is nobody equal to him." (Letter to Richard Peters, November, 1845, in Swisher, *Roger B. Taney* 442 [1935].) Particularizing on the Chief Justice's eulogy, American commentators then and later stressed the contributions Story's scholarship and gift for comparative law had afforded. This was especially true in bringing a wide admiralty and equity jurisdiction into the somewhat hostile environment of the jury-oriented American law. Equity, for which he drew the Supreme Court rules in 1842, was the particular beneficiary of his judicial and extra-judicial activism. He had worked for its adoption as a state legislator, had sounded its virtues in the pages of *The North American Review,* and had demonstrated its superiority in the diversity jurisdiction of his circuit court (which suitors changed their residence to obtain) in comparison to the common law bound state tribunal in the same city.

Yet appraisal of his legal efforts could well find their most significant consequences written in economic and political, then purely juridical, terms. On the first count is the enormous part Story played in the development of the American business corporation. Here the foundation stone is his concurring opinion in the *Dartmouth College* case where he revised the ancient division of corporate organization from governmental-charitable to public-private, invested the latter group with all constitutional protections flowing to vested rights, and explicitly included business corporations within it. Contemporary reaction, both approving and critical, recognized the line of departure as arch-Federalist James Kent hailed the new and interesting views while Jacksonian David Henshaw denounced the concurrence as a bold exposition of corporate privilege.

Almost as important was the circuit opinion in *Wood* v. *Dummer,* 30 Fed. Cas. 435 (No. 17,944) (C.C.D. Me. 1824), where Story applied the ancient law of trusts to the emerging form of business enterprise with corporate capital becoming a trust fund for the successive benefit of its creditors and its stockholders, the directors becoming trustees, and the firm itself becoming an entity distinct from its "members." Paralleling this structural innovating was the operational one he propounded in *Bank of the United States* v. *Dandridge,* 12 Wheat. 64 (1827), in which, contrary to Coke and Blackstone and over John Marshall's dissent, he overturned the ancient doctrine of the common seal in favor of a rule of law permitting corporations to conduct their affairs on the same basis as unincorporated associations and private individuals. And in terms of interstate extension, these simplified operations received significant impetus from a theory of comity expressed in his *Commentaries on Conflicts* and written into case law through Chief Justice Taney in *Bank of Augusta* v. *Earle,* 13 Pet. 519 (1839).

Two other elements were involved in this task of bringing law to the aid of economic development. One was his work in the law of finance and its instruments where scholarship was fortified by a practical experience gained in the presidency of the Merchants Bank of Salem from 1815 through 1837 and a vice-presidency of the Salem Institute for Savings over much the same period. Noteworthy here are not only his opinions and commentaries developing the law of negotiable instruments as such, but also their significant consequences otherwise. Thus his opinion in *Bank of the United States* v. *Bank of Georgia,* 10 Wheat. 333 (1825), which not only imported into American law the rule of *Price* v. *Neal* which made banks absolutely liable for recognition of the authenticity of signatures on their own instruments, but it also made them the terminal—and indispensable—points of settlement indispensable to an increasingly commercial society. And as a technological complement to this work were his threshold structurings of American patent law where his efforts have been recognized from his first decade on the Court down to modern times. In perhaps only one area were his efforts essentially unrewarded. This concerned his career-long quest for a federal bankruptcy law. A statute, which was but one of several versions he had drafted over the years, was finally adopted in 1841 but repealed in 1843.

Yet even Story's towering work in American economic development is overshadowed by his efforts in laying the juristic framework of American nationhood. For it was his sustained constitutional exegesis in *Martin* v. *Hunter's Lessee* of a Union which antedated and transcended the Constitution itself which has reappeared in successive and historic restatements—in Marshall's reiteration in *Cohens* v. *Virginia,* 8 Wheat. 266 (1823); in Webster's reply to Hayne; in Jackson's anti-nullification proclamation; in Story's own *Commentaries on the Constitution* (including its popularized versions for adult and juvenile lay readers, the *Familiar Exposition* and *Constitutional Class Book*); and finally the war message which President Lincoln (who himself had owned a set of the *Commentaries on the Constitution*) delivered on July 4, 1861. There have been a host of counter-polemics ranging from Abel Upshur's *A Brief Inquiry into the True Nature and Character of Our Federal Government Being a Review of Judge Story's Commentaries on the Constitution* (1840) to Edgar Lee Masters' *Lincoln the Man* (1931). Yet in a recent and significant roster, "Representative Books Reflecting American Life and Thought," no counter-polemics appear, while the *Commentaries on the Constitution* is listed as "a legal classic of continuing importance and reputation." (Library of Congress, 1960)

Yet for all of his immense influence and scholarship and quite apart from the still provocative nature of some of his political and social views, Story's most attractive aspect is his outgoing and warm-hearted personality. His affectionate nature was doubtless expressed with difficulty on some occasions, for he was repeatedly beset by family tragedies. He lost not only his first wife, but five of the seven children of his second marriage and, in addition, suffered some minor physical infirmities which were a continuing source of discomfort.

To be sure, even these personal traits have their shortcomings. Story was a compulsive conversationalist, and his teaching has been cuttingly criticized as vanity which took the form of lecturing awe-stricken boys who sneezed when he took snuff. Moreover, his educational activities have been singled out for especial censure for an uncritically kind heart which too often bestowed undeserved or exaggerated praise on students and also for structuring a curriculum tinged with commercial banality.

Yet when all idiosyncrasies are allowed, there emerges a picture of an extraordinary man possessed of fantastic drive, persistence and application, beset both personally and politically with a foreboding sense of apprehension and yet persistently rising above it and manifesting in his personal life a democracy which he denied in political theory. Two tributes appropriately exemplify his character. One was by a writer who came to him as a penniless immigrant with a plan for an encyclopedia and sought some legal articles. "The only condition this kindhearted man made," said Francis Lieber, "was that I should not publish the fact that he had contributed the articles . . . until some period subsequent to their appearance." (Quoted in Harley, *Francis Lieber* 57 [1899].) The other came from his colleague and occasional opponent on the Supreme Court, Chief Justice Roger Taney:

> *[I]t is here on this bench . . . that his loss is most severely and painfully felt. For we have not only known him as a learned and able associate in the labors of this court, but he was also endeared to us as a man, by his kindness of heart, his frankness, and his high and pure integrity.* [Proceedings, 4 How. vii (1846).]

SELECTED BIBLIOGRAPHY

It has been well said that of all of Story's vast output, the book we miss the most is the one he planned but never wrote—his memoirs. An anticipatory synopsis of them appears in an autobiographical letter to his son written in 1831, which is reproduced in Story's *Miscellaneous Writings* (W. W. Story ed., Boston, 1852) and also, in fragmented fashion, in the son's W. W. Story's *Life and Letters of Joseph Story* (Boston, 1851). The latter carries all the limitations of a filial memorial but is nonetheless solid, generally accurate, and remains the authoritative work on Story. Readers unwilling to essay its prolixities or those of the *Miscellaneous Writings* may find more to their taste the writings by and about Story collected, together with an extensive bibliography, in J. Hogan & D. Schwartz, eds., *Joseph*

Story (New York, 1959). Hogan has also retrieved and reprinted numerous Story writings which are listed in the bibliography.

While a modern, definitive biography is lacking, two relatively short but admirable studies have been done in recent years. One is Henry Steele Commager's 1941 Bacon lecture, "Joseph Story," which is reprinted in *The Gaspar G. Bacon Lectures on the Constitution of the United States 1940–1950* (Boston, 1953). The other is in Perry Miller's posthumous *The Life of the Mind in America* (Boston, 1966). An earlier somewhat unsystematic effort which occasioned favorable comment is that by William Schofield, appearing in 3 *Great American Lawyers* (Lewis ed., Philadelphia, 1907). And, of necessity, any book dealing with the Supreme Court or its membership during the first half of the nineteenth century must treat Story in fairly substantial measure.

A portrait of Story as legal educator is contained in Charles Warren, *History of the Harvard Law School* (Cambridge, 1908) and Arthur Sutherland, *The Law at Harvard* (Cambridge, 1967). An indication of Story's influence as lawgiver may be seen in the multiple references in S. E. Baldwin, *Two Centuries Growth in American Law 1701–1901* (New York, 1901). Other analyses of Story's work are contained in McClellan, "Joseph Story and the American Constitution" unpublished doctoral dissertation (University of Virginia, 1964) and Newmeyer, "Joseph Story: A Political and Constitutional Study" unpublished dissertation (University of Nebraska, 1959).

In addition, a growing number of periodical articles on Story have been appearing. See, for example, G. Dunne, "Joseph Story: The Germinal Years," 75 *Harvard Law Review* 707 (1962); "Joseph Story: 1812 Overture," 77 *Harvard Law Review* 240 (1963); "Joseph Story: The Great Term," 79 *Harvard Law Review* 877 (1966); R. Pound, "The Place of Judge Story in the Making of American Law," 48 *American Law Review* 676 (1914) and F. Prager, "The Influence of Mr. Justice Story on American Patent Law," 5 *American Journal of Legal History* 254 (1961).

Joseph Story

REPRESENTATIVE OPINIONS

MARTIN v. HUNTER'S LESSEE, 1 WHEAT. 304 (1816)
SWIFT v. TYSON, 16 PET. 1 (1842)

Selection of the "typical" Story opinion involves an exceedingly difficult choice which is somewhat reduced when two are selected. Within the latter range and notwithstanding surface diversity, *Martin* v. *Hunter's Lessee* and *Swift* v. *Tyson* are a felicitously "matched pair" comprehending between them almost the whole of Story's jurisprudential philosophy. One involved public, the other private law. One came toward the beginning, the other near the end of his judicial career. Both involve his view of the nature of the law and the function of the federal judiciary under the Constitution. More specifically, both involve the power of the federal judiciary to pronounce their judgments irrespective of the contrary views of state courts.

Martin v. *Hunter's Lessee* concerned not only the power to pronounce but to override. The issue of the case arose in conflicting titles to Virginia land, one based on confiscatory legislation of the Revolutionary period while the other looked to an Anglo-American treaty. Heard once on the merits and decided in favor of the treaty claimants, *Fairfax's Devisee* v. *Hunter's Lessee,* 7 Cranch 603 (1813), the case came back on the principal issue of whether the Supreme Court might constitutionally bear such an appeal from a state court or whether its jurisdiction in constitutional matters was limited to federal tribunals. Story, in a somewhat uncharacteristic epigram ("It is *the case,* then, and not *the Court* that gives the jurisdiction"), thereby laid the cornerstone for the Supreme Court's power of judicial review for the entire constitutional design. Specific details on the case may be found in 1 Charles Warren, *The Supreme Court in United States History,* 443–450 (Boston, 1937) and 4 Albert Beveridge, *The Life of John Marshall,* 144–166 (New York, 1919). Other comments may be found in 4 Henry Adams, *A History of the United States during the Administration of James*

Madison, bk. IX, 190–192 (*New York, 1930*); Robert Harris, *The Judicial Power of the United States* (Louisiana, 1940) 100–102; and G. Dunne, *Joseph Story: 1812 Overture,* 77 *Harvard Law Review,* 275–277 (1963).

Swift v. *Tyson* involved a narrower compass, namely, when passing on a question of "general" commercial law, were federal courts bound by state-decided precedent? Story held in the negative and thereby made his tribunal a great commercial court, enunciating "a nationally uniform commercial law" (see G. Gilmore, *Article 9: What It Does,* 26 *Louisiana Law Review* 287 [1966]). The literature on the case is very large. In the most general sense, this would include opposing and overruling judicial views—e.g., Justice Holmes' dissent in *Black & White Taxicab and Transfer Co.* v. *Brown and Yellow Taxicab and Transfer Co.,* 276 U.S. 518, 535 (1928), and Justice Brandeis' reversing opinion in *Erie R. Co.* v. *Tompkins,* 304 U.S. 64 (1938). A reconciling synthesis is undertaken in Judge Henry J. Friendly's 1964 Cardozo lecture, "In Praise of Eric—And of the New Federal Common Law," reprinted in 39 *N. Y. U. Law Review* 383 (1964), whose citations may be consulted for other published material. An unusual and refreshing review of *Swift* v. *Tyson* is contained in the late Karl Llewellyn's *The Common Law Tradition* 414–416 (1960).

STORY, J., delivered the opinion of the court. This is a writ of error from the court of appeals of Virginia, founded upon the refusal of that court to obey the mandate of this court, requiring the judgment rendered in this very cause, at February term 1813, to be carried into due execution. The following is the judgment of the court of appeals rendered on the mandate: "The court is unanimously of opinion, that the appellate power of the supreme court of the United States does not extend to this court, under a sound construction of the constitution of the United States; that so much of the 25th section of the act of congress to establish the judicial courts of the United States, as extends the appellate jurisdiction of the supreme court to this court, is not in pursuance of the constitution of the United States; that the writ of error, in this cause, was improvidently allowed, under the authority of that act; that the proceedings thereon in the supreme court were *coram non judice,* in relation to this court, and that obedience to its mandate be declined by the court."

The questions involved in this judgment are of great importance and delicacy. Perhaps, it is not too much to affirm, that, upon their right decision, rest some of the most solid principles which have hitherto been supposed to sustain and protect the constitution itself. The great respectability, too, of the court whose decisions we are called upon to review, and the entire deference which we entertain for the learning and ability of that court, add much to the difficulty of the task which has so unwelcomely fallen upon us. It is, however, a source of consolation, that we have had the assistance of most able and learned arguments to aid our inquiries; and that the opinion which is now to be pronounced has been weighed with every solicitude to come to a correct result, and matured after solemn deliberation.

Before proceeding to the principal questions, it may not be unfit to dispose of some preliminary considerations which have grown out of the arguments at the bar.

The constitution of the United States was ordained and established, not by the states in their sovereign capacities, but emphatically, as the preamble of the constitution declares, by "the People of the United States."[1] There can be no doubt, that it was competent to the people to invest the general government with all the powers which

[1] *The preamble to the constitution is constantly referred to, by statesmen and jurists, to aid them in the exposition of its provisions. On the proper construction of the words quoted in the opinion of the court, the two great political parties into which the country is divided, have based their respective principles of government.*

they might deem proper and necessary; to extend or restrain these powers according to their own good pleasure, and to give them a paramount and supreme authority. As little doubt can there be, that the people had a right to prohibit to the states the exercise of any powers which were, in their judgment, incompatible with the objects of the general compact; to make the powers of the state governments, in given cases, subordinate to those of the nation, or to reserve to themselves those sovereign authorities which they might not choose to delegate to either. The constitution was not, therefore, necessarily carved out of existing state sovereignties, nor a surrender of powers already existing in state institutions, for the powers of the states depend upon their own constitutions; and the people of every state had the right to modify and restrain them, according to their own views of policy or principle. On the other hand, it is perfectly clear, that the sovereign powers vested in the state governments, by their respective constitutions, remained unaltered and unimpaired, except so far as they were granted to the government of the United States. These deductions do not rest upon general reasoning, plain and obvious as they seem to be. They have been positively recognised by one of the articles in amendment of the constitution, which declares, that "the powers not delegated to the United States by the constitution, nor prohibited by it to the states, are reserved to the states respectively, or to the people."

The government, then, of the United States can claim no powers which are not granted to it by the constitution, and the powers actually granted, must be such as are expressly given, or given by necessary implication. On the other hand, this instrument, like every other grant, is to have a reasonable construction, according to the import of its terms; and where a power is expressly given, in general terms, it is not to be restrained to particular cases, unless that construction grow out of the context, expressly, or by necessary implication. The words are to be taken in their natural and obvious sense, and not in a sense unreasonably restricted or enlarged.

The constitution unavoidably deals in general language. It did not suit the purposes of the people, in framing this great charter of our liberties, to provide for minute specifications of its powers, or to declare the means by which those powers should be carried into execution. It was foreseen, that this would be perilous and difficult, if not an impracticable, task. The instrument was not intended to provide merely for the exigencies of a few years, but was to endure through a long lapse of ages, the events of which were locked up in the inscrutable purposes of Providence. It could not be foreseen, what new changes and modifications of power might be indispensable to effectuate the general objects of the charter; and restrictions and specifications, which, at the present, might seem salutary, might, in the end, prove the overthrow of the system itself. Hence, its powers are expressed in general terms, leaving to the legislature, from time to time, to adopt its own means to effectuate legitimate objects, and to mould and model the exercise of its powers, as its own wisdom, and the public interests, should require.

With these principles in view, principles in respect to which no difference of opinion ought to be indulged, let us now proceed to the interpretation of the constitution, so far as regards the great points in controversy.

The third article of the constitution is that which must principally attract our attention. The 1st section declares, "the judicial power of the United States shall be vested in one supreme court, and in such other inferior courts as the congress may, from time to time, ordain and establish." The 2d section declares, that "the judicial power shall extend to all cases in law or equity, arising under this constitution, the laws of the United States, and the treaties made, or which shall be made, under their authority; to all cases affecting ambassadors, other public ministers and consuls; to all cases of admiralty and maritime jurisdiction; to controversies to which the United States shall be a party; to controversies between two or more states; between a state and citizens of another state; between citizens of different states; between citizens of the same state, claiming lands under the grants of different states; and between a state, or the citizens thereof, and foreign states, citizens or subjects." It then proceeds to declare, that "in all cases affecting ambassadors, other public ministers and consuls, and those in which a state shall be a party, the supreme court shall have original jurisdiction. In all the other cases before mentioned, the supreme court shall have appellate jurisdiction, both as to law and fact, with such exceptions, and under such regulations, as the congress shall make."

Such is the language of the article creating and defining the judicial power of the United States. It is the voice of the whole American people, solemnly declared, in establishing one great department of that government which was, in many respects, national, and in all, supreme. It is a part of the very same instrument which was to act, not merely upon individuals, but upon states; and to deprive them altogether of the exercise of some powers of sovereignty, and to restrain and regulate them in the exercise of others.

Let this article be carefully weighed and considered. The language of the article throughout is manifestly designed to be mandatory upon the legislature. Its obligatory force is so imperative, that congress could not, without a violation of its duty, have refused to carry it into operation. The judicial power of the United States *shall* be vested (not *may* be vested) in one supreme court, and in such inferior courts as congress may, from time to time, ordain and establish. Could congress have lawfully refused to create a supreme court, or to vest in it the constitutional jurisdiction? "The judges, both of the supreme and inferior courts, shall hold their offices during good behavior, and shall, at stated times, receive, for their services, a compensation which shall not be diminished during their continuance in office." Could congress create or limit any other tenure of the judicial office? Could they refuse to pay, at stated times, the stipulated salary, or diminish it during the continuance in office? But one answer can be given to these questions: it must be in the negative. The object of the constitution was to establish three great departments of government; the legislative, the executive and the judicial departments. The first was to pass laws, the second, to approve and execute them, and the third, to expound and enforce them. Without the latter, it would be impossible to carry into effect some of the express provisions of the constitution. How, otherwise, could crimes against the United States be tried and punished? How could causes between two states be heard and determined? The judicial power must, therefore, be vested in some court, by congress; and to suppose, that it was not an obligation binding on them, but might, at their pleasure, be omitted or declined, is to suppose, that, under the sanction of the constitution, they might defeat the constitution itself; a construction which would lead to such a result cannot be sound.

The same expression, "shall be vested," occurs in other parts of the constitution, in defining the powers of the other co-ordinate branches of the government. The first article declares that "all legislative powers herein granted shall be vested in a congress of the United States." Will it be contended that the legislative power is not absolutely vested? that the words merely refer to some future act, and mean only that the legislative power may hereafter be vested? The second article declares that "the executive power shall be vested in a president of the United States of America." Could congress vest it in any other person; or, is it to await their good pleasure, whether it is to vest at all? It is apparent, that such a construction, in either case, would be utterly inadmissible. Why, then, is it entitled to a better support, in reference to the judicial department?

If, then, it is a duty of congress to vest the judicial power of the United States, it is a duty to vest the whole judicial power. The language, if imperative as to one part, is imperative as to all. If it were otherwise, this anomaly would exist, that congress might successively refuse to vest the jurisdiction in any one class of cases enumerated in the constitution, and thereby defeat the jurisdiction as to all; for the constitution has not singled out any class on which congress are bound to act in preference to others.

The next consideration is, as to the courts in which the judicial power shall be vested. It is manifest, that a supreme court must be established; but whether it be equally obligatory to establish inferior courts, is a question of some difficulty. If congress may lawfully omit to establish inferior courts, it might follow, that in some of the enumerated cases, the judicial power could nowhere exist. The supreme court can have original jurisdiction in two classes of cases, only, viz., in cases affecting ambassadors, other public ministers and consuls, and in cases in which a state is a party. Congress cannot vest any portion of the judicial power of the United States, except in courts ordained and established by itself; and if in any of the cases enumerated in the constitution, the state courts did not then possess jurisdiction, the appelate jurisdiction of the supreme court (admitting that it could act on state courts) could not reach those cases, and consequently, the injunction of the constitution, that the judicial power "shall be vested," would be disobeyed. It would seem, therefore, to follow, that congress are bound to create some inferior courts, in which to vest all that jurisdiction which, under the constitution, is exclusively vested in the

United States, and of which the supreme court cannot take original cognisance. They might establish one or more inferior courts; they might parcel out the jurisdiction among such courts, from time to time, at their own pleasure. But the whole judicial power of the United States should be, at all times, vested, either in an original or appellate form, in some courts created under its authority.

This construction will be fortified by an attentive examination of the second section of the third article. The words are "the judicial power shall extend," &c. Much minute and elaborate criticism has been employed upon these words. It has been argued, that they are equivalent to the words "may extend," and that "extend" means to widen to new cases not before within the scope of the power. For the reasons which have been already stated, we are of opinion, that the words are used in an imperative sense; they import an absolute grant of judicial power. They cannot have a relative signification applicable to powers already granted; for the American people had not made any previous grant. The constitution was for a new government, organized with new substantive powers, and not a mere supplementary charter to a government already existing. The confederation was a compact between states; and its structure and powers were wholly unlike those of the national government. The constitution was an act of the people of the United States to supersede the confederation, and not to be engrafted on it, as a stock through which it was to receive life and nourishment.

If, indeed, the relative signification could be fixed upon the term "extend," it could not (as we shall hereafter see) subserve the purposes of the argument in support of which it has been adduced. This imperative sense of the words "shall extend," is strengthened by the context. It is declared, that "in all cases affecting ambassadors, &c., that the supreme court shall have original jurisdiction." Could congress withhold original jurisdiction in these cases from the supreme court? The clause proceeds —"in all the other cases before mentioned the supreme court shall have appellate jurisdiction, both as to law and fact, with such exceptions, and under such regulations, as the congress shall make." The very exception here shows that the framers of the constitution used the words in an imperative sense. What necessity could there exist for this exception, if the preceding words were not used in that sense? Without such exception, congress would, by the preceding words, have possessed a complete power to regulate the appellate jurisdiction, if the language were only equivalent to the words "may have" appellate jurisdiction. It is apparent, then, that the exception was intended as a limitation upon the preceding words, to enable congress to regulate and restrain the appellate power, as the public interests might, from time to time, require.

Other clauses in the constitution might be brought in aid of this construction; but a minute examination of them cannot be necessary, and would occupy too much time. It will be found, that whenever a particular object is to be effected, the language of the constitution is always imperative, and cannot be disregarded, without violating the first principles of public duty. On the other hand, the legislative powers are given in language which implies discretion, as from the nature of legislative power such a discretion must ever be exercised.

It being, then, established, that the language of this clause is imperative, the question is, as to the cases to which it shall apply. The answer is found in the constitution itself; the judicial power shall extend to all the cases enumerated in the constitution. As the mode is not limited, it may extend to all such cases, in any form, in which judicial power may be exercised. It may, therefore, extend to them in the shape of original or appellate jurisdiction, or both; for there is nothing in the nature of the cases which binds to the exercise of the one in preference to the other.

In what cases (if any) is this judicial power exclusive, or inclusive, at the election of congress? It will be observed, that there are two classes of cases enumerated in the constitution, between which a distinction seems to be drawn. The first class includes cases arising under the constitution, laws and treaties of the United States; cases affecting ambassadors, other public ministers and consuls, and cases of admiralty and maritime jurisdiction. In this class, the expression is, and that the judicial power shall extend to all cases; but in the subsequent part of the clause, which embraces all the other cases of national cognisance, and forms the second class, the word "all" is dropped, seemingly *ex industriâ*. Here, the judicial authority is to extend to controversies (not to all controversies) to which the United States shall be a party, &c. From this difference of phraseology, perhaps, a difference of constitutional intention may, with propriety, be inferred. It is hardly to be presumed, that the variation in the language could have been accidental. It must have been the result of some determinate reason; and it is not very difficult to find a reason sufficient to support the apparent change of intention. In respect to the first class, it may well have been the intention of the framers of the constitution imperatively to extend the judicial power, either in an original or appellate form, to *all* cases; and in the latter class, to leave it to congress to qualify the jurisdiction, original or appellate, in such manner as public policy might dictate.

The vital importance of all the cases enumerated in the first class to the national sovereignty, might warrant such a distinction. In the first place, as to cases arising under the constitution, laws and treaties of the United States. Here, the state courts could not ordinarily possess a direct jurisdiction. The jurisdiction over such cases could not exist in the state courts, previous to the adoption of the constitution, and it could not afterwards be directly conferred on them; for the constitution expressly requires the judicial power to be vested in courts ordained and established by the United States. This class of cases would embrace civil as well as criminal jurisdiction, and affect, not only our internal policy, but our foreign relations. It would, therefore, be perilous to restrain it in any manner whatsoever, inasmuch as it might hazard the national safety. The same remarks may be urged as to cases affecting ambassadors, other public ministers and consuls, who are emphatically placed under the guardianship of the law of nations; and as to cases of admiralty and maritime jurisdiction, the admiralty jurisdiction embraces all questions of prize and salvage, in the correct adjudication of which foreign nations are deeply interested; it embraces also maritime torts, contracts and offences, in which the principles of the law and comity of nations often form an essential inquiry. All these cases, then, enter into the national policy, affect the national rights, and may compromit the national sovereignty. The original or appellate jurisdiction ought not, therefore, to be restrained, but should be commensurate with the mischiefs intended to be remedied, and of course, should extend to all cases whatsoever.

A different policy might well be adopted in reference to the second class of cases; for although it might be fit, that the judicial power should extend to all controversies to which the United States should be a party, yet this power might not have been imperatively given, lest it should imply a right to take cognisance of original suits brought against the United States as defendants in their own courts. It might not have been deemed proper to submit the sovereignty of the United States, against their own will, to judicial cognisance, either to enforce rights or to prevent wrongs; and as to the other cases of the second class, they might well be left to be exercised under the exceptions and regulations which congress might, in their wisdom, choose to apply. It is also worthy of remark, that congress seem, in a good degree, in the establishment of the present judicial system, to have adopted this distinction. In the first class of cases, the jurisdiction is not limited, except by the subject-matter; in the second, it is made materially to depend upon the value in controversy.

We do not, however, profess to place any implicit reliance upon the distinction which has here been stated and endeavored to be illustrated. It has the rather been brought into view, in deference to the legislative opinion, which has so long acted upon, and enforced, this distinction. But there is, certainly, vast weight in the argument which has been urged, that the constitution is imperative upon congress to vest all the judicial power of the United States, in the shape of original jurisdiction, in the supreme and inferior courts created under its own authority. At all events, whether the one construction or the other prevail, it is manifest, that the judicial power of the United States is, unavoidably, in some cases, exclusive of all state authority, and in all others, may be made so, at the election of congress. No part of the criminal jurisdiction of the United States can, consistently with the constitution, be delegated to state tribunals. The admiralty and maritime jurisdiction is of the same exclusive cognisance; and it can only be in those cases where, previous to the constitution, state tribunals possessed jurisdiction, independent of national authority, that they can now constitutionally exercise a concurrent jurisdiction. Congress, throughout the judicial act, and particularly in the 9th, 11th and 13th sections, have legislated upon the supposition, that in all the cases to which the judicial powers of the United States extended, they might rightfully vest exclusive jurisdiction in their own courts.

But, even admitting that the language

of the constitution is not mandatory, and that congress may constitutionally omit to vest the judicial power in courts of the United States, it cannot be denied, that when it is vested, it may be exercised to the utmost constitutional extent.

This leads us to the consideration of the great question, as to the nature and extent of the appellate jurisdiction of the United States. We have already seen, that appellate jurisdiction is given by the constitution to the supreme court, in all cases where it has not original jurisdiction; subject, however, to such exceptions and regulations as congress may prescribe. It is, therefore, capable of embracing every case enumerated in the constitution, which is not exclusively to be decided by way of original jurisdiction. But the exercise of appellate jurisdiction is far from being limited, by the terms of the constitution, to the supreme court. There can be no doubt, that congress may create a succession of inferior tribunals, in each of which it may vest appellate as well as original jurisdiction. The judicial power is delegated by the constitution, in the most general terms, and may, therefore, be exercised by congress, under every variety of form of appellate or original jurisdiction. And as there is nothing in the constitution which restrains or limits this power, it must, therefore, in all other cases, subsist in the utmost latitude of which, in its own nature, it is susceptible.

As, then, by the terms of the constitution, the appellate jurisdiction is not limited as to the supreme court, and as to this court, it may be exercised in all other cases than those of which it has original cognisance, what is there to restrain its exercise over state tribunals, in the enumerated cases? The appellate power is not limited by the terms of the third article to any particular courts. The words are, "the judicial power (which includes appellate power) shall extend to all cases," &c., and "in all other cases before mentioned the supreme court shall have appellate jurisdiction." It is the case, then, and not the court, that gives the jurisdiction. If the judicial power extends to the case, it will be in vain to search in the letter of the constitution for any qualification as to the tribunal where it depends. It is incumbent, then, upon those who assert such a qualification, to show its existence, by necessary implication. If the text be clear and distinct, no restriction upon its plain and obvious import ought to be admitted, unless the inference be irresistible.

If the constitution meant to limit the appellate jurisdiction to cases pending in the courts of the United States, it would necessarily follow, that the jurisdiction of these courts would, in all the cases enumerated in the constitution, be exclusive of state tribunals. How, otherwise, could the jurisdiction extend to *all* cases arising under the constitution, laws and treaties of the United States, or to *all* cases of admiralty and maritime jurisdiction? If some of these cases might be entertained by state tribunals, and no appellate jurisdiction as to them should exist, then the appellate power would not extend to *all,* but to *some,* cases. If state tribunals might exercise concurrent jurisdiction over all or some of the other classes of cases in the constitution, without control, then the appellate jurisdiction of the United States might, as to such cases, have no real existence, contrary to the manifest intent of the constitution. Under such circumstances, to give effect to the judicial power, it must be construed to be exclusive; and this not only when the *casus fœderis* should arise directly, but when it should arise, incidentally, in cases pending in state courts. This construction would abridge the jurisdiction of such courts far more than has been ever contemplated in any act of congress.

On the other hand, if, as has been contended, a discretion be vested in congress, to establish, or not to establish, inferior courts, at their own pleasure, and congress should not establish such courts, the appellate jurisdiction of the supreme court would have nothing to act upon, unless it could act upon cases pending in the state courts. Under such circumstances, it must be held, that the appellate power would extend to state courts; for the constitution is peremptory, that it shall extend to certain enumerated cases, which cases could exist in no other courts. Any other construction, upon this supposition, would involve this strange contradiction, that a discretionary power, vested in congress, and which they might rightfully omit to exercise, would defeat the absolute injunctions of the constitution in relation to the whole appellate power.

But it is plain, that the framers of the constitution did contemplate that cases within the judicial cognisance of the United States, not only might, but would, arise in the state courts, in the exercise of their ordinary jurisdiction. With this view, the sixth article declares, that "this constitution, and the laws of the United States which shall be made in pursuance thereof, and all treaties made, or which shall be made, under the authority of the United States, shall be the supreme law of the land, and the judges in every state shall be bound thereby, anything in the constitution or laws of any state to the contrary notwithstanding." It is obvious, that this obligation is imperative upon the state judges, in their official, and not merely in their private, capacities. From the very nature of their judicial duties, they would be called upon to pronounce the law applicable to the case in judgment. They were not to decide merely according to the laws or constitution of the state, but according to the constitution, laws and treaties of the United States—"the supreme law of the land."

A moment's consideration will show us the necessity and propriety of this provision, in cases where the jurisdiction of the state courts is unquestionable. Suppose, a contract for the payment of money is made between citizens of the same state, and performance thereof is sought in the courts of that state; no person can doubt, that the jurisdiction completely and exclusively attaches, in the first instance, to such courts. Suppose, at the trial, the defendant sets up in his defence a tender under a state law, making paper-money a good tender, or a state law, impairing the obligation of such contract, which law, if binding, would defeat the suit. The constitution of the United States has declared, that no state shall make any thing but gold or silver coin a tender in payment of debts, or pass a law impairing the obligation of contracts. If congress shall not have passed a law providing for the removal of such a suit to the courts of the United States, must not the state court proceed to hear and determine it? Can a mere plea in defence be, of itself, a bar to further proceedings, so as to prohibit an inquiry into its truth or legal propriety, when no other tribunal exists to whom judicial cognisance of such cases is confided? Suppose, an indictment for a crime, in a state court, and the defendant should allege in his defence, that the crime was created by an *ex post facto* act of the state, must not the state court, in the exercise of a jurisdiction which has already rightfully attached, have a right to pronounce on the validity and sufficiency of the defence? It would be extremely difficult, upon any legal principles, to give a negative answer to these inquiries. Innumerable instances of the same sort might be stated in illustration of the position; and unless the state courts could sustain jurisdiction in such cases, this clause of the sixth article would be without meaning or effect, and public mischiefs, of a most enormous magnitude, would inevitably ensue.

It must, therefore, be conceded, that the constitution not only contemplated, but meant to provide for cases within the scope of the judicial power of the United States, which might yet depend before state tribunals. It was foreseen, that in the exercise of their ordinary jurisdiction, state courts would incidentally take cognisance of cases arising under the constitution, the laws and treaties of the United States. Yet, to all these cases, the judicial power, by the very terms of the constitution, is to extend. It cannot extend, by original jurisdiction, if that was already rightfully and exclusively attached in the state courts, which (as has been already shown) may occur; it must, therefore, extend by appellate jurisdiction, or not at all. It would seem to follow, that the appellate power of the United States must, in such cases, extend to state tribunals; and if, in such cases, there is no reason why it should not equally attach upon all others, within the purview of the constitution.

It has been argued, that such an appellate jurisdiction over state courts is inconsistent with the genius of our governments, and the spirit of the constitution. That the latter was never designed to act upon state sovereignties, but only upon the people, and that if the power exists, it will materially impair the sovereignty of the states, and the independence of their courts. We cannot yield to the force of this reasoning; it assumes principles which we cannot admit, and draws conclusions to which we do not yield our assent.

It is a mistake, that the constitution was not designed to operate upon states, in their corporate capacities. It is crowded with provisions which restrain or annul the sovereignty of the states, in some of the highest branches of their prerogatives. The tenth section of the first article contains a long list of disabilities and prohibitions imposed upon the states. Surely, when such essential portions of state sovereignty are taken away, or prohibited to be exercised, it cannot be correctly asserted, that the constitution does not act upon the states. The language of the constitution is also imperative upon the states, as to the performance of many duties. It is imperative upon the state legislatures, to make laws prescribing the time, places and manner of holding elections for senators and representatives, and for electors of president and vice-president. And in these, as well as some other cases, congress have a right to revise, amend or supersede the laws which may be passed by state legislatures. When, therefore, the states are stripped of some of the highest attributes of sovereignty, and the same are given to the United States; when the legislatures of the states are, in some respects, under the control of congress, and in every case are, under the constitution, bound by the paramount authority of the United States; it is certainly difficult to support the argument, that the appellate power over the decisions of state courts is contrary to the genius of our institutions. The courts of the United States can, without question, revise the proceedings of the executive and legislative authorities of the states, and if they are found to be contrary to the constitution, may declare them to be of no legal validity. Surely, the exercise of the same right over judicial tribunals is not a higher or more dangerous act of sovereign power.

Nor can such a right be deemed to impair the independence of state judges. It is assuming the very ground in controversy, to assert that they possess an absolute independence of the United States. In respect to the powers granted to the United States, they are not independent; they are expressly bound to obedience, by the letter of the constitution; and if they should unintentionally transcend their authority, or misconstrue the constitution, there is no more reason for giving their judgments an absolute and irresistible force, than for giving it to the acts of the other co-ordinate departments of state sovereignty.

The argument urged from the possibility of the abuse of the revising power, is equally unsatisfactory. It is always a doubtful course, to argue against the use or existence of a power, from the possibility of its abuse. It is still more difficult, by such an argument, to ingraft upon a general power, a restriction which is not to be found in the terms in which it is given. From the very nature of things, the absolute right of decision, in the last resort, must rest somewhere—wherever it may be vested, it is susceptible of abuse. In all questions of jurisdiction, the inferior, or appellate court, must pronounce the final judgment; and common sense, as well as legal reasoning, has conferred it upon the latter.

It has been further argued against the existence of this appellate power, that it would form a novelty in our judicial institutions. This is certainly a mistake. In the articles of confederation, an instrument framed with infinitely more deference to state rights and state jealousies, a power was given to congress to establish "courts for revising and determining, finally, appeals in all cases of captures." It is remarkable, that no power was given to entertain original jurisdiction in such cases; and consequently, the appellate power (although not so expressed in terms) was altogether to be exercised in revising the decisions of state tribunals. This was, undoubtedly, so far a surrender of state sovereignty; but it never was supposed to be a power fraught with public danger, or destructive of the independence of state judges. On the contrary, it was supposed to be a power indispensable to the public safety, inasmuch as our national rights might otherwise be compromitted, and our national peace be endangered. Under the present constitution, the prize jurisdiction is confined to the courts of the United States; and a power to revise the decisions of state courts, if they should assert jurisdiction over prize causes, cannot be less important, or less useful, than it was under the confederation.

In this connection, we are led again to the construction of the words of the constitution, "the judicial power shall extend," &c. If, as has been contended at the bar, the term "extend" have a relative signification, and mean to widen an existing power, it will then follow, that, as the confederation gave an appellate power over state tribunals, the constitution enlarged or widened that appellate power to all the other cases in which jurisdiction is given to the courts of the United States. It is not presumed, that the learned counsel would choose to adopt such a conclusion.

It is further argued, that no great public mischief can result from a construction which shall limit the appellate power of the United States to cases in their own courts: first, because state judges are bound by an oath to support the constitution of the United States, and must be presumed to be men of learning and integrity; and secondly, because congress must have an unquestionable right to remove all cases within the scope of the judicial power from the state courts to the courts of the United States, at any time before final judgment, though not after final judgment. As to the first reason—admitting that the judges of the state courts are, and always will be, of as much learning, integrity and wisdom, as those of the courts of the United States (which we very cheerfully admit), it does not aid the argument. It is manifest, that the constitution has proceeded upon a theory of its own, and given or withheld powers according to the judgment of the American people, by whom it was adopted. We can only construe its powers, and cannot inquire into the policy or principles which induced the grant of them. The constitution has presumed (whether rightly or wrongly, we do not inquire), that state attachments, state prejudices, state jealousies, and state interests, might sometimes obstruct, or control, or be supposed to obstruct or control, the regular administration of justice. Hence, in controversies between states; between citizens of different states; between citizens claiming grants under different states; between a state and its citizens, or foreigners, and between citizens and foreigners, it enables the parties, under the authority of congress, to have the controversies heard, tried and determined before the national tribunals. No other reason than that which has been stated can be assigned, why some, at least, of those cases should not have been left to the cognisance of the state courts. In respect to the other enumerated cases—the cases arising under the constitution, laws and treaties of the United States, cases affecting ambassadors and other public ministers, and cases of admiralty and maritime jurisdiction—reasons of a higher and more extensive nature, touching the safety, peace and sovereignty of the nation, might well justify a grant of exclusive jurisdiction.

This is not all. A motive of another kind, perfectly compatible with the most sincere respect for state tribunals, might induce the grant of appellate power over their decisions. That motive is the importance, and even necessity of uniformity of decisions throughout the whole United States, upon all subjects within the purview of the constitution. Judges of equal learning and integrity, in different states, might differently interpret the statute, or a treaty of the United States, or even the constitution itself: if there were no revising authority to control these jarring and discordant judgments, and harmonize them into uniformity, the laws, the treaties and the constitution of the United States would be different, in different states, and might, perhaps, never have precisely the same construction, obligation or efficiency, in any two states. The public mischiefs that would attend such a state of things would be truly deplorable; and it cannot be believed, that they could have escaped the enlightened convention which formed the constitution. What, indeed, might then have been only prophecy, has now become fact; and the appellate jurisdiction must continue to be the only adequate remedy for such evils.

There is an additional consideration, which is entitled to great weight. The constitution of the United States was designed for the common and equal benefit of all the people of the United States. The judicial power was granted for the same benign and salutary purposes. It was not to be exercised exclusively for the benefit of parties who might be plaintiffs, and would elect the national *forum,* but also for the protection of defendants who might be entitled to try their rights, or assert their privileges, before the same *forum.* Yet, if the construction contended for be correct, it will follow, that as the plaintiff may always elect the state court, the defendant may be deprived of all the security which the constitution intended in aid of his rights. Such a state of things can, in no respect, be considered as giving equal rights. To obviate this difficulty, we are referred to the power which, it is admitted, congress possesses to remove suits from state courts to the national courts; and this forms the second ground upon which the argument we are considering has been attempted to be sustained.

This power of removal is not to be found in express terms in any part of the constitution; if it be given, it is only given by implication, as a power necessary and proper to carry into effect some express power. The power of removal is certainly not, in strictness of language, an exercise of original jurisdiction; it presupposes an exercise of original jurisdiction to have attached elsewhere. The existence of this power of removal is familiar in courts acting according to the course of the common law, in criminal as well as civil cases, and it is exercised before as well as after judgment. But this is always deemed, in both cases, an exercise of appellate, and not of original jurisdiction. If, then, the right of removal be included in the appellate jurisdiction, it is only because it is one mode of exercising that power, and as congress is not limited by the constitution to any particular mode, or time, of exercising it, it may authorize a removal, either before or after judgment. The time, the process and the manner must be subject to its absolute legislative control.

A writ of error is, indeed, but a process which removes the record of one court to the possession of another court, and enables the latter to inspect the proceedings, and give such judgment as its own opinion of the law and justice of the case may warrant. There is nothing in the nature of the process, which forbids it from being applied by the legislature to interlocutory as well as final judgments. And if the right of removal from state courts exist, before judgment, because it is included in the appellate power, it must, for the same reason, exist, after judgment. And if the appellate power, by the constitution, does not include cases pending in state courts, the right of removal, which is but a mode of exercising that power, cannot be applied to them. Precisely the same objections, therefore, exist as to the right of removal before judgment, as after, and both must stand or fall together. Nor, indeed, would the force of the arguments on either side materially vary, if the right of removal were an exercise of original jurisdiction. It would equally trench upon the jurisdiction and independence of state tribunals.

The remedy, too, of removal of suits, would be utterly inadequate to the purposes of the constitution, if it could act only on the parties, and not upon the state courts. In respect to criminal prosecutions, the difficulty seems admitted to be insurmountable; and in respect to civil suits, there would, in many cases, be rights, without corresponding remedies. If state courts should deny the constitutionality of the authority to remove suits from their cognisance, in what manner could they be compelled to relinquish the jurisdiction? In respect to criminal cases, there would at once be an end of all control, and the state decisions would be paramount to the constitution; and though, in civil suits, the courts of the United States might act upon the parties, yet the state courts might act in the same way; and this conflict of jurisdictions would not only jeopardize private rights, but bring into imminent peril the public interests.

On the whole, the court are of opinion, that the appellate power of the United States does extend to cases pending in the state courts; and that the 25th section of the judiciary act, which authorizes the exercise of this jurisdiction in the specified cases, by a writ of error, is supported by the letter and spirit of the constitution. We find no clause in that instrument which limits this power; and we dare not interpose a limitation, where the people have not been disposed to create one.

Strong as this conclusion stands, upon the general language of the constitution, it may still derive support from other sources. It is an historical fact, that this exposition of the constitution, extending its appellate power to state courts, was, previous to its adoption, uniformly and publicly avowed by its friends, and admitted by its enemies, as the basis of their respective reasonings, both in and out of the state conventions. It is an historical fact, that at the time when the judiciary act was submitted to the deliberations of the first congress, composed, as it was, not only of men of great learning and ability, but of men who had acted a principal part in framing, supporting or opposing that constitution, the same exposition was explicitly declared and admitted by the friends and by the opponents of that system. It is an historical fact, that the supreme court of the United States have, from time to time, sustained this appellate jurisdiction, in a great variety of cases, brought from the tribunals of many of the most important states in the Union, and that no state tribunal has ever breathed a judicial doubt on the subject, or declined to obey the mandate of the supreme court, until the present occasion. This weight of contemporaneous exposition by all parties, this acquiescence of enlightened state courts, and these judicial decisions of the supreme court, through so long a period, do, as we think, place the doctrine upon a foundation of authority which cannot be shaken, without delivering over the subject to perpetual and irremediable doubts.

The next question which has been argued, is, whether the case at bar be within the purview of the 25th section of the judiciary act, so that this court may rightfully sustain the present writ of error? This section, stripped of passages unimportant in this inquiry, enacts, in substance, that a final judgment or decree, in any suit in the highest court of law or equity of a state, where is drawn in question the validity of a treaty or statute of, or an authority exercised under, the United States, and the decision is against their validity; or where is drawn in question the validity of a statute of, or an authority exercised under, any state, on the ground of their being repugnant to the constitution, treaties or laws of the United States, and the decision is in favor of such their validity; or of the constitution, or of a treaty or statute of, or commission held under, the United States, and the decision is against the title, right, privilege or exemption specially set up or claimed by either party, under such clause of the said constitution, treaty, statute or commission, may be re-examined, and reversed or affirmed, in the supreme court of the United States, upon a writ of error, in the same manner, and under the same regulations, and the writ shall have the same effect, as if the judgment or decree complained of had been rendered or passed in a circuit court, and the proceeding upon the reversal shall also be the same, except that the supreme court, instead of remanding the cause for a final decision, as before provided, may, at their discretion, if the cause shall have been once remanded before, proceed to a final decision of the same, and award execution. But no other error shall be assigned or regarded as a ground of reversal, in any such case as aforesaid, than such as appears upon the face of the record, and immediately respects the before-mentioned question of validity or construction of the said constitution, treaties, statutes, commissions or authorities in dispute.

That the present writ of error is founded upon a judgment of the court below, which drew in question and denied the validity of a statute of the United States, is incontrovertible, for it is apparent upon the face of the record. That this judgment is final upon the rights of the parties, is equally true; for if well founded, the former judgment of that court was of conclusive authority, and the former judgment of this court utterly void. The decision was, therefore, equivalent to a perpetual stay of proceedings upon the mandate, and a perpetual denial of all the rights acquired under it. The case, then, falls directly within the terms of the act. It is a final judgment in a suit in a state court, denying the validity of a statute of the United States; and unless a distinction can be made between proceedings under a mandate, and proceedings in an original suit, a writ of error is the proper remedy to revise that judgment. In our opinion, no legal distinction exists between the cases.

In causes remanded to the circuit courts, if the mandate be not correctly executed, a writ of error or appeal has always been supposed to be a proper remedy, and has been recognised as such, in the former decisions of this court. The statute gives the same effect to writs of error from the judgments of state courts as of the circuit courts; and in its terms provides for proceedings where the same cause may be a second time brought up on writ of error before the supreme court. There is no limitation or description of the cases to which the second writ of error may be applied; and it ought, therefore, to be co-extensive with the cases which fall within the mischiefs of the statutue. It will hardly be denied, that this cause stands in that predicament; and if so, then the appellate jurisdiction of this court has rightfully attached.

But it is contended, that the former judgment of this court was rendered upon a case, not within the purview of this section of the judicial act, and that, as it was pronounced by an incompetent jurisdiction, it was utterly void, and cannot be a sufficient foundation to sustain any subsequent proceedings. To this argument, several answers may be given. In the first place, it is not admitted, that, upon this writ of error, the former record is before us. The error now assigned is not in the former proceedings, but in the judgment rendered upon the mandate issued after the former judgment. The question now litigated is not upon the construction of a treaty, but upon the constitutionality of a statute of the United States, which is clearly within our jurisdiction. In the next place, in ordinary cases, a second writ of error has never been supposed to draw in question the propriety of the first judgment, and it is difficult to perceive how such a proceeding could be sustained, upon principle. A final judgment of this court is supposed to be conclusive upon the rights which it decides, and no statute has provided any process by which this court can revise its own judgments. In several cases which have been formerly adjudged in this court, the same point was argued by counsel, and expressly overruled. It was solemnly held, that a final judgment of this court was conclusive upon the parties, and could not be re-examined.

In this case, however, from motives of a public nature, we are entirely willing to waive all objections, and to go back and re-examine the question of jurisdiction, as it stood upon the record formerly in judgment. We have great confidence, that our jurisdiction will, on a careful examination, stand confirmed, as well upon principle as authority. It will be recollected, that the action was an ejectment for a parcel of land in the Northern Neck, formerly belonging to Lord Fairfax. The original plaintiff claimed the land under a patent granted to him by the state of Virginia, in 1789, under a title supposed to be vested in that state by escheat or forfeiture. The original defendant claimed the land as devisee under the will of Lord Fairfax. The parties agreed to a special statement of facts, in the nature of a special verdict, upon which the district court of Winchester, in 1793, gave a general judgment for the defendant, which judgment was afterwards reversed in 1810, by the court of appeals, and a general judgment was rendered for the plaintiff; and from this last judgment, a writ of error was brought to the supreme court. The statement of facts contained a regular deduction of the title of Lord Fairfax, until his death, in 1781, and also the title of his devisee. It also contained a regular deduction of the title of the plaintiff, under the state of Virginia, and further referred to the treaty of peace of 1783, and to the acts of Virginia respecting the lands of Lord Fairfax, and the supposed escheat or forfeiture thereof, as component parts of the case. No facts disconnected with the titles thus set up by the parties were alleged on either side. It is apparent, from this summary explanation, that the title thus set up by the plaintiff might be open to other objections; but the title of the defendant was perfect and complete, if it was protected by the treaty of 1783. If, therefore, this court had authority to examine into the whole record, and to decide upon the legal validity of the title of the defendant, as well as its application to the treaty of peace, it would be a case within the express purview of the 25th section of the act; for there was nothing in the record upon which the court below could have decided, but upon the title as connected with the treaty; and if the title was otherwise good, its sufficiency must have depended altogether upon its protection under the treaty. Under such circumstances, it was strictly a suit where was drawn in question the construction of a treaty, and the decision was against the title specially set up or claimed by the defendant. It would fall, then, within the very terms of the act.

The objection urged at the bar is, that this court cannot inquire into the title, but simply into the correctness of the construction put upon the treaty by the court of appeals; and that their judgment is not re-examinable here, unless it appear on the face of the record, that some construction was put upon the treaty. If, therefore, that court might have decided the case upon the invalidity of the title (and *non constat,* that they did not), independent of the treaty, there is an end of the appellate jurisdiction of this court. In support of this objection, much stress is laid upon the last clause of the section, which declares, that no other cause shall be regarded as a ground of reversal than such as appears on the face of the record and immediately respects the construction of the treaty, &c., in dispute.

If this be the true construction of the section, it will be wholly inadequate for the purposes which it professes to have in view, and may be evaded at pleasure. But we see no reason for adopting this narrow construction; and there are the strongest reasons against it, founded upon the words as well as the intent of the legislature. What is the case for which the body of the section provides a remedy by writ of error? The answer must be, in the words of the section, a suit where is drawn in question the construction of a treaty, and the decision is against the title set up by the party. It is, therefore, the decision against the title set up, with reference to the treaty, and not the mere abstract construction of the treaty itself, upon which the statute intends to found the appellate jurisdiction. How, indeed, can it be possible to decide, whether a title be within the protection of a treaty, until it is ascertained what that title is, and whether it have a legal validity? From the very necessity of the case, there must be a preliminary inquiry into the existence and structure of the title, before the court can construe the treaty in reference to that title. If the court below should decide, that the title was bad, and therefore, not protected by the treaty, must not this court have a power to decide the title to be good, and therefore, protected by the treaty? Is not the treaty, in both instances, equally construed, and the title of the party, in reference to the treaty, equally ascertained and decided? Nor does the clause relied on in the objection, impugn this construction. It requires, that the error upon which the appellate court is to decide, shall appear on the face of the record, and immediately respect the questions before mentioned in the section. One of the questions is, as to the construction of a treaty, upon a title specially set up by a party, and every error that immediately respects that question must, of course, be within the cognisance of the court. The title set up in this case is apparent upon the face of the record, and immediately respects the decision of that question; any error, therefore, in respect to that title must be re-examinable, or the case could never be presented to the court.

The restraining clause was manifestly

intended for a very different purpose. It was foreseen, that the parties might claim under various titles, and might assert various defences, altogether independent of each other. The court might admit or reject evidence applicable to one particular title, and not to all, and in such cases, it was the intention of congress, to limit what would otherwise have unquestionably attached to the court, the right of revising all the points involved in the cause. It, therefore, restrains this right to such errors as respect the questions specified in the section; and in this view, it has an appropriate sense, consistent with the preceding clauses. We are, therefore, satisfied, that, upon principle, the case was rightfully before us, and if the point were perfectly new, we should not hesitate to assert the jurisdiction.

But the point has been already decided by this court upon solemn argument. In *Smith* v. *State of Maryland* (6 Cranch 286), precisely the same objection was taken by counsel, and overruled by the unanimous opinion of the court. That case was, in some respects, stronger than the present; for the court below decided, expressly, that the party had no title, and therefore, the treaty could not operate upon it. This court entered into an examination of that question, and being of the same opinion, affirmed the judgment. There cannot, then, be an authority which could more completely govern the present question.

It has been asserted at the bar, that, in point of fact, the court of appeals did not decide either upon the treaty, or the title apparent upon the record, but upon a compromise made under an act of the legislature of Virginia. If it be true (as we are informed), that this was a private act, to take effect only upon a certain condition, viz., the execution of a deed of release of certain lands, which was matter *in pais,* it is somewhat difficult to understand, how the court could take judicial cognisance of the act, or of the performance of the condition, unless spread upon the record. At all events, we are bound to consider, that the court did decide upon the facts actually before them. The treaty of peace was not necessary to have been stated, for it was the supreme law of the land, of which all courts must take notice. And at the time of the decision in the court of appeals, and in this court, another treaty had intervened, which attached itself to the title in controversy, and of course, must have been the supreme law to govern the decision, if it should be found applicable to the case. It was in this view that this court did not deem it necessary to rest its former decision upon the treaty of peace, believing that the title of the defendant was, at all events, perfect, under the treaty of 1794.

The remaining questions respect more the practice than the principles of this court. The forms of process, and the modes of proceeding in the exercise of jurisdiction, are, with few exceptions, left by the legislature, to be regulated and changed, as this court may, in its discretion, deem expedient. By a rule of this court, the return of a copy of a record of the proper court, under the seal of that court, annexed to the writ of error, is declared to be "a sufficient compliance with the mandate of the writ." The record, in this case, is duly certified by the clerk of the court of appeals, and annexed to the writ of error. The objection, therefore, which has been urged to the sufficiency of the return, cannot prevail.

Another objection is, that it does not appear that the judge who granted the writ of error did, upon issuing the citation, take the bond required by the 22d section of the judiciary act. We consider that provision as merely directory to the judge; and that an omission does not avoid the writ of error. If any party be prejudiced by the omission, this court can grant him summary relief, by imposing such terms on the other party as, under all the circumstances, may be legal and proper. But there is nothing in the record, by which we can judicially know whether a bond has been taken or not; for the statute does not require the bond to be returned to this court, and it might, with equal propriety, be lodged in the court below, who would ordinarily execute the judgment to be rendered on the writ. And the presumption of the law is, until the contrary appears, that every judge who signs a citation has obeyed the injunctions of the act.

We have thus gone over all the principal questions in the cause, and we deliver our judgment with entire confidence, that it is consistent with the constitution and laws of the land. We have not thought it incumbent on us to give any opinion upon the question, whether this court have authority to issue a writ of *mandamus* to the court of appeals, to enforce the former judgments, as we did not think it necessarily involved in the decision of this cause.

It is the opinion of the whole court, that the judgment of the court of appeals of Virginia, rendered on the mandate in this cause, be reversed, and the judgment of the district court, held at Winchester, be, and the same is hereby affirmed.

SWIFT v. TYSON, 16 PET. 1 (1842)

MR. JUSTICE STORY delivered the opinion of the Court.

This cause comes before us from the Circuit Court of the southern district of New York, upon a certificate of division of the judges of that Court.

The action was brought by the plaintiff, Swift, as endorsee, against the defendant, Tyson, as acceptor, upon a bill of exchange dated at Portland, Maine, on the first day of May, 1836, for the sum of one thousand five hundred and forty dollars, thirty cents, payable six months after date and grace, drawn by one Nathaniel Norton and one Jairus S. Keith upon and accepted by Tyson, at the city of New York, in favour of the order of Nathaniel Norton, and by Norton endorsed to the plaintiff. The bill was dishonoured at maturity.

At the trial the acceptance and endorsement of the bill were admitted, and the plaintiff there rested his case. The defendant then introduced in evidence the answer of Swift to a bill of discovery, by which it appeared that Swift took the bill before it became due, in payment of a promissory note due to him by Norton and Keith; that he understood that the bill was accepted in part payment of some lands sold by Norton to a company in New York; that Swift was a bona fide holder of the bill, not having any notice of any thing in the sale or title to the lands, or otherwise, impeaching the transaction, and with the full belief that the bill was justly due. The particular circumstances are fully set forth in the answer in the record; but it does not seem necessary farther to state them. The defendant then offered to prove, that the bill was accepted by the defendant as part consideration for the purchase of certain lands in the state of Maine, which Norton and Keith represented themselves to be the owners of, and also represented to be of great value, and contracted to convey a good title thereto; and that the representations were in every respect fraudulent and false, and Norton and Keith had no title to the lands, and that the same were of little or no value. The plaintiff objected to the admission of such testimony, or of any testimony, as against him, impeaching or showing a failure of the consideration, on which the bill was accepted, under the facts admitted by the defendant, and those proved by him, by reading the answer of the plaintiff to the bill of discovery. The judges of the Circuit Court thereupon divided in opinion upon the following point or question of law; whether, under the facts last mentioned, the defendant was entitled to the same defence to the action as if the suit was between the original parties to the bill, that is to say, Norton, or Norton and Keith, and the defendant; and whether the evidence so offered was admissible as against the plaintiff in the action. And this is the question certified to us for our decision.

There is no doubt, that a bonâ fide holder of a negotiable instrument for a valuable consideration, without any notice of facts which impeach its validity as between the antecedent parties, if he takes it under an endorsement made before the same becomes due, holds the title unaffected by these facts, and may recover thereon, although as between the antecedent parties the transaction may be without any legal validity. This is a doctrine so long and so well established, and so essential to the security of negotiable paper, that it is laid up among the fundamentals of the law, and requires no authority or reasoning to be now brought in its support. As little doubt is there, that the holder of any negotiable paper, before it is due, is not bound to prove that he is a bonâ fide holder for a valuable consideration, without notice; for the law will presume that, in the absence of all rebutting proofs, and therefore it is incumbent upon the defendant to establish by way of defence satisfactory proofs of the contrary, and thus to overcome the primâ facie title of the plaintiff.

In the present case, the plaintiff is a bonâ fide holder without notice for what the law deems a good and valid consideration, that is, for a pre-existing debt; and the only real question in the cause is, whether, under the circumstances of the present case, such a pre-existing debt constitutes a valuable consideration in the sense of the general rule applicable to negotiable instruments. We say, under the circumstances of the present case, for the acceptance having been made in New York, the argument on behalf of the defendant is, that the contract is to be treated as a New York contract, and therefore to be governed by the laws of New York, as expounded by its Courts, as well upon general principles, as by the express provisions of the thirty-fourth section of the judiciary act of 1789, ch. 20. And then it is further contended, that by the law of New York, as thus expounded by its Courts, a pre-existing debt does not constitute, in the sense of the general rule, a valuable consideration applicable to negotiable instruments.

In the first place, then, let us examine into the decisions of the Courts of New York upon this subject. In the earliest case, *Warren* v. *Lynch,* 5 Johns. R. 289, the Supreme Court of New York appear to have held, that a pre-existing debt was a sufficient consideration to entitle a bonâ fide holder without notice to recover the amount of a note endorsed to him, which might not, as between the original parties, be valid. The same doctrine was affirmed by Mr. Chancellor Kent in *Bay* v. *Coddington,* 5 Johns. Chan. Rep. 54. Upon that occasion he said, that negotiable paper can be assigned or transferred by an agent or factor or by any other person, fraudulently, so as to bind the true owner as against the holder, provided it be taken in the usual course of trade, and for a fair and valuable consideration without notice of the fraud. But he added, that the holders in that case were not entitled to the benefit of the rule, because it was not negotiated to them in the usual course of business or trade, nor in payment of any antecedent and existing debt, nor for cash, or property advanced, debt created, or responsibility incurred, on the strength and credit of the notes; thus directly affirming, that a pre-existing debt was a fair and valuable consideration within the protection of the general rule. And he has since affirmed the same doctrine, upon a full review of it, in his Commentaries, 3 Kent. Comm. sect. 44, p. 81. The decision in the case of *Bay* v. *Coddington* was afterwards affirmed in the Court of Errors, 20 Johns, R. 637, and the general reasoning of the chancellor was fully sustained. There were indeed peculiar circumstances in that case, which the Court seem to have considered as entitling it to be treated as an exception to the general rule, upon the ground either because the receipt of the notes was under suspicious circumstances, the transfer having been made after the known insolvency of the endorser, or because the holder had received it as a mere security for contingent responsibilities, with which the holders had not then become charged. There was, however, a considerable diversity of opinion among the members of the Court upon that occasion, several of them holding that the decree ought to be reversed, others affirming that a pre-existing debt was a valuable consideration, sufficient to protect the holders, and others again insisting, that a pre-existent debt was not sufficient. From that period, however, for a series of years, it seems to have been held by the Supreme Court of the state, that a pre-existing debt was not a sufficient consideration to shut out the equities of the original parties in favour of the holders. But no case to that effect has ever been decided in the Court of Errors. The cases cited at the bar, and especially *Roosa* v. *Brotherson,* 10 Wend. R. 85; *The Ontario Bank* v. *Worthington,* 12 Wend. R. 593; and *Payne* v. *Cutler,* 13 Wend. R. 605, are directly in point. But the more recent cases, *The Bank of Salina* v. *Babcock,* 21 Wend. R. 490, and *The Bank of Sandusky* v. *Scoville,* 24 Wend. R. 115, have greatly shaken, if they have not entirely overthrown those decisions, and seem to have brought back the doctrine to that promulgated in the earliest cases. So that, to say the least of it, it admits of serious doubt, whether any doctrine upon this question can at the present time be treated as finally established; and it is certain, that the Court of Errors have not pronounced any positive opinion upon it.

But, admitting the doctrine to be fully settled in New York, it remains to be considered, whether it is obligatory upon this Court, if it differs from the principles established in the general commercial law. It is observable that the Courts of New York do not found their decisions upon this point upon any local statute, or positive, fixed, or ancient local usage: but they deduce the doctrine from the general principles of commercial law. It is, however, contended, that the thirty-fourth section of the judiciary act of 1789, ch. 20, furnishes a rule obligatory upon this Court to follow the decisions of the state tribunals in all cases to which they apply. That section provides "that the laws of the several states, except where the Constitution, treaties, or statutes of the United States shall otherwise require or provide, shall be regarded as rules of decision in trials at common law in the Courts of the United States, in cases where they apply." In order to maintain the argument, it is essential, therefore, to hold, that the word "laws," in this section, includes within the scope of its meaning the decisions of the local tribunals. In the ordinary use of language it will hardly be contended that the decisions of Courts constitute laws. They are, at most, only evidence of what the laws are; and are not of themselves laws. They are often re-examined, reversed, and qualified by the Courts themselves, whenever they are found to be either defective, or ill-founded, or otherwise incorrect. The laws of a state are more usually understood to mean the rules and enactments promulgated by the legislative authority thereof, or long established local customs having the force of laws. In all the various cases which have hitherto come before us for decision, this Court have uniformly supposed, that the true interpretation of the thirty-fourth section limited its application to state laws strictly local, that is to say, to the positive statutes of the state, and the construction thereof adopted by the local tribunals, and to rights and titles to things having a permanent locality, such as the rights and titles to real estate, and other matters immovable and intraterritorial in their nature and character. It never has been supposed by us, that the section did apply, or was designed to apply, to questions of a more general nature, not at all dependent upon local statutes or local usages of a fixed and permanent operation, as, for example, to the construction of ordinary contracts or other written instruments, and especially to questions of general commercial law, where the state tribunals are called upon to perform the like functions as ourselves, that is, to ascertain upon general reasoning and legal analogies, what is the true exposition of the contract or instrument, or what is the just rule furnished by the principles of commercial law to govern the case. And we have not now the slightest difficulty in holding, that this section, upon its true intendment and construction, is strictly limited to local statutes and local usages of the character before stated, and does not extend to contracts and other instruments of a commercial nature, the true interpretation and effect whereof are to be sought, not in the decisions of the local tribunals, but in the general principles and doctrines of commercial jurisprudence. Undoubtedly, the decisions of the local tribunals upon such subjects are entitled to, and will receive, the most deliberate attention and respect of this Court; but they cannot furnish positive rules, or conclusive authority, by which our own judgments are to be bound up and governed. The law respecting negotiable instruments may be truly declared in the language of Cicero, adopted by Lord Mansfield in *Luke* v. *Lyde,* 2 Burr. R. 883, 887, to be in a great measure, not the law of a single country only, but of the commercial world. Non erit alia lex Romæ, alia Athenis, alia nunc, alia posthac, sed et apud omnes gentes, et omni tempore, una eademque lex obtenebit.

It becomes necessary for us, therefore, upon the present occasion to express our own opinion of the true result of the commercial law upon the question now before us. And we have no hesitation in saying, that a pre-existing debt does constitute a valuable consideration in the sense of the general rule already stated, as applicable to negotiable instruments. Assuming it to be true (which, however, may well admit of some doubt from the generality of the language) that the holder of a negotiable instrument is unaffected with the equities between the antecedent parties, of which he has no notice, only where he receives it in the usual course of trade and business for a valuable consideration, before it becomes due; we are prepared to say, that receiving it in payment of, or as security for a pre-existing debt, is according to the known usual course of trade and business. And why upon principle should not a pre-existing debt be deemed such a valuable consideration? It is for the benefit and convenience of the commerical world to give as wide an extent as practicable to the credit and circulation of negotiable paper, that it may pass not only as security for new purchases and advances, made upon the transfer thereof, but also in payment of and as security for pre-existing debts. The creditor is thereby enabled to realize or to secure his debt, and thus may safely give a prolonged credit, or forbear from taking any legal steps to enforce his rights. The debtor also has the advantage of making his negotiable securities of equivalent value to cash. But establish the opposite conclusion, that negotiable paper cannot be applied in payment of or as security for pre-existing debts, without letting in all the equities between the original and antecedent parties, and the value and circulation of such securities must be essentially diminished, and the debtor driven to the embarrassment of making a sale thereof, often at a ruinous discount, to some third person, and then by circuity to apply the proceeds to the payment of his debts. What, indeed, upon such a doctrine would become of that large class of cases, where new notes are given by the same or by other parties, by way of renewal or security to banks, in lieu of old securities discounted by them, which have arrived at maturity? Probably more than one-half of all bank transactions in our country, as well as those of other countries, are of this nature. The doctrine would strike a fatal blow at all discounts of negotiable securities for pre-existing debts.

This question has been several times before this Court, and it has been uniformly held, that it makes no difference whatsoever as to the rights of the holder, whether the debt for which the negotiable instrument is transferred to him is a pre-existing debt, or is contracted at the time of the transfer. In each case he equally gives credit to the instrument. The cases of *Coolidge* v. *Payson,* 2 Wheaton, R. 66, 70, 73, and *Townsley* v. *Sumrall,* 2 Peters, R. 170, 182, are directly in point.

In England the same doctrine has been uniformly acted upon. As long ago as the case of *Pillans and Rose* v. *Van Meirop and Hopkins,* 3 Burr. 1664, the very point was made and the objection was overruled. That, indeed, was a case of far more stringency than the one now before us; for the bill of exchange, there drawn in discharge of a pre-existing debt, was held to bind the party as acceptor, upon a mere promise made by him to accept before the bill was actually drawn. Upon that occasion Lord Mansfield, likening the case to that of a letter of credit, said, that a letter of credit may be given for money already advanced, as well as for money to be advanced in future: and the whole Court held the plaintiff entitled to recover. From that period downward there is not a single case to be found in England in which it has ever been held by the Court, that a pre-existing debt was not a valuable consideration, sufficient to protect the holder, within the meaning of the general rule, although incidental dicta have been sometimes relied on to establish the contrary, such as the dictum of Lord Chief Justice Abbott in *Smith* v. *De Witt,* 6 Dowl. & Ryland, 120, and *De la Chaumette* v. *The Bank of England,* 9 Barn. & Cres., 209, where, however, the decision turned upon very different considerations.

Mr. Justice Bayley, in his valuable work on bills of exchange and promissory notes, lays down the rule in the most general terms. "The want of consideration," says he, "in toto or in part, cannot be insisted on, if the plaintiff or any intermediate party between him and the defendant took the bill or note bonâ fide and upon a valid consideration." Bayley on Bills, p. 499, 500, 5th London edition, 1830. It is observable that he here uses the words "valid consideration," obviously intending to make the distinction, that it is not intended to apply solely to cases, where a present consideration for advances of money on goods or otherwise takes place at the time of the transfer and upon the credit thereof. And in this he is fully borne out by the authorities. They go farther, and establish, that a transfer as security for past, and even for future responsibilities, will, for this purpose, be a sufficient, valid, and valuable consideration. Thus, in the case of *Bosanquet* v. *Dudman,* 1 Starkie, R. 1, it was held by Lord Ellenborough, that if a banker be under acceptances to an amount beyond the cash balance in his hands, every bill he holds of that customer's bona fide, he is to be considered as holding for value; and it makes no difference though he hold other collateral securities, more than sufficient to cover the excess of his acceptances. The same doctrine was affirmed by Lord Eldon in Ex parte Bloxham, 8 Ves. 531, as equally applicable to past and to future acceptances. The subsequent cases of *Heywood* v. *Watson,* 4 Bing. R. 496, and *Bramah* v. *Roberts,* 1 Bing. New Ca. 469, and *Percival* v. *Frampton,* 2 Cromp. Mees. & Rose, 180, are to the same effect. They directly establish that a bona fide holder, taking a negotiable note in payment of or as security for a pre-existing debt, is a holder for a valuable consideration, entitled to protection against all the equities between the antecedent parties. And these are the latest decisions, which our researches have enabled us to ascertain to have been made in the English Courts upon this subject.

In the American Courts, so far as we have been able to trace the decisions, the same doctrine seems generally but not universally to prevail. In *Brush* v. *Scribner,* 11 Conn., R. 388, the Supreme Court of Connecticut, after an elaborate review of the English and New York adjudications, held, upon general principles of commercial law, that a pre-existing debt was a valuable consideration, sufficient to convey a valid title to a bona fide holder against all the antecedent parties to a negotiable note. There is no reason to doubt, that the same rule has been adopted and constantly adhered to in Massachusetts; and certainly there is no trace to be found to the contrary. In truth, in the silence of any adjudications upon the subject, in a case of such frequent and almost daily occurrence in the commercial states, it may fairly be presumed, that whatever constitutes a valid and valuable consideration in other cases of contract to support titles of the most solemn nature, is held à fortiori to be sufficient in cases of negotiable instruments, as indispensable to the security of holders, and the facility and safety of their circulation. Be this as it may, we entertain no doubt, that a bonâ fide holder, for a pre-existing debt, of a negotiable instrument, is not affected by any equities between the antecedent parties, where he has received the same before it became due, without notice of any such equities. We are all, therefore, of opinion, that the question on this point, propounded by the Circuit Court for our consideration, ought to be answered in the negative; and we shall accordingly direct it so to be certified to the Circuit Court.

Smith Thompson

☆ 1768(?)–1843 ☆

APPOINTED BY

JAMES MONROE

YEARS ON COURT

1823–1843

Smith Thompson

by

GERALD T. DUNNE

SMITH THOMPSON, longtime exponent of the doctrine of concurrent powers, frontrunner in the judicial reaction to John Marshall's centralist federalism, and one of the most politically active and ambitious Justices ever to sit on the Supreme Court, was born in Dutchess County, New York. The exact place and time is uncertain. Both the towns of Amenia and Stanford have been named as his birthplace. One source names the date as January 17, 1768; another suggests it was a year later. Of New England stock, he was one of nine children of Ezra and Rachel (Smith) Thompson. His father was a prosperous farmer, a prominent Anti-Federalist and a delegate to the New York ratification convention of 1788. After attending common school he went to Princeton, from which he graduated in 1788. Thereafter he supported himself by teaching school while reading law in the Poughkeepsie office of James Kent, another distinguished son of Dutchess County and one of the great American jurists, a man whose career would be episodically intertwined with that of Thompson's.

Thompson completed his law apprenticeship in 1792, opened an office in Troy and returned to Poughkeepsie the following year to become associated in practice with Kent and Gilbert Livingston, an old political ally of his father and a member of one of the lesser branches of the powerful Livingston family. In 1794 he married Gilbert Livingston's daughter, Sarah, a union which both effected and symbolized professional, political, and family ties and one which was to form a dominant and continuing force in his public life.

Its significance became quickly apparent with the state political battles at the close of the eighteenth century, in which Thompson participated, being by both inheritance and marriage virtually a charter member of what was formally

GERALD T. DUNNE is Vice-President of the Federal Reserve Bank, St. Louis. He is the author of Monetary Decisions of the Supreme Court *and occasional contributions to various periodicals on American legal history.*

the anti-Federalist Republican party but was in fact the loose and shifting coalition made up of the followers of Aaron Burr and the adherents of the Clinton and Livingston families. As a rising member of the Livingston faction, Thompson was elected to the New York legislature in 1800 and also was a delegate to the state constitutional convention called the following year to exploit the Republican dominance in state affairs. The Livingston faction's power as well as Thompson's share in the fruits of the convention's work appeared soon after in his successive designations as district attorney for the middle district of New York and as a judge of the state supreme court. The honors came in such close sequence that Thompson mounted the bench on January 28, 1802, without having had the opportunity to serve as district attorney, and thus began a judicial career which, save for five years in the presidential Cabinet, was to last the rest of his life.

The familial overtones of New York politics were graphically shown in the appointments to the state judiciary which accompanied that of Thompson. One was that of Brockholst Livingston, a cousin of his wife and his future predecessor on the United States Supreme Court. The other was that of Morgan Lewis, like himself a Livingston in-law. By felicitous coincidence, however, there also was an association with the incumbent bench, for one of them was his old preceptor, James Kent, who had been on the court since 1798.

This unusual combination of relationships between congenial but strong-minded men, who freely set out their ideas on the law, doubtless underlies the controversy which permeated the early reports of the court. Thompson, like most of his colleagues, frequently submitted separate statements of his views. Yet the supposed diversity of outlook seems more the procedural consequence of giving short, *seriatim* opinions rather than being a reflection of fundamental divisions of juristic attitudes. Rather, in what well might be an institutional manifestation of a renewed federalism with its profound respect for the judicial process, Kent in New York, like Marshall in Washington, brought a group of rather formidable colleagues into an orchestral *per curiam* performance by a combination of intellect, will, and personal charm exerted in an environment hospitable to his views. In distinction from the national tribunal, however, only a small number of New York cases involved basic constitutional issues and even here the bench seldom divided along party lines. Instead, the New York court rose to great heights in resolving the disputes of a prospering and dynamic state. In fact, the very vigor of its judicial activism seems to have provoked a reaction which caused its virtual dissolution and reorganization at the New York constitutional convention of 1823. A measure of both its success and its fall can be found in the contemporary and doleful statement of Thompson's future colleague on the United States Supreme Court, Justice Joseph Story, that he had "no expectation of ever seeing, in my day, Judges of more learning, talent, and fidelity in any part of the Union."

Ironically, Thompson would part company with Story repeatedly on the Supreme Court in leading a reaction against Chief Justice Marshall's ideas on the preemptive nature of federalist centralism. In New York, however, it was Thompson's role to fulfill rather than revise, for he succeeded to the leadership of the state bench when Kent became chancellor in 1814, and the change of chief justices seemed to be without substantial effect on the ongoing work of the court. The difference between his roles in New York and Washington came down to the fact that the core ideas of his judicial and constitutional thought—a states' rights mercantilism tempered with a humanitarian overlay—were far more congenial to one environment than the other. In more specific terms, this meant a disposition to view the constitutional grants of power to the federal government—whether exercised or not—as nonetheless allowing the individual states a generous measure of concurrent authority. Here, unquestionably, the basic strain of this philosophy was expressed in his opinion in *Livingston* v. *Van Ingen,* 9 Johns. R. 507 (1812) involving the Livingston-Fulton steamboat monopoly on New York waters. In a powerful and comprehensive opinion Thompson held the state's grant of a monopoly did not contravene its own constitution and, further, involved no constitutional collision with the congressional power to grant patents or regulate interstate and foreign commerce. (His opinion was later undercut by John Marshall's famed decision in *Gibbons* v. *Ogden* 9 Wheat. [1824] which held that such a monopoly did in fact collide with the congressional commerce power.) In his conclusion he concurred with Kent, and while it is difficult to discern a common pattern between his views and Kent's, it is interesting to note that he also sided with Kent in *People* v. *Croswell,* 3 Johns. C. 337 (1804), where he concurred in the view that a defendant in a criminal libel proceeding might base his defense on the truth and good faith of the controverted publication. On the other hand, he differed with Kent in construing the scope and sanction of the full faith and credit clause. In *Hitchcock* v. *Aicken,* 1 Cai. R. 460 (1803), Thompson and Livingston, both future United States Supreme Court Justices, argued unsuccessfully for a rigorous reading of the clause while the majority of the court under Kent's leadership read it as giving outstate judgments only a *prima facie* validity. And, indicative of the persistence of his views on concurrent powers, was his opinion toward the end of his career on the state bench in *Hallett* v. *Novion,* 14 Johns. R. 273 (1817), where, declaring "not the place but the case which determines jurisdiction," he held that a controversy which was both a maritime and a domestic tort did not necessarily fall under the exclusive federal admiralty jurisdiction but might be adjudicated in its latter character under New York law.

Thompson also sat on the Council of Revision, consisting of the Governor, Chancellor, and Supreme Court judges, a group which held a veto power over legislation. Here, too, certain positions were suggested of the line both his political and judicial course would take. Thus his mercantilist conservatism was suggested in 1804 by his concurrence in the veto message that "charters of incorporation . . . were not to be essentially affected without the consent of the parties concerned." Yet this view was tempered by what would be a persistent concern that debtors be protected from undue oppression, and this was first shown by his authorship of a veto message in 1806 which disapproved a proposed creditor's remedy on the grounds that it was "too dangerous and unguarded." In still another issue he split with Kent, who objected to a law attempting to inhibit duelling through special penalties on legislators who fought in such duels. Thompson supported the measure. His antipathy toward the Clinton family—a feeling which would be a powerful influence in his career—led to his unsuccessful opposition on the Council to DeWitt Clinton's 1817 plan for the Erie Canal.

One New Yorker, also a longtime anti-Clintonian "Bucktail" who shrewdly acceded on the question of the Erie Canal, was Martin Van Buren, and his contrasting position of accommodation next to Thompson's opposition was an appropriate symbol of their ironically star-crossed careers. Each man reached for the position the other succeeded in gaining. One was the ambitious, would-be politician, completely disabled by secretive attitudes and austere personality from ever playing the part; the other was the politician *par excellence*. They began the closest of friends, and their names were literally linked together, for Van Buren named his youngest son after Smith Thompson. They became enemies in a clash of ambition, but the interconnection of their careers lasted, literally, beyond Thompson's life.

Yet none of this was foreseen in the congenial association that linked the state's chief justice and the rising young politician from Kinderhook as early as 1816 when the latter was discussing the possibility of running Thompson as an at-large elector. The incident was doubly meaningful not only as an index of the Thompson–Van Buren alliance but also of the deep involvement of the New York Supreme Court in partisan maneuverings notwithstanding its judicial pre-eminence. There seems some question as to who was the dominant partner in the Thompson–Van Buren relationship. Van Buren, writing in the sunset of his life, insisted that he "had been wery instrumental in giving [Thompson] the political prominence he possessed." And Van Buren's judgment is substantiated by a modern historian who calls Thompson Van Buren's "lieutenant on the New York Supreme Court." (A. Steinberg, *The First Ten,* 350 [1967].)

Thus it would seem highly probable that Thompson owed his move from the New York bench to the national cabinet to Van Buren's influence. It should also be noted, however, that like so many of the critical events of Thompson's career, the circumstances of his appointment as Secretary of the Navy in 1818 are shrouded in obscurity. The primary factor was President Monroe's announced intention to keep a sectional balance in his Cabinet and, more specifically, the appointment of John Quincy Adams of Massachusetts as Secretary of State, which meant the eventual termination of the services of the holdover Secretary of the Navy Benjamin Crowninshield, also from that state. Following Crowninshield's resignation in 1818, the President announced his intention to fill the vacancy from the middle Atlantic states and from a slate which included a former governor of Pennsylvania and a general from New York, and Thompson, who was personally unknown to Monroe but believed by him to be a man "whose reputation stood very high, and who was represented as having kept entirely aloof from all the intrigues of the New York parties." Whatever the accuracy of the President's assessment, Thompson was nominated in November of 1818, assumed office January 1, 1819, and attended his first Cabinet meeting shortly thereafter.

He entered the national scene at a turbulent and exciting time. One controversy involved Missouri's disputed admission to the Union as a slave state. Another concerned Jackson's invasion of Spanish Florida. A third centered about American relationships with Spain's former colonies. Thompson cautiously reserved his position on the Missouri and Florida questions, although almost from the first he seems to have supported Secretary of State John Quincy Adams in the view of Latin American relations which later became explicated in the Monroe Doctrine. However, in a significant datum of his own future judicial attitudes, he differed somewhat sharply with Adams on the maritime slave trade. Here, in the interest of effective suppression of the traffic, he was willing to grant the Royal Navy a right of search of American ships provided discovered American offenders could be tried in federal courts under constitutional guarantees. Doubtless this attitude underlay his announced opposition to "executive interference" when the French slaver, *La Jeune Eugenie,* was impounded before the United States Circuit Court for Massachusetts, *United States* v. *The La Jeune Eugenie,* 26 Fed. Cas. 832 (No. 15,551) (C.C.D. Mass., 1822).

Compared to the responsibilities which devolved from Monroe's use of the Cabinet as a consultative council and the President's custom of calling on the secretaries for their opinions on all matters of national policy, Thompson's administrative duties seemed relatively light and mainly involved the award of midshipmen's warrants and the naming of ships. Far more to his taste were the political opportunities his position afforded, and here considerations of both national and New York politics manifested themselves. Thus it is suggested that he had a hand in unseating the incumbent Speaker of the House, a New York politician named John W. Taylor, when the Seventeenth Congress convened in late 1821. Patronage also received his attention as he worked with Van Buren on state positions in Dutchess County and proved himself an especial Tartar when the Monroe administration sought to appoint (successfully as things eventually turned out) a postmaster over his opposition.

There was another element in Thompson's political activity which gradually became apparent. This was his own aspiration to the presidency, a quest which was not unique with him but, on the contrary, occupied the attention of the entire Cabinet, each member concerned with his own ambitions. As early as spring of 1822 Thompson's efforts seemed to have produced at least the compliment of being noticed when one contemporary asserted that of New York possibilities ". . . [Rufus] King & Thompson & [Daniel] Tompkins are out of the question." (Letter from John Speed Smith to Henry Clay, April 30, 1822, 3 *The Papers of Henry Clay* 203 [1963].) Astonishingly, however, in a field which included Adams, Calhoun, Clay, and Jackson, the appraisals were not all negative. "In conversation today," another informant wrote Clay, "a Senator from New Jersey, somewhat to my surprize, [says] he is in favor of Mr. Smith Thompson as next President." (Letter from Francis Johnson to Henry Clay, December 10, 1822, 3 *Clay* 334.)

In 1823 two interrelated developments profoundly complicated not only Thompson's position in the already complex presidential race but his entire subsequent public career. In early February he solicited the support of his old ally now Senator, Martin Van Buren. Later that month Justice Brockholst Livingston of the United States Supreme Court and Thompson's onetime colleague on the New York bench suffered what was obviously a fatal illness. Almost immediately Thompson was spoken of as a possible successor, even though the Secretary had other laurels in view, and the resulting complications as well as the ultimate resolution were summed up by Daniel Webster in a letter to Justice Story:

> *You will naturally be anxious to know whether any thing is done here as yet in relation to the appointment of your associate upon the Bench. No appointment has been made. Mr. Thompson will be appointed if he chuses* [sic] *to take the office, but he has not made up his mind, as I understand, as yet to do so. If called on* now *to decide, it is said he will* decline. *I cannot account for his hesitation but on a supposition, which I have heard suggested but cannot credit, that he thinks it* possible *events may throw another & a higher office in his way.*
>
> *When a man finds himself in a situation he hardly ever dreamed of, he is apt to take it for granted that he is a favorite of fortune, & to presume that his blind patroness may have yet greater things in reserve for him. . . .*
>
> *On the whole my expectation is that the appointment will be delayed, & that, in the end, Mr. Thompson will take it.* [*Letter of April 6, 1823, in* 14 Mass. Hist. Soc. Proc. (2nd Ser.) 404 (*1901*).]

Possibly Webster's tone would have been even more critical had he suspected what seems to have been the case—that Thompson was using the judicial vacancy as a ploy to elicit Van Buren's support in the presidential race but all the while secretly holding a string on the Supreme Court seat as his own consolation prize in the event his presidential hopes miscarried. To be sure, Thompson's effort to outmaneuver the man variously named "The Red Fox" and "The Little Magician" indicate a psychological overreaching greater than his political one, as the unfolding of events abundantly proved.

Apparently Thompson hoped to use Van Buren's endorsement to pick up additional support in the closing session of the Seventeenth Congress, and, reportedly, was irked that "Van Buren keeps himself dark on this matter." Van Buren stayed silent on the presidency as congressional adjournment came and went and responded with unhelpful suggestions that Thompson set his sights either on the Supreme Court or the vice-presidency. Thompson responded that he was not interested in the Court, had abjured any ambition in this direction to the President, and was in fact busily engaged in advancing Van Buren's cause for the vacant seat. Yet it would have taken a far wilier person than Thompson to win this battle of maneuver, and in a significant exchange of letters Van Buren forced Thompson's hand. In April of 1823, Van Buren, writing in his inimitable style, forthrightly asked Thompson "whether your declension has been definite & whether Mr. Monroe so understands it." Almost shamefacedly, Thompson replied, "I am not certain that I told him absolutely." Rufus King described Thompson's behavior as "intentionally crooked," and Thompson virtually admitted the charge when he asked Van Buren whether he could "with propriety" now seek the judicial office for himself and received a reply absolving him of any obligation. Thompson accordingly abandoned his presidential ambitions in favor of a return to the bench.

Other candidates seemingly complicated the field, but these were essentially distracting irrelevancies. One was that of Nathaniel Macon of North Carolina, whose strong states' rights views sufficed to send Story and Marshall into an apprehensive exchange of correspondence. ("You alarm me respecting the successor of our much lamented friend. I too had heard a rumour which I hoped was impossible.") (Letter from Marshall to Story, July 2, 1823, in 14 *Mass. Hist. Soc. Proc.* [2nd Ser.] 333 [1901].) Another candidate was promoted by Attorney General William Wirt. This was James Kent, who had been swept off the bench by the New York constitutional convention of 1822. Ostensibly retired for reasons of age, Kent was in fact at the height of his powers, which were now employed in lectures at Columbia and in service as office counsel for New York practitioners.

Through this maze ran still another ambition which may have been dispositive of the judicial succession. This was the quest of John C. Calhoun for the Presidency, and the subsequent sequence of events could possibly be read as consistent with a charge made by one of Clay's correspondents—that President Monroe secretly supported Calhoun's ambitions by putting Thompson on the Supreme Court so as to open the way for the appointment to the Cabinet of Samuel Southard, senator from New Jersey and strong Calhoun supporter. Yet were this the plan, implementation was slow enough. By mid-summer of 1823, Thompson was obviously the presidential choice, but neither he nor Monroe showed any inclination toward speedy action, and the President announced that Thompson should remain in the Cabinet until a successor in the Navy Department had been decided upon. When this had been done with the selection of Senator Southard, Thompson's judicial career began anew. After a recess appointment in September, his name went to the Senate in December, 1823, and confirmation quickly followed. Yet even this did not wholly end the matter, for the Clay camp apparently considered Thompson a vice-presidential possibility as late as the following spring.

The delayed appointment was a source of credit to none of the parties involved. Unquestionably Thompson tried to use Van Buren in pretending to advance the latter's name instead of his own to the vacant seat. On the other hand, John Quincy Adams, observing the maneuvering from the State Department, viewed Van Buren as the dissembler who played a deep game in seeking, alternatively, the Supreme Court and the ministry to France by "distant and disguised grasping . . . both at that office and at a mission abroad."

Neither did Monroe do himself any particular good, immediate or historical, in the matter. If he did use the judicial appointment as a lever to bring a Calhoun supporter into the Cabinet—and this is at least an open question—the effort ironically miscarried, for Calhoun did not win the succession, and Monroe's one appointment to the Supreme Court passed over the candidate many believed the most eminently qualified man, James Kent. Conceivably Monroe could have been dissuaded by Kent's age alone and certainly could not have foreseen that Kent's vigor would continue unimpaired for so many years. More probably, and as a Monroe biographer, D. C. Gilman, has suggested, partisan considerations were decisive in passing over Kent's name, for the President could well have felt that Kent's strong federalism would more than offset any talents he could bring to the Supreme Court.

Perhaps Van Buren came off the best of all, and he has certainly left the most complete comment on the episode:

> *On referring to my correspondence with Secretary Thompson . . . I find that, previously, to the offer of his influence in obtaining the Judgeship (of the Supreme Court) for me, he had solicited in his strait forward way my support of himself for the Presidency, and had become not a little impatient of my silence. This circumstance, which, for the slight impression that it made on me, had altogether escaped from my memory, may throw some light upon the course and disposition of the judicial appointment after it was ascertained that my inclinations in regard to the Presidential Question were not in that direction. I cannot say that I have at this moment any decided opinion as to the source from whence the obstacles arose which prevented my appointment. The correspondence which accompanies this memoir will be found to possess interest from the light it throws upon the ways of men and of several distinguished individuals in particular. I have myself fancied on reading it now that I could discover traces and views of feelings on the part of others which from the unsuspicious character of my mind did not occur to me at the time."* [*M. Van Buren,* Autobiography (1920) 141n.]

In any event, Van Buren seemed the most charitable. Thus Henry Clay noted that Thompson went on the Supreme Court "in the place Chancellor Kent should have filled." Van Buren was a little more cordial in saying (prophetically, as things worked out) that Thompson moved up to an office "for which, by the way, he was as eminently qualified as he was unfit for political life."

The illness of his infant daughter delayed Thompson's taking his seat on the United States Supreme Court and also served to mask the significance of that event. He joined the Court February 10, 1824, and thereafter took no part in the adjudication of cases argued before that date. One of these was the old steamboat monopoly controversy, now presented under the style of *Gibbons* v. *Ogden,* 9 Wheat. 1 (1824). In a sense the adjudication of the case might be said to be the high water mark of the centralism of the Marshall Court, for not only did Marshall find the monopoly unconstitutional as conflicting with the federal coasting statutes—and thereby override New York judgments to the opposite effect—but the Court's previous exponent of concurrent powers, Justice William Johnson of South Carolina, contributed a concurring opinion of an even more centralist character. Yet any question as to whether Thompson's views in *Van Ingen* had undergone modification would seem set at rest by the way he characterized Jefferson's bitter protest over the Supreme Court's burgeoning jurisdiction —"every word [of Jefferson] contained a volume of meaning."

Yet far from shattering the institutional unity of the Marshall Court, Thompson's appearance rather seemed to reinforce it, particularly in view of his concurrence in *Osborn* v. *Bank of the United States,* 9 Wheat. 738 (1824), with its strong affirmation of federal legislative and judicial jurisdiction. Indeed, his first opinion, *Renner* v. *Bank of Columbia,* 9 Wheat. 581 (1824), was a learned disquisition on negotiable instruments and seemed to suggest only that, as in the case of Brockholst Livingston, the high federal tribunal was being fortified by the learning of the New York bench. (Coincidentally there, too, Thompson's first opinion in New York—where he was also late in taking his seat—also dealt with this subject, *Carpenter* v. *Butterfield,* 3 Johns. C. 145 [1802].) And perhaps nothing would be better calculated to continue the illusion of legal scholarship than Thompson's authorship at the following year's term of the Court's opinion in *Bank of the United States* v. *Halstead,* 10 Wheat. 51 (1825). For here in a companion piece to Marshall's product in *Wayman* v. *Southard,* 10 Wheat. 1 (1825), he construed the ambiguous federal process statutes (providing for execution on judgments secured in federal courts) as not incorporating debtor-relief provisions contained in a comprehensive program of Kentucky legislation which did not permit sale of property taken under executions for less than three-fourths of its appraised value.

However, with the advent of the 1827 term, a series of decisions underlined the significance of Thompson's appointment. He broke into dissent (with "some reluctance, and very considerable diffidence,") from the Chief Justice's opinion in *Brown* v. *Maryland,* 12 Wheat. 419 (1827), that a state could not tax merchandise carried in interstate commerce as long as the goods were in the original package. But he did far more than dissent. In *Ogden* v. *Saunders,* 12 Wheat. 213 (1827), it was his appointment that provided the margin of validation for a state insolvency statute which protected the property of insolvents from liability for debts contracted subsequent to its passage, and thereby overruled contrary implications in *Sturges* v. *Crowninshield,* 4 Wheat. 122 (1819), which declared unconstitutional state insolvency laws affecting debts entered into prior to the passage of the law. The *Ogden* case sent Chief Justice Marshall into dissenting position on a constitutional question for the first and only time, and in it Thompson's concurring opinion sharply attacked Marshall's canonization of the institution of contract. One countering argument was constitutional—that the bankruptcy powers of the federal government implied that abrogation of contracts could, under some circumstances, be desirable. A second was pragmatic and drew on his New York experience—"such [insolvency] laws are useful, if not absolutely necessary, in a commercial community." Hence his states' rights commitments combined with a lively humanity to frame a thesis of concurrent powers whereby the constitutional grant of bankruptcy powers could well be supplemented by parallel state legislation—"A bankrupt system deals with commercial men, but this affords no reason why a state should not exercise its sovereign power in relieving the necessities of men who do not fall within the class of traders, and who, from like misfortune, have become incapable of performing their contracts." In this he showed a strong sense of *stare decisis,* for he might well have applied these principles to both prospective and retroactive legislation had he been willing to reverse *Crowninshield* outright. For what he would do when he saw his way clear was shown at the same term when he wrote the majority opinion in *Mason* v. *Haile,* 12 Wheat. 370 (1827), and denied there existed any constitutional requirement for the continuation of imprisonment for debt—this remedy, he asserted, might be abolished by a state for both existing and future obligations. This remedy was not, he claimed, part of any contract whose obligation was being impaired. And it was during the 1837 term that he spoke for the Court in *Jackson ex dem. St. John* v. *Chew,* 12 Wheat. 153 (1827), where, implying that a different rule would obtain were "general" law involved and thereby foreshadowing *Swift* v. *Tyson,* 16 Pet. 1 (1842), he held that state decisions were "laws" which the federal courts must follow in adjudicating purely local controversies.

"Only once in forty years," wrote D. S. Alexander, "did Thompson's love for the judiciary give way to political preferment, and then Martin Van Buren defeated him for governor." While certainly true, the statement is highly misleading. Throughout his state judicial career and in the early part of his federal one, Thompson was deeply but covertly involved in political intrigue. In 1807 he was offered, and declined, the mayoralty of New York City (then an appointive office); and after the War of 1812 he seems to have been a persistent possibility for the governor's chair. His prospective candidacies fell short of universal appeal. ("All admitted the Chief Justice to be honest and sincere, but it was thought he did not understand the feeling of the party sufficiently, and might quarrel with it before his term of office expired." Van Buren, *Autobiography,* 94.) Nonetheless in 1820 he looked like a very strong candidate to oppose the Clinton forces, and Van Buren unsuccessfully attempted to undertake the role. Others shared the estimate of his ability to unite the anti-Clintonians of both parties into a victorious coalition, and one political figure, William Coleman, felt no doubt of his availability: ". . . *Thompson can be had,*" (Letter to Morris Miller, June 20, 1819, in Shaw Livermore, *The Twilight of Federalism* 137n. [1962]).

As events turned out, Thompson could not be had, but the suggestion of his running for governor was resurrected with the advent of the 1828 election. This time the moving spirit appeared to be the sometime Speaker of the House of Representatives, John W. Taylor, who called on President Adams, and after indicating that the New York gubernatorial contest would doubtless determine the selection of presidential electors in that state in the forthcoming 1828 election, proposed that Thompson head the state ticket of the "friends of the Administration." Significantly, the President not only thought Thompson "would be an excellent candidate . . . [and] prove an able Governor" but saw no necessity for him to resign from the Court inasmuch as "in event of failure he would still hold his present office. . . ."

Although he claimed it all happened contrary to his intention and against his will, Thompson accordingly found himself nominated by one of the fissioning groups claiming the standard of the old Democratic-Republican party in what many called the most exciting election in the history of the state. It was the first popular choice of presidential electors. Two tickets competed for the presidency and three for the governorship, the latter development being a consequence of a contemporary controversy over Masonry.

It was a bitter and complex campaign as Van Buren announced for Jackson and thus united gubernatorial and presidential efforts within a single political framework on one side with Thompson and John Quincy Adams appearing to be in a *de facto* alliance in the other. Unquestionably, the acerbity was increased by memories of the Supreme Court succession issue of 1823 and what one observer claimed was Thompson's "deep-rooted hatred for Mr. V[an] Buren and his immediate adherents . . ." (Letter of William B. Rochester to Henry Clay, May 29, 1824, in 3 Clay 768). Another inflaming element was Thompson's failure to resign from the Court, notwithstanding John Quincy Adams' seemingly matter-of-fact acceptance of the fact of a campaigning judge as well as the precedent of Chief Justice John Jay, who sought the New York governorship in 1795 from the Bench of the Supreme Court without any particular criticism. However, 1828 was not 1795, and Martin Van Buren appropriately perhaps summed up the result: ". . . I was elected by a plurality of more than 30,000 over my quondam friend, Smith Thompson" (Van Buren, *Autobiography,* 220).

While Thompson's candidacy opposed Van Buren on the state level and Andrew Jackson on the national one, the resulting anti-Jacksonian stance did not mean a juridical *rapprochement* with Marshall. On the contrary, his basic states' rights views were vigorously restated the following year. In *Weston* v. *City Council of Charleston,* 2 Pet. 449 (1829), he dissented (1. c. 473) from Marshall's opinion which outlawed a nondiscriminatory local tax on government securities. And one year later he once more dissented (1. c. 445) from a Marshall judgment which struck down an exercise of local power, this time the invalidation of certain state-issued loan certificates as constitutionally prohibited bills of credit, *Craig* v. *Missouri,* 4 Pet. 410 (1830).

Rather, it was singularly appropriate that what is probably Thompson's greatest judicial work found him holding a view opposed to that of both Marshall and Jackson. This came in *Cherokee Nation* v. *Georgia,* 5 Pet. 1 (1831), when the plaintiff sought to invoke the original jurisdiction of the Supreme Court against hostile state legislation (which had the full sympathy of the Jackson administration) on the grounds that they were a "foreign State" within the meaning of the Constitution. Marshall, speaking for the Supreme Court, held to the contrary, and Thompson, dissenting (1. c. 50), spoke for the Indians in "an opinion of immense power." Reproduced *infra,* it is a felicitous example of the humanitarian leavening which Thompson manifested in *Ogden* v. *Saunders* and *Mason* v. *Haile, supra,* even though it somewhat traverses his states' rights sentiments and possibly modified some of his earlier views. See *Jackson ex dem. Sparkman* v. *Porter,* 13 Fed. Cas. 235 (No. 7,143) (C.C.N.D. N.Y., 1825).

In fact, the sharp difference between Thompson's essentially states' rights–mercantilistic views to both Marshall's centralism and Jacksonian *laissez faire* was graphically shown at the great trilogy of opinions at the 1837 "turnabout" term which radically tempered previous Marshall doctrine constricting state commerce, monetary, and corporate authority. Here Thompson saw his views vindicated twice and overridden once as he contributed two concurrences and joined one dissent. He wrote a concurring opinion (1. c. 327) in *Briscoe* v. *The Bank of the Commonwealth of Kentucky,* 11 Pet. 257 (1837), which could be read as sanctioning a view of state currency authority which he had unsuccessfully sought in *Craig* v. *Missouri.* He wrote another (1. c. 143) in *City of New York* v. *Miln,* 11 Pet. 102 (1837), which upheld local registration of immigrants and thus sharply cut the thrusts of *Brown* v. *Maryland* from which Thompson had dissented and *Gibbons* v. *Ogden* from which he certainly would have dissented had he taken his seat on time. Not all was triumph, however. In a position predictable from his *Van Ingen* opinion, he associated himself with Story's dissent in *Charles River Bridge* v. *Warren Bridge,* 11 Pet. 420 (1837), which held that corporate charters held no constitutional protection against infringement of implied prerogatives.

Chancellor Kent had a comment on his old student's position on the *Briscoe* case. "It absolutely overwhelms me," he wrote Justice Story, who had dissented; ". . . I am astonished that Judge Thompson should have deserted you, *but he had married a wife and could not come to the rescue.*" It was true enough that at the 1837 term Thompson was attended by a young wife "whom he gallantly attended in the midst of the social life of the Capital." Nonetheless Kent's tasteless and churlish comment, which was typical of the irascibility he increasingly manifested during the Jacksonian ascendancy, suggested that President Monroe may have been well advised when he passed over the New York jurist for the Supreme Court. On the other hand, the comment seems to have mirrored a general view of Thompson's second marriage as "an aging folly." Yet the general judgment could perhaps have been a shade more charitable. His first wife died September 22, 1833, and six months later Charles Sumner noted that "Judge Thompson is . . . somewhat depressed from the loss of his wife." In November, 1836, he remarried. His second wife was Eliza Livingston, the first cousin of his first wife. Two sons and two daughters were born of his first marriage (one of his daughters married the son of Vice-President Daniel Tompkins) and one son and two daughters of his second.

The coincidence which the Age of Jackson thus provided for Thompson's second marriage and his revisionary work at the 1837 term were preludes, however, for Thompson's most significant single opinion and, next to his dissent in the *Cherokee* case, what is probably his best judicial writing. This came the following year at the 1838 term when he authored the majority opinion in *Kendall* v. *United States ex rel. Stokes,* 12 Pet. 524 (1838). This was a suit for payment from the post office which grew out of the party battles of the Jackson Cabinet and turned on the power of the Circuit Court of the District of Columbia to compel by *mandamus* an officer of the executive branch to perform a ministerial duty. An unusual aspect of the case lies in the difference between the opinion as read from the bench and as printed in the reports. The omission probably was a rejoinder to the proposition implied in Jackson's veto message of the rechartering of the second bank and allegedly argued by one of the counsel—that the entire executive establishment constituted a coordinate branch of the government immune from any judicial control and bound by the President's (rather than the Court's) construction of the statutes and the Constitution.

The following passage in Thompson's oral opinion responded to this point:

> *It was urged at the bar that the Postmaster-General was alone subject to the direction and control of the President with respect to the execution of the duties imposed upon him by this law; and the right of the President is claimed as growing out of the obligation imposed upon him by the Constitution to take care that the laws be faithfully executed. This is a doctrine that cannot receive the sanction of this Court. It would be vesting in the President a dispensing power which has no countenance for its support in any part of the Constitution, and is asserting a principle which, if carried out in its results to all cases falling within it, would be clothing the President with a power entirely to control the legislation of Congress and paralyze the administration of justice. [Quoted in 2 C. Warren,* The Supreme Court in United States History 46 (1937).]

The passage, however, does not appear in the reports as a consequence of a subsequent plea of the Attorney General that no such theory had been urged in argument and urged that the passage be omitted from the written report. While the recollection of several members of the Court was to the contrary, the plea was granted. Even with the excision the opinion came under fire, and, typical of the star-crossed relationship between the two, the now President Martin Van Buren vigorously attacked the judicial ambitions of his onetime associate. "[A] decision which has resulted," wrote the President in his annual message to Congress, "in the judgment of money out of the National Treasury, for the first time since the establishment of the Government, by judicial compulsion exercised by the common law writ of *mandamus* . . . a decision founded upon a process of reasoning which, in my judgment, renders further legislative provision indispensable. . . ." Yet also typical of the *impasse* which attended their relationship, the presidential recommendation—repeal of the power of the Circuit Court of the District of Columbia to issue the writ of *mandamus*—went unheeded by Congress.

Thompson's second marriage, in effect reaffirming his alliance with the

Livingstons, was also an appropriate symbol of the way the times and events were overtaking him. The ascendancy of the Livingston family had now passed and other forces now controlled New York politics. New forces also controlled national politics, and the rising crisis over the slavery question forced Thompson's continuing concern with respect to concurrent powers into new and perplexing channels. Two occurred at the 1841 term. *United States* v. *The Schooner Amistad,* 15 Pet. 518 (1841), concerned a group of Africans illegally imported into Cuba, who had revolted, seized a ship and then had been captured in turn by an American naval vessel. Thompson heard the issues at his Connecticut Circuit Court, decided that existing treaties imposed an obligation to return the fugitives and ordered them taken to Africa and freed. (He gave no opinion in the *Amistad* itself, but noted his views in a collateral proceeding.) The federal government appealed the case, the extra-judicial allegations for the appeal being variously stated as Thompson's personal anti-slavery views, the abolitionist temper of Connecticut, and President Van Buren's desire to straddle the slavery issue. On appeal Thompson's views were not only upheld but extended with the captives being freed forthwith instead of being sent to Africa.

At the same 1841 term Thompson wrote the majority opinion in *Groves* v. *Slaughter,* 15 Pet. 449 (1841), a suit for the purchase price of slaves brought into Mississippi in possible violation of a provision of the state's constitution. The root issue turned on the extent to which the commerce power of the federal government disabled state legislation prohibiting the importation of slaves. Thompson wrote the majority opinion of a bitterly divided Bench, holding that the state constitutional provision was inoperative without further legislation and thereby avoiding a constitutional question in the case. Yet the issue could not be avoided, and what could well stand as the closing opinion of his long judicial career was a statement of views which were essentially the same as those he had expounded in the *Van Ingen* case on the New York bench. The occasion was *Prigg* v. *Pennsylvania,* 16 Pet. 539 (1842), which upheld the federal fugitive slave law and struck down all state legislation, friendly or hostile, which bore on the subject. Chief Justice Taney concurred in the result—quashing a Pennsylvania indictment for kidnapping—but dissented on the question of federal preemption. Thompson concurred in the concurrence "principally to guard against the conclusion, that, by my silence, I assent to the doctrine that all legislation on this subject is vested exclusively in Congress; and that all State legislation, in the absence of any law of Congress, is unconstitutional and void."

Thus forty years after his first judicial appointment and on the thirtieth anniversary of *Van Ingen,* Thompson expounded his consistent view of concurrent powers as the *finis* to his career. True enough, he had part of a term left, but a cryptic note of the reporter tells its fragmentary character: ". . . Mr. Justice Thompson being compelled to leave Washington on the 6th of February, did not hear any arguments after that day." Probably his departure was for reasons of health. He fell seriously ill toward the end of the year and died at his home, "Rust Plaetz" (Resting Place), December 18, 1843, and, continuing into death the associations which characterized his life, was interred in the nearby Livingston burying grounds.

The recurrence of prior patterns unfolded further yet, as the vacant Supreme Court seat once more became a ploy in a presidential election. The Whigs, scenting victory in 1844, heard of his illness with dismay. "If we could keep him alive for a couple of winters, even if unable to sign his name, we would hold fasts and prayers for it," wrote one. Justice Story returned to the apprehensive lamentations which he had expressed just prior to Thompson's appointment. ("What the President will do, we cannot determine. I have my own wishes on the subject, strong and warm, but I have no hope that they will be gratified. I want an associate of the *highest* integrity. . . ." Letter to James Kent, March 2, 1844, in 2 Story, *Life and Letters of Joseph Story,* 480.) Almost unbelievably, President Tyler considered the appointment of his most likely opponent in the election of 1844—Martin Van Buren. The tender was never made; the President was advised that if he wished to give the country the heartiest laugh it had ever had, he should make the nomination. Nonplussed, the President named John C. Spencer, a New York Whig, who was then rejected by the Senate. It was then offered to Silas Wright twice as well as to Horace Binney and John Sergeant of Philadelphia. All declined. Tyler then nominated Chancellor Walworth of New York, withdrew the nomination, and finally named another Chief Justice from the New York Supreme Court, Samuel Nelson. An eminently respected jurist, Nelson was confirmed by the Senate and took his seat March 5, 1844.

While on the Supreme Court, Thompson wrote its opinion in eighty-five cases, and in addition delivered five concurring opinions and eleven dissents. Relatively few are of constitutional importance. Given his long judicial background, it is not surprising that a significant number of his opinions deal with pleading, practice, and procedure. Again, given the commercial docket of his New York bench, it is to be expected that another group of opinions would deal with negotiable instruments and an example of his influence in this field might be found in *Renner* v. *Bank of Columbia, supra,* where he prevailed over Story in asserting that days of grace were to be determined by local usage rather than a uniform and general law. And still a third group of cases clusters around his cabinet service, e.g., his dissent in *United States* v. *Arredondo,* 6 Pet. 691, 749 (1832).

Surprisingly, however, he also wrote a number of opinions in equity, a jurisdiction which in New York was not held by his old court, but instead was committed to that of the chancellor. A significant if not typical Thompson equity opinion came in *Inglis* v. *Sailor's Snug Harbor,* 3 Pet. 99 (1830), an immensely complicated proceeding involving both expatriation and the statute of uses. Here, possibly because he had dealt with the matter on the New York Council of Revision, he carried the court with him over the opposition of Story.

Individually noteworthy opinions, in addition to those previously mentioned, would include his dissents in *Wheaton* v. *Peters,* 8 Pet. 591, 668 (1834) and *Beers* v. *Haughton,* 9 Pet. 329, 363 (1835). Both suggest that his basic states' rights concepts derived from a *laissez faire* federalism. Thus, in *Wheaton,* he expounded as to copyrights a point he had implied in *Van Ingen* as to patents—that the existence of a positive protective authority in the federal government did not automatically deprive the states of their residual common law powers to uphold the rights of their citizens in intellectual property. Again in *Beers* he unsuccessfully protested a circuit court's adoption, under its rule-making power, of a state statute abolishing imprisonment for debt and thereby logically complemented his earlier position in *Bank of the United States* v. *Halstead, supra.* Of historical interest and also illustrating his common law—or more precisely, English law—framework of reference was his *Arredondo* dissent, *supra,* and his opinions dealing with federal equity jurisdiction in civil law Louisiana, *Livingston* v. *Story,* 9 Pet. 632 (1835) and *Gaines* v. *Relf,* 15 Pet. 9 (1841).

While persistently concerned with tempering oppressive elements in the law, Thompson was something less than an ardent reformer. Primarily, his instinctive caution found its judicial outlet in a strong veneration of *stare decisis,* or to use his own words "the boundaries prescribed by the adjudged cases," *Lewis* v. *Few,* 5 Johns. R. 1 (1809). Yet it is difficult to frame him in a categorical reference. Thus as his judicial relationship with Kent creates an elusive pattern of accord and disagreement, so the libertarian side of his jurisprudence traces out a complicated pattern. Typical would be variant attitudes implicit in the *Cherokee* litigation and the slavery cases which came before him. There were differences, and this notwithstanding Beveridge's assertion that Thompson held "bitter" anti-slavery views and a modern historian who found his enforcement of the anti-slave trade statutes the work of a "vigorous proponent of practical law."

To be sure, one of his first opinions on the Supreme Court, *The Emily and the Caroline,* 9 Wheat. 381 (1824), would justify the latter conclusion but its logic is equally consistent with the common sense statutory construction on which Thompson prided himself. Otherwise it is difficult to piece out personal attitudes—besides an occasional concern for property and states' rights—in the other cases in which he considered the institutional by-products of slavery, e.g., *In re Martin,* 16 Fed. Cas. 881 (No. 9, 154) (C.C. S.D. N.Y. 1835), and *Lee* v. *Lee,* 8 Pet. 44 (1834). And while serving as Secretary of the Navy, it is not without significance that when he finally took a position on the Missouri question, he was the only non-Southerner in the cabinet to hold the view that Congress could not bar slavery in the future as a condition of a new state's admission to the Union.

The same somewhat enigmatic character overshadows Thompson generally. It is difficult to tell whether he was a real man of stature whose devious traits arrested his full potential or whether Webster was right in implying he was but a lucky mediocrity. Notwithstanding his historic significance, there are relatively few references in informal contemporary records, and most are slighting comments by his enemies. There are a few offsets, however, such as Marshall's mentioning his help in caring for the aged and infirm Justice Duvall. On balance, however, he was a man whose passing seemed to be scarcely noticed or mourned save by some Whig politicians concerned with a high-level judicial appointment. Thus, John Quincy Adams entered the fact of Thompson's death in his diary without further comment, and the only authentic passage in the few newspaper obituaries were references to "surmises about City Hall" as to his successor. Certainly, the notices of his death compared poorly to those given the contemporary passing of Attorney General Legare.

What notice was taken, however, did emphasize two points. One was his modesty and plainness in deportment. The other was his participation in the New York decisions which helped lay "deep and broad, the foundations of American jurisprudence." Thompson had other distinctions. As a onetime schoolteacher he was doubtless pleased with his honorary doctorates in law which Yale (1824), Princeton (1824), and Harvard (1835) awarded him as well as by his appointment (1813) to the state Board of Regents. A lifelong Presbyterian, he was a longtime member of the American Bible Society, took particular pleasure as Secretary of the Navy in furthering its work in the fleet, and at the time of his death was its oldest vice-president.

Principally, however, Justice Thompson's historic credentials rest on the role he both foreshadowed and played in tempering the centralizing federalism of the Marshall Court. Often more a matter of limiting rather than contradicting, Thompson's views were both supplement and reaction which brought a complex of germinal constitutional doctrines to a new level of development. For in their own way, Thompson's careful, historically articulated, fact-oriented opinions form a logical complement to the more categorical logic of Marshall and Story in undertaking "those delicate and difficult inquiries of conflicting powers between the general and state governments," *Weston* v. *City Council of Charleston,* 2 Pet. 449, 474 (1829) (dissenting), which constitute the heart of constitutional freedom.

SELECTED BIBLIOGRAPHY

Well-written, generally sympathetic, and systematic, Donald M. Roper's unpublished doctoral dissertation, *Mr. Justice Thompson and the Constitution* (Indiana University, 1963) is by far the best work on Thompson. A sketch of Thompson's life appears in 25 *Dutchess County Historical Society Yearbook* 26 (1940). In addition, Roper's article, "Justice Smith Thompson," 51 *The New York Historical Society Quarterly* 119 (1967), may be consulted. It is impossible to write New York political history without mentioning Thompson. See, e.g., J. Hammond, *The History of Political Parties in the State of New York* (Albany, 1842). J. Q. Adams, *Memoirs* C. F. Adams ed. (Philadelphia, 1874–1877) contains a running picture of Thompson's cabinet service. Unfortunately for Thompson, only his political enemies seem to have written about his aspirations to the presidency and the Supreme Court, and the works cited *supra* are characteristic.

Thompson's Supreme Court service is touched on, again sketchily and unsystematically, in A. Beveridge, *Life of John Marshall* (Boston and New York, 1919); and C. Swisher, *Roger B. Taney* (New York, 1935). His New York opinions are in *Coleman's Cases, Coleman's & Caines' Cases,* and the first seventeen volumes of *Johnson's Supreme Court Reports*. For his federal service, his circuit court opinions are in Paine's *Circuit Court Reports,* keyed at page 2460 of the *Federal Cases* series in its thirtieth (appendix) volume and his Supreme Court opinions are contained in 9 Wheaton to 16 Peters inclusive.

Smith Thompson

REPRESENTATIVE OPINIONS

THE CHEROKEE NATION v. THE STATE OF GEORGIA, 5 PET. 1 (1831)

While it is almost commonplace to suggest that opinions of the Supreme Court are the products of a particular historic context, lesser recognition is given to the fact that the estimate which posterity affords them is similarly conditioned. Thus, at various times in the past suggestions as to Thompson's most memorable Supreme Court opinion could well have included his views in *Ogden* v. *Saunders,* 12 Wheat. 213, 292 (1827) (on the validity of state insolvency laws) and *Kendall* v. *United States ex. rel. Stokes,* 12 Pet. 524 (1838) (holding that the federal courts might compel by *mandamus* the performance of purely ministerial duties enjoined by law upon members of the executive establishment). Yet, distinct from what the estimates of earlier periods might have been, the heightening sense of the nation's social conscience around the last third of the twentieth century would award the palm to Thompson's dissent in *Cherokee Nation* v. *Georgia,* 5 Pet. 1, 50 (1831).

In its narrowest compass, the case turned on a technical point of jurisdiction. In its largest sense, however, it epitomized the entire Indian tragedy. At issue was the question of whether the Cherokees were a foreign nation within the meaning of Article III of the Constitution so as to give the Supreme Court jurisdiction of their plea for protection against the repressive state legislation. This in turn involved, on one hand, the ancient doctrines of international law, the generalities of the constitutional text, and the contradictions of federal policy and, on the other, the scope of the judicial authority, the boundaries of presidential power, and the general equilibrium between state and national sovereignty.

The case itself grew out of conflicting commitments the federal government had made to the Cherokees and to the state of Georgia. In repeated treaties the Indians were not only confirmed in their lands, but accorded many of the characteristics of national sovereignty, including certain recognition of their laws and provision for the equivalent of passports for Americans crossing their hunting grounds. Yet Georgia had also been given commitments. In return for cession of Western claims, the federal government had solemnly promised to acquire the Cherokee lands within the state and remove the Indians from it.

The conflict epitomized the more general ambiguity concerning the status of the Indians, who in some senses held the aspects of sovereignty and in others were regarded as both alien but subordinate bodies occupying the territory of states, themselves quasi-sovereign. In the 42nd Federalist Paper Madison called this juridical status "a question of frequent perplexity and contention," and it came into sharp focus with the confrontation of the Cherokee nation and the state of Georgia in the late 1820's. The Cherokees, not only still unremoved but, despite Georgia pressure, rapidly adjusting to European culture, adopted a formal constitution patterned on the federal model, a code of laws, and asserted a formal sovereignty over their tribal lands. The state responded with a collection of repressive statutes which extended its own governmental framework to the Cherokee lands and forbade the functioning of the new Cherokee government and also of their federally guaranteed treaty rights. Complicating (or, really, resolving) this tangle was the election in 1828 of Andrew Jackson, who differed from his predecessors in office by being a long-time advocate of removing the Indians to the land west of the Mississippi.

The latter circumstance was decisive, for it meant that the Cherokee-Georgia controversy, in which the Indians' federal guarantees were their only hope, took place under conditions where the President was avowedly hostile to the Indian claims, where the Congress followed close behind the executive branch with enactment of an Indian Removal Act, and where only the Supreme Court seemed available as a recourse. Accordingly, the Cherokees sought its protective jurisdiction in a threefold pattern of litigation. The first, a petition for a stay of execution of a Cherokee tried for murder under the newly extended Georgia jurisdiction, was rendered moot when the defendant was executed in the face of restraining process from the Supreme Court. The second, a sweeping plea for injunctive relief from the Georgia legislation, was denied on jurisdictional grounds. The third, an appeal by a missionary imprisoned under that legislation, came to nought when the executive branch declined to enforce the Supreme Court's mandate of reversal.

The second case involved four opinions. Chief Justice Marshall, for the Court, denied the Cherokees were a foreign nation and, hence, dismissed the case for want of power to hear the case as a matter of original jurisdiction. Justices Baldwin and Johnson concurred in this judgment of dismissal in separate opinions. Thompson, Story concurring, held for the Indians and dissented. Reprinted in full, Thompson's dissent follows a brief extract from the majority opinion which somberly states the historic and constitutional context of the case:

Mr. Chief Justice Marshall delivered the opinion of the court:

This bill is brought by the Cherokee Nation, praying an injunction to restrain the State of Georgia from the execution of certain laws of that State, which as it is alleged, go directly to annihilate the Cherokees as a political society, and to seize, for the use of Georgia, the lands of the nation which have been assured to them by the United States in solemn treaties repeatedly made and still in force.

If the courts were permitted to indulge their sympathies, a case better calculated to excite them can scarcely be imagined. A people once numerous, powerful, and truly independent, found by our ancestors in the quiet and uncontrolled possession of an ample domain, gradually sinking beneath our superior policy, our arts and our arms, have yielded their lands by successive treaties, each of which contains a solemn guarantee of the residue, until they retain no more of their formerly extensive territory than is deemed necessary to their comfortable subsistence. To preserve this remnant the present application is made.

Before we can look into the merits of the case, a preliminary inquiry presents itself. Has this court jurisdiction of the cause?

* * * *

The court has bestowed its best attention on this question, and, after mature deliberation, the majority is of opinion that an Indian tribe or nation within the United States is not a foreign state in the sense of the Constitution, and cannot maintain an action in the courts of the United States.

* * * *

Mr. Justice Thompson, dissenting: Entertaining different views of the questions now before us in this case, and having arrived at a conclusion different from that of a majority of the court, and considering the importance of the case and the constitutional principle involved in it, I shall proceed, with all due respect for the opinion of others, to assign the reasons upon which my own has been formed.

In the opinion pronounced by the court, the merits of the controversy between the State of Georgia and the Cherokee Indians have not been taken into consideration. The denial of the application for an injunction has been placed solely on the ground of want of jurisdiction in this court to grant the relief prayed for. It became, therefore, unnecessary to inquire into the merits of the case. But thinking as I do that the court has jurisdiction of the case, and may grant relief, at least in part, it may become necessary for me, in the course of my opinion, to glance at the merits of the controversy; which I shall, however, do very briefly, as it is important so far as relates to the present application.

Before entering upon the examination of the particular points which have been made and argued, and for the purpose of guarding against any erroneous conclusions, it is proper that I should state that I do not claim for this court the exercise of jurisdiction upon any matter properly falling under the denomination of political power. Relief to the full extent prayed by the bill may be beyond the reach of this court. Much of the matter therein contained by way of complaint would seem to depend for relief upon the exercise of political power; and as such appropriately devolving upon the executive, and not the judicial department of the government. This court can grant relief so far only as the rights of person or property are drawn in question, and have been infringed.

It would very ill become the judicial station which I hold to indulge in any remarks upon the hardship of the case, or the great injustice that would seem to have been done to the complainants, according to the statement in the bill, and which, for the purpose of the present motion, I must assume to be true. If they are entitled to other than judicial relief, it cannot be admitted that in a government like ours, redress is not to be had in some of its departments; and the responsibility for its denial must rest upon those who have the power to grant it. But believing as I do that relief to some extent falls properly under judicial cognizance, I shall proceed to the examination of the case under the following heads:

1. Is the Cherokee Nation of Indians a competent party to sue in this court?

2. Is a sufficient case made out in the bill to warrant this court in granting any relief?

3. Is an injunction the fit and appropriate relief?

1. By the Constitution of the United States it is declared (Art. 3, sec. 2) that the judicial power shall extend to all cases in law and equity arising under this Constitution, the laws of the United States, and treaties made or which shall be made under their authority, etc., to controversies between two or more States, etc., and between

a State or the citizens thereof; and foreign states, citizens or subjects.

The controversy in the present case is alleged to be between a foreign state and one of the States of the Union, and does not, therefore, come within the eleventh amendment of the Constitution, which declares that the judicial power of the United States shall not be construed to extend to any suit in law or equity commenced or prosecuted against one of the United States by citizens of another State, or by citizens or subjects of any foreign state. This amendment does not, therefore, extend to suits prosecuted against one of the United States by a foreign state. The Constitution further provides that in all cases where a State shall be a party, the Supreme Court shall have original jurisdiction. Under these provisions in the Constitution, the complainants have filed their bill in this court in the character of a foreign state, against the State of Georgia; praying an injunction to restrain that State from committing various alleged violations of the property of the nation, claimed under the laws of the United States, and treaties made with the Cherokee Nation.

That a State of this Union may be sued by a foreign state when a proper case exists and is presented, is too plainly and expressly declared in the Constitution to admit of doubt; and the first inquiry is, whether the Cherokee Nation is a foreign state within the sense and meaning of the Constitution.

The terms "state" and "nation" are used in the law of nations, as well as in common parlance, as importing the same thing; and imply a body of men united together to procure their mutual safety and advantage by means of their union. Such a society has its affairs and interests to manage; it deliberates, and takes resolutions in common, and thus becomes a moral person, having an understanding and a will peculiar to itself, and is susceptible of obligations and laws. Vattel, 1. Nations being composed of men naturally free and independent, and who before the establishment of civil societies, live together in the state of nature, nations or sovereign states, are to be considered as so many free persons living together in a state of nature. Vattel 2, sec. 4. Every nation that governs itself, under what form soever, without any dependence on a foreign power, is a sovereign State. Its rights are naturally the same as those of any other State. Such are moral persons who live together in a natural society, under the law of nations. It is sufficient if it be really sovereign and independent; that is, it must govern itself by its own authority and laws. We ought, therefore, to reckon in the number of sovereigns those States that have bound themselves to another more powerful, although by an unequal alliance. The condition of these unequal alliances may be infinitely varied; but whatever they are, provided the inferior ally reserves to itself the sovereignty or the right to govern its own body, it ought to be considered an independent State. Consequently, a weak State, that, in order to provide for its safety, places itself under the protection of a more powerful one without stripping itself of the right of government and sovereignty, does not cease on this account to be placed among the sovereigns who acknowledge no other power. Tributary and feudatory States do not thereby cease to be sovereign and independent States so long as self-government and sovereign and independent authority is left in the administration of the State. Vattel, c. 1, pp. 16, 17.

Testing the character and condition of the Cherokee Indians by these rules, it is not perceived how it is possible to escape the conclusion that they form a sovereign State. They have always been dealt with as such by the government of the United States, both before and since the adoption of the present Constitution. They have been admitted and treated as a people governed solely and exclusively by their own laws, usages and customs within their own territory, claiming and exercising exclusive dominion over the same; yielding up by treaty, from time to time, portions of their land, but still claiming absolute sovereignty and self-government over what remained unsold. And this has been the light in which they have, until recently, been considered from the earliest settlement of the country by the white people. And, indeed, I do not understand it is denied by a majority of the court that the Chereokee Indians form a sovereign State according to the doctrine of the law of nations; but that, although a sovereign State, they are not considered a foreign state within the meaning of the Constitution.

Whether the Cherokee Indians are to be considered a foreign state or not, is a point on which we cannot expect to discover much light from the law of nations. We must derive this knowledge chiefly from the practice of our own government, and the light in which the nation has been viewed and treated by it.

That numerous tribes of Indians, and among others the Cherokee Nation, occupied many parts of this country long before the discovery by Europeans, is abundantly established by history; and it is not denied but that the Cherokee Nation occupied the territory now claimed by them long before that period. It does not fall within the scope and object of the present inquiry to go into a critical examination of the nature and extent of the rights growing out of such occupancy, or the justice and humanity with which the Indians have been treated or their rights respected.

That they are entitled to such occupancy, so long as they choose quietly and peaceably to remain upon the land, cannot be questioned. The circumstance of their original occupancy is here referred to merely for the purpose of showing that if these Indian communities were then, as they certainly were, nations, they must have been foreign nations to all the world; not having any connection, or alliance of any description, with any power on earth. And if the Cherokees were then a foreign nation, when or how have they lost that character, and ceased to be a distinct people, and become incorporated with any other community?

They have never been, by conquest, reduced to the situation of subjects to any conqueror, and thereby lost their separate national existence and the rights of self-government, and become subject to the laws of the conqueror. Whenever wars have taken place, they have been followed by regular treaties of peace, containing stipulations on each side according to existing circumstances; the Indian nation always preserving its distinct and separate national character. And notwithstanding we do not recognize the right of the Indians to transfer the absolute title of their lands to any other than ourselves; the right of occupancy is still admitted to remain in them, accompanied with the right of self-government, according to their own usages and customs; and with the competency to act in a national capacity, although placed under the protection of the whites, and owing a qualified subjection so far as is requisite for public safety. But the principle is universally admitted that this occupancy belongs to them as a matter of right, and not by mere indulgence. They cannot be disturbed in the enjoyment of it, or deprived of it, without their free consent; or unless a just and necessary war should sanction their dispossession.

In this view of their situation, there is as full and complete recognition of their sovereignty, as if they were the absolute owners of the soil. The progress made in civilization by the Cherokee Indians cannot surely be considered as in any measure destroying their national or foreign character, so long as they are permitted to maintain a separate and distinct government; it is their political condition that constitutes their foreign character, and in that sense must the term "foreign" be understood as used in the Constitution. It can have no relation to local, geographical, or territorial position. It cannot mean a country beyond sea. Mexico or Canada is certainly to be considered a foreign country in reference to the United States. It is the political relation in which one government or country stands to another, which constitutes it foreign to the other. The Cherokee territory, being within the chartered limits of Georgia, does not affect the question. When Georgia is spoken of as a State, reference is had to its political character, and not to boundary; and it is not perceived that any absurdity or inconsistency grows out of the circumstance that the jurisdiction and territory of the State of Georgia surround or extend on every side of the Cherokee territory. It may be inconvenient to the State, and very desirable that the Cherokees should be removed; but it does not at all affect the political relation between Georgia and those Indians. Suppose the Cherokee territory had been occupied by Spaniards or any other civilized people, instead of Indians, and they had from time to time ceded to the United States portions of their lands precisely in the same manner as the Indians have done, and in like manner retained and occupied the part now held by the Cherokees, and having a regular government established there: would it not only be considered a separate and distinct nation or State, but a foreign nation, with reference to the State of Georgia or the United States? If we look to lexicographers, as well as approved writers, for the use of the term "foreign," it may be applied with the strictest propriety to the Cherokee Nation.

In a general sense it is applied to any person or thing belonging to another nation or country. We call an alien a foreigner, because he is not of the country in which we reside. In a political sense we call every country foreign which is not within the jurisdiction of the same government. In this sense, Scotland before the union was foreign to England, and Canada and Mexico foreign to the United States. In the United States all transatlantic countries are foreign to us. But this is not the only sense in which it is used.

It is applied with equal propriety to an adjacent territory, as to one more remote. Canada or Mexico is as much foreign to us as England or Spain. And it may be laid down as a general rule that when used in relation to countries in a political sense, it refers to the jurisdiction or government of the country. In a commercial sense, we call all goods coming from any country not within our own jurisdiction foreign goods.

In the diplomatic use of the term, we call every minister a foreign minister who comes from another jurisdiction or government. And this is the sense in which it is judicially used by this court, even as between the different States of this Union. In the case of *Buckner* v. *Finley,* 2 Peters, 590, it was held that a bill of exchange drawn in one State of the Union on a person living in another State, was a foreign bill, and to be treated as such in the courts of the United States. The court says, that in applying the definition of a foreign bill to the political character of the several States of this Union in relation to each other, we are all clearly of opinion that bills drawn in one of these States upon persons living in another of them, partake of the character of foreign bills, and ought to be so treated. That for all national purposes embraced by the federal Constitution the States and the citizens thereof are one; united under the same sovereign authority, and governed by the same laws. In all other respects, the States are necessarily foreign to, and independent of each other; their constitutions and forms of government being, although republican, altogether different, as are their laws and institutions. So in the case of *Warder* v. *Arrell,* decided in the Court of Appeals of Virginia, 2 Wash. 298. The court in speaking of foreign contracts, and saying that the laws of the foreign country where the contract was made must govern, add: The same principle applies, though with no greater force, to the different States of America; for though they form a confederated government, yet the several States retain their individual sovereignties; and, with respect to their municipal regulations, are to each other foreign.

It is manifest from these cases that a foreign State, judicially considered, consists in its being under a different jurisdiction or government, without any reference to its territorial position. This is the marked distinction, particularly in the case of *Buckner* v. *Finley*. So far as these States are subject to the laws of the Union they are not foreign to each other. But so far as they are subject to their own respective State laws and government, they are foreign to each other. And if, as here decided, a separate and distinct jurisdiction or government is the test by which to decide whether a nation be foreign or not, I am unable to perceive any sound and substantial reason why the Cherokee Nation should not be so considered. It is governed by its own laws, usages and customs; it has no connection with any other government or jurisdiction, except by way of treaties entered into with like form and ceremony as with other foreign nations. And this seems to be the view taken of them by Mr. Justice Johnson in the case of *Fletcher* v. *Peck,* 6 Cranch 146; 2 Peters's Cond. Rep. 308.

In speaking of the state and condition of the different Indian nations, he observes, "that some have totally extinguished their national fire, and submitted themselves to the laws of the States; others have by treaty acknowledged that they hold their national existence at the will of the State within which they reside; others retain a limited sovereignty, and the absolute proprietorship of their soil. The latter is the case of the tribes to the west of Georgia, among which are the Cherokees. We legislate upon the conduct of strangers or citizens within their limits, but innumerable treaties formed with them acknowledge them to be an independent people; and the uniform practice of acknowledging their right of soil by purchasing from them, and restraining all persons from encroaching upon their territory, makes it unnecessary to insist upon their rights of soil."

Although there are many cases in which one of these United States has been sued by another, I am not aware of any instance in which one of the United States has been sued by a foreign state. But no doubt can be entertained that such an action might be sustained upon a proper case being presented. It is expressly provided for in the Constitution, and this provision is certainly not to be rejected as entirely nugatory.

Suppose a State, with the consent of Congress, should enter into an agreement with a foreign power (as might undoubtedly be done, Constitution, Art. 1, Sec. 10) for a loan of money; would not an action be sustained in this court to enforce payment thereof? Or suppose the State of Georgia, with the consent of Congress, should purchase the right of the Cherokee Indians to this territory, and enter into a contract for the payment of the purchase money; could there be a doubt that an action could be sustained upon such a contract? No objection would certainly be made for want of competency in that nation to make a valid contract. The numerous treaties entered into with the nation would be a conclusive answer to any such objection. And if an action could be sustained in such case, it must be under that provision in the Constitution which gives jurisdiction to this court in controversies between a State and a foreign state. For the Cherokee Nation is certainly not one of the United States.

And what possible objection can lie to the right of the complainants to sustain an action? The treaties made with this nation purport to secure to it certain rights. These are not gratuitous obligations assumed on the part of the United States. They are obligations founded upon a consideration paid by the Indians by cession of part of their territory. And if they, as a nation, are competent to make a treaty or contract, it would seem to me to be a strange inconsistency to deny to them the right and power to enforce such a contract. And where the right secured by such treaty forms a proper subject for judicial cognizance, I can perceive no reason why this court has not jurisdiction of the case. The Constitution expressly gives to the court jurisdiction in all cases of law and equity arising under treaties made with the United States. No suit will lie against the United States upon such treaty, because no possible case can exist where the United States can be sued. But not so with respect to a State; and if any right secured by treaty has been violated by a State, in a case proper for judicial inquiry, no good reason is perceived why an action may not be sustained for violation of a right secured by treaty, as well as by contract under any other form. The judiciary is certainly not the department of the government authorized to enforce all rights that may be recognized and secured by treaty. In many instances these are mere political rights with which the judiciary cannot deal. But when the question relates to a mere right of property, and a proper case can be made between competent parties, it forms a proper subject for judicial inquiry.

It is a rule which has been repeatedly sanctioned by this court, that the judicial department is to consider as sovereign and independent States or nations those powers that are recognized as such by the executive and legislative departments of the government, they being more particularly intrusted with our foreign relations. 4 Cranch 214; 2 Peters's Cond. Rep. 98; 3 Wheat. 634; 4 Wheat. 64.

If we look to the whole course of treatment by this country of the Indians from the year 1775 to the present day, when dealing with them in their aggregate capacity as nations or tribes, and regarding the mode or manner in which all negotiations have been carried on and concluded with them, the conclusion appears to me irresistible that they have been regarded by the executive and legislative branches of the government not only as sovereign and independent, but as foreign nations or tribes, not within the jurisdiction nor under the government of the States within which they were located. This remark is to be understood, of course, as referring only as such as live together as a distinct community, under their own laws, usages and customs; and not to the mere remnant of tribes which are to be found in many parts of our country, who have become mixed with the general population of the country; their national character extinguished, and their usages and customs in a great measure abandoned; self-government surrendered; and who have voluntarily, or by the force of circumstances which surrounded them, gradually become subject to the laws of the States within which they are situated.

Such, however, is not the case with the Cherokee Nation. It retains its usages and customs and self-government, greatly improved by the civilization which it has been the policy of the United States to encourage and foster among them. All negotiations carried on with the Cherokees and other Indian nations have been by way of treaty, with all the formality attending the making of treaties with any foreign power. The journals of Congress, from the year 1775 down to the adoption of the present Constitution, abundantly establish this fact. And since that period such negotiations have been carried on by the treaty-making power, and uniformly under the denomination of treaties.

What is a treaty as understood in the law of nations? It is an agreement or contract between two or more nations or sovereigns, entered into by agents appointed for that purpose, and duly sanctioned by the supreme power of the respective parties. And where is the authority, either in the

Constitution or in the practice of the government, for making any distinction between treaties made with the Indian nations and any other foreign power? They relate to peace and war; the surrender of prisoners; the cession of territory; and the various subjects which are usually embraced in such contracts between sovereign nations.

A recurrence to the various treaties made with the Indian nations and tribes in different parts of the country will fully illustrate this view of the relation in which our government has considered the Indians as standing. It will be sufficient, however, to notice a few of the many treaties made with this Cherokee Nation.

By the Treaty of Hopewell of the 28th November, 1785 (1 Laws U. S. 322), mutual stipulations are entered into to restore all prisoners taken by either party, and the Cherokees stipulate to restore all negroes and all other property taken from the citizens of the United States; and a boundary line is settled between the Cherokees and the citizens of the United States, and this embraced territory within the chartered limits of Georgia. And by the sixth article it is provided that if any Indian or person residing among them, or who shall take refuge in their nation, shall commit a robbery, or murder, or other capital crime on any citizen of the United States or person under their protection, the nation or tribe to which such offender may belong shall deliver him up to be punished according to the ordinances of the United States. What more explicit recognition of the sovereignty and independence of this nation could have been made? It was a direct acknowledgment that this territory was under a foreign jurisdiction. If it had been understood that the jurisdiction of the State of Georgia extended over this territory, no such stipulation would have been necessary. The process of the courts of Georgia would have run into this as well as into any other part of the State. It is a stipulation analogous to that contained in the Treaty of 1794 with England (1 Laws U. S. 220), by the twenty-seventh article of which it is mutually agreed that each party will deliver up to justice all persons who, being charged with murder or forgery committed within the jurisdiction of either, shall seek an asylum within any of the countries of the other. Upon what ground can any distinction be made as to the reason and necessity of such stipulation, in the respective treaties? The necessity for the stipulation in both cases must be because the process of one government and jurisdiction will not run into that of another; and separate and distinct jurisdiction, as have been shown, is what makes governments and nations foreign to each other in their political relations.

The same stipulation, as to delivering up criminals who shall take refuge in the Cherokee Nation, is contained in the Treaty of Holston of the 2d of July, 1791. 1 Laws U. S. 327. And the eleventh article fully recognizes the jurisdiction of the Cherokee Nation over the territory occupied by them. It provides that if any citizen of the United States shall go into the territory belonging to the Cherokees and commit any crime upon, or trespass against the person or property of any friendly Indian, which, if committed within the jurisdiction of any State would be punishable by the laws of such State, shall be subject to the same punishment, and proceeded against in the same manner as if the offense had been committed within the jurisdiction of the State. Here is an explicit admission that the Cherokee territory is not within the jurisdiction of any State. If it had been considered within the jurisdiction of Georgia, such a provision would not only be unnecessary but absurd. It is a provision looking to the punishment of a citizen of the United States for some act done in a foreign country. If exercising exclusive jurisdiction over a country is sufficient to constitute the State or power so exercising it a foreign state, the Cherokee Nation may assuredly with the greatest propriety be so considered.

The phraseology of the clause in the Constitution giving to Congress the power to regulate commerce, is supposed to afford an argument against considering the Cherokees a foreign nation. The clause reads thus: "To regulate commerce with foreign nations, and among the several States, and with the Indian tribes." Constitution, Art. 1, Sec. 8. The argument is that if the Indian tribes are foreign nations, they would have been included without being specially named, and being so named imports something different from the previous term "foreign nations."

This appears to me to partake too much of a mere verbal criticism, to draw after it the important conclusion that Indian tribes are not foreign nations. But the clause affords, irresistibly, the conclusion that the Indian tribes are not there understood as included within the discription of the "several States," or there could have been no fitness in immediately thereafter particularizing "the Indian tribes."

It is generally understood that every separate body of Indians is divided into bands or tribes, and forms a little community within the nation to which it belongs; and as the nation has some particular symbol by which it is distinguished from others, so each tribe has a badge by which it is denominated, and each tribe may have rights applicable to itself.

Cases may arise where the trade with a particular tribe may require to be regulated, and which might not have been embraced under the general description of the term "nation," or it might at least have left the case somewhat doubtful; as the clause was intended to vest in Congress the power to regulate all commercial intercourse, this phraseology was probably adopted to meet all possible cases; and the provision would have been imperfect if the term "Indian tribes" had been omitted.

Congress could not then have regulated the trade with any particular tribe that did not extend to the whole nation. Or, it may be, that the term "tribe" is here used as importing the same thing as that of "nation," and adopted merely to avoid the repetition of the term "nation"; and the Indians are specially named, because there was a provision somewhat analogous in the confederation; and entirely omitting to name the Indian tribes, might have afforded some plausible grounds for concluding that this branch of commercial intercourse was not subject to the power of Congress.

On examining the journals of the old Congress, which contain numerous proceedings and resolutions respecting the Indians, the terms "nation" and "tribe" are frequently used indiscriminately, and as importing the same thing; and treaties were sometimes entered into with the Indians, under the description or denomination of tribes, without naming the nation. See Journals 30th June and 12th July, 1775; 8th March, 1776; 20th October, 1777, and numerous other instances.

But whether any of these suggestions will satisfactorily account for the phraseology here used or not, it appears to me to be of too doubtful import to outweigh the considerations to which I have referred to show that the Cherokees are a foreign nation. The difference between the provision in the Constitution and that in the confederation on this subject appears to me to show very satisfactorily that, so far as related to trade and commerce with the Indians wherever found in tribes, whether within or without the limits of a State, was subject to the regulation of Congress.

The provision in the confederation (Art. 9, 1 Laws U. S. 17) is, that Congress shall have the power of regulating the trade and management of all affairs with the Indians not members of any of the States, provided that the legislative right of any State within its own limits be not infringed or violated. The true import of this provision is certainly not very obvious. See "The Federalist," No. 42. What were the legislative rights intended to be embraced within the proviso is left in great uncertainty. But whatever difficulty on that subject might have arisen under the confederation, it is entirely removed by the omission of the proviso in the present Constitution; thereby leaving this power entirely with Congress, without regard to any State right on the subject, and showing that the Indian tribes were considered as distinct communities although within the limits of a State.

The provision, as contained in the confederation, may aid in illustrating what is to be inferred from some parts of the Constitution (Art. 1, Sec. 1, par. 3), as to the apportionment of representatives, and acts of Congress in relation to the Indians, to wit, that they are divided into two distinct classes. One composed of those who are considered members of the State within which they reside, and the other not; the former embracing the remnant of the tribes who had lost their distinctive character as a separate community and had become subject to the laws of the States, and the latter such as still retain their original connection as tribes, and live together under their own laws, usages and customs, and, as such, are treated as a community independent of the State. No very important conclusion, I think, therefore, can be drawn from the use of the term "tribe" in this clause of the Constitution, intended merely for commercial regulations. If considered as importing the same thing as the term "nation," it might have been adopted to avoid the repetition of the word "nation."

Other instances occur in the Constitution where different terms are used importing the same thing. Thus, in the clause giving jurisdiction to this court, the term "foreign states" is used instead of "foreign nations," as in the clause relating to commerce. And again, in Art. 1, Sec. 10, a still different phraseology is employed: "No State, without the consent of Congress, shall enter into any agreement or compact with a 'foreign power.' " But each of these terms —nation, state, power—as used in different parts of the Constitution, imports the same thing, and does not admit of a different interpretation. In the treaties made with the Indians they are sometimes designated under the name of "tribe," and sometimes that of "nation." In the Treaty of 1804 with the Delaware Indians, they are denominated the "Delaware tribe of Indians." 1 Laws U. S. 305. And in a previous treaty with the same people in the year 1778, they are designated by the name of "the Delaware Nation." 1 Laws U. S. 302.

As this was one of the earliest treaties made with the Indians, its provisions may serve to show in what light the Indian nations were viewed by Congress at that day.

The territory of the Delaware Nation was within the limits of the States of New York, Pennsylvania, and New Jersey. Yet we hear of no claim of jurisdiction set up by those States over these Indians. This treaty, both in form and substance, purports to be an arrangement with an independent sovereign power. It even purports to be articles of confederation. It contains stipulations relative to peace and war, and for permission to the United States troops to pass through the country of the Delaware Nation. That neither party shall protect in their respective States, servants, slaves, or criminals, fugitives from the other; but secure and deliver them up. Trade is regulated between the parties. And the sixth article shows the early pledge of the United States to protect the Indians in their possessions against any claims or encroachments of the States. It recites that whereas the enemies of the United States have endeavored to impress the Indians in general with an opinion that it is the design of the States to extirpate the Indians and take possession of their country, to obviate such false suggestions, the United States do engage to guaranty to the aforesaid nation of Delawares and their heirs, all their territorial rights, in the fullest and most ample manner, as it has been bounded by former treaties, etc. And provision is even made for inviting other tribes to join the confederacy and to form a State, and have a representation in Congress, should it be found conducive to the mutual interest of both parties. All which provisions are totally inconsistent with the idea of these Indians being considered under the jurisdiction of the States, although their chartered limits might extend over them.

The recital, in this treaty, contains a declaration and admission of Congress of the rights of Indians in general; and that the impression which our enemies were endeavoring to make—that it was the design of the States to extirpate them and take their lands—was false. And the same recognition of their rights runs through all the treaties made with the Indian nations or tribes from that day down to the present time.

The twelfth article of the Treaty of Hopewell contains a full recognition of the sovereign and independent character of the Cherokee Nation. To impress upon them full confidence in the justice of the United States respecting their interest, they have a right to send a deputy of their choice to Congress. No one can suppose that such deputy was to take his seat as a member of Congress, but that he would be received as the agent of that nation. It is immaterial what such agent is called, whether minister, commissioner or deputy; he is to represent his principal.

There could have been no fitness or propriety in any such stipulation, if the Cherokee Nation had been considered in any way incorporated with the State of Georgia, or as citizens of that State. The idea of the Cherokees being considered citizens is entirely inconsistent with several of our treaties with them. By the eighth article of the Treaty of the 26th December, 1817 (6 Laws U. S. 706), the United States stipulate to give 640 acres of land to each head of any Indian family residing on the lands now ceded, or which may hereafter be surrendered to the United States, who may wish to become citizens of the United States; so also the second article of the Treaty with the same nation, of the 10th of March, 1819, contains the same stipulation in favor of the heads of families who may choose to become citizens of the United States; thereby clearly showing that they were not considered citizens at the time those stipulations were entered into, or the provision would have been entirely unnecessary, if not absurd. And if not citizens, they must be aliens or foreigners, and such must be the character of each individual belonging to the nation. And it was, therefore, very aptly asked on the argument (and I think not very easily answered) how a nation composed of aliens or foreigners can be other than a foreign nation.

The question touching the citizenship of an Oneida Indian came under the consideration of the Supreme Court of New York in the case of *Jackson* v. *Goodel,* 20 Johns.

193. The lessor of the plaintiff was the son of an Oneida Indian who had received a patent for the lands in question as an officer in the Revolutionary War; and although the Supreme Court, under the circumstances of the case, decided he was a citizen, yet Chief Justice Spencer observed, "we do not mean to say that the condition of the Indian tribes (alluding to the Six Nations), at former and remote periods, has been that of subjects or citizens of the State; their condition has been gradually changing, until they have lost every attribute of sovereignty, and become entirely dependent upon and subject to our government." But the cause being carried up to the Court of Errors, Chancellor Kent, in a very elaborate and able opinion on that question, came to a different conclusion as to the citizenship of the Indian, even under the strong circumstances of that case.

"The Oneidas," he observed, "and the tribes composing the Six Nations of Indians, were originally free and independent nations, and it is for the counsel to contend that they have now ceased to be a distinct people and become completely incorporated with us, to point out the time when that event took place. In my view they have never been regarded as citizens, or members of our body politic. They have always been, and still are, considered by our laws as dependent tribes, governed by their own usages and chiefs; but placed under our protection, and subject to our coercion so far as the public safety required it, and no farther. The whites have been gradually pressing upon them, as they keep receding from the approaches of civilization. We have purchased the greater part of their lands, destroyed their hunting-grounds, subdued the wilderness around them, overwhelmed them with our population, and gradually abridged their native independence. Still they are permitted to exist as distinct nations, and we continue to treat with their sachems in a national capacity, and as being the lawful representatives of their tribes. Through the whole course of our colonial history, these Indians were considered dependent allies. The colonial authorities uniformly negotiated with them, and made and observed treaties with them as sovereign communities exercising the right of free deliberation and action; but, in consideration of protection, owing a qualified subjection in a national capacity to the British crown. No argument can be drawn against the sovereignty of these Indian nations from the fact of their having put themselves and their lands under the protection of the British crown; such a fact is of frequent occurrence between independent nations. One community may be bound to another by a very unequal alliance, and still be a sovereign State. Vatt. B. 1, ch. 16, sec. 194. The Indians, though born within our territorial limits are considered as born under the dominion of their own tribes. There is nothing in the proceedings of the United States during the Revolutionary War which went to impair, and much less to extinguish, the national character of the Six Nations, and consolidate them with our own people. Every public document speaks a different language, and admits their distinct existence and competence as nations, but placed in the same state of dependence, and calling for the same protection which existed before the war. In the treaties made with them we have the forms and requisites peculiar to the intercourse between friendly and independent States; and they are conformable to the received institutes of the law of nations. What more demonstratable proof can we require of existing and acknowledged sovereignty."

If this be a just view of the Oneida Indians, the rules and principles have applied to that nation may with much greater force be applied to the character, state, and condition of the Cherokee Nation of Indians; and we may safely conclude that they are not citizens, and must of course be aliens; and, if aliens in their individual capacities, it will be difficult to escape the conclusion that, as a community, they constitute a foreign nation or State, and thereby become a competent party to maintain an action in this court, according to the express terms of the Constitution.

And why should this court scruple to consider this nation a competent party to appear here?

Other departments of the government, whose right it is to decide what powers shall be recognized as sovereign and independent nations, have treated this nation as such. They have considered it competent, in its political and national capacity, to enter into contracts of the most solemn character; and if these contracts contain matter proper for judicial inquiry, why should we refuse to entertain jurisdiction of the case? Such jurisdiction is expressly given to this court in cases arising under treaties. If the executive department does not think proper to enter into treaties or contracts with the Indian nations, no case with them can arise calling for judicial cognizance. But when such treaties are found containing stipulations proper for judicial cognizance, I am unable to discover any reasons satisfying my mind that this court has not jurisdiction of the case.

The next inquiry is, whether such a case is made out in the bill as to warrant this court in granting any relief.

I have endeavored to show that the Cherokee Nation is a foreign state; and, as such, a competent party to maintain an original suit in this court against one of the United States. The injuries complained of are violations committed and threatened upon the property of the complainants secured to them by the laws and treaties of the United States. Under the Constitution, the judicial power of the United States extends expressly to all cases in law and equity arising under the laws of the United States, and treaties made, or which shall be made, under the authority of the same.

In the case of *Osborn* v. *The United States Bank,* 9 Wheat. 819, the court says that this clause in the Constitution enables the judicial department to receive jurisdiction to the full extent of the Constitution, laws, and treaties of the United States, when any question respecting them shall assume such a form that the judicial power is capable of acting on it. That power is capable of acting only when the subject is submitted to it by a party who asserts his rights in the form presented by law. It then becomes a case, and the Constitution authorizes the application of the judicial power.

The question presented in the present case is, under the ordinary form of judicial proceedings, to obtain an injunction to prevent or stay a violation of the rights of property claimed and held by the complainants, under the treaties and laws of the United States; which, it is alleged, have been violated by the State of Georgia. Both the form and the subject matter of the complaint, therefore, fall properly under judicial cognizance.

What the rights of property in the Cherokee Nation are, may be discovered from the several treaties which have been made between the United States and that nation between the years of 1785 and 1819. It will be unnecessary to notice many of them. They all recognize, in the most unqualified manner, a right of property in this nation, to the occupancy at least, of the lands in question. It is immaterial whether this interest is a mere right of occupancy, or an absolute right to the soil. The complaint is for a violation, or threatened violation, of the possessory right. And this is a right in the enjoyment of which they are entitled to protection, according to the doctrine of this court in the cases of *Fletcher* v. *Peck,* 6 Cranch 87; 2 Peters's Cond. Rep. 308, and Johnson v. M'Intosh, 8 Wheat. 592. By the fourth article of the Treaty of Hopewell, as early as the year 1785 (1 Laws U. S. 323), the boundary line between the Cherokees and the citizens of the United States within the limits of the United States is fixed.

The fifth article provides for the removal and punishment of citizens of the United States or other persons, not being Indians, who shall attempt to settle on the lands so allotted to the Indians; thereby not only surrendering the exclusive possession of these lands to this nation, but providing for the protection and enjoyment of such possession. And, it may be remarked, in corroboration of what has been said in a former part of this opinion, that there is here drawn a marked line of distinction between the Indians and citizens of the United States; entirely excluding the former from the character of citizens.

Again, by the Treaty of Holston in 1791 (1 Laws U. S. 325) the United States purchase a part of the territory of this nation, and a new boundary line is designated, and provision made for having it ascertained and marked. The mere act of purchasing and paying a consideration for these lands is a recognition of the Indian right. In addition to which, the United States, by the seventh article, solemnly guarantee to the Cherokee Nation all their lands not ceded by that treaty. And by the eighth article it is declared, that any citizens of the United States, who shall settle upon any of the Cherokee lands, shall forfeit the protection of the United States; and the Cherokees may punish them or not as they shall please.

This treaty was made soon after the adoption of the present Constitution. And in the last article it is declared that it shall take effect, and be obligatory upon the contracting parties as soon as the same shall have been ratified by the President of the United States, with the advice and consent of the Senate; thereby showing the early opinion of the government of the character of the Cherokee Nation. The contract is made by way of treaty, and to be ratified in the same manner as all other treaties made with sovereign and independent nations; and which has been the mode of negotiating in all subsequent Indian treaties.

And this course was adopted by President Washington upon great consideration, by and with the previous advice and concurrence of the Senate. In his message sent to the Senate on that occasion, he states that the white people had intruded on the Indian lands, as bounded by the Treaty of Hopewell, and declares his determination to execute the power intrusted to him by the Constitution to carry that treaty into faithful execution; unless a new boundary should be arranged with the Cherokees, embracing the intrusive settlements, and compensating the Cherokees therefor. And he puts to the Senate this question: Shall the United States stipulate solemnly to guaranty the new boundary which shall be arranged? Upon which the Senate resolved that in case a new or other boundary than that stipulated by the Treaty of Hopewell shall be concluded with the Cherokee Indians, the Senate do advise and consent solemnly to guaranty the same, 1 Executive Journal, 60. In consequence of which the Treaty of Holston was entered into, containing the guarantee.

Further cessions of land have been made at different times by the Cherokee Nation to the United States for a consideration paid therefor, and, as the treaties declare, in acknowledgment of the protection of the United States (see Treaty of 1798, 1 Laws U. S. 332); the United States always recognizing, in the fullest manner, the Indian right of possession; and in the Treaty of the 8th of July, 1817, art. 5 (6 Laws U.S. 702), all former treaties are declared to be in full force; and the sanction of the United States is given to the proposition of a portion of the nation to begin the establishment of fixed laws and a regular government, thereby recognizing in the nation a political existence, capable of forming an independent government, separate and distinct from and in no manner whatever under the jurisdiction of the State of Georgia; and no objection is known to have been made by that State.

And, again, in 1819 (6 Laws U. S. 748), another treaty is made sanctioning and carrying into effect the measures contemplated by the Treaty of 1817; beginning with a recital that the greater part of the Cherokees have expressed an earnest desire to remain on this side of the Mississippi, and being desirous, in order to commence those measures which they deem necessary to the civilization and preservation of their nation that the treaty between the United States and them of the 8th of July, 1817, might without further delay be finally adjusted, have offered to make a further cession of land, etc.

This cession is accepted, and various stipulations entered into, with a view to their civilization and the establishment of a regular government, which has since been accomplished. And by the fifth article it is stipulated that all white people who have intruded, or who shall thereafter intrude on the lands reserved for the Cherokees, shall be removed by the United States, and proceeded against according to the provisions of the Act of 1802, entitled "An Act to regulate trade and intercourse with the Indian tribes, and to preserve peace on the frontiers." 3 Laws U. S. 460.

By this act the boundary lines established by treaty with the various Indian tribes are required to be ascertained and marked; and among others, that with the Cherokee Nation, according to the Treaty of the 2d of October, 1798.

It may be necessary here briefly to notice some of the provisions of this Act of 1802 (so far as it goes to protect the rights of property of the Indians), for the purpose of seeing whether there has been any violation of those rights by the State of Georgia which falls properly under judicial cognizance. By this act it is made an offense punishable by fine and imprisonment, for any citizen or other person resident of the United States, or either of the territorial districts, to cross over or go within the boundary line, to hunt or destroy the game, or drive stock to range or feed on the Indian lands, or to go into any country allotted to the Indians, without a passport; or to commit therein any robbery, larceny, trespass, or other crime, against the person or property of any friendly Indian, which would be punishable, if committed within the jurisdiction of any State against a citizen of the United States; thereby necessarily implying that the Indian territory secured by treaty was not within the jurisdiction of any State. The act further provides that when property is taken or destroyed, the offender shall forfeit and pay twice the value of the property so taken or destroyed. And by the fifth section it is declared that if any citizen of the United States, or other person, shall make a settlement on any lands belonging or secured, or guaranteed, by treaty with the United States to any Indian tribe; or shall survey or attempt to survey such lands, or designate any of the boundaries by marking trees or otherwise, such offender shall forfeit a sum not exceeding one thousand dollars, and suffer imprisonment not exceeding twelve months.

This act contains various other provisions for the purpose of protecting the Indians in the free and uninterrupted enjoyment of their lands: and authority is given (sec. 16) to employ the military force of the United States to apprehend all persons who shall be found in the Indian country in violation of any of the provisions of the act, and to deliver them up to the civil authority, to be proceeded against in due course of law.

It may not be improper here to notice some diversity of opinion that has been entertained with respect to the construction of the nineteenth section of this act, which declares that nothing therein contained shall be construed to prevent any trade or intercourse with the Indians living on lands surrounded by settlements of citizens of the United States, and being within the ordinary jurisdiction of any of the individual States. It is understood that the State of Georgia contends that the Cherokee Nation come within this section, and are subject to the jurisdiction of that State. Such a construction makes the act inconsistent with itself, and directly repugnant to the various treaties entered into between the United States and the Cherokee Indians. The act recognizes and adopts the boundary line as settled by treaty. And by these treaties, which are in full force, the United States solemnly guaranty to the Cherokee Nation all their lands not ceded to the United States; and these lands lie within the chartered limits of Georgia: and this was a subsisting guaranty under the Treaty of 1791, when the Act of 1802 was passed. It would require the most unequivocal language to authorize a construction so directly repugnant to these treaties.

But this section admits of a plain and obvious interpretation, consistent with other parts of the act, and in harmony with these treaties. The reference undoubtedly is to that class of Indians which has already been referred to, consisting of the mere remnants of tribes, which have become almost extinct; and who have in a great measure lost their original character and abandoned their usages and customs, and become subject to the laws of the State, although in many parts of the country living together and surrounded by the whites. They cannot be said to have any distinct government of their own, and are within the ordinary jurisdiction and government of the State where they are located.

But such was not the condition and character of the Cherokee Nation in any respect whatever in the year 1802, or at any time since. It was a numerous and distinct nation, living under the government of their own laws, usages, and customs, and in no sense under the ordinary jurisdiction of the State of Georgia; but under the protection of the United States, with a solemn guaranty by treaty of the exclusive right to the possession of their lands. This guaranty is to the Cherokees in their national capacity. Their land is held in common, and every invasion of their possessory right is an injury done to the nation, and not to any individual. No private or individual suit could be sustained: the injury done being to the nation, the remedy sought must be in the name of the nation. All the rights secured to these Indians, under any treaties made with them, remain unimpaired. These treaties are acknowledged by the United States to be in full force by the proviso to the seventh section of the Act of the 28th of May, 1830, which declares that nothing in this act contained shall be construed as authorizing or directing the violation of any existing treaty between the United States and any Indian tribes.

That the Cherokee Nation of Indians have, by virtue of these treaties, an exclusive right of occupancy of the lands in question, and that the United States are bound under their guarantee to protect the nation in the enjoyment of such occupancy, cannot, in my judgment, admit of a doubt; and that some of the laws of Georgia set out in the bill are in violation of, and in conflict with those treaties and the Act of 1802, is to my mind equally clear. But a majority of the court having refused the injunction, so that no relief whatever can be granted, it would be a fruitless inquiry for me to go at large into an examination of the extent to which relief might be granted by this court, according to my own view of the case.

I certainly, as before observed, do not claim, as belonging to the judiciary, the exercise of political power. That belongs to another branch of the government. The protection and enforcement of many rights secured by treaties, most certainly do not belong to the judiciary. It is only where the rights of persons or property are involved, and when such rights can be presented under some judicial form of proceedings, that courts of justice can interpose relief.

This court can have no right to pronounce an abstract opinion upon the constitutionality of a State law. Such law must be brought into actual or threatened operation upon rights properly falling under judicial cognizance, or a remedy is not to be had here.

The laws of Georgia set out in the bill, if carried fully into operation, go the length of abrogating all of the laws of the Cherokees, abolishing their government, and entirely subverting their national character. Although the whole of these laws may be in violation of the treaties made with this nation, it is probable this court cannot grant relief to the full extent of the complaint. Some of them, however, are so directly at variance with these treaties and the laws of the United States touching the rights of property secured to them, that I can perceive no objection to the application of judicial relief. The State of Georgia certainly could not have intended these laws as declarations of hostility, or wish their execution of them to be viewed in any manner whatever as acts of war; but merely as an assertion of what is claimed as a legal right; and in this light ought they to be considered by this court.

The Act of the 2d of December, 1830, is entitled "An Act to authorize the governor to take possession of the gold and silver and other mines lying and being in that section of the chartered limits of Georgia commonly called the Cherokee country, and those upon all other unappropriated lands of the State, and for punishing persons who may be found trespassing on the mines." The preamble to this act asserts the title to these mines to belong to the State of Georgia; and by its provisions twenty thousand dollars are appropriated and placed at the disposal of the governor to enable him to take possession of those mines; and it is made a crime, punishable by imprisonment in the penitentiary of Georgia at hard labor, for the Cherokee Indians to work these mines. And the bill alleges that under the laws of the State in relation to the mines, the governor has stationed at the mines an armed force who are employed in restraining the complainants in their rights and liberties in regard to their own mines, and in enforcing the laws of Georgia upon them. These can be considered in no other light than as acts of trespass, and may be treated as acts of the State, and not of the individuals employed as the agents. Whoever authorizes or commands an act to be done may be considered a principal, and held responsible, if he can be made a party to a suit, as the State of Georgia may undoubtedly be. It is not perceived on what ground the State can claim a right to the possession and use of these mines. The right of occupancy is secured to the Cherokees by treaty, and the State has not even a reversionary interest in the soil. It is true, that by the compact with Georgia of 1802, the United States have stipulated to extinguish for the use of the State the Indian title to the lands within her remaining limits, "as soon as it can be done peaceably and upon reasonable terms." But until this is done, the State can have no claim to the lands.

The very compact is a recognition by the State of a subsisting Indian right, and which may never be extinguished. The United States have not stipulated to extinguish it until it can be done "peaceably and upon reasonable terms;" and whatever complaints the State of Georgia may have against the United States for the nonfulfillment of this compact, it cannot affect the right of the Cherokees. They have not stipulated to part with that right; and until they do, their right to the mines stands upon the same footing as the use and enjoyment of any other part of the territory.

Again, by the Act of 21st December, 1830, surveyors are authorized to be appointed to enter upon the Cherokee territory and lay it off into districts and sections, which are to be distributed by lottery among the people of Georgia; reserving to the Indians only the present occupancy of such improvements as the individuals of their nation may now be residing on, with the lots on which such improvements may stand, and even excepting from such reservation improvements recently made near the gold mines.

This is not only repugnant to the treaties with the Cherokees, but directly in violation of the Act of Congress of 1802; the fifth section of which makes it an offense punishable with fine and imprisonment, to survey or attempt to survey or designate any of the boundaries, by marking trees or otherwise, of any land belonging to or secured by treaty to any Indian tribe: in the face of which, the law of Georgia authorizes the entry upon, taking possession of and surveying and distributing by lottery, these lands guaranteed by treaty to the Cherokee

Nation; and even gives authority to the governor to call out the military force to protect the surveyors in the discharge of the duty assigned them.

These instances are sufficient to show a direct and palpable infringement of the rights of property secured to the complainants by treaty, and in violation of the Act of Congress of 1802. These treaties and this law, are declared by the Constitution to be the supreme law of the land: it follows, as matter of course, that the laws of Georgia, so far as they are repugnant to them, must be void and inoperative. And it remains only very briefly to inquire whether the execution of them can be restrained by injunction according to the doctrine and practice of courts of equity.

According to the view which I have already taken of the case, I must consider the question of right as settled in favor of the complainants. This right rests upon the laws of the United States, and treaties made with the Cherokee Nation. The construction of these laws and treaties are pure questions of law, and for the decision of the court. There are no grounds, therefore, upon which it can be necessary to send the cause for a trial at law of the right, before awarding an injunction; and the simple question is, whether such a case is made out by the bill as to authorize the granting an injunction.

This is a prohibitory writ to restrain a party from doing a wrong or injury to the rights of another. It is a beneficial process for the protection of rights, and is favorably viewed by courts of chancery, as its object is to prevent rather than redress injuries; and has latterly been more liberally awarded than formerly, 7 Ves., Jun. 307.

The bill contains charges of numerous trespasses by entering upon the lands of the complainants and doing acts greatly to their injury and prejudice, and to the disturbance of the quiet enjoyment of their land, and threatening a total destruction of all their rights. And although it is not according to the course of chancery to grant injunctions to prevent trespasses when there is a clear and adequate remedy at law, yet it will be done when the case is special and peculiar, and when no adequate remedy can be had at law, and particularly when the injury threatens irreparable ruin, 6 Ves. 147; 7 Eden, 307. Every man is entitled to be protected in the possession and enjoyment of his property; and the ordinary remedy by action of trespass may generally be sufficient to afford such protection. But, where from the peculiar nature and circumstances of the case, this is not an adequate protection, it is a fit case to interpose the preventive process of injunction. This is the principle running through all the cases on this subject, and is founded upon the most wise and just considerations; and this is peculiarly such a case. The complaint is not of a mere private trespass, admitting of compensation in damages; but of injuries which go to the total destruction of the whole rights of the complainants. The mischief threatened is great and irreparable. 7 Johns. Ch. 330. It is one of the most beneficial powers of a court of equity to interpose and prevent an injury before any has actually been suffered; and this is done by a bill which is sometimes called a bill quia timet. Mitford, 120.

The doctrine of this court in the case of Osborn v. The United States Bank, 9 Wheat. 738, fully sustains the present application for an injunction. The bill in that case was filed to obtain an injunction against the auditor of the State of Ohio to restrain him from executing a law of that State, which was alleged to be to the great injury of the bank, and to the destruction of rights conferred by their charter. The only question of doubt entertained by the court in that case was as to issuing an injunction against an officer of the State to restrain him from doing an official act enjoined by statute, the State not being made a party. But even this was not deemed sufficient to deny the injunction. The court considered that the Ohio law was made for the avowed purpose of expelling the bank from the State and depriving it of its chartered privileges; and they say if the State could have been made a party defendant, it would scarcely be denied that it would be a strong case for an injunction; that the application was not to interpose the writ of injunction, to protect the bank from a common and casual trespass of an individual, but from a total destruction of its franchise, of its chartered privileges, so far as respected the State of Ohio. In that case, the State could not be made a party according to the eleventh amendment of the Constitution; the complainants being mere individuals and not a sovereign State. But, according to my view of the present case, the State of Georgia is properly made a party defendant; the complainants being a foreign state.

The laws of the State of Georgia in this case go as fully to the total destruction of the complainants' rights as did the law of Ohio to the destruction of the rights of the bank in that State; and an injunction is as fit and proper in this case to prevent the injury as it was in that.

It forms no objection to the issuing of the injunction in this case that the lands in question do not lie within the jurisdiction of this court. The writ does not operate in rem, but in personam. If the party is within the jurisdiction of the court, it is all that is necessary to give full effect and operation to the injunction; and it is immaterial where the subject matter of the suit, which is only affected consequentially, is situated. This principle is fully recognized by this court in the case of *Massie* v. *Watts,* 6 Cranch 157, when this general rule is laid down that in a case of fraud of trust or of contract, the jurisdiction of a court of chancery is sustainable wherever the person may be found, although lands not within the jurisdiction of the court may be affected by the decree. And reference is made to several cases in the English chancery recognizing the same principle. In tha case of *Penn* v. *Lord Baltimore,* 1 Ves. 444, a specific performance of a contract respecting lands lying in North America was decreed; the chancellor saying the strict primary decree of a court of equity is in personam, and may be enforced in all cases when the person is within its jurisdiction.

Upon the whole, I am of opinion:

1. That the Cherokees compose a foreign State within the sense and meaning of the Constitution, and constitute a competent party to maintain a suit against the State of Georgia.

2. That the bill presents a case for judicial consideration, arising under the laws of the United States, and treaties made under their authority with the Cherokee Nation, and which laws and treaties have been and are threatened to be still further violated by the laws of the State of Georgia referred to in this opinion.

3. That an injunction is a fit and proper writ to be issued to prevent the further execution of such laws, and ought therefore to be awarded.

And I am authorized by my brother Story to say that he concurs with me in this opinion.

Robert Trimble

☆ 1776–1828 ☆

APPOINTED BY

JOHN QUINCY ADAMS

YEARS ON COURT

1826–1828

Robert Trimble

by

FRED L. ISRAEL

ON APRIL 11, 1826, President John Quincy Adams appointed Robert Trimble to the Supreme Court. This was Adams' first and only Court nomination. The Senate confirmed Trimble on May 9, 1826, by a twenty-seven to five vote. And, at the age of fifty, Trimble, a distinguished Kentucky lawyer and jurist described by a contemporary as "robust and strong," took his seat on the then seven-man tribunal dominated by John Marshall. Twenty-seven months later Trimble was dead. But, although he is today one of the virtually forgotten men who sat on the Court, his two-year record indicates the beginning of what might have been an important judicial career. "We are persuaded that, if he had lived ten years longer, in the discharge of the same high duties, from the expansibility of his talents, and his steady devotion to jurisdiction," wrote Joseph Story, "he would have gained a still higher rank."

Robert Trimble was born in Berkeley County, Virginia, (now part of West Virginia) on November 17, 1776. His father, William Trimble, as described by a family friend, "was honest, respectable, and pious; but never wealthy. He was one of those hardy and enterprising adventurers who first settled in Kentucky. His object, like that of others, was to improve his fortune by obtaining a grant of land." (1 *American Jurist* 149 [1829].) The elder Trimble probably came to Kentucky County in 1778 when the area consisted of but a few military garrisons composed of several cabins grouped together for defense against the Indians. There was no money, except the small sums which new settlers brought. Because of wild animals, cattle, sheep, and hogs could not be raised in sufficient numbers for food supply and these early Kentucky pioneers cultivated wheat and hunted deer and elk. The only hope for improvement of this hand to mouth existence was an increase in land values—and this came, but very slowly. An entry in an old Jefferson County, Kentucky record book states that one William

FRED L. ISRAEL, Associate Professor of History at the City College of New York, is the author of Nevada's Key Pittman.

Trimble received title to 750 acres "at the fork of Howards Creek" on May 5, 1780—and other entries through 1784 indicate that he surveyed and entered nine claims totaling more than 8,000 acres. Young Trimble "became accustomed to engage in hunting game and scouting in search of Indians. In his youth he was active and athletic beyond his years, and he exhibited both bodily and mental activity above his fellows, and was recognised among them as a leader" (*Ibid.,* p. 157).

The first newspaper printed in Kentucky, the *Kentucky Gazette,* published an advertisement on December 27, 1787, announcing a new school in Lebanon, Fayette County. The subjects taught included: "Latin and Greek languages, together with such branches of the sciences as are usually taught in public seminaries." Trimble undoubtedly attended such a school, paying for his tuition in pork or produce. By the time he reached adulthood, he possessed "a powerful mind developed by self-training." In order to obtain money to continue his education, the future Justice taught school at Canebridge and Mt. Sterling, but the exact sequence of his later education cannot be determined because of conflicting accounts. Most probably, in the early 1790's, he studied at Bourbon Academy in Bourbon County and at the Kentucky Academy in Pisgah, later to become Transylvania University. And, after completing his studies, Trimble read law under the direction of George Nicholas, first Professor of Law at Transylvania, and James Brown, later Minister to France, 1823–1829. About 1800, Trimble began his own law practice in Paris, Kentucky, a town of approximately 500 located about eighty miles east of Louisville. The young lawyer gained an excellent reputation and "his great candor and fairness secured him the attentive ear of the court; and his sound judgment, which was his most distinguished characteristic, generally saved his client from being deceived or disappointed. His arguments in court, though less brilliant than those of some others, were sound, logical, forcible and interesting" (*Ibid.,* p. 153). In 1802, Trimble, now twenty-six, was elected to the Kentucky House of Representatives from Bourbon County but little is known of his service there. He probably found politics distasteful and financially unrewarding as he declined to run again—and, in fact, Trimble declined every future opportunity to enter politics although he could have been elected to the United States Senate in 1812. Private practice proved to be more lucrative and the need for financial security became an overriding consideration after his marriage to Nancy Timberlake on August 18, 1803, as the couple had at least ten children.

On April 13, 1807, Trimble accepted appointment as Justice of the Kentucky Court of Appeals, serving through December, 1808. The Court consisted of three judges plus a chief justice—two of Trimble's colleagues later had distinguished political careers; Ninian Edwards served as governor of the Territory of Illinois (1809–1818) and then the state's first senator (1818–1824); Felix Grundy served as United States senator from Tennessee (1829–1838; 1839–1840) and Attorney General of the United States (1838–39). The Court convened in Frankfort for fall and spring terms, each lasting approximately three months. Disputed land claims were the principal litigations and numerous such cases crowded the calendar. Most decisions were anonymous at this time, although this practice began to change during the spring 1808 term. A tabulation for the fall 1808 term shows that Trimble wrote four of the eighteen signed opinions—each is quite dull but illustrates his logical reasoning (4 Kentucky *Reports,* 1; 8; 41; 53 [1808]). Trimble had reluctantly accepted the Court appointment, questioning the low yearly salary—$1,000. Although in 1807, the average Kentucky lawyer's financial rewards were not high—with bonds for cows, calves, and pigs being usual fees—Trimble apparently had a very successful practice as he considered his judicial terms a "financial sacrifice." He resigned after the 1808 sessions, claiming that he could not support his growing family on his meager judicial salary. The same financial reasons made him decline the Chief Justiceship of Kentucky in 1810 and an 1813 offer to resume his duties on the Court of Appeals. Although he refused these appointments, Trimble, nevertheless, rendered other public services. For many years, he acted as a trustee of Transylvania University though declining several offers to accept the law professorship. In the elections of 1808, 1812, and 1816, Trimble was a presidential elector—voting for James Madison twice and in 1816 for James Monroe. From 1813 to 1817, he supervised the state district attorney's office, but this did not interfere with his own practice. Together with John J. Crittenden, Trimble represented Kentucky in negotiations with Tennessee officials, negotiations which settled the disputed boundary between the two states.

Trimble's private practice flourished—in 1810, after ten years as a practicing lawyer, he owned nine slaves worth a total value of about $9,000. His fees were reasonable and, we are told, he "never extorted from poverty or distress. . . . He might, with better economy, have amassed a greater fortune." In January, 1817, after having accumulated a sizable sum of money, certainly sufficient to support and educate his children, Trimble decided to accept President James Madison's nomination to be the Federal District Judge for Kentucky. The Senate confirmed his appointment on January 31, 1817, and Trimble served until his elevation to the Supreme Court on May 9, 1826.

Trimble's eight years as Kentucky's federal judge, 1817–1826, coincided with an extremely bitter state-federal jurisdictional dispute, climaxing with a complete and controversial reorganization of the state's courts. During this period, financial panics, too many state banks, excess of paper money, creditor-defrauding, and the crucial determination of state-federal relationship almost exasperated Kentuckians. The federal courts insisted on federal jurisdiction in admiralty over Kentucky's inland waters; the Court invalidated Kentucky's laws protecting settlers who had made improvements on disputed land claims and voided the state's bankruptcy laws; and, finally, the Supreme Court sustained the obnoxious centralized Bank of the United States (*Osborn* v. *Bank of the United States,* 9 Wheat. 738 [1824]). And so, as Charles Warren wrote: "Kentucky was thus brought to the verge of open rebellion against the Court." Vituperative statements aside, the conflict centered around John Marshall's assertion of federal supremacy and the resulting claims of state sovereignty. In December, 1823, the Kentucky legislature urged changes in the entire federal judicial system and the state's congressional delegation repeatedly introduced bills providing for radical abrogation of the Supreme Court's assumed appellate powers. The controversy apparently involved Trimble's district court. Unfortunately, however, Trimble's federal court reports have not been preserved and it is necessary to make assumptions based on scanty secondary accounts. Trimble undoubtedly supported the supremacy of the federal government as a July, 1821, editorial in the *Kentucky Gazette* attacked him for questioning the omnipotence of the state legislature, warning that his overt disregard for Kentucky's sovereignty might lead to his impeachment. And, when Justice Thomas Todd of Kentucky died in February, 1826, President Adams chose Trimble because, like Todd, he unswervingly believed in federal court supremacy over the state processes. The five senators who cast their votes against Trimble's confirmation on May 9, 1826, opposed him for this reason.

When Trimble took his Supreme Court seat for the January, 1827, term, Chief Justice Marshall was at the height of his influence. The Court then met in a small room in the Capitol basement which later became a library when the Court took over the old Senate chambers in 1860. One observer left this caustic description:

> *The apartment is not in a style which comports with the dignity of that body, or which wears a comparison with the other Halls of the Capitol. The room is in the basement story in an obscure part of the north wing. In arriving at it, you pass a labyrinth, and almost need the clue of Ariadne to guide you to the sanctuary of the blind goddess. A stranger might traverse the dark avenues of the Capitol for a week, without finding the remote corner in which Justice is administered to the American Republic.*

The seven judges sat on a long bench at the east end of the room on a raised platform, with a lawyer's table directly in front and beneath them. Chief Justice Marshall sat in the middle with Justices Story, Thompson, and Duvall on his right and Justices Washington, Johnson, and Trimble on his left.

Trimble agreed with Marshall in almost every case—the main exception is Marshall's minority opinion in *Ogden* v. *Saunders,* 12 Wheat. 213 (1827). During the 1827 session, the Court delivered forty-eight opinions—with Trimble speaking for the Court nine times. The following year, the Court rendered fifty-five opinions—and Trimble authored seven. The tall gaunt Chief Justice outperformed his colleagues in these two years by writing thirty-nine majority and two dissenting opinions. Most of the cases assigned to Trimble involved technical land litigation and procedural matters.

Perhaps Trimble wrote his most important opinion in *Ogden* v. *Saunders.* Eight years earlier, in *Sturges* v. *Crowninshield,* 4 Wheat. 122 (1819), the Court decided that state bankruptcy laws were permissible in the absence of a federal statute, provided these laws did not violate other constitutional rights. The New York law in question, however, was declared void because it released a man from his agreement to pay another man a sum of money which had been borrowed before the law in question was passed, and thus impaired the obligation of contracts, forbidden by the Constitution. The economic depression following the Panic of 1819 caused several states to seek a loophole in *Sturges* v. *Crowninshield* by enacting bankruptcy laws applying only to debts contracted after the statute's passage. Such a clause, so it was reasoned, would place a limitation on subsequent contracts and would circumvent Marshall's ruling that state power over bankruptcy was limited by the contract clause. "It is probable that Congress will soon pass a general bankrupt law," observed one New York newspaper, "if Congress declines . . . and the States are prohibited from adopting laws for themselves, the commercial state of the country will present a spectacle not found in history. The debtor, the merchant whose fortune has been swept away by events beyond his control, will be pursued by unrelenting creditors without cessation." And so, when a case testing a New York bankruptcy law was brought before the Court in 1824, the business community anxiously awaited the decision. Delays, however, postponed a final argument until January 18, 1827. Four weeks later, on February 18th, the Court delivered its four to three decision, with the majority holding that the New York insolvency law which discharged both the person of the debtor and his future property acquisitions did not impair the obligation of contracts entered into after the law's passage. Chief Justice Marshall and Justices Story and Duvall dissented, maintaining that the Constitution protected all contracts, past or future, from state legislation which, in any manner, impaired their obligation. The majority decision, observed Marshall, would cause the contract clause of the Constitution to "be prostrate and be construed into an inanimate, inoperative and an unmeaning clause." This decision in *Ogden* v. *Saunders* was the first and only time the Court voted against Marshall on an important constitutional issue and became the first case to modify the contract clause interpretations penned by the earlier Marshall Court.

Trimble's opinion in this case, which is printed below, broadly held that the law in question did not impair contract obligations. "Such a power seems to be almost indispensible to the very existence of the states, and is necessary to the safety and welfare of the people," he reasoned. In taking direct issue with Marshall's conservative and narrow view on the contract clause, Trimble wrote:

> *The construction insisted upon by those who maintain that prospective laws of the sort now under consideration are unconstitutional, would, so I think, transform a special limitation upon the general powers of the states, into a general restriction. It would convert, by construction, the exception into a general rule, against the best settled rules of construction. The people of the states, under every variety of circumstances, must remain unalterably, according to this construction, under the dominion of this supposed universal law, and the obligations resulting from it.*

Except for brief intermittent periods totaling sixteen years prior to 1898, there was no comprehensive federal bankruptcy law until the very end of the nineteenth century—hence the majority ruling in *Ogden* v. *Saunders* prevailed for many years. Trimble's opinion is important, not only from the major economic issue humanely and fairly settled, but because Trimble departed from his conviction of federal supremacy over states' rights to uphold a broad construction of the right of states to act in this matter. Unlike Marshall and Story, Trimble did not allow philosophical beliefs to lead him to a retrogressive conclusion.

Undoubtedly, Trimble's most interesting decision was his opinion for the Court in *The Antelope Case,* 12 Wheat. 546 (1827). During the 1820's, criminal cases involving violations of the federal slave trade ban crowded lower federal court calendars. In 1825, the Supreme Court was confronted for the first time with the double question of whether international law had outlawed the slave trade and, if so, what disposition should be made of slaves brought into the United States by an American revenue cutter which had captured a foreign ship carrying African slaves. The Court had reluctantly decided in the 1825 *Antelope Case,* 10 Wheat. 66, that, although the slave trade was immoral, the Court had to adhere to international law as then formulated and international law did not regard the slave trade as piracy. "Whatever might be the answer of a moralist to this question," wrote Marshall, "a jurist must search for its legal solution in those principles of action which are sanctioned by the usages, the national acts, and the general assent of that portion of the world of which he considers himself as a part, and to whose law the appeal is made." Trimble's 1827 decision, reprinted below, concerned the final settlement of the case. In 1825, the Court decreed that those captured slaves which Spanish or Portuguese authorities claimed, were to be returned to them and the remaining Africans were to be "disposed of" according to American law. Trimble ruled that the Court's decree had been fully carried out and he approved of the methods used in determining Spanish ownership, thus closing the case.

Trimble died on August 25, 1828, of a "malignant bilious fever," having served two full terms on the Court. *Niles Weekly Register* reported that the Supreme Court Justices resolved to wear black crepe on their left arms for the entire 1829 term as "evidence of their respect for the virtues and talents of the late Judge." Joseph Story eulogized that "perhaps no man ever on the bench gained so much in so short a period of his judicial career . . . no man could bestow more thought, more caution, more candor, or more research upon any legal investigation than he did. . . . He loved the Union with an unfaltering love and was ready to make any sacrifice to ensure its perpetuity. He was a patriot in the pure sense."

SELECTED BIBLIOGRAPHY

There are no collections of Trimble papers. A sound contemporary biographical sketch of Trimble is an anonymous article, "Memoir of Judge Trimble," 1 *American Jurist* 149 (1829). See also: Alan Neil Schneider, "Robert Trimble," 12 *Kentucky State Bar Journal* 21 (1947) and John S. Goff, "Mr. Justice Trimble of the United States Supreme Court," 58 *Register of the Kentucky Historical Society* 6 (1960). The Supreme Court's tribute to Trimble is in 2 Pet. 3 (1829).

Robert Trimble

REPRESENTATIVE OPINIONS

THE ANTELOPE CASE, 12 WHEAT. 546 (1827)

The Court had decided in the 1825 Antelope Case, 10 Wheat. 66, that, although the slave trade was personally reprehensible and immoral to the Justices, international law, nevertheless, had not outlawed it. Therefore, the Court ruled slave trading was not piracy if engaged in by nations still sanctioning such practices. In this instance, a slave ship first captured by a privateer in violation of American neutrality, then recaptured by an American revenue cutter and brought into port, had to be restored—slaves and all—after proof of ownership was demonstrated. In the 1825 opinion, the Court decreed that those captured slaves which Spanish or Portuguese authorities claimed were to be returned, with the remaining Africans to be "disposed of" according to American law. Trimble's 1827 decision concerned the final settlement of the case. He ruled that the Court's decree had been fully carried out and he approved of the methods used in determining ownership. Of interest in his opinion is the prevalent attitude that African slaves were subhuman objects, chattel property to be bought and sold. Although this case is but an historical footnote, it is interesting to note that the same generation which had produced the Bill of Rights, rationalized and justified "man's inhumanity to man."

Mr. Justice Trimble delivered the opinion of the Court.

This case having been before this Court, and a decree rendered therein at February term, 1825, and again brought up, and an explanatory decree made therein at February term, 1826, the reports of the case in 10 *Wheat. Rep.* 66. and 11 *Wheat. Rep.* 413., are referred to for the general history of its facts and circumstances, and for the principles settled in it by the former decrees of this Court. The case was remanded to the Circuit Court, with directions to make a final disposition of the controversy between the parties, pursuant to the principles of the decrees of 1825 and 1826 of this Court.

The Circuit Court, in order to enable it

to decree finally in the case, directed the register to take and report an account of the costs, and also of the expenses of keeping, maintaining, &c. of the Africans, by the marshal, and which account was accordingly reported. Exceptions were filed to the report by both the Portuguese and Spanish claimants.

The Circuit Court also caused proofs to be taken for the purpose of identifying individually the Africans to be delivered to the Spanish claimants, as directed by the decree of 1826.

Thus circumstanced, the case came on for final hearing before the Circuit Court. The Court decreed that the Portuguese claimant should not be made liable for costs, or any proportion of the expenses and charges of the marshal for maintaining, &c. the Africans; and being of opinion that thirty-nine of the Africans were sufficiently identified by proof, as being the property of the Spanish claimants, directed the thirty-nine Africans, so identified, to be delivered to the Spanish claimants, upon their paying a proportion of the costs and expenses reported by the registrar, in the ratio of the number of Africans delivered, to the whole number; and the Circuit Court was further of opinion, that the residue of the Africans not directed to be delivered to the Spanish claimants, should be delivered to the United States, to be disposed of according to law; but, on the question whether they shall be delivered absolutely, or on condition of payment of the balance of the expenses which will remain unsatisfied after charging the Africans adjudged to the Spanish claimants in their due ratio, the judges of the Circuit Court being divided in opinion, ordered this difference of opinion to be certified to this Court.

The case comes up on this certificate of division, and, also, upon an appeal prayed by the District Attorney on behalf of the United States, and allowed, "From so much of the said final order of the Circuit Court, as relates to the apportionment among the several parties of the costs and expenses, in the preservation, maintenance, and custody, of the said Africans, and of the costs and expenses of the various proceedings which have been had in relation to the said Africans, and, also, from so much of said order as decrees thirty-nine of the said Africans to the Spanish claimants."

We will first consider the question arising upon the certificate of division of opinion between the judges of the Circuit Court.

It appears, from the opinion delivered by the Circuit Court, and from the registrar's report, that, in making up that report as to the amount of expenses, sixteen cents *per diem* was allowed the marshal for the custody, maintenance, &c. of the Africans; and the Spanish claimants were charged, as a condition precedent, with the proportion of expenses of the marshal, after this rate, in the ratio of the number of Africans to be delivered to them. The residue of the marshal's expenses, at the same rate *per diem*, is supposed to be meant by the term "expenses," in the question on which the judges were opposed in opinion; and it is supposed the question upon which the judges were opposed in opinion was, whether the Africans not directed to be delivered to the Spanish claimants, should be delivered by the marshal to the United States, absolutely and unconditionally, to be disposed of according to law, or whether it should be imposed on the United States as a condition precedent to their delivery, that the United States should pay to the marshal his claim for expenses at the rate aforesaid, in the ratio of the number of Africans to be delivered to the United States.

The Spanish claimants have not appealed from the decree of the Circuit Court. As the Court had decided that they ought to bear some proportion of the expenses, it was necessary, for the purpose of ascertaining the amount which they were to pay, to fix upon some data for making up the account of expenses so far as related to them. But, as they do not complain, this Court is not called upon to decide whether they were overcharged or not, nor to determine whether the rate of sixteen cents *per diem* was warranted by law, as the Circuit Court supposed, so far as the Spanish claimants are concerned.

As relates to the United States, the question propounded by the judges of the Circuit Court, and upon which they were divided in opinion, does not necessarily draw in question the data or rate of the marshal's allowance for expenses; but whether the payment of his expenses, at any rate, or to any amount, ought to be made a precedent condition to the delivery of the Africans to the United States. It may well be doubted, however, whether the State law does, as supposed by the Court, authorize the marshal to charge, as matter of right, sixteen cents *per diem*, for keeping, maintaining, &c. the Africans; although it might furnish some guide, in an appeal to the sound discretion and justice of the government, in making him a reasonable compensation. It is true, the first section of the "Act for providing compensation for the marshal," (3d vol. ch. 125.) after declaring the fees and compensation to be allowed the marshal for certain enumerated services, &c. adds, "For all other services not herein enumerated, such fees or compensation as are allowed in the Supreme Court of the State where the services are rendered." This has generally been construed, and, we think, rightly, to mean, that where the services performed are not enumerated in the act of Congress, but such services are enumerated, and a fixed allowance made therefor in the State laws, they shall fix the rule of compensation. The case under consideration is wholly unprovided for by the laws and usages of the State. The Africans to be delivered to the United States, are neither slaves in contemplation of law, nor prisoners of war, nor persons charged with crimes. The compensations allowed by the laws of the State to sheriffs and jailors, in these cases, do not, therefore, furnish any positive rule of law or right, as to the compensation which ought to be allowed the marshal in the peculiar circumstances attending these Africans. He is, no doubt, entitled to a reasonable compensation; but that must depend upon the circumstances of the case, and not any positive rule. But be that as it may, it could not legally enter into the judgment and decree of the Court, so far as that judgment or decree was to affect the rights of the United States, or the rights of the marshal as against the United States. It is a general rule, that no Court can make a direct judgment or decree against the United States, for costs and expenses, in a suit to which the United States is party, either on behalf of any suitor, or any officer of the government. As to the officers of the government, the law expressly provides a different mode.

The third section of the "Act for regulating process," &c. (vol. 2. ch. 137.) makes provision for the fees and compensation to be allowed the marshal, similar to the "Act for providing for compensation to marshals," &c. above cited. The fourth section makes some further regulations concerning the fees and compensation to be allowed clerks and marshals, and then provides, "that the same having been examined and certified by the Court, or one of the judges of it, in which the services shall have been rendered, shall be passed in the usual manner at, and the amount thereof paid out of, the treasury of the United States," &c.

These provisions show, we think, incontestably, that, whether the marshal's fees and compensation for services rendered the United States be fixed by some positive statutory rule, as in enumerated services, or depends upon what is reasonable and just under the circumstances of the case, as in non-enumerated services, they must be certified to, and paid out of, the treasury, and cannot lawfully constitute any part of the judgment or decree in the cause. It would, indeed, be extraordinary, if the marshal who is the servant of the government, and holds possession of the Africans merely by its authority, could obstruct the operations of the government by a claim for compensation for his services. The laws give the marshal no lien on the Africans, and we can discover no principle which will justify the Court in creating a lien, in effect, by its decree. There is no necessity for such a proceeding.

The seventh section of "An act in addition to the acts prohibiting the slave trade," appropriates one hundred thousand dollars to carry the law into effect. The second section of the act authorizes the President of the United States to make "such regulations and arrangements as he may deem expedient for the safe keeping, support, and removal, beyond the limits of the United States, of all such negroes," &c. (5 vol. ch. 511.)

It is not to be doubted, that if a reasonable account for expenses were certified according to law, that arrangements would be made to pay it out of the fund appropriated for carrying into effect the laws prohibiting the slave trade.

We are of opinion it ought to be certified to the Circuit Court, that all the Africans captured in the Antelope, except those directed to be delivered to the Spanish claimants, should be decreed to be delivered to the United States, absolutely and unconditionally, without the precedent payment of expenses.

In that part of the case brought up by appeal, it is insisted on behalf of the United States, that so much of the decree of the Circuit Court "as relates to the apportionment among the several parties of the costs and expenses in the preservation, maintenance, and custody of the Africans, and the costs and expenses of the various proceedings which have been had in relation to said Africans," is erroneous. It is contended, that these costs and expenses were occasioned by the prosecution of a groundless claim by the Portuguese and Spanish claimants, and that they should have been decreed to pay them.

It may well be doubted whether these questions are now open to discussion. By a former order and decree of the Circuit Court, made before the former appeals, the ordinary costs and charges were regulated, and they were paid accordingly; that order is not now before this Court in this appeal. By the former decree of the Circuit Court, rendered before the former appeals, a principle was established as to the ratio in which the Spanish and Portuguese claimants should be chargeable with the expenses of maintenance, &c. The principle was, that they should be charged in the ratio of the number of Africans to be delivered to them respectively.

There was no appeal from that part of the former decree of the Circuit Court; or if there was, it was virtually affirmed by the former decree of this Court.

In the application of the principle to the case as it now stands, it seems to follow, necessarily, that as none of the Africans are to be delivered to the Portuguese claimant, he should pay none of the expenses of keeping them; and that the Spaniard should pay in the ratio of thirty-nine, the number to be delivered to him. The condition of the Portuguese consul, too, is very peculiar. Under the circumstances in which these Africans were captured, and brought into the United States, it was his duty to interpose a claim for part of them, on behalf of the subjects of his majesty the King of Portugal. That claim was sustained in the District and Circuit Courts, and the general propriety of the claim was also recognised by the former decree of this Court, but as no individual Portuguese claimant of the property appeared before the hearing of the appeal, the claim of the Vice Consul of Portugal was dismissed on that ground. It would be too much to visit him with the extraordinary expenses under such circumstances, and he has heretofore paid his proportion of the ordinary expenses of the suit.

We think there is no just ground of complaint on the part of the United States, that the Spanish claimants have not been burdened with more than a rateable proportion of the expense of keeping the Africans.

It only remains to be inquired, whether the Circuit Court erred in directing thirty-nine of the Africans to be delivered to the Spanish claimants.

It has been argued, that there is no credible and competent evidence to identify them, or any of them.

We are not of that opinion. We think, that under the peculiar and special circumstances of the case, the evidence of identity is competent, credible, and reasonably satisfactory, to identify the whole thirty-nine.

It ought not to be forgotten, that in the original cause it had been established to the satisfaction of this Court, that ninety-three of the Africans brought in with the Antelope, were the property of the Spanish claimants; but, as many of the Africans had died, it was the opinion of this Court, that number should be reduced according to the whole number living. The Circuit Court, proceeding upon this principle, fixed the whole number to which the Spanish claimants were entitled at fifty, and then proceeded to inquire as to their identity.

Grondona, who had been examined as a witness in the original cause, was second officer on board the Antelope when the Spanish Africans were purchased, and put on board the Antelope, on the coast of Africa.

It appears, that the Africans captured, and brought in with the Antelope, were put into the possession of Mr. William Richardson; and that he had about fifty of them employed at work upon the fortifications at Savannah; that while there, Grondona came out with the marshal for the purpose of identifying the Spanish Africans; that the fifty Africans were drawn up in a line; that Grondona made signs, and spoke to the negroes, and they to him, and they generally appeared to recognise him as an acquaintance. On cross-examination, he says, he cannot say that every one of the negroes recognised the sign made by the person accompanying the marshal to the fortifications, but that they generally did.

The Africans of the Antelope being paraded in front of the court house, Mr. Richardson was directed by the Court to point out, and designate, individually, the Africans who had worked on the fortifications, and he designated thirty-four. It is proved by Mr. Morel, the marshal, that Grondona recognised five others, who were with other persons, and that they appeared to recognise Grondona as an acquaintance. These five are described by name, and pointed out by other witnesses.

Before these proofs were taken in open Court, for the purpose of identifying the Africans claimed by the Spaniards, Grondona had disappeared, and it is suggested was dead. He had, however, in his examination as a witness in chief in the cause, shown, that he was an officer on board, and knew the Africans belonging to the Spanish claimants. Grondona, and the Africans, both spoke languages not understood by the witnesses; yet it could well be seen by them that Grondona and the Africans knew and understood each other; and Mr. Richardson swears, that many of them appeared to know him very well, and that he claimed them as part of the Africans originally put on board the Antelope by the Spanish owners.

We think this evidence was sufficient, under the very peculiar circumstances of this case, reasonably to satisfy the mind of the identity of thirty-nine of the Africans as belonging to the Spanish claimants.

DECREE and CERTIFICATE. This cause came on, &c. On consideration whereof, this Court is of opinion, that there is no error in the decree of the Circuit Court so far as the same proceeds, and that it be AFFIRMED; and upon the question on which the judges of the Circuit Court were divided in opinion; it is the opinion of this Court, that all the Africans, not to be delivered to the Spanish claimants, ought to be decreed to be delivered to the United States, unconditionally, and without the precedent payment of expenses, to be by them disposed of according to law.

OGDEN v. SAUNDERS, 12 WHEAT. 212 (1827)

The question posed in *Ogden* v. *Saunders* was did the states have the right to enact bankruptcy laws or did such laws impair the obligation of contracts. Since the Constitution granted Congress the right to establish "uniform laws on the subject of bankruptcies throughout the limited States," did the several states have the right to enact their own bankruptcy laws pending congressional action? The 1801 and 1813 New York acts in question provided that a debtor may be discharged from all his debts, upon assigning his property to trustees for the use of his creditors. The Court had already decided in *Sturges* v. *Crowninshield,* 4 Wheat. 122 (1819), that state bankruptcy laws could apply only to debts contracted after the passage of such law. With Chief Justice Marshall and Justices Duvall and Story dissenting, the Court, speaking through Trimble, upheld the state bankruptcy enactments as not impairing the obligation of contracts in so far as the laws adhered to the principle enunciated in the *Sturges* case. Prior to 1898, Congress exercised the power to establish uniform bankruptcy laws only infrequently; 1801–1803, 1841–1843, 1867–1878. Thus, Trimble's 1827 opinion prevailed for many years.

Mr. Justice TRIMBLE. The question raised upon the record in this case, and which has been discussed at the bar, may be stated thus: Has a State, since the adoption of the constitution of the United States, authority to pass a bankrupt or insolvent law, discharging the bankrupt or insolvent from all contracts made within the State after the passage of the law, upon the bankrupt or insolvent surrendering his effects, and obtaining a certificate of discharge from the constituted authorities of the State?

The counsel for the defendant in error have endeavoured to maintain the negative of the proposition, on two grounds:

First. That the power conferred on Congress by the constitution, "to establish uniform laws on the subject of bankruptcies throughout the United States," is, in its nature, an exclusive power; that, consequently, no State has authority to pass a bankrupt law; and that the law under consideration is a bankrupt law.

Secondly. That it is a law impairing the

obligation of contracts, within the meaning of the constitution.

In the case of *Sturges* v. *Crowninshield* (4 *Wheat. Rep.* 122.) this Court expressly decided, "that since the adoption of the constitution of the United States, a State has authority to pass a bankrupt law, provided such law does not impair the obligation of contracts, within the meaning of the constitution, and provided there be no act of Congress in force to establish a uniform system of bankruptcy conflicting with such law."

This being a direct judgment of the Court, overruling the first position assumed in argument, that judgment ought to prevail, unless it be very clearly shown to be erroneous.

Not having been a member of the Court when that judgment was given, I will content myself with saying, the argument has not convinced me it is erroneous; and that, on the contrary, I think the opinion is fully sustained by a sound construction of the constitution.

There being no act of Congress in force to establish a uniform system of bankruptcy, the first ground of argument must fail.

It is argued, that the law under consideration is a law impairing the obligation of contracts within the meaning of the constitution. The 10th section of the 1st art. of the constitution is in these words: "no State shall enter into any treaty, alliance, or confederation, grant letters of marque and reprisal; coin money; emit bills of credit; make any thing but gold and silver coin a tender in payment of debts; pass any bill of attainder, *ex post facto* law, or law impairing the obligation of contracts; or grant any title of nobility."

In the case of *Sturges* v. *Crowninshield*, the defendant in the original suit had been discharged in New York, under an insolvent law of that State, which purported to apply to past as well as future contracts; and being sued on a contract made within the State prior to the passage of the law, he pleaded his certificate of discharge in bar of the action. In answer to the 3d and 4th questions, certified from the Circuit Court to this Court for its final decision, drawing in question the constitutionality of the law, and the sufficiency of the plea in bar founded upon it, this Court certified its opinion, "that the act of New-York, pleaded in this case, so far as it attempts to discharge the contract on which this suit was instituted, is a law impairing the obligation of contracts, within the meaning of the constitution of the United States; and that the plea of the defendant is not a good and sufficient bar of the plaintiff's action."

In the case of *M'Millan* v. *M'Neal* (4 *Wheat. Rep.* 209.) the defendant in the Court below pleaded a discharge obtained by him in Louisiana, on the 23d of August, 1815, under the insolvent law of that State, passed in 1808, in bar of a suit instituted against him upon a contract made in South Carolina, in the year 1813. This Court decided that the plea was no bar to the action; and affirmed the judgment given below for the plaintiff.

These cases do not decide the case at bar. In the first, the discharge was pleaded in bar to a contract made prior to the passage of the law; and in the second, the discharge obtained in one State under its laws, was pleaded to a contract made in another State. They leave the question open, whether a discharge obtained in a State, under an insolvent law of the State, is a good bar to an action brought on a contract made within the State after the passage of the law.

In presenting this inquiry, it is immaterial whether the law purports to apply to past as well as future contracts, or is wholly prospective in its provisions.

It is not the terms of the law, but its effect, that is inhibited by the constitution. A law may be in part constitutional, and in part unconstitutional. It may, when applied to a given case, produce an effect which is prohibited by the constitution; but it may not, when applied to a case differently circumstanced, produce such prohibited effect. Whether the law under consideration, in its effects and operation upon the contract sued on in this case, be a law impairing the obligation of this contract, is the only necessary inquiry.

In order to come to a just conclusion, we must ascertain, if we can, the sense in which the terms, "obligation of contracts," is used in the constitution. In attempting to do this, I will premise, that in construing an instrument of so much solemnity and importance, effect should be given, if possible, to every word. No expression should be regarded as a useless expletive; nor should it be supposed, without the most urgent necessity, that the illustrious framers of that instrument had, from ignorance or inattention, used different words, which are, in effect, merely tautologous.

I understand it to be admitted in argument, and if not admitted, it could not be reasonably contested, that, in the nature of things, there is a difference between a *contract,* and the *obligation* of the contract. The terms contract, and obligation, although sometimes used loosely as convertible terms do not properly impart the same idea. The constitution plainly presupposes that a contract and its obligation are different things. Were they the same thing, and the terms, contract and obligation convertible, the constitution, instead of being read as it now is, "that no State shall pass any law impairing the obligation of contracts," might, with the same meaning, be read, "that no State shall pass any law impairing the *obligation* of *obligations,"* or, "the contract of contracts"; and to give to the constitution the same meaning which either of these readings would import, would be ascribing to its framers a useless and palpably absurd tautology. The illustrious framers of the constitution could not be ignorant that there were, or might be, many contracts without obligation, and many obligations without contracts. "A contract is defined to be, an agreement in which a party undertakes to do, or not to do, a particular thing." *Sturges* v. *Crowninshield* (4 *Wheat. Rep.* 197.)

This definition is sufficient for all the purposes of the present investigation, and its general accuracy is not contested by either side.

From the very terms of the definition, it results incontestibly, that the contract is the sole act of the parties, and depends wholly on their will. The same words, used by the same parties, with the same objects in view, would be the same contract, whether made upon a desert island, in London, Constantinople, or New-York. It would be the *same contract,* whether the law of the place where the contract was made, recognised its validity, and furnished remedies to enforce its performance, or prohibited the contract, and withheld all remedy for its violation.

The language of the constitution plainly supposes that the *obligation* of a contract is something not wholly depending upon the will of the parties. It incontestibly supposes the obligation to be something which attaches to, and lays hold of the contract, and which, by some superior external power, regulates and controls the conduct of the parties in relation to the contract; it evidently supposes that superior external power to rest in the will of the legislature.

What, then, is the obligation of contracts, within the meaning of the constitution? From what source does that obligation arise?

The learned Chief Justice, in delivering the opinion of the Court in *Sturges* v. *Crowninshield,* after having defined a contract to be "an agreement wherein a party undertakes to do, or not to do, a particular thing," proceeds to define the obligation of the contract in these words: "the *law* binds him to perform his engagement, and *this* is, of course, the obligation of the contract."

The *Institutes,* lib. 3. tit. 4. (Cooper's translation,) says, "an obligation is the *chain of the law,* by which we are necessarily bound to make some payment, according to the law of the land."

Pothier, in his treatise concerning obligations, in speaking of the obligation of contracts, calls it *"vinculum legis,"* the chain of the law. *Paley,* p. 56. says, "to be obliged, is to be urged by a violent motive, resulting from the command of another." From these authorities, and many more might be cited, it may be fairly concluded, that the obligation of the contract consists in the *power and efficacy* of the law which applies to, and enforces performance of the contracts, or the payment of an equivalent for non-performance. The obligation does not inhere, and subsist in the contract itself, *proprio vigore,* but in the law applicable to the contract. This is the sense, I think, in which the constitution uses the term "obligation."

From what law, and how, is this obligation derived, within the meaning of the constitution? Even if it be admitted that the moral law necessarily attaches to the agreement, that would not bring it within the meaning of the constitution. Moral obligations are those arising from the admonitions of conscience and accountability to the Supreme Being. No human lawgiver can impair them. They are entirely foreign from the purposes of the constitution. The constitution evidently contemplates an obligation which might be impaired by a law of the State, if not prohibited by the constitution.

It is argued, that the obligation of contracts is founded in, and derived from, general and universal law; that, by these laws, the obligation of contracts is co-extensive with the duty of performance, and, indeed, the same thing; that the obligation is not derived from, nor depends upon, the civil or municipal laws of the State; and that this general universal duty, or obligation, is what the constitution intends to guard and protect against the unjust encroachments of State legislation. In support of this doctrine, it is said, that no State, perhaps, ever declared by statute or positive law that contracts shall be obligatory; but that all States, assuming the pre-existence of the obligation of contracts, have only superadded, by municipal law, the means of carrying the pre-existing obligation into effect.

This argument struck me, at first, with great force; but, upon reflection, I am convinced it is more specious than solid. If it were admitted, that, in an enlarged and very general sense, obligations have their foundation in natural, or what is called, in the argument, universal law; that this natural obligation is, in the general, assumed by States as pre-existing, and, upon this assumption, they have not thought it necessary to pass declaratory laws in affirmance of the principles of universal law: yet nothing favourable to the argument can result from these admissions, unless it be further admitted, or proved, that a State has no authority to regulate, alter, or in any wise control, the operation of this universal law within the State, by its own peculiar municipal enactions. This is not admitted, and, I think, cannot be proved.

I admit that men have, by the laws of nature, the right of acquiring, and possessing property, and the right of contracting engagements. I admit, that these natural rights have their correspondent natural obligations. I admit, that, in a state of nature, when men have not submitted themselves to the controlling authority of civil government, the natural obligation of contracts is co-extensive with the duty of performance. This natural obligation is founded solely in the principles of natural or universal law. What is this natural obligation? All writers who treat on the subject of obligations, agree, that it consists in the right of the one party, to demand from the other party what is due; and if it be withheld, in his right, and supposed capacity to enforce performance, or to take an equivalent for non-performance, by his own power. This natural obligation exists among sovereign and independent States and nations, and amongst men, in a State of nature, who have no common superior, and over whom none claim, or can exercise, a controlling legislative authority.

But when men form a social compact, and organize a civil government, they necessarily surrender the regulation and control of these natural rights and obligations into the hands of the government. Admitting it, then, to be true, that, in general, men derive the right of private property, and of contracting engagements, from the principles of natural, universal law; admitting that these rights are, in the general, not derived from, or created by society, but are brought into it; and that no express, declaratory, municipal law, be necessary for their creation or recognition; yet, it is equally true, that these rights, and the obligations resulting from them, are subject to be regulated, modified, and, sometimes, absolutely restrained, by the positive enactions of municipal law. I think it incontestibly true, that the *natural* obligation of *private* contracts between individuals in society, ceases, and is converted into a *civil* obligation, by the very act of surrendering the right and power of enforcing performance into the hands of the government. The right and power of enforcing performance exists, as I think all must admit, only in the law of the land, and the obligation resulting from this condition is a civil obligation.

As, in a state of nature, the natural obligation of a contract consists in the right and potential capacity of the individual to take, or enforce the delivery of the thing due to him by the contract, or its equivalent; so, in the social state, the obligation of a contract consists in the efficacy of the civil law, which attaches to the contract, and enforces its performance, or gives an equivalent in lieu of performance. From these principles it seems to result as a necessary corollary, that the obligation of a contract made within a sovereign State, must be precisely that allowed by the law of the State, and none other. I say *allowed,* because, if there be nothing in the municipal law to the contrary, the civil obligation being, by the very nature of government, substituted for, and put in the place of, natural obligation, would be co-extensive with it; but if by positive enactions, the civil obligation is regulated and modified so as that it does not correspond with the natural obligation, it is plain the extent of the obligation must depend wholly upon the municipal law. If the positive law of the State declares the contract shall have no obligation, it can have no obligation, whatever may be the principles of natural law in relation to such a contract. This doctrine has been held and maintained by all States and nations. The power of controlling, modifying, and even of taking away, all obligation from such contracts as, independent of positive enactions to the contrary, would have been obligatory, has been exercised by all independent sovereigns; and it has been universally held, that the Courts of one sovereign will, upon principles of comity and common justice, enforce contracts made within the dominions of another sovereign, so far as they were obligatory by the law of the country where made; but no instance is recollected, and none is believed to exist, where the Courts of one sovereign have held a contract, made within the dominions of another, obligatory against, or beyond the obligation assigned to it by the municipal law of its proper country. As a general proposition of law, it cannot be maintained, that the obligation of contracts depends upon, and is derived from, universal law, independent of, and against, the civil law of the State in which they are made. In relation to the States of this Union, I am persuaded, that the position that the obligation of contracts is derived from universal law, urged by the learned counsel in argument, with great force, has been stated by them much too broadly. If true, the States can have no control over contracts. If it be true that the "obligation of contracts," within the meaning of the constitution, is derived solely from general and universal law, independent of the laws of the State, then it must follow, that all contracts made in the same or similar terms, must, whenever, or wherever made, have the same obligation. If this universal natural obligation is that intended by the constitution, as it is the same, not only everywhere, but at all times, it must follow, that every description of contract which could be enforced, at any time or place, upon the principles of universal law, must, necessarily, be enforced at all other times, and in every State, upon the same principles, in despite of any positive law of the State to the contrary.

The arguments, based on the notion of the obligation of universal law, if adopted, would deprive the States of all power of legislation upon the subject of contracts, other than merely furnishing the remedies or means of carrying this obligation of universal law into effect. I cannot believe that such consequences were intended to be produced by the constitution.

I conclude, that, so far as relates to private contracts between individual and individual, it is the civil obligation of contracts; that obligation which is recognised by, and results from, the law of the State in which the contract is made, which is within the meaning of the constitution. If so, it follows, that the States have, since the adoption of the constitution, the authority to prescribe and declare, by their laws, prospectively, what shall be the obligation of all contracts made within them. Such a power seems to be almost indispensable to the very existence of the States, and is necessary to the safety and welfare of the people. The whole frame and theory of the constitution seems to favour this construction. The States were in the full enjoyment and exercise of all the powers of legislation on the subject of contracts, before the adoption of the constitution. The people of the States, in that instrument, transfer to, and vest in the Congress, no portion of this power, except in the single instance of the authority given to pass uniform laws on the subject of bankruptcies throughout the United States; to which may be added, such as results by necessary implication in carrying the granted power into effect. The whole of this power is left with the States, as the constitution found it, with the single exception, that in the exercise of their general authority they shall pass no law "impairing the obligation of contracts."

The construction insisted upon by those who maintain that prospective laws of the sort now under consideration are unconstitutional, would, as I think, transform a special limitation upon the general powers of the States, into a general restriction. It would convert, by construction, the exception into a general rule, against the best settled rules of construction. The people of the States, under every variety of change of circumstances, must remain unalterably, according to this construction, under the dominion of this supposed universal law, and the obligations resulting from it. Upon no acknowledged principle can a special exception, out of a general authority, be extended by construction so as to annihilate or embarrass the exercise of the general authority. But, to obviate the force of this view of the subject, the learned counsel admit, that the legislature of a State has authority to provide by law what contracts shall not be obligatory, and to declare that no remedy shall exist for the enforcement of such as the legislative wisdom deems injurious. They say, the obligation of a contract is coeval with its existence; that the moment an agreement is made, obligation attaches to it; and they endeavour to maintain a distinction between such laws as declare that certain contracts shall not be obligatory at all, and such as declare they shall not be obligatory, or (what is the same thing in effect) shall be discharged, upon the happening of a future event. The former, they say, were no contracts in contemplation of law, were wholly forbidden, and, therefore, never obligatory; the latter were obligatory at their creation, and that *obligation* is protected by the constitution from being impaired by any future operation of the law.

This course of reasoning is ingenious and perplexing; but I am greatly mistaken if it will not be found, upon examination, to be unsatisfactory and inconclusive. If it were admitted, that, generally, the civil obligation of a contract made in a State attaches to it when it is made, and that this obligation, whatever it be, cannot be defeated by any effect or operation of law, which does not attach to it at its creation, the admission would avail nothing. It is as well a maxim of political law, as of reason, that the whole must necessarily contain all the parts; and, consequently, a power competent to declare a contract shall have no obligation, must necessarily be competent to declare it shall have only a conditional or qualified obligation.

If, as the argument admits, a contract never had any obligation, because the pre-existing law of the State, declaring it should have none, attached to it at the moment of its creation, why will not a pre-existing law, declaring it shall have only a qualified obligation, attach to it in like manner at the moment of its creation? A law, declaring that a contract shall not be enforced, upon the happening of a future event, is a law declaring the contract shall have only a qualified or conditional obligation. If such law be passed before the contract is made, does not the same attach to it the moment it is made; and is not the obligation of the contract, whatever may be its terms, qualified from the beginning by force and operation of the existing law? If it is not, then it is absolute in despite of the law, and the obligation does not result from the law of the land, but from some other law.

The passing of a law declaring that a contract shall have *no obligation,* or shall have obligation generally, but cease to be obligatory in specified events, is but the exertion of the same power. The difference exists, not in the character of the power, but the degree of its exertion, and the manner of its operation.

In the case at bar, the contract was made in the State, and the law of the State at the time it was made, in effect, provided that the obligation of the contract should not be absolute, but qualified by the condition that the party should be discharged upon his becoming insolvent, and complying with the requisitions of the insolvent law. This qualification attached to the contract, by law, the moment the contract was made, became inseparable from it, and travelled with it through all its stages of existence, until the condition was consummated by the final certificate of discharge.

It is argued that this cannot be so, because the contract would be enforced, and must necessarily be enforced, in other States, where no such insolvent law exists. This argument is founded upon a misapprehension of the nature of the qualification itself. It is in nature of a condition subsequent, annexed by operation of law to the contract at the moment of its creation.

The condition is, that upon the happening of all the events contemplated by the law, and upon their verification, in the manner prescribed by the law itself, by the constituted authorities of the State, the contract shall not thereafter be obligatory. Unless all these take place; unless the discharge is actually obtained within the State, according to its laws, the contingency has not happened, and the contract remains obligatory, both in the State and elsewhere.

It has been often said, that the laws of a State in which a contract is made, enter into, and make part of the contract; and some who have advocated the constitutionality of prospective laws of the character now under consideration, have placed the question on that ground. The advocates of the other side, availing themselves of the infirmity of this argument, have answered triumphantly, "admitting this to be so, the constitution is the supreme law of every State, and must, therefore, upon the same principle, enter into every contract, and overrule the local laws." My answer to this view of both sides of the question is, that the argument, and the answer to it, are equally destitute of truth.

I have already shown that the contract is nothing but the agreement of the parties; and that if the parties, in making their agreement, use the same words, with the same object in view, where there is no law, or where the law recognises the agreement, and furnishes remedies for its enforcement, or where the law forbids, or withholds all remedy for the enforcement of the agreement, it is the very same contract in all these predicaments. I have endeavoured to show, and I think successfully, that the obligation of contracts, in the sense of the constitution, consists not in the contract itself, but in a superior external force, controlling the conduct of the parties in relation to the contract; and that this superior external force is the law of the State, either tacitly or expressly recognising the contract, and furnishing means whereby it may be enforced. It is this superior external force, existing potentially, or actually applied, "which binds a man to perform his engagements"; which, according to Justinian, is "the chain of the law, by which we are necessarily bound to make some payment—*according to the law of the land*"; and which, according to Paley, being "a violent motive, resulting from the command of another," obliges the party to perform his contract. The law of the State, although it constitutes the obligation of the contract, is no part of the contract itself; nor is the constitution either a part of the contract, or the supreme law of the State, in the sense in which the argument supposes. The constitution is the supreme law of the land upon all subjects upon which it speaks. It is the sovereign will of the whole people. Whatever this sovereign will enjoins, or forbids, must necessarily be supreme, and must counteract the subordinate legislative will of the United States, and of the States.

But on subjects, in relation to which the sovereign will is not declared, or fairly and necessarily implied, the constitution cannot, with any semblance of truth, be said to be the supreme law. It could not, with any semblance of truth, be said that the constitution of the United States is the supreme law of any State in relation to the solemnities requisite for conveying real estate, or the responsibilities or obligations consequent upon the use of certain words in such conveyance. The constitution contains *no law*, no declaration of the sovereign will, upon these subjects; and cannot, in the nature of things, in relation to them, be the supreme law. Even if it were true, then, that the law of a State in which a contract is made, is part of the contract, it would not be true that the constitution would be part of the contract. The constitution nowhere professes to give the law of contracts, or to declare what shall or shall not be the obligation of contracts. It evidently presupposes the existence of contracts by the act of the parties, and the existence of their obligation, not by authority of the constitution, but by authority of law; and the pre-existence of both the contracts and their obligation being thus supposed, the sovereign will is announced, that "no State shall pass any law impairing the obligation of contracts."

If it be once ascertained that a contract existed, and that an obligation, general or qualified, of whatsoever kind, had once attached, or belonged to the contract, by law, then, and not till then, does the supreme law speak, by declaring *that* obligation shall not be impaired.

It is admitted in argument, that statutes of frauds and perjuries, statutes of usury, and of limitation, are not laws impairing the obligation of contracts. They are laws operating prospectively upon contracts thereafter made. It is said, however, they do not apply, in principle, to this case; because the statutes of frauds and perjuries apply only to the remedies, and because, in that case, and under the statutes of usury, the contracts were void from the beginning, were not recognised by law as contracts, and had no obligation; and that the statutes of limitation create rules of evidence only.

Although these observations are true, they do not furnish the true reason, nor, indeed, any reason, why these laws do not impair the obligation of contracts. The true and only reason is, that they operate on contracts made after the passage of the laws, and not upon existing contracts. And hence the Chief Justice very properly remarks, of both usury laws, and laws of limitation, in delivering the opinion in *Sturges* v. *Crowninshield,* that if they should be made to operate upon contracts already entered into, they would be unconstitutional and void. If a statute of frauds and perjuries should pass in a State formerly having no such laws, purporting to operate upon existing contracts, as well as upon those made after its passage, could it be doubted, that so far as the law applied to, and operated upon, existing contracts, it would be a law "impairing the obligation of contracts?" Here, then, we have the true reason and principle of the constitution. The great principle intended to be established by the constitution, was the inviolability of the *obligation* of contracts, as the obligation existed and was recognised by the laws in force at the time the contracts were made. It furnished to the legislatures of the States a simple and obvious rule of justice, which, however theretofore violated, should, by no means, be thereafter violated; and whilst it leaves them at full liberty to legislate upon the subject of all future contracts, and assign to them either no obligation, or such qualified obligation as, in their opinion, may consist with sound policy, and the good of the people; it prohibits them from retrospecting upon existing obligations, upon any pretext whatever. Whether the law professes to apply to the contract itself, to fix a rule of evidence, a rule of interpretation, or to regulate the remedy, it is equally within the true meaning of the constitution, if it, in effect, impairs the obligation of existing contracts; and, in my opinion, is out of its true meaning, if the law is made to operate on future contracts only. I do not mean to say, that every alteration of the existing remedies would impair the obligation of contracts; but I do say, with great confidence, that a law taking away all remedy from existing contracts, would be, manifestly, a law impairing the obligation of contracts. The moral obligation would remain, but the legal, or civil obligation, would be gone, if such a law should be permitted to operate. The natural obligation would be gone, because the laws forbid the party to enforce performance by his own power. On the other hand, a great variety of instances may readily be imagined, in which the legislature of a State might alter, modify, or repeal existing remedies, and enact others in their stead without the slightest ground for a supposition that the new law impaired the obligation of contracts. If there be intermediate cases of a more doubtful character, it will be time enough to decide them when they arise.

It is argued, that as the clause declaring that "no State shall pass any law impairing the obligation of contracts," is associated in the same section of the constitution with the prohibition to "coin money, emit bills of credit," or "make any thing but gold and silver coin a legal tender in payment of debts"; and as these all evidently apply to legislation in reference to future, as well as existing contracts, and operate prospectively, to prohibit the action of the law, without regard to the time of its passage, the same construction should be given to the clause under consideration.

This argument admits of several answers. First, as regards the prohibition to coin money, and emit bills of credit. The constitution had already conferred on Congress the whole power of coining money, and regulating the current coin. The grant of this power to Congress, and the prohibitions upon the States, evidently take away from the States all power of legislation and action on the subject, and must, of course, apply to the future action of laws, either then made, or to be made. Indeed, the language plainly indicates, that it is the *act* of "coining money," and the *act* of emitting bills of credit, which is forbidden, without any reference to the time of passing the law, whether before or after the adoption of the constitution. The other prohibition, to "make any thing but gold or silver coin a tender in payment of debts," is but a member of the same subject of currency committed to the general government, and prohibited to the States. And the same remark applies to it already made as to the other two. The prohibition is not, that no State shall *pass* any law; but that even if a law does exist, the "State shall not make any thing but gold and silver coin a legal tender." The language plainly imports, that the prohibited tender shall not be made a *legal* tender, whether a law of the State exists or not. The whole subject of tender, except in gold and silver, is withdrawn from the States. These cases cannot, therefore, furnish a sound rule of interpretation for that clause which prohibits the States from *passing* laws "impairing the obligation of contracts." This clause relates to a subject confessedly left wholly with the States, with a single exception; they relate to subjects wholly withdrawn from the States, with the exception that they may pass laws on the subject of tender in gold and silver coin only.

The principle, that the association of one clause with another of like kind, may aid in its construction, is deemed sound; but I think it has been misapplied in the argument. The principle applied to the immediate associates of the words under consideration, is, I think, decisive of this question. The immediate associates are the prohibitions to pass bills of attainder, and *ex post facto* laws. The language and order of the whole clause is, no State shall "pass any bill of attainder, *ex post facto* law, or law impairing the obligation of contracts." If the maxim *noscitur a sociis,* be applied to this case, there would seem to be an end of the question. The two former members of the clause undeniably prohibit retroactive legislation upon the existing state of things, at the passage of the prohibited laws. The associated idea is, that the latter member of the same clause should have a similar effect upon the subject matter to which it relates. I suppose this was the understanding of the American people when they adopted the constitution. I am justified in this supposition by the contemporary construction given to the whole of this clause by that justly celebrated work, styled the Federalist, written at the time, for the purpose of recommending the constitution to the favour and acceptance of the people. In No. 44. (p. 281.) commenting upon this very clause, and all its members, the following observations are made: "Bills of attainder, *ex post facto* laws, and laws impairing the obligation of contracts, are contrary to the first principles of the social compact, and to every principle of sound legislation. The two former are expressly prohibited by the declarations prefixed to some of the State constitutions, and all of them are prohibited by the spirit and scope of these fundamental charters."

Did the American people believe, could they believe, these heavy denunciations were levelled against laws which fairly prescribed, and plainly pointed out, to the people, rules for their *future* conduct; and the rights, duties and obligations, growing out of their future words or actions? They must have understood, that these denunciations were just, as regarded bills of attainder, and *ex post facto* laws, because they were exercises of arbitrary power, perverting the justice and order of existing things by the reflex action of these laws. And would they not naturally and necessarily conclude, the denunciations were equally just as regarded laws passed to impair the obligation of existing contracts, for the same reason?

The writer proceeds: "Our own experience has taught us, nevertheless, that additional fences against these dangers ought not to be omitted. Very properly, therefore, have the Convention added this constitutional bulwark in favour of personal security and private rights; and I am much deceived, if they have not, in so doing, as faithfully consulted the genuine sentiments, as the undoubted interests of their constituents. The sober people of America are weary of the fluctuating policy which has directed the public councils. They have seen with regret, and with indignation, that sudden changes, and legislative interferences, in cases affecting personal rights, become jobs in the hands of enterprising and influential speculators; and snares to the more industrious and less informed part of the community. They have seen, too, that one legislative interference is but the link of a long chain of repetitions; every subsequent interference being naturally produced by the effects of the preceding. They very rightly infer, therefore, that some thorough reform is wanting, which will banish speculations on public measures, inspire a general prudence and industry, and give a regular course to the business of society."

I cannot understand this language otherwise than as putting bills of attainder, *ex post facto* laws, and laws impairing the obligation of contracts, all upon the same footing, and deprecating them all for the same cause. The language shows, clearly, that the whole clause was understood at the time of the adoption of the constitution to have been introduced into the instrument in the very same spirit, and for the very same purpose, namely, for the protection of personal security and of private rights. The language repels the idea, that the member of the clause immediately under consideration was introduced into the constitution upon any grand principle of national policy, independent of the protection of private rights, so far as such an idea can be repelled, by the total omission to suggest any such independent grand principle of national policy, and by placing it upon totally different ground.

It proves that the sages who formed and recommended the constitution to the favour and adoption of the American people, did not consider the protection of private *rights,* more than the protection of personal security, as too insignificant for their serious regard, as was urged with great earnestness in argument. In my judgment, the language of the authors of the Federalist proves that they, at least, understood, that the protection of personal security, and of private rights, from the despotic and iniquitous operation of retrospective legislation, was, itself, and alone, the grand principle intended to be established. It was a principle of the utmost importance to a free people, about to establish a national government, "to establish justice," and, "to secure to themselves and their posterity the blessings of liberty." This principle is, I think, fully and completely sustained by the construction of the constitution which I have endeavoured to maintain.

In my judgment, the most natural and obvious import of the words themselves, prohibiting the passing of laws "impairing the obligation of contracts;" the natural association of that member of the clause with the two immediately preceding members of the same clause, forbidding the passing of "bills of attainder," and "*ex post facto* laws"; the consecutive order of the several members of the clause; the manifest purposes and objects for which the whole clause was introduced into the constitution, and the contemporary exposition of the whole clause, all warrant the conclusion, that a State has authority, since the adoption of the constitution, to pass a law, whereby a contract made within the State, after the passage of the law, may be discharged, upon the party obtaining a certificate of discharge, as an insolvent, in the manner prescribed by the law of the State.

John McLean

☆ 1785–1861 ☆

APPOINTED BY

ANDREW JACKSON

YEARS ON COURT

1829–1861

John McLean

by

FRANK OTTO GATELL

THE BELIEF THAT service on the Supreme Court should be divorced from active involvement in the political process is one of America's engaging fictions. It gains little support from the career of John McLean. The future "Politician on the Supreme Court" was born in the northern part of New Jersey on March 11, 1785. His father Fergus McLean (originally McLain) was an Ulsterman who came to New Jersey in 1775 and fitted the Scotch-Irish stereotype in several ways: he was a weaver by trade, and, of course, he was a Presbyterian. In America he married Sophia Blackford of Middlesex County, New Jersey. Later the family made the great move westward, and, after several stopovers in western Virginia and Kentucky, they settled in Warren County, Ohio, on a farm about forty miles from Cincinnati. That was in 1797, and despite the frontier environment of early nineteenth century Ohio, John was able to obtain a fair amount of schooling. At first he attended the neighborhood Warren County school, and later, with money earned working as a farmhand for neighbors, he studied with two schoolmasters who were also Presbyterian ministers.

In 1804, McLean began to study law. He began a two-year apprenticeship with John S. Gano, a prominent Cincinnati lawyer who was also clerk of the Hamilton County Court of Common Pleas. Through work in Gano's office, McLean learned about the law in practice; through concurrent study in the office of Arthur St. Clair, Jr., he learned about the law in theory.

Upon the completion of the apprenticeship, McLean embarked upon a new career which almost took him out of the legal profession. He purchased a printing office in Lebanon, Ohio, shortly after marrying Rebecca Edwards of Newport, Kentucky. The marriage was probably the chief factor in his decision to

FRANK O. GATELL, Professor of History at the University of California, Los Angeles, is the author of John Gorham Palfrey and the New England Conscience.

enter private business at that time. Within a year, McLean began issuing a newspaper, the Lebanon *Western Star,* and this and a part-time law practice provided him his living. The editorship also propelled him into politics. Very few newspapers of the day were "independent" of politics, and even those that were usually had some issue or commitment to sustain. McLean's paper was of the political-weekly, garden variety. He supported the Jeffersonian party, and in 1810 he was able to turn the printshop over to a brother, Nathaniel, and concentrate exclusively on his law practice while working at the county clerk's office. A year later, his political activities brought him an appointment as examiner of the U.S. Land Office at Cincinnati.

At this time McLean underwent a significant religious conversion. Despite his Presbyterian family background and schooling, he had remained a skeptical young man. But in 1811, an evangelist named John Collins arrived at Lebanon. Collins was an effective Methodist circuit rider. Among many others, he converted McLean and his brother to the Wesleyan faith. Unlike many such quick conversions which later prove temporary, McLean never wavered in his newfound beliefs. From his conversion to his death, McLean remained a devout Methodist, and after his political and judicial rise it would be fair to say that he became the leading Methodist layman in the country. He was active in church affairs and later wrote a series of articles on the Bible for church magazines. In 1849, he was named honorary president of the American Sunday School Union.

McLean had been rising steadily in the southern Ohio community, and in 1812, at age twenty-seven, he won election to the U.S. House of Representatives. Thus he just missed membership in the famed War Hawk Congress of 1811–1812. The first meeting of the Thirteenth Congress was an extra session in the summer of 1813. McLean supported the administration's war measures, on one occasion noting that more than one nation in ancient history had been destroyed because of internal discord. He called for national unity to save the Republic, at a time when opposition to the war was mounting and spreading even beyond the political opposition. McLean was a western hawk, who aggressively supported the Madison administration, and in 1814 he won reelection and soon became chairman of the House committee on accounts. In that capacity he consistently backed finance bills made necessary by the war, such as the retention of the wartime direct tax and appropriations for the speedy rebuilding of public buildings in Washington which the British had burned. During the session of 1815, he also fought for a change in the handling of private pension claims in a way which demonstrated his awareness of the realities of egalitarian politics. When the Compensation Bill came up he pressed for compensation based on loss incurred rather than rank, which had previously been used as the standard.

McLean's support for the war did not mean complete commitment to nationalist measures, however. His votes on bills to charter a second Bank of the United States demonstrate this. Although he voted in favor of resolutions calling for the reestablishment of a national institution in 1814 and for the bank bill of the following year, in 1816 he opposed the measure that did in fact create the Second National Bank. His objections were along orthodox Jeffersonian lines, but had more to do with the details of funding the bank than with constitutional scruples. He did not think that holders of depreciated government securities should be allowed to use that paper to purchase B.U.S. stock at par. The incident showed that although McLean believed in certain general principles of government and constitutionalism, his final decisions on measures could not automatically be deduced from those principles.

One of McLean's last acts in Congress came during the Republican congressional caucus of 1816. He worked hard for the nomination of James Monroe, and this would later have an important effect on McLean's career when Monroe, as President, remembered the friends who acted on his behalf.

In 1816, both the limited financial attractiveness of congressional service and the desire to be closer to his growing family caused McLean to resign his seat. His strong support for the administration earned him the confidence of the Republican leaders in Ohio, and the legislature elected him a judge of the state supreme court.

McLean was to serve on the state court for six years, and he was one of four members. The Ohio Supreme Court was chiefly, though not exclusively, an appeals court. Under it were the courts of common pleas, and the high court had original jurisdiction in cases involving large sums of money, or capital offenses. It was a hard-working but underpaid court, holding meetings once a year in each county. To cover the court's work the state was divided into two parts, and a pair of judges constituted a quorum in the counties nearest their residences. Thus the supreme court judges spent much time on circuit, and McLean regretted "that, from the peculiar organization of our court, every question, however important, must be viewed with haste, and often decided without much reflection." Attempts to achieve a fair and geographically convenient distribution of circuit assignments took up a good deal of the judges' time and the problem was never fully resolved. These conditions and a salary of $1,000 a year did not make a seat on the Ohio Supreme Court one of the legal-political plums of the early nineteenth-century America.

In the second year on the bench, McLean read an opinion of significance as a portent of his stand forty years later in *Dred Scott*. A Negro named Lunsford had applied for a writ of *habeas corpus*. As a Kentucky slave, Lunsford had been mortgaged and sold to a Cincinnati resident who had Lunsford work in Cincinnati by day, but cross the river to slavery each night. McLean decided that Lunsford should be discharged from the defendant's custody since the previous sale ended his legal control over the Negro. That point settled, the opinion need not have continued. "It is not strictly necessary that an opinion on any other point should be suggested," admitted McLean, "but as there is much solicitude on another point by the citizens of Kentucky, who live adjacent to our state, it may not be improper to give some intimation of my present impressions on the subject." He continued that in the abstract he would incline toward granting freedom to all slaves "according to the immutable principles of natural justice." But as a judge his opinions could not become only reflections of personal opinion. Although he would not say that any slave introduced into free territory by his master was automatically free, he did contend that if a master used slave labor in a free state, "by such act he forfeits the right of property in slaves."

The lobbying during the congressional caucus of 1816 bore fruit in 1822 when President Monroe appointed McLean to the office of Commissioner of the General Land Office. Not only did this treble his salary, but it brought him back to Washington. His ambitions to return to the capital were probably heightened by his unsuccessful candidacy for U.S. senator in 1822 when the legislature chose Ethan A. Brown, a former colleague on the state supreme court. The Land Office, like land sales, was booming, and McLean had his first extended experience with the scramble for clerkships, a degrading but inescapable aspect of pre–civil service-reform politics which became even more acute the next year when McLean moved on to a higher post.

In 1823, Monroe appointed McLean Postmaster General. In this office McLean proved an extremely energetic administrator. He expanded the postal service significantly, greatly increasing the number of routes and deliveries. Within two years he had established as many new post offices as had been in existence twenty years before. Of course, this was a reflection of the nation's tremendous growth in this period, as Americans spilled over the Appalachian mountains in great numbers, but it should be noted that McLean, a westerner himself, responded to the needs and opportunities and helped close the gap in postal service which had existed before he took office. McLean did not let his office "run itself." He worked hard, and maintained a frequent correspondence with first-class postmasters and those lower in the department scale in an effort to improve service. By 1828, the department employed nearly 27,000 persons, making it the largest section of the executive branch. And the expansion came about with an increase in the amount of revenue collected; in one report McLean made the happy but premature prediction that the Post Office might some day be able to support itself on revenues collected alone. McLean did his job well. In the opinion of President John Quincy Adams, McLean was an "able and efficient worker," probably the most efficient Postmaster General to serve up to that time. This may help account for the decision that the Postmaster General, then occupying a sub-Cabinet status, be paid the same salary as Cabinet members and prepared the way for his elevation to full Cabinet rank.

Even before this, the Postmaster General was the "Cabinet politician." He made an average of five to ten appointments daily and apportioned large sums of money to postmasters and postal contractors. McLean established as policy regarding removals of postmasters the rule that no dismissal would occur without substantial cause and only after the postmaster in question had had ample time to answer charges made against him. McLean knew that a hasty removal would terminate public confidence in the man involved, and he sought to maintain respect for his officers, as much for postmasters as for other federal workers.

This rationalization of a very touchy aspect of department business worked well. The postmasters knew where they stood, and McLean established a good rapport with his subordinates.

The administrator also played the game of politics, but outside of his department. Originally, McLean supported John C. Calhoun for the Presidency in 1824. Calhoun had helped obtain McLean's appointment, but when the South Carolinian settled for the vice-presidency, McLean directed his loyalty toward Adams. The latter had retained him as Postmaster General, though McLean's influence was not so great as it had been under Monroe. For one thing, Adams' second in command was Henry Clay, a westerner McLean did not care for. When national politics reduced itself by 1828 to Adams versus Jackson, McLean straddled adroitly. He cultivated many of the Jacksonians and at the same time gave the Adams administration no cause to dump him. Clay urged such a punitive course on the President, but Adams, though believing McLean a double-dealer, could find no specific act to justify dismissal. McLean had parried requests that he use the federal patronage at his disposal for more openly partisan purposes. In an exchange of letters with Edward Everett, he took the lofty ground of public good overriding political expediency. Such action did not endear him to the Adams' men, but his solid position with several pro-Adams senators from the West, and his reputed influence among Methodist voters, also meant that another branch of political expediency dictated McLean's survival in an administration he did little to aid.

When Jackson became President in 1829, McLean also came in for a promotion. Robert Trimble of Kentucky had died in September, 1828, and John Quincy Adams had offered the vacant seat to Charles Hammond of Ohio and then to Henry Clay, both of whom declined. John Crittenden's name was then submitted to the Senate which was controlled by the Democrats which then decided to wait until Jackson was inaugurated. McLean's ostensibly nonpolitical game worked, but, motives aside, it was nevertheless a "good and satisfactory appointment." McLean's biographer saw the nomination in broader terms: it came in response to his personal popularity, administrative skill, political adroitness, and geographical considerations. Whatever the reasons, McLean accepted, and started a term on the bench which would last thirty-one years.

Despite the new duties, McLean did not abandon hopes for the ultimate political prize. Initially, Jackson was supposed to have served but one term, and McLean's name figured prominently in early speculating concerning the election of 1832. But these expectations did not prove well-founded. For one thing, McLean's judicial status did not allow him to pursue his political goal with that combination of coquettishness and desire which marks our prenomination charades. And for another, McLean began to lose the little favor he had with Jackson. McLean was one of the Washington figures who cut Mrs. Peggy Eaton socially, much to Jackson's disgust. On more substantial grounds, McLean favored nationally supported internal improvements and a protective tariff—two major ingredients of the Adams-Clay American System. On the Bench, McLean's reactions to the Georgia Indian cases did not sit well with the President who was totally unsympathetic to their claims. In *Cherokee Nation* v. *Georgia,* 5 Pet. 1 (1831), an action to enjoin Georgia from enforcing its laws within the Cherokee nation, McLean concurred in Marshall's opinion that although the Indians' complaint was a valid one, as a domestic, dependent nation they could not sue in the federal courts. But a year later in *Worcester* v. *Georgia,* 6 Pet. 515 (1832), Marshall ruled that the Cherokee nation was entirely out of the jurisdiction of Georgia law and the state had no power to pass laws affecting the Cherokees or their territories. McLean concurred and this time expressed himself in strongly nationalistic terms. McLean stated that the Georgians had undoubtedly acted under the conviction of doing right, and that the federal government had been too dilatory in implementing its removal policy, enunciated thirty years before. But on the questions of jurisdiction and national power, nothing remained in doubt. National power must be effective: "It is vain, and worse than vain, that the national legislature enact laws, if those laws are to remain on the statute book as monuments of the imbecility of the national power. . . . No one can deny that the Constitution of the United States is the supreme law of the land; and consequently, no act of any state legislature, or of Congress, which is repugnant to it, can be of any validity."

Such sentiments did not mean that McLean had no respect for local power, however. In two cases in the 1830's he upheld the rights of local interests as opposed to the constitutional prohibition against a state's issuance of bills of credit. In *Craig* v. *Missouri,* 4 Pet. 40 (1830), McLean dissented, despite Chief Justice Marshall's majority opinion that certain certificates issued by the state of Missouri were bills of credit. Since the state had not enforced the circulation of the certificates, and its object was to relieve the distress caused by several bank failures, McLean felt that where doubt existed (and McLean harbored such doubts as to the applicability of the constitutional prohibition) the judgment of state courts and all branches of the state government should be accepted. Separation of state and national powers was very difficult; "like the colors of the rainbow, they seem to intermix, so as to render a separation extremely difficult." But each had to exercise great forbearance.

Some of this forbearance came through seven years later in *Briscoe* v. *Commonwealth Bank of Kentucky,* 11 Pet. 257 (1837). The legality of state bank notes hung in the balance here, an issue of the utmost importance since they then comprised the bulk of the country's circulating medium. Were these notes the prohibited "bills of credit"? McLean, speaking for the Court, said they were not; that a bill of credit must be issued by a state on the credit of the state. Thus such notes issued by the bank, operating on its own capital, did not fall under the category of bills of credit. The state may have been the sole stockholder, but it exercised no special powers in that capacity. McLean in this decade was conscientiously seeking a working compromise between the state and federal power. Failure to find one would lead to a "most injurious conflict of jurisdiction."

McLean decided a crucial case in the field of copyright which is still a fundamental part of that area of the law, *Wheaton* v. *Peters,* 8 Pet. 591 (1834). Henry Wheaton was the official reporter of the Supreme Court from 1816 to 1827. He claimed copyright on his reports and his title was eventually conveyed to one Robert Donaldson. Richard Peters, Wheaton's successor as reporter, published a condensed version of Wheaton's cases. Wheaton sued, claiming infringement of his rights, primarily under the common law, since it appeared he had not fully complied with the Copyright Act. McLean, for the Court, followed the great English case of *Donaldson* v. *Beckett,* 4 Burr. 2408, which held that an author's common law right in his literary property disappears upon publication of his work and all his rights then derive from the copyright law itself. The common law of Pennsylvania would follow this rule, said McLean, while "there can be no common law of the United States" in this context. Thus only the copyright law was relevant. Since it was not clear whether Wheaton had complied with all the statutory requirements of notice and deposit of copies, the case was remanded to discover these facts. McLean added that there could be no copyright in the Court's opinions themselves.

Following Marshall's death in 1835, there was some speculation that McLean might be promoted to the Chief Justiceship, but Jackson was reserving that honor for a more reliable man. Two years later, Taney, the new Chief Justice, handed down his famed opinion in *Charles River Bridge* v. *Warren Bridge,* 11 Pet. 420 (1837), and McLean filed a dissent. Although he was the only Justice to hold that the Court had no jurisdiction, he opined that on the merits of the case the vested rights of the Charles River Bridge Company proprietors had been impaired. But he felt that if the national judiciary took jurisdiction, it would open Pandora's box concerning such appropriations of property for public use in every state. Massachusetts should have made adequate compensation to the owners of the original bridge, who nevertheless did not have recourse to the federal courts.

In a series of important cases dealing with the commerce clause McLean shifted to a more nationalistic position than he had adopted in his early years on the Court. Originally, in *City of New York* v. *Miln,* 11 Pet. 102 (1837), he had joined the majority upholding the state's use of the police power which was being contested as an infringement upon congressional power in regulating commerce. The New York law required ship captains to furnish data on passengers and to return impoverished or undesirable immigrants, if so ordered by the mayor. The Supreme Court agreed that this represented a reasonable exercise of the local police power and was not in violation of the commerce clause. But ten years later, McLean had moved toward declaring the federal commerce power an exclusive one, and toward a more expanded view of that power. In the *License Cases,* 5 How. 504 (1847), which involved the legality of state laws controlling the sale of liquor, McLean asserted the exclusive right of Congress to regulate interstate commerce, although at the same time he denied that these particular New England licensing laws came under that category. They were also legitimate uses of the police power. Two years later in the *Passenger Cases,* 7 How. 283 (1849), he did not find such legitimacy. Here the state required a payment of several dollars for each immigrant landed, the money to be used to provide medical facilities for those newcomers who needed it. McLean, and the Court majority, struck down the laws as unconstitutional since the tax on passengers entering from a foreign port constituted regulation of foreign commerce.

This view of exclusiveness emerged clearly in McLean's dissent in *Cooley* v. *Board of Wardens,* 12 How. 299 (1852). Congressional power was exclusive. Congress might adopt a state law, such as dealing with pilotage in harbors (the issue in this case), but it could not assign to states its own legislative power. Pilotage by the admission of the Court majority was part of foreign commerce, and this was enough in McLean's mind to take it out of the realm of state legislation. Allow the states to so act, and McLean feared a "race of legislation between Congress and the States, and between the States." It would invite the kind of commercial conflicts which existed before the adoption of the Constitution. McLean resisted Curtis' pragmatic response to the problem, causing Curtis to label him and Wayne, the other *Cooley* dissenter, "the most high-toned federalists on the bench."

Whether the description was accurate or not, McLean did believe in the judicial protection of property rights and, when applicable, through the use of the contract clause. The Democratic administration of his own state of Ohio had in 1851 passed a law taxing the state banks. The state supreme court upheld the law, denying that the bank charters exempted them from such taxation. Lawyers for the Piqua branch of the State Bank of Ohio appealed the case to the Supreme Court, claiming that the charter, issued under a previous state law which stipulated the amount of taxes to be levied, was a contract which could not be subsequently modified by the state. McLean agreed, *Piqua Branch of State Bank of Ohio* v. *Knoop,* 16 How. 369 (1854). He brushed aside the doctrine that the state's taxing power was not subject to federal oversight, stating that laws impairing the obligation of contract would render such intervention necessary. And in another Ohio case, involving the Ohio Life Insurance and Trust Company, *Ohio Life Insurance and Trust Co.* v. *Debolt,* 16 How. 416 (1854), McLean again tried to protect private property from what he considered to be the anti-banking prejudices of the Democratic members of the legislature. The Trust Company's charter provided that no higher taxes would be levied upon it than on the regular banks of the state. McLean thought (in dissent) that when the taxing law of 1851 passed, all the existing Ohio banks were governed by the law of 1845, and that the Trust Company by the terms of its charter must come under the tax schedule of the 1845 law and no other. Taney, on the other hand, interpreting the charter very rigidly, found for the applicability of the law of 1851.

The Dorr Rebellion in Rhode Island was one of the great political-constitutional issues of the 1840's. McLean spoke for the Court in 1844, in *Ex parte Dorr,* 3 How. 103 (1844), refusing to grant Thomas Dorr a writ of *habeas corpus.* Once a man indicted for treason was in custody of state officials, he was beyond the power of the federal courts. This decision was unanimous. In 1849 in the follow-up case, *Luther* v. *Borden,* 7 How. 1 (1849), all the Justices except Woodbury agreed that the basic question of which of the contending governments in Rhode Island was legal was a political question with which the Court would not interfere.

As already noted, McLean was a prominent Methodist layman. Sectional squabbling within his denomination produced the case of the Methodist Book Concern. When the Methodists split into northern and southern factions in 1844, the property of the Book Concern was also to be divided, but the northerners declared that no profits would be allowed the Methodist Church, South. Southern ministers brought suit, and when the case reached the circuit court in Ohio, McLean excused himself. Before the issue could reach the Supreme Court, McLean did all he could to bring about a settlement. In 1853, the Court unanimously upheld the southerner's claims, *Smith* v. *Swormstedt,* 16 How. 288 (1853). Again, McLean did not participate. Western Methodists grumbled for a while, but McLean insisted on a moderate and fair approach to these questions, devout Methodist though he was. Several years before, he had joined the Court in upholding Stephen Girard's will which established an academy and prohibited the presence of any clergy, *Vidal et al.* v. *Philadelphia,* 2 How. 127 (1844). Although those attempting to break the will argued that it represented a flagrant attack upon religion, McLean and his colleagues upheld Girard's right to so dispose of his property, although they doubtless had little sympathy with his anticlericalism.

McLean had never abandoned his presidential ambitions. He watched every political movement closely, waiting for the opportune moment, never quite seeing it, and finally convincing his would-be supporters that his timidity more than matched his ambitiousness. In the 1830's, he first hoped that a moderate Democratic candidate would be called for. There followed a lengthy and chaste flirtation with the anti-Masons, again with no result. Then he became one of the many anti–Martin Van Buren stalking horses of the mid and late 1830's. Van Buren had little trouble disposing of this and similar threats. In McLean's case, he was a poor candidate. He was personally reserved at a time when most contenders began with conviviality and built upon that advantage. His judicial station made political maneuverings a "delicate" matter. Also, during the thirties banking was the key issue, and McLean's anti-bank vote in 1816 embarrassed him among the anti-Jacksonians. So McLean continued his flirtations, went on riding the circuit, went on reading opinions in Washington, and went on dreaming.

The temporary anarchy in American national politics caused by the death of Harrison and accession of John Tyler to the presidency brought an offer of a Cabinet post. Tyler wanted him to take over the War Department, but McLean decided against it. The peacetime War Department held less attraction for him than the Supreme Court. During the 1840's he again figured prominently in preconvention speculations about presidential nominees, but the only nomination actually open to him, or at least possible, was the Free Soil nomination in 1848. McLean hedged as usual, and the Free Soilers chose Van Buren. The Whigs had intimated that if McLean ignored the Free Soilers, he would be the Whig choice four years later. McLean found that prospect pleasing, but nothing came of it.

Although McLean had rejected the offer to associate himself with the Free Soil Party, he gravitated toward the Free Soil position politically in the 1850's. There had never been any doubt that McLean was an anti-slavery man. At the start of his judicial career he had made that clear, at the same time trying to keep his opinions separate from his judicial duties. Natural justice and freedom, he felt, were one and the same, but the United States Constitution provided otherwise in some respects. By the 1850's he was less sure that they could be so compartmentalized. In 1848 he had declared in an open letter that "a slave is free when taken beyond the operation of the law which sanctions slavery. The relation of master and slave is created by law, and this relation is dissolved whenever the slave, with the consent of his master, goes beyond the operation of the law which makes him a slave. My view is that the Wilmot Proviso is already in the constitution, and must prohibit slavery, as effectually, as if it were adopted expressly."

McLean's pro-freedom bias in cases concerning Negroes in free states or territories who were allegedly slaves had already been well established by the time *Dred Scott* was decided. In the fugitive slave case, *Prigg* v. *Pennsylvania,* 16 Pet. 539 (1842), he argued that states might prevent the seizure of alleged fugitive slaves: "In a State where slavery is allowed, every colored person is presumed to be a slave; and on the same principle, in a non-slaveholding State, every person is presumed to be free, without regard to color." Yet his position was by no means doctrinaire. In *Jones* v. *Van Zandt,* 5 How. 215 (1847), McLean agreed with the majority in upholding the conviction of Van Zandt, who had broken a federal law against harboring fugitive slaves. He defended Justice Woodbury's opinion, and in fact he had presided over the conviction in circuit court. McLean would go for freedom as far as the law would permit, but he declined to accept the "higher law than the Constitution" philosophy, as argued by one of Van Zandt's appeal attorneys, William H. Seward.

The Byzantine politics of the *Dred Scott* decision are both too intricate and too well-known to require restatement. The combination of principle, expediency, and poor timing which caused the decision to emerge from the Court a few days after Buchanan's inauguration, and the opinions to range further than they might have, were a mirror of the tortured politics of the 1850's. McLean's role was, of course, crucial in that respect. The case had originally been argued in February, 1856, and discussed in conference in April. Further argument was called for in December, 1856, on the question of the Court's jurisdiction. The Justices met to discuss the case again in February, 1857, when a majority decided to dispose of the case on the narrow ground that Dred Scott's status must be determined by Missouri law. Since he would be considered a slave when he returned to that state he could not sue in the federal courts.

McLean, however, decided to go beyond the narrow jurisdictional point. In dissent, he denied that it had been sufficiently established that the Court had no jurisdiction. Citizenship derived from state citizenship, and a Negro who was a citizen of a state could sue in federal courts under diversity of citizenship. The Negro's social status was "more a matter of taste than of law." Congress, he felt, had the power to exclude slaves or free Negroes from the territories. And slaveholders might not take their chattels into a territory the same as a horse or other property, a contention made by the majority. He found many precedents for the "rule of freedom" governing the status of slaves voluntarily introduced into free territory. Both McLean and Curtis firmly asserted that a free Negro was a citizen, and on the basis of interstate comity, McLean argued that the Missouri court which had ruled against Scott should have given more weight to the constitution and laws of Illinois, his temporary place of residence. He concluded that the lower court's order should be reversed.

McLean's desire to speak out on the question of slavery in the territories certainly shaped the content of the "proslavery opinions." In response to his dissent, the five pro-slavery Justices (Taney, Catron, Wayne, Campbell, and Daniel) decided to meet the issue squarely, holding that a Negro could not be a citizen and Congress could not legislate about slavery in the territories. The result was the most serious of the "self-inflicted wounds"—in Chief Justice Hughes' words—in the Court's history.

As the political furor which followed in the wake of the *Dred Scott* decision mounted, McLean's political stock in the North rose. Anti-slavery men forgot their previous disappointments with him and hailed McLean as the champion of freedom. An Ohio newspaper declared that "the monstrous opinion of Judge Taney will be read with surprise, and the able one of Judge McLean with admiration." The praise came a year too late to influence a presidential nomination, but there was always 1860 to look forward to. Thaddeus Stevens tried to advance McLean's fortunes at the Republican Convention in Chicago, but the leading Ohio Republicans blocked the move. During the secession crisis McLean played a moderate but not an active role. He hoped that a political accommodation would be found to avoid war, but at this time his health had begun to fail. He travelled from Washington to Cincinnati in March, 1861, already ill, and died of pneumonia within a few days, on April 4, 1861.

McLean was a large man physically and a man of large ambitions, but he cannot be accounted one of the leading Justices of the Supreme Court. His tenure on the Court was long, and his work was conscientiously undertaken and completed. But he lacked the genius which has illuminated some judicial careers. Many observers intimated that his having one eye cocked toward the White House distracted him, thus preventing a full application of his powers to the legal problems at hand; and that the constant political availability reduced his effectiveness and tarnished his image both at the time and in perspective. Perhaps; but it may have been that the quality and significance of his judicial utterances would have been precisely what they were, even if he had never allowed a vision of political sugar plums to dance in his head.

SELECTED BIBLIOGRAPHY

The Library of Congress possesses a large collection of McLean manuscripts. To no one's surprise, there are a great many political letters. And McLean's replies are readily found in the collections of his political friends. (For example, to cite but one, the Elisha Whittlesey Papers, at the Western Reserve Historical Society, Cleveland, contains dozens of McLean items.) The standard biography of McLean is: Francis P. Weisenburger, *The Life of John McLean: A Politician on the United States Supreme Court* (Columbus, 1937). A new biography would be welcome, especially one which more adequately analyzed McLean's judicial career. Some letters McLean wrote to John Teasdale were printed in LVI *Bibliotheca Sacra* (Oberlin, Ohio, 1899). Other references must be sought in such monographs as those dealing with the *Dred Scott* case or with Ohio Whig and Republican political history of that day.

John McLean

REPRESENTATIVE OPINIONS

DRED SCOTT v. SANDFORD, 19 HOW. 393 (1857)

McLean's dissent in the *Dred Scott* case was perhaps the most important of all the opinions written in the case. Although the majority originally decided to dispose of the case on narrow jurisdictional grounds, McLean's dissent which focused directly on the Negro's legal status and congressional power to legislate about slavery produced a counterattack on the Court in the form of Taney's pro-slavery opinion which was supported by the other southern Justices and Justice Grier. McLean's dissent expressed the northern consensus on the slavery question and was eventually written into the Constitution by the Civil War and the Fourteenth Amendment.

Mr. Justice McLEAN dissenting.

This case is before us on a writ of error from the Circuit Court for the district of Missouri.

An action of trespass was brought, which charges the defendant with an assault and imprisonment of the plaintiff, and also of Harriet Scott, his wife, Eliza and Lizzie, his two children, on the ground that they were his slaves, which was without right on his part, and against law.

The defendant filed a plea in abatement, "that said causes of action, and each and every of them, if any such accrued to the said Dred Scott, accrued out of the jurisdiction of this court, and exclusively within the jurisdiction of the courts of the State of Missouri, for that to wit, said plaintiff, Dred Scott, is not a citizen of the State of Missouri, as alleged in his declaration, because he is a negro of African descent, his ancestors were of pure African blood, and were brought into this country and sold as negro slaves; and this the said Sandford is ready to verify; wherefore he prays judgment whether the court can or will take further cognizance of the action aforesaid."

To this a demurrer was filed, which, on argument, was sustained by the court, the plea in abatement being held insufficient; the defendant was ruled to plead over. Under this rule he pleaded: 1. Not guilty; 2. That Dred Scott was a negro slave, the property of the defendant; and 3. That Harriet, the wife, and Eliza and Lizzie, the daughters of the plaintiff, were the lawful slaves of the defendant.

Issue was joined on the first plea, and replications of *de injuria* were filed to the other pleas.

The parties, agreed to the following

facts: In the year 1834, the plaintiff was a negro slave belonging to Dr. Emerson, who was a surgeon in the army of the United States. In that year, Dr. Emerson took the plaintiff from the State of Missouri to the post of Rock Island, in the State of Illinois, and held him there as a slave until the month of April or May, 1836. At the time last mentioned, Dr. Emerson removed the plaintiff from Rock Island to the military post at Fort Snelling, situate on the west bank of the Mississippi river, in the territory known as Upper Louisiana, acquired by the United States of France, and situate north of latitude thirty-six degrees thirty minutes north, and north of the State of Missouri. Dr. Emerson held the plaintiff in slavery, at Fort Snelling, from the last-mentioned date until the year 1838.

In the year 1835, Harriet, who is named in the second count of the plaintiff's declaration, was the negro slave of Major Taliaferro, who belonged to the army of the United States. In that year, Major Taliaferro took Harriet to Fort Snelling, a military post situated as hereinbefore stated, and kept her there as a slave until the year 1836, and then sold and delivered her as a slave, at Fort Snelling, unto Dr. Emerson, who held her in slavery, at that place, until the year 1838.

In the year 1836, the plaintiff and Harriet were married at Fort Snelling, with the consent of Dr. Emerson, who claimed to be their master and owner. Eliza and Lizzie, named in the third count of the plaintiff's declaration, are the fruit of that marriage. Eliza is about fourteen years old, and was born on board the steamboat Gipsey, north of the north line of the State of Missouri, and upon the river Mississippi. Lizzie is about seven years old, and was born in the State of Missouri, at the military post called Jefferson Barracks.

In the year 1838, Dr. Emerson removed the plaintiff and said Harriet and their daughter Eliza from Fort Snelling to the State of Missouri, where they have ever since resided.

Before the commencement of the suit, Dr. Emerson sold and conveyed the plaintiff, Harriet, Eliza, and Lizzie, to the defendant, as slaves, and he has ever since claimed to hold them as slaves.

At the times mentioned in the plaintiff's declaration, the defendant, claiming to be the owner, laid his hands upon said plaintiff, Harriet, Eliza, and Lizzie, and imprisoned them; doing in this respect, however, no more than he might lawfully do, if they were of right his slaves at such times.

In the first place, the plea to the jurisdiction is not before us, on this writ of error. A demurrer to the plea was sustained, which ruled the plea bad, and the defendant, on leave, pleaded over.

The decision on the demurrer was in favor of the plaintiff; and as the plaintiff prosecutes this writ of error, he does not complain of the decision on the demurrer. The defendant might have complained of this decision, as against him, and have prosecuted a writ of error, to reverse it. But as the case, under the instruction of the court to the jury, was decided in his favor, of course he had no ground of complaint.

But it is said, if the court, on looking at the record, shall clearly perceive that the Circuit Court had no jurisdiction, it is a ground for the dismissal of the case. This may be characterized as rather a sharp practice, and one which seldom, if ever, occurs. No case was cited in the argument as authority, and not a single case precisely in point is recollected in our reports. The pleadings do not show a want of jurisdiction. This want of jurisdiction can only be ascertained by a judgment on the demurrer to the special plea. No such case, it is believed, can be cited. But if this rule of practice is to be applied in this case, and the plaintiff in error is required to answer and maintain as well the points ruled in his favor, as to show the error of those ruled against him, he has more than an ordinary duty to perform. Under such circumstances, the want of jurisdiction in the Circuit Court must be so clear as not to admit of doubt. Now, the plea which raises the question of jurisdiction, in my judgment, is radically defective. The gravamen of the plea is this: "That the plaintiff is a negro of African descent, his ancestors being of pure African blood, and were brought into this country, and sold as negro slaves."

There is no averment in this plea which shows or conduces to show an inability in the plaintiff to sue in the Circuit Court. It does not allege that the plaintiff had his domicil in any other State, nor that he is not a free man in Missouri. He is averred to have had a negro ancestry, but this does not show that he is not a citizen of Missouri, within the meaning of the act of Congress authorizing him to sue in the Circuit Court. It has never been held necessary, to constitute a citizen within the act, that he should have the qualifications of an elector. Females and minors may sue in the Federal courts, and so may any individual who has a permanent domicil in the State under whose laws his rights are protected, and to which he owes allegiance.

Being born under our Constitution and laws, no naturalization is required, as one of foreign birth, to make him a citizen. The most general and appropriate definition of the term citizen is "a freeman." Being a freeman, and having his domicil in a State different from that of the defendant, he is a citizen within the act of Congress, and the courts of the Union are open to him.

It has often been held, that the jurisdiction, as regards parties, can only be exercised between citizens of different States, and that a mere residence is not sufficient; but this has been said to distinguish a temporary from a permanent residence.

To constitute a good plea to the jurisdiction, it must negative those qualities and rights which enable an individual to sue in the Federal courts. This has not been done; and on this ground the plea was defective, and the demurrer was properly sustained. No implication can aid a plea in abatement or in bar; it must be complete in itself; the facts stated, if true, must abate or bar the right of the plaintiff to sue. This is not the character of the above plea. The facts stated, if admitted, are not inconsistent with other facts, which may be presumed, and which bring the plaintiff within the act of Congress.

The pleader has not the boldness to allege that the plaintiff is a slave, as that would assume against him the matter in controversy, and embrace the entire merits of the case in a plea to the jurisdiction. But beyond the facts set out in the plea, the court, to sustain it, must assume the plaintiff to be a slave, which is decisive on the merits. This is a short and an effectual mode of deciding the cause; but I am yet to learn that it is sanctioned by any known rule of pleading.

The defendant's counsel complain, that if the court take jurisdiction on the ground that the plaintiff is free, the assumption is against the right of the master. This argument is easily answered. In the first place, the plea does not show him to be a slave; it does not follow that a man is not free whose ancestors were slaves. The reports of the Supreme Court of Missouri show that this assumption has many exceptions; and there is no averment in the plea that the plaintiff is not within them.

By all the rules of pleading, this is a fatal defect in the plea. If there be doubt, what rule of construction has been established in the slave States? In *Jacob* v. *Sharp,* (Meigs's Rep., Tennessee, 114,) the court held, when there was doubt as to the construction of a will which emancipated a slave, "it must be construed to be subordinate to the higher and more important right of freedom."

No injustice can result to the master, from an exercise of jurisdiction in this cause. Such a decision does not in any degree affect the merits of the case; it only enables the plaintiff to assert his claims to freedom before this tribunal. If the jurisdiction be ruled against him, on the ground that he is a slave, it is decisive of his fate.

It has been argued that, if a colored person be made a citizen of a State, he cannot sue in the Federal court. The Constitution declares that Federal jurisdiction "may be exercised between citizens of different States," and the same is provided in the act of 1789. The above argument is properly met by saying that the Constitution was intended to be a practical instrument; and where its language is too plain to be misunderstood, the argument ends.

In *Chiræ* v. *Chiræ,* (2 Wheat., 261; 4 Curtis, 99,) this court says: "That the power of naturalization is exclusively in Congress does not seem to be, and certainly ought not to be, controverted." No person can legally be made a citizen of a State, and consequently a citizen of the United States, of foreign birth, unless he be naturalized under the acts of Congress. Congress has power "to establish a uniform rule of naturalization."

It is a power which belongs exclusively to Congress, as intimately connected with our Federal relations. A State may authorize foreigners to hold real estate within its jurisdiction, but it has no power to naturalize foreigners, and give them the rights of citizens. Such a right is opposed to the acts of Congress on the subject of naturalization, and subversive of the Federal powers. I regret that any countenance should be given from this bench to a practice like this in some of the States, which has no warrant in the Constitution.

In the argument, it was said that a colored citizen would not be an agreeable member of society. This is more a matter of taste than of law. Several of the States have admitted persons of color to the right of suffrage, and in this view have recognised them as citizens; and this has been done in the slave as well as the free States. On the question of citizenship, it must be admitted that we have not been very fastidious. Under the late treaty with Mexico, we have made citizens of all grades, combinations, and colors. The same was done in the admission of Louisiana and Florida. No one ever doubted, and no court ever held, that the people of these Territories did not become citizens under the treaty. They have exercised all the rights of citizens, without being naturalized under the acts of Congress.

There are several important principles involved in this case, which have been argued, and which may be considered under the following heads:

1. The locality of slavery, as settled by this court and the courts of the States.

2. The relation which the Federal Government bears to slavery in the States.

3. The power of Congress to establish Territorial Governments, and to prohibit the introduction of slavery therein.

4. The effect of taking slaves into a new State or Territory, and so holding them, where slavery is prohibited.

5. Whether the return of a slave under the control of his master, after being entitled to his freedom, reduces him to his former condition.

6. Are the decisions of the Supreme Court of Missouri, on the questions before us, binding on this court, within the rule adopted.

In the course of my judicial duties, I have had occasion to consider and decide several of the above points.

1. As to the locality of slavery. The civil law throughout the Continent of Europe, it is believed, without an exception, is, that slavery can exist only within the territory where it is established; and that, if a slave escapes, or is carried beyond such territory, his master cannot reclaim him, unless by virtue of some express stipulation. (Grotius, lib. 2, chap. 15, 5, 1; lib. 10, chap. 10, 2, 1; Wicqueposts Ambassador, lib. 1, p. 418; 4 Martin, 385; Case of the Creole in the House of Lords, 1842; 1 Phillimore on International Law, 316, 335.)

There is no nation in Europe which considers itself bound to return to his master a fugitive slave, under the civil law or the law of nations. On the contrary, the slave is held to be free where there is no treaty obligation, or compact in some other form, to return him to his master. The Roman law did not allow freedom to be sold. An ambassador or any other public functionary could not take a slave to France, Spain, or any other country of Europe, without emancipating him. A number of slaves escaped from a Florida plantation, and were received on board of ship by Admiral Cochrane; by the King's Bench, they were held to be free. (2 Barn. and Cres., 440.)

In the great and leading case of *Prigg* v. *The State of Pennsylvania,* (16 Peters, 594; 14 Curtis, 421,) this court say that, by the general law of nations, no nation is bound to recognise the state of slavery, as found within its territorial dominions, where it is in opposition to its own policy and institutions, in favor of the subjects of other nations where slavery is organized. If it does it, it is as a matter of comity, and not as a matter of international right. The state of slavery is deemed to be a mere municipal regulation, founded upon and limited to the range of the territorial laws. This was fully recognised in Somersett's case, (Lafft's Rep., 1; 20 Howell's State Trials, 79,) which was decided before the American Revolution.

There was some contrariety of opinion among the judges on certain points ruled in Prigg's case, but there was none in regard to the great principle, that slavery is limited to the range of the laws under which it is sanctioned.

No case in England appears to have been more thoroughly examined than that of Somersett. The judgment pronounced by Lord Mansfield was the judgment of the Court of King's Bench. The cause was argued at great length, and with great ability, by Hargrave and others, who stood among the most eminent counsel in England. It was held under advisement from term to term, and a due sense of its importance was felt and expressed by the Bench.

In giving the opinion of the court, Lord Mansfield said:

"The state of slavery is of such a nature that it is incapable of being introduced on any reasons, moral or political, but only by positive law, which preserves its force long after the reasons, occasion, and time itself, from whence it was created, is erased from the memory; it is of a nature that nothing can be suffered to support it but positive law."

He referred to the contrary opinion of Lord Hardwicke, in October, 1749, as Chancellor: "That he and Lord Talbot, when Attorney and Solicitor General, were of opinion that no such claim, as here presented, for freedom, was valid."

The weight of this decision is sought to be impaired, from the terms in which it was described by the exuberant imagination of Curran. The words of Lord Mansfield, in giving the opinion of the court, were such as were fit to be used by a great judge, in a most important case. It is a sufficient answer to all objections to that judgment, that it was pronounced before the Revolution, and that it was considered by this court as the highest authority. For near a century, the decision in Somersett's case has remained the law of England. The case of the slave Grace, decided by Lord Stowell in 1827, does not, as has been supposed, overrule the judgment of Lord Mansfield. Lord Stowell held that, during the residence of the slave in England, "No dominion, authority, or coercion, can be exercised over him." Under another head, I shall have occasion to examine the opinion in the case of Grace.

To the position, that slavery can only exist except under the authority of law, it is objected, that in few if in any instances has it been established by statutory enactment. This is no answer to the doctrine laid down by the court. Almost all the principles of the common law had their foundation in usage. Slavery was introduced into the colonies of this country by Great Britain at an early period of their history, and it was protected and cherished, until it became incorporated into the colonial policy. It is immaterial whether a system of slavery was introduced by express law, or otherwise, if it have the authority of law. There is no slave State where the institution is not recognised and protected by statutory enactments and judicial decisions. Slaves are made property by the laws of the slave States, and as such are liable to the claims of creditors; they descend to heirs, are taxed, and in the South they are a subject of commerce.

In the case of *Rankin* v. *Lydia,* (2 A. K. Marshall's Rep.,) Judge Mills, speaking for the Court of Appeals of Kentucky, says: "In deciding the question, (of slavery,) we disclaim the influence of the general principles of liberty, which we all admire, and conceive it ought to be decided by the law as it is, and not as it ought to be. Slavery is sanctioned by the laws of this State, and the right to hold slaves under our municipal regulations is unquestionable. But we view this as a right existing by positive law of a municipal character, without foundation in the law of nature, or the unwritten and common law."

I will now consider the relation which the Federal Government bears to slavery in the States:

Slavery is emphatically a State institution. In the ninth section of the first article of the Constitution, it is provided "that the migration or importation of such persons as any of the States now existing shall think proper to admit, shall not be prohibited by the Congress prior to the year 1808, but a tax or duty may be imposed on such importation, not exceeding ten dollars for each person."

In the Convention, it was proposed by a committee of eleven to limit the importation of slaves to the year 1800, when Mr. Pinckney moved to extend the time to the year 1808. This motion was carried—New Hampshire, Massachusetts, Connecticut, Maryland, North Carolina, South Carolina, and Georgia, voting in the affirmative; and New Jersey, Pennsylvania, and Virginia, in the negative. In opposition to the motion, Mr. Madison said: "Twenty years will produce all the mischief that can be apprehended from the liberty to import slaves; so long a term will be more dishonorable to the American character than to say nothing about it in the Constitution." (Madison Papers.)

The provision in regard to the slave trade shows clearly that Congress considered slavery a State institution, to be continued and regulated by its individual sovereignty; and to conciliate that interest, the slave trade was continued twenty years, not as a general measure, but for the "benefit of such States as shall think proper to encourage it."

In the case of *Groves* v. *Slaughter,* (15 Peters, 449; 14 Curtis, 137,) Messrs. Clay and Webster contended that, under the commercial power, Congress had a right to regulate the slave trade among the several States; but the court held that Congress had no power to interfere with slavery as it exists in the States, or to regulate what is called the slave trade among them. If this trade were subject to the commercial power, it would follow that Congress could abolish or establish slavery in every State of the Union.

The only connection which the Federal Government holds with slaves in a State, arises from that provision of the Constitution which declares that "No person held to service or labor in one State, under the laws thereof, escaping into another, shall, in consequence of any law or regulation therein, be discharged from such service or labor, but shall be delivered up, on claim of the party to whom such service or labor may be due."

This being a fundamental law of the Federal Government, it rests mainly for its execution, as has been held, on the judicial power of the Union; and so far as the rendition of fugitives from labor has become a subject of judicial action, the Federal obligation has been faithfully discharged.

In the formation of the Federal Constitution, care was taken to confer no power on the Federal Government to interfere with this institution in the States. In the provision respecting the slave trade, in fixing the ratio of representation, and providing for the reclamation of fugitives from labor, slaves were referred to as persons, and in no other respect are they considered in the Constitution.

We need not refer to the mercenary spirit which introduced the infamous traffic in slaves, to show the degradation of negro slavery in our country. This system was imposed upon our colonial settlements by the mother country, and it is due to truth to say that the commercial colonies and States were chiefly engaged in the traffic. But we know as a historical fact, that James Madison, that great and good man, a leading member in the Federal Convention, was solicitous to guard the language of that instrument so as not to convey the idea that there could be property in man.

I prefer the lights of Madison, Hamilton, and Jay, as a means of construing the Constitution in all its bearings, rather than to look behind that period, into a traffic which is now declared to be piracy, and punished with death by Christian nations. I do not like to draw the sources of our domestic relations from so dark a ground. Our independence was a great epoch in the history of freedom; and while I admit the Government was not made especially for the colored race, yet many of them were citizens of the New England States, and exercised the rights of suffrage when the Constitution was adopted, and it was not doubted by any intelligent peson that its tendencies would greatly ameliorate their condition.

Many of the States, on the adoption of the Constitution, or shortly afterward, took measures to abolish slavery within their respective jurisdictions; and it is a well-known fact that a belief was cherished by the leading men, South as well as North, that the institution of slavery would gradually decline, until it would become extinct. The increased value of slave labor, in the culture of cotton and sugar, prevented the realization of this expectation. Like all other communities and States, the South were influenced by what they considered to be their own interests.

But if we are to turn our attention to the dark ages of the world, why confine our view to colored slavery? On the same principles, white men were made slaves. All slavery has its origin in power, and is against right.

The power of Congress to establish Territorial Governments, and to prohibit the introduction of slavery therein, is the next point to be considered.

After the cession of western territory by Virginia and other States, to the United States, the public attention was directed to the best mode of disposing of it for the general benefit. While in attendance on the Federal Convention, Mr. Madison, in a letter to Edmund Randolph, dated the 22d April, 1787, says: "Congress are deliberating on the plan most eligible for disposing of the western territory not yet surveyed. Some alteration will probably be made in the ordinance on that subject." And in the same letter he says: "The inhabitants of the Illinois complain of the land jobbers, &c., who are purchasing titles among them. Those of St. Vincent's complain of the defective criminal and civil justice among them, as well as of military protection." And on the next day he writes to Mr. Jefferson: "The government of the settlements on the Illinois and Wabash is a subject very perplexing in itself, and rendered more so by our ignorance of the many circumstances on which a right judgment depends. The inhabitants at those places claim protection against the savages, and some provision for both civil and criminal justice."

In May, 1787, Mr. Edmund Randolph submitted to the Federal Convention certain propositions, as the basis of a Federal Government, among which was the following:

"Resolved, That provision ought to be made for the admission of States lawfully arising within the limits of the United States, whether from a voluntary junction of government and territory or otherwise, with the consent of a number of voices in the National Legislature less than the whole."

Afterward, Mr. Madison submitted to the Convention, in order to be referred to the committee of detail, the following powers, as proper to be added to those of general legislation:

"To dispose of the unappropriated lands of the United States. To institute temporary Governments for new States arising therein. To regulate affairs with the Indians, as well within as without the limits of the United States."

Other propositions were made in reference to the same subjects, which it would be tedious to enumerate. Mr. Gouverneur Morris proposed the following:

"The Legislature shall have power to dispose of and make all needful rules and regulations respecting the territory or other property belonging to the United States; and nothing in this Constitution contained shall be so construed as to prejudice any claims either of the United States or of any particular State."

This was adopted as a part of the Constitution, with two verbal alternations—Congress was substituted for Legislature, and the word *either* was stricken out.

In the organization of the new Government, but little revenue for a series of years was expected from commerce. The public lands were considered as the principal resource of the country for the payment of the Revolutionary debt. Direct taxation was the means relied on to pay the current expenses of the Government. The short period that occurred between the cession of western lands to the Federal Government by Virginia and other States, and the adoption of the Constitution, was sufficient to show the necessity of a proper land system and a temporary Government. This was clearly seen by propositions and remarks in the Federal Convention, some of which are above cited, by the passage of the Ordinance of 1787, and the adoption of that instrument by Congress, under the Constitution, which gave to it validity.

It will be recollected that the deed of cession of western territory was made to the United States by Virginia in 1784, and that it required the territory ceded to be laid out into States, that the land should be disposed of for the common benefit of the States, and that all right, title, and claim, as well of soil as of jurisdiction, were ceded; and this was the form of cession from other States.

On the 13th of July, the Ordinance of 1787 was passed, "for the government of the United States territory northwest of the river Ohio," with but one dissenting vote. This instrument provided there should be organized in the territory not less than three nor more than five States, designating their boundaries. It was passed while the Federal Convention was in session, about two months before the Constitution was adopted by the Convention. The members of the Convention must therefore have been well acquainted with the provisions of the Ordinance. It provided for a temporary Government, as initiatory to the formation of State Governments. Slavery was prohibited in the territory.

Can any one suppose that the eminent men of the Federal Convention could have overlooked or neglected a matter so vitally important to the country, in the organization of temporary Governments for the vast territory northwest of the river Ohio? In the 3d section of the 4th article of the Constitution, they did make provision for the admission of new States, the sale of the public lands, and the temporary Government of the territory. Without a temporary Government, new States could not have been formed, nor could the public lands have been sold.

If the third section were before us now for consideration for the first time, under the facts stated, I could not hesitate to say there was adequate legislative power given in it. The power to make all needful rules and regulations is a power to legislate. This no one will controvert, as Congress cannot make "rules and regulations," except by legislation. But it is argued that the word territory is used as synonymous with the word land; and that the rules and regulations of Congress are limited to the disposition of lands and other property belonging to the United States. That this is not the true construction of the section appears from the fact that in the first line of the section "the power to dispose of the public lands" is given expressly, and, in addition, to make all needful rules and regulations. The power to dispose of is complete in itself, and requires nothing more. It authorizes Congress to use the proper means within its discretion, and any further provision for this purpose would be a useless verbiage. As a composition, the Constitution is remarkably free from such a charge.

In the discussion of the power of Congress to govern a Territory, in the case of the *Atlantic Insurance Company* v. *Canter,* (1 Peters, 511; 7 Curtis, 685,) Chief Justice Marshall, speaking for the court, said, in regard to the people of Florida, "they do not, however, participate in political power; they do not share in the Government till Florida shall become a State; in the mean time, Florida continues to be a Territory of the United States, governed by virtue of that clause in the Constitution which empowers Congress 'to make all needful rules and regulations respecting the territory or other property belonging to the United States.' "

And he adds, "perhaps the power of governing a Territory belonging to the United States, which has not, by becoming a State, acquired the means of self-government, may result necessarily from the fact that it is not within the jurisdiction of any particular State, and is within the power and jurisdiction of the United States. The right to govern may be the inevitable consequence of the right to acquire territory; whichever may be the source whence the power is derived, the possession of it is unquestioned." And in the close of the opinion, the court say, "in legislating for them [the Territories,] Congress exercises the combined powers of the General and State Governments."

Some consider the opinion to be loose and inconclusive; others, that it is *obiter dicta;* and the last sentence is objected to as recognising absolute power in Congress over Territories. The learned and eloquent Wirt, who, in the argument of a cause before the court, had occasion to cite a few sentences from an opinion of the Chief Justice, observed, "no one can mistake the style, the words so completely match the thought."

I can see no want of precision in the language of the Chief Justice; his meaning cannot be mistaken. He states, first, the third section as giving power to Congress to govern the Territories, and two other grounds from which the power may also be implied. The objection seems to be, that the Chief Justice did not say which of the grounds stated he considered the source of the power. He did not specifically state this, but he did say, "whichever may be the source whence the power is derived, the possession of it is unquestioned." No opinion of the court could have been expressed with a stronger emphasis; the power in Congress is unquestioned. But those who have undertaken to criticise the opinion, consider it without authority, because the Chief Justice did not designate specially the power. This is a singular objection. If the power be unquestioned, it can be a matter of no importance on which ground it is exercised.

The opinion clearly was not *obiter dicta.* The turning point in the case was, whether Congress had power to authorize the Territorial Legislature of Florida to pass the law under which the Territorial court was established, whose decree was brought before this court for revision. The power of Congress, therefore, was the point in issue.

The word "territory," according to Worcester, "means land, country, a district of country under a temporary Government." The words "territory or other property," as used, do imply, from the use of the pronoun other, that territory was used as descriptive of land; but does it follow that it was not used also as descriptive of a district of country? In both of these senses it belonged to the United States—as land, for the purpose of sale; as territory, for the purpose of government.

But, if it be admitted that the word territory as used means land, and nothing but land, the power of Congress to organize a temporary Government is clear. It has power to make all needful regulations respecting the public lands, and the extent of those "needful regulations" depends upon the direction of Congress, where the means are appropriate to the end, and do not conflict with any of the prohibitions of the Constitution. If a temporary Government be deemed needful, necessary, requisite, or is wanted, Congress has power to establish it. This court says, in *McCulloch* v. *The State of Maryland,* (4 Wheat., 316,) "If a certain means to carry into effect any of the powers expressly given by the Constitution to the Government of the Union be an appropriate measure, not prohibited by the Constitution, the degree of its necessity is a question of legislative discretion, not of judicial cognizance."

The power to establish post offices and post roads gives power to Congress to make contracts for the transportation of the mail, and to punish all who commit depredations upon it in its transit, or at its places of distribution. Congress has power to regulate commerce, and, in the exercise of its discretion, to lay an embargo, which suspends commerce; so, under the same power, harbors, lighthouses, breakwaters, &c., are constructed.

Did Chief Justice Marshall, in saying that Congress governed a Territory, by exercising the combined powers of the Federal and State Governments, refer to unlimited discretion? A Government which can make white men slaves? Surely, such a remark in the argument must have been inadvertently uttered. On the contrary, there is no power in the Constitution by which Congress can make either white or black men slaves. In organizing the Government of a Territory, Congress is limited to means appropriate to the attainment of the constitutional object. No powers can be exercised which are prohibited by the Constitution, or which are contrary to its spirit; so that, whether the object may be the protection of the persons and property of purchasers of the public lands, or of communities who have been annexed to the Union by conquest or purchase, they are initiatory to the establishment of State Governments, and no more power can be claimed or exercised than is necessary to the attainment of the end. This is the limitation of all the Federal powers.

But Congress has no power to regulate the internal concerns of a State, as of a Territory; consequently, in providing for the Government of a Territory, to some extent, the combined powers of the Federal and State Governments are necessarily exercised.

If Congress should deem slaves or free colored persons injurious to the population of a free Territory, as conducing to lessen the value of the public lands, or on any other ground connected with the public interest, they have the power to prohibit them from becoming settlers in it. This can be sustained on the ground of a sound national policy, which is so clearly shown in our history by practical results, that it would seem no considerate individual can question it. And, as regards any unfairness of such a policy to our Southern brethren, as urged in the argument, it is only necessary to say that, with one-fourth of the Federal population of the Union, they have in the slave States a larger extent of fertile territory than is included in the free States; and it is submitted, if masters of slaves be restricted from bringing them into free territory, that the restriction on the free citizens of non-slaveholding States, by bringing slaves into free territory, is four times greater than that complained of by the South. But, not only so; some three or four hundred thousand holders of slaves, by bringing them into free territory, impose a restriction on twenty millions of the free States. The repugnancy to slavery would probably prevent fifty or a hundred freemen from settling in a slave Territory, where one slaveholder would be prevented from settling in a free Territory.

This remark is made in answer to the argument urged, that a prohibition of slavery in the free Territories is inconsistent with the continuance of the Union. Where a Territorial Government is established in a slave Territory, it has uniformly remained in that condition until the people form a State Constitution; the same course where the Territory is free, both parties acting in good faith, would be attended with satisfactory results.

The sovereignty of the Federal Government extends to the entire limits of our territory. Should any foreign power invade our jurisdiction, it would be repelled. There is a law of Congress to punish our citizens for crimes committed in districts of country where there is no organized Government. Criminals are brought to certain Territories or States, designated in the law, for punishment. Death has been inflicted in Arkansas and in Missouri, on individuals, for murders committed beyond the limit of any organized Territory or State; and no one doubts that such a jurisdiction was rightfully exercised. If there be a right to acquire territory, there necessarily must be an implied power to govern it. When the military force of the Union shall conquer a country, may not Congress provide for the government of such country? This would be an implied power essential to the acquisition of new territory. This power has been exercised, without doubt of its constitutionality, over territory acquired by conquest and purchase.

And when there is a large district of country within the United States, and not within any State Government, if it be necessary to establish a temporary Government to carry out a power expressly vested in Congress—as the disposition of the public lands—may not such Government be instituted by Congress? How do we read the Constitution? Is it not a practical instrument?

In such cases, no implication of a power can arise which is inhibited by the Constitution, or which may be against the theory of its construction. As my opinion rests on the third section, these remarks are made as an intimation that the power to establish a temporary Government may arise, also, on the other two grounds stated in the opinion of the court in the insurance case, without weakening the third section.

I would here simply remark, that the Constitution was formed for our whole country. An expansion or contraction of our territory required no change in the fundamental law. When we consider the men who laid the foundation of our Government and carried it into operation, the men who occupied the bench, who filled the halls of legislation and the Chief Magistracy, it would seem, if any question could be settled clear of all doubt, it was the power of Congress to establish Territorial Governments. Slavery was prohibited in the entire Northwestern Territory, with the approbation of leading men, South and North; but this prohibition was not retained when this ordinance was adopted for the government of Southern Territories, where slavery existed. In a late republication of a letter of Mr. Madison, dated November 27, 1819, speaking of this power of Congress to prohibit slavery in a Territory, he infers there is no such power, from the fact that it has not been exercised. This is not a very satisfactory argument against any power, as there are but few, if any, subjects on which the constitutional powers of Congress are exhausted. It is true, as Mr. Madison states, that Congress, in the act to establish a Government in the Mississippi Territory, prohibited the importation of slaves into it from foreign parts; but it is equally true, that in the act erecting Louisiana into two Territories, Congress declared, "it shall not be lawful for any person to bring into Orleans Territory, from any port or place within the limits of the United States, any slave which shall have been imported since 1798, or which may hereafter be imported, except by a citizen of the United States who settles in the Territory, under the penalty of the freedom of such slave." The inference of Mr. Madison, therefore, against the power of Congress, is of no force, as it was founded on a fact supposed, which did not exist.

It is refreshing to turn to the early incidents of our history, and learn wisdom from the acts of the great men who have gone to their account. I refer to a report in the House of Representatives, by John Randolph, of Roanoke, as chairman of a committee, in March, 1803—fifty-four years ago. From the Convention held at Vincennes, in Indiana, by their President, and from the people of the Territory, a petition was presented to Congress, praying the suspension of the provision which prohibited slavery in that Territory. The report stated "that the rapid population of the State of Ohio sufficiently evinces, in the opinion of your committee, that the labor of slaves is not necessary to promote the growth and settlement of colonies in that region. That this labor, demonstrably the dearest of any, can only be employed to advantage in the cultivation of products more valuable than any known to that quarter of the United States; that the committee deem it highly dangerous and inexpedient to impair a provision wisely calculated to promote the happiness and prosperity of the Northwestern country, and to give strength and security to that extensive frontier. In the salutary operation of this sagacious and benevolent restraint, it is believed that the inhabitants will, at no very distant day, find ample remuneration for a temporary privation of labor and of emigration." (1 vol. State Papers, Public Lands, 160.)

The judicial mind of this country, State and Federal, has agreed on no subject, within its legitimate action, with equal unanimity, as on the power of Congress to establish Territorial Governments. No court, State or Federal, no judge or statesman, is known to have had any doubts on this question for nearly sixty years after the power was exercised. Such Governments have been established from the sources of the Ohio to the Gulf of Mexico, extending to the Lakes on the north and the Pacific Ocean on the west, and from the lines of Georgia to Texas.

Great interests have grown up under the Territorial laws over a country more than five times greater in extent than the original thirteen States; and these interests, corporate or otherwise, have been cherished and consolidated by a benign policy, without any one supposing the law-making power had united with the Judiciary, under the universal sanction of the whole country, to usurp a jurisdiction which did not belong to them. Such a discovery at this late date is more extraordinary than anything which has occurred in the judicial history of this or any other country. Texas, under a previous organization, was admitted as a State; but no State can be admitted into the Union which has not been organized under some form of government. Without temporary Governments, our public lands could not have been sold, nor our wildernesses reduced to cultivation, and the population protected; nor could our flourishing States, West and South, have been formed.

What do the lessons of wisdom and experience teach, under such circumstances, if the new light, which has so suddenly and unexpectedly burst upon us, be true? Acquiescence; acquiescence under a settled construction of the Constitution for sixty years, though it may be erroneous; which has secured to the country an advancement and prosperity beyond the power of computation.

An act of James Madison, when President, forcibly illustrates this policy. He had made up his opinion that Congress had no power under the Constitution to establish a National Bank. In 1815, Congress passed a bill to establish a bank. He vetoed the bill, on objections other than constitutional. In his message, he speaks as a wise statesman and Chief Magistrate, as follows:

"Waiving the question of the constitutional authority of the Legislature to establish an incorporated bank, as being precluded, in my judgment, by the repeated recognitions under varied circumstances of the validity of such an institution, in acts of the Legislative, Executive, and Judicial branches of the Government, accompanied by indications, in different modes, of a concurrence of the general will of the nation."

Has this impressive lesson of practical wisdom become lost to the present generation?

If the great and fundamental principles of our Government are never to be settled, there can be no lasting prosperity. The Constitution will become a floating waif on the billows of popular excitement.

The prohibition of slavery north of thirty-six degrees thirty minutes, and of the State of Missouri, contained in the act admitting that State into the Union, was passed by a vote of 134, in the House of Representatives, to 42. Before Mr. Monroe signed the act, it was submitted by him to his Cabinet, and they held the restriction of slavery in a Territory to be within the constitutional powers of Congress. It would be singular, if in 1804 Congress had power to prohibit the introduction of slaves in Orleans Territory from any other part of the Union, under the penalty of freedom to the slave, if the same power, embodied in the Missouri compromise, could not be exercised in 1820.

But this law of Congress, which prohibits slavery north of Missouri and of thirty-six degrees thirty minutes, is declared to have been null and void by my brethren. And this opinion is founded mainly, as I understand, on the distinction drawn between the ordinance of 1787 and the Missouri compromise line. In what does the distinction consist? The ordinance, it is said, was a compact entered into by the confederated States before the adoption of the Constitution; and that in the cession of territory authority was given to establish a Territorial Government.

It is clear that the ordinance did not go into operation by virtue of the authority of the Confederation, but by reason of its modification and adoption by Congress under the Constitution. It seems to be supposed, in the opinion of the court, that the articles of cession placed it on a different footing from territories subsequently acquired. I am unable to perceive the force of this distinction. That the ordinance was intended for the government of the Northwestern Territory, and was limited to such Territory, is admitted. It was extended to Southern Territories, with modifications, by acts of Congress, and to some Northern Territories. But the ordinance was made valid by the act of Congress, and without such act could have been of no force. It rested for its validity on the act of Congress, the same, in my opinion, as the Missouri compromise line.

If Congress may establish a Territorial Government in the exercise of its discretion, it is a clear principle that a court cannot control that discretion. This being the case, I do not see on what ground the act is held to be void. It did not purport to forfeit property, or take it for public purposes. It only prohibited slavery; in doing which, it followed the ordinance of 1787.

I will now consider the fourth head, which is: "The effect of taking slaves into a State or Territory, and so holding them, where slavery is prohibited."

If the principle laid down in the case of *Prigg* v. *The State of Pennsylvania* is to be maintained, and it is certainly to be maintained until overruled, as the law of this court, there can be no difficulty on this point. In that case, the court says: "The state of slavery is deemed to be a mere municipal regulation, founded upon and limited to the range of the territorial laws." If this be so, slavery can exist nowhere except under the authority of law, founded on usage having the force of law, or by statutory recognition. And the court further says: "It is manifest, from this consideration, that if the Constitution had not contained the clause requiring the rendition of fugitives from labor, every non-slaveholding State in the Union would have been at liberty to have declared free all runaway slaves coming within its limits, and to have given them entire immunity and protection against the claims of their masters."

Now, if a slave abscond, he may be reclaimed; but if he accompany his master into a State or Territory where slavery is prohibited, such slave cannot be said to have left the service of his master where his services were legalized. And if slavery be limited to the range of the territorial laws, how can the slave be coerced to serve in a State or Territory, not only without the authority of law, but against its express provisions? What gives the master the right to control the will of his slave? The local law, which exists in some form. But where there is no such law, can the master control the will of the slave by force? Where no slavery exists, the presumption, without regard to color, is in favor of freedom. Under such a jurisdiction, may the colored man be levied on as the property of his master by a creditor? On the decease of the master, does the slave descend to his heirs as property? Can the master sell him? Any one or all of these acts may be done to the slave, where he is legally held to service. But where the law does not confer this power, it cannot be exercised.

Lord Mansfield held that a slave brought into England was free. Lord Stowell agreed with Lord Mansfield in this respect, and that the slave could not be coerced in England; but on her voluntary return to Antigua, the place of her slave domicil, her former status attached. The law of England did not prohibit slavery, but did not authorize it. The jurisdiction which prohibits slavery is much stronger in behalf of the slave within it, than where it only does not authorize it.

By virtue of what law is it, that a master may take his slave into free territory, and exact from him the duties of a slave? The law of the Territory does not sanction it. No authority can be claimed under the Constitution of the United States, or any law of Congress. Will it be said that the slave is taken as property, the same as other property which the master may own? To this I answer, that colored persons are made property by the law of the State, and no such power has been given to Congress. Does the master carry with him the law of the State from which he removes into the Territory? and does that enable him to coerce his slave in the Territory? Let us test this theory. If this may be done by a master from one slave State, it may be done by a master from every other slave State. This right is supposed to be connected with the person of the master, by virtue of the local law. Is it transferable? May it be negotiated, as a promissory note or bill of exchange? If it be assigned to a man from a free State, may he coerce the slave by virtue of it? What shall this thing be denominated? Is it personal or real property? Or is it an indefinable fragment of sovereignty, which every person carries with him from his late domicil? One thing is certain, that its origin has been very recent, and it is unknown to the laws of any civilized country.

A slave is brought to England from one of its islands, where slavery was introduced and maintained by the mother country. Although there is no law prohibiting slavery in England, yet there is no law authorizing it; and, for near a century, its courts have declared that the slave there is free from the coercion of the master. Lords Mansfield and Stowell agree upon this point, and there is no dissenting authority.

There is no other description of property which was not protected in England, brought from one of its slave islands. Does not this show that property in a human being does not arise from nature or from the common law, but, in the language of this court, "it is a mere municipal regulation, founded upon and limited to the range of the territorial laws?" This decision is not a mere argument, but it is the end of the law, in regard to the extent of slavery. Until it shall be overturned, it is not a point for argument; it is obligatory on myself and my brethren, and on all judicial tribunals over which this court exercises an appellate power.

It is said the Territories are common property of the States, and that every man has a right to go there with his property. This is not controverted. But the court say a slave is not property beyond the operation of the local law which makes him such. Never was a truth more authoritatively and justly uttered by man. Suppose a master of a slave in a British island owned a million of property in England; would that authorize him to take his slaves with him to England? The Constitution, in express terms, recognises the *status* of slavery as founded on the municipal law: "No person held to serve or labor in one State, *under the laws thereof,* escaping into another, shall," &c. Now, unless the fugitive escape from a place where, by the municipal law, he is held to labor, this provision affords no remedy to the master. What can be more conclusive than this? Suppose a slave escape from a Territory where slavery is not authorized by law, can he be reclaimed?

In this case, a majority of the court have said that a slave may be taken by his master into a Territory of the United States, the same as a horse, or any other kind of property. It is true, this was said by the court, as also many other things, which are of no authority. Nothing that has been said by them, which has not a direct bearing on the jurisdiction of the court, against which they decided, can be considered as authority. I shall certainly not regard it as such. The question of jurisdiction, being before the court, was decided by them authoritatively, but nothing beyond that question. A slave is not a mere chattel. He bears the impress of his Maker, and is amenable to the laws of God and man; and he is destined to an endless existence.

Under this head I shall chiefly rely on the decisions of the Supreme Courts of the Southern States, and especially of the State of Missouri.

In the first and second sections of the sixth article of the Constitution of Illinois, it is declared that neither slavery nor involuntary servitude shall hereafter be introduced into this State, otherwise than for the punishment of crimes whereof the party shall have been duly convicted; and in the second section it is declared that any violation of this article shall effect the emancipation of such person from his obligation to service. In Illinois, a right of transit through the State is given the master with his slaves. This is a matter which, as I suppose, belongs exclusively to the State.

The Supreme Court of Illinois, in the case of *Jarrot* v. *Jarrot,* (2 Gilmer, 7,) said:

"After the conquest of this Territory by Virginia, she ceded it to the United States, and stipulated that the titles and possessions, rights and liberties, of the French settlers, should be guarantied to them. This, it has been contended, secured them in the possession of those negroes as slaves which they held before that time, and that neither Congress nor the Convention had power to deprive them of it; or, in other words, that the ordinance and Constitution should not be so interpreted and understood as applying to such slaves, when it is therein declared that there shall be neither slavery nor involuntary servitude in the Northwest Territory, nor in the State of Illinois, otherwise than in the punishment of crimes. But it was held that those rights could not be thus protected, but must yield to the ordinance and Constitution."

The first slave case decided by the Supreme Court of Missouri, contained in the reports, was *Winny* v. *Whitesides,* (1 Missouri Rep., 473,) at October term, 1824. It appeared that, more than twenty-five years before, the defendant, with her husband, had removed from Carolina to Illinois, and brought with them the plantiff; that they continued to reside in Illinois three or four years, retaining the plaintiff as a slave; after which, they removed to Missouri, taking her with them.

The court held, that if a slave be detained in Illinois until he be entitled to freedom, the right of the owner does not revive when he finds the negro in a slave State.

That when a slave is taken to Illinois by his owner, who takes up his residence there, the slave is entitled to freedom.

In the case of *Lagrange* v. *Chouteau,* (2 Missouri Rep., 20, at May term, 1828,) it was decided that the ordinance of 1787 was intended as a fundamental law for those who may choose to live under it, rather than as a penal statute.

That any sort of residence contrived or permitted by the legal owner of the slave, upon the faith of secret trusts or contracts, in order to defeat or evade the ordinance, and thereby introduce slavery *de facto,* would entitle such slave to freedom.

In *Julia* v. *McKinney,* (3 Missouri Rep., 279,) it was held, where a slave was settled in the State of Illinois, but with an intention on the part of the owner to be removed at some future day, that hiring said slave to a person to labor for one or two days, and receiving the pay for the hire, the slave is entitled to her freedom, under the second section of the sixth article of the Constitution of Illinois.

Rachel v. *Walker* (4 Missouri Rep., 350, June term, 1836) is a case involving, in every particular, the principles of the case before us. Rachel sued for her freedom; and it appeared that she had been bought as a slave in Missouri, by Stockton, an officer of the army, taken to Fort Snelling, where he was stationed, and she was retained there as a slave a year; and then Stockton removed to Prairie du Chien, taking Rachel with him as a slave, where he continued to hold her three years, and then he took her to the State of Missouri, and sold her as a slave.

"Fort Snelling was admitted to be on the west side of the Mississippi river, and north of the State of Missouri, in the territory of the United States. That Prairie du Chien was in the Michigan Territory, on the east side of the Mississippi river. Walker, the defendant, held Rachel under Stockton."

The court said, in this case:

"The officer lived in Missouri Territory, at the time he bought the slave; he sent to a slaveholding country and procured her; this was his voluntary act, done without any other reason than that of his convenience; and he and those claiming under him must be holden to abide the consequences of introducing slavery both in Missouri Territory and Michigan, contrary to law; and on that ground Rachel was declared to be entitled to freedom."

In answer to the argument that, as an officer of the army, the master had a right to take his slave into free territory, the court said no authority of law or the Government compelled him to keep the plaintiff there as a slave.

"Shall it be said, that because an officer of the army owns slaves in Virginia, that when, as officer and soldier, he is required to take the command of a fort in the non-slaveholding States or Territories, he thereby has a right to take with him as many slaves as will suit his interests or convenience? It surely cannot be law. If this be true, the court say, then it is also true that the convenience or supposed convenience of the officer repeals, as to him and others who have the same character, the ordinance and the act of 1821, admitting Missouri into the Union, and also the prohibition of the several laws and Constitutions of the non-slaveholding States."

In *Wilson* v. *Melvin,* (4 Missouri R., 592,) it appeared the defendant left Tennessee with an intention of residing in Illinois, taking his negroes with him. After a month's stay in Illinois, he took his negroes to St. Louis, and hired them, then returned to Illinois. On these facts, the inferior court instructed the jury that the defendant was a sojourner in Illinois. This the Supreme Court held was error, and the judgment was reversed.

The case of *Dred Scott* v. *Emerson* (15 Missouri R., 682, March term, 1852) will now be stated. This case involved the identical question before us, Emerson having, since the hearing, sold the plaintiff to Sandford, the defendant.

Two of the judges ruled the case, the Chief Justice dissenting. It cannot be improper to state the grounds of the opinion of the court, and of the dissent.

The court say: "Cases of this kind are not strangers in our court. Persons have been frequently here adjudged to be entitled to their freedom, on the ground that their masters held them in slavery in Territories or States in which that institution is prohibited. From the first case decided in our court, it might be inferred that this result was brought about by a presumed assent of the master, from the fact of having voluntarily taken his slave to a place where the relation of master and slave did not exist. But subsequent cases base the right to 'exact the forfeiture of emancipation,' as they term it, on the ground, it would seem, that it was the duty of the courts of this State to carry into effect the Constitution and laws of other States and Territories, regardless of the rights, the policy, or the institutions, of the people of this State."

And the court say that the States of the Union, in their municipal concerns, are regarded as foreign to each other; that the courts of one State do not take notice of the laws of other States, unless proved as facts, and that every State has the right to determine how far its comity to other States shall extend; and it is laid down, that when there is no act of manumission decreed to the free State, the courts of the slave States cannot be called to give effect to the law of the free State. Comity, it alleges, between States, depends upon the discretion of both, which may be varied by circumstances. And it is declared by the court, "that times are not as they were when the former decisions on this subject were made." Since then, not only individuals but States have been possessed with a dark and fell spirit in relation to slavery, whose gratification is sought in the pursuit of measures whose inevitable consequence must be the overthrow and destruction of our Government. Under such circumstances, it does not behoove the State of Missouri to show the least countenance to any measure which might gratify this spirit. She is willing to assume her full responsibility for the existence of slavery within her limits nor does she seek to share or divide it with others.

Chief Justice Gamble dissented from the other two judges. He says:

"In every slaveholding State in the Union, the subject of emancipation is regulated by statute; and the forms are prescribed in which it shall be effected. Whenever the forms required by the laws of the State in which the master and slave are resident are complied with, the emancipation is complete, and the slave is free. If the right of the person thus emancipated is subsequently drawn in question in another State, it will be ascertained and determined by the law of the State in which the slave and his former master resided; and when it appears that such law has been complied with, the right to freedom will be fully sustained in the courts of all the slaveholding States, although the act of emancipation may not be in the form required by law in which the court sits.

"In all such cases, courts continually administer the law of the country where the right was acquired; and when that law becomes known to the court, it is just as much a matter of course tc decide the rights of the parties according to its requirements, as it is to settle the title of real estate situated in our State by its own laws."

This appears to me a most satisfactory answer to the argument of the court. Chief Justice continues:

"The perfect equality of the different States lies at the foundation of the Union. As the institution of slavery in the States is one over which the Constitution of the United States gives no power to the General Government, it is left to be adopted or rejected by the several States, as they think best; nor can any one State, or number of States, claim the right to interfere with any other State upon the question of admitting or excluding this institution.

"A citizen of Missouri, who removes with his slave to Illinois, has no right to complain that the fundamental law of that State to which he removes, and in which he makes his residence, dissolves the relation between him and his slave. It is as much his own voluntary act, as if he had executed a deed of emancipation. No one can pretend ignorance of this constitutional provision, and," he says, "the decisions which have heretofore been made in this State, and in many other slaveholding States, give effect to this and other similar provisions, on the ground that the master, by making the free State the residence of his slave, has submitted his right to the operation of the law of such State; and this," he says, "is the same in law as a regular deed of emancipation."

He adds:

"I regard the question as conclusively settled by repeated adjudications of this court, and, if I doubted or denied the propriety of those decisions, I would not feel myself any more at liberty to overturn them, than I would any other series of decisions by which the law of any other question was settled. There is with me," he says, "nothing in the law relating to slavery which distinguishes it from the law on any other subject, or allows any more accommodation to the temporary public excitements which are gathered around it."

"In this State," he says, "it has been recognised from the beginning of the Government as a correct position in law, that a master who takes his slave to reside in a State or Territory where slavery is prohibited, thereby emancipates his slave." These decisions, which come down to the year 1837, seemed to have so fully settled the question, that since that time there has been no case bringing it before the court for any reconsideration, until the present. In the case of *Winny* v. *Whitesides,* the question was made in the argument, "whether one nation would execute the penal laws of another," and the court replied in this language, (Huberus, quoted in 4 Dallas,) which says, "personal rights or disabilities obtained or communicated by the laws of any particular place are of a nature which accompany the person wherever he goes"; and the Chief Justice observed, in the case of *Rachel* v. *Walker,* the act of Congress called the Missouri compromise was held as operative as the ordinance of 1787.

When Dred Scott, his wife and children, were removed from Fort Snelling to Missouri, in 1838, they were free, as the law was then settled, and continued for fourteen years afterwards, up to 1852, when the above decision was made. Prior to this, for nearly thirty years, as Chief Justice Gamble declares, the residence of a master with his slave in the State of Illinois, or in the Territory north of Missouri, where slavery was prohibited by the act called the Missouri compromise, would manumit the slave as effectually as if he had executed a deed of emancipation; and that an officer of the army who takes his slave into that State or Territory, and holds him there as a slave, liberates him the same as any other citizen—and down to the above time it was settled by numerous and uniform decisions; and that on the return of the slave to Missouri, his former condition of slavery did not attach. Such was the settled law of Missouri until the decision of Scott and Emerson.

In the case of *Sylvia* v. *Kirby,* (17 Misso. Rep., 434,) the court followed the above decision, observing it was similar in all respects to the case of Scott and Emerson.

This court follows the established construction of the statutes of a State by its Supreme Court. Such a construction is considered as a part of the statute, and we follow it to avoid two rules of property in the same State. But we do not follow the decisions of the Supreme Court of a State beyond a statutory construction as a rule of decision for this court. State decisions are always viewed with respect and treated as authority; but we follow the settled construction of the statutes, not because it is of binding authority, but in pursuance of a rule of judicial policy.

But there is no pretence that the case of *Dred Scott* v. *Emerson* turned upon the construction of a Missouri statute; nor was there any established rule of property which could have rightfully influenced the decision. On the contrary, the decision overruled the settled law for nearly thirty years.

This is said by my brethren to be a Missouri question; but there is nothing which gives it this character, except that it involves the right to persons claimed as slaves who reside in Missouri, and the decision was made by the Supreme Court of that State. It involves a right claimed under an act of Congress and the Constitution of Illinois, and which cannot be decided without the consideration and construction of those laws. But the Supreme Court of Missouri held, in this case, that it will not regard either of those laws, without which there was no case before it; and Dred Scott, having been a slave, remains a slave. In this respect it is admitted this is a Missouri question—a case which has but one side, if the Act of Congress and the Constitution of Illinois are not recognised.

And does such a case constitute a rule of decision for this court—a case to be followed by this court? The course of decision so long and so uniformly maintained established a comity or law between Missouri and the free States and Territories where slavery was prohibited, which must be somewhat regarded in this case. Rights sanctioned for twenty-eight years ought not and cannot be repudiated, with any semblance of justice, by one or two decisions, influenced, as declared, by a determination to counteract the excitement against slavery in the free States.

The courts of Louisiana having held, for a series of years, that where a master took his slave to France, or any free State, he was entitled to freedom, and that on bringing him back the status of slavery did not attach, the Legislature of Louisiana declared by an act that the slave should not be made free under such circumstances. This regulated the rights of the master from the time the act took effect. But the decision of the Missouri court, reversing a former decision, affects all previous decisions, technically, made on the same principles, unless such decisions are protected by the lapse of time or the statute of limitations. Dred Scott and his family, beyond all controversy, were free under the decisions made for twenty-eight years, before the case of *Scott* v. *Emerson*. This was the undoubted law of Missouri for fourteen years after Scott and his family were brought back to that State. And the grave question arises, whether this law may be so disregarded as to enslave free persons. I am strongly inclined to think that a rule of decision so well settled as not to be questioned, cannot be annulled by a single decision of the court. Such rights may be inoperative under the decision in future; but I cannot well perceive how it can have the same effect in prior cases.

It is admitted, that when a former decision is reversed, the technical effect of the judgment is to make all previous adjudications on the same question erroneous. But the case before us was not that the law had been erroneously construed, but that, under the circumstances which then existed, that law would not be recognised; and the reason for this is declared to be the excitement against the institution of slavery in the free States. While I lament this excitement as much as any one, I cannot assent that it shall be made a basis of judicial action.

In 1816, the common law, by statute, was made a part of the law of Missouri; and that includes the great principles of international law. These principles cannot be abrogated by judicial decisions. It will require the same exercise of power to abolish the common law, as to introduce it. International law is founded in the opinions generally received and acted on by civilized nations, and enforced by moral sanctions. It becomes a more authoritative system when it results from special compacts, founded on modified rules, adapted to the exigencies of human society; it is in fact an international morality, adapted to the best interests of nations. And in regard to the States of this Union, on the subject of slavery, it is eminently fitted for a rule of action, subject to the Federal Constitution. "The laws of nations are but the natural rights of man applied to nations." (Vattel.)

If the common law have the force of a statutory enactment in Missouri, it is clear, as it seems to me, that a slave who, by a residence in Illinois in the service of his master, becomes entitled to his freedom, cannot again be reduced to slavery by returning to his former domicil in a slave State. It is unnecessary to say what legislative power might do by a general act in such a case, but it would be singular if a freeman could be made a slave by the exercise of a judicial discretion. And it would be still more extraordinary if this could be done, not only in the absence of special legislation, but in a State where the common law is in force.

It is supposed by some, that the third article in the treaty of cession of Louisiana to this country, by France, in 1803, may have some bearing on this question. The article referred to provides, "that the inhabitants of the ceded territory shall be incorporated into the Union, and enjoy all the advantages of citizens of the United States, and in the mean time they shall be maintained and protected in the free enjoyment of their liberty, property, and the religion they profess."

As slavery existed in Louisiana at the time of the cession, it is supposed this is a guaranty that there should be no change in its condition.

The answer to this is, in the first place, that such a subject does not belong to the treaty-making power; and any such arrangement would have been nugatory. And, in the second place, by no admissible construction can the guaranty be carried further than the protection of property in slaves at that time in the ceded territory. And this has been complied with. The organization of the slave States of Louisiana, Missouri, and Arkansas, embraced every slave in Louisiana at the time of the cession. This removes every ground of objection under the treaty. There is therefore no pretence, growing out of the treaty, that any part of the territory of Louisiana, as ceded, beyond the organized States, is slave territory.

Under the fifth head, we were to consider whether the status of slavery attached to the plaintiff and wife, on their return to Missouri.

This doctrine is not asserted in the late opinion of the Supreme Court of Missouri, and up to 1852 the contrary doctrine was uniformly maintained by that court.

In its late decision, the court say that it will not give effect in Missouri to the laws of Illinois, or the law of Congress called the Missouri compromise. This was the effect of the decision, though its terms were, that the court would not take notice, judicially, of those laws.

In 1851, the Court of Appeals of South Carolina recognised the principle, that a slave, being taken to a free State, became free. (*Commonwealth* v. *Pleasants,* 10 Leigh Rep., 697.) In *Betty* v. *Horton,* the Court of Appeals held that the freedom of the slave was acquired by the action of the laws of Massachusetts, by the said slave being taken there. (5 Leigh Rep., 615.)

The slave States have generally adopted the rule, that where the master, by a residence with his slave in a State or Territory where slavery is prohibited, the slave was entitled to his freedom everywhere. This was the settled doctrine of the Supreme Court of Missouri. It has been so held in Mississippi, in Virginia, in Louisiana, formerly in Kentucky, Maryland, and in other States.

The law, where a contract is made and is to be executed, governs it. This does not depend upon comity, but upon the law of the contract. And if, in the language of the Supreme Court of Missouri, the master, by taking his slave to Illinois, and employing him there as a slave, emancipates him as effectually as by a deed of emancipation, is it possible that such an act is not matter for adjudication in any slave State where the master may take him? Does not the master assent to the law, when he places himself under it in a free State?

The States of Missouri and Illinois are bounded by a common line. The one prohibits slavery, the other admits it. This has been done by the exercise of that sovereign power which appertains to each. We are bound to respect the institutions of each, as emanating from the voluntary action of the people. Have the people of either any right to disturb the relations of the other? Each State rests upon the basis of its own sovereignty, protected by the Constitution. Our Union has been the foundation of our prosperity and national glory. Shall we not cherish and maintain it? This can only be done by respecting the legal rights of each State.

If a citizen of a free State shall entice or enable a slave to escape from the service of his master, the law holds him responsible, not only for the loss of the slave, but he is liable to be indicted and fined for the misdemeanor. And I am bound here to say, that I have never found a jury in the four States which constitute my circuit, which have not sustained this law, where the evidence required them to sustain it. And it is proper that I should also say, that more cases have arisen in my circuit, by reason of its extent and locality, than in all other parts of the Union. This has been done to vindicate the sovereign rights of the Southern States, and protect the legal interests of our brethren of the South.

Let these facts be contrasted with the case now before the court. Illinois has declared in the most solemn and impressive form that there shall be neither slavery nor involuntary servitude in that State, and that any slave brought into it, with a view of becoming a resident, shall be emancipated. And effect has been given to this provision of the Constitution by the decision of the Supreme Court of that State. With a full knowledge of these facts, a slave is brought from Missouri to Rock Island, in the State of Illinois, and is retained there as a slave for two years, and then taken to Fort Snelling, where slavery is prohibited by the Missouri compromise act, and there he is detained two years longer in a state of slavery. Harriet, his wife, was also kept at the same place four years as a slave, having been purchased in Missouri. They were then removed to the State of Missouri, and sold as slaves, and in the action before us they are not only claimed as slaves, but a majority of my brethren have held that on their being returned to Missouri the status of slavery attached to them.

I am not able to reconcile this result with the respect due to the State of Illinois. Having the same rights of sovereignty as the State of Missouri in adopting a Constitution, I can perceive no reason why the institutions of Illinois should not receive the same consideration as those of Missouri. Allowing to my brethren the same right of judgment that I exercise myself, I must be permitted to say that it seems to me the principle laid down will enable the people of a slave State to introduce slavery into a free State, for a longer or shorter time, as may suit their convenience; and by returning the slave to the State whence he was brought, by force or otherwise, the status of slavery attaches, and protects the rights of the master, and defies the sovereignty of the free State. There is no evidence before us that Dred Scott and his family returned to Missouri voluntarily. The contrary is inferable from the agreed case: "In the year 1838, Dr. Emerson removed the plaintiff and said Harriet, and their daughter Eliza, from Fort Snelling to the State of Missouri, where they have ever since resided." This is the agreed case; and can it be inferred from this that Scott and family returned to Missouri voluntarily? He was removed; which shows that he was passive, as a slave, having exercised no volition on the subject. He did not resist the master by absconding or force. But that was not sufficient to bring him within Lord Stowell's decision; he must have acted voluntarily. It would be a mockery of law and an outrage on his rights to coerce his return, and then claim that it was voluntary, and on that ground that his former status of slavery attached.

If the decision be placed on this ground, it is a fact for a jury to decide, whether the return was voluntary, or else the fact should be distinctly admitted. A presumption against the plaintiff in this respect, I say with confidence, is not authorized from the facts admitted.

In coming to the conclusion that a voluntary return by Grace to her former domicil, slavery attached, Lord Stowell took great pains to show that England forced slavery upon her colonies, and that it was maintained by numerous acts of Parliament and public policy, and, in short, that the system of slavery was not only established by Great Britain in her West Indian colonies, but that it was popular and profitable to many of the wealthy and influential people of England, who were engaged in trade, or owned and cultivated plantations in the colonies. No one can read his elaborate views, and not be struck with the great difference between England and her colonies, and the free and slave States of this Union. While slavery in the colonies of England is subject to the power of the mother country, our States, especially in regard to slavery, are independent, resting upon their own sovereignties, and subject only to international laws, which apply to independent States.

In the case of Williams, who was a slave in Granada, having run away, came to England, Lord Stowell said: "The four judges all concur in this—that he was a slave in Granada, though a free man in England, and he would have continued a free man in all other parts of the world except Granada."

Strader v. *Graham* (10 Howard, 82, and 18 Curtis, 305) has been cited as having a direct bearing in the case before us. In that case the court say: "It was exclusively in the power of Kentucky to determine, for itself, whether the employment of slaves in another State should or should not make them free on their return." No question was before the court in that case, except that of jurisdiction. And any opinion given on any other point is *obiter dictum,* and of no authority. In the conclusion of his opinion, the Chief Justice said: "In every view of the subject, therefore, this court has no jurisdiction of the case, and the writ of error must on that ground be dismissed."

In the case of *Spencer* v. *Negro Dennis,* (8 Gill's Rep., 321,) the court say: "Once free, and always free, is the maxim of Maryland law upon the subject. Freedom having once vested, by no compact between the master and the liberated slave, nor by any condition subsequent, attached by the master to the gift of freedom, can a state of slavery be reproduced."

In *Hunter* v. *Bulcher,* (1 Leigh, 172:)

"By a statute of Maryland of 1796, all slaves brought into that State to reside are declared free; a Virginian-born slave is carried by his master to Maryland; the master settled there, and keeps the slave there in bondage for twelve years, the statute in force all the time; then he brings him as a slave to Virginia, and sells him there. Adjudged, in an action brought by the man against the purchaser, that he is free."

Judge Kerr, in the case, says:

"Agreeing, as I do, with the general view taken in this case by my brother Green, I would not add a word, but to mark the exact extent to which I mean to go. The law of Maryland having enacted that slaves carried into that State for sale or to reside shall be free, and the owner of the slave here having carried him to Maryland, and voluntarily submitting himself and the slave to that law, it governs the case."

In every decision of a slave case prior to that of *Dred Scott* v. *Emerson,* the Supreme Court of Missouri considered it as turning upon the Constitution of Illinois, the ordinance of 1787, or the Missouri compromise act of 1820. The court treated these acts as in force, and held itself bound to execute them, by declaring the slave to be free who had acquired a domicil under them with the consent of his master.

The late decision reversed this whole line of adjudication, and held that neither the Constitution and laws of the States, nor acts of Congress in relation to Territories, could be judicially noticed by the Supreme Court of Missouri. This is believed to be in conflict with the decisions of all the courts in the Southern States, with some exceptions of recent cases.

In *Marie Louise* v. *Morat et al.,* (9 Louisiana Rep., 475,) it was held, where a slave having been taken to the kingdom of France or other country by the owner, where slavery is not tolerated, operates on the condition of the slave, and produces immediate emancipation; and that, where a slave thus becomes free, the master cannot reduce him again to slavery.

Josephine v. *Poultney,* (Louisiana Annual Rep., 329,) "where the owner removes with a slave into a State in which slavery is prohibited, with the intention of residing there, the slave will be thereby emancipated, and their subsequent return to the State of Louisiana cannot restore the relation of master and slave." To the same import are the cases of *Smith* v. *Smith,* (13 Louisiana Rep., 441; *Thomas* v. *Generis,* Louisiana Rep., 483; *Harry et al.* v. *Decker and Hopkins,* Walker's Mississippi Rep., 36.) It was held that, "slaves within the jurisdiction of the Northwestern Territory became freemen by virtue of the ordinance of 1787, and can assert their claim to freedom in the courts of Mississippi." (*Griffith* v. *Fanny,* 1 Virginia Rep., 143.) It was decided that a negro held in servitude in Ohio, under a deed executed in Virginia, is entitled to freedom by the Constitution of Ohio.

The case of *Rhodes* v. *Bell* (2 Howard, 307; 15 Curtis, 152) involved the main principle in the case before us. A person residing in Washington city purchased a slave in Alexandria, and brought him to Washington. Washington continued under the law of Maryland, Alexandria under the law of Virginia. The act of Maryland of November, 1796, (2 Maxcy's Laws, 351,) declared any one who shall bring any negro, mulatto, or other slave, into Maryland, such slave should be free. The above slave, by reason of his being brought into Washington city, was declared by this court to be free. This, it appears to me, is a much stronger case against the slave than the facts in the case of Scott.

In *Bush v. White,* (3 Monroe, 104,) the court say:

"That the ordinance was paramount to the Territorial laws, and restrained the legislative power there as effectually as a Constitution in an organized State. It was a public act of the Legislature of the Union, and a part of the supreme law of the land; and, as such, this court is as much bound to take notice of it as it can be of any other law."

In the case of *Rankin* v. *Lydia,* before cited, Judge Mills, speaking for the Court of Appeals of Kentucky, says:

"If, by the positive provision in our code, we can and must hold our slaves in the one case, and statutory provisions equally positive decide against that right in the other, and liberate the slave, he must, by an authority equally imperious, be declared free. Every argument which supports the right of the master on one side, based upon the force of written law, must be equally conclusive in favor of the slave, when he can point out in the statute the clause which secures his freedom."

And he further said:

"Free people of color in all the States are, it is believed, quasi citizens, or, at least, denizens. Although none of the States may allow them the privilege of office and suffrage, yet all other civil and conventional rights are secured to them; at least, such rights were evidently secured to them by the ordinance in question for the government of Indiana. If these rights are vested in that or any other portion of the United States, can it be compatible with the spirit of our confederated Government to deny their existence in any other part? Is there less comity existing between State and State, or State and Territory, than exists between the despotic Governments of Europe?"

These are the words of a learned and great judge, born and educated in a slave State.

I now come to inquire, under the sixth and last head, "whether the decisions of the Supreme Court of Missouri, on the question before us, are binding on this court."

While we respect the learning and high intelligence of the State courts, and consider their decisions, with others, as authority, we follow them only where they give a construction to the State statutes. On this head, I consider myself fortunate in being able to turn to the decision of this court, given by Mr. Justice Grier, in *Pease* v. *Peck,* a case from the State of Michigan, (18 Howard, 589,) decided in December term, 1855. Speaking for the court, Judge Grier said:

"We entertain the highest respect for that learned court, (the Supreme Court of Michigan,) and in any question affecting the construction of their own laws, where we entertain any doubt, would be glad to be relieved from doubt and responsibility by reposing on their decision. There are, it is true, many dicta to be found in our decisions, averring that the courts of the United States are bound to follow the decisions of the State courts on the construction of their own laws. But although this may be correct, yet a rather strong expression of a general rule, it cannot be received as the annunciation of a maxim of universal application. Accordingly, our reports furnish many cases of exceptions to it. In all cases where there is a settled construction of the laws of a State, by its highest judicature established by admitted precedent, it is the practice of the courts of the United States to receive and adopt it, without criticism or further inquiry. When the decisions of the State court are not consistent, we do not feel bound to follow the last, if it is contrary to our own convictions; and much more is this the case where, after a long course of consistent decisions, some new light suddenly springs up, or an excited public opinion has elicited new doctrines subversive of former safe precedent."

These words, it appears to me, have a stronger application to the case before us than they had to the cause in which they were spoken as the opinion of this court; and I regret that they do not seem to be as fresh in the recollection of some of my brethren as in my own. For twenty-eight years, the decisions of the Supreme Court of Missouri were consistent on all the points made in this case. But this consistent course was suddenly terminated, whether by some new light suddenly springing up, or an excited public opinion, or both, it is not necessary to say. In the case of *Scott* v. *Emerson,* in 1852, they were overturned and repudiated.

This, then, is the very case in which seven of my brethren declared they would not follow the last decision. On this authority I may well repose. I can desire no other or better basis.

But there is another ground which I deem conclusive, and which I will re-state.

The Supreme Court of Missouri refused to notice the act of Congress or the Constitution of Illinois, under which Dred Scott, his wife and children, claimed that they are entitled to freedom.

This being rejected by the Missouri court, there was no case before it, or least it was a case with only one side. And this is the case which, in the opinion of this court, we are bound to follow. The Missouri court disregards the express provisions of an act of Congress and the Constitution of a sovereign

State, both of which laws for twenty-eight years it had not only regarded, but carried into effect.

If a State court may do this, on a question involving the liberty of a human being, what protection do the laws afford? So far from this being a Missouri question, it is a question, as it would seem, within the twenty-fifth section of the judiciary act, where a right to freedom being set up under the act of Congress, and the decision being against such right, it may be brought for revision before this court, from the Supreme Court of Missouri.

I think the judgment of the court below should be reversed.

Henry Baldwin

☆ 1780–1844 ☆

APPOINTED BY

ANDREW JACKSON

YEARS ON COURT

1830–1844

Henry Baldwin

by

FRANK OTTO GATELL

HENRY BALDWIN was the son of Michael and Theodora Wolcot Baldwin, of New Haven, Connecticut. He was born in that city on January 14, 1780, and his New England heritage extended back into the early seventeenth century. One of his several half-brothers, Abraham Baldwin, a prominent Georgia statesman, served as a member of both the Continental Congress, 1785–88, and the Constitutional Convention of 1787, and was a United States senator from Georgia, 1799–1807. Henry's brother, Michael, also achieved some prominence, this time in Ohio's political life, though he did not attain such eminence as Abraham. Young Henry lived for some time on a farm outside of New Haven, but he returned to the city to enter Yale College. He was graduated with the Class of 1797, at age seventeen, after having compiled an outstanding scholastic record.

As for Henry's profession, it was decided that he study law. The young man was fortunate to obtain a clerkship in the office of one of Philadelphia's leading lawyers, Alexander J. Dallas. Upon completion of these studies, Baldwin was admitted to the bar. Shortly thereafter, he headed west, ostensibly to join his brother Michael in Ohio. But Baldwin completed only half of the journey. He settled instead in Pittsburgh, which in 1799 was a promising but not yet thriving town of fifteen hundred people, already calling itself a "great western emporium." Commercial activity along the Ohio River to Cincinnati was growing rapidly, and much more would follow in the ensuing decades. Considering Baldwin's age, the ambitious young man could not have chosen a better place to practice his profession. A hardened, professional elite had not yet formed in Pittsburgh and the opportunities seemed unlimited.

Baldwin joined the Allegheny County Bar in 1801. An agreeable fellow, he

FRANK O. GATELL, Professor of History at the University of California, Los Angeles, is the author of John Gorham Palfrey and the New England Conscience.

quickly formed many professional and personal friendships. One of the most important in his first years was with Tarleton Bates, a capable lawyer who had come from Virginia. Another young lawyer, Walter Forward, joined the pair, and this "Great Triumvirate of Early Pittsburgh" practiced with much success until Bates' death in 1806. Despite this loss, Baldwin's firm gained an increasingly prominent place in western Pennsylvania's legal hierarchy. And it was well-earned, according to the testimony of contemporaries. Henry M. Brackenridge, a friend of Baldwin's and later a Congressman from Pennsylvania, 1840–41, recalled that Baldwin's courtroom arguments were cogent and eloquent, but without "any ornament of unnecessary verbiage." While many lawyers, especially in rural or semi-urban settings, relied on flamboyant oratory rather than legal erudition to win cases, Baldwin was noted for his carefully prepared briefs, many of which he complied by referring to his large and well-selected personal library. Whatever his preferences, Baldwin could not remain a local, scholarly recluse. Most of his practice took place in Allegheny County, but certainly not all. Travelling through nearby counties was a regular feature of a Pittsburgh lawyer's life at that time. Baldwin, physically strong and a convivial sort, did not find such trips as oppressive as the constant complaints of his contemporary lawyers and judges might lead us to believe.

In 1802 Baldwin married a third cousin, Marianna Norton. A year later, she gave birth to Baldwin's only child, a son named Henry, but within a month the mother died. Baldwin's second marriage, in 1805, was to Sally Ellicott, daughter of Major Andrew Ellicott, a well-known engineer and surveyor. Baldwin met her in Meadville, while organizing the circuit court for Erie County, and the Baldwins continued to reside in both Meadville and Pittsburgh. They built a home in Meadville in 1841, shortly before Baldwin's death.

In addition to their legal practices, Bates, Forward, and Baldwin became political leaders of one of the several Republican factions in western Pennsylvania, and even acquired a newspaper, *The Tree of Liberty,* to expound their opinions. The party, although split into factions supporting or opposing Governor Thomas McKean (1799–1808), afforded opportunities for rapid political advancement to young aggressive lawyers. Although still in his mid-twenties, Baldwin was already an acknowledged leader in the Pittsburgh community, and before long he had acquired such local nicknames as the "Idol of Pennsylvania" and the "Pride of Pittsburgh." He was a member of most committees and councils which looked after Pittsburgh affairs. During the War of 1812, he served on the local Public Safety Council, although it is curious that despite his relative youth he did not become actively involved in the military struggle, especially since participation in militia activities was then almost a *sine qua non* for young lawyer-politicians.

But the same reticence cannot be detected in Baldwin's business activities. Here, there was involvement to spare. As part owner of at least three rolling mills in the western part of the state, including the Union Rolling Mill, near Pittsburgh, the largest in that region, his business interests soon extended into

Ohio, where he was a partner in a lucrative Steubenville woolen mill, the first built west of the mountains at the then terminus of the Cumberland Road. Ownership in this establishment was probably the reason why Baldwin, and his Pittsburgh partner, James Ross, did not protest when Congress decided to bypass Pittsburgh in voting to extend the Cumberland Road.

In 1816 Baldwin won election to the United States House of Representatives from Crawford County, Pennsylvania. Manufacturing interests in the Pittsburgh area had become restive because of the removal of the double duties in the wartime tariff schedule and leading businessmen decided to send Baldwin, one of their own, to Washington to work for a still higher tariff than the one passed in 1816. Baldwin ran as a factional maverick, receiving organizational support from Independent Republicans and Federalists. He was not the candidate of the agrarian-based Republican regulars, but his popularity throughout the region placed the regular leaders in a quandary as they could not attack Baldwin openly without endangering the success of their entire ticket. The election was also important as an indication of conflict between the urban and rural Republicans in western Pennsylvania. The Pittsburghers were tired of having each township in the county exert an equal amount of influence in the nominating process. Supporters of the regular nominee, Walter Lowrie, charged that the city folk wanted to establish "a species of aristocracy in which certain rich individuals in the *city* shall have a predominating influence; an aristocracy . . . to give the city of Pittsburgh the whole management of elections and appointments." For their part, the Baldwinites attacked the functioning of the party machinery, as then set up—an attack on "caucus nominations, which they would later transfer to the national scene during the rise of Andrew Jackson. It was a process Baldwin was to further and draw benefits from. Important as the organizational arguments were, the overriding consideration bearing upon this election was the economic growth of Pittsburgh. The rising manufacturing interest was not to be denied. Baldwin defeated Lowrie, and three-fourths of his majority of 800 votes came from the city. Pittsburgh now had a spokesman who would seek national governmental protection and support for its already established pattern of economic growth.

Baldwin took his House seat in December, 1817, and immediately became a member of the committee on manufactures. Of course, he urged the protective tariff as a national measure, one that would benefit all sections, and all segments of the economy. But for the next few years his efforts did not produce spectacular results. Some duties were raised by the tariff of 1818, but the happy days of the double duties did not come back. He did enough for his district in other matters, such as the establishment of a federal district court in Pittsburgh, however, to enable him to repel the attempt made to unseat him in the 1818 election. Locked in a power struggle with the clique led by Senator Abner Lacock of Beaver County, Baldwin was accused of conflict-of-interests arising from his investments in iron and textile mills. This charge, and the recurrent one of party irregularity (or neo-federalism), were not enough to defeat him. Baldwin won his second contest, and once again demonstrated that shadow may be as serviceable as substance, so far as election results are concerned. No real substantial differences emerged between Baldwin and the Lacock faction man, but the latter had been saddled with the aura of caucus and party management; Baldwin remained the untrammeled man of the people.

During his second term, Baldwin continued to press for tariff revision, but without much success, as Congress was then engrossed with the Missouri Compromise debates. The tariff honeymoon of 1816 was over; in that year many southern politicians had accepted the rigid protective tariff schedules on a temporary basis, citing reasons of national security. They had not come over permanently to the protective position. Thus, the reargument of the tariff at a time of sectional crisis over the admission of Missouri and Maine was considered highly inexpedient if not downright dangerous. Baldwin had been one of the northerners opposed to the attempts to pass anti-slavery provisos for the territories, as well as conditional admission of new states. He hoped that, by this stand, the South in return would support a higher tariff. Although he ran the risk of being called a northern "doughface," Baldwin was one of eighteen men from the nonslave states who voted for the compromises.

The *quid pro quo* never materialized. In 1820, Baldwin's committee on manufactures presented a clearly protective tariff bill. But southerners, in and out of Congress, objected so strongly that many in the North thought the reaction was revenge for the northern attempt to restrict slavery. A divided northern vote, and almost total opposition from the South, sent the Baldwin bill down to defeat in the Senate by one vote. The protection forces would have to wait until later in the 1820's for their victories. Instead of a new tariff bill, Baldwin returned home with little to show for his efforts, and with a pro-South albatross round his neck. His compromise votes became an issue in the campaign, but not a fatal one. His supporters toasted him along predictable lines: "Henry Baldwin, Esq.—The Nation looks to him as the champion of her industry; and England dreads his tariff more than our ships of battle." The last statement may have been an unintentionally adverse judgment upon the state of our navy.

While in Congress, Baldwin was an outspoken defender of Andrew Jackson. When the General's military actions in Florida (1818), came into question, the Pennsylvanian made a speech exonerating him of misconduct. Baldwin's factional rival, Senator Lacock, was a member of the committee to investigate Jackson and his seizure of East Florida; thus Baldwin's speech had more than one object in view. Baldwin contended that the sooner Congress dropped the investigation, the sooner it could attend to substantive matters—such as upward tariff revision. In this instance, he was wrong about what Congress would do once it finished with the Seminole inquiry, but in the process Baldwin established an enduring political alliance with the General from Tennessee.

Baldwin resigned from the House in 1822 because of ill health. Within two years, with his health restored, he resumed his accustomed position of leadership in Allegheny County. In that unofficial capacity, he was instrumental in assuring that the Pennsylvania Canal's western terminus be established at Pittsburgh, as well as in other matters touching his city's welfare. Throughout this period, Baldwin continued to push the Jackson candidacy. Several Tennessee politicians had supported Jackson with local, state-oriented ends in mind, but the idea of the candidacy, especially the spread of "Jackson-fever" in Pennsylvania, ran away from the plans of the Nashville Junto, and made Jackson a leading candidate in his own right. Baldwin was one of the prominent "feverish" Pennsylvanians. In 1824, John Quincy Adams, who within a year would be President, described Baldwin as "a Crawfordite under a Jackson mask." This was not the only time Adams erred politically. Whatever his apparent commitment to the components of the American System (which should have made him a Clay man, not a Crawfordite), Baldwin did not veer from his Jacksonism. Late in 1823, he had urged Jackson to declare himself a presidential candidate, several months before the move could be considered politically expedient. But Baldwin was not active in the pro-Jackson campaign of 1824. In fact, he considered the enthusiasm for Jackson in Pittsburgh excessive, and although his general stand had been made public, he left the actual legwork to a second wave of ambitious young lawyers, such as Robert J. Walker.

In the years following Adams' election in 1825, Baldwin kept in close touch with the Jacksonian leadership, advising on political movements in western Pennsylvania. On numerous public occasions, Baldwin described Jackson as not being hostile to tariff protection, indeed, a crucial issue in an important state needed by the General. The Jackson victory in 1828 made Baldwin a likely candidate for a federal office. His coterie expected the Treasury Department, but Vice-President Calhoun exerted enough influence to have a Pennsylvanian friendly to him, Samuel D. Ingham, appointed instead. Baldwin returned from the Inauguration ceremony empty-handed, but he refused repeated invitations to whine publicly about Jackson's apparent mistreatment of a friend.

Baldwin soon obtained his reward. In November 1829, Justice Bushrod Washington died. Three Pennsylvanians were in contention for the seat: Horace Binney, supported by the Philadelphia bar; John Bannister Gibson, the state's chief justice and Calhoun's nominee; and Baldwin. The Calhounites spoke out strongly against Baldwin, Duff Green running an unfavorable editorial in his *United States Telegraph*. Van Buren, then battling with Calhoun for Jackson's mantle, admitted a Baldwin appointment was "a step which will create no inconsiderable sensation." When Jackson named Baldwin, unfriendly editors immediately commented upon Calhoun's waning prestige. The nomination went through with only token opposition from South Carolina's senators. If legal talents alone had determined the choice, Binney would have obtained the position. But even the anti-Jacksonians seemed relieved with Baldwin, since they feared Gibson was a radical Democratic "agrarian," and opposed to any form of federal judicial review. Justice Joseph Story wrote privately, "the appointment is quite satisfactory to those who wish well to the country and the Court." Webster, happy that Gibson had been sidetracked, observed that "Baldwin is supposed to be . . . a sound man, he is undoubtedly a man of some talents."

The new Justice's judicial tenure almost ended before it had fairly begun. In the summer of 1831 rumors began circulating that Baldwin was already unhappy with life on the Court and the tenor of its decisions. Van Buren explained: "Judge Baldwin is dissatisfied with the situation, for reasons which it is unnecessary to explain further than they grow out of opposition to what he regards as an unwarrantable extension of its powers by the Court, and has given the President notice of his intention to resign." During the term of 1831, Baldwin had dissented seven times. In one instance, *Ex parte Crane,* 5 Pet. 190 (1831), in which the Court upheld its power to issue an original writ of *mandamus* to a circuit court, he had severely scored the Court (in an opinion by Marshall) for what he deemed a clearly untenable extension of federal jurisdiction. Such actions, he warned would bring "consequences of the most alarming kind," should the Court encroach upon state powers. He called for a "discreet exercise of the powers of this court." The Secretary of the Treasury, Louis McLane, was ready to step up to the Court if Baldwin carried out his intention, but President Jackson prevailed upon his appointee to remain on the bench.

Perhaps Jackson had second thoughts shortly thereafter. The President's crusade against the Bank of the United States brought with it foot-dragging on the part of some Jacksonian leaders, and Baldwin was among that number. While on circuit in Pennsylvania, Baldwin had delivered an opinion in which he accepted the legality of drafts issued by branches of the National Bank which were passing for money. This was in direct conflict with the Jackson administration's views. Benton, and other Democratic spokesmen, including Roger Taney, attacked the branch drafts as a species of fraud. Taney later recalled that Baldwin "was known to be warmly in favor of the renewal of the charter and had held earnest and repeated conversations with me at my office, endeavoring to persuade me to advise the President not to veto the recharter bill." A minor Cabinet crisis occurred in late 1832 concerning Justice Baldwin, and emanating as well from the enmity felt between Taney, then Secretary of the Treasury, and McLane, who had become Secretary of State. Jackson had asked for advice on whether to proceed against the Bank legally, seeking revocation of its charter, or to withhold federal funds from the Bank and await the expiration of the charter. Taney argued against the legal action (the issuance of a *scire facias*), partly because the case would be tried in Philadelphia, the Bank's "lair," and because the unreliable Justice Baldwin would preside and perhaps use the occasion to chastise the administration for its bank policy. It was already well known that Baldwin had begun to suffer lapses of sanity. McLane reprimanded Taney for mentioning this as disrespectful to the Justice, and Taney replied that Baldwin's condition, though unfortunate, could not be ignored since no change of venue was possible. In the end, the President decided to remove the deposits. These were particularly bad months for Baldwin. He was then confined to a hospital and missed the first court term of 1833.

Jackson's first two appointees, McLean and Baldwin, had not hewn closely to the Jacksonian line. Baldwin's Bank War apostasy must be accounted a major disappointment. Nor had he opposed Chief Justice Marshall in the Georgia Indian suits. In the first, *Cherokee Nation* v. *Georgia,* 5 Pet. 1 (1831), he concurred in dismissing the suit on grounds that Indians could not appear as plaintiffs; and in the second, *Worcester* v. *Georgia,* 6 Pet. 515 (1832), he concurred without a separate opinion that federal control over the Indian tribes was exclusive. Also in 1832, Baldwin wrote the opinion in *United States* v. *Arredondo,* 6 Pet. 691 (1831), reaffirming previous holdings that courts must protect claims to land titles, whenever possible, even though such claims be founded on apparently flimsy pretexts. Thus a grant made in Florida by a Spanish public official, and in accordance with law, was valid until the government could establish otherwise. A prominent historian of the Court, Charles Warren, called this opinion "superb," "for in this case the Court established the public land policy of the Government on the basis of the most scrupulous respect for treaties, preferring to preserve the honor, rather than the property of the government."

Several similar cases, arising in the next few years, were settled on those principles. To place the burden of proof upon the claimant, rather than the government, would in Baldwin's opinion have been "an entire novelty in our jurisprudence." The administration had fought these cases stubbornly, and the Whig press crowed that Jackson "sent for Judge Baldwin, who drew up the opinion of the Court, and gave him a lecture." True or not, Jackson was certainly displeased with Baldwin, as he drew closer to Marshall. When the Chief Justice died in 1835, Story noted: "I rejoice that Judge Baldwin took such an interest in the Chief Justice's dying hours. I had no doubt he would, for there is no person on earth (I believe) for whom he felt so much reverence and respect."

The term beginning in January, 1837, proved of great importance to Baldwin. The Court then decided four cases in a manner which provoked the Justice into writing separate opinions, although he concurred in the result reached by the Court. The cases were the famous holdovers from the Marshall Court, *Charles River Bridge* v. *Warren Bridge,* 11 Pet. 420 (1837), *City of New York* v. *Miln,* 11 Pet. 102 (1837), the Tennessee boundary case, *Poole* v. *Lessee of John Fleeger,* 11 Pet. 185 (1837), and *Briscoe* v. *Bank of Kentucky,* 11 Pet. 257 (1837). Although Baldwin had not taken a prominent part in the settlement of the cases, he decided to speak out. Originally, he intended to publish his views as an appendix to *Peter' Reports,* but resorted to separate pamphlet publication instead, to avoid delaying the regular issuance of the *Reports*. It appeared as *A General View of the Origin and Nature of the Constitution and Government of the United States. . . . Together with Opinions in the Cases decided at January Term, 1837, Arising on the Restraints on the Powers of the States.* Baldwin opened with a nonapologetic explanation: "If there are any cases, in which the judges of a Court of the last resort may, without apology, present the grounds of their judgment in detail, they are those which arise on an alleged repugnance between a law or act of a state, and the constitution of the United States." Only safe principles would serve as guides in such cases, and happily "these principles are few and simple," like the operating principles of a machine. The liberating, simplistic, major premise was that the Constitution is "the grant of the people of the several states"; this provided "an easy solution of all questions arising under it." But the machine broke down once the interpreter took it "as the grant of the people of the United States in the aggregate." Baldwin proceeded to a "full explanation of what may be deemed my peculiar views of the constitution."

He noted that when the cases had first been argued, in the early 1830's, he stood in the minority in every instance; in *Charles River Bridge* he had stood alone. But changes of opinion and personnel had produced but one dissenter in three cases (Justice Story). Baldwin lamented that half a century of constitutional construction had not yet settled the prime issues of contention. And further that the political tone of constitutional debate had increased markedly. Everyone had become his own constitutional lawyer, even many who had no claim to the public's ear, and certainly not the legal profession's, on such subjects.

There were three schools of constitutional thought. The first two, which Baldwin located at polar extremes, he found wanting: first, the nationalist school, which feared the centrifugal tendencies of confederation and were willing to allow the growth of national power, even when such accretions might clearly impinge on the acknowledged rights of the states; and, second, the school which predicted the ineluctable growth of national power toward the end of consolidation, leaving the states as subordinate administrative units. In defense, they of course argued for narrow construction. These two groups were easily defined. According to Baldwin, the third view, his own, tried "to take the Constitution with its amendments as it is, and to expound it by the accepted rules of interpretation; whatever might be the result on the powers granted, restricted, excepted or reserved; if it was the meaning and intention of the Supreme Law of the land, it was their rule of action." No doubt Baldwin established his intellectual middle ground to his own satisfaction, but clearly his move into the gray zone was more indicative of a general state of mind and purpose than it was a clear indication of the specifics of permissible constitutional construction. The controlling axiom which he thought infused some interpretive precision was the view that the Constitution was a grant of the sovereign people of the several states. Thus "we can understand the federal and state systems . . . as the work of the same hand; which, in the institution of one government for state purposes separately, and another for the federal purposes of thirteen united or confederated states, has acted in separate bodies; and can ascertain what it had granted, how far it has restrained itself, and measure the grant by its exceptions and reservations." It was because Baldwin deemed that the cases (even where he concurred with the Court's judgment, *Charles River Bridge,* for example) had not been decided with sufficient consideration of his constitutional maxim, that he had composed his collected concurrences and submitted them to the public.

Baldwin's action in publishing the pamphlet produced mixed reactions.

Justice Story was not overly happy about several critical remarks Baldwin had made about Story's *Commentaries on the Constitution.* A year later, Story remarked of a Baldwin opinion: "It was full of his elaborate citations and comments in his own peculiar way." Baldwin had acquired a reputation for eccentricity, to employ a euphemism, and a newspaperman from Boston wrote: "I expected to find a little, cross, crabbed old man. He is, on the contrary, a large, full favored, black haired, quaker looking gentleman, of the most prepossessing exterior—industrious, attentive, careful, and I should think, exceedingly agreeable and obliging." He had doubtless seen Baldwin on one of his better days. John C. Calhoun wrote approvingly from South Carolina of the *General View:* "Your exposition of the origin, the nature and character of our system is demonstrated very clearly; so much so as to place them beyond the sphere of controversy. . . . As explained by you, it is one of great beauty and harmony." And, added Calhoun, it provided sound arguments in support of state interposition. He closed by suggesting the two men discuss the points further when they met.

In several subsequent cases, Baldwin continued to adhere to his policy of speaking for himself, whatever the decision of the Court may have been. In *Bank of Augusta* v. *Earle,* 13 Pet. 519 (1839), he wrote a separate concurring opinion which was not reported, however. And in *Groves* v. *Slaughter,* 15 Pet. 449 (1841), Baldwin, though among the majority, again voiced his views. He thought that states could not regulate interstate commerce, and that since slaves were both persons and articles of commerce, no state could prohibit their movement in interstate commerce. Baldwin did not care if no other Justices agreed with him. Slaves were property, and the right was anterior to the Constitution, which merely recognized and protected certain aspects of the right to hold property in slaves. The privileges and immunities clause required that state regulations intended to apply to citizens of other states place the latter on the same equality of treatment as its own citizens. In this early judicial reference to the due process clause of the Fifth Amendment as a protection of property rights, Baldwin concluded: "any power of Congress over the subject is . . . conservative in its character, for the purpose of protecting the property of the citizens of the United States, which is a lawful subject of commerce among the States, from any state law which affects to prohibit its transmission for sale from one state to another, through a third or more States." Baldwin also agreed with the Court's decision in *Prigg* v. *Pennsylvania,* 16 Pet. 539 (1842), which upheld the Fugitive Slave Law and declared invalid all state laws in opposition or in support of it, but dissented vigorously from the principles laid down in the majority opinion of Justice Story. The defendant who had been accused of kidnapping a Negro woman and taking her back to Maryland could not be guilty of the crime, Baldwin said, since the person abducted was a slave. No discussion of federal exclusivity was necessary.

In *Holmes* v. *Jennison,* 14 Pet. 540 (1840), a *habeas corpus* and federal-state relations case, Baldwin reaffirmed his views of constitutional restraint. He attacked the unceasing tendency of the Court to assume powers of "a vagrant nature, to be exercised under such of the various items specified, as may be suggested by a train of ingenious, refined, and subtle reasoning, from one implication to another, till there can be found some hook whereby to connect this with some granted power." This strong prose also demonstrates the touch of harshness which could influence Baldwin when stirred by an issue. In this case he lectured the Court, a bit presumptuously, on its duties regarding the internal police powers of the states.

Baldwin did not work harmoniously with the fellow members of his Court. Some contemporary observers claimed that he functioned better on circuit than in Washington. It was not so much what Baldwin said. That was acceptable, even if the specific points might produce disagreements. But Baldwin's manner, what has been described as his "nonconformity in writing opinions and his peculiar mannerisms during his last years on the Court," more often than not damaged, if they did not destroy, a judicial meeting of the minds with his colleagues. Of course, his temporary derangements were in a different category altogether. In his last years, the twin misfortunes of recurrent illness (his death was anticipated at least a year before it actually took place on April 21, 1844), and embarrassed finances, robbed this period of any of the gratifications that might have been predicted in 1830 when this talented man took his place on the nation's highest Court. Biographers and memorialists of "second-string" judges often begin their concluding sections with disclaimers about the limitations of their man, but then proceed to extol certain aspects of his career. In Baldwin's case, the limitations, self-imposed and otherwise, were too numerous and too pervasive to allow for a happy peroration.

SELECTED BIBLIOGRAPHY

Henry Baldwin's historiographical anonymity is almost complete. There is, of course, his own apologia, Henry Baldwin, *A General View of the Origin and Nature of the Constitution and Government of the United States* . . . (Philadelphia, 1837). And his Pittsburgh years have been the subject of a master's thesis, which appeared in print as: Flavia M. Taylor, "The Political and Civic Career of Henry Baldwin, 1799–1830," 24 *Western Pennsylvania Historical Magazine* 37 (1941). There matters rest. But a few years ago, Professor Gerald Gunther of the Stanford University Law School uncovered some interesting Baldwin items in the Supreme Court papers deposited in the National Archives. They consisted of notes on cases made by Baldwin during the 1830's, notes which indicated a different picture of the final years of the Marshall Court than previously presented.

Henry Baldwin

REPRESENTATIVE OPINIONS

HOLMES v. JENNISON, 14 PET. 540 (1840)

George Holmes had been indicted for murder by a grand jury in Quebec. He crossed the border into Vermont where he was arrested. The governor, Silas Jennison, ordered him to be delivered to the Canadian authorities, but he petitioned the Vermont courts for a writ of *habeas corpus,* claiming the state had no power to deal with a foreign government in any way, even to surrender fugitives. The Vermont Supreme Court upheld the governor's actions and the case was appealed to the Supreme Court which split four-four, thus affirming the Vermont court's decision. Taney, Story, McLean, and Wayne would have reversed the decision below, on the ground that any agreement between the Vermont governor and the Canadian government was forbidden by the Constitution. Thompson, Barbour and Catron voted to dismiss the appeal since, in their view, the Supreme Court had no jurisdiction in the case. Baldwin also voted not to interfere with the judgment of the Vermont court in the opinion which follows:

Opinion of Mr. Justice BALDWIN.

Concurring most fully and cordially in the opinions delivered by those of my brethren, who are opposed to any action by this Court on this case, I have nothing to add to the reasons assigned by them respectively, lest it might imply my want of confidence in the grounds which they have taken; and in my mind maintained with conclusive force. There are, however, two subjects of high consideration involved in this case, which I feel constrained to notice; as my opinion would have been governed by them had there been no other grounds for my declining to interfere with the order of the Supreme Court of Vermont, remanding the relator to the custody, whence he was brought before them by the writ of habeas corpus.

1. The Constitution of the United States confers no power on any department of the federal government, to prevent a state or its officers from sending out of its territory a person in the situation of Holmes the relator.

2. That a writ of error does lie from this to a state Court, to revise their proceedings on a writ of habeas corpus.

That the treaty-making power of the Constitution, is competent to bind the states by a stipulation to surrender fugitives from justice, is not denied by any; nor that where such power is executed by a treaty, a state is under an obligation to surrender: but that while such power remains dormant or contingent, the obligation does not exist, and that Congress have no power to impose it, has been too clearly extablished by my brethren, to leave it in my power to add to the weight of their reasoning. But while I admit the competency of the treaty-making power to compel, I utterly deny its power to prevent the expulsion of a fugitive from justice from the territory of a state, pursuant to its laws, or the general authority vested in its executive or other appropriate officers, to administer and enforce its regulations of internal police.

This distinction between the power to compel, and the power to prevent the surrender of a fugitive, is visible in the whole frame of the Constitution, as well in the general lines which it designates, in separating the powers of the federal and state governments, by grants, prohibitions, and separations, as by its more specific provisions.

There cannot be found a clause in the whole instrument, which in terms or by any fair construction, can be made to bring the power to compel a state not to surrender, within any enumerated subject over which Congress can legislate; unless it is sought as one of a vagrant nature, to be exercised under such of the various items specified, as may be suggested by a train of ingenious, refined, and subtle reasoning, from one implication to another, till there is found some hook whereby to connect this with some granted power. Nay, it is cautiously omitted in the prohibition on the states, to use any language, which can be tortured into a reference to the subject matter; and as the nature of the treaty-making power precludes any enumeration of the subjects of its exercise, it is left with no other prescribed limitation, than, that treaties to have their constitutional effect, must be made "under the authority of the United States." This power must then be called into action, and act on the subject, before a state can be deprived of the right to surrender, or retain a fugitive at its pleasure; a right which each state possessed in its plenitude, on the dissolution of the articles of confederacy, and which remained unimpaired, till it became party to the Constitution, on its adoption by the people thereof, whereby they held the power subject to such restraints, as treaty stipulations might impose in future. Without such stipulation the whole subject matter of fugitives of any description, from a foreign nation, or any of its colonies or dependencies, is reserved to the respective states, as fully as before the Constitution; but, with such stipulation in a treaty, I admit the state is as much bound to make the surrender, as if it had been a subject of express delegation of power to the President and Senate; or as if the same provision had been made in relation to foreign fugitives from justice, or service, as those from the respective states, but which is guardedly omitted.

In the second clause of the second section of the fourth article, the Constitution provides, that "A person charged in any state with treason, felony, or other crime, who shall flee from justice and be found in another state, shall on demand of the executive authority of the state from which he fled, be delivered up to be removed to the state from which he fled." A corresponding provision is made for fugitives from service or labour; and Congress, by the act of 1793, have prescribed the mode in which the provision of the Constitution shall be carried into effect. 1 Story, 284,285.

It will not be pretended that these provisions do not impose upon the states of this Union, an obligation as imperative, and impair their reserved rights to the same extent, as a similar stipulation in a treaty between the United States and any foreign state; let it then be assumed that there was such a treaty with Great Britain, in relation to fugitives from justice in Canada; and a stronger case cannot be supposed; the question it involves is not difficult of solution.

The object and great purpose of the Constitution and Congress, in one case, and of the treaty in the other, is to make it the duty of the state and its officers to make the surrender on a demand; but it does not follow that it may not be done voluntarily or without demand; to take the fugitive to the border and force him to pass the line, whether the authorities of the adjacent states or provinces are desirous, or even willing to receive him or not, is but an ordinary police power. This is the true point in issue; whether a state is prohibited by the Constitution, from doing of its own accord, an act which it is bound to do, whenever demanded pursuant to a law or a treaty of the United States; and which it might do or refuse, if the subject was neither within the law or treaty-making power of the United States.

Had no provision been made for the reclamation of fugitives from the states, there could be no pretence for denying to the states an unlimited discretion over the whole subject; the Constitution has put one single limitation on this discretion, in case of a demand from the executive of another state; leaving that discretion as free and full where no demand is made, as if the Constitution had been wholly silent on the subject. And if it had been so silent, the only difference would have been, that though there would have been no obligation to surrender on a demand, there would have been the same right and power to do it, as now exists in each state in respect to their respective fugitives; or as would exist under a treaty-making provision for the reciprocal delivery of fugitives from the Canadas, or the states.

No injunction of the Constitution can be violated, nor the faith of treaties impaired, by each state or province refusing to be made a Botany Bay, an asylum or even the receptacle of the vagabonds, the criminals, or convicts of the other; any duty of state to state, of state to the Union, and the United States to foreign powers; is fully and faithfully executed by the performance of the duties and stipulations imposed or made. But no political community, no municipal corporation, can be under any obligation to suffer a moral pestilence to pollute its air, or contagion, of the most corrupting and demoralizing influence, to spread among its citizens, by the conduct and example of men, who, having forfeited the protection of their own government by their crimes, claim to be rescued from the consequences, by an appeal to the same Constitution and laws, under which our own citizens are not, and cannot be screened from punishment, when it is merited by their conduct. No state can be compelled to admit, retain, or support foreign paupers, or those from another state; they may be removed or sent where they came; not because poverty is a crime, but because it is a misfortune not to be mitigated or relieved by the compulsory contributions of those among whom they throw themselves, or are cast by their governments for maintenance.

Every state has acknowledged power to pass, and enforce quarantine, health, and inspection laws, to prevent the introduction of disease, pestilence, or unwholesome provisions; such laws interfere with no powers of Congress or treaty stipulations; they relate to internal police, and are subjects of domestic regulation within each state, over which no authority can be exercised by any power under the Constitution, save by requiring the consent of Congress to the imposition of duties on exports and imports, and their payment into the treasury of the United States. 11 Pet. 102. 130, &c. 9 Wheat. 203, &c. 12 Wheat. 436, &c. Vide section 10, article 1, clause 2. "These laws form a portion of that immense mass of legislation, which embraces every thing within the territory of a state, not surrendered to the general government," &c. 9 Wheat. 203. "No direct general power over these subjects is granted to Congress, and consequently they remain subject to state legislation." Ib. "The constitutionality of such laws, has never, so far as we have been informed, been denied, (Ib. 205;) and are considered as flowing from the acknowledged power of a state, to provide for the health of its citizens." Ib.

"The power to direct the removal of gunpowder, is a branch of the police power, which unquestionably remains with the states." 12 Wheat. 443. "We are not sure that this may not be classed among inspection laws. The removal or destruction of infectious or unsound articles, is undoubtedly an exercise of that power; and forms an express exception to the prohibition we are considering. Indeed, the laws of the United States expressly sanction the health laws of a state." Ib. 444. These principles were reaffirmed in the city of New York *vs.* Miln, in language worthy of repetition, and most appropriate to this case in all its bearings.

"That the state of New York possessed power to pass this law (respecting foreign paupers) before the adoption of the Constitution of the United States, might probably be taken as a truism, without the necessity of proof. But as it may tend to present it in a clearer point of view, we will quote a few passages from a standard writer upon public law, showing the origin and character of this power."

Vattel, book 2, chap. 7, sect. 94. "The sovereign may forbid the entrance of his territory, either to foreigners in general, or in particular cases, or to certain persons, or for certain particular purposes, according as he may think it advantageous to the state."

Vattel, book 2, chap. 8, sect. 100. "Since the lord of the territory, may, whenever he thinks proper, forbid its being entered; he has, no doubt, a power to annex what conditions he pleases, to the permission to enter."

"The power then of New York to pass this law, having undeniably existed at the formation of the Constitution, the simple inquiry is, whether by that instrument it was taken from the state, and granted to Congress; for if it were not, it yet remains with them."

"If, as we think, it be a regulation, not of commerce, but of police; then it is not taken from the states. To decide this, let us examine its purpose, the end to be attained; and the means of its attainment."

"It is apparent, from the whole scope of the law, that the object of the legislature was to prevent New York from being burdened by an influx of persons brought thither in ships, either from foreign countries, or from any other of the states; and for that purpose, a report was required of the names, places of birth, &c., of all passengers; that the necessary steps might be taken by the city authorities; to prevent them from becoming chargeable as paupers."

"The power reserved to the several states, will extend to all the objects which in the ordinary course of affairs, concern the liberties, lives, and properties of the people; and the internal order, improvement, and prosperity of the state." 11 Pet. 132, 133.

After a review of Gibbons *vs.* Ogden, and Brown *vs.* Maryland; and showing that their opinion is not in collision with the principles of either of those cases; the Court say:—"But we do not place our opinion on this ground. We choose rather to plant ourselves on what we consider an impregnable position. They are these,—That a state has the same undeniable, and unlimited jurisdiction, over all persons and things within its territorial limits, as any foreign nation; where that jurisdiction is not surrendered or restrained by the Constitution of the United States. That by virtue of this, it is not only the right, but the bounden and solemn duty of a state, to advance the safety, happiness, and prosperity of its people; and to provide for its general welfare, by any and every act of legislation which it may deem conducive to these ends; where the power over the particular subject, or the manner of its exercise, is not surrendered or restrained in the manner just stated. That all those powers which relate to merely municipal regulations, or what may, perhaps, more properly be called 'internal police,' are not thus surrendered or restrained; and that consequently, in relation to these, the authority of a state is complete, unqualified, and exclusive." 11 Pet. 139.

"We think it as competent, and as necessary for a state to provide precautionary measures against the moral pestilence of paupers, vagabonds, and possibly convicts; as it is to guard against the physical pestilence, which may arise from unsound and infectious articles imported; or from a ship, the crew of which may be labouring under an infectious disease." Ib. 143.

These principles were not declared for the first time in the case of Miln; they flowed from those which were established as unquestionable in the United States *vs.* Bevans, where this language is used:—

"What then is the extent of jurisdiction which a state possesses?

"We answer without hesitation, the jurisdiction of a state is coextensive with its territory; coextensive with its legislative power.

"The place described, is unquestionably within the original territory of Massachusetts. It is then within the jurisdiction of Massachusetts; unless that jurisdiction has been ceded to the United States (3 Wheat. 386, 387,) by a cession of territory; or, which is essentially the same, of general jurisdiction." Ib. 388.

"It is not questioned, that whatever may be necessary to the full and unlimited exercise of admiralty and maritime jurisdiction is in the government of the Union. Congress may pass all laws which are necessary and proper for giving the most complete effect to this power. Still the general jurisdiction over the place, subject to this grant of power, adheres to the territory as a portion of sovereignty not yet given away. The residuary powers of legislation are still in Massachusetts. Suppose, for example, the power of regulating trade had not been given to the general government. Would this extension of the judicial power to all cases of admiralty and maritime jurisdiction, have divested Massachusetts of the power to regulate the trade of her bay?" Ib. 389.

It would be at least superfluous, if not presumptuous in me, to attempt to illustrate or enforce the soundness of these principles, which this Court declare to be impregnable positions, on which they plant their opinion. That they may neither be shaken or impaired by any future collision between them, and any opinions which may be founded on a contrary construction of the Constitution; is most ardently to be desired, by all who wish to see the federal and state governments move within their respective orbits, with the same harmony for the future, as they have done for the past. The continuance of this harmony, will, in my opinion, be in imminent danger, not only of interruption, but of extinction; whenever the course of this Court shall be such, as to subvert the great principles of constitutional jurisprudence, on which it has defined the line of separation between the powers which are granted to the United States, and those prohibited or reserved to the states, or the people thereof respectively. Nor is there one among these latter powers, which it is so dangerous to attempt to impair, as that of internal police; and especially that portion of it which relates to fugitives, vagabonds, criminals, or convicts, whether they have fled from justice before, or after trial: for if a state cannot expel from her territory this species of pestilence, so infectious, contagious, and fatal to the morals of the community, in which they are suffered to mix and move unmolested; her power of police is a shadow, a farce, while this most feculent mass of corruption remains a public nuisance, which the power of a state is incompetent to abate.

It is but a poor and meagre remnant of the once sovereign power of the states, a miserable shred and patch of independence, which the Constitution has not taken from them, if in the regulation of its internal police, state sovereignty has become so shorn of authority, as to be competent only to exclude paupers, who may be a burden on the pockets of its citizens; unsound, infectious articles, or diseases, which may affect their bodily health; and utterly powerless to exclude those moral ulcers on the body political, which corrupt its vitals, and demoralize its members. If there is any one subject, on which this Court should abstain from any course of reasoning, tending to expand the granted powers of the Constitution, so as to bring internal police within the law or treaty-making power of the United States, by including it within the prohibition on the states, it is the one now before us. Nay, if such construction is not unavoidable, it ought not to be given: lest we introduce into the Constitution a more vital and pestilential disease than any principle on which the relator could be rescued from the police power of Vermont, would fasten on its institutions, dangerous as it might be, or injurious its effects. Should an adjudication so fearful in its consequences, be made in a case of a kindred nature with this, the people and states of this Union will "plant themselves" on the "impregnable positions," taken in the opinions of this Court, in the cases quoted; and standing on grounds thus consecrated, refuse to surrender those rights which we had declared to be "complete, unqualified, and exclusive."

The power of this Court is moral, not physical; it operates by its influence, by public confidence in the soundness and uniformity of the principles on which it acts; not by its mere authority as a tribunal, from which there is no appeal; and if ever its solemn decisions should be overlooked by itself, or we should cease to respect those of our predecessors, the people and the states will still adhere to them; and our successors will refuse to follow our deviations from the ancient path. It may be the doctrine of the day, that the reserved rights of the states are too broad, and the powers of Congress too narrow; but it will not withstand the scrutiny of time, or the deliberate consideration of the principles on which the cases referred to have been decided, and those therein promulgated. If they shall ever be disregarded in public opinion, and their reversal follow; it will not be done by the establishment of those principles on which it is now attempted to enlarge the prohibitions on the states, and to expand the powers of Congress, by implication upon implication, to effect both objects by ingenious or farfetched suppositions or assumptions. Ingenuity, talents, and subtlety, can work a countermine under the Constitution, by which the contrary effect may be produced; whereby the reserved powers of the states may absorb as much of the granted powers of the general government, as the adoption of the grounds on which the relator's case has been placed would take from those which have neither been granted by, or prohibited to the states. Equally dreading and avoiding both extremes, I am content to take the Constitution as it has hitherto been expounded by this Court, on all subjects connected with the cause now before us; in my opinion it leaves no open point, even admitting what is known not to exist, that there was a treaty stipulation on the subject. But without such stipulation, the relator's case is most bald and barren of merits; it rests upon doctrines not to be sanctioned consistently with past adjudications, which, in the United States *vs.* Bevans, asserted the jurisdiction and legislative power of a state to be coextensive with its territory, over all subjects not delegated to the general government; and in Gibbons *vs.* Ogden, Brown *vs.* Maryland, and New York *vs.* Miln, declared that no power over the internal police of a state had been so delegated by the Constitution; but was reserved exclusively to the states. I deem it wholly unnecessary to make a detailed application of those cases to the present; their affinity is too visible on a comparison, to require any thing more than a reference to them respectively, as they are reported; police is in every feature; the moral and physical health of the people is the common object of police regulations in all their ramifications, as applied to the vast variety of subjects which they embrace, and none of which are confided to any other than state power; and all of which must remain under its exclusive control, till the Constitution is changed.

The states are enjoined by the Constitution, to surrender a fugitive from another state on a demand; they will be obliged to do it under a treaty stipulation to a foreign power; and thus far, but no farther, has there been, or can be any abridgment of their power over the subject: they cannot be deprived of their right of expelling from their territory those fugitives who have no privileges within it; or be compelled to retain them, when they are not entitled to the protection of its Constitution or laws. Any refugee crosses the border at his peril; his government may not desire to reclaim him for punishment, and be unwilling to receive him again; but that matters not to the state to which he flies; the right and power to remove, expel, and voluntarily to surrender the fugitive, is as perfect as if it was a duty prescribed by a power paramount to that of the state.

This is, in my opinion, the turning point of this case; and this right to determine what persons fleeing from abroad shall be suffered to remain a burden on its citizens for their support, or a dangerous example to the community, is so peculiarly and appropriately a subject of state jurisdiction, as to be incapable of delegation to any other power. Any action of Congress upon it, would be not only an assumption of ungranted power, but a direct usurpation of powers reserved to the states; and if exercised by means of coercion, to compel a state to retain the vagabonds from other states, or the border provinces, would operate more fatally on the morals of the people, than pestilence upon their health, or gunpowder on their property, and their lives. Happily, such power is not visible in the Constitution; nor has it been infused into it by construction; whenever internal police is the object, the power is excepted from every grant, and reserved to the states, in whom it remains in as full and unimpaired sovereignty as their soil, which has not been granted to individuals, or ceded to the United States; as a right of jurisdiction over the land and waters of a state, it adheres to both, so as to be impracticable of exercise, by any other power, without cession or usurpation. Such is the power which the governor, as chief magistrate of Vermont, has exercised over this fugitive; in my opinion, it was properly exercised; and that no department of this government is competent, on subjects of police, to control him, or any other state officer, in the execution of his or their offices.

By the course which has been taken, all danger of interfering with the relations of the United States and foreign powers, either on matters of commercial intercourse, or diplomatic concern is avoided; such interference could happen only on the refusal to deliver up the fugitive, on the demand or request of the authorities of Canada; for a compliance with either, would rather add strength to, than tend to weaken the pre-existing relations of amity and comity between the two nations. On the other hand, if the delivery was spontaneous, and made in the true spirit of border peace, and mutual safety from crime, the boon would be the more acceptable; or if the authorities of the state should send the fugitive back whence he came, those of Canada would have no cause of complaint, because they had made no reclamation, or because Vermont was unwilling to incorporate among its citizens a foreigner whom his own government was disposed not to take back. The United States cannot complain, for neither their rights or power can be affected, unless some department of their government shall put itself in the place of Vermont, to determine on what subject its internal system of police shall operate, and how it shall be executed; but on any other ground or pretext, there can be no colourable argument or reason for such interference. That the case before us is one in any way affecting our foreign relations, seems to me wholly supposititious; and the untoward consequences which seem to be apprehended from affirming the exercise of the power of the governor, appear as wholly conjectural, and without any rational foundation in fact or principle. But be this as it may, we have no warrant from the Constitution, and Congress can give us none, to authorize us to interfere with the exercise of a power, which comes within every definition which this Court has given of a regulation of the internal police of a state; or to examine whether it has been exerted under the authority of a state law, or by the constitutional power of its chief executive magistrate. It suffices for all the purposes of this case, that the subject matter is not of federal cognisance; but is excluded from the jurisdiction of the United States to its full extent, and reserved for the action of another sovereignty, whose power over it must remain untouched, till an amendment to the Constitution shall displace it. That this may never be done is, in my opinion, devoutly to be wished by every friend to the permanency of our institutions.

The other ground on which I am opposed to any interference with the proceeding of the Supreme Court of Vermont in this matter is, that it is not within the appellate jurisdiction of this Court, under the twenty-fifth section of the Judiciary Act; because the order of that Court on a habeas corpus, is not a judgment on which a writ of error can be brought.

I cannot so well define the nature and object of the writ of habeas corpus, or so well explain the proceedings upon it, as in the language of this Court:—"It has been demonstrated at the bar, that the question brought forward on a habeas corpus, is always distinct from that which is involved in the cause itself. The question whether the individual shall be imprisoned, is always distinct from the question whether he shall be convicted or acquitted of the charge on which he is to be tried; and therefore these questions are separated and may be decided in different Courts."

"The decision that the individual shall be imprisoned, must always precede the application for a writ of habeas corpus; and this writ must always be for the purpose of revising that decision, and therefore appellate in its nature." 4 Cranch. 101. "This being a mere inquiry, which without deciding upon guilt, precedes the institution of a prosecution, the question to be determined is, whether the accused shall be discharged or held to trial; and if the latter, in what place they are to be tried, and whether they shall be confined or admitted to bail. If, &c. upon inquiry it manifestly appears, that no such crime has been committed, or that the suspicion entertained of the prisoner was wholly groundless, in such cases only is it lawful totally to discharge him, otherwise he must either be committed to prison, or give bail." Ib. 125, 126.

"The Judicial Act (sect. 14) authorizes this Court, and all the Courts of the United States, and the judges thereof, to issue the writ for the purpose of inquiring into the cause of commitment." 3 Pet. 201. "It is a high prerogative writ, known to the common law, the great object of which is the liberation of those who may be imprisoned without sufficient cause." "It is in the nature of a writ of error to examine the legality of the commitment." Ib. 202.

It lies to a Circuit Court of the United States, sitting in a state, (3 Dall. 17,) or to the Circuit Court of this District, (3 Cranch. 448. 4 Cranch. 101,) it is an exercise of appellate jurisdiction, and "we are but revising the effect of their process, &c. under which the prisoner is detained." 7 Pet. 573. But it does not lie in favour of persons committed for treason or felony, plainly expressed in the warrant, convicted of a contempt, (9 Wheat. 39,) or a crime, by a Court of competent jurisdiction, (3 Pet. 202, 208,) or persons in execution, (Ib.;) nor will the Court upon the writ look beyond the judgment, and re-examine the charges on which it was rendered, (Ib. 202;) for if this Court cannot directly revise the judgment of a Circuit Court in a criminal case, they cannot do it indirectly. Ib. 208. The power to issue this writ being concurrent in this Court, the Circuit, and District Courts, and every judge of either, the action upon the writ when the party is before a Court or judge, is directed to the same object, "for the purpose of inquiring into the cause of commitment," in order to ascertain whether he shall be remanded to prison, discharged on bail, or without bail; in doing which this Court has no more power than any district judge; the nature of the power and the rules by which it must be exercised, are the same. 4 Cranch. 96.

This Court has declared this power to be appellate, and not original; so I shall take it on its authority, though if the point was new, it would seem to me to be the exercise of a special authority given by the Judiciary Act, for the specific purpose therein set forth: and that from the very nature of a high prerogative writ, it must be issued, and acted upon by prerogative, and not appellate power; especially by the Courts of the United States, whose jurisdiction is special, and limited to the cases specified in the Constitution and Judiciary Act. Taking however the power to issue the writ, and the action upon it to be appellate, then every district judge can exercise it to the same extent that this or a Circuit Court can; consequently he can revise the process of either Court, by which a person has been committed, by inquiring into the cause of commitment, and proceeding thereupon in the same manner, as if the commitment had been by a justice of the peace. This inquiry is confined to the question of recommitment, or discharge, the result of which depends on the discretion of the judge or Court before whom the prisoner is brought; the warrant of commitment must be inspected to see whether it sets out a proper cause for imprisonment; the evidence is examined for probable cause of prosecution; and if the warrant and evidence are sufficient, then the question of bail and its amount necessarily arises, which is, confessedly, a matter purely discretionary, subject only to the provision of the eighth Amendment to the Constitution, the thirty-third section of the Judiciary Act, (1 Story, 66;) and the fourth section of the act of 1793. 1 Story, 311.

On this view of the nature and object of the writ of habeas corpus, with the proceeding upon it, considered as the exercise of appellate jurisdiction; the first inquiry is, whether the manner in which it has been exercised, can be revised by a writ of error, to any Court or Judge of the United States.

That a writ of error will not lie upon any proceeding before a judge of this Court, or a district judge, in vacation, is too clear for discussion; there is no Court, no record to remove, no judgment to revise, the judge acts by a summary order, which affects only the question of imprisonment, discharge, or bail; the very nature of such action by an appellate power, by a judge out of Court, precludes its revision by another appellate power; which can act only by a writ of error, directed to a Court of record, to remove their final judgment and proceedings in the case. This Court cannot issue a writ of error to a District Court, in any case where a special authority to do it is not expressly given by law; nor to a Circuit Court, unless by the provision of the Judiciary Act, (7 Cranch 108, 287. 2 Wheat. 259, 395. 6 Pet. 495, 496. 12 Pet. 143. 13 Pet. 290;) nor can the Circuit Court issue a writ of error to a District Court, in any other than the specified cases provided for; "or issue compulsory process to remove a cause before final judgment." Such process (as a certiorari) is void, and may be disregarded (2 Wheat. 225, 226) as a nullity.

By the twenty-second section of the Judiciary Act, final judgments and decrees, in civil actions in the District Courts, may be re-examined in the Circuit Courts on a writ of error; whereby the power of the Circuit Court rests on two things; the judgment must be final, and must be rendered in a civil action, neither of which can exist in a habeas corpus issued under the fourteenth section, which gives authority to issue and act upon this writ, in two classes of cases. 1. To all the Courts of the United States, where it is necessary for the exercise of their respective jurisdictions, and agreeable to the principles and usages of law. 2. To either of the justices of the Supreme Court, as well as judges of the District Court, "for the purpose of an inquiry into the cause of commitment." Provided that writs of habeas corpus shall in no case extend to prisoners in gaol; unless they are in custody under the authority of the United States, committed for trial before some Court of the same, or to testify, &c. 1 Story, 59.

On a full consideration of this section, this Court, in the case of Bollman and Swartwout held, that it applied to the great writ of habeas corpus ad subjiciendum, providing the "means by which this great constitutional privilege should receive life and activity," that the generic term habeas corpus, when used singly and without additions, means the great writ now applied for; "and in that sense it is used in the Constitution." 4 Cranch. 94–100. It was also held, that it did not apply to a habeas corpus ad respondendum, to process from a state Court, to a habeas corpus cum causa, or the mode of bringing causes into a Court of the United States, from a state Court, (Ib. 96, 98;) consequently this great writ issues only in cases where a party is imprisoned on the charge of some criminal offence against the United States; and not in a civil action, to which they may be a party, as is apparent from the view taken by the Court in connecting the thirty-third and fourteenth sections.

The thirty-third section directs, that, "upon all arrests in criminal cases, bail shall be admitted, except where the punishment may be death; in which cases it shall not be admitted, but by the Supreme or a Circuit Court, or by a justice of the Supreme Court, or a judge of a District Court; who shall exercise their discretion therein, regarding the nature and circumstances of the offence, and of the evidence, and the usages of law." Vide 1 Story, 66; on which the Court remark:—

"The appropriate process of bringing up a prisoner not committed by the Court itself, to be bailed, is by the writ now applied for; of consequence a Court possessing the power to bail prisoners not committed by itself, may award a writ of habeas corpus for the exercise of that power"; and the thirty-third section was held to be explanatory of the fourteenth. 4 Cranch, 99, 100.

Hence there are, in my opinion, three objections to a writ of error from a Circuit to a District Court, to revise their proceedings on a writ of habeas corpus ad subjiciendum: 1. It is not a civil action. 2. The order to recommit, to bail, or discharge is not a final judgment or decree. 3. The action of the Court is discretionary, depending on the nature of the case, the evidence, and the usages of law. These objections apply with greater force to a writ of error from this to a Circuit Court under the twenty-second section, which provides that "upon a like process, may final judgments and decrees in civil actions, and suits in equity, in a Circuit Court, brought there by original process, or removed there from Courts of the several states, or removed there by appeal from a District Court, be re-examined in the Supreme Court. Independent then of the three objections above mentioned, others arise from the additional provisions in relation to the writ of error from the Supreme Court. It lies only from a final judgment, in a civil action, &c. brought in a Circuit Court by original process, or removed there from a state, or District Court; consequently it lies not upon a proceeding on a habeas corpus; which is the exercise of appellate power, commencing on petition, affidavit, and motion for the writ, and terminating by an order which the Court makes according to its discretion. This order, from its nature and effect, is not and cannot be final; for it only discharges the party from any further confinement, under the process under which he was arrested, "but not from any other process which may be issued against him, under the same indictment." 9 Pet. 710. The inquiry being merely preliminary to a trial, the order is only interlocutory, and can extend no farther than to the specific subjects of the inquiry, which can have no bearing on the final result of the prosecution, as to guilt or innocence.

By using the term "original process" the law excludes that which is appellate, it relates to the writ, by which a plaintiff brings a defendant into the Circuit Court, to answer a demand made in a civil action for a debt or damages; but surely not to a writ issued for persons in confinement under a criminal charge, directed to the officer or person who has him in custody under the authority of the United States, the object of which is to procure the liberation of the prisoner. The same conclusion results from the reference to civil actions in the Circuit Court, "removed there from Courts of the several states"; these actions are described in the twelfth section, which prescribes the mode of removal, and declares that when removed, "the cause shall proceed in the same manner, as if it had been brought there by original process." So as to civil actions removed there by appeal from a District Court, which are defined in the twenty-first section, and confined to final decrees "in causes of admiralty and maritime jurisdiction"; whence it follows, that the proceeding of the Circuit Court on a writ of habeas corpus, cannot be comprehended within either of the three classes of cases, to which a writ of error is confined by the terms of the twenty-second section of the Judiciary Act.

The provisions of the twenty-third and twenty-fourth sections lead to the same conclusion, by pointing only to those cases in which an execution can issue, or be superseded by the writ of error, and where, upon affirmance, the Court may decree just damages to the respondent in error for his delay, and single or double costs at their discretion; and by directing the mode of proceeding by the Supreme Court on affirming or reversing, and sending a special mandate to the Circuit Court, to award execution thereupon, (Vide 1 Story, 61), which will be hereafter considered in connection with the twenty-fifth. An application of these provisions to a writ of error on a writ of habeas corpus, makes it manifest that the law contemplated no such case, no execution issues, the order for recommitment or to give bail, or for a discharge, cannot be superseded; no damages can accrue by delay, and no mandate for execution can be awarded, for no final judgment exists on which an execution could issue. Had it been intended to embrace a habeas corpus, some provision appropriate to the case omission affords the most conclusive evidence to the contrary; or if any thing is wanting to remove all doubt, it will be found in the nature and object of this great writ, this constitutional privilege. It was designed to afford a speedy remedy to a party unjustly accused of a crime, without obstructing or delaying public justice; both of which objects would be defeated, by the delays consequent upon a writ of error, as it may be taken out by either party; if it can be by one, the Court can make no distinction between them, as it is a writ of right. Vide 7 Wheat. 42. For these reasons I am fully convinced, that no writ of error can be issued by this, or a Circuit Court, under the authority of the Judiciary Act, to revise a proceeding on a writ of habeas corpus, by any judge or Court of the United States: the next inquiry is, whether it can issue on a similar proceeding in a state Court.

By the twenty-fifth section it is provided, "That a final judgment or decree in any suit in the highest Court of law or equity of a state, in which a decision of the suit could be had," &c. (enumerating the particular classes of cases) "may be re-examined, and reversed or affirmed in the Supreme Court of the United States, upon a writ of error," &c. "in the same manner, and under the same regulations, and the writ shall have the same effect, as if the judgment or decree complained of had been rendered or passed in a Circuit Court; and the proceeding upon the reversal shall be the same, except, that the Supreme Court, instead of remanding the cause for a final decision as before provided, may at their discretion, if the cause has once been remanded before, proceed to a final decision of the same, and award execution." 1 Story, 61, 62. 1 Wheat. 353. This section differs from the twenty-second, only in using the term "any suit," in place of "civil actions," the effect of which is, that the writ of error lies to remove an indictment from a state Court, as held in Cohens *vs.* Virginia. 6 Wheat. 390, 391, 407, 410, &c. and to a prohibition, in Weston *vs.* The City, &c. of Charleston, (2 Pet. 463, 464,) but the nature of the judgment to be re-examined is the same, it must be a final one. The twenty-third section applies to the writ of error to a state Court, in all respects as to a Circuit Court. So does the twenty-fourth, unless so far as its provisions come within the exception of the twenty-fifth, which it becomes necessary to consider. The twenty-fourth section directs, that when a judgment or decree of the Circuit Court shall be reversed by the Supreme Court, it shall proceed to render such judgment, or pass such decree, as the Circuit Court should have rendered or passed; except when the reversal is in favour of the plaintiff or petitioner in the original suit, and the damages to be assessed or matter to be decreed are uncertain, in which case they shall remand the cause for a final decision. And the Supreme Court shall not issue execution in causes that are removed before them by writs of error, but shall send a special mandate to the Circuit Court to award execution thereupon."

Connecting this section with the exception in the twenty-fifth, we have the precise case provided for in the latter; "where the damages to be assessed," (in a suit at law), "or the matter to be decreed," (in a suit in equity), "are uncertain"; then the Supreme Court may "proceed to a final decision, and award execution," if the cause had been before remanded. Now it is most evident, that neither the exception in the twenty-fourth or twenty-fifth section, can apply to a proceeding on the writ of habeas corpus, for two conclusive reasons; 1. That if the reversal is in favour of the petitioner or plaintiff in this writ, there are no damages to be assessed, nor any matter to be decreed, which is uncertain; the judgment to be rendered is certain, and can be none other, than for the discharge of the prisoner, on, or without bail; and is not, nor can be a final decision of the cause. 2. The original suit is on the warrant of commitment, and a decision which precedes the application for the writ of habeas corpus, the issuing of which, and the proceeding upon it are, as has been held uniformly by this Court, the exercise of appellate jurisdiction and power.

A third reason is equally apparent in both sections, the final judgment must have been one, on which an execution could be awarded by the Circuit Court on a special mandate from this, under the twenty-fourth; or by this Court, in a case coming within the exception of the twenty-fifth; and in either case, there must have been a final decision of the cause, before any execution could be awarded.

The terms "original suit," and "cause," are used in the same sense, in the twenty-fourth section, so in the twenty-fifth; "suit" and "the cause" mean the same thing, both terms referring to the final action of this Court, whether they "remand the cause for a final decision," by the Circuit Court, and send them a special mandate to award execution under the twenty-fourth; or themselves, "proceed to a final decision of the same (the cause), and award execution," under the twenty-fifth section.

These considerations bring this inquiry to a narrow space, presenting to my mind stronger objections to the jurisdiction of this Court over the present case, than would apply to a writ of error to a Court of the

United States; while all the reasons which apply in the latter case, operate with full force on this; unless some distinction can be found between the terms "civil actions," and "any suit," or "the cause"; in which a final judgment has been rendered, which will justify a writ of error to a state Court, in a case where it would not lie to a Court of the United States, by reason of its not being a final decision or judgment; or on any other ground than that it was not a civil action. The only distinction between the two classes of cases, consist singly in this; that the term "any suit," in the twenty-fifth section, is broader than the term "civil actions," &c., in the twenty-second; whereby criminal cases may be revised by this Court, on a writ of error to a state Court; though they are excluded from the appellate jurisdiction of this, over Circuit Courts; unless they are certified by a Circuit Court, on a division of opinion between the judges thereof, under the sixth section of the act of 1802 (2 Story, 856); if such action as is therein prescribed, can be called the exercise of appellate power, and not a mere special, statutory authority.

In following to its consequences the settled principle of this Court, that in issuing and acting upon a writ of habeas corpus under the fourteenth section, it is by appellate power; it will appear that the reasons for so considering this power, are most conclusive against the exercise of their appellate jurisdiction over writs of error to the proceedings of a state or Circuit Court, on such a writ issued by either. In defining appellate power in such cases, the Court say:—"It is the revision of a decision of an inferior Court, by which a citizen has been committed to jail"; the question on a habeas corpus "is always distinct from that which is involved in the cause itself (4 Cranch. 100); these questions are separted, and may be decided by different Courts." "The decision that the individual shall be imprisoned must always precede the application for the writ of habeas corpus; and this writ must always be for the purpose of revising that decision; and therefore appellate in its nature." Ib. 101. The case on a habeas corpus, is "a mere inquiry, &c., whether the accused shall be discharged, or held to bail." Ib. 125. The law which gives authority to issue the writ, defines its object, "for the purpose of inquiring into the cause of commitment," (3 Pet. 201); "its legality, and the sufficiency of that cause." Ib. 202. "Considering then as we do, that we are but revising the effect of the process awarded by the Circuit Court, under which the prisoner is detained, we cannot say that it is the exercise of an original jurisdiction."

A discharge under this writ, discharges the party only from such process, and not "from any other process under the same indictment," (9 Pet. 710); or a new one. 4 Cranch. 136.

Let then whatever term, action, case, cause, suit, be given to a writ of habeas corpus, and the proceedings upon it; let the final action of the Court upon it be called a decision, an award, a judgment, or order, the character or nature of either, and the effect are the same; nothing is revised but the process of arrest, and the decision on which the process issued, and the arrest is made; the inquiry is limited to the cause of commitment; and every question arising is always so distinct from "the cause itself," that this inquiry can be determined by one Court, and the cause by another.

There can then be no final decision of "any suit," the "original suit," or "the cause," on a writ of habeas corpus, the subject matter in controversy remains unaffected by the mere inquiry into the cause of commitment, its sufficiency or the legality of the process, as fully as if no habeas corpus had been issued; any judgment rendered by any Court affects only the process; nor can it be in any sense deemed a "final judgment in a suit," on "the cause itself," or "a final decision of the same." So as to make it cognisable in this Court, by any appellate jurisdiction, on a writ of error to a Circuit Court, under the twenty-second, or a state Court, under the twenty-fifth section of the Judiciary Act.

Another objection equally fatal to the writ of error in this case is, that though the awarding the writ of habeas corpus is a matter of right, and "is granted ex debito justitiæ," yet the action of the Court is governed by its sound discretion, exercised on the whole circumstances of the case, according to which "the relief is allowed or refused on a motion." But a rule or order, denying the motion, is not a judgment, "it is only a decision on a collateral, or interlocutory point, which has never been deemed the foundation of a writ of error," which lies "only upon a final judgment or determination of a cause." "A very strong case illustrating the doctrine is, that error will not lie to the refusal of a Court to grant a peremptory mandamus," &c., as held by the House of Lords, (Vide 6 Pet. 656, 657;) and cases cited, 9 Pet. 4. 6. No principle is, or can be better settled by this Court, than that no writ of error lies upon any proceeding in a cause, depending on the discretion of the Court. 1 Pet. 168. 6 Pet. 217. 656. 7 Pet. 149. 13 Pet. 15. There can be no case more peculiarly and exclusively of that description, than one involving only the question of discharge, or recommitment on a habeas corpus; which is declared to be "the appropriate process" for that purpose. 4 Cranch. 100. "A mere inquiry, without deciding upon guilt," (Ib. 125;) "always distinct from the question, whether he shall be convicted, or acquitted," (Ib. 101;) and directed only to process, (7 Pet. 573. 9 Pet. 710;) not to the final determination of the cause, (6 Pet. 657;) but to a decision on a mere interlocutory, collateral point, cautiously excluded from revision on error, by the Judiciary Act.

The same result is found in "the principles and usages of (the common) law," as laid down in the time of Coke, without a single deviation to this time. In 8 Co. 127[b], 128[a], it was declared, that no writ of error could lie upon a habeas corpus; because it was "festinum remedium." S. P. Strange, 539. It will not lie upon a writ of procedendo; the refusal of a prohibition, or mandamus for the party, shall not be hung up on error, (Strange, 391. 543;) nor on a judgment quod computet, in account, Quod partitio fiat, in partition, by default in trespass; on awards of inquiry, on awards interlocutory, and not definitive, nor till the "last judgment" is rendered, on "all the matter within the original," the "whole matter of the cause"; because till then, the judgment or award is not final. 11 Co. 38[b]—40[a]. Vide Com. Dig. Pleader, Error, B. When an interlocutory judgment or award works a forfeiture, then error lies to be relieved therefrom. 11 Co. 41[a]. But this is only an exception to a universal rule, that error lies only on a final judgment which determines the whole subject matters in a cause; from which this Court has never yet departed, by any direct adjudication in error under either the twenty-second, or twenty-fifth sections of the Judiciary Act, or on the rules of the common law.

That the course of opinions delivered in this case by the majority, if not all the other judges, is different from mine is apparent; but as no judgment has been rendered by the Court, this point cannot be judicially settled: it is yet open to argument by counsel whenever a similar case arises; and of consequence, remains open for the consideration of this Court, or any of its members, here or elsewhere, as it has hitherto been considered. My reference to the Judiciary Act and the opinions of this Court, have been more in detail than to the principles of the common law, or the adjudged cases; because the former appeared to me to be conclusive, as to what the law of the land and of the Court has been, is, and ought to be in future. If it admitted of doubt, as to the latter, it sufficed for the case, to show by a brief reference, what the common law has been for centuries, and now is, without ever so far departing from what I deem my judicial duty, as to even inquire what it ought to be; as if it was in my power to abrogate, or vary from its rules on this or any other subject. When a point is decided by the adjudged cases, or laid down as settled in the books of acknowledged authority; I take it, and feel bound to act upon it, as the common law, which is infused into our jurisprudence; unless some act of Congress, some local law, or some decision of this Court, prescribes another rule. When this Court declare that "we are entirely satisfied to administer the law as we find it," (7 Wheat. 45. 3 Wheat. 209;) I feel bound to endeavour to find, and when found to follow it in all its course; and in searching among the fountains, rather than the rivulets of the law, for its true principle, I have found no safer guide than its forms, which from ancient times have embodied and preserved, unchanged, those principles which time has consecrated, by the certainty of the law, and the security and repose which an adherence to its rule affords to the rights of property and person.

Forms of writs, process, proceedings in suits, judgments, and executions, in all their various applications to matters of jurisprudence, were devised of old, and are yet followed, in order to practically apply the rules and principles of the law they enforce upon persons, property, and rights of all description; and when these forms are overlooked, the principles to which they give life, activity, and effect, will be forgotten or disregarded; nor is there a more effectual mode of producing both results, than at this day to look beyond those rules which have prevailed for centuries, and been respected as the land-marks of the law, to the reasons on which they were originally founded, of which this case affords a strong illustration.

It is admitted that in the whole course of the common law, there is no one precedent of a writ of error, upon the proceeding on a writ of habeas corpus; yet it has been earnestly contended at the bar, that error lies in such case on general principles; and that the contrary course of the English Courts has arisen from the mere omission to enter on the proceeding by habeas corpus, the purely technical words, "ideo consideratum est" in the order or award made by the Court.

Had the learned counsel of the relator disclosed to the Court the result of an inquiry, why these (so called) technical words were deemed so important, the reasons would have been found to be most decisive in a case of habeas corpus or mandamus; for before the statute of no record was made of the proceedings on those writs, no judgment was rendered on them, and consequently there was no record to remove from an inferior to a Superior Court, by a writ of error.

The omission of the term 'ideo consideratum est," which is the appropriate and only form known to the common law to denote the judgment of a Court, on a matter of record, in contradistinction to an order or award in granting or refusing a motion; was deemed good evidence that the law did not recognise a decision in which these words were not used, as a final judgment on which a writ of error could be brought; especially when, by the common law, such a decision was not made a matter of record, or so considered. However these reasons may operate on the minds of others, they satisfy mine that they are founded in the best established principles of the common law, and that when they are not found in the forms it has adopted, to denote the action of a Court, on a matter before them, their decision is not a judgment of record, cognisable in error, or in the words of Coke and this Court; "that without a judgment or an award in the nature of a judgment, no writ of error doth lie," (6 Pet. 656;) nor on decisions on motions "addressed to the sound discretion of the Court, and as a summary relief which the Court is not compellable to allow." Ib. 657. The refusal to quash an execution, is not in the sense of the common law, a judgment; much less a final judgment. It is a mere interlocutory order. Even at the common law, error lies only from a final judgment; and by the express provisions of the Judiciary Act, &c., sec. 22, a writ of error lies in this Court only on final judgments. Ib. A writ of error will not lie to a writ of error coram vobis, granted by the Circuit Court to correct its own errors; "it is subject to the same exceptions which have always been sustained in this Court, against revising the interlocutory acts and orders of the inferior Courts." 7 Pet. 147. 1 Pet. 340. "It is not one of those remedies over which the supervising power of this Court is given." Ib. 148. "The writ of error (coram vobis) was but a substitution for a motion in the Court below." Ib. No judgment in the cause is brought up by the writ, but merely a decision on a collateral motion, which may be renewed. 7 Pet. 149. S. P. 9 Wheat. 578, cited. In both cases the writ of error was dismissed, "because it was a case proper for the exercise of that discretion, and not coming within the description of an error in the principal judgment." Ib. Ib. "The decision of the Court upon a rule or motion is not of that character," (a final judgment,) this point which is clear by the words of the (Judiciary) Act, has been often adjudged by this Court." The cases in 6 Pet. 648, and 9 Pet. 4 are noted with approbation, and their principles reaffirmed. Vide 9 Pet. 602. These are the reasons why a writ of error will not lie at common law, or under the Judiciary Act in such cases, and these are the general principles of all law, and the foundation of the universal rule; that where power is given to any tribunal, to be exercised at its discretion, whether it is legislative, executive, judicial, or special, the decision of such tribunal is revisable only by some other tribunal, to which a supervisory power is given. 6 Pet. 729, 730. S. P. 7 Cranch. 42, &c. 1 Pet. 340, 2 Pet. 163. 3 Pet. 203. 10 Pet. 472, &c. 12 Pet. 611. The forms and modes of expression, by which any tribunal pronounces its discretion to have been exercised, does not affect the nature or character of its decision; that depends on what it has decided and its effect, whether it is a final judgment, or an interlocutory one, or a mere summary order, direction, or decision, on a rule or motion, which is not in law a judgment, though it may be expressed in the words appropriate to a judgment. The law looks to the thing done, as the true test of whether it is cognisable in error. To make it so, there must be a consideration of the record, on the matter of law, not of discretion; a final judgment of the whole matters of law in the suit, by determining the controversy, and the cause; which by the forms of the common law, always is expressed in the dead language of the old forms of judgment—"Ideo consideratum est," which has exposed this term to the imputation of technicality; but when its sense and meaning is expressed in the living language of this Court, and applied to the varied subjects and modes of its action, a very different character must be attributed to the significant and appropriate terms in which their decision is announced, according to the case before them.

Thus, in awarding the writ of habeas corpus: "The motion is granted," 4 Cranch. 101; or, "On consideration of the petition," &c. "Whereupon it is considered ordered and adjudged, that a writ of habeas corpus be forthwith granted," &c. 7 Pet. 583. So, where the party is discharged: "It is therefore the opinion of the Court," &c., "that there is not sufficient evidence," &c. "to justify his commitment," (Ib. 134,) "and, therefore, as the crime has not been committed," the Court can only direct them to be discharged. Ib. 136. Or, after reciting the return of the marshal: "On consideration whereof," &c. "it is now here considered," &c., that—be discharged from the writs "in the said return mentioned," (7 Pet. 585;) in other words, the motion is granted. On the refusal to award the habeas corpus: "On consideration of the rule granted in this case," &c., "it is considered, ordered, and adjudged by the Court, that the rule be discharged, and that the prayer of the petitioner for a writ of habeas corpus be and the same is hereby refused." 3 Pet. 209. Or "Upon the whole it is the opinion of the Court that the motion be overruled." "Writ denied." 7 Wheat. 45. "The rule therefore to show cause is denied, and the motion for the habeas corpus is overruled," (9 Pet. 710); the motion is not granted. When this Court decides on a certificate of division of opinion of the judges of a Circuit Court, the form is: "This cause came on to be heard on the transcript of the record," &c. "on the questions and points," &c. "certified to this Court. On consideration whereof, it is the opinion of this Court," that, &c. (3 Pet. 189), the point is decided. On an appeal in a suit in equity: "This cause came on," &c. on "consideration whereof, it is ordered and decreed," &c. 3 Pet. 221. On a writ of error to a Circuit Court: "This cause came on to be heard on the transcript of the record, &c. on consideration whereof, it is ordered and adjudged by the Court, &c." 3 Pet. 241. On a writ of error to a state Court: "This cause," &c. "on consideration whereof, it is considered and declared," &c. "It is therefore considered and adjudged," &c. (3 Pet. 267,) or, "On consideration whereof, it is ordered and adjudged," &c. (3 Pet. 291,) that the decree or judgment be reversed or affirmed. On a rule to show cause why a mandamus should not issue: "On consideration whereof, it is now here considered and ordered by this Court, that the rule prayed for be and is hereby granted," 6 Pet. 776. On the motion for a peremptory mandamus after the return: "The Court doth therefore direct that a mandamus be awarded," &c. (7 Pet. 648;) or, "On consideration of the rule, &c., it is now here considered, ordered, and adjudged by this Court." 8 Pet. 304–306. On a motion for an attachment for not obeying a peremptory mandamus: "The motion is dismissed," 8 Pet. 590. On refusal to grant the rule to show cause: "The rule is therefore refused," (11 Pet. 174:) or on a motion for a mandamus being denied: "On consideration of the motion, &c., it is now here ordered and adjudged," &c., and "the same is hereby overruled," (12 Pet. 344, 475,) or, "The motion for the mandamus is denied." 13 Pet. 290. In applying these varied forms to the substance, it is apparent that this Court adheres to those of the common law and its principles, having, it is true, less regard to mere terms, but leaving no difficulty in ascertaining their meaning, in their use, and application to their action on the case before them. Thus, in deciding on a rule or motion, in a case of a habeas corpus or mandamus, they use or omit as the case may be, the terms appropriate to a judgment, or those of a mere order directing or declaring the result of their opinion; yet on referring to the subject matter which they have decided, the Court in using the terms denoting judgment, always conclude on consideration of the rule, motion, petition, or return; and never leave their action open to any doubt as to the character of their decision, whether it finally disposes of the cause, or is a mere summary order, on some matter of an intermediate nature. But when the Court proceeds to render a final decree, or judgment, on an appeal, or writ of error, it is always done in the appropriate language of judgment; "This cause came on to be heard on the transcript of the record of the ——— Court, &c.," on consideration whereof, &c.; showing that they act upon the cause itself, on a judicial inspection of the record, and decide on all the matters of law therein contained, (5 Pet. 199;) and not on preliminary matters which leave the cause undecided. This action is also on a final judgment or decree of the Court below; which decided the whole cause, and would have been conclusive on it, had no appeal or writ of error been taken, or if the law had allowed none; the appellate power can act only on such decrees and judgments; in appeals it acts on the facts as well as the law of the case; in writs of error, it acts only on the matters of law. 1 Wheat. 335. 2 Wheat. 142. 6 Pet. 49. 7 Pet. 149, 282. 12 Pet. 331. 13 Pet. 164.

These forms lead to the true rules and principle of law which are the test of what judgments, decrees, orders, or awards in the nature thereof, are cognisable in error, and what are not; what are so, has been seen; what are not, is most distinctly declared by this Court. "We have only to say, that a judge must exercise his discretion in those intermediate proceedings, which take place between the institution and the trial of a suit; and if in the performance of his duty, he acts oppressively, it is not to this Court that application is to be made," (8 Pet. 590. S. P. 9 Pet. 604); "the appropriate redress, if any, is to be obtained by an appeal, after the final decree shall be had in the cause." 13 Pet. 408.

No language can apply more forcibly to a proceeding on the writ of habeas corpus. It is intermediate between the institution and trial of the suit or prosecution; it is within the discretion of the Court, to remand or discharge; their order therein, is interlocutory in its nature, not definitive of the suit, but on the mere collateral questions of bail, commitment, or discharge from process of arrest; and whether terms of judgment are used, or omitted, in granting, or refusing the motion, the substance is the same; no final judgment in the suit is, or can be rendered; it remains open for trial as fully as before the habeas corpus was awarded.

The cases in this Court on habeas corpus, are decisive of the point, that no order or judgment rendered in them are final in their nature or effect; and in the very common and familiar case of a question of freedom or slavery, which is decided on the writ of habeas corpus on a motion to discharge; it has never been doubted that the question of right, was perfectly upon a writ of homine replegiando, let the decisions on the habeas corpus have been either way.

On the review of the forms and principles of the common law, as adopted by this Court, there is (as is admitted) no precedent of a writ of error on a habeas corpus, being sustained, which is powerful evidence that those which are unquestioned, forbid it; and no principle exists which can justify it; while I am utterly unable to comprehend, by what sound rule of jurisprudence prescribed to the Courts of the United States, a double appellate power in the same Court, ever can be exercised over the same suit, and the same subject matter, 1. By the writ of habeas corpus ad subjiciendum; 2. By writ of error.

When appellate power is once exerted, it is spent by the judgment of the appellate Court, unless another Court is authorized to revise such judgment; if a Circuit Court exerts this power by a writ of habeas corpus, and the granting or refusing the motion to discharge is a final judgment and decision of the cause; it follows that it is not a case for this writ; for if the defendant is remanded to custody, he is in, on an execution of the judgment; or if he is discharged, he cannot be again arrested on the same process; the writ does not lie when he is at large without bail; if under bail, that is imprisonment in law. On the contrary, if the order for recommitment, or discharge, is not a final judgment in the suit, it is interlocutory, in an intermediate proceeding, depending on the discretion of the Court, in deciding a collateral point; leaving the points and matters of law, on which the last and final judgment is to be rendered, entirely open; and of consequence, presenting no matter to which a writ of error can attach; by excluding from the cognisance of the appellate Court the only questions which it can revise. In the first case, a writ of error lies, and in the second the great writ of habeas corpus lies, if any appellate power can reach the suit in that state of things; the suit, or cause, is the same, whether the party remains in prison under the original commitment, or after being brought up on that writ, he is remanded by the Court; if this exercise of its discretion is revisable by any other Court, it must be by a revision of the same subjects which had been before revised. The "cause of commitment," its "legality," its "sufficiency," "the nature and circumstances of the offence, the evidence, and the principles and usages of law;" are the subject matters of such revision by appellate power, on any writ whatever; of error, if the judgment is final; of habeas corpus, if it is only interlocutory or collateral; or (no judgment at all) if the granting or denying the motion is a mere intermediate proceeding by summary order. But if a second writ of habeas corpus is not grantable to relieve the party from even the oppression of the Court, in remanding him on the first; "it is not to this Court that application must be made," (8

Pet. 590;) "and the appropriate remedy, if any is to be obtained by an appeal (a writ of error) after the final decree (judgment) shall be had in the cause." 13 Pet. 408.

To sustain a writ of error, on a proceeding on a writ of habeas corpus under the Judiciary Act, a mere inquiry must be construed to mean a final judgment, a final decision; the cause of commitment becomes the cause of action, or prosecution, the suit, the original suit, the cause; and an authority resting alone on a statute, conferred "for the purpose of inquiring" only, by the fourteenth section, by one writ, must be assumed under the twenty-second, or twenty-fifth by another writ, whose office, the action upon it, and the subjects of action are wholly different. The past decisions of this Court must also be radically revised, in order to so shape their definitions, and action, as to meet this altered condition of the law; the process of revision must also be applied to the Judiciary Act, whereby the refusal to grant a rule, or motion to discharge, will be made to mean the final judgment, the determination of the suit, and a recognisance of bail for the appearance of the party at the trial thereof, to be an award of execution, or à contra. By an order of discharge before trial, "proceed to a final decision of the cause," though not even the indictment is found, and thus convict or acquit the party in a writ of error, to a Court, on the proceeding of mere inquiry into the cause of his commitment; for it must be remembered, that when this Court decides on a writ of error, the judgment below must be either affirmed or reversed; this Court must give the same judgment as the Court below should have done, unless in the excepted cases, which cannot arise on the habeas corpus. And when this is done, there remains the further act of directing a special mandate to another Court, to award execution of the judgment of this; or for this Court to do it, in the case provided for. 1 Wheat. 353, &c.

There must also be infused into the law, some mode or process by which the order for commitment, bail, or discharge, may be superseded by the party suing out the writ of error; some provision must be also made, as to the progress of the prosecution during the pendency of the writ of error. Now process may be issued, or a new indictment may be found for the same offence, nay, a trial may be had, before this Court can decide on the sufficiency of the first cause of commitment; and when they shall have done this by "a final decision of the cause" or suit, and sent their "special mandate to award execution thereupon," the return to that mandate may be, that the party has been arrested on other process, convicted of the offence, or is at liberty after an acquittal. This Court can award no execution till the cause has been once remanded, under the twenty-fifth section as it now reads. So, in a case coming within the exception of the twenty-fourth, for in all other cases, they must, on reversing, render the same judgment which ought to have been rendered below.

Now if we had reversed the judgment of the Supreme Court of Vermont, we could have rendered a judgment of discharge, for there are no damages to be assessed, and nothing uncertain to be adjudged; yet we could award no execution till a mandate had been first sent, and returned unexecuted, or not returned, or returned with the above or the same reasons, as are to be found on the return to the mandate in Hunter *vs.* Martin, 7 Cranch. 628. 1 Wheat. 305, 306. "That the writ of error in this cause was improvidently allowed under the authority of that act; (the twenty-fifth section) "that the proceedings thereon in the Supreme Court were "coram non judice" in relation to this Court, and that obedience to its mandate be declined by the Court."

If such an occurrence has actually happened in a case, where this Court had undoubted jurisdiction, it may be expected in future cases of a writ of error in one like the present; which can be brought within the law, only by a successive train of implication upon implication, till ingenious reasoning may fasten it to some expression, which may be thought to justify the assumption of the power. But more than jurisdiction must be assumed, before this Court could exert it to the extent which such a case requires; for though resistance to its mandate may be contingent, or merely possible, it ought to be well considered, whether, when it should happen, the Court felt assured that they would be sustained by the law and Constitution, in enforcing obedience by mandamus, attachment, and the imprisonment of the judges of the highest Court of a state.

It is not enough that the term "any suit" may embrace a case of habeas corpus; it must be one which in all other respects admits of the action prescribed in the Judiciary Act, in all its provisions relative to the appellate jurisdiction of this Court; if it is, there will be found no defect of power to execute its final mandate, or execution, by the authority of this Court. If it is not, then if the Court assumes jurisdiction, it must usurp power to carry into effect a judgment which the law does not recognise, and consequently makes no provision for its execution. It is dangerous, at least, if not unwise or rash, to exercise a power which may be given by the Constitution; but which Congress has given no authority to execute, or given in terms so obscure, that to so construe them, is in substance the exercise of legislative power, by the judicial department. However desirable it may be thought to enlarge jurisdiction, and expand its exercise so as to embrace cases not yet known to the law, or by so construing the Constitution and law, as to make it by reasoning what it ought to have been in the text; and giving inference and incident the effect of ordinance and enactment, increase the ostensible power of the Court; yet assuredly it will continue to lose, in public confidence, that moral strength, which can alone insure its efficient and quiet action, in the same proportion as it extends ungranted jurisdiction. No course appears to me to lead more certainly to such results, than that which the Court has been urged to take in this case; had we reversed the (so called) final judgment, and our mandate had encountered new process, &c. &c. our own solemn judgment would have had a most ludicrous effect, as a final decision, of what? not the suit, cause, or prosecution, but on the legality of the original process, which is a most conclusive reason why a decision on mere process is not the subject of a writ of error. Or had the matter remained as it was, our reversal would have respected only the refusal to discharge the party from the process; our mandate to discharge, would, if executed, leave him liable to arrest on new process, without affecting the suit; which is an equally conclusive reason to show that a final decision in error on the habeas corpus is not such as is contemplated by the twenty-fourth or twenty-fifth sections, or provided for by either.

Or should that Court refuse obedience to our mandate, the predicament of this Court would be precisely the same as in Hunter *vs.* Martin; they must at the next term proceed in one of the following modes.

1. Follow the precedent of Hunter *vs.* Martin—issue "a writ of error" to the Supreme Court of Vermont, "founded" on their "refusal to obey the mandate of this Court"; raise that refusal to the dignity of a final judgment, (Vide 1 Wheat. 305,) and then reverse it, and affirm "the judgment of the District Court." Ib. 262. This however would not be a course appropriate to the present case; there is no judgment of any inferior Court, or if there was, this Court would have no power by the twenty-fifth section, to affirm or reverse it, because the decision complained of was had in the highest Court of law of the state, (6 Pet. 49;) nor could any mandate be directed to any other Court, (1 Wheat. 353. 8 Pet. 314;) and it requires no reasoning to show that this Court ought not, and would not deal with the jailor or other person who had the custody of the relator. 7 Pet. 282.

2. "Proceed to a final decision of the cause and award execution," as specially authorized by the twenty-fifth section; but this would be abortive, as there could be no final decision of the cause of prosecution, on a mere inquiry into the cause of commitment; nor could any execution be awarded against person or property; and the nature of the case precludes any efficient action, save by a mandate to be directed to the Court, most certainly not to the jailor.

3. Issue a peremptory mandamus to the judges, to carry the mandate into effect, (Vide 5 Cranch. 115. 7 Pet. 648. 8 Pet. 305,) which is expressly authorized by the fourteenth section of the Judiciary Act, and is most appropriate to this case; it being necessary for the exercise of the appellate jurisdiction of this Court, and agreeable to the principles and usages of law—the common law. 12 Pet. 492, 493. And if that mandamus is not obeyed, then on the authority of the seventeenth section, award an attachment, and if no sufficient cause is shown to avert it; "punish by fine and imprisonment," this "contempt of authority." Vide 1 Story, 59, 60. Vide 8 Pet. 588, 590.

Such is the power with which this Court is invested by the Constitution and laws, so it may, and ought to be exerted, whenever it becomes necessary to exercise its appellate jurisdiction, in vindicating its authority to enforce the law in its majesty, upon any tribunal, which has rendered a judgment under state authority in violation of the Constitution, a law, or treaty of the United States; and refuses to obey the mandate of reversal.

On every case which lawfully invokes the action of these powers, this Court, I trust, will not hesitate to exert it, that it will, by so doing, "plant" itself in public opinion and confidence, on an "impregnable position," (11 Pet. 139,) I cannot doubt; nor, that when this Court deliberately takes the first step in exercising jurisdiction on a writ of error to a state Court, they will be prepared, and resolved to take the last, should the exigencies of the case invoke it. But if the Court is not well assured that the law of the case will fully justify the last, the time for reflection is before the first step is taken: otherwise they may be induced, if not compelled, to halt, to retrace their steps by retrogression, or to stop the progress of the cause to final judgment and execution, from a doubt whether they have, or the conviction that they have not, the legitimate power to finish what they had begun.

James M. Wayne

☆ 1790–1867 ☆

APPOINTED BY

ANDREW JACKSON

YEARS ON COURT

1835–1867

James M. Wayne

by

FRANK OTTO GATELL

ONE OF THE pre–Civil War Supreme Court Justices who best illustrates the difficulties of trying to reconcile a belief in effective, delegated national powers with the concept of state sovereignty was James Moore Wayne. Wayne, born in 1790, was the twelfth of thirteen children of Richard Wayne and Elizabeth Clifford. His father was a Yorkshireman, a Major in the British Army who came to America in 1759. He later settled in Charleston, South Carolina, where he married Miss Clifford, whose family had lived in South Carolina for several generations. Richard Wayne vacillated during the Revolution, finally casting his lot with the Loyalist side. Had it not been for the influence of his wife's family, his property would have been confiscated and he himself banished. He moved to Savannah, Georgia, in 1789.

In Savannah, the Waynes quickly established themselves among the leading families of that town. They had a rice plantation a few miles above Savannah, a place called "Argyle Island." The family lived there, but were close enough to Savannah to enjoy the social and commercial benefits of their status. James' early education was at the hands of a tutor who lived with the family. And at age fourteen, he entered the freshman class of Princeton (then called the College of New Jersey). There he was not a lonely exile among the Yankees, since the college attracted many sons of the Georgia aristocracy. He was graduated in the prescribed four years, in 1808, with the degree of Bachelor of Arts.

From Princeton, Wayne proceeded to study law. First a prominent Savannah attorney instructed him and then Judge Charles Chauncey of New Haven, Connecticut. He returned to Georgia in 1810, and a year later was admitted to the bar. His progress as a fledgling lawyer was quite methodical. He went from study with yet another attorney, his brother-in-law Richard Stites, to a partnership with a young lawyer, and finally in 1816 to his own practice.

FRANK O. GATELL, Professor of History at the University of California, Los Angeles, is the author of John Gorham Palfrey and the New England Conscience.

In 1813, he married Mary Johnson Campbell. The union lasted fifty-four years and produced three children. Also, during the War of 1812 with Britain, Wayne prepared to do his bit in his country's defense. He became Captain of a volunteer militia unit, the "Chatham Light Dragoons," a fact which attests to his solid standing in the community at a time when such militia posts were a fairly accurate gauge of a man's popularity and power. The Dragoons girded themselves bravely for an anticipated British assault on Savannah, but unlike their Baltimore counterparts they never had to face the reality of shots fired in anger.

In 1815, Wayne entered politics. He was elected a representative in the Georgia legislature from Chatham County. Legislation favoring debtors—easing the terms of debt repayment—was then an important issue in Georgia politics. In response to the hard times brought on by the Jefferson Embargo, the legislature of 1808 had passed several laws intended to soften the rigors of debt status. The posting of security could postpone forced sales of property for six months, or payment of one-third the amount of such sales could also stop the disposition of the property. A few years later several state supreme court justices opined that the laws were unconstitutional, thus precipitating the controversy. In the legislature, the majority of members agreed to repeal the relief laws, but at the same time declared that the judges had assumed a power they did not possess: the power to deem such laws unconstitutional. This was a power which rested solely with the General Assembly. Wayne was happy to join in repealing the laws (he had been elected in Savannah by those favoring repeal), but he would not join the majority in their attack upon judicial review.

After two terms in the legislature, Wayne moved back to political service in his native city. He was mayor of Savannah for two years (1817–19), a tenure which proved more troublesome than satisfying. At twenty-seven, the office may have gratified his personal ambitions, but it did little to aid him financially, so he resigned to resume his law practice, this time with Richard R. Cuyler as his partner. Wayne pursued his career actively and became well known among the bench and bar of that region in handling suits in both state and federal courts.

Late in 1819, the General Assembly elected him to a judgeship, sitting in Savannah's Court of Common Pleas. Although the new post was much more than a sinecure, Wayne was able to pursue his law practice at the same time. Yet a judgeship in one of the state's superior courts, the real stepping-stone to political advancement, was more appealing. Wayne had hopes for such an appointment as early as 1821, but the job went to another man with greater influence with the governor. A year later he obtained the position. Georgia politics at that time was a tangle of factionalism and personal politics. Wayne had to tread warily to avoid giving more offense to individuals than was healthy for political success. He was already committed to one or another form of the political game, and Georgia of the 1820's was the perfect training ground for the neophyte, perhaps even better training than one might receive in New York or Virginia, the highly "politicized" states, where adherence to the ruling machine all but prescribed the tempo of political advancement.

Meanwhile, Wayne kept busy with his judicial duties. Stepping-stone or not, the superior court judgeship involved plenty of work. His Eastern Circuit Court handled a great many cases, embracing all of the varieties which came under local and state jurisdiction. Wayne worked hard, tried for as impartial a mind and manner as a human being can achieve, and he generally earned the respect of the adversaries and their counsel who came before him. He was no back-slapper, but seemed to be a popular judge—so far as the judicial function will allow a man to seek popular approval. But he did have ample opportunity to make himself known. His court's semiannual sessions were more than legal affairs. The leading men of the counties comprising Wayne's circuit welcomed the legal corps which rode out from Savannah, and this made the sessions as important to the social and political life of the state as they were to the maintenance of the rule of law.

Wayne had been harboring expanded political ambitions for many years. In the early 1820's he coveted a seat in Congress, and the desire became a reality in 1828. By that time Wayne, who had previously been a member of the William H. Crawford-George Troup faction, had with the rest of the Crawfordites switched his allegiance to Andrew Jackson. And like all Georgians, he believed that land then occupied by Indians belonged solely to the state. He opposed the attempt of the Cherokees to establish a sovereign state within the boundaries of Georgia. Thus Jackson's policy of refusal to accept the creation of such an Indian nation and his concurrent efforts to force the Indians to emigrate west of the Mississippi made him attractive to Georgians.

Wayne's congressional career began in December, 1829. Among other issues, the tariff figured prominently in the political reshufflings which the Jackson years would bring. Anti-tariff sentiment was strong in Georgia, but not nearly so strong as in the neighboring state of South Carolina. Both states, in common with political opinion in most of the South, stigmatized the protective tariff as a cause of their apparent commercial decline. But when South Carolina took the matter beyond the realm of protest and petition, out of the normal channels of legislative give-and-take and into the extreme of nullification, southern unity broke down. Georgians, it turned out, would be equally negative about the tariff *and* nullification. Wayne in a public letter branded the South Carolina scheme "false in theory, and in practice disastrous to our country." As a Unionist, Wayne took a careful middle position between the extremes of nullification and consolidation, and his constituents rewarded him with an overwhelming vote for reelection late in 1832. A month later, South Carolina proceeded with its Ordinance of Nullification, but did so without much hope of aid from Georgia or other southern states.

Wayne further strengthened his position with the Jackson Administration by supporting the Force Bill. He was the only member of the Georgia delegation to do so, since the law gave the President the authority to use the armed forces to collect the federal revenue, if necessary. It was Jackson's strong response to nullification, and although southern politicians might oppose South Carolina's action many still thought it unwise to accept the President's militant position as expressed in the Force Bill. But Wayne went ahead, despite protests and veiled threats from state rights politicians. From two standpoints, that of his principles, and the fact that the nullifiers were relatively weak in Georgia, Wayne felt confident about his stand.

There were other points of harmony with the Jacksonian position. Wayne's views on internal improvements were orthodox: he favored the deepening of rivers and harbors (including, presumably, that of Savannah), but he opposed federal appropriations for constructing canals and highways. The establishment of post roads, often used as a vehicle for expansion of federal efforts in that sphere, Wayne interpreted to mean nothing more than the right to select routes on roads already existing. In that regard he was a bit more orthodox than the President. But on the Bank, the "Monster Bank" of Nicholas Biddle, there was no divergence of opinion. Wayne preached the Jacksonian line in all its stark simplicity, and he did so ardently and frequently. Nor had Wayne been forced to learn these sentiments in Washington. Georgia had a strong record of anti-Bank sentiment. Wayne opposed recharter in 1832, and he opposed restoration of the deposits in 1834. To him, the Bank was the "fourth department of our Government, stronger than the other three, wielded by the capitalists of the nation, without responsibility to the people."

Such principles and practices inevitably made him *persona grata* with the leading Jacksonians. Senator Benton considered Wayne one of the most reliable Democrats in the House, and the White House also took proper notice of his efforts. In 1834, with both his Nullification and Bank stands to run on, he won reelection to Congress, defeating the candidate of the States' Rights party. Wayne emerged as a leading Unionist Democrat and began to be mentioned as the man who might fill a then-vacant seat in the U.S. Senate. Shortly after the campaign of 1834, Justice William Johnson of the Supreme Court died. Johnson was a South Carolinian, but that state had lost favor with Jackson, to put it mildly. Sectional balance on the Court would be maintained, but the administration decided to skip over South Carolina and select Wayne of Georgia. In January, 1835, Jackson sent his name to the Senate for confirmation.

Jackson's judicial appointments were then a matter of great contention, but Wayne's did not provoke too much controversy. As one Whig newspaper admitted: "Few Whigs would hesitate to acknowledge that Judge Wayne is preferable for the bench of the Supreme Court to some other candidate of the Jackson Party." And a New York editor added: "The appointment seems to be acceptable generally." There was more than a grain of truth to the Democratic claim of the *New York Post* that: "Mr. Wayne's character as a Republican of talent, education, firmness and honesty is well known." It was a fine testament to Wayne that despite his close involvement with some of the fundamentally disturbing political issues of the day he still retained the respect of those political opponents who were willing to judge him with some objectivity.

During the Nullification struggle, Wayne had shown that he thought the national government possessed substantive powers in certain clearly delegated spheres. This conviction came out clearly in Wayne's opinions concerning the commerce clause. As a member of the Taney Court (Chief Justice Marshall had died in the same year Wayne took his seat as Associate Justice), Wayne participated in the uneven course pursued by that Court in attempting to formulate a consensus on the extent of federal power in the field of interstate and foreign commerce. But although indecision might mark the deliberations of some of his colleagues on that problem, Wayne came to adhere to a straight-line view in favor of national power which would later cause a Massachusetts Whig Justice, Benjamin R. Curtis, to refer to him as one of the "most high-toned Federalists on the bench." Wayne argued that Congress had exclusive power to regulate such forms of commerce, and that the constitutional grant had erased all right of the states to legislate on the subject.

Wayne's initial exposure to the problem came in *City of New York* v. *Miln,* 11 Pet. 102 (1837). Here, Wayne concurred in the Court's decision that a New York law requiring ship captains to report on immigrants and to post bonds to cover expenses of passengers who became public charges was constitutional. Wayne agreed that this legislation was not prohibited by the commerce clause and was a valid exercise of the state police power. As mayor of Savannah, Wayne had sponsored similar legislation for his port city. In 1847, the Court decided the *License Cases,* 5 How. 504 (1847), dealing with state attempts to regulate imported liquors through licensing. There was unanimity in upholding the laws, but most Justices issued separate opinions. Significantly, Wayne remained silent.

But two years later in the *Passenger Cases,* 7 How. 283 (1849), Wayne spoke out. Again, the problem of regulating immigrants arose, this time because of state taxes for each newcomer levied by New York and Massachusetts. A bare majority of the Justices agreed to strike down the laws and Wayne was among them. His opinion rested on the axiom that the commerce power was "exclusively vested in Congress." If states legislated in that sphere, "whatever may be the motive for such enactments . . . if they practically operate as regulations of commerce, or as restraints upon navigation, they are unconstitutional." There could be no "exception from the entireness of the power in Congress to regulate [interstate and foreign] commerce." Wayne's ultra position was more a portent of things to come in constitutional interpretation than a reflection of legal realities at the time. When the case of *Cooley* v. *Board of Wardens,* 12 How. 299, came up in 1852, the Court tried to solve this particularly vexing question of divided sovereignty and commerce. A local pilotage law was at issue, and Justice Curtis offered a flexible verbal formula stating that federal exclusivity should apply only to those instances when the specific case demanded it. Otherwise local authorities could legislate, although it might impinge on the federal commerce power. Neither Justices McLean or Wayne would accept the solution. Wayne's dissent reiterated his views of the *Passenger Cases,* views which he continued to maintain for the remainder of his judicial career.

Another major area of constitutional interpretation which needed "tidying up" by the Taney Court after the groundbreaking, but perhaps overly expanded, decisions of Marshall, was that of the contract clause. By the time Wayne and his colleagues came to grapple with the issue, the corporate form of business organization had won the field, and the legal relation of the private corporation to state government was a question which had to be settled and which had important bearings on American economic growth as well as federal-state relations. Specifically, the Court had final judgment on attempts of state legislatures to alter conditions of previously granted corporate rights. In *Charles River Bridge* v. *Warren Bridge,* 11 Pet. 420 (1837), Chief Justice Taney rejected the idea that any but explicit privileges could be read into corporate charters. and Wayne agreed wholeheartedly with his chief, as he did two years later in *Bank of Augusta* v. *Earle,* 13 Pet. 519 (1839), where the Court upheld the power of a corporation chartered in one state to enter into contracts in another unless explicitly forbidden to do so by the latter.

Wayne was a friend of corporate enterprise. He thought that courts should listen attentively to the cases brought by corporate investors, and that for purposes of federal jurisdiction corporations should be treated as citizens of the state which had granted the charter. Appeals for application of the contract clause of the Constitution, forbidding state legislatures from passing laws impairing the obligations of contracts, found a friend in Wayne. In several cases (*Gordon* v. *Appeal Tax Court,* 3 How. 133 [1845] and *Planters' Bank* v. *Sharp,* 6 How. 301 [1848], among others) Wayne voted to invalidate state laws he thought impaired the state's charter-contracts with banks. And he was the lone though silent dissenter in the well-known case, *West River Bridge Co.* v. *Dix,* 6 How. 507 (1848), which allowed the application of eminent domain against a monopoly franchise. And in several Ohio banking law cases, Wayne held in 1856 that a state could not escape its contractual obligations by means of a constitutional amendment which was in effect another form of impairing legislation. See *Dodge* v. *Woolsey,* 18 How. 331 (1856). But Wayne's views were not so ultra as to be ludicrous. Thus the statutory *per diem* allowed Pennsylvania's officials was not a contract which subsequent legislatures might not tamper with, to cite one example of Wayne's own "rule of reason" in applying the contract clause, *Butler* v. *Pennsylvania,* 10 How. 402 (1851). (Opinion by Justice Daniel, joined in by Wayne.) But in general, Wayne could be found on the side of private rights in such cases.

In the process of specialization which inevitably takes place on the Supreme Court, Wayne emerged as an expert on admiralty law. One contemporary judge thought that whatever favorable reputation Wayne earned from his written opinions came primarily from his admiralty decisions. In 1847 he spoke for the Court in a case (*Waring* v. *Clarke,* 5 How. 441) involving a ship collision on the Mississippi considerably above New Orleans but at a point where the river was still subject to tides. Wayne upheld the federal courts admiralty jurisdiction, and in so doing leaned upon the arguments of British admiralty courts rather than the limiting concepts of the common law courts. The federal power extended beyond the "high sea" to "arms of the sea, waters flowing from it into ports and havens, and as high upon rivers as the tide ebbs and flows." And a few years later such jurisdiction was extended even further in cases involving shipping on the Great Lakes, and in one case above Mississippi tide water.

Several other important cases bore upon the question of federal jurisdiction. In *Louisville Railroad Co.* v. *Letson,* 2 How. 497 (1844), the issue was whether a federal court had jurisdiction over cases involving corporations as parties. Previously, Marshall had ruled that corporations could sue in federal courts if all the stockholders were citizens of a state other than the defendant's. This severely limited the legal maneuverability of all but a few locally owned corporations. Wayne overturned the precedents. He averred that "a corporation created by a State to perform its function under the authority of that State, and only suable there, though it may have members out of that State, seems to us to be a person, though an artificial one, inhabiting and belonging to that State, and therefore entitled, for the purpose of suing and being sued, to be deemed a citizen of that State." Thus the state citizenship and residence of the many stockholders became irrelevant, and through diversity, corporations operating nationwide could seek legal redress in federal courts. And in *Dobbins* v. *Erie County,* 16 Pet. 435 (1842), Wayne repudiated the attempt of a state, Pennsylvania, through use of its taxing power to reduce the salary of a federal officer. Such an unwarranted invasion of federal power occurred "when taxation by a State acts upon the instruments, emoluments and persons, which the United States may use and employ as necessary and proper means to execute their sovereign powers."

Federal jurisdiction in allotted spheres, including diversity of citizenship, was all-important to Wayne. Not because he was without respect for state sovereignty, but because the federal system demanded that ". . . the people [must] think and feel, though residing in different states of the Union, that their relations to each other were protected by the strictest justice, administered in courts independent of all local control or connection with the subject matter of the controversy . . ." (*Dodge* v. *Woolsey,* 18 How. 331 [1856]).

As was the case with all branches of the American governmental process, the slavery issue intruded more and more significantly into the Court's councils as time wore on. As both a constitutionalist and a southerner, Wayne of course believed that the institution of slavery enjoyed full constitutional protection. In an 1854 speech, he explained that extensions of federal power in certain spheres, commerce for example, did not imply that the national government could alter or regulate slavery as a subsidiary function of the prescribed regulatory power. No federal power could be used "in such a way as to dissolve, or even disquiet, the fundamental organization" of the states. In short, Washington could not meddle with slavery. It could only "deal with it kindly, in such a manner that the integrity of the state may be preserved," and it should aid the slave states to repel any encroachment, whatever the source. The Constitution, if applied correctly and fairly, was the South's greatest bulwark and guarantor of its rights.

From the start of his Supreme Court career, Wayne participated in cases dealing with the laws of slavery. But in most instances the cases were primarily concerned with other aspects of the litigation, and they did not yet represent an effort by the legal branch to resolve basic political problems. In 1842, Wayne, himself a slaveholder, concurred with Story of Massachusets in *Prigg* v. *Pennsylvania,* 16 Pet. 539 (1842), that the federal power regarding fugitive slave laws was exclusive. Each man saw the result through his own telescope: Story, who thought he had struck a blow for freedom, desired that nonslave states be unable to pass laws to *aid* the return of fugitives; Wayne feared that if states could legislate they would pass laws hindering surrender of fugitives.

Wayne's sentiments on certain federal powers may have brought accusations from extreme states' rights men that he had abandoned southern principles, but on the questions of the Negro and slavery, Wayne gave no offense. He never entertained the notion that Negroes could or should be allowed citizenship. The Negroes' inferior status, whether slave or free, was in the nature of things and the law should be firm in maintaining that status. Decades before, while serving as a Savannah alderman, he supported legislation to outlaw schools for Negroes, and he later sentenced a person who broke that ordinance. Free Negroes were subordinate, without "hope that their posterity here can become more elevated than themselves." It was unthinkable that "they can be made partners of the political and civil institutions of the States, or of those of the United States." By the middle 1850's, Wayne had sold his plantation, and retained only nine slaves (who were hired out), but his convictions that the rights of slaveholders were neither to be disparaged nor curtailed held firm. And one of these rights, to be used if the owner so wished, was that of taking his slaves into the territories. Wayne did not join the growing chorus of "Positive Good" southerners, who extolled the institution as beneficial equally to slaves as to masters (if not more so), but mild regrets once expressed, he saw no manageable way out. And to abrogate the vested rights created by slavery would be both unwise and illegal.

Wayne thought that the Court should use the *Dred Scott* case, 19 How. 393 (1857), as a vehicle for settling the territorial question conclusively. He urged this course on Chief Justice Taney and several other colleagues but received mixed reactions. There then took place the backstairs conferences over timing, extent of the decision, and the worries over the "Free Soil" opinions sure to come from McLean and Curtis, which ultimately brought the majority into line in favor of an expanded decision. In any case, Wayne did not have to be convinced or frightened into his course of action. At one of the conferences, Wayne argued that "public expectation has been aroused" on the issues raised by the case. A decision on jurisdiction alone "will be condemned as failing in our duty." And Wayne also wanted agreement that Taney should prepare the majority opinion.

Contrary to Wayne's wishes, the Chief Justice did not speak for all the majority Justices—those who agreed that Congress could not prohibit slavery in the territories. But Wayne did state, in his short concurring opinion, that he agreed entirely with Taney's document, "without any qualification of its reasoning or its conclusions." He was the only member who put himself behind Taney and his views so explicitly. One student has suggested, based on an examination of the style of Taney's opinion, that Wayne in fact wrote major portions of it. (Hogan, "The Role of Chief Justice Taney in the Decision of the Dred Scott Case," 58 *Cas. & Com.* 3 [1953].) Wayne was fully cognizant of the combustible materials with which the Court had dealt. His opinion went so far as to contain an aside, remarkable for the Court's (any court's) necessary fiction of detachment, that the Supreme Court "had neither sought nor made the case." He was realist enough to acknowledge that he and his fellow Justices had settled the question only "so far as it is practicable for this Court to accomplish such an end." Those elements of the political establishment as wished to accept Dred Scott as the final word joined to praise the sentiments of Taney, Wayne, et al. Pennsylvania Democrats, in convention, declared it "a model of constitutional wisdom, of sound legal learning, and of calm unanswerable reasoning." Even the Republicans, who, of course, flayed Taney's opinion, were less scathing with Wayne, another indication of his ability to retain the respect of adversaries.

With more and more Americans accepting polar positions regarding slavery, Wayne tried to maintain his Unionism. It was an increasingly uncomfortable stance, one sure to provoke acrimony whatever his views. In 1859, Wayne, as part of his circuit court duties, presided over the trial of the slave traders who sailed and owned the *Wanderer*. His charge to the grand jury left no doubt where he stood. He upheld the wisdom and necessity of the constitutional prohibition against the international slave trade, and urged the jurors not to flinch in upholding the Constitution. His charge to the trial jury was explicit: the defendants were "pretty plainly and conclusively shown to be connected with" the slave trade, and the severity of the death penalty was not a concern for the jury. The Savannah jurors heard him out, and soon came back to acquit the men.

With the election of Lincoln and the onset of the secession crisis, Wayne had to make a painful decision. His son, an army major, resigned his commission and returned to Georgia to serve his state. Wayne did not disapprove of the act, but he himself decided to remain on the federal bench. He thought that the South, and the Unionist cause, needed a voice in the judicial department more than ever. When secession actually came, Justice Campbell of Alabama resigned from the Court, but Wayne kept to his plan. Constitutional secession was to him a contradiction, although he did not discount the theoretically acceptable last resort, revolution. The crisis was a terrible blow for an old, consistent Unionist, then closing out a public career. He was, of course, denounced in his native state, and in 1862 a Confederate court branded him an enemy alien and confiscated his property in Georgia. Wayne's son, then state adjutant general, was able to recover the property, but only by agreeing to limiting conditions.

To a consistent Unionist, the Civil War was torture. And to a southerner, one who had chosen to remain in the national, or enemy, camp, the agony was all the more hard to bear. Northerners praised Wayne's adherence to the Union;

the press of Georgia, when it noticed him at all, dismissed the turncoat: "Georgia does not claim him, and he is no more of us." But Wayne would not budge from his principles, however painfully out of place they might seem during those unhappy years. Toward the end of the war he commented on the events, and the imperishability of the Union, despite the fact that the country had become "distracted by rebellion and scourged by civil war."

Such consistency demanded that he uphold the war measures of the Lincoln Administration. He certainly did not wish the Republicans well politically, but the government had been constitutionally installed, and that was enough. In 1862, the Court was asked to rule on the naval blockade of southern ports in the *Prize Cases,* 2 Black 635 (1862). The President had declared such a blockade by executive order, employing the constitutional war powers. The Court split five to four, upholding the President. Wayne was one of the five, despite the fact that the dissenters included such men as Taney, Catron, and Clifford—those with whom he was most closely associated. A trio of Republicans had joined the Court in 1862, breaking the hold on the Court which by and large had been enjoyed by the southern Democrat-"Doughface" coalition in the prewar decades.

Wayne, of course, still considered himself a Georgian. When the Confederacy collapsed, he returned home immediately. The situation was undoubtedly difficult, but as in most of the South, readjustment began quickly, remarkably so in view of four years of civil war. Although he considered the war a rebellion, Wayne opposed a punitive policy in dealing with the South. In two significant cases of 1867 involving test oaths, *Cummings* v. *Missouri,* 4 Wall. 277 (1867), and *Ex parte Garland,* 4 Wall. 333 (1867), Wayne joined a majority of five in striking down the laws as unconstitutional. Military Reconstruction did not gain his support, and he would not hold circuit court in states where such rule existed. But Wayne did not have to witness the playing out of the Reconstruction tragedy. He died in Washington on July 5, 1867, and was buried in Savannah.

Wayne's political and judicial career, if not brilliant, was nevertheless admirably consistent. He defended a balanced view of the nature of the Union, one which reflected the realities of power, at least for the early part of the nineteenth century. The Constitution was not to him a "rope of sand." But the tragedy of Wayne's life proved to be the tragedy of the Union itself. The precarious balance he sought between state and national power could not be maintained, and the shift to preponderant national power came during a blood bath which made southern Constitutional Unionists such as Wayne resemble old fogies, men deprived of even the dubious compensation of extremism to console them.

SELECTED BIBLIOGRAPHY

No large collection of Wayne papers exists. Wayne's biographer, Alexander Lawrence, nevertheless expressed the hope that they had not been destroyed and yet might turn up. An early biographical sketch is, John Livingston, "Hon. James M. Wayne, of Georgia . . .," 5 *United States Monthly Law Magazine* 382 (1852). (It also appeared in John Livingston, I *Biographical Sketches of Distinguished American Lawyers* 158–75 [1854].) The modern biography is Alexander A. Lawrence, *James Moore Wayne, Southern Unionist* (Chapel Hill, 1943).

James M. Wayne

REPRESENTATIVE OPINIONS

DODGE v. WOOLSEY, 18 HOW. 331 (1856)

The state of Ohio had granted corporate charters to various banks, containing very generous exemptions from taxation. Later legislatures repealed these exemptions, going so far as to amend their state constitution to insure that new taxes could be levied uniformly. The State Bank of Ohio refused to pay the tax, insisting that a charter, like any contract, could not be impaired by the state even by constitutional amendment. Wayne, speaking for the Court, upheld the bank, the first time a state constitutional provision was declared invalid. Justices Campbell, Catron and Daniel dissented denouncing "these extraordinary pretensions of corporations . . ."

Mr. Justice WAYNE delivered the opinion of the court.

It must often happen, under such a government as that of the United States, that constitutional questions will be brought to this court for decision, demanding extended investigation and its most careful judgment.

This is one of that kind; but fortunately it involves no new principles, nor any assertion of judicial action which has not been repeatedly declared to be within the constitutional and legislative jurisdiction of the courts of the United States, and by way of appeal or by writ of error, as the case may be, within that of the supreme court.

It is a suit in chancery, which was brought by John M. Woolsey, in the circuit court of the United States for the district of Ohio, seeking to enjoin the collection of a tax assessed by the State of Ohio on the Commercial Branch Bank of Cleveland, a branch of the State Bank of Ohio. He makes George C. Dodge, the tax collector, the directors of the bank, and the bank itself, defendants.

Woolsey avers that he is a citizen of the State of Connecticut, that he is the owner of thirty shares in the Branch Bank of Cleveland, that Dodge and the other defendants are all citizens of the State of Ohio, and that the Commercial Bank of Cleveland, is a corporation, and was made such, as a branch of the State Bank of Ohio, by an act of the general assembly of that State, passed the 24th of February, 1845, entitled "An act to incorporate the State Bank of Ohio and other banking companies." He alleges that the Commercial Bank has in all things complied with the requirements of its charter, and that, by the 60th section of the act, it is declared that each banking company organized under it and complying with its provisions, shall, semi-annually, on the 1st of May and 1st of November of each year, those being the days for declaring dividends, set off to the State of Ohio six per cent. on the profits, deducting therefrom the expenses and ascertained losses of the company, for six months next preceding each dividend day; and that the sums so set off shall be in lieu of all taxes to which said company, or the stockholders thereof, on account of stock owned therein, would otherwise be subject; and that the cashier of such company shall, within ten days thereafter, inform the auditor of the State of Ohio of the amount set off, and shall pay the same to the treasurer of the State on the order of the auditor.

It is averred that the Bank of Cleveland had at all times complied with the requirements of the act. That, in the year 1853, it set off to the State six per cent. on the two semi-annual dividends which had been made in that year, on the first day of May and the first day of November, which amounted in the aggregate to the sum of $3,206^{65}/_{100}$. That the same had been notified to the auditor, and that the bank had always been ready to pay the same when demanded. The complainant then avers, that three years before bringing his suit, having full confidence that the State of Ohio would observe good faith towards the bank, in respect to its franchises and privileges conferred upon it by the act of incorporation, and that it would adhere with fidelity to the rule of taxation provided for in the charter, he had purchased thirty shares of the capital stock of the bank, and that he was then the owner of the same. He further states, after he had made such purchases, that on the 17th of June, 1851, a draft of a new constitution had been submitted to the electors of the State for their acceptance or rejection, which, if accepted by a majority of the electors who should vote, was to take effect as the constitution of the State, on the 1st of September, 1851. It is admitted that it was accepted, that it became and now is the constitution of the State of Ohio. It is provided in sections two and three of the 12th article of that constitution, that laws shall be passed, taxing by an uniform rule, all moneys, credits, investments in bonds, stock, joint-stock companies, or otherwise; and that the general assembly shall provide by law for taxing the notes and bills discounted or purchased, money loaned, and all other property, effects, or dues whatever, without deduction, of all banks now existing, or hereafter created, and of all bankers, so that all property employed in banking shall always bear a burden of taxation equal to that imposed on the property of individuals. And in the 4th section of the 13th article of the constitution of 1851, it is further declared, that the property of corporations now existing, or hereafter created, shall be subject to taxation, as the property of individuals.

It appears also by the bill, that the general assembly of the State of Ohio passed an act on the 13th of April, 1852, for the assessment and taxation of all property in the State, and for levying taxes on the same according to its true value in money, in which it is declared to be the duty of the president and cashier of every bank, or banking company, "that shall have been, or may hereafter be, incorporated by the laws of the State, and having the right to issue bills for circulation as money, to make and return, under oath, to the auditor of the county in which such banks may be, in the month of May, annually, a written statement containing, first, the average amount of notes and bills discounted or purchased, which amount shall include all the loans or discounts, whether originally made, or renewed during the year, or at any time previous; whether made on bills of exchange, notes, bonds, mortgages, or other evidence of indebtedness, at their actual cost value in money; whether due previous to, during, or after the period aforesaid, and on which said banking company has, at any time, recovered or received, or is entitled to receive, any profit or other consideration whatever, either in the shape of interest, discount, exchange, or otherwise; and secondly, the average amount of all other moneys, effects, or dues of every description, belonging to such bank, or banking company, loaned, invested, or otherwise used or employed, with a view to profit, or upon which such bank, or banking company receives, or is entitled to receive, interest.

The act then makes it the duty of the auditors, in the counties in which a bank or banking companies may be, to receive from them returns of notes and bills discounted, and all other moneys and effects or dues, as provided for in the 19th section of the act, to enter the same for taxation upon the grand duplicate of the property of the county, and upon the city duplicate for city taxes, in cases where the city tax is not returned upon the grand duplicate, but is collected by city officers; which amounts so returned and entered shall be taxed for the same purposes and to the same extent that personal property is, or may be taxed, in the place where such bank or banking company is situated. It is then averred that the president and cashier of the Commercial Bank of Cleveland, fearing the penalty imposed by the act for a refusal or neglect to make a return according to the act, did, in the month of May, in the year 1852, make a return, protesting against the right of the State to assess a tax upon the bank, other than that which was provided for, in the charter of its incorporation of the 24th February, 1845. But it appears that the return so coerced from the president and directors of the bank had been assessed by the auditor, for the tax of 1852, at $\$10{,}197\frac{55}{100}$, exceeding by $\$7{,}526\frac{72}{100}$ the amount of tax for which the bank was liable under its charter, which George C. Dodge, as collector of taxes, seized and collected by distress on its moneys. It is also shown by the bill, that there has been another entry of taxation against the bank for the year 1853, of $\$14{,}771\frac{87}{100}$, exceeding the sum to which it is liable under its charter by $\$11{,}665\frac{22}{100}$ for that year.

It is against the collection of this tax that John M. Woolsey, as a stockholder in the bank, has brought this suit, claiming an exemption from it as a stockholder, upon the ground that the act of the general assembly of the State of Ohio, and the tax assessed under it upon the bank, are in violation of the 10th section of the 1st article of the constitution of the United States, which declares that no State shall pass any law impairing the obligation of contracts. And he seeks the aid of the circuit court to enjoin Dodge, the defendant, from collecting the same from the bank, as collector of taxes, as he had threatened to do by distress, and as he had done for the assessed tax for the year 1852.

The complainant gives a further aspect to his suit which it is also proper to notice. It is, if the taxes are permitted to be assessed and collected from the bank, under the act of the 13th of April, 1852, it will virtually destroy and annul the contract between the State and the bank, in respect to the tax which the State imposed upon it by the charter of its incorporation, in lieu of all other taxes upon the bank or the stockholders thereof, on account of stock owned therein; that his stock will be thereby lessened in value, his dividends diminished; and that the tax is so onerous upon the bank, that it will compel a suspension and final cessation of its business. He finally declares that as a stockholder, on his own behalf, he had requested the directors of the bank to take measures, by suit or otherwise, to assert the franchises of the bank against the collection of what he believes to be an unconstitutional tax, and that they had refused to do so.

To this bill the defendant, George C. Dodge, filed an answer. The other defendants did not answer. He admits the material allegations of the bill, except the allegation that the tax law of April 13, 1852, is unconstitutional; says that the act is in conformity with the constitution of Ohio, which took effect September 1, 1851, and that it is in harmony with the constitution of the United States. He denies that any application was made by Woolsey to the directors of the bank, to take measures, by suit or otherwise, to prevent the collection of the tax, and insists that this averment was inserted merely for the purpose of giving color to a proceeding in chancery. That the complainant would not have sustained an irreparable injury even if he had, as treasurer, proceeded to distrain for the tax; for that the bank would have had a remedy at law against him for all damages which might have been sustained in consequence of such distress, as he is worth, at a reasonable estimate, eighty thousand dollars after the payment of all his debts. And he insists that the complainant had not exhibited such a case as entitled him to the interposition of a court of equity. To this answer a general replication was filed. But it was agreed by the counsel in the cause, that the complainant had, by his attorney, addressed a letter to the Commercial Bank of Cleveland, to institute proper proceedings to prevent the collection of the tax by Dodge, in the same manner as had been done by the attorney of a stockholder in the Canal Bank of Cleveland, for a tax assessed upon it under the same act, and that the action of the board of the Commercial Bank, in answer to Woolsey's application, was the same as had been given by the directors of the Canal Bank. That resolution was in these words: "Resolved, that we fully concur in the views expressed in said letter as to the illegality of the tax therein named, and believe it to be in no way binding upon the bank; but, in consideration of the many obstacles in the way of testing the law in the courts of the

State, we cannot consent to take the action which we are called upon to take, but must leave the said Kleman to pursue such measures as he may deem best in the premises."

Upon the foregoing pleadings and admission, the circuit court rendered a final decree for the complainant, perpetually enjoining the treasurer against the collection of the tax, under the act of the 13th February, 1852, and subjecting the defendant, Dodge, to the payment of the costs of the suit. From that decision the defendant, Dodge, has appealed to this court.

His counsel have relied upon the following points to sustain the appeal:—

1. The complainant does not show himself to be entitled to relief in a court of chancery, because the charter of the bank provides, that its affairs shall be managed by a board of directors, and that they are not amenable to the stockholders for an error of judgment merely. And that in order to make them so, it should have been averred that they were in collusion with the tax collector in their refusal to take legal steps to test the validity of the tax.

2. It was urged that this suit had been improperly brought in the circuit court of the United States for the district of Ohio, because it is a contrivance to create a jurisdiction, where none fairly exists, by substituting an individual stockholder in place of the Commercial Bank as complainant, and making the directors defendants; the stockholder being made complainant, because he is a citizen of the State of Connecticut, and the directors being made defendants to give countenance to his suit.

3d. It was said, if the foregoing points were not available to defeat the action, that it might be contended that the defendant was in the discharge of his official duty when interrupted by the mandate of the circuit court, and that the tax had been properly assessed by a law of the State, in conformity with its constitution, of the 1st September, 1851.

We will consider the points in their order. The first comprehends two propositions, namely; that courts of equity have no jurisdiction over corporations, as such, at the suit of a stockholder for violations of charters, and none for the errors of judgment of those who manage their business ordinarily.

There has been a conflict of judicial authority in both. Still, it has been found necessary, for prevention of injuries for which common-law courts were inadequate, to entertain in equity such a jurisdiction in the progressive development of the powers and effects of private corporations upon all the business and interests of society.

It is now no longer doubted, either in England or the United States, that courts of equity, in both, have a jurisdiction over corporations, at the instance of one or more of their members; to apply preventive remedies by injunction, to restrain those who administer them from doing acts which would amount to a violation of charters, or to prevent any misapplication of their capitals or profits, which might result in lessening the dividends of stockholders, or the value of their shares, as either may be protected by the franchises of a corporation, if the acts intended to be done create what is in the law denominated a breach of trust. And the jurisdiction extends to inquire into, and to enjoin, as the case may require that to be done, any proceedings by individuals, in whatever character they may profess to act, if the subject of complaint is an imputed violation of a corporate franchise, or the denial of a right growing out of it, for which there is not an adequate remedy at law. 2 Russ. & Mylne Ch. R., Cunliffe *v.* Manchester and Bolton Canal Company, 480, *n.;* Ware *v.* Grand Junction Water Company, 2 Russ. & Mylne, 470; Bagshaw *v.* Eastern Counties Railway Company, 7 Hare Ch. R. 114; Angell & Ames, 4th ed. 424, and the other cases there cited.

It was ruled in the case of Cunliffe *v.* The Manchester and Bolton Canal Company, 2 Russ. & Mylne Ch. R. 481, that where the legal remedy against a corporation is inadequate, a court of equity will interfere, and that there were cases in which a bill in equity will lie against a corporation by one of its members. "It is a breach of trust towards a shareholder in a joint-stock incorporated company, established for certain definite purposes prescribed by its character, if the funds or credit of the company are, without his consent, diverted from such purpose, though the misapplication be sanctioned by the votes of a majority; and, therefore, he may file a bill in equity against the company in his own behalf, to restrain the company by injunction from any such diversion or misapplication. In the case of Ware *v.* Grand Junction Water Company, 2 Russell & Mylne, a bill filed by a member of the company against it, Lord Brougham said: "It is said this is an attempt on the part of the company to do acts which they are not empowered to do by the acts of parliament," meaning the charter of the company; "so far I restrain them by injunction." "Indeed, an investment in the stock of a corporation must, by every one, be considered a wild speculation, if it exposed the owners of the stock to all sorts of risk in support of plausible projects not set forth and authorized by the act of incorporation, and which may possibly lead to extraordinary losses." The same jurisdiction was invoked and applied in the case of Bagshaw *v*. The Eastern Counties Railway Company; so, also, in Coleman *v*. The same company, 10 Beavan's Ch. Reports, 1. It appeared in that case that the directors of the company, for the purpose of increasing their traffic, proposed to guarantee certain profits, and to secure the capital of an intended steam-packet company, which was to act in connection with the railway. It was held, such a transaction was not within the scope of their powers, and they were restrained by injunction. And in the second place, that in such a case one of the shareholders in the railway company was entitled to sue in behalf of himself and all the other shareholders, except the directors, who were defendants, although some of the shareholders had taken shares in the steam-packet company. It was contended in this case that the corporation might pledge, without limit, the funds of the company for the encouragement of other transactions, however various and extensive, provided the object of that liability was to increase the traffic upon the railway, and thereby increase the traffic to the shareholders. But the master of the rolls, Lord Langdale, said, "there was no authority for any thing of that kind."

But further, it is not only illegal for a corporation to apply its capital to objects not contemplated by its charter, but also to apply its profits. And therefore a shareholder may maintain a bill in equity against the directors and compel the company to refund any of the profits thus improperly applied. It is an improper application for a railway company to invest the profits of the company in the purchase of shares in another company. The dividend (says Lord Langdale, in Solamons *v*. Laing, 14 Jurist for December, 1850), which belongs to the shareholders, and is divisible among them, may be applied severally as their own property; but the company itself or the directors, or any number of shareholders, at a meeting or otherwise, have no right to dispose of his shares of the general dividends, which belong to the particular shareholder, in any manner contrary to the will, or without the consent or authority of, that particular shareholder.

We do not mean to say that the jurisdiction in equity over corporations at the suit of a shareholder has not been contested. The cases cited in this argument show it to have been otherwise; but when the case of Hodges *v*. The New England Screw Company et al. was cited against it—(we may say the best argued and judicially considered case which we know upon the point, both upon the original hearing and rehearing of that cause,)—the counsel could not have been aware of the fact that, upon the rehearing of it, the learned court, which had decided that courts of equity have no jurisdiction over corporations as such at the suit of a stockholder for violations of charter, reviewed and recalled that conclusion. The language of the court is: "We have thought it our duty to review in this general form this new and unsettled jurisdiction, and to say, in view of the novelty and importance of the subject, and the additional light which has been thrown upon it since the trial, we consider the jurisdiction of this court over corporations for breaches of charter, at the suit of shareholders, and how far it shall be extended, and subject to what limits, is still an open question in this court. 1 Rhode Island Reports, 312—rehearing of the case September term, 1853."

The result of the cases is well stated in Angell & Ames, paragraphs 391, 393. "In cases where the legal remedy against a corporation is inadequate, a court of equity will interfere, is well settled, and there are cases in which a bill in equity will lie against a corporation by one of its members." "Though the result of the authorities clearly is, that in a corporation, when acting within the scope of and in obedience to the provisions of its constitution, the will of the majority, duly expressed at a legally constituted meeting, must govern; yet beyond the limits of the act of incorporation, the will of the majority cannot make an act valid; and the powers of a court of equity may be put in motion at the instance of a single shareholder, if he can show that the corporation are employing their statutory powers for the accomplishment of purposes not within the scope of their institution. Yet it is to be observed, that there is an important distinction between this class of cases and those in which there is no breach of trust, but only error and misapprehension, or simple negligence on the part of the directors."*

We have then the rule and its limitation. It is contended that this case is within the limitation; or that the directors of the Commercial Bank of Cleveland, in their action in respect to the tax assessed upon it, under the act of April 18, 1852, and in their refusal to take proper measures for testing its validity, have committed an "error of judgment merely."

It is obvious, from the rule, that the circumstances of each case must determine the jurisdiction of a court of equity to give the relief sought. That the pleadings must be relied upon to collect what they are, to ascertain in what character, and to what end a shareholder invokes the interposition of a court of equity, on account of the mismanagement of a board of directors. Whether such acts are out of or beyond the limits of the act of incorporation, either of commission contrary thereto, or of negligence in not doing what it may be their chartered duty to do.

This brings us to the inquiry, as to what the directors have done in this case, and what they refused to do upon the application of their co-corporator, John M. Woolsey. After a full statement of his case, comprehending all of his rights and theirs also, alleging in his bill that his object was to test the validity of a tax upon the ground that it was unconstitutional, because it impaired the obligation of a contract made by the State of Ohio with the Commercial Bank of Cleveland, and the stockholders thereof; he represents in his own behalf, as a stockholder, that he had applied to the directors, requesting them to take measures, by suit or otherwise, to prevent the collection of the tax by the treasurer, and that they refused to do so, accompanying, however, their refusal with the declaration that they fully concurred with Woolsey in his views as to the illegality of the tax; that they believed it in no way binding upon the bank, but that, in consideration of the many obstacles in the way of resisting the collection of the tax in the courts of the State, they could not consent to take legal measures for testing it. Besides this refusal, the papers in the case disclose the fact that the directors had previously made two protests against the constitutionality of the tax, because it was repugnant to the constitution of the United States, and to that of Ohio also, both concluding with a resolution that they would not, as then advised, pay the tax, unless compelled by law to do so, and that they were determined to rely upon the constitutional and legal rights of the bank under its charter. Now, in our view, the refusal upon the part of the directors, by their own showing, partakes more of disregard of duty, than of an error of judgment. It was a non-performance of a confessed official obligation, amounting to

* *So it has been repeatedly decided, that a private corporation may be sued at law by one of its own members. The text upon this subject is so well expressed, with authorities to support it, that we will extract the paragraph 390 from Angell & Ames entire. A private corporation may be sued by one of its own members. This point came directly before the court, in the State of South Carolina in an action of assumpsit against the Catawba Company. The plea in abatement was, that the plaintiff himself was a member of that company, and therefore could maintain no action against it in his individual capacity. The court, after hearing argument, overruled the plea as containing principles subversive of justice; and they moreover said, that the point had been settled by two former cases, wherein certain officers were allowed to maintain actions for their salaries due by the company. In this respect, the cases of incorporated companies are entirely dissimilar from those of ordinary copartnerships, or unincorporated joint-stock companies. In the former, the individual members of the company are entirely distinct from the artificial body endowed with corporate powers. A member of a corporation who is a creditor, has the same right as any other creditor to secure the payment of his demands, by attachment or by levy upon the property of the corporation, although he may be personally liable by statute to satisfy other judgments against the corporation. An action was maintained against a corporation on a bond securing a certain sum to the plaintiff, a member of the corporation, the member being deemed by the court a stranger. Pierce & Partridge, 3 Met. Mass. 44; so of notes and bonds, accounts and rights to dividends. Hill* v. *Manchester and Salford Water-works, Adol. & Ellis, 866; Dunson* v. *Imperial Glass Company, 3 B. & Adol. 125; Geer* v. *School District, 6 Vermont, 186; Methodist Episcopal Society, 18 Ib. 5 405; Robers* v. *Danby Universalist Society, 19 Ib. 187.*

what the law considers a breach of trust, though it may not involve intentional moral delinquency. It was a mistake, it is true, of what their duty required from them, according to their own sense of it, but, being a duty by their own cofession, their refusal was an act outside of the obligation which the charter imposed upon them to protect what they conscientiously believed to be the franchises of the bank. A sense of duty and conduct contrary to it, is not "an error of judgment merely," and cannot be so called in any case. It amounted to an illegal application of the profits due to the stockholders of the bank, into which a court of equity will inquire to prevent its being made.

Thinking, as we do, that the action of the board of directors was not "an error of judgment merely" but a breach of duty, it is our opinion that they were properly made parties to the bill, and that the jurisdiction of a court of equity reaches such a case to give such a remedy as its circumstances may require. This conclusion makes it unnecessary for us to notice further the point made by the counsel that the suit should have been brought in the name of the corporation, in support of which they cited the case of the Bank of the United States *v.* Osborn. The obvious difference between this case and that is, that the Bank of the United States brought a bill in the circuit court of the United States for the district of Ohio, to resist a tax assessed under an act of that State, and executed by its auditor, and here the directors of the Commercial Bank of Cleveland, by refusing to do what they had declared it to be their duty to do, have forced one of its corporators, in self-defence, to sue. If the directors had done so in a state court of Ohio, and put their case upon the unconstitutionality of the tax act, because it impaired the obligation of a contract, and had the decision been against such claim, the judgment of the state court could have been reëxamined, in that particular, in the supreme court of the United States, under the same authority or jurisdiction by which it reversed the judgment of the supreme court of Ohio, in the case of the Piqua Branch of the State Bank of Ohio *v.* Jacob Knoop, treasurer of Miami county, 16 How. 369.

But it was said in the argument, that this suit had been improperly brought in the circuit court of the United States, because it was a contrivance by Woolsey, or between him and the directors of the bank, to give that court jurisdiction, on account of their residence and citizenship being in different States. That the subject-matter of the suit was within the exclusive jurisdiction of the state courts, and that, if the jurisdiction in the courts of the United States was sustained, it would make inoperative to a great extent the 7th amendment of the constitution of the United States and the 16th section of the Judiciary Act of 1789, this last being a declaratory act, settling the law, as to cases of equity jurisdiction, in the nature of a proviso, limitation, or exception to its exercise. And further, that it would make the judiciary of the United States paramount to that of the individual States, and the legislative and executive departments of the federal government paramount to the same departments of the individual States.

We first remark as to the imputation of contrivance, that it is the assertion of a fact which does not appear in the case, one which the defendants should have proved if they meant to rely upon it to abate or defeat the complainant's suit, and that, not having done so, as they might have attempted to do, we cannot presume its existence. Mr. Woolsey's right, as a citizen of the State of Connecticut, to sue citizens of the State of Ohio in the courts of the United States, for that State, cannot be questioned. The papers in the case also show, that the directors and himself occupy antagonist grounds in respect to the controversy which their refusal to sue forced him to take in defence of his rights as a shareholder in the bank. Nor can the counsel for the defendant assume the existence of such a fact in the argument of their case in this court, in the absence of any attempt on their part to prove it in the circuit court.

We remark, as to the subject-matter of the suit being within the exclusive jurisdiction of the state courts, that the courts of the United States and the courts of the States have concurrent jurisdiction in all cases between citizens of different States, whatever may be the matter in controversy, if it be one for judicial cognizance. Such is the constitution of the United States, and the legislation to congress "in pursuance thereof." And when it was urged that the jurisdiction of the case belonged exclusively to the state courts of Ohio, under the 7th article of the amendments to the constitution, and the 16th section of the judiciary act of 1789 was invoked to sustain the position, it seems it was forgotten that this court and other courts of the United States had repeatedly decided that the equity jurisdiction of the courts of the United States is independent of the local law of any State, and is the same in nature and extent as the equity jurisdiction of England, from which it is derived, and that it is no objection to this jurisdiction, that there is a remedy under the local law. Gordon *v*. Hobart, 2 Sumner, C. C. Rep. 401.

It was also said by both of the counsel for the defendant, and argued with some zeal, that if the court sustained the jurisdiction in this case, it would be difficult to determine whether any thing, and how much of state sovereignty may hereafter exist. We shall give to this observation our particular consideration, regretting that it should be necessary, but not doubting that such a jurisdiction exists at the suit of a shareholder, and that the appellate jurisdiction of this court may be exercised in the matter, rights of the States, but, by doing so, giving not only without taking away any of the additional securities for their preservation, to the great benefit of the people of the United States. If it does not exist and was not exercised, we should indeed have a very imperfect national government, altogether unworthy of the wisdom and foresight of those who framed it; incompetent, too, to secure for the future those advantages hitherto secured by it to the people of the United States, and which were in their contemplation, when, by their conventions in the several States, the constitution was ratified.

Impelled then by a sense of duty to the constitution, and the administration of so much of it as has been assigned to the judiciary, we proceed with the discussion.

The departments of the government are legislative, executive, and judicial. They are coördinate in degree to the extent of the powers delegated to each of them. Each, in the exercise of its powers, is independent of the other, but all, rightfully done by either, is binding upon the others. The constitution is supreme over all of them, because the people who ratified it have made it so; consequently, any thing which may be done unauthorized by it is unlawful. But it is not only over the departments of the government that the constitution is supreme. It is so, to the extent of its delegated powers, over all who made themselves parties to it; States as well as persons, within those concessions of sovereign powers yielded by the people of the States, when they accepted the constitution in their conventions. Nor does its supremacy end there. It is supreme over the people of the United States, aggregately and in their separate sovereignties, because they have excluded themselves from any direct or immediate agency in making amendments to it, and have directed that amendments should be made representatively for them, by the congress of the United States, when two thirds of both houses shall propose them; or where the legislatures of two thirds of the several States shall call a convention for proposing amendments, which, in either case, become valid, to all intents and purposes, as a part of the constitution, when ratified by the legislatures of three fourths of the several States, or by conventions in three fourths of them, as one or the other mode of ratification may be proposed by congress. The same article declares that no amendment, which might be made prior to the year 1808, should, in any manner, affect the first and fourth clauses in the ninth section of the first article, and that no State, without its consent, shall be deprived of its equal suffrage in the senate. The first being a temporary disability to amend, and the other two permanent and unalterable exceptions to the power of amendment.

Now, whether such a supremacy of the constitution, with its limitations in the particulars just mentioned, and with the further restriction laid by the people upon themselves, and for themselves, as to the modes of amendment, be right or wrong politically, no one can deny that the constitution is supreme, as has been stated, and that the statement is in exact conformity with it.

Further, the constitution is not only supreme in the sense we have said it was, for the people in the ratification of it have chosen to add that "this constitution and the laws of the United States which shall be made in pursuance thereof; and all treaties made, or which shall be made, under the laws of the United States which shall be supreme law of the land, and the judges in every State shall be bound thereby, any thing in the constitution or laws of any State to the contrary notwithstanding." And, in that connection, to make its supremacy more complete, impressive, and practical, that there should be no escape from its operation, and that its binding force upon the States and the members of congress should be unmistakable, it is declared that "the senators and representatives, before mentioned, and the members of the state legislatures, and all executive and judicial officers, both of the United States and of the several States, shall be bound by an oath or affirmation to support this constitution.

Having stated, not by way of argument or inference, but in the words of the constitution, the particulars in which it is declared to be supreme, we proceed to show that it contains an interpreter, or has given directions for determining what is its meaning and operation, what "laws are made in pursuance thereof," and to fix the meaning of treaties which had been made, or which shall be made, under the authority of the United States, when either the constitution, the laws of congress, or a treaty, are brought judicially in question, in which a State, or a citizen of the United States, or a foreigner, shall claim rights before the courts of the United States, or in the courts of the States, either under the constitution or the laws of the United States, or from a treaty.

All legislative powers in the constitution are vested in a congress of the United States, which shall consist of a senate and house of representatives. Then stating of whom the house shall be composed, how they shall be chosen by the people of the several States, the qualification of electors, the age of representatives, the time of their citizenship, and their inhabitancy in the State in which they shall be chosen; how representatives and direct taxes shall be apportioned, how the senate shall be composed, with sundry other provisions relating to the house and the senate, the powers of congress are enumerated affirmatively. The 9th section then declares what the congress shall not have power to do, and it is followed by the 10th, consisting of three paragraphs, all of them prohibitions upon the States from doing the particulars expressed in them.

Our first suggestion now is, as all the legislative powers are concessions of sovereignty from the people of the States, and the prohibitions upon them in the 10th section are likewise so, both raise an obligation upon the States not to legislate upon either; each, however, conferring rights, according to what may be the constitutional legislation of congress upon the first; and the second giving rights of equal force, without legislation in respect to such of them as execute themselves, on account of their being prohibitions of what the States shall not do. For instance, no legislation by congress is wanted to make more binding upon the States what they have bound themselves in absolute terms not to do. As where it is said "no State shall enter into any treaty, alliance, or confederation, grant letters of marque and reprisal, coin money, emit bills of credit, make any thing but gold and silver coin a tender in payment of debts, pass any bill of attainder, *ex post facto* law, or law impairing the obligation of contracts, or grant any title of nobility."

Our next suggestion is, that the grants of legislative powers, and the negation of the exercise of other powers by the States, some of them being declarations that they would not legislate upon those matters which had been exclusively given up for the legislation of congress, do not imply that the States would be wilfully disregardful of the obligations solemnly placed upon them by their people; but that there might be interferences from their legislation in some of those particulars, either with the constitution, or between their enactments and those of congress. But this apprehension (not without cause) was founded upon the legislation of some of the States during the continuance of the articles of confederation, affecting the rights and interests of persons in their contracts, from which they could get no relief, unless it was granted by the same State legislatures which passed the acts. This suggested the necessity, or rather made it obvious, that our national union would be incomplete and altogether insufficient for the great ends contemplated, unless a constitutional arbiter was provided to give certainty and uniformity, in all of the States, to the interpretation of the constitution and the legislation of congress; with powers also to declare judicially what acts of the legislatures of the States might be in conflict with either. Had this not been done, there would have been no mutuality of constitutional obligation between the States, either in respect to the constitution or the laws of congress, and each of them would have determined for itself the operation of both, either by legislation or judicial action. In either way, exempting itself and its citizens from engagements which it had not made by itself, but in common with other States of the union, equally sovereign; by which they bound their sovereignties to each other, that neither of them should assume to settle a principle or interest for itself, in a matter which was the common interest of all of them. Such is certainly the common sense view of the people, when any number of them enter into a contract for their mutual benefit, in the same proportions of interest. In such a case, neither should assume the right to bind his compeers by his judgment, as to the stipulations of their contract. If one of them did so, any other of them might call in the aid of the law to settle their differences, and its judgment would terminate the controversy. It must not be said that the illustration is inappropriate, because individuals have no other mode to settle their disputes, and that States and nations, from their equal sovereignty, have no tribunal to terminate authoritatively their differences, each having the right to judge and do so for itself.

But ours is not such a government. The States, or rather the people forming it, though sovereign as to the powers not delegated to the United States by the constitution, nor prohibited by it to the States, are not independent of each other, in respect to the powers ceded in the constitution.

Their union, by the constitution, was made by each of them conceding portions of their equal sovereignties for all of them, and it acts upon the States conjunctively and separately, and in the same manner upon their citizens, aggregately in some things, and in others individually, in many of their relations of business, and also upon their civil conduct, so far as their obedience to the laws of congress is concerned.

In such a union, the States are bound by all of those principles of justice which bind individuals to their contracts. They are bound by their mutual acquiescence in the powers of the constitution, that neither of them should be the judge, or should be allowed to be the final judge of the powers of the constitution, or of the interpretation of the laws of congress. This is not so, because their sovereignty is impaired; but the exercise of it is diminished in quantity, because they have, in certain respects, put restraints upon that exercise, in virtue of voluntary engagements. (Vattel, Ch. 1, section 10.)

We will now give two illustrations—one from the constitution, and the other from one of the cases decided in this court, upon a tax act of the State of Ohio—to show that the framers of the constitution, and the conventions which ratified it, were fully aware of the necessity for and meant to make a department of it, to which was to be confided the final decision judicially of the powers of that instrument, the conformity of laws with it, which either congress or the legislatures of the States may enact, and to review the judgments of the state courts, in which a right is decided against, which has been claimed in virtue of the constitution or the laws of congress.

The third clause of the 2d section of the 1st article of the constitution is, "that representatives and direct taxes shall be apportioned among the several States, according to their respective numbers, which shall be determined by adding to the whole number of free persons, including those bound to service for a term of years, and excluding Indians not taxed, three fifths of all other persons." We will suppose that congress shall again impose a direct tax, and that a citizen liable to assessment should dispute its application to a kind of his property, alleging it not to be a direct tax, in the sense of that provision of the constitution; and that he should apply to a state court for relief from an execution which had been levied upon his property for its collection, making the United States collector of the tax a party to his suit; and that the court should enjoin him from further proceedings to collect the tax. It is plain, if such a judgment was final, and could not be reviewed by any other court, or by the supreme court of the United States, in virtue of its appellate jurisdiction, as that has been given by the act of congress, the result would be, that the citizens of the State in which the judgment was given, would be exempted from the payment of a tax which had been intended by congress to be apportioned upon the property of all of the citizens of the United States, in conformity with the constitution. This would practically defeat the rule of apportionment if it was acquiesced in by the government of the United States, and the constitutional collection of the tax could not be made in any State according to the act. We do not mean that the officers of the United States could not collect the tax in those States in which no such judgment had been given; but if the judgment could not be reviewed, that the constitutional rule for the imposition of direct taxes could not be executed by any legislation of congress which a State legislature or a state court might not say was unconstitutional. We should not then have a more perfect union than we had under the articles of confederation. Each State then paid the requisition of congress, when it pleased to do so. Had it been continued, the union would be more feeble for all national purposes than it had been. Then the States only disregarded their obligations to suit their convenience. Had it not been corrected, as it has been done in the constitution, we have no reason to believe that there would not be like results, or that the courts of the States would not be resorted to, to determine the constitutionality of taxes laid by congress. This was certainly not meant by the framers of the constitution, nor can its disallowance be brought under the 10th article of its amendments, which declares "that the powers not delegated to the United States by the constitution, nor prohibited by it to the states, are reserved to the States respectively, or to the people."

The illustration given, and its results, have been drawn from the constitution of the United States, also from what might be the action of the state legislatures and state courts, which could not be prevented unless the supreme court of the United States had the power to review the action of the state courts upon a matter exclusively of national interest, made so by the legislation of congress.

Hitherto, no such case as we have supposed has happened, but a reference to the case of Hylton *v*. The United States, 3 Dallas, 171, in which an attempt was made to test the constitutionality of a tax assessed by the United States, will show that a case of the kind is not unlikely to occur, when congress shall impose a tax apportioning representation and direct taxation; or, under the general declaration in the 8th section of the 1st article of the constitution, that "congress shall have power to lay and collect taxes, duties, imposts, and excises, but that all duties shall be uniform throughout the United States." Let it be understood, too, that the power is not only to impose duties and taxes, but to collect them, and from the power to collect must necessarily be inferred the disability of the legislatures of the States, or of the courts of the States, in any way to interfere with its execution, as that may be directed by congress. If the courts of the States, or their legislatures, could finally determine against the constitutionality of a tax laid by congress, there would be no certainty or uniformity of taxation upon the citizens of the United States, or of the apportionment of representation and direct taxation according to the constitution.

Other illustrations of the propriety and necessity for a judicial tribunal of the United States to settle such questions finally, might be made from other clauses of the constitution. We will, however, cite but one of them in addition to such as have been already mentioned. It is the power of congress to regulate commerce, and we refer to the case of Brown *v*. The State of Maryland, as an instance of the attempt of that State to lay a tax upon imports, which this court pronounced to be unconstitutional.

We will now give other illustrations, in which the rights of property are involved, to show the cautious wisdom of that provision of the constitution which secures to the citizens of the different States a right to sue in the courts of the United States, and to claim either in them, or in the courts of the States, the protection either of the constitution or of the laws of congress.

The legislature of Ohio passed an act in 1803, incorporating the proprietors of the half-million of acres of land south of Lake Erie called the "Sufferers' Land." This act required the appointment of directors, who were authorized to extinguish the Indian title, to survey the land into townships, or otherwise make partition among the owners; and, among other things provided, "that, to defray all necessary expenses of the company in purchasing and extinguishing the Indian claim of title to the land, surveying, locating, and making partition, and all other necessary expenses of said company, power is hereby vested in the said directors, and their successors in office, to levy a tax or taxes on said land, and enforce the collection thereof." It was also provided that the directors should have power and authority to do whatever it shall appear to them to be necessary and proper to be done for the well-ordering and interest of the proprietors, not contrary to the laws of the State. Subsequently, the legislature of Ohio imposed a tax upon these lands as a part of the revenue to be raised for the State. The directors assessed a tax upon the share of each proprietor, to pay the tax to the State. A sale of a part of the land was made for that purpose, and the question subsequently raised in the circuit court of the United States for the district of Ohio, in a suit at the instance of the heirs of one of the proprietors whose land had been sold, was, whether the sale conveyed a title to the land to the purchaser. It was determined by this court, that it did not, because the directors had not power to make an assessment upon the lands to pay the state tax, and that the tax, as laid by the State, had been done in violation of the corporate powers given to the directors. In this case the plaintiffs sought protection against the tax laid by Ohio, and acquiesced in by the directors of the corporation, because that tax was contrary to the contract which the State had made with the corporation for the benefit of the proprietors of the land. The State, without being a party to the record, was interested in the question. It was a suit between citizens of different States, brought by the plaintiffs in the United States circuit court for Ohio; and the motive for seeking that tribunal was, that his rights might be tried in one not subject either to State or local influences. It placed both parties upon an equality, in fact and in appearances; and whatever might have been the result, neither could complain of the disinterestedness of the court which adjudged their rights. Beatty *v*. The Lessee of Knowles, 4 Peters, 152.

The foundation of the right of citizens of different States to sue each other in the courts of the United States, is not an unworthy jealousy of the impartiality of the state tribunals. It was a higher aim and purpose. It is to make the people think and feel, though residing in different States of the Union, that their relations to each other were protected by the strictest justice, administered in courts independent of all local control or connection with the subject-matter of the controversy between the parties to a suit.

Men unite in civil society, expecting to enjoy peaceably what belongs to them, and that they may regain it by the law when wrongfully withheld. That can only be accomplished by good laws, with suitable provisions for the establishment of courts of justice, and for the enforcement of their decisions. The right to establish them flows from the same source which determines the extent of the legislative and executive powers of government. Experience has shown that the object cannot be attained without a supreme tribunal, as one of the departments of the government, with defined powers in its organic structure, and the mode for exercising them to be provided legislatively. This has been done in the constitution of the United States. Its framers were well aware of their responsibilities to secure justice to the people; and well knew, as the object of all trials in courts was to determine the suits between citizens, that it could not be done satisfactorily to them, unless they had the privilege to appeal from the first tribunal which had jurisdiction of a suit to another which should have authority to pronounce definitively upon its merits. (Vattel, 9th chapter, on justice and polity.) Without such a court the citizens of each State could not have enjoyed all the privileges and immunities of citizens in the several States, as they were intended to be secured by the second section of the 4th article of the constitution. Nor would the judicial power have been extended in fact to "all cases in law and equity arising under the constitution, the laws of the United States, and treaties made or which shall be made under their authority, to all cases affecting ambassadors and other public ministers and consuls; to all cases of admiralty and maritime jurisdiction; to controversies to which the United States shall be a party; to controversies between two or more States; to those between citizens of different States, or between citizens of the same State, claiming lands under grants of different States; and between a State and the citizens thereof and foreign States, citizens or subjects." Article 3d, section 1st.

Without the supreme court, as it has been constitutionally and legislatively constituted, neither the constitution nor the laws of congress passed in pursuance of it, nor treaties, would be in practice or in fact the supreme law of the land, and the injunction that the judges in every State should be bound thereby, any thing in the constitution or laws of any State to the contrary notwithstanding, would be useless, if the judges of state courts, in any one of the States, could finally determine what was the meaning and operation of the constitution and laws of congress, or the extent of the obligation of treaties.

But let it be remembered, that the appellate jurisdiction of the supreme court, as it is, is one of perfect equality between the States and the United States. It acts upon the constitution and laws of both, in the same way, to the same extent, for the same purposes, and with the same final result. Neither the dignity nor the independence of either are lessened by its organization or action.

The same electors choose the members of the house of representatives who choose the members of the most popular branch of the state legislatures. The senators of the United States are chosen by the legislatures of the States. The senate and house of representatives of the United States exercise their legislative powers independently of each other, their concurrence being necessary to pass laws. The States are represented in the one, the people in the other and in both. But as it was thought that they and the state legislatures might pass laws conflicting with the letter or the spirit of the constitution under which they legislated, it became necessary to make a judicial department for the United States, with a jurisdiction best suited to preserve harmony between the States, severally and collectively, with the national government, and which would give the people of all of the States that confidence and security under it anticipated by them when they announced, "that we, the people of the United States, in order to form a more perfect union, establish justice and domestic tranquillity, provide for the common defence, and promote the general welfare, and secure the blessings of liberty to ourselves and our posterity, do ordain this constitution for the United States." Without a judicial department, just such as it is, neither the powers of the constitution nor the purposes for which they were given could have been attained.

We do not know a case more appropriate to show the necessity for such a jurisdiction than that before us.

A citizen of the United States, residing in Connecticut, having a large pecuniary interest in a bank in Ohio, with a board of directors opposed, in fact, to the only course which could be taken to test the constitutional validity of a law of that State bearing upon the franchises of their corporation, is told by the directors, that though they fully concur with him in believing the tax law of Ohio unconstitutional and in no way binding upon the bank, they will not institute legal proceedings to prevent the collection of the tax, "in consideration of the many obstacles in the way of resisting the tax in the state courts." Without partaking, ourselves, in their uncertainty of relief in the courts of Ohio, it must be admitted their declaration was calculated to diminish this suitor's confidence in such a result, and to induce him to resort to the only other tribunal which there was to take cognizance of his cause. Besides, it was not his interest alone which would be affected by the result. Hundreds, citizens of the State of Ohio and citizens of other States, are concerned in the question. Millions of money in that State, and millions upon millions of banking capital in the other States, are to be affected by its judicial decision; all depending upon the assertion, in opposition to the claim of the complainant, that a new constitution of a State supersedes every legislative enactment touching its own internal policy, and bearing upon the interest of persons, which may have been the subject of legislation under a preceding constitution. In the words of the counsel for the defendant, that all such legislation must give way when found to contravene the will of the sovereign people, subsequently expressed in a new state constitution. The assertion may be met and confuted, without further argument, by what was said by Mr. Madison, in the 43d number of The Federalist, upon the 6th article of the constitution, which is: "All debts and engagements entered into before the adoption of this constitution shall be as valid against the United States under this constitution as under the confederation." His remark is, "This can only be considered as a declaratory proposition, and may have been inserted, among other reasons, for the satisfaction of foreign creditors, who cannot be strangers to the pretended doctrine, that a change in the political form of civil society has the magical effect of dissolving its moral obligations."

And here we will cite another passage from the writings of that great statesman, and venerated man by every citizen of the United States who knows how much his political wisdom contributed to the establishment of our American popular institutions. He says, in the 22d number of The Federalist: "A circumstance which shows the defects of the confederation remains to be mentioned—the want of a judiciary power. Laws are a dead letter without courts to expound and define their true meaning and operation. The treaties of the United States, to have any force at all, must be considered as a part of the law of the land. Their true import, as regards individuals, must, like all other laws, be ascertained by judicial determinations. To produce uniformity in these determinations, they ought to be submitted to a supreme tribunal; and this tribunal ought to be instituted under the same authorities which form the treaties themselves. These ingredients are both indispensable. If there is in each State a court of final jurisdiction, there may be as many different final determinations on the same point as there are courts. These are endless diversities in the opinions of men. We often see not only different courts, but the judges of the same court, differing from each other. To avoid the confusion which would unavoidably result from the contradictory decisions of a number of independent judicatures, all nations have found it necessary to establish one tribunal paramount to the rest, possessing a general superintendence, and authorized to settle and declare in the last resort a uniform rule of civil justice. This is the more necessary where the frame of the government is so compounded that the laws of the whole are in danger of being contravened by the laws of the parts. In this case, if the particular tribunals are invested with a right of ultimate decision, besides the contradictions to be expected from difference of opinion, there will be much to fear from the bias of local views and prejudices, and from the interference of local institutions. As often as such an interference should happen, there would be reason to apprehend that the provisions of the particular laws might be preferred to those of the general laws, from the deference which men in office naturally look up to that authority to which they owe their official existence."

Hitherto we have shown from the constitution itself that the framers of it meant to provide a jurisdiction for its final interpretation, and for the laws passed by Congress, to give them an equal operation in all of the States.

But there are considerations out of the constitution which contribute to show it, which we will briefly mention. Without such a judicial tribunal there are no means provided by which the conflicting legislation of the States with the constitution and the laws of congress may be terminated, so as to give to either a national operation in each of the States. In such an event no means have been provided for an amicable accommodation; none for a compromise; none for mediation; none for arbitration; none for a congress of the States as a mode of conciliation. The consequence of which would be a permanent diversity of the operation of the constitution in the States, as well in matters exclusively of public concern as in those which secure individual rights. Fortunately it is not so. A supreme tribunal has been provided, which has hitherto, by its decisions, settled all differences which have arisen between the authorities of the States and those of the United States. The legislation under which its appellate power is exercised has been of sixty-seven years' duration, without any countenanced attempt to repeal it. It is rather late to question it; and in continuing to exercise it, this court complies with the decisions of its predecessors, believing, after the fullest examination, that its appellate jurisdiction is given in conformity with the constitution.

The last position taken by the counsel for the defendant, now the appellant here, is, that George C. Dodge was in the discharge of his official duty as treasurer of Cuyahoga county, in the State of Ohio, when interrupted by the mandate of the circuit court; that the tax in his hands for collection against the bank was regularly assessed under a valid law of the State, passed April 18, 1852, in conformity with the requisitions of the constitution, adopted June 17, 1851, which took effect 1st September, 1851.

It was admitted, in the argument of it, that the only difference between this case and that of the Piqua Branch of the State of Ohio *v.* Jacob Knoop, 16 Howard, 369, is, that the latter was a claim for a tax under a law of Ohio, of March 21, 1851, under the former constitution of Ohio, of 1802; and that the tax now claimed is assessed under the act of April 18, 1852, under the new constitution of Ohio.

Both acts, in effect, are the same in their operation upon the charter of the bank, as that was passed by the general assembly of Ohio, in the year 1845. Each of them is intended to collect, by way of tax, a larger sum than the bank was liable to pay, under the charter of 1845. This is admitted. It is not denied, the record shows that the tax assessed for the year 1853 exceeds the sum to which it was liable, under its charter, \$11,565 22/100. The tax assessed is \$14,771 87/100. The tax which it would have paid, under the act of 1845, would have been \$3,206 65/100.

The fact raises the question whether the tax now claimed has not been assessed in violation of the 10th section of the 1st article of the constitution, which declares that no State shall pass any law impairing the obligation of contracts.

The law of 1845 was an agreement with the bank, *quasi ex contractu*—and also an agreement separately with the shareholders, *quasi ex contractu*—that neither the bank as such, nor the shareholders as such, should be liable to any other tax larger than that which was to be levied under the 60th section of the act of 1845.

That 60th section is, "that each banking company under the act, on accepting thereof and complying with its provisions, shall semiannually, on the days designated for declaring dividends, set off to the State six per cent. on the profits, deducting therefrom the expenses and ascertained losses of the company for the six months next preceding, which sum or amount so set off shall be in lieu of all taxes to which the company, or the stockholders therein, would otherwise be subject. The sum so set off to be paid to the treasurer, on the order of the auditor of the State." The act under which the tax of 1853 has been assessed is: "That the president and cashier of every bank and banking company that shall have been, or may hereafter be, incorporated by the laws of this State, and having the right to issue bills of circulation as money, shall make and return, under oath, to the auditor of the county in which such bank or banking company may be situated, in the month of May annually, a written statement containing, first, the average amount of notes and bills discounted or purchased, which amount shall include all the loans or discounts, whether originally made or renewed during the year aforesaid, or at any previous time, whether made on bills of exchange, notes, bonds, or mortgages, or any other evidence of indebtedness, at their actual cost value in money, whether due previous to, during, or after the period aforesaid, and on which such banking company has at any time reserved or received, or is entitled to receive, any profit or other consideration whatever; and, secondly, the average amount of all other moneys, effects, or dues of every description belonging to the bank or banking company, loaned, invested, or otherwise used with a view to profit, or upon which the bank, &c., receives, or is entitled to receive, interest."

The two acts have been put in connection, that the difference between the modes of taxation may be more obvious; and it will be readily seen, that the second is not intended to tax the profits of the bank, but its entire business, capital, circulation, credits, and debts due to it, being professed to be intended to equalize the tax to be paid by the bank with that required to be paid upon personal property. A careful examination of the two acts and of the tabular returns annexed to this opinion, will prove that such equality of taxation has not been attained. It will show that the bank is taxed more than three times the number of mills upon the dollars that is assessed upon personal property, whatever may be comprehended under that denomination by the act of the 13th April, 1852. But if it did not, it could make no difference in our conclusion. For the tax to be paid by the bank under the act of 24th February, 1824, is a legislative contract, equally operative upon the State and upon the bank, and the stockholders of the bank, until the expiration of its charter, which will be in 1866. No critical examination of the words, "that on the days designated for declaring dividends, to wit, on the first Monday in May and November of each year, the bank shall set off to the said State of Ohio six per cent. on the profits, deducting therefrom the expenses and ascertained losses of said company for six months next preceding each dividend day, and that the sums or amounts so set off shall be in lieu of all taxes to which said company or the stockholders thereof on account of stock owned therein would otherwise be subject," could make them more exact in meaning than they are. The words "would otherwise be subject," relate to the legislative power to tax, and is a relinquishment of it, binding upon that legislature which passed the act, and upon succeeding legislatures as a contract not to tax the bank during its continuance with more than six per cent. upon its semiannual profits. A change of constitution cannot release a State from contracts made under a constitution which permits them to be made. The inquiry is, is the contract permitted by the existing constitution? If so, and that cannot be denied in this case, the sovereignty which ratified it in 1802 was the same sovereignty which made the constitution of 1851, neither having more power than the other to impair a contract made by the state legislature with individuals. The moral obligations never die. If broken by states and nations, though the terms of reproach are not the same with which we are accustomed to designate the faithlessness of individuals, the violation of justice is not the less.

This case is coincident with that of the Piqua Branch of the State Bank of Ohio *v.* Knoop, 16 How. 369, decided by this court in the year 1853. It rules this in every particular; and to the opinion then given we have nothing to add, nor any thing to take away. We affirm the decree of the circuit court, and direct a mandate accordingly.

LOUISVILLE RAILROAD CO. v. LETSON, 2 HOW. 497 (1844)

The legal status of corporations was an issue of great importance in the years before the Civil War: were they "persons" as far as the Constitution was concerned? of what state were they a citizen?

could they sue in the federal courts? could a state bar them from suing in their courts? When a New York citizen sued a South Carolina corporation in the federal courts of South Carolina, the defendant corporation denied jurisdiction, claiming that some of its members were citizens of North Carolina and therefore the case was not between "a citizen" of one state and "a citizen of another." Wayne speaking for the Court held for the plaintiff. The fact that some members may reside in a different state did not divest the federal courts of jurisdiction since the relevant issue is the state where the corporation is located.

Mr. Justice WAYNE delivered the opinion of the court.

The jurisdiction of the court is denied in this case upon the grounds that two members of the corporation sued are citizens of North Carolina; that the state of South Carolina is also a member, and that two other corporations in South Carolina are members, having in them members who are citizens of the same state with the defendant in error.

The objection, that the state of South Carolina is a member, cannot be sustained. Cases have been already decided by this court which overrule it. The doctrine is, if the state be not necessarily a defendant, though its interest may be affected by the decision, the courts of the United States are bound to exercise jurisdiction. United States *v*. Peters, 5 Cranch. 115. In the case of the Bank of the United States *v*. Planters' Bank of Georgia, this court ruled "that when a government becomes a partner in a trading concern, it divests itself, so far as it concerns the transactions of that company, of its sovereign character and takes that of a private citizen. Instead of communicating to the company its privileges and its prerogatives, it descends to a level with those with whom it associates itself, and takes the character which belongs to its associates and to the business which is to be transacted. Thus, many states of this Union, who have an interest in banks, are not suable even in their own courts, yet they never exempt the corporation from being sued. The state of Georgia, by giving to the bank the capacity to sue and be sued, voluntarily strips itself of its sovereign character, so far as respects the transactions of the bank, and waives all the privileges of that character." 9 Wheat. 907. South Carolina stands in the same attitude in the case before us, that Georgia did in the case in 9 Wheat. It is no objection, then, to the jurisdiction of the court, on account of the averment in the plea, that the state of South Carolina is a member of the Louisville, Cincinnati, and Charleston Railroad Company. The true principle is, that the jurisdiction of the Circuit Courts of the United States cannot be decreed or taken away on account of a state having an interest in a suit, unless the state is a party on the record. Osborne and the Bank of the United States, 9 Wheat. 852. This must be the rule under our system, whether the jurisdiction of the court is denied on account of any interest which a state may have in the subject-matter of the suit, or when it is alleged that jurisdiction does not exist on account of the character of the parties.

We will here consider that averment in the plea which alleges that the court has not jurisdiction, "because the Louisville, Cincinnati, and Charleston Rail-road Company is not a corporation whose members are citizens of South Carolina, but that some of the members of the said corporation are citizens of South Carolina, and some of them, namely, John Rutherford and Charles Baring, are and were at the time of commencing the said action, citizens of North Carolina."

The objection is equivalent to this proposition, that a corporation in a state cannot be sued in the Circuit Courts of the United States, by a citizen of another state, unless all the members of the corporation are citizens of the state in which the suit is brought.

The suit, in this instance, is brought by a citizen of New York in the Circuit Court of the United States for the district of South Carolina, which is the locality of the corporation sued.

Jurisdiction is decreed, because it is said, it is only given, when "the suit is between a citizen of the state where the suit is brought and a citizen of another state." And it is further said that the present is not such a suit, because two of the corporators are citizens of a third state.

The point in this form has never before been under the consideration of this court. We are not aware that it ever occurred in either of the circuits, until it was made in this case. It has not then been directly ruled in any case. Our inquiry now is, what is the law upon the proposition raised by the plea.

Our first remark is, that the jurisdiction is not necessarily excluded by the terms, when, "the suit is between a citizen of the state where the suit is brought and a citizen of another state," unless the word citizen is used in the Constitution and the laws of the United States in a sense which necessarily excludes a corporation.

A corporation aggregate is an artificial body of men, composed of divers constituent members *ad instar corporis humani,* the ligaments of which body politic, or artificial body, are the franchises and liberties thereof, which bind and unite all its members together; and in which the whole frame and essence of the corporation consist. Bac. Abr. Cor. (A). It must of necessity have a name, for the name is, as it were, the very being of the constitution, the heart of their combination, without which they could not perform their corporate acts, for it is nobody to plead and be impleaded, to take and give, until it hath gotten a name. Bac. Abr. Cor. (C).

Composed of persons, it may be that the members are citizens—and if they are, though the corporation can only plead and be impleaded by its name, or the name by which it may sue or be sued, if a controversy arises between it and a plaintiff who is a citizen of another state, and the residence of the corporation is in the state in which the suit is brought, is not the suit substantially between citizens of different states, or, in the words of the act giving to the courts jurisdiction, "a suit between a citizen of the state where the suit is brought and a citizen of another state?"

Jurisdiction, in one sense, in cases of corporations, exists in virtue of the character of members, and must be maintained in the courts of the United States, unless citizens can exempt themselves from their constitutional liability to be sued in those courts, by a citizen of another state, by the fact, that the subject of controversy between them has arisen upon a contract to which the former are parties, in their corporate and not in their personal character.

Constitutional rights and liabilities cannot be so taken away, or be so avoided. If they could be, the provision which we are here considering could not comprehend citizens universally, in all the relations of trade, but only those citizens in such relations of business as may arise from their individual or partnership transactions.

Let it then be admitted, for the purposes of this branch of the argument, that jurisdiction attaches in cases of corporations, in consequence of the citizenship of their members, and that foreign corporations may sue when the members are aliens—does it necessarily follow, because the citizenship and residence of the members give jurisdiction in a suit at the instance of a plaintiff of another state, that all of the corporators must be citizens of the state in which the suit is brought?

The argument in support of the affirmative of this inquiry is, that in the case of a corporation in which jurisdiction depends upon the character of the parties, the court looks beyond the corporation to the individuals of which it is composed for the purpose of ascertaining whether they have the requisite character, and for no other purpose.

The object would certainly be to ascertain the character of the parties, but not to the extent of excluding all inquiry as to what the effect will be, when it has been ascertained that the corporators are citizens of different states from that of the locality of the corporation, where by its charter it can only be sued.

Then the question occurs, if the corporation be only suable where its locality is, and those to whom its operations are confided are citizens of that state, and a suit is brought against it by a citizen of another state, whether by a proper interpretation of the terms given to the Circuit Court jurisdiction, it is not a suit between citizens of the state where the suit is brought and a citizen of another state. The fact that the corporators do live in different states does not aid the solution of the question.

The first, obvious, and necessary interpretation of the terms by which jurisdiction is given, is, that the suit need not be between citizen and citizen, but may be between citizens. Then, do the words, "of the state where the suit is brought," limit the jurisdiction to a case in which all the defendants are citizens of the same state?

The constitutional grant of judicial power extends to controversies "between citizens of different states." The words in the legislative grant of jurisdiction, "of the state where the suit is brought and a citizen of another state," are obviously no more than equivalent terms to confine suits in the Circuit Courts to those which are "between citizens of different states." The words in the Constitution then are just as operative to ascertain and limit jurisdiction as the words in the statute. It is true, that under these words "between citizens of different states," Congress may give the courts jurisdiction between citizens in many other forms than that in which it has been conferred. But in the way it is given, the object of the legislature seems exclusively to have been to confer jurisdiction upon the court, strictly in conformity to the limitation as it is expressed in the Constitution, "between citizens of different states."

A suit then brought by a citizen of one state against a corporation by its corporate name in the state of its locality, by which it was created and where its business is done by any of the corporators who are chosen to manage its affairs, is a suit, so far as jurisdiction is concerned, between citizens of the state where the suit is brought and a citizen of another state. The corporators as individuals are not defendants in the suit, but they are parties having an interest in the result, and some of them being citizens of the state where the suit is brought, jurisdiction attaches over the corporation,—nor can we see how it can be defeated by some of the members, who cannot be sued, residing in a different state. It may be said that the suit is against the corporation, and that nothing must be looked at but the legal entity, and then that we cannot view the members except as an artificial aggregate. This is so, in respect to the subject-matter of the suit and the judgment which may be rendered; but if it be right to look to the members to ascertain whether there be jurisdiction or not, the want of appropriate citizenship in some of them to sustain jurisdiction, cannot take it away, when there are other members who are citizens, with the necessary residence to maintain it.

But we are now met and told that the cases of Strawbridge and Curtis, 3 Cranch. 267, and that of the Bank of the United States and Deveaux, 5 Cranch. 84—hold a different doctrine.

We do not deny that the language of those decisions do not justify in some degree the inferences which have been made from them, or that the effect of them has been to limit the jurisdiction of the Circuit Courts in practice to the cases contended for by the counsel for the plaintiff in error. The practice has been, since those cases were decided, that if there be two or more plaintiffs and two or more joint-defendants, each of the plaintiffs must be capable of suing each of the defendants in the courts of the United States in order to support the jurisdiction, and in cases of corporation to limit jurisdiction to cases in which all the corporators were citizens of the state in which the suit is brought. The case of Strawbridge and Curtis was decided without argument. That of the Bank and Deveaux after argument of great ability. But never since that case has the question been presented to this court, with the really distinguished ability of the arguments of the counsel in this—in no way surpassed by those in the former. And now we are called upon in the most imposing way to give our best judgments to the subject, yielding to decided cases every thing that can be claimed for them on the score of authority except the surrender of conscience.

After mature deliberation, we feel free to say that the cases of Strawbridge and Curtis and that of the Bank and Deveaux were carried too far, and that consequences and inferences have been argumentatively drawn from the reasoning employed in the latter which ought not to be followed. Indeed, it is difficult not to feel that the case of the Bank of the United States and the Planters' Bank of Georgia is founded upon principles irreconcilable with some of those on which the cases already adverted to were founded. The case of the Commercial Bank of Vicksburg and Slocomb was most reluctantly decided upon the more authority of those cases. We do not think either of them maintainable upon the true principles of interpretation of the Constitution and the laws of the United States. A corporation created by a state to perform its functions under the authority of that state and only suable there, though it may have members out of the state, seems to us to be a person, though an artificial one, inhabiting and belonging to that state, and therefore entitled, for the purpose of suing and being sued, to be deemed a citizen of that state. We remark too, that the cases of Strawbridge and Curtis and the Bank and Deveaux have never been satisfactory to the bar, and that they were not, especially the last, entirely satisfactory to the court that made them. They have been followed always most reluctantly and with dissatisfaction. By no one was the correctness of them more questioned than by the late chief justice who gave them. It is within the knowledge of several of us, that he repeatedly expressed regret that those decisions had been made, adding, whenever the subject was mentioned, that if the point of jurisdiction was an original one, the conclusion would be different. We think we may safely assert, that a majority of the members of this court have at all times partaken of the same regret, and that whenever a case has occurred on the circuit, involving the application of the case of the Bank and Deveaux, it was yielded to, because the decision had been made, and not because it was thought to be right. We have already said that the case of the Bank of Vicksburg and Slocomb, 14 Peters, was most reluctantly given, upon mere authority. We are now called upon, upon the authority of those cases alone, to go further in this case than has yet been done. It has led to a review of the principles of all the cases. We cannot follow further, and upon our maturest deliberation we do not think that the cases relied upon for a doctrine contrary to that which this court will here announce, are sustained by a sound and comprehensive course of professional reasoning. Fortunately a departure from them involves no change in a rule of property. Our conclusion, too, if it shall not have universal acquiescence, will be admitted by all to be coincident with the policy of the Constitution and the condition of our country. It is coincident also with the recent legislation of Congress, as that is shown by the act of the 28th of February, 1839, in amendment of the acts respecting the judicial system of the United States. We do not hesitate to say, that it was passed exclusively with an intent to rid the courts of the decision in the case of Strawbridge and Curtis.

But if in all we have said upon jurisdiction we are mistaken, we say that the act of 28th of February, 1839, enlarges the jurisdiction of the courts, comprehends the case before us, and embraces the entire result of the opinion which we shall now give.

The first section of that act provides, "that wherein any suit at law or in equity, commenced in any court of the United States, there shall be several defendants, any one or more of whom shall not be inhabitants of, or found within the district where the suit is brought, or shall not voluntarily appear thereto, it shall be lawful for the court to entertain jurisdiction, and proceed to the trial and adjudication of such suit between the parties who may be properly before it; but the judgment or decree rendered therein, shall not conclude or prejudice other parties, not regularly served with process, or not voluntarily appearing to answer." We think, as was said in the case of the Commercial Bank of Vicksburg *v.* Slocomb, that this act was intended to remove the difficulties which occurred in practice, in cases both in law and equity, under that clause in the 11th section of the Judiciary act, which declares, "that no civil suit shall be brought before either of said courts against an inhabitant of the United States, by any original process, in any other district than that whereof he is an inhabitant, or in which he shall be found at the time of serving the writ," but a re-examination of the entire section will not permit us to re-affirm what was said in that case, that the act did not contemplate a change in the jurisdiction of the courts as it regards the character of the parties. If the act, in fact, did no more than to make a change, by empowering the courts to take cognisance of cases other than such as were permitted in that clause of the 11th section, which we have just cited, it would be an enlargment of jurisdiction as to the character of parties. The clause, that the judgment or decree rendered shall not conclude or prejudice other parties, who have not been regularly served with process, or who have not voluntarily appeared to answer, is an exception, exempting parties so situated from the enactment and must be so strictly applied. It is definite as to the persons of whom it speaks, and contains no particular words, as a subsequent clause, by which the general words of the statute can be restrained. The general words embrace every suit at law or in equity, in which there shall be several defendants, "any one or more of whom shall not be inhabitants of, or found within the district where the suit is brought, or who shall not voluntarily appear thereto." The words, "shall not be inhabitants of," applies as well to corporators as to persons who are not so; and if, as corporators, they are not suable individually and cannot be served with process, or voluntarily appear in an action against the corporation of which they are members, the conclusion should be that they are not included in the exception, but are within the general terms of the statute. Or, if they are viewed as defendants in the suit, then, as corporators, they are regularly served with process in the only way the law permits them to be, when the corporation is sued by its name.

The case before us might be safely put upon the foregoing reasoning and upon the statute, but hitherto we have reasoned upon this case upon the supposition, that in order to found the jurisdiction in cases of corporations, it is necessary there should be an averment, which, if contested, was to be supported by proof, that some of the corporators are citizens of the state by which the corporation was created, where it does its business, or where it may be sued. But this has been done in deference to the doctrines of former cases in this court, upon which we have been commenting. But there is a broader ground upon which we desire to be understood, upon which we altogether rest our present judgment, although it might be maintained upon the narrower ground already suggested. It is, that a corporation created by and doing business in a particular state, is to be deemed to all intents and purposes as a person, although an artificial person, an inhabitant of the same state, for the purposes of its incorporation, capable of being treated as a citizen of that state, as much as a natural person. Like a citizen it makes contracts, and though in regard to what it may do in some particulars it differs from a natural person, and in this especially, the manner in which it can sue and be sued, it is substantially, within the meaning of the law, a citizen of the state which created it, and where its business is done, for all the purposes of suing and being sued. And in coming to this conclusion, as to the character of a corporation, we only make a natural inference from the language of this court upon another occasion, and assert no new principle. In the case of Dartmouth College *v.* Woodward, 4 Wheat. 636, this court says, "a corporation is an artificial being, invisible, intangible, and existing only in contemplation of law. Being the mere creature of law, it possesses only those properties which the charter of its creation confers upon it, either expressly or as incidental to its very existence. These are such as were supposed best calculated to effect the object for which it was created. Among the most important are immortality, and if the expression may be allowed, individuality—properties, by which a perpetual succession of many persons are considered as the same and may act as a single individual. They enable a corporation to manage its own affairs, and to hold property without the perplexing intricacies, the hazardous and endless necessity, of perpetual conveyances for the purpose of transmitting it from hand to hand. It is chiefly for the purpose of clothing bodies of men in succession with these qualities and capacities, that corporations were invented and are in use. By these means a perpetual succession of individuals are capable of acting for the promotion of the particular object like one immortal being." Again, the Providence Bank and Billings, 4 Peters, 514, it is said, "the great object of an incorporation is to bestow the character and properties of individuality on a collective and changing body of men. This capacity is always given to such a body. Any privileges which may exempt it from the burdens common to individuals do not flow necessarily from the charter, but must be expressed in it, or they do not exist." In that case the bank was adjudged to be liable to a tax on its property as an individual. Lord Coke, says, "every corporation and body politic residing in any county, riding, city or town corporate, or having lands or tenements in any shire, *qua propriis manibus et sumptibus possident et habent,* are said to be inhabitants there, within the purview of the statute." In the case of King *v.* Gardner, in Cowper, a corporation was decided by the Court of King's Bench, to come within the description of occupiers or inhabitants. In the Bank and Deveaux, the case relied upon most for the doctrines contended for by the plaintiff in error, it is said of a corporation, "this ideal existence is considered as an inhabitant, when the general spirit and purposes of the law requires it." If it be so for the purposes of taxation, why is it not so for the purposes of a suit in the Circuit Court of the United States, when the plaintiff has the proper residence? Certainly the spirit and purposes of the law require it. We confess our inability to reconcile these qualities of a corporation—residence, habitancy, and individuality, with the doctrine that a corporation aggregate cannot be a citizen for the purposes of a suit in the courts of the United States, unless in consequence of a residence of all the corporators being of the state in which the suit is brought. When the corporation exercises its powers in the state which chartered it, that is its residence, and such an averment is sufficient to give the Circuit Courts jurisdiction.

Our conclusion makes it unnecessary for us to consider that averment in the plea which denies jurisdiction on the ground that citizens of the same state with the plaintiff are members of corporations in South Carolina, which are members of the Louisville, Cincinnati, and Charleston Rail-road Company.

The judgment of the Circuit Court below is affirmed.

ORDER

This cause came on to to be heard on the transcript of the record from the Circuit Court of the United States for the district of South Carolina, and was argued by counsel. On consideration whereof, It is now here ordered and adjudged by this court, that the judgment of the said Circuit Court in this cause be, and the same is hereby affirmed with costs and damages at the rate of six per centum per annum.

Roger B. Taney

☆ 1777–1864 ☆

APPOINTED BY

ANDREW JACKSON

YEARS ON COURT

1836–1864

Roger B. Taney

by
FRANK OTTO GATELL

ROGER TANEY's reputation has been subject to the cyclical variations that have influenced the retrospective evaluation of many of our political figures. In Taney's case the disability has been increased by the fact that this remarkable jurist always labored to escape the shadow of his predecessor, John Marshall. When the historiographical apotheosis of Marshall took place in the post–Civil War era, Taney's reputation (which had been building steadily until *Dred Scott*) fell accordingly. The Marylander's Jacksonianism, a term which became a code word for some or many unspecified brands of radicalism and agrarian negativism, supposedly put him beyond the pale of judicial respect. But by the second quarter of our century this simple view of constitutional history (Marshall the Builder versus Taney the Destroyer) could not be sustained. The work of Carl Swisher and others showed clearly that Taney had not played Samson, pulling down the temple round him. The revisionism was welcome, yet at the same time it created the danger that a new view would emerge that might all but obliterate the differences between Taney's jurisprudence and Marshall's. If so, this would again put Taney within the range of Marshall's shadow, but this time in the role of camp follower. Taney and his like-minded associates would not have accepted that. If the term radicalism is inappropriate when applied to Roger Taney, he nevertheless came to the Supreme Court determined to apply "Jacksonian reform" to the last holdout branch of the federal government.

Taney descended from a prominent Maryland tidewater family which first settled there in the 1660's. The Taneys were tobacco planters, and Roger was born in Calvert County on March 17, 1777. Following his elementary education in the usual one-room, one-tutor local schools, he was sent to a grammar school.

FRANK O. GATELL, Professor of History at the University of California, Los Angeles, is the author of John Gorham Palfrey and the New England Conscience.

This and private tutoring by a Princeton College student prepared him for matriculation at Dickinson College in Pennsylvania at age fifteen. He graduated in 1795, and was his class valedictorian.

Next came reading in law in the office of Judge Jeremiah Chase, who was on the bench of the Maryland General Court. The Maryland bench and bar of the turn of the century were of very high quality, and Taney's exposure to them, both in court and at Chase's office in Annapolis, provided valuable training to the apprentice lawyer. After three years' study, Taney was admitted to the bar. He actually won his first case two days before, but the victorious young lawyer was unhappy with his timid performance. Taney was unable to sustain himself in Annapolis. There were too many experienced lawyers in town, so the young man returned home—at this point still his only secure point of operations. Within a year he had been sent back to the state capital, this time as a representative to the state assembly or House of Delegates.

In keeping with his family alignment, Taney's politics were Federalist. In the legislature he sided with the rural area representatives then battling with the Baltimoreans over the construction of a canal between Chesapeake and Delaware bays. Baltimore opposed the canal, fearing loss of trade to the merchants of Philadelphia. Taney voted with the rural forces in favor of the canal. However, he opposed a proposal supported by his party for the introduction of the secret ballot. The planter squirearchy wanted open elections where their social prestige could more easily be converted into a political power. Voters should be "rewarded" on election day with drink and food, and they should vote "right." This had been part of Taney's own election. In 1800, however, the matter became temporarily academic for Taney. The Jeffersonian victory of that year put him on the shelf after only one year in the legislature.

In 1801, Taney moved to the town of Frederick, which was to be his home for twenty years. Within the limited confines of county seat law and politics, Taney rose to a position of leadership by building up a successful law practice. When the Court of Appeals sat there he was often called on to handle the more important cases. He had not entirely abandoned politics, nor changed his partisan affiliation, however. In 1803 he sought to return to the House of Delegates as a Federalist candidate. The election turned more upon the personality of the candidates than upon issues, but there was an element present which would radically alter the tone if not the substance of American politics. Taney's opponents scored him for his allegedly aristocratic airs. This was one of the first elections in Frederick by secret ballot and without a property qualification for voting. Taney lost by a greater margin than Federalists running in the preceding years. This victim of universal manhood suffrage may have reflected ruefully on the fact that is was his father, Michael Taney, who six years before in the legislature had introduced a universal manhood suffrage bill.

The Taney family was Roman Catholic. When Roger married Anne Key, an Episcopalian, in 1806, they agreed upon a unique arrangement: sons born to them would be raised as Catholics; daughters would become Episcopalians. The new Mrs. Taney was the daughter of a wealthy farmer, John Ross Key, and the sister of Francis Scott Key. The Taneys had six children who survived, all daughters, and all but one remained a member of the Episcopalian church.

Most of Taney's time still went to his legal practice, but he continued playing a prominent if unsuccessful role as Federalist leader and candidate. Several times he ran for the state senate and once on the slate of presidential electors. As the international crisis preceding the War of 1812 heightened, a significant rift developed within the Maryland Federalist party. With the declaration of war those who accepted the more general Federalist position of total opposition to the Madison administration found that a group of Federalists, Taney among them, reacted to the issue in nonpartisan terms. The faction was known as the "Coodies," and Taney acquired the nickname of "King Coody." He confirmed his maverick status in 1816 when he refused to support DeWitt Clinton of New York, the anti-caucus Republican who had been endorsed by many Federalists. Taney was saved either from expulsion from his party or the alternative of amalgamation with the Republicans by the fact that hardline Federalist opposition to the war had left the party politically vulnerable. The former Coodies were able to exert some influence, and in the elections to the state senate in 1816, a lower house controlled by Federalists elected Taney to a senate term of five years.

During his years in the state senate, Taney and his colleagues were vitally concerned with questions of finance and banking. At this juncture Taney, representing his rural constituency, believed that the Baltimore banks were monopolizing the state's credit facilities. This was the period of Baltimore's most spectacular economic growth, a process viewed with some apprehension outside of the city. Taney seemed interested in countering this with some countervailing power. He helped establish a bank at Hagerstown, specifically designed to extend credit to farmers, and he also served on the board of the Farmers Bank of Maryland. Another possible counter was the revived national bank. Taney favored recharter of the second Bank of the United States in 1816, and during the Panic of 1819 he remained a supporter of the national institution. He did not vote for the bill which put a prohibitive tax on the operations of the Bank's Baltimore branch, the law which led eventually to *McCulloch* v. *Maryland,* 4 Wheat. 316 (1819). But the disclosure of speculation and fraud at the Baltimore branch began the process of turning Taney against the Bank. In the end, of course, he became (after Jackson) its bitterest enemy.

The Federalist party, where it still existed, was in a confused state. Taney's politics mirrored this situation. Although he supported the second national bank in its first few years of operation, in other respects Taney remained a states' rights man. This was particularly so on the ever-touchy issue of slavery. Frederick was not in Maryland's area of heaviest slave concentration. Taney joined the Colonization Society and freed those slaves he inherited. Yet he would not support any proposals which called for the federal government to limit the institution. Each state had complete control over slavery, and whatever problems arose must be solved by the states. The Missouri debates had demonstrated graphically and ominously the dangers of a prolonged sectional argument over slavery.

Taney's senate service ended with the expiration of his single term in 1821. Two years later, he left Frederick for Baltimore. Once again, it was a case of his measured ambition calling on him to take the next logical step leading to his advancement. Taney did very well professionally among the Baltimore lawyers, and at the same time he found a new political home. Even before the end of his senate term, Federalist power had disintegrated. Like many other Federalists adrift in Maryland and in other states, Taney jumped on the Jackson bandwagon. But unlike most of these Federalist-Jacksonians, Taney thus made a lifelong political commitment. He supported Jackson in 1824, and for three years was chairman of the Jackson Central Committee for Maryland. This was the organizational basis for the Jackson campaign in the Free State in 1828, the year Jackson won the Presidency. The general did not carry the state, but he ran strongly, receiving five of its eleven electoral votes (electors were then chosen by districts). Taney had already established himself as among the top Democratic leaders. In 1826 he was chosen state attorney general, a post he was to hold for five years.

To the horror of incumbent National Republicans, the initial stage of Jacksonian reform largely involved the removal of politically unreliable office holders. Although there was no clean sweep, enough of a turnover took place to earn for the Jacksonians their merited association with the spoils system. State politicians demonstrated less delicacy or worry about public opinion than those at Washington. Taney, advising on federal patronage in Maryland, successfully urged a purging of custom house officers and postmasters for the good of the country and the party. The administration took note of his political orthodoxy and partisan sternness, two qualities which they would later ask Taney to employ during the height of the Bank War. In 1831 when the first Jackson Cabinet dissolved in the wake of the Peggy Eaton fiasco, Taney moved to Washington and into the office of Attorney General.

As Attorney General, Taney rendered opinions which indicated the nature of his constitutional beliefs and his later judicial precepts. He continued to express strong views on the division of powers between the state and federal governments. In federal-state relations, he, like Jackson, adhered firmly to the idea of divided sovereignty. Thus Taney fully supported his chief's Nullification Proclamation, although it was another Jacksonian, Edward Livingston, who acted as principal draftsman of that important state paper. Since state and national governments shared many powers concurrently, Taney believed that it was the Supreme Court's role to decide which powers should indeed be shared, and which were to be reserved to one or the other locus of sovereignty. Slavery, however, was not an area to be disputed. Taney reiterated his views that this was basically a state problem. The federal government might, of course, involve itself in such interstate questions involving slavery as the problem of fugitive slaves (upholding the property rights of southerners in so doing), but the local and municipal details of maintaining the legal and statutory basis of the slave society rested solely in the hands of each state.

During Jackson's first administration, Taney was not the most "visible" Democrat. At first, attention focused on Calhoun and Van Buren as they sparred for the succession. But at the same time the "invisibles," those stigmatized as the Kitchen Cabinet, prepared to assume power under Jackson (and later Van Buren) and the newly reorganized Democratic party. Taney was part of that group, and his conduct during the Bank War shot him into national prominence with a vengeance. He supported Jackson's veto of the Bank recharter bill in 1832, of course, helping draft the veto message, although not authoring it as previously thought. Next year came the real crisis. Once nullification had been disposed of successfully, Jackson decided upon his next blow at the Bank; he would remove the deposits of federal money from the "Monster's" vaults. Several impediments remained in the way in the form of recalcitrant Secretaries of the Treasury. Louis McLane and William J. Duane would not cooperate, and since the Secretary, not the President, possessed statutory authority to remove the deposits, Jackson had to find a reliable man to do the job. He chose Taney, shifting him from Justice to the Treasury. Taney did not disappoint him. As of the first of October, 1833, the Bank of the United States ceased to be the depository for federal funds.

Removal was easy enough (given one's political courage), but what would be substituted as the government's financial policy? The administration in the summer of 1833 decided upon a network of depository state banks, soon called "pet banks," and Secretary Taney became the head of this loosely-knit system. He worked closely with Amos Kendall, fourth auditor of the Treasury, and principal member of the Kitchen Cabinet. Also, a friendship Taney had made in Baltimore a decade previously figured importantly in this deposit question. Thomas Ellicott, president of the Union Bank of Maryland, was one of the state bankers who readily accepted appointment as a pet banker; but more, he also helped convince the administration that removal was financially practicable. Taney had worked as attorney for the Union Bank in the 1820's and he held some of the bank's stock. His connection with Ellicott gave the Baltimore banker's urgings increased force with Jackson, although the President certainly needed no convincing as to the national bank's iniquity. When Taney named the Union Bank one of the deposit banks, opposition men pointed to the apparent conflict of interest and accused Taney of seeking to profit personally from the operations of the bank.

Taney weathered that storm, and the pet banks sustained themselves during the "Biddle Panic" winter of 1833–34 when the national bank contracted loans sharply (perhaps with political intent). But the storm in the Senate in the spring of 1834 proved another case. Taney had been administering the Treasury on an interim appointment. Jackson, anticipating the reaction which would take place when the Senate finally received Taney's nomination, held off as long as possible.

He sent it in toward the end of the Session, but the delay did not help. Clay and Calhoun led the attack, and the Senate rejected Taney's nomination. The Secretary resigned (to be replaced by Levi Woodbury).

It appeared that Taney had been retired to the limited realm of state politics. He returned to Maryland, where he tried to defend the administration's banking policies as best he could. But the reaction to the Jacksonian program, especially among the political leadership and among many of the merchants who had been tied to the Democratic party, was very severe. This resulted in a Whig victory in the state in 1834 and the apparent destruction of Taney's political prospects. Taney resumed his legal practice in Baltimore and bided his time. Democratic successes in other states meant that by 1835 the Senate majority no longer rested in the hands of the opposition. Several vacancies then occurred in the United States Supreme Court. For example, in 1835 the Senate confirmed the appointment of James M. Wayne of Georgia. Like Taney, Wayne had been an anti-Bank stalwart, and his confirmation indicated that the opposition would not be able to block Jacksonian appointments indefinitely.

Also in 1835, Justice Gabriel Duvall resigned due to old age. Jackson immediately responded to this opportunity by nominating Taney, and the Senate discussed the possibility of his appointment but did not make an immediate decision. Late in the session, however, Daniel Webster recommended an indefinite postponement of the nomination, rather than outright rejection. This move received the approval of the Senate by a close vote. It was tantamount to a rejection of Taney, but Jackson would not give up easily. When Chief Justice Marshall died in July, 1835, Jackson threw down the gauntlet once more, nominating Taney for the position of Chief Justice. At the same time the President also submitted the name of Philip P. Barbour of Virginia as Associate Justice. The Senate, those in opposition at least, delayed as long as possible but finally after an executive session of which no records were kept, both Taney and Barbour were confirmed on March 16, 1836.

Taney came to the Court amid the severest predictions of doom from his political opponents. The over-reaction in the Whig camp can scarcely be understood in view of the man's subsequent judicial career. One New York City newspaper claimed that the "pure ermine of the Supreme Court is sullied by the appointment of a political hack." Even those Whigs who appreciated Taney's legal abilities, complained that his intimate connection with the Jackson administration, and especially the manner in which Jackson had used Taney as his hatchet man during the Bank struggle, prejudiced Taney's judicial role. It is interesting to note that although old Federalists and Whigs mourned Marshall's loss and contrasted the new Chief Justice unfavorably with the old, Marshall himself had privately tried to get Taney on the bench in 1833 when he was first rejected. And, of course, Marshall also had come from the Cabinet into the Chief Justiceship. The Whig uproar about Taney the partisan politician was thus a bit disingenuous. Like his predecessor, Taney did not cease all political activity nor hide his political sympathies as a result of his new status. He continued to advise Maryland politicians on local political affairs; he continued to advise the President on such matters as the annual message to Congress. And after 1837, Taney maintained close relations with the Van Buren administration even on such purely political items as patronage.

If any additional proof is needed that the radical charge against Taney is ridiculous, his reaction to riots which occurred in Baltimore in 1835 furnishes such evidence. The disturbances arose out of the banking situation in the city of Baltimore. The Bank of Maryland, which had been mismanaged in 1832 and 1833, failed the following year. Many of the Bank of Maryland creditors were working men whose savings had been lured from them by the innovation of interest paid on deposits. These people grew increasingly restive as month after month went by without any payment of their claims. In the summer of 1835, the resentment boiled over. More than a year of frustration and fear produced a noisy public protest by creditors, a protest which soon degenerated into mob action. For several days, the rioters had their way, destroying, among other things, homes of persons connected with the bank, while the bumbling city administration stood aside.

Taney was vacationing in Virginia at the time. He reacted strongly to the riots and their judicial aftermath, and wrote his son-in-law:

> *There ought not to have been a moment's hesitation about the use of fire-arms, and the firm and free use of them the moment that force was attempted by the mob. The first stone thrown at those who had assembled under the orders of the mayor, should have been the signal to fire. And if this had been made known before hand, no stone would have been thrown, and there would have been no idle spectators in the way of being shot. Such a contest ought always to be treated as one in which the existence of free government is put to hazard, and should be met like men who are resolved to maintain it at every sacrifice. I wish I had been in Baltimore. I think I would have induced my poor friend Mayor Hunt to do his duty, in the only effectual way in which it can ever be done, on such an occasion. Talk about putting an end to such scenes by pacific measures!*

If Whig America had then read these letters, it might have reacted less apprehensively to the idea of Chief Justice Taney—a man whose "radicalism" they thought threatened the basic order of society. Whatever Taney, the Democrat, thought of the common man, he certainly was no friend of the mob.

The political furor attending the appointment of Taney to the Chief Justiceship aroused fears, exaggerated ones, among judicial nationalists that the new Taney Court would quickly proceed to dismantle John Marshall's nationalism. The first three decisions handed down by the Taney Court seemed to justify some of the Whig apprehension. Yet in viewing the total effect of the change to a Jacksonian Court, it is clear now that Marshall's ideas, although altered, were certainly not discarded. The Marshall Court had already outlined the basic contours of national judicial power and the Taney Court contributed by refining these powers within broader limitations. Nevertheless, there was a change in political philosophy, or ideology, which can be extracted from the Taney decisions. Taney was not willing to extend the federal power any further than had already been done by Marshall. He preferred to leave a wide range of powers exclusively in the hands of the states and to include much under the aegis of concurrent powers or shared sovereignty. The Taney Court granted to the states much more autonomy in commerce and it also qualified the rights of corporations which were, in this period, becoming extra-political national institutions. The decisions rendered often acted as a moderating force, that is, a grant of local police power, between the extreme nationalism of Marshall and Story and the equally extreme sectionalism of the old Republican states' rights men.

Thus the Taney Court's decisions bolstered the Jacksonian idea of divided sovereignty. The three important cases of 1837, those which so frightened the Whigs, subsequently helped create the historiographical misinterpretation of the nature of the Taney Court, as one which differed *fundamentally* with Marshall's dicta. It was no accident that the nationalist historians of the late nineteenth century were called the "Whig school" of American historiography; in this particular regard they adopted the earlier views of their Whig forebears almost precisely.

All the cases had first been argued during the final years of the Marshall Court. But they had been continued, in some instances because of the resignations and deaths then taking place among the Justices. *City of New York* v. *Miln,* 11 Pet. 102 (1837) was one of these cases. A New York law required that ship captains report upon all passengers brought into the port of New York. The question at issue was whether the law interfered with the federal commerce power. Justice Barbour answered for the Taney Court and upheld the right of state regulation. The ideological line within the Court was drawn very sharply in a dissenting opinion by Justice Story which argued that the commerce power rested exclusively in the hands of the federal government. And in *Briscoe* v. *Bank of Kentucky,* 11 Pet. 257 (1837), the Court again diverged from the Marshall-nationalistic interpretation. Marshall had argued that states could not emit bills of credit since this was specifically prohibited by the Constitution. The Court did not disagree directly with Marshall's earlier opinion, but felt that although the Bank of Kentucky was a state-owned institution, it was not in fact the state itself. Furthermore, the emission of bank notes was an important function which should not be denied to any bank.

But the most important decision of 1837, of course, was *Charles River Bridge Co.* v. *Warren Bridge Co.,* 11 Pet. 420 (1837). In this case, Taney wrote the opinion himself and the document stands as one of the most revealing and significant pronouncements of Jacksonianism in the 1830's. The bridge controversy had become a *cause célèbre* of Massachusetts politics in the 1820's, and during the next decade it aroused a great deal of attention when the issue came up before the United States Supreme Court. The Massachusetts legislature had granted a charter to the Charles River Bridge Company in 1785. This bridge proved extremely profitable and as Boston and its environs grew at a tremendous rate so did the profits from the bridge. Agitation began for the granting of a second charter to a competitive bridge company, and astute politicians seized upon the issue. By the late 1820's some of them even ran for office under the banner of a Free Bridge Party. In 1828 the organization known as the Warren Bridge Company obtained permission to build another bridge from Boston to Charlestown. The original Charles River Bridge proprietors, of course, objected. The case went into the state courts when the Charles River Bridge Company in 1829 sought an injunction against the construction of the second bridge on the ground that its charter rights had been violated. The state supreme court divided on the issue and the case then went up to the United States Supreme Court.

Four years before, in 1833, Taney, while Attorney General, had been asked to give an opinion in a New Jersey Railroad case, an opinion which subsequently had great bearing upon his Charles River Bridge case decision. The New Jersey legislature had granted a railroad charter, stipulating as well that no one else should be permitted to operate competing transportation services. Taney wrote that the legislative body did not possess the entire sovereignty of the state. This resided in the people, and when the legislature overstepped its bounds, its actions were void. He referred specifically to "other limitations necessarily to be implied from the nature of other institutions and the principles of free representative government." Legislatures could not limit or restrict the legislative power of their successors. For if they could "the single improvident act of legislation, may entail lasting and incurable ills on the people of a state." He concluded that the monopoly grant to the railroad was void, for it was "inconsistent with the principles upon which all our political institutions are founded." Nothing occurred in the next four years to make him change his mind; in fact, the nature of the political struggle undoubtedly confirmed Taney's views with regard to public policy and monopoly grants.

Counsel for the Charles River Bridge interests argued that the company's charter granted exclusive rights which could not be withdrawn or limited. And they maintained that even in governmental grants, implications drawn from the nature of the grant might be valid. On the other hand, counsel for the newer, competing bridge had as its strongest point the fact that the bridge had already paid for itself and was already owned by the commonwealth. They contended that *any* property was subject to public use, and that property might be sacrificed or even destroyed if the public good required it. They also urged the acceptance of the use of the all-important police power: "Among the essential powers of government, are not only the power of taxation, and defense, but that of providing safe and convenient ways for the public necessity; and the right of taking property for public use."

As is true with many great Supreme Court decisions, Taney began his opinion with a disclaimer. The Chief Justice opened with an assurance that the Court was aware of its duty "to deal with these great and extensive interests with the utmost caution." Taney's decision turned upon his interpretation of the Charles River Bridge Company's charter. He cited opinions of English courts which declared that rights of entrepreneurs must sometimes bow to those of the public. And since American law was based upon English principles there seemed no reason why this principle should not also apply. "It would present a singular spectacle," Taney observed in mock disbelief, "if, while the courts in England are restraining the spirit of monopoly and exclusive privilege in the nature of monopolies, and confining corporations to the privileges plainly given them in their charters, that the courts of this country should be found enlarging these privileges by implication, and interpreting a statute more unfavorable to the public."

As for American precedents, Taney stressed a case involving a bank chartered in Rhode Island, *Providence Bank* v. *Billings,* 4 Pet. 514 (1830). Here, the bank had claimed that the state, by the very nature of the charter, had given up the right to tax, since power to tax meant power to destroy. Marshall had rejected this absurd resort to his famed *McCulloch* v. *Maryland* dictum. He said that the community was vitally interested in retaining the taxing power, and that if the power had not been specifically waived, its abandonment could not be inferred. Going beyond this, Taney argued that the taxing power was but one of the several essential powers of government which were not to be taken away by inference. The police power of the state "to promote the happiness and prosperity of the community," also represented one of these vital powers. And although "the rights of private property are sacredly guarded, we must not forget that the community also have rights, and that the happiness and well-being of every citizen depend on their faithful preservation."

The charter of the Charles River Bridge Company contained no section granting exemption from competition. To infer such an exemption "would be a strong exertion of judicial power, acting upon its own views of what justice required . . . , a sort of judicial coercion, creating an implied contract." Taney would not make such a jump from the wording of the charter to the plea of the proprietors. The opinion closed with a comment on the harmful effects a decision in favor of the Charles River Company would have on established internal improvement enterprises which had come into parallel competition with originally chartered companies.

The Court's decision created a furor, especially within the legal profession, which is always so basically conservative. But Taney had only held that the Court would not read charters inferentially. He did not challenge Marshall's basic constitutional principle on contracts, namely, that a government charter is a binding contract. Yet he gave the Marshall dictum a flexibility that it very much needed and which it probably would not have received from Marshall himself.

Those who seek in the workings of the Taney Court new constitutional principles with regard to property rights naturally emphasize the *Charles River Bridge* case and particularly the sentence about community rights. But as Benjamin Wright has observed "the simple fact is that the contract clause was more secure and a broader base for the defense of property rights in 1864 than it had been in 1835." *Charles River Bridge* was the really significant break with part of the Marshall tradition, yet the influence of this decision would be felt later. The era was one of consolidation and application. Taney adopted most of Marshall's contract clause principles, and there was no indication that the Court viewed the just rights of private property with hostility. On the contrary, the Court interpreted grants to public utilities so as to open channels of commerce. This was as much in the interest of private investors as it was of the public welfare.

Another area of limitation upon the application of the contract clause was with regard to the doctrine of the inalienability of the right of eminent domain. Although this had not determined the Charles River Bridge case, it seemed to be the consensus that the power of the state to take property for public use, with proper compensation, should not be abridged. The case of *West River Bridge Company* v. *Dix,* 6 How. 507 (1848), presented this issue squarely. The state of Vermont decided in 1839 to build a comprehensive road system and to take over with compensation those franchises whose functions might better be served through state action. Justice Daniel spoke for the Court and agreed that although the charter was a contract it must bow to the indisputable right of every sovereign community to guard its existence and promote its interests, that is, the right of eminent domain. Taney concurred.

The principal reason for the inclusion of the contract clause in the Constitution was to prohibit the kind of pro-debtor legislation which had prevailed in some states during the Confederation period. Several cases arose in which such laws were declared void. *Bronson* v. *Kinzie,* 1 How. 311 (1843), involved two Illinois laws of 1841. Individuals who had been foreclosed could redeem their property by repaying the money with 10% interest, and no sales were to be made under court order unless the property realized two-thirds of its appraised value. Both laws were to apply retroactively. Kinzie, a Chicago property holder, obtained a loan from a New York banker, offering land as security. The loan was made before the laws had been passed. Taney stated that there was no constitutional objection to the state's changing the remedy for contract enforcement, so long as it did not involve an impairment of the obligation of contract. If the law embraced such an impairment the effect or the goal of the legislation became irrelevant. The obligation could not be ignored or reduced legislatively. It was the Court's duty to establish a line between mere alteration of remedy and impairment. Then Taney spoke in words which Marshall would certainly have approved: "It would be unjust to the memory of the distinguished men who framed it [the contract clause], to suppose that it was designed to protect a barren and abstract right without any practical application upon the business of life. It was undoubtedly adopted as a part of the Constitution for a great and useful purpose. It was to maintain the integrity of contracts, and to secure their faithful execution throughout the Union, by placing them under the protection of the Constitution of the United States." Thus contracts entered into before 1841 could not be altered, although subsequent contracts were subject to the new conditions. For once, Justice Story was enthusiastic about a Taney decision. He wrote to his Chief: "These are times in which the Court is called upon to support every sound constitutional doctrine in support of the rights of property and creditors."

Four years later, in *Cook* v. *Moffat,* 5 How. 295 (1847), the Court decided another contract clause case. Cook, a bankrupt Baltimore merchant, who had purchased goods from a New Yorker, sought relief under the insolvency laws of Maryland which provided that with the surrender of his available goods, the debtor was relieved of all previous obligations. Justice Grier, for the majority, rejected the contention that the contract in the case was performed in Maryland, since the notes and payments for the goods were made in New York, and held that the Maryland laws did not apply. Taney delivered a separate opinion assenting, but with some misgivings. He felt that if a state might pass a bankruptcy law, as provided in *Sturges* v. *Crowninshield,* then the federal courts sitting within that state should respect them. Nevertheless, he joined the majority and on the rule of *stare decisis* the Court affirmed the judgment of the lower court which Taney himself had written. And in all of the opinions, the Justices showed no enmity toward property rights.

Another important case involving the status of corporations was *Bank of Augusta* v. *Earle,* 13 Pet. 519 (1839). At that time the only bank in Alabama was state-owned and the state permitted no private institution to operate within its borders. This case stemmed from the right of banks outside of Alabama to issue bills of credit on cotton exports. The Alabama banks felt that the issuing of bills of credit was exclusively a banking privilege and therefore they had the sole right to issue such bills on the lucrative cotton trade, although the state constitution had not mentioned bills of exchange specifically. Intersectional commerce, particularly in the handling of cotton sales, depended upon the use of such bills. The Bank of Augusta, Georgia, was one of the outside banks which continued to purchase bills in Alabama. When some of the makers of these instruments, citizens of Alabama, refused to pay, claiming that under Alabama law they had not made valid contracts, the case went into the federal court. The case aroused much interest especially after a circuit court judge ruled that a corporation chartered in one state had no right to operate in another without special permission.

Chief Justice Taney delivered the Supreme Court's opinion. The first question to be settled was the contention that a corporation composed of citizens of other states was entitled to the benefit of the Constitution's privileges and immunities clause. Taney rejected the idea that the Court must regard the members of a corporation as individuals simply carrying on business in a corporate name. He ruled that this interpretation would give citizens of other states greater privileges than those enjoyed by citizens of the state itself. The contract had been made by a corporation, not by individuals. The corporation could claim only those rights specifically granted to it. It was true that a corporation could have no legal existence outside of the boundaries which created it, or as Taney put it: "it must dwell in the place of its creation and can not migrate to another sovereignty." But although it could not intrude its presence in other areas, other sovereignties might recognize it. The corporation "is indeed a mere artificial being, invisible and intangible; yet it is a person, for certain purposes in contemplation of law, and has been recognized as such by the decisions of this Court." Every power of the corporation in another state depended upon the laws of sovereignty in which in effect it had become a guest. "It is needless to enumerate here the instances in which, by the general practice of civilized countries, the laws of one will be recognized and executed in another."

As for the contention that such a doctrine of comity did not apply to the states, Taney held otherwise. "The intimate union of these states, as members of the same great political family, the deep and vital interests which bind them so closely together, should lead us, in the absence of proof to the contrary, to presume a greater degree of comity, and friendship, and kindness toward one another, than between foreign nations." As sovereign entities, the states could legislate on the issue, but in the absence of such a declaration of state policy toward outside corporations, there was no reason to deny the doctrine of comity. Alabama banking legislation was not clear on the question of bills of exchange, and it was not for the Court to settle the state's policy by interpretation. Thus Taney rendered judgment against Earle, the Alabama defaulter. Although the outcome favored the corporation, Taney also stated the doctrine that states could exclude corporations altogether or prescribe conditions for their operation within their boundaries. Thus, in this instance, Taney showed a due regard for both the rights of corporations and the rights of the states.

The Bank of Augusta case was prelude to several additional decisions demonstrating a favorable attitude toward corporations. Throughout this period the corporate form of organization became increasingly popular. This created a need for precise definition of the corporation's legal status. In *Louisville Railroad Co.* v. *Letson,* 2 How. 497 (1844), Justice Wayne pronounced a broad view of corporate responsibility and rights. Especially important was his statement that legally, a corporation might be considered a person, an inhabitant of the same state in which that corporation had been chartered. Yet the court had not been unanimous in this instance. And Taney, who was absent from the bench because of illness, may well have joined those who dissented from Wayne's broad, pro-corporation interpretation. Certainly Justice Daniel, the most agrarian of the Justices, remained unalterably opposed to the idea that corporations were citizens. Taney's stand was a characteristic attempt to achieve a middle ground. Marshall, in *Bank of the United States* v. *Deveaux,* 5 Cranch 61 (1809), had stated that a corporation "is certainly not a citizen; and consequently can not sue and be sued in the courts of the United States, unless the rights of the members can be exercised in their corporate name." This limited such suits to those in which all members of a corporation were citizens of states other than the citizen being sued. The irony, which Marshall might have appreciated, came when the Taney Court expanded federal court jurisdiction in this respect. The Court assumed that the stockholders of a corporation were citizens of the state in which the corporation had been formed. It did not matter if they happened to be citizens of the same state as the other party in the litigation. And by virtue of this corporate citizenship, federal courts could assume jurisdiction in cases between corporations of one state and citizens of another.

Following the Miln case, a decade elapsed before the next significant commerce clause cases. The *License Cases,* 5 How. 504 (1847), involved state licensing laws regulating the sale of liquor. Two dealt with the sale of alcohol imported from abroad and a third with liquor brought in from a neighboring state. They were grouped together for convenience in the Court term of 1847, but the attempt to simplify matters fell apart when it came to writing opinions. Although all Justices agreed that the licensing provisions of the states were valid, six of them produced nine separate opinions.

Taney's opinion was the most significant. In 1827 he had argued for the state in *Brown* v. *Maryland,* 12 Wheat. 419, the "original package" case, but "further and more mature reflection has convinced me that the rule laid down by the Supreme Court is a just and safe one, and perhaps the best that could have been adopted for preserving the rights of the United States on the one hand, and of the states on the other, and preventing collision between them." Obviously the states could not pass laws regulating the importation of liquor but the licensing laws in question dealt with retail and domestic trade. If a state deemed internal traffic in spirits injurious to its citizens, Taney would allow such regulation and he saw nothing in the Constitution to prevent it. Each state must act to protect its own health and safety. Taney restated his views of the police powers: "They are nothing more or less than the powers of government inherent in every sovereignty to the extent of its dominions. And whatever state passes a quarantine law, or a law to punish offences, or to establish courts of justice, or to regulate commerce within its own limits, in every case it exercises these powers; the power of sovereignty, the power to govern men and things within the limits of its dominion."

The *Passenger Cases,* 7 How. 283, came before the Court in 1849, and again illustrated Taney's balanced states' rights views. The cases dealt with state laws which levied taxes on immigrants, taxes which in some cases were prohibitive. Justice McLean spoke for a Court which declared these state laws unconstitutional by a five to four margin. They involved, he said, the regulation of foreign commerce, a sphere which properly belonged to the federal government.

Taney, true to his Jacksonian states' rights position, dissented. His opinion referred disapprovingly to the overturning of the License Cases decision: "I had supposed the question to be settled, so far as any question upon the construction of the constitution ought to be regarded as closed by the decision of this Court. I do not, however, object to the revision of it, and am quite willing that it be regarded hereafter as the law of this Court, that its opinion upon the construction of the constitution is always open to discussion when it is supposed to have been founded in error." If such state laws were invalidated, then the state could not protect itself against disease and pauperism. To knock down laws was easy, but nothing had been suggested to replace those which would protect the interest of commerce and at the same time support the obligations of humanity. The states did have the right to exclude unwanted and undesirable persons from their borders. Yet Taney carefully distinguished the right to regulate aliens from the right to deny entrance to citizens of the United States. Regarding the levy on the passengers, Taney contended that taxing was a concurrent power, yet he emphasized that the state taxing power could not apply to passengers from other states. Free passage of citizens from one state to another could not be impeded, "for all the great purposes for which the federal government was formed, we are one people, with one common country." Two years later in *Cooley* v. *Board of Wardens,* 12 How. 299 (1852), the Court accepted the compromise which Taney had been seeking—an accommodation between an exclusive national commerce power and a complete reliance upon a state's police power.

In its handling of cases involving slavery the Taney Court suffered a severe loss of prestige, and Taney himself came close to being relegated to judicial oblivion. In 1841, the Court decided *Groves* v. *Slaughter,* 15 Pet. 449 (1841), which dealt with the financial implications of the interstate slave trade and which also took on importance in the anti-slavery struggle. The constitution of Mississippi prohibited the importation of slaves from other states, not from any antislavery sentiment, of course, but because so much of the state's capital was going into slave purchases from other states. The controversy arose over the validity of a note for the payment of such imported slaves. The majority of the Court, Taney included, ruled that the state constitution's provisions were not self-operative. And, therefore, the absence of specific Mississippi laws on the subject did not invalidate the note in question. The decision avoided the question of the right to sell slaves across state lines, and the exclusiveness of the congressional power over this branch of commerce. The Groves case became increasingly important as ammunition for debates on slavery when the heat of the issue increased in the 1840's. It was used often by proslavery men as authority for sustaining a state's sovereign control over slavery.

A few years later the supreme court of Mississippi, ignoring the Groves case, ruled that the constitutional provision was operative. The new case came to the Supreme Court as *Rowan* v. *Runnels,* 5 How. 134 (1847). Counsel for the Mississippi interest argued that established interpretations of state courts should rule Supreme Court decision, unless an obvious violation of the federal Constitution or U.S. laws existed. Thus the counsel argued that the Supreme Court ought to review the Groves case. Taney said no. There was no reason for change; he wrote, "We can hardly be required by any comity or respect for the state courts, to surrender our judgment. Undoubtedly this Court will always feel itself bound to respect the decisions of state courts, and from the time they are made regard them as conclusive in all cases upon the construction of their own constitution and laws. But we ought not to give them a retroactive effect and allow them to render invalid contracts entered into with citizens of other states, which in the judgment of this court were lawfully made." Taney felt that if comity were pushed to this length, the constitutional rights of citizens of other states to sue in federal courts would be negated.

Several important cases involved fugitive slaves. In *Prigg* v. *Pennsylvania,* 16 Pet. 539 (1842), Taney assumed an attitude of concern for maintaining federal law as well as for the rights of the owner over his property. The case involved a Maryland slave who had escaped from her master and gone to Pennsylvania. Prigg had been sent to return her to Maryland, but a Pennsylvania law of 1826, which denied to anyone but the owner the right to remove a runaway slave, defined this act as kidnapping. Justice Story upheld the federal fugitive slave law, at the same time declaring that the federal government might not require the cooperation of state officials in the rendition of fugitives. In so deciding, Story invalidated the Pennsylvania law as unconstitutional and argued for an exclusive federal power regarding fugitive slaves. Taney agreed with his colleagues that the Pennsylvania law was unconstitutional since it inhibited the effectiveness of the federal fugitive slave act. But he did not agree that Congress had exclusive power in the matter. Although the federal government did not prohibit states from passing laws to protect personal property rights in the form of runaway slaves, the fugitive slave law depended upon the states' cooperation for its effectiveness. Taney argued that it was the duty of each state to protect the property of slaveowners which came within its boundaries. The decisions in the Prigg case did not discuss the abstract rights to freedom that a slave might have, rights which state or federal courts could not take away. Taney had concentrated upon the rights and duties of both federal and state legislatures to protect the property rights of the owners.

In 1851 another important case dealing with the rights of slaves, *Strader* v. *Graham,* 10 How. 82, came before the Court. Graham, a Kentuckian, had contracted with the owner of a minstrel show to train two Negro slaves. When the boys escaped in 1841 to Ohio and then to Canada, Graham sued Strader, the owner of the vessel the minstrel band traveled on. The Kentucky courts ruled in favor of the slaveowner. Strader's attorney had argued that once the youths touched the soil of Indiana or Ohio, with the consent of their master, they became free. But Attorney General John J. Crittenden of Kentucky took the other side. He said that there was no question of residence and that the slaves had crossed the Ohio River for one night stands many years before the successful escape. The Supreme Court had no jurisdiction to review the action of the state court since Kentucky law was the only one applicable. Taney agreed on the key question of jurisdiction. Kentucky law, alone, decided the domestic conditions of slaves within that state. The Northwest Ordinance did not have relevance to this case. The Ordinance was no longer effective except insofar as its provisions had been incorporated into state constitutions.

These cases, and several others, involving the status of slaves (many of them runaways) were a prelude to *Dred Scott*. Originally, Taney had planned to deliver an opinion which simply followed the precedent of *Strader* v. *Graham*. But, as is well known, Justice McLean's announced intention of issuing an anti-slavery opinion changed Taney's strategy. Also, he may well have begun to believe that a comprehensive opinion, one tinged with the judicial finality that many politicians had been demanding for years, would alleviate and perhaps put an end to the acrimonious sectional debate over the constitutionality of slavery extension.

Taney and each of his colleagues read a separate opinion on March 7, 1857, three days after the inauguration of James Buchanan. Thus there was no "official" majority decision, but Taney's is usually regarded as such. Only three Justices, Taney, Wayne, and Daniel, gave a flat negative on the question of whether Scott or any Negro descended from slaves could be a citizen. A clear majority, headed by Taney, found that the status of a slave was fixed by the laws of the state in which he lived when the question was raised, not upon the law of the area where he had resided temporarily. With a majority agreeing that Missouri law controlled Scott's condition, that is, that his status was that of a slave, there could be no right to sue, no federal jurisdiction. The case could have stopped there. But the majority pushed on, with only Justice Nelson declining to explore additional questions. The six adventurers went on to conclude that Congress could not legally exclude slaves from any territory. This voided the Missouri Compromise.

Taney's argument in support of this contention ran as follows: "Whenever the United States acquired new territory, it held it for the common benefit of the entire nation. The federal government administered the areas during their territorial stage, but did so as trustees for the people. All citizens must enjoy equality of rights in the territories. Though Congress could acquire territories and prepare them for statehood it did not have a broad police power within the areas. No word can be found in the Constitution which gives Congress a greater power over slave property, or which entitles property of that kind to less protection, than property of any other description." Congress could not prohibit slavery, for such exclusion would violate the due process clause of the Fifth Amendment. It could not take away vested property rights, but on the contrary Congress had the power and the duty of protecting the slaveowner in his rights. Thus all territorial restrictions on slavery were to be blown away.

The anti-slavery part of the North seized upon Taney's decision as political ammunition. Abolitionists, of course, had expected nothing less. And they seized upon the sentences in Taney's opinion concerning the Negroes' lack of legal rights. Taney, describing what he termed the universal sentiments of American colonists in the century before the Declaration of Independence and the Constitution, declared that Negroes "had been regarded as beings of an inferior order, and altogether unfit to associate with the white race, either in social or political relations; and so far inferior, they had no rights which the white man was bound to respect." However accurate this may have been historically, and unfortunately it *was* accurate, these words spoken at the height of the anti-slavery debate proved injurious in the extreme. The Court was accused of having made a corrupt bargain. Taney and Buchanan were pictured in the North as having conspired in advance for the benefit of southern slaveholders. The prestige of the Court dropped in direct proportion to the rise in power of anti-slavery politics in the North. The Chicago *Tribune* wrote an open letter to President Buchanan: "You may 'cheerfully submit'—of course you will, to whatever the five slaveholders and two or three doughfaces on the Supreme Court may be ready to utter on this subject; but not one man who really desires the triumph of freedom over slavery in the territories will do so. This is a country in which the people make both laws and judges and they will try their strength on the issues here presented." The case split the Court as well, when an acrimonious correspondence took place between Taney and Justice Curtis over the publication of the opinions. Curtis resigned shortly thereafter.

Taney did not consider slavery a positive good, far from it. In the same year as the *Dred Scott* case, he explained his position to a Massachusetts minister who had questioned him on the subject: "I am not a slaveholder. More than thirty years ago I manumitted every slave I ever owned except two who were too old when they became my property to provide for themselves. These two I supported in comfort as long as they lived." Yet Taney would have agreed with Jefferson's comment of 1820 about the South having the wolf by the ears. "Every intelligent person whose life has been passed in a slaveholding state, and who has carefully observed the character and capacity of the African race, will see that a general and sudden emancipation would be absolute ruin to the Negroes, as well as to the white population." Like other southerners, Taney believed abolition had impeded the tendency to improve the slave's lot. The agitation had made the master more sensitive to criticism and fearful of the loyalty of his slaves. The bonds had been drawn tighter, since the master believed that slaves were "for the most part weak, credulous, and easily misled by stronger minds."

In *Ableman* v. *Booth,* 21 How. 506 (1859), Taney again strongly upheld national powers, but once again in the service of the "slave power." The case involved the attempt of Wisconsin citizens, the legislature, and even the state courts, to hamper the application of the federal fugitive slave law of 1850. Taney spoke for a unanimous court in declaring that the action of the Wisconsin courts violated the established relationship between federal and state judiciaries. If the state courts had the power they claimed, then permission to prosecute offences against the laws of the United States lay entirely in the hands of the state judiciary. If this were admitted, no logical reason remained why this power could not extend to all crimes against laws of the United States. Taney then employed dual sovereignty to prevent this invasion of the jurisdiction of federal courts by those of a state: "The sphere of action appropriated to the United States is as far beyond the reach of the judicial process issued by a state judge or a state court as if the line of division was traced by landmarks and monuments visible to the eye. And the state of Wisconsin has no more power to authorize these proceedings, than it would have had if the prisoner had been confined in

Michigan, or in any other state in the Union, for an offense against the laws of the state in which he was imprisoned."

Taney then went on to defend federal judicial supremacy in terms which some claim went beyond even the views of Marshall. "Now it certainly be no humiliation to a citizen of a republic to yield a ready obedience to the laws as administered by the constituted authorities. Nor can it be inconsistent with the dignity of a sovereign state to observe faithfully, and in the spirit of sincerity and truth, the compact into which it voluntarily entered when it became a state of this union." Even if the federal commissioners had acted wrongly in this case, or if there were defects in the law, these were subject to correction in federal courts, not state tribunals. All the provisions of the federal fugitive slave act of 1850 were in accordance with the Constitution.

If the years immediately preceding the Civil War had been a period of tribulation to Taney, the war years themselves were no better. The Court met in December, 1860, a month after Lincoln's election, and rumors circulated that Taney was about to resign. *Dred Scott,* and other decisions, had linked Taney inextricably with the Buchanan administration. It was obvious, however, that there would be no similar link with Lincoln.

The central area of conflict between Taney and President Lincoln was the issue of political dissent and antiwar feeling. Lincoln realized that it was essential that border states should be kept from joining the Confederacy. In order to curb pro-southern sympathy among residents of border states and to keep the secession movement from spreading, Lincoln suspended such civil liberties as the writ of *habeas corpus* in the areas. This action in Maryland brought him into direct conflict with Taney, who also served as a circuit judge in the federal court system in Maryland.

The activities of Confederate sympathizers in Maryland had become so dangerous to the movement of Union troops that in April, 1861, Lincoln suspended *habeas corpus,* or rather gave General Winfield Scott the authority to do so if required to maintain public safety. Characteristically, the Constitution is vague as to exactly *who* has the power to suspend *habeas corpus*. But it should be noted that the clause appears in the legislative article of the document. Thus it might be inferred that the Founders intended that Congress, not the President, should suspend.

Taney became embroiled in the controversy in May, 1861. He issued a writ of *habeas corpus* directing Union General Cadwalader to bring before him an alleged Confederate sympathizer, John Merryman, who had been detained. On the appointed day neither Merryman nor General Cadwalader appeared. Instead a colonel from the General's staff brought a paper stating in essence that the military would obey only the orders of the President. Taney, enraged, then threatened legal action against General Cadwalader, and rather overdramatically he feared that he himself would be arrested. When his marshal could not gain admission to Fort McHenry to serve the second writ, Taney exploded and made comments from the bench of a sensational character. He explained that he had ordered the writ of attachment because the President could not constitutionally suspend *habeas corpus* and because persons who were not subject to military justice, if arrested by the military, must be turned over to civil authorities. If, he continued, General Cadwalader were before him at that moment he would imprison him. And he vowed further to send the President a copy of "these proceedings . . . and call upon him to perform his constitutional duty and enforce the laws. In other words, to enforce the process of this court." The Lincoln administration won this dispute through inaction; there was nothing that Taney could do. Later, Attorney General Bates published an opinion upholding the President's right to suspend the writ. There the matter rested until a year after the southern surrender; in *Ex parte Milligan,* 4 Wall. 2 (1866), Taney and constitutional liberty won a tardy vindication from a Republican Supreme Court.

But in the meantime the Republican press roasted the Chief Justice. It scored him as a "apologist for treason." Taney would have preferred to allow the South to secede rather than to do permanent damage to civil liberties. Lincoln preferred to sidestep the Constitution and preserve the Union. Taney viewed the dissolution of the Union as less of a disaster than the reign of coercion which he thought would be necessary to save it. Meanwhile, other pro-southern Marylanders joined Merryman in federal prisons, where they were held without knowledge of specific charges against them. About sixty of these cases were on the federal dockets, but Taney declined to hear them because he was convinced that Maryland was under martial law. Taney felt that trials held in such an unfavorable atmosphere would serve no useful purpose. These events mirrored the extent of Taney's pessimism. It was not his war. To the best of his ability, he had tried to prevent it. And to the best of his ability, he tried to see that it was waged with respect for the Constitution. Thus he joined the anti-administration dissenters in the *Prize Cases,* 2 Black 635 (1863). Taney probably accounted his judicial career a failure when he died in Washington, on October 12, 1864.

Like every other American politician, Taney considered himself a constitutional unionist. In politics, Andrew Jackson had implemented the dual sovereignty of the Constitution. On the bench, Roger Taney tried to do the same thing. His ideas on federalism and constitutional theory are consistent expressions of his belief in dual sovereignty. Inevitably, the Court was drawn into politics. Taney had never been one to shirk political battles and unfortunately for him and his Court's reputation, he is most remembered for his *Dred Scott* decision. There, a bit of shirking, or judicial restraint, would have served his purposes better than his unfortunate attempt to resolve the nation's insoluble problem of the 1850's. But Taney's greatest contribution was to preserve, and at the same time to refine, the main lines of Marshall's constitutional law. He pared down some of Marshall's more extreme positions, but under Taney there was no massive assault on the basic principle: that the national government possessed substantive powers under the Constitution. Taney did this not because he accepted Marshall's pro-nationalist point of departure, but because he sincerely believed in dual sovereignty.

SELECTED BIBLIOGRAPHY

Most of Taney's personal papers have apparently been lost. There is a small group of valuable letters written by Taney at the Library of Congress, but they fall mainly into the pre-judicial period. Many Taney letters can be found in other collections, particularly in the Maryland Historical Society, Baltimore. Early biographies by Samuel Tyler, *Memoir of Roger Brooke Taney, LL.D.* (Baltimore, 1872) and Benjamin C. Steiner, *Life of Roger Brooke Taney* (Baltimore, 1922) were superseded by Carl Brent Swisher, *Roger B. Taney* (New York, 1935). See also Charles W. Smith, Jr., *Roger B. Taney: Jacksonian Jurist* (Chapel Hill, 1936) and Walker Lewis, *Without Fear or Favor: A Biography of Chief Justice Roger Brooke Taney* (Boston, 1965). But Swisher remains the prime secondary source. There are many monographs and interpretative pieces, including: George W. Biddle, *Constitutional Development in the United States as Influenced by Chief Justice Taney* (New York, 1890); Albert G. Mallison, "The Political Theories of Roger B. Taney," 1 *Southwestern Political Science Quarterly* 219 (1920); Wallace Mendelson, "Chief Justice Taney—Jacksonian Judge," 12 *University of Pittsburgh Law Review* 381 (1951); Robert J. Harris, "Chief Justice Taney: Prophet of Reform and Reaction," 10 *Vanderbilt Law Review* 227 (1957); Gerald Garvey, "The Constitutional Revolution of 1837 and the Myth of Marshall's Monolith," 18 *Western Political Quarterly* 27 (1965).

Roger B. Taney

REPRESENTATIVE OPINIONS

CHARLES RIVER BRIDGE v. WARREN BRIDGE, 11 PET. 420 (1837)

Like John Marshall, who made one of his great constitutional pronouncements almost immediately upon joining the Court (*Marbury* v. *Madison*), Taney began his term as Chief Justice with one of the greatest of his decisions. The original Charles River Bridge was an extremely valuable thoroughfare. In 1828 a charter was granted by the Massachusetts legislature allowing a new bridge to be built over the Charles River. But was this new grant an impairment of the original charter granted to the Charles River Bridge interests? John Marshall would have answered yes. But Taney, steeped in Jacksonianism, would not tie the hands of the state government in legislating for the welfare of the people.

Mr. Chief Justice TANEY delivered the opinion of the Court.

The questions involved in this case are of the gravest character, and the Court have given to them the most anxious and deliberate consideration. The value of the right claimed by the plaintiffs is large in amount; and many persons may no doubt be seriously affected in their pecuniary interests by any decision which the Court may pronounce; and the questions which have been raised as to the power of the several states, in relation to the corporations they have chartered, are pregnant with important consequences; not only to the individuals who are concerned in the corporate franchises, but to the communities in which they exist. The Court are fully sensible that it is their duty, in exercising the high powers conferred on them by the constitution of the United States, to deal with these great and extensive interests with the utmost caution; guarding, as far as they have the power to do so, the rights of property, and at the same time carefully abstaining from any encroachment on the rights reserved to the states.

It appears, from the record, that in the year 1650, the legislature of Massachusetts, granted to the president of Harvard college "the liberty and power," to dispose of the ferry from Charlestown to Boston, by lease or otherwise, in the behalf and for the behoof of the college: and that, under that grant, the college continued to hold and keep the ferry by its lessees or agents, and to receive the profits of it until 1785. In the last mentioned year, a petition was presented to the legislature, by Thomas Russell and others, stating the inconvenience of the transportation by ferries, over Charles river, and the public advantages that would result from a bridge; and praying to be incorporated for the purpose of erecting a bridge in the place where the ferry between Boston and Charlestown was then kept. Pursuant to this petition, the legislature, on the 9th of March, 1785, passed an act incorporating a company, by the name of "The Proprietors of the Charles River Bridge," for the purposes mentioned in the petition. Under this charter the company were empowered to erect a bridge, in "the place where the ferry was then kept;" certain tolls were granted, and the charter was limited to forty years, from the first opening of the bridge for passengers; and from the time the toll commenced, until the expiration of this term, the company were to pay two hundred pounds, annually, to Harvard college; and at the expiration of the forty years the bridge was to be the property of the commonwealth; "saving (as the law expresses it) to the said college or university, a reasonable annual compensation, for the annual income of the ferry, which they might have received had not the said bridge been erected."

The bridge was accordingly built, and was opened for passengers on the 17th of June, 1786. In 1792, the charter was extended to seventy years, from the opening of the bridge; and at the expiration of that time it was to belong to the commonwealth. The corporation have regularly paid to the college the annual sum of two hundred pounds, and have performed all of the duties imposed on them by the terms of their charter.

In 1828, the legislature of Massachusetts incorporated a company by the name of "The Proprietors of the Warren Bridge," for the purpose of erecting another bridge over Charles river. This bridge is only sixteen rods, at its commencement, on the Charlestown side, from the commencement of the bridge of the plaintiffs; and they are about fifty rods apart at their termination on the Boston side. The travellers who pass over either bridge, proceed from Charlestown square, which receives the travel of many great public roads leading from the country; and the passengers and travellers who go to and from Boston, used to pass over the Charles River Bridge, from and through this square, before the erection of the Warren Bridge.

The Warren Bridge, by the terms of its charter, was to be surrendered to the state, as soon as the expenses of the proprietors in building and supporting it should be reimbursed; but this period was not, in any event, to exceed six years from the time the company commenced receiving toll.

When the original bill in this case was filed, the Warren Bridge had not been built; and the bill was filed after the passage of the law, in order to obtain an injunction to prevent its erection, and for general relief. The bill, among other things, charged as a ground for relief, that the act for the erection of the Warren Bridge impaired the obligation of the contract between the commonwealth and the proprietors of the Charles River Bridge; and was therefore repugnant to the constitution of the United States. Afterwards, a supplemental bill was filed, stating that the bridge had then been so far completed, that it had been opened for travel, and that divers persons had passed over, and thus avoided the payment of the toll, which would otherwise have been received by the plaintiffs. The answer to the supplemental bill admitted that the bridge had been so far completed, that foot passengers could pass; but denied that any persons but the workmen and the superintendents had passed over with their consent. In this state of the pleadings, the cause came on for hearing in the supreme judicial court for the county of Suffolk, in the commonwealth of Massachusetts, at November term, 1829; and the court decided that the act incorporating the Warren Bridge, did not impair the obligation of the contract with the proprietors of the Charles River Bridge, and dismissed the complainants' bill: and the case is brought here by writ of error from that decision. It is, however, proper to state, that it is understood that the state court was equally divided upon the question; and that the decree dismissing the bill upon the ground above stated, was pronounced by a majority of the court, for the purpose of enabling the complainants to bring the question for decision before this Court.

In the argument here, it was admitted, that since the filing of the supplemental bill, a sufficient amount of toll had been received by the proprietors of the Warren Bridge to reimburse all their expenses, and that the bridge is now the property of the state, and has been made a free bridge; and that the value of the franchise granted to the proprietors of the Charles River Bridge, has by this means been entirely destroyed.

If the complainants deemed these facts material, they ought to have been brought before the state court, by a supplemental bill; and this Court, in pronouncing its judgment, cannot regularly notice them. But in the view which the Court take of this subject these additional circumstances would not in any degree influence their decision. And as they are conceded to be true, and the case has been argued on that ground, and the controversy has been for a long time depending, and all parties desire a final end of it; and as it is of importance to them, that the principles on which this Court decide should not be misunderstood; the case will be treated in the opinion now delivered, as if these admitted facts were regularly before us.

A good deal of evidence has been offered to show the nature and extent of the ferry right granted to the college; and also to show the rights claimed by the proprietors of the bridge at different times, by virtue of their charter; and the opinions entertained by committees of the legislature, and others, upon that subject. But as these circumstances do not affect the judgment of this Court, it is unnecessary to recapitulate them.

The plaintiffs in error insist, mainly, upon two grounds: 1st. That by virtue of the grant of 1650, Harvard college was entitled, in perpetuity, to the right of keeping a ferry between Charlestown and Boston; that this right was exclusive; and that the legislature had not the power to establish another ferry on the same line of travel, because it would infringe the rights of the college; and that these rights, upon the erection of the bridge in the place of the ferry, under the charter of 1785, were transferred to, and became vested in "the proprietors of the Charles River Bridge;" and that under, and by virtue of this transfer of the ferry right, the rights of the bridge company were as exclusive in that line of travel, as the rights of the ferry. 2d. That independently of the ferry right, the acts of the legislature of Massachusetts of 1785, and 1792, by their true construction, necessarily implied that the legislature would not authorize another bridge, and especially a free one, by the side of this, and placed in the same line of travel, whereby the franchise granted to the "proprietors of the Charles River Bridge" should be rendered of no value; and the plaintiffs in error contend, that the grant of the ferry to the college, and of the charter to the proprietors of the bridge, are both contracts on the part of the state; and that the law authorizing the erection of the Warren Bridge in 1828, impairs the obligation of one or both of these contracts.

It is very clear, that in the form in which this case comes before us; being a writ of error to a state court; the plaintiffs in claiming under either of these rights, must place themselves on the ground of contract, and cannot support themselves upon the principle, that the law divests vested rights. It is well settled by the decisions of this Court, that a state law may be retrospective in its character, and may divest vested rights; and yet not violate the constitution of the United States, unless it also impairs the obligation of a contract. In 2 Peters, 413; Satterlee v. Mathewson; this Court, in speaking of the state law then before them, and interpreting the article in the constitution of the United States which forbids the states to pass laws impairing the obligation of contracts, uses the following language. "It (the state law) is said to be retrospective; be it so. But retrospective laws which do not impair the obligation of contracts, or partake of the character of ex post facto laws, are not condemned or forbidden by any part of that instrument," (the constitution of the United States). And in another passage in the same case, the Court say; "the objection, however, most pressed upon the Court, and relied upon by the counsel for the plaintiff in error, was, that the effect of this act was to divest rights which were vested by law in Satterlee. There is certainly no part of the constitution of the United States, which applies to a state law of this description; nor are we aware of any decision of this, or of any circuit court, which has condemned such a law upon this ground, provided its effect be not to impair the obligation of a contract." The same principles were reaffirmed in this Court, in the late case of Watson and others v. Mercer, decided in 1834, 8 Pet. 110; "as to the first point, (say the Court,) it is clear that this Court has no right to pronounce an act of the state legislature void, as contrary to the constitution of the United States, from the mere fact that it divests antecedent vested rights of property. The constitution of the United States does not prohibit the states from passing retrospective laws, generally; but only ex post facto laws."

After these solemn decisions of this Court, it is apparent that the plaintiffs in error cannot sustain themselves here, either upon the ferry right, or the charter to the bridge; upon the ground that vested rights of property have been divested by the legislature. And whether they claim under the ferry right, or the charter to the bridge, they must show that the title which they claim, was acquired by contract, and that the terms of that contract, have been violated by the charter to the Warren Bridge. In other words, they must show that the state had entered into a contract with them, or those under whom they claim, not to establish a free bridge at the place where the Warren Bridge is erected. Such, and such only, are the principles upon which the plaintiffs in error can claim relief in this case.

The nature and extent of the ferry right granted to Harvard college, in 1650, must depend upon the laws of Massachusetts; and the character and extent of this right has been elaborately discussed at the bar. But in the view which the Court take of the case before them, it is not necessary to express any opinion on these questions. For assuming that the grant to Harvard college, and the charter to the Bridge company, were both contracts, and that the ferry right was as extensive and exclusive as the plaintiffs contend for; still they cannot enlarge the privileges granted to the bridge, unless it can be shown, that the rights of Harvard college in this ferry have, by assignment, or in some other way, been transferred to the proprietors of the Charles River Bridge, and still remain in existence, vested in them, to the same extent with that in which they were held and enjoyed by the college before the bridge was built.

It has been strongly pressed upon the Court, by the plaintiffs in error, that these rights are still existing, and are now held by the proprietors of the bridge. If this franchise still exists, there must be somebody possessed of authority to use it, and to keep the ferry. Who could now lawfully set up a ferry where the old one was kept? The bridge was built in the same place, and its abutments occupied the landings of the ferry. The transportation of passengers in boats, from landing to landing, was no longer possible; and the ferry was as effectually destroyed, as if a convulsion of nature had made there a passage of dry land. The ferry then, of necessity, ceased to exist, as soon as the bridge was erected; and when the ferry itself was destroyed, how can rights which were incident to it, be supposed to survive? The exclusive privileges, if they had such, must follow the fate of the ferry, and can have no legal existence without it—and if the ferry right had been assigned by the college, in due and legal form, to the proprietors of the bridge, they themselves extinguished that right, when they erected the bridge in its place. It is not supposed by any one, that the Bridge company have a right to keep a ferry. No such right is claimed for them, nor can be claimed for them, under their charter to erect a bridge—and it is difficult to imagine how ferry rights can be held by a corporation, or an individual, who have no right to keep a ferry. It is clear, that the incident must follow the fate of the principal, and the privilege connected with property, cannot survive the destruction of the property; and if the ferry right in Harvard college was exclusive, and had been assigned to the proprietors of the bridge, the privilege of exclusion could not remain in the hands of their assignees, if those assignees destroyed the ferry.

But upon what ground can the plaintiffs in error contend that the ferry rights of the college have been transferred to the proprietors of the bridge? If they have been thus transferred, it must be by some mode of transfer known to the law; and the evidence relied on to prove it, can be pointed out in the record. How was it transferred? It is not suggested that there ever was, in point of fact, a deed of conveyance executed by the college to the Bridge company. Is there any evidence in the record from which such a conveyance may, upon legal principle, be presumed? The testimony before the Court, so far from laying the foundation for such a presumption, repels it in the most positive terms. The petition to the legislature, in 1785, on which the charter was granted, does not suggest an assignment, nor any agreement or consent on the part of the college; and the petitioners do not appear to have regarded the wishes of that institution, as by any means necessary to ensure their success. They place their application entirely on considerations of public interest and public convenience, and the superior advantages of a communication across Charles river by a bridge, instead of a ferry. The legislature, in granting the charter, show, by the language of the law, that they acted on the principles assumed by the petitioners. The preamble recites that the bridge "will be of great public utility;" and that is the only reason they assign, for passing the law which incorporates this company. The validity of the charter is not made to depend on the consent of the college, nor of any assignment or surrender on their part; and the legislature deal with the subject, as if it were one exclusively within their own power, and as if the ferry right were not to be transferred to the Bridge company, but to be extinguished and they appear to have acted on the principle, that the state by virtue of its sovereign powers and eminent domain, had a right to take away the franchise of the ferry; because, in their judgment, the public interest and convenience would be better promoted by a bridge in the same place; and upon that principle they proceed to make a pecuniary compensation to the college, for the franchise thus taken away: and as there is an express reservation of a continuing pecuniary compensation to the college, when the bridge shall become the property of the state, and no provision whatever for the restoration of the ferry right, it is evident that no such right was intended to be reserved or continued. The ferry, with all its privileges was intended to be forever at an end, and a compensation in money was given in lieu of it. The college acquiesced in this arrangement, and there is proof, in the record, that it was all done with their consent. Can a deed of assignment to the Bridge company which would keep alive the ferry rights in their hands, be presumed under such circumstances? Do not the petition, the law of incorporation, and the consent of the college to the pecuniary provision made for it in perpetuity, all repel the notion of an assignment of its rights to the Bridge company, and prove that every party to this proceeding, intended that its franchises, whatever they were, should be resumed by the state, and to be no longer held by any individual, or corporation? With such evidence before us, there can be no ground for presuming a conveyance to the plaintiffs. There was no reason for such a conveyance. There was every reason against it; and the arrangements proposed by the charter to the bridge, could not have been carried into full effect, unless the rights of the ferry were entirely extinguished.

It is however said, that the payment of the two hundred pounds a year to the college, as provided for in the law, gives to the proprietors of the bridge an equitable claim to be treated as the assignees of their interest; and by substitution, upon chancery principles, to be clothed with all their rights.

The answer to this argument is obvious. This annual sum was intended to be paid out of the proceeds of the tolls, which the company were authorized to collect. The amount of the tolls, it must be presumed, was graduated with a view to this incumbrance, as well as to every other expenditure to which the company might be subjected, under the provisions of their charter. The tolls were to be collected from the public, and it was intended that the expense of the annuity to Harvard college should be borne by the public; and it is manifest that it was so borne, from the amount which it is admitted they received, until the Warren Bridge was erected. Their agreement, therefore, to pay that sum, can give them no equitable right to be regarded as the assignees of the college, and certainly can furnish no foundation for presuming a conveyance; and as the proprietors of the bridge are neither the legal nor equitable assignees of the college, it is not easy to perceive how the ferry franchise can be invoked in aid of their claims, if it were even still a subsisting privilege; and had not been resumed by the state, for the purpose of building a bridge in its place.

Neither can the extent of the pre-existing ferry right, whatever it may have been, have any influence upon the construction of the written charter for the bridge. It does not, by any means, follow, that because the legislative power in Massachusetts, in 1650, may have granted to a justly favoured seminary of learning, the exclusive right of ferry between Boston and Charlestown, they would, in 1785, give the same extensive privilege to another corporation, who were about to erect a bridge in the same place. The fact that such a right was granted to the college, cannot by any sound rule of construction, be used to extend the privileges of the Bridge company beyond what the words of the charter naturally and legally import. Increased population longer experienced in legislation, the different character of the corporations which owned the ferry from that which owned the bridge, might well have induced a change in the policy of the state in this respect; and as the franchise of the ferry, and that of the bridge, are different in their nature, and were each established by separate grants, which have no words to connect the privileges of the one with the privileges of the other; there is no rule of legal interpretation, which would authorize the Court to associate these grants together, and to infer that any privilege was intended to be given to the Bridge company, merely because it had been conferred on the ferry. The charter to the bridge is a written instrument which must speak for itself, and be interpreted by its own terms.

This brings us to the act of the legislature of Massachusetts, of 1785, by which the plaintiffs were incorporated by the name of "The Proprietors of the Charles River Bridge;" and it is here, and in the law of 1792, prolonging their charter, that we must look for the extent and nature of the franchise conferred upon the plaintiffs.

Much has been said in the argument of the principles of construction by which this law is to be expounded, and what undertakings, on the part of the state, may be implied. The Court think there can be no serious difficulty on that head. It is the grant of certain franchises by the public to a private corporation, and in a matter where the public interest is concerned. The rule of construction in such cases is well settled, both in England, and by the decisions of our own tribunals. In 2 Barn. & Ado. 793, in the case of the Proprietors of the Stourbridge Canal against Wheely and others, the court say, "the canal having been made under an act of parliament, the rights of the plaintiffs are derived entirely from that act. This, like many other cases, is a bargain between a company of adventurers and the public, the terms of which are expressed in the statute; and the rule of construction in all such cases, is now fully established to be this; that any ambiguity in the terms of the contract, must operate against the adventures, and in favour of the public, and the plaintiffs can claim nothing that is not clearly given them by the act." And the doctrine thus laid down is abundantly sustained by the authorities referred to in this decision. The case itself was as strong a one, as could well be imagined, for giving to the canal company, by implication, a right to the tolls they demanded. Their canal had been used by the defendants, to a very considerable extent, in transporting large quantities of coal. The rights of all persons to navigate the canal, were expressly secured by the act of parliament; so that the company could not prevent them from using it, and the toll demanded was admitted to be reasonable. Yet, as they only used one of the levels of the canal, and did not pass through the locks; and the statute, in giving the right to exact toll, had given it for articles which passed *"through any one or more of the locks,"* and had said nothing as to toll for navigating one of the levels; the court held that the right to demand toll, in the latter case, could not be implied, and that the company were not entitled to recover it. This was a fair case for an equitable construction of the act of incorporation, and for an implied grant; if such a rule of construction could ever be permitted in a law of that description. For the canal had been made at the expense of the company; the defendants had availed themselves of the fruits of their labours, and used the canal freely and extensively for their own profit. Still the right to exact toll could not be implied, because such a privilege was not found in the charter.

Borrowing, as we have done, our system of jurisprudence from the English law; and having adopted, in every other case, civil and criminal, its rules for the construction of statutes; is there any thing in our local situation, or in the nature of our political institutions, which should lead us to depart from the principle where corporations are concerned? Are we to apply to acts of incorporation, a rule of construction differing from that of the English law, and, by implication, make the terms of a charter in one of the states, more unfavourable to the public, than upon an act of parliament, framed in the same words, would be sanctioned in an English court? Can any good reason be assigned for excepting this particular class of cases from the operation of the general principle; and for introducing a new and adverse rule of construction in favour of corporations, while we adopt and adhere to the rules of construction known to the English common law, in every other case, without exception? We think not; and it would present a singular spectacle, if, while the courts in England are restraining, within the strictest limits, the spirit of monopoly, and exclusive privileges in nature of monopolies, and confining corporations to the privileges plainly given to them in their charter; the courts of this country should be found enlarging these privileges by implication; and construing a statute more unfavorably to the public, and to the rights of the community, than would be done in a like case in an English court of justice.

But we are not now left to determine, for the first time, the rules by which public grants are to be construed in this country. The subject has already been considered in this Court; and the rule of construction, above stated, fully established. In the case of the United States v. Arrendondo, 8 Pet. 738, the leading cases upon this subject are collected together by the learned judge who delivered the opinion of the Court; and the principle recognised, that in grants by the public, nothing passes by implication.

The rule is still more clearly and plainly stated in the case of Jackson v.

Lamphire, in 3 Pet. 289. That was a grant of land by the state; and in speaking of this doctrine of implied covenants in grants by the state, the Court use the following language, which is strikingly applicable to the case at bar:—"The only contract made by the state, is the grant to John Cornelius, his heirs and assigns, of the land in question. The patent contains no covenant to do, or not to do any further act in relation to the land; and we do not feel ourselves at liberty, in this case, to create one by implication. The state has not, by this act, impaired the force of the grant; it does not profess or attempt to take the land from the assigns of Cornelius, and give it to one not claiming under him; neither does the award produce that effect; the grant remains in full force; the property conveyed is held by his grantee, and the state asserts no claim to it."

The same rule of construction is also stated in the case of Beatty v. The Lessee of Knowles, 4 Pet. 168; decided in this Court in 1830. In delivering their opinion in that case, the Court say:—"That a corporation is strictly limited to the exercise of those powers which are specifically conferred on it, will not be denied. The exercise of the corporate franchise being restrictive of individual rights, cannot be extended beyond the letter and spirit of the act of incorporation."

But the case most analogous to this, and in which the question came more directly before the Court, is the case of the Providence Bank v. Billings & Pittmann, 4 Pet. 514; and which was decided in 1830. In that case, it appeared that the legislature of Rhode Island had chartered the bank, in the usual form of such acts of incorporation. The charter contained no stipulation on the part of the state, that it would not impose a tax on the bank, nor any reservation of the right to do so. It was silent on this point. Afterwards, a law was passed, imposing a tax on all banks in the state; and the right to impose this tax was resisted by the Providence Bank, upon the ground, that if the state could impose a tax, it might tax so heavily as to render the franchise of no value, and destroy the institution; that the charter was a contract, and that a power which may in effect destroy the charter is inconsistent with it, and is impliedly renounced by granting it. But the Court said that the taxing power was of vital importance, and essential to the existence of government; and that the relinquishment of such a power is never to be assumed. And in delivering the opinion of the Court, the late Chief Justice states the principle, in the following clear and emphatic language. Speaking of the taxing power, he says, "as the whole community is interested in retaining it undiminished, that community has a right to insist that its abandonment ought not to be presumed, in a case in which the deliberate purpose of the state to abandon it does not appear." The case now before the Court, is, in principle, precisely the same. It is a charter from a state. The act of incorporation is silent in relation to the contested power. The argument in favour of the proprietors of the Charles River Bridge, is the same, almost in words, with that used by the Providence bank; that is, that the power claimed by the state, if it exists, may be so used as to destroy the value of the franchise they have granted to the corporation. The argument must receive the same answer; and the fact that the power has been already exercised so as to destroy the value of the franchise, cannot in any degree affect the principle. The existence of the power does not, and cannot depend upon the circumstance of its having been exercised or not.

It may, perhaps, be said, that in the case of the Providence Bank, this Court were speaking of the taxing power; which is of vital importance to the very existence of every government. But the object and end of all government is to promote the happiness and prosperity of the community by which it is established; and it can never be assumed, that the government intended to diminish its power of accomplishing the end for which it was created. And in a country like ours, free, active, and enterprising, continually advancing in numbers and wealth; new channels of communication are daily found necessary, both for travel and trade; and are essential to the comfort, convenience, and prosperity of the people. A state ought never to be presumed to surrender this power, because, like the taxing power, the whole community have an interest in preserving it undiminished. And when a corporation alleges, that a state has surrendered for seventy years, its power of improvement and public accommodation, in a great and important line of travel, along which a vast number of its citizens must daily pass; the community have a right to insist, in the language of this Court above quoted, "that its abandonment ought not to be presumed, in a case, in which the deliberate purpose of the state to abandon it does not appear." The continued existence of a government would be of no great value, if by implications and presumptions, it was disarmed of the powers necessary to accomplish the ends of its creation; and the functions it was designed to perform, transferred to the hands of privileged corporations. The rule of construction announced by the Court, was not confined to the taxing power; nor is it so limited in the opinion delivered. On the contrary, it was distinctly placed on the ground that the interests of the community were concerned in preserving, undiminished, the power then in question; and whenever any power of the state is said to be surrendered or diminished, whether it be the taxing power or any other affecting the public interest, the same principle applies, and the rule of construction must be the same. No one will question that the interests of the great body of the people of the state, would, in this instance, be affected by the surrender of this great line of travel to a single corporation, with the right to exact toll, and exclude competition for seventy years. While the rights of private property are sacredly guarded, we must not forget that the community also have rights, and that the happiness and well being of every citizen depends on their faithful preservation.

Adopting the rule of construction above stated as the settled one, we proceed to apply it to the charter of 1785, to the proprietors of the Charles River Bridge. This act of incorporation is in the usual form, and the privileges such as are commonly given to corporations of that kind. It confers on them the ordinary faculties of a corporation, for the purpose of building the bridge; and establishes certain rates of toll, which the company are authorized to take. This is the whole grant. There is no exclusive privilege given to them over the waters of Charles river, above or below their bridge. No right to erect another bridge themselves, nor to prevent other persons from erecting one. No engagement from the state, that another shall not be erected; and no undertaking not to sanction competition, nor to make improvements that may diminish the amount of its income. Upon all these subjects the charter is silent; and nothing is said in it about a line of travel, so much insisted on in the argument, in which they are to have exclusive privileges. No words are used, from which an intention to grant any of these rights can be inferred. If the plaintiff is entitled to them, it must be implied, simply, from the nature of the grant; and cannot be inferred from the words by which the grant is made.

The relative position of the Warren Bridge has already been described. It does not interrupt the passage over the Charles River Bridge, nor make the way to it or from it less convenient. None of the faculties or franchises granted to that corporation, have been revoked by the legislature; and its right to take the tolls granted by the charter remains unaltered. In short, all the franchises and rights of property enumerated in the charter, and there mentioned to have been granted to it, remain unimpaired. But its income is destroyed by the Warren Bridge; which, being free, draws off the passengers and property which would have gone over it, and renders their franchise of no value. This is the gist of the complaint. For it is not pretended, that the erection of the Warren Bridge would have done them any injury, or in any degree affected their right of property; if it had not diminished the amount of their tolls. In order then to entitle themselves to relief, it is necessary to show, that the legislature contracted not to do the act of which they complain; and that they impaired, or in other words, violated that contract by the erection of the Warren Bridge.

The inquiry then is, does the charter contain such a contract on the part of the state? Is there any such stipulation to be found in that instrument? It must be admitted on all hands, that there is none—no words that even relate to another bridge, or to the diminution of their tolls, or to the line of travel. If a contract on that subject can be gathered from the charter, it must be by implication; and cannot be found in the words used. Can such an agreement be implied? The rule of construction before stated is an answer to the question. In charters of this description, no rights are taken from the public, or given to the corporation, beyond those which the words of the charter, by their natural and proper construction, purport to convey. There are no words which import such a contract as the plaintiffs in error contend for, and none can be implied; and the same answer must be given to them that was given by this Court to the Providence Bank. The whole community are interested in this inquiry, and they have a right to require that the power of promoting their comfort and convenience, and of advancing the public prosperity, by providing safe, convenient, and cheap ways for the transportation of produce, and the purposes of travel, shall not be construed to have been surrendered or diminished by the state;

unless it shall appear by plain words, that it was intended to be done.

But the case before the Court is even still stronger against any such implied contract, as the plaintiffs in error contend for. The Charles River Bridge was completed in 1786. The time limited for the duration of the corporation by their original charter, expired in 1826. When, therefore, the law passed authorizing the erection of the Warren Bridge, the proprietors of Charles River Bridge held their corporate existence under the law of 1792, which extended their charter for thirty years; and the rights, privileges, and franchises of the company, must depend upon the construction of the last mentioned law, taken in connection with the act of 1785.

The act of 1792, which extends the charter of this bridge, incorporates another company to build a bridge over Charles river; furnishing another communication with Boston, and distant only between one and two miles from the old bridge.

The first six sections of this act incorporate the proprietors of the West Boston Bridge, and define the privileges, and describe the duties of that corporation. In the seventh section there is the following recital: "And whereas the erection of Charles River Bridge was a work of hazard and public utility, and another bridge in the place of West Boston bridge may diminish the emoluments of Charles River Bridge; therefore, for the encouragement of enterprise," they proceed to extend the charter of the Charles River Bridge, and to continue it for the term of seventy years from the day the bridge was completed; subject to the conditions prescribed in the original act, and to be entitled to the same tolls. It appears, then, that by the same act that extended this charter, the legislature established another bridge, which they knew would lessen its profits; and this, too, before the expiration of the first charter, and only seven years after it was granted; thereby showing, that the state did not suppose that, by the terms it had used in the first law, it had deprived itself of the power of making such public improvements as might impair the profits of the Charles River Bridge; and from the language used in the clauses of the law by which the charter is extended, it would seem, that the legislature were especially careful to exclude any inference that the extension was made upon the ground of compromise with the Bridge Company, or as a compensation for rights impaired.

On the contrary, words are cautiously employed to exclude that conclusion; and the extension is declared to be granted as a reward for the hazard they had run, and "for the encouragement of enterprise." The extension was given because the company had undertaken and executed a work of doubtful success; and the improvements which the legislature then contemplated, might diminish the emoluments they had expected to receive from it. It results from this statement, that the legislature in the very law extending the charter, asserts its rights to authorize improvements over Charles river which would take off a portion of the travel from this bridge and diminish its profits; and the Bridge Company accept the renewal thus given, and thus carefully connected with this assertion of the right on the part of the state. Can they, when holding their corporate existence under this law, and deriving their franchises altogether from it; add to the privileges expressed in their charter an implied agreement, which is in direct conflict with a portion of the law from which they derive their corporate existence? Can the legislature be presumed to have taken upon themselves an implied obligation, contrary to its own acts and declarations contained in the same law? It would be difficult to find a case justifying such an implication, even between individuals; still less will it be found where sovereign rights are concerned, and where the interests of a whole community would be deeply affected by such an implication. It would, indeed, be a strong exertion of judicial power, acting upon its own views of what justice required, and the parties ought to have done; to raise, by a sort of judicial coercion, an implied contract, and infer it from the nature of the very instrument in which the legislature appear to have taken pains to use words which disavow and repudiate any intention, on the part of the state, to make such a contract.

Indeed, the practice and usage of almost every state in the Union, old enough to have commenced the work of internal improvement, is opposed to the doctrine contended for on the part of the plaintiffs in error. Turnpike roads have been made in succession, on the same line of travel; the later ones interfering materially with the profits of the first. These corporations have, in some instances, been utterly ruined by the introduction of newer and better modes of transportation, and travelling. In some cases, rail roads have rendered the turnpike roads on the same line of travel so entirely useless, that the franchise of the turnpike corporation is not worth preserving. Yet in none of these cases have the corporations supposed that their privileges were invaded, or any contract violated on the part of the state. Amid the multitude of cases which have occurred, and have been daily occurring for the last forty or fifty years, this is the first instance in which such an implied contract has been contended for, and this Court called upon to infer it from an ordinary act of incorporation, containing nothing more than the usual stipulations and provisions to be found in every such law. The absence of any such controversy, when there must have been so many occasions to give rise to it, proves that neither states, nor individuals, nor corporations, ever imagined that such a contract could be implied from such charters. It shows that the men who voted for these laws, never imagined that they were forming such a contract; and if we maintain that they have made it, we must create it by a legal fiction, in opposition to the truth of the fact, and the obvious intention of the party. We cannot deal thus with the rights reserved to the states; and by legal intendments and mere technical reasoning, take away from them any portion of that power over their own internal police and improvement, which is so necessary to their well being and prosperity.

And what would be the fruits of this doctrine of implied contracts on the part of the states, and of property in a line of travel by a corporation, if it should now be sanctioned by this Court? To what results would it lead us? If it is to be found in the charter to this bridge, the same process of reasoning must discover it, in the various acts which have been passed, within the last forty years, for turnpike companies. And what is to be the extent of the privileges of exclusion on the different sides of the road? The counsel who have so ably argued this case, have not attempted to define it by any certain boundaries. How far must the new improvement be distant from the old one? How near may you approach without invading its rights in the privileged line? If this Court should establish the principles now contended for, what is to become of the numerous rail roads established on the same line of travel with turnpike companies; and which have rendered the franchises of the turnpike corporations of no value? Let it once be understood that such charters carry with them these implied contracts, and give this unknown and undefined property in a line of travelling; and you will soon find the old turnpike corporations awakening from their sleep, and calling upon this Court to put down the improvements which have taken their place. The millions of property which have been invested in rail roads and canals, upon lines of travel which had been before occupied by turnpike corporations, will be put in jeopardy. We shall be thrown back to the improvements of the last century, and obliged to stand still, until the claims of the old turnpike corporations shall be satisfied; and they shall consent to permit these states to avail themselves of the lights of modern science, and to partake of the benefit of those improvements which are now adding to the wealth and prosperity, and the convenience and comfort, of every other part of the civilized world. Nor is this all. This Court will find itself compelled to fix, by some arbitrary rule, the width of this new kind of property in a line of travel; for if such a right of property exists, we have no lights to guide us in marking out its extent, unless, indeed, we resort to the old feudal grants, and to the exclusive rights of ferries, by prescription, between towns; and are prepared to decide that when a turnpike road from one town to another, had been made, no rail road or canal, between these two points, could afterwards be established. This Court are not prepared to sanction principles which must lead to such results.

Many other questions, of the deepest importance, have been raised and elaborately discussed in the argument. It is not necessary, for the decision of this case, to express our opinion upon them; and the Court deem it proper to avoid volunteering an opinion on any question, involving the construction of the constitution, where the case itself does not bring the question directly before them, and make it their duty to decide upon it.

Some questions, also, of a purely technical character, have been made and argued, as to the form of proceeding and the right to relief. But enough appears on the record to bring out the great question in contest; and it is the interest of all parties concerned, that the real controversy should be settled without further delay: and as the opinion of the Court is pronounced on the main question in dispute here, and disposes of the whole case, it is altogether unnecessary to enter upon the examination of the forms of proceeding, in which the parties have brought it before the Court.

The judgment of the supreme judicial court of the commonwealth of Massachusetts, dismissing the plaintiffs' bill, must, therefore, be affirmed, with costs.

DRED SCOTT v. SANDFORD, 19 HOW. 393 (1857)

It is difficult to see now what Taney hoped to accomplish in his wide-sweeping decision in the *Dred Scott* case. The Court had carefully avoided all the emotional issues of slavery over the years, deciding on narrow jurisdictional grounds or on points of state law whenever such cases had come before it. In *Strader* v. *Graham,* 10 How. 82 (1852), the Court concluded that a Negro's legal status must be determined by the law of the state in which he resided and the federal courts were bound by that finding. Dred Scott's status as a Missouri resident could have been decided in the same way (i.e., he was a slave under Missouri law) and indeed an opinion by Justice Nelson was prepared along those lines. But Taney opened the Pandora's box of the Negro's legal status under the Constitution and Congress' power to legislate about slavery after Justices McLean and Curtis announced they would raise these issues in dissent. Perhaps Taney hoped, as President Buchanan had urged, that a comprehensive opinion by the Supreme Court would settle the matter. Taney's political sense must surely have been dulled by 1857 when he was eighty years old and he let himself be persuaded to adopt that view. In his opinion he insisted that slaves could not be citizens but were only property which could not be regulated by Congress. Thus the Missouri Compromise of 1820 which prohibited slavery above 36° 30′ was beyond the power of Congress. This was only the second act of Congress declared unconstitutional by the Court, but the repercussions were far different than those following the *Marbury* case.

Mr. Chief Justice TANEY delivered the opinion of the court.

This case has been twice argued. After the argument at the last term, differences of opinion were found to exist among the members of the court; and as the questions in controversy are of the highest importance, and the court was at that time much pressed by the ordinary business of the term, it was deemed advisable to continue the case, and direct a re-argument on some of the points, in order that we might have an opportunity of giving to the whole subject a more deliberate consideration. It has accordingly been again argued by counsel, and considered by the court; and I now proceed to deliver its opinion.

There are two leading questions presented by the record:

1. Had the Circuit Court of the United States jurisdiction to hear and determine the case between these parties? And

2. If it had jurisdiction, is the judgment it has given erroneous or not?

The plaintiff in error, who was also the plaintiff in the court below, was, with his wife and children, held as slaves by the defendant, in the State of Missouri; and he brought this action in the Circuit Court of the United States for that district, to assert the title of himself and his family to freedom.

The declaration is in the form usually adopted in that State to try questions of this description, and contains the averment necessary to give the court jurisdiction; that he and the defendant are citizens of different States; that is, that he is a citizen of Missouri, and the defendant a citizen of New York.

The defendant pleaded in abatement to the jurisdiction of the court, that the plaintiff was not a citizen of the State of Missouri, as alleged in his declaration; being a negro of African descent, whose ancestors were of pure African blood, and who were brought into this country and sold as slaves.

To this plea the plaintiff demurred, and the defendant joined in demurrer. The court overruled the plea, and gave judgment that the defendant should answer over. And he thereupon put in sundry pleas in bar, upon which issues were joined; and at the trial the verdict and judgment were in his favor. Whereupon the plaintiff brought this writ of error.

Before we speak of the pleas in bar, it will be proper to dispose of the questions which have arisen on the plea in abatement.

That plea denies the right of the plaintiff to sue in a court of the United States, for the reasons therein stated.

If the question raised by it is legally before us, and the court should be of opinion that the facts stated in it disqualify the plaintiff from becoming a citizen, in the sense in which that word is used in the Constitution of the United States, then the judgment of the Circuit Court is erroneous, and must be reversed.

It is suggested, however, that this plea is not before us; and that as the judgment in the court below on this plea was in favor of the plaintiff, he does not seek to reverse it, or bring it before the court for revision by his writ of error; and also that the defendant waived this defence by pleading over, and thereby admitted the jurisdiction of the court.

But, in making this objection, we think the peculiar and limited jurisdiction of courts of the United States has not been adverted to. This peculiar and limited jurisdiction has made it necessary, in these courts, to adopt different rules and principles of pleading, so far as jurisdiction is concerned, from those which regulate courts of common law in England, and in the different States of the Union which have adopted the common-law rules.

In these last-mentioned courts, where their character and rank are analogous to that of a Circuit Court of the United States; in other words, where they are what the law terms courts of general jurisdiction; they are presumed to have jurisdiction, unless the contrary appears. No averment in the pleadings of the plaintiff is necessary, in order to give jurisdiction. If the defendant objects to it, he must plead it specially, and unless the fact on which he relies is found to be true by a jury, or admitted to be true by the plaintiff, the jurisdiction cannot be disputed in an appellate court.

Now, it is not necessary to inquire whether in courts of that description a party who pleads over in bar, when a plea to the jurisdiction has been ruled against him, does or does not waive his plea; nor whether upon a judgment in his favor on the pleas in bar, and a writ of error brought by the plaintiff, the question upon the plea in abatement would be open for revision in the appellate court. Cases that may have been decided in such courts, or rules that may have been laid down by common-law pleaders, can have no influence in the decision in this court. Because, under the Constitution and laws of the United States, the rules which govern the pleadings in its courts, in questions of jurisdiction, stand on different principles and are regulated by different laws.

This difference arises, as we have said, from the peculiar character of the Government of the United States. For although it is sovereign and supreme in its appropriate sphere of action, yet it does not possess all the powers which usually belong to the sovereignty of a nation. Certain specified powers, enumerated in the Constitution, have been conferred upon it; and neither the legislative, executive, nor judicial departments of the Government can lawfully exercise any authority beyond the limits marked out by the Constitution. And in regulating the judicial department, the cases in which the courts of the United States shall have jurisdiction are particularly and specifically enumerated and defined; and they are not authorized to take cognizance of any case which does not come within the description therein specified. Hence, when a plaintiff sues in a court of the United States, it is necessary that he should show, in his pleading, that the suit he brings is within the jurisdiction of the court, and that he is entitled to sue there. And if he omits to do this, and should, by any oversight of the Circuit Court, obtain a judgment in his favor, the judgment would be reversed in the appellate court for want of jurisdiction in the court below. The jurisdiction would not be presumed, as in the case of a common-law English or State court, unless the contrary appeared. But the record, when it comes before the appellate court, must show, affirmatively, that the inferior court had authority, under the Constitution, to hear and determine the case. And if the plaintiff claims a right to sue in a Circuit Court of the United States, under that provision of the Constitution which gives jurisdiction in controversies between citizens of different States, he must distinctly aver in his pleading that they are citizens of different States; and he cannot maintain his suit without showing that fact in the pleadings.

This point was decided in the case of Bingham *v.* Cabot, (in 3 Dall., 382,) and even since adhered to by the court. And in Jackson *v.* Ashton, (8 Pet., 148,) it was held that the objection to which it was open could not be waived by the opposite party, because consent of parties could not give jurisdiction.

It is needless to accumulate cases on this subject. Those already referred to, and the cases of Capron *v.* Van Noorden, (in 2 Cr., 126,) and Montalet *v.* Murray, (4 Cr., 46,) are sufficient to show the rule of which we have spoken. The case of Capron *v.* Van Noorden strikingly illustrates the difference between a common-law court and a court of the United States.

If, however, the fact of citizenship is averred in the declaration, and the defendant does not deny it, and put it in issue by plea in abatement, he cannot offer evidence at the trial to disprove it, and consequently cannot avail himself of the objection in the appellate court, unless the defect should be apparent in some other part of the record. For if there is no plea in abatement, and the want of jurisdiction does not appear in any other part of the transcript brought up by the writ of error, the undisputed averment of citizenship in the declaration must be taken in this court to be true. In this case, the citizenship is averred, but it is denied by the defendant in the manner required by the rules of pleading, and the fact upon which the denial is based is admitted by the demurrer. And, if the plea and demurrer, and judgment of the court below upon it, are before us upon this record, the question to be decided is, whether the facts stated in the plea are sufficient to show that the plaintiff is not entitled to sue as a citizen in a court of the United States.

We think they are before us. The plea in abatement and the judgment of the court upon it, are a part of the judicial proceedings in the Circuit Court, and are there recorded as such; and a writ of error always brings up to the superior court the whole record of the proceedings in the court below. And in the case of the United States *v.* Smith, (11 Wheat., 172,) this court said, that the case being brought up by writ of error, the whole record was under the consideration of this court. And this being the case in the present instance, the plea in abatement is necessarily under consideration; and it becomes, therefore, our duty to decide whether the facts stated in the plea are or are not sufficient to show that the plaintiff is not entitled to sue as a citizen in a court of the United States.

This is certainly a very serious question, and one that now for the first time has been brought for decision before this court. But it is brought here by those who have a right to bring it, and it is our duty to meet it and decide it.

The question is simply this: Can a negro, whose ancestors were imported into this country, and sold as slaves, become a member of the political community formed and brought into existence by the Constitution of the United States, and as such become entitled to all the rights, and privileges, and immunities, guaranteed by that instrument to the citizen? One of which rights is the privilege of suing in a court of the United States in the cases specified in the Constitution.

It will be observed, that the plea applies to that class of persons only whose ancestors were negroes of the African race, and imported into this country, and sold and held as slaves. The only matter in issue before the court, therefore, is, whether the descendants of such slaves, when they shall be emancipated, or who are born of parents who had become free before their birth, are citizens of a State, in the sense in which the word citizen is used in the Constitution of the United States. And this being the only matter in dispute on the pleadings, the court must be understood as speaking in this opinion of that class only, that is, of those persons who are the descendants of Africans who were imported into this country, and sold as slaves.

The situation of this population was altogether unlike that of the Indian race. The latter, it is true, formed no part of the colonial communities, and never amalgamated with them in social connections or in government. But although they were uncivilized, they were yet a free and independent people, associated together in nations or tribes, and governed by their own laws. Many of these political communities were situated in territories to which the white race claimed the ultimate right of dominion. But that claim was acknowledged to be subject to the right of the Indians to occupy it as long as they thought proper, and neither the English nor colonial Governments claimed or exercised any dominion over the tribe or nation by whom it was occupied, nor claimed the right to the possession of the territory, until the tribe or nation consented to cede it. These Indian Governments were regarded and treated as foreign Governments, as much so as if an ocean had separated the red man from the white; and their freedom has constantly been acknowledged, from the time of the first emigration to the English colonies to the present day, by the different Governments which succeeded each other. Treaties have been negotiated with them, and their alliance sought for in war; and the people who compose these Indian political communities have always been treated as foreigners not living under our Government. It is true that the course of events has brought the Indian tribes within the limits of the United States under subjection to the white race; and it has been found necessary, for their sake as well as our own, to regard them as in a state of pupilage, and to legislate to a certain extent over them and the territory they occupy. But they may, without doubt, like the subjects of any other foreign Government, be naturalized by the authority of Congress, and become citizens of a State, and of the United States; and if an individual should leave his nation or tribe, and take up his abode among the white population, he would be entitled to all the rights and privileges which would belong to an emigrant from any other foreign people.

We proceed to examine the case as presented by the pleadings.

The words "people of the United States" and "citizens" are synonymous terms, and mean the same thing. They both describe the political body who, according to our republican institutions, form the sovereignty, and who hold the power and conduct the Government through their representatives. They are what we familiarly call the "sovereign people," and every citizen is one of this people, and a constituent member of this sovereignty. The question before us is, whether the class of persons described in the plea in abatement compose a portion of this people, and are constituent members of this sovereignty? We think they are not, and that they are not included, and were not intended to be included, under the word "citizens" in the Constitution, and can therefore claim none of the rights and privileges which that instrument provides for and secures to citizens of the United States. On the contrary, they were at that time considered as a subordinate and inferior class of beings, who had been subjugated by the dominant race, and, whether emancipated or not, yet remained subject to their authority, and had no rights or privileges but such as those who held the power and the Government might choose to grant them.

It is not the province of the court to decide upon the justice or injustice, the policy or impolicy, of these laws. The decision of that question belonged to the political or law-making power; to those who formed the sovereignty and framed the Constitution. The duty of the court is, to interpret the instrument they have framed, with the best lights we can obtain on the subject, and to administer it as we find it, according to its true intent and meaning when it was adopted.

In discussing this question, we must not confound the rights of citizenship which a State may confer within its own limits, and the rights of citizenship as a member of the Union. It does not by any means follow, because he has all the rights and privileges of a citizen of a State, that he must be a citizen of the United States. He may have all of the rights and privileges of the citizen of a State, and yet not be entitled to the rights and privileges of a citizen in any other State. For, previous to the adoption of the Constitution of the United States, every State had the undoubted right to confer on whomsoever it pleased the character of citizen, and to endow him with all its rights. But this character of course was confined to the boundaries of the State, and gave him no rights or privileges in other States beyond those secured to him by the laws of nations and the comity of States. Nor have the several States surrendered the power of conferring these rights and privileges by adopting the Constitution of the United States. Each State may still confer them upon an alien, or any one it thinks proper, or upon any class of description of persons; yet he would not be a citizen in the sense in which that word is used in the Constitution of the United States, nor entitled to sue as such in one of its courts, nor to the privileges and immunities of a citizen in the other States. The rights which he would acquire would be restricted to the State which gave them. The Constitution has conferred on Congress the right to establish an uniform rule of naturalization, and this right is evidently exclusive, and has always been held by this court to be so. Consequently, no State, since the adoption of the Constitution, can by naturalizing an alien invest him with the rights and privileges secured to a citizen of a State under the Federal Government, although, so far as the State alone was concerned, he would undoubtedly be entitled to the rights of a citizen, and clothed with all the rights and immunities which the Constitution and laws of the State attached to that character.

It is very clear, therefore, that no State can, by any act or law of its own, passed since the adoption of the Constitution, introduce a new member into the political community created by the Constitution of the United States. It cannot make him a member of this community by making him a member of its own. And for the same reason it cannot introduce any person, or description of persons, who were not intended to be embraced in this new political family, which the Constitution brought into existence, but were intended to be excluded from it.

The question then arises, whether the provisions of the Constitution, in relation to the personal rights and privileges to which the citizen of a State should be entitled, embraced the negro African race, at that time in this country, or who might afterwards be imported, who had then or should afterwards be made free in any State; and to put it in the power of a single State to make him a citizen of the United States, and endue him with the full rights of citizenship in every other State without their consent? Does the Constitution of the United States act upon him whenever he shall be made free under the laws of a State, and raised there to the rank of a citizen, and immediately clothe him with all the privileges of a citizen in every other State, and in its own courts?

The court think the affirmative of these propositions cannot be maintained. And if it cannot, the plaintiff in error could not be a citizen of the State of Missouri, within the meaning of the Constitution of the United States, and, consequently, was not entitled to sue in its courts.

It is true, every person, and every class and description of persons, who were at the time of the adoption of the Constitution recognised as citizens in the several States, became also citizens of this new political body; but none other; it was formed by them, and for them and their posterity, but for no one else. And the personal rights and privileges guarantied to citizens of this new sovereignty were intended to embrace those only who were then members of the several State communities, or who should afterwards by birthright or otherwise become members, according to the provisions of the Constitution and the principles on which it was founded. It was the union of those who were at that time members of distinct and separate political communities into one political family, whose power, for certain specified purposes, was to extend over the whole territory of the United States. And it gave to each citizen rights and privileges outside of his State which he did not before possess, and placed him in every other State upon a perfect equality with its own citizens as to rights of person and rights of property; it made him a citizen of the United States.

It becomes necessary, therefore, to determine who were citizens of the several States when the Constitution was adopted. And in order to do this, we must recur to the Governments and institutions of the thirteen colonies, when they separated from Great Britain and formed new sovereignties, and took their places in the family of independent nations. We must inquire who, at that time, were recognised as the people or citizens of a State, whose rights and liberties had been outraged by the English Government; and who declared their independence, and assumed the powers of Government to defend their rights by force of arms.

In the opinion of the court, the legislation and histories of the times, and the language used in the Declaration of Independence, show, that neither the class of persons who had been imported as slaves, nor their descendants, whether they had become free or not, were then acknowledged as a part of the people, nor intended to be included in the general words used in that memorable instrument.

It is difficult at this day to realize the state of public opinion in relation to that unfortunate race, which prevailed in the civilized and enlightened portions of the world at the time of the Declaration of Independence, and when the Constitution of the United States was framed and adopted. But the public history of every European nation displays it in a manner too plain to be mistaken.

They had for more than a century before been regarded as beings of an inferior order, and altogether unfit to associate with the white race, either in social or political relations; and so far inferior, that they had no rights which the white man was bound to respect; and that the negro might justly and lawfully be reduced to slavery for his benefit. He was bought and sold, and treated as an ordinary article of merchandise and traffic, whenever a profit could be made by it. This opinion was at that time fixed and universal in the civilized portion of the white race. It was regarded as an axiom in morals as well as in politics, which no one thought of disputing, or supposed to be open to dispute; and men in every grade and position in society daily and habitually acted upon it in their private pursuits, as well as in matters of public concern, without doubting for a moment the correctness of this opinion.

And in no nation was this opinion more firmly fixed or more uniformly acted upon than by the English Government and English people. They not only seized them on the coast of Africa, and sold them or held them in slavery for their own use; but they took them as ordinary articles of merchandise to every country where they could make a profit on them, and were far more extensively engaged in this commerce than any other nation in the world.

The opinion thus entertained and acted upon in England was naturally impressed upon the colonies they founded on this side of the Atlantic. And, accordingly, a negro of the African race was regarded by them as an article of property, and held, and bought and sold as such, in every one of the thirteen colonies which united in the Declaration of Independence, and afterwards formed the Constitution of the United States. The slaves were more or less numerous in the different colonies, as slave labor was found more or less profitable. But no one seems to have doubted the correctness of the prevailing opinion of the time.

The legislation of the different colonies furnishes positive and indisputable proof of this fact.

It would be tedious, in this opinion, to enumerate the various laws they passed upon this subject. It will be sufficient, as a sample of the legislation which then generally prevailed throughout the British colonies, to give the laws of two of them; one being still a large slaveholding State, and the other the first State in which slavery ceased to exist.

The province of Maryland, in 1717, (ch. 13, s. 5,) passed a law declaring "that if any free negro or mulatto intermarry with any white woman, or if any white man shall intermarry with any negro or mulatto woman, such negro or mulatto shall become a slave during life, excepting mulattoes born of white women, who, for such intermarriage, shall only become servants for seven years, to be disposed of as the justices of the county court, where such marriage so happens, shall think fit; to be applied by them towards the support of a public school within the said county. And any white man or white woman who shall intermarry as aforesaid, with any negro or mulatto, such white man or white woman shall become servants during the term of seven years, and shall be disposed of by the justices as aforesaid, and be applied to the uses aforesaid."

The other colonial law to which we refer was passed by Massachusetts in 1705, (chap. 6.) It is entitled "An act for the better preventing of a spurious and mixed issue," &c.; and it provides, that "if any negro or mulatto shall presume to smite or strike any person of the English or other Christian nation, such negro or mulatto shall be severely whipped, at the discretion of the justices before whom the offender shall be convicted."

And "that none of her Majesty's English or Scottish subjects, nor of any other Christian nation, within this province, shall contract matrimony with any negro or mulatto; nor shall any person, duly authorized to solemnize marriage, presume to join any such in marriage, on pain of forfeiting the sum of fifty pounds; one moiety thereof to her Majesty, for and towards the support of the Government within this province, and the other moiety to him or them that shall inform and sue for the same, in any of her Majesty's courts of record within the province, by bill, plaint, or information."

We give both of these laws in the words used by the respective legislative bodies, because the language in which they are framed, as well as the provisions contained in them, show, too plainly to be misunderstood, the degraded condition of this unhappy race. They were still in force when the Revolution began, and are a faithful index to the state of feeling towards the class of persons of whom they speak, and of the position they occupied throughout the thirteen colonies, in the eyes and thoughts of the men who framed the Declaration of Independence and established the State Constitutions and Governments. They show that a perpetual and impassable barrier was intended to be erected between the white race and the one which they had reduced to slavery, and governed as subjects with absolute and despotic power, and which they then looked upon as so far below them in the scale of created beings, that intermarriages between white persons and negroes or mulattoes were regarded as unnatural and immoral, and punished as crimes, not only in the parties, but in the person who joined them in marriage. And no distinction in this respect was made between the free negro or mulatto and the slave, but this stigma, of the deepest degradation, was fixed upon the whole race.

We refer to these historical facts for the purpose of showing the fixed opinions concerning that race, upon which the statesmen of that day spoke and acted. It is necessary to do this, in order to determine whether the general terms used in the Constitution of the United States, as to the rights of man and the rights of the people, was intended to include them, or to give to them or their posterity the benefit of any of its provisions.

The language of the Declaration of Independence is equally conclusive.

It begins by declaring that, "when in the course of human events it becomes necessary for one people to dissolve the political bands which have connected them with another, and to assume among the powers of the earth the separate and equal station to which the laws of nature and nature's God entitle them, a decent respect for the opinions of mankind requires that they should declare the causes which impel them to the separation."

It then proceeds to say: "We hold these truths to be self-evident: that all men are created equal; that they are endowed by their Creator with certain unalienable rights; that among them is life, liberty, and the pursuit of happiness; that to secure these rights, Governments are instituted, deriving their just powers from the consent of the governed."

The general words above quoted would seem to embrace the whole human family, and if they were used in a similar instrument at this day would be so understood. But it is too clear for dispute, that the enslaved African race were not intended to be included, and formed no part of the people who framed and adopted this declaration; for if the language, as understood in that day, would embrace them, the conduct of the distinguished men who framed the Declaration of Independence would have been utterly and flagrantly inconsistent with the principles they asserted; and instead of the sympathy of mankind, to which they so confidently appealed, they would have deserved and received universal rebuke and reprobation.

Yet the men who framed this declaration were great men—high in literary acquirements—high in their sense of honor, and incapable of asserting principles inconsistent with those on which they were acting. They perfectly understood the meaning of the language they used, and how it would be understood by others; and they knew that it would not in any part of the civilized world be supposed to embrace the negro race, which, by common consent, had been excluded from civilized Governments and the family of nations, and doomed to slavery. They spoke and acted according to the then established doctrines and principles, and in the ordinary language of the day, and no one misunderstood them. The unhappy black race were separated from the white by indelible marks, and laws long before established, and were never thought of or spoken of except as property, and when the claims of the owner or the profit of the trader were supposed to need protection.

This state of public opinion had undergone no change when the Constitution was adopted, as is equally evident from its provisions and language.

The brief preamble sets forth by whom it was formed, for what purposes, and for whose benefit and protection. It declares that it is formed by the *people* of the United States; that is to say, by those who were members of the different political communities in the several States; and its great object is declared to be to secure the blessings of liberty to themselves and their posterity. It speaks in general terms of the *people* of the United States, and of *citizens* of the several States, when it is providing for the exercise of the powers granted or the privileges secured to the citizen. It does not define what description of persons are intended to be included under these terms, or who shall be regarded as a citizen and one of the people. It uses them as terms so well understood, that no further description or definition was necessary.

But there are two clauses in the Constitution which point directly and specifically to the negro race as a separate class of persons, and show clearly that they were not regarded as a portion of the people or citizens of the Government then formed.

One of these clauses reserves to each of the thirteen States the right to import slaves until the year 1808, if it thinks proper. And the importation which it thus sanctions was unquestionably of persons of the race of which we are speaking, as the traffic in slaves in the United States had always been confined to them. And by the other provision the States pledge themselves to each other to maintain the right of property of the master, by delivering up to him any slave who may have escaped from his service, and be found within their respective territories. By the first above-mentioned clause, therefore, the right to purchase and hold this property is directly sanctioned and authorized for twenty years by the people who framed the Constitution. And by the second, they pledge themselves to maintain and uphold the right of the master in the manner specified, as long as the Government they then formed should endure. And these two provisions show, conclusively, that neither the description of persons therein referred to, nor their descendants, were embraced in any of the other provisions of the Constitution; for certainly these two clauses were not intended to confer on them or their posterity the blessings of liberty, or any of the personal rights so carefully provided for the citizen.

No one of that race had ever migrated to the United States voluntarily; all of them had been brought here as articles of merchandise. The number that had been emancipated at that time were but few in comparison with those held in slavery; and they were identified in the public mind with the race to which they belonged, and regarded as a part of the slave population rather than the free. It is obvious that they were not even in the minds of the framers of the Constitution when they were conferring special rights and privileges upon the citizens of a State in every other part of the Union.

Indeed, when we look to the condition of this race in the several States at the time, it is impossible to believe that these rights and privileges were intended to be extended to them.

It is very true, that in that portion of the Union where the labor of the negro race was found to be unsuited to the climate and unprofitable to the master, but few slaves were held at the time of the Declaration of Independence; and when the Constitution was adopted, it had entirely worn out in one of them, and measures had been taken for its gradual abolition in several others. But this change had not been produced by any change of opinion in relation to this race; but because it was discovered, from experience, that slave labor was unsuited to the climate and productions of these States: for some of the States, where it had ceased or nearly ceased to exist, were actively engaged in the slave trade, procuring cargoes on the coast of Africa, and transporting them for sale to those parts of the Union where their labor was found to be profitable, and suited to the climate and productions. And this traffic was openly carried on, and fortunes accumulated by it, without reproach from the people of the States where they resided. And it can hardly be supposed that, in the States where it was then countenanced in its worst form—that is, in the seizure and transportation—the people could have regarded those who were emancipated as entitled to equal rights with themselves.

And we may here again refer, in support of this proposition, to the plain and unequivocal language of the laws of the several States, some passed after the Declaration of Independence and before the Constitution was adopted, and some since the Government went into operation.

We need not refer, on this point, particularly to the laws of the present slaveholding States. Their statute books are full of provisions in relation to this class, in the same spirit with the Maryland law which we have before quoted. They have continued to treat them as an inferior class, and to subject them to strict police regulations, drawing a broad line of distinction between the citizen and the slave races, and legislating in relation to them upon the same principle which prevailed at the time of the Declaration of Independence. As relates to these States, it is too plain for argument, that they have never been regarded as a part of the people or citizens of the State, nor supposed to possess any political rights which the dominant race might not withhold or grant at their pleasure. And as long ago as 1822, the Court of Appeals of Kentucky decided that free negroes and mulattoes were not citizens within the meaning of the Constitution of the United States; and the correctness of this decision is recognised, and the same doctrine affirmed, in 1 Meigs's Tenn. Reports, 331.

And if we turn to the legislation of the States where slavery had worn out, or measures taken for its speedy abolition, we shall find the same opinions and principles equally fixed and equally acted upon.

Thus, Massachusetts, in 1786, passed a law similar to the colonial one of which we have spoken. The law of 1786, like the law of 1705, forbids the marriage of any white person with any negro, Indian, or mulatto, and inflicts a penalty of fifty pounds upon any one who shall join them in marriage; and declares all such marriages absolutely null and void, and degrades thus the unhappy issue of the marriage by fixing upon it the stain of bastardy. And this mark of degradation was renewed, and again impressed upon the race, in the careful and deliberate preparation of their revised code published in 1836. This code forbids any person from joining in marriage any white person with any Indian, negro, or mulatto, and subjects the party who shall offend in this respect, to imprisonment, not exceeding six months, in the common jail, or to hard labor, and to a fine of not less than fifty nor more than two hundred dollars; and, like the law of 1786, it declares the marriage to be absolutely null and void. It will be seen that the punishment is increased by the code upon the person who shall marry them, by adding imprisonment to a pecuniary penalty.

So, too, in Connecticut. We refer more particularly to the legislation of this State, because it was not only among the first to put an end to slavery within its own territory, but the first to fix a mark of reprobation upon the African slave trade. The law last mentioned was passed in October, 1788, about nine months after the State had ratified and adopted the present Constitution of the United States; and by that law it prohibited its own citizens, under severe penalties, from engaging in the trade, and declared all policies of insurance on the vessel or cargo made in the State to be null and void. But, up to the time of the adoption of the Constitution, there is nothing in the legislation of the State indicating any change of opinion as to the relative rights and position of the white and black races in this country, or indicating that it meant to place the latter, when free, upon a level with its citizens. And certainly nothing which would have led the slaveholding States to suppose, that Connecticut designed to claim for them, under the new Constitution, the equal rights and privileges and rank of citizens in every other State.

The first step taken by Connecticut upon this subject was as early as 1774, when it passed an act forbidding the further importation of slaves into the State. But the section containing the prohibition is introduced by the following preamble:

"And whereas the increase of slaves in this State is injurious to the poor, and inconvenient."

This recital would appear to have been carefully introduced, in order to prevent any misunderstanding of the motive which induced the Legislature to pass the law, and places it distinctly upon the interest and convenience of the white population—excluding the inference that it might have been intended in any degree for the benefit of the other.

And in the act of 1784, by which the issue of slaves, born after the time therein mentioned, were to be free at a certain age, the section is again introduced by a preamble assigning a similar motive for the act. It is in these words:

"Whereas sound policy requires that the abolition of slavery should be effected as soon as may be consistent with the rights of individuals, and the public safety and welfare"—showing that the right of property in the master was to be protected, and that the measure was one of policy, and to prevent the injury and inconvenience, to the whites, of a slave population in the State.

And still further pursuing its legislation, we find that in the same statute passed in 1774, which prohibited the further importation of slaves into the State, there is also a provision by which any negro, Indian, or mulatto servant, who was found wandering out of the town or place to which he belonged, without a written pass such as is therein described, was made liable to be seized by any one, and taken before the next authority to be examined and delivered up to his master—who was required to pay the charge which had accrued thereby. And a subsequent section of the same law provides, that if any free negro shall travel without such pass, and shall be stopped, seized, or taken up, he shall pay all charges arising thereby. And this law was in full operation when the Constitution of the United States was adopted, and was not repealed till 1797. So that up to that time free negroes and mulattoes were associated with servants and slaves in the police regulations established by the laws of the State.

And again, in 1833, Connecticut passed another law, which made it penal to set up or establish any school in that State for the instruction of persons of the African race not inhabitants of the State, or to instruct or teach in any such school or institution, or board or harbor for that purpose, any such person, without the previous consent in writing of the civil authority of the town in which such school or institution might be.

And it appears by the case of Crandall *v.* The State, reported in 10 Conn. Rep., 340, that upon an information filed against Prudence Crandall for a violation of this law, one of the points raised in the defence was, that the law was a violation of the Constitution of the United States; and that the persons instructed, although of the African race, were citizens of other States, and therefore entitled to the rights and privileges of citizens in the State of Connecticut. But Chief Justice Dagget, before whom the case was tried, held, that persons of that description were not citizens of a State, within the meaning of the word citizen in the Constitution of the United States, and were not therefore entitled to the privileges and immunities of citizens in other States.

The case was carried up to the Supreme Court of Errors of the State, and the question fully argued there. But the case went off upon another point, and no opinion was expressed on this question.

We have made this particular examination into the legislative and judicial action of Connecticut, because, from the early hostility it displayed to the slave trade on the coast of Africa, we may expect to find the laws of that State as lenient and favorable to the subject race as those of any other State in the Union; and if we find that at the time the Constitution was adopted, they were not even there raised to the rank of citizens, but were still held and treated as property, and the laws relating to them passed with reference altogether to the interest and convenience of the white race, we shall hardly find them elevated to a higher rank anywhere else.

A brief notice of the laws of two other States, and we shall pass on to other considerations.

By the laws of New Hampshire, collected and finally passed in 1815, no one was permitted to be enrolled in the militia of the State, but free white citizens; and the same provision is found in a subsequent collection of the laws, made in 1855. Nothing could more strongly mark the entire repudiation of the African race. The alien is excluded, because, being born in a foreign country, he cannot be a member of the community until he is naturalized. But why are the African race, born in the State, not permitted to share in one of the highest duties of the citizen? The answer is obvious; he is not, by the institutions and laws of the State, numbered among its people. He forms no part of the sovereignty of the State, and is not therefore called on to uphold and defend it.

Again, in 1822, Rhode Island, in its revised code, passed a law forbidding persons who were authorized to join persons in marriage, from joining in marriage any white person with any negro, Indian, or mulatto, under the penalty of two hundred dollars, and declaring all such marriages absolutely null and void; and the same law was again re-enacted in its revised code of 1844. So that, down to the last-mentioned period, the strongest mark of inferiority and degradation was fastened upon the African race in that State.

It would be impossible to enumerate and compress in the space usually allotted to an opinion of a court, the various laws, marking the condition of this race, which were passed from time to time after the Revolution, and before and since the adoption of the Constitution of the United States. In addition to those already referred to, it is sufficient to say, that Chancellor Kent, whose accuracy and research no one will question, states in the sixth edition of his Commentaries, (published in 1848, 2 vol., 258, note *b,*) that in no part of the country except Maine, did the African race, in point of fact, participate equally with the whites in the exercise of civil and political rights.

The legislation of the States therefore shows, in a manner not to be mistaken, the inferior and subject condition of that race at the time the Constitution was adopted, and long afterwards, throughout the thirteen States by which that instrument was framed; and it is hardly consistent with the respect due to these States, to suppose that they regarded at that time, as fellow-citizens and members of the sovereignty, a class of beings whom they had thus stigmatized; whom, as we are bound, out of respect to the State sovereignties, to assume they had deemed it just and necessary thus to stigmatize, and upon whom they had impressed such deep and enduring marks of inferiority and degradation; or, that when they met in convention to form the Constitution, they looked upon them as a portion of their constituents, or designed to include them in the provisions so carefully inserted for the security and protection of the liberties and rights of their citizens. It cannot be supposed that they intended to secure to them rights, and privileges, and rank, in the new political body throughout the Union, which every one of them denied within the limits of its own dominion. More especially, it cannot be believed that the large slaveholding States regarded them as included in the word citizens, or would have consented to a Constitution which might compel them to receive them in that character from another State. For if they were so received, and entitled to the privileges and immunities of citizens, it would exempt them from the operation of the special laws and from the police regulations which they considered to be necessary for their own safety. It would give to persons of the negro race, who were recognised as citizens in any one State of the Union, the right to enter every other State whenever they pleased, singly or in companies, without pass or passport, and without obstruction, to sojourn there as long as they pleased, to go where they pleased at every hour of the day or night without molestation, unless they committed some violation of law for which a white man would be punished; and it would give them the full liberty of speech in public and in private upon all subjects upon which its own citizens might speak; to hold public meetings upon political affairs, and to keep and carry arms wherever they went. And all of this would be done in the face of the subject race of the same color, both free and slaves, and inevitably producing discontent and insubordination among them, and endangering the peace and safety of the State.

It is impossible, it would seem, to believe that the great men of the slaveholding States, who took so large a share in framing the Constitution of the United States, and exercised so much influence in procuring its adoption, could have been so forgetful or regardless of their own safety and the safety of those who trusted and confided in them.

Besides, this want of foresight and care would have been utterly inconsistent with the caution displayed in providing for the admission of new members into this political family. For, when they gave to the citizens of each State the privileges and immunities of citizens in the several States, they at the same time took from the several States the power of naturalization, and confined that power exclusively to the Federal Government. No State was willing to permit another State to determine who should or should not be admitted as one of its citizens, and entitled to demand equal rights and privileges with their own people, within their own territories. The right of naturalization was therefore, with one accord, surrendered by the States, and confided to the Federal Government. And this power granted to Congress to establish an uniform rule of *naturalization* is, by the well-understood meaning of the word, confined to persons born in a foreign country, under a foreign Government. It is not a power to raise to the rank of a citizen any one born in the United States, who, from birth or parentage, by the laws of the country, belongs to an inferior and subordinate class. And when we find the States guarding themselves from the indiscreet or improper admission by other States of emigrants from other countries, by giving the power exclusively to Congress, we cannot fail to see that they could never have left with the States a much more important power—that is, the power of transforming into citizens a numerous class of persons, who in that character would be much more dangerous to the peace and safety of a large portion of the Union, than the few foreigners one of the States might improperly naturalize. The Constitution upon its adoption obviously took from the States all power by any subsequent legislation to introduce as a citizen into the political family of the United States any one, no matter where he was born, or what might be his character or condition; and it gave to Congress the power to confer this character upon those only who were born outside of the dominions of the United States. And no law of a State, therefore, passed since the Constitution was adopted, can give any right of citizenship outside of its own territory.

A clause similar to the one in the Constitution, in relation to the rights and immunities of citizens of one State in the other States, was contained in the Articles of Confederation. But there is a difference of language, which is worthy of note. The provision in the Articles of Confederation was, "that the *free inhabitants* of each of the States, paupers, vagabonds, and fugitives from justice, excepted, should be entitled to all the privileges and immunities of free citizens in the several States."

It will be observed, that under this Confederation, each State had the right to decide for itself, and in its own tribunals, whom it would acknowledge as a free inhabitant of another State. The term *free inhabitant,* in the generality of its terms, would certainly include one of the African race who had been manumitted. But no example, we think, can be found of his admission to all the privileges of citizenship in any State of the Union after these Articles were formed, and while they continued in force. And, notwithstanding the generality of the words "free inhabitants," it is very clear that, according to their accepted meaning in that day, they did not include the African race, whether free or not: for the fifth section of the ninth article provides that Congress should have the power "to agree upon the number of land forces to be raised, and to make requisitions from each State for its quota in proportion to the number of *white* inhabitants in such State, which requisition should be binding."

Words could hardly have been used which more strongly mark the line of distinction between the citizen and the subject; the free and the subjugated races. The latter were not even counted when the inhabitants of a State were to be embodied in proportion to its numbers for the general defence. And it cannot for a moment be supposed, that a class of persons thus separated and rejected from those who formed the sovereignty of the States, were yet intended to be included under the words "free inhabitants," in the preceding article, to whom privileges and immunities were so carefully secured in every State.

But although this clause of the Articles of Confederation is the same in principle with that inserted in the Constitution, yet the comprehensive word *inhabitant,* which might be construed to include an emancipated slave, is omitted; and the privilege is confined to *citizens* of the State. And this alteration in words would hardly have been made, unless a different meaning was intended to be conveyed, or a possible doubt removed. The just and fair inference is, that as this privilege was about to be placed under the protection of the General Government, and the words expounded by its tribunals, and all power in relation to it taken from the State and its courts, it was deemed prudent to describe with precision and caution the persons to whom this high privilege was given—and the word *citizen* was on that account substituted for the words *free inhabitant.* The word citizen excluded, and no doubt intended to exclude, foreigners who had not become citizens of some one of the States when the Constitution was adopted; and also every description of persons who were not fully recognised as citizens in the several States. This, upon any fair construction of the instruments to which we have referred, was evidently the object and purpose of this change of words.

To all this mass of proof we have still to add, that Congress has repeatedly legislated upon the same construction of the Constitution that we have given. Three laws, two of which were passed almost immediately after the Government went into operation, will be abundantly sufficient to show this. The two first are particularly worthy of notice, because many of the men who assisted in framing the Constitution, and took an active part in procuring its adoption, were then in the halls of legislation, and certainly understood what they meant when they used the words "people of the United States" and "citizen" in that well-considered instrument.

The first of these acts is the naturalization law, which was passed at the second session of the first Congress, March 26, 1790, and confines the right of becoming citizens *"to aliens being free white persons."*

Now, the Constitution does not limit the power of Congress in this respect to white persons. And they may, if they think proper, authorize the naturalization of any one, of any color, who was born under allegiance to another Government. But the language of the law above quoted, shows that citizenship at that time was perfectly understood to be confined to the white race; and that they alone constituted the sovereignty in the Government.

Congress might, as we before said, have authorized the naturalization of Indians, because they were aliens and foreigners. But, in their then untutored and savage state, no one would have thought of admitting them as citizens in a civilized community. And, moreover, the atrocities they had but recently committed, when they were the allies of Great Britain in the Revolutionary war, were yet fresh in the recollection of the people of the United States, and they were even then guarding themselves against the threatened renewal of Indian hostilities. No one supposed then that any Indian would ask for, or was capable of enjoying, the privileges of an American citizen, and the word white was not used with any particular reference to them.

Neither was it used with any reference to the African race imported into or born in this country; because Congress had no power to naturalize them, and therefore there was no necessity for using particular words to exclude them.

It would seem to have been used merely because it followed out the line of division which the Constitution has drawn between the citizen race, who formed and held the Government, and the African race, which they held in subjection and slavery, and governed at their own pleasure.

Another of the early laws of which we have spoken, is the first militia law, which was passed in 1792, at the first session of the second Congress. The language of this law is equally plain and significant with the one just mentioned. It directs that every "free able-bodied white male citizen" shall be enrolled in the militia. The word *white* is evidently used to exclude the African race, and the word "citizen" to exclude unnaturalized foreigners; the latter forming no part of the sovereignty, owing it no allegiance, and therefore under no obligation to defend it. The African race, however, born in the country, did owe allegiance to the Government, whether they were slave or free; but it is repudiated, and rejected from the duties and obligations of citizenship in marked language.

The third act to which we have alluded is even still more decisive; it was passed as late as 1813, (2 Stat., 809,) and it provides: "That from and after the termination of the war in which the United States are now engaged with Great Britain, it shall not be lawful to employ, on board of any public or private vessels of the United States, any person or persons except citizens of the United States, *or* persons of color, natives of the United States."

Here the line of distinction is drawn in express words. Persons of color, in the judgment of Congress, were not included in the word citizens, and they are described as another and different class of persons, and authorized to be employed, if born in the United States.

And even as late as 1820, (chap. 104, sec. 8,) in the charter to the city of Washington, the corporation is authorized "to restrain and prohibit the nightly and other disorderly meetings of slaves, free negroes, and mulattoes," thus associating them together in its legislation; and after prescribing the punishment that may be inflicted on the slaves, proceeds in the following words: "And to punish such free negroes and mulattoes by penalties not exceeding twenty dollars for any one offence; and in case of the inability of any such free negro or mulatto to pay any such penalty and cost thereon, to cause him or her to be confined to labor for any time not exceeding six calendar months." And in a subsequent part of the same section, the act authorizes the corporation "to prescribe the terms and conditions upon which free negroes and mulattoes may reside in the city."

This law, like the laws of the States, shows that this class of persons were governed by special legislation directed expressly to them, and always connected with provisions for the government of slaves, and not with those for the government of free white citizens. And after such an uniform course of legislation as we have stated, by the colonies, by the States, and by Congress, running through a period of more than a century, it would seem that to call persons thus marked and stigmatized, "citizens" of the United States, "fellow-citizens," a constituent part of the sovereignty, would be an abuse of terms, and not calculated to exalt the character of an American citizen in the eyes of other nations.

The conduct of the Executive Department of the Government has been in perfect harmony upon this subject with this course of legislation. The question was brought officially before the late William Wirt, when he was the Attorney General of the United States, in 1821, and he decided that the words "citizens of the United States" were used in the acts of Congress in the same sense as in the Constitution; and that free persons of color were not citizens, within the meaning of the Constitution and laws; and this opinion has been confirmed by that of the late Attorney General, Caleb Cushing, in a recent case, and acted upon by the Secretary of State, who refused to grant passports to them as "citizens of the United States."

But it is said that a person may be a citizen, and entitled to that character, although he does not possess all the rights which may belong to other citizens; as, for example, the right to vote, or to hold particular offices; and that yet, when he goes into another State, he is entitled to be recognised there as a citizen, although the State may measure his rights by the rights which it allows to persons of a like character or class resident in the State, and refuse to him the full rights of citizenship.

This argument overlooks the language of the provision in the Constitution of which we are speaking.

Undoubtedly, a person may be a citizen, that is, a member of the community who form the sovereignty, although he exercises no share of the political power, and is incapacitated from holding particular offices. Women and minors, who form a part of the political family, cannot vote; and when a property qualification is required to vote or hold a particular office, those who have not the necessary qualification cannot vote or hold the office, yet they are citizens.

So, too, a person may be entitled to vote by the law of the State, who is not a citizen even of the State itself. And in some of the States of the Union foreigners not naturalized are allowed to vote. And the State may give the right to free negroes and mulattoes, but that does not make them citizens of the State, and still less of the United States. And the provision in the Constitution giving privileges and immunities in other States, does not apply to them.

Neither does it apply to a person who, being the citizen of a State, migrates to another State. For then he becomes subject to the laws of the State in which he lives, and he is no longer a citizen of the State from which he removed. And the State in which he resides may then, unquestionably, determine his *status* or condition, and place him among the class of persons who are not recognised as citizens, but belong to an inferior and subject race; and may deny him the privileges and immunities enjoyed by its citizens.

But so far as mere rights of person are concerned, the provision in question is confined to citizens of a State who are temporarily in another State without taking up their residence there. It gives them no political rights in the State, as to voting or holding office, or in any other respect. For a citizen of one State has no right to participate in the government of another. But if he ranks as a citizen in the State to which he belongs, within the meaning of the Constitution of the United States, then, whenever he goes into another State, the Constitution clothes him, as to the rights of person, with all the privileges and immunities which belong to citizens of the State. And if persons of the African race are citizens of a State, and of the United States, they would be entitled to all of these privileges and immunities in every State, and the State could not restrict them; for they would hold these privileges and immunities under the paramount authority of the Federal Government, and its courts would be bound to maintain and enforce them, the Constitution and laws of the State to the contrary notwithstanding. And if the States could limit or restrict them, or place the party in an inferior grade, this clause of the Constitution would be unmeaning, and could have no operation; and would give no rights to the citizen when in another State. He would have none but what the State itself chose to allow him. This is evidently not the construction or meaning of the clause in question. It guaranties rights to the citizen, and the State cannot withhold them. And these rights are of a character and would lead to consequences which make it absolutely certain that the African race were not included under the name of citizens of a State, and were not in the contemplation of the framers of the Constitution when these privileges and immunities were provided for the protection of the citizen in other States.

The case of Legrand *v.* Darnall (2 Peters, 664) has been referred to for the purpose of showing that this court has decided that the descendant of a slave may sue as a citizen in a court of the United States; but the case itself shows that the question did not arise and could not have arisen in the case.

It appears from the report, that Darnall was born in Maryland, and was the son of a white man by one of his slaves, and his father executed certain instruments to manumit him, and devised to him some landed property in the State. This property Darnall afterwards sold to Legrand, the appellant, who gave his notes for the purchase-money. But becoming afterwards apprehensive that the appellee had not been emancipated according to the laws of Maryland, he refused to pay the notes until he could be better satisfied as to Darnall's right to convey. Darnall, in the mean time, had taken up his residence in Pennsylvania, and brought suit on the notes, and recovered judgment in the Circuit Court for the district of Maryland.

The whole proceeding, as appears by the report, was an amicable one; Legrand being perfectly willing to pay the money, if he could obtain a title, and Darnall not wishing him to pay unless he could make him a good one. In point of fact, the whole proceeding was under the direction of the counsel who argued the case for the appellee, who was the mutual friend of the parties, and confided in by both of them, and whose only object was to have the rights of both parties established by judicial decision in the most speedy and least expensive manner.

Legrand, therefore, raised no objection to the jurisdiction of the court in the suit at law, because he was himself anxious to obtain the judgment of the court upon his title. Consequently, there was nothing in the record before the court to show that Darnall was of African descent, and the usual judgment and award of execution was entered. And Legrand thereupon filed his bill on the equity side of the Circuit Court, stating that Darnall was born a slave, and had not been legally emancipated, and could not therefore take the land devised to him, nor make Legrand a good title; and praying an injunction to restrain Darnall from proceeding to execution on the judgment, which was granted. Darnall answered, averring in his answer that he was a free man, and capable of conveying a good title. Testimony was taken on this point, and at the hearing the Circuit Court was of opinion that Darnall was a free man and his title good, and dissolved the injunction and dismissed the bill; and that decree was affirmed here, upon the appeal of Legrand.

Now, it is difficult to imagine how any question about the citizenship of Darnall, or his right to sue in that character, can be supposed to have arisen or been decided in that case. The fact that he was of African descent was first brought before the court upon the bill in equity. The suit at law had then passed into judgment and award of execution, and the Circuit Court, as a court of law, had no longer any authority over it. It was a valid and legal judgment, which the court that rendered it had not the power to reverse or set aside. And unless it had jurisdiction as a court of equity to restrain him from using its process as a court of law, Darnall, if he thought proper, would have been at liberty to proceed on his judgment, and compel the payment of the money, although the allegations in the bill were true, and he was incapable of making a title. No other court could have enjoined him, for certainly no State equity court could interfere in that way with the judgment of a Circuit Court of the United States.

But the Circuit Court as a court of equity certainly had equity jurisdiction over its own judgment as a court of law, without regard to the character of the parties; and had not only the right, but it was its duty—no matter who were the parties in the judgment—to prevent them from proceeding to enforce it by execution, if the court was satisfied that the money was not justly and equitably due. The ability of Darnall to convey did not depend upon his citizenship, but upon his title to freedom. And if he was free, he could hold and convey property, by the laws of Maryland, although he was not a citizen. But if he was by law still a slave, he could not. It was therefore the duty of the court, sitting as a court of equity in the latter case, to prevent him from using its process, as a court of common law, to compel the payment of the purchase-money, when it was evident that the purchaser must lose the land. But if he was free, and could make a title, it was equally the duty of the court not to suffer Legrand to keep the land, and refuse the payment of the money, upon the ground that Darnall was incapable of suing or being sued as a citizen in a court of the United States. The character or citizenship of the parties had no connection with the question of jurisdiction, and the matter in dispute had no relation to the citizenship of Darnall. Nor is such a question alluded to in the opinion of the court.

Besides, we are by no means prepared to say that there are not many cases, civil as well as criminal, in which a Circuit Court of the United States may exercise jurisdiction, although one of the African race is a party; that broad question is not before the court. The question with which we are now dealing is, whether a person of the African race can be a citizen of the United States, and become thereby entitled to a special privilege, by virtue of his title to that character, and which, under the Constitution, no one but a citizen can claim. It is manifest that the case of Legrand and Darnall has no bearing on that question, and can have no application to the case now before the court.

This case, however, strikingly illustrates the consequences that would follow the construction of the Constitution which would give the power contended for to a State. It would in effect give it also to an individual. For if the father of young Darnall had manumitted him in his lifetime, and sent him to reside in a State which recognised him as a citizen, he might have visited and sojourned in Maryland when he pleased, and as long as he pleased, as a citizen of the United States; and the State officers and tribunals would be compelled, by the paramount authority of the Constitution, to receive him and treat him as one of its citizens, exempt from the laws and police of the State in relation to a person of that description, and allow him to enjoy all the rights and privileges of citizenship, without respect to the laws of Maryland, although such laws were deemed by it absolutely essential to its own safety.

The only two provisions which point to them and include them, treat them as property, and make it the duty of the Government to protect it; no other power, in relation to this race, is to be found in the Constitution; and as it is a Government of special, delegated, powers, no authority beyond these two provisions can be constitutionally exercised. The Government of the United States had no right to interfere for any other purpose but that of protecting the rights of the owner, leaving it altogether with the several States to deal with this race, whether emancipated or not, as each State may think justice, humanity, and the interests and safety of society, require. The States evidently intended to reserve this power exclusively to themselves.

No one, we presume, supposes that any change in public opinion or feeling, in relation to this unfortunate race, in the civilized nations of Europe or in this country, should induce the court to give to the words of the Constitution a more liberal construction in their favor than they were intended to bear when the instrument was framed and adopted. Such an argument would be altogether inadmissible in any tribunal called on to interpret it. If any of its provisions are deemed unjust, there is a mode prescribed in the instrument itself by which it may be amended; but while it remains unaltered, it must be construed now as it was understood at the time of its adoption. It is not only the same in words, but the same in meaning, and delegates the same powers to the Government, and reserves and secures the same rights and privileges to the citizen; and as long as it continues to exist in its present form, it speaks not only in the same words, but with the same meaning and intent with which it spoke when it came from the hands of its framers, and was voted on and adopted by the people of the United States. Any other rule of construction would abrogate the judicial character of this court, and make it the mere reflex of the popular opinion or passion of the day. This court was not created by the Constitution for such purposes. Higher and graver trusts have been confided to it, and it must not falter in the path of duty.

What the construction was at that time, we think can hardly admit of doubt. We have the language of the Declaration of Independence and of the Articles of Confederation, in addition to the plain words of the Constitution itself; we have the legislation of the different States, before, about the time, and since, the Constitution was adopted; we have the legislation of Congress, from the time of its adoption to a recent period; and we have the constant and uniform action of the Executive Department, all concurring together, and leading to the same result. And if anything in relation to the construction of the Constitution can be regarded as settled, it is that which we now give to the word "citizen" and the word "people."

And upon a full and careful consideration of the subject, the court is of opinion, that, upon the facts stated in the plea in abatement, Dred Scott was not a citizen of Missouri within the meaning of the Constitution of the United States, and not entitled as such to sue in its courts; and, consequently, that the Circuit Court had no jurisdiction of the case, and that the judgment on the plea in abatement is erroneous.

We are aware that doubts are entertained by some of the members of the court, whether the plea in abatement is legally before the court upon this writ of error; but if that plea is regarded as waived, or out of the case upon any other ground, yet the question as to the jurisdiction of the Circuit Court is presented on the face of the bill of exception itself, taken by the plaintiff at the trial; for he admits that he and his wife were born slaves, but endeavors to make out his title to freedom and citizenship by showing that they were taken by their owner to certain places, hereinafter mentioned, where slavery could not by law exist, and that they thereby became free, and upon their return to Missouri became citizens of that State.

Now, if the removal of which he speaks did not give them their freedom, then by his own admission he is still a slave; and whatever opinions may be entertained in favor of the citizenship of a free person of the African race, no one supposes that a slave is a citizen of the State or of the United States. If, therefore, the acts done by his owner did not make them free persons, he is still a slave, and certainly incapable of suing in the character of a citizen.

The principle of law is too well settled to be disputed, that a court can give no judgment for either party, where it has no jurisdiction; and if, upon the showing of Scott himself, it appeared that he was still a slave, the case ought to have been dismissed, and the judgment against him and in favor of the defendant for costs, is, like that on the plea in abatement, erroneous, and the suit ought to have been dismissed by the Circuit Court for want of jurisdiction in that court.

But, before we proceed to examine this

part of the case, it may be proper to notice an objection taken to the judicial authority of this court to decide it; and it has been said, that as this court has decided against the jurisdiction of the Circuit Court on the plea in abatement, it has no right to examine any question presented by the exception; and that anything it may say upon that part of the case will be extra-judicial, and mere obiter dicta.

This is a manifest mistake; there can be no doubt as to the jurisdiction of this court to revise the judgment of a Circuit Court, and to reverse it for any error apparent on the record, whether it be the error of giving judgment in a case over which it had no jurisdiction, or any other material error; and this, too, whether there is a plea in abatement or not.

The objection appears to have arisen from confounding writs of error to a State court, with writs of error to a Circuit Court of the United States. Undoubtedly, upon a writ of error to a State court, unless the record shows a case that gives jurisdiction, the case must be dismissed for want of jurisdiction in *this court*. And if it is dismissed on that ground, we have no right to examine and decide upon any question presented by the bill of exceptions, or any other part of the record. But writs of error to a State court, and to a Circuit Court of the United States, are regulated by different laws, and stand upon entirely different principles. And in a writ of error to a Circuit Court of the United States, the whole record is before this court for examination and decision; and if the sum in controversy is large enough to give jurisdiction, it is not only the right, but it is the judicial duty of the court, to examine the whole case as presented by the record; and if it appears upon its face that any material error or errors have been committed by the court below, it is the duty of this court to reverse the judgment, and remand the case. And certainly an error in passing a judgment upon the merits in favor of either party, in a case which it was not authorized to try, and over which it had no jurisdiction, is as grave an error as a court can commit.

The plea in abatement is not a plea to the jurisdiction of this court, but to the jurisdiction of the Circuit Court. And it appears by the record before us, that the Circuit Court committed an error, in deciding that it had jurisdiction, upon the facts in the case, admitted by the pleadings. It is the duty of the appellate tribunal to correct this error; but that could not be done by dismissing the case for want of jurisdiction here—for that would leave the erroneous judgment in full force, and the injured party without remedy. And the appellate court therefore exercises the power for which alone appellate courts are constituted, by reversing the judgment of the court below for this error. It exercises its proper and appropriate jurisdiction over the judgment and proceedings of the Circuit Court, as they appear upon the record brought up by the writ of error.

The correction of one error in the court below does not deprive the appellate court of the power of examining further into the record, and correcting any other material errors which may have been committed by the inferior court. There is certainly no rule of law—nor any practice—nor any decision of a court—which even questions this power in the appellate tribunal. On the contrary, it is the daily practice of this court, and of all appellate courts where they reverse the judgment of an inferior court for error, to correct by its opinions whatever errors may appear on the record material to the case; and they have always held it to be their duty to do so where the silence of the court might lead to misconstruction or future controversy, and the point has been relied on by either side, and argued before the court.

In the case before us, we have already decided that the Circuit Court erred in deciding that it had jurisdiction upon the facts admitted by the pleadings. And it appears that, in the further progress of the case, it acted upon the erroneous principle it had decided on the pleadings, and gave judgment for the defendant, where, upon the facts admitted in the exception, it had no jurisdiction.

We are at a loss to understand upon what principle of law, applicable to appellate jurisdiction, it can be supposed that this court has not judicial authority to correct the last-mentioned error, because they had before corrected the former; or by what process of reasoning it can be made out, that the error of an inferior court in actually pronouncing judgment for one of the parties, in a case in which it had no jurisdiction, cannot be looked into or corrected by this court, because we have decided a similar question presented in the pleadings. The last point is distinctly presented by the facts contained in the plaintiff's own bill of exceptions, which he himself brings here by this writ of error. It was the point which chiefly occupied the attention of the counsel on both sides in the argument—and the judgment which this court must render upon both errors is precisely the same. It must, in each of them, exercise jurisdiction over the judgment, and reverse it for the errors committed by the court below; and issue a mandate to the Circuit Court to conform its judgment to the opinion pronounced by this court, by dismissing the case for want of jurisdiction in the Circuit Court. This is the constant and invariable practice of this court, where it reverses a judgment for want of jurisdiction in the Circuit Court.

It can scarcely be necessary to pursue such a question further. The want of jurisdiction in the court below may appear on the record without any plea in abatement. This is familiarly the case where a court of chancery has exercised jurisdiction in a case where the plaintiff had a plain and adequate remedy at law, and it so appears by the transcript when brought here by appeal. So also where it appears that a court of admiralty has exercised jurisdiction in a case belonging exclusively to a court of common law. In these cases there is no plea in abatement. And for the same reason, and upon the same principles, where the defect of jurisdiction is patent on the record, this court is bound to reverse the judgment, although the defendant has not pleaded in abatement to the jurisdiction of the inferior court.

The cases of Jackson *v.* Ashton and of Capron *v.* Van Noorden, to which we have referred in a previous part of this opinion, are directly in point. In the last-mentioned case, Capron brought an action against Van Noorden in a Circuit Court of the United States, without showing, by the usual averments of citizenship, that the court had jurisdiction. There was no plea in abatement put in, and the parties went to trial upon the merits. The court gave judgment in favor of the defendant with costs. The plaintiff thereupon brought his writ of error, and this court reversed the judgment given in favor of the defendant, and remanded the case with directions to dismiss it, because it did not appear by the transcript that the Circuit Court had jurisdiction.

The case before us still more strongly imposes upon this court the duty of examining whether the court below has not committed an error, in taking jurisdiction and giving a judgment for costs in favor of the defendant; for in Capron *v.* Van Noorden the judgment was reversed, because it did *not appear* that the parties were citizens of different States. They might or might not be. But in this case it *does appear* that the plaintiff was born a slave; and if the facts upon which he relies have not made him free, then it appears affirmatively on the record that he is not a citizen, and consequently his suit against Sandford was not a suit between citizens of different States, and the court had no authority to pass any judgment between the parties. The suit ought, in this view of it, to have been dismissed by the Circuit Court, and its judgment in favor of Sandford is erroneous, and must be reversed.

It is true that the result either way, by dismissal or by a judgment for the defendant, makes very little, if any, difference in a pecuniary or personal point of view to either party. But the fact that the result would be very nearly the same to the parties in either form of judgment, would not justify this court in sanctioning an error in the judgment which is patent on the record, and which, if sanctioned, might be drawn into precedent, and lead to serious mischief and injustice in some future suit.

We proceed, therefore, to inquire whether the facts relied on by the plaintiff entitled him to his freedom.

The case, as he himself states it, on the record brought here by his writ of error, is this:

The plaintiff was a negro slave, belonging to Dr. Emerson, who was a surgeon in the army of the United States. In the year 1834, he took the plaintiff from the State of Missouri to the military post at Rock Island, in the State of Illinois, and held him there as a slave until the month of April or May, 1836. At the time last mentioned, said Dr. Emerson removed the plaintiff from said military post at Rock Island to the military post at Fort Snelling, situate on the west bank of the Mississippi river, in the Territory known as Upper Louisiana, acquired by the United States of France, and situate north of the latitude of thirty-six degrees thirty minutes north, and north of the State of Missouri. Said Dr. Emerson held the plaintiff in slavery at said Fort Snelling, from said last-mentioned date until the year 1838.

In the year 1835, Harriet, who is named in the second count of the plaintiff's declaration, was the negro slave of Major Taliaferro, who belonged to the army of the United States. In that year, 1835, said Major Taliaferro took said Harriet to said Fort Snelling, a military post, situated as hereinbefore stated, and kept her there as a slave until the year 1836, and then sold and delivered her as a slave, at said Fort Snelling, unto the said Dr. Emerson hereinbefore named. Said Dr. Emerson held said Harriet in slavery at said Fort Snelling until the year 1838.

In the year 1836, the plaintiff and Harriet intermarried, at Fort Snelling, with the consent of Dr. Emerson, who then claimed to be their master and owner. Eliza and Lizzie, named in the third count of the plaintiff's declaration, are the fruit of that marriage. Eliza is about fourteen years old, and was born on board the steamboat Gipsey, north of the north line of the State of Missouri, and upon the river Mississippi. Lizzie is about seven years old, and was born in the State of Missouri, at the military post called Jefferson Barracks.

In the year 1838, said Dr. Emerson removed the plaintiff and said Harriet, and their said daughter Eliza, from said Fort Snelling to the State of Missouri, where they have ever since resided.

Before the commencement of this suit, said Dr. Emerson sold and conveyed the plaintiff, and Harriet, Eliza, and Lizzie, to the defendant, as slaves, and the defendant has ever since claimed to hold them, and each of them, as slaves.

In considering this part of the controversy, two questions arise: 1. Was he, together with his family, free in Missouri by reason of the stay in the territory of the United States hereinbefore mentioned? And 2. If they were not, is Scott himself free by reason of his removal to Rock Island, in the State of Illinois, as stated in the above admissions?

We proceed to examine the first question.

The act of Congress, upon which the plaintiff relies, declares that slavery and involuntary servitude, except as a punishment for crime, shall be forever prohibited in all that part of the territory ceded by France, under the name of Louisiana, which lies north of thirty-six degrees thirty minutes north latitude, and not included within the limits of Missouri. And the difficulty which meets us at the threshold of this part of the inquiry is, whether Congress was authorized to pass this law under any of the powers granted to it by the Constitution; for if the authority is not given by that instrument, it is the duty of this court to declare it void and inoperative, and incapable of conferring freedom upon any one who is held as a slave under the laws of any one of the States.

The counsel for the plaintiff has laid much stress upon that article in the Constitution which confers on Congress the power "to dispose of and make all needful rules and regulations respecting the territory or other property belonging to the United States"; but, in the judgment of the court, that provision has no bearing on the present controversy, and the power there given, whatever it may be, is confined, and was intended to be confined, to the territory which at that time belonged to, or was claimed by, the United States, and was within their boundaries as settled by the treaty with Great Britain, and can have no influence upon a territory afterwards acquired from a foreign Government. It was a special provision for a known and particular territory, and to meet a present emergency, and nothing more.

A brief summary of the history of the times, as well as the careful and measured terms in which the article is framed, will show the correctness of this proposition.

It will be remembered that, from the commencement of the Revolutionary war, serious difficulties existed between the States, in relation to the disposition of large and unsettled territories which were included in the chartered limits of some of the States. And some of the other States, and more especially Maryland, which had no unsettled lands, insisted that as the unoccupied lands, if wrested from Great Britain, would owe their preservation to the common purse and the common sword, the money arising from them ought to be applied in just proportion among the several States to pay the expenses of the war, and ought not to be appropriated to the use of the State in whose chartered limits they might happen to lie, to the exclusion of the other States, by whose combined efforts and common expense the territory was defended and preserved against the claim of the British Government.

These difficulties caused much uneasiness during the war, while the issue was in some degree doubtful, and the future boundaries of the United States yet to be defined by treaty, if we achieved our independence.

The majority of the Congress of the Confederation obviously concurred in opinion with the State of Maryland, and desired to obtain from the States which claimed it a cession of this territory, in order that Congress might raise money on this security to carry on the war. This appears by the resolution passed on the 6th of September, 1780, strongly urging the States to cede these lands to the United States, both for the sake of peace and union among themselves, and to maintain the public credit; and this was followed by the resolution of October 10th, 1780, by which Congress pledged itself, that if the lands were ceded, as recommended by the resolution above mentioned, they should be disposed of for the common benefit of the United States, and be settled and formed into distinct republican States, which should become members of the Federal Union, and have the same rights of sovereignty, and freedom, and independence, as other States.

But these difficulties became much more serious after peace took place, and the boundaries of the United States were established. Every State, at that time, felt severely the pressure of its war debt; but in Virginia, and some other States, there were large territories of unsettled lands, the sale of which would enable them to discharge their obligations without much inconvenience; while other States, which had no such resource, saw before them many years of heavy and burdensome taxation; and the latter insisted, for the reasons before stated, that these unsettled lands should be treated as the common property of the States, and the proceeds applied to their common benefit.

The letters from the statesmen of that day will show how much this controversy occupied their thoughts, and the dangers that were apprehended from it. It was the disturbing element of the time, and fears were entertained that it might dissolve the Confederation by which the States were then united.

These fears and dangers were, however, at once removed, when the State of Virginia, in 1784, voluntarily ceded to the United States the immense tract of country lying northwest of the river Ohio, and which was within the acknowledged limits of the State. The only object of the State, in making this cession, was to put an end to the threatening and exciting controversy, and to enable the Congress of that time to dispose of the lands, and appropriate the proceeds as a common fund for the common benefit of the States. It was not ceded, because it was inconvenient to the State to hold and govern it, nor from any expectation that it could be better or more conveniently governed by the United States.

The example of Virginia was soon afterwards followed by other States, and, at the time of the adoption of the Constitution, all of the States, similarly situated, had ceded their unappropriated lands, except North Carolina and Georgia. The main object for which these cessions were desired and made, was on account of their money value, and to put an end to a dangerous controversy, as to who was justly entitled to the proceeds when the lands should be sold. It is necessary to bring this part of the history of these cessions thus distinctly into view, because it will enable us the better to comprehend the phraseology of the article in the Constitution, so often referred to in the argument.

Undoubtedly the powers of sovereignty and the eminent domain were ceded with the land. This was essential, in order to make it effectual, and to accomplish its objects. But it must be remembered that, at that time, there was no Government of the United States in existence with enumerated and limited powers; what was then called the United States, were thirteen separate, sovereign, independent States, which had entered into a league or confederation for their mutual protection and advantage, and the Congress of the United States was composed of the representatives of these separate sovereignties, meeting together, as equals, to discuss and decide on certain measures which the States, by the Articles of Confederation, had agreed to submit to their decision. But this Confederation had none of the attributes of sovereignty in legislative, executive, or judicial power. It was little more than a congress of ambassadors, authorized to represent separate nations, in matters in which they had a common concern.

It was this Congress that accepted the cession from Virginia. They had no power to accept it under the Articles of Confederation. But they had an undoubted right, as independent sovereignties, to accept any cession of territory for their common benefit, which all of them assented to; and it is equally clear, that as their common property, and having no superior to control them, they had the right to exercise absolute dominion over it, subject only to the restrictions which Virginia had imposed in her act of cession. There was, as we have said, no Government of the United States then in existence with special enumerated and limited powers. The territory belonged to sovereignties, who, subject to the limitations above mentioned, had a right to establish any form of government they pleased, by compact or treaty among themselves, and to regulate rights of person and rights of property in the territory, as they might deem proper. It was by a Congress, representing the authority of these several and separate sovereignties, and acting under their authority and command (but not from any authority derived from the Articles of Confederation,) that the instrument usually called the ordinance of 1787 was adopted; regulating in much detail the principles and the laws by which this territory should be governed; and among other provisions, slavery is prohibited in it. We do not question the power of the States, by agreement among themselves, to pass this ordinance, nor its obligatory force in the territory, while the confederation or league of the States in their separate sovereign character continued to exist.

This was the state of things when the Constitution of the United States was formed. The territory ceded by Virginia belonged to the several confederated States as common property, and they had united in establishing in it a system of government and jurisprudence, in order to prepare it for admission as States, according to the terms of the cession. They were about to dissolve this federative Union, and to surrender a portion of their independent sovereignty to a new Government, which, for certain purposes, would make the people of the several States one people, and which was to be supreme and controlling within its sphere of action throughout the United States; but this Government was to be carefully limited in its powers, and to exercise no authority beyond those expressly granted by the Constitution, or necessarily to be implied from the language of the instrument, and the objects it was intended to accomplish; and as this league of States would, upon the adoption of the new Government, cease to have any power over the territory, and the ordinance they had agreed upon be incapable of execution, and a mere nullity, it was obvious that some provision was necessary to give the new Government sufficient power to enable it to carry into effect the objects for which it was ceded, and the compacts and agreements which the States had made with each other in the exercise of their powers of sovereignty. It was necessary that the lands should be sold to pay the war debt; that a Government and system of jurisprudence should be maintained in it, to protect the citizens of the United States who should migrate to the territory, in their rights of person and of property. It was also necessary that the new Government, about to be adopted, should be authorized to maintain the claim of the United States to the unappropriated lands in North Carolina and Georgia, which had not then been ceded, but the cession of which was confidently anticipated upon some terms that would be arranged between the General Government and these two States. And, moreover, there were many articles of value besides this property in land, such as arms, military stores, munitions, and ships of war, which were the common property of the States, when acting in their independent characters as confederates, which neither the new Government nor any one else would have a right to take possession of, or control, without authority from them; and it was to place these things under the guardianship and protection of the new Government, and to clothe it with the necessary powers, that the clause was inserted in the Constitution which gives Congress the power "to dispose of and make all needful rules and regulations respecting the territory or other property belonging to the United States." It was intended for a specific purpose, to provide for the things we have mentioned. It was to transfer to the new Government the property then held in common by the States, and to give to that Government power to apply it to the objects for which it had been destined by mutual agreement among the States before their league was dissolved. It applied only to the property which the States held in common at that time, and has no reference whatever to any territory or other property which the new sovereignty might afterwards itself acquire.

The language used in the clause, the arrangement and combination of the powers, and the somewhat unusual phraseology it uses, when it speaks of the political power to be exercised in the government of the territory, all indicate the design and meaning of the clause to be such as we have mentioned. It does not speak of *any* territory, nor of *Territories,* but uses language which, according to its legitimate meaning, points to a particular thing. The power is given in relation only to *the* territory of the United States—that is, to a territory then in existence, and then known or claimed as the territory of the United States. It begins its enumeration of powers by that of disposing, in other words, making sale of the lands, or raising money from them, which, as we have already said, was the main object of the cession, and which is accordingly the first thing provided for in the article. It then gives the power which was necessarily associated with the disposition and sale of the lands—that is, the power of making needful rules and regulations respecting the territory. And whatever construction may now be given to these words, every one, we think, must admit that they are not the words usually employed by statesmen in giving supreme power of legislation. They are certainly very unlike the words used in the power granted to legislate over territory which the new Government might afterwards itself obtain by cession from a State, either for its seat of Government, or for forts, magazines, arsenals, dock yards, and other needful buildings.

And the same power of making needful rules respecting the territory is, in precisely the same language, applied to the *other* property belonging to the United States—associating the power over the territory in this respect with the power over movable or personal property—that is, the ships, arms, and munitions of war, which then belonged in common to the State sovereignties. And it will hardly be said, that this power, in relation to the last-mentioned objects, was deemed necessary to be thus specially given to the new Government, in order to authorize it to make needful rules and regulations respecting the ships it might itself build, or arms and munitions of war it might itself manufacture or provide for the public service.

No one, it is believed, would think a moment of deriving the power of Congress to make needful rules and regulations in relation to property of this kind from this clause of the Constitution. Nor can it, upon any fair construction, be applied to any property but that which the new Government was about to receive from the confederated States. And if this be true as to this property, it must be equally true and limited as to the territory, which is so carefully and precisely coupled with it—and like it referred to as property in the power granted. The concluding words of the clause appear to render this construction irresistible; for, after the provisions we have mentioned, it proceeds to say, "that nothing in the Constitution shall be so construed as to prejudice any claims of the United States, or of any particular State."

Now, as we have before said, all of the States, except North Carolina and Georgia, had made the cession before the Constitution was adopted, according to the resolution of Congress of October 10, 1780. The claims of other States, that the unappropriated lands in these two States should be applied to the common benefit, in like manner, was still insisted on, but refused by the States. And this member of the clause in question evidently applies to them, and can apply to nothing else. It was to exclude the conclusion that either party, by adopting the Constitution, would surrender what they deemed their rights. And when the latter provision relates so obviously to the unappropriated lands not yet ceded by the States, and the first clause makes provision for those then actually ceded, it is impossible, by any just rule of construction, to make the first provision general, and extend to all territories, which the Federal Government might in any way afterwards acquire, when the latter is plainly and unequivocally confined to a particular territory; which was a part of the same controversy, and involved in the same dispute, and depended upon the same principles. The union of the two provisions in the same clause shows that they were kindred subjects; and that the whole clause is local, and relates only to lands, within the limits of the United States, which had been or then were claimed by a State; and that no other territory was in the mind of the framers of the Constitution, or intended to be embraced in it. Upon any other construction it would be impossible to account for the insertion of the last provision in the place where it is found, or to comprehend why, or for what object, it was associated with the previous provision.

This view of the subject is confirmed by the manner in which the present Government of the United States dealt with the subject as soon as it came into existence. It must be borne in mind that the same States that formed the Confederation also formed and adopted the new Government, to which so large a portion of their former sovereign powers were surrendered. It must also be borne in mind that all of these same States which had then ratified the new Constitution were represented in the Congress which passed the first law for the government of this territory; and many of the members of that legislative body had been deputies from the States under the Confederation—had united in adopting the ordinance of 1787, and assisted in forming the new Government under which they were then acting, and whose powers they were then exercising.

And it is obvious from the law they passed to carry into effect the principles and provisions of the ordinance, that they regarded it as the act of the States done in the exercise of their legitimate powers at the time. The new Government took the territory as it found it, and in the condition in which it was transferred, and did not attempt to undo anything that had been done. And, among the earliest laws passed under the new Government, is one reviving the ordinance of 1787, which had become inoperative and a nullity upon the adoption of the Constitution. This law introduces no new form or principles for its government, but recites, in the preamble, that it is passed in order that this ordinance may continue to have full effect, and proceeds to make only those rules and regulations which were needful to adapt it to the new Government, into whose hands the power had fallen. It appears, therefore, that this Congress regarded the purposes to which the land in this Territory was to be applied, and the form of government and principles of jurisprudence which were to prevail there, while it remained in the Territorial state, as already determined on by the States when they had full power and right to make the decision; and that the new Government, having received it in this condition, ought to carry substantially into effect the plans and principles which had been previously adopted by the States, and which no doubt the States anticipated when they surrendered their power to the new Government. And if we regard this clause of the Constitution as pointing to this Territory, with a Territorial Government already established in it, which had been ceded to the States for the purposes hereinbefore mentioned—every word in it is perfectly appropriate and easily understood, and the provisions it contains are in perfect harmony with the objects for which it was ceded, and with the condition of its government as a Territory at the time. We can, then, easily account for the manner in which the first Congress legislated on the subject—and can also understand why this power over the Territory was associated in the same clause with the other property of the United States, and subjected to the like power of making needful rules and regulations. But if the clause is construed in the expanded sense contended for, so as to embrace any territory acquired from a foreign nation by the present Government, and to give it in such territory a despotic and unlimited power over persons and property, such as the confederated States might exercise in their common property, it would be difficult to account for the phraseology used, when compared with other grants of power—and also for its association with the other provisions in the same clause.

The Constitution has always been remarkable for the felicity of its arrangement of different subjects, and the perspicuity and appropriateness of the language it uses. But if this clause is construed to extend to territory acquired by the present Government from a foreign nation, outside of the limits of any charter from the British Government to a colony, it would be difficult to say, why it was deemed necessary to give the Government the power to sell any vacant lands belonging to the sovereignty which might be found within it; and if this was necessary, why the grant of this power should precede the power to legislate over it and establish a Government there; and still more difficult to say, why it was deemed necessary so specially and particularly to grant the power to make needful rules and regulations in relation to any personal or movable property it might acquire there. For the words, *other property* necessarily, by every known rule of interpretation, must mean property of a different description from territory or land. And the difficulty would perhaps be insurmountable in endeavoring to account for the last member of the sentence, which provides that "nothing in this Constitution shall be so construed as to prejudice any claims of the United States or any particular State," or to say how any particular State could have claims in or to a territory ceded by a foreign Government, or to account for associating this provision with the preceding provisions of the clause, with which it would appear to have no connection.

The words "needful rules and regulations" would seem, also, to have been cautiously used for some definite object. They are not the words usually employed by statesmen, when they mean to give the powers of sovereignty, or to establish a Government, or to authorize its establishment. Thus, in the law to renew and keep alive the ordinance of 1787, and to reestablish the Government, the title of the law is: "An act to provide for the government of the territory northwest of the river Ohio." And in the Constitution, when granting the power to legislate over the territory that may be selected for the seat of Government independently of a State, it does not say Congress shall have power "to make all needful rules and regulations respecting the territory"; but it declares that "Congress shall have power to exercise exclusive legislation in all cases whatsoever over such District (not exceeding ten miles square) as may, by cession of particular States and the acceptance of Congress, become the seat of the Government of the United States.

The words "rules and regulations" are usually employed in the Constitution in speaking of some particular specified power which it means to confer on the Government, and not, as we have seen, when granting general powers of legislation. As, for example, in the particular power to Congress "to make rules for the government and regulation of the land and naval forces, or the particular and specific power to regulate commerce"; "to establish an uniform *rule* of naturalization"; "to coin money and *regulate* the value thereof." And to construe the words of which we are speaking as a general and unlimited grant of sovereignty over territories which the Government might afterwards acquire, is to use them in a sense and for a purpose for which they were not used in any other part of the instrument. But if confined to a particular Territory, in which a Government and laws had already been established, but which would require some alterations to adapt it to the new Government, the words are peculiarly applicable and appropriate for that purpose.

The necessity of this special provision in relation to property and the rights or property held in common by the confederated States, is illustrated by the first clause of the sixth article. This clause provides that "all debts, contracts, and engagements entered into before the adoption of this Constitution, shall be as valid against the United States under this Government as under the Confederation." This provision, like the one under consideration, was indispensable if the new Constitution was adopted. The new Government was not a mere change in a dynasty, or in a form of government, leaving the nation or sovereignty the same, and clothed with all the rights, and bound by all the obligations of the preceding one. But, when the present United States came into existence under the new Government, it was a new political body, a new nation, then for the first time taking its place in the family of nations. It took nothing by succession from the Confederation. It had no right, as its successor, to any property or rights of property which it had acquired, and was not liable for any of its obligations. It was evidently viewed in this light by the framers of the Constitution. And as the several States would cease to exist in their former confederated character upon the adoption of the Constitution, and could not, in that character, again assemble together, special provisions were indispensable to transfer to the new Government the property and rights which at that time they held in common; and at the same time to authorize it to lay taxes and appropriate money to pay the common debt which they had contracted; and this power could only be given to it by special provisions in the Constitution. The clause in relation to the territory and other property of the United States provided for the first, and the clause last quoted provided for the other. They have no connection with the general powers and rights of sovereignty delegated to the new Government, and can neither enlarge nor diminish them. They were inserted to meet a present emergency, and not to regulate its powers as a Government.

Indeed, a similar provision was deemed necessary in relation to treaties made by the Confederation; and when in the clause next succeeding the one of which we have last spoken, it is declared that treaties shall be the supreme law of the land, care is taken to include, by express words, the treaties made by the confederated States. The language is: "and all treaties made, or which shall be made, under the authority of the United States, shall be the supreme law of the land."

Whether, therefore, we take the particular clause in question, by itself, or in connection with the other provisions of the Constitution, we think it clear, that it applies only to the particular territory of which we have spoken, and cannot, by any just rule of interpretation, be extended to territory which the new Government might afterwards obtain from a foreign nation. Consequently, the power which Congress may have lawfully exercised in this Territory, while it remained under a Territorial Government, and which may have been sanctioned by judicial decision, can furnish no justification and no argument to support a similar exercise of power over territory afterwards acquired by the Federal Government. We put aside, therefore, any argument, drawn from precedents, showing the extent of the power which the General Government exercised over slavery in this Territory, as altogether inapplicable to the case before us.

But the case of the American and Ocean Insurance Companies *v.* Canter (1 Pet. 511) has been quoted as establishing a different construction of this clause of the Constitution. There is, however, not the slightest conflict between the opinion now given and the one referred to; and it is only by taking a single sentence out of the latter and separating it from the context, that even an appearance of conflict can be shown. We need not comment on such a mode of expounding an opinion of the court. Indeed it most commonly misrepresents instead of expounding it. And this is fully exemplified in the case referred to, where, if one sentence is taken by itself, the opinion would appear to be in direct conflict with that now given; but the words which immediately follow that sentence show that the court did not mean to decide the point, but merely affirmed the power of Congress to establish a Government in the Territory, leaving it an open question, whether that power was derived from this clause in the Constitution, or was to be necessarily inferred from a power to acquire territory by cession from a foreign Government. The opinion on this part of the case is short and we give the whole of it to show how well the selection of a single sentence is calculated to mislead.

The passage referred to is in page 542, in which the court, in speaking of the power of Congress to establish a Territorial Government in Florida until it should become a State, uses the following language:

"In the mean time Florida continues to be a Territory of the United States, governed by that clause of the Constitution which empowers Congress to make all needful rules and regulations respecting the territory or other property of the United States. Perhaps the power of governing a Territory belonging to the United States, which has not, by becoming a State, acquired the means of self-government, may result, necessarily, from the facts that it is not within the jurisdiction of any particular State, and is within the power and jurisdiction of the United States. The right to govern may be the inevitable consequence of the right to acquire territory. *Whichever may be the source from which the power is derived, the possession of it is unquestionable.*"

It is thus clear, from the whole opinion on this point, that the court did not mean to decide whether the power was derived from the clause in the Constitution, or was the necessary consequence of the right to acquire. They do decide that the power in Congress is unquestionable, and in this we entirely concur, and nothing will be found in this opinion to the contrary. The power stands firmly on the latter alternative put by the court—that is, as *"the inevitable consequence of the right to acquire territory."*

And what still more clearly demonstrates that the court did not mean to decide the question, but leave it open for future consideration, is the fact that the case was decided in the Circuit Court by Mr. Justice Johnson, and his decision was affirmed by the Supreme Court. His opinion at the circuit is given in full in a note to the case, and in that opinion he states, in explicit terms, that the clause of the Constitution applies only to the territory then within the limits of the United States, and not to Florida, which had been acquired by cession from Spain. This part of his opinion will be found in the note in page 517 of the report. But he does not dissent from the opinion of the Supreme Court; thereby showing that, in his judgment, as well as that of the court, the case before them did not call for a decision on that particular point, and the court abstained from deciding it. And in a part of its opinion subsequent to the passage we have quoted, where the court speak of the legislative power of Congress in Florida, they still speak with the same reserve. And in page 546, speaking of the power of Congress to authorize the Territorial Legislature to establish courts there, the court say: "They are legislative courts, created in virtue of the general right of sovereignty which exists in the Government, or in virtue of that clause which enables Congress to make all needful rules and regulations respecting the territory belonging to the United States."

It has been said that the construction given to this clause is new, and now for the first time brought forward. The case of which we are speaking, and which has been so much discussed, shows that the fact is otherwise. It shows that precisely the same question came before Mr. Justice Johnson, at his circuit, thirty years ago—was fully considered by him, and the same construction given to the clause in the Constitution which is now given by this court. And that upon an appeal from his decision the same question was brought before this court, but was not decided because a decision upon it was not required by the case before the court.

There is another sentence in the opinion which has been commented on, which even in a still more striking manner shows how one may mislead or be misled by taking out a single sentence from the opinion of a court, and leaving out of view what precedes and follows. It is in page 546, near the close of the opinion, in which the court say: "In legislating for them," (the territories of the United States,) "Congress exercises the combined powers of the General and of a State Government." And it is said, that as a State may unquestionably prohibit slavery within its territory, this sentence decides in effect that Congress may do the same in a Territory of the United States, exercising there the powers of a State, as well as the power of the General Government.

The examination of this passage in the case referred to, would be more appropriate when we come to consider in another part of this opinion what power Congress can constitutionally exercise in a Territory, over the rights of person or rights of property of a citizen. But, as it is in the same case with the passage we have before commented on, we dispose of it now, as it will save the court from the necessity of referring again to the case. And it will be seen upon reading the page in which this sentence is found, that it has no reference whatever to the power of Congress over rights of person or rights of property—but relates altogether to the power of establishing judicial tribunals to administer the laws constitutionally passed, and defining the jurisdiction they may exercise.

The law of Congress establishing a Territorial Government in Florida, provided that the Legislature of the Territory should have legislative powers over "all rightful objects of legislation; but no law should be valid which was inconsistent with the laws and Constitution of the United States."

Under the power thus conferred, the Legislature of Florida passed an act, erecting a tribunal at Key West to decide cases of salvage. And in the case of which we are speaking, the question arose whether the Territorial Legislature could be authorized by Congress to establish such a tribunal, with such powers; and one of the parties, among other objections, insisted that Congress could not under the Constitution authorize the Legislature of the Territory to establish such a tribunal with such powers, but that it must be established by Congress itself; and that a sale of cargo made under its order, to pay salvors, was void, as made without legal authority, and passed no property to the purchaser.

It is in disposing of this objection that the sentence relied on occurs, and the court begin that part of the opinion by stating with great precision the point which they are about to decide.

They say: "It has been contended that by the Constitution of the United States, the judicial power of the United States extends to all cases of admiralty and maritime jurisdiction; and that the whole of the judicial power must be vested 'in one Supreme Court, and in such inferior courts as Congress shall from time to time ordain and establish.' Hence it has been argued that Congress cannot vest admiralty jurisdiction in courts created by the Territorial Legislature."

And after thus clearly stating the point before them, and which they were about to decide, they proceed to show that these Territorial tribunals were not constitutional courts, but merely legislative, and that Congress might, therefore, delegate the power to the Territorial Government to establish the court in question; and they conclude that part of the opinion in the following words: "Although admiralty jurisdiction can be exercised in the States in those courts only which are established in pursuance of the third article of the Constitution, the same limitation does not extend to the Territories. In legislating for them, Congress exercises the combined powers of the General and State Governments."

Thus it will be seen by these quotations from the opinion, that the court, after stating the question it was about to decide in a manner too plain to be misunderstood, proceeded to decide it, and announced, as the opinion of the tribunal, that in organizing the judicial department of the Government in a Territory of the United States, Congress does not act under, and is not restricted by, the third article in the Constitution, and is not bound, in a Territory, to ordain and establish courts in which the judges hold their offices during good behaviour, but may exercise the discretionary power which a State exercises in establishing its judicial department, and regulating the jurisdiction of its courts, and may authorize the Territorial Government to establish, or may itself establish, courts in which the judges hold their offices for a term of years only; and may vest in them judicial power upon subjects confided to the judiciary of the United States. And in doing this, Congress undoubtedly exercises the combined power of the General and a State Government. It exercises the discretionary power of a State Government in authorizing the establishment of a court in which the judges hold their appointments for a term of years only, and not during good behaviour; and it exercises the power of the General Government in investing that court with admiralty jurisdiction, over which the General Government had exclusive jurisdiction in the Territory.

No one, we presume, will question the correctness of that opinion; nor is there anything in conflict with it in the opinion now given. The point decided in the case cited has no relation to the question now before the court. That depended on the construction of the third article of the Constitution, in relation to the judiciary of the United States, and the power which Congress might exercise in a Territory in organizing the judicial department of the Government. The case before us depends upon other and different provisions of the Constitution, altogether separate and apart from the one above mentioned. The question as to what courts Congress may ordain or establish in a Territory to administer laws which the Constitution authorizes it to pass, and what laws it is or is not authorized by the Constitution to pass, are widely different—are regulated by different and separate articles of the Constitution, and stand upon different principles. And we are satisfied that no one who reads attentively the page in Peters's Reports to which we have referred, can suppose that the attention of the court was drawn for a moment to the question now before this court, or that it meant in that case to say that Congress had a right to prohibit a citizen of the United States from taking any property which he lawfully held into a Territory of the United States.

This brings us to examine by what provision of the Constitution the present Federal Government, under its delegated and restricted powers, is authorized to acquire territory outside of the original limits of the United States, and what powers it may exercise therein over the person or property of a citizen of the United States, while it remains a Territory, and until it shall be admitted as one of the States of the Union.

There is certainly no power given by the Constitution to the Federal Government to establish or maintain colonies bordering on the United States or at a distance, to be ruled and governed at its own pleasure; nor to enlarge its territorial limits in any way, except by the admission of new States. That power is plainly given; and if a new State is admitted, it needs no further legislation by Congress, because the Constitution itself defines the relative rights and powers, and duties of the State, and the citizens of the State, and the Federal Government. But no power is given to acquire a Territory to be held and governed permanently in that character.

And indeed the power exercised by Congress to acquire territory and establish a Government there, according to its own unlimited discretion, was viewed with great jealousy by the leading statesmen of the day. And in the Federalist (No. 38), written by Mr. Madison, he speaks of the acquisition of the Northwestern Territory by the confederated States, by the cession from Virginia, and the establishment of a Government there, as an exercise of power not warranted by the Articles of Confederation, and dangerous to the liberties of the people. And he urges the adoption of the Constitution as a security and safeguard against such an exercise of power.

We do not mean, however, to question the power of Congress in this respect. The power to expand the territory of the United States by the admission of new States is plainly given; and in the construction of this power by all the departments of the Government, it has been held to authorize the acquisition of territory, not fit for admission at the time, but to be admitted as soon as its population and situation would entitle it to admission. It is acquired to become a State, and not to be held as a colony and governed by Congress with absolute authority; and as the propriety of admitting a new State is committed to the sound discretion of Congress, the power to acquire territory for that purpose, to be held by the United States until it is in a suitable condition to become a State upon an equal footing with the other States, must rest upon the same discretion. It is a question for the political department of the Government, and not the judicial; and whatever the political department of the Government shall recognise as within the limits of the United States, the judicial department is also bound to recognise, and to administer in it the laws of the United States, so far as they apply, and to maintain in the Territory the authority and rights of the Government, and also the personal rights and rights of property of individual citizens, as secured by the Constitution. All we mean to say on this point is, that, as there is no express regulation in the Constitution defining the power which the General Government may exercise over the person or property of a citizen in a Territory thus acquired, the court must necessarily look to the provisions and principles of the Constitution, and its distribution of powers, for the rules and principles by which its decision must be governed.

Taking this rule to guide us, it may be safely assumed that citizens of the United States who migrate to a Territory belonging to the people of the United States, cannot be ruled as mere colonists, dependent upon the will of the General Government, and to be governed by any laws it may think proper to impose. The principle upon which our Governments rest, and upon which alone they continue to exist, is the union of States, sovereign and independent within their own limits in their internal and domestic concerns, and bound together as one people by a General Government, possessing certain enumerated and restricted powers, delegated to it by the people of the several States, and exercising supreme authority within the scope of the powers granted to it, throughout the dominion of the United States. A power, therefore, in the General Government to obtain and hold colonies and dependent territories, over which they might legislate without restriction, would be inconsistent with its own existence in its present form. Whatever it acquires, it acquires for the benefit of the people of the several States who created it. It is their trustee acting for them, and charged with the duty of promoting the interests of the whole people of the Union in the exercise of the powers specifically granted.

At the time when the Territory in question was obtained by cession from France, it contained no population fit to be associated together and admitted as a State; and it therefore was absolutely necessary to hold possession of it, as a Territory belonging to the United States, until it was settled and inhabited by a civilized community capable of self-government, and in a condition to be admitted on equal terms with the other States as a member of the Union. But, as we have before said, it was acquired by the General Government, as the representative and trustee of the people of the United States, and it must therefore be held in that character for their common and equal benefit; for it was the people of the several States, acting through their agent and representative, the Federal Government, who in fact acquired the Territory in question, and the Government holds it for their common use until it shall be associated with the other States as a member of the Union.

But until that time arrives, it is undoubtedly necessary that some Government should be established, in order to organize society, and to protect the inhabitants in their persons and property; and as the people of the United States could act in this matter only through the Government which represented them, and through which they spoke and acted when the Territory was obtained, it was not only within the scope of its powers, but it was its duty to pass such laws and establish such a Government as would enable those by whose authority they acted to reap the advantages anticipated from its acquisition, and to gather there a population which would enable it to assume the position to which it was destined among the States of the Union. The power to acquire necessarily carries with it the power to preserve and apply to the purposes for which it was acquired. The form of government to be established necessarily rested in the discretion of Congress. It was their duty to establish the one that would be best suited for the protection and security of the citizens of the United States, and other inhabitants who might be authorized to take up their abode there, and that must always depend upon the existing condition of the Territory, as to the number and character of its inhabitants, and their situation in the Territory. In some cases a Government, consisting of persons appointed by the Federal Government, would best subserve the interests of the Territory, when the inhabitants were few and scattered, and new to one another. In other instances, it would be more advisable to commit the powers of self-government to the people who had settled in the Territory, as being the most competent to determine what was best for their own interests. But some form of civil authority would be absolutely necessary to organize and preserve civilized society, and prepare it to become a State; and what is the best form must always depend on the condition of the Territory at the time, and the choice of the mode must depend upon the exercise of a discretionary power by Congress, acting within the scope of its constitutional authority, and not infringing upon the rights of person or rights of property of the citizen who might go there to reside, or for any other lawful purpose. It was acquired by the exercise of this discretion, and it must be held and governed in like manner, until it is fitted to be a State.

But the power of Congress over the person or property of a citizen can never be a mere discretionary power under our Constitution and form of Government. The powers of the Government and the rights and privileges of the citizen are regulated and plainly defined by the Constitution itself. And when the Territory becomes a part of the United States, the Federal Government enters into possession in the character impressed upon it by those who created it. It enters upon it with its powers over the citizen strictly defined, and limited by the Constitution, from which it derives its own existence, and by virtue of which alone it continues to exist and act as a Government and sovereignty. It has no power of any kind beyond it; and it cannot, when it enters a Territory of the United States, put off its character, and assume discretionary or despotic powers which the Constitution has denied to it. It cannot create for itself a new character separated from the citizens of the United States, and the duties it owes them under the provisions of the Constitution. The Territory being a part of the United States, the Government and the citizen both enter it under the authority of the Constitution, with their respective rights defined and marked out; and the Federal Government can exercise no power over his person or property, beyond what that instrument confers, nor lawfully deny any right which it has reserved.

A reference to a few of the provisions of the Constitution will illustrate this proposition.

For example, no one, we presume, will contend that Congress can make any law in a Territory respecting the establishment of religion, or the free exercise thereof, or abridging the freedom of speech or of the press, or the right of the people of the Territory peaceably to assemble, and to petition the Government for the redress of grievances.

Nor can Congress deny to the people the right to keep and bear arms, nor the right to trial by jury, nor compel any one to be a witness against himself in a criminal proceeding.

These powers, and others, in relation to rights of person, which it is not necessary here to enumerate, are, in express and positive terms, denied to the General Government; and the rights of private property have been guarded with equal care. Thus the rights of property are united with the rights of person, and placed on the same ground by the fifth amendment to the Constitution, which provides that no person shall be deprived of life, liberty, and property, without due process of law. And an act of Congress which deprives a citizen of the United States of his liberty or property, merely because he came himself or brought his property into a particular Territory of the United States, and who had committed no offence against the laws, could hardly be dignified with the name of due process of law.

So, too, it will hardly be contended that Congress could by law quarter a soldier in a house in a Territory without the consent of the owner, in time of peace; nor in time of war, but in a manner prescribed by law. Nor could they by law forfeit the property of a citizen in a Territory who was convicted of treason, for a longer period than the life of the person convicted; nor take private property for public use without just compensation.

The powers over person and property of which we speak are not only not granted to Congress, but are in express terms denied, and they are forbidden to exercise them. And this prohibition is not confined to the States, but the words are general, and extend to the whole territory over which the Constitution gives it power to legislate, including those portions of it remaining under Territorial Government, as well as that covered by States. It is a total absence of power everywhere within the dominion of the United States, and places the citizens of a Territory, so far as these rights are concerned, on the same footing with citizens of the States, and guards them as firmly and plainly against any inroads which the General Government might attempt, under the plea of implied or incidental powers. And if Congress itself cannot do this—if it is beyond the powers conferred on the Federal Government—it will be admitted, we presume, that it could not authorize a Territorial Government to exercise them. It could confer no power on any local Government, established by its authority, to violate the provisions of the Constitution.

It seems, however, to be supposed, that there is a difference between property in a slave and other property, and that different rules may be applied to it in expounding the Constitution of the United States. And the laws and usages of nations, and the writings of eminent jurists upon the relation of master and slave and their mutual rights and duties, and the powers which Governments may exercise over it, have been dwelt upon in the argument.

But in considering the question before us, it must be borne in mind that there is no law of nations standing between the people of the United States and their Government, and interfering with their relation to each other. The powers of the Government, and the rights of the citizen under it, are positive and practical regulations plainly written down. The people of the United States have delegated to it certain enumerated powers, and forbidden it to exercise others. It has no power over the person or property of a citizen but what the citizens of the United States have granted. And no laws or usages of other nations, or reasoning of statesmen or jurists upon the relations of master and slave, can enlarge the powers of the Government, or take from the citizens the rights they have reserved. And if the Constitution recognises the right of property of the master in a slave, and makes no distinction between that description of property and other property owned by a citizen, no tribunal, acting under the authority of the United States, whether it be legislative, executive, or judicial, has a right to draw such a distinction, or deny to it the benefit of the provisions and guarantees which have been provided for the protection of private property against the encroachments of the Government.

Now, as we have already said in an earlier part of this opinion, upon a different point, the right of property in a slave is distinctly and expressly affirmed in the Constitution. The right to traffic in it, like an ordinary article of merchandise and property, was guaranteed to the citizens of the United States, in every State that might desire it, for twenty years. And the Government in express terms is pledged to protect it in all future time, if the slave escapes from his owner. This is done in plain words—too plain to be misunderstood. And no word can be found in the Constitution which gives Congress a greater power over slave property, or which entitles property of that kind to less protection than property of any other description. The only power conferred is the power coupled with the duty of guarding and protecting the owner in his rights.

Upon these considerations, it is the opinion of the court that the act of Congress which prohibited a citizen from holding and owning property of this kind in the territory of the United States north of the line therein mentioned, is not warranted by the Constitution, and is therefore void; and that neither Dred Scott himself, nor any of his family, were made free by being carried into this territory; even if they had been carried there by the owner, with the intention of becoming a permanent resident.

We have so far examined the case, as it stands under the Constitution of the United States, and the powers thereby delegated to the Federal Government.

But there is another point in the case which depends on State power and State law. And it is contended, on the part of the plaintiff, that he is made free by being taken to Rock Island, in the State of Illinois, independently of his residence in the territory of the United States; and being so made free, he was not again reduced to a state of slavery by being brought back to Missouri.

Our notice of this part of the case will be very brief; for the principle on which it depends was decided in this court, upon much consideration, in the case of Strader et al. *v.* Graham, reported in 10th Howard, 82. In that case, the slaves had been taken from Kentucky to Ohio, with the consent of the owner, and afterwards brought back to Kentucky. And this court held that their *status* or condition, as free or slave, depended upon the laws of Kentucky, when they were brought back into that State, and not of Ohio; and that this court had no jurisdiction to revise the judgment of a State court upon its own laws. This was the point directly before the court, and the decision that this court had not jurisdiction turned upon it, as will be seen by the report of the case.

So in this case. As Scott was a slave when taken into the State of Illinois by his owner, and was there held as such, and brought back in that character, his *status,* as free or slave, depended on the laws of Missouri, and not of Illinois.

It has, however, been urged in the argument; that by the laws of Missouri he was free on his return, and that this case, therefore, cannot be governed by the case of Strader et al. *v.* Graham, where it appeared, by the laws of Kentucky, that the plaintiffs continued to be slaves on their return from Ohio. But whatever doubts or opinions may, at one time, have been entertained upon this subject, we are satisfied, upon a careful examination of all the cases decided in the State courts of Missouri referred to, that it is now firmly settled by the decisions of the highest court in the State, that Scott and his family upon their return were not free, but were, by the laws of Missouri, the property of the defendant; and that the Circuit Court of the United States had no jurisdiction, when, by the laws of the State, the plaintiff was a slave, and not a citizen.

Moreover, the plaintiff, it appears, brought a similar action against the defendant in the State court of Missouri, claiming the freedom of himself and his family upon the same grounds and the same evidence upon which he relies in the case before the court. The case was carried before the Supreme Court of the State; was fully argued there; and that court decided that neither the plaintiff nor his family were entitled to freedom, and were still the slaves of the defendant; and reversed the judgment of the inferior State court, which had given a different decision. If the plaintiff supposed that this judgment of the Supreme Court of the State was erroneous, and that this court had jurisdiction to revise and reverse it, the only mode by which he could legally bring it before this court was by writ of error directed to the Supreme Court of the State, requiring it to transmit the record to this court. If this had been done, it is too plain for argument that the writ must have been dismissed for want of jurisdiction in this court. The case of Strader and others *v.* Graham is directly in point; and, indeed, independent of any decision, the language of the 25th section of the act of 1789 is too clear and precise to admit of controversy.

But the plaintiff did not pursue the mode prescribed by law for bringing the judgment of a State court before this court for revision, but suffered the case to be remanded to the inferior State court, where it is still continued, and is, by agreement of parties, to await the judgment of this court on the point. All of this appears on the record before us, and by the printed report of the case.

And while the case is yet open and pending in the inferior State court, the plaintiff goes into the Circuit Court of the United States, upon the same case and the same evidence, and against the same party, and proceeds to judgment, and then brings here the same case from the Circuit Court, which the law would not have permitted him to bring directly from the State court. And if this court takes jurisdiction in this form, the result, so far as the rights of the respective parties are concerned, is in every respect substantially the same as if it had in open violation of law entertained jurisdiction over the judgment of the State court upon a writ of error, and revised and reversed its judgment upon the ground that its opinion upon the question of law was erroneous. It would ill become this court to sanction such an attempt to evade the law, or to exercise an appellate power in this circuitous way, which it is forbidden to exercise in the direct and regular and invariable forms of judicial proceedings.

Upon the whole, therefore, it is the judgment of this court, that it appears by the record before us that the plaintiff in error is not a citizen of Missouri, in the sense in which that word is used in the Constitution; and that the Circuit Court of the United States, for that reason, had no jurisdiction in the case, and could give no judgment in it. Its judgment for the defendant must, consequently, be reversed, and a mandate issued, directing the suit to be dismissed for want of jurisdiction.

LICENSE CASES, 5 HOW. 504 (1847)

When Massachusetts and New Hampshire laws regulating intoxicating beverages were challenged in the *License Cases,* the Court had no difficulty upholding the statutes in question. However, there were six separate opinions delivered in the case. Taney's opinion focused directly on the police power of the states. He held that the laws were part of the normal exercise of sovereignty, "the power to govern men and things within the limits of its dominion." There was no collision with the commerce clause since importation was not forbidden by the states. However, traffic in the beverages once they arrived in the state could be regulated by local authorities.

Mr. Chief Justice TANEY. In the cases of Thurlow *v*. The State of Massachusetts, of Fletcher *v*. The State of Rhode Island, and of Peirce et al. *v*. The State of New Hampshire, the judgments of the respective State courts are severally affirmed.

The justices of this court do not, however, altogether agree in the principles upon which these cases are decided, and I therefore proceed to state the grounds upon which I concur in affirming the judgments. The first two of these cases depend upon precisely the same principles; and although the case against the State of New Hampshire differs in some respects from the others, yet there are important principles common to all of them, and on that account it is more convenient to consider them together. Each of the cases has arisen upon State laws, passed for the purpose of discouraging the use of ardent spirits within their respective territories, by prohibiting their sale in small quantities, and without licenses previously obtained from the State authorities. And the validity of each of them has been drawn in question, upon the ground that it is repugnant to that clause of the constitution of the United States which confers upon Congress the power to regulate commerce with foreign nations and among the several States.

The cases have been separately and fully and ably argued, and the questions which they involve are undoubtedly of the highest importance. But the construction of this clause in the constitution has been so fully discussed at the bar, and in the opinions delivered by the court in former cases, that scarcely any thing can be suggested at this day calculated to throw much additional light upon the subject, or any argument offered which has not heretofore been considered, and commented on, and which may not be found in the reports of the decisions of this court.

It is not my purpose to enter into a particular examination of the various passages in different opinions of the court, or of some of its members, in former cases, which have been referred to by counsel, and relied upon as supporting the construction of the constitution for which they are respectively contending. And I am the less inclined to do so because I think these controversies often arise from looking to detached passages in the opinions, where general expressions are sometimes used, which, taken by themselves, are susceptible of a construction that the court never intended should be given to them, and which in some instances would render different portions of the opinion inconsistent with each other. It is only by looking to the case under consideration at the time, and taking the whole opinion together, in all its bearings, that we can correctly understand the judgment of the court.

The constitution of the United States declares that that constitution, and the laws of the United States which shall be made in pursuance thereof, and all treaties made, or which shall be made, under the authority of the United States, shall be the supreme law of the land. It follows that a law of Congress regulating commerce with foreign nations, or among the several States, is the supreme law; and if the law of a State is in conflict with it, the law of Congress must prevail, and the State law cease to operate so far as it is repugnant to the law of the United States.

It is equally clear, that the power of Congress over this subject does not extend further than the regulation of commerce with foreign nations and among the several States; and that beyond these limits the States have never surrendered their power over trade and commerce, and may still exercise it, free from any controlling power on the part of the general government. Every State, therefore, may regulate its own internal traffic, according to its own judgment and upon its own views of the interest and well-being of its citizens.

I am not aware that these principles have ever been questioned. The difficulty has always arisen on their application; and that difficulty is now presented in the Rhode Island and Massachusetts cases, where the question is how far a State may regulate or prohibit the sale of ardent spirits, the importation of which from foreign countries has been authorized by Congress. Is such a law a regulation of foreign commerce, or of the internal traffic of the State?

It is unquestionably no easy task to mark by a certain and definite line the division between foreign and domestic commerce, and to fix the precise point, in relation to every imported article, where the paramount power of Congress terminates, and that of the State begins. The constitution itself does not attempt to define these limits. They cannot be determined by the laws of Congress or the States, as neither can by its own legislation enlarge its own powers, or restrict those of the other. And as the constitution itself does not draw the line, the question is necessarily one for judicial decision, and depending altogether upon the words of the constitution.

This question came directly before the court for the first time in the case of Brown *v*. The State of Maryland, 12 Wheat. 419. And the court there held that an article authorized by a law of Congress to be imported continued to be a part of the foreign commerce of the country while it remained in the hands of the importer for sale, in the original bale, package, or vessel in which it was imported; that the authority given to import necessarily carried with it the right to sell the imported article in the form and shape in which it was imported, and that no State, either by direct assessment or by requiring a license from the importer before he was permitted to sell, could impose any burden upon him or the property imported beyond what the law of Congress had itself imposed; but that when the original package was broken up for use or for retail by the importer, and also when the commodity had passed from his hands into the hands of a purchaser, it ceased to be an import, or a part of foreign commerce, and became subject to the laws of the State, and might be taxed for State purposes, and the sale regulated by the State, like any other property. This I understand to be substantially the decision in the case of Brown *v*. The State of Maryland, drawing the line between foreign commerce, which is subject to the regulation of Congress, and internal or domestic commerce, which belongs to the States, and over which Congress can exercise no control.

I argued the case in behalf of the State, and endeavoured to maintain that the law of Maryland, which required the importer as well as other dealers to take out a license before he could sell, and for which he was to pay a certain sum to the State, was valid and constitutional; and certainly I at that time persuaded myself that I was right, and thought the decision of the court restricted the powers of the State more than a sound construction of the constitution of the United States would warrant. But further and more mature reflection has convinced me that the rule laid down by the Supreme Court is a just and safe one, and perhaps the best that could have been adopted for preserving the right of the United States on the one hand, and of the States on the other, and preventing collision between them. The question, I have already said, was a very difficult one for the judicial mind. In the nature of things, the line of division is in some degree vague and indefinite, and I do not see how it could be drawn more accurately and correctly, or more in harmony with the obvious intention and object of this provision in the constitution. Indeed, goods imported, while they remain in the hands of the importer, in the form and shape in which they were brought into the country, can in no just sense be regarded as a part of that mass of property in the State usually taxed for the support of the State government. The immense amount of foreign products used and consumed in this country are imported, landed, and offered for sale in a few commercial cities, and a very small portion of them are intended or expected to be used in the State in which they are imported. A great (perhaps the greater) part imported, in some of the cities, is not owned or brought in by citizens of the State, but by citizens of other States, or foreigners. And while they are in the hands of the importer for sale, in the form and shape in which they were introduced, and in which they are intended to be sold, they may be regarded as merely *in transitu,* and on their way to the distant cities, villages, and country for which they are destined, and where they are expected to be used and consumed, and for the supply of which they were in truth imported. And a tax upon them while in this condition, for State purposes, whether by direct assessment, or indirectly, by requiring a license to sell, would be hardly more justifiable in principle than a transit duty upon the merchandise when passing through a State. A tax in any shape upon imports is a tax on the consumer, by enhancing the price of the commodity. And if a State is permitted to levy it in any form, it will put it in the power of a maritime importing State to raise a revenue for the support of its own government from citizens of other States, as certainly and effectually as if the tax was laid openly and without disguise as a duty on imports. Such a power in a State would defeat one of the principal objects of forming and adopting the constitution. It cannot be done directly, in the shape of a duty on imports, for that is expressly prohibited. And as it cannot be done directly, it could hardly be a just and sound construction of the constitution which would enable a State to accomplish precisely the same thing under another name, and in a different form.

Undoubtedly a State may impose a tax upon its citizens in proportion to the amount they are respectively worth; and the importing merchant is liable to this assessment like any other citizen, and is chargeable according to the amount of his property, whether it consists of money engaged in trade, or of imported goods which he proposes to sell, or any other property of which he is the owner. But a tax of this description stands upon a very different footing from a tax on the thing imported, while it remains a part of foreign commerce, and is not introduced into the general mass of property in the State. Nor, indeed, can it even influence materially the price of the commodity to the consumer, since foreigners, as well as citizens of other States, who are not chargeable with the tax, may import goods into the same place and offer them for sale in the same market, and with whom the resident merchant necessarily enters into competition.

Adopting, therefore, the rule as laid down in Brown *v*. The State of Maryland, I proceed to apply it to the cases of Massachusetts and Rhode Island. The laws of Congress regulating foreign commerce authorize the importation of spirits, distilled liquors, and brandy, in casks or vessels not containing less than a certain quantity, specified in the laws upon this subject. Now, if the State laws in question came in collision with those acts of Congress, and prevented or obstructed the importation or sale of these articles by the importer in the original cask or vessel in which they were imported, it would be the duty of this court to declare them void.

It has, indeed, been suggested, that, if a State deems the traffic in ardent spirits to be injurious to its citizens, and calculated to introduce immorality, vice, and pauperism into the State, it may constitutionally refuse to permit its importation, notwithstanding the laws of Congress; and that a State may do this upon the same principles that it may resist and prevent the introduction of disease, pestilence, or pauperism from abroad. But it must be remembered that disease, pestilence, and pauperism are not subjects of commerce, although sometimes among its attendant evils. They are not things to be regulated and trafficked in, but to be prevented, as far as human foresight or human means can guard against them. But spirits and distilled liquors are universally admitted to be subjects of ownership and property, and are therefore subjects of exchange, barter, and traffic, like any other commodity in which a right of property exists. And Congress, under its general power to regulate commerce with foreign nations, may prescribe what article of merchandise shall be admitted, and what excluded; and may therefore admit, or not, as it shall deem best, the importation of ardent spirits. And inasmuch as the laws of Congress authorize their importation, no State has a right to prohibit their introduction.

But I do not understand the law of Massachusetts or Rhode Island as interfering with the trade in ardent spirits while the article remains a part of foreign commerce, and is in the hands of the importer for sale, in the cask or vessel in which the laws of Congress authorize it to be imported. These State laws act altogether upon the retail or domestic traffic within their respective borders. They act upon the article after it has passed the line of foreign commerce, and become a part of the general mass of property in the State. These laws may, indeed, discourage imports, and diminish the price which ardent spirits would otherwise bring. But although a State is bound to receive and to permit the sale by the importer of any article of merchandise which Congress authorizes to be imported (it is not bound to furnish a market for it), nor to abstain from the passage of any law which it may deem necessary or advisable to guard the health or morals of its citizens, although such law may discourage importation, or diminish the profits of the importer, or lessen the revenue of the general government. And if any State deems the retail and internal traffic in ardent spirits injurious to its citizens, and calculated to produce idleness, vice, or debauchery, I see nothing in the constitution of the United States to prevent it from regulating and restraining the traffic, or from prohibiting it altogether, if it thinks proper. Of the wisdom of this policy, it is not my province or my purpose to speak. Upon that subject, each State must decide for itself. I speak only of the restrictions which the constitution and laws of the United States have imposed upon the States. And as these laws of Massachusetts and

Rhode Island are not repugnant to the constitution of the United States, and do not come in conflict with any law of Congress passed in pursuance of its authority to regulate commerce with foreign nations and among the several States, there is no ground upon which this court can declare them to be void.

I come now to the New Hampshire case, in which a different principle is involved,—the question, however, arising under the same clause in the constitution, and depending on its construction.

The law of New Hampshire prohibits the sale of distilled spirits, in any quantity, without a license from the selectmen of the town in which the party resides. The plaintiffs in error, who were merchants in Dover, in New Hampshire, purchased a barrel of gin in Boston, brought it to Dover, and sold it in the cask in which it was imported, without a license from the selectmen of the town. For this sale they were indicted, convicted, and fined, under the law above mentioned.

The power to regulate commerce among the several States is granted to Congress in the same clause, and by the same words, as the power to regulate commerce with foreign nations, and is coextensive with it. And, according to the doctrine in Brown *v.* Maryland, the article in question, at the time of the sale, was subject to the legislation of Congress.

The present case, however, differs from Brown *v.* The State of Maryland in this,—that the former was one arising out of commerce with foreign nations, which Congress had regulated by law; whereas the present is a case of commerce between two States, in relation to which Congress has not exercised its power. Some acts of Congress have indeed been referred to in relation to the coasting trade. But they are evidently intended merely to prevent smuggling, and do not regulate imports or exports from one State to another. This case differs also from the cases of Massachusetts and Rhode Island; because, in these two cases, the laws of the States operated upon the articles after they had passed beyond the limits of foreign commerce, and consequently were beyond the control and power of Congress. But the law of New Hampshire acts directly upon an import from one State to another, while in the hands of the importer for sale, and is therefore a regulation of commerce, acting upon the article while it is within the admitted jurisdiction of the general government, and subject to its control and regulation.

The question, therefore, brought up for decision is, whether a State is prohibited by the constitution of the United States from making any regulations of foreign commerce, or of commerce with another State, although such regulation is confined to its own territory, and made for its own convenience or interest, and does not come in conflict with any law of Congress. In other words, whether the grant of power to Congress is of itself a prohibition to the States, and renders all State laws upon the subject null and void. This is the question upon which the case turns; and I do not see how it can be decided upon any other ground, provided we adopt the line of division between foreign and domestic commerce as marked out by the court in Brown *v.* The State of Maryland. I proceed, therefore, to state my opinion upon it.

It is well known that upon this subject a difference of opinion has existed, and still exists, among the members of this court. But with every respect for the opinion of my brethren with whom I do not agree, it appears to me to be very clear, that the mere grant of power to the general government cannot, upon any just principles of construction, be construed to be an absolute prohibition to the exercise of any power over the same subject by the States. The controlling and supreme power over commerce with foreign nations and the several States is undoubtedly conferred upon Congress. Yet, in my judgment, the State may nevertheless, for the safety or convenience of trade, or for the protection of the health of its citizens, make regulations of commerce for its own ports and harbours, and for its own territory; and such regulations are valid unless they come in conflict with a law of Congress. Such evidently I think was the construction which the constitution universally received at the time of its adoption, as appears from the legislation of Congress and of the several States; and a careful examination of the decisions of this court will show, that, so far from sanctioning the opposite doctrine, they recognize and maintain the power of the States.

The language in which the grant of power to the general government is made certainly furnishes no warrant for a different construction, and there is no prohibition to the States. Neither can it be inferred by comparing the provision upon this subject with those that relate to other powers granted by the constitution to the general government. On the contrary, in many instances, after the grant is made, the constitution proceeds to prohibit the exercise of the same power by the States in express terms; in some cases absolutely, in others without the consent of Congress. And if it was intended to forbid the States from making any regulations of commerce, it is difficult to account for the omission to prohibit it, when that prohibition has been so carefully and distinctly inserted in relation to other powers, where the action of the State over the same subject was intended to be entirely excluded. But if, as I think, the framers of the constitution (knowing that a multitude of minor regulations must be necessary, which Congress amid its great concerns could never find time to consider and provide) intended merely to make the power of the federal government supreme upon this subject over that of the States, then the omission of any prohibition is accounted for, and is consistent with the whole instrument. The supremacy of the laws of Congress, in cases of collision with State laws, is secured in the article which declares that the laws of Congress, passed in pursuance of the powers granted, shall be the supreme law; and it is only where both governments may legislate on the same subject that this article can operate. For if the mere grant of power to the general government was in itself a prohibition to the States, there would seem to be no necessity for providing for the supremacy of the laws of Congress, as all State laws upon the subject would be *ipso facto* void, and there could therefore be no such thing as conflicting laws, nor any question about the supremacy of conflicting legislation. It is only where both may legislate on the subject, that the question can arise.

I have said that the legislation of Congress and the States has conformed to this construction from the foundation of the government. This is sufficiently exemplified in the laws in relation to pilots and pilotage, and the health and quarantine laws.

In relation to the first, they are admitted on all hands to belong to foreign commerce, and to be subject to the regulations of Congress, under the grant of power of which we are speaking. Yet they have been continually regulated by the maritime States, as fully and entirely since the adoption of the constitution as they were before; and there is but one law of Congress making any specific regulation upon the subject, and that passed as late as 1837, and intended, as it is understood, to alter only a single provision of the New York law, leaving the residue of its provisions entirely untouched. It is true, that the act of 1789 provides that pilots shall continue to be regulated by the laws of the respective States then in force, or which may thereafter be passed, until Congress shall make provision on the subject. And undoubtedly Congress had the power, by assenting to the State laws then in force, to make them its own, and thus make the previous regulations of the States the regulations of the general government. But it is equally clear, that, as to all future laws by the States, if the constitution deprived them of the power of making any regulations on the subject, an act of Congress could not restore it. For it will hardly be contended that an act of Congress can alter the constitution, and confer upon a State a power which the constitution declares it shall not possess. And if the grant of power to the United States to make regulations of commerce is a prohibition to the States to make any regulation upon the subject, Congress could no more restore to the States the power of which it was thus deprived, than it could authorize them to coin money, or make paper-money a tender in the payment of debts, or to do any other act forbidden to them by the constitution. Every pilot law in the commercial States has, it is believed, been either modified or passed since the act of 1789 adopted those then in force; and the provisions since made are all void, if the restriction on the power of the States now contended for should be maintained; and the regulations made, the duties imposed, the securities required, and penalties inflicted by these various State laws are mere nullities, and could not be enforced in a court of justice. It is hardly necessary to speak of the mischiefs which such a construction would produce to those who are engaged in shipping, navigation, and commerce. Up to this time their validity has never been questioned. On the contrary, they have been repeatedly recognized and upheld by the decisions of this court; and it will be difficult to show how this can be done, except upon the construction of the constitution which I am now maintaining. So, also, in regard to health and quarantine laws. They have been continually passed by the States ever since the adoption of the constitution, and the power to pass them recognized by acts of Congress, and the revenue officers of the general government directed to assist in their execution. Yet all of these health and quarantine laws are necessarily, in some degree, regulations of foreign commerce in the ports and harbours of the State. They subject the ship, and cargo, and crew to the inspection of a health-officer appointed by the State; they prevent the crew and cargo from landing until the inspection is made, and destroy the cargo if deemed dangerous to health. And during all this time the vessel is detained at the place selected for the quarantine ground by the State authority. The expenses of these precautionary measures are also usually, and I believe universally, charged upon the master, the owner, or the ship, and the amount regulated by the State law, and not by Congress. Now, so far as these laws interfere with shipping, navigation, or foreign commerce, or impose burdens upon either of them, they are unquestionably regulations of commerce. Yet, as I have already said, the power has been continually exercised by the States, has been continually recognized by Congress ever since the adoption of the constitution, and constantly affirmed and supported by this court whenever the subject came before it.

The decisions of this court will also, in my opinion, when carefully examined, be found to sanction the construction I am maintaining. It is not my purpose to refer to all of the cases in which this question has been spoken of, but only to the principal and leading ones; and,—

First, to Gibbons *v*. Ogden, because this is the case usually referred to and relied on to prove the exclusive power of Congress and the prohibition to the States. It is true that one or two passages in that opinion, taken by themselves, and detached from the context, would seem to countenance this doctrine. And, indeed, it has always appeared to me that this controversy has mainly arisen out of that case, and that this doctrine of the exclusive power of Congress, in the sense in which it is now contended for, is comparatively a modern one, and was never seriously put forward in any case until after the decision of Gibbons *v*. Ogden, although it has been abundantly discussed since. Still, it seems to me to be clear, upon a careful examination of that case, that the expressions referred to do not warrant the inference drawn from them, and were not used in the sense imputed to them; and that the opinion in that case, when taken altogether and with reference to the subject-matter before the court, establishes the doctrine that a State may, in the execution of its powers of internal police, make regulations of foreign commerce; and that such regulations are valid, unless they come into collision with a law of Congress. Upon examining that opinion, it will be seen that the court, when it uses the expressions which are supposed to countenance the doctrine of exclusive power in Congress, is commenting upon the argument of counsel in favor of equal powers on this subject in the States and the general government, where neither party is bound to yield to the other; and is drawing the distinction between cases of concurrent powers and those in which the supreme or paramount power was granted to Congress. It therefore very justly speaks of the States as exercising their own powers in laying taxes for State purposes, although the same thing is taxed by Congress; and as exercising the powers granted to Congress when they make regulations of commerce. In the first case, the State power is concurrent with that of the general government,—is equal to it, and is not bound to yield. In the second, it is subordinate and subject to the superior and controlling power conferred upon Congress. And it is solely with reference to this distinction, and in the midst of this argument upon it, that the court uses the expressions which are supposed to maintain an absolute prohibition to the States. But it certainly did not mean to press the doctrine to that extent. For it does not decide the case on that ground (although it would have been abundantly sufficient, if the court had entertained the opinion imputed to it), but, after disposing of the argument which had been offered in favor of concurrent powers, it proceeds immediately, in a very full and elaborate argument, to show that there was a conflict between the law of New York and the act of Congress, and explicitly puts its decision upon that ground. Now the whole of this part of the opinion would have been unnecessary and out of place, if the State law was of itself a violation of the constitution of the United States, and therefore utterly null and void, whether it did or did not come in conflict with the law of Congress.

Moreover, the court distinctly admits, on pages 205, 206, that a State may, in the execution of its police and health laws, make regulations of commerce, but which Congress may control. It is very clear, that, so far as these regulations are merely internal, and do not operate on foreign commerce, or commerce among the States, they are altogether independent of the power of the general government and cannot be controlled by it. The power of control, therefore, which the court speaks of, presupposes that they are regulations of foreign commerce, or commerce among the States. And if a State, with a view to its police or health, may make valid regulations of commerce which yet fall within the controlling power of the general government, it follows that the State is not absolutely prohibited from making regulations of foreign commerce within its own territorial limits, provided they do not come in conflict with the laws of Congress.

It has been said, indeed, that quarantine and health laws are passed by the States, not by virtue of a power to regulate commerce, but by virtue of their police powers, and in order to guard the lives and health of their citizens. This, however, cannot be said of the pilot laws, which are yet admitted to be equally valid. But what are the police powers of a State? (They are nothing more or less than the powers of government inherent in every sovereignty to the extent of its dominions.) And whether a State passes a quarantine law, or a law to punish offences, or to establish courts of justice, or requiring certain instruments to be recorded, or to regulate commerce within its own limits, in every case it exercises the same power; that is to say, the power of sovereignty, the power to govern men and things within the limits of its dominion. It is by virtue of this power that it legislates; and its authority to make regulations of commerce is as absolute as its power to pass health laws, except in so far as it has been restricted by the constitution of the United States. And when the validity of a State law making regulations of commerce is drawn into question in a judicial tribunal, the authority to pass it cannot be made to depend upon the motives that may be supposed to have influenced the legislature, nor can the court inquire whether it was intended to guard the citizens of the State from pestilence and disease, or to make regulations of commerce for the interests and convenience of trade.

Upon this question the object and motive of the State are of no importance, and cannot influence the decision. It is a question of power. Are the States absolutely prohibited by the constitution from making any regulations of foreign commerce? If they are, then such regulations are null and void, whatever may have been the motive of the State, or whatever the real object of the law; and it requires no law of Congress to control or annul them. Yet the case of Gibbons *v.* Ogden unquestionably affirms that such regulations may be made by a State, subject to the controlling power of Congress. And if this may be done, it necessarily follows that the grant of power to the federal government is not an absolute and entire prohibition to the States, but merely confers upon Congress the superior and controlling power. And to expound the particular passages herein before mentioned in the manner insisted upon by those who contend for the prohibition would be to make different parts of that opinion inconsistent with each other,—an error which I am quite sure no one will ever impute to the very eminent jurist by whom the opinion was delivered.

And that the meaning of the court in the case of Gibbons *v.* Ogden was such as I have insisted on is, I think, conclusively proved by the case of Willson et al. *v.* The Blackbird Creek Marsh Company, 2 Peters, 251, 252. In that case a dam authorized by a State law had been erected across a navigable creek, so as to obstruct the commerce above it. And the validity of the State law was objected to, on the ground that it was repugnant to the constitution of the United States, being a regulation of commerce. But the court says,—"The repugnancy of the law of Delaware to the constitution is placed entirely on its repugnancy to the power to regulate commerce with foreign nations, and among the several States; a power which has not been so exercised as to affect the question," and then proceeds to decide that the law of Delaware could not "be considered as repugnant to the power to regulate commerce in its dormant State, or as being in conflict with any law passed on the subject."

The passages I have quoted show that the validity of the State law was maintained because it was not in conflict with a law of Congress, although it was confessedly within the limits of the power granted. And it is worthy of remark, that the counsel for the plaintiff in error in that case relied upon Gibbons *v.* Ogden as conclusive authority to show the unconstitutionality of the State law, no doubt placing upon the passages I have mentioned the construction given to them by those who insist upon the exclusiveness of the power. This case, therefore, was brought fully to the attention of the court. And the decision in the last case, and the grounds on which it was placed, in my judgment show most clearly what was intended in Gibbons *v.* Ogden; and that in that case, as well as in the case of Willson *v.* The

Blackbird Creek Marsh Company, the court held that a State law was not invalid merely because it made regulations of commerce, but that its invalidity depended upon its repugnancy to a law of Congress passed in pursuance of the power granted. And it is worthy, also, of remark, that the opinion in both of these cases was delivered by Chief Justice Marshall; and I consider his opinion in the latter one as an exposition of what he meant to decide in the former.

In the case of the City of New York *v.* Miln, 11 Peters, 130, the question as to the power of the States upon this subject was very fully discussed at the bar. But no opinion was expressed upon it by the court, because the case did not necessarily involve it, and there was great diversity of opinion on the bench. Consequently the point was left open, and has never been decided in any subsequent case in this court.

For my own part, I have always regarded the cases of Gibbons *v.* Ogden, and Willson *v.* The Blackbird Creek Marsh Company, as abundantly sufficient to sanction the construction of the constitution which in my judgment is the true one. Their correctness has never been questioned; and I forbear, therefore, to remark on the other cases in which this subject has been mentioned and discussed.

It may be well, however, to remark, that in analogous cases, where, by the constitution of the United States, power over a particular subject is conferred on Congress without any prohibition to the States, the same rule of construction has prevailed. Thus, in the case of Houston *v.* Moore, 5 Wheat. 1, it was held, that the grant of power to the federal government to provide for organizing, arming, and disciplining the militia did not preclude the States from legislating on the same subject, provided the law of the State was not repugnant to the law of Congress. And every State in the Union has continually legislated on the subject, and I am not aware that the validity of these laws has ever been disputed, unless they came in conflict with the law of Congress.

The same doctrine was held in the case of Sturges *v.* Crowninshield, 4 Wheat. 196, under the clause in the constitution which gives to Congress the power to establish uniform laws on the subject of bankruptcies throughout the United States.

And in the case of Chirac *v.* Chirac, 2 Wheat. 269, which arose under the grant of power to establish a uniform rule of naturalization, where the court speaks of the power of Congress as exclusive, they are evidently merely sanctioning the argument of counsel stated in the preceding sentence, which placed the invalidity of the naturalization under the law of Maryland, not solely upon the grant of power in the constitution, but insisted that the Maryland law was "virtually repealed by the constitution of the United States, and the act of naturalization enacted by Congress." Undoubtedly it was so repealed, and the opposing counsel in the case did not dispute it. For the law of the United States covered every part of the Union, and there could not, therefore, by possibility be a State law which did not come in conflict with it. And, indeed, in this case it might well have been doubted whether the grant in the constitution itself did not abrogate the power of the States, inasmuch as the constitution also provided, that the citizens of each State should be entitled to all the privileges and immunities of citizens in the several States; and it would seem to be hardly consistent with this provision to allow any one State, after the adoption of the constitution, to exercise a power, which, if it operated at all, must operate beyond the territory of the State, and compel other States to acknowledge as citizens those whom it might not be willing to receive.

In referring to the opinions of those who sat here before us, it is but justice to them, in expounding their language, to keep in mind the character of the case they were deciding. And this is more especially necessary in cases depending upon the construction of the constitution of the United States; where, from the great public interests which must always be involved in such questions, this court has usually deemed it advisable to state very much at large the principles and reasoning upon which their judgment was founded, and to refer to and comment on the leading points made by the counsel on either side in the argument. And I am not aware of any instance in which the court has spoken of the grant of power to the general government as excluding all State power over the subject, unless they were deciding a case where the power had been exercised by Congress, and a State law came in conflict with it. In cases of this kind, the power of Congress undoubtedly excludes and displaces that of the State; because, wherever there is collision between them, the law of Congress is supreme. And it is in this sense only, in my judgment, that it has been spoken of as exclusive in the opinions of the court to which I have referred. The case last mentioned is a striking example; for there the language of the court, affirming in the broadest terms the exclusiveness of the power, evidently refers to the argument of counsel stated in the preceding sentence.

Upon the whole, therefore, the law of New Hampshire is, in my judgment, a valid one. For, although the gin sold was an import from another State, and Congress has clearly the power to regulate such importations, under the grant of power to regulate commerce among the several States, yet, as Congress has made no regulation on the subject, the traffic in the article may be lawfully regulated by the State as soon as it is landed in its territory, and a tax imposed upon it, or a license required, or the sale altogether prohibited, according to the policy which the State may suppose to be its interest or duty to pursue.

The judgment of the State courts ought, therefore, in my opinion, to be affirmed in each of the three cases before us.

BANK OF AUGUSTA v. EARLE, 13, PET. 519 (1839)

Taney's ability to compromise legitimate but opposing interests, to give corporate enterprise the opportunity to expand while upholding the power of the state to regulate its internal affairs for the best welfare of the people is exemplified in his *Bank of Augusta* decision. Justice McKinley on circuit had concluded that corporate entities were artificial creations of one state and could therefore not act or do business outside the limits of its home territory. Thus the defense raised by the maker of a note that a foreign corporation could not sue outside its home state was upheld by McKinley. Taney speaking for the Supreme Court on appeal reversed that decision. While he accepted much of McKinley's approach, he concluded that reasons of comity between the states, which he presumed to be greater than between foreign nations, compelled the conclusion that one state would permit a corporation from another state to act within its borders unless it explicitly declared otherwise. Thus silence would be construed as consent. In the case at issue, since no excluding legislation had been passed, the foreign bank could collect on its note.

Mr. Chief Justice TANEY delivered the opinion of the Court.

These three cases involve the same principles, and have been brought before us by writs of error directed to the Circuit Court and southern district of Alabama. The two first have been fully argued by counsel; and the last submitted to the Court upon the arguments offered in the other two. There are some shades of difference in the facts as stated in the different records, but none that can affect the decision. We proceed therefore to express our opinion on the first case argued, which was the Bank of Augusta *vs.* Joseph B. Earle. The judgment in this case must decide the others.

The questions presented to the Court arise upon a case stated in the Circuit Court in the following words:—

"The defendant defends this action upon the following facts, that are admitted by the plaintiffs: that plaintiffs are a corporation, incorporated by an act of the legislature of the state of Georgia, and have power usually conferred upon banking institutions, such as to purchase bills of exchange, &c. That the bill sued on was made and endorsed, for the purpose of being discounted by Thomas M'Gran, the agent of said bank, who had funds of the plaintiffs in his hands for the purpose of purchasing bills, which funds were derived from bills and notes discounted in Georgia by said plaintiffs, and payable in Mobile; and the said M'Gran, agent as aforesaid, did so discount and purchase the said bill sued on, in the city of Mobile, state aforesaid, for the benefit of said bank, and with their funds, and to remit said funds to the said plaintiffs.

"If the Court shall say that the facts constitute a defence to this action, judgment will be given for the defendant, otherwise for plaintiffs, for the amount of the bill, damages, interest, and cost; either party to have the right of appeal or writ of error to the Supreme Court upon this statement of facts, and the judgment thereon."

Upon this statement of facts the Court gave judgment for the defendant; being of opinion that a bank incorporated by the laws of Georgia, with a power among other things to purchase bills of exchange, could not lawfully exercise that power in the state of Alabama; and that the contract for this bill was therefore void, and did not bind the parties to the payment of the money.

It will at once be seen that the questions brought here for decision are of a very grave character, and they have received from the Court an attentive examination. A multitude of corporations for various purposes have been chartered by the several states; a large portion of certain branches of business has been transacted by incorporated companies, or through their agency; and contracts to a very great amount have undoubtedly been made by different corporations out of the jurisdiction of the particular state by which they were created. In deciding the case before us, we in effect determine whether these numerous contracts are valid, or not. And if, as has been argued at the bar, a corporation, from its nature and character, is incapable of making such contracts; or if they are inconsistent with the rights and sovereignty of the states in which they are made, they cannot be enforced in the Courts of justice.

Much of the argument has turned on the nature and extent of the powers which belong to the artificial being called a corporation; and the rules of law by which they are to be measured. On the part of the plaintiff in error, it has been contended that a corporation composed of citizens of other states are entitled to the benefit of that provision in the Constitution of the United States which declares that "The citizens of each state shall be entitled to all privileges and immunities of citizens in the several states;" that the Court should look behind the act of incorporation, and see who are the members of it; and, if in this case it should appear that the corporation of the Bank of Augusta consists altogether of citizens of the state of Georgia, that such citizens are entitled to the privileges and immunities of citizens in the state of Alabama: and as the citizens of Alabama may unquestionably purchase bills of exchange in that state, it is insisted that the members of this corporation are entitled to the same privilege, and cannot be deprived of it even by express provisions in the Constitution or laws of the state. The case of the Bank of the United States *vs.* Deveaux, 5 Cranch, 61, is relied on to support this position.

It is true, that in the case referred to, this Court decided that in a question of jurisdiction they might look to the character of the persons composing a corporation; and if it appeared that they were citizens of another state, and the fact was set forth by proper averments, the corporation might sue in its corporate name in the Courts of the United States. But in that case the Court confined its decision, in express terms, to a question of jurisdiction; to a right to sue; and evidently went even so far with some hesitation. We fully assent to the propriety of that decision; and it has ever since been recognised as authority in this Court. But the principle has never been extended any farther than it was carried in that case; and has never been supposed to extend to contracts made by a corporation; especially in another sovereignty. If it were held to embrace contracts, and that the members of a corporation were to be regarded as individuals carrying on business in their corporate name, and therefore entitled to the privileges of citizens in matters of contract, it is very clear that they must at the same time take upon themselves the liabilities of citizens, and be bound by their contracts in like manner. The result of this would be to make a corporation a mere partnership in business, in which each stockholder would be liable to the whole extent of his property for the debts of the corporation; and he might be sued for them, in any state in which he might happen to be found. The clause of the Constitution referred to certainly never intended to give to the citizens of each state the privileges of citizens in the several states, and at the same time to exempt them from the liabilities which the exercise of such privileges would bring upon individuals who were citizens of the state. This would be to give the citizens of other states far higher and greater privileges than are enjoyed by the citizens of the state itself. Besides, it would deprive every state of all control over the extent of corporate franchises proper to be granted in the state; and corporations would be chartered in one, to carry on their operations in another. It is impossible upon any sound principle to give such a construction to the article in question. Whenever a corporation makes a contract, it is the contract of the legal entity; of the artificial being created by the charter; and not the contract of the individual members. The only rights it can claim are the rights which are given to it in that character, and not the rights which belong to its members as citizens of a state: and we now proceed to inquire what rights the plaintiffs in error, a corporation created by Georgia, could lawfully exercise in another state; and whether the purchase of the bill of exchange on which this suit is brought was a valid contract, and obligatory on the parties.

The nature and character of a corporation created by a statute, and the extent of the powers which it may lawfully exercise, have upon several occasions been under consideration in this Court.

In the case of Head and Amory *vs.* the Providence Insurance Company, 2 Cranch, 127, Chief Justice Marshall, in delivering the opinion of the Court, said, "without ascribing to this body, which in its corporate capacity is the mere creature of the act to which it owes its existence, all the qualities and disabilities annexed by the common law to ancient institutions of this sort, it may correctly be said to be precisely what the incorporating act has made it; to derive all its powers from that act, and to be capable of exerting its faculties only in the manner which that act authorizes.

"To this source of its being, then, we must recur to ascertain its powers; and to determine whether it can complete a contract by such communications as are in this record."

In the case of Dartmouth College *vs.* Woodward, 4 Wheat. 636, the same principle was again decided by the Court. "A corporation," said the Court, "is an artificial being, invisible, intangible, and existing only in contemplation of law. Being a mere creature of the law, it possesses only those properties which the charter of its creation confers upon it, either expressly, or as incidental to its very existence."

And in the case of the Bank of the United States *vs.* Dandridge, 12 Wheat. 64, where the questions in relation to the powers of corporations and their mode of action, were very carefully considered; the Court said, "But whatever may be the implied powers of aggregate corporations by the common law, and the modes by which those powers are to be carried into operation; corporations created by statute, must depend both for their powers and the mode of exercising them, upon the true construction of the statute itself."

It cannot be necessary to add to these authorities. And it may be safely assumed that a corporation can make no contracts, and do no acts either within or without the state which creates it, except such as are authorized by its charter; and those acts must also be done, by such officers or agents, and in such manner as the charter authorizes. And if the law creating a corporation, does not, by the true construction of the words used in the charter, give it the right to exercise its powers beyond the limits of the state, all contracts made by it in other states would be void.

The charter of the Bank of Augusta authorizes it, in general terms, to deal in bills of exchange; and, consequently, gives it the power to purchase foreign bills as well as inland; in other words, to purchase bills payable in another state. The power thus given, clothed the corporation with the right to make contracts out of the state, in so far as Georgia could confer it. For whenever it purchased a foreign bill, and forwarded it to an agent to present for acceptance, if it was honoured by the drawee, the contract of acceptance was necessarily made in another state; and the general power to purchase bills without any restriction as to place, by its fair and natural import, authorized the bank to make such purchases, wherever it was found most convenient and profitable to the institution; and also to employ suitable agents for that purpose. The purchase of the bill in question was, therefore, the exercise of one of the powers which the bank possessed under its charter; and was sanctioned by the law of Georgia creating the corporation, so far as that state could authorize a corporation to exercise its powers beyond the limits of its own jurisdiction.

But it has been urged in the argument, that notwithstanding the powers thus conferred by the terms of the charter, a corporation, from the very nature of its being, can have no authority to contract out of the limits of the state; that the laws of a state can have no extra-territorial operation; and that as a corporation is the mere creature of a law of the state, it can have no existence beyond the limits in which that law operates; and that it must necessarily be incapable of making a contract in another place.

It is very true that a corporation can have no legal existence out of the boundaries of the sovereignty by which it is created. It exists only in contemplation of law, and by force of the law; and where that law ceases to operate, and is no longer obligatory, the corporation can have no existence. It must dwell in the place of its creation, and cannot migrate to another sovereignty. But although it must live and have its being in that state only, yet it does not by any means follow that its existence there will not be recognised in other places; and its residence in one state creates no insuperable objection to its power of contracting in another. It is indeed a mere artificial being, invisible and intangible; yet it is a person, for certain purposes in contemplation of law, and has been recognised as such by the decisions of this Court. It was so held in the case of The United States *vs.* Amedy, 11 Wheat. 412, and in Beaston *vs.* The Farmer's Bank of Delaware, 12 Peters, 135. Now, natural persons through the intervention of agents, are continually making contracts in countries in which they do not reside; and where they are not personally present when the contract is made; and nobody has ever doubted the validity of these agreements. And what greater objection can there be to the capacity of an artificial person, by its agents, to make a contract within the scope of its limited powers, in a sovereignty in which it does not reside; provided such contracts are permitted to be made by them by the laws of the place?

The corporation must no doubt show, that the law of its creation gave it authority to make such contracts, through such agents. Yet, as in the case of a natural person, it is not necessary that it should actually exist in the sovereignty in which the contract is made. It is sufficient that its existence as an artificial person, in the state of its creation, is acknowledged and recognised by the law of the nation where the dealing takes place; and that it is permitted by the laws of that place to exercise there the powers with which it is endowed.

Every power, however, of the description of which we are speaking, which a corporation exercises in another state, depends for its validity upon the laws of the sovereignty in which it is exercised; and a corporation can make no valid contract without their sanction, express or implied. And this brings us to the question which has been so elaborately discussed; whether, by the comity of nations and between these states, the corporations of one state are permitted to make contracts in another. It is needless to enumerate here the instances in which, by the general practice of civilized countries, the laws of the one, will, by the comity of nations, be recognised and executed in another, where the right of individuals are concerned. The cases of contracts made in a foreign country are familiar examples; and Courts of justice have always expounded and executed them, according to the laws of the place in which they were made; provided that law was not repugnant to the laws or policy of their own country. The comity thus extended to other nations is no impeachment of sovereignty. It is the voluntary act of the nation by which it is offered; and is inadmissible when contrary to its policy, or prejudicial to its interests. But it contributes so largely to promote justice between individuals, and to produce a friendly intercourse between the sovereignties to which they belong; that Courts of justice have continually acted upon it, as a part of the voluntary law of nations. It is truly said, in Story's Conflict of Laws, 37, that "In the silence of any positive rule, affirming, or denying, or restraining the operation of foreign laws, Courts of justice presume the tacit adoption of them by their own government; unless they are repugnant to its policy, or prejudicial to its interests. It is not the comity of the Courts, but the comity of the nation which is administered, and ascertained in the same way, and guided by the same reasoning by which all other principles of municipal law are ascertained and guided."

Adopting, as we do, the principle here stated, we proceed to inquire whether, by the comity of nations, foreign corporations are permitted to make contracts within their jurisdiction; and we can perceive no sufficient reason for excluding them, when they are not contrary to the known policy of the state, or injurious to its interests. It is nothing more than the admission of the existence of an artificial person created by the law of another state, and clothed with the power of making certain contracts. It is but the usual comity of recognising the law of another state. In England, from which we have received our general principles of jurisprudence, no doubt appears to have been entertained of the right of a foreign corporation to sue in its Courts; since the case Henriquez *vs.* The Dutch West India Company, decided in 1729, 2 L. Raymond, 1532. And it is a matter of history, which this Court are bound to notice, that corporations, created in this country, have been in the open practice for many years past, of making contracts in England of various kinds, and to very large amounts; and we have never seen a doubt suggested there of the validity of these contracts, by any Court or any jurist. It is impossible to imagine that any Court in the United States would refuse to execute a contract, by which an American corporation had borrowed money in England; yet if the contracts of corporations made out of the state by which they were created, are void, even contracts of that description could not be enforced.

It has, however, been supposed that the rules of comity between foreign nations do not apply to the states of this Union; that they extend to one another no other rights than those which are given by the Constitution of the United States; and that the Courts of the general government are not at liberty to presume, in the absence of all legislation on the subject, that a state has adopted the comity of nations towards the other states, as a part of its jurisprudence; or that it acknowledges any rights but those which are secured by the Constitution of the United States. The Court think otherwise. The intimate union of these states, as members of the same great political family; the deep and vital interests which bind them so closely together; should lead us, in the absence of proof to the contrary, to presume a greater degree of comity, and friendship, and kindness towards one another, than we should be authorized to presume between foreign nations. And when (as without doubt must occasionally happen) the interest or policy of any state requires it to restrict the rule, it has but to declare its will, and the legal presumption is at once at an end. But until this is done, upon what grounds could this Court refuse to administer the law of international comity between these states? They are sovereign states; and the history of the past, and the events which are daily occurring, furnish the strongest evidence that they have adopted towards each other the laws of comity in their fullest extent. Money is frequently borrowed in one state, by a corporation created in another. The numerous banks established by different states are in the constant habit of contracting and dealing with one another. Agencies for corporations engaged in the business of insurance and of banking have been established in other states, and suffered to make contracts without any objection on the part of the state authorities. These usages of commerce and trade have been so general and public, and have been practised for so long a period of time, and so generally acquiesced in by the states, that the Court cannot overlook them when a question like the one before us is under consideration. The silence of the state authorities, while these events are passing before them, show their assent to the ordinary laws of comity which permit a corporation to make contracts in another state. But we are not left to infer it merely from the general usages of trade, and the silent acquiescence of the states. It appears from the cases cited in the argument, which it is unnecessary to recapitulate in this opinion; that it has been decided in many of the state Courts, we believe in all of them where the question has arisen, that a corporation of one state may sue in the Courts of another. If it may sue, why may it not make a contract? The right to sue is one of the powers which it derives from its charter. If the Courts of another country take notice of its existence as a corporation, so far as to allow it to maintain a suit, and permit it to exercise that power; why should not its existence be recognised for other purposes, and the corporation permitted to exercise another power which is given to it by the same law and the same sovereignty—where the last mentioned power does not come in conflict with the interest or policy of the state? There is certainly nothing in the nature and character of a corporation which could justly lead to such a distinction; and which should extend to it the comity of suit, and refuse to it the comity of contract. If it is allowed to sue, it would of course be permitted to compromise, if it thought proper, with its debtor; to give him time; to accept something else in satisfaction; to give him a release; and to employ an attorney for itself to conduct its suit. These are all matters of contract, and yet are so intimately connected with the right to sue, that the latter could not be effectually exercised if the former were denied.

We turn in the next place to the legislation of the states.

So far as any of them have acted on this subject, it is evident that they have regarded the comity of contract, as well as the comity of suit, to be a part of the law of the state, unless restricted by statute. Thus a law was passed by the state of Pennsylvania, March 10, 1810, which prohibited foreigners and foreign corporations from making contracts of insurance against fire, and other losses mentioned in the law. In New York, also, a law was passed, March 18, 1814, which prohibited foreigners and foreign corporations from making in that state insurances against fire; and by another law, passed April 21, 1818, corporations chartered by other states are prohibited from keeping any office of deposit for the purpose of discounting promissory notes, or carrying on any kind of business which incorporated banks are authorized by law to carry on. The prohibition of certain specified contracts by corporations in these laws, is by necessary implication an admission that other contracts may be made by foreign corporations in Pennsylvania, and New York; and that no legislative permission is necessary to give them validity. And the language of these prohibitory acts most clearly indicates that the contracts forbidden by them might lawfully have been made before these laws were passed.

Maryland has gone still farther in recognising this right. By a law passed in 1834, that state has prescribed the manner in which corporations not chartered by the state, "which shall transact or shall have transacted business" in the state, may be sued in its Courts upon contracts made in the state. The law assumes in the clearest manner, that such contracts were valid, and provides a remedy by which to enforce them.

In the legislation of Congress, also, where the states and the people of the several states are all represented, we shall find proof of the general understanding in the United States, that by the law of comity among the states, the corporations chartered by one were permitted to make contracts in the others. By the act of Congress of June 23, 1836, (4 Story's Laws, 2445,) regulating the deposits of public money, the Secretary of the Treasury was authorized to make arrangements with some bank or banks, to establish an agency in the states and territories where there was no bank, or none that could be employed as a public depository, to receive and disburse the public money which might be directed to be there deposited. Now if the proposition be true that a corporation created by one state cannot make a valid contract in another, the contracts made through this agency in behalf of the bank, out of the state where the bank itself was chartered, would all be void, both as respected the contracts with the government and the individuals who dealt with it. How could such an agency, upon the principles now contended for, have performed any of the duties for which it was established?

But it cannot be necessary to pursue the argument further. We think it is well settled, that by the law of comity among nations, a corporation created by one sovereignty is permitted to make contracts in another, and to sue in its Courts; and that the same law of comity prevails among the several sovereignties of this Union. The public and well known, and long continued usages of trade; the general acquiescence of the states; the particular legislation of some of them, as well as the legislation of Congress; all concur in proving the truth of this proposition.

But we have already said that this comity is presumed from the silent acquiescence of the state. Whenever a state sufficiently indicates that contracts which derive their validity from its comity are repugnant to its policy, or are considered as injurious to its interests; the presumption in favour of its adoption can no longer be made. And it remains to inquire, whether there is any thing in the constitution or laws of Alabama, from which this Court would be justified in concluding that the purchase of the bill in question was contrary to its policy.

The constitution of Alabama contains the following provisions in relation to banks. "One state bank may be established, with such number of branches as the General Assembly may from time to time deem expedient, provided that no branch bank shall be established, nor bank charter renewed, under the authority of this state, without the concurrence of two-thirds of both houses of the General Assembly; and provided also that not more than one bank or branch bank shall be established, nor bank charter renewed, but in conformity to the following rules:

"1. At least two-fifths of the capital stock shall be reserved for the state.

"2. A proportion of power, in the direction of the bank, shall be reserved to the state, equal at least to its proportion of stock therein.

"3. The state and individual stockholders shall be liable respectively for the debts of the bank, in proportion to their stock holden therein.

"4. The remedy for collecting debts shall be reciprocal, for and against the bank.

"5. No bank shall commence operations until half of the capital stock subscribed for be actually paid in gold and silver; which amount shall, in no case, be less than one hundred thousand dollars."

Now from these provisions in the constitution, it is evidently the policy of Alabama to restrict the power of the legislature in relation to bank charters, and to secure to the state a large portion of the profits of banking, in order to provide a public revenue; and also to make safe the debts which should be contracted by the banks. The meaning too in which that state used the word bank, in her constitution, is sufficiently plain from its subsequent legislation. All of the banks chartered by it, are authorized to receive deposits of money, to discount notes, to purchase bills of exchange, and to issue their own notes payable on demand to bearer. These are the usual powers conferred on the banking corporations in the different states of the Union; and when we are dealing with the business of banking in Alabama, we must undoubtedly attach to it the meaning in which it is used in the constitution and laws of the state. Upon so much of the policy of Alabama, therefore, in relation to banks as is disclosed by its constitution, and upon the meaning which that state attaches to the word bank, we can have no reasonable doubt. But before this Court can undertake to say that the discount of the bill in question was illegal, many other inquiries must be made, and many other difficulties must be solved. Was it the policy of Alabama to exclude all competition with its own banks by the corporations of other states? Did the state intend, by these provisions in its constitution, and these charters to its banks, to inhibit the circulation of the notes of other banks, the discount of notes, the loan of money, and the purchase of bills of exchange? Or did it design to go still further, and forbid the banking corporations of other states from making a contract of any kind within its territory? Did it mean to prohibit its own banks from keeping mutual accounts with the banks of other states, and from entering into any contract with them, express or implied? Or did she mean to give to her banks the power of contracting within the limits of the state with foreign corporations, and deny it to individual citizens? She may believe it to be the interest of her citizens to permit the competition of other banks in the circulation of notes, in the purchase and sale of bills of exchange, and in the loan of money. Or she may think it to be her interest to prevent the circulation of the notes of other banks; and to prohibit them from sending money there to be employed in the purchase of exchange, or making contracts of any other description.

The state has not made known its policy upon any of these points. And how can this Court, with no other lights before it, undertake to mark out by a definite and distinct line the policy which Alabama has adopted in relation to this complex and intricate question of political economy? It is true that the state is the principal stockholder in her own banks. She has created seven; and in five of them the state owns the whole stock; and in the others two-fifths. This proves that the state is deeply interested in the successful operation of her banks, and it may be her policy to shut out all interference with them. In another view of the subject, however, she may believe it to be her policy to extend the utmost liberality to the banks of other states; in the expectation that it would produce a corresponding comity in other states towards the banks in which she is so much interested. In this respect it is a question chiefly of revenue, and of fiscal policy. How can this Court, with no other aid than the general principles asserted in her constitution, and her investments in the stocks of her own banks, undertake to carry out the policy of the state upon such a subject in all of its details, and decide how far it extends, and what qualifications and limitations are imposed upon it? These questions must be determined by the state itself, and not by the Courts of the United States. Every sovereignty would without doubt choose to designate its own line of policy; and would never consent to leave it as a problem to be worked out by the Courts of the United States, from a few general principles, which might very naturally be misunderstood or misapplied by the Court. It would hardly be respectful to a state for this Court to forestall its decision, and to say, in advance of her legislation, what her interest or policy demands. Such a course would savour more of legislation than of judicial interpretation.

If we proceed from the constitution and bank charters to other acts of legislation by the state, we find nothing that should lead us to a contrary conclusion. By an act of Assembly of the state, passed January 12th, 1827, it was declared unlawful for any person, body corporate, company, or association, to issue any note for circulation as a bank note, without the authority of law; and a fine was imposed upon any one offending against this statute. Now this act protected the privileges of her own banks, in relation to bank notes only; and contains no prohibition against the purchase of bills of exchange, or against any other business by foreign banks, which might interfere with her own banking corporations. And if we were to form our opinion of the policy of Alabama from the provisions of this law, we should be bound to say that the legislature deemed it to be the interest and policy of the state not to protect its own banks from competition in the purchase of exchange, or in any thing but the issuing of notes for circulation. But this law was repealed by a subsequent law, passed in 1833, repealing all acts of Assembly not comprised in a digest then prepared and adopted by the legislature. The law of 1827 above mentioned was not contained in this digest, and was consequently repealed. It has been said at the bar, in the argument, that it was omitted from the digest by mistake, and was not intended to be repealed. But this Court cannot act judicially upon such an assumption. We must take their laws and policy to be such as we find them in their statutes. And the only inference that we can draw from these two laws, is, that after having prohibited under a penalty any competition with their banks by the issue of notes for circulation, they changed their policy, and determined to leave the whole business of banking open to the rivalry of others. The other laws of the state, therefore, in addition to the constitution and charters, certainly would not authorize this Court to say, that the purchase of bills by the corporations of another state was a violation of its policy.

The decisions of its judicial tribunals lead to the same result. It is true that in the case of The State *vs.* Stebbins, 1 Stewart's Alabama Reports, 312, the Court said that since the adoption of their constitution, banking in that state was to be regarded as a franchise. And this case has been much relied on by the defendant in error.

Now we are satisfied, from a careful examination of the case, that the word franchise was not used, and could not have been used by the Court in the broad sense imputed to it in the argument. For if banking includes the purchase of bills of exchange, and all banking is to be regarded as the exercise of a franchise, the decision of the Court would amount to this—that no individual citizen of Alabama could purchase such a bill. For franchises are special privileges conferred by government upon individuals, and which do not belong to the citizens of the country, generally, of common right. It is essential to the character of a franchise that it should be a grant from the sovereign authority, and in this country no franchise can be held which is not derived from a law of the state.

But it cannot be supposed that the constitution of Alabama intended to prohibit its merchants and traders from purchasing or selling bills of exchange; and to make it a monopoly in the hands of their banks. And it is evident that the Court of Alabama, in the case of The State *vs.* Stebbins, did not mean to assert such a principle. In the passage relied on they are speaking of a paper circulating currency, and asserting the right of the state to regulate and to limit it.

The institutions of Alabama, like those of the other states, are founded upon the great principles of the common law; and it is very clear that at common law, the right of banking in all of its ramifications, belonged to individual citizens; and might be exercised by them at their pleasure. And the correctness of this principle is not questioned in the case of The State *vs.* Stebbins. Undoubtedly, the sovereign authority may regulate and restrain this right: but the constitution of Alabama purports to be nothing more than a restriction upon the power of the legislature, in relation to banking corporations; and does not appear to have been intended as a restriction upon the rights of individuals. That part of the subject appears to have been left, as is usually done, for the action of the legislature, to be modified according to circumstances; and the prosecution against Stebbins was not founded on the provisions contained in the constitution, but was under the law of 1827 above mentioned, prohibiting the issuing of bank notes. We are fully satisfied that the state never intended by its constitution to interfere with the right of purchasing or selling bills of exchange; and that the opinion of the Court does not refer to transactions of that description, when it speaks of banking as a franchise.

The question then recurs—Does the policy of Alabama deny to the corporations of other states the ordinary comity between nations? or does it permit such a corporation to make those contracts which from their nature and subject matter, are consistent with its policy, and are allowed to individuals? In making such contracts a corporation no doubt exercises its corporate franchise. But it must do this whenever it acts as a corporation, for its existence is a franchise. Now it has been held in the Court of Alabama itself, in 2 Stewart's Alabama Reports, 147, that the corporation of another state may sue in its Courts; and the decision is put directly on the ground of national comity. The state therefore has not merely acquiesced by silence, but her judicial tribunals have declared the adoption of the law of international comity in the case of a suit. We have already shown that the comity of suit brings with it the comity of contract; and where the one is expressly adopted by its Courts, the other must also be presumed according to the usages of nations, unless the contrary can be shown.

The cases cited from 7 Wend. 276, and from 2 Rand. 465, cannot influence the decision in the case before us. The decisions of these two state Courts were founded upon the legislation of their respective states, which was sufficiently explicit to enable their judicial tribunals to pronounce judgment on their line of policy. But because two states have adopted a particular policy in relation to the banking corporations of other states, we cannot infer that the same rule prevails in all of the other states.

Each state must decide for itself. And it will be remembered, that it is not the state of Alabama which appears here to complain of an infraction of its policy. Neither the state, nor any of its constituted authorities, have interfered in this controversy. The objection is taken by persons who were parties to those contracts; and who participated in the transactions which are now alleged to have been in violation of the laws of the state.

It is but justice to all the parties concerned to suppose that these contracts were made in good faith, and that no suspicion was entertained by either of them that these engagements could not be enforced. Money was paid on them by one party, and received by the other. And when we see men dealing with one another openly in this manner, and making contracts to a large amount, we can hardly doubt as to what was the generally received opinion in Alabama at that time, in relation to the right of the plaintiffs to make such contracts. Every thing now urged as proof of her policy, was equally public and well known when these bills were negotiated. And when a Court is called on to declare contracts thus made to be void upon the ground that they conflict with the policy of the state; the line of that policy should be very clear and distinct to justify the Court in sustaining the defence. Nothing can be more vague and indefinite than that now insisted on as the policy of Alabama. It rests altogether on speculative reasoning as to her supposed interests; and is not supported by any positive legislation. There is no law of the state which attempts to define the rights of foreign corporations.

We, however, do not mean to say that there are not many subjects upon which the policy of the several states is abundantly evident, from the nature of their institutions, and the general scope of their legislation; and which do not need the aid of a positive and special law to guide the decisions of the Courts. When the policy of a state is thus manifest, the Courts of the United States would be bound to notice it as a part of its code of laws; and to declare all contracts in the state repugnant to it, to be illegal and void. Nor do we mean to say whether there may not be some rights under the Constitution of the United States, which a corporation might claim under peculiar circumstances, in a state other than that in which it was chartered. The reasoning, as well as the judgment of the Court, is applied to the matter before us; and we think the contracts in question were valid, and that the defence relied on by the defendants cannot be sustained.

The judgment of the Circuit Court in these cases, must therefore be reversed with costs.

Philip Pendleton Barbour

☆ 1783–1841 ☆

APPOINTED BY

ANDREW JACKSON

YEARS ON COURT

1836–1841

Philip Pendleton Barbour

by

FRANK OTTO GATELL

VIRGINIA PARTICULARISM, the defense of state sovereignty and southern rights in the early nineteenth century, proved a failure. The perspective of more than a century puts the movement and its leaders almost in the same camp as their ideological opposites, the New England Federalists. As anachronisms, the men of both the Essex Junto and the Richmond Junto seem to have been by-passed by American history, as the United States emerged as a democratic, urban society well beyond the calculations of either group. For the Virginians, the name of Judge Spencer Roane is frequently cited, taking up what little of the historical limelight is available. Other Virginians of like mind and similar politics have not fared so well. Among the forgotten confederates were many men prominent in their day, upholders of Old Republican principles, traditionalists at a time when the country was probably in its period of greatest economic and social change. Philip P. Barbour was as representative a Virginia strict constructionist as can be found.

Barbour's ancestry was old-line Virginian. His great-grandfather, James Barbour, was a Scottish merchant who settled in Virginia in the seventeenth century. Philip's father, Thomas Barbour, married Mary Pendleton Thomas, thus the important family connection which gave Philip his middle name. Thomas Barbour was a wealthy planter of Orange County, a member of the House of Burgesses and a signer of the 1769 Virginia Association which banned the importation of British goods. Philip was born on May 25, 1783, but by that time his family's finances were not what they had been. Thomas had spent money too liberally, and Philip did not receive the kind of schooling usually afforded to a son of the Virginia aristocracy. Nevertheless, in the local schools he displayed a remarkable talent for his studies, especially in languages and in the classics. Justice Story, eulogizing Barbour in 1841, wrote: "Even in the

FRANK O. GATELL, Professor of History at the University of California, Los Angeles, is the author of John Gorham Palfrey and the New England Conscience.

performance of the tasks of a country school, he manifested that precision of information and depth of research, which, on a broader theatre, and carried to higher subjects, won for him a wide-spread and enduring reputation."

After a short period of studying law, Barbour moved to Kentucky in 1800. Here the self-taught lawyer attempted to practice his profession, but within a year he was back in Virginia. He borrowed some money and attended William and Mary College for a few months. In 1802 he resumed his law practice, this time in his native state. With all respect to Barbour's brilliance and scholarly aptitudes, his easy entrance into the legal profession reveals much about the liberal admission standards for lawyers which prevailed at that time. He did well enough at his work to marry, two years later, Frances Johnson, the daughter of an Orange County planter. For the next eight years Barbour occupied himself with an increasingly successful law practice.

In 1812, at the age of 29, Barbour entered politics. He was elected a member of the House of Delegates from Orange County. He had apparently acquired enough of a reputation to earn for himself several important committee assignments. In two years of service in the legislature he was a member of the judiciary and finance committees. And since Barbour's assembly terms coincided with the War of 1812, he also took a prominent part in the legislature's responses to that conflict. Barbour, along with other delegates who were elated over some American naval victories, proposed that the state lend the federal government funds to build a large ship of the line, but the bill did not pass. In the legislative special session of 1813, Barbour served on a committee formed to consider defense measures. The legislature did agree to end the exemption from military service then allowed to college students, but happily for the state no British invasion materialized.

Barbour's elevation to national office came with his election to the United States House of Representatives in 1814. Thus after only two years in politics he had moved from the state to the national level. He did this more quickly than most politicians of his era, since it was then more customary than now for a man to spend half a dozen or so years in the state legislature before moving up to Congress. When Barbour took his seat that year the hegemony of the Virginia dynasty still did not appear threatened. Virginians had occupied the Presidency for all but four years of the nation's short history, and President Monroe's two terms lay ahead. The Virginia delegation to Congress in 1814 was an impressive one, and despite changes in the economy which pointed to the rise of rival states, especially those outside of the South, many people thought that a new generation of Virginia statesmen would arise to maintain the state's domination over the country's political affairs. Among the Virginia members of Congress was Senator James Barbour, Philip's older brother. The two men were to take different paths politically in the 1820's, but at this time both were still states' rights Republicans, and it is reasonable to presume that James Barbour, who had been governor during the two years Philip served in the legislature, had aided his younger brother's rapid political climb.

A sign that times were changing, even within the Virginia dynasties, was that leading national officeholders, including Presidents Madison and later Monroe, began to support or acquiesce in elements of national legislation which were then coming to be known as the American System. From other states, such outstanding leaders as Henry Clay and John C. Calhoun supported measures giving the federal government and its agencies increased power, and in some cases Virginia's Presidents did little to oppose them. The Barbour family itself split, with James supporting nationalistic programs, a policy which eventually earned him a place in John Quincy Adams' Cabinet. But Philip remained true to his conception of pure Virginia principles. Strict construction, respect for the reserved rights of the sovereign states, and fear of federal encroachment were the guiding views of the Old Republicans. John Taylor of Caroline supplied the philosophy; Spencer Roane the judicial pronouncements; Thomas Ritchie the journalistic reiteration; and Philip Barbour, among others in Congress, the vigilance which was the price of Virginia liberty.

Barbour's constitutional conservatism emerged clearly in his response to the issue of federally sponsored internal improvement projects. Most of his congressional speeches stressed the constitutional questions involved in the subject. This was certainly true of the 1817 Bonus Bill which would have subsidized a network of roads and canals by setting aside the government's bonus paid by the Bank of the United States. One of the specific projects was a road from Buffalo to New Orleans, through Washington. Barbour ridiculed the measure, calling it "a bill to construct a road from the liberties of the country by way of Washington to despotism." He admitted the desirability of improvement projects as such, but since the federal government did not possess the power to undertake such ventures, matters of expediency should not be allowed to outweigh what he considered to be a clear constitutional prohibition. Although the bill passed the House and the Senate by narrow votes, President Madison vetoed it on constitutional grounds.

In January, 1819, the House debated a motion to censure General Andrew Jackson for his overly energetic military actions in Spanish Florida. Barbour spoke to the issue and against the censure resolution. He promised that whenever a case arose of a military man trampling the Constitution to gratify personal ambition he would lead the movement to punish the offender: "for I, too, love my country, I, too, love its Constitution . . . the ark of our political salvation." But in the present instance, the issues were anything but simple, as evidenced by the division in the House: "the officer concerned [Jackson] was called upon to decide, in the wilds of Florida, upon a state of things not anticipated . . . in which that officer whose distinguished services have identified his name with the character of his country, has . . . no ambition, but one, to serve his country . . . ; in such a case as this . . . I will not vote for censure, for I weigh the acts of every moral agent by the intention." As for the two British subjects, Arbuthnot and Ambrister, hanged by Jackson, they had aided the Indians in waging war against the United States, and it was Arbuthnot who had "poured the secret poison of discontent in the minds of the Indians." The men could not have been tried either in the United States or England. Their punishment, so well merited, had to be severe and swiftly administered at the spot. Barbour's apologia for Jackson continued, with suitable quotations and citations from Vattel and other authorities. He would not censure Jackson because "he has only executed the sentence of the law; because he has carried into effect the public justice of the country; and because an act conformable to law, and in accordance with the principles of justice, even if you call it stern justice, cannot be *morally wrong.*"

Barbour was one of the chief spokesmen in defense of southern rights during the early stages of the debate over the admission of Missouri. He and Henry Clay rushed to counter the arguments of restrictionist northerners such as James Talmadge and John W. Taylor, the New Yorkers who were leading the attempt in the House of Representatives to keep slavery out of the incoming state of Missouri. The first part of Barbour's major speech, delivered in February, 1819, dealt with the constitutionality of the proposed restriction. Needless to say, Barbour considered the measure unconstitutional. Congress could admit new states, but not a species of semi-sovereign or limited states. "This term State," he explained, "has a fixed and determinate meaning; in itself, it imports the existence of a political community, free and independent, and entitled to exercise all the rights of sovereignty, of every description whatever." The American states had, it was true, given up something in forming the Union, they were "shorn of many of their beams of sovereignty," such as declaring war, or coining money, but the question of the existence or nonexistence of slavery was preeminently a matter for the individual states to decide.

The anti-slavery restriction on one incoming state would be the unwise precedent for further encroachments. Barbour also specifically dismissed the applicability of the Confederation government's 1787 Northwest Ordinance. It did not bind the states north of the Ohio River, which might introduce slavery within their boundaries at any time. This was sound constitutional doctrine, and equally interesting was the fact that in these territorial debates, southern spokesmen such as Barbour seemed to be allowing full congressional power to regulate local matters in territories, a position which an increasing number of southerners would spurn in the 1850's.

Following the constitutional disquisition, Barbour marshalled anti-restrictionist arguments which were based on "every consideration of humanity, of justice, and sound policy." This might be called the sociological section of the speech. He echoed Clay's words concerning the desirability of diffusing slavery over all the country's area, or at a minimum over half of it. This was best for all, and mostly for the slaves themselves, who "although they were held as property, yet they were considered and treated as the most valuable, as the most favored property; their masters remembered that they were men, and although certainly degraded in the scale of society . . . we felt for them those sympathies which bind one man to another, though the other may be our inferior." Thus if the master moved westward, he would take his slaves with him, both from affection and the need for labor in the wilderness.

To prohibit slavery in Missouri meant effectively to prohibit the emigration of southerners to that state. But apparently the affection the owner felt for his slave had not created a state of perfect reciprocity, because Barbour then went on to discuss slave insurrection. Diffusion would act to protect American society from that threat, reducing the dangerous concentrations of blacks which existed in some regions. A scattered slave population would be less prone to revolt and easier to suppress should such insurrection occur. Not that Barbour himself felt threatened; he reported "no alarm upon that subject at present," and he "slept quietly in his bed, notwithstanding the apprehension which some gentlemen seemed to entertain." But no one could tell what the future might bring. "We have no power to enact the proposed [restriction] amendment," he concluded, "and if we had, it would be highly impolitic and unjust."

Barbour was happiest while upholding the constitutionality of the South's position, not while defending the particulars of slavery as a social system. In February, 1820, during the second Missouri debate he warned: "This is neither the time nor the occasion for the discussion of the abstract justice or injustice of slavery. . . . We are the creatures of the Constitution, not its creators; we are called here to execute, not to make one. Let gentlemen, then, remember that it is not sufficient for them to show that slavery cannot be justified in itself; . . . they will yet fail to maintain their ground, unless they can also show that the Constitution gives us power over it." The proposed restriction of slavery in Missouri, he argued, would violate both the Constitution and the Louisiana Purchase treaty of 1803—the latter point would be developed by Justice John Catron thirty-seven years later in his *Dred Scott* opinion.

It was Barbour's contention that the arguments of the northern restrictionists were an indication of the dangerous current of constitutional latitudinarianism abroad in the land. Delegated powers were coming to mean authorization for anything the federal government wished to undertake. There was no end in sight. Every accretion of power, every expansion of a specified grant pointed to an ever greater role for the national government. He concluded by warning that state sovereignty, within its constituted spheres, was the cement of the Union. To tamper with this threatened the whole structure: "Let it not be supposed that I come here as the apostle of disunion. . . . But, whilst I deprecate disunion as the most tremendous evil, I cannot shut my eyes against the light of experience." The western territories represented opportunity but peril as well. Barbour predicted that they might become "the theatre on which the title to itself may be decided, not by Congressional debate . . . but by that force which always begins when constitutions end."

Such pessimistic views about the declining power of the states undoubtedly were based partially on reactions to some of the decisions of the Marshall Court. Barbour was one of two counsel who appeared for his state in the celebrated case, *Cohens* v. *Virginia,* 6 Wheat. 264 (1821). The state senate had resolved that the counsel for Virginia were to argue only the question of jurisdiction. State courts had convicted two Baltimoreans for illegally selling tickets for a District of Columbia lottery in Virginia, in defiance of state law which banned sale of "foreign" lottery tickets. Before the Supreme Court, Barbour argued that it was not reasonable to regard a law passed for the District to meet local needs as a law of the United States to have effect in all the states. He also maintained that since a state was a party in the case, the Court had no jurisdiction in view of the Eleventh Amendment which prohibited a suit against a state without its consent. He and his co-counsellor, Alexander Smythe, contended that there was no constitutional authority for considering the federal judiciary superior to the state judiciary. Since the lottery law was not meant to extend to Virginia, the Court had no jurisdiction. Marshall, of course, decided that the Court had jurisdiction on the basis of national supremacy, although Virginia "won" the case against the lottery sellers. In terms of a state's rights the net effect of the decision was clear, and three years later, during House debates on a judiciary reform bill, Barbour had still not surrendered to Marshall. According to Webster, that day he "re-argued Cohens' case."

During one of his congressional terms, Barbour served as Speaker of the House. Following Clay's remarkable decade of building up the power of the Speaker, the office went to John W. Taylor of New York in 1820. But southern restiveness over Taylor's nationalistic leanings and support for Adams brought about Barbour's election in 1821. His constitutional orthodoxy, his opposition to the Missouri restriction attempt and to the protective tariff gained him enough votes from his section to secure the election over Taylor. One Washington newspaper spoke of the result as a complete victory for the South, but this overstatement ignored the fact that the election also reflected the battle between the Adams and Crawford factions with Barbour and most of the southerners favoring the latter. One historian of the office of Speaker dismissed Barbour's term as "narrow and partisan," without giving any substantiation. In any case, it was short. In 1823, Clay reclaimed his office as part of his drive for higher office, and there was little that Barbour could do to parry the Kentuckian's political power and obvious qualifications for the post.

The competition between the two southerners extended into the floor debates. Clay's great speech of January, 1824, in support of internal improvements, was to some extent a reply to Barbour's position in the negative. The clash attracted considerable attention, and a friend of Clay wrote to ask, "How does Mr. Barbour feel towards you after the prodigious beating you gave him?" It is doubtful that Barbour believed he had received a beating, although this exchange, and a similar one on the tariff, did nothing to endear the two men to each other.

Barbour did not stand for reelection to the House in 1824. He returned very briefly to private life. Within a year, Jefferson offered him a law professorship at the newly founded University of Virginia, but Barbour declined. Almost immediately thereafter he accepted a judgeship in the state judicial system, becoming a member of the General Court for the Eastern District of Virginia. He held this post nearly two years, until the solicitations of his Orange County constituents caused him to resign and accept an unopposed nomination for his old seat in Congress. When he returned to the House in December, 1827, he was again a candidate for Speaker. Barbour had much more strength among his colleagues than shown in the vote which elected his fellow Virginian, Andrew Stevenson (Stevenson obtained 104 votes; Barbour 4). Many southerners actually preferred Barbour, but in order to concentrate as many votes as possible against John W. Taylor, the Missouri bill restrictionist from New York, they went along with the Stevenson nomination.

As a member of the Richmond Junto, the Virginia Republican machine, Barbour had with other members of his group switched his political allegiance from Crawford to Jackson. This followed the fall of Crawford's fortunes because of physical disability and the phenomenal rise of Andrew Jackson. Despite the fact that his brother was a member of Adams' Cabinet, Philip Barbour remained an unceasing critic of the administration. A year before the presidential election, in December, 1827, he sought to make the Bank of the United States an issue by introducing a resolution calling on the federal government to sell its one fifth interest in the Bank. His purpose was to demonstrate that the Bank was merely a private institution, enjoying government privileges and investment, not an actual agency of the government. Many pro-Bank observers thought that the introduction of the resolution indicated the start of an anti-Bank campaign by the Jackson men. But Barbour had been premature. His resolution went down overwhelmingly, 174 to 9. The Bank did not become an issue in the campaign of 1828, but Barbour's stand would be remembered later when to a large degree Jacksonian orthodoxy came to be measured by attitudes toward the Bank.

In the wake of Jackson's 1828 victory, Barbour became one of those deserving Democrats frequently mentioned for higher office. His name figured in calculations concerning the makeup of the first Jackson Cabinet. But instead of choosing the prominent southerners who supposedly were in line for Cabinet offers, Jackson's personal desires weighed heavily in the selections. In 1830, Barbour did accept a federal appointment, however, as judge of the Federal District Court for Eastern Virginia. A year later he was once again the subject of speculation over the Cabinet when Jackson reorganized the body in the wake of the Peggy Eaton affair and the Calhoun defection. The post of Attorney General was open, but it went to Roger Taney, soon to become Barbour's chief on the Supreme Court.

During this period, a constitutional convention took place in Virginia with Barbour playing a prominent part. The convention met at Richmond in October, 1829. Barbour became chairman of the committee on the executive department, and when the convention president, ex-President Monroe, resigned because of ill health, the delegates chose Barbour president *pro tem* and then president of the convention. Occupying the place of presiding officer may have cut down on

Barbour's participation in the debates because he was not one of the convention's most frequent speakers.

But during the times he did speak, and in his votes, Barbour was definitely in the conservative camp of the eastern planters. On representation, he showed little sympathy for the contentions and complaints of the westerners. In a speech delivered shortly after the convention opened, he opposed apportionment based solely on white population. Instead he supported a motion that it be based on white population and taxable property combined. He denied that because all men were admitted to be "by nature, equally free," that it followed therefore that "all men are entitled to an equal share of political power." Too many men had confused civil rights with political rights, since, after all, such groups as women, children, aliens, and paupers enjoyed the former but were denied the latter. Government operated upon both persons and property, and it was logical that both persons and property should be represented. "We must rest [the foundation of this constitution] on two great columns: Persons and property. Withdraw either, and you have a weak and tottering edifice, which can never endure the shocks of time."

On suffrage, also, Barbour sought a conservative balance. Restrictions on the exercise of voting rights were certainly legal, but what was desirable? "Is not," he asked rhetorically, "some landed qualification the best surety for such a permanent interest in the community as justly entitles any citizen to the exercise of this right?" Landed wealth differed from other forms. The wealth of Stephen Girard, the Philadelphia merchant and banker, did not belong to the state of Pennsylvania. It could be transferred elsewhere momentarily. But landed property was "visible, tangible, immovable." The relative ease with which a fair amount of property could be acquired in America disposed of the charge that voting qualifications based on real property meant the rise of an American aristocracy. "It places the elective franchise within the reach of every man in the community, who possesses ordinary industry and economy. From such an arrangement, no danger can arise to the liberties of the people." The conservatives gave up some ground on the representation and suffrage questions, but not much. Barbour and his convention associates retained enough control to check the men from the valley and the mountains, at least for several decades.

During the 1832 election, Barbour's loyalty to Jackson underwent a very severe test. Barbour had not dallied with the Calhoun brand of southern orthodoxy, and during the Nullification crisis he assured the administration that Virginia would not follow South Carolina's lead in repudiating Jackson's unionism. The President himself received the prediction from Barbour elatedly, and he wrote to Van Buren that Judge Barbour was "in ecstasy with my message" on nullification. It was Van Buren, not Calhoun, who provided the basis for a possible break between Barbour and Jackson. The President had clearly indicated that he wished Van Buren to succeed him in the White House, and in 1832 this aim could best be served by nominating the New Yorker for the vice-presidency. Most Jacksonians went along, but in the South anti-Van Buren feeling did not disappear easily. Much as Van Buren might point to a political record of Republicanism and due regard for the rights of the states, he remained suspect, perhaps simply because he was a northerner and had been too successful. In Virginia, Barbour's friends in the party's legislative caucus tried unsuccessfully to nominate him for vice-president in March, 1832. But in an informal popular vote Barbour won, and delegates favoring him named a Jackson-Barbour ticket at a meeting in Charlottesville.

The party regulars could not accept this, however. Thomas Ritchie, the editor of the *Richmond Enquirer,* responded by praising Barbour, but he also pointed out that a split Democratic vote would throw the election of vice-president into the Senate and give the choice to the anti-Jackson forces. He tried to induce Barbour to scotch the movement at the start, but Barbour seems to have been biding his time, hoping perhaps that Jackson would reconsider his demand that Van Buren be the man. All through the 1832 summer Barbour remained silent while the boomlet spread to North Carolina, but the pressure applied by the regulars began to tell. In October, Barbour instructed the chairman of his own Jackson-Barbour committee to support the regular nomination. The movement collapsed, and Van Buren had succeeded once again.

By 1835 it was clear that the Marshall Era of Supreme Court history would soon come to an end. Rumors of the Chief Justice's resignation began to circulate as early as 1831, while constitutional nationalists trembled at the thought of who might be named to replace him. John Quincy Adams feared that "if he should be now withdrawn, some shallow-pated wild-cat like Philip P. Barbour, fit for nothing but to tear the Union to rags and tatters, would be appointed in his place." Adams was probably reacting as much to Barbour's anti-administration politics in Congress during 1827–29 as to his judicial qualifications. But such proposals as one made by Barbour in 1829, that a vote of five members of the Supreme Court (there were then seven Justices) be required for decisions in constitutional cases, made him suspect among the nationalists. These negative feelings never entirely disappeared. As late as 1838, a Whig paper referred to "such small lights as have been recently placed on the bench—such shallow metaphysical hair-splitters as P. P. Barbour."

In March, 1836, the apparent reconstruction of the Court which the nationalists had dreaded occurred when the Senate confirmed the nominations of Barbour as Associate Justice and Taney as Chief Justice. Taney's confirmation, coming as it did a year after a negative vote on him as Associate Justice by a Senate controlled by Whigs and Calhoun men, aroused more controversy and received more attention than Barbour's. There were more negative votes in Taney's case. Neither man pleased the Whigs. "But if Mr. Barbour's appointment is extremely objectionable, what can be said of the appointment of Mr. Taney?" asked an exasperated Boston editor. Democrats welcomed the double victory in the Senate. Ritchie in the *Enquirer* extolled Taney, and added, "Barbour, too, the pride of the Democracy of Virginia, is now seated upon the bench of the Supreme Court, which he is so eminently fitted to adorn with his talents and enlighten with his inflexible and uncompromising states' rights principles."

Barbour did not sit on the Court long enough to compile a distinctive and forceful judicial record. In general, he agreed with Chief Justice Taney's lead, the modification of Marshall's judicial nationalism which had contemporary conservatives of the nationalist stamp quaking in their boots, but which in retrospect appears to be anything but revolutionary. Barbour was part of the majority in such cases as *Charles River Bridge* v. *Warren Bridge,* 11 Pet. 420 (1837), and *Briscoe* v. *Bank of Kentucky,* 11 Pet. 257 (1837). In those instances Taney and McLean wrote the opinions.

But it was Barbour who spoke for the Court in *City of New York* v. *Miln,* 11 Pet. 102 (1837). At issue was a New York law providing that masters of ships entering the port of New York from overseas or another state file a report giving information on all persons brought in as passengers. Miln refused, was fined, and his attorneys attacked the state law as an unwarranted regulation of foreign and interstate commerce, subjects for congressional regulation exclusively. Initially, Taney assigned the task of preparing the Court's opinion to Justice Smith Thompson, but when a conference revealed that the majority differed in some points with Thompson, Justice Barbour took on the job.

The heart of Barbour's opinion lay in the contention that the New York law was valid as an exercise of the police power to protect the health and safety of the community. This basic local power was not in dispute, and its exercise by the state sovereignty was accepted by all. But did it apply here? Barbour listed several self-styled "impregnable positions," namely that a state possessed the same unlimited jurisdiction over persons and things, within its territorial limits, as a foreign state; where jurisdiction had not been surrendered constitutionally to the federal government, the state was bound to provide for its general welfare; and that the internal police power had not been surrendered or restrained. "Consequently, in relation to these, the authority of a state is complete, unqualified, and exclusive." The police power, the proper concern with "the welfare of the whole people of a state . . . and upon the persons and things within its jurisdiction," which had received such an important boost from Taney in *Charles River Bridge,* was made additionally secure by Barbour's opinion.

The Miln opinion was the most significant one from Barbour's pen. In 1838, he joined in dissent with Taney and Catron in *Kendall* v. *United States ex rel. Stokes,* 12 Pet. 524 (1838), an important case dealing with judicial supervision of executive acts. The old point of *Marbury* v. *Madison,* a writ of *mandamus* to an executive officer, arose again. The Court upheld the power of circuit courts to issue writs of *mandamus* to government officers compelling them to perform their legally defined duties. The three dissenters demurred at issuing the writ on jurisdictional grounds. In *Holmes* v. *Jennison,* 14 Pet. 540 (1840), the issue was whether the governor of Vermont could deliver over an alleged criminal to Canadian justice. The Court split four to four, thus upholding the state authorities, and in concurring, Barbour expressed clearly his conviction that the Constitution did not define obligations of states to foreign countries. Since no Vermont law or federal treaty was here applicable, the governor (who had the backing of his state supreme court) had complete discretion.

In February, 1841, death came suddenly to Barbour. He had been feeling ill early in the month, but seemed much improved. On the 24th he was back at work, and attended a conference which lasted until ten in the evening. That night he died in his sleep of a heart attack. His colleague, Joseph Story, wrote a very affecting account of Barbour's death to Mrs. Story, a few days later. This judicial nationalist, the direct heir to Marshall's legacy, nevertheless could see in Barbour "a man of great integrity, of a very solid and an acute understanding, of considerable legal attainments (in which he was daily improving), and altogether a very conscientious, upright, and laborious judge, whom we all respected for his talents and virtues, and his high sense of duty."

SELECTED BIBLIOGRAPHY

Philip Barbour awaits the appearance of a biographer, but the absence of a concentrated collection of personal papers will probably deter those interested in undertaking such a worthwhile project. One inadequate article is in print, P. P. Cynn, "Philip Pendleton Barbour," 4 *John P. Branch Historical Papers of Randolph-Macon College* 67 (1913). See also, 15 Peters ii for a biographical eulogy on Barbour by Justice Joseph Story. His legislative career can be traced in the relevant volumes of the congressional debates, and in the report of debates at the Virginia constitutional convention of 1829–1830. Other specific references in print are sketchy and repetitious.

Philip P. Barbour

REPRESENTATIVE OPINIONS

CITY OF NEW YORK v. MILN, 11 PET. 102 (1837)

A New York state law required the masters of all ships to report various information on all passengers landing in the port. The law was challenged on the ground that it regulated foreign commerce and thus was invalid under the commerce clause of the Constitution. Barbour's opinion upheld the law as a legitimate use of the state's police power.

Mr. Justice BARBOUR delivered the opinion of the Court.

This case comes before this Court upon a certificate of division of the circuit court of the United States for the southern district of New York.

It was an action of debt brought in that court by the plaintiff, to recover of the defendant, as consignee of the ship called the Emily, the amount of certain penalties imposed by a statute of New York, passed February 11th, 1824; entitled, An act concerning passengers in vessels coming to the port of New York.

The statute, amongst other things, enacts, that every master or commander of any ship, or other vessel, arriving at the port of New York, from any country out of the United States, or from any other of the United States than the state of New York, shall, within twenty-four hours after the arrival of such ship or vessel in the said port, make a report in writing, on oath or affirmation, to the mayor of the city of New York, or, in case of his sickness, or absence, to the recorder of the said city, of the name, place of birth, and last legal settlement, age and occupation, of every person who shall have been brought as a passenger in such ship or vessel, on her last voyage from any country out of the United States into the port of New York, or any of the United States, and from any of the United States other than the state of New York, to the city of New York, and of all passengers who shall have landed, or been suffered or permitted to land, from such ship, or vessel, at any place, during such her last voyage, or have been put on board, or suffered, or permitted to go on board of any other ship or vessel, with the intention of proceeding to the said city, under the penalty on such master or commander, and the owner or owners, consignee or consignees of such ship or vessel, severally and respectively, of seventy-five dollars for every person neglected to be reported as aforesaid, and for every person whose name, place of birth, and last legal settlement, age, and occupation, or either or any of such particulars, shall be falsely reported as aforesaid, to be sued for and recovered as therein provided.

The declaration alleges that the defendant was consignee of the ship Emily, of which a certain William Thompson was master; and that in the month of August, 1829, said Thompson, being master of such ship, did arrive with the same in the port of New York, from a country out of the United States, and that one hundred passengers were brought in said ship on her then last voyage, from a country out of the United States, into the port of New York; and that the said master did not make the report required by the statute, as before recited.

The defendant demurred to the declaration.

The plaintiff joined in the demurrer, and the following point, on a division of the court, was thereupon certified to this Court, viz.

"That the act of the legislature of New York, mentioned in the plaintiff's declaration, assumes to regulate trade and commerce between the port of New York and foreign ports, and is unconstitutional and void."

It is contended by the counsel for the defendant, that the act in question is a regulation of commerce; that the power to regulate commerce is, by the constitution of the United States, granted to congress; that this power is exclusive, and that consequently, the act is a violation of the constitution of the United States.

On the part of the plaintiff it is argued, that an affirmative grant of power previously existing in the states to congress, is not exclusive; except 1st, where it is so expressly declared in terms, by the clause giving the power; or 2dly, where a similar power is prohibited to the states; or 3dly, where the power in the states would be repugnant to, and incompatible with, a similar power in congress: that this power falls within neither of these predicaments; that it is not, in terms, declared to be exclusive; that it is not prohibited to the states; and that it is not repugnant to, or incompatible with, a similar power in congress; and that having preexisted in the states, they therefore have a concurrent power in relation to the subject; and that the act in question would be valid, even if it were a regulation of commerce, it not contravening any regulation made by congress.

But they deny that it is a regulation of commerce: on the contrary, they assert that it is a mere regulation of internal police, a power over which is not granted to congress; and which therefore, as well upon the true construction of the constitution, as by force of the tenth amendment to that instrument, is reserved to, and resides in the several states.

We shall not enter into any examination of the question whether the power to regulate commerce, be or be not exclusive of the states, because the opinion which we have formed renders it unnecessary: in other words, we are of opinion that the act is not a regulation of commerce, but of police; and that being thus considered, it was passed in the exercise of a power which rightfully belonged to the states.

That the state of New York possessed power to pass this law before the adoption of the constitution of the United States, might probably be taken as a truism, without the necessity of proof. But as it may tend to present it in a clearer point of view, we will quote a few passages from a standard writer upon public law, showing the origin and character of this power.

Vattel, book 2d, chap. 7th, sec. 94. "The sovereign may forbid the entrance of his territory, either to foreigners in general, or in particular cases, or to certain persons, or for certain particular purposes, according as he may think it advantageous to the state."

Ibid. chap. 8, sec. 100. "Since the lord of the territory may, whenever he thinks proper, forbid its being entered, he has, no doubt, a power to annex what conditions he pleases, to the permission to enter."

The power then of New York to pass this law having undeniably existed at the formation of the constitution, the simple inquiry is, whether by that instrument it was taken from the states, and granted to congress; for if it were not, it yet remains with them.

If, as we think, it be a regulation, not of commerce, but police; then it is not taken from the states. To decide this, let us examine its purpose, the end to be attained, and the means of its attainment.

It is apparent, from the whole scope of the law, that the object of the legislature was, to prevent New York from being burdened by an influx of persons brought thither in ships, either from foreign countries, or from any other of the states; and for that purpose a report was required of the names, places of birth, &c. of all passengers, that the necessary steps might be taken by the city authorities, to prevent them from becoming chargeable as paupers.

Now, we hold that both the end and the means here used, are within the competency of the states, since a portion of their powers were surrendered to the federal government. Let us see what powers are left with the states. The Federalist, in the 45th number, speaking of this subject, says; the powers reserved to the several states, will extend to all the objects, which in the ordinary course of affairs, concern the lives, liberties, and properties of the people; and the internal order, improvement, and prosperity of the state.

And this Court, in the case of Gibbons *v.* Ogden, 9 Wheat. 203, which will hereafter be more particularly noticed, in speaking of the inspection laws of the states, say; they form a portion of that immense mass of legislation which embraces every thing within the territory of a state, not surrendered to the general government, all which can be most advantageously exercised by the states, themselves. Inspection laws, quarantine laws, health laws of every description, as well as laws for regulating the internal commerce of a state, and those which respect turnpike roads, ferries, &c., are component parts of this mass.

Now, if the act in question be tried by reference to the delineation of power laid down in the preceding quotations, it seems to us that we are necessarily brought to the conclusion, that it falls within its limits. There is no aspect in which it can be viewed in which it transcends them. If we look at the place of its operation, we find it to be within the territory, and, therefore, within the jurisdiction of New York. If we look at the person on whom it operates, he is found within the same territory and jurisdiction. If we look at the persons for whose benefit it was passed, they are the people of New York, for whose protection and welfare the legislature of that state are authorized and in duty bound to provide.

If we turn our attention to the purpose to be attained, it is to secure that very protection, and to provide for that very welfare. If persons whose rights and whose duties are rightfully prescribed and controlled by the laws of the respective states within whose territorial limits they are found: in that, say the Court, the act of a state came into direct collision with an act of the United States; in this, no such collision exists.

Nor is there the least likeness between the facts of this case, and those of Brown against The State of Maryland. The great grounds upon which the Court put that case were:—that sale is the object of all importation of goods; that, therefore, the power to allow importation, implied the power to authorize the sale of the thing imported: that a penalty inflicted for selling an article in the character of importer, was in opposition to the act of congress, which authorized importation under the authority to regulate commerce: that a power to tax an article in the hands of the importer the instant it was landed, was the same in effect as a power to tax it whilst entering the port; that, consequently, the law of Maryland was obnoxious to the charge of unconstitutionality, on the ground of its violating the two provisions of the constitution; the one giving to congress the power to regulate commerce, the other forbidding the states from taxing imports.

In this case, it will be seen that the discussion of the Court had reference to the extent of the power given to congress to regulate commerce, and to the extent of the prohibition upon the states from imposing any duty upon imports. Now it is difficult to perceive what analogy there can be between a case where the right of the state was inquired into, in relation to a tax imposed upon the sale of imported goods, and one where, as in this case, the inquiry is as to its right over persons within its acknowledged jurisdiction; the goods are the subject of commerce, the persons are not: the Court did indeed extend the power to regulate commerce, so as to protect the goods imported from a state tax after they were landed, and were yet in bulk; but why? Because they were the subjects of commerce; and because, as the power to regulate commerce, under which the importation was made, implied a right to sell; that right was complete, without paying the state for a second right to sell, whilst the bales or packages were in their original form. But how can this apply to *persons?* They are not the subject of commerce; and, not being *imported goods,* cannot fall within a train of reasoning founded upon the construction of a power given to congress to regulate commerce, and the prohibition to the states from imposing a duty on imported goods.

Whilst, however, neither of the points decided in the cases thus referred to, is the same with that now under consideration, and whilst the general scope of the reasoning of the Court in each of them, applies to questions of a different nature; there is a portion of that reasoning in each which has a direct bearing upon the present subject, and which would justify measures on the part of states, not only approaching the line which separates regulations of commerce from those of police, but even those which are almost identical with the former class, if adopted in the exercise of one of their acknowledged powers. In Gibbons against Ogden, 9 Wheaton, 204, the Court say, if a state, passing laws on a subject acknowledged to be within its control, and, with a view to those subjects, shall adopt a measure of the same character with one which congress may adopt; it does not derive its authority from the particular power which has been granted, but from some other which remains with the state, and may be executed by the same means. All experience shows that the same measures, or measures scarcely distinguishable from each other, may flow from distinct powers; but this does not prove that the powers are identical. Although the means used in their execution may sometimes approach each other, so nearly as to be confounded, there are other situations in which they are sufficiently distinct to establish their individuality.

In page 209, the Court say:—Since, however, in regulating their own purely internal affairs, whether of trading or of police, the states may sometimes enact laws, the validity of which depends on their interfering with, and being contrary to an act of congress passed in pursuance of the constitution; they would inquire whether there was such collision in that case, and they came to the conclusion that there was.

From this it appears, that whilst a state is acting within the legitimate scope of its power as to the end to be attained, it may use whatsoever means, being appropriate to that end, it may think fit; although they may be the same, or so nearly the same, as scarcely to be distinguishable from those adopted by congress acting under a different power: subject, only, say the Court, to this limitation, that in the event of collision, the law of the state must yield to the law of congress. The Court must be understood, of course, as meaning that the law of congress is passed upon a subject within the sphere of its power.

Even then, if the section of the act in question could be considered as partaking of the nature of a commercial regulation, the principle here laid down would save it from condemnation, if no such collision exist.

It has been contended, at the bar, that there is that collision; and in proof of it we have been referred to the revenue act of 1799, and to the act of 1819, relating to passengers. The whole amount of the provision in relation to this subject, in the first of these acts, is to require, in the manifest of a cargo of goods, a statement of the names of the passengers, with their baggage, specifying the number and description of packages belonging to each respectively: now it is apparent, as well from the language of this provision, as from the context, that the purpose was to prevent goods being imported without paying the duties required by law, under the pretext of being the baggage of passengers.

The act of 1819, contains regulations obviously designed for the comfort of the passengers themselves: for this purpose it prohibits the bringing more than a certain number proportioned to the tonnage of the vessel, and prescribes the kind and quality of provisions, or sea stores, and their quantity, in a certain proportion to the number of the passengers.

Another section requires the master to report to the collector a list of all passengers, designating the age, sex, occupation, the country to which they belong, &c.; which list is required to be delivered to the secretary of state, and which he is directed to lay before congress.

The object of this clause, in all probability, was to enable the government of the United States, to form an accurate estimate of the increase of population by emigration; but whatsoever may have been its purpose, it is obvious, that these laws only affect, through the power over navigation, the passengers whilst on their voyage, and until they shall have landed. After that, and when they have ceased to have any connexion with the ship, and when, therefore, they have ceased to be *passengers;* we are satisfied, that acts of congress, applying to them as such, and only professing to legislate in relation to them *as such,* have then performed their office, and can, with no propriety of language, be said to come into conflict with the law of a state, whose operation only begins when that of the laws of congress ends; whose operation is not even on the same subject, because although the person on whom it operates is the same, yet having ceased to be a *passenger,* he no longer stands in the only relation in which the laws of congress either professed or intended to act upon him.

There is, then, no collision between the law in question, and the acts of congress just commented on; and, therefore, if the state law were to be considered as partaking of the nature of a commercial regulation; it would stand the test of the most rigid scrutiny, if tried by the standard laid down in the reasoning of the Court, quoted from the case of Gibbons against Ogden.

But we do not place our opinion on this ground. We choose rather to plant ourselves on what we consider impregnable positions. They are these: That a state has the same undeniable and unlimited jurisdiction over all persons and things, within its territorial limits, as any foreign nation; where that jurisdiction is not surrendered or restrained by the constitution of the United States. That, by virtue of this, it is not only the right, but the bounden and solemn duty of a state, to advance the safety, happiness and prosperity of its people, and to provide for its general welfare, by any and every act of legislation, which it may deem to be conducive to these ends; where the power over the particular subject, or the manner of its exercise is not surrendered or restrained, in the manner just stated. That all those powers which relate to merely municipal legislation, or what may, perhaps, more properly be called *internal police,* are not thus surrendered or restrained; and that, consequently, in relation to these, the authority of a state is complete, unqualified, and exclusive.

We are aware, that it is at all times difficult to define any subject with proper precision and accuracy; if this be so in general, it is emphatically so in relation to a subject so diversified and multifarious as the one which we are now considering.

If we were to attempt it, we should say, that every law came within this description which concerned the welfare of the whole people of a state, or any individual within it; whether it related to their rights, or their duties; whether it respected them as men, or as citizens of the state; whether in their public or private relations; whether it related to the rights of persons, or of property, of the whole people of a state, or of any individual within it; and whose operation was within the territorial limits of the state, and upon the persons and things within its jurisdiction. But we will endeavour to illustrate our meaning rather by exemplification, than by definition. No one will deny, that a state has a right to punish any individual found within its jurisdiction, who shall have committed an offence within its jurisdiction, against its criminal laws. We speak not here of foreign ambassadors, as to whom the doctrines of public law apply. We suppose it to be equally clear, that a state has as much right to guard, by anticipation, against the commission of an offence against its laws, as to inflict punishment upon the offender after it shall have been committed. The right to punish, or to prevent crime, does in no degree depend upon the citizenship of the party who is obnoxious to the law. The alien who shall just have set his foot upon the soil of the state, is just as subject to the operation of the law, as one who is a native citizen. In this very case, if either the master, or one of the crew of the Emily, or one of the passengers who were landed, had, the next hour after they came on shore, committed an offence, or indicated a disposition to do so; he would have been subject to the criminal law of New York, either by punishment for the offence committed, or by prevention from its commission where good ground for apprehension was shown, by being required to enter into a recognisance with surety, either to keep the peace, or be of good behaviour, as the case might be; and if he failed to give it, by liability to be imprisoned in the discretion of the competent authority. Let us follow this up to its possible results. If every officer, and every seaman belonging to the Emily, had participated in the crime, they would all have been liable to arrest and punishment; although, thereby, the vessel would have been left without either commander or crew. Now why is this? For no other reason than this, simply, that being within the territory and jurisdiction of New York, they were liable to the laws of that state, and amongst others, to its criminal laws; and this too, not only for treason, murder, and other crimes of that degree of atrocity, but for the most petty offence which can be imagined.

It would have availed neither officer, seaman, or passenger, to have alleged either of these several relations in the recent voyage across the Atlantic. The short but decisive answer would have been, that we know you now only as offenders against the criminal laws of New York, and being now within her jurisdiction, you are now liable to the cognisance of those laws. Surely the officers and seamen of the vessel have not only as much, but more concern with navigation than a passenger; and yet, in the case here put, any and every one of them would be held liable. There would be the same liability, and for the same reasons, on the part of the officers, seamen, and passengers to the civil process of New York, in a suit for the most trivial sum; and if, according to the laws of that state, the party might be arrested and held to bail, in the event of his failing to give it, he might be imprisoned until discharged by law.

Here, then, are the officers and seamen, the very agents of navigation, liable to be arrested and imprisoned under civil process, and to arrest and punishment under the criminal law.

But the instrument of navigation, that is, the vessel, when within the jurisdiction of the state, is also liable by its laws to execution. If the state have a right to vindicate its criminal justice against the officers, seamen, and passengers who are within its jurisdiction, and also, in the administration of its civil justice, to cause process of execution to be served on the body of the very agents of navigation, and also on the instrument of navigation, under which it may be sold, because they are within its jurisdiction and subject to its laws; the same reasons, precisely, equally subject the master, in the case before the Court, to liability for failure to comply with the requisitions of the section of the statute sued upon. Each of these laws depends upon the same principle for its support; and that is, that it was passed by the state of New York, by virtue of her power to enact such laws for her internal police as it deemed best; which laws operate upon the persons and things within her territorial limits, and therefore within her jurisdiction.

Now in relation to the section in the act immediately before us, that is obviously passed with a view to prevent her citizens from being oppressed by the support of multitudes of poor persons, who come from foreign countries without possessing the means of supporting themselves. There can be no mode in which the power to regulate internal police could be more appropriately exercised. New York, from her particular situation, is, perhaps more than any other city in the Union, exposed to the evil of thousands of foreign emigrants arriving there, and the consequent danger of her citizens being subjected to a heavy charge in the maintenance of those who are poor. It is the duty of the state to protect its citizens from this evil; they have endeavoured to do so, by passing, amongst other things, the section of the law in question. We should, upon principle, say that it had a right to do so.

Let us compare this power with a mass of power, said by this Court in Gibbons against Ogden, not to be surrendered to the general government. They are inspection laws, quarantine laws, health laws of every description, as well as laws for regulating the internal commerce of a state, &c. To which it may be added, that this Court, in Brown against The State of Maryland, admits the power of a state to direct the removal of gunpowder, as a branch of the police power, which unquestionably remains, and ought to remain with the states.

It is easy to show, that if these powers, as is admitted, remain with the states, they are stronger examples than the one now in question. The power to pass inspection laws, involves the right to examine articles which are imported, and are, therefore, directly the subject of commerce; and if any of them are found to be unsound, or infectious, to cause them to be removed, or even destroyed. But the power to pass these inspection laws, is itself a branch of the general power to regulate internal police.

Again, the power to pass quarantine laws, operates on the ship which arrives, the goods which it brings, and all persons in it, whether the officers and crew, or the passengers; now the officers and crew are the agents of navigation; the ship is an instrument of it, and the cargo on board is the subject of commerce: and yet it is not only admitted, that this power remains with the states, but the laws of the United States expressly sanction the quarantines, and other restraints which *shall be required and established by the health laws of any state;* and declare that they shall be duly observed by the collectors and all other revenue officers of the United States.

We consider it unnecessary to pursue this comparison further; because we think, that if the stronger powers under the necessity of the case, by inspection laws and quarantine laws to delay the landing of a ship and cargo, which are the subjects of commerce and navigation, and to remove or even to destroy unsound and infectious articles, also the subject of commerce, can be rightfully exercised; then, that it must follow as a consequence, that powers less strong, such as the one in question, which operates upon no subject either of commerce or navigation, but which operates alone within the limits and jurisdiction of New York upon a person, at the time not even engaged in navigation, is still more clearly embraced within the general power of the states to regulate their own internal police, and to take care that no detriment come to the commonwealth.

We think it as competent and as necessary for a state to provide precautionary measures against the moral pestilence of paupers, vagabonds, and possibly convicts as it is to guard against the physical pestilence, which may arise from unsound and infectious articles imported, or from a ship, the crew of which may be labouring under an infectious disease.

As to any supposed conflict between this provision and certain treaties of the United States, by which reciprocity as to trade and intercourse is granted to the citizens of the governments, with which those treaties were made; it is obvious to remark, that the record does not show that any person in this case was a subject or citizen of a country to which treaty stipulation applies: but, moreover, those which we have examined, stipulate that the citizens and subjects of the contracting parties shall submit themselves to the laws, decrees, and usages to which native citizens and subjects are subjected.

We are therefore of opinion, and do direct it to be certified to the circuit court for the southern district of New York, that so much of the section of the act of the legislature of New York, as applies to the breaches assigned in the declaration, does not assume to regulate commerce between the port of New York and foreign ports; and that so much of said section is constitutional.

We express no opinion on any other part of the act of the legislature of New York; because no question could arise in the case in relation to any part of the act, except that declared upon.

John Catron

☆ 1786(?)–1865 ☆

APPOINTED BY

ANDREW JACKSON

YEARS ON COURT

1837–1865

John Catron

by

FRANK OTTO GATELL

THERE IS A DEARTH of information about John Catron's early years. Not even the date or place of his birth have been clearly established. The best that can be said is that he was probably born about 1786 in Pennsylvania, of German ancestry on his father's side. He spent some childhood years in Virginia and then moved to Kentucky where he stayed until 1812. His background was apparently one of poverty, and whatever education he obtained was either self-taught or came late in life. He next went to Tennessee, in the area near the Cumberland Mountains. After service during the War of 1812 under General Jackson, Catron was admitted to the bar in 1815. He combined both general practice with service as a prosecuting attorney in one of the circuits of his region. Three years later, in 1818, he moved to Nashville and became one of the leaders of that ambitious corps of lawyer-politicians, the Davidson County bar.

Tennessee's highest court was then called the Supreme Court of Errors and Appeals. In 1824 the legislature increased the number of judges on this court and then elected Catron to the seat. Tradition had it that an impasse among the judges over land laws, and the knowledge on the part of the legislature of Catron's views on such litigation, produced both the court's expansion and the specific appointment. Whatever the cause, Catron had already built up a solid reputation in this specialty of the law, and land litigation represented probably the most important issue in the courts of Tennessee at that time. In his years on the state bench, Catron helped establish principles of judicial response to these questions and thus ensure a satisfactory resolution of the problems arising from conflicting claims to land. When in 1831 the legislature created the office of Chief Justice of the state supreme court, Catron received the honor. He held this

FRANK O. GATELL, Professor of History at the University of California, Los Angeles, is the author of John Gorham Palfrey and the New England Conscience.

seat until 1834. In that year, the new state constitution reorganized the judicial system, abolishing the Court of Errors and Appeals. Catron resigned and briefly left the bench for private practice.

During the 1820's, Catron had been busy in more fields than the law. As a businessman, he invested a good deal of his money in the iron industry. In 1827, Catron, his brother, and another partner purchased the Buffalo Iron Works. George Catron acted as manager, but John was the real moving spirit, and he supplied most of the capital. The business was profitable, partly because the state government encouraged the industry's spread through land and tax subsidies. The Works had the use of ten thousand acres, and when Catron sold out his interest in 1833 he received close to $20,000 for it. He later reinvested in a smaller amount, but did not become as intimately involved in the operation as had been previously the case. On the political front, Catron worked hard at the intricate and shifting politics of Tennessee, both before and after his election to the state court. He emerged as one of the leading Jackson men, not at the absolute top rank but important enough to have his counsels heard if not always heeded.

One of Catron's better-known state court opinions was *State* v. *Smith,* 9 Tenn. 228 (1829), a case concerning duelling. The defendant, an attorney, had accepted a challenge to a duel in Tennessee, and went to Kentucky for the affair, where he killed his opponent. The circuit court had disbarred him, but Smith appealed to the supreme court which affirmed the lower court's judgment. There was just cause for such disbarment, wrote Catron in a stinging opinion against duelling. The state had every right and even a duty to "restrain the blind and criminal passions that drive to ruin the fearless and valuable man; to restrain the wicked vanity of the noisy coxcomb; and to protect from his misguided fears of giddy and idle ridicule the physically weak and nervous man." For such commendable reasons, and more, "have mankind generally, and Tennessee in particular, legislated to punish duelling. . . ." He ridiculed the contention that death in a duel, or inflicting it, was no more than "a kind of honorable homicide! The law knows it as a wicked and wilful murder, and it is our duty to treat it as such. We are placed here firmly and fearlessly to execute the laws of the land, not visionary codes of honor, framed to subserve the purposes of destruction."

Another case in the field of social customs was *State* v. *Smith and Lane,* 10 Tenn. 272, also decided in 1829. Here, Catron ruled that selling tickets for a private lottery violated the state laws against illegal forms of gambling, and in doing so, his style transcended the norms of judicial writing to achieve what must be described as oratorical flights on the printed page. For example: "Like other passions, which agitate the great mass of the community, it [the passion to gamble] lies dormant until once aroused, and then, with the contagion and fury of pestilence, it sweeps morals, motives to honest pursuits and industry into the vortex of vice; unhinges the principles of religion and common honesty; the mind becomes ungovernable, and is destroyed to all useful purposes; chances of successful gambling alone are looked to for prosperity in life . . . ; trembling anxiety for success in lotteries, at the faro bank or loo table, exclude all other thoughts . . . the highly excited and desperate feelings are kindled by drunkenness, from which arises a wretch, with a wrecklessness and desolation of feeling, that the genius of a Shakespeare or a Milton could not, nor can any man describe. . . . The most profligate and abandoned wickedness and profanity, not elsewhere known or heard of . . . are heard at the gaming table . . .; moral man and savage beast seem there to be reduced to a level. . . ." Enough. Even Thomas Hart Benton, the Missouri Democrat and uncrowned king of bombastic rhetoric, could not have bested Catron in this *argumentum ad horrendum.*

A more important case, *Fisher's Negroes* v. *Dabbs,* 14 Tenn. 119 (1834), had to do with the right of emancipation, and the status of free Negroes. The manumission clauses of wills were valid, Catron wrote, but the deed created "an imperfect right, until the State, the community of which such emancipated person is to become a member, assents to the contract between the master and the slave." Emancipation was serious business, and society as a whole had an interest in it. "Degraded by their color and condition in life, the free negroes are a very dangerous and most objectionable population where slaves are numerous. Therefore no slave can be safely freed but with the assent of the government where the manumission takes place." What status then did the free Negro possess in Tennessee? Socially, it was intolerable, since "the slave, who receives the protection and care of a tolerable master, holds a condition here, superior to the negro who is freed from domestic slavery. . . . The free black man lives amongst us without motive and without hope." Thus Catron declared that the manumission granted in the will under examination would be allowed only if the freed Negroes were sent to Liberia. Removal to other states of the Union, even supposing that other states would accept the South's emancipated Negroes, was no answer: "Nothing can be more untrue than that the free negro is more respectable as a member of society in the non-slaveholding, than in the slaveholding States. In each, he is a degraded outcast, and his fancied freedom a delusion. . . . Generally, and almost universally, society suffers, and the negro suffers by manumission."

Catron's judicial status did not prevent him from entering into one of the touchiest political imbroglios of his day, the fight against the Bank of the United States. Several months before Jackson sent to Congress his first message which criticized the Bank, Catron published a series of newspaper articles in Nashville, leaving no doubt about the judge's anti-Bank feelings. The articles appeared in June, 1829, in the form of a series of letters addressed to "the cultivators of the soil and laboring people of Tennessee." Catron's targets were the loan practices and alleged usury of the Nashville branch of the Bank. In attacking the institution, Catron ran through a commercial and financial chamber of horrors: the Bank charged up to 10% per month; it squeezed money out of the State of Tennessee for the benefit of easterners at an alarming rate; it owned enormous parcels of property; it held tyrannical sway over the supply of specie in the state;

it was exempt from state taxation. In short, the Bank could control, if it did not in fact already do so, the economic well-being of the citizens of Tennessee. This was exploitation by a foreign money power. A possible remedy lay in the fact that the question of recharter would come up soon. Biddle was immensely anxious to obtain a recharter, wrote Catron, before the expiration date of 1836. Specifically, Catron pointed out that the Tennessee legislature might vote on a resolution regarding recharter of the Bank at the next session. Thus the issue should be aired and resolved in the context of the next legislative elections.

Catron was not entirely negative. He opposed the Bank of the United States, but a truly national banking institution seemed feasible at the time. His substitute plan, not surprisingly, gave more power to the states. Branches were to be established, for example, only with permission of the host states; and branch capital should come from within the host state only. Also the state legislatures should appoint the directors of branches, and the same legislatures could tax the branches at reasonable rates fixed by charter. The Bank issue had been relatively quiet during the second half of the 1820's, and as if to anticipate and parry the charge of gratuitously stirring up conflicts, Catron argued that the conflict with the Bank had never died out; "Some of us, gentlemen, have for years been pledged to stand together boldly and firmly, when the day should arrive for the execution of a policy new in these States, and which is to be great in effect, I grant, but we have counted the cost."

The response of political opponents and friends of the Bank was immediate and predictable. The National Republican press attacked Catron's plan and commentaries as a transparent attempt to influence the forthcoming elections in favor of Jacksonian candidates. Also Catron was accused of echoing Jackson's anti-Bank views because several judgeships, either in the federal system or the chief justiceship of the state supreme court were the objects of his ambition. All of this took place before Jackson's anti-Bank message in December. That summer, Judge Catron's articles sounded out popular sentiment on the Bank and prepared the ground for the later assault against Biddle and his institution. He probably acted in concert with the principal Jacksonians of Tennessee in making this exploratory probe. Whatever the validity of the "inside" details, Catron did shortly thereafter become chief justice of the state supreme court.

The Indian controversies of Jackson's first administration are usually associated almost exclusively with the state of Georgia. But the Cherokee Nation's lands also included portions of other states, and Tennessee was one of them. In Georgia, the state legislature had extended its jurisdiction into the Indian areas despite adverse rulings by the United States Supreme Court. Georgia's defiance and Jackson's advocacy of Indian removal beyond the Mississippi combined to prevent enforcement of the Court's decisions. Tennessee emulated its neighbor state. In November, 1833, in the face of Marshall's decision in *Worcester* v. *Georgia,* 6 Pet. 515 (1832), the Tennessee legislature passed laws assuming state jurisdiction over the Indian area in the southeastern corner of the state. According to a legislative report, "the general controlling authority over the

Indians," was a state matter, certainly so in such questions as crimes and contracts, Chief Justice Marshall notwithstanding. Two years later, in 1835, the state supreme court decided *State* v. *Foreman,* 16 Tenn. 256 (1835), and addressed itself to this issue of federal relations. The defendant in a murder case denied that state courts had jurisdiction since both he and the dead man were Indians and the act had been committed within the Indian territory. Thus the plea was entered that the state law of 1833 was unconstitutional.

Catron upheld the state law in a massive opinion which takes up one hundred and fourteen pages in Yerger's *Tennessee Reports.* The Chief Justice read the Indians a history lesson about the white man's rights on this continent: "In 1497, John Cabot, a Venetian, then residing in England. . . ." etc., etc. No European powers had allowed the aborigines political rights; their claims to sovereignty were enforced by the sword. "From the opening of the first crusade, to this day, it is amongst the most curious and most prominent truths in the history of man." The civilizing process was not to be denied nor disparaged, since "it was more just that the country should be peopled by Europeans, than continue the haunts of savage beasts, and of men yet more fierce and savage." Civilized men should not be misled by misapplied pity for "mere wandering tribes of savages," who had failed to cultivate the soil in their possession; such creatures "deserve to be exterminated as savage and pernicious beasts." Progress demanded that these people, acting as roadblocks to civilization, be pushed aside. These are strong words, and probably hateful ones, for a twentieth century reader; but there can be little doubt that Chief Justice Catron in speaking so frankly was not out of step with the majority of his fellow Tennesseeans. He was not totally unaware of the humanitarian counterarguments to these views, but these he rejected as impracticable: "The philosopher and jurist of the quiet city, may easily prove, that such a people had undoubted rights of soil and of sovereignty; and sympathy and eloquence may, as in the Cherokee case, powerfully urge their adoption on the courts of justice," the latter a reference to *Worcester* v. *Georgia, supra.* But these sophistries overlooked the prime consideration, that for the European it had been a matter of conquer or perish. The rejection of the second alternative was neither unwise nor immoral. "Our claim is based on the right to coerce obedience. The claim may be denounced by the moralist. We answer, it is the law of the land. Without its assertion and vigorous execution, this continent never could have been inhabited by our ancestors."

These repeated statements show that the moral objections to "conquer-or-perish" troubled Catron. But what was left if it were to be abandoned? Logic would then demand a confession of usurpation and a return to Europe. What Catron failed to do here, despite his history lesson, was to speak of changed conditions of life among some of the Indian tribes. Charges of unmitigated barbarism and ferocity against the Cherokees of the 1830's simply did not reflect the reality of tribal adaptation, especially to the need for cultivation of the soil which Catron extolled as the apparent hallmark of civilized status. The Cherokees, he argued, could not be separated from all the other tribes, particularly the savages of the trans-Mississippi West. The Cherokees' "is not a case of conscience before this court, but a case of law." By this time, the reader must respectfully decline to accept the validity of the justice's pleading. The case seems less one of law than of the rationalization of power.

Then, in page after page, Catron defended the state's authority over the lands within its boundaries. The states had full jurisdiction over Indians when they entered the Union. All they had delegated to Congress in the Constitution was the right to regulate commerce with Indian tribes. Commerce here, as in the case of all delegated powers, must be construed strictly, applying only to actual commercial traffic and intercourse. But "in the execution of this power, congress had extended its legislation not to the Indian boundary, but over the Indian nation; assuming jurisdiction, not only over the regulation of commerce, but for the general punishment of crime." Also, the constitutional prohibition against the creation of a new state—that is, a new sovereignty—within a state's territory without consent of that state, meant that an Indian sovereignty could not be created within Tennessee. Congressional encroachment upon state jurisdiction could not be permitted. Catron did refer to the status of the Cherokees at that moment in history, but disparagingly: "The Cherokees are overrun by the whites, their government is broken up and suppressed by Georgia, their few people within our limits are so scattered and feeble, as not only to be incapable of self-government, but they are wholly incapable of protecting themselves, or the whites among them. . . . Theirs is, emphatically, a land without law, if our laws do not reach it, and so to all appearance it must remain." The legislature had acted within its powers to prevent lawlessness in part of the state. This was the judicial gloss on the frontier's *fait accompli.*

Catron's handling of this case conformed perfectly to his Jacksonian political views, but was at variance with an opinion handed down several years before. In *Cornet* v. *Winton,* 10 Tenn. 143 (1826), which involved title to land originally owned by an Indian, Catron had made several appreciative comments on Cherokee civilization: "The Cherokees have at all times, since we knew any thing of their history, had a government of their own . . . ; and in 1819 were, and now are, far removed from the mere wandering and wild savage." "They are in truth a nation of people under the tutelage of the Government of the United States." Even stronger was Catron's conclusion which attacked "the early notions of the Spaniards and others" that Indians were mere beasts without rights of any kind. These "have long since been exploded, as the result of avarice, fraud, and rapacity." The Cherokees did have rights, "which rights, I am proud to say, have for the last thirty years, been respected with that good faith on our part, that became us as honest men and christians." But in *State* v. *Foreman, supra,* Catron ignored *his* previous opinion to cite Judge John Haywood's dissenting opinion which had held against the Indians' rights! The passage of nine years, and the intervening politics of Indian removal had a marked effect on Catron's jurisprudence. He fully expected the *Foreman* case to go up to the United States Supreme Court, and suggested to Governor Newton Cannon that the legislature prepare for such an appeal and appoint counsel. But the final agreement by the remaining Cherokees to move westward removed the opportunity and necessity for such an appeal. What the Taney Court would have done with the case remains a tantalizing uncertainty.

The year's respite from the bench gave Catron the chance to give undivided attention to political matters. During the election of 1836 he directed Martin Van Buren's campaign in Tennessee. The year before, Catron had appealed directly to Jackson to shelve the vice-presidential candidacy of Richard M. Johnson because of Johnson's well-known relationship with a female slave: "We must not in this great and I trust final battle against thirty-five millions of money [the Bank of the United States], against uncompromising nullification, against a scheme of protection, and of its correlative, waste by internal improvements, think of humoring third rate politicians from a state flatly against us." Van Buren did win the election, Johnson or no, and Catron's hard work and political loyalty earned him a nomination to the United States Supreme Court, one of Jackson's final acts as President. On his last day in office, March 3, 1837, Jackson announced Catron's appointment and that of another man, John McKinley, in response to congressional enlargement of the Court from seven to nine members. Catron was then fifty-one years old.

Catron just missed participating in the cases decided at the famous term of 1837, but the issues confronted at that time had not been settled definitively and would reappear in later years. On the commerce clause, Catron followed a reasonable line between the federal and state power, with a preferential bias in favor of the latter. In the *License Cases,* 5 How. 504 (1847), he presented two separate opinions, one for each case, upholding the state laws in question. The laws sought to limit the importation of liquor both from foreign countries and other states. According to him "the police power was not touched by the Constitution, but left to the States as the Constitution found it." Subjects which were legitimate objects of such local legislation could be regulated, congressional action to the contrary notwithstanding. Even on subjects clearly within the operation of the federal commerce power, if the national government had failed to act, the states might proceed to regulate. If the Framers had intended that the federal commerce power be exclusive, they would have declared so plainly in the Constitution. Not only should an exclusive power not be inferred constitutionally, but as a practical matter, thought Catron, it would have seriously damaging consequences since for over sixty years the states had been acting in the field. Such a course would "expunge more State laws and city corporate regulations than Congress is likely to make in a century on the same subject." Likewise, regarding foreign commerce, Catron argued that once resale or repackaging took place the imports were subject to state regulation. The state laws in the *License Cases* had encroached on no laws of Congress, and were thus valid.

That Catron took seriously his view of the critical importance of congressional action can be seen in his response to the *Passenger Cases,* 7 How. 283 (1849). He was with the majority which invalidated state laws taxing immigrants because of conflict with acts of Congress. He also wrote that state laws passed as revenue acts in the field of commerce, were regulatory as well, and if they conflicted with federal laws they must be held invalid. Three years later, in *Cooley* v. *Board of Wardens,* 12 How. 299 (1851), Catron agreed with Curtis' majority opinion that uniform regulation was necessary only in areas which required an exclusive federal power. Otherwise, the states could act although they might incidentally operate upon foreign or interstate commerce.

Corporate powers was another area in which Catron sought to protect state rights, although his reaction here was a bit delayed. He concurred, without a separate opinion, in *Bank of Augusta* v. *Earle,* 13 Pet. 519 (1839) and in *Louisville Railroad Co.* v. *Letson,* 2 How. 497(1844), two cases which greatly aided in giving national scope to the operations of corporations. But in cases involving canal and railroad companies in 1852 and 1853, he dissented from what he considered an excessive view of expanding corporate rights. (*Rundle* v. *The Delaware and Raritan Canal Co.,* 14 How. 79 [1852] and *Marshall* v. *Baltimore & Ohio Railroad Co.,* 16 How. 314 [1853]. Justices Daniel and Campbell attacked federal jurisdiction in corporation cases, *per se,* but Catron strove to reach a middle ground. He did not accept the notion that all stockholders of a corporation could be regarded as a collective citizen. The president and board members were the potential litigants, and should be responsible for the acts of the corporation. Moreover, if these officers were citizens of the chartering state, they should be allowed recourse to federal courts in suits against citizens of other states. This reasonable use of federal jurisdiction also furthered the cause of justice, since federal courts were less biased regarding local interests than the state courts, whose "judges and juries . . . are inhabitants of the cities where the suit must be tried, . . . [*and where litigants must*] contend with powerful corporations, in local courts, where the chances of impartial justice would be greatly against them; and where no prudent man would engage with such an antagonist, if he could help it." Catron also took the opportunity in the second case, *Marshall* v. *Baltimore & Ohio Railroad Co.,* to declare that he had "at all times denied that a corporation is a citizen within the sense of the Constitution."

The Ohio Bank cases of 1854 provided further opportunity for expressions concerning the subordination of corporate rights to state sovereignty and the popular will. When in *Piqua Branch of the State Bank of Ohio* v. *Knoop,* 16 How. 369 (1854), the majority held that charter terms constituted a contract between the state and the bank, Catron and two others dissented: "The sovereign political power is not the subject of contract so as to be vested in an irrepealable charter of incorporation, and taken away from, and placed beyond the reach of future legislatures." The taxing power he described as "a political power of the highest class," not to be alienated by one legislature. Only a constitutional exception could do that. And in *Ohio Life Insurance and Trust Company* v. *Debolt,* 16 How. 416 (1854), the Court ruled that exemption from taxation could not be inferred. Catron observed that "the unparalleled increase of corporations throughout the Union . . . ; the ease with which charters containing exclusive privileges and exemptions are obtained; the vast amount of property, power, and exclusive benefits, prejudicial to other classes of society that are vested in and held by these numerous bodies of associated wealth," made it all-important that corporations not be allowed to "stand above the state government creating them." *Dodge* v. *Woolsey,* 18 How. 331 (1856), provoked another dissent. A constitutional amendment repealing all previous tax exemptions was held to be an impairment of the obligation of contract. Catron concurred in Campbell's strong dissent from this ruling.

Concerning slavery and the judicial problems which arose from the apprehension and rendition of fugitive slaves, Catron consistently upheld the federal power. His apparently complete concurrence with Story's opinion in *Prigg* v. *Pennsylvania,* 16 Pet. 539 (1842), suggests that at that time he considered the federal power to be exclusive, but if so, this he modified in opinions of the early 1850's. *Norris* v. *Crocker,* 13 How. 429 (1851), declared that the Fugitive Slave Act of 1850 had superseded the old law of 1793, and *Moore* v. *Illinois,* 14 How. 13 (1852), declared that state laws regarding fugitives could stand if they did not conflict with the federal statutes. Catron joined in both decisions of the Court.

Catron's role in the *Dred Scott* case was an important one. He was, of course, a member of the "pro-southern" majority. Late in 1856, during the rehearing of the case, he responded to argument of counsel by querying Jefferson Davis, the Secretary of War, concerning Scott's stay in free territory with the army surgeon who was his master. Catron wanted to know if any regulations existed concerning the presence of slave servants on army posts, and Davis replied that the use of any type of servant, slave or free, had been allowed without distinction, and with the usual compensation to the officer. Catron's involvement with the administration then deepened. Early in February, President-elect James Buchanan sent an inquiry to Catron concerning the disposition of the case. The two men knew each other well. Justice Catron had given active support to Buchanan during the presidential campaign, even going to the length of attempting to prove that in 1844 Jackson had favored Buchanan for the Democratic nomination. If Catron believed this at the time, it must be ascribed to a faulty memory, for in 1844 Jackson's aid to Polk had been essential to his fellow Tennesseean. In any case, on the eve of his inauguration, Buchanan wished to be able to announce that the territorial problem, the vexing question which had ruined the administration of his predecessor and fellow Democrat, Franklin Pierce, had finally been resolved judicially. Catron replied that disposition of the matter, especially its timing, lay with Chief Justice Taney. A leak of information following the case's first hearing, a breach of confidence ostensibly committed by a Court member, made Taney all the more touchy about the security problem. Catron promised that he would find out all he could and relay the information shortly. Ever the politician, Catron concluded his letter with a patronage recommendation.

That was on the sixth of February, 1857. Four days later, the tenth, Catron reported that a decision was imminent, probably on the fifteenth, but he warned that it would settle nothing, since the Justices would avoid the territorial question. Catron then proceeded to give Buchanan his views. There certainly existed congressional power over the territories, and to deny it altogether would ignore long-standing precedents and create a political storm. But the Louisiana Purchase treaty guaranteed that all inhabitants of that territory retained their rights, that of property included. The treaty provision was thus a limitation on the congressional power. Once admitted to statehood the inhabitants could legislate for themselves on slavery however they wished. Thus for Catron the Purchase treaty terms invalidated the Missouri Compromise.

It all appeared simple. On February fourteenth, the Justices in conference seemed agreed that constitutionality of the Compromise need not be entered into, and Justice Nelson was asked to prepare a limited opinion. But McLean and Curtis demurred, expressing their intention to develop the apparently suppressed themes. Still Catron was not worried. A third letter to Buchanan promised that "the question involving the constitutionality of the Missouri Compromise line is presented to the appropriate tribunal to decide; . . . It is due to its high and independent character to suppose that it will decide and settle a controversy which has so long and seriously agitated the country, and which *must* ultimately be decided by the Supreme Court." With McLean and Curtis so obviously "unsound" on the question, Catron then took a giant step further. He urged Buchanan to write Justice Grier, another Pennsylvanian, reminding him of the importance of the case, "and how good an opportunity it is to settle the agitation by an affirmative decision of the Supreme Court, the one way or the other." Grier had the right instincts and views, Catron thought, but he had to be prodded gently. Buchanan complied, and in his inaugural address on March fourth he promised to abide by the Court's decision, adding disingenuously, "whatever this may be."

Nelson, of course, never delivered the opinion of a united Court. Each Justice spoke for himself in the end, but on the question of Scott's status in view of his stay in the Illinois territory, Catron agreed entirely with Nelson. Such status, and any alleged change in status, was a subject for determination by the courts of Missouri alone. The opinion followed closely the reasoning of Catron's letter to Buchanan. Federal power did obtain in the territories. "It is asking much of a judge who has been exercising jurisdiction, from the western Missouri line to the Rocky Mountains, and on this understanding of the Constitution inflicting the extreme penalty of death for crimes committed where the direct legislation of Congress was the only rule, to agree that he had been all the while acting in mistake, and as an usurper." But such governing must be in accord with the terms of the treaty of cession. Thus Congress might not abridge the property rights of slaveholding citizens in any part of that territory. "The third article of the treaty of 1803 . . . stands protected by the constitution, and cannot be repealed." In addition, the Missouri Compromise line violated the constitutional guarantee of equal privileges and immunities to citizens of all states. Such a guarantee was the "leading feature of the constitution—a feature on which the Union depends, and which secures to the respective States and their citizens an entire EQUALITY of rights. . . ." Dred Scott was a slave when he filed his suit and a slave when the case was decided. Of the seven majority Justices, Catron was one of four who did not take up the question of whether a free Negro was barred from citizenship.

The outburst that followed the reading of opinions may have surprised Catron and shaken his hopes for a resolution of the question. He had put much into the case, both officially and *sub rosa,* and he was gratified that Justice Wayne of Georgia had come to support his views of treaty obligations, despite a previous opinion in another direction. But the general divergence of views produced sounds of the uncertain trumpet. There was no denying that the Court's attempted master stroke had been costly in political and personal terms. One Republican newspaperman, James S. Pike, ran through the Court with much sarcasm and incisiveness. He described Catron as a "robust, unintellectual man . . . . whose erroneous opinions would, as a general rule, more often result from obtuseness than from original sin." Only stupidity caused Catron to "reject the Jesuitism, the sophistries, and the falsehoods by which Judge Taney would instinctively attempt to support the same conclusion."

Obtuseness implies stubbornness, but says nothing about which principles are to be held tenaciously. Republicans no doubt concluded from Catron's *Dred Scott* opinion and from his southern background that the Justice would support the South in any action it attempted. If so, they could not have been more wrong. When the Supreme Court adjourned on March 14, 1861, ten days after Lincoln's inaugural, Catron rushed from Washington to perform his circuit duties in Kentucky, Tennessee, and Missouri. In all three states secession sentiment ran high, although only Tennessee would ultimately join the Confederacy. Catron felt that the maintenance of federal judicial power in the disaffected states was all-important, whatever the risk. Following his work in Kentucky, Catron proceeded to Nashville, fully intending to hold circuit, despite a military commitment by the Tennessee legislature to the Confederate government. The federal marshal in Nashville warned Catron that his very life was in danger if he proceeded with his plan to open the court. The marshal would give no assistance, so Catron had to leave Tennessee. In St. Louis he did meet his court, and there he denounced the secessionists as rebels while denying writs of *habeas corpus* to several men then being held as traitors by federal officials. Catron's Unionism was unshakable. Had Jefferson Davis appeared before him, he doubtless would have liked to do what Andrew Jackson once threatened to do with John C. Calhoun: hang him higher than Haman.

Catron's courageous though only partially successful mission on his circuit was the act of a brave and principled man. It was a pity that Jackson was not alive to see the actions of Catron, his real judicial protégé. But there was a price to be paid. When Catron returned to Nashville, his statements and acts in St.

Louis did invoke the possibility of vigilante justice against him. He was ordered either to resign his seat on the Court or quit Nashville within twenty-four hours, the time limit which seems customary in such situations. Catron decided to leave, although he had to go without his ailing wife, and although he himself was over seventy years old. In Kentucky, in the fall of 1861, Catron cooperated fully with military authorities in exercising judicial restraint with regard to issuance of writs of *habeas corpus*. The situation there was critical. All of the governmental authorities agreed that a literal, or overly libertarian view on *habeas corpus* in that area, and at that time, might lose Kentucky to the Union. Catron, unlike his colleague Taney in the Maryland circuit, gave the authorities little trouble. His expulsion from Tennessee undoubtedly made Catron suppress whatever tender feelings he might have retained about the secessionists as individuals. Vocal Southern sympathizers would find no friend in Catron, who kept in touch with President Lincoln to be sure that new district judges were sent out or appointed to replace several men who had chosen to support the Confederacy. He also reaffirmed his devotion to the Union, and informed the President in detail of the financial burden his patriotic stand entailed, namely forfeiture of property in Nashville and elsewhere worth about $100,000. But unpleasant though this was, his primary duty was clear: "I have to punish Treason, & will."

Catron's Unionism did not mean that he blindly accepted all that the government did to suppress the rebellion. In the *Prize Cases,* 2 Black 635 (1863), he aligned himself with the dissenters, Justice Nelson acting as spokesman, who declined to accept Lincoln's presidential initiative in waging a personal war through blockade in the first months of the war before Congress met. But in most instances Catron supported the government, as he did in the case of *United States* v. *Republican Banner Officers,* 27 Fed. Cases 783 (No. 16, 148) (C.C.D. Tenn. 1863). There, on circuit, he upheld the federal confiscation act against a disloyal newspaper, because "there being then a formidable rebellion in progress, the intention of Congress in enacting this law must have been to deter persons from so using and employing their property as to aid and promote the insurrection."

Catron did his part, and more, for the Union, but toward the end of the war it was clear that he was already an anachronism. A new Court was forming around him, to be made up of Lincoln appointees. The Old Jacksonians had had their day. In 1864, the Attorney General, Edward Bates, noted in his diary (and not too sadly) that Taney, Wayne, Catron, or Grier seemed feeble and ready to resign if adequate pensions were provided. Bates did not have to wait long in two of the cases: Taney died that same year, and Catron died the next spring, on May 30, 1865, shortly after the preservation of the Union had been assured by the Confederate surrender.

When the term "Jacksonian jurist" appears it is most often associated with Roger Taney. No one will deny that Taney fits the description, but John Catron does so even more. That both Jackson and Catron came from Tennessee is the most obvious but not the most important element in the comparison. Catron, like Jackson, was zealous in guarding the rights of the states and in opposing the "Monsters" of accumulated wealth and privilege. When the crisis of secession came he acted in accordance with his political chief's legacy. He too believed, "The Federal Union—it must be preserved."

SELECTED BIBLIOGRAPHY

Catron is often mentioned in monographs on national politics in the antebellum period, but usually only in passing. For some biographical notes, see Joshua W. Caldwell, *Sketches of the Bench and Bar of Tennessee* (Knoxville, 1898), 85–92. A more up-to-date and scholarly treatment of Justice Catron is Edmund C. Gass, "The Constitutional Opinions of Justice John Catron," 8 *East Tennessee Historical Society's Publications* 54 (1936).

John Catron

REPRESENTATIVE OPINIONS

LICENSE CASES, 5 HOW. 504 (1847)

The states of New Hampshire and Massachusetts had each passed various laws regulating the importation of liquor into the respective state. When certain merchants were indicted for failure to acquire the licenses required by the state laws, they claimed the laws were inconsistent with the commerce clause and therefore invalid. The Court speaking with six voices upheld the state laws. Catron's opinion focused on the long existence of such laws and the need for state police power to regulate matters such as liquor importation.

Mr. Justice CATRON.

PIERCE AND ANOTHER *v.* NEW HAMPSHIRE

Andrew Pierce and two others were indicted for selling one barrel of gin, contrary to a statute of New Hampshire, passed in 1838, which provides, that if any person shall, without license from the selectmen of the town where such person resides, sell any wine, rum, gin, brandy, or other spirits, in any quantity, or shall sell any mixed liquors, part of which are spirituous, such person so offending, for each offence, on conviction upon an indictment, shall forfeit and pay a sum not exceeding fifty dollars, nor less than twenty-five dollars, for the use of the county.

The barrel of gin had been purchased by the defendants at Boston, in the Commonwealth of Massachusetts, and was brought coastwise by water near to Dover, in New Hampshire, where it was sold in the same barrel and condition that it had been when purchased in Boston. Part of the regular business of the defendants was to sell ardent spirits in large quantities.

The defendants' counsel contended, on the trial, that the statute of 1838 was unconstitutional and void, because the same is in violation of certain public treaties of the United States with Holland, France, and other countries, containing stipulations for the admission of spirits into the United States, and because it is repugnant to the two following clauses in the constitution of the United States, viz.:—

"No State shall, without the consent of

the Congress, lay any imposts or duties on imports or exports, except what may be absolutely necessary for executing its inspection laws."

"The Congress shall have power to regulate commerce with foreign nations, and among the several States, and with the Indian tribes."

In answer to these objections, the court instructed the jury, that the statute of July 4, 1838, was not entirely void, if it might have an operation constitutionally in any case; and that, as far as this case was concerned, it could not be in violation of any treaty with any foreign power which had been referred to, permitting the introduction of foreign spirits into the United States, because the liquor in question here was proved to be American gin.

The court further instructed the jury, that this statute, as it regarded this case, was not repugnant to the clause in the constitution of the United States providing that no State shall, without the consent of Congress, lay any duty on imports or exports, because the gin in this case was not a foreign article, and was not imported into, but had been manufactured in, the United States.

The court further instructed the jury, that this State could not regulate commerce between this and other States; that this State could not prohibit the introduction of articles from another State with such a view, nor prohibit a sale of them with such a purpose; but that, although the State could not make such laws with such views and for such purposes, she was not entirely forbidden to legislate in relation to articles introduced from foreign countries or from other States; that she might tax them the same as other property, and might regulate the sale to some extent; that a State might pass health and police laws which would, to a certain extent, affect foreign commerce, and commerce between the States; and that this statute was a regulation of that character, and constitutional.

The jury found the defendants guilty, and the Court of Common Pleas fined them thirty dollars; from which they prosecuted their writ of error to the Superior Court of Judicature of New Hampshire, where the judgment was affirmed. The present writ of error is prosecuted, under the twenty-fifth section of the Judiciary Act of 1789, to reverse the judgment of the State court of New Hampshire, on the grounds above stated. And the question and the case presented for our consideration are, whether the State laws, and the judgment founded on them, are repugnant to the constitution of the United States. The court below having decided in favor of their validity, this is the only question that comes within our jurisdiction, although divers others were presented to and adjudged by the State court.

The importance of this case, as regards its bearing on the commerce among the States, and on the relations and rights of their citizens and inhabitants, is not to be disguised. To my mind it presents most delicate and difficult considerations.

The first objection, that the statute of New Hampshire violated certain treaties with Holland, France, &c., providing for the admission of ardent spirits, has no application to the case, as the spirits sold were not foreign, but American gin.

The second objection relies on the first article and tenth section of the constitution, which provides, that "no State shall lay any imposts or duties on imports or exports, nor any duty on tonnage," unless with the assent of Congress, &c. These are negative restrictions, where the constitution operates by its own force; but as no duty or tax was imposed on the gin introduced into New Hampshire from Massachusetts, either directly or indirectly, these prohibitions on the State power to not apply.

The third objection proceeds on the clause, that "the Congress shall have power to regulate commerce with foreign nations, and among the several States, and with the Indian tribes," to which it is insisted the State statute is opposed. The power given to Congress is unrestricted, and broad as the subjects to which it relates; it extends to all lawful commerce with foreign nations, and in the same terms to all lawful commerce among the States; and "among" means between two only, as well as among more than two; if it was otherwise, than an intermediate State might interdict and obstruct the transportation of imports over it to a third State, and thereby impair the general power. The article in question was introduced from one State directly into another, and the first question is, Was it a subject of lawful commerce among the States, that Congress can regulate? That ardent spirits have been for ages, and now are, subjects of sale and of lawful commerce, and that of a large class, throughout a great portion of the civilized world, is not open to controversy; so our commercial treaties with foreign powers declare them to be, and so the dealing in them among the States of this Union recognizes them to be. But this condition of the subject-matter was met by the State decision on the ground, and on this only, "that the State might pass health and police laws which would, to a certain extent, affect foreign commerce and commerce between the States; and that the statute [of New Hampshire] was a regulation of that character, and constitutional."

This was the charge to the jury, and on it the verdict and judgment are founded, and which the State court of last resort affirmed. The law and the decision apply equally to foreign and to domestic spirits, as they must do on the principles assumed in support of the law. The assumption is, that the police power was not touched by the constitution, but left to the States as the constitution found it. This is admitted; and whenever a thing, from character or condition, is of a description to be regulated by that power in the State, then the regulation may be made by the State, and Congress cannot interfere. But this must always depend on facts, subject to legal ascertainment, so that the injured may have redress. And the fact must find its support in this, whether the prohibited article belongs to, and is subject to be regulated as part of, foreign commerce, or of commerce among the States. If, from its nature, it does not belong to commerce, or if its condition, from putrescence or other cause, is such when it is about to enter the State that it no longer belongs to commerce, or, in other words, is not a commercial article, then the State power may exclude its introduction. And as an incident to this power, a State may use means to ascertain the fact. And here is the limit between the sovereign power of the State and the federal power. That is to say, that which does not belong to commerce is within the jurisdiction of the police power of the State; and that which does belong to commerce is within the jurisdiction of the United States. And to this limit must all the general views come, as I suppose, that were suggested in the reasoning of this court in the cases of Gibbons *v.* Ogden, Brown *v.* The State of Maryland, and New York *v.* Miln.

What, then, is the assumption of the State court? Undoubtedly, in effect, that the State had the power to declare what should be an article of lawful commerce in the particular State; and, having declared that ardent spirits and wines were deleterious to morals and health, they ceased to be commercial commodities there, and that then the police power attached, and consequently the powers of Congress could not interfere. The exclusive State power is made to rest, not on the fact of the state or condition of the article, nor that it is property usually passing by sale from hand to hand, but on the declaration found in the State laws, and asserted as the State policy, that it shall be excluded from commerce. And by this means the sovereign jurisdiction in the State is attempted to be created, in a case where it did not previously exist.

If this be the true construction of the constitutional provision, then the paramount power of Congress to regulate commerce is subject to a very material limitation; for it takes from Congress, and leaves with the States, the power to determine the commodities, or articles of property, which are the subjects of lawful commerce. Congress may regulate, but the States determine what shall or shall not be regulated.

Upon this theory, the power to regulate commerce, instead of being paramount over the subject, would become subordinate to the State police power; for it is obvious that the power to determine the articles which may be the subjects of commerce, and thus to circumscribe its scope and operation, is, in effect, the controlling one. The police power would not only be a formidable rival, but, in a struggle, must necessarily triumph over the commercial power, as the power to regulate is dependent upon the power to fix and determine upon the subjects to be regulated.

The same process of legislation and reasoning adopted by the State and its courts could bring within the police power any article of consumption that a State might wish to exclude, whether it belonged to that which was drank, or to food and clothing; and with nearly equal claims to propriety, as malt liquors and the produce of fruits other than grapes stand on no higher grounds than the light wines of this and other countries, excluded, in effect, by the law as it now stands. And it would be only another step to regulate real or supposed extravagance in food and clothing. And in this connection it may be proper to say, that the three States whose laws are now before us had in view an entire prohibition from use of spirits and wines of every description, and that their main scope and object is to enforce exclusive temperance as a policy of State, under the belief that such a policy will best subserve the interests of society; and that to this end, more than to any other, has the sovereign power of these States been exerted;

for it was admitted, on the argument, that no licenses are issued, and that exclusion exists, so far as the laws can produce the result,—at least, in some of the States,—and that this was the policy of the law. For these reasons, I think the case cannot depend on the reserved power in the State to regulate its own police.

Had the gin imported been "an import" from a foreign country, then the license law prohibiting its sale by the importer would be void. The reasons for this conclusion are given in my opinion on the case of Thurlow *v.* The Commonwealth of Massachusetts, and need not be repeated, and are founded on the case of Brown *v.* The State of Maryland. The next inquiry is, did it stand on the foot of "an import," coming, as it did, from another State? If it be true, as the State courts held it was, that Congress has the exclusive power to regulate commerce among the States (the States having none), and the gin introduced being an article of commerce, and the State license law being a regulation of commerce (as it was held by this court to be in the case of Brown *v.* The State of Maryland), then the State law is void, because the State had no power to act in the matter by way of regulation to any extent.

This narrows the controversy to the single point, whether the States have power to regulate their own mode of commerce among the States, during the time the power of Congress lies dormant, and has not been exercised in regard to such commerce.

Although some regulations have been made by Congress affecting the coasting trade, requiring manifests of cargoes where they exceed a certain value, to prevent smuggling, and for other purposes, still, no regulation exists affecting, in any degree, such an import as the one under consideration. It must find protection against the State law under the constitution, or it can have none. This is also true as respects similar articles of commerce passing from State to State by land. Congress has left the States to proceed in this regard as they were proceeding when the constitution was adopted.

Is, then, the power of Congress exclusive? The advocates of this construction insist that it has been settled by this court that the power to regulate commerce is exclusive, and can be exercised by Congress alone. And the inquiry in advance of further discussion is, Has the construction been thus settled? The principle case relied on is that of Gibbons *v.* Ogden, 9 Wheat. 1, in support of the assumption. In that case a monopoly had been granted to the inventers of machinery propelled by steam, which, when applied to vessels, forced them through the water. The law of monopoly of New York extended to the tide-waters, and for navigating these with two steamboats belonging to Gibbons, a bill was filed against him, and he was enjoined by the State courts of New York; and in his answer he relied on licenses granted under the act of 18th February, 1793, for enrolling and licensing ships and vessels to be employed in the coasting trade, and for regulating the same. This was the sole defence. The court first held that the power to regulate commerce included the power to regulate navigation also, as an incident to, and part of, commerce.

After discussing many topics connected with, or supposed to be connected with, the subject, the power of taxation was considered by the court, and the powers to tax in the States and the United States compared with the power to regulate commerce, and in this connection the chief justice, delivering the opinion of the court, said,—"But, when a State proceeds to regulate commerce with foreign nations, or among the several States, it is exercising the very power granted to Congress, and is doing the very thing which Congress is authorized to do. There is no analogy, then, between the power of taxation and the power of regulating commerce. In discussing the question, whether this power is still in the States, in the case under consideration, we may dismiss from it the inquiry, whether it is surrendered by the mere grant to Congress, or is retained until Congress shall exercise the power. We may dismiss that inquiry, because it has been exercised, and the regulations Congress deemed proper to make are now in full operation. The sole question is, Can a State regulate commerce with foreign nations, and among the States, while Congress is regulating it?"

And then the court proceeds to discuss the effect of the licenses set up in Gibbons' answer, and gives a decree of reversal, on that sole question, in his favor. The decree says,—"This court is of opinion, that the several licenses to the steamboats the Stoudinger and the Bellona to carry on the coasting trade, which are set up by the appellant, Thomas Gibbons, in his answer, which were granted under an act of Congress passed in pursuance of the constitution of the United States, gave full authority to those vessels to navigate the waters of the United States, by steam or otherwise, for the purpose of carrying on the coasting trade; any law of the State of New York to the contrary notwithstanding." And then the State law is declared void, as repugnant to the constitution and laws of the United States. 9 Wheat. 240.

This case, then, decides that navigation was within the commercial power of the United States, and that a coasting license granted pursuant to an act of Congress, in the exercise of the power, was an authority under the supreme law to navigate the public waters of New York, notwithstanding the State law granting the monopoly. This decision was made in 1824. Three years after (1827) the case of Brown *v.* The State of Maryland came before the court. 12 Wheat. 419.

Brown, an importing merchant, had been indicted for selling packages of dry goods in the form they were imported, without taking out a license to sell by wholesale. To this he demurred, and the demurrer was sustained, on the ground that "imports" could be sold by the importer regardless of the State law, on which the indictment was founded. Two propositions were stated by the court, and the decision of the cause proceeded on them both, and was favorable to Brown:—First, The provision of the constitution which declares, that "no State shall, without the consent of Congress, lay any imposts or duties on imports or exports." And, second, That which declares Congress shall have power to regulate commerce with foreign nations, and among the several States, and with the Indian tribes.

The first proposition has no application to the controversy before us, as here no tax or duty was imposed.

2. The court proceeds (p. 446) to inquire of the extent of the power, and says,—"It is complete in itself, and acknowledges no limitations, and is coextensive with the subject on which it operates." And for this Gibbons *v.* Ogden is referred to, as having asserted the same postulates. The opinion then urges the necessity that Congress should have power over the whole subject, and the power to protect the imported article in the hands of the importer, and proceeds to say,—"We think it cannot be denied what can be the meaning of an act of Congress which authorized importation, and offers the privilege for sale at a fixed price to every person who chooses to become a purchaser." "We think, then, that if the power to authorize a sale exists in Congress, the conclusion that the right to sell is connected with the law permitting importation, as an inseparable incident, is inevitable."

Two points were decided on the second proposition:—1st. That a tax on the importer was a tax on the import.

2d. That "an import," which had paid a tax to the United States according to the regulations of commerce made by Congress, could not be taxed a second time in the hands of the importer.

Neither of these cases touch the question of exclusive power, nor do I suppose it was intended by the writer of the opinions to approach that question, as he studiously guarded the opinion in the leading case of Gibbons *v.* Ogden against such an inference, and professedly followed the doctrines there laid down in Brown *v.* The State of Maryland.

The next case that came before the court was that of Willson et al. *v.* The Blackbird Creek Marsh Company, in 1829, 2 Peters, 257. The chief justice again delivered the opinion of the court, as he had done in the two previous cases. The company was authorized to make a dam across the creek under a State charter. The creek was a navigable tide-water; the dam was constructed, and the licensed sloop of Willson not being enabled to pass, he broke the dam, and the company sued him for damages; to which he pleaded, that the creek was a navigable highway, where the tide ebbed and flowed, and that he only did so much damage as to allow his vessel to pass. The plea was demurred to, and there was a judgment against Willson in the State court. It was insisted on his behalf in this court that the power to regulate commerce included navigation; and that navigable streams are the waters of the United States, and subject to the power of Congress; and the case of Gibbons *v.* Ogden was relied on. The chief justice in the opinion said:—"The counsel for the plaintiff in error insists that it comes in conflict with the powers of the United States to regulate commerce with foreign nations, and among the several States.

"If Congress had passed any act which bore upon the case, any act in execution of the power to regulate commerce, the object of which was to control State legislation over those small navigable creeks into which the tide flows, and which abound throughout the lower country of the Middle and Southern States, we should feel not much difficulty in saying, that a State law coming in conflict with such act would be void. But Congress has passed no such act. The repugnancy of the law of Delaware to the constitution is placed entirely on its repugnancy to the power to regulate commerce with foreign nations and among the several States; a power which has not been so exercised as to affect the question.

"We do not think that the act empowering the Blackbird Creek Marsh Company to place a dam across the creek can, under all the circumstances of the case, be considered as repugnant to the power to regulate commerce in its dormant state, or as being in conflict with any law passed on the subject."

Here the adjudications end. But judges, who were of the court when the three cases cited were determined, differ as to the true meaning of the chief justice in the language employed in the case of Gibbons *v*. Ogden, in illustrating the constitution in aspects supposed to bear more or less on the questions before the court; such, for instance, as that the commercial power was a unit, and covered the entire subject-matter of commerce with foreign nations and among the States; and that navigation was included in the power. In the case of New York *v*. Miln, 11 Peters, 102, Mr. Justice Thompson and Mr. Justice Story differed entirely as to what the language employed in the opinion in Gibbons *v*. Odgen meant, in regard to the true exposition of the constitution;—one contending that the language used had reference to the power of Congress, and to a case where it had been fully exercised; the other insisting that the opinion maintained the exclusive power in Congress to regulate commerce, and that the States had no authority to legislate, but were altogether excluded from interfering. This was Mr. Justice Story's opinion. I think it must be admitted that Chief Justice Marshall understood himself as Mr. Justice Thompson understood him, otherwise he could not have held as he did in the last case, in 1829, of Willson *v*. The Blackbird Creek Marsh Company. And as this case was an adjudication on the precise question whether the constitution of the United States, in itself, extinguished the powers of the States to interfere with navigation on tide-water, and as it was adjudged, in the case of Gibbons *v*. Ogden, that the power to regulate commerce included navigation as fully as if the clause had expressed it in terms, it is difficult to say that this case does not settle the question favorably to the exercise of jurisdiction on the part of the States, until Congress shall act on the same subject and suspend the State law in its operation. But, owing to the conflicting opinions of individual judges, it is deemed proper to treat the question as though it was an open one, in the aspect that this case presents it; and then the consideration arises,—Can a State, by its general laws, operating on all persons and property within its jurisdiction, regulate articles coming into the State from other States, and prohibit their sale, unless a license is obtained by the person bringing them in; and where no tax or duty is demanded of the person, or imposed on the article?

In this proposition, it is not intended to involve the consideration, that where Congress regulates a particular commerce by general laws, as where a tax is levied on some articles on being introduced from abroad, and others permitted to come in free, that all are regulated; this I admit in the instance put, and in all others of a like character. But as no general law of Congress has regulated commerce among the States, such a rule cannot apply here.

To a true understanding of the power conferred on Congress to regulate commerce among the States, it may be proper briefly to refer to their condition and acts before the constitution was adopted, in this respect. The prominent evil was, that they taxed the commerce of each other directly and indirectly; and to secure themselves from undue and opposing taxes, the constitution first provides, that Congress shall lay no tax on articles exported from any State; second, that no State shall lay any imposts or duties on imports or exports; nor, third, lay any duty on tonnage, without the consent of Congress, except so much as may be necessary for executing its inspection laws. These are prohibitions, to which the States have conformed.

But, as many general and all necessary local regulations existed when the constitution was adopted, and this, in all the States, affecting the end of commerce within their respective limits, the local regulations were continued, so far as the constitution left them in force. And they have been added to and accumulated to a great extent up to this time in the maritime States, not only as regards commerce among the States, but affecting foreign commerce also; the States, within their harbours and inland waters, have done almost every thing, and Congress next to nothing. So minute and complicated are the wants of commerce when it reaches its port of destination, that even the State legislatures have been incapable of providing suitable means for its regulation between ship and shore, and therefore charters, granted by the State legislatures, have conferred the power on city corporations. Owing to situation and climate, every port and place where commerce enters a State must have peculiarity in its regulations; and these it would be exceedingly difficult for Congress to make; nor could it depute the power to corporations, as the States do. The difficulties standing in the way of Congress are fast increasing with the increase of commerce and the places where it is carried on. And where it enters States through their inland borders, by land and water, the complication is not less, and especially on the large rivers. There, too, Congress has the undisputed power to regulate commerce coming from State to State; but as every village would require special legislation, and constant additions as it grew and its commerce increased, to deal with the subject on the part of Congress would be next to impossible in practice. I admit that this condition of things does not settle the question of contested power; but it satisfactorily shows that Congress cannot do what the States have done, are doing, and must continue to do, from a controlling necessity, even should the exclusive power in Congress be maintained by our decision. And this state of things was too prominently manifest for the convention to overlook it. Nor do I suppose they did so, for the following reasons.

The general rules of construction applicable to the negative and affirmative powers of grant in the constitution are commented on in the 32d number of the Federalist, in these terms:—"That, notwithstanding the affirmative grants of general authorities, there has been the most pointed care, in those cases where it was deemed improper that the like authorities should reside in the States, to insert negative clauses prohibiting the exercise of them by the States. The tenth section of the first article consists altogether of such provisions. This circumstance is a clear indication of the sense of the convention, and furnishes a rule of interpretation out of the body of the act, which justifies the position I have advanced, and refutes every hypothesis to the contrary." That is, in favor of the State power. These remarks were made to quiet the fears of the people, and to clear up doubts on the meaning of the constitution, then before them for adoption by the State conventions. And it is an historical truth, never, so far as I know, denied, that these papers were received by the people of the States as the true exponents of the instrument submitted for their ratification. Proceeding on the principle of construction applicable to affirmative statutes,—that they stood together as a general rule, if there were no negative words,—and taking the doctrine laid down in the Federalist to be the true rule of interpretation,—that where the States were intended to be prohibited negative words had been used,—the States continued to do what they had previously done, and were not by negation prohibited from doing; that is to say, to exercise the powers conferred on Congress in arming, and organizing and disciplining the militia, to pass bankrupt laws, and to regulate the details of commerce within their limits, coming from other States and foreign countries.

The exercise of the powers to regulate the militia, and to pass bankrupt laws, has not the approval of this court in the cases of Houston *v.* Moore, and in Ogden *v.* Saunders.

As to the existence of the power in the States in these two instances, there is no further controversy here or elsewhere.

And in regard to the third, Congress has stood by for nearly sixty years, and seen the States regulate the commerce of the whole country, more or less, at the ports of entry and at all their borders, without objection, and for this court now to decide that the power did not exist in the States, and that all they had done in this respect was void from the beginning, would overthrow and annul entire codes of State legislation on the particular subject. We would by our decision expunge more State laws and city corporate regulations than Congress is likely to make in a century on the same subject, and on no better assumption than that Congress and the State legislatures had been altogether mistaken as to their respective powers for fifty years and more. If long usage, general acquiescence, and the absence of complaint can settle the interpretation of the clause in question, then it should be deemed as settled in conformity to the usage by the courts.

And as Congress and the courts have conceded that the States may pass laws regulating the militia, and on the subject of bankruptcies, and that the affirmative grants of power to Congress in these instances did not deprive the States from exercising the power until Congress acted, it is now too late, under existing circumstances, for this court to say that the similar affirmative power to regulate commerce with foreign nations and among the States shall be held an exclusive power in Congress; as it could no more be done with consistency of interpretation, than with safety to the existing state of the country.

In proceeding on this moderate, and, as I think, prudent and proper construction, all further difficulty will be obviated in regard to the admission of property into the States; this the States may regulate, so they do not tax; and if the States (or any one of them) abuse the power, Congress can interfere at pleasure, and remedy the evil; nor will the States have any right to complain. And so the courts can interfere if the States assume to exercise an excess of power, or act on a subject of commerce that is regulated by Congress. As already stated, it is hardly possible for Congress to deal at all with the details of this complicated matter.

The case before us presents a fair illustration of the difficulty; all venders of spirits produced in New Hampshire are compelled to be licensed before they can lawfully sell; this is not controverted, and cannot be. To hold that the State license law was void, as respects spirits coming in from other States as articles of commerce, would open the door to an almost entire evasion, as the spirits might be introduced in the smallest divisible quantities that the retail trade would require; the consequence of which would be, that the dealers in New Hampshire would sell only spirits produced in other States, and that the products of New Hampshire would find an unrestrained market in the neighbouring States having similar license laws to those of New Hampshire.

For the sake of convenience, the views on which this opinion proceeds will be briefly restated.

1. It is maintained, that spirits and wines are articles belonging to foreign commerce and commerce among the States; and that Congress can regulate their introduction and transmission into and through the States so long as they belong to either class of such commerce, but no further.

2. That any State law whose provisions are repugnant to the existing regulations of Congress (within the above limit) is void, so far as it is opposed to the legislation of Congress.

3. That the police power of the States was reserved to the States, and that it is beyond the reach of Congress; but that such police power extends to articles only which do not belong to foreign commerce, or to commerce among the States, at the time the police power is exercised in regard to them; and that the fact of their condition is a subject proper for judicial ascertainment.

4. That the power to regulate commerce among the States may be exercised by Congress at pleasure, and the States cut off from regulating the same commerce at the same time it stands regulated by Congress; but that, until such regulation is made by Congress, the States may exercise the power within their respective limits.

5. That the law of New Hampshire was a regulation of commerce among the States in regard to the article for selling of which the defendants were indicted and convicted; but that the State law was constitutionally passed, because of the power of the State thus to regulate; there being no regulation of Congress, special or general, in existence to which the State law was repugnant.

And, for these reasons, I think the judgment of the State court should be affirmed.

THURLOW *v.* MASSACHUSETTS.

The statute of Massachusetts provides, that no person shall presume to be a retailer or seller of wine, brandy, rum, or other spirituous liquors, in a less quantity than twenty-eight gallons, and that delivered and carried away all at one time, unless he is first licensed as a retailer of wine and spirits, as is provided in this chapter, on pain of forfeiting twenty dollars for each offence.

The plaintiff, Thurlow, was found guilty by a jury for violating this law, on which verdict the Supreme Judicial Court of Massachusetts pronounced judgment; and from which a writ of error was prosecuted to this court under the twenty-fifth section of the Judiciary Act of 1789. The bill of exceptions shows that some of the sales charged in the indictment were of foreign liquors; in regard to which the court directed the jury that the license law applied as well to imported spirits as to domestic. It was proved that the defendant below had sold in quantities of gallons, quarts, and pints. And the question submitted for our consideration is, whether the State law, and the judgment founded on it, are repugnant to the acts of Congress authorizing the importation of wines, brandies, and other foreign spirits;

and it is proper to remark, that our jurisdiction and power to interfere involve the question merely of repugnance or no repugnance; if repugnance is found to exist, we must reverse, and if not, we must affirm. It follows, that the judicial ascertainment of the fact will end the controversy.

For the plaintiff in error it is insisted, that the State law and the judgment founded on it are repugnant to the acts of Congress authorizing the importation of foreign wines and spirits, and to their introduction into the United States on paying a prescribed tax. That the laws of the States cannot control the retail trade in such liquors; that if they can to any extent, they may prohibit their sale altogether, and by this means do that indirectly which cannot be done directly, that is to say, prohibit their introduction; that the purposes of wholesale importation being retail distribution, the two must go together; if not, the first is of no value; that importations reach our country in large masses for the sole purposes of diffusion and consumption, and unless Congress has the control of distribution until the imported article reaches the consumer, the power to admit and to regulate commerce in regard to it will be worthless, and little better than a barren theory, leaving us where we began in 1789. That any law, therefore, that prohibits consumption necessarily destroys importation; and the retail process being the ordinary means to consumption, and indispensable to it, to refuse this means would wholly defeat the end Congress has protected; that is to say, consumption. On the soundness of this reasoning, the result of the controversy depends.

To this argument we answer, that under the power to regulate foreign commerce, Congress can protect every article belonging to foreign commerce, so long as it does belong to it, from the operation of a tax or a license, imposed by a State law, that obstructs or hinders the commerce. But the true inquiry here is, how long does the imported article so continue? The acts of Congress protect "imports," and prescribe the quantity and measure in which they shall be made; the question of more or less is within the competency of Congress, but how long the imported article continues to be "an import" is a different question, for so soon as it ceases to be so, then it is beyond the power conferred on Congress "to regulate foreign commerce," and that power cannot afford it further protection. This is the line of jurisdiction where the powers of Congress end, and where the powers of the States begin, when dealing respectively with the imported article. And such is the limit established in the case of Brown *v*. The State of Maryland. I do not mean to say that Congress may not protect an import for the purposes of transmission over land, in the form it was imported, from one State to another, for the purposes of distribution and sale by the importer, as this can be done under the power to regulate commerce among the States. The question under examination is, not what Congress may do, but what it has done. It has not permitted spirituous liquors to be imported in the quantities that they were sold by the plaintiff in error. And when the article passes by sale from the hands of the importer into the hands of another, either for the purposes of resale or of consumption, or is divided into smaller quantities, by breaking up the casks, packages, &c., by the importer, the article ceases to be a protected "import," according to the legislation of Congress as it now stands, and therefore the liquors sold in this instance did not belong to "foreign commerce," when sold at the retail house by single gallons, quarts, &c. When thus divided and sold in the body of the State, the foreign liquors became a part of its property, and were subject to be taxed, or to be regulated by licenses, like any other property owned within the State.

But while foreign liquors, imported according to the regulations of Congress, remain in the cask, bottle, &c., in the original form, then the importer may sell them in that form at the port of entry, or in any other part of the United States, nor can any State law hinder the importer from doing so; nor does it make any difference whether the imported article paid a tax on its introduction, or was admitted as a free article; until it passes from the hands of the importer, is "an import," and belongs to regulated "foreign commerce," and is protected.

It follows from the principles stated, that the spirituous liquors sold by the defendant stood on no higher ground than domestic spirits did, and that domestic spirits are subject to the State authority as objects of taxation, or of license in restraint of their sale, is not a matter of controversy, and certainly cannot be here, under the twenty-fifth section of the Judiciary Act.

I admit as inevitable, that, if the State has the power of restraint by licenses to any extent, she has the discretionary power to judge of its limit, and may go to the length of prohibiting sales altogether, if such be her policy; and that if this court cannot interfere in the case before us, so neither could we interfere in the extreme case of entire exclusion, except to protect imports belonging to foreign commerce, as already defined. The reasons are obvious. We have no power to inquire into abuses (if such there be) inflicted by State authority on the inhabitants of the State, unless such abuses are repugnant to the constitution, laws, or treaties of the United States.

For the reasons above set forth, I think the judgment of the State court should be affirmed.

And as the case of Joel Fletcher against the State of Rhode Island depends on the same principles, to every extent, I think it must be affirmed also.

PIQUA BRANCH OF THE STATE BANK OF OHIO v. KNOOP, 16 HOW. 369 (1854)

The Ohio legislature had granted a series of tax exemptions to various corporations over the years. Later statutes tried to remove these exemptions and levy uniform taxes on all business entities. A branch of the State Bank of Ohio protested against the levying of a tax on it in the light of a specific exemption in its charter. The Court through Justice McLean upheld the bank, concluding that the charter was a contract which could not be impaired by the state. Catron dissented, writing in strong words against any interpretation which would allow the state's taxing power to be alienated.

Mr. Justice CATRON.

This is a contest between the State of Ohio and a portion of her banking institutions, organized under a general banking law, passed in 1845. She was then a wealthy and prosperous community, and had numerous banks which employed a large capital, and were taxed by the general laws five per cent. on their dividends, being equal to thirty cents on each hundred dollars' worth of stock, supposing it to be at par value. But this was merely a State tax, payable into the State treasury. The old banks were liable to taxes for county purposes, besides; and when located in cities or towns, for corporation taxes also. These two items usually amounted to much more than the State tax.

Such was the condition of Ohio when the general banking law was passed in 1845. By this act, any number of persons not less than five might associate together, by articles, to carry on banking.

The State was laid off into districts, and the law prescribes the amount of stock that may be employed in each. Every county was entitled to one bank, and some to more. Commissioners were appointed to carry the law into effect. It was the duty of this Board of Control to judge of the articles of association, and other matters necessary to put the banks into operation. Any company might elect to become a branch of the State Bank, or to be a separate bank, disconnected with any other. Fifty thousand dollars was the minimum, and five hundred thousand the maximum, that could be employed in any one proposed institution.

By the fifty-first section, each of the banking companies authorized to carry on business was declared to be a body corporate with succession to the first day of May, 1866, with general banking powers; with the privilege to issue notes of one dollar and upwards, to one hundred dollars; and each bank was required to have "on hand in gold and silver coin, or their equivalent, one half at least of which shall be in gold and silver coin in its vault, an amount equal to thirty per cent. of its outstanding notes of circulation"; and whenever the specie on hand, or its equivalent, shall fall below twenty per cent of the outstanding notes, then no more notes shall be circulated. The equivalent to specie, meant deposits that might be drawn against in the hands of eastern banks, or bankers of good credit. In this provision constituted the great value of the franchise.

The 59th section declares that semi-annual dividends shall be made by each bank of its profits, after deducting expenses;

and the 60th section provides, that six per cent. per annum of these profits shall be set off to the State, "which sum or amount so set off shall be in lieu of all taxes to which such company, or the stockholders thereof on account of stock owned therein, would otherwise be subject." This was equal to thirty-six cents per annum on each hundred dollars of stock subscribed, supposing it to yield six per cent. interest.

By an act of 1851, it was declared that bank stock should be assessed at its true value, and that it should be taxed for State, county, and city purposes, to the same extent that personal property was required to be taxed at the place where the bank was located. As this rate was much more than that prescribed by the 60th section of the act of 1845, the bank before us refused to pay the excess, and suffered herself to be sued by the tax collector, relying on the 60th section, above recited, as an irrepealable contract, which stood protected by the Constitution of the United States.

It is proper to say that the trifling sum in dispute in this cause is the mere ground of raising the question between the State of Ohio and some fifty of her banks, claiming exemption under the act of 1845.

The taxable property of these banks is about eighteen millions of dollars, according to the auditor's report of last year, and which was used on the argument of this cause, by both sides. Of course, the State officers, and other tax payers, assailed the corporations claiming the exemption, and various cases were brought before the Supreme Court of Ohio, drawing in question the validity of the act of 1851 in so far as it increased the taxes of the banks beyond the amount imposed by the 60th section of the act of 1845. The State court sustained the act of 1851, from which decision a writ of error was prosecuted, and the cause brought to this court.

The opinions of the State court have been laid before us, for our consideration; and on our assent or dissent to them, the case depends.

The first question made and decided in the Supreme Court of Ohio was, whether the 60th section of the act of 1845, purported to be in its terms, a contract not further to tax the banks organized under it during the entire term of their existence? The court held that it imported no such contract; and with this opinion I concur.

The question was examined by the judge who delivered the unanimous opinion of the court, in the case of *Debolt* v. *The Ohio Life Insurance and Trust Company,* 1 Ohio St., 564, with a fairness, ability, and learning, calculated to command the respect of all those who have his opinion to review; and which opinion has, as I think, construed the 60th section truly. But, as my brother Campbell has rested his opinion on this section without going beyond it, and as I concur in his views, I will not further examine that question, but adopt his opinion in regard to it.

The next question, decided by the State court is of most grave importance; I give it in the language of the State court: "Had the general assembly power, under the constitution then in force, permanently to surrender, by contract, within the meaning and under the protection of the Constitution of the United States, the right of taxation over any portion of the property of individuals, otherwise subject to it?" On which proposition the court proceeds to remark:

"Our observations and conclusions upon this question, must be taken with reference to the unquestionable facts, that the act of 1851 was a *bonâ fide* attempt to raise revenue by an equal and uniform tax upon property, and contained no covert attack upon the franchises of these institutions. That the surrender did not relate to property granted by the State, so as to make it a part of the grant for which a consideration was paid; the State having granted nothing but the franchise, and the tax being upon nothing but the money of individuals invested in the stock; and that no bonus or gross sum was paid in hand for the surrender, so as to leave it open to controversy, that reasonable taxes, to accrue in future, were paid in advance of their becoming due. What effect a different state of facts might have, we do not stop to inquire. Indeed, if the attempt has here been made, it is a naked release of sovereign power without any consideration or attendant circumstance to give it strength or color; and, so far as we are advised, is the first instance where the rights and interests of the public have been entirely overlooked."

"Under these circumstances, we feel no hesitation in saying the general assembly was incompetent to such a task. This conclusion is drawn from a consideration of the limited authority of that body, and the nature of the power claimed to be abridged.

"That political sovereignty, in its true sense, exists only with the people, and that government is 'founded on their sole authority,' and subject to be altered, reformed, or abolished only by them, is a political axiom upon which all the American governments have been based, and is expressly asserted in the bill of rights. Such of the sovereign powers with which they were invested, as they deem necessary for protecting their rights and liberties, and securing their independence, they have delegated to governments created by themselves, to be exercised in such manner and for such purposes as were contemplated in the delegation. That these powers can neither be enlarged or diminished by these repositories of delegated authority, would seem to result, inevitably, from the fundamental maxim referred to, and to be too plain to need argument or illustration.

"If they could be enlarged, government might become absolute; if they could be diminished or abridged, it might be stripped of the attributes indispensable to enable it to accomplish the great purposes for which it was instituted. And, in either event, the constitution would be made, either more or less, than it was when it came from the hands of its authors; being changed and subverted without their action or consent. In the one event its power for evil might be indefinitely enlarged; while in the other its capacity for good might be entirely destroyed; and thus become either an engine of oppression, or an instrument of weakness and pusillanimity.

"The government created by the constitution of this State, (Ohio,) although not of enumerated, is yet one of limited powers. It is true, the grant to the general assembly of 'legislative authority' is general; but its exercise within that limit is necessarily restrained by the previous grant of certain powers to the federal government, and by the express limitations to be found in other parts of the instrument. Outside of that boundary, it needed no express limitations, for nothing was granted. Hence this court held, in *Cincinnati, Wilmington, &c. R. R.* v. *Clinton Co.,* 1 Ohio St., 77, that any act passed by the general assembly not falling fairly within the scope of 'legislative authority,' was as clearly void as though expressly prohibited. So careful was the convention to enforce this principle, and to prevent the enlargement of the granted powers by construction or otherwise, that they expressly declared in art. 8, § 28—'To guard against the transgression of the high powers we have delegated, we declare that all powers, not hereby delegated, remain with the people.' When, therefore, the exercise of any power by that body is questioned, its validity must be determined from the nature of the power, connected with the manner and purpose of its exercise. What, then, is the taxing power? And to what extent, and for what purposes has it been conferred upon the legislature? That it is a power incident to sovereignty—'a power of vital importance to the very existence of every government'—has been as often declared as it has been spoken of. Its importance is not too strongly represented by Alexander Hamilton, in the 30th number of the Federalist, when he says: 'Money is with propriety considered as the vital principle of the body politic; as that which sustains its life and motion, and enables it to perform its most important functions. A complete power, therefore, to procure a regular and adequate supply of revenue, as far as the resources of the community will permit, may be regarded as an indispensable ingredient in every constitution. From a deficiency in this particular, one of two evils must ensue; either the people must be subjected to continual plunder, as a substitute for a more eligible mode of supplying the public wants, or the government must sink into a fatal atrophy, and in a short course of time perish.'

"This power is not to be distinguished, in any particular material to the present inquiry, from the power of eminent domain. Both rest upon the same foundation—both involve the taking of private property—and both, to a limited extent, interfere with the natural right guaranteed by the constitution, of acquiring and enjoying it. But, as this court has already said, in the case referred to, 'neither can be classed amongst the independent powers of government, or included in its objects and ends.' No government was ever created for the purpose of taking, taxing, or otherwise interfering with the private property of its citizens. 'But charged with the accomplishment of great objects necessary to the safety and prosperity of the people, these rights attach as incidents to those objects, and become indispensable means to the attainment of those ends.' They can only be called into being to attend the independent powers, and can never be exercised without an existing necessity.

"To sustain this power in the general assembly, would be to violate all the great principles to which I have alluded. It would affirm its right to deal in, and barter away the sovereign right of the State, and thereby, in effect to change the constitution. When the general assembly of 1845 convened, it found the State in the unquestionable possession of the sovereign right of taxation, for the accomplishment of its lawful objects, extending to 'all the persons and property belonging to the body politic.' "

When its successor convened, in 1846, under the same constitution, and to legislate for the same people, if this defence is available, it found the State shorn of this power over fifteen or twenty millions of property, still within its jurisdiction and protected by its laws. This and each succeeding legislature had the same power to surrender the right, as to any and all other property; until at length the government, deprived of every thing upon which it could operate, to raise the means to attain its necessary ends, by the exercise of its granted powers, would have worked its own inevitable destruction, beyond all power of remedy, either by the legislature or the people. It is no answer to this to say that confidence must be reposed in the legislative body, that it will not thus abuse the power.

"But, in the language of the court, in *McCulloch* v. *Maryland,* 4 Wheat., 316, 'is this a case of confidence?' "

"For every surrender of the right to tax particular property not only tends to paralyze the government, but involves a direct invasion of the rights of property, of the balance of the community; since the deficiency thus created must be made up by larger contributions from them, to meet the public demand."

The foregoing are some of the reasonings of the State court on the consideration here involved. With these views I concur, and will add some of my own. The first is, "That acts of parliament derogatory from the power of subsequent legislatures, are not binding. Because, (as Blackstone says,) the legislature being in truth the sovereign power, is always equal, always absolute; and it acknowledges no superior on earth, which the prior legislature must have been if its ordinances could bind a subsequent parliament. And upon the same principle Cicero, in his letters to Atticus, treats with proper contempt these restraining clauses which endeavor to tie up the hands of succeeding legislatures. When you repeal the law itself, says he, you at the same time repeal the prohibitory clause which guards against repeal."

If this is so under the British government, how is it in Ohio? Her Supreme Court holds that the State constitution of 1802 expressly prohibited one legislature from restraining its successors by the indirect means of contracts exempting certain property, from taxation. The court says,—Power to exempt property, was reserved to the people; they alone could exempt, by an organic law. That is to say, by an amended constitution. The clause mainly relied on declares, "that all powers not delegated, remain with the people." Now it must be admitted that this clause has a meaning; and it must also be conceded (as I think) that the Supreme Court of Ohio has the uncontrollable right to declare what that meaning is; and that this court has just as little right to question that construction as the Supreme Court of Ohio has to question our construction of the Constitution of the United States.

In my judgment the construction of the court of Ohio is proper; but if I believed otherwise I should at once acquiesce. Let us look at the matter fairly and truly as it is, and see what a different course on part of this court would lead to; nay, what Ohio is bound to do in self-defence and for self-preservation, under the circumstances.

In 1845 a general banking law is sought at the hands of the legislature, where five dollars in paper can be circulated for every dollar in specie in the bank, or on deposit, in eastern banks or with brokers. One dollar notes are authorized; every county in the State is entitled to a bank, and the large ones to several; the tempting lure is held out of six per cent. interest on five hundred dollars for every hundred dollars paid in as stock: thus obtaining a profit of twenty-four dollars on each hundred dollars actually paid in. That such a bill would have advocates enough to pass it through the legislature, all experience attests; and that the slight tax of thirty-six cents on each hundred dollars' worth of stock, subscribed and paid, was deemed a privilege, when the existing banks and other property were taxed much higher, is plainly manifest. As was obvious, when the law passed, banks sprang up at once—some fifty in number having a taxable basis last year of about eighteen millions. The elder and safer banks were, of course, driven out, and new organizations sought under the general law, by the stockholders. From having constructed large public works, and made great expenditures, Ohio has become indebted so as to require a very burdensome tax on every species of property; this was imposed by the act of 1851, and on demanding from these institutions their equal share, the State is told that they were protected by a contract made with the legislature of 1845, to be exempt from further taxation, and were not bound by the late law, and, of course, they were sued in their own courts. The Supreme Court holds that by the express terms of the State constitution no such contract could be made by the legislature of 1845, to tie up the hands of the legislature of 1851. And then the banks come here and ask our protection against this decision, which declares the true meaning of the State constitution. It expressly guarantees to the people of Ohio the right to assemble, consult, "and instruct their representatives for the common good"; and then "to apply to the legislature for a redress of grievances." It further declares, that all powers not conferred by that constitution on the legislature are reserved to the people. Now, of what consequence or practical value will these attempted securities be if one legislature can restrain all subsequent ones by contracting away the sovereign power to which instructions could apply?

The question, whether the people have reserved this right so as to hold it in their own hands, and thereby be enabled to regulate it by instructions to a subsequent legislature (or by a new constitution,) is a question that has been directly raised only once, in any State of the Union, so far as I know. In the case of *Brewster* v. *Hough,* 10 N. H., 139, it was raised, and Chief Justice Parker, in delivering the opinion of the court in a case in all respects like the one before us, says, "That it is as essential that the public faith should be preserved inviolate as it is that individual grants and contracts should be maintained and enforced. But there is a material difference between the right of a legislature to grant lands, or corporate powers, or money, and a right to grant away the essential attributes of sovereignty or rights of eminent domain. These do not seem to furnish the subject-matter of a contract."

This court sustained the principle announced by the Supreme Court of New Hampshire, in the West River Bridge case. A charter for one hundred years, incorporating a bridge company, had been granted; the bridge was built and enjoyed by the company. Then another law was passed authorizing public roads to be laid out, and free bridges to be erected; the commissioners appropriated the West River Bridge and made it free; the Supreme Court of Vermont sustained the proceeding on a review of that decision. And this court held that the first charter was a contract securing the franchises and property in the bridge to the company; but that the first legislature could not cede away the sovereign right of eminent domain, and that the franchises and property could be taken for the uses of free roads and bridges, on compensation being made.

Where the distinction lies, involving a principle, between that case and this, I cannot perceive, as every tax-payer is compensated by the security and comfort government affords. The political necessities for money are constant and more stringent in favor of the right of taxation; its exercise is required daily to sustain the government. But in the essential attributes of sovereignty the right of eminent domain and the right of taxation are not distinguishable.

If the West River Bridge case be sound constitutional law (as I think it is), then it must be true that the Supreme Court of Ohio is right in holding that the legislature of 1845 could not deprive the legislature of 1851 of its sovereign powers or of any part of them.

It is insisted, that the case of the *State of Ohio* v. *The Commercial Bank of Cincinnati,* 7 Ohio, 125, has held otherwise. This is clearly a mistake. The State in that case raised no question as to the right of one legislature to cede the sovereign power to a corporation, and tie up the hands of all subsequent legislatures: no such constitutional question entered into the decision; nor is any allusion made to it in the opinion of the court. It merely construed the acts of assembly, and held that a contract did exist on the ground that by the charter the bank was taxed four per cent.; and therefore the charter must be enforced, as this rate of taxation adhered to the charter, and excluded a higher imposition.

It would be most unfortunate for any court, and especially for this one, to hold that a decision affecting a great constitutional consideration, involving the harmony of the Union, (as this case obviously does,) should be concluded by a decision in a case where the constitutional question was not raised by counsel; and so far from being considered by the court, was never thought of: such a doctrine is altogether inadmissible. And in this connection I will say, that there are two cases decided by this court, (and relied on by the plaintiff in error,) in regard to which similar remarks apply. The first one is that of *New Jersey* v. *Wilson,* 7

Cranch, 164. An exchange of lands took place in 1758 between the British colony of New Jersey and a small tribe of Indians residing there. The Indians had the land granted to them by an act of the colonial legislature, which exempted it from taxes. They afterwards sold it, and removed. In 1804, the State legislature taxed these lands in the hands of the purchasers; they were proceeded against for the taxes, and a judgment rendered, declaring the act of 1804 valid. In 1812, the judgment was brought before this court, and the case submitted on the part of the plaintiff in error without argument; no one appearing for New Jersey. This court held the British contract with the Indians binding; and, secondly, that it run with the land which was exempt from taxation in the hands of the purchasers.

No question was raised in the Supreme Court of New Jersey, nor decided there, or in this court, as to the constitutional question of one legislature having authority to deprive a succeeding one of sovereign power. The question was not considered, nor does it seem to have been thought of in the State court or here.

The next case is *Gordon's case,* 3 How., 144. What questions were there presented on the part of the State of Maryland, does not appear in the report of the case, but I have turned to them in the record, to see how they were made in the State courts. They are as follows:

"1st. That at the time of passing the general assessment law of 1841, there was no contract existing between the State and the banks, or any of them, or the stockholders therein or any of them, by which any of the banks or stockholders can claim an exemption from the taxation imposed upon them by the said act of 1841."

"2d. That the contract between the State and the old banks, if there be any contract, extends only to an exemption from further 'taxes or burdens,' of the corporate privileges of banking; and does not exempt the property, either real or personal, of said banks or the individual stockholders therein."

"3d. That even if the contract should be construed to exempt the real and personal property of the old banks, and the property of the stockholders therein, yet such exemption does not extend to the new banks, or those chartered since 1830, and, moreover, that the power of revocation, in certain cases in these charters, reserves to the State the power of passing the general assessment law."

"4th. That the imposition of a tax of 20 cents upon every one hundred dollars' worth of property, upon both the old and new banks, under the said assessment law, is neither unequal nor oppressive, nor in violation of the bill of rights."

"5th. That taxation upon property within the State, wherever the owners may reside, is not against the bill of rights."

On these legal propositions the opinion here given sets out by declaring that, "The question, however, which this court is called on to decide, and to which our decision will be confined, is—Are the shareholders in the old and new banks, liable to be taxed under the act of 1841, on account of the stock which they owned in the banks?"

The following paragraph is the one relied on as adjudging the question, that the taxing power may be embodied in a charter and contracted away as private property, to wit: "Such a contract is a limitation on the taxing power of the legislature making it, and upon succeeding legislatures, to impose any further tax on the franchise."

"But why, when bought, as it becomes property, may it not be taxed as land is taxed which has been bought from the State, was repeatedly asked in the course of the argument. The reason is, that every one buys land, subject in his own apprehension to the great law of necessity, that we must contribute from it and all of our property something to maintain the State. But a franchise for banking, when bought, the price is paid for the use of the privilege whilst it lasts, and any tax upon it would substantially be an addition to the price."

As the case came up from the Supreme Court of Maryland, this court had power merely to reëxamine the questions raised in the court below, and decided there. All that is asserted in the opinion beyond this is outside of the case of which this court had jurisdiction, and is only so far to be respected as it is sustained by sound reasoning; but its dicta are not binding as authority; and so the Supreme Court of Maryland held in the case of the *Mayor &c. of Baltimore* v. *The Baltimore and Ohio Railroad Company,* 6 Gill (Md.), 288.

The State of Maryland merely asked to have her statutes construed, and if, by their true terms, she had promised to exempt the stockholders of her banks from taxation, then she claimed no tax of them. She took no shelter under constitutional objections, but guardedly avoided doing so.

If an expression of opinion is authority that binds, regardless of the case presented, then we are as well bound the other way, by another quite equal authority. In the case of *East Hartford* v. *Hartford Bridge Co.*, 10 How., 535, Mr. Justice Woodbury, delivering the opinion of the court, says: The case of *Goszler* v. *The Corporation of Georgetown*, 6 Wheat., 596, 598, "appears to settle the principle that a legislative body cannot part with its powers by any proceeding so as not to be able to continue the exercise of them. It can, and should, exercise them again and again, as often as the public interests require." . . . .

"Its members are made, by the people, agents or trustees for them, on this subject, and can possess no authority to sell or grant their power over the trust to others."

The *Hartford case* was brought here from the Supreme Court of Connecticut, by writ of error, on the ground that East Hartford held a ferry right secured by a legislative act that was a private contract. But this court held, among other things, that, by a true construction of the State laws, no such contract existed; so that this case cannot be relied on as binding authority more than *Gordon's case*. If fair reasoning and clearness of statement are to give any advantage, then the *Hartford case* has that advantage over *Gordon's case*.

It is next insisted that the State legislatures have in many instances, and constantly, discriminated among the objects of taxation; and have taxed and exempted according to their discretion. This is most true. But the matter under discussion is aside from the exercise of this undeniable power in the legislature. The question is whether one legislature can, by contract, vest the sovereign power of a right to tax, in a corporation as a franchise, and withhold the same power that legislature had to tax, from all future ones? Can it pass an irrepealable law of exemption?

General principles, however, have little application to the real question before us, which is this: Has the constitution of Ohio withheld from the legislature the authority to grant, by contract with individuals, the sovereign power; and are we bound to hold her constitution to mean as her Supreme Court has construed it to mean? If the decisions in Ohio have settled the question in the affirmative that the sovereign political power is not the subject of an irrepealable contract, then few will be so bold as to deny that it is our duty to conform to the construction they have settled; and the only objection to conformity that I suppose could exist with any one is, that the construction is not settled. How is the fact?

The refusal of some fifty banks to pay their assessed portion of the revenue for the year 1851, raised the question for the first time in the State of Ohio; since then the doctrine has been maintained in various cases, supported unanimously by all the judges of the Supreme Court of that State, in opinions deeply considered, and manifesting a high degree of ability in the judges, as the extract from one of them, above set forth, abundantly shows. If the construction of the State constitution is not settled, it must be owing to the recent date of the decisions. An opinion proceeding on this hypothesis will, as I think, involve our judgment now given in great peril hereafter; for if the courts of Ohio do not recede, but firmly adhere to their construction until the decisions, now existing, gain maturity and strength by time, and the support of other adjudications conforming to them, then it must of necessity occur that this court will be eventually compelled to hold that the construction is settled in Ohio; when it must be followed to avoid conflict between the judicial powers of that State and the Union, an evil that prudence forbids.

1. The result of the foregoing opinion is, that the sixtieth section of the general banking law of 1845 is, in its terms, no contract professing to bind the Legislature of Ohio not to change the mode and amount of taxation on the banks organized under this law; and for this conclusion I rely on the reasons stated by my brother Campbell, in his opinion, with which I concur.

2. That, according to the constitutions of all the States of this Union, and even of the British Parliament, the sovereign political power is not the subject of contract so as to be vested in an irrepealable charter of incorporation, and taken away from, and placed beyond the reach of, future legislatures; that the taxing power is a political power of the highest class, and each successive legislature having vested in it, unimpaired, all the political powers previous legislatures had, is authorized to impose taxes on all property in the State that its constitution does not exempt.

It is undeniably true that one legislature may by a charter of incorporation exempt from taxation the property of the corporation in part, or in whole, and with or without consideration; but this exemption will only last until the necessities of the State require its modification or repeal.

3. But if I am mistaken in both these conclusions, then, I am of opinion that, by the express provisions of the constitution of Ohio, of 1802, the legislature of that State had withheld from its powers the authority to tie up the hands of subsequent legislatures in the exercise of the powers of taxation, and this opinion rests on judicial authority that this court is bound to follow; the Supreme Court of Ohio having held by various solemn and unanimous decisions, that the political power of taxation was one of those reserved rights intended to be delegated by the people to each successive legislature, and to be exercised alike by every legislature according to the instructions of the people. This being the true meaning of the nineteenth and twenty-eighth sections of the bill of rights, forming part of the constitution of 1802; one section securing the right of instructing representatives, and the other protecting reserved rights held by the people.

Whether this construction given to the State constitution is the proper one, is not a subject of inquiry in this court; it belongs exclusively to the State courts, and can no more be questioned by us than State courts and judges can question our construction of the Constitution of the United States. For these reasons I am of opinion that the judgment of the Supreme Court of Ohio should be affirmed.

John McKinley

☆ 1780–1852 ☆

APPOINTED BY

MARTIN VAN BUREN

YEARS ON COURT

1837–1852

John McKinley

by

FRANK OTTO GATELL

JOHN McKINLEY was one of the many Virginians, born in the late eighteenth century, who moved westward to populate the New Southwest. Culpeper County, Virginia, was his birthplace and the event occurred on May 1, 1780. He was the son of Andrew and Mary Logan McKinley. Soon after the boy's birth the family moved to Lincoln County, Kentucky. John was fortunate that his family had a professional background. His father was a physician, and the younger McKinley began to study law. He was admitted to the bar in 1800, practicing law in Frankfort, then Louisville, before moving to Huntsville, Alabama, in 1818.

In his new state, McKinley joined the growing corps of lawyer-merchant-politicians who were then shaping the malleable politics of the new area. McKinley lost no time in attempting to make his mark. As he himself put it in 1819: "I am at length a citizen of Alabama, and got here just in time to be run for Judge of one of the circuits laid off by the late legislature. . . . Do congratulate me on my debut. . . ." He lost that judicial contest, but next year he did win election to the legislature. Two years later, in 1822, his political stature had risen sufficiently for him to be run as a candidate for the United States Senate, although another man beat him out.

In presidential politics, McKinley had initially supported Henry Clay. During the campaign of 1824, Clay had asked McKinley to keep him posted on political developments in Alabama, and the latter had responded with reports of the growing Jackson sentiment in his state. Although "a majority of the most intelligent" Alabamians might favor Clay, there could be no doubt that the electorate as a whole had swung over to Jackson. These facts strained previously established political loyalties and commitments, and many an American poli-

FRANK O. GATELL, Professor of History at the University of California, Los Angeles, is the author of John Gorham Palfrey and the New England Conscience.

tician had to make adjustments. McKinley was no exception. In 1826, he still toyed with Clay, sending expressions of approval for the doomed Adams administration, but by the end of the year, McKinley acknowledged himself to be a Jackson man.

Whatever the principles involved—and steady adherence to professed principles was *not* the hallmark of Alabama politics in this early factional stage—McKinley's switch served his personal interests as well. By hitching his wagon to the rising political star, McKinley obtained a coveted seat in the United States Senate in November, 1826, filling the vacancy caused by the death of Henry Chambers. He explained in a public letter, a form then in vogue as a means of establishing one's political stand, that he had yielded his previous, but sincere, preference for Clay because of the will of the people of Alabama. It was a clear statement of support for the doctrine of popular sovereignty as an operating principle, a position which had not yet gained widespread acceptance. McKinley also wrote in favor of a constitutional amendment to allow the people to elect the President directly, and thus avoid cabals in the House of Representatives which might produce "corrupt bargains" in the style of Adams and Clay. The extent of the realignments which came in the wake of Jackson's rise in Alabama can be gauged by the fact that both major candidates for the Senate seat, McKinley and Clement C. Clay, had been Henry Clay supporters in 1824. Two years later, both were claiming precedence as Jackson men. In his second attempt, McKinley won the election and the trip to Washington.

Like most new members of the Senate "Club," McKinley seldom spoke during his first session. He did, however, take a particular interest in land legislation, upholding the rights of small purchasers as against those of speculators who bought large tracts. Actual settlers, those who had begun the process of taming the land, and who might be temporarily in arrears in land payments, he reasoned, should have special consideration from the government. And, during debate on a bankruptcy bill, in which he again defended the debtor interest, the senator scored the Supreme Court's recently delivered opinion in *Sturges* v. *Crowninshield,* 4 Wheat. 122 (1819), a contract clause case in which Chief Justice Marshall restricted state action on bankruptcy as "judicial legislation." McKinley added, "Such appears to be the political bias of a majority of that Court, and the great authority of its decisions upon constitutional law, that the powers of the Federal Government are, by mere construction, made to overshadow State powers, and render them almost contemptible." McKinley wanted the moderating terms of bankruptcy laws applied to the entire population, without regard to occupation, and he condemned Marshall's interpretation as an umbrella of privilege for the merchants. He also feared that bankruptcy proceedings, as interpreted by the court, might press too heavily and immediately on the farmer who was chronically in debt but by no means necessarily insolvent.

McKinley also evinced a strong interest in the public lands within his own state. In 1828 he sponsored a bill transferring title of the public domain within Alabama to the state. Its avowed purpose was the improvement of waterways and roads, and if properly carried out, the program would revitalize all aspects of the Alabama economy. The bill which passed was more limited than what McKinley had originally asked for, but it did grant a large parcel for improvement of Muscle Shoals. Finally, McKinley was an early advocate of graduation in the price of public lands within territories, and of cession of lands within the states. He adhered to the orthodox states' rights view that the states, in 1776, had acquired all rights to lands within their boundaries. Retention by the federal government was unconstitutional, since it was a denial of the sovereignty of the states. Possession of the lands by the states did not, of course, work against the interests of the United States; whatever added to the prosperity of one state, added to the prosperity of the nation as a whole. But McKinley would not accept a theory of national government wherein the whole, or the nation, was equal to more than the sum of the parts, the states. Both these strict constructionist and anti-speculator views combined to produce a strongly worded oratorical effort from McKinley, but Congress that session was not interested in the kind of comprehensive and liberalizing reform he and others argued for.

The sincerity of McKinley's conversion to Jacksonianism remained a point for partisan contention for several years. The Democratic press in Alabama had to counteract suspicions about his reliability, averring that no better Jackson man existed and that Clay no longer wielded any influence over McKinley. Anti-Jacksonians were not to be deterred by the reality of events after 1826; any weapon usable against McKinley was fair tactics. The Democrats soon learned that McKinley was sound, however uncertain may have been his initial commitment and however studied his previous hesitation. With the approach of the election of 1828, the rematch between Adams and Jackson had been shifted from the House of Representatives back to the popularly chosen presidential electors and McKinley had little doubt of the outcome. "The people" would see that Jackson prevailed over Adams' wilting administration. In Alabama there was hardly a contest; Jackson won the state handily, with McKinley doing his part to stimulate the proper turnout of voters.

McKinley was present in the Senate in December, 1829, to witness the Jacksonians coming to power. Like many of his party men, he thought that the selection of a cabinet had not shown the new President at his best, nor had the patronage been distributed in a manner entirely satisfactory. "Such a scramble for office never was seen before as that which took place . . . after General Jackson's arrival," he observed to the melee of deserving Democrats. But again in common with most of his fellow Democrats, specific criticisms of Jackson's first few months did not alter his high opinion of the man, nor his belief that most wrong decisions could be traced to bad advice from the wrong advisers. For his part, McKinley continued to press for the kind of land legislature which would spur westward settlement, protect states' rights, and give fairness precedence over revenue-raising considerations. He was by then chairman of the Senate committee on public lands, and as strong as preemptionist as could be found in the chamber. Specifically, he wanted the government price reduced from $1.25

per acre to fifty cents, since most of the unsold lands were of poor quality, and thus almost automatically slated to go into the hands of small farmers. A realistic land policy would effectively solve the problem of squatters ("pioneers of all the new settlements in the West and Southwest," he called them), by making it feasible for them to purchase their lands legally.

The maverick quality of many of the western Jacksonians can be seen in McKinley's vote for the Maysville Road Bill (May, 1830). This piece of legislation, of course, provoked one of Jackson's best-known vetoes as the turnpike project, claimed the President, was local in character. But Senator McKinley went against the views of his party leader and, apparently, against his own as well. His rationale was that federal aid for internal improvement projects was permissible if a state requested specific funds to carry out an intrastate project. Alabama had received such monies for improvement of the Tennessee River, and Kentucky's request for similar help in building the sixty mile road should have been honored. McKinley believed that his action was in conformity with the instructions of the Alabama legislature.

In 1830, with reelection coming up, McKinley made faint stabs at playing the reluctant candidate. Officeholding was a great personal sacrifice; a senator earned little but unceasing abuse from much of the public; but he would not "turn tail under fire." Reluctant or not, McKinley entered into the campaign, truncated though such campaigns were in the era before direct popular election of senators. His principal appeal to the electorate hinged upon his efforts to reform the federal land laws. The opposition's chief arguing point, that McKinley remained an uncertain Jacksonian, did not seriously threaten the senator, but the candidacy of his opponent, Gabriel Moore, former representative and now governor, was another matter. There were factional as well as personal reasons for this move: Moore had closer ties with the Calhoun Democrats than McKinley, but essentially Moore was incensed over the failure of Alabama's senators to obtain a judicial appointment for his nephew. An unedifying war of words ensued between the two men, and the legislature barely chose Moore. President Jackson himself took note of the outcome, ascribing it, with characteristic certainty, to the machinations of John C. Calhoun, the "great nullifyer."

McKinley's next political post was in the same legislature which had rejected his senatorial claims. He had moved to the town of Florence in Lauderdale County, and his neighbors elected him to the legislature in 1831. Earlier, Jackson and other political friends had urged him to run for governor, but McKinley settled for the relative quiet of an elder statesman in the state legislature. As a former United States senator, he naturally assumed a more prominent position than any other first term legislator. It was McKinley who prepared the legislature's petition to Congress attacking the Bank of the United States as an "unjust monopoly" which was "inconsistent with our free institutions, and dangerous to the peace and safety of the union." The Bank should be replaced by an enlarged institution, in which the federal government would have a controlling interest and direction. The suggestions were not a complete surrender of

McKinley's states' rights position; although he did not object to the existence of a national financial agency in constitutional terms, he would not allow the establishment of a branch of the Bank without consent of the host state. He also helped keep the Alabama Democrats in line against South Carolina's attempt to nullify the tariff, phrasing the issue: "Jackson and the union, or Calhoun and disunion." As chairman of the nominations committee which chose the state's presidential electors, McKinley adhered to Jackson's wishes in supporting Martin Van Buren for vice-president, despite strong efforts of many southern Democrats to put Philip P. Barbour of Virginia on the ballot.

Such stalwart political action resulted in his return to Congress, this time to the House of Representatives. He won his election in 1832, and this enabled him to participate in the "Panic Session" of 1833–34. He worked closely with James K. Polk of Tennessee in blunting the Whig attempt to order the federal deposits returned to the Bank of the United States, and in protecting the state banks which had accepted the deposits from the political sniping which marked the session. At the same time, McKinley displayed an awareness of the dangers inherent in the economic boom which quickly replaced the temporary recession of the Panic Winter. He urged a reduction in government spending, particularly in the many internal improvement projects in western states which crowded in upon Congress. And, as a portent of things to come, his final speech as a member of the House in 1834 warned against accepting petitions for the abolition of slavery in the District of Columbia. McKinley said he would take his property where he wished within the Union; Congress had no right to interfere.

One term in Congress satisfied McKinley. He did not run for reelection, returning to the state legislature in 1836. Unlike many southerners, he supported Van Buren loyally that year. Gabriel Moore, however, had consistently opposed Van Buren, and the price he had to pay for this apostasy was a reversal of the senatorial election in 1830. This time McKinley, the orthodox, administration Democrat, was elected, and Moore was not even in the running.

Gratifying though the election must have been, McKinley did not serve his second term in the Senate. In March, 1837, on Jackson's last day in office, Congress approved a bill increasing the number of Justices of the United States Supreme Court from seven to nine and expanding the circuits. One of the new seats was offered by Jackson to William Smith of Alabama, but Smith declined. The offer (by Van Buren who had since taken his oath of office) next went to McKinley, who desired the post, one he described as "certainly the most onerous and laborious of any in the United States. Should I perform all the duties of the office I shall have to hold eight circuit courts, and assist in holding the Supreme court, [note that McKinley listed the circuit duties before the meetings in Washington] and travel upwards of five thousand miles every year." Nevertheless, he accepted and took his seat on the Court in January, 1838.

McKinley had barely missed participating in *Charles River Bridge* v. *Warren Bridge,* 11 Pet. 420 (1837), but within a year of joining the Court he played an important part in another contract clause case. *Bank of Augusta* v.

Earle, 13 Pet. 519 (1839) arose out of the tangled situation then existing in state banking. Alabama wished to protect the near-monopoly status of its own state bank. When an Alabama merchant refused to pay a bill of exchange of a Georgia bank on the ground that a "foreign" corporation had no legal right to make a contract within a "sovereign" state, the Bank of Augusta, Georgia, sued in federal court under the diversity of citizenship jurisdiction. In the federal circuit court, McKinley declared against the Georgia bank, stating that a corporation could not make contracts or operate in another state, directly or through an agent, unless the host state specifically granted permission. The effect of this limiting doctrine on interstate commerce at the time of the establishment of an effective national economic system can be imagined. Justice Story's horrified comment was exaggerated but warranted: the circuit opinion had "frightened half the lawyers and all the corporations of the country out of their proprieties." Story's fear at that moment was that the new Jacksonian Justices (Catron of Tennessee had been appointed with McKinley) would uphold the lower court decision. Actually there were three separate cases, the so-called Comity Cases of 1839, the chief of which was *Bank of Augusta* v. *Earle*—but one of the three involved the United States Bank of Pennsylvania (Nicholas Biddle's state-chartered institution), leading a Philadelphia Whig paper to warn that "the importance of this case does not appear to be duly estimated. . . . If this is a covert attack on the dead monster, we suspect that it proceeds from the infusion of Democracy into the Judiciary. . . ."

Before the Supreme Court, attorneys for the Bank of Augusta lashed out at McKinley's decision. Daniel Webster scored it as "anti-commercial, and anti-social, new and unheard of in our system, and calculated to break up the harmony which has so long prevailed among the states and people of the Union." A corporation's right to do business on an interstate basis was guaranteed by the privileges and immunities clause, since, Webster contended, corporations were but groups of citizens. The counsel for Earle had called for effective curbing of corporate powers, cannily phrasing his argument along lines similar to Taney's views in *Charles River Bridge;* that is, that corporate charters must be construed narrowly, especially where the public welfare was concerned. In response, the Chief Justice in his majority opinion travelled a middle course between the pleas of the attorneys. Although corporations were not citizens, they or their agents might do business in other states in the absence of specific exclusion. The absence of prohibition created the assumption that such interstate business might proceed. Ultimately, the Supreme Court's assumption after 1880 that corporations were legal persons within the meaning of the Fourteenth Amendment sapped the vitality of the Taney precedent.

McKinley, however, heard nothing in Washington to cause him to change his mind. His dissent was based on the compact theory of government, as well as the banking provisions of the Alabama constitution. A corporation existed only by virtue of state action and within the boundaries of the sovereign which had created it. Thus the creation of one sovereignty could not force itself upon another unless permitted, positively and not by inference, to do so. No competent branch of Alabama government had ever granted such permission to the plaintiffs. In so arguing, McKinley also rejected the contention that the principle of comity between nations should be applicable. He did not think it of use in considering relations between states, although his own strong views on state sovereignty might have been used to argue in the affirmative, as indeed the Chief Justice did. He saw no other possible conclusion but that "Alabama, as an independent foreign state; owing no duty, nor being under any obligation to . . . the states by whose corporations she was invaded; was the sole and exclusive judge of what was proper or improper to be done; and consequently had a right to . . . determine whether she could grant a favour to . . . those states without injury to herself." Alabama had passed laws intended to keep the profits from banking within her boundaries. Profits from the operation of the state bank and its branches had made direct state taxes unnecessary. Whatever other states and their bankers thought of this system, it was for Alabama to decide upon its continuation.

Understandably, McKinley's lone dissent received strong support from the Alabama authorities. The governor remonstrated against the Court in a message to the legislature calling the decision a direct encroachment on the state's sovereignty, and describing the federal judicial power as "the most portentous power. . . . It is the sleeping lion of the Constitution," which had to be arrested. The state legislature responded by passing such a specific prohibition as Taney's opinion had declared necessary to curtail such interstate operations, and Alabama continued its policy of "isolation."

The Justice's adherence to principle in the Georgia bank case, or what others called his sheer stubbornness, proved to be an anomaly as far as lone dissent was concerned. He was the odd man out only one more time in his judicial career, falling far behind his colleague, Justice Daniel of Virginia, in that category. Of course there were other occasions in which he dissented, twenty-five in all, but in the company of associates. One of these was *Groves* v. *Slaughter,* 16 Pet. 449 (1841). Here the state of Mississippi had amended its constitution to curb the overimportation of slaves from other states. A Mississippian refused, in 1839, to pay for some slaves, contending the purchase was void, being in violation of the state constitutional provision. A majority of the Court held that specific state legislation was necessary to enforce the state constitutional stipulation; therefore the contract was valid. This narrow decision upholding the Mississippi provision, obviated the need for taking up the vexing question of the exclusivity or non-exclusivity of the federal commerce power affecting the movement of slaves across state lines. But Justice McLean insisted on reading an opinion arguing for the exclusive character of the federal commerce power, that states could not regulate interstate commerce whether Congress had legislated on the subject or not. McKinley's judicial bedfellow in this case was Story, the man who had lamented the Bank of Augusta circuit opinion. Both men considered the contract void, believing that supplementary legislation was not needed to validate Mississippi's constitutional prohibition. But here they parted company. The Massachusetts jurist supported an exclusive federal view of the commerce power; the Alabamian, although he did not go into the question in *Groves* v. *Slaughter,* did not.

At the end of that decade, the Court decided the *Passenger Cases,* 7 How. 283 (1849), but with a multitude of aggregate voices constituting the majority. Both New York and Massachusetts were raising revenue through head taxes upon alien passengers arriving in the states' ports. The money raised would be used to cope with problems created by immigrants, citing the local police power as justification. Five Justices agreed that the laws were an unconstitutional state regulation of commerce, but each man had his separate say. McKinley prepared an opinion, although he agreed "in the whole reasoning upon the main question" because he felt the Court had not adequately dealt with the constitutional clause which prohibited congressional interference, before 1808, with the migration or importation of such persons as the states wished to admit. He thought "migration" and "importation" referred to separate categories, the latter covering slaves and articles of commerce. Thus, after 1808, migrants could not be subjected to restrictions by the states, since federal jurisdiction obtained through an enumerated power; "it therefore follows, that passengers can never be subject to state laws until they become a portion of the population of the state." When the Court expounded its doctrine of selective exclusiveness in 1852, in *Cooley* v. *Board of Wardens,* 12 How. 299, McKinley was absent and near death.

Two cases decided in 1845, although not themselves overly important, are useful in highlighting McKinley's constitutional views. In *Lane* v. *Vick,* 3 How. 464 (1845), he dissented (Chief Justice Taney was another dissenter) from an opinion which he thought expanded the jurisdiction and power of the federal courts far too much. The Court was called on to interpret various provisions of a will bequeathing certain land in Mississippi. The Court held that the construction of the will made by the Mississippi Supreme Court was not binding on it. Concurrent jurisdiction existed in many categories of civil cases, and he tended to the belief that in most, the state court's interpretation should be followed by federal courts. There was no precise boundary line, but McKinley leaned in favor of the state decisions unless the need for federal uniformity was clearly undeniable. And in *Pollard* v. *Hagan,* 3 How. 212 (1845), McKinley returned to his favorite subject while in Congress, the power of the federal government over the public lands. The federal government could not exercise sovereignty over the lands because it merely held them as trustee for states which would ultimately be created from those lands. Thus the states-to-be, if they were to stand on a basis of equality with the original states, must be considered the sovereignties. The compact among sovereigns could have no effective meaning if the central agency were to pass beyond the bounds allotted to it by the member sovereigns. Finally, since the national government had not exercised sovereignty within the original states, except where the states had so granted such exercise (as in military posts, or in the District of Columbia), it could not do so within the new states. It should be noted that McKinley was not in this instance speaking as a doctrinal voice in the wilderness, since a clear majority of the Court accepted this view.

The Court term of 1845 was the highwater mark of McKinley's judicial effectiveness. That year, he wrote a total of ten opinions, his largest output for a single term. After that, chronic bad health curtailed his activities, and he descended from a relatively prominent role to one of virtual obscurity during the next seven years. He had by this time moved to Lexington, Kentucky, and the farflung circuit he had to travel did little to aid in the restoration of his health. In 1838, the Justices were asked to report on the number of miles they had travelled annually to meet with district judges as a federal circuit court. McKinley, who was assigned to cover Alabama, Mississippi, Louisiana, and Arkansas, reported in sorrow that this meant at least ten thousand miles of travelling. Other Justices were in the vicinity of two thousand miles in their estimates (Taney had to put up with a mere 458 miles); McKinley had fewer cases than Taney, but was far and away the champion traveller, although anything but an enchanted one. He cut down on travel by neglecting to go to Arkansas.

When McKinley died at Lexington on July 19, 1852, Chief Justice Taney called him "a sound lawyer, faithful and assiduous in the discharge of his duties," although he added at once, "while his health was sufficient to undergo the labor." Taney's biographer, Carl B. Swisher, has written that McKinley was a "man of moderate ability who achieved neither distinction nor notoriety," and with this judgment there is little or no basis for quarrel. Other southerners, both jurists and non-jurists, were saying the same things as McKinley, and saying them with more bite and with more eloquence, but no one was saying them with more consistency or conviction.

SELECTED BIBLIOGRAPHY

McKinley remains virtually unknown, and the paucity of scholarly writing on antebellum Alabama does not indicate any change in the near future. Jimmie Hicks, "Associate Justice John McKinley: A Sketch," 18 *Alabama Review* 227 (1965) is, as its title indicates, little more than a sketch. John M. Martin, "John McKinley: Jacksonian Phase," 28 *Alabama Historical Quarterly* 7 (1966) is more detailed but covers only the congressional career as revealed in the *Register of Debates*.

John McKinley

REPRESENTATIVE OPINIONS

POLLARD'S LESSEE v. HAGAN, 3 HOW. 212 (1845)

Ownership of the public lands of the United States was often contested by the states and the federal government before the Civil War. One typical case arose in Alabama where the claimant of certain land in the city of Mobile traced his ownership to a patent of the federal government. To decide whether his claim was valid, the Court was compelled to determine the nature of the relationship between the federal government and both the original thirteen states and later states entering the Union. McKinley held for the Court that the federal government held all public lands out of which later states were created in trust for the new states and their governments had the same power of sovereignty over their territory as the original thirteen colonies. Thus Alabama's claim to the land in question was superior to that of the federal government.

Mr. Justice McKINLEY delivered the opinion of the court.

This case comes before this court upon a writ of error to the Supreme Court of Alabama.

An action of ejectment was brought by the plaintiffs against the defendants, in the Circuit Court of Mobile county, in said state; and upon the trial, to support their action, "the plaintiffs read in evidence a patent from the United States for the premises in question, and an act of Congress passed the 6th day of July, 1836, confirming to them the premises in the patent mentioned, together with an act of Congress passed the 20th of May, 1824. The premises in question were admitted by the defendants to be comprehended within the patent; and there was likewise an admission by both parties that the land lay between Church street and North Boundary street, in the city of Mobile; and there the plaintiffs rested their case."

"The defendants, to maintain the issue on their part, introduced a witness to prove that the premises in question, between the years 1819 and 1823, were covered by water of the Mobile river at common high tide;" to which evidence the plaintiffs by their counsel objected; but the court overruled the objection, and permitted the evidence to go to the jury. "It was also in proof, on the part of the defendant, that at the date of the Spanish grant to Panton, Leslie & Co., under which they claim, the waters of the Mobile bay, at high tide, flowed over what is now Water street, and over about one-third of the lot west of Water street, conveyed by the Spanish grant to Panton, Leslie & Co.; and that the waters continued to overflow Water street, and the premises sued for, during all the time up to 1822 or 1823; to all which admissions of evidence, on part of the defendants, the plaintiffs excepted." "The court charged the jury, that if they believed the premises sued for were below usual high water-mark, at the time Alabama was admitted into the union, then the act of Congress, and the patent in pursuance thereof, could give the plaintiffs no title, whether the waters had receded by the labor of man only, or by alluvion; to which the plaintiffs excepted. Whereupon a verdict and judgment were rendered in favor of the defendants, and which judgment was afterwards affirmed by the Supreme Court of the state."

This question has been heretofore raised, before this court, in cases from the same state, but they went off upon other points. As now presented, it is the only question necessary to the decision of the case before us, and must, therefore, be decided. And we now enter into its examination with a just sense of its great importance to all the states of the union, and particularly to the new ones. Although this is the first time we have been called upon to draw the line that separates the sovereignty and jurisdiction of the government of the union, and the state governments, over the subject in controversy, many of the principles which enter into and form the elements of the question have been settled by previous, well considered, decisions of this court, to which we shall have occasion to refer in the course of this investigation.

The counsel for the plaintiffs insisted, in argument, that the United States derived title to that part of Alabama, in which the land in controversy lies, from the King of Spain; and that they succeeded to all his rights, powers, and jurisdiction, over the territory ceded, and therefore hold the land and soil, under navigable waters, according to the laws and usages of Spain; and by those laws and usages the rights of a subject to land derived from the crown could not extend beyond high watermark, on navigable waters, without an express grant; and that all alluvion belonged to the crown, and might be granted by this king, together with all land between high water and the channel of such navigable waters; and by the compact between the United States and Alabama, on her admission into the union, it was agreed, that the people of Alabama for ever disclaimed all right or title to the waste or unappropriated lands lying within the state, and that the same should remain at the sole disposal of the United States; and that all the navigable waters within the state should for ever remain public highways, and free to the citizens of that state and the United States, without any tax, duty, or impost, or toll therefor, imposed by that state. That by these articles of the compact, the land under the navigable waters, and the public domain above high water, were alike reserved to the United States, and alike subject to be sold by them; and to give any other construction to these compacts, would be to yield up to Alabama, and the other new states, all the public lands within their limits.

We think a proper examination of this subject will show, that the United States never held any municipal sovereignty, jurisdiction, or right of soil in and to the territory, of which Alabama, or any of the new states were formed; except for temporary purposes, and to execute the trusts created by the acts of the Virginia and Georgia legislatures, and the deeds of cession executed by them to the United States, and the trust created by the treaty with the French republic, of the 30th of April, 1803, ceding Louisiana.

All that part of Alabama which lies between the thirty-first and thirty-fifth degree of north latitude, was ceded by the state of Georgia to the United States, by deed bearing date the 24th day of April, 1802, which is substantially, in all its principles and stipulations, like the deed of cession executed by Virginia to the United States, on the 1st day of March, 1784, by which she ceded to the United States the territory north-west of the river Ohio. Both of these deeds of cession stipulated, that all the lands within the territory ceded and not reserved or appropriated to other purposes, should be considered as a common fund for the use and benefit of all the United States, to be faithfully and *bona fide* disposed of for that purpose, and for no other use or purpose whatever. And the statute passed by Virginia authorizing her delegates to execute this deed, and which is recited in it, authorizes them, in behalf of the state, by a proper deed to convey to the United States, for the benefit of said states, all the right, title, and claim, as well of soil as jurisdiction, "upon condition that the territory so ceded shall be laid out and formed into states, containing a suitable extent of territory, not less than 100, nor more than 150 miles square, or as near thereto as circumstances will admit: and that the states so formed shall be republican states and admitted members of the federal union, having the same rights of sovereignty, freedom, and independence, as the other states." And the delegates conclude the deed thus: "Now know ye, that we, the said Thomas Jefferson, Samuel Hardy, Arthur Lee, and James Monroe, by virtue of the power and authority committed to us by the act of the said general assembly of Virginia before recited, and in the name and for and on behalf of the said commonwealth, do by these presents convey, transfer, assign, and make over unto the United States in Congress assembled, for the benefit of said states, Virginia inclusive, all right, title, and claim, as well of soil as of jurisdiction, which the said commonwealth hath to the territory or tract of country within the limits of the Virginia charter, situate, lying, and being to the north-west of the river Ohio, to and for the uses and purposes, and on the conditions of the said recited act."

And in the deed of cession by Georgia it is expressly stipulated, "That the territory thus ceded shall form a state and be admitted as such into the union as soon as it shall contain sixty thousand free inhabitants, or at an earlier period if Congress shall think it expedient, on the same conditions and restrictions, with the same privileges, and in the same manner, as is provided in the ordinance of Congress of the 13th day of July, 1787, for the government of the north-western territory of the United States, which ordinance shall in all its parts extend to the territory contained in the present act of cession, that article only excepted which forbids slavery." The manner in which the new states were to be admitted into the union, according to the ordinance of 1787, as expressed therein, is as follows: "And whenever any of the said states shall have sixty thousand free inhabitants therein, such state shall be admitted by its delegates into the Congress of the United States, on an equal footing with the original states in all respects whatever." Thus it appears that the stipulations, trusts, and conditions, are substantially the same in both of these deeds of cession; and the acts of Congress, and of the state legislatures in relation thereto, are founded in the same reasons of policy and interest, with this exception, however—the cession made by Virginia was before the adoption of the Constitution of the United States, and that of Georgia afterwards. Taking the legislative acts of the United States, and the states of Virginia and Georgia, and their deeds of cession to the United States, and giving to each, separately, and to all jointly, a fair interpretation, we must come to the conclusion that it was the intention of the parties to invest the United States with the eminent domain of the country ceded, both national and municipal, for the purposes of temporary government, and to hold it in trust for the performance of the stipulations and conditions expressed in the deeds of cession and the legislative acts connected with them. To a correct understanding of the rights, powers, and duties of the parties to these contracts, it is necessary to enter into a more minute examination of the rights of eminent domain, and the right to the public lands. When the United States accepted the cession of the territory, they took upon themselves the trust to hold the municipal eminent domain for the new states, and to invest them with it, to the same extent, in all respects, that it was held by the states ceding the territories.

The right which belongs to the society, or to the sovereign, of disposing, in case of necessity, and for the public safety, of all the wealth contained in the state, is called the *eminent domain*. It is evident that this right is, in certain cases, necessary to him who governs, and is, consequently, a part of the empire, or sovereign power. Vat. Law of Nations, section 244. This definition shows, that the eminent domain, although a sovereign power, does not include all sovereign power, and this explains the sense in which it is used in this opinion. The compact made between the United States and the state of Georgia, was sanctioned by the Constitution of the United States; by the 3d section of the 4th article of which it is declared, that "New states may be admitted by the Congress into this union; but no new state shall be formed or erected within the jurisdiction of any other state, nor any state be formed by the junction of two or more states or parts of states, without the consent of the legislatures of the states concerned, as well as of Congress."

When Alabama was admitted into the union, on an equal footing with the original states, she succeeded to all the rights of sovereignty, jurisdiction, and eminent domain which Georgia possessed at the date of the cession, except so far as this right was diminished by the public lands remaining in the possession and under the control of the United States, for the temporary purposes provided for in the deed of cession and the legislative acts connected with it. Nothing remained to the United States, according to the terms of the agreement, but the public lands. And, if an express stipulation had been inserted in the agreement, granting the municipal right of sovereignty and eminent domain to the United States, such stipulation would have been void and inoperative: because the United States have no constitutional capacity to exercise municipal jurisdiction, sovereignty, or eminent domain, within the limits of a state or elsewhere, except in the cases in which it is expressly granted.[1]

By the 16th clause of the 8th section of the 1st article of the Constitution, power is given to Congress "to exercise exclusive legislation in all cases whatsoever, over such district (not exceeding ten miles square) as may by cession of particular states, and the acceptance of Congress, become the seat of government of the United States, and to exercise like authority over all places purchased, by the consent of the legislature of the state in which the same may be, for the erection of forts, magazines, arsenals, dock-yards, and other needful buildings." Within the District of Columbia, and the other places purchased and used for the purposes above mentioned, the national and municipal powers of government, of every description, are united in the government of the union. And these are the only cases, within the United States, in which all the powers of government are united in a single government, except in the cases already mentioned of the temporary territorial governments, and there a local government exists. The right of Alabama and every other new state to exercise all the powers of government, which belong to and may be exercised by the original states of the union, must be admitted, and remain unquestioned, except so far as they are, temporarily, deprived of control over the public lands.

We will now inquire into the nature and extent of the right of the United States to these lands, and whether that right can in any manner affect or control the decision of the case before us. This right originated in voluntary surrenders, made by several of the old states, of their waste and unappropriated lands, to the United States, under a resolution of the old Congress, of the 6th of September, 1780, recommending such surrender and cession, to aid in paying the public debt, incurred by the war of the Revolution. The

[1] *The statement, that the United States government has no power to take lands within the boundaries of a state by the exercise of the right of eminent domain, has been overruled by the Supreme Court of the United States,* (Kohl *v.* United States, *1 Otto, 367*), *without any reference to this statement. A quotation of a single sentence from Cooley on Constitutional Limitations is made by the court, and relied upon: "So far, however, as the general government may deem it important to appropriate lands or other property for its own purposes and to enable it to perform its functions,—as must sometimes be necessary in the case of forts, light-houses, military posts or roads, and other conveniences and necessities of government—the general government may still exercise the authority, as well within the state as within the territory under its exclusive jurisdiction, and its right to do so may be supported by the same reasons which support the right in any case; that is to say, the absolute necessity that means in the government for performing its functions and perpetuating its existence should not be liable to be controlled or defeated by the want of consent of private parties, or of any other authority."* Cooley Const. Lim., *651, (5 ed.) In* Gilmer *v.* Lime Point, *18 Cal., 229, it was held that the state might take property by the exercise of the right of eminent domain and devote it to the general government for its use. So in* Burt *v.* Merchants' Ins. Co., *106 Mass., 356;* s. c. *115 Mass., 1;* Burt *v.* Wigglesworth, *117 Id., 302. So it might pass an act authorizing the general government to take land for public use under the clause in the constitution of the state authorizing the state to take land for the public use.* Reddall *v.* Bryon, *14 Md., 444. See* Ash *v.* Cummings, *50 N. H., 591. But in* People ex rel. Twombly *v.* Auditor General, *23 Mich., 471, it was held that the state could not thus take and appropriate lands, for the general government had the power to take such lands when it deemed it necessary, and therefore, the state had no authority to do so; and in* Darlington *v.* United States, *82 Pa. St., 382, the act of Congress authorizing such a taking was upheld.*

object of all the parties to these contracts of cession, was to convert the land into money for the payment of the debt, and to erect new states over the territory thus ceded; and as soon as these purposes could be accomplished, the power of the United States over these lands, as property, was to cease.

Whenever the United States shall have fully executed these trusts, the municipal sovereignty of the new states will be complete, throughout their respective borders, and they, and the original states, will be upon an equal footing, in all respects whatever. We, therefore, think the United States hold the public lands within the new states by force of the deeds of cession, and the statutes connected with them, and not by any municipal sovereignty which it may be supposed they possess, or have reserved by compact with the new states, for that particular purpose. The provision of the Constitution above referred to shows that no such power can be exercised by the United States within a state. Such a power is not only repugnant to the Constitution, but it is inconsistent with the spirit and intention of the deeds of cession. The argument so much relied on by the counsel for the plaintiffs, that the agreement of the people inhabiting the new states, "that they for ever disclaim all right and title to the waste or unappropriated lands lying within the said territory; and that the same shall be and remain at the sole and entire disposition of the United States," cannot operate as a contract between the parties, but is binding as a law. Full power is given to Congress "to make all needful rules and regulations respecting the territory or other property of the United States." This authorized the passage of all laws necessary to secure the rights of the United States to the public lands, and to provide for their sale, and to protect them from taxation.

And all constitutional laws are binding on the people, in the new states and the old ones, whether they consent to be bound by them or not. Every constitutional act of Congress is passed by the will of the people of the United States, expressed through their representatives, on the subject-matter of the enactment; and when so passed it becomes the supreme law of the land, and operates by its own force on the subject-matter, in whatever state or territory it may happen to be. The proposition, therefore, that such a law cannot operate upon the subject-matter of its enactment, without the express consent of the people of the new state where it may happen to be, contains its own refutation, and requires no farther examination. The propositions submitted to the people of the Alabama territory for their acceptance or rejection, by the act of Congress authorizing them to form a constitution and state government for themselves, so far as they related to the public lands within that territory, amounted to nothing more nor less than rules and regulations respecting the sales and disposition of the public lands. The supposed compact relied on by the counsel for the plaintiffs, conferred no authority, therefore, on Congress to pass the act granting to the plaintiffs the land in controversy.

And this brings us to the examination of the question, whether Alabama is entitled to the shores of the navigable waters, and the soils under them, within her limits. The principal argument relied on against this right, is, that the United States acquired the land in controversy from the King of Spain. Although there was no direct reference to any particular treaty, we presume the treaty of the 22d of February, 1819, signed at Washington, was the one relied on, and shall so consider the argument. It was insisted that the United States had, under the treaty, succeeded to all the rights and powers of the King of Spain; and as by the laws and usages of Spain, the king had the right to grant to a subject the soil under navigable waters, that, therefore, the United States had the right to grant the land in controversy, and thereby the plaintiffs acquired a complete title.

If it were true that the United States acquired the whole of Alabama from Spain, no such consequences would result as those contended for. It cannot be admitted that the King of Spain could, by treaty or otherwise, impart to the United States any of his royal prerogatives; and much less can it be admitted that they have capacity to receive or power to exercise them. Every nation acquiring territory, by treaty or otherwise, must hold it subject to the constitution and laws of its own government, and not according to those of the government ceding it. Vat. Law of Nations, b. 1, c. 19, s. 210, 244, 245, and b. 2, c. 7, s. 80.

The United States have never claimed any part of the territory included in the states of Mississippi or Alabama, under any treaty with Spain, although she claimed at different periods a considerable portion of the territory in both of those states. By the treaty between the United States and Spain, signed at San Lorenzo el Real, on the 27th of October, 1795, "The high contracting parties declare and agree, that the line between the United States and East and West Florida, shall be designated by a line, beginning on the river Mississippi, at the northernmost part of the thirty-first degree of north latitude, which from thence shall be drawn due east to the middle of the Chatahouchee river," &c. This treaty declares and agrees, that the line which was described in the treaty of peace between Great Britain and the United States, as their southern boundary, shall be the line which divides their territory from East and West Florida. The article does not import to be a cession of territory, but the adjustment of a controversy between the two nations. It is understood as an admission that the right was originally in the United States.

Had Spain considered herself as ceding territory, she could not have neglected to stipulate for the property of the inhabitants, a stipulation which every sentiment of justice and of national honor would have demanded, and which the United States would not have refused. But, instead of requiring an article to this effect, she expressly stipulated to withdraw the settlements then within what the treaty admits to be the territory of the United States, and for permission to the settlers to take their property with them. "We think this an unequivocal acknowledgement that the occupation of the territory by Spain was wrongful, and we think the opinion thus clearly indicated was supported by the state of facts. It follows, that Spanish grants made after the treaty of peace can have no intrinsic validity." *Henderson* v. *Poindexter,* 12 Wheat., 535.

Previous to the cession made by Georgia, the United States, by the act of Congress of the 7th of April, 1798, had established the Mississippi territory including the territory west of the Chatahouchee river, to the Mississippi river, above the 31st degree of north latitude, and below the Yazous river, subject to the claim of Georgia to any portion of the territory. And the territory thus erected was subjected to the ordinance of the 13th of July, 1787, for its government, that part of it excepted which prohibited slavery: 1 Story's Laws, 494. And by the act of the 1st of March, 1817, having first obtained consent of Georgia to make two states instead of one within the ceded territory, Congress authorized the inhabitants of the western part of the Mississippi territory to form for themselves a constitution and state government, "to consist of all the territory included within the following boundaries, to wit: Beginning on the river Mississippi at the point where the southern boundary line of the state of Tennessee strikes the same; thence east along the said boundary line to the Tennessee river; thence up the same to the mouth of Bear creek: thence by a direct line, to the north-west corner of Washington county; thence due south to the Gulf of Mexico; thence westwardly, including all the islands within six leagues of the shore, to the junction of Pearl river with Lake Borgne; thence up said river to the thirty-first degree of north latitude; thence west along said degree of latitude to the Mississippi river; thence up the same to the beginning." 3 Story's Laws, 1620. And on the 3d of March, 1817, Congress passed an act declaring "That all that part of the Mississippi territory which lies within the following boundaries, to wit: Beginning at the point where the line of the thirty-first degree of north latitude intersects the Perdido river; thence east to the western boundary line of the state of Georgia; thence along said line to the southern boundary line of the state of Tennessee; thence west, along said boundary line, to the Tennessee river; thence up the same to the mouth of Bear creek; thence by a direct line to the north-west corner of Washington county; thence due south to the Gulf of Mexico; thence eastwardly, including all the islands within six leagues of the shore to the Perdido river; thence up the same to the beginning; shall, for the purposes of temporary government, constitute a separate territory, and be called Alabama."

And by the 2d section of the same act it is enacted, "That all offices which exist, and all laws which may be in force when this act shall go into effect, shall continue to exist and be in force until otherwise provided by law." 3 Story's Laws, 1634, 1635. And by the 2d article of the compact contained in the ordinance of 1787, which was then in force in the Mississippi territory, among other things, it was provided, that "the inhabitants of the said territory shall always be entitled to the benefits of the writ of habeas corpus, and of the trial by jury, and of judicial proceedings according to the course of the common law." And by the proviso to the 5th section of the act of the 2d of March, 1819, authorizing the people of the Alabama territory to form a constitution and state government, it is enacted, "That the constitution, when formed, shall be republican, and not repugnant to the ordinance of the 13th of July, 1787, between the states and the people of the territory north-west of the Ohio river, so far as the same has been extended to the said territory [of Alabama] by the articles of agreement between the United States and the state of Georgia." By these successive acts on part of the United States, the common law has been extended to all the territory within the limits of the state of Alabama, and therefore excluded all other law, Spanish or French.

It was after the date of the treaty of the 22d of February, 1819, between the United States and Spain, but before its ratification, the people of the Alabama territory were authorized to form a constitution; and the state was admitted into the union, according to the boundaries established when the country was erected into a territorial government. But the United States have never admitted that they derived title from the Spanish government to any portion of the territory included within the limits of Alabama. Whatever claim Spain may have asserted to the territory above the thirty-first degree of north latitude, prior to the treaty of the 27th of October, 1795, was abandoned by that treaty, as has been already shown. We will now inquire whether she had any right to territory below the thirty-first degree of north latitude, after the treaty between France and the United States, signed at Paris on the 30th of April, 1803, by which Louisiana was ceded to the United States. The legislative and executive departments of the government have constantly asserted the right of the United States to this portion of the territory under the 1st article of this treaty; and a series of measures intended to maintain the right have been adopted. Mobile was taken possession of, and erected into a collection district, by act of the 24th of February, 1804, chap. 13, (2 Story's Laws, 914.) In the year 1810, the President issued his proclamation, directing the governor of the Orleans territory to take possession of the country, as far as the Perdido, and hold it for the United States. In April, 1812, Congress passed an act to enlarge the limits of Louisiana. This act includes part of the country claimed by Spain, as West Florida. And in February, 1813, the President was authorized to occupy and hold all that tract of country called West Florida, which lies west of the river Perdido, not then in the possession of the United States. And these measures having been followed by the erection of Mississippi territory into a state, and the erection of Alabama into a territory, and afterwards into a state, in the year 1819, and extending them both over this territory: could it be doubted that these measures were intended as an assertion of the title of the United States to this country?

In the case of *Foster* and *Elam* v. *Neilson,* 2 Pet., 253, the right of the United States to this country underwent a very able and thorough investigation. And Chief Justice Marshall, in delivering the opinion of the court, said: "After these acts of sovereign power over the territory in dispute, asserting the American construction of the treaty, by which the government claims it, to maintain the opposite construction in its own courts would certainly be an anomaly in the history and practice of nations. If those departments, which are intrusted with the foreign intercourse of the nation, which assert and maintain its interests against foreign powers, have unequivocally asserted its rights of dominion over a country of which it is in possession, and which it claims under a treaty; if the legislature has acted on the construction thus asserted, it is not in its own courts that this construction is to be denied." The chief justice then discusses the validity of the grant made by the Spanish government, after the ratification of the treaty between the United States and France, and it is finally rejected on the ground that the country belonged to the United States, and not to Spain, when the grant was made. The same doctrine was maintained by this court in the case of *Garcia* v. *Lee,* 12 Pet., 511. These cases establish, beyond controversy, the right of the United States to the whole of this territory, under the treaty with France.

Alabama is therefore entitled to the sovereignty and jurisdiction over all the territory within her limits, subject to the common law, to the same extent that Georgia possessed it before she ceded it to the United States. To maintain any other doctrine, is to deny that Alabama has been admitted into the union on an equal footing with the original states, the constitution, laws, and compact, to the contrary notwithstanding. But her rights of sovereignty and jurisdiction are not governed by the common law of England as it prevailed in the colonies before the Revolution, but as modified by our own institutions. In the case of *Martin and others* v. *Waddell,* 16 Pet., 410, the present chief justice, in delivering the opinion of the court, said: "When the Revolution took place, the people of each state became themselves sovereign; and in that character hold the absolute right to all their navigable waters, and the soils under them for their own common use, subject only to the rights since surrendered by the Constitution." Then to Alabama belong the navigable waters, and soils under them, in controversy in this case, subject to the rights surrendered by the Constitution to the United States; and no compact that might be made between her and the United States could diminish or enlarge these rights.

The declaration, therefore, contained in the compact entered into between them when Alabama was admitted into the union, "that all navigable waters within the said state shall for ever remain public highways, free to the citizens of said state, and of the United States, without any tax, duty, impost, or toll therefor, imposed by the said state," would be void if inconsistent with the Constitution of the United States. But is this provision repugnant to the Constitution? By the 8th section of the 1st article of the Constitution, power is granted to Congress "to regulate commerce with foreign nations, and among the several states." If, in the exercise of this power, Congress can impose the same restrictions upon the original states, in relation to their navigable waters, as are imposed, by this article of the compact, on the state of Alabama, then this article is a mere regulation of commerce among the several states, according to the Constitution, and, therefore, as binding on the other states as Alabama.

In the case of *Gibbons* v. *Ogden,* 9 Wheat., 196, after examining the preliminary questions respecting the regulation of commerce with foreign nations, and among the states, as connected with the subject-matter there in controversy, Chief Justice Marshall said: "We are now arrived at the inquiry: What is this power?

"It is the power to regulate, that is, to prescribe the rule by which commerce is to be governed. This power, like all others vested in Congress, is complete in itself, may be exercised to its utmost extent, and acknowledges no limitations other than are prescribed in the Constitution. These are expressed in plain terms, and do not affect the questions which arise in this case. If, as has been always understood, the sovereignty of Congress, though limited to specified objects, is plenary as to those objects, the power over commerce with foreign nations, and among the several states, is vested in Congress as absolutely as it would be in a single government having in its constitution the same restrictions on the exercise of the power as are found in the Constitution of the United States." As the provision of what is called the compact between the United States and the state of Alabama does not, by the above reasoning, exceed the power thereby conceded to Congress over the original states on the same subject, no power or right was, by the compact, intended to be reserved by the United States, nor to be granted to them by Alabama.

This supposed compact is, therefore, nothing more than a regulation of commerce, to that extent, among the several states, and can have no controlling influence in the decision of the case before us. This right of eminent domain over the shores and the soils under the navigable waters, for all municipal purposes, belongs exclusively to the states within their respective territorial jurisdictions and they, and they only, have the constitutional power to exercise it. To give to the United States the right to transfer to a citizen the title to the shores and the soils under the navigable waters, would be placing in their hands a weapon which might be wielded greatly to the injury of state sovereignty, and deprive the states of the power to exercise a numerous and important class of police powers. But in the hands of the states this power can never be used so as to affect the exercise of any national right of eminent domain or jurisdiction with which the United States have been invested by the Constitution. For, although the territorial limits of Alabama have extended all her sovereign power into the sea, it is there, as on the shore, but municipal power, subject to the Constitution of the United States, "and the laws which shall be made in pursuance thereof."[1]

By the preceding course of reasoning we have arrived at these general conclusions: First, The shores of navigable waters, and the soils under them, were not granted by the Constitution to the United States, but were reserved to the states respectively. Secondly, The new states have the same rights, sovereignty, and jurisdiction over this subject as the original states. Thirdly, The right of the United States to the public lands, and the power of Congress to make all needful

[1] *Quoted.* Gilman *v.* Philadelphia, *3 Wall., 726.*

rules and regulations for the sale and disposition thereof, conferred no power to grant to the plaintiffs the land in controversy in this case. The judgement of the Supreme Court of the state of Alabama is therefore, affirmed.

BANK OF AUGUSTA v. EARLE, 13 PET. 519 (1839)

A Georgia bank had purchased a bill of exchange and then sued the maker of the bill (a citizen of Alabama) in his home state. One of the defenses raised was that the bank, created under the laws of Georgia, could not act beyond its borders. This defense was upheld by McKinley, sitting on circuit in Alabama. His opinion, in Justice Story's words, "frightened half the lawyers and all the corporations of the country out of their proprieties." On appeal to the Supreme Court, the decision was reversed, but McKinley in dissent defended his position in a violently anti-corporate opinion.

McKinley, Justice. (*Dissenting.*)—I dissent from so much of the opinion of the majority of the court as decides that the law of nations furnishes a rule by which validity can be given to the contracts in these cases; and from so much as decides that the contracts, which were the subjects of the suits, were not against the policy of the laws of Alabama.

This is the first time since the adoption of the constitution of the United States, that any federal court has, directly or indirectly, imputed national power to any of the states of the Union; and it is the first time that validity has been given to such contracts, which, it is acknowledged, would otherwise have been void, by the application of a principle of the necessary law of nations. This principle has been adopted and administered by the court as part of the municipal law of the state of Alabama, although no such principle has been adopted or admitted by that state. And whether the law of nations still prevails among the states, notwithstanding the constitution of the United States? or the right and authority to administer it in these cases are derived from that instrument? are questions not distinctly decided by the majority of the court. But whether attempted to be derived from one source or the other, I deny the existence of it anywhere, for any such purpose.

Because the municipal laws of nations cannot operate beyond their respective territorial limits, and because one nation has no right to legislate for another; certain rules, founded in the law of nature and the immutable principles of justice have, for the promotion of harmony and commercial intercourse, been adopted by the consent of civilized nations. But no necessity exists for such a law among the several states. In their character of states, they are governed by written constitutions and municipal laws. It has been admitted by the counsel, and decided by the majority of the court, that without the authority of the statutes of the states, chartering these banks, they would have no power whatever to purchase a bill of exchange, even in the state where they are established. If it requires the exertion of the legislative power of Pennsylvania, for instance, to enable the United States Bank to purchase a bill of exchange in that state; why should it not require the same legislative authority, to enable it to do the same act in Alabama? It has been contended in argument, that the power granted to the bank to purchase a bill of exchange at Philadelphia, in Pennsylvania, payable at Mobile, in Alabama, would be nugatory, unless the power existed also to make contracts at both ends of the line of exchange. The authority to deal in exchange may very well be exercised, by having command of one end of the line of exchange only. To buy and sell the same bill at the bank, is dealing in exchange, and may be exercised with profit to the bank; but not perhaps as conveniently as if it could make contracts in Alabama as well as at the bank.

But if it has obtained authority to command but one end of the line of exchange, it certainly has no right to complain that it cannot control the other, when that other is within the jurisdiction of another state, whose authority or consent it has not even asked for. The bill of exchange which is the subject of controversy between the Bank of Augusta and Earle, and that which is the subject of controversy between the United States Bank and Primrose, were both drawn at Mobile, and made payable at New York. Neither of the banks had authority from any state, to make a contract at either end of the line of exchange here established. Here, then, they claim, and have exercised, all the rights and privileges of natural persons, independent of their charters; and claim the right, by the comity of nations, to make original contracts everywhere, because they have a right, by their charters, to make like contracts in the states where they were created, and have "a local habitation and a name."

It is difficult to conceive of the exercise of national comity, by a state having no national power. Whatever national power the old thirteen states possessed, previous to the adoption of the constitution of the United States, they conferred, by that instrument, upon the federal government. And to remove all doubt upon the question, whether the power thus conferred was exclusive or concurrent, the states are, by the tenth section of the first article of the constitution, expressly prohibited from entering into any treaty, alliance or confederation; and without the consent of congress, from entering into any agreement or compact with another state, or with a foreign power. By these provisions, the states have, by their own voluntary act, and for wise purposes, deprived themselves of all national power, and of all the means of international communication; and cannot even enter into an agreement or compact with a sister state, for any purpose whatever, without the consent of congress. The comity of nations is defined by Judge STORY, in his Conflict of Laws, to be the obligations of the laws of one nation in the territories of another, derived altogether from the voluntary consent of the latter. And in the absence of any positive rule, affirming, or denying, or restraining, the operation of foreign laws, courts of justice presume the tacit adoption of them by their own government, unless they are repugnant to its policy or prejudicial to its interests. Conflict of Laws 37.

Now, I ask again, what is the necessity for such a rule of law as this? Have not the states full power to adopt or reject what laws of their sister states they please? And why should the courts interfere in this case, when the states have full power to legislate for themselves, and to adopt or reject such laws of their sister states as they think proper? If Alabama had adopted these laws, no difficulty could have arisen in deciding between these parties. This court would not then have been under the necessity of resorting to a doubtful presumption for a rule to guide its decision. But when the court have determined that they have the power to presume that Alabama has adopted the laws of the states chartering these banks, other difficult questions arise. How much of the charter of each bank has been adopted? This is a question of legislative discretion, which, if submitted to the legislature of the state, would be decided upon reasons of policy and public convenience. And the question of power, to pass such a law, under the constitution of Alabama, would have to be considered and decided. These are very inconvenient questions for a judicial tribunal to determine. As the majority of the court have not expressly stated whether Alabama has adopted the whole charters of the banks, or what parts they have adopted there is now no certainty what the law of Alabama is on the subject of these charters.

But these are not all the difficulties that arise in the exercise of this power by the judiciary. Many questions very naturally present themselves in the investigation of this subject, and the first is—to what government does this power belong? Secondly, has it been conferred upon the United States? or has it been reserved to the states by the tenth amendment of the constitution? If it be determined, that the power belongs to the United States, in what provision of the constitution is it to be found? And how is it to be exercised? By the judiciary or by congress? The counsel for the banks contended, that the power of congress to regulate commerce among the several states, deprives Alabama of the power to pass any law restraining the sale and purchase of a bill of exchange; and by consequence, the whole power belongs to congress. The court, by the opinion of the majority, does not recognise this doctrine, in terms. But if the power which the court exercised, is not derived from that provision of the constitution, in my opinion, it does not exist.

If ever congress shall exercise this power, to the broad extent contended for, the power of the states over commerce, and contracts relating to commerce, will be reduced to very narrow limits. The creation of banks, the making and indorsing of bills of exchange and promissory notes, and the damages on bills of exchange, all relate, more or less, to the commerce among the several states. Whether the exercise of these powers amounts to regulating the commerce among the several states, is not a question for my determination on this occasion. The majority of the court have decided that the comity of nations gives validity to these contracts.

And what are the reasons upon which this doctrine is now established? Why, the counsel for the banks say—we are obliged to concede, that these banks had no authority to make these contracts in the state of Alabama, in virtue of the laws of the states creating them, or by the laws of Alabama; therefore, unless this court will extend to them the benefit of the comity of nations, they must lose all the money now in controversy, they will be deprived hereafter of the benefit of a very profitable branch of their business as bankers, and great public inconvenience will result to the commerce of the country. And besides all this, there are many corporations in the north, which were created for the purpose of carrying on various branches of manufactures, and particularly that of cotton. Those engaged in the manufacture of cotton will be unable to send their agents to the south, to sell their manufactured articles, and to purchase cotton to carry on their business; and may lose debts already created. This is the whole amount of the argument, upon which the benefit of this doctrine is claimed. Because banks cannot make money in places and by means not authorized by their charters; because they may lose by contracts made in unauthorized places; because the commerce of the country may be subjected to temporary inconvenience; and because corporations in the north, created for manufacturing purposes only, cannot, by the authority of their charters, engage in commerce also; this doctrine, which has not heretofore found a place in our civil code, is to be established. Notwithstanding, it is conceded, that the states hold ample legislative power over the same subject, it is deemed necessary, on this occasion, to settle this doctrine by the supreme tribunal. The majority of the court having, in their opinion, conceded, that Alabama might make laws to prohibit foreign banks to make contracts, thereby admitted, by implication, that she could make laws to permit such contracts. I think it would have been proper to have left the power there, to be exercised or not, as Alabama, in her own sovereign discretion, might judge best for her interest or her comity. The majority of the court thought and decided otherwise. And here arises the radical and essential difference between them and me.

They maintain a power in the federal government, and in the judicial department of it, to do that which, in my judgment, belongs, exclusively, to the state governments; and to be exercised by the legislative and not the judicial departments thereof. A difference so radical and important, growing out of the fundamental laws of the land, has imposed on me the unpleasant necessity of maintaining, single-handed, my opinion, against the opinion of all the other members of the court. However unequal the conflict, duty impels me to maintain it firmly; and, although I stand alone here, I have the good fortune to be sustained, to the whole extent of my opinion, by the very able opinion of the court of appeals of Virginia, in the case of the *Marietta Bank* v. *Pindall,* 2 Rand. 465. If congress have the power to pass laws on this subject, it is an exclusive power; and the states would then have no power to prohibit contracts of any kind, within their jurisdictions. If the government of the United States have power to restrain the states, under the power to regulate commerce, whether it be exerted by the legislative or the judicial department of the government, is not material; it being the paramount law, it paralyzes all state power on the same subject. And this brings me to the consideration of the second ground on which I dissent.

It was contended by the counsel for the banks, that all the restraints imposed by the constitution of Alabama, in relation to banking, were designed to operate upon the legislature of the state, and not upon the citizens of that or any other state. To comprehend the whole scope and intention of that instrument, it will be necessary to ascertain, from the language used, what was within the contemplation and design of the convention. The provision in the constitution on the subject of banking is this: "One state bank may be established, with such number of branches as the general assembly may, from time to time, deem expedient; provided, that no branch bank shall be established, nor bank charter renewed, under the authority of this state, without the concurrence of two-thirds of both houses of the general assembly; and provided also, that not more than one bank nor branch bank shall be established, nor bank charter renewed, at any one session of the general assembly, nor shall any bank or branch bank be established, or bank charter renewed, but in conformity with the following rules: 1. At least two-fifths of the capital stock shall be reserved for the state. 2. A proportion of power in the direction of the bank shall be reserved to the state, equal at least to its proportion of stock therein. 3. The state, and the individual stockholders, shall be liable respectively, for the debts of the bank, in proportion to their stock holden therein. 4. The remedy for collecting debts shall be reciprocal for and against the bank. 5. No bank shall commence operations until half of the capital stock subscribed for shall be actually paid in gold or silver, which amount shall in no case be less than $100,000."

There are a few other unimportant rules laid down, but they are not material to the present inquiry. The inquiry naturally suggests itself to the mind—Why did Alabama introduce into her constitution these very unusual and specific rules? If they had not been deemed of great importance, they would not have been found there. Can any one say, therefore, that this regularly organized system, to which all banks within the state of Alabama were to conform, did not establish for the state, her legislature, or other authorities, a clear and unequivocal policy on the subject of banking? It has been conceded in the argument, and by the opinion of the majority of the court, that these constitutional provisions do restrict and limit the power of the legislature of the state. Then, the legislature cannot establish a bank in Alabama, but in conformity with the rules here laid down. They have established seven banks; five of them belonging exclusively to the state, and two-fifths of the stock of the other two, with a proportionate power in the direction, reserved to the state. Each of these banks is authorized to deal in exchange.

It is proper to stop here, and inquire whether the subject of exchange is proper to enter into the policy of the legislation of a state; and whether it is a part of the customary and legitimate business of banking. All the authorities on the subject show that, in modern times, it is a part of the business of banking. See Postlethwaite's Commercial Dictionary, tit. Bank; Tomlin's Law Dictionary, tit. Bank; Rees' Cyclopædia, tit. Bank; Vattel 105. This last author quoted, after showing that it is the duty of the sovereign of a nation to furnish for his subjects a sufficiency of money, for the purposes of commerce, to preserve it from adulteration, and to punish those who counterfeit it, proceeds to say, "There is another custom more modern, and of no less use to commerce, than the establishment of money, namely, exchange, for the business of the bankers; by means of whom a merchant remits immense sums from one end of the world to the other, with very little expense, and, if he pleases, without danger. For the same reasons that sovereigns are obliged to protect commerce, they are obliged to protect this custom by good laws, in which every merchant, foreigner or citizen may find security." From these authorities, it appears, that exchange is a part of modern banking, or at least so intimately connected with it, that all modern banks have authority to deal in it. And it also appears, that it is as much the duty of a state to provide for exchange, as for money or a circulating medium, for its subjects or citizens.

When the state of Alabama reserved to herself, by her fundamental law, at least two-fifths of the capital and control of all banks to be created in the state, and, by her laws, has actually appropriated to herself the whole of the capital, management and profits of five out of seven banks, and two-fifths of the other two; had she not the same right to appropriate the banking right, to deal in exchange, to herself, to the same extent? While performing her duty, under the constitution, by providing a circulating medium for the citizens, she was not unmindful of her duty in relation to exchange, and that is also provided for. Has she not provided increased security and safety to the merchant, by making herself liable for the payment of every bill of exchange sold by the five banks belonging to her, and for two-fifths of all sold by the other two? And has she not also provided by law, that all the profits derived from thus dealing in bills of exchange shall go into the public treasury, for the common benefit of the people of the state? And has she not, by the profits arising from her banking, including the profits on exchange, been enabled to pay the whole expenses of the government, and thereby to abolish all direct or other taxation? See Aikin's Digest 651.

It was not the intention of the legislature, by conferring the power upon these banks to purchase and sell bills of exchange, to deprive the citizens of the state, or any other natural person, of the right to do the same thing. But it was the intention to exclude all accumulated bank capital which did not belong to the state, in whole or in part, according to the constitution, from dealing in exchange; and such is the inevitable and legal effect of those laws. Let us test this principle. It is admitted by the majority of the court, in their opinion, that these constitutional provisions were intended as a restraint upon the legislature of the state. If so intended, the legislature can pass no law contrary to the spirit and intention of the constitution; nor contrary to the spirit and intention of the charters of the banks, created in pursuance of its provisions. Now, were the laws chartering the banks which are parties to this suit, contrary to the spirit and intention of the constitution and laws of Alabama? That is the precise question.

It must be borne in mind, that these were banks, and nothing but banks, that made the contracts in Alabama; and in that character, and that only, have they been considered in the opinion of the majority of the court. Were those banks chartered by the legislature of Alabama, two-thirds of both houses concurring? Was, at least, two-fifths of the capital stock, and of the management of these banks reserved to the state? Did the profits arising from the purchase of these bills of exchange go into the treasury of Alabama? All these questions must be answered in the negative. Then, these are not constitutional banks in Alabama, and cannot contract there. The majority of the court have decided these causes upon the presumption, that Alabama had adopted the laws of Georgia, Louisiana and Pennsylvania chartering these banks. And this presumption rests for its support upon the fact, that there is nothing in the laws or the policy of the laws of Alabama to resist this presumption. I suppose, it will not be contended, that the power of this court, to presume that Alabama had adopted these laws, is greater than the power of Alabama to adopt the laws for herself? Suppose, these banks had made a direct application to the legislature of Alabama, to pass a law to authorize them to deal in bills of exchange in that state, could the legislature have passed such a law, without violating the constitution of the state?

An incorporated bank, in Alabama, is not only the mere creature of the law creating it, as banks are in other states; but it is the creature of a peculiar fundamental law; and if its charter is not in conformity to the provisions of the fundamental law, it is void. It must be recollected, that the banks, which are the plaintiffs in these suits, when they present themselves to the legislature, asking permission to use their corporate privileges there, are not demanding a right, but asking a favor, which the legislature may grant or refuse as it pleases. If it should refuse, it would violate no duty, incur no responsibility. If, however, the court exercise the power, it is upon the positive obligation of Alabama, that the presumption must arise, or the right does not exist. A positive rule of law cannot arise out of an imperfect obligation, by presumption or implication. But to put it on the foot of bare repugnance of the law, presumed to be adopted, to the laws of the country adopting, if there be any repugnance, the court ought not to presume the adoption. Story's Conflict of Laws 37. The charter of every bank, not created in conformity with the constitution of Alabama, must, at least, be repugnant to it. The presumption is, that the charters of all these banks were repugnant, there being no reason or inducement to make them conform, in the states where they were created. The power of the court to adopt the laws creating these banks, as they actually existed, and the power of the legislature of Alabama to adopt them in a modified form, or to grant the banks a mere permission to do a specified act, present very different questions, and involve very different powers. If, therefore, the legislature could not adopt the charters, in the least objectionable form, nor authorize the banks to deal in exchange, without violating the constitution of Alabama, how can it be said, that the contracts in controversy are not against the policy of the laws of Alabama? And by what authority does the majority of this court presume, that Alabama has adopted those laws? The general rule is, that slight evidence and circumstances shall defeat a mere legal presumption of law. This case will be a signal exception to that rule.

In the case of *Pennington* v. *Townsend,* 7 Wend. 278, the Protection and Lombard Bank, chartered by New Jersey, by agents, undertook to do banking business in New York, and there discounted the check which was the subject of the suit, in violation of the restraining acts of 1813 and 1818; the first of which enacts, that no person, unauthorized by law, shall become a member of any association for the purpose of issuing notes or transacting any other business which incorporated banks may or do transact. The act of 1818 enacts, that it shall not be lawful for any person, association or body corporate to keep any office of deposit for discounting, or for carrying on any kind of banking business, and affixes a penalty of $1000, to be recovered, &c. Under these laws, the contract between the parties was held to be void; and the court says, "The protection against the evil intended to be remedied, to wit, preventing banking without the authority of the legislature of the state, is universal in its application within the state and without exception; unless qualified by the same power which enacted it, or by some other paramount law. Such is not the law incorporating this bank."

Is there anything in these laws which more positively prohibits banking in New York, without the authority of the legislature of that state, than there is in the constitution of Alabama, prohibiting all banking, except in the manner prescribed by the constitution? Can it be believed, that she intended to protect herself against the encroachments of her own legislature only, and to leave herself exposed to the encroachments of all her sister states? Does the language employed in these provisions of the constitution justify any such construction? It is general, comprehensive, and not only restrictive, but expressly prohibitory. Whatever is forbidden by the constitution of Alabama, can be done by no one, within her jurisdiction; and it was sufficient for her to know, that no bank could do any valid banking act there, without violating her constitution. It was contended, by the counsel for the banks, that no law could be regarded as declaring the policy of the state, unless it was penal; and inflicted some punishment for its violation. This doctrine is as novel as it is unfounded in principle. I know of no such exclusive rule by which to reach the mind and intention of the legislature. If the language used shows clearly that particular acts were intended to be prohibited, and the act is afterwards done, it is against the policy of the law and void. Suppose, the legislature of Alabama were to establish a bank disregarding all the conditions and restrictions imposed by the constitution; would it not violate that instrument, and therefore, the act be void? And can Georgia, Louisiana or Pennsylvania, by their respective legislatures, do in Alabama, what her own legislature cannot do? The relations which these states hold towards each other, in their individual capacity of states, under the constitution of the United States, is that of perfect independence. In the case of *Buckner* v. *Finley,* 2 Pet. 590, Chief Justice MARSHALL said, "For all national purposes embraced by the federal constitution, the states and the citizens thereof are one, united under the same sovereign authority, and governed by the same laws. In all other respects the states are necessarily foreign to, and independent of each other." It is in this foreign and independent relation, that these four states stand before this court in these cases. The condition of Alabama, taken with a view to this relation, cannot be worse than that of an independent nation, in like circumstances. What that would be, we will see from authority.

"Nations being free and independent of each other in the same manner as men are naturally free and independent the second general law of their society is, that each nation ought to be left in the peaceable enjoyment of that liberty it has derived from nature. The natural society of nations cannot subsist, if the rights which each has received from nature are not respected. None would willingly renounce its liberty; it would rather break off all commerce with those that should attempt to violate it. From this liberty and independence, it follows, that every nation is to judge of what its conscience demands, of what it can or cannot do, of what is proper or improper to be done; and consequently, to examine and determine whether it can perform any office for another, without being wanting in what it owes to itself. In all cases, then, where a nation has the liberty of judging what its duty requires, another cannot oblige it to act in such or such a manner. For the attempting this would be doing an injury to the liberty of nations. A right to offer constraint to a free person can only be invested in us in such cases, where that person is bound to perform some particular thing for us, or from a particular reason that does not depend on his judgment; or, in a word, where we have a complete authority over him." Vattel 53-4.

Now, apply these just and reasonable principles to Alabama, in her relation of a foreign and independent state, reposing upon the rights reserved to her by the tenth amendment of the constitution of the United States; and then show the power that can compel her to pass penal laws to guard and protect those perfect, ascertained, constitutional rights from the illegal invasion of a bank created by any other state. If this power exists at all, it can be shown, and the authority by which it acts. But not even a reasonable pretence for any such power or authority has been shown. The conclusion must, therefore, be, that Alabama, as an independent foreign state, owing no duty, nor being under any obligation to either of the states, by whose corporations she was invaded, was the sole and exclusive judge of what was proper or improper to be done; and consequently, had a right to examine and determine whether she could grant a favor to either of those states, without injury to herself; unless, indeed, there be a controlling power, in this court, derived from some provision of the constitution of the United States. As none such has been set up, or relied upon, in the opinion of the majority of the court, for the present, I have a right to conclude, that none such exists. And without considering any of the minor points discussed in the argument, or noticed in the opinion, I dismiss the subject.

Peter V. Daniel

☆ 1784–1860 ☆

APPOINTED BY

MARTIN VAN BUREN

YEARS ON COURT

1841–1860

Peter V. Daniel

by

FRANK OTTO GATELL

VIRGINIA LEGAL conservatism had many able spokesmen when the nineteenth century began. By the middle of the century, however, both the effectiveness of that body of thought and the state itself were in decline. It was Peter V. Daniel's misfortune that his career line placed him precisely in the center of this historical process. He was born too late to be a Founding Father and he was born too early to modernize. Neither John Taylor of Caroline, the philosopher of agrarian Virginia, nor Spencer Roane, the Old Dominion's Judge, had to cope with the problems of a country fast nationalizing in spite of itself. Particularist doctrines of constitutional law and the pursuit of Virginia's state interest as part of a sectional bloc found increasingly rough going. For Daniel, service on the Supreme Court in support of those interests became a protracted holding action.

A year after the American Revolutionary settlement had been made by the Treaty of Paris, Peter Vivian Daniel was born in Stafford County, Virginia, on April 24, 1784. His family had lived in Virginia for several generations, and his grandfather, another Peter Daniel, was one of the early settlers of Stafford County. Justice Daniel was the son of Travers Daniel and Frances Moncure, the daughter of a clergyman. The Daniel family lived on a plantation called "Crow's Nest," where Peter grew up and received his primary education from a series of private tutors. This informal but effective schooling was followed in 1802 by a brief stay at Princeton (then called the College of New Jersey) where Daniel was allowed to enter the junior class at the age of eighteen. But the pleasures of the academy were not for him, and after returning home without a degree, Daniel went to Richmond in 1805 to study law. He was able to do so in the office of one of the best-known members of the Virginia bar, Edmund Randolph,

FRANK O. GATELL, Professor of History at the University of California, Los Angeles, is the author of John Gorham Palfrey and the New England Conscience.

who had been Washington's Attorney General. After three years of study, Daniel was ready for his profession. He gained admittance to the bar in 1808.

Daniel's clerkship had other results as well. He followed the classic pattern by marrying his mentor's daughter. Lucy Randolph became his wife in April, 1810, and by this step Daniel became part of the ruling group of Virginia. Although his antecedents were quite "respectable," the marriage was a definite move upward for him in the social hierarchy of Virginia. It would prove a great boon to his career, which was already on the ascendant as shown by the fact that in 1809, at age twenty-five, Stafford County electors sent him to the state legislature as their representative.

During the years 1812–15, Daniel's most important public service was his contribution to the prosecution of the second war with Great Britain. Federalists, whether from New England or the South, might oppose the conflict, and denigrate the effort as "Mr. Madison's War," but Daniel, as a Virginia Republican, did what he could to aid the national administration and the Virginia Dynasty's President. During the session of 1812–13, the Virginia legislature passed an act to supplement the state's militia system in view of the lack of the federal government's defensive measures. But in 1813 the governor suspended the law because of mounting resistance to state regulars and the lessening of enemy pressure which made the law seem less necessary at that time. Daniel, who had become a member of the Virginia Privy Council in 1812, strongly opposed the suspension of the law for two reasons: first because the executive had no power to suspend the law, and second because he believed the regular Virginia force afforded the state a sound defense. Early in 1814, a proposal for augmenting the size of the militia for the defense of Richmond was lost, and Daniel again protested, arguing the necessity for stronger measures of self-defense. Daniel would have proved an accurate prophet, although to the great cost of his state, if the British, emulating their Revolutionary War example, had mounted a campaign in Virginia and burned Richmond instead of Washington.

In October, 1818, Daniel became lieutenant governor of Virginia. Although he did not abandon his law practice, by this time he was clearly moving into the more political phase of his career. He became a member of the informal but cohesive political group known as the Richmond Junto. This was the inner circle of the state's Republican party, and since the turn of the century it had determined party affairs, and consequently the state's affairs. It radiated political power throughout the state from its central energizing point in the state capital, Richmond. Daniel, "on duty" at the Richmond headquarters, was thus one of the handful of individuals who helped give the state a unified political voice. They performed a valuable and much-needed function in view of Virginia's political topography—the many counties and the absence of cities or many large towns. Virginia's "agrarian" politics was by definition decentralized, and without an effective coordinating agency the state could not have wielded as much political power for as long as it did.

An important element in Virginia politics of the 1820's was the reestablishment of a working coalition with the Republican party of New York. The Richmond Junto and Martin Van Buren's Albany Regency agreed to work together to further the ends of the party which would soon be called the Democratic party. Daniel established a friendship with Van Buren, which was to last for many years, to be disturbed later by Van Buren's free soilism of 1848. But before that, Daniel was to receive from his friend the highest award available to a lawyer-politician, a seat on the United States Supreme Court. Throughout the 1820's and 1830's, Daniel and Van Buren saw eye to eye on nearly all public issues, political and constitutional. Much more of a meeting of the minds existed between them than between Van Buren and Thomas Ritchie, editor of the Junto's newspaper, the *Richmond Enquirer*. Thus Van Buren's choice of Daniel, made in the final days of his troubled administration, came as no surprise because in the previous decades Daniel had established himself as the leading Van Buren supporter in Virginia, a state in which Van Buren was not universally loved.

Daniel's connection with Van Buren also involved, of course, a political commitment to Andrew Jackson. He supported the President throughout, and during Jackson's first administration, when tension mounted over Calhoun's alienation with Jackson, Daniel attacked the South Carolinian as an enemy of Virginia interests. He urged publicly that the issue be left to the people's judgment, never doubting that Jackson had little to fear in that regard. At the first Democratic national convention, which met at Baltimore in May, 1832, Daniel was one of the presiding officers, holding the post of first vice-president. With Jackson's renomination assured, the question of the vice-presidential nomination was the only doubtful point. Van Buren was Jackson's choice, and Daniel, the strong Van Buren supporter, was instrumental in making sure that the convention made the desired endorsement.

Another factor in consolidating Daniel's position as a good Jacksonian was his course in the Bank controversy. At a time when many Democrats either treaded water or actually bolted the party over Jackson's attack on the national bank, Daniel remained firm. Recharter of the second Bank of the United States became the key issue of the election of 1832. Daniel favored a society free of all banks, both state and federal. Throughout his public career, Daniel maintained an adherence to a strict view of Old Republicanism (or early Jeffersonianism) regarding banking. Bank charters were the worst form of artificial economic privilege, and Daniel pushed this view to its logical if increasingly unrealistic extreme, contending that the entire form of corporate business enterprise menaced the country. Banks were but the most vicious example of great corporate monopolies, cancerous growths which would destroy the country if not cut out.

Daniel's display of loyalty during the Bank war brought him an offer of a cabinet post. When Roger B. Taney moved from the Justice to the Treasury Department and ordered removal of federal funds from the national bank in 1833, Jackson offered Daniel the Attorney Generalship. Daniel declined reluctantly. The inadequate salary which the post carried meant that he would have to sacrifice his family's interests if he accepted.

Although Daniel could not enter the cabinet at that time, he did not retire from the political battle then raging. He assured the administration that he supported its policies wholeheartedly. Jackson needed as much help as he could get in Virginia. Nullification, and then the removal of deposits, shook the party structure profoundly. Early in 1834, both houses of the legislature condemned the removal of deposits, and instructed the state's congressional representatives to vote for restoration. Several important Democrats wavered, but not Daniel. In the legislature he continued to uphold the President's course, and to urge the winding up of all bank charters. He soon paid the price for such outspoken ultraism from an exposed position. In January, 1835, the legislature, then in Whig hands, terminated his service on the Council after a tenure of twenty-three years, seventeen of them as lieutenant governor.

Loyal political service, especially if it is costly to the lieutenant, deserves immediate reward. Jackson cherished political loyalty. Within a year, he appointed Daniel to the federal bench, as Judge of the United States District Court of Eastern Virginia. In the interim, Daniel had been busy working for the Richmond Junto's central committee, trying to counter the Whig tide in Virginia, and trying to prepare the national Democratic party for Van Buren's presidential bid in 1836.

As the federal courts were then constituted, judges served in a dual capacity: as judges of district courts, and as members of circuit courts of appeals, sitting with a Justice of the United States Supreme Court. Daniel often served alone. He was the only judge of the district court, and in circuit should Justice Barbour be absent, Judge Daniel himself then became the second step in the tripartite federal judicial hierarchy. Thus, in many cases, the system meant an appeal to a higher court, but to the same individual, with Daniel asked to review a case he had decided in the lower court.

Daniel went on the bench firmly convinced that latitudinarian judicial constructions, if allowed to continue unchecked, would at worst destroy the country or at best dissolve the Union. There was a good deal of self-righteousness involved in his attitudes and approaches. Self-confidence is, of course, necessary for anyone undertaking a public charge, but in Daniel's case he seemed to believe in constitutional fundamentalism in judicial practice as well as judicial principles. Judges should expound the Constitution and laws instead of making decisions for partisan reasons. Stripped of verbiage this meant that judges should expound the Constitution and laws narrowly, especially when it came to national powers. Daniel never explained how he would guard himself against the danger of improper interpretation or partisan leanings. Apparently he thought that constitutional conservatism was in itself ample assurance of judicial objectivity, or at least an important first step in that direction. Federal encroachment—the threat of consolidated government—was his *bête noire*. He thought the admiralty and commerce powers were being used as improper vehicles for adding to national power. Corporations were also using the federal courts to shield them from proper controls by the states' political and judicial processes. And, most pertinent to his anxieties grounded in states' rights beliefs, the protection of a state's jurisdiction in all that pertained to slavery might be eroded through the unwarranted growth of national judicial power.

The five years' service Daniel performed on the district and circuit courts were not particularly demanding, either in time or in intellectual effort. The total number of cases he heard during that period was small. Most of the cases involved suits by the federal government arising from tariff violations or other breaches of federal statutes. Petty smuggling and much post office litigation occupied a good deal of Daniel's time. Criminal cases were very rare, and there were scattered admiralty cases, usually dealing with small boats engaged in coastal or river trades. In circuit, issues were considerably more substantial. These cases often resulted from the suits brought by the citizen of one state against a Virginian to secure payment of sums owed northern businessmen and banks. Later, Daniel contended that corporations should not be allowed to sue in federal courts, but as circuit court judge he made no such objections. Daniel established no new benchmarks of judicial interpretation as district and circuit judge. Important constitutional questions can very often arise in cases which present the simplest and humblest details, but in the case of Daniel as a member of the lower federal courts, particularly in the district court, it was a case of both modest accomplishment and modest materials to work with.

In 1841 Daniel moved up to the High Court. In February of that year, and with a week left in his presidential term, Martin Van Buren further rewarded his friend and political supporter by naming him to the Supreme Court. Justice Barbour had died, and Van Buren responded immediately to prevent the nomination's falling into Whig hands. The President dispensed with the usual recommendation and selection process, and Daniel had the nomination before Barbour could be buried, while Whigs feigned horror over such disrespect for the dead. Two days before Harrison's inauguration, Daniel took the oath as Associate Justice of the Supreme Court.

Six months before, during the unsuccessful attempt to reelect President Van Buren, Judge (and soon-to-become Justice) Daniel addressed a Democratic county convention. The occasion provided the opportunity for him to outline his basic political-constitutional beliefs, beliefs he would thereafter employ as the underpinning for his judicial pronouncements. Daniel lauded the Virginia and Kentucky Resolutions of 1798 as the bulwark of proper federal-state relations. They remained the "best commentary upon the Constitution and the best defense of our reserved rights." He would have no part of the organic theory of constitutional origin. The document was clearly a compact among the states, and the central government had no powers other than those clearly granted to it. Within the partisan setting of the address, Daniel commented on specific political programs and issues of the day, including an attack on the fallen Bank of the United States and a warning against any plans for a substitute national bank, but the thread running through the entire oration was that of strict construction, with its exaltation of state sovereignty and its apprehensions regarding federal encroachment. It was Old Republicanism, in all its purity.

These principles, never abandoned and hardly modified, made Daniel the Court's extreme agrarian, the sworn enemy of consolidation, corporations, and banks; the extreme defender of states' rights, and finally the extreme sectionalist and radical partisan in the slavery question. Daniel took his seat in 1841, a strong advocate of Democratic party unity. His entire political career had taken place within the context of the New York–Virginia political axis, and the commitment to Jeffersonian Republicanism that this represented. But during the 1840's, and especially after the election of Taylor and Fillmore in 1848, and the impact of the anti-slavery movements on northern politics, Daniel quickly withdrew into a position of extreme southern sectionalism. His hostility to the threats from the North, real and imagined, became a passion with him. He could see little hope, especially after the very man who had forged the sectional coalition, Van Buren, turned traitor to the principles of sectional accommodation and ran for the presidency on the Free Soil ticket in 1848.

One of the most important areas of constitutional development with which the Taney Court had to grapple was that of federal control of commerce. Marshall had laid the foundations for a broad view of federal powers in foreign and interstate commerce where these seemed to impinge on local control and the exercise of the police power by the state. Once again, Daniel insisted that the national government had far exceeded its constitutionally limited grant of power, and he invariably declared himself on the side of the state as against any view of a purely national power. This issue of federal exclusiveness was the heart of the problem in the cases arising from application of the commerce clause to regulate interstate commerce.

The issue came before Daniel and his colleagues in several cases. The first were a group lumped together in 1847 as the *License Cases,* 5 How. 504 (1847) in which several New England states had attempted to prevent the importation of liquors through a licensing system for retail sale. The suits charged that the states were infringing upon interstate commerce, and the Court upheld these instances of local regulation. In the *License Cases,* Daniel supported the view that the commerce clause had not created an exclusive power and that all imports were subject to state regulation and taxation as soon as title had been vested in someone within the state. Once the goods were out of the custom house and became the sole property of the importer or his customer, they might be taxed or their sale regulated by the state. Two years later, in the *Passenger Cases,* 7 How. 559 (1849), the Court went against state regulation, this time by a tax on immigrants instead of on intoxicants. After four years of arguments, and the achievement of anything but consensus, the narrow majority for state regulation in the *License Cases* became a narrow majority against state regulation. Daniel dissented strongly. He thought the majority had "trampled down some of the strongest defenses of the safety and independence of the states." Federal exclusiveness in commerce, or in anything, was the greatest threat and Daniel spoke plainly to his fellow Justices and the country from that constitutional point of departure.

This ultraism, or unswerving devotion to a principle, came out again clearly in a case decided in 1851, *Pennsylvania* v. *Wheeling Bridge,* 13 How. 518 (1851). Here the state of Pennsylvania, in support of the commercial interests of Pittsburgh, sought an abatement of the nuisance allegedly caused by a bridge over the Ohio River at Wheeling, Virginia. The Court upheld the complaint, and Justice McLean ordered the bridge razed. Taney and Daniel dissented, Daniel in especially strong terms. He claimed that the commerce power was being used to promote a monopoly of one means of transportation over another (the river over the bridge) and he denied that the state had the power to bring action in behalf of a local interest. Steamboats should shorten their smokestacks if necessary, and the federal government should stay out of matters in which it had no legal concern.

The Taney Court finally came to a resting ground on the question of the commerce clause with the promulgation of the doctrine of selective exclusiveness in the case of *Cooley* v. *Board of Wardens,* 12 How. 299 (1852). The issue at hand was whether or not the federal government had exclusive power over pilotage in harbors and could thus *permit* the states to regulate pilotage; or whether the states themselves could pass such regulatory statutes. Pennsylvania had passed a law requiring shippers to use the services of local pilots or pay a fee to be used as a fund for retired or "decayed" pilots. The Court majority agreed that the exclusiveness or non-exclusiveness of the commerce clause would depend on the specific application. Pilotage did not fall into the exclusive category, a definition whose flexibility did not please the polar extremes of Court opinion: neither on the one hand the exclusive nationalists like McLean and Wayne, nor on the other the localist Daniel, who was this time in concurrence but not for the reasons stated in the majority opinion. Daniel believed that the regulation of pilotage was not a regulation of interstate or foreign commerce, and that it was an inherent prerogative of the states. It was an area of regulation barred to federal intervention, whatever the disposition of the national government.

Daniel's fight for state supremacy within the federal system extended into the field of federal jurisdiction. He tried to keep as many cases as possible out of the federal courts. The prime example of his view was the question of the right of a corporation to sue or be sued in federal courts. Since a corporation was legally "an artificial person" and not a "citizen," and since only citizens could sue in federal courts, he declared that corporations therefore had no access to federal courts on the basis of diversity of citizenship. He denied jurisdiction in every case in which a corporation claimed such diversity of citizenship. See his dissenting opinions in *Rundle* v. *Delaware & Raritan Canal Co.,* 14 How. 80 (1852), *Northern Indiana R.R.* v. *Michigan State R.R.,* 15 How. 233 (1853), and *Marshall* v. *Baltimore & Ohio Railroad Co.,* 16 How. 314 (1853). Daniel maintained this opinion, the doctrine that corporations were *persona non standi* in federal courts, against the majority of his associates. His judicial attitude stemmed partly from his opposition to corporations. The growth of corporations was rapid in those times, and many states were granting them expanded legal rights. But Daniel's agrarian point of view insisted upon keeping corporations amenable to the states, the sovereignties which had created them, and to do that it was necessary to deny them full rights of citizenship and thus prevent their recourse to federal courts.

The contract clause of the Constitution, the chief restriction upon legislative regulation of business before the due process revolution of the late nineteenth century, afforded Daniel another avenue for judicial dissent. In *Planters' Bank of Mississippi* v. *Sharp,* 6 How. 301 (1848), among others, he opposed the application of the contract clause to corporate charters. He felt that the clause was not an absolute restriction and that it remained subject to the police power. Even the sanctity of contract must sometimes yield to the public good, where the specific situation overwhelmingly demanded it.

In 1849 Daniel enjoyed the unaccustomed luxury of speaking for the majority in a contract clause case. This exceptional instance, Daniel's leading constitutional opinion, occurred in the case of *West River Bridge Co.* v. *Dix,* 6 How. 507 (1849). At issue was the application of the power of eminent domain, as an implied reservation in the original corporate franchise. Daniel could see no difference between corporate or unincorporated property when it came to the power of eminent domain and held that a state must have the power to condemn any property for public use. This did not mean that the Court had come over to Daniel's ultra position on the contract clause, but in this instance it agreed that to some undefined extent, the contract clause was subject to the police power, and the sanctity of contract might have to yield before imperative public necessity. This opinion joined Taney's *Charles River Bridge* opinion as the twin pillars of the Taney Court redefinition of Marshall's contract clause interpretations.

Another form of assault on states' rights agrarianism, in Daniel's eyes, was the anti-slavery crusade. For him the maintenance of the South's socio-economic system was bound up with the very foundations of constitutional government. In *Prigg* v. *Pennsylvania,* 16 Pet. 539 (1842), the issue was the proper relationship of state fugitive slave laws to the federal law covering that subject. Although the majority of the Court opined that federal power to enact laws relating to fugitive slaves was exclusive, Daniel contended that it was concurrent.

In his opinion in *Prigg,* he anticipated *Dred Scott* in contending that Congress had no constitutional power to restrict the introduction of slaves into the territories. The Missouri Compromise was thus wholly unconstitutional and void. The question of the existence of slavery was a matter to be determined solely by the people of each territory without any interference by the federal government. If Daniel had had his way, the Court would have declared the restrictionist aspects of the Compromise unconstitutional long before 1857. Ten years before, he had written Van Buren: "I have ever regarded what has been called the Missouri Compromise, as utterly without warrant from the Constitution. The people of this nation may in practice observe it if they so please, but so far as any *authority* for it is to be sought in the Constitution no foundation for it whatsoever can be discovered there. Congress never had the power to ordain or establish it."

When the Court finally faced the issue of slavery and territories in the *Dred Scott* case (19 How. 393), and attempted a definitive solution, Daniel had no trouble responding to the challenge. Starting as he did with the premise that the Missouri Compromise was unconstitutional, and his basic views on the status of the Negro, Daniel was, of course, one of the majority Justices. Paralleling Taney's famed commentary upon the African's status, Daniel wrote "that the African Negro race never had been acknowledged as belonging to the family of nations . . . ; that this race has been by all the nations of Europe regarded as subjects of capture or purchase; as subjects of commerce or traffic; and that the introduction of that race into every section of this country was not as members of civil or political society, but as slaves. . . ." Daniel held that all Negroes came to the United States as slaves, strictly the property of their owner. In that capacity as property the Negro could not be a citizen. A slaveowner could by his own act of emancipation make a free man, but he could not create a citizen. Only the state could do that. Thus since Scott was not a citizen, the Court had no jurisdiction. The Compromise had been nothing more than unwarranted political tampering with citizens' property rights, "a means of forfeiting that equality of rights and immunities which are the birthright . . . of every citizen of the United States." The territories, as national domain, could not be set aside for "any one class or portion of the people."

Daniel believed that yet another threat to the fabric of *his* Constitution lay in the prospect of expanding the admiralty jurisdiction of federal courts. He generally resisted such a tendency toward judicial expansiveness. A controversy arose as to where admiralty cases should be tried. Federal courts assumed jurisdiction when cases resulted from disputes arising on the high seas and tried the cases in federal district courts without juries. State courts heard controversies arising in inland waterways through the use of jury trials. Daniel opposed federal admiralty jurisdiction primarily because he objected to federal courts judging disputes between citizens of the same state, and also because he felt that the absence of a jury trial did not comport with our common law institutions. Under the common law, federal admiralty jurisdiction would have been confined to tidal waters, but Congress extended federal jurisdiction over internal navigable waters in order to provide for uniform control over shipping using such waters. The Court approved such an extension in *Propellor Genessee Chief* v. *Fitzhugh,* 12 How. 443 (1852), despite a sharp dissent from Daniel warning against constitutional latitudinarianism for expedient reasons. He declined to "construe the Constitution by mere geographical considerations." From reprimand, Daniel switched to ridicule in another case of that term with a mock prediction that soon the Court, on the same principle, would allow federal control over the brawls of Washington urchins who fished in the creeks of the Potomac.

In view of the preceding constitutional positions, it can be taken for granted that Daniel had no sympathy for programs of internal improvement financed by the federal government. Such projects involved expenditures which in turn would inevitably lead to the imposition of high tariffs to raise revenue. The well-travelled and highly valued Cumberland Road provided an example of such an allegedly unconstitutional internal improvement subsidized by the federal government. According to Daniel in 1845, "neither Congress nor the Federal Government in the exercise of all or any of its powers or attributes possesses the power to construct roads, nor any other description of what have been called internal improvements, within the limits of the States." The views of national powers expressed in this opinion (*Searight* v. *Stokes,* 3 How. 151 [1845]) rank among the narrowest ever voiced by a Justice of the Supreme Court.

During his Supreme Court service, Daniel's constitutional opinions were not numerous. For the most part he spoke for the Court in matters of land titles and procedural questions. In his final years on the Bench, the Court's most important case was that of *Ableman* v. *Booth,* 21 How. 169 (1859). Here, he was with a unanimous Court which put down Wisconsin's open rebellion against the Fugitive Slave Law of 1850 and against the decisions of the federal courts. But Daniel's general pattern of dissent had continued to the end. On the final day of the 1858–59 term, he submitted his last dissenting opinion in *Barber* v. *Barber,* 21 How. 582 (1859), where he insisted that federal courts had no jurisdiction in matters of divorce and alimony.

After the Court adjournment, Daniel returned to Richmond with his second wife and two small children. (The first Mrs. Daniel had died in 1847; in 1853, at age 67, he had married Elizabeth Harris of Philadelphia.) Peter V. Daniel died in Richmond, on May 31, 1860, a few days after Virginia voters had ratified a secession ordinance. There is no doubt where Daniel would have stood on the issue if his health had permitted him to register his opinion.

"Principled anachronism" might have been an appropriate caption for his epitaph. No one could have accused Daniel of having played the "pliable" judge. He maintained his original principles while many men around him were trying to adjust theirs to changing times. Daniel thought that they were merely losing their heads, and he had early in life decided to keep his intact and uncluttered by what passed for modernism in law and politics as America passed from its agrarian to its industrial age.

SELECTED BIBLIOGRAPHY

Despite the fact that Peter Daniel is little remembered today, his career has been the subject of two scholarly works. Lawrence Burnette, Jr., contributed an interpretive essay, "Peter V. Daniel: Agrarian Justice," 62 *Virginia Magazine of History and Biography* 289 (1954). The other is a full-scale biography of very recent vintage: John P. Frank, *Justice*

Daniel Dissenting: A Biography of Peter V. Daniel, 1784–1860 (Cambridge, 1964). Both pieces capably develop the central theme of agrarianism, and in tandem they have seemingly "fixed" Daniel's position and relative importance as politician and jurist.

Peter V. Daniel

REPRESENTATIVE OPINIONS

SEARIGHT v. STOKES, 3 HOW. 151 (1845)

The *Searight* case showed Daniel in his most extreme states' rights position. In that case he denied the power of the federal government to make internal improvements of any kind, whether for roads or canals. Daniel claimed in dissent that the states held their land "by title paramount to the Constitution, [which] cannot be taken," except for forts, arsenals and the like. It was therefore his position that the state of Pennsylvania could tax vehicles carrying the federal mails on the Cumberland Road, a contention rejected by the majority of the Court.

Mr. Justice DANIEL. With the profoundest respect for the opinions of my brethren, I find myself constrained openly to differ from the decision which, on behalf of the majority of the court, has just been pronounced. This case, although in form a contest between individuals, is in truth a question between the government of the United States and the government of Pennsylvania. It is, to a certain extent, a question of power between those two governments; and, indeed, so far as it is represented to be a question of compact, the very consideration on which the interests of the federal government are urged involves implications affecting mediately or directly what are held to be great and fundamental principles in our state and federal systems. It brings necessarily into view the operation and effect of the compact insisted upon as controlled and limited by the powers of both the contracting parties. In order to show more plainly the bearing of the principles above mentioned upon the case before us, they will here be more explicitly, though cursorily, referred to.

I hold, then, that neither Congress nor the federal government in the exercise of all or any of its powers or attributes possesses the power to construct roads, nor any other description of what have been called internal improvements, within the limits of the states. That the territory and soil of the several states appertain to them by title paramount to the Constitution, and cannot be taken, save with the exceptions of those portions thereof which might be ceded for the seat of the federal government and for sites permitted to be purchased for forts, arsenals, dock-yards, &c., &c. That the power of the federal government to acquire, and that of the states to cede to that government portions of their territory, are by the Constitution limited to the instances above adverted to, and that these powers can neither be enlarged nor modified but in virtue of some new faculty to be imparted by amendments of the Constitution. I believe that the authority vested in Congress by the Constitution to establish post-roads, confers no right to open new roads, but implies nothing beyond a discretion in the government in the regulations it may make for the Post-office Department for the selection amongst various routes, whilst they continue in existence, of those along which it may deem it most judicious to have the mails transported. I do not believe that this power given to Congress expresses or implies any thing peculiar in relation to the means or modes of transporting the public mail, or refers to any supposed means or modes of transportation beyond the usual manner existing and practised in the country, and certainly it cannot be understood to destroy or in any wise to affect the proprietary rights belonging to individuals or companies vested in those roads. It guaranties to the government the right to avail itself of the facilities offered by those roads for the purposes of transportation, but imparts to it no exclusive rights—it puts to the government upon the footing of others who would avail themselves of the same facilities.

In accordance with the principles above stated, and which with me are fundamental, I am unable to perceive how the federal government could acquire any power over the Cumberland road by making appropriations, or by expending money to any amount for its construction or repair, though these appropriations and expenditures may have been made with the assent, and even with the solicitation of Pennsylvania. Neither the federal government separately, nor conjointly with the state of Pennsylvania, could have power to repeal the Constitution. Arguments drawn from convenience or inconvenience can have no force with me in questions of constitutional power; indeed, they cannot be admitted at all, for if once admitted, they sweep away every barrier erected by the Constitution against implied authority, and may cover every project which the human mind may conceive. It matters not, then, what or how great the advantage which the government of the United States may have proposed to itself or to others in undertaking this road; such purposes or objects could legitimate no acts either expressly forbidden or not plainly authorized. If the mere appropriation or disbursement of money can create rights in the government, they may extend this principle indefinitely, and with the very worst tendencies—those tendencies would be the temptation to prodigality in the government and a dangerous influence with respect to others.

In my view, then, the federal government could erect no toll-gates nor make any exaction of tolls upon this road; nor could that government, in consideration of what it had done or contributed, constitutionally and legally demand of the state of Pennsylvania the regulation of tolls either as to the imposition of particular rates or the exemption of any species of transportation upon it. As a matter of constitutional and legal power and authority, this appertained to the state of Pennsylvania exclusively. Independently, then, of any stipulations with respect to them, vehicles of the United States, or vehicles transporting the property of the United States, and that property itself, would, in passing over this road, be in the same situation precisely with vehicles and property appertaining to all other persons; they would be subject to the tolls regularly imposed by law. There can be no doubt if the road were vested in a company or in a state, that either the company or the state might stipulate for any rate of toll within the maximum of their power, or might consent to an entire exemption; and such stipulation, if made for a valuable or a legal consideration, would be binding.

The United States may contract with companies or with communities for the transportation of their mails, or any of their property, as well as with carriers of a different description; and consequently could contract with the state of Pennsylvania. But what is meant to be insisted on here is, that the government could legally claim no power to collect tolls, no exemption from tolls, nor any diminution of tolls in their favour, purely in consequence of their having expended money on the road, and without the recognition by Pennsylvania of that expenditure as a condition in any contract they might make with that state. Without such recognition, the federal government must occupy the same position with other travellers or carriers, and remain subject to every regulation of her road laws which the state could legally impose on others.

This brings us to an examination of the statutes of Pennsylvania, and to an inquiry into any stipulations which the state is said to have made with the federal government, as declared in those statutes. That examination will, however, be premised by some observations, which seem to be called for on this occasion. These acts of the Pennsylvania legislature have been compared with the acts of other legislative bodies relative to this road, and it has been supposed that the Pennsylvania laws should be interpreted in conjunction with those other state laws, and farther, that all these separate state enactments should be taken, together with the acts of Congress passed as to them respectively, as forming one, or as parts of one entire compact with the federal government. I cannot concur in such a view of this case. On the contrary, I must consider each of the states that have legislated in respect to this road, as competent to speak for herself; as speaking in reference to her own interests and policy, and independently of all others; and unshackled by the proceedings of any others. By this rule of construction let us examine the statutes of Pennsylvania. The act of April 4th, 1831, which may be called the compact law, as it contains all that Pennsylvania professed to undertake, begins by stating the doubts which were entertained upon the authority of the United States to erect toll-gates and to collect tolls on the Cumberland road; doubts which, with the government as well as with others, seem to have ripened into certainties, inasmuch as, notwithstanding its large expenditures upon this road, the government had never exacted tolls for travelling or for transportation upon it. The statute goes on next to provide, that if the government of the United States will make such farther expenditures as shall put the road lying within the limits of Pennsylvania in complete repair, Pennsylvania will erect toll-gates and collect tolls upon the road, to be applied to the repairs and preservation of it. The same act invests the commissioners it appoints to superintend the road, with power to increase or diminish the tolls to be levied; limiting the increase by the rates which the state had authorized upon an artificial road that she had established from the Susquehanna, opposite the borough of Harrisburg, to Pittsburg. Then in the act of 1831 are enumerated the subjects of toll, and the rates prescribed as to each of those subjects. Amongst the former are mentioned chariots, coaches, coachees, stages, wagons, phaetons, chaises. In the 3d proviso to the 2d section it is declared, "that no toll shall be received or collected for the passage of any wagon or carriage laden with the property of the United States, or any cannon or military stores belonging to the United States, or to any of the states belonging to this union." On the 13th of June, 1836, was passed by the legislature of Pennsylvania, "An act relating to the tolls on that part of the Cumberland road which passes through Pennsylvania." The 1st section of this act is in the following words: "All wagons, carriages, or other modes of conveyance, passing upon that part of the Cumberland road which passes through Pennsylvania, carrying goods, cannon, or military stores, belonging to the United States, or to any individual state of the union, which are excepted from the payment of toll by the second section of an act passed the fourth of April, anno Domini eighteen hundred and thirty-one, shall extend only so far as to relieve such wagons, carriages, and other modes of conveyance, from the payment of toll to the proportional amount of such goods so carried, belonging to the United States, or to any of the individual states of the union; and that in all cases of wagons, carriages, stages, or other modes of conveyance, carrying the United States mail, with passengers or goods such wagon, stage, or other mode of conveyance, shall pay half-toll upon such modes of conveyance."

Upon the construction to be given to the 1st and 2d sections of the statute of 1831, and to the 1st section of the statute of 1836, depends the decision of the case before us. By the defendant in error it is insisted that, by the sections of the act of 1831 above cited, stages or stage-coaches, transporting the mail of the United States, are wholly exempted by compact from the payment of tolls, although the mails may constitute but a small portion of their lading; and those vehicles may be at the same time freighted for the exclusive profit of the mail contractors, with any number of passengers, or with any quantity of baggage or goods, which can be transported in them, consistently with the transportation of the mail; and that the 1st section of the act of 1836, which declares that "in all cases of wagons, carriages, stages, or other modes of conveyance, carrying the United States mail, with passengers or goods, such wagon, stage, or other mode of conveyance, shall pay half-toll upon such mode of conveyance," is a violation of the compact. Let us pause here, and inquire what was the natural and probable purpose of the exemption contained in the act of 1831? Was that exemption designed as a privilege or facility to the government, or as a donation for private and individual advantage? Common sense would seem to dictate the reply, that the former only was intended by the law; and even if the privilege or facility to the government could be best secured by associating it with individual profit, certainly that privilege or facility could, on no principle of reason or fairness, be so sunk, so lost sight of, so entirely perverted, as to make it a mean chiefly of imposition and gain on the part of individuals, and the cause of positive and serious public detriment; and such must be the result of the practice contended for by the defendants in error, as it would tend to impede the celerity of transportation, and to destroy the road itself, by withholding the natural and proper fund for its maintenance. Passing then from what is believed to be the natural design of these enactments, let their terms and language be considered. By those of the 2d section of the law of 1831, every stage or wagon is made expressly liable to toll, without regard to the subjects it might transport, and without regard to the ownership of the vehicle itself. The terms of the law are universal; they comprehend all stages and all wagons; they would necessarily, therefore, embrace stages and wagons of the United States, or the like vehicles of others carrying the property of the United States or of private persons. If, then, either the vehicles of the United States, or of others carrying the property of the United States, have been withdrawn from the operation of the act of 1831, this can have been done only by force of the 3d proviso of the 2d section of that act. The proviso referred to declares that no toll shall "be collected for the passage of any wagon or carriage laden with the property of the United States," &c., &c. Can this proviso be understood as exempting stages, whether belonging to the government or to individuals, which were intended purposely to carry the MAIL? It is not deemed necessary, in interpreting this proviso, to discuss the question, whether the United States have a property in mails which they carry. It may be admitted that the United States and all their contractors have in the mails that property which vests by law in all common carriers; it may be admitted that the United States have an interest in the mails even beyond this. These admissions do not vary the real inquiry here, which is, whether by this proviso the mails of the United States, or the carriages transporting them, were intended to be exempted from tolls? This law, like every other instrument, should be interpreted according to the common and received acceptation of its words; and artificial or technical significations of words or phrases should not be resorted to, except when unavoidable, to give a sensible meaning to the instrument interpreted; or when they may be considered as coming obviously within the understanding and contemplation of the parties. According to this rule of interpretation, what would be commonly understood by "the property of the United States," or by the phrase "wagons and carriages laden with the property of the United States?" Would common intendment apply those terms to the *mail* of the United States, or to vehicles carrying that mail? The term "mail" is perhaps universally comprehended as being that over which the government has the management for the purposes of conveyance and distribution; and it would strike the common understanding as something singular, to be told that the money or letters belonging to the citizen, and for the transportation of which he pays, was not his property, but was the property of the United States. The term "mail," then, having a meaning clearly defined and universally understood, it is conclusive to my mind, that in a provision designed to exempt that mail, or the vehicle for its transportation, the general and equivocal term "property" would not have been selected, but the terms "mail," and "stages carrying the mail"—terms familiar to all—would have been expressly introduced.

Farther illustration of the language and objects of the legislature of Pennsylvania may be derived from the circumstance, that, in the law of 1831, they couple the phrase "property of the United States" with "property of the states." The same language is used in reference to both; they are both comprised in the same sentence; the same exemption is extended to both. Now the states have no mails to be transported. It then can by no means follow, either by necessary or even plausible interpretation, that by "property of the United States" was meant the "mails of the United States," any more than by "property of the states" was meant the "mails" of those states; on the contrary, it seems far more reasonable that the legislature designed to make no distinction with regard to either, but intended that the term "property" should have the same signification in reference both to the state and federal governments.

In the acceptation of the term "property," insisted on for the defendants in error, the mails committed to the contractor are the property of that contractor also. Yet it would hardly have been contended that in a provision for exempting the "property" of a mail contractor from tolls, either a vehicle belonging to the United States, and in the use of such a contractor, or the mail which he carried in it, would be so considered as his property as to bring them within that exemption; yet such is the conclusion to which the interpretation contended for by the defendants would inevitably lead. That construction I deem to be forced and artificial, and not the legitimate interpretation of the statute, especially when I consider that there are various other subjects of property belonging to the United States, and belonging to them absolutely and exclusively, which from their variety could not well be specifically enumerated, and which, at some period or other, it might become convenient to the government and beneficial to the country to transport upon this road. But if, by any interpretation, the words "wagon or carriage laden with the property of the United States," can be made to embrace stages carrying the mail, and employed purposely for that service, they surely cannot, by the most forced construction, be made to embrace stages laden with every thing else, by comparison, except the mail of the United States, and in which the mail was a mere pretext for the transportation of passengers and merchandise, or property of every description and to any amount, free of toll. They must at all events be laden with the mail. The term laden cannot be taken here as a mere expletive, nor should it be wrested from its natural import—be made identical in signification with the terms "carrying" or "transporting." Such a departure would again be a violation of common intendment, and should not be resorted to; and the abuses just shown, which such a departure would let in and protect, furnish another and most cogent reason why the common acceptation of the phrase, "property of the United States," should be adhered to. Fairness and equality with respect to all carriers and travellers upon this road, and justice to the state which has undertaken to keep it in repair from the tolls collectable upon it, require this adherence.

If the interpretation here given of the act of 1831 be correct, then admitting that act to be a compact between Pennsylvania and the United States, the former has, by the 1st section of the act of 1836, infracted no stipulation in that compact. Pennsylvania never did, according to my understanding of her law of 1831, agree to the exemption from tolls for stages, wagons, or vehicles of any kind, intended for carrying the mails of the United States. These stood upon the like footing with other carriages. If this be true, then by the act of 1836, in which she has subjected to half-tolls only, stages, wagons, &c., carrying the mails, and at the same time transporting passengers or goods, so far from violating her compact, or inflicting a wrong upon the government or upon mail contractors, that state has extended to them a privilege and an advantage which, under the 3d proviso of the act of 1831, they did not possess. My opinion is, that the plaintiff in the court below had an undoubted right of recovery.

WEST RIVER BRIDGE CO. v. DIX, 6 HOW. 507 (1848)

In the 1840's the fight between corporations and the state governments was in full swing. Whatever legislation was passed which effected corporate enterprise was attacked as an impairment of the contract between the state and the corporation as contained in the charter, in keeping with John Marshall's decision in the Dartmouth College case. The corporate claims reached so far as to deny any power of eminent domain over corporate property. This contention was rejected by the Court in the *West River Bridge* case in an opinion by Justice Daniel.

Mr. Justice DANIEL delivered the opinion of the court.

The West River Bridge Company, Plaintiffs, *vs.* Joseph Dix and the Towns of Brattleborough and Dummerston, Defendants, upon a writ of error to the Supreme

Court of Judicature of the State of Vermont, sitting in certain proceedings as a court of law,

and

The same Plaintiffs, *vs.* The Towns of Brattleborough and Dummerston, and Joseph Dix, Asa Boyden, and Phineas Underwood, upon a writ of error to the Supreme Court of Judicature, and to the Chancellor of the First Circuit of the State of Vermont.

These two causes have been treated in the argument as one,—and such they essentially are. Though prosecuted in different forms and in different forums below, they are merely various modes of endeavouring to attain the same end, and a decision in either of the only question they raise for the cognizance of this court disposes equally of that question in the other.

They are brought before us under the twenty-fifth section of the Judiciary Act, in order to test the conformity with the Constitution of the United States of certain statutes of Vermont; laws that have been sustained by the Supreme Court of Vermont, but which it is alleged are repugnant to the tenth section of the first article of the Constitution, prohibiting the passage of State laws impairing the obligation of contracts.

It appears from the records of these causes, that, in the year 1795, the plaintiffs in error were, by act of the legislature of Vermont, created a corporation, and invested with the exclusive privilege of erecting a bridge over West River, within four miles of its mouth, and with the right of taking tolls for passing the same. The franchise granted this corporation was to continue for one hundred years, and the period originally prescribed for its duration has not yet expired. The corporation erected their bridge, have maintained and used it, and enjoyed the franchise granted to them by law, until the institution of the proceeding now under review.

By the general law of Vermont relating to roads, passed 19th November, 1839 (*vide* Revised Laws of Vermont, p. 553), the County Courts are authorized, upon petition, to appoint commissioners to lay out highways within their respective counties, and to assess the damages which may accrue to landholders by the opening of roads, and these courts, upon the reports of the commissioners so appointed, are empowered to establish roads within the bounds of their local jurisdiction. A similar power is vested in the Supreme Court, to lay out and establish highways extending through several counties.

By an act of the legislature of Vermont, passed November 19th, 1839, it is declared, that "whenever there shall be occasion for any new highway in any town or towns of this State, the Supreme and County Courts shall have the same power to take any real estate, easement, or franchise of any turnpike or other corporation, when in their judgment the public good requires a public highway, which such courts now have, by the laws of the State, to lay out highways over individual or private property; and the same power is granted, and the same rules shall be observed, in making compensation to all such corporations and persons whose estates, easement, franchise, or rights shall be taken, as are now granted and provided in other cases." Under the authority of these statutes, and in the modes therein prescribed, a proceeding was instituted in the County Court of Windham, upon the petition of Joseph Dix and others, in which, by the judgment of that court, a public road was extended and established between certain termini, passing over and upon the bridge of the plaintiffs, and converting it into a free public highway. By the proceedings and judgment just mentioned, compensation was assessed and awarded to the plaintiffs for this appropriation of their property, and for the consequent extinguishment of their franchise. The judgment of the County Court, having been carried by certiorari before the Supreme Court of the State, was by the latter tribunal affirmed.

Pending the proceedings at law upon the petition of Dix and others, a bill was presented by the plaintiffs in error to the chancellor of the first judicial circuit of the State of Vermont, praying an injunction to those proceedings so far as they related to the plaintiffs or to the real estate, easement, or franchise belonging to them. This bill, having been demurred to, was dismissed by the chancellor, whose decree was affirmed on appeal to the Supreme Court, and a writ of error to the last decision brings up the case on the second record.

In considering the question propounded in these causes, there can be no doubt, nor has it been doubted in argument, on either side of this controversy, that the charter of incorporation granted to the plaintiffs in 1793, with the rights and privileges it declared or implied, formed a contract between the plaintiffs and the State of Vermont, which the latter, under the inhibition in the tenth section of the first article of the Constitution, could have no power to impair. Yet this proposition, though taken as a postulate on both sides, determines nothing as to the real merits of these causes. True, it furnishes a guide to our inquiries, yet leaves those inquiries still open, in their widest extent, as to the real position of the parties with reference to the State legislation or to the Constitution. Following the guide thus furnished us, we will proceed to ascertain that position. No State, it is declared, shall pass a law impairing the obligation of contracts; yet, with this concession constantly yielded, it cannot be justly disputed that in every political sovereign community there inheres necessarily the right and the duty of guarding its own existence, and of protecting and promoting the interests and welfare of the community at large. This power and this duty are to be exerted not only in the highest acts of sovereignty, and in the external relations of governments; they reach and comprehend likewise the interior polity and relations of social life, which should be regulated with reference to the advantage of the whole society. This power, denominated the *eminent domain* of the State, is, as its name imports, paramount to all private rights vested under the government, and these last are, by necessary implication, held in subordination to this power, and must yield in every instance to its proper exercise.

The Constitution of the United States, although adopted by the sovereign States of this Union, and proclaimed in its own language to be the supreme law for their government, can, by no rational interpretation, be brought to conflict with this attribute in the States; there is no express delegation of it by the Constitution; and it would imply an incredible fatuity in the States, to ascribe to them the intention to relinquish the power of self-government and self-preservation. A correct view of this matter must demonstrate, moreover, that the right of eminent domain in government in no wise interferes with the inviolability of contracts; that the most sanctimonious regard for the one is perfectly consistent with the possession and exercise of the other.

Under every established government, the tenure of property is derived mediately or immediately from the sovereign power of the political body, organized in such mode or exerted in such way as the community or State may have thought proper to ordain. It can rest on no other foundation, can have no other guarantee. It is owing to these characteristics only, in the original nature of tenure, that appeals can be made to the laws either for the protection or assertion of the rights of property. Upon any other hypothesis, the law of property would be simply the law of force. Now it is undeniable, that the investment of property in the citizen by the government, whether made for a pecuniary consideration or founded on conditions of civil or political duty, is a contract between the State, or the government acting as its agent, and the grantee; and both the parties thereto are bound in good faith to fulfil it. But into all contracts, whether made between States and individuals or between individuals only, there enter conditions which arise not out of the literal terms of the contract itself; they are superinduced by the preëxisting and higher authority of the laws of nature, of nations, or of the community to which the parties belong; they are always presumed, and must be presumed, to be known and recognized by all, are binding upon all, and need never, therefore, be carried into express stipulation, for this could add nothing to their force. Every contract is made in subordination to them, and must yield to their control, as conditions inherent and paramount, wherever a necessity for their execution shall occur. Such a condition is the right of eminent domain. This right does not operate to impair the contract effected by it, but recognizes its obligation in the fullest extent, claiming only the fulfilment of an essential and inseparable condition. Thus, in claiming the resumption or qualification of an investiture, it insists merely on the true nature and character of the right invested. The impairing of contracts inhibited by the Constitution can scarcely, by the greatest violence of construction, be made applicable to the enforcing of the terms or necessary import of a contract; the language and meaning of the inhibition were designed to embrace proceedings attempting the interpolation of some new term or condition foreign to the original agreement, and therefore inconsistent with and violative thereof. It, then, being clear that the power in question not being within the purview of the restriction imposed by the tenth section of the first article of the Constitution, it remains with the States to the full extent in which it inheres in every sovereign government, to be exercised by them in that degree that shall by them be deemed commensurate with public necessity. So long as they shall steer clear of the single predicament denounced by the Constitution, shall avoid interference with the obligation of contracts, the wisdom, the modes, the policy, the hardship of any exertion of this power are subjects not within the proper cognizance of this court. This is, in truth, purely a question of power; and, conceding the power to reside in the State government, this concession would seem to close the door upon all further controversy in connection with it. The instances of the exertion of this power, in some mode or other, from the very foundation of civil government have been so numerous and familiar, that it seems somewhat strange, at this day, to raise a doubt or question concerning it. In fact, the whole policy of the country, relative to roads, mills, bridges, and canals, rests upon this single power, under which lands have been always condemned; and without the exertion of this power, not one of the improvements just mentioned could be constructed. In our country, it is believed that the power was never, or, at any rate, rarely, questioned, until the opinion seems to have obtained, that the right of property in a chartered corporation was more sacred and intangible than the same right could possibly be in the person of the citizen; an opinion which must be without any grounds to rest upon, until it can be demonstrated either that the ideal creature is more than a person, or the corporeal being is less. For, as a question of the power to appropriate to public uses the property of private persons, resting upon the ordinary foundations of private right, there would seem to be room neither for doubt nor difficulty. A distinction has been attempted, in argument, between the power of a government to appropriate for public uses property which is corporeal, or may be said to be in being, and the like power in the government to resume or extinguish a franchise. The distinction thus attempted we regard as a refinement which has no foundation in reason, and one that, in truth, avoids the true legal or constitutional question in these causes; namely, that of the right in private persons, in the use or enjoyment of their private property, to control and actually to prohibit the power and duty of the government to advance and protect the general good. We are aware of nothing peculiar to a franchise which can class it higher, or render it more sacred, than other property. A franchise is property, and nothing more; it is incorporeal property, and is so defined by Justice Blackstone, when treating, in his second volume, chap. 3, page 20, of the Rights of Things. It is its character of property only which imparts to it value, and alone authorizes in individuals a right of action for invasions or disturbances of its enjoyment. *Vide* Bl. Comm., Vol. III., chap. 16, p. 236, as to injuries to this description of private property, and the remedies given for redressing them. A franchise, therefore, to erect a bridge, to construct a road, to keep a ferry, and to collect tolls upon them, granted by the authority of the State, we regard as occupying the same position, with respect to the paramount power and duty of the State to promote and protect the public good, as does the right of the citizen to the possession and enjoyment of his land under his patent or contract with the State, and it can no more interpose any obstruction in the way of their just exertion. Such exertion we hold to be not within the inhibition of the Constitution, and no violation of a contract. The power of a State, in the exercise of eminent domain to extinguish immediately a franchise it had granted, appears never to have been directly brought here for adjudication, and consequently has not been heretofore formally propounded from this court; but in England, this power, to the fullest extent, was recognized in the case of the Governor and Company of the Cast Plate Manufacturers *v.* Meredith, 4 Term Reports, 794, and Lord Kenyon, especially in that case, founded solely upon this power the entire policy and authority of all the road and canal laws of the kingdom.

The several State decisions cited in the argument, from 3 Paige's Chancery Reports, p. 45, from 23 Pickering, p. 361, from 17 Connecticut Reports, p. 454, from 8 New Hampshire Reports, p. 398, from 10 New Hampshire Reports, p. 371, and 11 New Hampshire Reports, p. 20, are accordant with the decision above mentioned, from 4 Durnford and East, and entirely supported by it. One of these State decisions, namely, the case of the Enfield Toll-Bridge Company *v.* The Hartford and New Haven Railroad Company, 17 Connecticut Reports, places the principle asserted in an attitude so striking, as seems to render that case worthy of a separate notice. The legislature of Connecticut, having previously incorporated the Enfield Bridge Company, inserted, in a charter subsequently granted by them to the Hartford and Springfield Railroad Company, a provision in these words,—"That nothing therein contained shall be construed to prejudice or impair any of the rights now vested in the Enfield Bridge Company." This provision, comprehensive as its language may seem to be, was decided by the Supreme Court of the State as not embracing any exemption of the Bridge Company from the legislative power of eminent domain, with respect to its franchise, but to declare this, and this only,—that, notwithstanding the privilege of constructing a railroad from Hartford to Springfield in the most direct and feasible route, granted by the latter charter, the franchise of the Enfield Bridge Company should remain as inviolate as the property of other citizens of the State. These decisions sustain clearly the following positions, comprised in this summary given by Chancellor Walworth, 3 Paige's Reports, p. 73, where he says, that, "notwithstanding the grant to individuals, the eminent domain, the highest and most exact idea of property, remains in the government, or in the aggregate body of the people in their sovereign capacity; and they have a right to resume the possession of the property in the manner directed by the constitution and laws of the State, whenever the public interest requires it. This right of resumption may be exercised, not only where the safety, but also where the interest, or even the expediency, of the State is concerned." In these positions, containing no exception with regard to property in a franchise (an exception which we should deem to be without warrant in reason), we recognize the true doctrines of the law as applicable to the cases before us. In considering the question of constitutional power,—the only question properly presented upon these records,—we institute no inquiry as to the adequacy or inadequacy of the compensation allowed to the plaintiffs in error for the extinguishment of their franchise; nor do we inquire into the conformity between the modes prescribed by the statutes of Vermont and the proceedings which actually were adopted in the execution of those statutes; these are matters regarded by this court as peculiarly belonging to the tribunals designated by the State for the exercise of her legitimate authority, and as being without the province assigned to this court by the Judiciary Act.

Upon the whole, we consider the authority claimed for the State of Vermont, and the exertion of that authority which has occurred under the provisions of the [illegible] above mentioned, by the extinguishment [illegible] the franchise previously granted the plaintiffs, as set forth upon the records before us, as presenting no instance of the impairing of a contract, within the meaning of the tenth section of the first article of the Constitution, and consequently no case which is proper for the interposition of this court. The decisions of the Supreme Court of Vermont are therefore affirmed.